CHICAGO PUBLIC LIBRARY
R00633 85134

HD
4802
.H36
1986
V. 1
Handbook of labor
economics
$110.00

DATE
D1266105

HANDBOOK OF LABOR ECONOMICS

VOLUME I

EHEHEHEHEHEHEHEHEHEHEHEHEHEHEHEHEHEHEHEHEHEHEHEHEHEHE

HANDBOOKS IN ECONOMICS

5

Series Editors

KENNETH J. ARROW

MICHAEL D. INTRILIGATOR

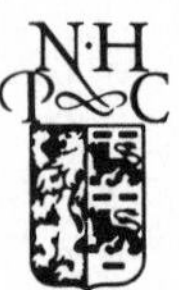

NORTH-HOLLAND
AMSTERDAM · NEW YORK · OXFORD · TOKYO

EHEHEHEHEHEHEHEHEHEHEHEHEHEHEHEHEHEHEHEHE

HANDBOOK OF LABOR ECONOMICS

VOLUME I

Edited by

ORLEY ASHENFELTER
Princeton University

and

RICHARD LAYARD
London School of Economics

1986

NORTH-HOLLAND
AMSTERDAM · NEW YORK · OXFORD · TOKYO

ISBN North-Holland for this set 0 444 87858 0
ISBN North-Holland for this volume 0 444 87856 4

Publishers
ELSEVIER SCIENCE PUBLISHERS B.V.
P.O. Box 1991
1000 BZ Amsterdam
The Netherlands

Sole distributors for the U.S.A. and Canada
ELSEVIER SCIENCE PUBLISHING COMPANY, INC.
52 Vanderbilt Avenue
New York, N.Y. 10017
U.S.A.

Library of Congress Cataloging-in-Publication Data

Handbook of labor economics.

(Handbooks in economics ; 5)
Includes bibliographies.
1. Labor economics. I. Ashenfelter, Orley, 1942- . II. Layard, R. III. Series.
HD4802.H36 1986 331 86-16730
ISBN 0-444-87858-0 (set)
ISBN 0-444-87856-4 (v. 1)
ISBN 0-444-87857-2 (v. 2)

PRINTED IN THE NETHERLANDS

INTRODUCTION TO THE SERIES

The aim of the *Handbooks in Economics* series is to produce Handbooks for various branches of economics, each of which is a definitive source, reference, and teaching supplement for use by professional researchers and advanced graduate students. Each Handbook provides self-contained surveys of the current state of a branch of economics in the form of chapters prepared by leading specialists on various aspects of this branch of economics. These surveys summarize not only received results but also newer developments, from recent journal articles and discussion papers. Some original material is also included, but the main goal is to provide comprehensive and accessible surveys. The Handbooks are intended to provide not only useful reference volumes for professional collections but also possible supplementary readings for advanced courses for graduate students in economics.

CONTENTS OF THE HANDBOOK

VOLUME I

PART 1 – SUPPLY OF LABOR

PART 2 – DEMAND FOR LABOR

PART 3 – WAGE STRUCTURE

VOLUME II

PART 4 – LABOR MARKET EQUILIBRIUM AND FRICTION

PREFACE TO THE HANDBOOK

The modern development of labor economics is a bold effort to use systematic theory to explain important empirical facts about the labor market. The results of this effort are topical, lively, and sometimes controversial, because the findings are relevant to both public and private decision-making. This Handbook brings together for the first time a systematic review of the research topics, empirical findings, and methods that comprise modern labor economics.

The chapters, which have all been written by leading contributors to the original research on each topic, are designed both to evaluate what has been learned *and* where further research may be profitable. We believe they will therefore be valuable to a wide range of readers, both those who wish an introduction to what has been done *and* those who wonder where things are heading.

The reader will find three common themes running through these chapters. In every case a guiding principle is the search for a parsimonious and systematic theoretical framework that both is consistent with the known facts about the labor market and that has further implications for empirical analyses. Also common to these chapters is a familiarity with some common empirical methods and empirical results and the clear perception that further empirical testing is necessary. Finally, a common theme that runs through the chapters is the presumption that an understanding of the way labor markets work will lead all of us to better decisions in both our public and private lives. In our view it is these common features of the chapters in this Handbook that represent the high standards set for the finest work in applied economics.

Volume I is concerned with the classic topics of labor supply and demand and their impact on the wage structure. These topics have been of interest to social scientists for many centuries, since they bear on two fundamental questions. First, what are the sources of income inequality, and second, what are the disincentive effects of attempts to produce a more equal income distribution? Labor supply is concerned with the incentives which individuals have to provide labor services, and labor demand is concerned with the incentives which firms have to use them. The more elastic the demand and supply, the greater the efficiency costs of interventionist policies. Thus, a key theme running through many of these chapters is just how big these elasticities are.

Until recently the data available to answer these questions were very limited, as were the computational facilities to handle them. But on the labor supply side this has changed drastically with the advent of large data sets on individuals, and

Frank Stafford (Chapter 7) shows the tremendous impact which this has had on the output of good empirical work in labor economics.

Labor supply has many dimensions. Even the apparently simple question of hours worked breaks down into hours per week, weeks per year, and years per lifetime. For most prime-age men the issue is less whether to work at all than how much to work. As John Pencavel (Chapter 1) shows, the evidence suggests that men's choice between hours of work and leisure is only weakly influenced by the available wages. For married women, there are more alternative uses of time than for men, since in the majority of households they do more of the household work. This has led many researchers to conclude that wages affect women's work more than men's. James Heckman and Mark Killingsworth (Chapter 2) examine the evidence using a host of different approaches to explain the division of women's time between paid work and other activities. Of course, much of the variation in female labor supply is not explained by wages and income, but by changes in family status. Montgomery and Trussell (Chapter 3) survey the connection between demography and labor economics this implies. Finally, Reuben Gronau (Chapter 4) surveys the whole range of different possible activities, including paid work and others, and attempts to explain it. Needless to say all the four chapters we have mentioned embed their analyses, where relevant, in a model of family decision-making.

A person's lifetime labor supply is much affected by when he stops (retires) and when he starts (quits education). The decision to retire is profoundly affected by the availability of social security and private pensions, which in turn raises the question of how private pensions are determined. The research on these issues is fully explored by Edward Lazear (Chapter 5). Turning to education, this is important not only for its effect on the duration of work-life but upon the skills of those people who are at work. Richard Freeman (Chapter 6) surveys the research on the productive role of education and its effect on earnings, and evaluates the effect of financial rewards in affecting the number of people wishing to stay in school.

We know less about labor demand than about labor supply, because we have less cross-section data on firms than on households. Thus, most work on labor demand is based on time-series analysis. Work has tended to fall into two rather distinct groups: that which mainly aims to estimate the effects of wages, and that which mainly aims to track the detailed quarter-by-quarter adjustment of employment to external shocks. Daniel Hamermesh (Chapter 8) surveys the theory and evidence about wage effects, where there are two rather separate issues: first the effects of relative wages on the skill- or age-mix of employment at given output, and second the effect of real wages on the aggregate level of output and employment. Stephen Nickell (Chapter 9) is concerned, in contrast, with the detailed path through which employment adjusts to a shock, given that full immediate adjustment is too costly.

The wage structure is determined as a first approximation by demand and supply, though Volume II also treats the impact of other institutional structures. There is a supply of workers with given characteristics to jobs of given quality, and there is a corresponding demand. Each depends on the wages paid for given worker and job characteristics. This wage structure adjusts until supply and demand are equal. The wage structure can thus be described by a functional relationship between the wage on the one hand and, on the other, the characteristics of the worker and of the job he is in.

Robert Willis (Chapter 10) surveys this relationship beginning with the famous human capital model. His review establishes the wide empirical applicability of this framework in a variety of circumstances. Yoram Weiss (Chapter 11) concentrates on one particular dimension of the wage structure: its variation over the life-cycle. He models this, allowing individuals to choose their rate of human capital investment at all points of time. Variation of wages over time to compensate for earlier human capital investment is but one example of the more general role of compensating differentials in the wage structure. Sherwin Rosen (Chapter 12) examines a whole range of other differences between jobs for which compensating differentials are paid – differences in risk to life and health, climatic conditions, convenience of hours, uncertainty of prospects and so on.

One glaring feature of the wage structure is the lower wages paid to women and blacks. This may be so even when they are compared with otherwise identical white males. If so, this raises the question of how such discrimination can persist in a competitive economic environment, and a host of possible explanations are surveyed by Glen Cain (Chapter 13).

The papers in Volume II generally proceed from the common observation that heterogeneity in worker skills and employer demands often tempers the outcomes that would be expected in frictionless labor markets. Donald Parsons (Chapter 14) surveys the burgeoning and very recent work that documents and attempts to explain the nature of long-term employment relationships. Much of this work has started from empirical observations on the length of employment relationships and attempted to present alternative theoretical set-ups that may justify alternative employment arrangements. The primary motives singled out for the nature of long-term employment relationships in this literature are employer and employee attitudes toward risk and the incomplete information they bring to employment bargains.

Much the same motivation underlies the models of search in the labor market that Dale Mortensen (Chapter 15) reviews, but the emphasis is different. Here the goal is to explore the determinants of the allocation of worker resources to searching across job opportunities.

Two chapters deal with the modern analysis of unemployment. George Johnson and Richard Layard (Chapter 16) explore the determination of the structure of unemployment. Here the goal is to describe the longer-term level and persistent unemployment structures that exist and to assess the various explanations for them. Another feature of unemployment in modern economies is the business cycle. David Lilien and Robert Hall (Chapter 17) review the broad evidence on the nature of the cyclical movements in unemployment and the theoretical explanations for why this puzzling phenomenon exists.

The last section of the Handbook deals explicitly with the institutional structures that are a part of modern labor markets. Henry Farber (Chapter 18) reviews the considerable work on trade union decision-making that has emerged in the last two decades. One particularly important aspect of trade union behavior is the strike activity that seems to insert inexplicable costs into the bargaining relationship. John Kennan (Chapter 19) reviews the empirical and theoretical work in this field with a view to establishing the extent to which the former is consistent with the latter.

In the following chapter, Gregg Lewis (Chapter 20) turns his hand to an updated survey of the impact of trade union bargaining on relative wages. Since the publication of his classic *Unionism and Relative Wages in the U.S.* over twenty years ago, both new data and new methods have been brought to the discussions of this topic. Lewis reviews this modern research with the same meticulous care and fine judgment he brought to this topic two decades ago.

Paul Taubman and Michael Wachter (Chapter 21) explicitly take up the discussion of earnings mobility and the extent to which social and familial class structures result in labor market outcomes nearer the Marxist than the classical explanations. The empirical work in this area concentrates on the extent of income mobility across families and over time, which is of considerable importance in the minds of many in establishing the operating characteristics of any society.

Ronald Ehrenberg and Joshua Schwarz (Chapter 22) survey the special characteristics of labor markets in the public sector. Recognizing that the motivations of public-sector employers may be more complex than in the private sector, the survey provides a wealth of information on the special structures in public-sector labor markets and the analyses of how they operate.

Like most good research, the material reviewed in this Handbook raises as many questions as it answers. Future research will no doubt continue to emphasize the interaction between systematic explanation and careful data analysis, which seems to us the key to continued success in economics.

CONTENTS OF VOLUME I

Chapter 2

Female Labor Supply: A Survey

MARK R. KILLINGSWORTH and JAMES J. HECKMAN 103

Chapter 3

Models of Marital Status and Childbearing

MARK MONTGOMERY and JAMES TRUSSELL 205

Chapter 6

Demand for Education

RICHARD B. FREEMAN

Chapter 7

Forestalling the Demise of Empirical Economics: The Role of Microdata in Labor Economics Research

FRANK STAFFORD

PART 2 – DEMAND FOR LABOR

Chapter 8

The Demand for Labor in the Long Run

DANIEL S. HAMERMESH

PART 3 – WAGE STRUCTURE

Chapter 10

Wage Determinants: A Survey and Reinterpretation of Human Capital Earnings Functions

ROBERT J. WILLIS 525

Chapter 11

The Determination of Life Cycle Earnings: A Survey

YORAM WEISS 603

PART 1

SUPPLY OF LABOR

With respect to hours of work, there is the work of Lewis (1957), Bry (1959), Jones (1961), and Finegan (1962).

Modern research on labor supply is characterized by a more careful attempt to separate the measurement of income from substitution effects. It dates from Mincer's (1962) paper on the labor force participation rate of married women and Kosters' (1966) dissertation on the hours worked by men. Since the mid-1960s, progress in computing technology – especially the development of more efficient methods of storing on magnetic tapes and processing information on individuals and the enormous reduction in the costs of applying multivariate statistical techniques to these data – has resulted in a vast outpouring of empirical research in labor supply. This literature has already been the subject of a number of very good surveys: Heckman and MaCurdy (1981); Heckman, Killingsworth and MaCurdy (1981); Keeley (1981); and Killingsworth (1981, 1983). Each of these tends to be a survey of the economics literature. This survey strives to be a little different, namely a survey of the topic and our knowledge of it as well as what economists have written about it. This is why I have devoted an important part, Section 2, to a summary statement of the major empirical regularities in male labor force participation and male hours of work. It is these and other regularities that economists' theories should be trying to explain and, if economics is indeed a science rather than a branch of applied mathematics, then it is the task of economists to confront the theories with the evidence. As will become clear, there has been a great deal of empirical work on male labor supply and much of it has been imbedded explicitly in the standard neoclassical allocation theory. In fact, one of the most pleasing aspects of labor supply research during the last 20 years has been its careful attention to the theoretical underpinnings. At the same time, the overwhelming proportion of this empirical work has not questioned the validity of the conventional model; this model has been treated as a maintained hypothesis. Empirical research has concentrated on quantifying the magnitude of the presumed relationships. Such quantification is naturally an important ingredient of any science, but in many laboratory sciences refined attempts at calibration represent a stage of research that usually follows, not precedes, the testing of hypotheses. In male labor supply research, very little formal testing of the standard model has been undertaken. Labor supply research cannot be indicated for "measurement without theory", but it can be described as "measurement without testing". The theory is by no means empty of refutable implications and, at least when asked, most economists would grant that ultimately the implications or assumptions of any economic theory must correspond with actual behavior. So why has the great volume of empirical work involved so little testing of the standard model?

I suspect that one reason can be attributed to the fact that not merely are we reluctant to *reject* a theory until we have a viable substitute close at hand – this is a familiar proposition in the sociology of science – but also we hesitate even to *test* a theory until an alternative, behavioral, hypothesis is available.[6] The answer "I don't know" is something that an economist will say after being pushed by careful questioning, but he will not readily volunteer this response.

A more substantive reason for the lack of hypothesis testing in labor supply research is that many economists view such tests as tantamount to questioning whether a consumer's income-compensated demand curve for a commodity slopes downwards with respect to its price. After all, so the argument would go, the neoclassical theory of labor supply is a straightforward extension of the consumer's allocation problem and surely we believe that demand curves slope downwards? Putting aside the issue of whether that basic proposition of consumer theory has itself been corroborated, it is usually agreed that, in the absence of adverse evidence, the confirmation of a hypothesis increases with the number of favorable test outcomes: if the theory of consumer behavior had been found to be an apt description of the demand for apples, oranges, cherries, bananas, and many other fruit, an economist will wager it also applies to the demand for pears. But it is by no means clear that the exchanges taking place in the labor market are well described by analogies to the individual's behavior with respect to the purchases of fruit, that the evidence about the demand curves for fruit is relevant to the supply of work effort. As Coase (1937), Phelps Brown (1960, pp. 289–293), Simon (1951), and others have emphasized, labor market transactions possess many dimensions – the wages to be paid, the level of work effort to be applied, the range of activities to which the employee may be directed, the duration of the contract, and so on – and the particular combination of wages and hours worked represents only a subset of the bundle of items involved in the exchange. It is not at all obvious that this subset may be siphoned off from the rest and appropriately characterized by the sort of allocation process that the conventional model applies. I am not suggesting that the preferences of workers have nothing to do with their market work decisions, only that what I call below the canonical model may not be the most useful characterization of the way in which preferences and opportunities come together to determine outcomes in the labor market.

Nevertheless, the research attempts to measure the relevant parameters precisely have resulted in some notable advances in our understanding of the issues. For instance, the economics and econometrics of hours of work as distinct from labor force participation decisions are much better understood than they were 20 years ago. Though the literature on nonlinear budget constraints is by no means recent, it has been only in the past ten years that their implications for empirical work have been fully explored. The development and application of tractable dynamic models of labor supply have also represented a major advance in our

[6] Cf. Lakatos (1970, p. 179, n. 2): "The reluctance of economists and other social scientists to accept Popper's methodology may have been partly due to the destructive effect of naive falsificationism on budding research programmes."

understanding of the issues. We have much more and much better information today on the major empirical regularities in work behavior and especially on the importance of unobserved variables in accounting for variations across individuals in their hours of work. In all these respects, the standards of enquiry and critical debate in labor supply research have risen tremendously compared with the state of affairs 20 years or so ago. It is in this sense that undeniable progress has been made.

An outline of this survey is as follows. In the next section, Section 2, I identify the major time-series and cross-section empirical regularities in male labor supply behavior. It is these that any economic theory should be designed to address. Section 3 presents first the canonical static model of labor supply and then it immediately proceeds to deal with the problems in applying this model at the aggregative level. The static model is then amended to handle the situation of nonlinear budget constraints. Section 3 concludes with an outline of the most popular life-cycle model of labor supply. Section 4 addresses the issues in and results from the estimation of the static model. In this section, problems in specifying the model are first considered and then the results are presented from the U.S. nonexperimental literature, the British literature, and the U.S. experimental literature. Section 5 discusses the estimates from the applications of the life-cycle model. Some conclusions and suggestions for further research are given in Section 6.

2. Empirical regularities

2.1. *Trends in work behavior*

For a century or so, at least in North America and West Europe, a declining fraction of a man's lifetime has been spent at market work. This decline has been manifested in a number of ways: more years have been spent at school and the age of entry into full-time market employment has advanced; workers have been wholly or partially retiring from the labor force at younger ages; fewer hours have been worked per day and per week; and there have been more holidays and longer vacations. In addition, I suspect that work effort per hour has decreased, although this is difficult to verify. Consider now these different dimensions of work behavior.

Changes during the last 80 years or so in the labor force participation rates of men of different ages are documented for the United States, Britain, Canada, and Germany in Tables 1.1, 1.2, 1.3, and 1.4. The age group that maintained the closest association with the labor market has been men aged 25 to 44 years; for all four countries in all these years, more than 90 percent of these men were classified as members of the labor force. However, from the turn of the century

Table 1.1
United States: Male labor force participation rates (expressed as a percentage) by age over time.

Age (in years)	1890	1900	1910	1920	1930	1940	1950	1960	1970(a)	1970(b)	1982
10–13	17.8	17.7	9.2	6.0	3.3						
14/16–19	57.1	61.1	56.2	52.6	41.1	34.4	39.9	38.1	47.8	58.4	58.1
20–24	92.0	91.7	91.1	90.9	89.9	88.0	82.8	86.2	80.9	86.6	86.0
25–44	97.6	96.3	96.6	97.1	97.5	95.0	92.8	95.2	94.4	96.8	95.1
45–64	95.2	93.3	93.6	93.8	94.1	88.7	87.9	89.0	87.3	89.4	81.0
≥ 65	73.9	68.3	58.1	60.1	58.3	41.5	41.6	30.6	25.0	26.8	17.8
All	87.4	87.3	86.3	86.5	84.1	79.0	79.0	77.4	76.8	80.6	77.2

Notes: The Censuses after 1930 did not count children aged less than 14 years in the labor force. The age category "14/16–19" relates to 14–19 years for the years from 1890 to 1960 and to 16–19 years thereafter. The age category "All" describes all males aged 14 years and over from 1890 to 1960 and all males aged 16 years and over thereafter. The data for the years 1890, 1900, 1910, 1920, 1930, 1940, and 1950 are from Long (1958, Table A-2, p. 287). The data for 1960 are from U.S. Department of Commerce, Bureau of the Census, *U.S. Census of Population 1960: Employment Status and Work Experience*, Subject Reports PC(2)-6A, Table 1. The data for 1970(a) are from U.S. Department of Commerce, Bureau of the Census, 1970 *Census of Population*: *Employment Status and Work Experience*, Subject Reports PC(2)-6A, Table 1. The data for 1970(b) and for 1982 are from the monthly Current Population Survey of households and are not strictly comparable with the decennial census data in the other columns. The data for 1970(b) are from *Employment and Earnings*, January 1971, Table A-1, page 115 and those for 1982 from *Employment and Earnings*, January 1983, Table 3, page 142.

Table 1.2
Great Britain: Male labor force participation rates (expressed as a percentage) by age over time.

Age (in years)	1891	1911	1931	1951	1966	1981
< 20			84.7	83.8	70.6	64.6
20–24	98.1	97.3	97.2	94.9	92.6	89.2
25–44	97.9	98.5	98.3	98.3	98.2	97.5
45–64	93.7	94.1	94.3	95.2	95.1	90.2
65 +	65.4	56.8	47.9	31.1	23.5	10.8
All			90.5	87.6	84.0	77.8

Notes: The category " < 20" relates to males aged 14–19 years in 1931, to males aged 15–19 years in 1951 and 1966, and to males aged 16–19 years in 1981. The category "All" relates to males aged 14 years and over in 1931, to males aged 15 years and over in 1951 and 1966, and to males aged 16 years and over in 1981. The data for the years 1891, 1911, 1931, 1951, and 1966 come from Department of Employment and Productivity, *British Labour Statistics Historical Abstract 1886–1968*, London, HMSO, 1971, Table 109, pp. 206–207. Those for 1981 are from Central Statistical Office, *Annual Abstract of Statistics 1983 Edition*, 1983, Table 6.16, p. 130.

Table 1.3
Canada: Male labor force participation rates (expressed as a percentage) by age over time.

Age (in years)	1911	1931	1951	1971	1980
14/15–19	64.6	51.4	48.1	46.6	51.9
20–24	92.2	92.3	91.8	86.5	79.7
25–44	97.1	97.6	96.3	92.7	92.2
45–64	94.4	94.8	90.6	85.9	83.3
65+	52.1	55.8	38.5	23.6	14.0

Notes: The youngest age category is 14–19 years in 1911, 1931, and 1951 and is 15–19 years in 1971 and 1980. For the years 1911, 1931, and 1951, the data are from Long (1958, Table A-11, p. 305). For the years 1971 and 1980, the sources are the International Labour Organization's *Yearbook of Labour Statistics* for 1975–76 and 1983, respectively.

for each and every age-group, the labor force participation rates of men in all these countries has fallen. The decline has been most marked for older men: for men aged 65 years and over, as recently as the early 1930s labor force participation rates of 58 percent, 48 percent, and 56 percent were recorded in the United States, Britain, and Canada, respectively. Twenty years later these rates had fallen by about the same 17 percentage points in each of these countries. A similar change was registered in Germany from 47 percent in 1925 to 27 percent in 1950. The post World War II period has witnessed further declines in each country in the labor force participation rates of older men. These declines have often been attributed to the expansion of government-organized social security

Table 1.4
Germany: Male labor force participation rates (expressed as a percentage) by age over time.

Age (in years)	1895	1907	1925	1939	1950	1970	1981
14/15–19	83.6	86.1	85.0	86.0	74.2	66.6	46.4
20–24	95.1	95.7	95.0	96.2	93.4	86.4	81.4
25–44	97.2	97.4	97.4	98.0	96.3	96.7	95.8
45–64	91.8	89.4	91.4	87.0	89.6	85.7	83.7
65+	58.8	50.2	47.4	29.7	26.7	16.0	7.0

Notes: Betwcen 1895 and 1950, the youngest age group is 14–19 years; for 1970 and 1981, the youngest age group is 15–19 years. For the years 1895, 1907, 1925, and 1939, "Germany" consists of that area defined by her post World War I frontiers without the Saar. For the other years, "Germany" means the Federal Republic of Germany, excluding Berlin. The source for the data for 1895, 1907, 1925, 1939, and 1950 is Long (1958, Table A-16, p. 313). For the years 1970 and 1981, the sources are the International Labour Organization's *Yearbook of Labour Statistics* for 1973 and 1983, respectively.

Table 1.5
United States and Britain: labor force participation rates (expressed as percentages) of males and females combined over time.

United States		Britain	
Year	Participation	Year	Participation
1890	54.0	1891	61.3
1900	54.8	1901	59.9
1910	55.7	1911	60.4
1920	55.6	1921	58.6
1930	54.6	1931	57.7
1940	52.2	1951	57.7
1950	53.4	1961	59.3
1960	55.4	1971	61.4
1970	55.7	1981	61.0

Notes: The U.S. data in all years describe males and females aged 14 years and older and the British data in all years describe males and females aged 20 years and older. The U.S. data come from the Decennial Censuses and the precise sources are the same as those given beneath Table 1.1. The sources for the British data are the same as those given beneath Table 1.2.

systems and, indeed, it is unlikely that the taxes and benefits associated with the operation of these systems have not affected the labor force participation rate of older people.[7] On the other hand, it should be noted that the participation rates of older men were already declining before the period of the great expansion of government social security.

At the same time as the labor force participation rates of men were falling, those of women were rising. Indeed, as Table 1.5 shows for the United States and Britain, these changes largely offset one another. The absence of a trend in the overall (male and female) labor force participation rate prompted Klein and Kosobud (1961) to classify it as one of the "great ratios of economics". Both in 1910 and in 1970, the participation rate of all people aged 14 years and over in the United States was 55.7 percent; in 1981 in Britain, the participation rate of all people aged 20 years and over differed by only three-tenths of one percent from the rate in 1891.

Year-to-year movements in the labor force participation rate reflect the state of the business cycle as well as underlying trends. A convenient and simple way of

[7]Parsons (1980) claims the Social Security disability program is responsible for the declines during the post World War II period in the labor force participation rate of men aged 45–54 years. This interpretation is challenged by Haveman and Wolfe (1984) and then defended by Parsons (1984).

describing these cycles and trends is to fit the following equation to annual U.S. data from 1955 to 1982 for the civilian labor force participation rates of different groups of males in the population:

$$\Delta L_{jt} = \alpha_j + \beta_j \Delta U_t^{\mathrm{r}} + \varepsilon_{jt}. \tag{1}$$

In this equation, $\Delta L_{jt} = L_{jt} - L_{jt-1}$ and L_{jt} is the civilian labor force participation rate (expressed as a percentage) of group j in year t and $\Delta U_t^{\mathrm{r}} = U_t^{\mathrm{r}} - U_{t-1}^{\mathrm{r}}$ and U_t^{r} is the unemployment rate (expressed as a percentage) of white males aged 35–44 years in year t. The unemployment rate of this group is a better indicator of the stage of the business cycle as it operates in the labor market than is the overall unemployment rate and the superscript "r" on U designates this as the "reference" group. The responsiveness of the participation rate to the business cycle is measured by β while α reflects a linear time trend. The equation error is represented by ε_t and the index j runs over nine age groups and two racial groups.

The consequences of estimating eq. (1) by ordinary least squares are shown in Table 1.6. According to these estimates, over the past 27 years there has been a downward trend of almost three-tenths of one percent per year in the participation rate of white men and of almost one-half of one percent per year in the participation of black men. These trends are especially marked for young black men and for older men, both black and white. Although most of the estimates of β are negative (suggesting the participation rate falls in a recession),[8] these effects are small and not statistically significant except for younger men.[9] In general, very little variation in annual movements of male participation rates is removed by this cyclical indicator and Mincer's (1966) summary diagnosis – "some net cycle elasticity plus much residual variation due to other factors" – remains apt.[10]

For Britain, a time series on the male labor force participation rate for different age-groups is not published for the entire post-war period.[11] So I constructed an annual series for the entire adult male labor force participation

[8]The phenomenon of the labor force contracting in a recession is sometimes described as "the discouraged worker effect", that is, the costs of searching for acceptable employment rises in a recession to a degree such that it no longer pays some individuals to continue searching.

[9]A finding of long standing is that school enrollment rates of young people rise in a recession. See, for example, Duncan (1956).

[10]Equation (1) was also estimated with a different cyclical indicator, namely, the inventory-sales ratio in manufacturing and wholesale and retail trade. Very similar results were obtained with this variable as those reported in Table 1.6. Note that this is also the case for white men aged 35–44 years for whom there is a real danger of a spurious correlation between L and U^{r} in eq. (1).

[11]A series exists on an important subset of the male labor force (namely, all except employers, the self-employed, some part-time employees, and the military), but for men this was discontinued in January 1971. Analyses of these series are in Corry and Roberts (1970, 1974).

Table 1.6
United States: Estimates of trend (α) and cycle (β) in male civilian labor force participation rates by race and age, 1955–1982.

Age (in years)	α	β	R^2	D–W
White				
Total,				
≥ 16	−0.284*(0.051)	−0.094(0.059)	0.09	1.59
16–17	0.181(0.246)	−1.103*(0.285)	0.37	1.61
18–19	0.078(0.229)	−0.800*(0.266)	0.26	1.29
20–24	0.015(0.158)	−0.201(0.184)	0.04	1.81
25–34	−0.057(0.038)	−0.121*(0.044)	0.22	1.78
35–44	−0.075*(0.027)	−0.042(0.031)	0.07	2.24
45–54	−0.169*(0.039)	0.056(0.046)	0.05	1.00
55–64	−0.651*(0.123)	0.008(0.143)	0.01	1.82
≥ 65	−0.796*(0.142)	−0.085(0.165)	0.01	1.49
Black and other				
Total,				
≥ 16	−0.492*(0.116)	−0.162(0.134)	0.05	1.48
16–17	−0.626*(0.388)	−1.105*(0.449)	0.19	2.44
18–19	−0.780*(0.329)	−0.634(0.382)	0.10	2.24
20–24	−0.438(0.222)	−0.711(0.257)	0.23	1.59
25–34	−0.256*(0.115)	−0.125(0.133)	0.03	2.41
35–44	−0.220*(0.097)	−0.090(0.112)	0.02	2.18
45–54	−0.319(0.212)	−0.215(0.245)	0.03	2.66
55–64	−0.686*(0.324)	0.008(0.375)	0.01	2.02
≥ 65	−0.861*(0.273)	−0.147(0.316)	0.01	2.17

Notes: Estimated standard errors are in parentheses next to their associated regression coefficients. "D–W" is the Durbin–Watson statistic. For ease of reading, an asterisk has been placed next to those point estimates more than twice their estimated standard errors. The data are taken from the *Employment and Training Report of the President 1981* and from recent issues of *Employment and Earnings*.

rate over the 31 years from 1951 to 1981[12] and estimated the cyclical and trend movements in this labor force participation rate by fitting eq. (1) to the data. As a cyclical indicator, however, I used the deviations of the index of industrial production from a linear time trend, positive deviations corresponding to a low level of aggregate business activity and negative deviations to a high level of business activity. The labor force participation rate (expressed as a percentage) and this cyclical indicator were first-differenced and then, as in eq. (1), an

[12] To be precise, I constructed the ratio of the male labor force (called in Britain the working population) to the male home population aged 15 years and over. Both numerator and denominator are measured at the same moment, the middle of each year, and both relate to Britain (not the United Kingdom). The sources for the data were issues of the *Annual Abstract of Statistics* published by the Central Statistical Office. The mean value of this male labor force participation rate over the 1951–81 period is 0.836 with a standard deviation of 0.047.

ordinary least-squares equation was fitted to the data over the years 1952–1981.[13] The resulting estimates (with estimated standard errors in parentheses) are as follows:

$$\hat{\alpha} = \underset{(0.094)}{-0.446^*}, \quad \hat{\beta} = \underset{(0.022)}{-0.015}, \quad R^2 = 0.02, \quad \text{D–W} = 1.36.$$

According to these estimates, the male labor force participation rate in Britain over the last 30 years displays a small procyclical movement that would not be deemed significantly different from zero by conventional criteria and a negative trend of almost one-half of a percentage point per year. A comparison of these estimates with those in Table 1.6 for the entire U.S. male labor force indicates that movements in the British male labor force participation rate look very similar to those in the United States.

Hours worked by men declined markedly during the first four decades of the twentieth century. For the United States, this is evident from the data in Table 1.7 which are taken from the decennial Censuses of Population and which relate to men working in manufacturing industry only. They show that, whereas in 1909, 92 percent of all males were working more than 48 hours per week, the percentage had fallen to 54 percent in 1929 and then to 7 percent in 1940. This dramatic decline between 1929 and 1940 was in part the consequence of the Fair Labor Standards Act of 1938 which required that all hours over a standard workweek be compensated at the rate of 1.5 times the regular wage. Initially the standard workweek was set at 44 hours; since 1940 it has been 40 hours.[14]

The U.S. trends from 1940 onwards are indicated by the data in Table 1.8 which are not restricted to manufacturing industry. This table suggests that there has not been a pronounced change in hours worked per week since 1940 except for a reduction in the fraction working 41–48 hours and a greater bunching in the

[13] If I_t is the index of industrial production in year t (published in issues of the *Monthly Digest of Statistics*) and if T_t is a linear time trend, then I fitted to the annual data for the years 1948–81 the following ordinary least-squares equation:

$$I_t = \underset{(2.28)}{64.28} + \underset{(0.114)}{2.277}\, T_t,$$

where the figures in parentheses are estimated standard errors. (The mean value of I_t over these years is 104.1.) I then formed as a cyclical indicator, C_t, the difference between the predicted value of the index, $\hat{I}_t$, and the actual value of the index, I_t: $C_t = \hat{I}_t - I_t$. Thus, when C_t is positive, a recession is implied while when C_t is negative a high level of aggregate business activity is implied. (Defining it in this way, C_t moves in the same direction as the unemployment rate, the cyclical indicator used in describing variations in U.S. labor force participation rates.) Then, in accordance with the specification in eq. (1), annual changes in the male labor force participation rate were regressed on ΔC_t, where $\Delta C_t = C_t - C_{t-1}$. The results are not altered if the cyclical indicator is formed from regressing I_t on a quadratic time trend nor if a linear time trend is added to eq. (1).

[14] Some evidence assessing the effects of the FLSA on hours worked (especially in the 1940s) is contained in Lewis (1958). More information gauging the importance of the overtime provisions for hours worked is found in Ehrenberg and Schumann (1981).

Table 1.7
United States: Percentage distribution of weekly hours in manufacturing industry by employed males from the decennial censuses of population.

Hours worked	1909	1919	1929	1940	1950	1960	1970
≤ 34	7.9	12.2	0.5	13.3	6.9	7.8	10.1
35–39				4.9	3.5	4.7	4.9
40			2.8	51.3	64.3	56.4	53.1
41–43			1.0	14.2	17.1	19.3	18.6
44–47		3.8	14.8	1.9			
48		32.6	26.9	7.4			
49–53	7.3	16.4	25.1	3.9	5.6	7.8	8.8
54	15.4	9.1	6.3				
55–59	30.2	13.7	15.1				
60	30.5	9.1	7.5	3.0	2.6	4.0	4.4
> 60	8.7	3.0					

Notes: The data relate to all employed males in 1960 and 1970 and to all employed wage and salary workers in the years earlier. The 1970 data describe males aged 16 years and over. In the years 1929–60, the data describe males aged 14 years and over. The Census collected data on "prevailing hours of labor" in 1909 and 1919 and on "customary hours of labor" in 1929. In the Census of 1940 and in subsequent years, the hours of work relate precisely to the census week. A small number of workers whose hours were not reported in 1929, 1940, and 1950 are not included in constructing the frequency distributions above. The 1970 data are from the *Industrial Characteristics* volume (Table 39) of the 1970 Census of Population. The 1960 data are from the *Industrial Characteristics* volume (Table 9) of the 1960 Census of Population. The 1950 data are from the *Industrial Characteristics* volume (Table 11) of the 1950 Census of Population. The 1940 data are from *Sixteenth Census of the United States 1940: Population Vol. III The Labor Force* Part I: U.S. Summary, Table 86, p. 259. The 1929 data are from *Fifteenth Decennial Census of the United States 1930: Manufactures 1929*, Vol. I, General Report, Table 5. The 1919 data are from the *Fourteenth Census of the United States Taken in the Year 1920*, Vol. VIII, Manufactures 1919, General Report and Analytic Tables, Table 17. The 1909 data are from the *Thirteenth Census of the United States Taken in the Year 1910*, Vol. VIII, Manufactures 1909, General Report and Analysis, Chapter XII, Table 8, p. 316.

distribution of hours worked at 40 hours. This spike at 40 hours per week is typically attributed to the overtime provisions of the Fair Labor Standards Act and the rising fraction of employees working these hours corresponds to the expansion of the Act's provisions: at the time of its implementation, less than one-fifth of all employees were covered by the overtime provisions; by the late 1970s, this figure had grown to approximately 58 percent.

The absence of a strong trend in hours worked during the post World War II period is consistent with the series on hours worked compiled from household interviews as part of the Current Population Survey (Table 1.9). These data are available on a consistent basis from 1955 and, as distinct from the data derived from the establishment surveys, they do not describe hours paid for, but hours worked by those at work. (Individuals on vacation, ill, or on strike are not covered by these hours of work data in Table 1.9.) The annual observations on hours worked per week by male wage and salary workers clearly reveal procycli-

Table 1.8
United States: Percentage distribution of hours worked of employed males during the Census week in 1940, 1950, 1960, and 1970.

Hours worked	1940	1950	1960	1970
1–14	1.59	2.02	4.42	4.54
15–29	5.79	4.75	4.60	5.71
30–34	4.47	3.37	3.09	5.03
35–39	4.56	2.86	4.48	4.91
40	33.53	41.45	41.59	43.06
41–48	29.37	19.29	19.59	17.41
49–59	8.87	10.69	10.36	9.99
≥ 60	11.83	15.57	11.87	9.35

Notes: These data describe all U.S. males aged 14 years and over who were employed during the Census week and who reported their hours of work. The 1940 data relate to wage and salary workers only. Also, in 1940, the categories labelled above as "1–14" and "15–29" are, in fact, less than 14 hours and 14–29 hours, respectively. The 1940 data are from *Sixteenth Census of the United States*: *1940*, *Vol. III*, *The Labor Force*, Part 1: U.S. Summary, Table 86, p. 259. The 1950 data are from *U.S. Census of Population 1950*, *Vol. IV*, *Special Reports*, Part I, Chapter A, Employment and Personal Characteristics, Table 13. The 1960 data are from *U.S. Census of Population 1960 Subject Reports*, Employment Status and Work Experience, Table 12. The 1970 data are from *U.S. Census of Population 1970 Subject Reports*, Employment Status and Work Experience, Table 17.

cal movements,[15] but after accounting for these cyclical effects there is little evidence of a trend over the past 27 years. These inferences come from fitting the following equation to the annual observations on weekly hours worked:

$$\Delta h_{jt} = \alpha_j + \beta_j \Delta U_t^{\mathrm{r}} + \varepsilon_{jt}, \tag{2}$$

where $\Delta h_{jt} = h_{jt} - h_{jt-1}$ and h_{jt} is the average weekly hours worked by group j in year t, $\Delta U_t^{\mathrm{r}} = U_t^{\mathrm{r}} - U_{t-1}^{\mathrm{r}}$ and U_t^{r} is the unemployment rate (expressed as a percentage) of white men aged 35–44 years in year t (the superscript "r" denoting my choice of these men as a reference group), and ε_{jt} is a stochastic error term. Any linear trend in hours worked is measured by α while β is supposed to reflect business cycle influences on hours. The index j runs over the six groups identified for the U.S. data in Table 1.9 and the ordinary least-squares estimates of the parameters α_j and β_j are given in Table 1.10. There are significant cyclical movements in hours worked for all workers except those in the older age groups. Most of the estimated trend terms (the α's) are negative, but none would be judged significant by conventional criteria except for that for

[15] For an analysis of weekly hours worked over the business cycle, see Bry (1959).

Table 1.9
United States, 1955–82, and United Kingdom, 1938–82:
Average weekly hours worked by male employees.

	United Kingdom: All adults	United States					
		All	14/16–17 years	18–24 years	25–44 years	45–64 years	≥ 65 years
1938	47.7						
1946–49	46.9						
1950–54	47.9						
1955–59	48.4	42.6	20.9	40.2	44.2	43.6	38.0
1960–64	47.5	42.5	18.4	39.9	44.5	43.7	35.7
1965–69	46.4	42.7	21.0	39.2	45.1	44.0	35.0
1970–74	45.2	41.8	22.5	38.1	44.1	43.3	32.5
1975–79	44.0	41.6	22.3	38.0	43.8	43.1	30.8
1980–82	43.0	40.8	20.6	37.1	43.0	42.2	30.6

Notes: The U.K. data relate to full-time manual workers and are taken from each October's earnings and hours enquiry of the major industries. The data are published in various issues of the *Ministry of Labour Gazette* and of the *Department of Employment Gazette*. The United States' data derive from household interviews in the Current Population Survey and they measure the average hours actually worked (not those paid for) of male employees in nonagricultural industries at work. (Consequently, those absent from work because of illness, vacation, or strike are not represented in these figures.) For the years 1955–58, the data are published in the *Current Population Reports*, Labor Force Series P-50, issues number 63 (Table 3), 72 (Table 18), 85 (Table 18), and 89 (Table 24). For the years 1959–64, the data are from *Special Labor Force Reports*, Table D-7 of each issue, Report numbers 4, 14, 23, 31, 43, and 52. For the years 1965–82, the data are taken from each January's issue of *Employment and Earnings* which give the figures for the preceding year. Before 1967, the youngest age group relates to those aged 14–17 years and from 1967 it relates to 16–17 years.

workers aged 65 years and over who reveal a declining trend of about 0.3 hours per year over the 1956–1982 period.

Although the downward trend in weekly hours worked in the United States seems to describe the data up to 1940 and not after that date, the length of the work year may have fallen because of increases in paid vacations and holidays. The only consistent time-series data relating to this dimension of work of which I am aware are the occasional surveys of employee compensation, a summary of which is presented in Table 1.11. Although the data in this table suggest that hours actually worked have fallen compared with hours paid for, the recorded changes are small.[16]

British long-term experience with weekly hours worked has been similar to that for the United States. The standard working week for manual workers set down in various collective bargaining agreements ranged from 48 to 60 hours or more

[16] There exist several studies investigating whether the absence of a trend during the post World War II period in weekly hours worked is spurious. Jones' (1974) study may be most thorough, but anyway the conclusions of Kniesner (1976b) and Owen (1979) are similar: hours worked have fallen little or not at all during this period and this influence survives adjustments for paid vacations and holidays.

Table 1.10
United States and Britain: Estimates of trend (α) and cycle (β) in weekly hours worked by male employees.

	α	β	R^2	D–W
Britain, 1949–1981				
All adult manual workers	−0.073(0.083)	−0.082*(0.020)	0.34	1.81
United States, 1956–1982				
All	−0.075(0.055)	−0.163*(0.062)	0.22	2.29
14/16–17 years	−0.088(0.197)	−0.731*(0.223)	0.30	1.29
18–24 years	−0.145(0.081)	−0.328*(0.091)	0.34	1.51
25–44 years	−0.044(0.066)	−0.194*(0.074)	0.21	2.19
45–64 years	0.003(0.321)	−0.525(0.363)	0.08	2.95
≥ 65 years	−0.329*(0.088)	0.103(0.100)	0.04	2.05

Notes: Estimated standard errors are given in parentheses next to their associated regression coefficients. "D–W" is the Durbin–Watson statistic. For ease of reading, an asterisk has been placed next to those point estimates more than twice their estimated standard errors. The data sources are given in the notes beneath Table 1.9.

before World War I. This fell further to 44 and 45 hours after World War II. A comprehensive survey of hours actually worked by British manual workers was conducted in October 1938 by the Ministry of Labour. In the principal industries, it found that the average hours worked by adult male manual workers were 47.7 while the frequency distribution of hours worked was as follows: 15.5 percent of these employees worked less than 44 hours, 16.4 percent worked from 44 hours to less than 47 hours, 27.6 percent worked between 47 and 48 hours (inclusive), and 39.2 percent worked more than 48 hours.

The movement since 1938 in weekly hours worked by male manual workers is given in the first column of Table 1.9. Again, to determine whether or not a trend exists in these post World War II data, eq. (2) was fitted to the annual observations on hours worked from 1949 to 1981. As was the case when eq. (1) was fitted to the British male labor force participation rate, eq. (2) was estimated using as a cyclical indicator the deviation of the index of industrial production from its fitted linear trend. The ordinary least-squares estimates of eq. (2) fitted to the British data are given in the first line of Table 1.10 and they are similar to the U.S. results: there is a strong procyclical variation in hours worked in Britain and no significant time trend. The strong cyclical influence on hours worked probably accounts for much of the difference in the frequency distribution of hours between September 1968 and April 1981 as shown in Table 1.12. That is to say, the fraction of male employees working between 35 and 39 hours increased from 18.5 percent in September 1968 to 22.0 percent in April 1977 and to 28.3 percent in April 1981 while the percentage working in each of the categories above 42 hours decreased uniformly from 1968 to 1977 to 1981. However, these

Table 1.11
United States: Paid leave hours as a percentage of total hours paid for, 1958, 1966, 1977.

	1958	1966	1977
Manufacturing:			
Nonoffice workers	6	6	8.4
Office workers		8	10.5
All workers		7	9.0
Nonmanufacturing:			
Nonoffice workers		4	5.5
Office workers		7	8.9
All workers		5	6.9
All nonfarm industries:			
Nonoffice workers		5	6.6
Office workers		7	9.2
All workers		6	7.6

Notes: The 1958 data are from U.S. Department of Labor, *Composition of Payroll Hours in Manufacturing, 1958*, Bureau of Labor Statistics Bulletin number 1283, October 1960. The 1966 data are from U.S. Department of Labor, *Employee Compensation in the Private Nonfarm Economy, 1966*, Bureau of Labor Statistics Bulletin number 1627, June 1969. The 1977 data are from U.S. Department of Labor, *Employee Compensation in the Private Nonfarm Economy, 1977*, Bureau of Labor Statistics, Summary 80-5, April 1980.

years exhibited a growing slack in the level of aggregate business activity as indicated, for instance, by the male unemployment rate (seasonally unadjusted and including school leavers) which stood at 3.2 percent in September 1968, at 7.0 percent in April 1977, and at 12.6 percent in April 1981.

What is not reflected in these data on hours worked in a given week is the increasing length of paid vacations in Britain over the post-war period. I know of no data that document the number of days paid for, but not worked in Britain. However, the information in Table 1.13 suggests that there has been a substantial increase in paid vacations. These data are taken from national collective bargaining agreements and they concern the length of paid vacations to which covered workers are entitled. Whereas, in fact, annual paid vacations were unusual for manual workers in Britain before World War II, the data in Table 1.13 indicate that there have been substantial increases in the length of paid vacations during the last 30 years. The increases in paid vacations were especially pronounced during periods of government-mandated wage controls and incomes policies that diverted attention to less visible ways (than cash) of increasing employee compensation.[17]

The discussion above has documented the trends this century in male labor

[17]See Department of Employment, *Employment Gazette*, Vol. 89, No. 4, April 1981, p. 184.

Table 1.12
Britain: Percentage distribution of weekly hours worked by male employees in 1968, 1977, and 1981.

	September 1968	April 1977	April 1981
$0 < h \leq 24$	2.0	1.8	1.6
$24 < h \leq 30$	2.1	2.0	2.1
$30 < h \leq 35$	4.2	5.5	6.8
$35 < h \leq 37$	7.3	11.2	12.4
$37 < h \leq 39$	11.2	10.8	15.9
$39 < h \leq 40$	20.1	26.2	27.6
$40 < h \leq 42$	7.1	5.3	5.4
$42 < h \leq 44$	8.0	7.3	6.1
$44 < h \leq 46$	6.6	6.0	5.0
$46 < h \leq 48$	7.0	5.9	4.3
$48 < h \leq 50$	5.2	4.3	3.1
$50 < h \leq 54$	7.0	5.3	3.7
$54 < h \leq 60$	7.0	4.9	3.4
$60 < h \leq 70$	4.0	2.5	1.8
$70 < h$	2.0	1.0	0.8

Notes: These data cover all men (both manual and nonmanual workers) whose pay for the survey period was not affected by absence. The 1968 data are from Department of Employment and Productivity, *New Earnings Survey 1968*, H.M.S.O., 1970, Table 83, p. 120. The 1977 data are from Department of Employment, *New Earnings Survey 1977, Part A: Report and Key Results*, H.M.S.O., 1977, Table 27, p. A35. The 1981 data are from Department of Employment, *New Earnings Survey 1981, Part A: Report and Key Results*, H.M.S.O., 1981, Table 27, p. A90.

force participation rates and hours worked. Just as men have spent a declining fraction of their lives at work for pay, so have they spent an increasing fraction at school. Some evidence of this is provided by the cohort analyses in Tables 1.14 and 1.15. These data are taken from surveys in 1970 and in 1971 of men of different ages and they document the striking association between the age of the cohort and the years spent at school.[18]

2.2. *Cross-sectional variations in work behavior*

Some important variations in labor force participation across individual men are documented by the linear probability estimates in Table 1.16. These are reproduced from Bowen and Finegan's (1969) monumental work on the 1960 Census of Population. As is evident from Table 1.16, there is a strong positive relation-

[18] They are a biased indicator of the degree to which schooling levels completed have risen over time insofar as mortality rates are associated with years of schooling. On this association, see Grossman (1975).

Table 1.13
United Kingdom: Manual workers' basic paid vacation entitlements as set down in national collective bargaining agreements, 1951–1982.

Year	Percentage of workers with basic vacations of					
	< 2 weeks	2 weeks	Between 2 and 3 weeks	3 weeks	Between 3 and 4 weeks	≥ 4 weeks
1951	31	66	2	1		
1955	1	96	2	1		
1960		97	1	2		
1965		75	22	3		
1970		41	7	49	3	
1975		1	1	17	51	30
1980				2	24	74
1982				2	5	93

Notes: Until 1965, the column given as "3 weeks" is, in fact, "3 weeks and over". In addition to these annual vacations, workers are usually entitled to payment of wages for public or statutory holidays or days in lieu of these payments. The data for 1951–65 are from the Department of Employment and Productivity, *British Labour Statistics Historical Abstract 1886–1968*, London, H.M.S.O., 1971, Table 34, p. 91. Data for 1970 onwards are from various issues of the Department of Employment's *Gazette*.

Table 1.14
United States: Schooling completed by the male population in 1970 by age.

Years of age in 1970	Year of birth	Median years school completed	Percentage of cohort whose highest schooling levels completed were				
			≥ 4 years of college	≥ 2 years of college	≥ 4 years of high school	≥ 8 years of elementary school	≥ 5 years of elementary school
≥ 75	≤ 1895	8.3	5.3	8.8	20.9	57.1	79.4
70–74	1896–1900	8.6	6.2	10.1	24.5	64.1	85.3
65–69	1901–1905	8.8	7.4	11.8	27.6	68.1	88.0
60–64	1906–1910	9.6	8.7	13.9	34.7	75.1	91.5
55–59	1911–1915	10.7	9.3	14.9	41.4	79.8	93.4
50–54	1916–1920	12.0	10.8	17.2	49.7	84.7	95.0
45–49	1921–1925	12.2	14.1	21.2	55.6	87.1	95.7
40–44	1926–1930	12.2	16.4	23.7	57.3	88.4	96.4
35–39	1931–1935	12.4	18.6	26.2	64.3	90.2	96.8
30–34	1936–1940	12.5	18.5	26.6	68.9	92.7	97.6
25–29	1941–1945	12.6	19.5	29.6	74.2	94.7	98.2

Notes: These data are constructed from those given in Table 199 of U.S. Department of Commerce, Bureau of the Census, *1970 Census of Population*, Volume I, Characteristics of the Population, Part 1, U.S. Summary, Section 2, June 1973.

ship between participation and schooling: for prime-age males (that is, those aged 25–54 years), a person with 17 or more years of schooling has almost a 9 percent higher probability of being in the labor force than someone with 0–4 years of schooling who is otherwise identical in his observable characteristics. This participation–schooling relationship among older men is especially strong. For prime-age males, ceteris paribus, a white man is almost 2 percent more likely

Table 1.15
Britain: Highest educational qualification attained by male population in 1971 by age.

Years of age in 1971	Year of birth	Percentage of cohort whose highest educational qualifications were at the level of		
		"Higher education"	"Middle education"	"Lower education"
≥ 65	≤ 1906	5.1	14.9	80.0
60–64	1907–1911	7.6	23.6	68.8
50–59	1912–1921	6.1	25.8	68.1
40–49	1922–1931	10.7	27.2	62.1
30–39	1932–1941	14.2	33.2	52.6
25–29	1942–1946	13.6	41.9	44.5

Notes: The level "Higher education" includes university degrees, equivalent professional qualifications, and other qualifications beyond the GCE "A" level standard. "Middle education" includes any subjects passed at the GCE "A" level and "0" level plus clerical and commercial qualifications and apprenticeships. "Lower education" means no qualifications attained. The data are from Office of Population Censuses and Surveys, Social Survey Division, *The General Household Survey 1971*, Introductory Report, H.M.S.O., Table 7.15.

to be in the labor force than a black man. A married man with his spouse present is much more likely to be in the labor force (8 percent more likely for prime-age males, other things equal) than a man with a different marital status. Greater nonwage income is associated with lower participation and participation probabilities form an inverted U-shape with respect to age: they rise until 25 years of age, then remain constant until the middle-to-late fifties at which point they decline rapidly.

Some empirical regularities with respect to the hours worked by men are evident from the ordinary least-squares regression results presented in Table 1.17. These estimates describe the work behavior of 23059 men aged from 25 to 55 years of age at the time of the 1980 Census of Population.[19] The column "weekly hours" relates to the number of hours usually worked during those weeks the person worked in 1979; the column "weeks per year" relates to the number of weeks during 1979 in which a person did any work for pay or profit (including paid vacation and paid sick leave); and the column "annual hours" relates to the product for any person of "weekly hours" in 1979 and "weeks per year" in 1979.

[19]The sample of 23059 men was determined as follows. There are 94025 dwelling units included in the Public Use Sample Tape "C" sample nationwide file. Of these, 8,021 units were rejected because they were vacant, another 25725 units were rejected because no male was listed as household head (or, if a woman was listed as the household head, no husband or live-in partner was listed), another 22198 units were rejected because the male was not aged between 25 and 55 years (inclusive), another 1097 were rejected because the male received some farm income, and another 12933 were rejected because either the male's labor income was truncated (being less than $-9,995 or more than $75000) or the male's data on labor supply were missing. This yields a sample of 24051 men of whom 992 had zero hours of work in 1979.

Table 1.16
Ordinary least-squares estimates of labor force participation equations fitted to data on individual men from the 1/1000 sample of the 1960 U.S. Census of Population.

	(1)	(2)	(3)	(4)
Age-group	18–24 years	25–54 years	55–64 years	65–74 years
nobs	3095.0	22 415.0	4967.0	3392.0
modv	94.0	96.7	85.2	38.7
Estimates of:				
Intercept	79.3	83.7	73.5	48.4
Years of schooling				
0–4	Reference	Reference	Reference	Reference
5–7	5.3(3.3)	4.1(0.7)	5.4(1.8)	5.9(2.3)
8	9.4(3.2)	5.2(0.7)	10.5(1.7)	14.5(2.3)
9–11	9.2(2.9)	6.3(0.6)	13.4(1.8)	17.9(2.7)
12	10.3(2.9)	6.9(0.6)	13.5(2.0)	20.4(2.9)
13–15	6.5(3.1)	8.1(0.7)	17.2(2.2)	25.1(3.5)
16	11.2(3.5)	8.5(0.7)	18.0(2.7)	31.9(4.5)
≥17	5.6(5.3)	8.8(0.7)	26.6(3.1)	39.7(5.5)
Ethnicity				
Black	Reference	Reference	} Reference	} Reference
Other nonwhite	1.2(4.9)	2.7(1.3)		
White	1.5(1.3)	1.8(0.4)	1.9(1.7)	0.5(2.8)
Marital status				
Never married	} −6.7(0.9)	} Reference	Reference	Reference
Separated or divorced			4.0(2.4)	1.7(4.0)
Widowed			0.7(2.7)	1.2(3.5)
Married spouse present	Reference	7.8(0.3)	12.6(1.7)	12.7(2.9)
Nonwage income				
< $500		Reference	Reference	Reference
$500–999		−4.1(0.5)	−19.0(1.6)	−31.1(2.3)
$1000–1999		−10.1(0.7)	−35.1(1.8)	−39.9(1.9)
$2000–2999		−13.9(1.2)	−34.0(2.6)	−44.8(2.5)
$3000–4999		−7.0(1.2)	−36.7(3.0)	−55.2(3.3)
≥ $5000		−13.2(1.4)	−30.3(3.1)	−40.9(4.3)
Years of age				
18/55/65	Reference		Reference	Reference
19/56/66	7.0(1.9)		−1.6(1.9)	0.5(2.9)
20/57/67	7.5(1.8)		−1.5(2.0)	−1.6(2.9)
21/58/68	10.5(1.8)		−2.0(2.0)	−2.4(3.0)
22/59/69	8.2(1.8)		−1.3(1.9)	−4.7(3.1)
23/60/70	11.3(1.8)		−5.5(2.0)	−6.4(3.1)
24/61/71	8.6(1.8)		−6.0(2.1)	−12.2(3.1)
62/72			−5.6(2.1)	−9.2(3.3)
63/73			−10.8(2.1)	−8.5(3.5)
64/74			−9.1(2.1)	−13.8(3.5)
25–34		Reference		
35–44		−0.4(0.3)		
45–54		−1.2(0.3)		
$\hat{F}$ ratio	10.5	92.2	45.4	40.0

Notes: These estimates are from Bowen and Finegan (1969, Tables A-38, A-1, A-14, and A-15). Standard errors are given in parentheses next to estimated coefficients. The number of observations is given by "nobs" and the mean of the dependent variable is given by "modv". All the variables above are in the form of dummy variables with "Reference" indicating the category omitted from the list of variables. Under the group of variables "Years of age" the first column (18,19,20,etc.) relates to the 18–24 year olds in column (1), the second column (55,56,57,etc.) relates to the 55–64 year olds in column (3), and the third column (65,66,67,etc.) relates to the 65–74 year olds in column (4). The group described as "Separated or divorced" under "Marital status" includes married men with their spouses absent. "Nonwage income" represents the sum of rental income, interest, dividends, alimony, pensions, and welfare payments.

Table 1.17
Ordinary least-squares estimates of male hours and weeks worked equations fitted to data from 1/1000 sample of the 1980 U.S. Census of Population.

Independent variable		Dependent variable		
Mean and standard deviation	Definition	Weekly hours	Weeks per year	Annual hours
	Constant	36.2	34.91	1194.88
9.53 (10.00)	Average hourly earnings in dollars	−0.226 (0.006)	−0.107 (0.005)	−13.78 (0.36)
0.477 (2.318)	Interest, dividend, and rental income in thousands of dollars	0.089 (0.026)	0.010 (0.022)	4.62 (1.57)
0.307 (1.502)	Other income of the individual in thousands of dollars	−0.214 (0.039)	−1.141 (0.034)	−55.38 (2.40)
5.978 (7.547)	Family income minus male head's in thousands of dollars	−0.027 (0.008)	0.001 (0.007)	−1.17 (0.52)
37.98 (8.89)	Age in years	0.385 (0.072)	0.471 (0.062)	38.33 (4.40)
1521.3 (704.0)	Age squared in years	−0.005 (0.001)	−0.005 (0.001)	−0.43 (0.06)
0.46 (0.50)	1 = Completed high school	1.098 (0.229)	2.200 (0.198)	132.61 (14.06)
0.46 (0.50)	1 = Completed any college education	2.152 (0.237)	3.020 (0.205)	219.20 (14.57)
0.43 (0.74)	1 = Any children aged 0–6 years	0.199 (0.090)	0.237 (0.078)	20.70 (5.55)
0.82 (1.06)	1 = Any children aged 7–16 years	0.133 (0.062)	0.044 (0.054)	7.55 (3.83)
0.84 (0.36)	1 = Married and spouse present	1.068 (0.197)	1.803 (0.170)	121.47 (12.09)
0.02 (0.15)	1 = Married and spouse absent	1.044 (0.424)	0.112 (0.366)	59.41 (26.04)
0.05 (0.21)	1 = Hispanic	−1.981 (0.284)	−1.711 (0.245)	−160.51 (17.44)
0.07 (0.26)	1 = Black	−2.736 (0.229)	−1.549 (0.198)	−190.34 (14.05)
0.02 (0.15)	1 = Not White nor Black nor Hispanic	−1.508 (0.390)	−1.489 (0.337)	−130.32 (23.94)
0.06 (0.24)	1 = Self-employed	4.473 (0.246)	−0.260 (0.213)	219.20 (15.12)
0.19 (0.39)	1 = Employed by local, state, or Federal government	−1.133 (0.152)	0.274 (0.131)	−43.94 (9.30)
0.05 (0.22)	1 = Health disability	−1.342 (0.262)	−5.312 (0.226)	−262.86 (16.05)
0.83 (0.38)	1 = Lived in a metropolitan area	−0.518 (0.160)	0.679 (0.138)	2.68 (9.79)
0.06 (0.23)	1 = Lived in New England	0.400 (0.289)	0.095 (0.250)	26.98 (17.76)

Table 1.17 continued

Independent variable		Dependent variable		
Mean and standard deviation	Definition	Weekly hours	Weeks per year	Annual hours
0.16	1 = Lived in Mid-Atlantic	−0.434	0.608	4.81
(0.37)	states	(0.213)	(0.183)	(13.04)
0.19	1 = Lived in East North	0.731	0.639	64.99
(0.39)	Central states	(0.205)	(0.177)	(12.60)
0.07	1 = Lived in West North	0.546	0.599	53.11
(0.26)	Central states	(0.267)	(0.231)	(16.40)
0.16	1 = Lived in South Atlantic	0.475	0.897	62.03
(0.37)	states	(0.214)	(0.185)	(13.14)
0.06	1 = Lived in East South	0.065	0.253	20.39
(0.23)	Central states	(0.290)	(0.251)	(17.85)
0.10	1 = Lived in West South	1.492	0.879	112.58
(0.30)	Central states	(0.241)	(0.208)	(14.82)
0.05	1 = Lived in Mountain states	0.143	0.251	21.34
(0.23)		(0.294)	(0.254)	(18.05)
	R^2	0.096	0.117	0.130

Notes: The mean (and standard deviation in parentheses) of weekly hours is 43.41 (9.26), that of weeks worked is 48.89 (8.08), and that of annual hours is 2131.07 (579.26). There are 23 059 observations in each regression equation. Another 992 observations had zero annual hours of work so the labor force participation rate of this group was 95.9 percent. The East North Central states are Ohio, Indiana, Illinois, Michigan, and Wisconsin. The West North Central states are Iowa, Minnesota, Missouri, Kansas, Nebraska, South Dakota, and North Dakota. The East South Central states are Kentucky, Tennessee, Alabama, and Mississippi. The West South Central states are Arkansas, Louisiana, Oklahoma, and Texas. The omitted region consists of California, Oregon, Washington, Alaska, and Hawaii.

The notes to Table 1.17 provide mean values and standard deviations of these variables. According to these estimates, a dollar higher average hourly earnings is associated with 14 fewer hours worked per year, the responsiveness of weekly hours being greater than the responsiveness of weeks per year. The behavioral implications of this negative hours–earnings association are not clear, however: the interviewees are asked their earnings (wage income plus self-employment income) in 1979 and the variable "average hourly earnings" consists of annual earnings divided by annual hours of work; consequently, any errors in measuring hours of work are communicated to the measure of average hourly earnings. Increases in interest, dividend, and rental income are positively (though weakly) associated with hours of work while other income of the individual (mainly public assistance and social security and, as such, it is typically work-related income) is negatively associated with work behavior. The hours–age relationship forms an inverted U-shape with the maximum occurring around 44 years of age. Men with higher schooling levels completed work longer hours as do fathers with

Table 1.18
Percentage distribution of hours worked in 1974 according to hours worked in 1967.

		Hours in 1967							
		0–1499	1500–1849	1850–2149	2150–2499	2500–2999	3000–3499	≥ 3500	
Percent of observations in 1967		5.5	7.0	29.0	23.7	19.3	9.4	6.0	100
Hours in 1974	0–1499	35.7	16.7	10.1	8.7	5.0	8.1	7.4	
	1500–1849	12.4	26.1	10.5	10.7	8.5	2.5	7.6	
	1850–2149	14.7	31.7	49.5	28.2	20.7	17.3	11.9	
	2150–2499	14.1	15.1	18.1	28.6	27.4	15.3	9.7	
	2500–2999	13.5	4.8	7.8	16.1	23.3	30.2	17.1	
	3000–3499	5.9	3.0	2.4	5.8	9.6	18.0	23.1	
	≥ 3500	3.7	2.6	1.6	1.8	5.6	8.6	23.2	
Total		100	100	100	100	100	100	100	

Notes: The underlying data consist of 2209 men all of whom were married in the first year of interview (1968) and all of whom worked no less than 250 hours in both 1967 and 1974.

younger children, married men, non-Hispanic white men, self-employed men, men who claimed a health disability, and men who were not government workers.[20] Some marked regional variations in hours worked are evident. It is important to observe that only between 9.7 percent and 13.0 percent of the sample variation in these measures of work behavior is accounted for by the least-squares combination of variables in Table 1.17. Indeed, the inability of empirical studies of working hours to remove anything more than a relatively small fraction of the observed variation in a large sample's hours is striking.

Notwithstanding the popular notion that, each and every year, virtually all men work 2000 hours per year (40 hours per week and 50 weeks per year), in fact there exists a substantial amount of variation across individuals in their hours of work and also important variations for many individuals from year to year. Some indication of the temporal variations in annual hours of work is provided by the data in Table 1.18 which are taken from a paper by Hill and Hoffman (1977) that also analyzes men from the Michigan Panel. The data in Table 1.18 describe 2209 men all of whom were married in the first year of interview (1968) and all of whom were at work for at least 250 hours in both the years 1967 and 1974. The first column of Table 1.18 shows that 5.5 percent of these men worked 0–1499 hours in 1967; of these men who worked 0–1499 hours in 1967, 35.7 percent also

[20] In the dummy variable categories, the omitted groups are men who did not complete high school, men without any children, unmarried men, non-Hispanic white men, men neither self-employed nor working for the government, men with no health disability, men not living in a metropolitan area, and men living in California, Oregon, Washington, Alaska, and Hawaii.

worked 0–1499 hours in 1974. The main diagonal in Table 1.18 tends to have larger entries than the off-diagonal terms, but this is by no means always the case: thus, of those who worked 2500–2999 hours in 1967, 23.3 percent worked the same hours in 1974, whereas 27.4 percent worked 2150–2499 hours, an indication of some regression towards the mean. The authors describe these changes as "pervasive" and, indeed, 51.1 percent of the variance of the logarithmic change in these men's annual earnings between 1967 and 1974 was attributable alone to the variance of the logarithmic change in hours worked.

3. Conceptual framework

3.1. *The canonical model*

The model that guides most economists' analyses of the determinants of the supply of working hours derives most directly from Hicks' (1946) paragraph 11 of his Mathematical Appendix. According to this characterization, the labor supply function is derived from a general model of consumer demand in which a fixed endowment of a commodity is divided into one part for sale on the market and another part reserved for direct consumption. In this instance, the endowment consists of a fixed block of time, T, that in the simplest of cases is to be divided between hours worked in the market, h, and hours spent in other activities, $l: T = h + l$. The *reservation demand* for hours of "leisure", l, simply consists of what is left over from market sales of h. In this canonical model, there is no savings decision to be made and the individual is fully informed of all the values of the relevant variables and parameters. An individual with personal characteristics A (such as his age or race) possesses a well-behaved (real-valued, continuous, quasi-concave) utility function defined over his consumption of commodities, x, and his hours of work, h:

$$U = U(x, h; A, \varepsilon), \tag{3}$$

where ε stands for the individual's "tastes". Whether ε is called a taste component or an individual's "ability in home production" or whatever, the essential point is that, unlike the variables in A, ε is unobserved to the researcher. In accordance with the empirical findings reported above whereby a substantial fraction of the variation in hours of work across individuals is not removed by variables observed by the economist, the presence of ε in the utility function allows for individuals to differ from one another in ways not observed by the researcher.

The partial derivative of U in eq. (3) with respect to x is assumed to be positive and that with respect to h is assumed to be negative, at least in the neighborhood of the observed hours of work.[21] If throughout the analysis the relative prices of the different commodities do not change, then x represents a Hicksian composite commodity. The individual sells his services to the consumer in the product market either directly when he is "self-employed" or indirectly when he is employed by a firm to contribute towards producing a commodity. In either case, the individual's total compensation, c, for his market work depends positively upon how much of his time is alloted to this activity: $c = c(h)$. In the simplest of cases, each hour of work is rewarded at the same fixed rate, w, and $c(h) = wh$. The average and marginal payment for his work time are now the same and, if p denotes the fixed per unit price of the bundle of commodities x and if y represents income independent of the working decision, then the individual's budget constraint is linear and homogeneous of degree zero in p, w, and y:

$$px = wh + y. \tag{4}$$

The individual is assumed to do the best he can given the constraints he faces. Or, more formally, the individual chooses values of $x > 0$ and $h \geq 0$ that maximize eq. (3) subject to the budget constraint (4).[22] Observe that this problem has been characterized in terms of a single individual's objective function and budget constraint. This is by no means necessary. Suppose this individual's utility depends upon his spouse's market work time (h_2) in addition to his own work time (h_1):

$$U = U(x_1, h_1, h_2;\ A, \varepsilon). \tag{5}$$

If his spouse's utility function contains the same arguments and if the two of them pool their incomes and expenditures,

$$p_1x_1 + p_2x_2 = w_1h_1 + w_2h_2 + y, \tag{6}$$

in the simple case of a linear budget constraint where w_1 and w_2 denote the

[21]Another characterization of the problem involves defining the utility function over activities that are produced by a household production function whose inputs are purchased goods and time. In Becker's (1965) formulation, time at market work does not directly enter the utility function at all and so the question does not arise of whether U is decreasing in h. See Atkinson and Stern (1979) and Chapter 4 by Gronan in this Handbook.

[22]The problem is sometimes written in terms of leisure, l, and the endowment of time, T, by having the individual select $x > 0$ and $l > 0 \leq T$ to maximize $U(x, l;\ A, \varepsilon)$ subject to $px + wl = wT + y = I$, where I is called full income. This formulation in an empirical context poses the problem of what value to assign to T, the results not being invariant to this assignment. I prefer the formulation of the problem in the text that involves variables whose counterparts in the data are more easily defined.

hourly wage rates paid to individuals 1 and 2, respectively, and x_1 and x_2 represent the consumption of commodities by individuals 1 and 2, respectively, then the problem becomes one of selecting x_1, x_2, h_1, and h_2 to maximize the utility functions of the two individuals subject to their joint budget constraint (6). As stated, this is a bargaining problem and typically the solution may be satisfied with many different combinations of x_1, x_2, h_1, and h_2. To determine which of the many possibilities will obtain requires the introduction of particular behavioral postulates that yield specific solutions.[23] The usual method of handling these problems is to assume that the social choice conditions for the existence of a well-behaved aggregate (household) utility function have been met or that the household's utility function is identical with that of the "head" of the household who integrates the welfare of all the household's members [see Samuelson (1956) and Becker (1974)]. Under these circumstances, x_1, x_2, h_1, and h_2 are chosen to maximize eq. (5) subject to the budget constraint (6). Clearly, in these household models, each individual's allocation of his work time depends upon not only his own wage rate, but also the wage rate of his spouse.

Return to the formulation whereby a single individual selects $x>0$ and $h\geq 0$ to maximize $U(x, h;\ A, \varepsilon)$ subject to a linear budget constraint $px = wh + y$. It is important to distinguish the characteristics of the interior solution for hours of work, $h>0$, from the corner solution, $h=0$. In the case of the individual selecting a positive number of hours to supply to the market, the first-order condition for a constrained maximum[24] requires that commodities and hours of work be chosen such that the negative of the marginal rate of substitution (m) of working hours for commodities equals the real wage (w/p):

$$\frac{w}{p} = -m(x, h;\ A, \varepsilon) = -\frac{\partial U/\partial h}{\partial U/\partial x}. \tag{7}$$

The reduced form equations, the commodity demand and working hours supply functions, are derived by solving eq. (7) jointly with the budget constraint (4):

$$\left.\begin{aligned} x &= x(p, w, y;\ A, \varepsilon)\\ h &= h(p, w, y;\ A, \varepsilon)\end{aligned}\right\},\quad \text{if } h>0. \tag{8}$$

The properties of this hours of work equation are discussed below. This interior solution for hours of work may be expressed differently by making use of the concept of the individual's reservation wage, w^*. The real reservation wage, w^*/p, is the slope of an indifference curve between commodity consumption and

[23] For instance, Manser and Brown (1979) assume a Nash solution to this bargaining problem.

[24] The assumption that the utility function is quasi-concave ensures the satisfaction of the second-order conditions for a constrained maximum.

hours at work evaluated at $h=0$ and, for any given individual, typically the value of this reservation wage will vary from one indifference curve to another, i.e. the reservation wage will depend upon x and so indirectly upon y for any given A and $\varepsilon: w^*(y, A, \varepsilon)$. Equivalently, the real reservation wage is equal to the negative of the marginal rate of substitution of working hours for commodities evaluated at $h=0$: $w^*/p = -m(x, 0;\ A, \varepsilon)$. The reservation wage is the individual's implicit value of his time when at the margin between participating in the labor market and not participating.[25] If, at that margin, the market's valuation of his time, w, exceeds the individual's implicit value of his time, w^*, then he will participate in the labor market and supply a positive number of hours of market work. Then eqs. (7) and (8) will hold enabling us to write:

$$\text{if } w > w^*, \quad \text{then } h = h(p, w, y;\ A, \varepsilon) > 0. \tag{9}$$

On the other hand, if at the margin between participating and not participating in the labor market the individual places a greater value on an extra unit of his time than does the market (that is, if $w^* > w$), then naturally the individual will reserve his entire allocation of time for himself and the solution to the constrained maximization problem will be a corner $h=0$. Consequently, we may write:

$$\text{if } w \leq w^*, \quad \text{then } h = 0. \tag{10}$$

Consider now the properties of the labor supply function $h = h(p, w, y;\ A, \varepsilon)$ derived in eq. (8). The zero homogeneity property that was introduced through the budget constraint carries over to the commodity demand and labor supply functions: a given proportionate change in p, w, and y leaves the optimizing values of x and h in eqs. (8) unchanged. A second property of the labor supply function so derived is manifested when examining the effect of a small increase in w on the supply of h: $\partial h/\partial w$. The Slutsky equation decomposes this effect into a substitution effect, s, and an income effect, $h \cdot \partial h/\partial y$:

$$\frac{\partial h}{\partial w} = s + h\frac{\partial h}{\partial y}. \tag{11}$$

The substitution effect, s, measures the utility-constant (or income-compensated) effect of an increase in the wage rate on the individual's hours of work and the theory of constrained utility maximization outlined above restricts s to be positive: an increase in the wage rate raises the price of an hour not worked in the market and, at the same level of utility, this induces less consumption of non-market time and more time allocated to market work. At the same time, an

[25] Or the real reservation wage, w^*/p is the value of the real wage such that hours of work are zero exactly, i.e. from eq. (8), $h(1, w^*/p, y;\ A, \varepsilon) = 0$.

increase in the wage rate augments the individual's wealth allowing him to consume more of those things that increase his utility and to consume less of those things that generate disutility (such as hours of market work). This is the income effect of a wage increase on hours of market work and it is given in eq. (11) by $h\cdot\partial h/\partial y$. This term is negative provided nonmarket time is a normal commodity. Consequently, the sign of the uncompensated effect of an increase in the individual's wage rate on his hours of work [the left-hand side of eq. (11)] is indeterminate in sign and depends on the relative magnitudes of the substitution and income effects.

As in other constrained maximizing problems where the constraint is linear, the optimizing eqs. (8) possess a symmetry property according to which $(\partial x/\partial w)_{\bar{u}}=-(\partial h/\partial p)_{\bar{u}}$, where the $\bar{u}$ subscript denotes that these derivatives involve "pure" price changes, i.e. they are evaluated with utility held constant. In addition, under these circumstances of an interior solution to the maximization problem where the constraint is linear and the utility function is quasi-concave, the derived hours of work equation will be a *continuous* function of the budget constraint variables.

Frequently, eq. (11) is expressed in terms of elasticities:

$$E=E^*+(mpe), \tag{12}$$

where $E=(\partial h/\partial w)(w/h)\gtrless 0$ is the uncompensated wage elasticity of hours of work, $E^*=(sw)/h>0$ is the income-compensated wage elasticity, and $mpe=w\cdot\partial h/\partial y$ is the marginal propensity to earn out of nonwage income. The second term on the right-hand side, mpe, is often described in the empirical literature as the "total income elasticity".[26] If both commodities and nonworking time are "normal" (i.e. if both $\partial x/\partial y>0$ and $-\partial h/\partial y>0$), then the mpe is less than zero but greater than minus unity.[27] If nonworking time is "inferior", then a dollar increase in nonwage income increases the consumption of commodities by more than one dollar.

Substitute the optimizing commodity demand and labor supply functions (8) into the utility function (3) to express the individual's maximized utility as an indirect function of commodity prices, the wage rate, and nonlabor income:

$$V=V(p,w,y;\;A,\varepsilon). \tag{13}$$

This indirect utility function also possesses the zero homogeneity property in p, w, and y: because an equiproportionate change in p, w, and y leaves the optimizing x and h unchanged according to (8), so must the maximized value of

[26] It may be written as the product of $(wh)/y$ and $(\partial h/\partial y)(y/h)$.

[27] Differentiating the budget constraint with respect to y (and in so doing recognizing the dependence of x and h on y) yields the Engel aggregation condition $p(\partial x/\partial y)-w(\partial h/\partial y)=1$.

utility be unaltered. It is straightforward to show that $\partial V/\partial p = -\lambda x$, $\partial V/\partial w = \lambda h$, and $\partial V/\partial y = \lambda$, where λ is the marginal utility of nonlabor income when evaluating the utility function at its optimum so that, combining these results,

$$
\begin{aligned}
-\frac{\partial V/\partial p}{\partial V/\partial y} &= x(p, w, y;\ A, \varepsilon),\\
\frac{\partial V/\partial w}{\partial V/\partial y} &= h(p, w, y;\ A, \varepsilon).
\end{aligned}
\tag{14}
$$

These equations, Roy's Identity, imply that the functional form of the commodity demand and labor supply equations may be derived relatively easily once a particular form of the indirect utility function, eq. (13), has been specified.[28]

3.2. Aggregation

The theory outlined above applies to a single individual. It has often been applied to data that have been aggregated across individuals. Thus, some claim to have estimated the income and substitution effects (or the net wage effect $\partial h/\partial w$) of eq. (8) by using data across industries or occupations and by specifying the dependent variable as the average hours worked of individuals in a given industry or occupation. [For instance, Metcalf, Nickell, and Richardson (1976) and S. Rosen (1969).] Others use time-series observations on average hours worked by all employees (both male and female) in the economy to fit eq. (8). [For instance, Abbott and Ashenfelter (1976, 1979), Barnett (1979, 1981), Darrough (1977), and Phlips (1978).]

There are two issues to address. The first one assumes all individuals occupy an interior solution to their constrained maximization problem and enquires into the conditions under which each individual's labor supply function can be aggregated into a macro labor supply function that possesses the properties of eq. (8). The second and more relevant issue looks into the aggregation problem when some individuals are at a corner solution and others are at an interior solution to their maximization problem.

[28] The dual to the budget-constrained utility maximization problem characterizes the individual as selecting x and h to minimize the net cost, $px - wh$, of attaining a prescribed level of utility. The reduced form equations corresponding to this problem are the utility-constant commodity demand and labor supply functions and if these functions are substituted back into the objective function, $px - wh$, the net expenditure function is derived.

The first issue is not identical to the standard problem in the consumer demand literature because in that literature all consumers are assumed to face the same commodity prices whereas in the labor supply context one price, the wage rate, varies across individuals. The papers listed above using aggregate data to estimate labor supply functions have specified as arguments some average of the wage rates of the workers and an average nonwage income. Therefore, consider the case in which the arithmetic mean of these variables is used in a macro labor earnings equation and in which the macro earnings equation is to be derived by aggregating each worker's labor earnings function. In these circumstances, each worker's *mpe* (marginal propensity to earn $= w \cdot \partial h / \partial y$) must be the same and it must be independent of the wage rate and nonwage income. In addition, the commodity demand functions must be linear in both wages and nonwage income. [See Deaton and Muellbauer (1980, pp. 159–161) and Muellbauer (1981).] These are nontrivial restrictions on the form of the labor supply and commodity demand equations although they do not rule out some interesting cases.[29]

The second aggregation problem has more serious implications and to appreciate these difficulties let us invoke a set of extreme assumptions, namely, that a population of individuals is identical in all characteristics observed by the economist (i.e. they have the same y and A and face the same p and w), but they have different values of the unobserved variable ε. Let $f(\varepsilon)$ be the density of ε in the population. These differences in ε generate a distribution of reservation wages across these individuals. Suppose this distribution of reservation wages is described by the density function $\phi(w^*)$ and suppose $\Phi(w^*)$ is the cumulative distribution corresponding to the density function. The cumulative distribution function $\Phi(\overline{w}^*)$ is interpreted as giving for any value $\overline{w}^*$ the probability of the event "$w^* \leq \overline{w}^*$". The proportion of these individuals who offer positive hours of work to the labor market consists of those whose values of w^* satisfy eq. (9), that is, those for whom $w^* < w$. Equivalently, the labor force participation rate (π) of this group is simply the cumulative distribution of w^* evaluated at $w^* = w$:

$$\pi(p, w, y, A) = \Phi(w; p, y, A),$$

where the dependence of the labor force participation rate on the variables assumed to be the same in this hypothetical population (namely, p, w, y, and A) has been made explicit. Because the cumulative distribution function is necessarily a monotone nondecreasing function [i.e. $\Phi(\underline{w}^*) \leq \Phi(\overline{w}^*)$ for $\underline{w}^* < \overline{w}^*$], an increase in the wage rate offered to these individuals cannot reduce the labor force participation rate:

$$\frac{\partial \pi}{\partial w} = \frac{\partial \Phi(w)}{\partial w} = \phi(w) \geq 0.$$

[29] The labor supply equation derived from a Stone–Geary utility function is a special case of the class of permissible functions that aggregate. The more general class accommodates a wider range of substitution possibilities than does the Stone–Geary.

Exactly how much the labor force participation rate increases (if at all) will depend upon the shape of the density function $\phi(w^*)$ in the neighborhood of $w^* = w$.[30]

The variable most often used in studies of labor supply with aggregated data measures the average hours worked per employee. This may be written

$$\mathscr{E}(h|w > w^*) = \frac{\int h(p, w, y; A, \varepsilon) f(\varepsilon) \mathrm{d}\varepsilon}{\pi(p, w, y, A)},$$

where the integration is over all those at work and where the hours of work function is that corresponding to the interior solution of the constrained utility maximization problem, eq. (8). Unless the conditioning event $w > w^*$ is satisfied for the entire population, i.e. unless $\pi = 1$, the partial derivatives of $\mathscr{E}(h|w > w^*)$ are not the same as the partial derivatives of eq. (8), $h(p, w, y; A, \varepsilon)$, and it is the latter to which the income and substitution effects outlined in Section 3.1 relate. Studies that regress average hours worked per worker on average wage rates and nonwage income and that interpret the resulting estimates in terms of income and substitution effects are compounding the effects of changes in these variables on (1) the hours worked by those who are at work both before and after these changes with the effects on (2) the composition of the population between workers and non-workers.

These problems of aggregating over individuals some of whom are occupying interior solutions to their constrained utility maximization problem and others corner solutions are likely to be more innocuous for studies restricted to prime-age males (for whom π does not fall far short of unity) than for those relating to young men, older men, and women. The aggregate time-series studies mentioned above, however, are fitted to data describing all workers, male and female, young and old, urban and rural and for the entire adult population, of course, the labor force participation rate has been substantially less than unity (see table 1.5). At this grand level of aggregation, there are the additional problems raised by the fact that the microeconometric evidence suggests differences in the utility functions of men and women even after allowing for differences in the unobserved components ε. So even though during this century the labor force participation rate of all adults in the United States has changed relatively little, the composition of the labor force has changed considerably: according to the U.S. decennial Censuses, whereas in 1900 some 18 percent of the labor force were women, in

[30] Thus, while an increase in w may increase or may decrease hours worked per employee, an increase in w cannot decrease the fraction of the population at work. On this, see Lewis (1967), Ben Porath (1973), and Heckman (1978). The distinction between the labor force and the number employed is not crucial to this argument. Whether hours spent searching for a job is included in the definition of the offer to sell hours or it is excluded (so that π measures the fraction of the population who are employed), this does not affect the substance of the argument.

1970 the figure had more than doubled to 37 percent. These problems of deriving meaningful behavioral parameters from aggregate time-series data are further aggravated by the difficulties that arise when individuals face different *nonlinear* budget constraints (discussed in Section 3.3) and when the conditions are almost certainly not satisfied for the identification from these data of a labor supply function – after all, while some are regressing hours per worker on the average wage rate and interpreting the results in the terms of the income and substitution effects of a labor supply equation, others are taking virtually the same aggregate data, running very similar regression equations, and interpreting the results in terms of the parameters of a structural labor demand function! Both groups of researchers tend to find a negative partial correlation between hours and wage rates: one group interprets this as a negatively-inclined labor supply function while the other group confirms the existence of an inelastic labor demand function![31] The inescapable conclusion is that the equations fitted to aggregate time-series data are not to be regarded as supplying meaningful evidence on the parameters of behavioral hours of work equations and so, in evaluating the empirical work in Section 4 below, I omit a discussion of the estimates from aggregated data.

A somewhat different set of aggregation issues arises in those few studies that use as the measure of labor supply not average hours worked, but the labor force participation rate of different cities. This procedure was employed by Mincer (1962) in his influential work on the labor supply of married women. He cast the wife's decision-making in a family context and he proposed and implemented a specification that distinguished more clearly than had previous researchers between the income and substitution effects operating on the wife's behavior. In his application, he used as his measure of labor supply the labor force participation rates of married women across different metropolitan areas of the United States. This use of aggregate participation rates as the measure of labor supply was followed in a number of subsequent studies, some of them dealing with the labor supply of men.[32] In these papers, the authors have often interpreted the coefficients on the wage rate and nonwage income variables in terms of the derivatives

[31]Some of the labor demand studies use hours per worker [e.g. Nadiri and Rosen (1974)] as the variable to be explained while others use total manhours [e.g. Sargent (1978)]. In either case an identification problem arises. As an example, compare the work of Abbott and Ashenfelter (1976, 1979) with that of Coen and Hickman (1970). Both use highly aggregated annual observations on variables covering a similar period – from 1929 to 1967 in the case of Abbott and Ashenfelter and from 1924 to 1965 (excluding 1941 to 1948) in the case of Coen and Hickman. Abbott and Ashenfelter maintain they are estimating a labor supply equation in a system of consumer demand equations while Coen and Hickman maintain they are estimating a labor demand equation in a system of input demand functions. In fact, both sets of authors seek to explain first-differences in hours worked, in labor earnings, or in manhours worked. Abbott and Ashenfelter (1979) estimate an uncompensated wage elasticity of the supply of hours worked of -0.07 for the linear expenditure system and of -0.14 for their form of the Rotterdam model. Coen and Hickman's preferred estimate of the elasticity of the demand for manhours with respect to wages is -0.19.

[32]See Ashenfelter and Heckman (1974), Bowen and Finegan (1964, 1969), Greenhalgh (1979), and Kosters (1966, 1969).

for the average individual of the hours of work eq. (8) expressed as a fraction of total time available. What justification can be provided for this?[33]

Assume that the period relevant to the constrained utility maximization problem is the individual's lifetime so that the budget constraint variables are defined in terms of their "permanent" values. The individual then determines the proportion of his life to be spent at market work, the particular timing of that participation being determined (it is assumed) by factors orthogonal to the labor supply problem. In this case, among a group of individuals with the same p, w, and y, the probability that one of them is at market work is the same as the proportion of available lifetime hours allocated to market work. What is crucial in this chain of reasoning is that the proportion of his lifetime supplied to market work (equal by assumption to the participation rate) should correspond to an interior solution to the constrained maximization problem for *all* individuals in the relevant population. Otherwise, instead of eq. (8) being applicable to all individuals, it holds for only a subset of the population with the remainder described by a corner solution, namely eq. (10). In fact, virtually all men in the United States are in the labor force at least part of their lives: according to the 1970 U.S. Census of Population, of all men aged 55 years and over who were not in the labor force during the Census week of 1970 and who responded to the question concerning their last year worked, a little over 1 percent had never worked at all. Although all but a tiny fraction of men work in the market at some stage in their life, there remain a number of heroic assumptions in this chain of reasoning – the particular timing of a person's participation is unlikely to be uncorrelated with the permanent budget constraint variables nor in many applications of this procedure do the authors exercise great care in distinguishing permanent budget constraint variables from their currently observed counterparts – such that it is difficult to accept the interpretation of the coefficients on the wage rate and nonwage income variables in cross-city labor force participation rate equations as the parameters on an hours of work function such as eq. (8).

3.3. *Nonlinear budget constraint*

Now return to the analysis of the individual's allocation of time and consumption. Section 3.1 assumed the simplest form for the budget constraint according to which each and every hour supplied by the individual to the market is rewarded at the fixed rate w. This assumption does not require that each employer does nothing more than specify for each job a fixed wage per hour, leaving the individual employee to choose how many hours he wishes to work. Even if each employer specified not merely the wage rate but also the number of hours each employee is expected to work, provided the wage offer does not vary

[33] The argument that follows is taken from Heckman (1978).

systematically with the stipulated hours and provided the entire range of hours of work is covered by the employers' offers, then a continuous linear budget constraint arises from the aggregation over many employers' wage-hours packages.

Nevertheless, there seem to be important instances in which a continuous, linear budget constraint does not accurately describe an individual's work-income opportunities and as a result the wage rate can no longer be assumed exogenous to the individual. For instance, the presence of quasi-fixed hiring and training costs that are more closely related to the number of employees rather than to their total hours worked encourages firms to offer higher wage rates for longer hours worked per employee [Lewis (1969)]. If this is the case, the wage-hours contract offered by each employer is such that relatively long work hours are tied to relatively high hourly wage rates and consequently the market hours–wage locus facing an individual worker is no longer linear. Even if the employer–employee contract should grant the employee considerable discretion over his hours of work, some payments systems will result in a nonlinear budget constraint. Such is the case when the employee is rewarded (at least in part) by what he produces on the job (such as with piece-rate systems or sales commissions) and this in turn is not a simple linear function of his hours worked. Furthermore, if it is his after tax compensation that is relevant to the individual's allocation decisions[34] and if the tax rates on his income are not independent of the amount of that income, then again the individual is no longer presented with a linear budget constraint. Even if statutory tax rates did not change with income, effective tax rates might vary because of systematic income tax evasion or because of the latitude exercised by administrators in the tax revenue and welfare disbursement agencies. Finally, there are fixed costs and benefits to working, that is, expenditures and compensation that do not vary over all values of an individual's hours of work. As an example of a fixed compensation, some health insurance schemes are available to each individual workers more cheaply when provided to all employees as a group and these benefits take the form of a lump-sum payment that does not depend upon an individual's precise hours worked (although they are sometimes available only if a certain minimum number of hours are regularly worked). Fixed money costs of work arise from travel expenses or necessary expenditures for the performance of the job; these costs must be incurred if any hours are worked in the market, but once the individual is at work they do not change with the number of hours worked.[35]

The modifications required by a nonlinear budget constraint for the theory of the allocation of time in Section 3.1 depend upon the particular form taken by the budget constraint. There are three cases to be considered: the first is when the budget constraint may be assumed to be fully differentiable and it forms a convex

[34] This has been tested in H. Rosen (1976), Hausman and Wise (1976), and Johnson and Pencavel (1984), all of whom could not reject the hypothesis that the relevant variable was after-tax wages not before-tax wages.

[35] Fixed time costs consist of the expenditure of time in travelling to and from work. For an analysis of these, see Moses and Williamson (1963), Oi (1976), and Cogan (1981).

set (so, if taxes are the cause of budget constraint nonlinearities, they are progressive at all levels of income) in which case the techniques of differential calculus may be applied and local comparisons of $-m$ with the slope of the budget constraint identify the individual's optimum allocation of consumption and work; the second is when the budget constraint forms a convex set, but it is piecewise linear with kinks at various levels of income; and the third is when the budget constraint set is nonconvex because of regressive tax rates or "lumpy" fixed costs. Consider each of these three cases in turn.

Where the budget constraint forms a convex set and where it is continuous throughout and fully differentiable, then once again Kuhn–Tucker methods can be applied to determine whether an individual works in the market and, if he works, the number of hours he chooses. In particular, let c be the individual's total compensation for his market work and let c be a positive function of hours worked, $h: c = c(h;\, B)$ with $c'(h;\, B) > 0$, $c''(h;\, B) < 0$, and where B stands for variables that affect the position of the compensation function and that are exogenous to the individual worker. The individual may now be characterized as choosing $x > 0$ and $h \geq 0$ to maximize $U(x, h;\, A, \varepsilon)$ subject to the budget constraint $px = c(h;\, B) + y$. For an interior solution, the negative of the marginal rate of substitution of working hours for commodities, $-m$, equals the real marginal rate of compensation:

$$\frac{c'(h;\, B)}{p} = -\frac{\partial U/\partial h}{\partial U/\partial x} = -m(x, h;\, A, \varepsilon).$$

An analogous modification is made to the condition that determines whether an individual will work: if $c'(0;\, B) \leq w^*$, then $h = 0$. For this type of budget constraint, a typical procedure is to replace the true nonlinear constraint with that artificial linear constraint which would induce the same hours of work by the individual. That is, if $\tilde{h}$ denotes the hours of work and $\tilde{x}$ the commodity consumption bundle that solve the constrained utility-maximization problem and if $\tilde{w} = c'(\tilde{h};\, B)$, then the linearized budget constraint is the equation $p\tilde{x} = \tilde{w}\tilde{h} + \tilde{y}$, where $\tilde{y}$ is known as "linearized nonwage income" or, sometimes, as "virtual" income [Burtless and Hausman (1978)] (see Figure 1.1). The hours of work eq. (8) may then be written as $h = h(p, \tilde{w}, \tilde{y};\, A, \varepsilon)$.[36]

The problem is only slightly less straightforward in the second case when the income tax system is progressive throughout, but the tax rate rises with income in discrete steps so the budget constraint has linear segments connected by kinks. Each segment of the budget constraint is defined by its real after-tax wage rate

[36] Observe that, because hours of work are affected in part by the unobserved variables ε and the artificial budget constraint is linearized around the observed hours of work, $\tilde{w}$ and $\tilde{y}$ are also going to be affected by ε. Consequently, in estimation, $\tilde{w}$ and $\tilde{y}$ cannot be treated correctly as exogenous variables. Hall (1973), Hausman and Wise (1976), and Rosen (1976) calculate the marginal wage rate and linearized nonwage income not in the manner described, but at the same number of working hours for everyone in their sample. This leads to an analogous sort of inconsistency that comes from not instrumenting the marginal wage and linearized nonwage income variables.

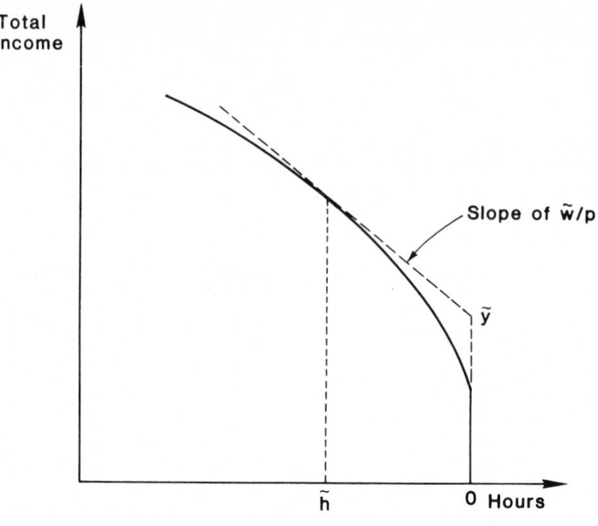

Figure 1.1

and by its real level of linearized nonwage income (i.e. by the height of the nonwage income axis if the slope of the budget constraint is extended to the vertical axis). The familiar tangency condition between the real net wage rate and $-m(x, h; A, \varepsilon)$ holds for any point chosen along one of the linear segments. An individual will locate at any kink if, at this point, his $-m(x, h,; A, \varepsilon)$ lies between the slopes of the budget constraint on either side of this kink. Once again, because the budget constraint is convex, local comparisons of $-m$ with the slope of the budget constraint are sufficient to identify the hours of work corresponding to maximum utility.

Local comparisons of the slope of the indifference curves with the slope of the budget constraint are not sufficient to identify the global utility optimum when the budget set is nonconvex, the third case. Examples of this are provided in Figures 1.2 and 1.3. In Figure 1.2, the income tax system is regressive as is the case when the implicit tax rate on welfare income (received at relatively low levels of total income) exceeds the explicit personal income tax rate. In Figure 1.3, there are fixed money costs of working of the amount ab' so that the budget constraint is $0ab$ if the individual works and $0ab'$ if the individual does not work in the market. For those who work, these fixed money costs are tantamount to a lower level of nonwage income. These fixed costs can be avoided altogether, however, by not working in the market and their lumpiness induces a discontinuity into the hours of work function: if only a relatively small number of hours are worked (relative, that is, to the market wage rate), then insufficient labor income will be earned to offset the fixed money expenditures of working, let alone to compensate for the disutility of market work; once the net wage rate rises sufficiently to

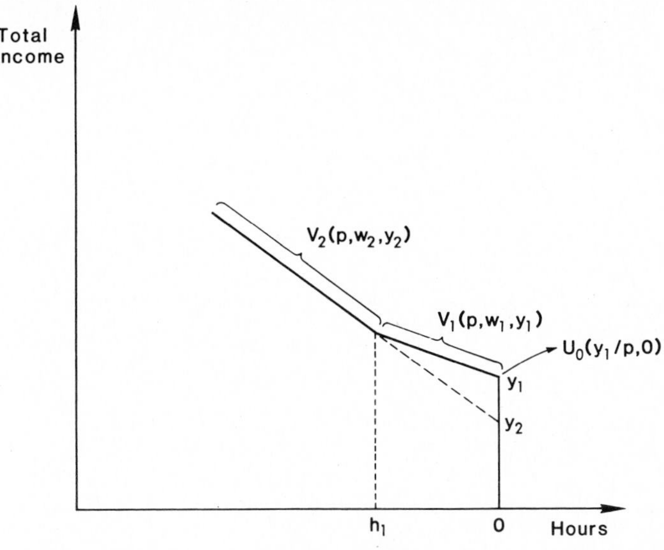

Figure 1.2

induce the individual to work, he works sufficient hours to generate enough labor income to pay the fixed costs of work and to offset the disutility of hours at work. These minimum hours of work are called reservation hours (h_r in Figure 1.3). When the budget constraint is nonconvex, the hours of work function may not be a continuous function of the slope of the budget constraint.

With a nonconvex budget constraint such as that in Figure 1.2, the individual must evaluate his utility at all locations along the frontier of his budget constraint. He is fully capable of doing this because he knows the form of his own utility function, he knows A and ε, and he knows the values of his budget constraint variables. He proceeds by dividing up his utility-maximizing problem into distinct stages, each stage corresponding to a particular corner or segment of his budget constraint. At the first stage he evaluates the utility of not working; in this case his consumption would be y_1/p and his utility would be $U_0(y_1/p,0;A,\varepsilon)$. At this next stage, he moves to the segment of his budget constraint between 0 and h_1 hours where w_1 is the slope of his budget constraint. Given p, w_1, and y_1 and conditional upon working between 0 and h_1 hours, he could determine whether a tangency condition (a local maximum) obtains between his indifference curve and his budget constraint. It may not, but if it does a maximum level of utility is given by $V_1(p,w_1,y_1;A,\varepsilon)$. He then proceeds to the segment of his budget constraint to the left of h_1 where the net wage is w_2 and linearized nonwage income is y_2. Again, given p, w_2, and y_2 and conditional upon working more than h_1 hours, the individual ascertains whether a tangency condition obtains. If it does, his maximum level of utility is given by

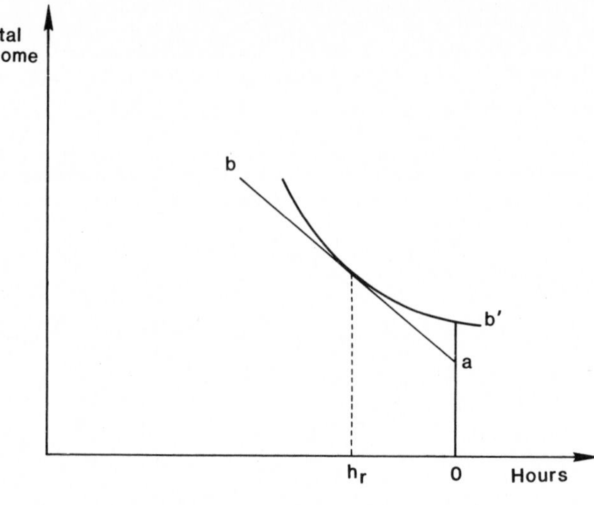

Figure 1.3

$V_2(p, w_2, y_2; A, \varepsilon)$.[37] Having determined the existence of any local maxima in the interior of his budget constraint, if there is more than one, he selects that with the greater utility. He checks to ensure that the utility associated with any interior local maximum exceeds U_0. If no local maximum exists in the interior of his budget constraint, his maximum in Figure 1.2 must be at zero hours of work. If the local maximum in the interior of his budget constraint dominates U_0, then his hours of work are determined by the application of Roy's Identity: $(\partial V_i/\partial w_i)/(\partial V_i/\partial y_i) = h(p, w_i, y_i; A, \varepsilon)$.

Even if the economist knows the form of the individual's utility function, he cannot replicate the individual's procedure exactly unless ε does not exist. This is, in fact, how Wales and Woodland (1979) proceed by presuming full knowledge of each individual's utility function (i.e. they suppress ε) and of his budget constraint, but assuming that there are errors in measuring hours of work, errors that are distributed independently of p, w, y, and A.

3.4. *Restrictions on hours of work by employers*

The models described to this point are characterized by the fact that an individual faces a budget constraint covering all possible hours of work. As mentioned at the beginning of the previous section, this does not necessarily

[37] If at a higher level of income, another segment of the budget constraint existed with a lower net wage than w_2 (a kink that bent out would exist), the direct utility function at this kink would have to be evaluated.

mean that each employer offers this continuum of possibilities, only that the market as a whole presents this set of opportunities. However, there exists a long tradition in economics of regarding this notion as fanciful and of characterizing the effective choices for the individual as those of working a "normal" or "standard" work schedule (hours per day, days per week, and weeks per year) or of not working at all. The employer may require overtime to be worked during a period of an unusually high level of business activity and may occasionally put his employees on short time when business is unusually slack, but at all times the employee's hours choices (if he works at all) are supplanted by his employer's discretionary actions.

Under these circumstances, the individual's constrained maximization problem consists simply of choosing x and h to maximize $U(x, h; A, \varepsilon)$ subject to the constraints $px = wh + y$, $x > 0$, and h equals either $\bar{h}$ or 0, where $\bar{h}$ denotes the employer's "take-it-or-leave-it" hours. The individual's choice degenerates into a simple comparison between his maximum utility if he works, $\bar{U} = U((w\bar{h} + y)/p, \bar{h}; A, \varepsilon)$ and his utility when not at work $U_0 = U(y/p, 0: A, \varepsilon)$. If it is the case that $\bar{U} > U_0$, $\bar{h}$ could exceed the hours he would choose (given the *same* values of the other exogenous variables) if the employer allowed any hours to be worked. Or, again, if $\bar{U} > U_0$, $\bar{h}$ might fall short of the hours the individual would choose (given the *same* values of the other exogenous variables) if the employer permitted him to work any number of hours the individual wishes. If this is the case, the individual's hours of work do not correspond to a situation in which the slope of the budget constraint is tangent to the individual's indifference curve. This attribute distinguishes this class of models from those in Sections 3.1 and 3.3.

Of course, in any labor market in which these hours of work restrictions are a permanent and regular feature, it is incorrect to specify the other variables constraining an individual's behavior to be the same in the presence of the hours constraints as in their absence. For, in evaluating the pecuniary and non-pecuniary net benefits of alternative jobs, individuals will gravitate towards those employers who fix working hours close to workers' preferences while employers who stipulate unpopular working hours will tend to experience difficulties in recruiting or retaining workers. In this manner, the wage rate will respond to these variations in the supply of workers to different employers and compensating wage differentials will arise. It would be an error, therefore, to estimate market equilibrium models in which workers are characterized as being constrained to work the number of hours mandated by their employers without at the same time treating the wage rate paid to these workers as jointly determined.[38]

Suppose these employer-mandated hours of work restrictions obtain and that an individual determines he is better off by working $\bar{h}$ hours than by not working at all. Let $h_0 = h(p, w, y; A, \varepsilon)$ be the hours this individual would work if the

[38] This is exactly how hours constraints are modelled in Abowd and Ashenfelter (1981).

employer allowed him to work any number of hours. Then the information required to help determine this individual's preferences for work and consumption (given p, w, y, and A) is h_0, but h_0 is not observed and only $\bar{h}$ is available. Under these circumstances, some economists have argued that time spent searching for the desired number of hours should be included in h_0 and they have used the sum of $\bar{h}$ and hours of unemployment, UN, as an estimate of h_0: $\bar{h}+UN=h_0$. [For instance, Cohen, Rea and Lerman (1970), Garfinkel (1973), Greenberg and Kosters (1973), and Hill (1973).] Or when only some unknown fraction, a, of reported hours of unemployment represent the offer to sell labor, observed hours of work ($\bar{h}$) may be expressed as a function of reported hours of unemployment (UN) plus a vector of variables believed to affect the hours an individual would choose to work in the absence of the employer's mandates:[39]

$$\bar{h}=h_0(p,w,y;A,\varepsilon)-a(UN). \tag{15}$$

Stochastic versions of this equation have been estimated by Dickinson (1974), Morgan (1979), Kalachek, Mellow and Raines (1978), Ashenfelter and Ham (1979), and Ashenfelter (1980). Whereas the earlier papers took account of unemployment in this way on the argument that they would measure more accurately or confidently conventional income and substitution effects, the more recent literature has interpreted the stochastic version of eq. (15) as "...a method for testing whether measured unemployment may be thought of as involuntary" [Ashenfelter (1978)]. According to this argument, "if, on the one hand, measured unemployment is simply another name for voluntary non-market time", then a should be zero; "if, on the other hand, measured unemployment is closely related to the extent to which workers face constraints on their labor market choices," then a should be positive. In fact, with cross-section data, a has been estimated as greater than unity [Dickinson (1974)], as almost exactly unity [Morgan (1979)], as 0.92 [Kalachek, Mellow and Raines (1978)], and as about 0.78 [Ashenfelter and Ham (1979)]; with aggregate time-series data [Ashenfelter (1980)],[40] the estimates of a ranged from 0.36 to 0.48 (with an estimated standard error of about 0.18) when the unemployment variable was treated as exogenous and to be equal to 0.04 (with a standard error of 0.23) when the unemployment variable was instrumented.

In view of the reams written on the subject of "voluntary" and "involuntary" unemployment, the proposal of resolving the empirical relevance of the issue simply by determining whether the coefficient a in eq. (15) is estimated to be zero

[39]It is unfortunate that the utility function and budget constraint underlying eq. (15) are not written down explicitly because it is not obvious how UN enters either the objective function or the constraint. Without knowing that, the behavioral interpretation of eq. (15) is difficult to discern.

[40]As Ashenfelter (1978) himself recognizes, the results from the aggregate time-series analysis were never in doubt: as the estimates of eq. (2) in Section 2.1 made clear, hours of work move closely with the unemployment rate over the business cycle whereas wage rates, nonlabor income, and commodity prices [the other right-hand side variables in eq. (15)] display considerably less business cycle variability. It is claimed that eq. (15) provides a structural explanation for this association.

must have considerable appeal to the profession.[41] Unfortunately, it is not so straightforward a matter for, according to the view that "measured unemployment is simply another name for voluntary non-market time", the duration of unemployment represents one part of the individual's optimal allocation of time and income and, as such, is jointly determined with hours of work and commodity consumption. According to this view, given the variations in individuals' hours of work left unaccounted for by the typical variables available to the economist, it is by no means surprising that, even after removing the influence of the variables p, w, y, and A, one object of choice in this allocation problem (hours of unemployment) is correlated with another dimension (hours of work). Would the existence of a partial correlation across households between expenditures on food and expenditures on clothing necessarily imply that clothing is rationed? The more relevant test is not whether a is zero, but rather a test of whether UN is endogenous.[42] However, this test comes up against the serious problem of an appropriate instrumental variable: what is the variable that can be validly excluded from an hours of work equation and that, at the same time, accounts for variations in the duration of unemployment? I do not know of one.[43] If this is so, then we are not capable of discriminating between the two different characterizations of unemployment.[44]

[41]When asked by some surveys, many individuals claim they would like to work a different number of hours from those they are currently working and some economists infer from this that the model in this section is the relevant one. This is surely an incorrect inference. It is not clear how the respondent interprets the question, but it is likely he answers the question assuming all other variables remain constant. In this case this may only mean that employers are not indifferent to the number of hours that their employees work. If the market offers tied wage-hours packages and the worker selects the best combination of wages and hours on his opportunity locus, then the relevant model is that in Section 3.3 above.

[42]Deaton (1982) also makes the argument that the relevant test in this context is an exogeneity test. In his case, he notes that, when commodities and hours of work are weakly separable in the utility function, the commodity demand equations may be written as a function of the prices of each commodity and of total income, $wh + y$, instead of as a function of w and y separately. When h is freely chosen, $wh + y$ is endogenous. Provided commodities and hours are weakly separable, the form of the commodity demand functions is the same whether hours are constrained or not. Using data on 1,617 households from the British Family Expenditure Survey, Deaton estimates such a system of hours-constrained commodity demand equations where an instrument for total income, $wh + y$, is provided by $w\hat{b} + y$, $\hat{b}$ being a parameter of the preference structure as estimated from the unconstrained version of the model. The results are ambiguous though Deaton infers they slightly favor the model characterizing hours of work as unconstrained. As he fully recognizes, there are a number of stringent assumptions in Deaton's application of this procedure and, indeed, the weak separability hypothesis is itself decisively rejected, but future work may be able to relax some of these assumptions and a modification of this methodology may yield some insights.

[43]In Ashenfelter's (1980) aggregate time-series study, the instrumental variables consisted of higher order terms of the wage rate, nonlabor income, and the prices of commodities. As he himself observes, the validity of these variables as instruments leans heavily on having identified correctly the functional form of the hours of work equation and, because we are not at all confident of the appropriate functional form, these variables are not very satisfactory instruments. In his study of individuals, Ham (1983) proposed using industry, occupation, and local unemployment rates as instruments for each individual's unemployment experience. Whether these are valid instruments depends upon the interpretation of the stochastic error term in the hours of work equation. In Ham's analysis (as in the model of labor supply in this survey paper), the error term represents variations in preferences that are unobserved to the researcher. It is unlikely that the distribution of these "tastes

A more fundamental issue that this rationing literature on hours of work does not address is the relevant wage rate at which individuals are being rationed. When dealing with rationed commodities where all consumers face the same prices, the price of a rationed commodity may be well defined. But in the case of individuals facing different wage rates, it is crucial that we identify the wage rate when rationed. In other words, in accounting for observed, rationed, hours of work $\bar{h}$ in eq. (15), what is the relevant wage rate, w, on the right-hand side? In aggregate studies such as Ashenfelter's, the wage rate used is the average wage received by all those at work and not unemployed so the implicit assumption is that rationed individuals and unrationed individuals face the same exogenous wage. In studies of this kind when data on individuals are used, for individuals experiencing some unemployment the wage rate that rations these men when unemployed is assumed to be the same as the wage rate they receive when employed. What is the appropriate rationed wage rate when an individual experiences no spell of employment and is always recorded as unemployed? Such individuals are deliberately excluded from these studies.[45] Because no exchange of labor services takes place while an individual is unemployed, no wage rate is recorded and observationally this is equivalent to the situation that arises when the reservation wage, w^*, exceeds the offered wage, w. In other words, the situation is observationally equivalent to what some economists call "voluntary unemployment".

3.5. *Life-cycle models*

All the models outlined above have been static, one-period descriptions of behavior. An important development in research on labor supply over the past

for work" parameters is independent of the unemployment experiences of these men; that is, those men with greater tastes for leisure will tend to take longer or more frequent spells of unemployment. Then, if industry, occupation, and local unemployment rates are correlated with the unemployment experiences of individual men (as Ham maintains), then these unemployment rates must also be correlated with the utility function parameters imbedded in the error term of the hours of work equation. In other words, these unemployment rates do not serve as appropriate instruments.

[44] A different procedure for testing for the presence of employer-mandated restrictions on hours of work is contained in Ham (1982). For a sample of prime-aged male workers experiencing no unemployment and claiming no underemployment, he estimates a labor supply function that allows for the possibility of sample selection bias resulting from excluding these unemployed and underemployed workers. He then tests whether the estimates that make no adjustment for the exclusion of the unemployed and underemployed differ significantly from those that do make that adjustment. He finds a significant difference and argues that the differences move in the direction suggested by the proposition that these unemployed and underemployed workers are constrained by employers' restrictions on hours of work.

[45] For example, Lundberg (1983) writes: "The sample was restricted to two-head households in which both husband and wife worked at some time.... The exclusion of these households was...to ensure a wage observation for each individual."

ten years has been the specification and estimation of life-cycle, multi-period, models according to which consumption and labor supply decisions in each period are made with regard to prices and wage rates in all periods. Utility is defined over lifetime consumption and lifetime hours of work and similarly the budget constraint incorporates incomes and expenditures in different periods plus the opportunity to reallocate incomes and expenditures across periods by borrowing and lending. Whereas in the static models discussed above interest and dividend income from previous savings decisions was treated as exogenous, in a life-cycle context it becomes endogenous and only inherited assets and unanticipated net returns on capital are genuinely exogenous. The life-cycle counterparts to eqs. (8) in Section 3.1 relate consumption and hours worked at age t to prices and to wage rates at each and every age where future budget constraint variables are appropriately discounted to the present.

The notion that an individual's or a household's consumption and working decisions are made with the future very much in view squares with some basic patterns of life-cycle behavior. The prototype is described by a young married couple starting out with few assets and working long hours, a portion of these hours representing on-the-job training; then moving to a higher asset position, continuing to work long hours (at least for the man) and starting to raise a family with the implied financial responsibilities for the future; and later in life working fewer hours and concomitantly running down their assets. Also, recall from Section 2.2 above that in U.S. cross-section data both male labor force participation probabilities and male hours of work display an inverted-U shape with respect to age. Hourly wage rates also map out an inverted-U shape with age although the peak in hours worked precedes the peak in wage rates.[46] The correspondence of the hours and wage profiles with respect to age conforms to the most basic implication of the life-cycle labor supply model, namely that an individual will supply more hours to the market during those periods when his wage rate is highest; this is the effect of evolutionary wage differences on hours worked. The hours–age and wage–age profiles of black men are flatter than those of white men with the peaks of both profiles occurring at younger ages for black men than for white men. Weekly hours and weekly wages also follow an inverted-U shape with respect to age in British data presented by Browning, Deaton and Irish (1983). They present these graphs separately for manual and nonmanual workers: for manual workers, wages peak a little later than hours; for nonmanual workers, the peaks in the two series are roughly coincident. At all ages, manual workers have higher hours and lower wages than nonmanual

[46]According to the life-cycle interpretation, the fact that the peak in hours worked precedes the peak in wage rates implies that the rate of interest exceeds the individual's rate of time preference. Weiss (1972) expresses this well: "The rate of interest induces an early work effort since labour earnings can be invested at a higher rate of return. The subjective discount rate induces the postponement of work since future effort seems less painful when viewed from the present."

workers. The life-cycle model of labor supply outlined below is an attempt to provide an explicit and formal characterization of these empirical regularities.[47]

The empirical implementation of the life-cycle model would appear to require a great volume of data: to understand an individual's labor supply today, the economist needs information on prices and wages throughout the individual's life! In fact, the empirical work on life-cycle labor supply has proceeded by placing sufficient restrictions on the form of the lifetime utility function that the parameters governing the dynamic allocation of consumption and hours can be estimated with relatively little data. To date, there exist two general approaches to this dynamic allocation problem. One derives from the literature on habit persistence and stock adjustment and specifies the individual's utility function in period t as conditional on the individual's consumption and hours of work in the previous period. The notion that the standards by which individuals gauge their welfare are molded by their prior experiences is, of course, an old one. Preferences displaying this state dependence in the labor supply literature have been estimated at the aggregative level by Philips (1978) and employed in aggregate business cycle simulations by Kydland and Prescott (1982) and they have been estimated with individual panel data by Hotz, Kydland and Sedlacek (1982) and Johnson and Pencavel (1984).[48] Whereas in this specification the lifetime utility function is intertemporally not (strongly) separable,[49] the opposite hypothesis is maintained in the second approach to the individual's life-cycle labor supply problem. Substantially more research has been conducted along the lines of the second approach and so I proceed to outline its central features in a little more detail.

Assume the lifetime utility function is additive over time and write the individual's utility in period t as a strictly concave function of commodities consumed in period t, x_t, and of hours worked in period t, h_t: $U_t(x_t, h_t; A_t, \varepsilon_t)$, where, as before, A_t denotes exogenous variables observed by the researcher while ε_t is a component unobserved by the researcher. Let the rate of time preference be given by ρ and suppose a fixed "lifetime" of $N+1$ periods. Then the individual's utility function is

$$\sum_{t=0}^{N} (1+\rho)^{-t} U_t(x_t, h_t; A_t, \varepsilon_t). \tag{16}$$

[47] The life-cycle model would attribute the greater hours with lower wages of British manual workers compared with nonmanual workers in terms of the greater life-cycle wealth of the latter.

[48] The interpretation of these models in the interesting special case of the Stone–Geary utility function is provided in the papers by Phlips and Spinnewyn (1982) and Pollak (1970).

[49] However, when a consumer fully recognizes the evolution of his tastes as he ages, Spinnewyn (1981) shows that the intertemporal model of consumer behavior with habit persistence can be transformed into a model without such persistence by a suitable redefinition of the cost of consumption and wealth.

The lifetime budget constraint is

$$K_0 + \sum_{t=0}^{N} (1+r)^{-t}(w_t h_t - p_t x_t) = 0, \tag{17}$$

where K_0 denotes initial wealth and r is the rate of interest which for convenience is assumed to be fixed. Bequests have been neglected although it is straightforward to permit a role for them. The individual selects $x_t > 0$ and $h_t \geq 0$ for each period to maximize (16) subject to the constraint (17), the first-order conditions for which are eq. (17) and

$$\frac{\partial U_t}{\partial x_t} = \theta^t \lambda_0 p_t, \qquad t = 0,\ldots, N, \tag{18}$$

$$-\frac{\partial U_t}{\partial h_t} \geq \theta^t \lambda_0 w_t, \quad t = 0,\ldots, N, \tag{19}$$

where $\theta = (1+\rho)/(1+r)$ and where λ_0 is the Lagrange multiplier attached to the budget constraint and is interpreted as the marginal utility of initial wealth when evaluating the utility function at its optimum. If eq. (19) is a strict inequality, the individual does not work in period t; if it is an equality, then some hours of work are supplied to the market. In what follows, given the high labor force participation rates of price–age men, I assume (19) is satisfied by an equality.

Now solve eqs. (18) and (19) for consumption and working hours in any period:

$$x_t = x\left(\lambda_0 \theta^t p_t, \lambda_0 \theta^t w_t; A_t, \varepsilon_t\right), \quad t = 0,\ldots, N, \tag{20}$$

$$h_t = h\left(\lambda_0 \theta^t p_t, \lambda_0 \theta^t w_t; A_t, \varepsilon_t\right), \quad t = 0,\ldots, N. \tag{21}$$

In these equations, λ_0 is endogenous, a function of the lifetime budget constraint variables and of A_t and ε_t. Indeed, it can be shown that $\partial\lambda_0/\partial K_0 < 0$, $\partial\lambda_0/\partial w_t \leq 0$, and $\partial\lambda_0/\partial p_t > 0$ [see Heckman (1974a, 1976a)]. Eqs. (20) and (21) have been called "λ_0-constant" functions or, more felicitously, Frisch demand and supply functions [Browning (1982)] in recognition of Ragnar Frisch's extensive use of additive utility functions. Given the assumed concavity of the utility function, these Frisch demand and supply functions possess many of the properties of conventional demand and supply functions: $\partial h_t/\partial(\lambda_0\theta^t w_t) > 0$ and $\partial x_t/\partial(\lambda_0\theta^t p_t) < 0$; there is a symmetry property $-\partial h_t/\partial(\lambda_0\theta^t p_t) =$

$\partial x_t/\partial(\lambda_0\theta' w_t) \gtrless 0$; and these functions are homogeneous of degree zero in λ_0^{-1}, p_t, and w_t[50] [see Heckman (1974a)].

Because the period-specific utility function represents one branch of the entire lifetime utility function, the Frisch labor supply eq. (21) is not independent of monotonic transformations of U_t. The important feature of these equations for empirical analysis is that they relate consumption and labor supply decisions in any period to variables outside that period only through λ_0 and that otherwise within-period prices and wage rates determine x_t and h_t. The variable λ_0 is a sufficient statistic in that it contains all the information concerning the lifetime budget constraint variables which is relevant to the current choice of consumption and hours of work. Moreover, although λ_0 varies across individuals in accordance with differences in their lifetime budget constraint variables and in other exogenous variables, for a given individual λ_0 is constant over his lifetime when future wages and prices are known with certainty. The derivative of h_t with respect to w_t in eq. (21) shows how an individual's hours respond to *evolutionary* wage changes, i.e. changes in wages along on individual's wage–age profile. As MaCurdy (1982) has emphasized, corresponding to the two classes of variables (the current period variables and the life cycle component, λ_0) in eqs. (20) and (21), the formulation of an empirically tractable model of life-cycle behavior naturally decomposes into two stages: the first is the specification of the Frisch equations and the second is the formulation of an equation to determine λ_0.

At the first stage, the immediate problem is, of course, that λ_0 is not directly observed. Moreover, λ_0 is not a random variable uncorrelated with wages and prices. Because it is not random, it cannot be consigned to some error term. However, as we shall see below, for certain forms of the Frisch equations, λ_0 (or a simple transformation of λ_0) may be expressed as an additive fixed effect that, in estimation with panel data, is easily accounted for by first-differencing the data over time.[51] The second stage of the estimation procedure relates λ_0 to its

[50] Instead of obtaining the Frisch equations by solving the first-order conditions from explicit constrained utility maximization, Browning (1982) shows they may be derived more simply by defining a consumer's within-period profit function as follows:

$$\Pi_t\left(\lambda_0^{-1}, \tilde{p}_t, \tilde{w}_t; A_t, \varepsilon_t\right) = \max_{x_t, h_t}\left\{\lambda_0^{-1} U_t\left(x_t, h_t; A_t, \varepsilon_t\right) - \tilde{p}_t x_t + \tilde{w}_t h_t\right\},$$

where $\tilde{p}_t = \theta' p_t$, $\tilde{w}_t = \theta' w_t$, and naturally λ_0^{-1} may be called "the price of utility". Then, by applying the envelope theorem to this profit function, the negative of eq. (20) is derived from $\partial\Pi_t/\partial\tilde{p}_t$ and eq. (21) is derived from $\partial\Pi_t/\partial\tilde{w}_t$. As is the case for a price-taking firm's profit function, this consumer's profit function is increasing the price of output (λ_0^{-1}), is decreasing in the prices of inputs ($\tilde{p}_t$ and $-\tilde{w}_t$), and is convex and linearly homogeneous in λ_0^{-1}, $\tilde{p}_t$, and $\tilde{w}_t$.

[51] If the Frisch hours eq. (21) is written with hours or earnings on the left-hand side (as distinct from some transformation of them such as their logarithms), then for λ_0 to be specified as an additive fixed effect the within-period utility function must be quasi-homothetic in commodities consumed and hours worked. See Browning, Deaton and Irish (1983).

determinants, namely the lifetime budget constraint variables, the rate of time preference, A_t, and ε_t. Observations on the entire budget constraint variables are, of course, not available so lifetime profiles must be simulated by using the observed income and wage data of people of different ages. Moreover, an explicit, closed-form solution for λ_0 is often not possible so instead the expression for λ_0 is approximated. Clearly, this second stage is less cleanly specified and estimated than the first stage, but knowledge of λ_0 is essential to describe an individual's labor supply response to *parametric* wage changes, i.e. wage changes that shift the entire wage–age profile.

A model involving decision-making over time would appear to require allowance for uncertainty about the future values of variables and an important aspect of this life-cycle model is that it accommodates such uncertainty in a tractable form. To see this, first rewrite the certainty model by defining by recursion $\lambda_0(1+\rho)^t/(1+r)^t = \lambda_t$ and so the first-order conditions eqs. (18) and (19) become:

$$\frac{\partial U_t}{\partial x_t} = \lambda_t p_t, \tag{22}$$

$$-\frac{\partial U_t}{\partial h_t} = \lambda_t w_t, \tag{23}$$

$$\lambda_t = \left(\frac{1+r}{1+\rho}\right)\lambda_{t+1}, \tag{24}$$

where λ_t is the marginal utility of wealth in period t. The Frisch demand and supply functions eqs. (20) and (21) are the same with λ_t replacing $\lambda_0\theta^t$:

$$x_t = x(\lambda_t p_t, \lambda_t w_t; A_t, \varepsilon_t), \quad t = 0,\dots,N, \tag{25}$$

$$h_t = h(\lambda_t p_t, \lambda_t w_t; A_t, \varepsilon_t), \quad t = 0,\dots,N. \tag{26}$$

Eq. (24) defines the optimal savings strategy and the lifetime problem decomposes into two levels. At the first level, an individual allocates his wealth over his life such that his marginal utility of wealth evolves as he ages according to eq. (24). At the second level, conditional upon wealth allocated to a given period, the within-period allocation problem is addressed. Strong separability of the lifetime utility function is more than sufficient to decentralize the life-cycle problem in this way.[52]

Now allow for uncertainty in the form of the individual being unsure of real wages or real rates of interest or even his preferences in the future. In these

[52] In fact, weak separability is sufficient and necessary. See Blackorby, Primont and Russell (1975).

circumstances, suppose the consumer revises his plans each period as new information on these variables is revealed and, in particular, suppose he maximizes his current and discounted expected utility subject to his period-by-period budget constraint. The first-order conditions describing the solution to this problem are identical to eqs. (22) and (23), but eq. (24) is now modified to read

$$\lambda_t = (1+\rho)^{-1}\mathscr{E}[(1+r)\lambda_{t+1}],$$

where r in this formula is the rate of return to be paid on each dollar of assets held at the beginning of period $t+1$. Because both r and λ_{t+1} are random, $\mathscr{E}[(1+r)\lambda_{t+1}]$ will typically involve the covariance between these two terms, but if a riskless rate of return exists, say, $\bar{r}$, then the previous equation may be written

$$\lambda_t \frac{1+\rho}{1+\bar{r}} = \mathscr{E}(\lambda_{t+1}) \tag{27}$$

or the expected (at period t) marginal utility of wealth in period $t+1$ is proportional to the marginal utility of wealth in period t, similar to a Martingale stochastic process [MaCurdy (1976)].[53] The consumer's savings policy implies that the means of all future values of λ are revised to account for all forecasting errors at the time they are realized. And because λ_t is a sub-Martingale, through eqs. (22) and (23), $(\partial U/\partial x_t)/p_t$ and $(\partial U/\partial h_t)/w_t$ also follow a sub-Martingale. So, according to this model, at the start of the life-cycle the consumer sets λ_0 so that it takes account of all the information on the future values of variables available at that time. As new information is acquired over time so λ_t is revised according to eq. (27). At each age, in order to satisfy eqs. (22), (23), and (27), the consumer requires knowledge of the variables observed in that period to determine his optimal consumption and hours of work and to update his marginal utility of wealth. Consequently, whereas eqs. (20) and (21) form the basis of empirical work of life-cycle labor supply under the assumption of perfect foresight, eqs. (25) and (26) constitute the analogous equations under conditions of uncertainty.

In the presence of uncertainty, when estimating an equation based on eq. (26), the error term will include forecast errors and, because w_t, A_t, and ε_t contain components unforeseen before their realization, w_t (even if measured without error), A_t, and ε_t will not be distributed independently of the equation's disturbance. Finding variables that are correlated with w_t and A_t and yet are uncorrelated with unanticipated components of these variables (i.e. finding genuine instruments) is difficult.

[53] This result and the conditions underlying it were derived by MaCurdy (1976). That all prices follow a Martingale or sub-Martingale process was conjectured by Alchian (1974).

Certain features of the life-cycle model have considerable appeal. For instance, anyone who has estimated static labor supply functions can testify to the awkward problems in deriving an accurate measure of nonwage income, that is, the income an individual would receive at $h = 0$. The life-cycle model avoids these difficulties. Whereas the static model has to be augmented with explanations in terms of family responsibilities in order to account for the age-pattern of hours of work, the life-cycle model addresses this empirical regularity explicitly.[54] Few would deny that there are circumstances in which the future values of certain variables affect current working decisions. The more pertinent issues are, first, whether these effects are sufficiently important to account for the key variations in male labor supply and, second, whether the particular model sketched above incorporates the essential features of intertemporal decision-making. We shall return to these two issues when the empirical work on life-cycle labor supply is discussed in Section 5 below.

4. Estimation of the static model

4.1. *Specification*

What guidance has the theory of labor supply outlined in the previous section provided for empirical work? As far as the conventional static model is concerned, I know of no attempts with individual data to specify all of the refutable implications of the theory – the positivity of the substitution effect, the symmetry condition, the zero homogeneity condition – as a series of research hypotheses that are either corroborated or refuted by the data.[55] This is surely surprising in view of the extensive literature that has been concerned with testing the predictions from the consumer's allocation problem (without the hours of work dimension) and that has done so by applying the theory to data aggregated over individuals. The availability of data sets containing observations on the actual decision-making units, the individual or the household, and on the same individu-

[54] The distinctive age-hours of work pattern is apparent in Current Population Survey data organized by Smith (1983). She presents data on annual hours of work by age, by sex, and by race from the four Surveys from 1977 to 1981. For instance, for all men in 1981 (unadjusted for all other characteristics) those aged 16–17 years were estimated to work an average of 715 hours, 18–19 years worked 1209 hours, 20–24 years worked 1634 hours, 25–34 years worked 2016 hours, 35–44 years worked 2126 hours, 45–54 years worked 2108 hours, 55–59 years worked 2037 hours, 60–64 years worked 1839 hours, and those 65 years and over worked 1241 hours.

[55] Occasionally one or other of these implications has been tested. For instance, Wales and Woodland (1976) determined in their husband and wife joint allocation model whether the matrix of compensated wage and price elasticities was correctly signed. For approximately half of their observations it was and for the other half it was not.

als over time means that the observable implications of the theory do not need to be augmented by a series of heroic aggregation assumptions in order to subject the theory to empirical scrutiny. Of course, many other problems remain in implementing the theory, but these turn out not to be specific to labor supply issues and they are rarely resolved except under exceptional circumstances by applying the theory to data aggregated over individuals.

While the implications of the conventional theory of labor supply have rarely been modelled as a series of testable hypotheses, researchers do not seem to be reluctant to treat the qualitative implications of the theory as maintained hypotheses. For instance, Burtless and Hausman (1978) estimate a labor supply model that allows for a distribution across individuals of values for the effect of nonwage income on hours, but in doing so they constrain this effect to be nonpositive. In fact, the estimates of this effect pile up close to zero and one wonders how many individuals would have positive values if the estimation scheme did not prohibit it.[56] In many studies, it seems as if estimates that do not generate positive substitution effects for hours of work or that suggest nonmarket time is an inferior good are not interpreted as refutations of the theory, but as indicating some error in implementing the theory. This is, of course, supposed to be an attribute of a discipline in its "normal science" phase although some would question quite legitimately whether the conventional model of labor supply had earned the right to this status.

Perhaps the primary contribution to date of the theory to empirical research on labor supply has been that of distinguishing the effects on hours of work of changes in wage rates from changes in nonwage income. Although this may appear a trivial contribution, it distinguishes the economist's approach to the topic of market work behavior from that of most other social scientists.[57] Moreover, as Mincer (1963) showed, the distinction may be usefully applied to understanding other patterns of behavior besides hours of work.

Although there have been a number of instances to the contrary, the general procedure has *not* been to specify a particular expression for the direct or indirect utility function (or expenditure function) and then to estimate the implied hours of work function. More often, an hours of work function convenient for estimation has been specified ab initio and the popular choice has been one that is linear in the parameters. That is, eq. (8) has been specified as follows:

$$h_i = \alpha_0 + \alpha_1\left(\frac{w}{p}\right)_i + \alpha_2\left(\frac{y}{p}\right)_i + \alpha_3 A_i + \varepsilon_i, \tag{28}$$

[56] They report that about one-fifth of the sample has an estimated elasticity of hours with respect to nonwage income of between -0.01 and zero. Their restriction on the effect of nonwage income on hours of work arises from the *global* requirement on their estimating technique that the substitution effect be non-negative for all individuals and for all values of the exogenous variables.

[57] For instance, see the interesting sociological study of labor supply in Smith-Lovin and Tickamyer (1978).

where i denotes individual i. In this form, ε_i is a stochastic disturbance term representing individual i's unobserved "tastes for work" and the zero homogeneity condition is a maintained hypothesis. Normalizing p to unity, the uncompensated wage effect is $\alpha_1 \lesseqgtr 0$ while, provided leisure is not an inferior good, $\alpha_2 \leq 0$. Consequently, the substitution effect, s, is given by $\alpha_1 - h\alpha_2$ which should be positive according to the allocation model outlined in Section 3.1 above. Provided $\alpha_1 > h\alpha_2$, eq. (28) implies a larger substitution effect for those who work longer hours.

Because any labor supply equation possessing all the properties of utility-maximizing hours of work functions implies a particular expression for the direct utility function, one may derive the form of the utility function when a linear hours of work equation such as (28) is specified:

$$U(x, h; A, \varepsilon) = \left(\frac{\alpha_2 h - \alpha_1}{\alpha_2^2}\right) \exp\left\{\frac{\alpha_2(\alpha_0 + \alpha_2 x + \alpha_3 A + \varepsilon) - \alpha_1}{\alpha_2 h - \alpha_1}\right\},$$

where $\alpha_1 > \alpha_2 h$.[58] Although x and h do not appear symmetrically in this unfamiliar utility function and although the error term occupies an unintuitive role, these will be small considerations if it is important to have a convenient hours of work estimating equation.

Questions concerning the form of the utility function, however, have received little attention compared with the research investigating the consequences of the error term, ε_i. The reason for this concern is that eq. (28) describes only those men whose optimizing problem is solved by working a positive number of hours; for others, the individual's problem is solved by setting h to zero. In other words, letting αX_i stand for the deterministic part of the right-hand side of eq. (28), the correct specification is as follows:

$$h_i = \alpha X_i + \varepsilon_i, \quad \text{if } w_i > w_i^*(p_i, y_i, A_i, \varepsilon_i), \tag{29}$$

$$h_i = 0, \quad \text{if } w_i \leq w_i^*(p_i, y_i, A_i, \varepsilon_i), \tag{30}$$

where the dependence of the reservation wage, w_i^*, on p_i, y_i, A_i, and ε_i has been made explicit. Clearly, if observations on only those men for whom $h_i > 0$ are used to estimate (28) by ordinary least squares, then $h_i > 0$ implies $\alpha X_i + \varepsilon_i > 0$ or $\varepsilon_i > -\alpha X_i$. Thus, when restricting the estimation of (28) to the sample of working men, ε_i is not distributed independently of X_i even though ε_i may be distributed randomly in the population; because $\mathscr{E}(\varepsilon_i | X_i) \neq 0$, one of the conditions under which ordinary least-squares provides a consistent estimator is violated. Expressed differently, when eq. (28) is fitted to the sample of working

[58] This is derived in Deaton and Muellbauer (1981, p. 96) and in Hausman (1981). Deaton and Muellbauer (1981) consider the case when the composite commodity theorem does not hold and the different components of x are identified.

men, observations are not selected from the population randomly, but systematically according to the requirement $\varepsilon_i > -\alpha X_i$ and a *sample selection bias* results.[59] The magnitude of the bias is likely to be less serious for those samples from populations for which most observations satisfy the criterion $w_i > w_i^*$. In other words, the least-squares selection bias is likely to be more important in describing the hours of work behavior of older and younger men than of prime-age males.[60]

An alternative and insightful characterization of this sample selection problem [attributable to Heckman (1976b)] recasts the issue as a conventional case of omitting a term from a least-squares regression equation. Define $\Delta w_i = w_i - w_i^*$ and observe that $\Delta w_i > 0$ if the individual works in the market [so that eq. (29) holds] while $\Delta w_i \leq 0$, if $h_i = 0$. Denote the determinants of Δw_i by Z_i which will include p_i, y_i, A_i, and ε_i as well as the variables influencing the offered wage rate:

$$\Delta w_i = \delta Z_i + u_i,$$

where u_i is a random variable assumed to have expectation zero and finite variance. Then, the regression of h_i given X_i over the sample of workers (i.e. over the sample for whom $\Delta w_i > 0$) is

$$\begin{aligned} \mathscr{E}(h_i|X_i, \Delta w_i > 0) &= \alpha X_i + \mathscr{E}(\varepsilon_i|u_i > -\delta Z_i) \\ &= \alpha X_i + \phi(\delta Z_i, \xi_i), \end{aligned} \tag{31}$$

where ξ_i denotes the parameters governing the joint density of ε_i and u_i. Because Z_i incorporates the effects of ε_i, the expected value of ε_i given $u_i > -\delta Z_i$ will not be zero. Applying ordinary least squares to (31) is equivalent to omitting the term ϕ, the conditional mean of ε_i, from the regression and thus the bias that results may be understood in terms of conventional omitted-variable bias arguments.

For instance, consider a variable such as nonwage income, y, that appears in both X_i and Z_i. A least-squares regression of h_i on X_i for a sample of workers that omits the conditional mean of ε_i, ϕ, results in estimates of the coefficient on nonwage income, say $\hat{\alpha}_2$ from eq. (24), that may be written approximately as

$$\hat{\alpha}_2 = \alpha_2 + \partial\phi/\partial y.$$

[59] The sample selection bias is not solved by Hall's (1973) procedure of fitting eq. (28) to workers and nonworkers together (setting h to zero for nonworkers). This procedure requires that eq. (29) hold not for $w > w^*$, but for $w \gtrless w^*$, a requirement that contradicts the theoretical structure.

[60] In the labor supply case, the sample selection problem is further complicated by the absence of observations on one of the independent variables, the wage rate facing (and not being accepted by) nonworkers. In his study of married women, Heckman (1974b) proposed and implemented a model that combines an equation determining wage rate offers with an equation determining the marginal rate of substitution of hours for commodities. Both equations were characterized by errors that were correlated with the exogenous variables because of sample selectivity problems.

The coefficient α_2 measures the effect of nonwage income on hours worked on the part of those already working and this is the derivative that figures in the analysis of interior solutions to the individual's constrained utility-maximization problem. This analysis suggests that, provided leisure is not an inferior good, $\alpha_2 \leq 0$. The term $\partial\phi/\partial y$ measures the effect of nonwage income in changing the sample of observations, i.e. the sample who work from the population. Suppose that those with greater nonwage income have tastes for work that are less inclined against work than those with little nonwage income (after controlling for the other determinants of work behavior). Then, as y is increased, so the composition of the sample is altered towards those with less aversion to work. Consequently, $\partial\phi/\partial y > 0$, $\hat{\alpha}_2 > \alpha_2$, and the estimated effect of nonwage income on hours of work will be biased in such a way as to indicate a less negative income effect than is really the case.

The sample selection bias can be addressed in a number of different ways. Perhaps the most common procedure is Heckman's (1976b) two-step estimator which replaces $\phi(\cdot)$, the conditional mean of ε_i, in eq. (31) with its value predicted from a previously-estimated equation. Although our understanding of the issues has been greatly enhanced by the large literature that has arisen on the subject of sample selection bias, I know of no evidence from empirical studies of male labor supply (whether old, young, or prime-age men) that documents grievous biases from a strategy of restricting estimation to the sample of workers and of not making any correction for this deliberate nonrandom selection of the observations.[61]

The following section presents the empirical results from fitting static labor supply functions. It is impossible for me to graph each fitted hours of work equation as a function of the observed values taken by the variables of interest. Yet this is exactly what is needed for a full understanding of the implications of any given set of estimates. Unfortunately, only rarely are such graphs presented. The normal substitute is to present the implied values of the behavior responses calculated at sample mean values or, less frequently, the average of the behavioral responses calculated for each observation.[62] Some papers do not even do this nor do they provide sufficient information for such calculations to be made by an interested reader. It is high time the editors and referees of all journals required that every empirical paper considered for publication present descriptive statistics on their samples analyzed.

[61] The paper by Wales and Woodland (1980) provides a convenient list of alternative methods. Also they report some sampling experiments with different estimators.

[62] These two methods of summarizing the behavior responses – either calculating the behavioral responses at the mean values of the variables or calculating the implied responses for each observation and then forming the average – may yield quite different values depending upon the form of the function and the distribution of the values of the variables. Although the latter may well be a preferable procedure, it is well nigh impossible to simulate all the studies to perform the calculations required.

The summary estimates I shall concentrate on are those measuring, first, the effect of a proportional increase in wage rates on the proportional change in hours worked and, second, the effect of a small increase in nonwage income on hours worked and, given wages, on earnings. The former is, of course, the uncompensated elasticity of hours of work with respect to wages (E) and the latter I call the marginal propensity to earn (*mpe*) out of nonwage income. Following eq. (12), the income-compensated elasticity of hours of work with respect to wages (E^*) is simply the difference between E and the *mpe*:

$$E = \frac{\partial h}{\partial w}\frac{w}{h}; \qquad mpe = w\frac{\partial h}{\partial y} \quad \text{and} \quad E^* = E - mpe.$$

Being independent of the units in which the budget constraint variables are measured, estimates of elasticities are more conveniently compared across different studies than are changes in hours worked over a given period of time (a year maybe or a week) per dollar or pound change in the wage rate. From the value of the *mpe* may be inferred how much of an increase in nonwage income is spent on the consumption of commodities. The consumption literature provides information on the marginal propensity to consume out of nonlabor income,[63] but this research focuses upon the division of an additional dollar of nonlabor income between consumption and saving holding labor income fixed, an issue involving intertemporal considerations. By contrast, the static model of time and consumption outlined in Section 3.1 takes such savings decisions as being determined at a prior stage of the individual's allocation problem and the question that arises from this model is the within-period division of an additional dollar of nonlabor income between the consumption of commodities and of leisure. Most of the estimates of this *mpe* come from the labor supply research to be surveyed shortly, but some educated guesses about the probable magnitude of this can be formed from measured effects of nonwage income on commodity consumption. Such estimates have been presented by Deaton (1982) using data on 1617 households from the British Family Expenditure Survey of 1973. In straightforward least-squares linear regressions that impose little prior structure on the data, he relates household expenditures on nine different categories of consumer goods to the husband's wage rate, nonwage income,[64] the number of children, the number of workers in the family, and a home ownership dummy variable. Nonwage income exerts a positive effect on the consumption of each category of goods and the sum of these marginal propensities to consume $\left(\sum p_i\,\partial x_i/\partial y\right)$ is about unity implying

[63] See, for instance, Holbrook and Stafford (1971).

[64] The husband's wage rate is defined as the ratio of "normal" weekly earnings to "normal" hours worked per week and then adjusted for income taxes. Nonwage income is, in fact, the net income of the household minus the husband's earnings.

a zero value for the *mpe*.[65] I know of no comparable study with U.S. data, but insofar as one may generalize from these results then a value of the *mpe* not far from zero is to be expected.

When comparing estimates of these behavioral responses from different research, it should be remembered that the points of evaluation differ across studies and, moreover, that for any given study these behavioral responses themselves vary from observation to observation. The manner in which these behavioral responses differ across observations is determined once the functional form for the estimating equation has been chosen. For example, when a linear hours of work equation is estimated both E and the *mpe* will necessarily be greater for individuals with relatively high wages. There is no strong prior reason to believe either that this should be true or that it should not be. Therefore, in specifying hours of work estimating equations, some economists feel more comfortable working with utility functions familiar from the research on consumer behavior. In research on labor supply, most of the (direct) utility functions posited have been additive in commodity consumption and in each individual's hours of work. The additivity assumption will necessarily bring with it restrictions on the relationship between E and the *mpe* and, in particular, analogous to Deaton's (1974) reasoning, additivity of the direct utility function can be shown to imply

$$E = (mpe) + \omega^{-1}\mu^{-1}[1 + (mpe)], \tag{32}$$

where $\mu = (wh)/y$ and $\omega = (\partial\lambda/\partial y)(y/\lambda) < 0$ is the elasticity of the marginal utility of nonwage income with respect to nonwage income.[66] In other words for someone for whom nonwage income is a very small fraction of total income (i.e. for someone whose value of μ^{-1} is very small), additivity of the direct utility function will restrict the estimated value of his *mpe* to be similar to his estimated value of the uncompensated elasticity of hours of work with respect to wages (E) and for this individual the compensated elasticity, $E^* = \omega^{-1}\mu^{-1}(mpe)[1 + (mpe)]$, will tend to be a small number. Of course in some data nonwage income appears for a number of people not to be such a small part of total income so for such individuals E will not approximate the *mpe*, but nevertheless eq. (32) shows that

[65] In fact, the estimates of the *mpe* after imposing more structure on the data are similar to these least squares regressions. See Atkinson and Stern (1980) and Deaton (1982).

[66] More generally, direct additivity of the household utility function $U = \phi[f_0(x) - f_1(h_1) - f_2(h_2)]$ implies the following relationships for the elasticity of hours of work of individual 1:

$$E_{1j} = \mu_1^{-1}(mpe)_1\left[\mu_j + \omega^{-1}(mpe)_j\right] + \delta_{1j}\omega^{-1}\mu_1^{-1}(mpe)_1, \quad j = 0,1,2,$$

where $\delta_{1j} = 1$ if $j = 1$ and $\delta_{1j} = 0$ otherwise, where $(mpe)_0 = p\,\partial x/\partial y$, and where E_{10} must be interpreted as the negative of the uncompensated elasticity of hours of work with respect to commodity prices. Note that, because a part of income is endogenous, ω here is different from the usual concept of Frisch's money flexibility.

additivity builds in restrictions among the behavioral responses that the data are unlikely to conform to.

It is useful as a reference for our discussion below to illustrate eq. (32) with a utility function (or a variant of it) that has been used relatively often in labor supply analysis. Abstracting from variations in personal characteristics A and in individual tastes ε, consider the following additive (strongly separable) utility function described by the parameters b, c, B, and ρ:

$$U(x, h) = \left[(1-B)(x-c)^{\rho} + B(b-h)^{\rho}\right]^{1/\rho}, \tag{33}$$

where $0 < B < 1$, $x > c$, $b > h$, and $\rho < 1$. This utility function goes by different names – sometimes the nonhomothetic constant-elasticity-of-substitution function, sometimes the one-branch utility tree – but I shall refer to it as the generalized Stone–Geary utility function [Pollak (1971)]. This function conveniently nests some special cases that have frequently been used in fitting labor supply functions.[67] The optimizing hours of work function from eq. (33) is

$$h = b - \frac{B^{\zeta} w^{-\zeta}(y + bw - cp)}{\left[(1-B)^{\zeta} p^{1-\zeta} + B^{\zeta} w^{1-\zeta}\right]}, \tag{34}$$

where $\zeta = (1-\rho)^{-1} > 0$ and the *mpe* and the uncompensated elasticity of hours of work with respect to wages (E) are as follows:

$$mpe = -\frac{B^{\zeta} w^{1-\zeta}}{(1-B)^{\zeta} p^{1-\zeta} + B^{\zeta} w^{1-\zeta}}$$

$$E = (1 - bh^{-1})\left\{\frac{[\zeta b + (1-\zeta)h]w}{(y + bw - cp)} - 1\right\}$$

$$= -1 + [1 + (mpe)][\zeta bh^{-1} + (1-\zeta)]. \tag{35}$$

The behavioral responses corresponding to the Stone–Geary utility function are obtained by letting ζ equal unity, whereas the conventional constant-elasticity-of-substitution function is obtained in eq. (33) by setting the "reference" parameters, c and b, to zero and replacing the term $B(b-h)^{\rho}$ with $-B^{*}h^{\rho}$. Chipman's (1965) "weakly homothetic" utility function results when $\rho \to -\infty$. With utility function (33), $\omega = -\zeta^{-1}y(y + bw - cp)^{-1}$, so that with the definitions of the *mpe* and E above, eq. (32) is easily derived.

[67]Within the class of empirical work making use of nonexperimental data on individual workers, eq. (33) covers the functional forms used by Betancourt (1971), Blundell and Walker (1981, 1983), Brown, Levin, Rosa, Ruffell and Ulph (1982–83), Hurd and Pencavel (1981), Rosen (1978), Wales (1973), and Wales and Woodland (1979). In addition, the hours of work equation derived from eq. (29) is similar to that estimated by Atkinson and Stern (1980, 1981).

In short, whether derived explicitly from a particular utility function or simply written down ab initio, the hours of work estimating equation involves selecting a specific functional form and the choice of this function inevitably embodies some assumptions about the differences in the behavioral responses (i.e. the differences in E and the *mpe*) across individuals. Unfortunately, at present an assessment of these assumptions is difficult because so little is known about these variations.

In most cases, the static model has been estimated by fitting a regression equation such as eq. (28) to cross-section data collected from a sample survey of households or of individuals. The precise questions asked vary from survey to survey, but normally an individual (or his spouse) is asked about his hours worked (and his weeks worked) in a given week (year) or in a typical week (year), his labor earnings during a specified period of time or his usual hourly earnings, and his income from other sources. The response to these questions form the basis of the observations on the purported labor supply function.

In an econometric exercise associating quantities (hours of work) and prices (wage rates), prior to estimation it is appropriate to enquire whether what is being estimated is a supply function, a demand function, or some hybrid. Suppose that a worker with a specific set of characteristics valued by firms faced a horizontal demand curve for his services, i.e. the worker may choose any hours to work at a given wage rate. Workers with different characteristics of varying values to firms would face horizontal demand curves at different levels of real wages. Provided some of these characteristics were not at the same time associated with these workers' preferences for income or leisure,[68] then in a cross-section of individuals the revealed wage–hours combinations would reflect the intersection of different horizontal demand curves with a fixed (for a given set of variables determining preferences) labor supply function. This provides one rationalization of the common presumption that a regression of hours worked on wage rates and other variables maps out a labor supply function.

As noted in Section 3.3 above, most firms appear not to be indifferent to the hours worked by each of their employees: the presence of quasi-fixed hiring and training costs that are more closely tied to the *number* of employees than to their hours worked encourages firms to offer higher wage rates for longer hours worked [Lewis (1969)]. If this is the case, the worker faces a wage–hours locus such that shorter hours of work are renumerated at a lower hourly wage rate. Once again, across workers with the same preferences, their labor supply function is traced out by a series of different (nonhorizontal) labor demand schedules, each demand curve indexed by a particular quality of labor. Provided identifying variables exist, the labor supply function can be estimated by a regression of hours worked

[68] What are the (identifying) variables that appear in the demand function for hours by employers and that do not enter the supply function for hours of work? Perhaps the most obvious candidates for such variables are indicators of the level of local labor market activity.

on wage rates, but now of course account must be taken of the fact that the wage offered by employers is no longer independent of each worker's own decisions.

4.2. Empirical results from U.S. nonexperimental data

A brief chronology of the major phases of modern empirical research on male labor supply may be listed as follows. Kosters' (1966, 1969) analysis of the hours worked of married men aged between 50 and 64 years old ranks as the first modern empirical study of this topic both by virtue of its close attention to its theoretical underpinnings and by virtue of his use of a sample of observations on individuals;[69] there soon followed many studies [a number of them being brought together in Cain and Watts (1973)] whose methods were similar to Kosters', but which analyzed other groups in the labor force; in response to the diversity of results from these studies and in an attempt to account for them, the next phase of research [as best illustrated by DaVanzo, DeTray and Greenberg (1973, 1976)] was the application of a variety of different procedures to a single body of data; the 1970s also saw increasing attention to the econometric implications of nonrandom sample selection [Heckman (1974b, 1976b)] and nonlinear budget constraints [Burtless and Hausman (1978), Wales and Woodland (1979)]; meanwhile, from the mid-1970s, new sources of information were becoming available, namely the results from the various negative income tax experiments and the estimates from British research; finally, the 1970s witnessed increasing attention to the life-cycle models of labor supply and, at the time of writing, this seems to be the most active area of male labor supply research.

In order to trace this chronology a little more closely, return to Kosters' original analysis of the hours worked by employed married men aged 50–64 years. His observations were drawn from the 1 in 1000 sample of the 1960 Census of Population and he estimated to these data ordinary least-squares equations linear in the logarithms of the variables. One such equation is the following which was estimated with 8467 observations:

$$\ln h_i = \underset{(0.0044)}{-\,0.094}\ \ln w_i - \underset{(0.0015)}{0.0073}\ \ln y_i + \cdots + \hat{\varepsilon}_i, \quad R^2 = 0.10,$$

where estimated standard errors are in parentheses beneath coefficients and where the dots indicate that 16 other variables were included in the regression equation. The income-compensated wage elasticity of hours of work (E^*)

[69]A number of studies preceded Kosters' that examined the issues at an aggregate level – Douglas (1934) had measured the association between hours worked and earnings at the industry level, Finegan (1962) at the occupational level, Winston (1966) at the national level – but Kosters appears to have been the first to apply the theory to the unit whose behavior it is meant to describe.

implied by the estimates is $+0.041$ when evaluated at the (geometric) mean values of the observations. The estimate of -0.094 for the uncompensated wage elasticity was robust with respect to changes in equation specification and, moreover, accorded well with previous estimates – with Douglas's (1934) preferred estimate "in all probability somewhere between -0.1 and -0.2" and with Winston's (1966) estimates of -0.07 to -0.10, though less so with Finegan's (1962) estimates of -0.25 to -0.35. On the other hand, the estimate of -0.0073 for the nonwage income elasticity of the supply of working hours appeared to be sensitive to changes in functional form and in the precise definition of nonwage income.

Kosters' procedures with relatively minor modifications were soon being applied by other researchers to different samples. A stimulus to this research was provided by the prominent public policy debate over the costs of welfare reform which were intimately tied to the labor supply effects of taxes and transfers. In part as a consequence of this emphasis on welfare reform, a number of studies that reported in early 1970s restricted their empirical work to samples of the relatively poor. In constructing such samples, observations were discarded on the basis of values taken by a variable (income) that is clearly related to the endogenous variable of interest (hours of work). This induces an analogous sort of sample selection bias as that discussed in Section 4.1 above.[70]

This feature of male labor supply studies of the early 1970s – that observations on relatively high income individuals or households were eliminated from their samples – represented only one dimension in which the various research papers differed from one another. They also differed in the precise definitions of the variables, the particular functional relationship posited, the assumptions made about commodity prices, and the set of nonbudget constraint variables included in the hours of work regression equations. These differences in the implementation of the labor supply model yielded sufficiently disparate estimates as to provide little practical assistance to questions of public policy. In view of these differences, it was important to address the question: "With respect to which set of assumptions and procedures are the hours of work estimates sensitive and with respect to which are they robust?" This was taken up by DaVanzo, DeTray and Greenberg (1973) who applied many different procedures to a single body of data, namely, 5294 white, married, male heads of households aged 25–54 years drawn from the 1967 Survey of Economic Opportunity (SEO). Their Rand report is full of valuable information for anyone embarking on his own labor supply

[70] For an elaboration of this point in the labor supply context, see Cain and Watts' (1973) lucid statement. For a more general treatment of the issue, see Goldberger (1981). Studies that imposed some sort of income criterion in defining their analysis sample included those of Boskin (1973), Fleischer, Parsons, and Porter (1973), Greenberg and Kosters (1973), Hall (1973), Hill (1973), Kalachek and Raines (1970), Kurz et al. (1974), and Rosen and Welch (1971).

study.[71] The same question was addressed by Masters and Garfinkel (1977) in their extensive analysis of data from the 1967 SEO and from the 1972 Michigan Panel Study of Income Dynamics (PSID). The differences in procedures among the studies and the consequences of these different procedures may be summarized as follows.

1. Problems in measuring the hours and wage rate variables. In studies based on data from the 1960 Census of Population or the 1967 Survey of Economic Opportunity, the hours of work variable combined one dimension of work behavior (namely, hours per week) in one year (in 1960 for the Census and in 1967 for the SEO) with another dimension of work (namely, weeks worked per year) in a different year (in 1959 for the Census and in 1966 for the SEO).[72] Then this dependent variable often appeared in the construction of the wage rate variable (i.e. for the Census data, annual labor income in 1959 was divided by this estimate of hours worked) so that any errors in measuring true hours worked in 1959 or in 1966 will appear in the wage rate variable inducing a spurious negative correlation between hours worked and wage rates. What contribution, if any, was this making to the frequent finding of a negatively-sloped labor supply curve? The answer, it seemed, was that the slope of the male ordinary least-squares estimated hours of work function was more negative when such a wage variable was used than when an alternative wage rate variable (such as an instrumented wage rate) was constructed. Evidence on this is contained in Bloch (1973), DaVanzo, DeTray and Greenberg (1973), Masters and Garfinkel (1977), and Borjas (1980). Nevertheless, even after trying to rid the wage variable of this spurious correlation, most studies found a negative (uncompensated) own-wage elasticity of hours of work at sample mean values: for instance, DaVanzo, DeTray and Greenberg (1973) report estimates between -0.15 and -0.09,[73] Masters and Garfinkel (1977) "best estimate" is -0.110, and Ashenfelter and Heckman's (1973) is -0.156.

[71] Much of their analysis was conducted with a sample of 2012 men who reported being unaffected by unemployment and by poor health and who received no work-related transfer payments. They then considered the consequences of adding to the original sample 3282 men who reported these characteristics.

[72] Many other definitions of the hours worked variable have been used. A common one is the product of the number of weeks worked in a given year and the average number of hours worked per week during those weeks in which the individual worked. Some studies add an estimate of hours spent unemployed to the number of hours worked.

[73] DaVanzo, DeTray and Greenberg's estimates reported here are derived from Tables 11 and 12 of their Rand study where the dependent variable is measured as annual hours of work and where the wage rate and nonwage income variables are instrumented. The sample in this case consists of those 2012 men who reported no unemployment or health disability nor receipt of any work-related transfer payments. Other variables included in these equations are age, age squared, schooling, household size, number of children less than six years of age, various variables denoting location of residence, the spouse's annual earnings, and the annual earnings of other family members.

2. The measurement of nonwage income. This variable was particularly difficult to measure accurately. Koster's procedure was to form this variable by deducting the husband's earnings from total household income, but this meant y included transfer income that was not independent of the husband's hours of work. Also, y excluded income in the form of the service flow from durable goods and housing. Moreover, this definition of nonwage income incorporated the earnings of the wife and of other members of the household and, therefore, it is not exogenous with respect to the husband's labor supply behavior if the work decisions of each member of the household are made jointly.[74] In other studies [e.g. Ashenfelter and Heckman (1973)], y is explicitly measured by aggregating the responses to the survey's questions about the net income received in the form of rents, dividends, interest, private transfers, and alimony payments. Another procedure [e.g. Fleisher, Parsons and Porter (1973)] is to assume that y is proportional to the household's net worth (where the factor of proportionality is given by the relevant rate of return). These different procedures generate markedly different estimates of the effect of nonwage income on hours of work. For instance, the *mpe* (i.e. $w \cdot \partial h / \partial y$) at sample mean values is estimated at -0.27 in Ashenfelter and Heckman (1973), -0.06 in Bloch (1973), -0.08 in Fleisher, Parsons, and Porter (1973), approximately -0.32 in Kalachek and Raines (1970), and -0.047 in Masters and Garfinkel (1977). However, these estimates are sensitive to the particular specification of the estimating equation and, indeed, it is by no means uncommon for a positive (partial) association to exist between nonwage income and hours of work. For instance, of the 57 different estimated coefficients on net worth reported in Tables 6, 9, 11, and 12 of DaVanzo, DeTray and Greenberg's Rand study, only 16 would be judged as significantly different from zero on conventional two-tailed t-tests and, of these 16, exactly one-half is positive and one-half is negative. Positive (partial) correlations between male hours worked and nonwage income are reported in Cohen, Rea and Lerman (1970), Dickinson (1974), Garfinkel (1973), Hill (1973), Kniesner (1976), and Masters and Garfinkel (1977) and they would probably have been calculated in Burtless and Hausman (1978), Hausman (1981), and Hurd and Pencavel (1981) if the estimation procedure had not prohibited it. In view of these widely varying estimates on nonwage income, when an equation such as eq. (24) is fitted and the substitution effect is calculated residually as $\alpha_1 - h\alpha_2$, given the negative (un-

[74] This raises another class of differences among the various empirical studies, namely, the treatment of the wife's labor earnings. Sometimes her earnings are incorporated into nonwage income in which case the tacit assumption is that these earnings produce an income effect on the husband's hours of work, but no substitution effect. On other occasions, the wife's wage rate is included as a separate independent variable, but often its estimated coefficient is insignificantly different from zero by conventional criteria. This was DaVanzo, DeTray and Greenberg's finding and, moreover, their estimates for the coefficient on the husband's wage rate were affected only trivially by different ways of specifying the wife's earnings.

compensated) effect of wages on hours of work that is typically estimated (i.e. given $\alpha_1 < 0$), it is by no means unusual for the implied substitution effects for male workers to be negative at the sample mean values of h. Such negative effects appear in the empirical work of, for instance, Cohen, Rea and Lerman (1970), DaVanzo, DeTray and Greenberg (1973), Fleisher, Parsons and Porter (1973), Hall (1973), Kniesner (1976), Kosters (1966), and Masters and Garfinkel (1977). This hardly constitutes a resounding corroboration of the conventional static model of labor supply.

3. The treatment of taxes. Sometimes, as in Kosters' study and in Ashenfelter and Heckman's (1973) study, no allowance was made for personal income taxes either in forming the wage rate or the nonwage income variable. On other occasions, as in Boskin (1973) and in Hall (1973), the budget constraint was assumed to be continuous and to form a convex set and budget constraint variables net of taxes were constructed, but then the joint determination of all these budget constraint variables with hours of work was ignored. There have been few instances [one is Kurz et al. (1974)][75] in which the budget constraint variables were adjusted for taxes and, in addition, they were treated as endogenous. In order to assess the effects of adjusting the budget constraint variables for taxes, we should like to see from the same body of data estimates of hours of work equations based on pre-tax budget constraint variables and instrumental variable estimates based on post-tax budget constraint variables. I know of no study that presents this information for men though Mroz (1984) has undertaken such a comparison for married women and found relatively small differences between the two sets of estimates.

Is the assumption that the after-tax budget constraints for most men are continuous and form a convex set an important departure from the truth? Some think so. Therefore, they have proposed and applied more elaborate algorithms that are designed to search over each segment of a piecewise-linear budget constraint in order to determine the parameters describing the utility-maximizing hours of work. For instance, Wales and Woodland (1979) assume they know without error each individual's net wage rate and nonwage income and they use these budget constraint variables together with the unknown parameters of the individual's constant-elasticity-of-substitution utility function (posited to be the same and nonstochastic for all individuals) to impute each individual's hours of work along each segment of his piecewise-linear budget constraint. For each individual, therefore, there is a relationship between the different possible values of the utility function's parameters and his imputed hours of work, given the values of his budget constraint. Among many possible values of the parameters

[75] However, the procedures of Kurz et al., do not yield a consistent estimator because nonlinear transformations of the imputed wage rate and nonwage income variables were used in the hours of work equations.

of the utility function, those are selected that minimize the sum over all individuals of the squared difference between the imputed hours and the actual hours. The only sources of error in their model are errors in maximization or the effects of random variables (examples of which, write Wales and Woodland, are unanticipated expenditures or illness) that cause the individual to work different hours from those given by his budget constraint variables and utility function. They applied their algorithm to a sample (from the Michigan PSID) of 226 married men whose wives did not work in the labor market and their estimates of the utility function parameters implied values of the (uncompensated) wage elasticity of hours of work of 0.14 and of the marginal propensity to earn of -0.70. This wage elasticity lies above the central tendency of estimates while the marginal propensity to earn is an even more noticeable outlier and one might be inclined to wonder whether the more conventional estimation methods have seriously misestimated these behavioral parameters. However, Wales and Woodland derived similar estimates when they applied the more conventional approach of linearizing the budget constraint around the observed hours of work for each man so that the more elaborate algorithm did not appear to be responsible for the estimates of the relatively high wage elasticity and aberrant marginal propensity to earn.

Other studies using these sorts of algorithms have also yielded odd estimates. For instance, Hausman's (1981) work is a generalization of Wales and Woodland's to allow for stochastic variation in preferences across individuals, but otherwise he proceeds on similar lines.[76] With a sample of 1085 married men from the 1975 Michigan PSID, Hausman has the benefit of almost five times as many observations as Wales and Woodland.[77] Fitting a linear hours of work function, Hausman estimated an (uncompensated) wage elasticity of male working hours of zero and a marginal propensity to earn of approximately -0.77.[78] Although this latter estimate is not without precedent, it differs sharply from the implications of estimates of nonwage income on consumption. Hausman's estimate implies that an additional dollar of nonwage income induces such a reduction in working hours that (at sample means) labor earnings fall by 77 cents and the consumption of commodities increases by only 23 cents. Income effects in consumption could be this small, but the prevailing evidence suggests the contrary.

[76] An excellent exposition of Hausman's work [and that of Burtless and Hausman (1978)] is contained in Heckman and MaCurdy (1981) and Heckman, Killingsworth and MaCurdy (1981).

[77] This increase in the size of the sample is not achieved costlessly, however. Whereas Wales and Woodland examined only those men whose wives did not work in the labor market, Hausman made no distinction between men whose wives were working and those who were not.

[78] This value is derived as follows. Hausman reports a mean gross wage rate of \$6.18 and predicted mean hours of 2181. This implies labor income of \$13 479. Suppose someone with this income faces a marginal tax rate of 25 percent. Then the mean net wage rate is approximately \$4.64 ($=$ \$6.18 $\times$ 0.75). Given his estimate of $\partial h/\partial y$ of -0.166, the *mpe* for such an individual is -0.77.

In short, these studies, using more elaborate computational algorithms, yield estimates of the key behavioral parameters that diverge from the central tendency of estimates and that are somewhat implausible. Because these studies pay greater attention to some issues (especially the piecewise-linear nature of the budget constraint and perhaps also its nonconvexity) at the cost of the neglect of others (e.g. they treat wage rates and nonwage income as exogenous and not measured with error), it is by no means evident that their estimates of the male labor supply function are to be regarded as preferable to those derived from more prosaic and perhaps more robust estimating methods.[79]

4. Assumptions about commodity prices. In most cross-section studies it was assumed that all individuals face the same prices for commodities so that variations in the money wage rate and money nonlabor income correspond to variations in the real values of the variables. There were a few studies [e.g. Bloch (1973), Boskin (1973)] that made use of some Bureau of Labor Statistics information on the cost of living in different regions and cities. If such geographic cost-of-living adjustments are not made, then this rationalizes the presence of region and city size dummy variables that often appear in estimated labor supply equations. When this BLS information on cost-of-living differences by city size and by region was used to deflate the wage rate variable, both DaVanzo, DeTray and Greenberg (1973) and Masters and Garfinkel (1977) report small changes in the estimated coefficient in the wage rate.

5. Issues of functional form. Kosters' linear-in-the-logarithms specification reported above is unusual in this literature. More frequently, as discussed in Section 4.1 linear equations along the lines of eq. (28) have been estimated. Occasionally the following semi-logarithmic specification in wage rates has been posited:

$$h_i = \alpha_0 + \alpha_1 \ln\left(\frac{w}{p}\right)_i + \alpha_2\left(\frac{y}{p}\right)_i + \alpha_3 A_i + \varepsilon_i,$$

which restricts the uncompensated wage effect to be smaller (in absolute value) for high wage individuals. There is, of course, no a priori reason to believe that the data will naturally conform to the restrictions on the behavioral parameters implied by these functions. In view of the prominent role occupied in introductory texts by the so-called backward-bending labor supply curve, it was natural for researchers to determine the empirical relevance of such a phenomenon. Normally this has been effected by adding quadratic terms in the wage rate to

[79]This conjecture about the robustness – that methods such as Hausman's and Wales and Woodland's are less robust with respect to small departures from the assumptions that underlie them as compared with the more conventional estimation methods – is also contained in Heckman (1983).

equations such as eq. (28) [e.g. Bloch (1973), DaVanzo, DeTray and Greenberg (1973), Hill (1973), Rosen and Welch (1971)] or by estimating a free form whereby the efficient α_1 is allowed to vary across different wage intervals [e.g. Cohen, Rea and Lerman (1970), DaVanzo, DeTray and Greenberg (1973), Garfinkel (1973), Greenberg and Kosters (1973), Hall (1973)]. There have been instances in which evidence for such a backward-bending hours of work function for males has been reported [e.g. Cohen, Rea and Lerman (1970)], but forward-bending curves have also been estimated [e.g. Hurd (1976), Kurz et al. (1974)], and from an overview of the empirical results, there does not appear to be powerful evidence for nonlinearities in the wage-hours relationship for men. However, most of this research on functional form has been incidental to other issues and a systematic empirical investigation of the variation of income and substitution effects across individuals has yet to be undertaken in labor supply research.[80]

6. Nonbudget constraint variables included in the hours of work equation. The various studies on male labor supply differ from each other in the set of control variables entered in the hours of work regression equation. For instance, some studies include a measure of the individual's educational attainment [e.g. Cohen, Rea and Lerman (1970), Garfinkel (1973), Hill (1973), Kniesner (1976), Kosters (1966), Rosen and Welch (1971)] while other studies exclude it [e.g. Ashenfelter and Heckman (1973), Bloch (1973), Boskin (1973), Hausman (1981), Hurd (1976), Masters and Garfinkel (1977)]. When such a variable is included, its estimated coefficient is almost always positive and significant by conventional criteria suggesting that, other things equal, more formally educated men work longer hours. Moreover, DaVanzo, DeTray, and Greenberg's investigation found that the size and sign of the wage coefficient was extremely sensitive to the presence of years of schooling in the estimated hours of work equation.[81] As another example, a measure of the number of dependents in the household is sometimes included in an equation accounting for variations in the working hours of men [e.g. Bloch (1973), Boskin (1973), Cohen, Rea and Lerman (1970), Hausman (1981), Masters and Garfinkel (1977)] and it is sometimes excluded [e.g. Ashenfelter and Heckman (1973), Fleisher, Parsons and Porter (1973), Garfinkel (1973) Rosen and Welch (1971)]. When a variable of this kind is included, it tends to reveal a significantly positive (partial) association with hours of work. In general, researchers have been somewhat cavalier in their choice of nonbudget constraint variables to be included in an hours of work equation, but unfortunately DaVanzo, DeTray, and Greenberg's experiment with their school-

[80]A start is contained in Dickinson (1979, 1980).

[81]Some researchers may well be seduced into omitting schooling from the hours of work regression equation because then they may claim it as an instrument for wage rates.

ing variable indicates that the presence or absence of certain nonbudget constraint variables may profoundly affect the inferences about the wage elasticity of hours of work. It is not unusual for no explicit reason to be given for the presence in the hours of work regression equation of these nonbudget constraint variables. Most researchers seem to have in mind that variables such as education or family size are systematically associated with differences in tastes for work (or, equivalently, differences in nonmarket productivity) so that they correspond to what I have denoted as the variables A in the description of the contrained maximization problem above. Nevertheless, as I have emphasized in Section 2, in addition to these taste variations that are believed to be associated with variables (such as education and family size) observed to the researcher, there is also a very important unobservable taste component (as represented by ε in Section 2). Usually this unobserved taste component is simply tacked on as the stochastic term to the hours of work equation, but there exist other ways of addressing the issue of variation in observed tastes. For instances, Greenberg and Kosters (1973) constructed a variable designed to represent differences in preferences for asset accumulation by measuring the difference between an individual's actual net assets and those net assets predicted on the basis of his age and wage rate from a prior regression equation and then expressing this difference as a fraction of total imputed wealth. This inclusion of this so-called preference variable changed their estimated coefficient on nonwage income in an hours of work regression equation from positive to negative. The problem with this variable, as Cain and Watts (1973) note, is that its construction makes use of information about the wage rate and nonwage income and thus it is natural to wonder whether it incorporates some part of the conventional wage and income effects of the budget constraint.

A number of the estimates from U.S. nonexperimental data of the static model's behavioral responses are brought together in Table 1.19 Although the major studies are included, this table is not exhaustive. In several cases [such as Wales and Woodland (1976, 1977)] insufficient information is provided in the publications with which to calculate the compensated wage-elasticities or the *mpe*. In other cases [e.g. Hall (1973)] many different estimates are presented and I gave up the attempt to summarize them adequately with a few numbers. I have also excluded studies such as those of Hausman (1981) and Hurd and Pencavel (1978) that in estimation restricted the effect of nonwage income on hours to be nonpositive. In drawing inferences from Table 1.19, the caveats given in Section 4.1 above should be kept in mind. These estimates are drawn from different estimating equations and from different functional forms and evaluating the estimated parameters at sample mean values of the variable provides only a very rough and inexact method of comparing behavioral responses. Table 1.19 reveals that, of the estimates presented, Wales and Woodland's (1979) are considerably different from the rest, a result I attribute both to the restriction between E and

Table 1.19
Estimates from U.S. nonexperimental data of behavioral responses for men.

	E	*mpe*	E^*
Ashenfelter and Heckman (1973)	−0.16	−0.27	0.12
Bloch (1973)	0.06	−0.06	0.12
Boskin (1973)	−0.29	−0.41	0.12
DaVanzo, DeTray and Greenberg (1973)	−0.15	−0.004	−0.14
Dickinson (1974)	−0.11	0.08	−0.19
Fleisher, Parsons and Porter (1973)	−0.19	−0.23	0.04
Garfinkel (1973)	0	0	0
Greenberg and Kosters (1973)	−0.09	−0.29	0.20
Ham (1982)	−0.16	−0.11	−0.05
Hausman and Ruud (1984)	−0.08	−0.63	0.55
Kniesner (1976a)	−0.17	−0.01	−0.16
Kosters (1966)	−0.09	−0.14	0.04
Masters and Garfinkel (1977)	−0.11	−0.05	−0.06
Wales and Woodland (1979)	0.14	−0.70	0.84

Notes: The estimates reported for DaVanzo, DeTray and Greenberg (1973) correspond to those given on the last line of Table 11 of their Rand report where both the wage rate and nonwage income variables were instrumented. Those for Ham (1982) correspond to those given in column (1) of Table IV of his paper. Those for Kniesner (1976a) apply to those men whose wives were not at work for pay. For Masters and Garfinkel (1977), I took what they described as their "best estimates" of E and the *mpe* even though the coefficients reported did not derive from the same regression equation. Boskin's (1973) results are those for white men only. Dickinson's (1974) *mpe* is calculated from his estimate coefficient on "other (nontransfer) family income". Hausman and Ruud's estimates are calculated for a household with an assumed marginal tax rate of 25 percent so the husband's net wage rate is \$4.31 and the wife's net wage rate is \$2.63.

the *mpe* implicit in their use of the CES function[82] and to their estimating method which may well not be robust with respect to small departures from the assumptions underlying its use. Of the remaining studies, the largest estimate of E is 0.06 [Bloch (1973)] and the smallest is -0.29 [Boskin (1973)]. The central tendency of estimates of E lies between -0.17 and -0.08 and a simple average of all the estimates of E in Table 1.19 (excluding Wales and Woodland's) is -0.12. Table 1.19's estimates of the *mpe* (again excluding Wales and Woodland's) range from a low of -0.63 [Hausman and Ruud (1984)] to a high of 0.08 [Dickinson (1974)]. The estimates of the *mpe* are more disparate than those for E and I hesitate to infer its value from such a varied set of estimates. Certainly, the large negative numbers seem very unlikely. In five cases in Table 1.19, the compensated wage elasticity of hours of work, E^*, is negative. Of the six positive

[82]As equation (35) makes clear, in the CES case when $b=0$, $E=-\zeta+(1-\zeta)(mpe)$.

values of $E*$ (excluding Wales and Woodland's and Hausman and Ruud's), the mean is 0.11. If E is -0.12 and $E*$ is 0.11, the *mpe* is -0.23.

4.3. Empirical results from British data

Modern British research on male hours of work got under way in the 1970s and from the beginning the work has consistently been concerned with the implications of the taxation of income on the supply of labor and so the studies invariably adjust each individual's budget constraint variables for such taxes.[83] The first papers were those of Brown, Levin and Ulph (1976) and Layard (1978). The data analyzed in the former study came from a survey conducted at the end of 1971 by a private market research firm. With a relatively small and perhaps unrepresentative sample[84] of 284 married men whose wives were not at work in the labor market, Brown, Levin and Ulph (1976) estimated (with a conventional ordinary least-squares regression linear in parameters but nonlinear in the budget constraint variables) an (uncompensated) own-wage elasticity of hours of work of between -0.085 and -0.131 at sample mean values.[85] This was derived from a curious specification in which both linearized nonwage income and a measure of "other income" were included.[86] Subsequent work by Brown (1981) and his associates using similar procedures yielded comparable wage elasticities and marginal propensities to earn of between -0.31 and -0.35. Other methods were also applied to these data including a study by Ashworth and Ulph (1981) that, independently of the work of Wales and Woodland (1979) and Burtless and Hausman (1978), proposed and implemented the procedure of searching over each individual's entire piecewise linear budget constraint to determine the utility-maximizing hours of work. With a generalized constant-elasticity-of-substitution indirect utility function applied to 335 married men, Ashworth and Ulph (1981) derived estimates that implied an uncompensated wage elasticity of hours of work of between -0.07 and -0.13 and a marginal propensity to earn of between -0.36 and -0.57.

Layard's (1978) study involved a much larger sample of 2700 married men from the General Household Survey of 1974 and, with a linear specification along

[83] The British studies of male workers always use weekly hours of work as the dependent variable.

[84] The authors themselves were aware of both the small size and possible nonrandom nature of their sample. A very informative discussion of these data is contained in Brown (1981).

[85] Although this wage elasticity is estimated to be negative at sample mean values, it becomes less negative as the wage rate rises and, indeed, it eventually takes on positive values. In other words, they estimate an hours of work function that is a mirror-image of the textbook backward-bending function.

[86] In a later study [Brown (1980, p. 60)], this is justified on the argument that "other income" is, in fact, dependent upon the male's labor supply. Of course, if this is the case, then it should be included in calculating the wage slope of the budget constraint.

the lines of eq. (24), he estimated an uncompensated wage elasticity of -0.13 and a small (in absolute value) marginal propensity to earn of -0.04. Indeed, with such an income effect, his implied compensated wage effect on hours of work was negative.

In Britain the availability of cross-section information from the Family Expenditure Survey (FES) on both hours of work and expenditures on different groups of commodities has permitted the joint estimation of labor supply and commodity demand equations as implied by eq. (8). Provided the allocation model underlying eq. (8) is correct, estimating such a system of equations has the advantage of generating much more efficient estimates. The greatest potential for these data is to *test* that allocation model, but curiously they have not been used for this purpose to date. Nevertheless, some indications of how these tests would fare are provided in the papers making use of these data. Consider, for instance, the work of Atkinson and Stern (1980, 1981) who specified a generalized Stone–Geary utility function where that generalization is the novel one involving explicit use of Becker's (1965) particular formulation of the household production approach to the allocation of time. In fact, when all the commodities may be aggregated into one composite, their hours of work function closely resembles eq. (30). They select a sample from the 1973 FES consisting of 1617 households with a male head employed full-time (not self-employed) and whose earnings placed him within the (fairly wide) range in which the slope of the after-tax budget constraint was approximately constant. They identify nine different categories of household consumption expenditures plus the hours of work of the men.[87] Their results suggested uncompensated wage elasticities (evaluated at their sample pre-tax mean values) ranging from -0.15 to -0.23 although, as in Brown, Levin and Ulph (1976), the estimated hours of work function is a forward-falling curve and at relatively high wages they estimate a positive wage elasticity. They tend to find that leisure is an inferior commodity and ultimately they impose the constraint that pure leisure is not valued for its own sake (i.e. it has value only insofar as it contributes to the production of utility-generating activities). As is often the case with the Stone–Geary specification, the extent of nonconvexity implied by the estimates is considerable and, in particular, many men work more hours than permitted by the estimates of the maximum amount remaining after allocating time to other activities.

Another study estimating a system of commodity demand and labor supply equations is Blundell and Walker's (1982). From the 1974 FES, they select a sample of only 103 households in which both the husband and the wife work, a term being included to account for this deliberate nonrandom selection of female

[87] The earnings of the wife and of others in the household are included in nonwage income.

workers. They also specified a generalized Stone–Geary utility function[88] in which six groups of commodities and the hours of work of the husband and of the wife appear as arguments. Their parameter estimates implied (at sample mean values) an uncompensated wage elasticity of male hours of work of -0.23 and a marginal propensity to earn of -0.36 with, therefore, an implied (compensated) wage elasticity for men of 0.13. Because the wife's marginal propensity to earn was estimated to be -0.22, their results implied that an additional dollar of nonwage income would raise consumption by only 42 cents (i.e. $1-0.36-0.22$). Blundell and Walker do not indicate how many of their 103 husbands and wives are working more hours than permitted by the estimated parameters describing the maximum feasible hours of work, but there are surely some although probably a smaller proportion of their sample than of Atkinson and Stern's. They test and reject the hypothesis that the husband and wife's time allocation decision is weakly separable from the household's decisions about the consumption of commodities, but maintained throughout the analysis is the hypothesis that expenditures on housing are separable from all other decisions. In a subsequent study of 308 working married couples drawn from the 1977 FES and specifying four categories of consumer goods (but excluding alcohol, tobacco, housing, and other durable goods (expenditures), Blundell and Walker (1983) report an uncompensated wage elasticity of male hours of work of -0.004 (evaluated at 39.6 weekly hours of work, the mean value for their earlier sample) and an *mpe* of -0.203.

The preliminary results from another British project financed by H. M. Treasury are becoming available at the time of writing this survey paper [Brown, Levin, Rosa, Ruffell and Ulph (1983)]. This new project involved both a new survey (conducted in late 1980) and a new sample of 3307 households who provided sufficient information for analysis. In an initial investigation of 810 one- and two-worker households, the researchers applied a similar algorithm to that used by Ashworth and Ulph (1981) and Wales and Woodland (1979) to search over each individual's entire piecewise linear budget constraint. Unfortunately, this algorithm did not identify a well-defined maximum of the likelihood function although the estimates of the parameters of the nonstochastic generalized Stone–Geary function [identical to eq. (33)] are described as being "in the right area". At the sample mean values of the wage rate and nonwage income, the worker in single-worker families is estimated to have an uncompensated wage elasticity of hours of work of -0.32, a compensated wage elasticity of 0.18, and a marginal propensity to earn of -0.50. In two-worker families, the husband

[88] The generalization takes the form of specifying the "subsistence" or "reference" quantities not as parameters, but as functions of commodity prices and of household structure. In fact, because all households are assumed to face the same prices for commodities, the only effective generalization is one which allows the subsistence quantities to vary across households with different numbers and ages of children.

Table 1.20
Estimates of the behavioral responses for British males.

		E	mpe	E^*
Ashworth and Ulph (1981)		−0.13	−0.36	0.23
Atkinson and Stern (1980)		−0.16	−0.07	−0.09
Blundell and Walker (1982)		−0.23	−0.36	0.13
Blundell and Walker (1983)		−0.004	−0.20	0.20
Brown, Levin, and Ulph (1976)		−0.13	−0.35	0.22
Brown et al. (1982–83)	Single worker	−0.33	−0.50	0.17
	Two workers	−0.14	−0.44	0.30
Layard (1978)		−0.13	−0.04	−0.09

Notes: The estimates for Brown, Levin and Ulph (1976) are those where the wife does not work for pay. The estimates for Brown et al. (1982–83) are those for a family with two children.

possesses an uncompensated wage elasticity of between −0.14 and −0.06 (the former estimate for husbands with two children and the latter for husbands with no children), a compensated wage elasticity of between 0.30 and 0.39, and a marginal propensity to earn to between −0.45 and −0.42. In these two-worker families, the wife's marginal propensity to earn is estimated at approximately −0.15 so that together these estimates imply a family's marginal propensity to earn of about −0.60 or, expressed differently, only 40 percent of a small increase in exogenous nonwage income is spent on the consumption of commodities.

A summary of these British estimates is contained in Table 1.20. All the estimates of the uncompensated wage elasticity of hours of work are negative and a simple average of the eight estimates is −0.16. Five of the eight estimates are between −0.16 and −0.13. As was the case with the studies with U.S. males, the variations in the *mpe* and in E^* among the studies is considerably greater than the variation in E. Of the six positive estimates of E^*, the average is 0.21.

4.4. *Empirical results from U.S. experimental data*

The fundamental implication of the allocation model outlined in Section 3.1 is that, for a population of individuals at a given time or for a given individual over time, other things equal, exogenous movements in budget constraints should induce movements in the supply of labor. This most basic proposition stood an excellent opportunity of being tested by the various negative income tax (NIT) experiments that were conducted in the United States in the decade from 1968 to 1978. With the laboratory sciences as a conscious example, these experiments selected a sample of households in a given locality and then introduced to a fraction of this sample (the experimental households) a different budget constraint while continuing to observe the other households (the controls). The consequences of changes in the budget constraint for the supply of labor could be inferred by contrasting the behavior of the experimental households with that of the control households during the experiment and/or by contrasting the behavior of the experimental families during the experiment with their behavior before (or after) the experiment.[89]

In fact, inferences from the experiments were much more difficult to draw. There were several reasons for this. First, the sample of (experimental and control) households studied was drawn selectively from the low-income population. This was a natural decision in view of the concern with welfare reform, but its effect was to introduce problems deriving from the truncation of a variable (income) directly related to the major variable of interest (labor supply). Second, this low-income sample of households was then not allocated randomly between the experimental and the control groups, but rather the allocation design was a more complicated one that partly tried to mitigate the budgetary costs of the experiment. Third, during each experiment, changes took place outside the experiment's control that affected the budget constraints of the participating households and that may have affected the control and experimental households differentially. For instance, in the middle of New Jersey's experiment, the state's welfare program was reformed in such a way that, for a number of experimental households, it now offered a more generous opportunity than the experiment's and so these households opted out of the experiment. As another example, the first NIT payments in Seattle were made (in November 1970) at a time when the area was experiencing a drastic and unprecedented rise in unemployment arising from the extensive layoffs in its aircraft industry and it was feared that an idiosyncratic labor market situation existed from which it was hazardous to extend inferences about the effects of a negative income tax to more typical labor market settings. Fourth, even if the sample of experimental households and the sample of control households had been the same at the outset, greater attrition of controls subsequently from the experiment rendered the two samples different from one another.[90] Fifth, as in all welfare and tax programs, incentives existed for individuals to misreport their incomes so that statutory and actual tax rates diverged. Indeed, it has been conjectured that the particular incentives created by the NIT experiments operated to exaggerate the magnitude of true labor supply

[89] This is the method prescribed in Orcutt and Orcutt's (1968) classic statement of the case for social experiments.

[90] Of course, the problem of attrition exists in all panel data, not merely in the NIT experimental data. A frequently-cited paper on the subject of attrition is that by Hausman and Wise (1977) who claimed that in the Gary experiment attrition bias was less with a "structural" model of earnings than with an analysis-of-variance (AOV) model. However, this inference was drawn from a comparison between, on the one hand, a "structural" model that included almost all the determinants of attrition in the earnings equation and, on the other hand, an AOV model that excluded many of the determinants of attrition from the earnings equation. The implied constraint in the AOV model was clearly not warranted and their comparison was thereby quite invalid.

effects.[91] Sixth, because most of the experimental households were eligible to receive NIT payments for three years,[92] it has been argued that the labor supply effects should be interpreted as those induced by *temporary* changes in net wage rates and nonwage income.[93] Seventh, because only a relatively small fraction of an area's population had their budget constraints altered by the experiments and because these changes were temporary, the inducements to make institutional adjustments in work schedules were considerably less than would be the case for a national and permanent NIT program. For instance, approximately two-thirds of the husbands in the Gary experiment worked in the steel mills on work schedules that permitted them little flexibility in working hours in their existing jobs. There would have been greater pressures on the employers and the unions to renegotiate different hours of work schedules if it had not been the case that only a relatively small fraction of all employees in these steel mills were enrolled in the experiment and if the experiment had lasted for more than three years. In this sense, the experimental–control differences would tend to understate the adjustments that would occur if the budget constraint changes were not confined to a relatively small population over a relatively short space of time. All these issues certainly impede drawing straightforward inferences from the experimental data although, given the size of the differences in NIT payments between experimental and control households in some of the experiments, it is unlikely that these problems entirely nullify simple experimental–control comparisons.

The NIT experiments were conducted on 1357 households in New Jersey and Pennsylvania from 1968 to 1972, 809 households in rural areas of North Carolina and Iowa from 1969 to 1973, 1800 households in Gary, Indiana, from 1970 to 1974, and 4800 households in Seattle and Denver from 1970 to 1980. Not only were many more households analyzed in the Seattle–Denver experiment compared with the others, but also it involved more generous NIT payments. For the typical male, in each case the experimental treatment meant changing his budget constraint from $0a_1a_2$ to $0b_1b_2a_2$ in Figure 1.4.[94] In other words the NIT experiment paid a grant (or support) of G dollars regardless of the household's income and then applied a relatively higher tax rate τ on all income in excess of G. The breakeven level of income, b_2 in Figure 1.4, occurred when the household's receipts in the form of the grant, G, equalled tax payments, $\tau(wh+y)$. For any individual located to the right of b_2 both before and after the introduction of the

[91] See Ashenfelter (1978), Greenberg, Moffit and Friedman (1981), and Welch (1978).

[92] Some households in Seattle and Denver experiment were eligible to receive payments for five years.

[93] The original work investigating this issue is Metcalf's (1973, 1974).

[94] Figure 1.4 assumes a pre-experimental budget constraint characterized by a continuously rising marginal tax rate. For some households (especially single heads of households), the non-experimental welfare programs (such as AFDC) generate budget constraints similar to the experimental budget constraint $0b_1b_2a_2$.

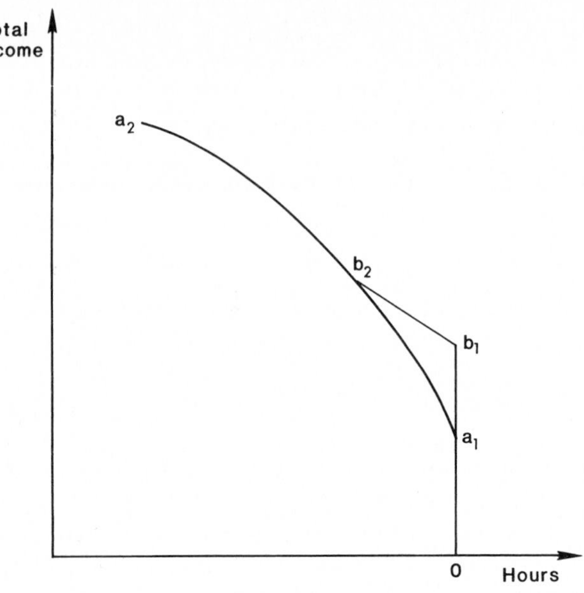

Figure 1.4

NIT experiment, his opportunities were enhanced and his pre-experimental budget constraint $px = wh + y$ became $px = G + (1-\tau)(wh + y)$, where τ is the differentially higher tax rate applied on income by the NIT experiment. There were also some individuals who were located on their pre-experimental budget constraints to the left of b_2, but who determined upon the introduction of the experiment they would be better off by so reducing their hours of work as to locate on b_1b_2 and become eligible for NIT payments. Other things equal, the flatter an individual's indifference curve (i.e. the greater an individual's elasticity of substitution between income and leisure), the greater the probability of his moving from above the breakeven level of income pre-experimentally to below the breakeven level of income during the experiment.[95] The values of G and τ differed across and within the four experiments[96] and once again the assignment of experimental households among the different NIT programs (each described

[95]Expressed differently, consider an experimental individual who is indifferent between a point on his budget constraint to the left of b_2 and a point to the right of b_2. For this individual, the experimentally-induced change in the budget constraint involves no income effect, only a substitution effect. This is essentially Ashenfelter's (1983) insight that the substitution effect can be measured from estimating the relationship between the fraction of individuals below the breakeven level of income and the slope of the arm b_1b_2.

[96]In the Seattle–Denver experiment, there were some "treatments" in which τ itself was not a constant, but instead fell as income rose.

by a particular combination of G and τ) was not random. In particular, there was a tendency for households with relatively low pre-experimental incomes to be assigned to the less generous NIT programs (i.e. those with relatively low G and high τ) thereby reducing the expected budgetary cost of the experiment.[97] This implies that the particular experimental parameters, G and τ, applied to each household depended upon its pre-experimental earnings and these in turn were not independent of its experimental labor supply insofar as there is correlation over time in a household's work behavior. In short, contrary to some claims, the experimental treatments were not genuinely exogenous both because each household decided whether to received NIT payments by being below the breakeven level of income b_2 and because the particular program parameters it faced were not assigned to it randomly.[98]

To determine whether the data collected by the NIT experiments conform to the basic notion that differences in work behavior are associated with differences in budget constraints, the following ordinary least-squares regression equation was estimated:

$$L_i = \beta_0 X_i + \beta_1 E_i + u_i, \tag{36}$$

where L_i stands for a dimension of individual i's work behavior[99] (such as his weekly hours of work or whether or not he was employed in the labor market), E_i takes the value of unity for an individual allocated to the experimental sample and of zero for an individual in the control sample, X_i measures other characteristics of the individual (and, in the Seattle–Denver research, X_i also includes the variables determining the assignment of individuals to different treatments), and u_i is a stochastic disturbance term. Sometimes eq. (36) was estimated with data

[97]An excellent analysis of the implications of the assignment process is contained in Keeley and Robins (1980) who advise including the variables determining the assignment of households to different NIT programs in equations designed to infer the labor supply effects of the experiments.

[98]This fact vitiates many of the original arguments in support of undertaking such social experiments. These arguments claimed that conventional income and substitution effects would be much easier to measure with experimental data because the experiment induced *exogenous* changes in the budget constraints of experimental households. As noted earlier, because of the nonrandom assignment of households between the control sample and the experimental sample and because of nonrandom assignment within the experimental sample of households to different treatments, the changes in the budget constraint were not truly exogenous to the households. Moreover, the nonlinearity of the budget constraints creates a further reason for the budget constraint variables to be endogenous. What appears to be a more convincing argument in defense of the experiments is that the within sample variations in the budget constraint variables (and especially in nonwage income) tend to be larger than in nonexperimental data and this holds out the hope of measuring the parameters associated with these budget constraint variables more precisely.

[99]Instead of work behavior, a few studies [such as Ashenfelter's (1978)] focus upon the experimental effect on net earnings. There is good reason for this in view of the fact that the NIT-induced change in earnings is proportional to the excess transfer cost of the program over the cost calculated on the basis of pre-experimental incomes alone.

drawn from midway during the experiment in which case X_i usually included some measure of an individual's pre-experimental labor supply. On other occasions, data were pooled from the experimental and the pre-experimental period and experimental–control differences during the experiment were distinguished from such differences before the experiment. The estimates of β_1 in eq. (36) were consistently (though not invariably) negative: for white husbands in the New Jersey–Pennsylvania experiment, the experimental group averaged 5.6 percent fewer hours of work per week than the control group [Rees (1974)]; for black husbands in Gary, the experimental group averaged 6.5 percent fewer hours of work per month than the control group [Moffitt (1979)]; and in the Seattle–Denver experiment, husbands in the experimental group worked 2.2 percent fewer hours per week than those in the control group [Keeley et al. (1978a)]. The differences among the NIT experiments in the point estimates of β_1 were less marked than the differences in their estimated standard errors: the experimental–control differences measured in the New Jersey–Pennsylvania, North Carolina–Iowa, and Gary experiments were often insignificantly different from zero by conventional criteria while those in the Seattle–Denver experiment were clearly significantly different from zero, a consequence of the substantially greater size of the Seattle–Denver experiment. Experimental husbands were also less likely than controls to be employed at any moment midway through the experiment – a 2.6 percent difference for white husbands in New Jersey–Pennsylvania [Rees (1974)], a 4.9 percent differential in Gary [Moffitt (1979)], and a 2.3 percent differential in Seattle–Denver [Pencavel (1982)]. These estimated experimental–control differences tend to understate the magnitude of the experimental labor supply response because the experimental–control dummy E_i in eq. (36) measures the effect of the experiment averaged over those experimental families who receive NIT payments by being below the breakeven level of income and those whose incomes place them above the breakeven level. In other words, β_1 in eq. (36) understates the experimental effects conditional upon being below the breakeven level of income.

The results reported in the previous paragraph were designed to answer the question of whether changes in budget constraints result in changes in work behavior. The evidence suggests that, beyond any pre-experimental differences, the changes introduced by the NIT experiments did induce differences between the experimental and control husbands' work behavior. Of course, the allocation model of Section 3.1 has implications beyond the simple one of maintaining that changes in budget constraints cause changes in work behavior; in any changes in budget constraints, this model distinguishes the effects of changes in wage rates from those attributable to changes in nonwage income. It is natural to determine, therefore, whether the experimentally-induced changes in net wage rates and in net nonwage income each generated effects on work behavior that are compatible with the neoclassical static allocation model. Moreover, distinguishing the effects on work behavior of the NIT tax rate from the effects of the guarantee level is essential if the purpose is to draw inferences from these experiments about how other welfare programs (with different program parameters) would operate.

There have been many different forms of specifying the net wage and nonwage income effects on work behavior induced by the NIT experiments although, as others have observed [e.g. Ashenfelter (1978)], many of the models used by analysts of the experimental data (especially those in New Jersey–Pennsylvania and in North Carolina–Iowa) were specified in ways that make it difficult to recover income and substitution effects from them. In those studies where these behavioral responses (or their transformations) are identified, most of the important differences among the studies have turned on the way in which each household's budget constraint has been measured. As Figure 1.4 makes clear, for both experimental and control households, the nonlinearity of the budget constraint renders the net wage rate endogenous to the labor supply decision. Hausman and Wise (1976) addressed this problem by measuring the budget constraint variables for each individual at the same number of working hours (namely, 1500 hours per year), but this has the effect of simply assigning the wrong budget constraint to all individuals except those who happen to be working 1500 hours. A procedure not so different from this is applied by Keeley et al. (1978a, 1978b) who take up Ashenfelter and Heckman's (1973) proposal of measuring the budget constraint variables in the second year of the Seattle–Denver experiment as those that would obtain at each individual's pre-experimental hours of work. Of course, these measures can only be correct if, in fact, each individual did not change his work behavior as a consequence of the NIT experiment or for any other reason. Johnson and Pencavel (1982) also measure the change in the budget constraint along these lines, but then they treat these variables so constructed as measured with error and apply an instrumental variable estimator. Moffitt (1979) measures the tax rate by averaging each individual's marginal tax rate over the entire length of his budget constraint. Johnson and Pencavel (1984) and MaCurdy (1983) linearize each individual's budget constraint around his observed hours of work during the Seattle–Denver experiment and then treat these budget constraint variables as endogenous by replacing them with their values predicted from a prior regression. Burtless and Hausman (1978) use a generalization of Wales and Woodland's (1979) procedure described in Section 4.3 where the generalization takes the form of permitting each individual's utility function to contain a component that is unobserved to the researcher and that varies (according to a specified distribution) across the population. Wales and Woodland's (1979) method of determining the unknown parameters of the hours of work function by searching over all segments of the piecewise linear budget constraint must now be specified such that each individual's location on a particular segment (given his net wage rate and net nonwage income) is known only probabilistically. As in Wales and Woodland's study,

Table 1.21
Estimates of the behavioral responses for men from the NIT experiments.

		E	mpe	E^*
Ashenfelter (1978a)		0.21	0.02	0.19
Ashenfelter (1978b)		0.17	−0.01	0.18
Burtless and Greenberg (1982)	3 Year	0.08	−0.04	0.12
	5 Year	−0.12	−0.18	0.06
Hausman and Wise (1977)		0.10	−0.01	0.11
Johnson and Pencavel (1982)		−0.16	−0.29	0.13
Johnson and Pencavel (1984)		0.02	−0.17	0.19
Keeley and Robins (1980)		−0.09	−0.14	0.05

Notes: Ashenfelter's estimates are from the North Carolina–Iowa rural experiment and Hausman and Wise's are from the New Jersey–Pennsylvania experiment. All the other estimates make use of data from the Seattle–Denver income maintenance experiment and all these estimates have been evaluated at the same number of hours of work (namely, 1880.97) and the same net wage rate ($2.293). These are the mean values of working experimental husbands in the pre-experimental year whose incomes in that year would have placed them below the breakeven level and they are taken from the sample analyzed by Keeley and Robins (1980). The earlier work by Keeley, Robins, Spiegelman and West (1978a, 1978b) uses the same estimating procedure as in Keeley and Robins (1980), but in the later study the sample includes Chicanos, unlike the earlier work. The difference between Ashenfelter's (a) and (b) estimates is explained in footnote 100.

Burtless and Hausman assume they measure each individual's budget constraint without error.

Table 1.21 summarizes the estimates of the *mpe* and the wage elasticities of hours of work from a number of the analyses of the hours of work of husbands in the NIT experiments. This table does not list every study that claims to be measuring these behavioral responses, but only those studies that satisfy two conditions: first, they provide sufficient structure on the estimated relationships that the results have some claim to correspond to the behavioral responses; and, second, they impose sufficiently few prior estimating restrictions as to supply an opportunity for the data to reveal whether they really conform to the implications of the static allocation model. This second condition implies that I have omitted, for example, Horner's (1977) paper with the New Jersey–Pennsylvania experimental data that measures the parameters of a Cobb–Douglas utility function and Burtless and Hausman's (1978) paper on the Gary experimental data that constrains no individual to have a positive *mpe*. The first condition means that I have excluded studies such as Watts' (1974) and Moffitt's (1979) that involved specifications in which the income and wage effects on hours of work were supposed to be gleaned from the estimated coefficients on the experimental tax rate and the guarantee level in an hours of work equation and where other variables also incorporating measures of wages and nonwage income were included in the regression.

Of the studies listed in Table 1.21, Hausman and Wise's (1977) makes use of the New Jersey–Pennsylvania experimental data, Ashenfelter's (1978) makes use of the North Carolina–Iowa experimental data,[100] and the rest make use of the Seattle–Denver experimental data. All the summary estimates in Table 1.21 relating to the Seattle–Denver experiment have been calculated at the same values of working hours and wage rates, as the notes to the table make clear. The point estimates of the uncompensated wage elasticity, E, range from a low of -0.159 [Johnson and Pencavel (1982)] to a high of $+0.015$ [Ashenfelter (1978)]. The point estimates of the *mpe* range from a low of -0.290 [Johnson and Pencavel (1982)] to a high of $+0.015$ [Ashenfelter (1978)]. The estimates of E^*, the compensated wage elasticity, in the different studies range from a low of 0.050 [Keeley and Robins (1980)] to a high of 0.192 [Ashenfelter (1978)]. This relatively narrow range of estimates of E^* comes about through offsetting values of E and the *mpe*, the range of estimates of E and *mpe* being considerably greater. The tendency is for the uncompensated hours of work function to be positively sloped with respect to wage rates at sample mean values. By estimating

[100] The two sets of estimates for Ashenfelter's analysis of the data from the rural experiment correspond to two different parameterizations of the experimentally-induced change in earnings. He posits an hours of work function for family member 1 as $h_1 = h_1(w_1, w_2, y)$, where w_2 is the net wage rate of family member 2. The experimentally-induced change in this person's earnings is

$$\begin{aligned} w_1\,\mathrm{d}h_1 &= w_1\frac{\partial h_1}{\partial w_1}\mathrm{d}w_1 + w_1\frac{\partial h_1}{\partial w_2}\mathrm{d}w_2 + w_1\frac{\partial h_1}{\partial y}\mathrm{d}y \\ &= -\left[w_1\left(w_1\frac{\partial h_1}{\partial w_1} + w_2\frac{\partial h_1}{\partial w_2}\right)\right]\tau + \left[w_1\frac{\partial h_1}{\partial y}\right](G-\tau y), \end{aligned}$$

where $\mathrm{d}w_1$ (the change in wage rates induced by the experiment) is given by $-\tau w_1$, $\mathrm{d}w_2 = -\tau w_2$, and $\mathrm{d}y$ (the change in nonwage income induced by the experiment) is $G-\tau y$. So what is designated in Table 1.21 as scheme (a) regresses the change in earnings on the tax rate τ and on $G-\tau y$. Observe that the coefficient on τ incorporates any cross-wage effects. The estimates under E for Ashenfelter (a) in Table 1.21 sets these cross wage effects to zero. Ashenfelter's second parameterization makes use of the Slutsky decomposition to write the previous equation

$$w_1\,\mathrm{d}h_1 = -w_1\left[w_1\left(\frac{\partial h_1}{\partial w_1}\right)^* + w_2\left(\frac{\partial h_1}{\partial w_2}\right)^*\right]\tau + w_1\frac{\partial h_1}{\partial y}[G-\tau(w_1h_1 + w_2h_2 + y)],$$

where the term $G-\tau(w_1h_1+w_2h_2+y)$ corresponds to the NIT payments and where the asterisk denotes compensated wage effects. Here the change in earnings is regressed on the tax rate τ and on NIT payments. Again the coefficient on τ reflects a cross-wage effect and again the estimates under E for Ashenfelter (b) in Table 1.21 sets these cross-wage effects to zero. This second parameterization is similar to that used by Keeley et al. (1978a, 1978b). They set cross-wage effects to zero and divide the last equation in this footnote by w_1.

the labor supply parameters separately for households on the three year experimental program from those on the five year program, Burtless and Greenberg (1982) derive values for E^* and the *mpe* that diverge in the manner that Metcalf (1973, 1974) conjectured: the compensated wage-elasticity is larger and the *mpe* is smaller (in absolute value) for the three year experimental husbands compared with the five year experimental husbands.

It is important to point out that the responses whose point estimates are presented in Table 1.21 are not normally estimated with much precision. For example, Hausman and Wise's point estimate of E of 0.095 comes with an estimated standard error of 0.043 so that a 95 percent confidence interval ranges from 0.001 to almost 0.180. Or the largest of the point estimates of E in Table 1.21, Ashenfelter's 0.207, has an estimated standard error of 0.122 so that a 95 percent confidence interval spans a range from -0.032 to $+0.446$. It is difficult to draw the inference from estimates such as these that the NIT experiments have permitted the relevant behavioral responses to have been measured with much precision.

4.5. *Conclusions*

If the estimates from Tables 1.19, 1.20, and 1.21 are put together, it appears that the estimates of E, the uncompensated wage elasticity of hours of work, from the American nonexperimental data tend to be more negative than those from the data collected in the NIT experiments. This difference between the estimates from the experimental and those from the nonexperimental data conforms to Metcalf's (1973, 1974) conjecture: the temporary nature of the NIT experiments will tend to cause the estimate of the *mpe* to be smaller (in absolute value) and the estimate of the compensated wage elasticity, E^*, to be larger when estimated from experimental data than their "permanent" values. If this is the case, then indeed we should expect the estimates of E to be larger when fitted to experimental then to nonexperimental data. British men appear to be similar to American men in their value for E, although this E decomposes into a more negative *mpe* and a larger E^* for the British. If a single number has to be attached to each of the behavioral responses, then for American prime-age men the (uncompensated) wage elasticity of hours of work is -0.10 and their *mpe* is -0.20.

The inferences in the previous paragraph are drawn from a comparison of the central tendency of the point estimates in Tables 1.19, 1.20 and 1.21. It would be misleading to present these summaries without at the same time emphasizing both the diversity of estimates and the imprecision with which these point estimates are measured. Moreover, if the estimates are interpreted as tests of the static model of labor supply (and no doubt some would not want to take this step), then the frequency of negative values for the income-compensated wage elasticity of hours of work casts serious doubt on its empirical relevance.

5. Estimation of the life-cycle model

The discussion of the Life-Cycle Models in Section 3.5 concentrated on those assuming strong separability of the lifetime utility function and the presentation of empirical work in this section restricts itself to this class of models. Also, as in the discussion of the empirical work on static models, I omit discussion of the estimation of life-cycle labor supply behavior at the macroeconomic level as in the work of Lucas and Rapping (1969) and others. The reason is in part because of major aggregation problems: such work normally seeks to explain movements in aggregate manhours worked and confuses individuals occupying a corner solution to their allocation problem with those at interior solutions. Indeed, the larger part of the movement in aggregate manhours over the business cycle is attributable to movements in the numbers of workers employed and not to movements in the hours worked of those continuous employed.[101] Because the microeconomic evidence reported below is restricted to individuals at interior solutions to their constrained optimization problem, it is not straightforward to go from these estimates to draw implications about corresponding parameters estimated with macroeconomic data.[102] It is not surprising, therefore, that as Altonji (1982) has shown the estimates of the macro parameters are by no means robust with respect to small changes in the assumptions underlying their calculation.

In the microeconomic research described in this section, it should be remembered that, although the life-cycle model has important refutable implications (for instance, the Frisch demand and supply functions possess symmetry, homogeneity, and sign properties), there has been virtually no work testing the

[101] For evidence on this, see Coleman (1983). By contrast, Hall (1980, p. 95) claims: "Both recessions of the 1970's saw pronounced reductions in average hours of work." As Coleman shows, Hall's inferences are in error. His index of aggregate hours is calculated using both the hours per worker and the number of workers series from the BLS establishment surveys. His series on total employment is from the household Current Population Survey. The ratio of aggregate hours from the establishment survey to numbers employed from the CPS yields a variable hours per worker series, but it does not correspond to anything observed in the U.S. economy. When Coleman uses either the ratio of hours to employment both from the establishment surveys or the ratio of hours to employment both from the CPS, the hours per worker series displays little annual variability. In other words, most of the cyclical variability in aggregate manhours is attributable to changes in the number of workers employed and not to changes in hours worked per employee.

[102] Often these macroeconomic models are described as if economic agents operate under uncertainty. As MaCurdy (1982) shows, this further aggravates the problems of identifying from aggregated data the effect on labor supply of parametric wage changes (which is what Lucas and Rapping maintain they are measuring).

empirical relevance of these implications. The life-cycle model has been characterized as the maintained hypothesis and empirical work has taken the form of gauging the parameters describing the presumed life-cycle allocation. Of course, the measurement of the parameters of well-specified models is a necessary ingredient of any science, but such information is not the same as that derived from offering the model good opportunities of being refuted and discovering it has survived such tests of its validity.

As we shall see, these life-cycle models are most convincingly estimated when the research makes use of successive observations over time of the same individuals (i.e. panel data). Because an important component of this work involves regressing changes (over time) in the hours worked of individuals on corresponding changes in their wage rates, it might be noted that the simple correlation between these two variables is negative at least in the U.S. data. For instance, Abowd and Card (1983) report that when changes in the logarithm of hours worked are regressed on changes in the logarithm of wages rates (controlling for no other variables) the estimated coefficient is -0.36 for 1531 prime-age male heads of households in ten years of the Michigan panel and it is -0.28 for 1321 men aged less than 65 years in 1975 in six survey years of the National Longitudinal Survey of Older Men.[103] However, in view of the problems documented in Section 4.2 in measuring hours and wages accurately, there is every reason to wonder how much of this negative correlation between the observed values of the variables is attributable to measurement errors and how much to an association between the true values of the variables. After all, often the wage rate variable is formed by dividing the respondent's annual earnings by hours worked so any error in measuring hours will produce a spurious negative correlation between hours and wage rates and this negative correlation will normally persist when taking first-differences in the variables.

In addition, both the measured hours and the measured wage rate variables do not precisely correspond to their counterparts in the economic model. That is, with respect to wage rates, there are all the problems described in Section 3.3 concerning nonlinear budget constraints (taxes, nonlinear compensation schedules, etc.) while hours of work are often computed as the product of two variables (average hours worked per week and weeks worked per year) and therefore are unlikely to correspond exactly to the true value of the variable. Also, according to one influential model, labor supply should exclude time spent in on-the-job training yet the hours reported rarely deduct such human capital investment. These problems concerning measurement error in wage rates and hours worked may well be exacerbated by first-differencing the variables because permanent components in these variables are thereby eliminated and "noise" components account for a relatively larger part of the measured total. Therefore, if only for

[103] Similar inferences can be drawn from data in Altonji's (1983) paper.

Table 1.22
Estimates of the intertemporal substitution elasticity, γ, for prime-age men.

Research	Equation estimated	Type of data	Other variables in equation	Instrumental variables used	$\hat{\gamma}$
MaCurdy (1981a)	Eq. (38) first-differenced	Panel data on individuals	None	Father's education, mother's education, parents' socio-economic status, schooling, age, interactions, year dummy variables	From 0.14 to 0.35 (0.07) (0.16)
MaCurdy (1981a)	As above	As above	Year dummy variables	As above	From 0.10 to 0.45 (0.13) (0.29)
Becker (1975)	Eq. (41)	Synthetic cohorts	Age, log of nonwage income, log of other family income, log of family size	Group means	0.45 for white men (0.11) 0.10 for nonwhite men (0.04)
Becker (1975)	Eq. (41) first-differenced	Synthetic cohorts	Changes in variables listed above	Group means	0.17 for white men (0.11) −0.06 for nonwhite men (0.08)
Smith (1977)	Eq. (41)	Synthetic cohorts	Age, log of wife's wage, number of young children	Group means	0.32 for white men (0.05) 0.23 for black men (0.11)
Browning, Deaton, and Irish (1983)	Eq. (42)	Synthetic cohort over time	Number of children, long-term interest rate, manual–nonmanual dummy, cohort and year dummies	Group means	About 0.05
Browning, Deaton, and Irish (1983)	Eq. (42) first-differenced	As above	Changes in above variables plus year dummies	Group means used plus age, age squared, lagged wages and prices	About 0.03
MaCurdy (1982)	Eq. (38) replacing λ_0 with age and age-invariant variables	Individual cross-section	Father's education, mother's education, parents' socio-economic status, age, own education	Father's education mother's education, parents' socio-economic status, age, own education, $(\text{age})^2$, $(\text{education})^2$	From −0.07 to 0.28 (0.23) (0.47)

Notes: Estimated standard errors are given in parentheses beneath coefficients. No standard errors are available for Browning, Deaton and Irish's estimates. MaCurdy's work uses the Michigan PSID. Becker makes use of the 1 in 1000 sample from the 1960 Census of Population. Smith uses the 1967 Survey of Economic Opportunity. Browning, Deaton and Irish use the British Family Expenditure Surveys.

purely statistical reasons, it would seem essential in this work to address explicitly the problems of measurement error in wages and hours. In fact, these reasons are compounded by economic considerations arising out of behavior under uncertainty. Consequently, the research surveyed below is restricted to that work taking explicit account of measurement error in these variables.[104] Table 1.22 contains a summary of estimates of the intertemporal substitution elasticity and other features of the research.

The archetypal study of male life-cycle labor supply was MaCurdy's (1981). He specified individual i's utility function at age t to be the addilog:

$$U_i(x_{it}, h_{it}; A_{it}, \varepsilon_{it}) = b_{it}(x_{it})^{\gamma_1} - \tilde{\gamma}^{-1}c_{it}(h_{it})^{\tilde{\gamma}}, \tag{37}$$

where

$$\tilde{\gamma} = \gamma^{-1} + 1, \quad \gamma > 0, \quad 0 < \gamma_1 < 1, \quad b_{it} > 0, \quad c_{it} = \exp[\gamma^{-1}(-\beta A_{it} - \varepsilon_{it})].$$

The objective function is thus not merely additive over time, it is also additive in consumption and hours within any given period. The Frisch hours of work equation for individual i at age t is

$$\ln h_{it} = \psi_i + \gamma \ln w_{it} + \beta A_{it} + \delta t + \varepsilon_{it}, \tag{38}$$

where $\psi_i = \gamma \ln \lambda_{0i}$ and $\delta = \gamma \ln \theta$. The first term on the right-hand side is invariant for a given individual over time and is different from individual to individual. The parameters of eq. (38) supply information on how an individual's hours of work differ over time in response to anticipated, evolutionary, wage changes, i.e. wage changes along a worker's wage–age profile. The proportional change in hours of work induced by a proportional increase in wage rates as a worker ages is measured in eq. (38) by $\gamma > 0$, the intertemporal substitution elasticity.[105]

To estimate eq. (38), MaCurdy used ten annual observations on 513 white, continuously-married, men from the Michigan PSID who were aged 25–46 years in 1967 and who were observed in each of the ten years from 1967 to 1976. The variables in A_{it} could be any whose values did not change over this ten-year period. The estimates of γ from first-differencing eq. (38) ranged from 0.14 to

[104]Abowd and Card (1983) do allow for measurement error in wages, but on the other hand they assume ε_{it} in eq. (16) to be zero, i.e. that the researcher knows each individual's utility function exactly. If their model is augmented to allow for unmeasured characteristics of individuals, then once these ε_{it} are permitted to be correlated for each individual over time Abowd and Card's variance components procedure no longer identifies the intertemporal substitution elasticity.

[105]Because the utility function has been assumed to be additive over time, the intertemporal substitution elasticity is equivalent to the specific substitution elasticity.

0.35 with standard errors on these coefficients of 0.07 and 0.16, respectively.[106] When yearly dummy variables were included in the first-differenced form of eq. (38), γ was estimated much less precisely although its point estimate changed little: the point estimates now ranged from 0.10 to 0.45 with standard errors of 0.125 and 0.29, respectively.[107] By including yearly dummy variables in the first-differenced equation, the coefficient on the wage rate cannot be interpreted as the response of labor supply to changes in wages induced by business cycle forces. So these point estimates implied that, as a male worker ages, a doubling of his wage rates induces a proportional increase in his hours worked of from ten percent to 45 percent.

These general inferences from the Michigan PSID have been confirmed by Altonji (1983) and by Ham (1983). The sample analyzed by Altonji is slightly different from MaCurdy's[108] and he also considers the consequences of using different sets of instrumental variables for the change in $\ln w_{it}$. The consequences for the estimated intertemporal substitution elasticity of the change in the sample are small: when Altonji uses the same variables MaCurdy used as instruments, his estimates of γ center around 0.27 with standard errors about two-thirds of this value. As an instrument for the change in $\ln w_{it}$ (where w_{it} is computed by dividing total earnings by hours worked), Altonji also uses an alternative measure of the wage variable derived by asking workers paid on an hourly basis about their hourly wage rate. Because this information is available for only a subset of workers, the use of this variable reduces his sample size by about 60 percent. The estimates of γ are now around 0.04 with estimated standard errors even larger than this. Similar results are derived when the lagged value of this alternative wage variable is used as an instrument. Ham (1983) uses eight years of data from the Michigan PSID from 1971 to 1979 (including men from the poverty subsample) to estimate a different functional form for the Frisch equation, namely, that postulated by Browning, Deaton and Irish (1983) in eq. (42) below. Evaluated near the mean values of wages and working hours, Ham's estimates of the intertemporal substitution elasticity are around 0.04.[109] In short, Altonji's and

[106] The higher of these estimates of γ come from adding $\gamma \ln h_{it}$ to both sides of eq. (38) and regressing changes in hours on changes in earnings.

[107] The coefficient on t is given by $\gamma \ln \theta \approx \gamma(\rho - r)$ so the coefficients on these yearly dummy variables (after division by γ) may be interpreted as the difference between the rate of time preference and the rate of interest. MaCurdy's estimates imply that on average r exceeds ρ by two to four percentage points.

[108] Altonji uses data from the 12 years of the panel from 1967 to 1978 on continuously married (to the same spouse) men aged 25–48 years in 1967. He includes observations even if they did not work in all 12 years, he includes nonwhites as well as whites, and he includes households from the more heavily sampled low income areas. The result is an increase in the total number of observations from 5,130 to over 8,000.

[109] Ham does not provide information on the mean wage and hours of work of the men in his sample. I have evaluated his point estimates in Table A1 of his paper at 2100 hours of work and at a wage of $6.00 per hour. These are approximately the average values of these variables for the Michigan panel in 1975, the midpoint in Ham's longitudinal data.

Ham's research with the Michigan PSID underscore MaCurdy's findings of an intertemporal substitution elasticity whose point estimate is less than 0.45 and that is not estimated with precision.[110]

Section 3.5 maintained that the Frisch labor supply equation may also be used as the basis for empirical work when agents make decisions under uncertainty. This is an important point and it is convenient to illustrate this by making use of the particular utility function (37) above. [The argument here draws liberally on MaCurdy (1982).] In this case, the first-order condition corresponding to eq. (28) may be written

$$\ln h_{it} = \gamma \ln \lambda_{it} + \gamma \ln w_{it} + \beta A_{it} + \varepsilon_{it}. \tag{39}$$

It can be shown that $\ln \lambda_{it}$ follows a stochastic process with drift and may be represented as

$$\ln \lambda_{it} = \sum_{j=0}^{t} \tilde{a}_j + \ln \lambda_{i0} + \sum_{j=1}^{t} \tilde{v}_{ij},$$

where $\tilde{v}_{ij}$ is the individual's forecast error at age j that arises from the values of variables at age j diverging from the values expected (at age $j-1$) to obtain at age j. Substituting this expression for $\ln \lambda_{it}$ into eq. (39) and first-differencing yields:

$$\Delta \ln h_{it} = a^* + \gamma \Delta \ln w_{it} + \beta \Delta A_{it} + \varepsilon_{it} - \varepsilon_{it-1} + v_{it}, \tag{40}$$

where $a^* = \gamma \tilde{a}$ and $v_{it} = \gamma \tilde{v}_{it}$. Compared with the equation derived by first-differencing eq. (38) (i.e. the certainty case), it is evident that under uncertainty assumptions have to be made about the nature of the forecast error v_{it}. Now the marginal utility of income in period t will depend upon wages, wealth, and the individual's characteristics in period t and also upon the future path of expected wages. So suppose $\gamma \ln \lambda_{it}$ in eq. (39) may be expressed as

$$\gamma \ln \lambda_{it} = \tilde{b}_{1t} A_{it} + \sum_{j=t}^{N} \tilde{c}_{tj} \mathscr{E}_{it}(\ln w_{ij}) + \tilde{b}_{2t} K_{it} + \xi_{it},$$

where K_{it} is the real value of the consumer's wealth at the start of period t and

[110]Altonji also tried to measure the intertemporal substitution elasticity from the within-period marginal rate of substitution between hours and food consumption. Because substitution within a branch of the lifetime utility function is being estimated (no essential use is made of intertemporal data), his period-specific preferences are estimated only up to a positive monotonic transformation and thus the degree of intertemporal substitutability cannot be inferred. This same problem exists (as they fully recognize) with Blundell and Walker's (1984) research: only the sign of the intertemporal substitution elasticity may be inferred, not its numerical magnitude.

the coefficients $\tilde{b}_{1t}$, $\tilde{c}_{tj}$, and $\tilde{b}_{2t}$ change as individuals age. The revision in $\gamma \ln \lambda_{it}$ at age t is

$$v_{it} = \tilde{b}_{1t}[A_{it} - \mathscr{E}_{it-1}(A_{it})] + \sum_{j=t}^{N} \tilde{c}_{tj}[\mathscr{E}_{it}(\ln w_{ij}) - \mathscr{E}_{it-1}(\ln w_{ij})] + \tilde{b}_{2t}[K_{it} - \mathscr{E}_{it-1}(K_{it})] + \xi_{it} - \mathscr{E}_{it-1}(\xi_{it}),$$

where $\mathscr{E}_{it-1}$ denotes individual i's expectations at age $t-1$ of the associated variables. It is implausible to assume that the economist knows each individual's expectations perfectly and consequently this further restricts the set of variables that may serve as instruments for $\Delta \ln w_{it}$ in eq. (40). These must be variables, of course, that are uncorrelated with unanticipated changes in wage rates, wealth, and preferences and yet that are associated with $\Delta \ln w_{it}$. Appropriate instruments are lagged values of wages and prices, variables known by the individual with certainty at the time that forecasts are made.

Now let us compare MaCurdy's estimates of the intertemporal substitution elasticity with those derived earlier by Becker (1975) and Smith (1977) who proceeded by constructing synthetic cohorts from individual observations drawn from the 1960 Census and the 1967 Survey of Economic Opportunity, respectively. That is, to say, they grouped individuals by age and averaged observations over individuals at the same age so that eq. (38) reads

$$\overline{\ln h_t} = \bar{\psi} + \gamma \overline{\ln w_t} + \beta \bar{A}_t + \delta t + \bar{\varepsilon}_t, \tag{41}$$

where t denotes each age and the bars indicate means. If the value of $\bar{\psi}$ is the same at all ages (i.e. there are no cohort effects), then group means act as instruments and the ordinary least-squares estimator applied to (41) yields consistent estimates. In Becker's work, λ was estimated for white men to be 0.448 (with an estimated standard error of 0.105) and for nonwhite men to be 0.098 (with a standard error of 0.040).[111] When eq. (41) was estimated in its level form to individuals sorted by years of schooling, there was a tendency for γ to fall with years of schooling. This tendency was not apparent when eq. (41) was estimated by first-differencing the variables between successive ages. Becker did not invariably estimate positive values for γ although, when negative effects were estimated, they tended to be small (in absolute value) relative to their estimated standard errors. In Smith's research the logarithm of the wife's wage rate (again averaged over individuals at the same age) was included on the right-hand side of eq. (41). This is consistent with preferences being defined over the hours worked of the wife as well as over the husband's hours and commodity consumption and with period-specific utility not being additive in the hours worked by the husband

[111] These results of Becker's correspond to his use of three-year moving averages of the underlying data. The estimates from the original observations are similar. Smith's results (to be reported shortly) also derive from forming three-year moving averages of all variables.

and by the wife. His estimates of γ for white married men were 0.322 (standard error of 0.047) and for black married men were 0.231 (standard error of 0.107). The estimate of the logarithm of the wife's wage rate (so the effect of an evolutionary increase in the wife's wage rate on the husband's hours of work) was negative though typically it was estimated very imprecisely. The effect of the logarithm of the husband's wage on the wife's hours of work was also negative though larger (in absolute value and also in relation to its estimated standard error). A formal test of the symmetry condition of the Frisch male and female labor supply equations was not conducted.

The most stringent assumption required for data on synthetic cohorts to identify the intertemporal substitution elasticity is that $\bar{\lambda}_0$ (or $\bar{\psi}$) be constant for all age groups or, if it is not, that it be distributed independently of $\overline{\ln w_t}$. In fact, if after controlling for other effects $\bar{\lambda}_0$ is lower for those age groups with currently lower average wage rates (e.g. if younger workers have greater lifetime wealth, but at present are facing lower wage rates than older workers), then the coefficient on $\overline{\ln w_t}$ in eq. (41) will not identify the intertemporal substitution elasticity, but will incorporate vintage effects. This cohort bias can be addressed if synthetic cohorts are constructed in several different calendar years and λ_0 is allowed to have a different value for each cohort. In this event, the variables in eq. (41) would bear a subscript t for the cohort and a subscript k for the calendar year that the cohort mean was observed. This was precisely how Browning, Deaton and Irish (1983) proceeded by constructing synthetic cohorts from successive British Family Expenditure Surveys. In other words, instead of one observation on each cohort that would derive from a single cross-section of individuals, Browning, Deaton and Irish had seven observations on each cohort starting with the tax year 1970/71 and ending with 1976/77. Their cohorts were categorized in 1970/71 into five-year age-groups from 18–23 years old to 54–58 years old (so there were eight cohorts in all) and for each cohort (and for manual and nonmanual workers separately) they formed averages for married men. The hours variable measured weekly hours worked and it was the response to the Survey's question concerning "normal hours". The wage variable was defined as the ratio of "normal" wage and salary income per week (after the payment of income taxes) to "normal hours", the left-hand side variable.

The particular form specified by Browning, Deaton and Irish for the Frisch labor supply equation was[112]

$$\bar{h}_{tk} = \gamma_0' \overline{\ln \lambda_0} + \gamma_1' C_t + \gamma_2' Y_k + \gamma_3' \overline{\ln w_{tk}} + \gamma_4' \overline{(p_k/w_{tk})^{1/2}} + \cdots + \bar{\varepsilon}_{tk}, \tag{42}$$

[112] This Frisch labor supply equation is derived by differentiating the consumer's profit function, Π, with respect to w where Π is given by

$$\Pi(\lambda, p, w) = a_0\lambda^{-1} - a_1 p + a_2 w + 2\gamma_4'(pw)^{1/2} - \delta_2' p \ln(p\lambda) + \gamma_3' w \ln(w\lambda),$$

and where a_1 and a_2 are permitted to depend upon variables other than p, w, and λ.

where the bar indicates the average value of the variable for cohort t in calendar year k. C denotes a vector of cohort dummy variables, Y a vector of calendar year dummy variables, and the dots indicate other variables included in the equation (see Table 1.22). All cohorts were assumed to face the same commodity prices, p_k, in any calendar year k. If γ_4' is zero, commodities and male labor supply are additive within periods. The intertemporal substitution elasticity [the derivative of the logarithm of $\bar{h}_{tk}$ in eq. (42) with respect to the logarithm of w_{tk}] is given by $h_{tk}^{-1}[\gamma_3' - (1/2)\gamma_4'(p_k/w_{tk})^{1/2}]$.

Their estimate of γ_3' in eq. (42) was 17.2 with an estimated standard error of 5.5 and their estimate of γ_4' was 26.0 with an estimated standard error of 10.5. Evaluated at approximate mean values, an intertemporal substitution elasticity of 0.05 was implied.[113] Unlike MaCurdy's results, these estimates were sensitive to the omission of the calendar year dummies. The estimate of γ_4' implies that, within each period, leisure time and commodity consumption are complements. The first-differenced (over calendar time) version of eq. (42) where $\overline{\Delta \ln w_{tk}}$ and $\overline{\Delta (p_k/w_{tk})^{1/2}}$ were instrumented yielded similar point estimates to those from fitting eq. (42) in level form although standard errors were larger and the test statistics fell slightly short of standard threshold levels. (See Table 1.22 for the instruments used.) Again the estimates were sensitive to the omission of the calendar year dummy variables.

Browning, Deaton and Irish's survey data also provided information on consumption expenditures though, unlike working hours, these represented actual and not "normal" consumption. They reported the consequences of estimating the Frisch commodity demand equation corresponding to eq. (42):

$$\bar{x}_{tk} = \delta_0' \overline{\ln \lambda_0} + \delta_1' C_t + \delta_2' \overline{\ln p_k} + \delta_3' \overline{(w_{tk}/p_k)^{1/2}} + \cdots + \bar{\varepsilon}_{tk}', \tag{43}$$

where symmetry would require δ_3' to equal $-\gamma_4'$ in eq. (42).[114] The estimated consumption intertemporal substitution elasticity, the effect of a proportional increase in p over the life cycle, is measured to be -1.38.[115] In the estimates of eq. (43) and of its first-differenced version, the value of δ_3' implied that within-period commodity consumption and leisure time are substitutes, a result contradicting the estimates of γ_4' in eq. (42). In the first-differenced equation, however, the estimate of δ_3' is less than its estimated standard error.

[113] These estimates are evaluated at mean weekly hours of work of 43.6 and the approximate mean of $\overline{(p_k/w_{tk})^{1/2}}$, namely 1.15.

[114] Because all cohorts are assumed to face the same commodity prices, the vector of year dummies (Y_k) and the term $\ln p_k$ cannot both be included in this equation. Including $\ln p$ and excluding Y is equivalent to including Y and restricting the coefficients on all the elements of Y to be the same. In fact, an F-test did not reject that constraint. Equation (43) may be derived from the consumer's profit function in footnote 112 by taking the derivative of the negative of Π with respect to p.

[115] The consumption intertemporal substitution elasticity is given by $x^{-1}[\delta_2' - (1/2)\delta_3'(w/p)^{1/2}]$. The statement in the text is derived by evaluating their estimated eqs. 5.10 and 6.5 at $x = 53.3$ and $(w/p)^{1/2} = 0.87$.

As shown in the discussion of Becker's and Smith's research above, a single cross-section of individuals may be used to compute the intertemporal substitution elasticity if synthetic cohorts are constructed from these data. However, under a string of exacting assumptions, the individual observations from a cross-section may be used more conventionally to estimate this elasticity. The essential idea here starts by recognizing that the unobserved variable λ_{0i} is a function of an individual's lifetime wage path and his initial wealth and it continues by noting that, if lifetime wages and initial wealth can be expressed as a function of age and age-invariant characteristics, then λ_{0i} in the Frisch labor supply equation may be replaced by these variables. In particular, MaCurdy (1982) replaced ψ_i in eq. (38) by variables measuring each individual's father's education, his mother's education, the socio-economic status of his parents, and the individual's own education and then fitted the resulting equation using observations on 561 white, continuously married, prime-age men from the Michigan PSID. He estimated this equation with each year's observations from 1967 to 1975 so there were nine separate estimates for the coefficient on $\ln w_{it}$, estimates of γ according to eq. (38). The estimates of γ ranged from a low of -0.07 in the 1975 cross-section to a high of 0.28 in the 1974 cross-section with estimated standard errors of 0.23 and 0.47, respectively. The simple average of these nine estimates of γ was 0.15. Only the age squared and education squared variables are identifying the variation in predicted wages, so it is not surprising that none of these nine coefficients passed the conventional thresholds of being significantly different from zero. These imprecise estimates are not very encouraging with respect to the use of individual observations from a single cross-section to measure the intertemporal substitution elasticity in this way.[116]

To summarize, the estimates to date of the male intertemporal substitution elasticity, γ, range from -0.07 to 0.45 with a central tendency of 0.20 (see Table 1.22). This means that evolutionary changes in wage rates generate relatively small changes in the hours worked of men aged from about 25 to 65 years: a 10 percent increase in his wages will induce about a 2 percent increase in his hours worked. The estimated standard errors surrounding these point estimates are also worthy of note: as often as not, the null hypothesis that life-cycle changes in wages have no effect on hours worked by prime-aged men cannot be rejected at conventional levels of significance. There is ample support here for someone whose research ignores the effects of evolutionary changes of wages on male hours worked.

It is important to note that the research described in the preceding paragraphs is directed towards only one part of the life-cycle characterization; it supplies

[116]MaCurdy (1983) uses cross-section consumption data from the Denver Income Maintenance Experiment to estimate the within-period marginal rate of substitution between commodity consumption and hours of work and then proceeded to the longitudinal dimension of the data to estimate a particular monotonic transformation of the utility function. The 121 men studied appear to display implausibly large wage elasticities though the reasons for the peculiar results are not apparent.

information on how an individual will allocate his working hours as he ages in response to evolutionary changes in his wage rates. In addition, there is the question of the response of labor supply at any age to changes in the entire wage profile. That is, two individuals both at age t' and facing the same wages at t' will supply different hours of work at t' (and at all other ages) if their entire life-cycle wage profiles differ (i.e. if their wages at ages other than t' differ). Answering this question requires relating each individual's marginal utility of wealth variable, λ_{0i}, or its transform such as ψ_i in eq. (38) to each individual's lifetime budget constraint variables, his rate of time preference, A_{it}, and ε_{it}. For male workers this second step seems to have been undertaken only by MaCurdy (1981) who relates his estimated fixed effects for different workers in eq. (38) to exogenous, age-invariant variables that determine each individual's lifetime budget constraint. These variables consist of family background characteristics, terms in the individual's own schooling, and estimated parameters describing the life-cycle growth in wage rates and initial nonwage income. His estimates suggest that, if a consumer experiences a ten percent increase in wage rates at all ages, he will increase his hours of work at all ages by between 0.5 and 1.3 percent. Again, the supply schedule of male hours of work is relatively inelastic with respect to the life-cycle wage profile.

Empirical research at the microeconomic level on male life-cycle labor supply is barely a few years old so surely it is premature to offer a confident evaluation of its performance. Some provisional judgments can be made, however. Does the extensively-used intertemporally additive model incorporate the essential features of life-cycle decision-making? The capacity of the model to take account of many aspects of intertemporal decision-making is really quite impressive. Not merely can it, in principle, be set in a context of uncertainty, but it can be generalized to allow for human capital investment, transactions costs associated with the purchase of consumer durables, and a variety of capital market imperfections (such as differential borrowing and lending rates of interest or transactions costs in financial capital markets). See MaCurdy (1981b). These are all prevalent features of the economy so their tractability within this life-cycle model adds to its appeal.

At the same time, the empirical implementation of this model already makes great demands on available data and augmenting the model to allow for these additional features probably exceeds the capacities of current data sets. If this is the case, then one response is to embark on the collection of more and more detailed information. Perhaps this should be done, but it should not proceed without some assessment of whether this extraordinary effort and expense will yield sufficiently high returns and this, in turn, requires some evaluation of whether the relationships emphasized in the life-cycle literature are important enough to account for the key variations in male labor supply.

At this stage of the research, the focus of the life-cycle research has been upon the labor supply responses to evolutionary movements in wages. The evidence to date indicates that these labor supply responses for prime-age men are very inelastic with respect to life-cycle changes in wages. Similarly, across male workers, the labor supply responses to differences in entire wage profiles appear to be small. In other words, the greater part of the variations in male labor supply across workers and over time is left unexplained by this research.[117] A great deal of effort has been brought to bear on what appears to be relationships of second-order of importance.

6. Conclusions

A great deal of research, much of it careful and some of it ingenious, has been undertaken on male labor supply during the past two decades. The vast proportion of that work – both that based on the static model and that based on the life-cycle model – indicates that the elasticities of hours of work with respect to wages are very small. In other words, the focus of most economists' research has been on behavioral responses that for men appear to be of a relatively small order of magnitude. In the case of applications of the static model of labor supply, there are a number of instances in which the income-compensated wage elasticity of hours of work is estimated to be negative. This, of course, violates an important (some would judge it to be "the" important) implication of that model and consequently it casts doubt on the empirical relevance of the model.

Of course, the static model can always be rescued from such a conclusion by arguing that what is at fault is not the allocation model itself, but rather the string of auxiliary hypotheses (assumptions about functional forms, measurement of the variables, etc.) that are required to apply the theory. Logically, this is a fully defensible position: that the theory's implications are at variance with observation means that at least one (and perhaps no more than one) of the hypotheses associated with the theory and its application is refuted. The problem with this defence is that, if the auxiliary hypotheses are continually being called upon to "save" the theory, then this comes close to denying the theory can ever be tested. It is not as if the model has already survived many different attempts to refute it. If this were the case, a few instances of its apparent failure might be attributed to the nonsatisfaction of the auxiliary assumptions. But, with this model, few scholars have conducted their research with the aim of testing the theory; most have been interested in quantifying a relationship whose existence is presumed to be true. As a by-product of this concern with measurement, they

[117]Some indication of this is provided by the consequences of fitting the hours of work equation whose estimates are reported in Table 1.17 above to the sample of 23,059 men stratified by years of age. In other words, I estimated 31 ordinary least-squares regressions, each one fitted to the hours worked and other data for men at each of the 31 years of age from 25 years to 55 years. All the right-hand side variables listed in Table 1.17 (except, of course, the age variables) were used as regressors. The size of the samples ranged from 514 men for those aged 55 years to 1,154 men for those aged 32 years. As illustrative of the poor explanatory power of the estimated linear combination of the right-hand side variables, the central tendency of the R^2s in these equations was 20% with a range extending from a high of 0.307 for men aged 45 years to a low of 0.135 for men aged 48 years.

have turned up a number of instances in which the behavioral responses take on values that violate the theory's predictions. Under these circumstances, the scientific procedure is surely to regard the theory as it has been formulated and applied to date as having been refuted by the evidence.

This does not mean that budget constraints have nothing to do with male hours of work. On the contrary, evidence from the Negative Income Tax experiments strongly suggests that changes in male work behavior are not independent of changes in their budget constraints. So prices and wages affect work decisions, but perhaps not in the particular way described by the familiar constrained utility-maximizing model. Or this model may be an apt description of some of the population, but a different characterization of behavior may be more appropriate for others. In this case, no *single* model of labor supply is adequate to account for the behavior of all individuals.

There is still much more work to be done with the canonical model. My severe judgments about its empirical relevance will have to be revised if it is shown that its apparent shortcomings to date are, in fact, the consequence of the manner in which it has been applied. If this is the case, then I hope more research with individual or household data will be conducted into the model's implications for the consumption of commodities and for savings. Consumption and savings behavior is supposed to be part of the same allocation process as hours of work and yet the empirical work on these issues has only recently explicitly recognized this. Also, I hope more will be done to integrate time spent in unemployment with decisions concerning hours of work. Current research treats unemployment in different ways: sometimes unemployment is classified as a state indistinguishable from being out of the labor force; sometimes time spent in unemployment is simply added to hours worked in the belief that both activities represent the supply of time to market activities; and sometimes time spent in unemployment is characterized as part of the optimal allocation of an individual's scarce resources, but as behaviorally distinct from hours worked. Little research has been directed towards determining which of these different treatments is the correct one. Furthermore, given the substantial resources that have already been directed towards measuring the effects of wages on work behavior and given the relatively small responses to wages that have been estimated for men, it would be useful if economists redirected some of these efforts into accounting more satisfactorily for variations in labor supply that are associated with other variables. In particular, because only a relatively small proportion of the variation in hours of work of prime-age men in the population is removed by the set of variables on which information is collected in most surveys, we need to know more about what this "unobserved heterogeneity" represents. Are these differences attributable to differences in the particular forms of the employment contracts under which individuals work? Are they associated with differences in discount rates among individuals? Are they attributable to attitudes and values that seem to be acquired from parents? There is a great deal that we do not know and that is waiting to be discovered.

References

Abbott, M. and O. Ashenfelter (1976) "Labour supply, commodity demand, and the allocation of time", *Review of Economic Studies*, 43(3):389–411.

Abbott, M. and O. Ashenfelter (1979) "Labour supply, commodity demand, and the allocation of time: correction", *Review of Economic Studies*, 46(3):567–569.

Abowd, John M. and Orley Ashenfelter (1981) "Anticipated unemployment, temporary layoffs, and compensating wage differentials", in: Sherwin Rosen, ed., *Studies in labor markets*. National Bureau of Economic Research, Univ. of Chicago Press, 141–170.

Abowd, John M. and David E. Card (1983) "Intertemporal substitution in the presence of long term contracts", Working Paper No. 166, Industrial Relations Section, Princeton University, September.

Ainsworth, R. B. (1949) "Earnings and working hours of manual wage-earners in the United Kingdom in October 1938", *Journal of the Royal Statistical Society, Series A*, 112:35–58.

Alchian, Armen A. (1974) "Information, martingales, and prices", *The Swedish Journal of Economics*, 76(1):3–11.

Altonji, Joseph G. (1982) "Intertemporal substitution model of labour market fluctuations: an empirical analysis", *Review of Economic Studies*, 49(159) Special Issue:783–824.

Altonji, Joseph G. (1983) "Intertemporal substitution in labor supply: evidence from micro data", Hoover Institution Conference on Labor Economics, January 1983.

Ashenfelter, Orley (1978) "The labor supply response of wage earners", in: John L. Palmer and Joseph A. Pechman, eds., *Welfare in rural areas: the North Carolina–Iowa income maintenance experiment*. Washington, D.C.: Brookings, 109–138.

Ashenfelter, Orley (1978), "Unemployment as a constraint on labour market behaviour", in: M. J. Artis and A. R. Nobay, eds., *Contemporary economic analysis*. The Association of University Teachers of Economics, 149–181.

Ashenfelter, Orley (1980) "Unemployment as disequilibrium in a model of aggregate labor supply", *Econometrica*, 48(3):547–564.

Ashenfelter, Orley (1983) "Determining participation in income-tested social programs", *Journal of the American Statistical Association*, 78(383):517–525.

Ashenfelter, Orley, and John Ham (1979) "Education, unemployment, and earnings", *Journal of Political Economy*, 87(5):99–116.

Ashenfelter, Orley and James Heckman (1973) "Estimating labor supply functions", in: G. G. Cain and H. W. Watts, *Income maintenance and labor supply*. Chicago: Markham, 265–278.

Ashenfelter, Orley and James Heckman (1974) "The estimation of income and substitution effects in a model of family labor supply", *Econometrica*, 42(1):73–85.

Ashworth, J. S. and D. T. Ulph (1981) "Endogeneity I: estimating labour supply with piecewise linear budget constraints", in C. V. Brown, ed., *Taxation and labour supply*. London: George Allen and Unwin, 53–68.

Atkinson, A. B. and N. H. Stern (1979) "A note on the allocation of time", *Economics Letters*, 3:119–123.

Atkinson, A. B. and N. H. Stern (1980) "On the switch from direct to indirect taxation", *Journal of Public Economics*, 14(2):195–224.

Atkinson, A. B. and N. H. Stern (1981) "On labour supply and commodity demands", in: Angus Deaton, ed., *Essays in the theory and measurement of consumer behaviour in honour of Sir Richard Stone*. Cambridge: Cambridge University Press, 265–296.

Bancroft, Gertrude (1958) *The American labor force: its growth and changing composition*. New York: Social Science Research Council.

Barmby, Tim, Richard Blundell and Ian Walker (1983) "Estimating a life cycle consistent model of family labour supply with cross-section data", unpublished paper, University of Manchester.

Barnett, William A. (1979) "The joint allocation of leisure and goods expenditure", *Econometrica*, 47(3):539–564.

Barnett, William A. (1981) *Consumer demand and labor supply*. Amsterdam: North-Holland.

Becker, Gary S. (1965) "A theory of the allocation of time", *Economic Journal*, 75:493–517.

Becker, Gary S. (1974) "A theory of social interactions", *Journal of Political Economy*, 82(6):1063–1093.

Becker, Gary S. (1975) "The allocation of time over the life cycle", in: G. R. Ghez and G. S. Becker, *The allocation of time and goods over the life cycle*. New York: National Bureau of Economic

Research, Columbia University Press, 83–132.
Ben-Porath, Yoram (1973) "Labor force participation rates and the supply of labor", *Journal of Political Economy*, 81(3):697–704.
Betancourt, Roger R. (1971) "The estimation of price elasticities from cross-section data under additive preferences", *International Economic Review*, 12(2):283–292.
Bloch, Farrell (1973) "The allocation of time to market and non-market work within a family unit", unpublished Ph.D. dissertation, Department of Economics, Stanford University.
Blundell, Richard and Ian Walker (1982) "Modelling the joint determination of household labour supplies and commodity demands", *Economic Journal*, 92(366):351–364.
Blundell, Richard and Ian Walker (1983) "Limited dependent variables in demand analysis: an application to modelling family labour supply and commodity demand behaviour", Discussion Paper ES126, Department of Econometrics and Social Statistics, University of Manchester.
Blundell, Richard and Ian Walker (1984) "A life-cycle consistent empirical model of family labor supply using cross-section data", unpublished paper, March.
Borjas, George J. (1980) "The relationship between wages and weekly hours of work: the role of division bias", *Journal of Human Resources*, 15(3):409–423.
Boskin, Michael J. (1973) "The economics of labor supply", in: G. G. Cain and H. W. Watts, *Income maintenance and labor supply*. Chicago: Markham, 163–181.
Bowen, William G. and T. Aldrich Finegan (1965) "Labor force participation and unemployment;, in: Arthur M. Ross, ed., *Employment policy and the labor market*. University of California Press, 115–161.
Bowen, William G. and T. Aldrich Finegan (1969) *The economics of labor force participation*. Princeton University Press.
Brown, C. V., E. Levin and D. T. Ulph (1976) "Estimates of labour hours supplied by married male workers in Great Britain", *Scottish Journal of Political Economy*, 23(3):261–277.
Brown, C. V. (1980) *Taxation and the incentive to work*. Oxford: Oxford University Press.
Brown, C. V., ed. (1981) *Taxation and labour supply*. London: George Allen and Unwin.
Brown, C. V., E. J. Levin, P. J. Rosa, P. J. Ruffell and D. T. Ulph (1982–83) "Direct taxation and short run labour supply", H. M. Treasury Project, Working Papers Nos. 1 to 12, Department of Economics, University of Stirling.
Browning, M. J. (1982) "Profit function representations for consumer preferences", mimeo, Bristol University.
Browning, Martin, Angus Deaton and Margaret Irish (1983) "A profitable approach to labor supply and commodity demands over the life-cycle", mimeo.
Bry, Gerhard (1959) *The average workweek as an economic indicator*, Occasional Paper 69, National Bureau of Economic Research.
Burtless, Gary and David Greenberg (1982) "Inferences concerning labor supply behavior based on limited duration experiment", *American Economic Review*, 72(3):488–497.
Burtless, Gary and Jerry A. Hausman (1978) "The effect of taxation on labor supply: evaluating the Gary negative income tax experiment", *Journal of Political Economy*, 86(6):1103–1130.
Cain, Glen G. and Harold W. Watts, eds. (1973) *Income maintenance and labor supply*. Chicago: Markham.
Chipman, John (1965) "A survey of the theory of international trade: Part 2, the neo-classical theory", *Econometrica*, 33(4):685–760.
Coase, R. H. (1937) "The nature of the firm", *Economica*, 4(16):386–405.
Coen, Robert M. and Bert G. Hickman (1970) "Constrained joint estimation of factor demand and production functions", *Review of Economics and Statistics*, 52(3):287–300.
Cogan, J. F. (1981) "Fixed costs and labor supply", *Econometrica*, 49(4):945–964.
Cohen, Malcolm S., Samuel A. Rea and Robert I. Lerman (1970) "A micro model of labor supply", BLS Staff Paper 4, U.S. Department of Labor.
Coleman, Thomas S. (1983) "Development and estimation of a dynamic model of labor supply", unpublished mimeo, University of Chicago.
Corry, B. A. and J. A. Roberts (1970) "Activity rates and unemployment: the evidence of the United Kingdom 1951–66", *Applied Economics*, 2(3):179–201.
Corry, B. A. and J. A. Roberts (1974) "Activity rates and unemployment. The U.K. experience: some further results", *Applied Economics*, 6(1):1–22.
Darrough, M. N. (1977) "A model of consumption and leisure in an intertemporal framework: a

systematic treatment using Japanese data", *International Economic Review*, 18(3):677–96.

DaVanzo, Julie, Dennis N. DeTray and David H. Greenberg (1973) "Estimating labor supply response: a sensitivity analysis", R-1372-OEO, The RAND Corporation.

Deardorff, A. V. and F. P. Stafford (1976) "Compensation of cooperating factors", *Econometrica*, 44(4):671–684.

Deaton, Angus (1974) "A reconsideration of the empirical implications of additive preferences", *Economic Journal*, 84(334):338–348.

Deaton, Angus (1982) "Model selection procedures, or, does the consumption function exist?", in: G. C. Chow and P. Crosi, eds., *Evaluating the reliability of macroeconomic models*. New York: John Wiley, 43–65.

Deaton, Angus and John Muellbauer (1980) *Economics and consumer behavior*. Cambridge: Cambridge University Press.

Deaton, Angus and John Muellbauer (1981) "Functional forms for labour supply and commodity demands with and without quantity restrictions", *Econometrica* 49(6):1521–1532.

Dickinson, Jonathan (1974) "Labor supply of family members", in: James N. Morgan, et al., eds., *Five thousand American families — patterns of economic progress*. Michigan, vol. I, 177–250.

Dickinson, Jonathan G. (1979) "Revealed preferences, functional form, and labor supply", unpublished mimeo.

Dickinson, Jonathan G. (1980) "Parallel preference structures in labor supply and commodity demand: an adaptation of the Gorman polar form", *Econometrica*, 48(7):1711–1725.

Douglas, Paul H. (1934) *The theory of wages*. New York: Macmillan.

Duncan, Beverly (1965) "Dropouts and the unemployed", *Journal of Political Economy*, 73(2):121–134.

Durand, John D. (1948) *The labor force in the United States, 1890–1960*. New York: Social Science Research Council.

Ehrenberg, Ronald G. and Paul L. Schumann (1981) "The overtime pay provisions of the fair labor standards act", in: Simon Rottenberg, ed., *The Economics of Legal Minimum Wages*. American Enterprise Institute, 264–295.

Finegan, T. A. (1962) "Hours of work in the United States—a cross-sectional analysis", *Journal of Political Economy*, 70(5):452–70.

Fleisher, Belton M., Donald O. Parsons and Richard D. Porter (1973) "Asset adjustments and labor supply of older workers", in: G. G. Cain and H. W. Watts, *Income maintenance and labor supply*. Chicago: Markham, 279–327.

Frain, LaRue (1929) "The relation between normal working time and hourly and weekly earnings", *Quarterly Journal of Economics*, 43(2):544–505.

Garfinkel, Irwin (1973) "On estimating the labor supply effects of a negative income tax", in: G. G. Cain and H. W. Watts, *Income maintenance and labor supply*. Chicago: Markham, 205–264.

Goldberger, Arthur S. (1981) "Linear regression after selection", *Journal of Econometrics*, 15(3):357–366.

Greenberg, David H. and Marvin Kosters (1973) "Income guarantees and the working poor: the effect of income-maintenance programs on the hours of work of male family heads", in: G. G. Cain and H. W. Watts, *Income maintenance and labour supply*. Chicago: Markham, 14–101.

Greenberg, David, Robert Moffitt and John Friedman (1981) "Underreporting and experimental effects on work effort: evidence from the Gary income maintenance experiment", *Review of Economics and Statistics*, 63(4):581–589.

Greenhalgh, Christine A. (1979) "Male labour force participation in Great Britain", *Scottish Journal of Political Economy*, 26(3):275–286.

Grossman, Michael (1975) "The correlation between health and schooling", in: Nestor E. Terleckyj, ed., *Household production and consumption*. New York: National Bureau of Economic Research, Columbia University Press, 147–211.

Hall, Robert E. (1973) "Wages, income, and hours of work in the U.S. labor force", in: G. G. Cain and H. W. Watts, *Income maintenance and labor supply*. Chicago: Markham, 102–162.

Hall, Robert E. (1980) "Employment fluctuations and wage rigidity", *Brookings Papers in Economy Activity*, 1:91–123.

Ham, John C. (1982) "Estimation of a labor supply model with censoring due to unemployment and underemployment", *Review of Economic Studies*, 49(157):335–354.

Ham, John C. (1983) "Testing whether unemployment represents life-cycle labor supply behavior", unpublished paper, Nov. 1983.

Hausman, Jerry A. (1981) "Labor supply", in: Henry J. Aaron and Joseph A. Pechman, eds., *How taxes affect economic behavior*. Washington, D.C.: The Brookings Institution, 27–72.

Hausman, Jerry and Paul Ruud (1984) "Family labor supply with taxes", *American Economic Review, Papers and Proceedings*, 74(2).

Hausman, J. A. and D. A. Wise (1976) "The evaluation of results from truncated samples: the New Jersey income maintenance experiment", *Annals of Economic and Social Measurement*, 5(4):421–46

Hausman, Jerry A. and David A. Wise (1977) "Social experimentation, truncated distributions, and efficient estimation", *Econometrica*, 45(4):919–938.

Hausman, Jerry A. and David A. Wise (1979) "Attrition bias in experimental and panel data: the Gary income maintenance experiment", *Econometrica*, 47(2):455–474.

Haveman, R. H. and B. L. Wolfe (1984) "The decline in male labor force participation: comment", *Journal of Political Economy*, 92(3):532–41.

Heckman, James J. (1974a) "Life cycle consumption and labor supply: an explanation of the relationship between income and consumption over the life cycle", *American Economic Review*, 64(1):188–194.

Heckman, James J. (1974b) "Shadow prices, market wages, and labor supply", *Econometrica*, 42(4):679–694.

Heckman, James J. (1976a) "A life-cycle model of earnings, learning, and consumption", *Journal of Political Economy*, Part 2, 84(4):11–44.

Heckman, James J. (1976b) "The common structure of statistical models of truncation, sample selection, and limited dependent variables and a simple estimator for such models", *Annals of Economic and Social Measurement*, 5(4):475–492.

Heckman, James J. (1978) "A partial survey of recent research on the labor supply of women", *American Economic Review Proceedings*, 68(2):200–207.

Heckman, James J. (1983) "Comment [on Hausman's paper]", in: Martin Feldstein, ed., *Behavioral simulation methods in tax policy analysis*. Chicago: National Bureau of Economic Research, University of Chicago Press, 70–82.

Heckman, James J., Mark Killingsworth and Thomas MaCurdy (1981) "Empirical evidence on static labour supply models: a survey of recent developments", in: Z. Hornstein, J. Grice and A. Webb, eds., *The economics of the labour market*. London: Her Majesty's Stationery Office, 74–122.

Heckman, James J. and Thomas E. MaCurdy (1981) "New methods for estimating labor supply functions: a survey", *Research in Labor Economics*, 4:65–102.

Hill, C. Russell (1973) "The determinants of labor supply for the working urban poor", in: G. G. Cain and H. W. Watts, *Income maintenance and labor supply*. Chicago: Markham, 182–204.

Hill, Daniel and Saul Hoffman (1977) "Husbands and wives", in: Gregg J. Duncan and James N. Morgan, eds., *Five thousand American families — patterns of economic progress*. Michigan, vol. V, 29–70.

Holbrook, Robert and Frank Stafford (1971) "The propensity to consume separate types of income: a generalized permanent income hypothesis", *Econometrica*, 39(1):1–22.

Horner, David (1977) "Labor supply of husbands", in: Harold Watts and Albert Rees, eds., *The New Jersey income maintenance experiment, Vol. II: labor supply responses*. New York: Academic Press.

Hotz, V. J., F. E. Kydland, and G. L. Sedlacek, "Intertemporal substitution and labor supply", unpublished paper, December 1982.

Hurd, Michael D. (1976) "The estimation of nonlinear labor supply functions with taxes from a truncated sample", Institute for Mathematical Studies in the Social Sciences, Technical Report No. 217, Stanford University.

Hurd, Michael D. and John Pencavel (1981) "A utility-based analysis of the wage subsidy program", *Journal of Public Economics*, 15:185–201.

Jevons, W. Stanley (1888) *The theory of political economy*. London: Macmillan.

Johnson, Terry R. and John Pencavel (1982) "Forecasting the effects of a negative income tax program", *Industrial and Labor Relations Review*, 35(2):221–234.

Johnson, Terry R. and John Pencavel (1984) "Dynamic hours of work functions for husbands, wives, and single females", *Econometrica*, 52(2):363–390.

Jones, Ethel B. (1961) "Hours of work in the United States, 1900–1957", unpublished Ph.D. dissertation, University of Chicago.

Jones, Ethel B. (1974) *An investigation of the stability of hours of work per week in manufacturing, 1947–1970*. College of Business Administration, University of Georgia.

Kalachek, Edward, Wesley Mellow and Frederic Raines (1978) "The male labor supply function reconsidered", *Industrial and Labor Relations Review*, 31(3):356–367.

Kalachek, Edward D. and Frederic Q. Raines (1970) "Labor supply of lower income workers and the negative income tax", *Technical studies, the President's commission on income maintenance programs*. Washington, D.C.: U.S. Government Printing Office, 159–186.

Keeley, Michael C. (1981) *Labor supply and public policy: a critical review*. New York: Academic Press.

Keeley, Michael C. and Philip K. Robins (1980) "The design of social experiments: a critique of the Conlisk-Watts assignment model", in: R. G. Ehrenberg, ed., *Research in labor economics*. Vol. 3, 293–333.

Keeley, Michael C., Philip K. Robins, Robert G. Spiegelman and Richard W. West (1978a) "The labor supply effects and costs of alternative negative income tax programs", *Journal of Human Resources*, 13(1):3–36.

Keeley, Michael C., Philip K. Robins, Robert G. Spiegelman and Richard W. West (1978b) "The estimation of labor supply models using experimental data", *American Economic Review*, 68(5):873–887.

Killingsworth, Mark R. (1981) "A survey of labor supply models: theoretical analyses and first-generation empirical results", *Research in Labor Economics*, 4:1–64.

Killingsworth, Mark R. (1983) *Labor supply*. Cambridge: Cambridge University Press.

Klein, L. R. and R. F. Kosobud (1961) "Some econometrics of growth: great ratios of economics", *Quarterly Journal of Economics*, 75(2):173–198.

Kniesner, Thomas J. (1976a) "An indirect test of complementarity in a family labor supply model", *Econometrica*, 44(4):651–669.

Kneisner, Thomas J. (1976b) "The full-time workweek in the United States, 1900–1970", *Industrial and Labor Relations Review*, 30(1):3–15.

Kosters, Marvin H. (1966) "Income and substitution effects in a family labor supply model", P-3339, The Rand Corporation.

Kosters, Marvin H. (1969) "Effects of an income tax on labor supply", in: Arnold C. Harberger and Martin J. Bailey, eds., *The taxation of income from capital*. Washington, D.C.: Studies of Government Finance, Brookings Institution, 301–324.

Kurz, Mordecai, Philip Robins, Robert Spiegelman, Richard West and Harlan Halsey (1974) "A cross sectional estimation of labor supply for families in Denver 1970", Research Memorandum 24, Center for the Study of Welfare Policy, Stanford Research Institute.

Kydland, Finn E. and Edward C. Prescott (1982) "Time to build and aggregate fluctuations", *Econometrica*, 50(6):1345–1370.

Lakatos, Imre (1970) "Falsification and the methodology of scientific research programmes", in: Imre Lakatos and Alan Musgrave, eds., *Criticism and the growth of knowledge*. Cambridge University Press, 1970, pp. 91–195.

Lau, Lawrence J., Wuu-Long Lin and Pan A. Yotopoulos (1978) "The linear logarithmic expenditure system: an application to consumption-leisure choice", *Econometrica*, 46(4): 843–868.

Layard, Richard (1978) "Hours supplied by British married men with endogenous overtime", Discussion Paper No. 30, Centre for Labour Economics, London School of Economics.

Lewis, H. Gregg (1957) "Hours of work and hours of leisure", in: *Proceedings of the Ninth Annual Meeting*. Industrial Relations Research Association, 196–206.

Lewis, H. Gregg (1967) "On income and substitution effects in labor force participation", unpublished paper, University of Chicago.

Lewis, H. Gregg (1969) "Employer interests in employee hours of work", unpublished paper.

Long, Clarence D. (1958) *The labor force under changing income and employment*. Princeton: National Bureau of Economic Research, Princeton University Press, General Series, No. 65.

Lundberg, Shelly (1983) "Is unemployment involuntary?", Hoover Institution Working Papers in Economics No. E-83-9, Stanford University.

MaCurdy, Thomas (1976) "A household life-cycle model under uncertainty with human capital investment", mimeo, Workshop in Applications of Economics, University of Chicago.

MaCurdy, Thomas (1981) "An empirical model of labor supply in a life-cycle setting", *Journal of Political Economy*, 89(6):1059–1085.

MaCurdy, Thomas (1981) "An intertemporal model of portfolio choice and human capital accumulation under uncertainty with extensions incorporating taxes, consumer durables, imperfections in capital markets, and nonseparable preferences", Hoover Institution Working Papers in Economics

No. E-81-18.

MaCurdy, Thomas E. (1982) "Interpreting empirical models of labor supply in an intertemporal framework with uncertainty", Research Paper No. 23, Stanford Workshop on Factor Markets.

MaCurdy, Thomas E. (1983) "A simple scheme for estimating an intertemporal model of labor supply and consumption in the presence of taxes and uncertainty", *International Economic Review*, 24(2): 265–289.

Manser, Marilyn and Murray Brown (1979) "Bargaining analyses of household decisions", in: C. B. Lloyd, E. S. Andrews and C. L. Gilroy, eds., *Women in the labor market*. New York: Columbia University Press, 3–26.

Masters, Stanley and Irwin Garfinkel (1977) *Estimating the labor supply effects of income-maintenance alternatives*. New York: Institute for Research on Poverty Monograph Series, Academic Press.

McElroy, Marjorie B. (1981) "Empirical results from estimates of joint labor supply functions of husbands and wives", in: R. G. Ehrenberg, ed., *Research in Labor Economics*, 4:53–64.

Metcalf, Charles E. (1973) "Making inferences from controlled income maintenance experiments", *American Economic Review*, 63(3):478–483.

Metcalf, Charles E. (1974) "Predicting the effects of permanent programs from a limited duration experiment", *Journal of Human Resources*, 9(4):530–555.

Metcalf, David, Stephen Nickell and Ray Richardson (1976) "The structure of hours and earnings in British manufacturing industry", *Oxford Economic Papers*, 28(3):284–303.

Mincer, Jacob (1962) "Labor force participation of married women: a study of labor supply", in: *Aspects of labor economics*. National Bureau of Economic Research, Princeton University Press, 63–105.

Mincer, Jacob (1963) "Market prices, opportunity costs, and income effects", in: Carl F. Christ, et al., *Measurement in economics: studies in mathematical economics and econometrics in memory of Yehuda Grunfeld*. Stanford University Press.

Mincer, Jacob (1966) "Labor force participation and unemployment: a review of recent evidence", in: R. A. Gordon and M. S. Gordon, eds., *Prosperity and unemployment*. 73–112.

Moffitt, Robert A. (1979) "The labor supply response in the Gary experiment", *Journal of Human Resources*, 14(4): 477–487.

Moffitt, Robert A. and Kenneth C. Kehrer (1981) "The effect of tax and transfer programs on labor supply: the evidence from the income maintenance experiments", in: R. G. Ehrenberg, ed., *Research in Labor Economics*, 4:103–150.

Morgan, James N. (1979) "Hours of work by family heads: constraints, marginal choices, and income goals", in: Greg J. Duncan and James N. Morgan, eds., *Five thousand American families – patterns of economic progress*. University of Michigan, vol. VII, 63–100.

Moses, Leon N. and Harold F. Williamson, Jr. (1963) "Value of time, choice of mode, and the subsidy issue in urban transportation", *Journal of Political Economy*, 71(3):247–264.

Mroz, Thomas A. (1984) "The sensitivity of an empirical model of married women's hours of work to economic and statistical assumptions", unpublished Ph.D. thesis, Stanford University.

Muellbauer, John (1981) "Linear aggregation in neoclassical labour supply", *Review of Economic Studies*, 48(1):21–36.

Nadiri, M. I. and S. Rosen (1974) *A disequilibrium model of demand for factors of production*. New York: National Bureau of Economic Research, Columbia University Press, General Series No. 99.

Oi, Walter (1976) "Residential location and labor supply", *Journal of Political Economy*, 84(4): Part 2, S221–S238.

Orcutt, Guy H. and Alice G. Orcutt (1968) "Incentive and disincentive experimentation for income maintenance policy purposes", *American Economic Review*, 58(4):754–727.

Owen, John D. (1979) *Working hours: an economic analysis*. Lexington, Mass.: Lexington Books.

Parsons, Donald O. (1980) "The decline in male labor force participation", *Journal of Political Economy*, 88(1):117–134.

Pencavel, John (1977) "Work effort, on-the-job screening, and alternative methods of remuneration", in: R. G. Ehrenberg, ed., *Research in Labor Economics*, 1:225–258.

Pencavel, John (1982) "Unemployment and the labor supply effects of the Seattle-Denver income maintenance experiments", *Research in Labor Economics*, 5:1–31.

Phelps Brown, E. H. (1960) *The growth of British industrial relations*. London.

Phlips, Louis (1978) "The demand for leisure and money", *Econometrica*, 6(5):1025–1044.

Pollak, Robert A. (1970) "Habit formation and dynamic demand functions", *Journal of Political Economy*, 78(4):745–63.

Pollak, Robert A. (1971) "Additive utility functions and linear Engel curves", *Review of Economic Studies*, 38(116):401–414.
Rees, Albert (1974) "An overview of the labor supply results", *Journal of Human Resources*, 9(2):158–180.
Rees, Albert (1979) "Douglas on wages and the supply of labor", *Journal of Political Economy*, 87(5): Part 1, 915–922.
Robbins, Lionel (1930) "On the elasticity of demand for income in terms of effort", *Economica*, 10(29):123–129.
Robins, Philip K. and Richard W. West (1980) "Program participation and labor supply response", *Journal of Human Resources*, 15(4):499–544.
Rosen, Harvey S. (1976) "Taxes in a labor supply model with joint wage-hours determination", *Econometrica*, 44(3):485–508.
Rosen, Harvey S. (1978) "The measurement of excess burden with explicit utility functions", *Journal of Political Economy, Supplement*, 86(2): Part 2, S121–S135.
Rosen, Sherwin (1969) "On the interindustry wage and hours structure", *Journal of Political Economy*, 77(2):249–273.
Rosen, Sherwin and Finis Welch (1971) "Labor supply and income redistribution", *Review of Economics and Statistics*, 53(3):278–282.
Samuelson, Paul A. (1956) "Social indifference curves", *Quarterly Journal of Economics*, 70(1):1–22.
Sargent, Thomas J. (1978) "Estimation of dynamic labor demand schedules under rational expectations", *Journal of Political Economy*, 86(6):1009–1044.
Schoenberg, E. and P. Douglas (1937) "Studies in the supply curve of labor: the relation in 1929 between average earnings in American cities and the proportion seeking employment", *Journal of Political Economy*, 45(1):45–79.
Simon, Herbert A. (1951) "A formal theory of the employment relationship", *Econometrica*, 19(3):293–305.
Smith, James P. (1975) "Assets and labor supply", R-1728-HEW, The Rand Corporation.
Smith, James P. (1977) "Family labor supply over the life cycle", *Explorations in Economic Research*, 4(2):205–276.
Smith, Shirley J. (1983) "Estimating annual hours of labor force activity", *Monthly Labor Review*, 106(2):13–22.
Smith-Lovin, Lynn and Ann R. Tickamyer (1978) "Nonrecursive models of labor force participation, fertility behavior, and sex role attitudes", *American Sociological Review*, 43(4):541–557.
Spinnewyn, Frans (1981) "Rational habit formation", *European Economic Review*, 15(1):91–109.
Teper, Lazare (1932) *Hours of labor*. Baltimore: Johns Hopkins Press.
U.S. Department of Labor, *Multiple jobholders in May 1979*, Bureau of Labor Statistics, Special Labor Force Report 239, January 1981.
Wales, Terence J. (1973) "Estimation of a labor supply curve for self-employed business proprietors", *International Economic Review*, 14(1):69–80.
Wales, Terence J. (1978) "Labour supply and commuting time: an empirical study", *Journal of Econometrics*, 8(2):215–226.
Wales, T. J. and A. D. Woodland (1976) "Estimation of household utility functions and labor supply response", *International Economic Review*, 17(2):397–410.
Wales, T. J. and A. D. Woodland (1977) "Estimation of the allocation of time for work leisure, and housework", *Econometrica*, 45(1):115–132.
Wales, T. J. and A. D. Woodland (1979) "Labour supply and progressive taxes", *Review of Economic Studies*, 46(1):83–95.
Wales, T. J. and A. D. Woodland (1980) "Sample selectivity and the estimation of labor supply functions", *International Economic Review*, 21(2):437–468.
Weiss, Yoram (1972) "On the optimal lifetime pattern of labour supply", *Economic Journal*, 82(328):1293–1315.
Welch, Finis (1978) "The labor supply response of farmers", in: John L. Palmer and Joseph A. Pechman, eds., *Welfare in rural areas: the North Carolina-Iowa income maintenance experiment*. Washington, D.C.: Brookings, 77–100.
Winston, Gordon C. (1966) "An international comparison of income and hours of work", *Review of Economics and Statistics*, 48(1):28–39.
Woytinsky, W. S. (1940) *Additional workers and the volume of unemployment in the depression*. New York: Social Science Research Council.

Chapter 2

FEMALE LABOR SUPPLY: A SURVEY

MARK R. KILLINGSWORTH

Rutgers University

JAMES J. HECKMAN*

University of Chicago

1. Introduction

This chapter surveys theoretical and empirical work on the labor supply of women, with special reference to women in Western economies, primarily the United States, in modern times.[1] The behavior of female labor supply has important implications for many other phenomena, including marriage, fertility, divorce, the distribution of family earnings and male–female wage differentials. The labor supply of women is also of interest because of the technical questions it poses. For example, since many women do not work, corner solutions are at least potentially a very important issue in both the theoretical and empirical analysis of female labor supply, even though in other contexts (e.g. studies of consumer demand) corner solutions are often ignored. [For recent discussions of this issue

*We thank Ricardo Barros, Bo Honoré, Tom Mroz and John Pencavel for invaluable comments and suggestions; Wolfgang Franz, Heather Joshi and Alice and Masao Nakamura for help in assembling data on the "stylized facts" about female labor supply presented in Section 2; Eileen Funck and Paul Rabideau for research assistance; and Orley Ashenfelter and Richard Layard for patience.

[1]For a general overview of women in the U.S. labor market, see Smith, ed. (1979); Fuchs (1984), Goldin (1980, 1983a, 1983b, 1984, 1986), Goldin and Sokoloff (1982) and Smith and Ward (1984a, 1984b) discuss historical and recent trends. The collection of papers in Layard and Mincer (1984), includes work on female labor supply in Australia, Britain, the Federal Republic of Germany, France, Israel, Italy, Japan, the Netherlands, the Soviet Union, Spain, Sweden, and the United States. See also Joshi (1985), Joshi and Owen (1984, 1985), and Martin and Roberts (1984) on Britain; Nakamura and Nakamura (1981), Nakamura, Nakamura and Cullen (1979), Smith and Stelcner (1985), Stelcner and Breslaw (1985), Stelcner and Smith (1985) and Robinson and Tomes (1985) on Canada; Franz (1981) and Franz and Kawasaki (1981) on the Federal Republic of Germany; Bourguignon (1985) on France; Hill (1983, 1984, 1985), Yamada and Yamada (1984, 1985) and Yamada, Yamada and Chaloupka (1985) on Japan; and Kapteyn, Kooreman and van Soest (1985), Kooreman and Kapteyn (1984a, 1985), Renaud and Siegers (1984) and van der Veen and Evers (1984) on the Netherlands.

Handbook of Labor Economics, Volume I, Edited by O. Ashenfelter and R. Layard

in the context of consumer demand studies, see Deaton (forthcoming) and Wales and Woodland (1983).]

The plan of this survey is as follows. We first present some "stylized facts" about female labor supply, and then discuss a number of theoretical models of special interest for understanding female labor supply. After considering empirical studies of the labor supply of women, we conclude with some suggestions for future research.

2. Female labor supply: Some stylized facts

This section presents some of the more important stylized facts about female labor supply. We first discuss major trends and cyclical patterns in time-series data, and then examine cross-sectional phenomena.

2.1. *Trends and cyclical patterns in time-series data*

Substantial secular increases in the labor force participation of women are a striking feature of the labor market in most developed economies in the twentieth century. Growth in participation began at different times and has proceeded at

Table 2.1
United States: Female civilian labor force participation rates (in percent) by age over time.

Age (in years)	1890	1900	1910	1920	1930	1940	1950	1960	1970	1980
10–13	5.4	6.1	3.9	2.9	1.5					
14/16–19[a]	24.4	26.8	28.1	28.4	22.8	18.8	22.5	23.9	35.3	45.7
20–24	30.8	32.1	35.5	38.1	42.5	45.1	42.5	44.9	56.3	67.8
25–44	15.6	18.0	21.0	22.5	25.4	30.2	33.0	39.1	47.8	64.9
45–64	12.6	14.1	17.1	17.1	18.7	19.8	28.6	41.6	48.2	50.5
≥ 65	8.3	9.1	8.6	8.0	8.0	5.9	7.6	10.4	10.0	8.7
All[b]	18.6	20.4	22.8	23.3	24.3	25.4	28.6	34.5	41.6	50.5

[a]14–19 years old (1890–1960) or 16–19 years old (1970, 1980).
[b]Age 14 or older (1890–1960) or age 16 or older (1970, 1980).
Sources:
1890–1950: Long (1958, Table A-2, p. 287).
1960: U.S. Department of Commerce, Bureau of the Census, *U.S. Census of the Population 1960: Employment Status and Work Experience*, Subject Reports PC(2)-6A, Table 1.
1970: U.S. Department of Commerce, Bureau of the Census, 1970 *Census of Population: Employment Status and Work Experience*, Subject Reports PC(2)-6A, Table 1.
1980: U.S. Department of Commerce, Bureau of the Census, 1980 *Census of Population*: Vol. 1, *Characteristics of the Population*, Chapter D, Detailed Population Characteristics, Part 1, United States Summary, Section A: United States, Table 272.

Table 2.2
Canada: Female labor force participation rates (in percent) by age over time.

Age (in years)	1911	1921	1931	1941	1951	1961	1971	1981
≤19[a]	26.9	24.0	21.7	25.8	37.2	33.0	36.9	61.2
20–24	23.8	35.0	42.3	41.8	46.8	49.3	62.8	44.5
25–44	13.5	14.5	17.9	21.0	23.1	30.2	44.2	65.2
45–64	9.4	10.1	10.7	12.1	17.9	29.7	40.0	46.3
≥ 65	5.2	6.3	6.1	5.5	5.1	6.7	8.2	6.0
All[b]	15.8	18.3	19.1	20.7	24.1	29.5	39.9	51.8

[a]14–19 years old (1911–31) or 15–19 years old (1941–81).
[b]Age 14 or older (1911–31) or age 15 or older (1941–81).
Sources:
1911–31: Long (1958, Table A-11, p. 305).
1941–61: 1961 *Census of Canada*, Vol. 3, Part 1, Table 2, pp. 2-1–2-2.
1971: 1971 *Census of Canada*, Vol. III, Part 7, Table 1, p. 1
1981: 1981 *Census of Canada*, Vol. I, National Series, Table 1 (for those 65 or older) and Table 3 (for other age groups).

different rates, but since the 1960s most advanced economies have seen considerable, and at times dramatic, rises in the proportion of women – particularly married women (especially those with small children) – in the labor force.

Tables 2.1–2.4 set out the time series of female participation rates for the United States, Canada, Great Britain and Germany, respectively [see also Sorrentino (1983)]. As shown there, participation rates have risen in all countries

Table 2.3
Great Britain: Female labor force participation rates (in percent) by age over time.

Age (in years)	1891	1901	1911	1921	1931[d]	1951	1961	1971	1981
< 20[a]				48.4	70.5	78.9	71.1	55.9	56.4
20–24[b]	58.4	56.7	61.9	62.4	65.1	65.4	62.0	60.1	69.3
25–44	29.5	27.2	24.3	28.4	30.9	36.1	40.8	50.7	59.5
45–64	24.6	21.1	21.6	20.1	19.6	28.7	37.1	50.2	51.9
≥ 65	15.9	13.4	11.5	10.0	8.2	5.3	5.4	6.4	3.7
All[c]				32.3	34.2	34.7	37.4	42.7	45.6

[a]12–19 years old (1921), 14–20 years old (1931), or 15–19 years old (1951–81).
[b]21–24 years old (1931) or 20–24 years old (1891–1921, 1951–81).
[c]Age 12 or older for 1921; age 14 or older for 1931; age 15 or older for 1951–81.
[d]No census conducted in 1941.
Sources:
1891–1961: Department of Employment and Productivity, *British Labour Statistics Historical Abstract 1886–1968*, London: HMSO, 1971, Table 109, pp. 206–207.
1971: *Census 1971*: *Great Britain*, *Economic Activity*, Part 1, Table 1.
1981: *Census 1981*: *Great Britain General Tables*, Table 12.

Table 2.4
Germany: Female labor force participation rates: (in percent) by age over time.

Age (in years)	1895[c]	1907[c]	1925[c]	1939[c]	1939[d]	1946[d]	1950[d]	1960[d]	1970[d]	1981[d]
14/15–19[a]	60.6	67.8	67.2	79.2	81.3	75.7	67.3	75.7	64.4	40.4
20–24	58.3	62.0	67.8	67.8	68.6	53.7	70.4	75.6	67.1	71.0
25–44	26.9	37.6	41.9	45.8	44.2	37.0	40.5	46.4	47.6	58.4
45–64	25.6	35.5	36.3	36.4	36.9	29.1	31.0	33.5	35.5	39.8
≥ 65	19.7	21.6	17.6	14.1	17.3	13.3	9.7	8.2	5.8	2.8
All[b]	36.2	44.1	45.7	45.5	46.1	38.0	39.3	41.5	38.2	39.8

[a]15–19 years old (1891–1950) or 15–19 years old (1960–81).
[b]Age 14 or over for 1891–1950; age 15 or over for 1960–81.
[c]Post-World War I boundaries, excluding Saar.
[d]Boundaries of Federal Republic of Germany, excluding Berlin.
Sources:
1895–1950: Long (1958, Table A-16, p. 313).
1960: *Statistiches Jahrbuch 1962*, Table 2, p. 143.
1970, 1981: ILO, *Yearbook of Labour Statistics*, 1975 (Table 4, p. 39) and 1982 (Table 4, p. 29).

Table 2.5
United States: Female labor force participation rates (in percent), by marital status and year.

	Married	Single	Widowed/Divorced
1890	4.6	43.1	29.9
1900	5.6	45.9	32.5
1910	10.7	54.0	34.1
1920	9.0	–	–
1930	11.7	55.2	34.4
1940	13.8	53.1	33.7
1950	21.6	53.6	35.5
1960	31.8	50.7	36.1
1970a	38.2	47.5	35.0
1970b	40.8	53.0	39.1
1980	40.8	61.5	44.0

Sources:
1890–1950: Long (1958, Table A-6, p. 297). Refers to persons age 16 or older.
1960: U.S. Department of Commerce, Bureau of the Census, *U.S. Census of Population 1960, Employment Status and Work Experience*, Table 4, p. 24. (Original data given for age 14 or older; figures in text calculated on assumption that half those age 14–17 were age 14–15 so as to refer to persons age 16 or older.)
1970a: U.S. Department of Commerce, Bureau of the Census, *U.S. Census of Population 1970, Employment Status and Work Experience*, Table 3, p. 37. Refers to persons age 16 or older.
1970b, 1980: U.S. Department of Labor, *Employment and Training Report of the President*, Table B-1, pp. 209–210. Data from March Current Population Survey for persons age 16 or older.

Table 2.6
Canada: Female labor force participation rates (in percent), by marital status and year.

	Married	Single	Widowed/Divorced
1921	21.5	48.1	21.7
1931	3.5	50.6	20.5
1941	3.8	60.1	20.2
1951	11.2	62.2	19.4
1961	22.0	54.2	23.0
1971	36.9	53.4	26.5
1981	51.9	61.8	31.3

Sources:
1921–51: Long (1958, Table A-12, p. 307). Refers to persons age 16 or older.
1961: *Census of Canada 1961*, Vol. III, Part 1, Table 17 (p. 17) and Vol. I, Part 3, Table 78 (p. 1). Refers to persons age 15 or older.
1971: *Census of Canada 1971*, Vol. III, Part 7, Table 6 (p. 1). Refers to persons age 15 or older.
1981: *Census of Canada 1981*, Vol. I – National Series, Table 1 (p. 1). Refers to persons age 15 or older.

and in almost all individual age groups (except for those 65 or over). Germany is to some extent an exception, for its aggregate female participation rate has changed little since 1946. The constancy of Germany's aggregate female participation rate is the net result of sizeable increases in participation among those age 25–64 accompanied by sizeable decreases for the young and the elderly.

Most of the increase in the aggregate female participation rate in recent years is attributable to an increase in the participation rate of married women, as shown in Tables 2.5–2.8, for the United States, Canada, Great Britain and Germany, respectively. Indeed, as shown in Tables 2.5 and 2.7, the participation rate of single women has actually declined somewhat in the United States and Britain, respectively. Table 2.8, for Germany, provides essentially the same evidence albeit for the more heterogeneous group of "nonmarried" (single, widowed or divorced) women. Moreover, as Tables 2.5–2.8 indicate, participation has increased markedly for married women, although the participation rate of married women remains lower than that of other women.

The substantial increase in participation among women, particularly married women, stands in sharp contrast with the secular decline in male participation rates. As Pencavel (Chapter 1 in this Handbook) notes, male participation rates in developed economies have generally been falling – both in the aggregate and for most age groups – since at least the first quarter of the twentieth century. (See Pencavel's Tables 1.1–1.4, analogous to our Tables 2.1–2.4.)

Table 2.7
Great Britain: Female labor force participation rates (in percent), by marital status and year.

	Married	Single	Widowed/Divorced
1911	9.6	70.1	29.4
1921	8.7	72.5	25.5
1931	10.1	74.0	21.2
1951	21.5	73.7	20.9
1961	30.1	69.4	22.8
1971	42.9	61.5	23.6
1981	47.2	60.8	22.9

Sources:
1911–51: Long (1958, Table A-10, p. 304). Refers to persons age 16 or older.
1961: *Census 1961 Great Britain Summary Tables*, Table 32, p. 76. Refers to persons age 15 or older.
1971: *Census 1971 Great Britain Advance Analysis*, Table 1, p. 1. Refers to persons age 15 or older.
1981: *Census 1981*: *Economic Activity Great Britain* (10 percent sample), Table 48. Refers to persons age 15 or older.

On the other hand, weekly hours by women workers appear to have been falling secularly, as shown for the United States in Tables 2.9 (for manufacturing) and 2.10 and 2.11 (for the entire economy) and for Britain in Table 2.12. This decline in weekly hours worked by women workers parallels the decline in weekly hours worked by men that is documented by Pencavel (see his Tables 1.7–1.9 and 1.12, analogous to our Tables 2.9–2.12).

Considered alongside the substantial secular increase in women's participation rates, these secular reductions in hours of work raise several interesting questions. First, has the secular reduction in weekly hours worked by women workers been enough to offset the secular increase in the female participation rate and reduce the total number of hours of market work of women? One may address this question using Owen's (1985) constructed measure of "total" weekly labor supply, "labor input per capita", computed as the product of the employment–population ratio and weekly hours worked by employed workers. The time series behavior of Owen's measure of female labor input per capita is presented in Table 2.13. As shown there, Owen's total female labor supply measure has approximately doubled among women age 25–64, has increased slightly among women age 20–24 and has declined only for the youngest (age 14–19) and oldest (65 or over) women.

Thus, the secular decline in female weekly hours worked has dampened, but has by no means fully offset, the effect of the secular increase in female

Table 2.8
Germany: Female labor force participation rates (in percent), by marital status and year.

<table>
<tr><th></th><th>Married</th><th>Single</th><th>Widowed/ Divorced</th></tr>
<tr><td>1895[a]</td><td>12.0</td><td colspan="2">60.7</td></tr>
<tr><td>1907[a]</td><td>26.0</td><td colspan="2">63.7</td></tr>
<tr><td>1925[a]</td><td>28.7</td><td colspan="2">64.7</td></tr>
<tr><td>1933[a]</td><td>29.2</td><td colspan="2">62.1</td></tr>
<tr><td>1939[a]</td><td>32.7</td><td colspan="2">62.5</td></tr>
<tr><td>1939[b]</td><td>30.6</td><td colspan="2">67.6</td></tr>
<tr><td>1950[b]</td><td>25.0</td><td colspan="2">57.7</td></tr>
<tr><td>1961[b]</td><td>32.4</td><td>37.5</td><td>23.3</td></tr>
<tr><td>1970[b]</td><td>35.6</td><td>27.0</td><td>21.6</td></tr>
<tr><td>1980[b]</td><td>40.6</td><td>28.2</td><td>19.3</td></tr>
</table>

[a]Post-World War I boundaries, excluding Saar.
[b]Boundaries of Federal Republic of Germany, excluding Berlin

Sources:
1895–1950: Long (1958, Table A-17, p. 314). Refers to persons age 16 or older.
1961: *Statistiches Jahrbuch 1963*, p. 140. Refers to persons age 14 or older.
1970: *Statistiches Jahrbuch 1971*, p. 122. Refers to persons age 15 or older.
1980: *Statistiches Jahrbuch 1981*, p. 94. Refers to persons age 15 or older.

participation in the labor force and in employment. On balance, the trend in total weekly labor input of women is clearly positive. Moreover, although participation and weekly hours of work are two of the most easily measured aspects of labor supply, they do not measure all aspects of labor supply. In particular, it is important to consider weeks worked per year as well. (We provide indirect evidence on this topic below.)

The fact that weekly hours worked by women workers have fallen even as women's labor force participation has risen also poses a subtle question concerning within-cohort as opposed to across-cohort effects. The most obvious and straightforward interpretation of the secular decline in women's weekly hours of work is that hours worked per week by women workers have indeed fallen across successive cohorts. However, the decline in weekly hours worked has been accompanied by a substantial increase in participation, and this raises the question of whether the decline in weekly hours worked may be at least partly a consequence of the addition of "low-hours" women, *within each cohort*, who would not be working had participation not increased. In other words, if increased participation amounts to an influx of part-time workers (e.g. because

Table 2.9
United States: Percentage distribution of weekly hours in manufacturing industry by employed females for the Decennial Censuses of Population, by year.

<table>
<tr><th>Hours worked</th><th>1940</th><th>1950</th><th>1960</th><th>1970</th><th>1980</th></tr>
<tr><td>≤ 34</td><td>21.4</td><td>13.1</td><td>16.5</td><td>19.2</td><td>14.9</td></tr>
<tr><td>35–39</td><td>8.8</td><td>8.1</td><td>12.4</td><td>10.9</td><td rowspan="2">70.0</td></tr>
<tr><td>40</td><td>51.2</td><td>68.8</td><td>60.4</td><td>59.2</td></tr>
<tr><td>41–48</td><td>17.7</td><td>8.7</td><td>9.1</td><td>8.3</td><td rowspan="3">15.1</td></tr>
<tr><td>49–59</td><td>0.7</td><td>1.0</td><td>1.2</td><td>1.7</td></tr>
<tr><td>≥ 60</td><td>0.3</td><td>0.3</td><td>0.5</td><td>0.7</td></tr>
</table>

Notes:
1940–50 data refer to wage and salary workers only;
1960–80 data refer to all employed persons.
1940–60 data refer to persons age 14 or older;
1970–80 data refer to persons age 16 or older.
"Hours worked" refers to hours worked during Census survey week.
Sources:
1940: *Sixteenth Census of the United States 1940*: *Population*, *Vol. III: The Labor Force*, Part I: U.S. Summary, Table 36, p. 259.
1950: 1950 Census of Population, *Industrial Characteristics*, Table 11.
1960: 1960 Census of Population, *Industrial Characteristics*, Table 9.
1970: 1970 Census of Population, *Industrial Characteristics*, Table 39.
1980: 1980 *Census of Population*, Vol. 1, *Characteristics of the Population*, Chapter D, Detailed Population Characteristics, Part 1, United States Summary, Section A: United States, Table 288.

greater availability of jobs with flexible hours has made work more attractive than before), then *average* hours worked may well fall even if hours worked by those *already* in the labor force stay the same or even rise.

Unfortunately, developing evidence on this issue is quite difficult: there are no data on the number of hours that a woman not now participating in the labor force *would* work *if* she were to work, must less data showing how this number has changed over time.

It does, however, seem clear that successive cohorts of women have generally supplied steadily increasing amounts of labor, where "labor supply" is defined as participation in the labor force, employment, weekly hours worked by the total population or annual hours worked (by either the working population or the total population). First, as shown in Table 2.14 and Figure 2.1, respectively, participation in the labor force and in paid employment have increased in successive cohorts of U.S. women: in general, more recent cohorts are more oriented

Table 2.10
United States: Percentage distribution of hours worked of employed females during the census week from the Decennial Census of Population, by Year.

Hours worked	1940[a]	1950	1960	1970	1980[b]
1–14	2.9	4.6	9.8	9.3	
15–29	8.3	10.0	11.4	13.5	30.8
30–34	7.0	6.0	6.5	8.7	
35–39	8.2	7.5	11.6	11.6	56.4
40	31.1	45.4	42.7	44.8	
41–48	27.7	17.2	11.8	7.7	
49–59	6.9	4.6	3.0	2.3	12.8
≥ 60	7.9	4.8	3.3	2.1	

[a]For 1940, figures refer to wage and salary workers only (for all other years, figures refer to all employed persons). The categories "1–14" and "15–29" for 1940 mean "under 14" and "14–29."

[b]For 1940–70, figures refer to persons age 14 or older; for 1980, figures refer to persons age 16 or older. In all cases, figures refer to persons employed during Census week.

Sources:

1940: *Sixteenth Census of the United States*: *1940*, *Vol. III*, *The Labor Force*, Part 1: U.S. Summary, Table 86, p. 259.

1950: *U.S. Census of Population 1950*, *Vol. IV*, *Special Reports*, Part I, Chapter A, Employment and Personal Characteristics, Table 13.

1960: *U.S. Census of Population 1960 Subject Reports*, Employment Status and Work Experience, Table 12.

1970: *U.S. Census of Population 1970 Subject Reports*, Employment Status and Work Experience, Table 17.

1980: 1980 *Census of Population*, Vol. 1, *Characteristics of the Population*, Chapter D, Detailed Population Characteristics, Part 1, United States Summary, Section A: United States, Table 288.

towards market work than were earlier cohorts. Moreover, among the most recent cohorts there appears to have been a dampening or even a disappearance of the decline in market activity at childbearing and childrearing ages that was characteristic of earlier cohorts. Table 2.15 and Figure 2.2 show data on employment rates by cohort for Britain that tell a story similar to the one in Table 2.14 and Figure 2.1, which refer to the United States.

A final piece of evidence on the behavior of successive cohorts appears in Tables 2.16 and 2.17, which present alternative measures of "total" labor supply (defined to include both employment and hours worked) for successive cohorts of U.S. women. [See also Smith (1983), who presents more detailed calculations for the shorter period 1977–81.] Table 2.16 presents Owen's (1985) series on total weekly labor input per capita by cohort, in which total labor supply is defined as the product of the employment rate and weekly hours worked by working women. Although it is obviously too early in the "lifetime" of the 1960 cohort to

Table 2.11
United States, 1955–82, and United Kingdom, 1939–82:
Average weekly hours worked.

	United Kingdom: All adults	United States: Females					
		All	14/16–17 years	18–24 years	25–44 years	45–64 years	≤ 65 years
1938	47.7						
1940–44	46.9						
1950–54	47.9						
1955–59	48.4	36.4	20.0	37.1	37.0	37.7	33.8
1960–64	47.5	35.3	16.2	35.9	35.8	37.1	31.9
1965–69	46.4	36.2	17.2	35.8	36.6	38.3	33.5
1970–74	45.2	34.2	18.8	33.1	34.8	35.9	29.0
1975–79	44.0	34.2	19.2	32.7	35.3	35.5	27.0
1980–82	43.0	34.1	18.4	32.5	35.4	35.2	27.5

Notes: The U.K. data relate to full-time manual workers and are taken from each October's earnings and hours enquiry of the major industries. The data are published in various issues of the *Ministry of Labour Gazette* and of the *Department of Employment Gazette*. The United States data derive from household interviews in the Current Population Survey and measure the average hours actually worked (not those paid for) of female employees in nonagricultural industries at work. (Consequently, those absent from work because of illness, vacation, or strike are not represented in these figures.) For the years 1955–58, the data are published in the *Current Population Reports*, Labor Force Series P-50, issues number 63 (Table 3), 72 (Table 18), 85 (Table 18), and 89 (Table 24). For the years 1959–64, the data are from *Special Labor Force Reports*, Table 0-7 of each issue, Report numbers 4, 14, 23, 31, 43, and 52. For the years 1965–82, the data are taken from each January's issue of *Employment and Earnings* which give the figures for the preceding year. Before 1967, the youngest age group relates to those aged 14–17 years and from 1967 it relates to 16–17 years.

be sure, Table 2.16 suggests that total weekly labor supply may well be higher (at least between the ages of 25 and 64) for more recent cohorts than it was for earlier cohorts.

Table 2.17 presents two series on cohort *annual* labor supply derived by Smith and Ward (1984, 1985). The first panel refers to annual hours worked by working women (calculated as the product of weekly hours worked times weeks worked per year among women who work). It suggests that, at a minimum, *annual* hours worked by working women have not fallen at the same rate as *weekly* hours worked: evidently, the secular downtrend in the latter has been offset to a considerable extent by a secular increase in weeks worked per year. The second panel of Table 2.17 provides analogous information by cohort on "total" annual labor supply, i.e. the product of the employment–population ratio and annual hours worked by working women. Although the changes in total annual labor supply across cohorts are somewhat uneven, there is some indication that total annual labor supply is higher among more recent cohorts (though the increase in

Table 2.12
Great Britain: Percentage distribution of weekly hours worked by female employees in 1968, 1977 and 1981.

	September 1968	April 1977	April 1981
$0 < h \leq 24$	20.4	22.7	24.3
$24 < h \leq 30$	10.7	12.4	11.7
$30 < h \leq 35$	10.9	13.1	13.3
$35 < h \leq 37$	9.9	16.5	16.7
$37 < h \leq 39$	15.8	10.7	17.1
$39 < h \leq 40$	15.4	18.9	12.0
$40 < h \leq 42$	9.2	1.9	1.6
$42 < h \leq 44$	3.1	1.4	1.1
$44 < h \leq 46$	1.8	0.8	0.7
$46 < h \leq 48$	1.4	0.6	0.6
$48 < h \leq 50$	0.5	0.3	0.3
$50 < h \leq 54$	0.5	0.3	0.3
$54 < h \leq 60$	0.3	0.2	0.2
$60 < h \leq 70$	0.1	0.1	0.1
$70 < h$	0.0	0.0	0.1

Notes: These data cover all women (both manual and nonmanual workers) whose pay for the survey period was not affected by absence.

Sources:

1968: Department of Employment and Productivity. *New Earnings Survey 1968*, H.M.S.O., 1970, Table 83, p. 120.

1977: Department of Employment, *New Earnings Survey 1977, Part A: Report and Key Results,* H.M.S.O., 1977, Table 27, p. A35.

1981: Department of Employment, *New Earnings Survey 1981, Part A: Report and Key Results*, H.M.S.O., 1981, Table 27, p. A90.

Table 2.13
United States: Female labor input per capita in selected years, 1920–77, by age.

Age	1920	1930	1940	1950	1955	1960	1965	1970	1977
14–19	12.4	9.0	6.2	9.3	8.4	6.8	6.2	6.8	8.0
20–24	17.6	18.3	17.3	16.6	16.5	16.0	17.1	18.7	20.8
25–44	10.1	10.7	11.0	13.2	13.7	13.6	14.5	15.3	19.5
45–64	8.1	8.3	8.4	12.1	14.3	15.9	16.8	17.1	16.5
≥ 65	3.9	3.7	2.8	3.4	3.7	3.4	3.0	2.8	2.1

Source: Owen (1985, Table 1.3). "Labor input per capita" calculated by multiplying proportion of population employed times weekly hours of work by employed workers.

Table 2.14
United States: Female labor force participation rates by age for successive female birth cohorts.

Birth Cohort	Ages									
	15–19	20–24	25–29	30–34	35–39	40–44	45–49	50–54	55–59	60–64
1886–90				19.8		21.1		21.2	*	20.6
1891–95			27.0		22.3		23.7	*	25.9	
1896–1900		37.5		23.6		26.0	*	30.8		29.4
1901–05	28.4		30.2		28.3	*	34.8		39.7	
1906–10		41.8		30.9	*	36.4		45.9		36.4
1911–15	22.8		35.5	*	33.8		47.4		47.6	
1916–20		45.6	*	31.0		45.3		52.4		41.4
1921–25	18.9	*	32.6		40.2		53.3		41.4	
1926–30		42.9		35.5		52.4		61.1		
1931–35	22.6		35.0		48.7		61.1			
1936–40		44.9		44.6		66.8				
1941–45	23.9		45.7		66.8					
1946–50		56.3		66.7						
1951–55	22.5		66.7							
1956–60		69.6								

Note: Birth cohorts 1916–20 to 1936–40 are mothers of the baby boom generations.
* Denotes ages of each birth cohort during World War II.
Source: Smith and Ward (1984, p. 8).

total annual labor supply, relative to earlier cohorts, is not nearly as dramatic as the increase in participation rates shown in Table 2.14).

Although the quantitative changes in female labor supply documented in Tables 2.1–2.17 are quite remarkable, the twentieth century has also seen striking qualitative changes in female labor supply, both in absolute terms and relative to men. In particular, in the United States the growth in the amount of female labor supply has been accompanied by a pronounced shift in its character: to a much greater extent than was true at the turn of the century, the representative woman worker today holds a white-collar – particularly a clerical – job. To some extent this simply reflects the economy-wide growth in the importance of white-collar work, but that is not the only factor, for the influx of women into white-collar (especially clerical) work occurred at a faster rate than did that of men.

Table 2.18 documents the changing occupational distribution of the male and female work force in the United States and shows that 20.2 percent of all women workers held white-collar jobs in 1900, versus 65.6 percent in 1980. Thus, the proportion of women in such jobs more than trebled over the period 1900–80, whereas the proportion of men in such jobs increased by a factor of only about 2.4. The proportion of men in clerical jobs increased by a factor of about 2.3, whereas the proportion of women in such jobs increased by almost ten-fold!

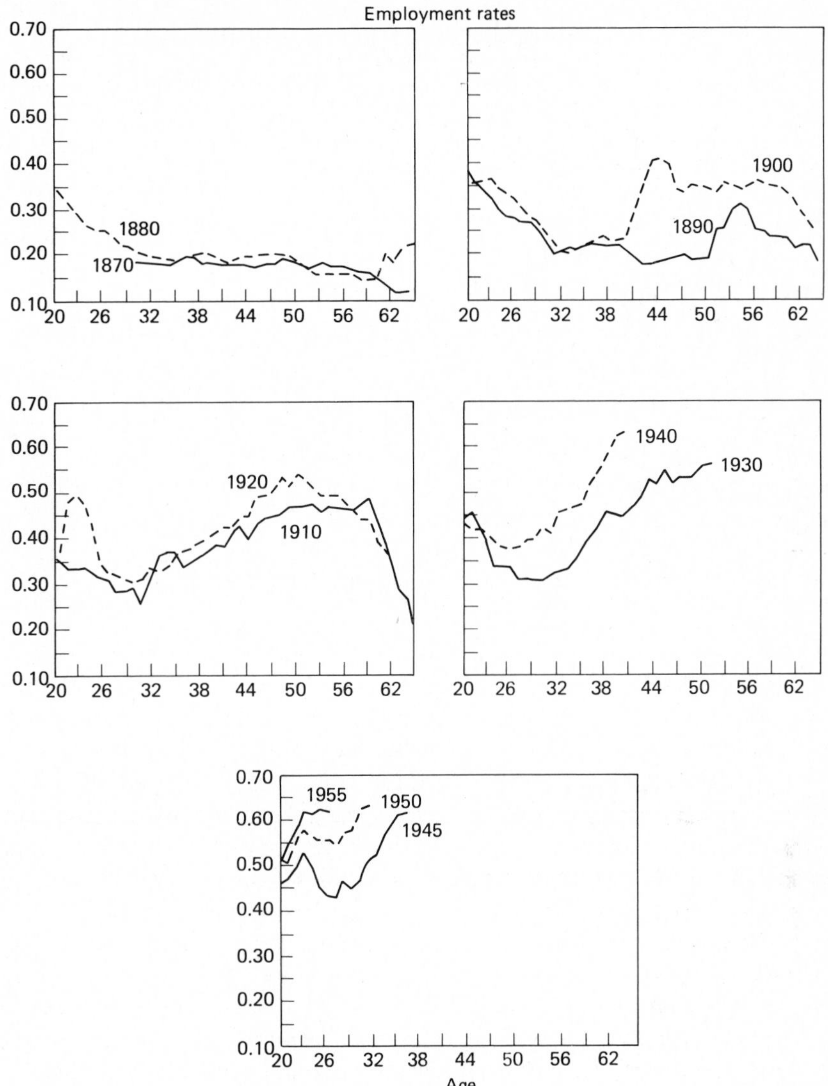

Figure 2.1. Employment–population ratios by age for successive female birth cohorts, 1870–1955, United States. *Source*: Smith and Ward (1984, p. 7).

Table 2.15
Great Britain: Employment–population ratios by age for successive female birth cohorts, 1920–60.

Birth cohort	Age 15–19	20–24	25–29	30–34	35–39	40–44	45–49	50–54	55–59
1920–24	90	71	40	37	46	55	63	66	55
1925–29	89	63	39	40	51	62	70	65	
1930–34	90	65	39	39	51	70	73		
1935–39	93	66	41	46	65	73			
1940–44	91	60	41	50	69				
1945–49	90	66	50	56					
1950–54	88	69	49						
1955–59	85[a]	63[a]							
1960–64	78								

[a]Age 16–19 only.
Source: Martin and Roberts (1984, Table 9.1, p. 117), derived from 1980 Department of Employment/Office of Population Censuses and Survey Women and Employment Survey. Full-time students excluded from all calculations.

Finally, note that the proportion of women in blue-collar and service jobs fell during 1900–80 while the proportion of men in both kinds of jobs rose. Thus, both in absolute terms and relative to men, the concentration of women in white-collar (especially clerical) jobs has increased, whereas the concentration of women in blue-collar and service jobs has decreased over the period 1900–80.

We conclude this discussion of secular trends in female labor supply by briefly considering educational attainment, marital status and fertility. First consider schooling. As shown in Tables 2.19 and 2.20, there has been a substantial increase in educational attainment of successive female cohorts in the United States and in Britain, respectively. Moreover, as Table 2.19 indicates, although median educational attainment for U.S. women has increased only slightly over time among cohorts born since 1926–30, the proportion of women with four or more years of college in successive cohorts born since that date has gone up by more than 50 percent.

If the phrase "dramatic trends" provides a nutshell characterization of women's educational attainment and labor supply, "dramatic fluctuations" provides a suitable description of the behavior of fertility and the distribution of women by marital status during the period 1890–1980. Table 2.21 documents the behavior of the distribution of women by marital status in the United States. There has clearly been a secular increase in the proportion of women in the "other" category (which consists for the most part of divorced women), but otherwise the most noteworthy feature of women's marital status distributions in the United States has been the degree to which they have fluctuated. In 1980, the proportion never married and the proportion currently married were both approximately

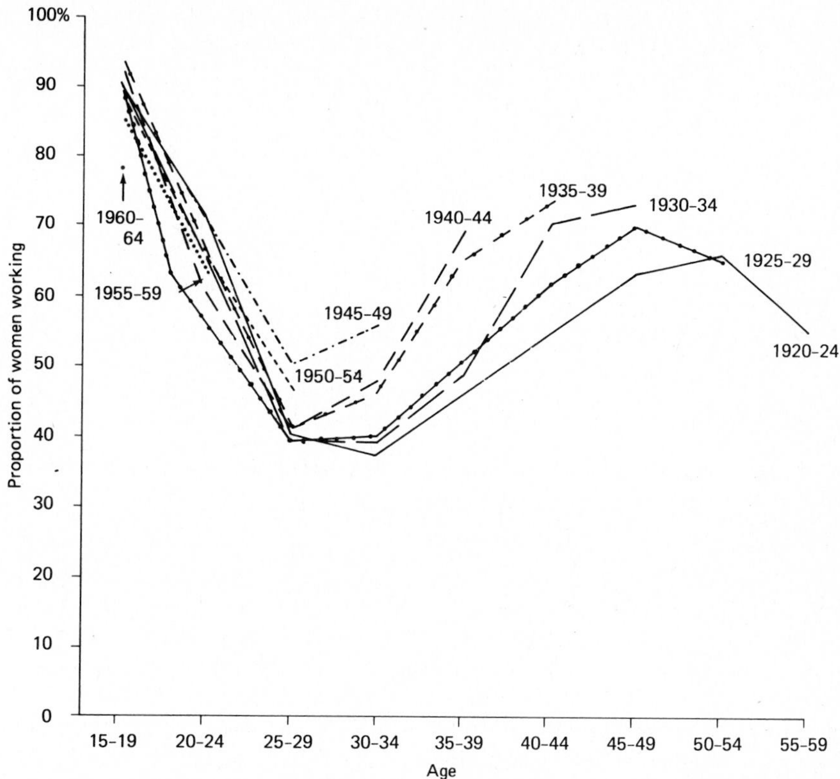

Figure 2.2. Employment–population ratios by age for successive female birth cohorts, 1920–60, Great Britain. *Source*: Martin and Roberts (1984, p. 119).

Table 2.16
United States: Labor input per capita by age for selected female cohorts.

Year entered labor force	14–19	20–24	25–44	45–64	> 65
1880	–	–	10.2	8.1	3.7
1900	14.1	18.6	10.1	8.4	3.4
1920	12.4	18.0	11.6	14.9	2.8
1940	6.2	17.9	13.7	16.5	–
1960	6.8	17.1	20.8	–	–
1977	8.0	–	–	–	–

Source: Owen (1985, Table 1.4). See notes to Table 2.13 for calculation of labor input per capita. Year of entry into labor force obtained by transforming age ranges as follows: 14–19 = 17; 20–24 = 22; 25–44 = 34; 45–64 = 54; 65 and over = 67. Estimates for intermediate years obtained by linear interpolation.

Table 2.17
United States: Annual hours worked, by age, selected female birth cohorts.

Birth Cohort	Age 16	20	25	30	35	40	45	50	55	60	64
	Annual hours worked by working women										
1902								1627	1580	1620	1633
1910						1496	1591	1565	1605	1511	1294
1918					1479	1456	1506	1636	1726	1620	
1926			1416	1402	1379	1471	1531	1524	1600		
1934	485	1339	1285	1296	1352	1483	1554				
1942	368	927	1382	1328	1391						
1950	298	1136	1426	1480							
	Annual hours worked by all women										
1902								774	789	742	639
1910						723	859	914	877	765	375
1918					686	765	895	900	929	693	
1926			716	627	679	832	942	895	924		
1934	169	861	656	626	800	930	1084				
1942	139	639	784	709	924						
1950	118	837	974	1081							

Source: Smith and Ward (1984, p. 85).

equal to what they were in 1890, but each of these ratios has varied substantially during the period 1890–1980. For example, in both 1890 and 1980 slightly less than half of the women age 20–24 were married, but in 1960 almost 70 percent of the women in this age group were married.

Figure 2.3 plots age-specific fertility rates for the ages between 20 and 30 for cohorts of U.S. women between 1890 and 1950. As shown there, fertility rates rose substantially starting with the 1920 cohort (the 1910 cohort was in the relevant age range during the years of the Great Depression, which is probably a major reason why its fertility was below that of the 1900 cohort). However, starting with the 1940 cohort, fertility began to fall again; indeed, the pattern of fertility by age for the 1950 cohort was almost identical to that of the 1910 cohort.

Although we have frequently referred to the patterns shown in Figures 2.1–2.3 and Tables 2.1–2.21 as "trends", they are actually just sets of time-series patterns and, as such, combine not only secular but also cyclical factors. For a rough and ready decomposition of observed time series into trend and cycle, we follow Pencavel (Chapter 1 in this Handbook) in regressing first differences in the labor force participation rate of a given female group (whites age 16–17, all nonwhites, etc.) on contemporaneous first differences in the unemployment rate of white males age 35–44, using annual data for 1955–82. As Pencavel notes, the intercept

Table 2.18
United States: Occupational distribution of workers by sex and year.

	1900	1910	1920	1930	1940	1950	1960	1970	1980
				Women					
White collar	20.2	26.0	38.5	44.3	44.9	52.3	55.3	60.5	65.6
Professional, technical	8.2	9.5	11.7	13.6	12.8	12.2	12.4	14.5	16.8
Managerial, administrative	1.6	2.0	2.4	2.7	3.3	4.3	5.0	4.5	6.9
Sales	4.4	5.0	6.3	6.8	7.4	8.6	7.7	7.0	6.8
Clerical	3.8	9.0	18.5	20.8	21.4	27.2	30.3	34.5	35.1
Blue collar	27.9	25.5	23.9	19.9	21.8	22.2	16.6	16.1	13.8
Craft	1.6	1.5	1.0	1.0	1.2	1.4	1.0	1.1	1.8
Operatives	24.0	23.0	20.0	17.2	19.3	20.1	15.2	14.5	10.7
Nonfarm laborers	3.3	1.5	2.4	1.4	1.2	0.7	0.4	0.5	1.2
Service	35.5	32.5	23.9	27.6	29.2	21.5	23.7	21.7	19.5
Farm	19.1	16.0	13.6	8.6	4.1	3.6	4.4	1.8	1.2
				Men					
White collar	17.6	20.1	21.4	25.2	26.7	30.5	37.4	41.0	42.4
Professional, technical	3.4	3.5	3.8	4.9	5.8	7.2	10.9	14.0	15.5
Managerial, administrative	6.9	7.8	7.8	8.7	8.6	10.5	13.6	14.2	14.4
Sales	4.5	4.6	4.5	6.2	6.5	6.4	5.8	5.6	6.0
Clerical	2.8	4.4	5.3	5.5	5.8	6.4	7.2	7.1	6.4
Blue collar	37.6	41.2	44.5	45.2	45.7	48.4	46.5	47.0	44.8
Craft	12.6	14.1	16.0	16.2	15.5	19.0	19.0	20.1	21.0
Operatives	10.4	12.5	14.5	15.4	18.1	20.5	19.6	19.6	16.8
Nonfarm laborers	14.7	14.6	14.1	13.6	12.2	8.7	7.9	7.3	7.0
Service	3.1	3.9	3.8	4.7	6.1	6.2	6.5	6.7	8.8
Farm	41.6	34.8	30.4	24.8	21.7	15.0	9.6	5.3	4.0
				Women / men					
White collar	1.15	1.29	1.80	1.76	1.68	1.71	1.48	1.48	1.55
Professional, technical	2.41	2.71	3.08	2.78	2.21	1.69	1.14	1.04	1.08
Managerial, administrative	0.23	0.25	0.31	0.31	0.38	0.41	0.37	0.33	0.48
Sales	0.98	1.09	1.40	1.10	1.14	1.34	1.33	1.25	1.13
Clerical	1.36	2.05	3.49	3.78	3.69	4.25	4.21	4.86	5.48
Blue collar	0.74	0.61	0.53	0.44	0.47	0.46	0.36	0.34	0.30
Craft	0.13	0.11	0.06	0.06	0.08	0.07	0.05	0.05	0.09
Operatives	2.31	1.84	1.38	1.12	1.06	0.98	0.77	0.73	0.64
Nonfarm laborer	0.22	0.10	0.17	0.10	0.10	0.08	0.05	0.07	0.17
Service	11.45	8.33	6.29	5.87	4.79	3.47	3.65	3.23	2.21
Farm	0.46	0.46	0.45	0.34	0.19	0.24	0.45	0.34	0.30

Note: Figures in the panel labelled "Women" ("Men") show the proportion of all women (men) in the indicated occupational category in the indicated year. Figures in the panel labelled "Women/Men" show the ratio of the female to the male proportion for the indicated occupational category for the indicated year.

Sources:

1900–50: *Employment and Training Report of the President 1976*, p. 387 (summary of Census data). Due to rounding, figures for individual categories may not sum to totals shown.

1960–80: *Statistical Abstract of the United States, 1981*, Table 673, p. 401 (summary of Census data).

Table 2.19
United States: Schooling completed by the female population, by age, 1980.

Years of age in 1980	Year of birth	Median years of school completed	Proportion of cohort whose highest schooling level completed was				
			≥ 4 years of college	≥ 2 years of college	≥ 4 years of high school	≥ 8 yrs of elementary school	≥ 5 years of elementary school
≥ 75	≤ 1905	8.9	6.4	12.3	34.3	72.8	89.6
70–74	1906–10	10.6	8.1	14.8	41.5	79.4	93.5
65–69	1911–15	11.4	7.6	13.9	46.0	82.8	94.8
60–64	1916–20	12.1	7.8	14.3	53.8	86.9	96.0
55–59	1921–25	12.3	8.2	15.7	60.8	89.5	96.6
50–54	1926–30	12.3	9.9	18.0	64.2	91.2	97.1
45–59	1931–35	12.4	11.2	19.7	69.1	92.6	97.5
40–44	1936–40	12.5	13.1	22.4	73.6	94.4	98.1
35–39	1941–45	12.6	16.4	26.9	78.5	95.8	98.6
30–34	1946–50	12.8	20.2	32.4	83.3	96.6	98.8
25–29	1951–55	12.8	20.5	34.0	84.7	97.3	99.0

Source: 1980 *Census of Population*, Vol. 1, *Characteristics of the Population*, Chapter D, Detailed Population Characteristics, Part 1, United States Summary, Section A: United States, Table 262.

in these regressions is an estimate of the secular trend in a given group's labor force participation rate, and the coefficient on the male unemployment variable is a measure of the group participation rate's cyclical sensitivity.

The results of this exercise appear in Table 2.22. In general, there is a strong secular uptrend in the participation rates of most female groups (as measured by the size and significance levels of the intercept parameter, a), especially among

Table 2.20
Great Britain: Highest educational qualification attained by female population in 1981 by age.

Age in 1981	Year of birth	Percentage of cohort whose highest educational qualifications were at the level of		
		Higher education	Middle education	Lower Education
≥ 65	≤ 1916	1.1	2.3	96.6
60–64	1917–21	1.2	3.3	95.5
50–59	1922–31	2.1	4.4	93.5
40–49	1932–41	3.6	6.3	90.1
30–39	1942–51	5.5	7.1	87.4
25–29	1952–66	8.1	8.1	83.8

Notes: "Higher education" includes university degrees and equivalent professional qualifications. "Middle education" includes qualifications beyond the GCE "A" level but below first degree level. "Lower education" means no qualifications attained beyond GCE "A" level.

Source: Office of Population Censuses and Surveys, *Census of 1981: Qualified Manpower Tables* (10 percent sample), Table 1.

Table 2.21
United States: Marital status of women by age and year, in percent.

Year	Ages 20–24 Never married	Ages 20–24 Currently married	Ages 20–24 Other	Ages 25–29 Never married	Ages 25–29 Currently married	Ages 25–29 Other
1890	51.8	46.7	1.4	25.4	71.4	3.2
1910	48.3	49.7	1.7	24.9	71.8	2.8
1930	46.0	51.6	2.1	21.7	74.3	3.8
1940	47.2	51.3	1.5	22.8	74.1	3.1
1950	32.3	65.6	2.1	13.3	83.3	3.4
1960	29.4	69.5	2.1	10.5	86.2	3.3
1970	36.3	60.5	3.2	12.2	82.5	5.4
1980	50.2	45.9	3.8	20.8	70.3	9.9

Source: Smith and Ward (1984, p. 15).

whites. Note that most of the intercept or secular coefficients a in Table 2.22 are larger in absolute value than are the analogous coefficients for men in Pencavel's Table 1.6.

Table 2.22 also suggests that female labor force participation is procyclical, in that the coefficient on the (change in the) male unemployment rate, b, is almost always negative and are larger in absolute value than the analogous coefficients for men reported by Pencavel. However, in most cases this relation is imprecisely estimated and would not be called significant at conventional test levels.

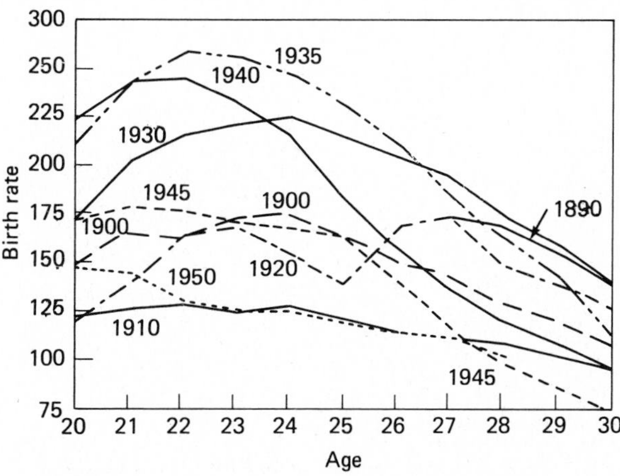

Figure 2.3. Age-specific birth rates for birth cohorts of 1890–1950, United States. *Source*: Smith and Ward (1984, p. 14).

Table 2.22
United States: Estimates of trend (a) and cycle (b) in female civilian labor force participation rates, by race and age, 1955–82.

Ages in years	*a*	*b*	R^2	D-W
		White		
Total ≥ 16	0.695* (0.080)	−0.102 (0.089)	0.05	1.09
16–17	0.652* (0.226)	−1.098* (0.297)	0.34	1.58
18–19	0.472* (0.204)	−0.198 (0.228)	0.03	1.74
20–24	0.988* (0.175)	−0.021 (0.196)	0.00	1.50
25–34	1.257* (0.183)	0.078 (0.204)	0.01	0.46
35–44	1.006* (0.136)	−0.024 (0.152)	0.00	0.74
45–54	0.781* (0.135)	−0.105 (0.150)	0.02	0.74
55–64	0.460* (0.151)	−0.189 (0.169)	0.05	0.95
≥ 65	−0.039 (0.075)	−0.085 (0.084)	0.04	1.36
		Black and other		
Total ≥ 16	0.292* (0.114)	−0.067 (0.127)	0.01	1.99
16–17	0.007 (0.444)	−0.226 (0.497)	0.01	2.58
18–19	0.312 (0.601)	−0.509 (0.672)	0.02	2.43
20–24	0.434 (0.326)	−0.439 (0.364)	0.05	1.51
25–34	0.709* (0.222)	−0.292 (0.248)	0.05	2.26
35–44	0.437* (0.202)	0.405 (0.226)	0.11	1.52
45–54	0.305 (0.217)	0.219 (0.242)	0.03	1.65
55–64	0.164 (0.270)	−0.500 (0.301)	0.10	2.24
≥ 65	−0.131 (0.170)	−0.085 (0.190)	0.01	2.53

Notes: Estimated standard errors are in parentheses next to their associated regression coefficients. "D-W" is the Durbin–Watson statistic. For ease of reading, an asterisk has been placed next to those point estimates more than twice their estimated standard errors. The data are taken from the *Employment and Training Report of the President 1981* and from recent issues of *Employment and Earnings*; 28 observations are used in each regression summarized above.

Thus, Table 2.22 and recent work by Clark and Summers (1981, 1982) and Coleman (1984) suggest that female labor force participation in the United States is not very sensitive to cyclical factors. [Joshi and Owen (1985) report similar findings for Britain.] In contrast, older work, most notably Mincer's (1966), found that participation – at least among married women – is strongly procyclical in the United States. A major difference between Mincer's work and the more recent work is that the latter controls either implicitly or explicitly for possible serial correlation (e.g. by first-differencing, as in our Table 2.22, or by maximum likelihood methods, as in Clark and Summers), whereas Mincer's work did not. Moreover, the recent results replicate Mincer's finding that the participation of teenage and prime-age women is relatively sensitive to cyclical variation; the finding of cyclical insensitivity in recent work has to do primarily with women age 45 or older.

2.2. *Cross-section patterns of female labor supply*

Most of the tables discussed in Section 2.1 present gross or unadjusted relationships between a measure of labor supply (e.g. labor force participation) and a single variable such as age or marital status. In this section we present a set of relatively simple adjusted relationships between labor supply and such variables in cross-section, where "adjusted" means that other factors have been held constant via simple statistical procedures. Although these adjusted relationships do not necessarily constitute a behavioral labor supply function, they do shed additional light on labor supply in the limited sense of documenting multivariate associations between labor supply and a number of variables of interest.

Table 2.23 presents labor force participation equations fitted to 1960 Census microdata by Bowen and Finegan (1969) for six different groups of single and married women in the age groups 25–54, 55–64 and 65–74 (the youngest group of married women includes women age 14–24 as well). Since Bowen and Finegan used least squares regression, the results shown in Table 2.23 may be interpreted as estimates of linear probability models.

In general, the results in Table 2.23 imply that labor force participation is strongly related to educational attainment, with greater schooling being associated with increases (at a decreasing rate) in the probability of labor force participation. White single women below the age of 65 have a somewhat higher probability of participation than do black single women under 65, other things being equal; however, older white single women and all white married women have lower participation probabilities than do their black counterparts, other things being equal. Being (or having previously been) married is associated with a lower participation probability; so is having a large amount of "other income" (i.e. income other than own earnings, including transfer income).

Table 2.23 also suggests that, other things (including marital status and number of children) being equal, there is a fairly pronounced inverted-U-shaped relation between the probability of participation and age, especially among married women: among younger women – single or married – being older is associated first with increased and then with reduced participation; among older women, participation tends to decline with age. Finally, for married women age 14–54 with spouse present, the presence of children (particularly children under the age of six) reduces the probability of participation.

2.3. *Some cautionary remarks*

Although this section has been concerned with stylized facts about labor supply, we want to emphasize, in concluding it, that the stylized facts presented here may not necessarily say much about structural, behavioral or "causal" labor supply functions. Wage–hours combinations observed either in cross-section or over time do not necessarily trace out a behavioral ("causal") supply schedule. Rather, in general such data are the result of the interaction of both supply and demand (see, for example Chapter 1 by Pencavel in this Handbook).

Thus, examination of stylized facts is only the beginning of a behavioral analysis, not the end. Accordingly, we now turn to theoretical models of labor supply and to empirical work aimed at deriving estimates of structural, behaviorally interpretable labor supply parameters.

3. Theoretical models and female labor supply

We now consider theoretical labor supply models that are or might be used in studying female labor supply. Thus, we do not attempt to discuss comprehensively all important labor supply models: Pencavel (Chapter 1 in this Handbook)

Table 2.23
Ordinary least squares estimates of labor force participation equations fitted to data on individual women from the 1/1000 sample of the 1960 U.S. Census of Population.

	(1) "Single", age 25–54	(2) Married, spouse present, age 14–54	(3) "Single", age 55–64	(4) Married, spouse present, age 55–64	(5) "Single", age 65–74	(6) Married, spouse present, age 65–74
Estimate of Intercept	82.2	57.3	71.7	56.8	60.8	27.4
Years of school						
0–4	Reference	Reference	Reference	Reference	Reference	Reference
5–7	−3.0(4.4)	8.5(2.3)	13.3(5.0)	1.7(3.1)	8.8(3.9)	1.3(2.1)
8	6.5(4.3)	10.2(2.2)	15.4(4.9)	7.2(3.0)	11.3(3.8)	−0.9(2.0)
9–11	7.4(4.1)	14.0(2.1)	18.1(5.0)	9.8(3.1)	12.4(4.3)	0.9(2.3)
12	12.3(4.0)	18.8(2.1)	24.2(5.1)	14.8(3.2)	15.2(4.2)	7.2(2.4)
13–15	11.1(4.4)	21.9(2.2)	28.3(5.7)	19.9(3.6)	18.7(5.1)	3.9(3.0)
16	14.8(4.7)	27.7(2.4)	28.3(6.1)	19.2(5.1)	22.9(5.8)	13.2(3.8)
≥17	15.8(4.7)	41.6(3.2)		33.5(7.8)		
Ethnicity						
Black	Reference	Reference	Reference	Reference	Reference	Reference
Other non-white		1.6(3.6)				
White	0.6(2.2)	−6.9(1.1)	1.8(4.1)	−4.4(3.0)	−1.9(4.4)	−6.6(2.8)
Marital status						
Never married	Reference	NA	Reference	NA	Reference	NA
Separated/divorced	−2.8(2.0)	NA	−4.3(4.1)	NA	−2.4(5.0)	NA
Widowed	−10.8(2.4)	NA	−7.2(3.1)	NA	−16.0(3.4)	NA
Married–spouse absent	−25.0(3.5)	NA	−13.4(6.1)	NA	−7.3(8.6)	NA
Employment status of husband						
Unemployed	NA	Reference	NA	Reference	NA	Reference
Working	NA	−6.1(1.7)	NA	6.9(4.2)	NA	−8.5(5.3)
Not in labor force	NA	−4.6(2.3)	NA	−7.4(1.9)	NA	−9.3(1.4)

Table 2.23 continued

	(1) "Single", age 25–54	(2) Married, spouse present, age 14–54	(3) "Single", age 55–64	(4) Married, spouse present, age 55–64	(5) "Single", age 65–74	(6) Married, spouse present, age 65–74
Other income						
< $0	Reference		Reference		Reference	
1–499	4.2(2.2)	Reference	−1.0(3.4)	Reference	−10.0(4.1)	Reference
500–999	−20.4(3.3)		−34.2(3.5)		−22.7(3.5)	
1000–1999		−5.6(2.4)	−48.0(4.0)	−10.5(4.1)	−34.5(3.7)	−4.6(2.8)
2000–2999		−2.3(2.2)	−54.1(6.2)	−14.2(4.1)	−41.2(5.6)	−3.9(2.8)
3000–3999		−4.2(2.1)		−15.5(4.1)	−43.8(5.8)	−9.5(3.0)
4000–4999		−5.0(2.1)		−20.0(4.1)		−11.9(3.2)
5000–5999		−9.0(2.0)		−18.2(4.1)		−8.3(3.3)
6000–6999	−21.1(3.2)	−12.5(2.1)		−25.5(4.2)		−5.7(3.6)
7000–8999		−18.9(2.1)	−63.3(6.1)	−26.7(4.1)	−44.7(6.9)	−9.6(3.2)
9000–10999		−23.4(2.2)		−34.3(4.5)		−11.1(4.0)
11000–14999		−27.4(2.3)		−32.5(4.5)		−6.5(3.7)
15000–24999		−36.7(2.5)		−34.0(5.0)		−7.9(4.0)
≥ 25000		−52.2(3.3)		−54.3(6.0)		
Age						
14–19/55/65	NA	Reference		Reference	Reference	
20–24/56/66	NA	9.9(2.2)	Reference	−4.0(3.1)		Reference
25–29/57/67	Reference	10.8(2.2)		−6.9(3.0)	−6.4(3.5)	
30–34/58/68	0.1(3.3)	10.0(2.2)		−8.5(3.2)		
35–39/59/69	3.4(3.2)	10.5(2.2)	−6.6(3.2)	−7.3(3.0)		−2.9(1.5)
40–44/60/70	2.0(3.0)	8.5(2.3)		−15.2(3.2)	−13.6(3.1)	
45–49/61/71	1.3(3.0)	3.6(2.3)	−11.6(3.0)	−15.9(3.2)		
50–54/62/72	2.4(2.9)	−5.4(2.3)		−15.9(3.4)		−4.9(1.6)
– /63/73	NA	NA	NA	−20.6(3.4)	−16.5(3.3)	
– /64/74	NA	NA	NA	−22.7(3.3)		
Presence (P) or absence (A) of children age < 6/6–13/14–17						
A/A/A	–	Reference	–	–	–	–
P/A/A	–	−42.8(1.1)	–	–	–	–
P/P/A	–	−41.1(1.2)	–	–	–	–
P/A/P	–	−32.5(2.2)	–	–	–	–
P/P/P	–	−35.4(1.5)	–	–	–	–
A/P/A	–	−19.9(1.3)	–	–	–	–
A/P/P	–	−19.6(1.2)	–	–	–	–
A/A/P	–	−2.7(1.0)	–	–	–	–
F-ratio	13.5	113.0	27.4	10.5	14.1	5.4
nobs	1,662	22,021	1,215	3,464	1,243	1,725
modv	86.8	35.8	62.9	28.2	24.6	7.4
Ref:						
page	664	670	694	698	696	701
table	A-5	A-8	A-16	A-18	A-17	A-19

Notes: Estimates are from Bowen and Finegan (1969); see row labelled "Ref." for page number and table number for each set of estimates. Standard errors appear in parentheses next to estimated coefficients. Number of observations = "nobs"; mean of dependent variable (labor force participation rate) = "modv." All variables above are in the form of dummy variables, with "reference" indicating the category omitted from the list of variables. Under the heading "Age", the categories in the first column (14–19, 20–24, 25–29, etc.) were used in the regressions reported in columns 1 and 2 (for single persons age 25–54 and married persons age 14–54, respectively); the categories in the second column (55, 56, 57, etc.) were used in the regressions reported in columns 3 and 4 (for single and married persons 55–64); and the categories in the third column (65, 66, 67, etc.) were used in the regressions reported in columns 5 and 6 (for single and married persons age 65–74). "Single" denotes all persons other than those who are married with spouse present (e.g. never married, widowed, divorced, separated). "Nonwage income" is the sum of rental income, interest, dividends, alimony, pensions, and welfare payments. Variables for presence or absence of children indicate the presence or absence of children in three age groups: under 6 years old, between 6 and 13 years old, and between 14 and 17 years old. Thus, for example, "A/A/A" denotes no children in any of the three categories; "P/A/A" denotes the presence of children under six but no children age 6–13 or 14–17; etc. NA = not applicable.

provides a most useful treatment of many such models; and in any case our focus is on female labor supply rather than labor supply generally.

Of course, there is no such thing as a distinct "model of female labor supply" per se: any theory worthy of the name ought to be just as applicable to men's as to women's labor supply. On the other hand, Section 3.1.1 points to a number of phenomena – marriage, the family, the occupational characteristics of labor supply – that seem to be important correlates of women's labor supply, and so are likely to be of particular interest for analyses of the labor supply of women. In analyzing the labor supply of women, it is therefore surely not unreasonable to focus on models that permit more than routine consideration of such factors.

3.1. *Static models*

We begin by considering static labor supply models in which decisionmakers are assumed to act as if actions taken today were irrelevant to tomorrow's economic environment, and in which accumulation of nonhuman and human wealth is ignored. From the standpoint of analyses of female labor supply, three kinds of topics seem particularly interesting: the role of the family; the allocation of time; and the heterogeneity of jobs.

3.1.1. *Models of family labor supply*

Family membership and its obligations seem to be very important correlates of levels of and trends in labor supply among women. (For example, the *level* of labor supply is generally lower but the positive *trend* in labor supply has usually been much stronger for married women than for single or other women.) Models that allow explicitly for the impact of family membership on decisions about hours of work, participation, etc. are therefore potentially quite useful for the analysis of female labor supply.

The conventional family labor supply model extends the analysis of the single individual by postulating a single decisionmaking unit, the family, which maximizes a twice-differentiable quasiconcave preference function

$$U = U(L_1, \dots, L_m, C), \tag{1}$$

where L_i is the "leisure" (nonmarket) time of family member i and C is the family's consumption of a composite consumer good. This maximization is subject to the constraint that total family income – the sum of its exogenous income R and the earnings of its m members – may not exceed the family's total expenditure on the consumer good:

$$PC \leq R + \sum_i W_i H_i, \tag{2}$$

where P is the price of one unit of the composite good, R is the amount of "exogenous" income (e.g. dividends) received by the family per period and W_i and H_i are the wage and hours of work of family member i per period, respectively. Available time is divided between market work and leisure, so that $H_i + L_i = T$, where T = total available time per period.

The first-order conditions for a maximum of (1) subject to (2) are

$$PC = R + \sum_i W_i H_i, \tag{3}$$

$$U_i - \mu W_i \geq 0, \quad \text{with } > \rightarrow H_i = 0, \tag{4a}$$

$$U_C - \mu P = 0, \tag{5}$$

where μ is a Lagrange multiplier that may be interpreted as the marginal utility or income to the family, U_C is the partial derivative of U with respect to C, and U_i is the partial derivative of U with respect to L_i. Note that (4a) allows for corner solutions, i.e. cases in which $L_i = T$ for at least some of the family members i. [Since the participation rate of married women is generally well below unity, this aspect of (4a) is particularly important.]

The comparative statics of the family labor supply model turn out to be very similar (often, identical) to those of the standard model of consumer behavior, in which an individual allocates a fixed income (and therefore does not treat labor supply or leisure as choice variables) among n different consumer goods. In particular, total differentiation of (3)–(5) yields the following results concerning (any pair of) family members i and j *when all members work*:

$$\mathrm{d}L_i/\mathrm{d}W_j = \mu(F_{ij}/|F|) - H_j(F_i/|F|), \tag{6}$$

$$\mathrm{d}L_i/\mathrm{d}R = -F_i/|F|, \tag{7}$$

$$\mathrm{d}L_i/\mathrm{d}P = \mu(F_{iC}/|F|) + C(F_i/|F|), \tag{8}$$

where F_i and F_{ij} are the cofactors of the elements $-W_i$ and U_{ij}, respectively, in the matrix F, the bordered Hessian matrix of the utility function (i.e. the matrix of second derivatives of U bordered by the $-W_i$ and $-P$), and where

$$F=\begin{bmatrix} 0 & -W_1 & \cdots & -W_m & -P \\ -W_1 & U_{11} & \cdots & U_{1m} & U_{1C} \\ \vdots & \vdots & & \vdots & \vdots \\ -W_m & U_{m1} & \cdots & U_{mm} & U_{mC} \\ -P & U_{C1} & \cdots & U_{Cm} & U_{CC} \end{bmatrix}. \tag{9}$$

The similarity between (6)–(8) and the analogous expressions obtained in the standard model of consumer behavior [see for example, Hicks (1946, esp. pp. 303–314)][2] is evident. The main difference between the two models has to do with the fact that, in the labor supply model, the commodity "time" is sold (in which case it is called work) as well as consumed (in which case it is called leisure), so that whereas in the consumer behavior model increases in commodity prices reduce utility, in the labor supply model an increase in the price of time raises utility.

The first term on the right-hand side (RHS) of (6) is called the compensated cross-substitution effect (or, when $j=i$, the compensated own-substitution effect) on i's leisure of an increase in j's wage. It refers to the effect on i's leisure time of an increase in j's wage with exogenous income R adjusted so as to keep family utility U constant. The total effects of wage changes – the sum of the two terms on the RHS of (6) – are uncompensated effects of wage changes. The leisure times of family members i and j are said to be substitutes or complements in the Hicks–Allen sense depending on whether the cross-substitution term in (6) is positive or negative, respectively. By the same token, the first-term on the RHS of (8) represents the cross-substitution or income-compensated effect of a rise in the price of market goods, P, on family member i's leisure time, L_i, and is positive or negative depending on whether C and L_i are substitutes or complements, respectively.

The second terms on the RHS of (6) and (8), and the sole term on the RHS of (7), is an income effect. By definition, an increase in exogenous income will increase i's leisure time if i's leisure is a "normal" good to the family, and will decrease i's leisure time if i's leisure time is an "inferior" good. By (6) and (8), increases in wages and prices, respectively, are to some extent akin to increases in exogenous income: at a given level of hours of work H_j, an increase in the wage W_j of family member j *increases* family income by H_j times as much as a \$1 increase in exogenous income R and so will have H_j times as big an income

[2]Although (6)–(8) refer to leisure, recall that it is assumed that $L_i + H_i = T$, so that – at least in this model – any change in leisure time is always accompanied by an opposite-signed change in hours of work of equal absolute magnitude. So one may readily convert (6)–(8) to expressions for changes in H_i by simply multiplying their RHS by -1.

effect; at a given level of consumption C, an increase in the price level P *reduces* family income (in real or constant purchasing-power terms) by C times as much as a \$1 *reduction* in exogenous income R and so will have C times as big an income effect.

The empirical content of the model consists of a number of properties that are implicit in constrained (family) utility maximization. The most important of these are homogeneity, symmetry, negativity and negative definiteness. First, the family's leisure and consumption demand functions are homogeneous of degree zero in all wages, exogenous income and the price level taken together: leisure and consumption decisions depend only on real (and not on nominal) variables; there is no money illusion.

Second, since F is symmetric because the utility function (1) is assumed to be twice differentiable, it follows that $F_{ij} = F_{ji}$, and thus that pairs of cross-substitution effects between the same two family members are equal – the property of *symmetry*. As Ashenfelter and Heckman (1974, p. 75) put it, symmetry means (among other things) that "an income compensated change in the husband's wage rate has the same effect on the wife's work effort as an income compensated change in the wife's rate has on the husband's work effort".

Third, F is negative definite, implying that $F_{ii}/|F| < 0$, and thus that all own-substitution effects of wage changes on leisure are negative – the property of *negativity*. The negative definiteness of F also implies that the *matrix* of own- and cross-substitution effects is *itself* negative definite; for example, in a family with just two members, 1 and 2, both of whom work, negative definiteness implies that, at the family's optimum,

$$\begin{vmatrix} s_{11} & s_{12} & s_{1C} \\ s_{21} & s_{22} & s_{2C} \\ s_{C1} & s_{C2} & s_{CC} \end{vmatrix} < 0, \tag{10}$$

$$\begin{vmatrix} s_{11} & s_{12} \\ s_{21} & s_{22} \end{vmatrix} > 0, \qquad \begin{vmatrix} s_{ii} & s_{iC} \\ s_{Ci} & s_{CC} \end{vmatrix} > 0 \quad (i = 1, 2), \tag{11}$$

where $s_{ij} = F_{ij}/|F|$ is the own- or cross-substitution effect on i of the price of j.

Recall that (6)–(8), (10) and (11) hold only if all family members work. In the general case in which some family members do *not* work, the leisure times of nonworking members do not change in response to sufficiently small changes in wages, exogenous income and the price level, so that expressions analogous to (6)–(8), (10) and (11) apply in the general case only to the subset of working family members. (Hence, in that case, F must be redefined to refer only to working members.) Families in which some members j have $H_j = 0$, $L_j = T$, may be said to be "rationed" – that is, such families are unable to "purchase" the amount of L_j they would desire to have if it were possible to ignore the constraint $L_j \leq T$.

It is interesting to note that such rationing has implications for the behavior of the family's "unrationed" members.[3] Much discussion of this notion relies on the Le Chatelier principle [see, for example, Samuelson (1947, pp. 36–46, 168–169)], which, in general terms, says that an individual with more options will have a more elastic supply (or demand) function in absolute value. Kniesner (1976) invoked this principle to argue that the substitution effect of a rise in the husband's wage on the husband's hours of work will always be more positive in families in which both spouses work than in families in which the wife does not work; and that if the spouses' leisure times are complements (substitutes) and are both normal, the negative income effect of a rise in the husband's wage on the husband's hours of work will be larger (smaller) in absolute value when both husband and wife work than when only the husband works. However, as Samuelson (1960) notes, such comparisons hold only at the identical consumption bundle, so that their usefulness in analyses of actual rationed and unrationed couples (whose consumption bundles are almost surely different) is somewhat limited.

By imposing additional structure on the problem (e.g. by assuming that the household utility function is quadratic in the vicinity of equilibrium), however, Heckman (1971, Essay III) was able to derive similar results for rationed and unrationed households with potentially *different* consumption bundles. For example, consider two households each facing the same wages and prices. One is unrationed, i.e. both husband and wife work; in the other, "rationed," household, the husband works but the wife does not. Then, under Heckman's assumptions, one can show (i) that the male compensated substitution effect will be smaller in the rationed than in the unrationed household; (ii) the income effect on consumption will be larger (smaller) for the unrationed household provided the wife's home time and consumption are net substitutes (complements); and (iii) the compensated or cross-substitution effect of a rise in the male wage on household demand for goods will be smaller (larger) in rationed households if one spouse's leisure is a net substitute for market goods whereas the other's is a net complement (if the spouses' leisure times are *both* either net complements *or* substitutes with market goods).

Like those discussed earlier, these propositions are consequences of the assumption that family members' decisions are the outcome of optimization of a well-defined family utility function. However, families are made up of individuals, and can either grow or dissolve: where, then, do family utility functions come from? There are several possible answers to this question. The first is that all family members simply conform to the preferences of one of the family's

[3] See Deaton and Muellbauer (1981), Hausman and Ruud (1984), Kooreman and Kapteyn (1984a), and Ransom (1985a, 1985b) for discussion of the implications of this kind of "rationing" for specification and estimation of family labor supply functions.

members, who may be called the family head. This answer begs the question of how a head is chosen and why other family members choose to obey the head. The second way to justify the family utility function is to assert that the social choice conditions for the existence of a well-behaved social (i.e. family) utility function are satisfied. The difficulty here is that such existence conditions are rather stringent [on this, see Samuelson (1956)], especially for families settling issues concerning multiple attributes [Mueller (1981)].

A third rationale for the family utility function relies on intrafamily resource transfers and an assumption that family members "care" for one another (in the sense that family member i's utility is affected by member j's consumption of goods and leisure). As Becker (1974, p. 331) puts it, "...if one member of a household – the 'head' – cares enough about all other members to transfer resources to them, this household would act *as if* it maximized the 'head's' preference function, even if the preferences of other members are quite different". (He later adds, p. 343: "In effect, transfers between members eliminate the conflict between different members' utility functions.")

The difficulty with this claim is that it is not generally true [Bergstrom (1984)]: In general, my acting so as to maximize my spouse's utility will not ensure that my own utility will be maximized even if my spouse cares for me (and is willing to transfer resources to me) to some extent; and my acting so as to maximize my own utility will not ensure that my spouse's utility will be maximized even if I care for my spouse (and so am willing to transfer resources to my spouse) to some extent.[4] At least in this sense, then, caring and intrafamily transfers are not generally sufficient to "eliminate the conflict between different [family] members' utility functions." That does not mean that being a family member can never be better than not being part of a family; but it does mean that an individual family member may have reason for questioning whether obeying the dictates of the family utility function will yield his or her potential optimum optimorum within the family – and that intrafamily conflict may well ensue.

Perhaps with these difficulties in mind, some researchers have developed alternatives to the family utility model [Pollak (1985)]. Leuthold (1968) casts family labor supply decisions in a framework that is formally rather similar to the analysis of duopoly [Allen (1938, esp. pp. 200–204)]: each individual family member maximizes his or her own individual utility, assumed to depend on the

[4] For example, consider a very simple model of a family of two persons, m and f, with *fixed* endowments of wealth Z_m and Z_f and utility functions $U_m = (Z_m - A)^a + (Z_f + A)^b$ and $U_f = (Z_m - A)^y + (Z_f + A)^z$, respectively, where A is the amount (negative *or* positive) that m transfers to f. (Note that since wealth is assumed fixed, labor supply is implicitly also assumed fixed, in the interest of simplification.) Then it is straightforward to show that, in general, maximizing m's utility will not simultaneously result in maximization of f's utility, and vice versa. [Equivalently, it can be shown that when the first order condition for a maximum of m's (f's) utility with respect to A is satisfied, the first order condition for a maximum of f's (m's) utility with respect to A is not generally satisfied.]

individual's own leisure time and on *family* consumption C, i.e.

$$U = U(L_i, C), \tag{12}$$

subject to the family budget constraint (2). Thus, the existence of the family is taken as given, and all consumption is implicitly assumed to be a public good. In the duopoly model, each firm seeks to maximize its own profit, but its actions affect the other firm's profit (and hence the other firm's behavior, and hence, indirectly, its *own* profit) because they share the same market. In the Leuthold model, each spouse seeks to maximize his or her own utility, but each family member's own actions affect the utility and behavior of all other members (and thus ultimately their own actions) because (i) each family member is assumed to derive utility from family consumption C, and (ii) all family members pool their incomes and are subject to the common budget constraint (2).

Specifically, in this formulation the leisure times and labor supplies of other family members j do not directly affect the utility of family member i, but they do have indirect effects through their impact on C. Thus, instead of the family utility model's cross-substitution effects, the individual utility model has what may be called indirect income effects. In other words, in the family utility model, the existence of a single family utility function means that a change in the wage of family member j has a cross-substitution effect on i's labor supply that is of indeterminate sign but equal in magnitude to the cross-substitution effect on j's labor supply of a change in i's wage. In contrast, in the individual utility model, each individual maximizes his or her own utility function, but changes in the wages of other family members still affect each member's behavior because all members pool their income. Hence, a change in j's wage generates what may be called an indirect income effect on i's labor supply that is necessarily negative (so long as leisure times are normal goods) but not necessarily equal to the indirect income effect of a change in i's wage on j's labor supply. Thus, whereas the family utility model provides predictions about the magnitudes but not the signs of its cross-substitution effects, the individual utility model provides predictions about the signs but not the magnitudes of its indirect income effects.[5]

Bargaining models of family behavior [e.g. Horney and McElroy (1978), Manser and Brown (1979, 1980), McElroy and Horney (1981)] provide an alternative formulation of family labor supply decisions.[6] The essential idea is to

[5]See Killingsworth (1983, esp. pp. 35–36) for further discussion. Bourguignon (1984) presents a modified version of the Leuthold model and discusses empirical tests of this model against conventional family-utility models of labor supply. For empirical analyses, see Ashworth and Ulph (1981), Kooreman and Kapteyn (1985) and Leuthold (1968).

[6]Mention should also be made of two somewhat less formal analyses of family labor supply decisions. Brown (1985) presents an institutional model of wives' labor supply decisions that

treat the decision of individual family members (and, indeed, the very existence of the family) in game-theoretic terms. For example, McElroy and Horney (1981) derive a Nash-bargained system of labor supply and commodity demand equations for each individual in a two-person household as the outcome of a constrained static, non-zero-sum game. This generalizes Leuthold's approach because it does not take the family as given and because it allows for private goods; unlike Leuthold, however, it ignores public goods.

Three features of such bargaining models are particularly noteworthy. First, because they explicitly treat alternatives to marriage as well as behavior within the family, bargaining models can be used in analyses of marriage and divorce. Second, within the family, differences in the distribution by recipient (husband, wife, etc.) of exogenous income may lead to differences in their bargaining strengths and, hence, their behavior, so that each *individual* family member's exogenous income appears as a *separate* argument in each demand equation (for leisure times, consumption, etc.). Third, some bargaining models [e.g. the Nash demand system developed by McElroy and Horney (1981)] retain some of the properties of the family utility model (e.g. homogeneity) and nest others (e.g. symmetry) as special cases. Thus, in principle, empirical analyses of hours of work can be used to test whether the bargaining model reduces to the conventional familiity utility case [for examples, see Horney and McElroy (1978) and Manser and Brown (1979, 1980); work based on bargaining models by Bjorn and Vuong (1984, 1985) considers labor force participation as opposed to hours of work].

Unfortunately, such tests are not necessarily straightforward [Ashenfelter (1979)]. One problem is that, precisely to the extent that bargaining models generalize the conventional model, one in effect abandons the sharp testable implications of the latter without necessarily putting alternative clearcut predictions in their place. The essential reason for this is that bargaining models are formally equivalent to Basemann's (1956) model with prices in the utility function, a situation in which testable restrictions of conventional theory frequently do not survive. A second problem is that, as a practical matter, it is likely to be

emphasizes interdependency of families and the role of an individual family's relative income position, à la Duesenberry (1952) and Veblen (1973). Grossbard-Shechtman (1984) adopts an individual utility function whose arguments include household time supplied by other persons and a budget constraint specifying that expenditures on market goods produced and on time supplied by other persons may not exceed the sum of nonwage income, earnings from market work and earnings from supplying household time to other individuals. Pay for market work w and implicit prices of household time p^* that the individual receives from or supplies to others are determined in labor and marriage markets, respectively; changes in exogenous factors (e.g. the relative size of the male or female population) affect marriage markets, the relative magnitudes and absolute levels of w and the p^* and, thus, labor supply decisions and marriage rates.

quite different to measure certain variables that play a key role in bargaining models, namely the exogenous income flows that are under the control of particular family members. A final difficulty is common to conventional and bargaining models of family behavior: as Samuelson (1947, pp. 111, 150; 1960, p. 13) observes, the fact that data do not come in infinitesimals means symmetry is not truly testable, and that the only propositions of utility maximization that are truly testable are propositions relating to revealed preference (which are formulated in terms of discrete, not infinitesimal, changes).

3.1.2. Models of the allocation of time

As noted in Section 3.1.1, the labor supply of women, especially married women seems to have increased secularly by appreciable amounts, whereas, in contrast, male labor supply seems to have fallen over time (see Pencavel, Chapter 1 in this Handbook). Also, as shown in Section 3.1.3 below, much – although by no means all – of the available empirical evidence suggests that (1) the own-wage uncompensated elasticity of labor supply of women is positive and fairly large, (2) the exogenous-income elasticities of both men and women are small and (3) the own-wage uncompensated labor supply elasticity of men is small and perhaps even negative. This being the case, it is certainly possible (especially if cross-wage effects are ignored) to devise a relatively simple explanation for the difference in secular trends of men's and women's market work: secular increases in exogenous income have had a minor negative effect on both groups; secular wage increases have reduced men's labor supply to a minor degree and have increased women's labor supply to a substantial degree.

However, this explanation begs an important question: Why is the female uncompensated wage elasticity of labor supply relatively high, as suggested in many empirical studies?

In principle, answering this question is also fairly straightforward. The first step is to apply to commodity demands the discussions of input demands of Hicks (1965, pp. 242–246), Marshall (1920, pp. 386, 852–853), and Pigou (1946, p. 682): the elasticity of demand for a good (in this case, leisure) with respect to its price (in this case, the wage rate) will be greater, the greater is the availability of alternatives to that good. The next step [Mincer (1962, 1963)] is to observe that women in effect have more alternative uses for their time – market work, home work and leisure – than do men, who for the most part divide their time between only two uses, market work and leisure. In other words, the substitution towards market work that men undertake when their wage rises is primarily a substitution away from leisure, whereas a wage increase leads women to substitute away for both leisure and home work. This argument does not explain why home work is primarily women's work. However, it does at least suggest, albeit informally,[7] why – when that is so – women's labor supply might be more wage-elastic than men's.

There remains the task of dressing these rather imprecise ideas in formal clothing. In doing so, researchers have moved away from a preoccupation with market work and the rather diffuse concept of "leisure", and towards a more general treatment of the allocation of time along a great variety of activities.

Becker (1965) remains the basic inspiration for much work along these lines. In his approach, the basic objects of choice are not consumer goods and leisure times, but rather *commodities* (sometimes called *activities*), Z_i, which are "produced" using consumer goods C_i and time as "inputs": time, cooking utensils and raw ingredients produce a cooked meal; time and a television set produce a form of entertainment; and so on. Hence, the family's utility U is now given by

$$U = U(Z_1, \ldots, Z_N), \tag{13}$$

where, in turn, Z_i is given by the *household production function*

$$Z_i = f^i(C_{1i}, \ldots, C_{zi}, L_{1i}, \ldots, L_{mi}), \tag{14}$$

where C_{ci} is the amount of the cth consumer good devoted to production of the ith commodity and L_{ki} is the amount of time of the kth family member devoted to production of Z_i. As before, maximization of utility, as given by (13), is subject to the usual family budget constraint, (2). The model yields a set of

[7]There is, however, a technical caveat to this argument. Leisure demand is simply the sum of demands for all different uses of nonmarket time (which, by Hicks' composite commodity theorem, can legitimately be aggregated to form a single composite, leisure, because the price of each use of nonmarket time is the wage rate); but an increase in the elasticity of demand for one component in this composite (e.g. nonmarket work) need not increase the elasticity of demand for the composite (total nonmarket time) itself. For example, assume that there are only two kinds of nonmarket time: nonmarket work, $L(1)$, and "pure" leisure, $L(2)$, with composite leisure L equal to $L(1)+L(2)$. It can be shown [Heckman (1971)] that the income-compensated elasticity of demand for L is equal to $s(LL) = s(11) + 2s(12) + s(22)$, where $s(ij)$ is the compensated elasticity of $L(i)$ with respect to the price of $L(j)$ $(i, j, = 1$ or $2)$ and where $s(LL)$ and $s(ii)$ are negative by concavity of preferences. It can also be shown that in the restricted case, when $L(1) = 0$ (as for the stereotypical male), the restricted compensated demand elasticity for L, $s(LL)^*$, is given by $s(LL)^* = s(11) - [s(12)^2/s(22)]$ $(<0$, again by concavity of preferences). Since both $s(LL)^*$ and $s(LL)$ are negative, we have $0 > s(LL)^* > s(LL)$ (i.e. the stereotypical male's compensated elasticity of total leisure demand is smaller in absolute value than that of the stereotypical female) if and only if $s(12) \leq -s(22)$. This condition always holds if $L(1)$ and $L(2)$ are net complements $(s(12) < 0)$, and will also hold if $L(1)$ and $L(2)$ are not "too substitutable". [If $L(1)$ and $L(2)$ were in fact strong substitutes in the sense that $s(12) > -s(22)$ (>0), then any restriction on performing home work $L(1)$ would – while reducing the compensated elasticity of demand for home work $s(11)$ – end up increasing the elasticity of demand for pure leisure $L(2)$ by so much that the elasticity of demand for total leisure, $L = L(1) + L(2)$, would actually increase.]

functions for the time devoted by each family member k to production of each activity i; k's hours of work are simply the residual, i.e. $H_k = T - \sum_i L_{ki}$.

The main advantage of the time allocation model lies in the fact that it treats explicitly the diverse uses to which nonmarket time may be put, thereby permitting quite detailed analyses of the nonmarket behavior of family members [see, for example, Gronau (1977) and Chapter 4 in this Handbook; Kooreman and Kapteyn (1984b)]. One study [Leibowitz (1974, pp. 246–247)] even finds that husbands' and wives' times are substitutable in the production of meals at the marginal rate of ten minutes of husband time for each five minutes of wife time! More generally, the model emphasizes a point that is implicit in conventional analyses but all too often ignored: goods prices as well as wage rates affect decisions about work and leisure; wage rates as well as goods prices affect decisions about consumption. [See, in particular, Mincer (1963) and Owen (1969, 1971).] In addition, the time allocation approach suggests ideas for specifying the functional form of empirical labor supply models [Wales and Woodland (1977)] and for elaboration of conventional models [see, for example, Atkinson and Stern (1981)].

Finally, the time allocation model provides a useful framework, largely absent from the quite abstract conventional labor supply model, for analyzing a variety of factors that may affect labor supply. For example, researchers since Long (1958, ch. 7) have discussed informally the labor supply effects of improvements in "household technology" – better stoves, refrigerators, etc.; and it is natural in the context of the time allocation model to treat such improvements as technical progress in the household production functions. [However, it should be noted that work such as that of Fisher and Shell (1971) provides a means of treating "quality change" or improvements in existing consumption goods within conventional consumer-behavior models.]

On the other hand, although the time allocation approach clearly represents a great advance in the analysis of *nonmarket* time, its potential for contributing to the understanding of *market* time – hours of work – should not be exaggerated. In this respect, the abstraction of the conventional model is perhaps misleading: even though the conventional model says nothing explicit about the different uses to which nonwork time may be put – meaning that the time allocation approach is clearly superior for analyses of *nonwork* time – virtually all of the time allocation model's predictions about *labor supply* can also be derived using the conventional approach. In this respect, there is little in the time allocation approach that is not also in the conventional approach, even if the former provides a much more detailed description of the setting in which labor supply decisions are made.

The main reason for this is that, in the time allocation model as in the conventional formulation, labor supply and consumption decisions ultimately depend on wages, prices and exogenous income, and utility can always be written as a function of leisure (nonmarket) times and consumption goods. To see why, note first that one can substitute the household production functions, (14), into the utility function, (13), to obtain:

$$U = U\left[Z_1(C_{11},\dots,C_{z1}, L_{11},\dots, L_{m1}),\dots, Z_n(C_{1n},\dots,C_{zn}, L_{1n},\dots, L_{mn})\right]. \tag{15}$$

Moreover, the opportunity cost of devoting an hour of family member i's time to *any* nonmarket activity is his or her wage, W_i; and the opportunity cost of devoting a unit of consumer good j to any nonmarket activity is likewise the price of that good, P_j. Thus, one may invoke the composite commodity theorem[8] and aggregate the nonmarket times of each family member i devoted to the various activities into a single composite leisure time, L_i; similarly, the amounts of each consumer good j devoted to the various activities may be aggregated into a single composite consumption good, C_j. Just to pursue this aggregation to the limit, one can then aggregate the individual composite consumption goods C_j into a single composite commodity C using the prices P_j of the individual goods C_j as weights. The end result, then, is that the utility function (15) reduces to relation giving utility as a function of the total leisure (or nonwork) times of the m different family members and of a composite good C – exactly as in the conventional model; and all of the major properties of labor supply and commodity demand functions found in the latter will also appear in this rewritten version of the time allocation model.[9]

[8] See Hicks (1946, pp. 312–313). As applied to labor supply models, the theorem asserts that if the prices of a set of consumption goods (or leisure times) always stay in the same relation to each other, then the set of consumption goods (or leisure times) can be treated as a single composite good for purposes of analysis (where the amount of the composite good may be measured as the relative price-weighted sum of the individual goods themselves). Thus, for example, if consumer goods prices stay in the same relation to each other, then instead of writing utility as a function of n different consumer goods and leisure, one may group the n goods into a single composite, C, and analyze the choice of C and L. In the present case, *any* hour of family member i's time always entails the *same* opportunity cost, namely i's wage rate W_i, so the price of i's time in any use relative to any other use is always unity. Hence, the nonwork or leisure hours that i devotes to different activities Z may all be aggregated into a single leisure composite L, which – since all relative prices are unity – is simply i's total leisure time.

[9] Becker (1965, p. 505) appears to think that this is not necessarily the case and, in particular, that the own-substitution effect of a wage increase on labor supply need not be positive in the time allocation model (as must be the case in the conventional model). However, this conjecture is incorrect [for example, see Atkinson and Stern (1981)]. It should be noted that the discussion in the text assumes an interior solution for leisure time for the household's members (since, if a household member does not work, the opportunity cost of his or her time exceeds the relevant real wage rate, and aggregation of the member's nonmarket time allocations using his or her real wage is inappropriate). Thus, it is possible that the time allocation model may offer insights into nonparticipation that do not appear, or are not as readily apparent, in the conventional approach. (We thank Ricardo Barros for pointing this out to us.)

To appreciate the nature of these issues in concrete terms, it is instructive to consider how one might use a very simple version of the time allocation model in analyzing the level and elasticity of women's labor supply [see Graham and Green (1984) for an empirical application similar to the one described here]. Consider a family consisting of two persons, m and f, whose well-behaved utility function depends on the family's consumption of just one activity Z, such that $U = Z^c$. Activity Z is produced via inputs of the family members times L_i and of a single consumer good C according to the constant-returns-to-scale Cobb–Douglas production function $Z = L_f^a L_m^b C^{1-a-b}$. The family maximizes utility subject to the constraints imposed by this production function and by the usual budget constraint, (2). A little manipulation of the first-order conditions for a maximum with respect to the L_i and C yields the following expression for the utility-maximizing level of L_i at an interior optimum:

$$L_i = A_i F/W_i, \quad \text{where } A_f = a,\ A_m = b, \tag{16}$$

and where $F = R + T(W_f + W_m)$, the family's "full income" (i.e. the maximum income attainable, reached if both m and f work all available hours T). Note that (16) implies that, even if m and f can earn equal market wages, f will devote *more* time to nonmarket work than m provided f is "better" at producing the nonmarket activity Z (i.e. provided $a > b$), and that this difference will be even greater if $W_f < W_m$. Here, then, is a simple explanation for married women's relatively low level of labor supply: in terms of the time allocation model, the reason is (at least, could be) a greater elasticity of output of activity Z with respect to married women's nonmarket time.

Exactly the same reasoning also provides a simple explanation for the relatively large elasticity of married women's labor supply. Use (16) and the fact that $H_i = T - L_i$ to obtain the equation for the labor supply H_i of each family member, and then use this labor supply equation to obtain the own-wage uncompensated elasticity of i's labor supply, e_{ii}:

$$e_{ii} = (A_i/H_i)[(F/W_i) - T]. \tag{17}$$

So long as f is "better" at nonmarket production than m (in the sense that $a > b$), $A_f/H_f > A_m/H_m$ and so $e_{ff} > e_{mm}$ even if $W_f = W_m$. These conclusions are reinforced if $W_f < W_m$. In other words, this simple version of the time allocation model implies that so long as wives are "better" at (have a higher output elasticity in) nonmarket production than husbands and earn wages no greater than those of (their) husbands, the *level* of labor supply will be lower but the *elasticity* of labor supply will be greater for wives than for husbands.

That such a simple model can account for two very important stylized facts about female labor supply noted in Section 3.1.1 seems, at first glance, quite impressive. Unfortunately, there is less to these results than meets the eye; in particular, they do not establish the superiority of the time allocation model over the conventional model for purposes of understanding the labor supply of (for example) wives. To see why, note that one would get *identical* conclusions by simply assuming a conventional Cobb–Douglas utility function,

$$U = L_f^{a*} L_m^{b*} C^{c*}, \tag{18}$$

where, in terms of the time allocation model, $a^* = ac$, $b^* = bc$ and $c^* = c(1-a-b)$. Maximization of (18) subject to (2) *also* yields the expressions (16) and (17) for the level of nonmarket time and the elasticity of labor supply of the two spouses; the only difference is that whereas the time allocation model would interpret differences between m and f in leisure and elasticity of labor supply as a result of household production function elasticity differences, the conventional model would interpret such differences as a consequence of different utility function parameters.[10] Moreover, much of the power of the household production function approach rests on some special assumptions – e.g. separability, the absence of joint production, etc. [Pollak and Wachter, (1974)] – which are not required for (and whose imposition could effectively restrict the scope of) analysis of labor supply per se. Finally, the key variable in the time allocation approach, "output" of the activity Z, is unobservable, which means that from an empirical standpoint the two models are indistinguishable for all practical purposes.

In sum, although the time allocation approach may be useful in analyses of different uses of *nonmarket* time, the novelty of the model and its potential usefulness for analyses of *market* time – labor supply – may be more apparent than real.

3.1.3. *Models of labor supply with heterogeneous jobs*

Not only the quantity, but also the qualitative nature of women's labor supply has changed substantially in the twentieth century. As shown in Section 3.1.1, women workers in the United States in the 1980s typically hold white-collar jobs – usually, clerical jobs – to a much greater extent than was the case in the 1890s. This shift in the occupational distribution of women workers has been substantial not only in absolute terms, but also – and of equal if not greater significance – relative to men.

[10] Note also that although $a > b$ could be interpreted as a technological relationship – e.g. that the elasticity of actual output of Z with respect to f's time is greater than the elasticity with respect to m's time – one could instead treat $a > b$ as meaning merely that, for reasons (psychological, cultural, etc.) that need have nothing to do with technology as such, the family is biased towards using f's rather than m's time in the production of Z. In other words, the parameters a and b *can* be interpreted in technological terms, but nothing about the model that *requires* that they be interpreted in this way.

This suggests that explicitly addressing the heterogeneity of work may be helpful for understanding secular trends in women's labor supply. It may also be important for analyzing cross-sectional labor supply patterns. The reason is that, when work is heterogeneous, observed combinations of wage rates and hours of work do not necessarily describe a labor supply schedule as such. Rather, such combinations may represent only a labor supply locus with little or no significance for questions about labor supply as such. In other words, a labor supply schedule is supposed to show the amount of labor that a given individual would supply at different wage rates, other things being equal. In contrast, a labor supply locus shows only the hours of work-wage rate combinations that a given individual would choose in conjunction with other attributes of jobs – fringe benefits, working conditions and the like. [As a special but possibly widespread case, Moffitt (1984a), consider a setting in which the hourly wage offered to workers by firms depends on the number of hours worked.]

Since these other attributes may be substitutable for wages and do not necessarily remain constant along the labor supply locus, there is no reason to expect that the labor supply locus necessarily provides much information about the structural parameters of the labor supply schedule (e.g. income and substitution effects). Indeed, considered as estimates of the labor supply function, estimates of the labor supply locus may be badly biased.

On the other hand, simply including job variables in labor supply functions may *also* result in problems, precisely because, like labor supply, they are choice variables.

As a simple example of both kinds of difficulties, consider the regression of hours of work H on the wage W, exogenous income R, a vector of background characteristics X and a "job variable" J (which may denote either some continuous job characteristic, or a discrete indicator of job actually held):

$$H = a + bW + cR + kX + jJ + e, \tag{19}$$

where e is an error term. Fitting (19) by least squares will not provide a consistent estimate of j because J is endogenous, in that it is chosen along with H. Also, to the extent that differences in J are accompanied by compensating wage differentials, W is also now a choice variable, so least squares estimates of (19) may also yield biased estimates of b. Finally, if the individual's choice of J depends on elements in X (e.g. age, schooling), then in general e and those elements in X will be correlated, *given* J; thus least squares estimates of (19) may also yield biased estimates of the coefficients k on those elements in X. In sum, explicit allowance for the heterogeneity of jobs [i.e. inclusion of J in labor supply functions such as (19)] requires revision or extension of existing estimation strategies.

On the other hand, if one simply ignores J, (19) becomes

$$H = a + bW + cR + kX + u, \tag{20}$$

where u, the composite error term, is given by $u = e + jJ$. Fitting (20) by least squares may result in biased estimates of *all* of its parameters. To see why, note that, in the conventional compensating differentials story, J and W are jointly determined; allowing for labor supply (which is usually ignored in compensating differentials models) simply adds H to the list of endogenous variables. If so, then the composite error term $u = e + jJ$ will be correlated with W, R and X. To put the point a bit differently, (19) is a labor supply function whereas (20) is a labor supply locus. Estimates of the parameters of (20) therefore cannot be regarded as (the equivalent of) estimates of the parameters of (19); for example, to a first approximation, estimates of the wage parameter b in (20) incorporate not only the ceteris paribus effect on labor supply of a wage change – the b of (19) – but also the effect of a change in J on labor supply, to the extent that J and W are correlated.

The basic issue raised by expressions such as (19) is behavioral rather than statistical, however. In a world of heterogenous jobs, hours, wages and jobs (or job characteristics) are all endogenously chosen. Thus, even if one had consistent estimates of the parameters of expressions such as (19), such estimates would refer only to choice of hours *given* choice of job (characteristics) J; they would reveal nothing about how exogenous changes are associated with changes in the set of endogenously-chosen variables H, W and J. For example, the coefficient c in (19) refers to the "direct" effect of a change in exogenous income on hours of work with W and J held constant; but in general a change in exogenous income will lead to changes in J and W, and thus to "indirect" as well as direct effects on H.

Despite its potential importance for labor supply analysis, surprisingly little has been done to allow explicitly for the heterogeneity of work in formal labor supply models. For the most part, studies in which job heterogeneity *has* been considered have been concerned with compensating wage differentials, i.e. with wages rather than labor supply per se. Such studies have typically been concerned with regressing wage rates on "job variables" – e.g. continuous variables measuring job characteristics, or dummy variables denoting "job held" – and on other variables, such as schooling, work experience and the like. Studies of this kind usually provide little or no information about preferences (which might be useful for understanding labor supply to heterogenous jobs); for the most part, they estimate the compensating wage differential required by the *marginal* individual in order to change the amount of a particular job characteristic or in order to change jobs per se [Smith (1979)]. Moreover, such studies usually ignore the fact that the "job variables" included in such regressions are endogenous.

Ironically (in view of the neglect of labor supply in such studies), analyzing labor supply in a model of job heterogeneity can also provide useful information on the forces that generate compensating wage differentials. By using information on labor supply as well as wages, one can estimate the supply (e.g. utility function) parameters that underly compensating wage differentials while allowing explicitly for the endogeneity of individuals' "job variables". Thus, studying labor supply in the context of a model of job heterogeneity not only improves understanding of labor supply as such, but also permits consistent estimation of compensating wage differentials and the supply parameters that underly such differentials. The reason for this is that data on labor supply within different jobs are generated by the same preference structure that generates job choice and compensating wage differentials. Analysis of all three outcomes – job choice, labor supply and wages – can therefore yield more information than analysis of wages alone.

Despite the potential importance of job heterogeneity, relatively little has been done to incorporate it into formal labor supply models. Tinbergen (1956) considered the choice of (variable) amounts of job characteristics – with "desirable" job characteristics assumed to reduce pecuniary income but raise utility – but assumed that all jobs (i.e. distinct combinations of job characteristics) require the same hours of work. Extending this approach to allow for variable labor supply is relatively straightforward, however. One approach is to consider the joint determination of labor supply (or leisure) and a set of continuous job characteristics. A second is to consider the joint determination of labor supply (or leisure) and the discrete choice among various distinct jobs.

Atrostic (1982) takes the first approach, specifying utility as a function of consumption of a composite consumer good C, leisure time L and the vector of characteristics of one's job, J. Since desirable (and undesirable) J may be expected to generate compensating wage differentials, the wage rate W is also a function of the J (instead of being given exogenously, as in most labor supply models). This leads to a model that is formally quite similar to the kind of demand system familiar to analysts of consumer expenditure; in effect, the J can be treated as consumer goods that in principle are little different from other consumer goods.

For a simple example, consider the following application of this approach to analysis of a single individual (extension to a family setting is straightforward). First, let W be a linear function of the J, implying that the budget constraint may be written as

$$PC \leq R + H\left[w_0 + \sum_i w_i J_i\right], \tag{21}$$

where the term inside square brackets is the wage *function*. Next, let the individual's utility be given by

$$U = U(C, L, HJ_1, \ldots, HJ_k]. \tag{22}$$

Then the resulting model effectively refers to the choice of labor supply H, leisure time $L = T - H$, the composite good C and a set of K *additional* consumption goods K ($= HJ$), with utility,

$$U = U(C, L, K_1, \ldots, K_k), \tag{23}$$

being maximized subject to the budget constraint

$$PC + \sum_i w_i K_i \leq R + w_0 H, \tag{24}$$

in which the w_i, $i = 1, \ldots, k$, play the role of prices, directly analogous to P. The parameter w_0 may be thought of as the individual's "potential wage", i.e. as the wage received when all the J (or, equivalently, K) are zero; the J, as nonpecuniary consumption *per hour* of work; the K, as total nonpecuniary consumption. Thus, this specification leads quite simply and conveniently to a model that closely resembles those used in the estimation of systems of consumer demand functions [Barten (1977), Brown and Deaton (1972), Deaton and Muellbauer (1980)]. However, it takes explicit account of the fact that the job characteristics J are endogenously chosen and that exogenous changes (e.g. in the general wage level, in w_0, in exogenous income, etc.) will affect the individual's W and J as well as H.

Killingsworth (1985) takes the second of the two approaches to analyzing heterogenous labor supply, considering the supply of work hours to discrete jobs (as opposed to choice of continuous job characteristics). In this framework, utility itself depends on the job one holds, other things (including the wage rate, exogenous income, etc.) being equal, as given by the (job-dependent) indirect utility function[11]

$$V_j = V_j[W_j, R], \tag{25}$$

where j indexes jobs, and where the wage rate W_j received by the individual when in any particular job j need not be the same as the wage that would be received if the individual were in any other job. Labor supply when in job j is given by direct application of Roy's Identity to (25); analysis of the individual's discrete job choice may be conducted using an index function model. (For example, in a simple world with just two jobs, the individual's discrete job choice could be analyzed using the binary probit or logit model.) Again, wages and job choice are treated as endogenous along with hours of work.

[11] See Pencavel (Chapter 1 in this Handbook) or Killingsworth (1983, pp. 15–16) for discussion. Since the optimal (i.e. utility-maximizing) consumption and leisure values C^* and L^* are functions of W, R and the price level P, *maximum* utility V – which depends on the *optimal* C and L – may be written as a function of W, R and P. [In other words, maximum utility $U^* = U(C^*, L^*) = V = V(W/P, R/P)$.] Roy's Identity asserts that labor supply H is given by the ratio of (i) the partial derivative of V with respect to the real wage W/P to (ii) the partial derivative of V with respect to real exogenous income R/P. (In the expression in the text, P is implicitly normalized to unity.)

Hill (1985) proceeds along similar lines, though without reference to an explicit utility function: she analyzes the labor force status of Japanese women using trinomial logit (where the three labor force categories are out of the labor force, working in family-owned enterprises or working in other paid employment); uses the logit results to derive inverse-Mills'-ratio-like variables analogous to those proposed by Heckman (1976b, 1979); and then includes these variables in regressions for labor supply and wage rates in the two employment sectors (i.e. family-owned and other enterprises).

Both the continuous job characteristics and the discrete job choice models of the supply of labor to heterogenous work have the potential of providing useful insights into important dimensions of female labor supply. Unfortunately, except in Hill's study (1985), such models have yet to be used to explore the structure of the occupational dimension of women's work effort [Atrostic (1982) and Killingsworth (1985) are concerned with male labor supply]. This is an important topic for future research.

3.2. *Dynamic models*

We now consider dynamic labor supply models, ones in which agents act as if today's decisions do in fact have future consequences and in which accumulation of nonhuman and/or human wealth is treated explicitly. We first discuss models in which wages at each moment are assumed to be given exogenously. We then examine models in which wages are endogenously determined, e.g. via human capital accumulation.

3.2.1. *Dynamic labor supply models with exogenous wages*

Until fairly recently, almost all work on labor supply either implicitly or explicitly adopted an essentially static analytical framework. In contrast, Mincer's (1962) pioneering work is noteworthy because it not only contributed significantly to development of that framework, but also introduced ideas of a fundamentally dynamic nature.[12]

A major motivation for Mincer's work was an apparent paradox concerning the labor supply of women, especially married women: in cross-sections, one typically observes *inverse* relations between women's labor force participation rates and males' wage rates, and between wives' labor force participation rates

[12]Among the most important early studies of labor supply are Douglas (1934), Durand (1948), Lewis (1957), Long (1958), and Schoenberg and Douglas (1937). Modern empirical work may be said to have begun in earnest with the studies by Cain (1966), Kosters (1966, 1969) and Mincer (1962). See Cain (1982) for an appreciation of Mincer's (1962) seminal paper in light of two decades of further research.

and husbands' earnings; but time-series data exhibit sustained increases in participation rates for women, especially married women – "one of the most striking phenomena in the history of the American labor force" [Mincer (1962, p. 64)] – despite substantial growth in real wage rates and real incomes.

In addressing this paradox, and the labor force participation of married women generally, Mincer considered a variety of essentially static topics (e.g. the importance of the family context and of household production in labor supply decisions), several of which are discussed in Section 3.1. However, his analysis also includes several fundamentally dynamic features, including the notion of life-cycle decisionmaking and the distinction [first developed by Friedman (1957)] between permanent and transitory components of income, earnings, wages, etc. These ideas are encapsulated in the following three paragraphs in Mincer's original paper (1962, p. 68; emphasis original):

> In a broad view, the quantity of labor supplied to the market by a wife is the fraction of her married life during which she participates in the labor force. Abstracting from the temporal distribution of labor force activities over a woman's life, this fraction could be translated into the probability of being in the labor force in a given period of time for an individual, hence into a labor force rate for a large group of women.
>
> If leisure and work preferences, long-run family incomes, and earning power were the same for all women, the total amount of market work would, according to the theory, be the same for all women. Even if that were true, however, the *timing* of market activities during the working life may differ from one individual to another. The life cycle induces changes in demands for and marginal costs of home work and leisure... There are life-cycle variations in family incomes and assets which may affect the timing of labor force participation, given a limited income horizon and a less than perfect capital market. Cyclical and random variations in wage rates, employment opportunities, income and employment of other family members, particularly of the head, are also likely to induce temporal variations in the allocation of time between home, market, and leisure. It is not surprising, therefore, that over short periods of observation, variation in labor force participation, or turnover, is the outstanding characteristic of labor force behavior of married women.
>
> To the extent that the temporal distribution of labor force participation can be viewed as a consequence of "transitory" variation in variables favoring particular timing, the distinction between "permanent" and current levels of the independent variables becomes imperative in order to adapt our model to family surveys in which the period of observation is quite short.

Subsequent researchers have drawn two major practical conclusions from these general remarks. First, some investigators have treated estimated wage and income coefficients obtained in empirical analysis of labor force participation as theoretically equivalent to wage and income coefficients estimated in analyses of hours of work, and so have used estimates of parameters affecting participation to retrieve measures of Hicks–Slutsky income and substitution effects. Second, some researchers have argued that, given the intertemporal considerations that underly labor supply decisions, it is essential to distinguish between temporary and permanent changes in wage rates, exogenous income, and other key determinants of labor supply.[13]

Although such ideas possess considerable intuitive appeal, they have not usually been derived – or even described – rigorously. This is unfortunate, for it has tended to limit quite severely the usefulness of work subsequent to Mincer's that has relied on these notions. In what follows, we develop them formally and then apply them to the analysis of female labor supply.

Perhaps the simplest way to embed Mincer's ideas in a formal model is to reinterpret the simple static analysis of labor supply in lifetime terms: since the single period of that model is of indeterminate length, there is no reason why the U, C, T, H, L, W and P of that model cannot be interpreted as lifetime variables. The only change necessary is to interpret R as the individual's initial real asset holdings (instead of her "exogenous income"). For simplicity, assume a zero market rate of interest (although even that is hardly essential, since all pecuniary variables such as W and P could be appropriately discounted); and introduce an unobserved "taste" or "household production" variable e that affects (lifetime) utility U and is independent of other variables, such that

$$U=U(C,L,e). \tag{26}$$

Note that this implicitly assumes that leisure times at different dates are perfect substitutes for each other (and similarly for consumption of goods at different dates).

The (lifetime) budget constraint subject to which utility is maximized is

$$PC \leq WH+R, \tag{27}$$

exactly as in the single-period static model. However, (27) does not require an assumption that the wage be constant over the worker's lifetime: the W in (27) is the "lifetime" wage, i.e. a kind of life-cycle *average* of (appropriately-discounted) single-period wage rates that may differ across periods.

To fix ideas, assume that the life cycle consists of T periods, and sort single-period real wage rates in descending order, so that $w(1)$ denotes the *highest*

[13] For examples of empirical studies that use analyses of participation to obtain measures of income and substitution effects, see Ashenfelter and Heckman (1974), Cain (1966) and Kosters (1966, 1969). For examples of empirical studies that pursue the distinction between permanent and transitory changes in wages and other labor supply determinants, see Kalachek and Raines (1970), Kalachek, Mellow and Raines (1978), Lillard (1978) and Watts, Poirier and Mallar (1977).

real wage and $w(T)$ the lowest. Then, as in the static model, a market wage-reservation wage comparison determines whether the individual will work sometime during her life. Specifically, the individual will work at least one period if $w(1)$ exceeds her (lifetime) reservation or "shadow" wage – i.e. the marginal rate of substitution evaluated at zero (lifetime) hours of work, $U_L(R,T,e)/U_C(R,T,e) = S(R,T,e)$:

$$U_L(R,T,e)/U_C(R,T,e) = S(R,T,e) \leq w^* \rightarrow H > 0. \tag{28}$$

The *total number* of periods the individual works can be expressed in terms of a similar comparison: the individual will work exactly k periods if, when the discounted real wage rates w are sorted in descending order,

$$w(k) \geq S(R,T,e) \geq w(k+1) \tag{29}$$

where, by virtue of the sort, $w(k) > w(k+1)$, and where at least one of the inequalities in (29) is strict.[14] By (29), the total number of periods worked, k, is a function of e, real initial wealth R and the "marginal wage" $w(k)$, i.e.

$$k = k[w(k), R, T, e]. \tag{30}$$

Once k and $w(k)$ are defined as "labor supply" and "the wage rate", respectively, this looks just like a conventional static labor supply function.

Finally, the proportion of all periods in the individual's *lifetime* that are devoted to work, h, is simply $h = k/T$. Since k is a function of $w(k)$, R and e by (30), h is also; thus, h may be expressed as

$$h = h[w(k), R, e], \tag{31}$$

where the $h(\cdot)$ function of (31) is proportional to the $k(\cdot)$ function of (30), with T being the factor of proportionality.

A practical difficulty with this model is that its estimation – e.g. fitting (30) or (31) – would seem to require data on labor supply over the entire life cycle (e.g. either k or h), which is surely an imposing hurdle for the empirical analyst. However, Mincer's discussion, quoted above, provides an ingenious way around this difficulty: abstracting from "transitory" factors (children, transitory variation in income or wages, etc.), the timing of work over the life cycle may be

[14] Note that (29) closely resembles expressions obtained in purely *static* models of labor supply under progressive taxation [see, for example, Heckman and MaCurdy (1984), Killingsworth (1983), Hausman (1983)]. In the latter setting, the single-period budget constraint consists of numerous segments, each corresponding to a different marginal rate of tax, with $w(k)$ referring to the value of the real wage *after taxes* on the kth budget line segment [where $w(k) > w(k+1)$ provided the marginal tax rate rises with income].

assumed to be random. If so, and if all individuals work at some point in their lives, then, as Heckman (1978) notes, one may estimate the parameters of (31) by simply replacing h, which refers to *lifetime* participation and is unobservable (or quite difficult to observe), with Z, i.e. a measure of participation *as of a given date*. In general, Z is easily measured: in aggregate time-series or cross-section data, Z would be a labor force participation rate; in microdata, Z would be a binary indicator variable denoting labor force participation or nonparticipation. In either case, then, in the absence of transitory factors, estimates of

$$Z = Z[w(k), R] + \text{error term} \tag{32}$$

serve as estimates of (31) and can be used to retrieve conventional income and substitution effects on labor supply. That is, given estimates of the parameters of (32), one can calculate the uncompensated effect of permanent wage change on labor supply as $\mathrm{d}Z[w(k), R]/\mathrm{d}[w(k)]$, and the income (more precisely, initial wealth) effect as $\{\mathrm{d}Z[w(k), R]/\mathrm{d}R\}Z$.

However, several serious difficulties stand in the way of this approach. Some of the difficulties are practical ones. For example, estimation of (32) requires a measure of the "marginal wage" $w(k)$ rather than of the wage prevailing as of the date referenced by the Z variable; and as (29) implies, to determine which period's wage is in fact the marginal wage, one will need information on at least part of the entire stream of wages over the life cycle. In other words, although one does not need data on lifetime labor supply to estimate (32), one does have to be able to determine which particular wage rate – of all the wages the individual will earn during her lifetime – happens to be the marginal wage rate [in the sense of (29)].

In addition to this practical problem, estimation of (32) must confront an analytical issue: using estimates of (32) to obtain measures of substitution and income effects is appropriate only when all individuals' lifetime labor supply H (or h) is positive, i.e. only when all individuals have an *interior solution* to their lifetime labor supply optimization problem. Although there is considerable controversy about the size of the female population that never works, there is at least some reason for thinking that some women do not, in fact, ever work [Ben-Porath (1973), Boothby (1984), Corcoran (1979), Heckman (1978), Heckman and Willis (1977, 1979), Mincer and Ofek (1979), Stewart and Greenhalgh (1984)]. If so, then analyses of labor force participation at a given date using expressions such as (32) will not provide useful evidence on income and substitution effects [Heckman (1978)].

To see why, note first that (32) is concerned with the probability that a given individual will work at some date t, given a vector of her characteristics X (which would include the sequence of wage rates, the value of R, etc.), which we will write as $\Pr\{H(t) > 0 | X\}$. Now, this probability may be expressed as the product of (i) the probability that this individual will ever work at any date in the life cycle, given her X, which we write as $\Pr\{h>0|X\}$; and (ii) the probability that this individual will work at t given her X *and* given that she works at some point in the life cycle, which we write as $\Pr\{H(t)>0|X,\ h>0\}$. Thus,

$$\Pr\{H(t)>0|X\}=\Pr\{h>0|X\}\Pr\{H(t)>0|X,h>0\}. \tag{33}$$

If the timing of participation over the life cycle is indeed "random" (or "random, leaving aside transitory factors"), then

$$\Pr\{H(t)>0|X,h>0\}=\mathrm{E}\{h|X,h>0\}, \tag{34}$$

where $\mathrm{E}\{x|y\}$ is the conditional expectation of x given y. (34) says that, under the randomness assumption, the probability that someone will work in any particular period t given that she works at some time during the life cycle (and given her X) is simply the proportion of the entire life cycle that she works. By (34), (33) becomes

$$\Pr\{H(t)>0|X\}=\Pr\{h>0|X\}\mathrm{E}\{h|X,h>0\}. \tag{35}$$

If everyone does work at some point in the life cycle, then $\Pr\{h>0|X\}=1$ and $\mathrm{E}\{h|X,h>0\}=\mathrm{E}\{h|X\}$, so (35) becomes

$$\Pr\{H(t)>0|X\}=\mathrm{E}\{h|X\}. \tag{36}$$

In this case, then, estimates of (32) – which is equivalent to the left-hand side of (36) – will indeed provide measures of theoretical substitution and income effects [which underly the right-hand side of (36)]. However, note also that if some individuals *never* work, labor force behavior at any date t is described by (33), *not* (36); and that in general the partial derivatives of the right-hand side of (33) with respect to W/P and R/P will not provide useful information about substitution and income effects because they will not be equivalent to the partial derivatives of the right-hand side of (36) with respect to the same variables.

It is worth noting at this point that – contrary to what has sometimes been asserted or conjectured – lifetime labor supply in this model, as given by expressions such as (31), *cannot* usually be written as a function of a "permanent wage" (or, alternatively, as a function of both "permanent" and "transitory" wages). Moreover, this model does not readily yield an expression for hours worked in any given period t, $H(t)$. To proceed further, it is helpful to use the formal model of life cycle behavior with exogenous wages summarized by Pencavel in Chapter 1 of this Handbook (note that we discuss endogenous wages in Section 3.2.2 below). That model explicitly considers $D+1$ distinct periods (e.g. "years") during the life cycle, with D assumed known and fixed, and specifies lifetime utility U as an additively-separable utility function

$$U=\sum_{t=0}^{D}(1+s)^{-t}u[C(t),L(t)], \tag{37}$$

where $C(t)$ and $L(t)$ are the individual's consumption of a composite good and leisure, respectively, in period t; s is the individual's subjective rate of time preference; and $u[\cdot]$ is the strictly concave single-period utility function. [Note that this is more general than (26) in that leisure times (or consumer goods) at different dates are not assumed to be perfect substitutes.] Lifetime utility is maximized subject to a lifetime budget constraint.

$$A(0)+\sum_{t=0}^{D}(1+r)^{-t}[W(t)H(t)-P(t)C(t)]\geq 0, \tag{38}$$

where $A(0)$ is the individual's initial asset holdings; r is the market rate of interest; and $P(t)$, $W(t)$ and $H(t)$ are the price level, wage rate and hours of work, respectively, during period t.[15] Now form the Lagrangian

$$L=\sum_{t=0}^{D}(1+s)^{-t}u[C(t),L(t)] + v\left\{A(0)+\sum_{t=0}^{D}(1+r)^{-t}[W(t)H(t)-P(t)C(t)]\right\}. \tag{39}$$

where v is a Lagrange multiplier, and obtain the first-order conditions for a

[15] We ignore bequests, and so the utility function (32) assumes that the only activities that affect utility are consumption and leisure. However, it is straightforward to allow for bequests by, for example, adding a *bequest function* $B[A(D)]$ to the right-hand side of (38), where $A(D)$ is the assets the individual has not spent as of the time of death, $t=D$. Note that (38) is separable in time, so that consumption or leisure at any date t does not affect the marginal utility of consumption or leisure at any *other* date t'. This assumption of intertemporal separability is fairly innocuous in many applications, but it does entail several rather specific behavioral assumptions. The main assumption implicit in intertemporal separability as specified in (38) is that, if leisure times at all dates are normal goods, then leisure times at different dates must be net substitutes (in the income-compensated or lifetime-utility-constant sense). See Brown and Deaton (1972, pp. 1165–1167) and Deaton (1974). Note also that the budget constraint (39), like the utility function (38), ignores bequests. In this case, (39) holds as an equality [see, for example, (42c)]. In the presence of bequests, (39) will usually hold as an inequality, with assets at the end of life $A(D)$ constituting the individual's bequest.

constrained maximum:

$$(1+s)^{-t}u_C(t) - v(1+r)^{-t}P(t) = 0,$$

$$(1+s)^{-t}u_L(t) - v(1+r)^{-t}W(t) \geq 0, \quad \text{with} > \rightarrow H(t) = 0,$$

$$A(0) + \sum_{t=0}^{D} (1+r)^{-t}[W(t)H(t) - P(t)C(t)] = 0,$$

where $u_i(t)$ is the partial derivative of the period-t utility function u with respect to i ($= C(t)$ or $L(t)$). Note that the second of these equations allows for the possibility that the individual may not work in period t, i.e. for a corner solution during at least part of the life cycle. Note also that v (which may be interpreted as the marginal utility of initial assets at the individual's optimum) is endogenous to the individual just like the $C(t)$ and $L(t)$; and that the value of v is determined along with the $D+1$ values of the $C(t)$ and the $D+1$ values of the $L(t)$ by solving the $2(D+1)+1$ equations above in terms of the exogenous givens of the model: the set of wage rates $W(t)$ and prices $P(t)$ and the level of initial assets, $A(0)$. Thus, when $A(0)$ or the $W(t)$ or $P(t)$ change, v as well as the $L(t)$ and $C(t)$ will change.

Next, to simplify notation, define

$$v(t) = [(1+r)/(1+s)]^{-t}v, \tag{40}$$

where $v(t)$ may be defined as the marginal utility of assets at period t, so as to rewrite the above first order conditions more compactly:

$$u_C(t) - v(t)P(t) = 0, \tag{41a}$$

$$u_L(t) - v(t)W(t) \geq 0, \quad \text{with} > \rightarrow H(t) = 0, \tag{41b}$$

$$A(0) + \sum_{t=0}^{D} (1+r)^{-t}[W(t)H(t) - P(t)C(t)] = 0. \tag{41c}$$

Thus far, our discussion has been concerned with equilibrium dynamics, i.e. with the characteristics of a given individual's lifetime equilibrium plan for her *sequence* of labor supply, leisure time and consumption values $H(t)$, $L(t)$ and $C(t)$ for $t = 0,1,\dots, D$, and for her shadow value of (initial) assets v. [Note also that (41) immediately yields $v(t)$ for $t = 1,2,\dots, D$ once v has been determined.] This equilibrium plan is formulated for a given *set* of wage rates and price levels $W(t)$ and $P(t)$, $t = 0,1,\dots, D$, and for a given initial asset level $A(0)$. To see how the equilibrium plans of *different* individuals will differ as a result of their facing a different $A(0)$ or a different set of $W(t)$, it is necessary to consider the comparative dynamics of the model, i.e. to analyze the way in which changes in exogenous variables such as the $W(t)$ lead to differences in choices [e.g. differences in v, $L(t)$ and $H(t)$].

In working out the model's comparative dynamics, we assume for the time being that equilibrium entails a lifetime interior solution, with positive hours of work $H(t)$ for all t. (We relax this assumption later, however.) Then one may write (41b) as an equality and solve the system (41a)–(41b) for $C(t)$ and $L(t)$ in terms of $v(t)P(t)$ and $v(t)W(t)$:

$$C(t) = C[v(t)P(t), v(t)W(t)], \tag{42a}$$

$$L(t) = L[v(t)W(t), v(t)P(t)]. \tag{42b}$$

These are often called "marginal utility of wealth-constant" or "Frisch" demand functions for C and L [Browning, Deaton and Irish (1985)].

Next, write (41b) as an equality and totally differentiate (41a)–(41b) to obtain:

$$\begin{aligned} \mathrm{d}C(t) &= \mathrm{d}[v(t)P(t)][u_{LL}(t)/\mathrm{d}(t)] - \mathrm{d}[v(t)W(t)][u_{CL}(t)/\mathrm{d}(t)] \\ &= \mathrm{d}P(t)\{[u_{LL}(t)v(t)]/\mathrm{d}(t)\} - \mathrm{d}W(t)\{[u_{CL}(t)v(t)]/\mathrm{d}(t)\} \\ &\quad + \mathrm{d}v(t)\{[u_{LL}(t)P(t) - u_{CL}(t)W(t)]/\mathrm{d}(t)\}, \end{aligned} \tag{43a}$$

$$\begin{aligned} \mathrm{d}L(t) &= \mathrm{d}[v(t)W(t)][u_{CC}(t)/\mathrm{d}(t)] - \mathrm{d}[v(t)P(t)][u_{CL}(t)/\mathrm{d}(t)] \\ &= \mathrm{d}W(t)\{[u_{CC}(t)v(t)]/\mathrm{d}(t)\} - \mathrm{d}P(t)\{[u_{CL}(t)v(t)]/\mathrm{d}(t)\} \\ &\quad + \mathrm{d}v(t)\{[u_{CC}(t)W(t) - u_{CL}(t)P(t)]/\mathrm{d}(t)\}, \end{aligned} \tag{43b}$$

where $u_{ij}(t)$, $i, j = C(t), L(t)$, is a second partial derivative of the period-t utility function u with respect to i and j; and $\mathrm{d}(t) = u_{CC}(t)u_{LL}(t) - u_{CL}(t)^2 > 0$ by concavity of u. The terms in braces that are multiplied times $\mathrm{d}v(t)$ in eqs. (43) are negative provided $C(t)$ and $L(t)$, respectively, are normal goods in the static one-period sense;[16] the terms in (43a) and (43b) that are multiplied times $\mathrm{d}P(t)$ and $\mathrm{d}W(t)$, respectively, are both negative by concavity of u.

Equations (43) show how differences in $v(t)$, $W(t)$ and $P(t)$ at any given date t lead to differences in consumption and leisure at that date. They can also be used to show how a difference in $W(t)$ *with* $v(t')$ *and* $P(t')$ *constant* will affect $a(t') = W(t')H(t') - P(t')C(t')$, the net increment to wealth made at any time

[16] By "normal in the static sense", we mean that if the individual were forced to maximize *single-period* utility u (instead of lifetime utility U) subject to the conventional *single-period* budget constraint $P(t)C(t) = W(t)H(t) + R(t)$, where $R(t)$ and $W(t)$ are exogenous income and the wage rate, then the income effects on $C(t)$ and $L(t)$ of a change in $R(t)$ would be proportional to $-[u_C u_{LL} - u_L u_{CL}]$ and $-[u_L u_{CC} - u_C u_{CL}]$, respectively. For example, see Cohen, Rea and Lerman (1970, esp. pp. 184–186).

t': by (43) [with $\mathrm{d}v(t') = \mathrm{d}P(t') = 0$],

$$\begin{aligned} \mathrm{d}a(t)/\mathrm{d}W(t) &= \mathrm{d}[W(t)H(t) - P(t)C(t)]/\mathrm{d}W(t) \\ &= H(t) - W(t)[\mathrm{d}L(t)/\mathrm{d}W(t)] - P(t)[\mathrm{d}C(t)/\mathrm{d}W(t)] \\ &= H(t) + Y_{LV}(t), \end{aligned} \tag{44a}$$

$$\mathrm{d}a(t')/\mathrm{d}W(t) = 0, \quad t' \neq t, \tag{44b}$$

where $Y_{LV}(t) = \{[u_C(t)u_{LC}(t) - u_L(t)u_{CC}(t)]/\mathrm{d}(t)\}$ and is positive provided leisure at t is normal in the static sense. Thus, *with $v(t)$ and $P(t)$ constant*, an increase in $W(t)$ will increase period t's addition to net worth provided $L(t)$ is normal; but so long as $v(s)$ and $P(s)$ are constant, an increase in $W(t)$ will not affect additions made at any other date $s = t$.

However, as noted above, a change in $W(t)$ will change not only $L(t)$ and $C(t)$ but also v [and thus, by (40), $v(t)$]: v and $v(t)$ are choice variables, just like $L(t)$ and $C(t)$. For example, it is intuitively plausible that, ceteris paribus, someone who enjoys a higher wage at any date t will feel better off and thus will have a lower v [and so, by (40), a lower $v(t)$ for *all* t] – that is, will regard assets as less "precious" or "scarce", and will begin to spend assets more freely. Indeed, as (44a) indicates, *unless* such a high-$W(t)$ individual changes her v [relative to the v chosen by a low-$W(t)$ individual], she will accumulate "excess assets", thereby violating the budget constraint (41c). Since there are no bequests (by assumption: see footnote 15) and since "you can't take it with you", that cannot be optimal. The appropriate response to higher $W(t)$ is to reduce v [and thus, by (40), to reduce $v(t)$ for *all* t]. To see why, consider the effect on $a(t)$ of increasing $v(t)$, ceteris paribus, as given by eqs. (43):

$$\begin{aligned} \mathrm{d}a(t)/\mathrm{d}v(t) &= -W(t)[\mathrm{d}L(t)/\mathrm{d}v(t)] - P(t)[\mathrm{d}C(t)/\mathrm{d}v(t)] \\ &= \{-W(t)^2 u_{CC}(t) - P(t)^2 u_{LL}(t) \\ &\quad + 2W(t)P(t)u_{CL}(t)\}/\mathrm{d}(t), \end{aligned} \tag{45}$$

which is positive by concavity of u. Thus, *reducing* v – which will reduce $v(t)$, by (40) – will reduce $a(t)$, thereby offsetting the increase in $a(t)$ associated with the ceteris paribus effects of the increase in $W(t)$ as given by (44). Hence, other things being equal, a greater $W(t)$ does indeed entail a lower v:

$$\mathrm{d}v/\mathrm{d}W(t) < 0. \tag{46a}$$

Moreover, by (40) and (46a), a higher $W(t)$ also entails a lower $v(t')$ at *all* dates

$t', t'=0,1,\ldots,t,\ldots,D$:

$$\begin{aligned} \mathrm{d}v(t')/\mathrm{d}W(t) &= [\mathrm{d}v(t')/\mathrm{d}v][\mathrm{d}v/\mathrm{d}W(t)] \\ &= [(1+r)/(1+s)]^{-t'}[\mathrm{d}v/\mathrm{d}W(t)] < 0. \end{aligned} \tag{46b}$$

Finally, (43b) and (46b) imply that the lower $v(t')$ at all dates t' caused by the greater $W(t)$ will increase leisure $L(t')$ at all t', provided $L(t')$ is normal in the static sense:

$$\begin{aligned} \mathrm{d}L(t')/\mathrm{d}W(t) &= [\mathrm{d}L(t')/\mathrm{d}v(t')][\mathrm{d}v(t')/\mathrm{d}W(t)] \\ &= \{[W(t')u_{CC}(t') - P(t')u_{CL}(t')]/\mathrm{d}(t')\} \\ &\quad \times [\mathrm{d}v(t')/\mathrm{d}W(t)], \end{aligned} \tag{47}$$

which is positive provided $L(t')$ is normal.

In sum, a greater value of $W(t)$ leads "directly," *with v constant*, to lower $L(t)$ and greater $H(t)$; that may be called the *v-constant* or Frisch effect of the greater $W(t)$, and is given by the first term after the second equals sign in (43b). However, if all leisure times and consumer goods are normal, then the greater $W(t)$ also leads to a smaller v, which leads "indirectly", *with v changing*, to greater $L(t)$ and smaller $H(t)$; that may be called the *v-variable* effect of the greater $W(t)$, and is given (for $t'=t$) by (47).

Thus, variation in the wage at any given date may have consequences not only at that date but also at other dates. Since Mincer (1962), many writers have focused on the labor supply effects of specific kinds of wage changes – "permanent" and "transitory". Their discussions raise both practical and conceptual issues that have rarely been tackled rigorously. Two seem particularly important. First, how should permanent and transitory wages (or wage changes) actually be defined? To our knowledge, this question has rarely been addressed formally. However, informal discussions seem ultimately to adopt essentially the same definition: the permanent wage W_P is defined as the present value of the stream of the individual's future wage rates $W(t)$ from period $t=0$ to period $t=D$, the age of death, so that

$$W_P = \sum_{t=0}^{D} (1+r)^{-t} W(t). \tag{48a}$$

Thus the transitory wage at t is the difference between the actual wage $W(t)$ and the permanent wage W_P:

$$w(t) = W(t) - W_P. \tag{48b}$$

This raises a second, practical, issue: since researchers rarely if ever have access to data on the entire set of future wage rates of any individual, how should (how can) the permanent wage actually be measured? As far as we can tell, each researcher who has considered this question has answered it differently; by and large, empirical measures of the permanent wage are constructed using essentially ad hoc procedures and depend to a considerable extent on the nature of the data that are available.

The final issue about permanent and transitory wages that has been discussed in the literature – again, not very rigorously – concerns whether transitory as well as permanent wage variation affects labor supply (e.g. hours of work, participation). In one view, which we will call "PO" for short, hours of work and labor force participation in any period t depend on the permanent wage *only*, apparently by analogy with Friedman's (1957) permanent income theory of consumption (according to which consumption depends on permanent, but not transitory, income). Thus, according to the PO hypothesis, one need not include the transitory wage $w(t)$ on the right hand side of expressions such as (32); alternatively, if $w(t)$ is included in such an expression, its coefficient will not be statistically different from zero.

The PO hypothesis has a rival, however, according to which one should include not only the permanent wage but also the transitory wage in estimating equations such as (32). In this alternative view, which we will call "PT" for short, changes in the permanent wage entail changes in both lifetime earning power and the opportunity cost of time, and therefore entail both substitution and income effects; whereas a transitory wage change at some date t does affect the opportunity cost of time at that date, and therefore generates a substitution effect, even though it does not entail any change in long-run earning power (and therefore does not generate an income effect). Thus, according to the PT hypothesis, one should include $w(t)$ as well as W_{P} in estimating expressions such as (32); moreover, the hypothesis implies that the coefficient on $w(t)$ will be positive and algebraically larger than the coefficient on W_{P}, since the latter represents the sum of a positive substitution effect and a negative income effect whereas the former represents a positive substitution effect only.[17]

Fortunately, it is straightforward to evaluate the rival hypotheses about permanent and transitory wages offered by PO and PT. Imagine two women, A and B, with the same permanent wage [as defined by (48a)] and identical in all other respects save one: their wage rates at two different dates, t^* and t', are different, so that their transitory wages at these two dates [$w(t^*)$ and $w(t')$, respectively]

[17]For studies that adopt PO, see Kalachek and Raines (1970) and Watts, Poirier and Mallar (1977). For studies that adopt PT, see Kalachek, Mellow and Raines (1978, p. 357) and Lillard (1978, p. 369); note that Mincer (1962, p. 68) contends that "'transitory' variation in variables [will favor] particular timing" of labor force participation, and thus implicitly adopts PT. For further discussion, see Killingsworth (1983, esp. pp. 286–296), who refers to PO and PT as "PT-1" and "PT-2," respectively.

are also different. Will these transitory wage differences lead to labor supply differences? If so, how will these two kinds of differences be related?

Let $dW(t^*)$ and $dW(t')$ denote the difference between A's and B's wage rates at t^* and at t', respectively. By (48) and the fact that A and B have the same permanent wage,

$$(1+r)^{-t^*}dW(t^*)+(1+r)^{-t'}dW(t')=0. \tag{49a}$$

For ease of reference, assume that $dW(t^*)>0$, i.e. A's wage is greater than B's at t^*. Then, by the above,

$$dW(t')=-(1+r)^{-(t^*-t')}dW(t^*)<0. \tag{49b}$$

Without loss of generality, let B's wage at both t' and t^* be equal to the permanent wage, W_P. By (48) and the assumption that the two women have the same permanent wage, this simply means that A has a positive transitory wage at t^* and a negative transitory wage at t'. Recall also that, by assumption, A and B are otherwise identical (e.g. both receive the same wage at all dates other than t' and t^*, have the same initial assets $A(0)$, etc.).

By (41c), (44) and (49), the v-constant effect of A's transitory wages at t^* and t' on the present value of her asset accumulation is

$$\begin{aligned} dz &= (1+r)^{-t^*}[da(t^*)/dW(t^*)]dW(t^*) \\ &\quad +(1+r)^{-t'}[da(t')/dW(t')]dW(t') \\ &= (1+r)^{-t^*}dW(t^*)\{H(t^*)+Y_{LV}(t^*)-H(t')-Y_{LV}(t')\}. \end{aligned} \tag{50}$$

That is, if A had the same value of v as B, the fact that her wage stream differs from B's – even though only in transitory respects – would mean that her life cycle asset accumulation would not be the same as B's [except for the special case in which the expression after either equals sign in (50) is zero]. In other words, even though they have the same permanent wage and initial assets, A will not be able to satisfy (41c) at the same value of v used by B. In general, then, A's value of v will differ from B's. By (45), A's value of v will be higher or lower than B's depending on whether the expression after either equals sign in (50) is negative or positive. If leisure is a normal good in the static sense, then, by (43b), the difference in v values will entail a negative or positive v-variable effect on on A's leisure time (relative to B's) at *all* dates t, including not only t^* and t' but all other dates as well. Moreover, by (43b), A's positive (negative) transitory wage at t^* (t') will have a negative (positive) v-constant effect on A's leisure time, relative to B's, at t^* (t').

In general, then, even transitory wage differences *will* lead to differences in leisure and labor supply – contrary to PO. Likewise, although A's positive transitory wage $dW(t^*)$ has a positive v-constant effect on her labor supply (relative to B's) at t^*, it will also have either a positive or a negative v-variable effect on her labor supply (relative to B's) at t^*, depending on the sign of the right-hand side of (50). Thus, on balance, labor supply and transitory wages at any given date such as t^* need not be positively correlated, even if other things (the permanent wage, initial asset level, etc.) remain the same – contrary to PT.

Thus far our discussion has assumed a lifetime interior solution for labor supply. However, the analysis carries over to the case of corner solutions without essential modification. The main caveat relevant to this case is the obvious one that changes in wages cannot have v-constant *or* v-variable effects on labor supply during any period t'' in which hours of work are zero.

For example, consider again our two workers, A and B, and this time suppose that (i) B works during t' but not during t^*; (ii) A and B have the same "permanent wage" as defined by (37), and (iii) A has a negative (positive) transitory wage at t' (t^*), as given by (49b). Thus, B has $L(t') < T$, $L(t^*) = T$ and, by (41a)–(41b), also has

$$u_L[C(t'), L(t')]/u_C[C(t'), L(t')] = W(t')/P(t'), \tag{51a}$$

$$u_L[C(t^*), T]/u_C[C(t^*), T] \geq W(t^*)/P(t^*). \tag{51b}$$

Now consider A's behavior. If her positive transitory deviation $dW(t^*)$ is sufficiently large, the inequality (51b) will not hold for her: that is, her wage at t^* may exceed her reservation wage [given by the left-hand side of (51b)], and she will work. In this case, A will be a labor force participant whereas B is not, even though both women have the same permanent wage – a contradiction of PO.

What if A's wage is not large enough to reverse the inequality (51b), so that A, like B, will not work at t^*? At time t', A has a negative transitory wage. However, contrary to PT, there is no reason why A must necessarily work fewer hours than B, or be more likely not to be a labor force participant.

To see why, note that if A's $L(t^*)$ is equal to T despite her transitory increase $dW(t^*)$, then this $dW(t^*)$ has no effect on $v(t^*)$ or $v(t')$. By (43a) and the assumption that $u_{CL} = 0$, A's $C(t')$ depends only on $v(t')$. By (43b), A's negative transitory wage $dW(t')$ raises her leisure at t' via the usual v-constant effect. However, the increase in $L(t')$ also reduces the asset accumulation A makes at t', $a(t')$, and this *reduces* $L(t')$ via the usual v-variable effect. In other words, the version of (50) relevant to A in this case is

$$dz = (1+r)^{-t'} dW(t')\{H(t') + Y_{LV}(t')\}. \tag{52}$$

Since $\mathrm{d}W(t') < 0$, $\mathrm{d}z$ is negative provided leisure at t^* is normal in the static sense. By (45), A will therefore have a higher v [i.e. will now act as if assets had a greater (shadow) value, so as to avoid having a negative net worth at or before death]. Hence, by (43b), the increase in $v(t')$ also has a negative v-variable effect on A's leisure at t' that may offset the positive v-constant or "direct" effect on $L(t')$ resulting from the $\mathrm{d}W(t') < 0$. Thus, here, as in other cases, it is not possible to gauge the net effect on A's leisure of a wage change. In particular, the negative transitory wage could lead either to less *or* more leisure.

Likewise, the negative transitory wage could lead either to a smaller *or* a greater probability of being a labor force participant. By (43a), the increase in $v(t')$ will have a negative v-variable effect on $C(t')$. Other things being equal, this *raises* the marginal utility of consumption and so *reduces* the reservation wage $u_L[C(t'),T]/u_C[C(t'),T]$ by an amount given by

$$\{-u_{CC}[C(t'),T](u_L[C(t'),T]/u_C[C(t'),T])+u_{LC}[C(t'),T]\} \\ \times\{1/u_C[C(t'),T]\}\{\mathrm{d}C(t')/\mathrm{d}v(t')\}, \tag{53}$$

where the first term in braces is positive provided leisure is a normal good in the static sense, the second term in braces is always positive and the third term is negative by (44a). Hence, the reservation wage falls as the offered wage falls; there is no particular reason to suppose that the decrease in $W(t')$ must be associated with a greater likelihood of nonparticipation.

In sum, the analysis of this section leads to a number of conclusions about dynamic labor supply analysis. Some are negative: for example, the analysis shows why the distinction between permanent and transitory wages embodied in eqs. (48) is not particularly useful from a theoretical standpoint. Other conclusions are more constructive, however. First, as a number of writers [e.g. Browning, Deaton, and Irish (1985), Heckman and MaCurdy (1980) Pencavel, Chapter 1 in this Handbook] have observed, the Frisch demand functions (42) provide a useful alternative to the kind of permanent–transitory approach embodied in eqs. (48). Indeed, in the Frisch framework, the marginal utility of assets (our v) constitutes a kind of "permanent wage"; and variations in the *observed* wage $W(t)$, *with v constant*, constitute a kind of "transitory" wage variation [since, with v constant, differences in $W(t)$ are always negatively correlated with differences in $L(t)$, by (41b)].

Although these concepts are relevant to dynamic labor supply in general, two implications of the Frisch framework seem especially useful for understanding female labor supply. The first concerns an important difference between the conventional static model and the dynamic exogenous-wage model. In the former, the reservation wage is independent of the real market wage rate W/P. In contrast, in the latter, the reservation wage in any given period is in general a function of all wage rates. To see why, note from eqs. (41) that, in the dynamic case, the reservation wage is given by

$$u_L[C(t),T]/u_C[C(t),T] = u_L[C(t),T]/v(t)P(t). \tag{54}$$

Moreover, as indicated above, $v(t)$ is in general a function of all wage rates [recall, for example, eqs. (46)]. This has somewhat unsettling implications about the merits of simple intuition derived from static labor supply models. For example, in such models, a higher current wage must always entail a greater probability of participation: a greater current wage does not affect the shadow or reservation wage but does affect the market opportunities against which home uses of time are compared. In contrast, in dynamic models, a higher current wage need not entail a greater participation probability: especially if wages are positively serially correlated, a higher current wage implies a generally higher wage *profile* (i.e. greater wages during *all* periods), and hence a lower v – which, other things being equal, tends to reduce (the probability of) participation. As Heckman (1978, p. 205) notes, this is relevant to findings by Olsen (1977) and Smith (1977a), according to which, among certain demographic groups, *lower* wage women are *more likely* to participate in the labor force: "It is significant that the 'perverse' association between wage rates and participation status is found in demographic groups with the greatest volume of lifetime labor supply – such as married black women. It is in such groups that income effects [from a higher wage profile] are likely to be the largest."

We conclude this discussion of dynamic exogenous-wage labor supply models by returning briefly to Mincer's (1962) pioneering work. Although it stimulated many subsequent attempts to develop a workable distinction between permanent and transitory wages, it is ironic that Mincer's paper itself was concerned with dividing not *wages* but rather the *income of other family members* into permanent and transitory components. In effect, Mincer was interested in a situation in which the individual receives an exogenous amount (possibly zero) of income in each period t, $Z(t)$, from sources other than work *or* assets. Can this $Z(t)$ be divided into permanent and transitory components, as Mincer contended? If so, how?

To introduce such income, it is necessary[18] to modify the budget constraint, (38) or (41c), which now must be written

$$A(0) + \sum_{t=0}^{D} (1+r)^{-t}[Z(t) + W(t)H(t) - P(t)C(t)] = 0. \tag{55}$$

[18] If $Z(t)$ is to be interpreted as the income of other family members, as Mincer (1962) interprets it, it is necessary to assume that there are no intrafamily cross-substitution effects of the kind discussed in Section 3.1. [In that case, earnings of other family members are analytically equivalent to exogenous income, because they entail income effects only, without (cross-) substitution effects.]

Since the $Z(t)$ are assumed exogenous, it is clear that their introduction does not entail any substantive change in the foregoing analysis. On the one hand, because the analysis implicitly assumes perfect foresight, the present value of the $Z(t)$ can be combined with initial assets $A(0)$ to rewrite the budget constraint still further:

$$A(0)' + \sum_{t=0}^{D} (1+r)^{-t}[W(t)H(t) - P(t)C(t)] = 0, \tag{56}$$

where

$$A(0)' = A(0) + \sum_{t=0}^{D} (1+r)^{-t}Z(t). \tag{57}$$

Clearly, none of the analysis of this section is thereby changed; all that is necessary is to note that $A(0)'$, not $A(0)$, is now the relevant "initial assets" variable. However, one can instead proceed as Mincer implicitly did, defining a permanent (exogenous) income variable Z_P as the amount of an annuity Z_P that, when received each period from $t = 0$ to $t = D$, would have a present value equal to the present value of the $Z(t)$. That is, permanent income satisfies the relation

$$\sum_{t=0}^{D} (1+r)^{-t}Z_P = \sum_{t=0}^{D} (1+r)^{-t}Z(t),$$

so that permanent and transitory income are given by

$$Z_P = \sum_{t=0}^{D} (1+r)^{-t}Z(t) \Big/ \sum_{t=0}^{D} (1+r)^{-t} \tag{58a}$$

$$z(t) = Z(t) - Z_P, \tag{58b}$$

respectively. So (41c) [or (55), or its equivalent] may *also* be written as

$$A(0) + \sum_{t=0}^{D} (1+r)^{-t}[Z_P + W(t)H(t) - P(t)C(t)] = 0. \tag{59}$$

Thus, Mincer's approach does not suffer from the difficulties inherent in attempts to divide wages into permanent and transitory components. As (55) and (59) indicate, one can write the budget constraint in terms of either actual exogenous income $Z(t)$ *or* "permanent" exogenous income Z_P. Moreover, (55), (58) and (59) show that behavior depends on permanent exogenous income only and *not* on "transitory" income $z(t)$, as Mincer (1962) in effect argued.

All this notwithstanding, many writers came to think of Mincer's permanent–transitory distinction as referring to wage rates as well as (or even instead of) exogenous income. Ironically, in the flurry of subsequent work aimed at measuring and estimating the effects of permanent and transitory wage rates, a different but closely related notion of Mincer's concerning the role of credit market constraints in labor supply decisions, was completely overlooked. As Mincer (1962, pp. 74–75) put it:

> According to [the permanent income] theory, aggregate family consumption is determined even in short periods by long-run levels of family income. Adjustment between planned consumption and income received in the short period of observation (current, or measured income) takes place via saving behavior, that is, via changes in assets in debts. However, if assets are low or not liquid, and access to the capital market costly or nonexistent, it might be preferable to make the adjustment to a drop on the family income on the money income side rather than on the money expenditure side. This is so because consumption requiring money expenditures may contain elements of short-run inflexibility such as contractual commitments. The greater short-run flexibility of nonmoney items of consumption (leisure, home production) may also be a cultural characteristic of a money economy. Under these conditions, a transitory increase in labor force participation of the wife may well be an alternative to dissaving, asset decumulation or increasing debt.

An obvious implication of this argument is that transitory as well as permanent components of exogenous income may affect labor supply in the presence of credit market constraints, short-run inflexibility of consumption commitments, etc. However, in general [for a few exceptions, see Johnson (1983) and Lundberg (1985)], little has been done to analyze these or other, related, ideas raised by Mincer's discussion. This is unfortunate, for such analysis may enhance understanding not only of purely microeconomic issues, but even of macroeconomic problems as well.

3.2.2. Dynamic labor supply models with endogenous wages

The notion that wages depend on labor supply (as well as the reverse) has long played an important role in research. The most obvious example concerns discussions of women's wages and of sex differentials in wages, in which labor supply – e.g. the consequences of intermittent or continuous participation in the job market – and human capital investment decisions are usually seen as playing a crucial role [for example, see Mincer and Polachek (1974)].

This being the case, someone who is looking at the life cycle literature for the first time, with an eye to what insights it can provide about the two-way relation between women's wages and labor supply, is likely to come away from that literature feeling somewhat disappointed. Formal theoretical life cycle models of the joint determination of labor supply and wages are generally quite abstract and provide little immediate insight into the dynamics of women's work and wages; for example, not infrequently such models assume an interior life cycle solution for labor supply (i.e. positive hours of work at each point in the life cycle), thereby ignoring the discontinuities in labor force participation that figure so prominently in discussions of women's wages. Empirical work on such dynamic issues has in general either implicitly [Mincer and Polachek (1974)] or explicitly [Heckman and MaCurdy (1980, 1982)] ignored the behavioral linkage between women's work and wages in a life cycle setting [for a recent exception, see Zabalza and Arrufat (1983)].

However, it may be that these difficulties are not really as serious as they seem at first glance. Even relatively simple and quite abstract life cycle models can yield at least some insight into the joint determination of women's work effort and wage rates. Moreover, models of the kind usually found in the literature may be made more concrete and directly applicable to female labor supply. To illustrate both points, we set up a conventional life cycle model modified so as to include a time-varying taste shifter $m(t)$. In our framework, a large (or growing) $m(t)$ denotes a large (or growing) taste for leisure time. It therefore serves as a simple means of representing explicitly (if quite crudely) in a formal analytical model a notion that has figured prominently in informal discussions of women's work and wages over the life cycle: that for a variety of reasons – biological, cultural, etc. – any given woman's desire for "leisure" (nonmarket time for childbirth and childrearing, for example) may first increase and then decrease over time. Of at least equal importance, however, is another rationale for introducing such a taste shifter: that, at any given date, different women will for a variety of reasons have different preferences for such leisure.

We begin by considering the formal structure of a model of an individual woman's life cycle.[19] We assume that she acts as if she enjoyed perfect foresight. Her earnings at any date t, $E(t)$, are given by

$$E(t) = E[H(t), K(t)], \tag{60}$$

where $H(t)$ is her hours of work at time t and $K(t)$ is her stock of "earning power" or "human capital" at t. Let the rate of change of $K(t)$, $\dot{K}(t)$, be given by the stock-flow relation

$$\dot{K}(t) = i[I(t), G(t), K(t)] - qK(t), \tag{61}$$

[19]For general discussion of dynamic endogenous-wage models, see Weiss (Chapter 11 in this Handbook) and McCabe (1983).

where $I(t)$ and $G(t)$ are time and goods, respectively, devoted to increasing one's earning power (to "human capital accumulation") at date t; where inclusion of $K(t)$ in the i or "gross investment" function implies that K is an input into its own production; and where q represents the rate of decay, depreciation or obsolescence of K. As just noted, we use a dot over a variable to denote its rate of change over time; thus, $\dot{X}(t) = \mathrm{d}X(t)/\mathrm{d}t$ for any variable X; note that for convenience, we now switch from the discrete-time approach of Section 3.2.1 to continuous time.

The dynamic or lifetime utility function may now be written

$$U = \int_0^D \mathrm{e}^{-st} u[C(t), m(t)L(t), K(t)]\,\mathrm{d}t, \tag{62}$$

where $m(t)$ is the taste shifter described earlier. This specifies lifetime utility U as the present value (discounted at the rate, s, at which the individual subjectively evaluates future amounts) of the stream of utilities u received at each instant t between now (time 0) and the end of life (time D).[20] Inclusion of $K(t)$ in the instantaneous utility function $u[\cdot]$ means that human capital contributes to well-being directly (e.g. helps one use leisure time efficiently) as well as indirectly (i.e. raises earning power). As in Section 3.2.1, we ignore bequests (see footnote 15).

It remains to specify the constraints subject to which lifetime utility, as given by (62), is maximized. The first constraint is that total available time at each moment is fixed at T and is allocated between investment $I(t)$, leisure $L(t)$ and hours of work $H(t)$, so that

$$T = I(t) + L(t) + H(t). \tag{63}$$

The relation between these theoretical constructs and empirically observable variables requires a bit of discussion at this point. The $H(t)$ in (60) and (63) refers to time actually devoted to work. However, in this model time spent *at* work (that is, at one's workplace) can also involve investment time, e.g. on-the-job training. Thus, for persons who have left school, the sum of investment time $I(t)$ and hours *of* work $H(t)$ (= "hours spent actually working") constitutes "labor supply" in the sense in which that term is normally used, i.e. hours spent *at* work. Likewise, the term "wage rate" is generally used to refer to average hourly earnings, i.e. earnings divided by the number of hours spent *at* work. Thus, in terms of the present model, average hourly earnings (= the "observed wage rate"), which as before we will denote by $W(t)$, is equal by definition to

$$W(t) = E(t)/[I(t) + H(t)]. \tag{64}$$

[20] The assumption that the utility function is additively separable in time is primarily just a simplification in the present context, but in other contexts it is not necessarily innocuous [see footnote 15, Hotz, Kydland and Sedlacek (1985) and Johnson and Pencavel (1984)].

The second constraint facing the individual is a dynamic budget constraint, requiring that she at least "break even" over her entire lifetime. For simplicity, we assume that capital markets are perfect, permitting borrowing and lending at market interest rate r. Then the dynamic or lifetime budget constraint may be written as

$$A(D) = A(0) + \int_0^D e^{-rt}[E(t) - P(t)C(t)]\,dt \geq 0. \tag{65}$$

This says that net worth at the end of life, $A(D)$ – i.e. initial wealth, $A(0)$, plus the (discounted) sum of increments to that initial stock made at each moment $t, e^{-rt}[E(t) - P(t)C(t)]$ – must be non-negative.

Further analysis is made somewhat easier by ignoring investment goods $G(t)$ in (61), and is facilitated greatly by introducing a simplification known as the "neutrality" assumption [Heckman (1976a)]. Under this assumption, human capital $K(t)$ acts like Harrod-neutral technical progress by "augmenting" *each* of the individual's inputs of time – leisure, work and investment – *equally*, in the sense that x percent more K would take the place of x percent less of each of L, H and I. Specifically, under the neutrality assumption, eqs. (60)–(62) become

$$E(t) = kH(t)K(t), \tag{66}$$

$$\dot{K}(t) = i[I(t)K(t)] - qK(t), \tag{67}$$

$$U = \int_0^D e^{-st}u[C(t), m(t)L(t)K(t)]\,dt, \tag{68}$$

where k may be thought of as the rental rate of human capital, assumed constant over time in the interest of simplification. In (67) we ignore investment goods $G(t)$, so the resulting human capital production function (or gross investment function) becomes $i[I(t)K(t)]$, with $i' > 0$ and $i'' < 0$ (i.e. i's first and second derivatives are positive and negative, respectively) on the assumption of positive but diminishing returns to IK in the production of (gross) increments to the human capital stock; assume further that $i[0] = 0$, i.e. when no investment occurs ($I = 0$), no gross increments to K are made. The instantaneous utility function u is now $u[C, mLK]$, and is assumed to be concave and increasing in its two arguments, C and mLK. Following Heckman (1976a), we refer to $H(t)K(t)$, $I(t)K(t)$ and $L(t)K(t)$ as effective hours of work, effective investment time and effective leisure, respectively; that is, to work, investment or leisure time as augmented by human capital K.

Letting $v(t)$ and $w(t)$ denote the shadow values (as of time t) of financial assets (A) and of human capital (K), respectively, one may write the first order conditions for a maximum of lifetime utility, (68), as follows:[21]

$$e^{-st}\{u_C(t)-v(t)P(t)\}=0, \tag{69}$$

$$e^{-st}\{v(t)kK(t)-u_L(t)K(t)m(t)\}\leq 0, \quad \text{with} < \rightarrow H(t)=0, \tag{70}$$

$$e^{-st}\{w(t)i'(t)K(t)-u_L(t)K(t)m(t)\}\leq 0, \quad \text{with} < \rightarrow I(t)=0, \tag{71}$$

where $u_j(t)$, $j=C$ or L, is the partial derivative of $u[C(t), m(t)L(t)K(t)]$ with respect to C or mLK; and $u_{jk}(t)$, $k=C$ or L, is the partial derivative of $u_j(t)$ with respect to C or mLK.

Equations (69)–(71) constitute a set of familiar marginal benefit–marginal cost rules. In each, the first term inside the braces is the marginal benefit of a particular activity – consumption, in (69); work, in (70); investment, in (71) – and the second is its marginal cost. In (69), the marginal benefit of consumption is simply its marginal utility; its marginal cost is the pecuniary price $P(t)$ of the consumer good converted into utility units by multiplication times $v(t)$, the shadow or utility value of an added dollar of wealth. In (70), the marginal benefit of work is the marginal utility of the additional earnings it generates [= the dollar amount of hourly earnings, $kK(t)$, converted to utility units by multiplication times $v(t)$], whereas its marginal cost is the marginal utility of leisure (i.e. the utility value of the leisure that must be given up). Finally, the marginal benefit of investment time is the utility value of the increment to the human capital stock caused by investment time [= the marginal product of investment time $I(t)$ in the production of human capital, $i'(t)K(t)$, multiplied times the shadow value of human capital, $w(t)$]; as with work, the marginal cost of investment time is the utility value of the leisure that must be forgone. Note that (70) and (71) allow for corner solutions for work and investment, respectively, in the sense that either activity's marginal cost may be so high relative to its marginal benefit that it may not be undertaken.

In addition to these marginal cost–marginal benefit rules, optimal behavior must satisfy several other requirements. First, by (62), bequests have no utility value, so assets at death must be zero:

$$A(D)=A(0)+\int_0^D e^{-rt}[E(t)-P(t)C(t)]\,dt=0. \tag{72}$$

[21] Formal discussion of endogenous-wage life-cycle models such as the one in the text is perhaps best undertaken as it has usually been undertaken in the literature, using optimal control theory. However, many readers may find control theory unfamiliar, and for us to attempt to familiarize readers with it would take us well beyond the scope of our topic. [For an admirably lucid introduction to the subject, see Arrow and Kurz (1972, ch. 2); for more detailed treatments, see Dixit, (1976) and Takayama (1985, ch. 8).] Accordingly, the discussion here will be intuitive and heuristic.

Second, the initial shadow value of assets, $v(0)$, and the *discounted* shadow value at any later date $t, v(t)$, must be equal, where the discount rate is the difference between the individual's subjective rate of time preference s and the market rate of interest r, i.e.

$$v(0)=\mathrm{e}^{-(s-r)t}v(t). \tag{73a}$$

Note that (73a) implies that

$$\dot{v}(t)=(s-r)v(t). \tag{73b}$$

It also implies that, so long as s and r remain the same, the value of v at any given date $t, v(t)$, will change *only* if $v(0)$ changes.

Finally, the individual equates the shadow value of human capital at any date t to the discounted stream of future benefits (measured in utility units) that would result from having an additional unit of human capital at that date. Specifically, optimal behavior requires

$$\begin{aligned} w(t) &= \int_t^D \mathrm{e}^{-(s+q)(z-t)}\big[m(z)u_L(z)L(z)+v(z)kH(z) \\ &\qquad + w(z)i'(z)I(z)\big]\,\mathrm{d}z \\ &= \int_t^D \mathrm{e}^{-(s+q)(z-t)}m(z)u_L(z)T\,\mathrm{d}z. \end{aligned} \tag{74a}$$

The terms after the first equals sign in (74a) represent the three distinct sources of benefits derived from an additional unit of human capital: human capital increases (i) effective leisure, (ii) market earnings and (iii) effective investment time, respectively.[22] Note that (74a) implies

$$\dot{w}(t)=(s+q)w(t)-m(t)u_L(t)T. \tag{74b}$$

This completes the construction of the formal model. What does it imply about women's labor supply, investment, wages, etc.? Here it is helpful to distinguish between equilibrium dynamics and comparative dynamics, or equivalently between responses to "evolutionary" changes and responses to "parametric" changes. In any dynamic model, "equilibrium" is of course an *intertemporal* equilibrium, in which the individual – faced with certain exogenous givens, e.g. initial wealth $A(0)$ and present and (expected) future price levels $P(t)$ – chooses a set of *time paths* for the relevant variables, e.g. $L(t)$, $I(t)$ and $H(t)$. Evolution-

[22] The second line of (74a) follows from the first by (63), (70), and (71). To see why, note that (70) and (71) imply that $H[vk-mu_L]=I[wi'-mu_L]=0$ always. For example, if H is nonzero, then (70) holds as an equality, but if (70) is an inequality, then $H=0$.

ary changes refer to the shape of these time paths, i.e. to the way the relevant variables change over time as the individual's intertemporal equilibrium unfolds – for short, to the individual's equilibrium dynamics.

Of course, if there were an unanticipated change in an exogenous given such as $A(0)$ or $P(t)$, then the individual would change her intertemporal equilibrium, or, equivalently, would change the time paths she had adopted for all choice variables such as $L(t)$, etc. Responses to such unanticipated or "parametric" changes in these exogenous givens entail *changes in* the individual's intemporal equilibrium and time paths, i.e. are aspects of the individual's comparative dynamics.

First consider equilibrium dynamics. Derivation of equilibrium dynamics results is greatly simplified if one assumes an interior solution for both H and I for all $t < D$.[23] Under this assumption (we consider corner solutions below), (70) and (71) hold as equalities, in which case eqs. (74) may be written as

$$w(t) = \int_t^D \mathrm{e}^{-(s+q)(z-t)} v(z) kT \mathrm{d}z, \tag{75a}$$

$$\dot{w}(t) = (s+q)w(t) - v(t)kT. \tag{75b}$$

Now define a new variable, $x(t) = w(t)/v(t)$, which may be interpreted as the money shadow value of human capital at time t (since it is the ratio of the marginal utility of human capital to the marginal utility of money at t). Since $w(D) = 0$ by (75a), eqs. (73)–(75) for $v(t)$ and $w(t)$ may be manipulated[24] to yield analogous expressions for $x(t)$:

$$x(t) = \int_t^D \mathrm{e}^{-(r+q)(z-t)} kT \mathrm{d}z = kT[1-\mathrm{e}^{-(r+q)(D-t)}]/(r+q), \tag{76a}$$

$$\dot{x}(t) = (r+q)x(t) - kT = -kT\mathrm{e}^{-(r+q)(D-t)}. \tag{76b}$$

Now consider equilibrium dynamics – that is, the individual's life-cycle paths – under the assumption of an interior solution for I and H. [To simplify notation, we now suppress the time index, (t), on variables except when doing so would cause confusion.] By (71) and the definition $x = w/v$, $xi' = k$; totally

[23] For example, Heckman (1976a) argues that periods of zero investment could be thought of as periods during which I is "low", periods of retirement or nonwork could be thought of as periods during which H is "low", periods of full-time schooling could be thought of as periods during which I is high relative to H, etc.

[24] Note that $\dot{x} = \mathrm{d}[w/v]/\mathrm{d}t = (\dot{v}w - \dot{w}v)/v^2 = [(\dot{w}/w) - (\dot{v}/v)]x$, which reduces to (76b) by (73) and (75). In turn, (76b) and the terminal condition $x(D) = 0$ form a differential equation system that may be solved to obtain the expression after the first equals sign in (76a), whose integral is the expression after the second equals sign in (76a).

differentiate this with respect to time to get

$$(\dot{IK}) = -(\dot{x}/x)(i'/i''). \tag{77}$$

To characterize the dynamic equilibrium path of IK, note first that, by (76)–(77), the fact that i depends only on IK and the assumption of an interior solution, the life-cycle path of IK is independent of m. By (67), it follows that the life-cycle path of K is also independent of m, and thus that $I = IK/K$ is also independent of m. In other words, knowing that period t is one of high or rising m tells us nothing about the behavior of I, K or IK at time t.

Next, note from (76) that $\dot{x}/x < 0$ throughout the life cycle. Since $i'/i'' < 0$ always, effective investment IK also falls throughout the life cycle. By (67), and our assumption that $i[0] = 0$, it follows that potential earning power $K(t)$ must also ultimately decline so long as depreciation occurs (i.e. so long as $q > 0$), even though $K(t)$ may (and, in reality, usually does) rise earlier in the life cycle.

Now consider the equilibrium behavior of C and LK over the life cycle. Write (70) as an equality to reflect the assumption of an interior solution for H and differentiate (69) and (70) with respect to time, solving for C and LK to obtain

$$\dot{C} = \{\dot{v}[mu_{LL}P - u_{CL}k]m + \dot{m}[M]mu_{CL}\}/d, \tag{78a}$$

$$\dot{LK} = \{\dot{v}[u_{CC}k - mu_{LC}P] + \dot{m}[mLKu_{LC}u_{LC} - Mu_{CC}]\}/d, \tag{78b}$$

where $d = m^2[u_{CC}u_{LL} - (u_{CL})^2]$, with $d > 0$ by concavity of u; $M = \mathrm{d}[mu_L]/\mathrm{d}m = u_L + mLKu_{LL}$; and where, to simplify, we assume P is constant.

The life-cycle path of consumption may be described using (78a). In (78a), the first term in square brackets inside the braces is negative if consumption is a normal good in the static one period sense.[25] Thus, if consumption is normal then, at least when m is not changing (so that $\dot{m} = 0$), consumption will rise or fall over time depending on whether v is negative or positive. In turn, (73b) indicates that v will be negative or positive depending on whether s is less or greater than r. Since a positive-sloped life-cycle consumption profile seems much more plausible on a priori grounds than a negative-sloped profile, we will henceforth assume that

$$s < r. \tag{79}$$

Of course, even if $s < r$ the time profile of consumption need not always be positive-sloped, for the life-cycle behavior of C also depends on the taste shifter m, as given by the second term inside braces in (78a). It might be plausible to

[25] See footnote 16. In the present case, the definition of "normal in the static sense" includes the requirement that the individual may not devote time to investment, i.e. must have $I(t) = 0$.

assume $u_{CL} > 0$ (which is sufficient, though not necessary, for both consumption and leisure to be normal goods in the static sense), i.e. that additional consumption raises the marginal utility of (effective) leisure. If so, then a rising m ($\dot{m} > 0$) increases the growth rate of C. Speaking somewhat more loosely, we may say that, provided $u_{CL} > 0$, consumption will tend to be high (or rising) during periods when m is high (or rising) – which might be interpreted as childbearing ages.[26]

Now consider the life-cycle path of effective leisure, as given by (78b). The first term inside the curly braces in (78b) is positive provided leisure is a normal good in the static one-period sense. Thus, if leisure is normal then, by (79) and (73b), during periods when m is constant, effective leisure LK will rise. Moreover, $M > 0$ provided increases in $m(t)$ over time do indeed amount to increases in the marginal utility of (effective) leisure,[27] and so the second term inside the curly braces in (78b) will be positive or negative depending on whether m is rising or falling. Hence a rising m ($\dot{m} > 0$) increases the rate of growth of LK. In less precise terms, one may say that effective leisure LK will tend to be high (or rising) during periods when $m(t)$ is high (or rising), such as the age of childbearing.

Finally, consider the equilibrium path of leisure, L. As noted earlier, the life-cycle path of K is independent of the life-cycle behavior of m. Thus, when $m(t)$ is high (or rising), not only effective leisure LK but also the *level* of leisure L will tend to be high (or rising). In other words, since $(\dot{LK}) = L\dot{K} + \dot{L}K$,

$$\dot{L} = [(\dot{LK}) - L\dot{K}]/K, \tag{80}$$

so that, by (78b), growth in m ($\dot{m} > 0$) increases the rate of growth of leisure, L, as well as the rate of growth of effective leisure, LK. In less formal language, one may say that not only effective leisure but also leisure itself will tend to be high (or rising) during periods when $m(t)$ is high (or rising), such as the child-bearing years.

This leads directly to several propositions concerning labor supply and wage rates. In a model of this kind, the equivalent of "labor supply" in the sense used in static models is "market time", $T - L(t) = I(t) + H(t)$, i.e. "hours spent *at* work". As shown above, $I(t)$'s behavior over time is independent of $m(t)$'s

[26] Both here and in what follows we abstract from the effects of concurrent changes in v [note from eqs. (78) that the growth rates of both C and LK depend on v as well as on m]. The phrase "tends to" as used in the text should thus be understood to mean, "tends to, leaving aside the effects of concurrent changes in v". The same caveat applies to our remarks in the text about the behavior of hours of leisure (L), actual work (H), and market time ($I + H$), and to our discussion of the "investment content" of an hour of market time ($I/(I + H)$).

[27] By (70), mu_L is the marginal utility of effective leisure LK, and is increasing with respect to m provided $M = \mathrm{d}[mu_L]/\mathrm{d}m = u_L + mLKu_{LL} > 0$. Note that $M > 0$ if the elasticity of the marginal utility of effective leisure with respect to effective leisure (LK) is less than unity in absolute value.

behavior, and growth in m ($\dot{m} > 0$) raises the rate of growth of L. Thus, growth in m reduces the growth rates of both hours actually worked, $H(t)$, and hours spent at work, $J(t) = H(t) + I(t)$: that is, growth in m will make the growth of H and J less positive, or else more negative.

Next consider the life-cycle path of the *observed* wage rate, i.e. earnings per hour spent *at* work, $E(t)/[H(t)+I(t)] = kK(t)H(t)/[H(t)+I(t)]$. As noted above, the paths of $I(t)$ and $K(t)$ are independent of $m(t)$ over the life cycle, whereas growth in $m(t)$ reduces the rate of growth of $H(t)$. Thus, growth in m reduces the rate of growth of the observed wage rate. Speaking somewhat more loosely, one may say that the observed wage rate will tend to grow relatively slowly (and could even fall) during periods when m is growing, such as the ages of childbearing and childrearing.

To the extent that the abstract taste shifter construct $m(t)$ can legitimately be given the concrete interpretation we give it – as a measure of the greater preference for "leisure" or nonmarket time $L(t)$ that a given woman may have during the age of childbearing and childrearing – the model described here provides a quite comprehensive and seemingly very satisfactory set of predictions about life-cycle patterns of women's work and wages. The model implies that, ceteris paribus, during the childbearing and childrearing ages leisure will be higher (or rising more rapidly), and both the wage rate and "labor supply" as conventionally defined will be lower (or rising less rapidly), than during other periods in the life cycle. At least in a gross sense, these predictions are clearly consistent with the stylized facts about the age pattern of female labor supply set out in Section 2.

In other respects, however, these predictions are at odds with casual theorizing about the female life cycle. The most obvious example concerns time devoted to investment in human capital, I, and human capital accumulation, K. A long tradition in discussions of women's life-cycle behavior [exemplified by, for example, Mincer and Polachek (1974)], which we will call the "Informal Theory", identifies the age of childbearing and childrearing as a period of reduced *investment* as well as of reduced *labor supply*; and links the low level of (or rate of growth in) women's wages during this period to the hypothesized low level of investment.

In contrast, in the present model, high or growing $m(t)$ – in effect, childbearing and childrearing – does not affect investment time or the human capital stock at all. Moreover, although the model does predict that the observed wage $E(t)/[H(t)+I(t)] = kK(t)H(t)/[H(t)+I(t)]$ will be low (rising slowly, falling) during the age of childbearing and childrearing, that is only because hours of actual work $H(t)$ are low: hours of investment time $I(t)$ and the human capital stock $K(t)$ at any age are completely independent of $m(t)$, i.e. of childbearing and childrearing. Indeed, in this model, the "investment content" of time spent *at* work – $I(t)/[H(t)+I(t)]$ – is relatively *high* during the age of childbearing and childrearing, even though the *amount* of time spent at work, $H(t)+I(t)$, is low (rising more slowly, falling).

It is certainly true that the model generating these results – in particular the neutrality assumption – is a rather special one. However, one cannot resolve the anomalies highlighted by this model by simply saying that its neutrality assumption is rather restrictive. Generalizing the model – e.g. allowing for possible non-neutrality – would certainly *permit* results more in keeping with the Informal Theory. However, any such generalization would almost certainly not *preclude* results of the kind just discussed. In other words, if even a special case of a formal model generates propositions that effectively call the Informal Theory into question, there is not much reason to suppose that propositions derived from a more general formal model would invariably conform to those of the Informal Theory.

In sum, in several important respects the implications of the formal life-cycle model developed here are at odds with the Informal Theory. Two caveats should be noted immediately, however. The first caveat is that the formal model and the Informal Theory agree about the behavior of observable variables (e.g. hours spent at work, average hourly earnings) and disagree only about the behavior of unmeasurable variables (e.g. investment time, the investment content of an hour spent at work, the human capital stock). Thus, it could be argued that the differences between the formal model and the Informal Theory (i) are much less important than are their similarities, and (ii) may not even be testable anyway.

The second caveat is that the Informal Theory is sufficiently informal that it should *not* necessarily be interpreted as we have thus far interpreted it, namely, as a set of statements about a given woman's behavior over the life cycle – i.e. equilibrium dynamics. Rather, it could be argued that the Informal Theory is really concerned more with cross-sectional differences among different women. To analyze such differences, one needs to consider the model's comparative dynamics: comparative dynamics is literally concerned with how a given individual responds to a change in some exogenous given, but it could equally well be taken to refer to *differences* between two individuals who have *different* values for the relevant exogenous givens. In particular, $m(t)$ need not be the same at any given date, and need not change in the same way over time, for different women. Likewise, different women need not have the same values for other exogenous givens [e.g. initial wealth, $A(0)$]. Do differences in $A(0)$, $m(t)$, etc. among different women lead to differences in labor supply, wages, and the like? If so, how and in what direction? Since the Informal Theory has often been invoked in discussions of questions of precisely this kind, there is ample reason for regarding it as referring at least to some extent to comparative dynamics.

It remains to consider the comparative dynamics of the formal model developed above. We will focus on effects of $m(t)$ and $A(0)$, starting with the comparative dynamics of investment and human capital accumulation [see

Heckman (1976) for a comprehensive discussion of many other comparative dynamics effects]. Because we have assumed an interior solution for both I and H, (70) and (71) hold as equalities, so that

$$k/i'[I(t)K(t)] = x(t). \tag{81}$$

By (76a), $x(t)$ is independent of both $A(0)$ and $m(t)$. It follows that, other things being equal, *women with different levels of initial wealth or tastes for leisure* (e.g. childbearing, marriage) *will nevertheless undertake the same amount of effective investment* $I(t)K(t)$. Since potential earnings $K(t)$ depend only on $I(t)K(t)$, and since $I(t) = I(t)K(t)/K(t)$, it follows that, other things being equal, women with different levels of initial wealth or tastes for leisure (e.g. childbearing, marriage) will nevertheless have the *same* human capital stock $K(t)$ and will devote the *same* amount of time to investment $I(t)$ at each age t.

Next consider how changes in $A(0)$ and $m(t)$ affect the time paths of consumption, leisure, etc. over the life cycle – or, equivalently, how differences in $A(0)$ and $m(t)$ among different persons lead to different levels of consumption, leisure, etc. at any point in the life cycle. Here again, as in the exogenous-wage model of Section 3.2.1, it is extremely helpful to use the Frisch demand system and to distinguish between (i) changes in time paths that would occur even if the shadow price of assets v remained unchanged, and (ii) changes that occur because changes in the relevant variables will in fact change the shadow price v. As in the exogenous-wage model, we will refer to these two kinds of changes as "shadow price-constant" and "shadow price-variable" effects, respectively. These are analogous to the substitution and income effects, respectively, of static labor supply models, but with one important difference: substitution and income effects refer to changes with the *level of utility* constant or variable, respectively; whereas shadow price-constant and shadow price-variable effects refer to changes with the *marginal utility of assets* constant or variable, respectively.

First consider the shadow price-constant effects on C and LK of changes in $A(0)$ and, *at a particular* t, in $m(t)$. By (69)–(70), a change in $A(0)$ will *not* change either $C(t)$ or $L(t)K(t)$ so long as the shadow price v remains unchanged. Thus, *the shadow price-constant effects on C and LK of a change in* $A(0)$ *are both zero*. To derive shadow price-constant effects of a change in $m(t)$, begin by differentiating (69) and (70) totally with respect to $v(t)$ and $m(t)$ *with t constant*, to obtain:

$$\begin{aligned} \mathrm{d}C(t) &= \mathrm{d}m(t)\{m(t)u_{CL}(t)[M(t)]/\mathrm{d}(t)\} \\ &\quad + \mathrm{d}v(t)\{m(t)[m(t)P(t)u_{LL}(t) - ku_{CL}(t)]/\mathrm{d}(t)\}, \end{aligned} \tag{82}$$

$$\begin{aligned} \mathrm{d}[L(t)K(t)] &= \mathrm{d}m(t)\{[-M(t)u_{CC}(t) + u_{CL}(t)^2 m(t)L(t)K(t)]/\mathrm{d}(t)\} \\ &\quad + \mathrm{d}v(t)\{[ku_{CC}(t) - m(t)P(t)u_{LC}(t)]/\mathrm{d}(t)\}, \end{aligned} \tag{83}$$

where $d(t)=m(t)^2[u_{CC}(t)u_{LL}(t)-u_{CL}(t)^2]$; $M(t)=d[m(t)u_L(t)]/dm(t)$; and $dC(t)$ and $d[L(t)K(t)]$ denote changes in consumption and effective leisure, respectively, at a *given* date t induced by changes in $m(t)$ and $v(t)$ at that date. If $v(t)$ is constant, $dv(t)=0$, so, by (82) and (83), the *shadow price-constant effects of a change in* $m(t)$ *on* $C(t)$ *and* $L(t)K(t)$ *are*

$$dC(t)/dm(t)=m(t)u_{CL}(t)[M(t)]/d(t), \tag{84}$$

$$d[L(t)K(t)]/dm(t)=\left[-M(t)u_{CC}(t)+u_{CL}(t)^2m(t)L(t)K(t)\right]/d(t). \tag{85}$$

So long as an increase in $m(t)$ at given t does indeed connote an increase in the marginal utility of effective leisure, $M(t)>0$ (recall footnote 15), and so an increase in $m(t)$ at given t *with the shadow value of initial assets constant* will increase effective leisure $L(t)K(t)$ at that date. If consumption raises the marginal utility of effective leisure ($u_{CL}(t)>0$), then a shadow value-constant increase in $m(t)$ at given t will also increase consumption $C(t)$ at that date.

These results refer only to the shadow price-constant effects of changes in $A(0)$ and $m(t)$. However, such changes will also lead to changes in the shadow prices $v(t)$ themselves. For example, it is intuitively plausible that, other things being equal, someone with greater initial assets will have a lower $v(t)$ at all dates $t\geq 0$ provided goods and leisure are normal – that is, will regard assets as less "precious" or "scarce" – than will someone with lower initial assets. It remains to establish that this conjecture is not merely plausible but also correct; to obtain an analogous result for the effect of greater $m(t)$ on $v(t)$; and then to derive the impact of either kind of change in $v(t)$ on $C(t)$ and $L(t)K(t)$ – the shadow price-variable changes described earlier.

To see how $v(t)$ at each t will change in response to an increase in initial assets $A(0)$, recall that with $v(t)$ constant a change in $A(0)$ has no effect on $C(t)$ or $L(t)K(t)$ [see (82)–(83)]; and note from (64) that, other things being equal, an increase in $A(0)$ will leave some assets unspent at the end of life. Since there are no bequests and since "you can't take it with you", that cannot be optimal. The appropriate response to an increase in $A(0)$ is reduce $v(t)$, i.e. to value assets less highly and spend them more freely. Indeed, as (82)–(83) indicate, at given values of $m(t)$, both $C(t)$ and $L(t)K(t)$ will fall when $v(t)$ is increased (provided consumption and leisure, respectively, are normal goods). That is,

$$dC(t)/dv(t)=m(t)[m(t)P(t)u_{LL}(t)-ku_{CL}(t)]/d(t), \tag{86}$$

$$d[L(t)K(t)]/dv(t)=[ku_{CC}(t)-m(t)P(t)u_{LC}(t)]/d(t), \tag{87}$$

where the expressions after the equals signs in (86)–(87) are negative provided C

and L, respectively, are normal goods in the static sense. Moreover, an increase in $v(t)$ will always *increase* net additions to wealth $a(t) = E(t) - P(t)C(t) = kTK(t) - kI(t)K(t) - kL(t)K(t) - P(t)C(t)$: since $\mathrm{d}K(t)/\mathrm{d}v(t) = \mathrm{d}I(t)/\mathrm{d}v(t) = 0$ by (81) and (67), $\mathrm{d}a(t)/\mathrm{d}v(t) = -k\{\mathrm{d}[L(t)K(t)]/\mathrm{d}v(t)\} - P(t)\{\mathrm{d}C(t)/\mathrm{d}v(t)\}$, so, by (86)–(87),

$$\mathrm{d}a(t)/\mathrm{d}v(t) = -\{k^2 u_{CC}(t) + [m(t)P(t)]^2 u_{LL}(t) - 2km(t)P(t)u_{CL}(t)\}/\mathrm{d}(t), \tag{88}$$

which is always positive by concavity of u. Thus, the disequilibrium caused by higher $A(0)$ – "excess" financial wealth at death, $A(D) > 0$ – is remedied by a *reduction* in $v(t)$. Provided C and L are normal, the reduction in v raises both consumption and effective leisure, thereby reducing earnings and increasing expenditure at each date, thereby exhausting the excess asset accumulation that would otherwise show up as $A(D) > 0$. It follows that

$$\mathrm{d}v(t)/\mathrm{d}A(0) < 0 \tag{89}$$

which, along with (86)–(87), implies that *the shadow price-variable effects on consumption and effective leisure of an increase in initial assets are both positive*. That is, the shadow price-variable effects of higher $A(0)$ are, respectively,

$$\{\mathrm{d}C(t)/\mathrm{d}v(t)\}\{\mathrm{d}v(t)/\mathrm{d}A(0)\} > 0, \tag{90}$$

$$\{\mathrm{d}[L(t)K(t)]/\mathrm{d}v(t)\}\{\mathrm{d}v(t)/\mathrm{d}A(0)\} > 0, \tag{91}$$

provided C and L are normal in the static sense.

Essentially the same reasoning leads to the proposition that *the shadow price-variable effects on consumption and effective leisure of a greater taste for leisure are both negative* – the opposite of the v-variable effects of a greater level of initial wealth. By (82)–(83), or equivalently (84)–(85), with $v(t)$ constant ($\mathrm{d}v(t) = 0$) a greater taste for leisure at any date t ($\mathrm{d}m(t) > 0$) will (i) increase consumption at that date provided $u_{CL}(t) > 0$; and (ii) increase effective leisure at that date provided $M(t) > 0$. Hence, net increments to wealth $a(t)$ fall due to the rise in $m(t)$: by (81) and (67), $\mathrm{d}K(t)/\mathrm{d}m(t) = 0$, so $\mathrm{d}a(t)/\mathrm{d}m(t) = -k\{\mathrm{d}[L(t)K(t)]/\mathrm{d}m(t)\} - P(t)\{\mathrm{d}C(t)/\mathrm{d}m(t)\}$. Thus, by (84)–(85):

$$\begin{aligned}\mathrm{d}a(t)/\mathrm{d}m(t) = -\{&M(t)[-ku_{CC}(t) + m(t)P(t)u_{CL}(t)]\\ &+ m(t)L(t)K(t)u_{LC}(t)\\ &\times[-m(t)P(t)u_{LL}(t) + ku_{LC}(t)]\}/\mathrm{d}(t),\end{aligned} \tag{92}$$

which is negative provided $M(t) > 0$, $u_{CL}(t) > 0$ and consumption and leisure are normal in the static sense. Thus, *with* $v(t)$ *constant*, a greater taste for leisure at any given date will lead to a shortfall of financial wealth that would violate (64). The remedy is to *increase* $v(t)$: by (88), an increase in $v(t)$ always increases net increments to wealth $a(t)$. Hence, if $M(t) > 0$, $u_{CL}(t) \geq 0$ and C and L are both normal,

$$\mathrm{d}v(t)/\mathrm{d}m(t) > 0, \tag{93}$$

which, along with (86)–(87), implies that *the shadow price-variable effects on consumption and effective leisure of an increase in the taste for leisure are both negative*. That is, if $M(t) > 0$, $u_{CL}(t) \geq 0$ and C and L are both normal, the shadow price-variable effects of higher $m(t)$ are, respectively,

$$\{\mathrm{d}C(t)/\mathrm{d}v(t)\}\{\mathrm{d}v(t)/\mathrm{d}m(t)\} < 0, \tag{94}$$

$$\{\mathrm{d}[L(t)K(t)]/\mathrm{d}v(t)\}\{\mathrm{d}v(t)/\mathrm{d}m(t)\} < 0. \tag{95}$$

In sum, women with a greater taste for leisure (e.g. a greater preference for activities such as childrearing) will (have to) put a greater shadow or implicit value on financial assets than will other women: the *v-constant* effect of greater m raises consumption and reduces earnings, which in turn requires greater caution with respect to earning and spending – an increase in v – so as to ensure that the lifetime budget constraint can still be satisfied. Thus, via the v-variable effect, consumption and effective leisure LK both fall. Since changes in v do not affect IK, K or I, the v-variable effect of greater m does not change IK, K or I but does reduce leisure time L ($= LK/K$). Hence the v-variable effect of greater m raises (i) actual hours of work $H = T - I - L$, (ii) hours *at* work $J = T - L = I + H$, and (iii) the observed wage $W = kKH/(I + H)$; and *reduces* the investment content of an hour spent at work $I/(I + H)$.

Now combine the shadow price-constant and shadow price-variable effects to derive the total effects of changes in $A(0)$ and $m(t)$ on consumption, leisure, etc. First consider the effects of greater $A(0)$. All shadow price-*constant* effects of greater $A(0)$ are zero, so the *total* effects of greater $A(0)$ are the same as the shadow price-*variable* effects of greater $A(0)$. Thus, ceteris paribus, a woman who has greater initial assets must necessarily have greater consumption and effective leisure than a woman with less initial assets. Also, other things being equal, the woman with higher initial assets will spend less time at work $J = T - L$, will spend less time actually working $H = T - I - L$, and will enjoy more leisure time L. Her observed wage $E/(I + H) = kKH/(I + H)$ will be lower, but the investment content of an hour of the time she spends at work $I/(I + H)$ will be higher, than for the woman with lower initial assets. Finally, ceteris paribus, the woman with higher initial assets will have the *same* potential earning power or human capital stock K as will a woman with lower initial assets; and both women will invest to the same extent (where investment refers either to investment time I or to effective investment IK).

Although these propositions of course refer in a literal sense to the effects of differences in initial assets, $A(0)$, it is important to note that they could also be interpreted as referring to the impact of marriage (especially if one ignores intrafamily cross-substitution effects of the kind described in Section 3.2): marriage seems to permit substantial economies of scale in consumption, and so to at least some extent is analogous to an increase in financial wealth (which, discounted back to time 0, is simply an increase in *initial* assets). If so, then marriage will (i) raise consumption and leisure time (and thus fertility?) at all ages; (ii) reduce hours *at* work, $J = T - L$, at all ages; and (iii) reduce the observed wage, $kKH/(I + H)$, at all ages.[28]

All this is very much in line with the intuition generated by the Informal Theory, and is certainly consistent with empirical findings on cross-section patterns of women's labor supply and wages by marital status. However, note that some of the implications of the formal model seem at odds with the reasoning of the Informal Theory: to the extent that marriage can indeed be regarded as akin to higher $A(0)$, the formal model implies that marriage does *not* affect investment time I, effective investment IK or human capital K. Moreover, in general no conclusions can be drawn from the formal model about the impact of marriage – higher $A(0)$ – on the *slope* of the earnings profile unless one adopts some specific assumptions about preferences [Heckman (1976, pp. S23, S41)]; in contrast, the Informal Theory has almost always associated marriage with flatter earnings profiles.

Now consider the comparative dynamics effects of greater $m(t)$, which are summarized in Table 2.24. To the extent that a greater $m(t)$ at any given date can be interpreted as a greater taste for leisure (for nonmarket as opposed to market work, for children, etc.), then the above indicates the following: (i) *with v constant*, a woman with a greater taste for raising children and other nonmarket activities will enjoy more consumer goods and leisure, will spend fewer hours at work (with, however, each hour having a higher investment content), and will

[28] Since these are comparative dynamics rather than equilibrium dynamics results, it is important to be clear about what they do and do not mean. They do *not* mean that, once a *given* woman marries, her leisure time, hours of work and wages will change in particular ways (relative to their levels at an earlier stage in the life cycle): changes of that kind refer to equilibrium dynamics, i.e. to the development of a given woman's *equilibrium lifetime plan* as she goes through the life cycle. Rather, these results refer to *differences in* lifetime plans between married and unmarried women who are similar in all other respects (e.g. initial human capital stocks, tastes for leisure, etc.). In effect, differences in initial nonhuman assets are treated here as proxies representing unobservable traits that lead otherwise observationally similar women to differ in terms of marital status and equilibrium life cycle paths. As such, the propositions discussed in the text are predictions about the ceteris paribus associations between marital status and other variables of interest (e.g. labor supply, leisure time or wage rates) that will be observed in cross-sections.

Table 2.24
Comparative dynamics effects of greater $m(t)$.

Variable	Effects of greater $m(t)$: v-constant effect	v-variable effect	Total effect
$I(T)K(T)$	0	0	0
$I(t), K(t)$	0	0	0
$C(t)$	$+^{a}$	$-^{c}$	?
$L(t)K(t), L(t)$	$+^{b}$	$-^{c}$	?
$H(t)$	$-$	$+$	?
$W(t)$	$-$	$+$	?
$I(t)/[H(t)+I(t)]$	$+$	$-$	?

[a] Provided $u_{CL} > 0$.
[b] Provided $M > 0$.
[c] Provided $u_{CL} > 0$, $M > 0$, and C and L both normal.

have a lower wage, than will a woman with a lesser taste for such nommarket activities; (ii) these reductions in hours of work and wages prompt the woman with a greater taste for nonmarket activities to place a greater implicit value on assets, and thus be more conservative about spending on consumption and leisure, implying (iii) that the *v-variable* effect of a greater taste for nonmarket activity will be to *increase* work and wages and *reduce* leisure time.

On balance, then, the *net* effects of a greater taste for nonmarket activity or "leisure" at any particular age t are generally indeterminate a priori (except as regards investment time and human capital accumulation, which are independent of m). For example, the v-constant effect of greater $m(t)$ acts to increase leisure $L(t)$, but the v-variable effect of greater $m(t)$ acts to reduce it.

It is nevertheless possible to derive some insight into the effects of greater $m(t)$ on individuals' life-cycle paths, thanks largely to the analytical distinction between the v-constant and v-variable effects of greater $m(t)$. On the one hand, the v-constant effects of greater $m(t)$ alter behavior *only* at age t, and not at any other age: since the lifetime utility function U is separable in time, consisting of an integral of instantaneous utility functions u, an increase in $m(t)$ with $v(t)$ constant *does* affect behavior *at time t* but does *not* affect behavior at any *other* date t'. [For example, note from (69)–(71) that $C(t)$, $L(t)K(t)$ and $I(t)K(t)$ are independent of $m(t')$ for all $t' \neq t$.] On the other hand, the v-variable effect of greater $m(t)$ affects behavior (e.g. leisure, the observed wage, hours at work) at *all* ages: the v-variable effects of greater $m(t)$ are spread over the individual's entire life cycle because borrowing and lending make it possible (for example) to earn and save during periods when $m(t)$ is low(er) and to borrow or live off past savings during periods when $m(t)$ is high(er). Thus, for all $t' \neq t$, the *only* effects of higher $m(t)$ are v-variable effects, whereas at t a higher level of $m(t)$ will have both v-variable *and* v-constant effects.

To the extent that the υ-variable effect of greater $m(t)$ at any given age is likely to be small, one would expect the υ-constant effect of greater $m(t)$ to dominate the υ-variable effect *at age t*. At *other* ages $t' \neq t$, higher $m(t)$ has a υ-variable effect *only*. Thus, so long as a greater $m(t)$ can indeed be interpreted as a greater taste for nonmarket work, childrearing, etc., the formal model developed here implies that, *during the childbearing and childrearing ages*, women with a greater taste for nonmarket work, childbearing and childrearing will tend to have (i) *lower* hours of actual work, hours at work, and observed wage rates, and (ii) *higher* hours of leisure and a *higher* investment content per hour spent at work, than will other women, ceteris paribus [provided – as seems reasonable a priori – υ-constant effects dominate during the periods t that $m(t)$ is high]. However, the model *also* implies that, at ages *other than* those of childbearing and childrearing, these patterns will be exactly reversed; then, women with a greater taste for nonmarket work, childbearing and childrearing will spend more time working, earn a higher observed wage, devote *less* time to leisure, and will work at jobs whose investment content is lower. Finally, the formal model implies that, at all ages, women with high tastes for nonmarket work, childrearing, etc. will have the same human capital stock K and will devote the same amount of time to investment I as other women, ceteris paribus.

Thus, the formal model's predictions about behavior during the age of childbearing and childrearing seem quite consistent with the intuition generated by the Informal Theory. However, its implications about behavior at ages other than those of childbearing and childrearing raise some questions about the Informal Theory. For the most part, the Informal Theory ignores the implicit substitution between high- and low-$m(t)$ periods that occurs in the formal model developed here.

The most noteworthy difference between the formal model and the Informal Theory is, of course, that in informal discussions marriage, childbearing, childrearing, etc. are usually assumed a priori to be associated with less investment (I) and human capital accumulation (K), whereas in the formal model developed here both investment and human capital are independent of marriage and children. An important reason for this is probably that the formal model presented above explicitly assumes a lifetime interior solution (i.e. positive H and I throughout the life cycle). Generalizing a model of this kind by allowing for corners (e.g. zero H and/or I during part of the life cycle) would permit explicit analysis of something that is suppressed by the assumption of a lifetime interior solution but that figures prominently in the Informal Theory: discontinuities in employment and work experience.

To sum up: although much informal discussion implicitly or explicitly emphasizes the interrelationships between women's work and wages in a life-cycle setting, rigorous analysis of such issues using formal life-cycle labor supply models with endogenous wages is still in its infancy. To some extent, even quite simple and abstract models have something to say about female labor supply over the life cycle; more important, relatively modest development of abstract models can yield additional insights and propositions about women's work and wages over the life cycle. To some extent, formal models confirm the intuition developed by informal theorizing; in other respects, however, the results of formal models raise questions about the merits of such simple intuition. Further research in this area is long overdue, and would seem to be eminently promising.

4. Empirical studies of female labor supply

We now discuss empirical analyses of female labor supply. We first describe some of the important problems that arise in such studies – concerning specification, measurement of variables, econometric technique, and the like – and then summarize the findings of recent empirical work. To motivate this discussion, we note at the outset that the results of some recent empirical studies of female labor supply differ appreciably from those of research conducted through the early 1980s. There has been a consensus of relatively long standing that compensated and uncompensated female labor supply wage elasticities are positive and larger in absolute value than those for men. In contrast, some recent studies appear to show that the compensated and uncompensated wage elasticities of women workers are little different from those of men; indeed, in this work, the female uncompensated elasticity is often estimated to be negative.

4.1. Empirical work on female labor supply: Methodological issues

As documented in Section 2, many women work – supply positive hours to the market – but many women do not. This simple fact has a number of very important implications for empirical work. First, in specifying the labor supply function, one must recognize that the labor supply of many women (those whose offered wage is well below the reservation level) will be completely insensitive to small changes in market wage rates, exogenous income or for that matter anything else. Many "first-generation" empirical studies of female labor supply conducted through the mid-1970s ignored this consideration because they specified the labor supply function as little different from other regression functions, e.g.

$$H = wa + Xb + Rc + e, \tag{96}$$

where H is hours of work per period, w is the real wage, R is real exogenous income, X is a vector of other (e.g. demographic) variables and e is a random error term. The difficulty in using such a relation to analyze the labor supply of all women is that, at best, (96) or functions like it refer only to *working* women rather than to the entire female population. Derivatives of H with respect to any variable are equal to the relevant parameter (a, b or c) only when the real offered or market wage rate w exceeds the real reservation wage w^*. In contrast, when $w < w^*$, all such derivatives are zero for (small) changes in all relevant variables. The same point is relevant to family labor supply models, in which any given family member's labor supply is (in general) a function of that family member's wage, the wages of all *other* family members and exogenous income: for example, the husband's (wife's) labor supply will be affected by small changes in the wife's (husband's) offered wage only if the wife (husband) is working.

A second problem arising from the usually-substantial extent of nonparticipation among women is that, in general, the market wages of nonworking women are not observed. Thus, even if (96) correctly specified the labor supply function, it could not be estimated using data on the entire female population, because measures of one of the relevant variables are usually not available for the entire population.

It might seem (and to many first generation researchers did in fact seem) that the easiest way to avoid both these problems – of specification and measurement – is to fit labor supply functions such as (96) to data on working women *only*. This avoids the specification problem because, among *working* women, changes in the relevant independent variables X will of course generally induce nonzero changes in labor supply; and it avoids the measurement problem because *working* women's wages are generally observed. Unfortunately, this attempted solution arises an econometric problem, variously known as "sample selection" or "selectivity" bias: if working women are not representative of *all* women, then using least squares regression methods to fit (96) to data restricted to working women may lead to bias in the estimated parameters b. Indeed, it may even lead to biased estimates of the structural parameters relevant to the behavior of *working* women!

To see why, consider the following simple argument [for further discussion, see Pencavel, Chapter 1 in this Handbook, or Killingsworth (1983, ch. 4)]. Working women have $w > w^*$. Thus, among all women who are capable of earning the same real market wage w, *working* women have relatively low *reservation* wages w^*. Similarly, among all women with the same reservation wage w^*, *working* women must have relatively high *market* wages w. Thus, on both counts – low reservation wages and high market wages – working women are likely to be unrepresentative of the entire female population. Least squares estimates of (96) derived from data restricted to working women may therefore suffer from bias. Indeed, they may even fail to provide unbiased measures of the behavioral responses of working women themselves.

The essential reason for this is that, unless wage rates and reservation wages depend only on observable variables and not on any unobservable factors, the labor supply error term e of working women may not be independent of their observed variables w, R and X. For example, consider the role of exogenous income, R. R is a determinant of hours of work H by (96), and is also a determinant of the reservation wage, w^*. To be concrete, let the reservation wage be a function of R, other observed variables Z and unobservables ("tastes for leisure") u, with

$$w^* = Zk + Rg + u. \tag{97}$$

Among working women, $w > w^*$, or, equivalently,

$$u < -[w - (Zk + Rg)]. \tag{98}$$

Thus, "other things" (the *observed* variables w, Z and R) being equal, working women have relatively low values of u. Moreover, if the labor supply error term e and the reservation wage error term u are correlated[29] then, in general, e will be correlated with R *within the group of working women* even if it is uncorrelated with R *in the female population as a whole*. Why? If leisure is a normal good, $c < 0$ and $g > 0$ (that is, greater exogenous income reduces labor supply and raises the reservation wage, ceteris paribus). Thus, by (98), women who have a high value of R *but who nevertheless work* will tend to have a relatively low value of u, "other things" (w and Z) being equal: in other words, women who work even though they receive large amounts of exogenous income must have a relatively low taste for leisure, ceteris paribus. If u and e are negatively correlated, as seems likely to be the case (see footnote 20), then e and R will be positively correlated *among working women* even if no such correlation exists in the female population as a whole. In this case, using conventional least squares regression to fit (96) to data on working women will yield a biased estimate of the exogenous income parameter c due to the correlation between e and R.

Several further remarks are in order at this point. First, similar arguments establish that the coefficient on any variable in X in (96) fitted to data on working women will be biased if it also appears in the vector Z in the reservation wage function (97). Second, if the observed wage rate w depends on unobservables v as well as observed characteristics (e.g. schooling) and if the wage unobservables v are correlated with the labor supply and reservation wage unobservables e and u, then the same reasoning establishes that the coefficient on w in (96) will also be biased when (96) is derived from data on working women. Finally, a straightforward extension of these arguments will demonstrate that a similar potential for bias can arise in analyses of family labor supply, e.g. when one estimates labor supply functions for wives using data restricted to wives whose husbands are employed.

[29] For example, a measure of "motivation" or "will to work" is unlikely to be available in any dataset, and may be determinant of both labor supply and the wage rate.

In general terms, the solution to these interrelated problems of specification, measurement and econometric technique is to estimate not only "the" labor supply function [that is, the structural relation determining hours of work, such as (96)] but also *other* behavioral functions relevant to work effort [e.g. the discrete choice of whether to supply any work at all, as given by a participation criterion such as (97)]. This approach has characterized so-called "second-generation" research on labor supply undertaken since the mid-1970s. Such estimation can take explicit account of the manner in which available data were generated (e.g. the fact that wages are observed only for workers) and of the fact that nonworkers' labor supply is insensitive to small changes in wages, exogenous income or other variables. Thus, measurement problems can be minimized, specification questions are addressed directly and the econometric bias problem can be avoided.

A variety of second-generation strategies for proceeding in this fashion have been developed in recent years. In lieu of a full description of all of them – which is well beyond the scope of this chapter, and which may be found elsewhere [see, for example, Killingsworth (1983, esp. ch. 3), Heckman and MaCurdy (1985), Wales and Woodland (1980)] – consider the following procedure due to Heckman (1976a, 1979) by way of example. Let the real wage w that an individual earns (or is capable of earning) be given by

$$w = Yh + v. \tag{99}$$

An individual works if $w > w^*$ and is a nonworker otherwise. Thus, by (97) and (99),

$$v - u > -(Yh - Zk - Rg) \leftrightarrow H > 0, \tag{100a}$$

$$v - u \leq -(Yh - Zk - Rg) \leftrightarrow H = 0, \tag{100b}$$

which are reduced-form expressions for the conditions under which an individual will or will not work, respectively. Likewise, by (96) and (99), the *reduced-form* function for the hours of work *of women who work* is

$$H = Yah + Xb + Rc + [av + e], \tag{101}$$

where the term in square brackets is a composite error term.

Now consider the estimation of (101) using data restricted to working women. The regression function corresponding to (101) is

$$\begin{aligned} &\mathrm{E}\{H | Y, X, R, Z, v - u > -(Yh - Zk - Rg)\} \\ &\quad = Yah + Xb + Rc + \mathrm{E}\{[av + e] | Y, X, R, Z, v - u > -(Yh - Zk - Rg)\} \\ &\quad = Yah + Xb + Rc + \mathrm{E}\{[av + e] | v - u > -(Yh - Zk - Rg)\}, \end{aligned} \tag{102a}$$

where the third line follows from the second because v and e are assumed to be independent of Y, X, R and Z. The last term on the right-hand side of this equality is the expectation of the composite error term $av+e$ *conditional on* positive hours of work (i.e. the mean of $av+e$ for someone with characteristics Y, Z and R who works). Its value depends on the variables Y, Z and R, the structural parameters h, k and g, and the parameters of the joint distribution of the random variables $av+e$ and $(v-u)$. Likewise, the regression function for the wages of workers is

$$\mathrm{E}\{w|Y, v-u>-(Yh-Zk-Rg)\} = Yh + \mathrm{E}\{v|v-u>-(Yh-Zk-Rg)\}, \tag{102b}$$

where the last term on the right-hand side of (103) is the conditional expectation of v, i.e. the mean value of v among workers.

To proceed further, researchers have typically assumed that the random variables v, e and u are jointly normally distributed (although other distributional assumptions and even nonparametric techniques could be used instead). In this case, it turns out [see, for example, Heckman (1979)] that the conditional mean of $av+e$ in (102a) and the conditional mean of v in (102b) can be written in a relatively simple fashion, i.e.

$$\mathrm{E}\{[av+e]|v-u>-(Yh-Zk-Rg)\} = [\sigma_{12}/\sigma_{22}^{0.5}]\lambda, \tag{103}$$

$$\mathrm{E}\{v|v-u>-(Yh-Zk-Rg)\} = [\sigma_{v2}/\sigma_{22}^{0.5}]\lambda, \tag{104}$$

where $\sigma_{12} = \mathrm{cov}[av+e, v-u]$, $\sigma_{v2} = \mathrm{cov}[v, v-u]$, $\sigma_{22} = \mathrm{var}[v-u]$, $\lambda = f[-I/\sigma_{22}^{0.5}]/\{1-F[-I/\sigma_{22}^{0.5}]\}$ and $I=(Yh-Zk-Rg)$. The important thing to note about (103) and (104) is that they express the conditional means of $av+e$ and of v in terms of observed variables and estimable parameters, thereby permitting estimation.

In the approach developed by Heckman (1976b, 1979), estimation proceeds in three steps. In the first, one estimates the parameters governing the decision to work or not to work, as given by eqs. (100), using probit analysis, i.e. by maximizing the probit likelihood function

$$1 = \Pi F[-I/\sigma_{22}^{0.5}]^{1-d}\{1-F[-I/\sigma_{22}^{0.5}]\}^{d}, \tag{105}$$

where d is a dummy variable equal to one if an individual works, and zero otherwise. This provides estimates of the parameter ratios $h/\sigma_{22}^{0.5}$, $k/\sigma_{22}^{0.5}$ and $g/\sigma_{22}^{0.5}$ which can be used to compute (estimates of) the λ for each working individual [recall the definition of λ in (103)–(104)]. Armed with these measures of working individuals' λ values, one can then estimate the reduced form hours and wage equations by using data for *working* individuals to fit the following functions by, for example, least squares:

$$H = Yah + Xb + Rc + \lambda m + y, \tag{106}$$

$$w = Yh + \lambda n + z, \tag{107}$$

where y and z are random error terms that are uncorrelated with the right-hand side variables in (106)–(107) by (103)–(104), and where, by (103)–(104), estimates of the parameters m and n are estimates of the ratios $\sigma_{12}/\sigma_{22}^{0.5}$ and $\sigma_{v2}/\sigma_{22}^{0.5}$, respectively.

We conclude this abbreviated methodological discussion with one further observation. It should already be clear that the error term plays a much more important role, and has been the focus of much more attention, in second- than in first-generation labor supply research. What may not immediately be clear is that, in general, three kinds of "error terms" (unobservables, measurement errors, etc.) may be relevant to labor supply: one kind has to do with the utility function (or other utility-related function such as the indifference curve, the marginal rate of substitution, etc.); another refers to the budget constraint; the third has to do with the optimum point (e.g. indifference curve–budget line tangency) itself. We refer to these as preference errors, budget constraint errors, and optimization errors, respectively.

Optimization errors (and errors in the measurement of hours of work) refer to discrepancies between optimal and actual (or between actual and *measured*) hours of work. Such discrepancies arise when, for example, individuals are unable to work as many hours as they desire due to unemployment, bad weather or other similar phenomena; or when data on hours of work do not accurately reflect the hours (optimal or not) that individuals are actually working. Preference errors refer to unobservable differences in utility (or utility-related) functions across individuals: for example, Burtless and Hausman (1978) and Hausman (1981) adopt a random-parameter utility function model in which the elasticity of hours of work with respect to exogenous income varies randomly across the population; and Heckman (1976b) assumes that the marginal rate of substitution is affected by unobservables as well as unobservables, as in (97). Finally, budget constraint errors refer to unobservable differences in budget constraints across individuals. For example, most recent work treats the wage as a function of unobserved as well as observed characteristics, as in (99); likewise, observationally identical individuals (with the same observed pretax wage rate, exogenous income, etc.) may not face the same marginal tax rate, meaning that their after-tax budget constraints differ due to unobservable factors (e.g. differences in consumption patterns that lead to different deductions, marginal tax rates, etc.).

4.2. *Estimates of female labor supply elasticities: An overview*

We now turn to estimates of female labor supply elasticities obtained in recent empirical analyses. We focus on the compensated (utility-constant) and uncompensated ("gross") elasticity of hours of work with respect to the wage rate and on the so-called "total-income" elasticity of annual hours (i.e. the difference between the uncompensated and compensated wage-elasticities of hours).[30] Details concerning the samples and variables used in these studies are summarized in Table 2.25; the results of the studies are set out in Table 2.26. All in all, most of the estimates suggest that female labor supply elasticities are large both in absolute terms and relative to male elasticities (on which see Pencavel, Chapter 1 in this Handbook). However, the range of estimates of the uncompensated wage elasticity of annual hours is dauntingly large: Dooley (1982), Nakamura and Nakamura (1981), and Nakamura, Nakamura and Cullen (1979) all report estimates of -0.30 or less, whereas Dooley (1982) and Heckman (1980) obtain estimates in excess of $+14.00$! Since most estimates of the uncompensated wage elasticity are positive and estimates of the total-income elasticity are almost always negative, it is not surprising that the compensated wage elasticities implied by the studies shown in Table 2.26 are generally positive; but even here it is the variability, rather than uniformity, of the estimates that is noteworthy. It is not uncommon for authors of empirical papers on female labor supply to point to results in other studies similar to the ones they have obtained but, as Table 2.26 suggests, such comparisons may not always be informative: it is all too easy to find at least one other set of results similar to almost any set of estimates one may have obtained!

The main exception to these generalizations concerns the results of studies of U.S. and Canadian data by Nakamura and Nakamura (1981), Nakamura, Nakamura and Cullen (1979), and Robinson and Tomes (1985).[31] Here, the uncompensated elasticity of labor supply with respect to wages is negative (so

[30] This discussion omits two kinds of studies: those based on the negative income tax (NIT) experiments, and those based on dynamic models of labor supply of the kind discussed in Section 3.2. One problem with studies based on the NIT experiments is that, as has recently been noted [Greenberg, Moffitt and Friedmann (1981), Greenberg and Halsey (1983)], participants in the experiments may have misreported their earnings and work effort (to an even greater extent than the "controls" who were not receiving experimental NIT payments). For discussions of studies based on the NIT experiments, see Killingsworth (1983, ch. 6), Moffitt and Kehrer (1981, 1983) and Robins (1984). There have been relatively few empirical studies based on formal dynamic labor models [see Altonji (1986), Blundell and Walker (1983), Heckman and MaCurdy (1980, 1982), Moffitt (1984b) and Smith (1977a, 1977b, 1977c, 1980)]; all but one [Moffitt (1984b)] treat the wage as exogenous (in the behavioral sense), and have produced somewhat mixed results. For a brief review, see Killingsworth (1983, ch. 5).

[31] See also Nakamura and Nakamura (1985a, 1985b), which differ from most other studies of female labor supply in that these analyses condition on labor supply in the year prior to the one being considered.

Table 2.25
Summary of samples and variables used in selected studies of female labor supply.

Study	Characteristics of sample	Construction of measures of H, W, R
Arrufat and Zabalza (1986)	Wives age < 60, neither unemployed nor self-employed, with working husbands < 65 who were not self-employed – GHS	H = hours of work per week W = hourly earnings, predicted from selecti bias-corrected regression R = husband's earnings + rent + dividends + interest + imputed rent (owner-occupie – mortgage interest + rent + property t rebates (after taxes calculated at zero hours of work for wife)
Ashworth and Ulph (1981)	Wives of husbands working ≥ 8 hours/week at salaried job, no other family members working; women with second job excluded if either (i) gross wage at second job > overtime rate on first job or (ii) did not want to work more overtime on first job than actually worked – BMRBS	H = hours of work per week W = marginal net wage (wage at first job, if constrained at first job; or lower of the wages on two jobs, otherwise), inclusive of overtime premium (if any) (linearized) R = net family income excluding own earnir (linearized)
Blundell and Walker (1982)	Working wives with working husbands, husband a manual worker, total weekly expenditures between £35 and £55 – FES	H = hours of work per week W = earnings/H (linearized) R = unearned income (linearized)
Cogan (1980a)	White wives age 30–44 – NLS	H = annual hours of work W = hourly wage R = husband's annual income
Cogan (1980b)	White wives not in school, disabled or retired, self and spouse not self-employed or farmer – PSID	H = annual hours of work W = hourly wage R = husband's earnings
Cogan (1981)	White wives age 30–44, self and spouse not self-employed or farmer – NLS	H = usual weekly hours × weeks worked in prior year W = earnings in prior year/hours worked in prior year R = husband's earnings
Dooley (1982)	Wives age 30–54 – USC	H = hours worked in survey week × weeks worked in prior year W = earnings in prior year/H R = other income exclusive of earnings of family members, self-employment inco Social Security, and public assistance benefits (separate variables included f husband's predicted income and actua predicted husband's income)
Franz and Kawasaki (1981)	Wives – M	H = hours worked in survey week W = hourly wage R = income of husband
Franz (1981)	Same as Franz and Kawasaki (1981)	Same as Franz and Kawasaki (1981)
Hanoch (1980)	White wives, husband a wage earner and nonfarmer – SEO	H = hours worked in survey week × weeks worked in prior year W = earnings in survey week/hours workec in survey week R = husband's earnings + property income transfer payments + other regular non-wage income

Table 2.25 continued

Study	Characteristics of sample	Construction of measures of H, W, R
Hausman (1980)	Black female household heads in Gary Income Maintenance Experiment, observed during experiment (households with preexperiment income > 2.4 times poverty line were excluded from experiment)	$H = 1$ if worked during middle two years of experiment, $= 0$ otherwise $W =$ hourly wage $R =$ nonlabor income
Hausman (1981)	Wives of husbands age 25–55 and not self-employed, farmers or disabled – PSID	$H =$ annual hours worked $W =$ hourly wage $R =$ imputed return to financial assets
Hausman and Ruud (1984)	Same as Hausman (1981)	Same as Hausman (1981)
Heckman (1976a)	White wives age 30–44 – NLS	$H =$ weeks worked $\times$ average hours worked per week $W =$ usual wage $R =$ assets
Heckman (1980)	White wives age 30–44, husband not a farmer – NLS	$H =$ annual earnings$/W$ $W =$ usual hourly wage $R =$ assets
Kooreman and Kapteyn (1984b)	Households in which both husband and wife are employed wage earners – TUS	$H =$ hours of work per week $W =$ net wage per hour $R =$ "unearned income" per week
Layard, Barton and Zabalza (1980)	Wives age ≤ 60, not self-employed – GHS hours	$H =$ annual weeks worked $\times$ usual weekly $W =$ predicted value of annual earnings$/H$, derived from OLS wage regression (linearized) $R =$ net annual unearned income, including imputed rent, interest and dividends (husband's W, derived as for wife's W, included as separate variable) (linearized)
Mroz (1985)	White wives age 30–60 in 1975 – PSID	$H =$ weeks worked in 1975 $\times$ usual hours of work per week $W =$ total earnings in 1975$/H$ $R =$ household income – wife's earnings
Moffitt (1984a)	Wives – NLS	$H =$ hours worked last week $W =$ hourly wage rate $R = 0.05 \times$ assets
Nakamura, Nakamura and Cullen (1979)	Wives with no nonrelatives in household – CC	$H =$ hours worked in survey week $\times$ weeks worked in prior year $W =$ annual earnings$/H$ $R =$ husband's earnings + asset income
Nakamura and Nakamura (1981)	Wives – CC, USC	$H =$ hours worked in survey week $\times$ weeks worked in prior year $W =$ annual earnings$/H$ (linearized) $R =$ husband's earnings + asset income – taxes payable at zero hours of wife's work
Ransom (1982)	Wives of husbands age 30–50 (neither spouse self-employed or working piecework) – PSID	$H =$ hours of work per week $W =$ predicted wage, derived from selection bias-corrected wage regression (linearized) $R =$ income other than earnings (linearized)
Renaud and Siegers (1984)	Wives age < 65 with husbands age < 65 and holding paid job – AVO	$H =$ hours of work per week $W =$ predicted net hourly wage rate derived from selection bias-corrected regression $R =$ net weekly income

Table 2.25 continued

Study	Characteristics of sample	Construction of measures of H, W, R
Robinson and Tomes (1985)	Single and married women reporting earnings on a per-hour basis ("hourly wage sample") or saying they were paid per hour ("hourly paid sample") – QLS	H = hours of work per week W = earnings per hour R = annual income of husband
Ruffell (1981)	Wives working ≥ 8 hours per week, no other working family members except husband – BMRBS	H = hours of work per week W = hourly wage, inclusive of overtime (if any) (linearized) R = nonemployment income + other family members' earnings (linearized)
Schultz (1980)	Wives, husband not full-time student or in armed forces – SEO	H = hours worked last week × weeks worke last year W = last week's earnings/last week's hours work (adjusted for regional cost of livin differences) (linearized) R = nonemployment income (linearized)
Smith and Stelcner (1985)	Wives age 20–54, not self-employed or family worker – CC	H = hours in survey week × weeks worked last year W = earnings last year/H (linearized) R = net nonlabor income + husband's earnings (linearized)
Stelcner and Breslaw (1985)	Wives age 20–54, Quebec residents, nonfarm, not new immigrant or full-time student or unpaid family worker or self-employed or permanently disabled – MDF	H = weeks worked in 1979 W = earnings last year/H (linearized) R = other family income (linearized)
Stelcner and Smith (1985)	Same as Smith and Stelcner (1985)	Same as Smith and Stelcner (1985)
Trussell and Abowd (1980)	Wives age 25–45 who between age 12 and 30 delivered at least one child – NSFG	H = annual hours of work W = hourly wage R = other family income
Yatchew (1985)	Same as Hausman's (1981) data for wives	Same as Hausman (1981)
Zabalza (1983)	Wives age < 60, not self-employed, with working husband age < 65 and not self-employed – GHS	H = hours worked in survey week (in intervals according to value of marginal W = tax rate hourly earnings, net of taxes R = husband's earnings + unearned income

Notes:
AVO = *Aanvullend Voorzieningsgebruik Onderzoek 1979*, Social and Cultural Planning Bureau, the Netherlands.
BMRBS = British Market Research Bureau survey, United Kingdom.
CC = Census of Canada, Statistics Canada.
FES = Family Expenditure Survey, Office of Population Censuses and Surveys, United Kingdom.
GHS = General Household Survey, Office of Population Censuses and Surveys, United Kingdom.
M = Microcensus, Statistiches Bundesamt, Federal Republic of Germany.
MDF = 1979 Micro Data File, Census Families Survey of Consumer Finances, Statistics Canada.
NLS = National Longitudinal Survey, Center for Human Resource Research, Ohio State University.
NSFG = National Survey of Family Growth, National Center for Health Statistics.
PSID = Panel Study of Income Dynamics, Survey Research Center, University of Michigan.
QLS = Quality of Life Survey, Institute for Behavioural Research, York University, Canada.
SEO = Survey of Economic Opportunity, U.S. Office of Economic Opportunity.
TUS = Time Use Survey, Survey Research Center, University of Michigan.
USC = U.S. Census, Bureau of the Census, U.S. Department of Commerce.

"Linearized" indicates that budget line is linearized at equilibrium hours of work and equilibrium marginal tax rate: linearized wage rate denotes wage rate × (1 – equilibrium marginal tax rate); linearized R = height of budget line when budget line is projected from equilibrium hours of work back to zero hours of work using linearized wage rate.

Table 2.26
Summary of labor supply estimates for women implied by results of selected studies of female labor supply.

Study	Sample, procedure used	Wage elasticity: Uncompensated	Wage elasticity: Compensated	Total-income elasticity
	Data for United States			
Heckman (1976b)	White wives age 30–44:			
	Procedure IV	1.46	1.48	−0.02
	Procedure VI	4.31	4.35	−0.04
Cogan (1980a)	White wives age 30–44:			
	Procedure II	1.14	1.17	−0.03
	Procedure III	3.50	3.60	−0.10
	Procedure VI	2.83	2.91	−0.09
Schultz (1980)	White wives age 35–44 (lbc):			
	Procedure I	0.16	0.21	−0.05
	Procedure II	0.13	0.19	−0.05
	Procedure III	0.65	0.83	−0.18
	Black wives age 35–44 (lbc):			
	Procedure I	0.60	0.34	0.26
	Procedure II	0.42	0.41	0.01
	Procedure III	1.04	0.56	0.48
Trussell and	White wives age 25–45 (Procedure VI)	4.50	n.a.	−0.41*
Abowd (1980)	Black wives age 25–45 (Procedure VI)	2.93	n.a.	≃ 0*
Heckman (1980)	White wives age 30–44:			
	Procedure IV	2.26	2.26	≃ 0
	Procedure VII	1.47	1.47	≃ 0
	Procedure IV(a)	14.79	14.79	≃ 0
	Procedure VII(a)	6.62	6.62	≃ 0
	Procedure V(a)	4.47	4.47	≃ 0
Hanoch (1980)	White wives age 30–44 (fc):			
	weeks worked < 52 (no "corner" in weeks worked)	0.64	0.81	−0.17
	weeks worked = 52 (with "corner" in weeks worked)	0.42	0.54	−0.13
Cogan (1980b)	White wives age 30–44:			
	Procedure VI	2.45	2.64	−0.19
	fixed costs of labor market entry model:			
	OLS	0.89	0.93	−0.04
	conditional ML	1.14	1.19	−0.05
Cogan (1981)	White wives age 30–44:			
	Procedure VI	2.10	2.18	−0.08
	fixed costs of labor market entry (conditional ML)	0.65	0.68	−0.03
Nakamura and Nakamura (1981)	Wives – Procedure VIII (lbc):			
	age 30–34	−0.27	0.11	−0.36
	age 35–39	−0.31	−0.12	−0.19
	age 40–44	−0.09	0.18	−0.27
Dooley (1982)	Wives – Procedure VII:			
	Whites: age 30–34	3.66	4.14	−0.48
	age 35–39	15.24	15.35	−0.11
	age 40–44	4.28	4.73	−0.45
	Blacks: age 30–34	0.67	1.01	−0.35
	age 35–39	−0.34	−0.17	−0.17
	age 40–44	−0.89	−1.06	0.18
Ransom (1982)	Wives, husband age 30–50 – ML, lbc (quadratic family duf)	0.40 to 0.42	0.46 to 0.50	−0.05 to −0.09

Table 2.26 continued

Study	Sample, procedure used	Wage elasticity: Uncompensated	Wage elasticity: Compensated	Total-income elasticity
Hausman (1980)	Black household heads – ML, fc, cbc (ep, eh) (linear lsf)	0.05	0.16	−0.11
Hausman (1981)	ML, fc, cbc (ep, eh) (linear lsf):			
	wives	0.91 to 1.00	n.a.	n.a.
	female household heads	0.46 to 0.53	0.58 to 0.77	−0.12 to −0.24
Moffitt (1984)	ML, cbc (eh) (linear lsf):			
	linear budget constraint	0.78	n.a.	−0.04*
	wage rate a quadratic function of hours worked:			
	response to change in wage at sample means	0.43	n.a.	−0.28*
	response to upward shift in entire budget constraint	0.21	n.a.	−0.18*
Hausman and Ruud (1984)	ML, cbc (eh) (iuf yielding lsf's quadratic in wages)	0.76	n.a.	−0.36*
Kooreman and Kapteyn (1984b)	first-stage ML for leisure times of husband and wife (eh), second-stage selection bias-corrected WLS regression of household ds (translog iuf)	0.27***	0.31***	0.00****
Yatchew (1985)	Wives – ML, cbc (ep) (translog iuf)	0.47	n.a.	−0.89*
	Data for Great Britain			
Layard, Barton and Zabalza (1980)	Wives age ≤ 60:			
	No allowance for taxes:			
	Procedure I (evaluated at overall means)	0.43	0.49	−0.06
	Procedure II (evaluated at workers' means)	0.08	0.09	−0.02
	Procedure III evaluated at overall means	0.78	0.97	−0.19
	Procedure III evaluated at workers' means	0.44	0.63	−0.19
	Lbc (eh, eb): Procedure II (evaluated at worker's means)	0.06	0.06	−0.10
Blundell and Walker (1982)	Wives – ML, lbc (family ds using Gpf, corrected for selection bias in requiring wife's $H > 0$):			
	Husband's H unrationed: No children	0.43	0.65	−0.22
	One child	0.10	0.32	−0.22
	Two children	−0.19	0.03	−0.22
	Husband's H rationed: No children	0.64	0.83	−0.19
	One child	0.09	0.28	−0.19
	Two children	−0.30	−0.11	−0.19
Zabalza (1983)	Wives – ML (ordered probit analysis), cbc (ep) (CES duf)	1.59	1.82	−0.23
Arrufat and Zabalza (1986)	Wives – ML (modified ordered probit analysis), cbc (ep, eh) (CES duf)	2.03	n.a.	−0.21*
Ashworth and Ulph (1981a)	Wives, husband < 65:			
	OLS – lbc (quadratic lsf)	−0.09 to −0.21	−0.04 to −0.23	0.02 to −0.05
	ML – lbc: CES iuf	−0.19	0.29	−0.48
	restricted generalized CES iuf	0.57	0.81	−0.24
	generalized CES iuf	0.32	0.55	−0.23

Table 2.26 continued

Study	Sample, procedure used	Wage elasticity: Uncompensated	Wage elasticity: Compensated	Total-income elasticity
Ruffell (1981)	Wives, husband < 65 (quadratic lsf):			
	OLS – lbc	−0.00	0.04	−0.04
	ML – cbc (eh)	0.43	0.51	−0.08
	MD – cbc (eh, eb)	0.72	0.77	−0.05
	Data for Canada			
Nakamura, Nakamura and Cullen (1979)	Wives – Procedure VII:			
	age 30–34	−0.17	0.00	−0.17
	age 35–39	−0.20	−0.16	−0.04
	age 40–44	−0.05	0.14	−0.19
Nakamura and Nakamura (1981)	Wives – Procedure VIII (lbc):			
	age 30–34	−0.27	0.23	−0.50
	age 35–39	−0.17	−0.12	−0.05
	age 40–44	−0.05	0.14	−0.19
Robinson and Tomes (1985)	Unmarried and married women: "hourly wage" sample:			
	Procedure II (actual wage used in lsf)	−0.22	−0.22	≃ 0
	Procedure II (instrument used for wage in lsf)	−0.85	−0.85	≃ 0
	Procedure II (actual wage used in lsf; selection biased-correction term, derived from probit analysis, included)	−0.23	−0.23	≃ 0
	Unmarried and married women: "hourly paid" sample:			
	Procedure II (actual wage used in lsf)	−0.19	−0.19	≃ 0
	Procedure II (instrument used for wage in lsf)	−0.44	−0.44	≃ 0
	Procedure II (actual wage used in lsf; selection bias-correction term, derived from probit analysis, included)	−0.20	−0.20	≃ 0
Smith and Stelcner (1985)	Wives: Procedure VII (lbc):			
	age 20–54	0.08	0.21	−0.13
	age 20–34	0.21	0.41	−0.20
	age 35–54	−0.04	0.06	−0.09
Stelcner and Smith (1985)	Wives: ML (probit analysis), ep (CES duf):			
	age 20–54	0.03	0.04	−0.01
	age 20–34	0.02	0.05	−0.03
	age 35–54	0.02	0.02	0.00
Stelcner and Breslaw (1985)	Wives in Quebec: Procedure VIII (lbc):			
	OLS with selection bias correction (no "tax illusion")	0.40	0.49	−0.09
	GLS with selection bias correction (no "tax illusion")	0.97	1.17	−0.20
	OLS with selection bias correction and "tax illusion"	0.40	0.49	−0.09
	GLS with selection bias correction and "tax illusion"	1.28	1.52	−0.24
	Data for Federal Republic of Germany			
Franz and Kawasaki (1981)	Wives – Procedure VII	1.08	1.28	−0.20
Franz (1981)	Wives – modified Procedure VII	1.37	1.66	−0.29
	Data for the Netherlands			
Renaud and Siegers (1984)	Wives – Procedure III	1.79	1.83	−0.04

Table 2.26 continued

Notes:

a = instrumental variable used for wife's work experience to allow for potential endogeneity of this variable.

* = elasticity of hours of work with respect to exogenous income (R).

** = elasticity of leisure with respect to wage rate (uncompensated).

*** = elasticity of leisure with respect to wage rate (compensated).

**** = elasticity of leisure with respect to exogenous income (R).

All elasticities are evaluated at sample means (reported by author(s)) of entire population of women, or are as reported (if available) directly by author(s). n.a. = not available (not enough information available to permit computation of elasticity). Total-income elasticity is defined as $W(\mathrm{d}H/\mathrm{d}R)$, equal to the difference between uncompensated and compensated elasticity of labor supply with respect to own wage rate. All calculations use structural labor supply parameters and therefore refer to labor supply response of a given individual (as opposed to, e.g., calculations using expected value of labor supply such as the Tobit expected-value locus).

Estimation technique:
- OLS = ordinary least squares
- GLS = generalized least squares
- WLS = weighted least squares
- ML = maximum likelihood
- MD = minimum distance

Basis of specification:
- Gpf = Gorman polar form of expenditure function
- duf = direct utility function
- iuf = indirect utility function
- ds = demand system
- lsf = labor supply function
- fc = allowance for fixed costs of labor market entry

Treatment of taxes:
- lbc = linearized budget constraint
- cbc = complete budget constraint

Error structure in cbc models:
- ep = variation (error term) in preferences (e.g. utility function or marginal rate of substitution function)
- eh = variation (errors of optimization and/or measurement) in hours of work
- eb = errors of measurement of budget constraint (e.g. wage rate or marginal tax rate)

Estimation procedure:
- I = Obtain predicted wage for all individuals from OLS estimates of wage equation using data on workers only; use predicted wage in OLS estimation of labor supply schedule with data on all individuals (nonworkers' labor supply set at zero).
- II = Obtain predicted wage for workers from OLS estimates of wage equation using data on workers only; use predicted wage in OLS estimation of labor supply schedule with data on workers only.
- III = Obtain predicted wage for all individuals from OLS estimates of wage equation using data on workers only; use predicted wage in Tobit estimation of labor supply schedule with data on all individuals.
- IV = Estimate wage equation by OLS using data for workers only; estimate reduced form labor supply equation using data on all individuals (with nonworkers' H set at zero); identify structural labor supply equation using reduced form estimates and estimates of wage equation.
- V = Estimate reduced form labor supply equation by Tobit; use Tobit estimates to compute a selection bias correction variable (inverse of Mills' ratio); include selection bias correction variable in estimation of wage equation by OLS (or GLS, etc.); identify structural labor supply equation using reduced form estimates and estimates of wage equation.
- VI = ML estimation of joint determination of wages and hours of work (extension of Tobit to simultaneous equation system).
- VII = "Heckit" for exactly-identified labor supply function: estimate reduced form equation for labor force participation by probit; use probit coefficients to compute a selection bias correction variable (inverse of Mills' ratio); include selection bias correction variable in estimation of wage and reduced form hours of work equations; identify structural labor supply equation using reduced form estimates and estimates of wage equation.
- VIII = "Heckit" for overidentified labor supply function: estimate reduced form equation for labor force participation by probit; use probit coefficients to compute a selection bias correction variable (inverse of Mills' ratio); include selection bias correction variable in estimation of wage equation; use estimates of structural wage equation to compute a predicted wage for working individuals; include predicted wage in OLS (or GLS, etc.) estimation of structural labor supply equation.

much so that even the implied compensated elasticity is also negative in some instances). Similarly, Smith and Stelcner (1985) and Stelcner and Smith (1985) obtain uncompensated (and compensated) elasticities that, although positive, are very small in magnitude.

It is tempting simply to dismiss such results as mere anomalies, particularly because the procedures used in these studies differ in some potentially important respects from those adopted in prior work.[32] The most useful evidence on female labor supply elasticities is likely to come from studies that conduct detailed sensitivity analyses, thereby highlighting the consequences of adopting different procedures for the same dataset. The one such analysis currently available is that of Mroz (1985), which offers some surprising and – to those[33] who heretofore thought that female labor supply elasticities were generally rather large – somewhat unsettling results that make it hard to dismiss out of hand results such as those of Nakamura et al.

Begin by considering the first line of Table 2.27, which summarizes results obtained by Heckman (1980) for data on white wives age 30–44 in the 1966 National Longitudinal Survey (NLS). The uncompensated wage elasticities shown there are higher (sometimes appreciably so) than those obtained by other authors, but they are certainly consistent with the notion that the uncompensated wage elasticity of female labor supply is greater than 0.50 or even 1.00.[34]

The second and third lines of Table 2.27 present the results of Mroz's (1985) replication of the Heckman (1980) paper using the same variables and statistical procedures (and alternative definitions of annual hours of work) for a different dataset: white wives age 30–60 in the 1976 Panel Study of Income Dynamics (PSID). The elasticities are uniformly lower in Mroz's (1985) results than in Heckman's (1980), especially when work experience is treated as statistically endogenous. Adding new variables (number of children age 7 or older and wife's age) to the labor supply equation results in larger implied elasticities (again, especially when work experience is treated as statistically endogenous), as shown

[32]For example, Robinson and Tomes (1985) include both single and married women in their analysis, whereas most other studies of female labor supply have considered married women separately; and the studies by Nakamura and Nakamura (1981) and Nakamura and Cullen (1979) do not include an education variable in the labor supply function, whereas many other studies have such a variable. Finally, in both the Robinson–Tomes and Nakamura et al. studies the labor supply function is overidentified (in the sense that more than one variable that does appear in the wage equation does not appear in the structural labor supply equation), whereas in most other work the labor supply function is exactly identified (in the sense that exactly one variable – usually, work experience – that does appear in the wage equation does not appear in the labor supply equation); hence Robinson–Tomes and Nakamura et al. use Procedure VIII, whereas much other work uses Procedure VII (see Table 2.26 for definition of these terms).

[33]See, for example, Heckman, Killingsworth and MaCurdy (1981, esp. pp. 107–109) and Killingsworth (1983, esp. p. 432).

[34]Recall the uncompensated elasticities shown in Table 2.26 that are implied by the results of other studies, e.g. 0.65 in Schultz (1980); 1.14 in Cogan (1980b); 0.65 in Cogan (1981); and 0.90–1.00 in Hausman (1981).

Table 2.27
Uncompensated wage elasticities of married women's labor supply implied by alternative estimates of Heckman (1980) model.

	Procedure IV	Procedure VII	Procedure IV[a]	Procedure VII[a]	Procedure VII[b]
Original Heckman (1980) results					
(white wives age 30–44, NLS)	2.49	2.00	2.93	6.61	n.a.
Mroz (1985) replication					
(white wives age 30–50, PSID)					
original Heckman variables					
H: definition 1	1.25	0.11	0.17	1.43	0.48
definition 2	1.33	0.22	0.24	0.62	0.63
with new variables added					
H: definition 1	1.51	1.09	1.75	1.68	1.60
definition 2	1.57	1.35	1.97	1.94	1.89

[a]Instrumental variables used for wife's work experience and (when applicable) selection bias-correction variable λ (which includes wife's work experience) to correct for possible endogeneity of wife's work experience.

[b]Instrumental variables used for wife's work experience in both labor supply function and (when applicable) estimation of probit equation for labor force participation (which is used in construction of selection bias variable λ) to correct for possible endogeneity of work experience.

Definitions of hours of work:
1 = (1975 earnings)/(hourly wage in 1976), if available; otherwise, definition 2.
2 = weeks worked in 1975 × usual hours worked per week.

Variables:
Wage equation = education, years of schooling, years of work experience.
Labor supply equation = years of work experience, years of schooling, husband's wage, nonlabor income, number of children age 6 or less.
New variables: age, number of children age 7 or more.

All elasticities evaluated at $H = 1300$ [= approximate mean of hours of work of working women in Heckman (1980) and Mroz (1985) data]. Elasticities obtained as in Heckman (1980), by computing ratio of coefficient on experience variable in labor supply equation to coefficient on experience variable in wage equation (the latter is set at 0.015 in all calculations) and dividing the result by 1300.

For a definition of the statistical procedures used, see Table 2.26.

in the last two lines of Table 2.27. However, the standard errors of the point estimates underlying this third set of elasticities are appreciably larger than those of the point estimates derived using the original Heckman variables. Moreover, it is hardly reassuring to find that (i) one can get to within hailing distance of the original Heckman (1980) results only by departing from the original Heckman (1980) specification or (ii) inclusion of the older children and age variables should have such a pronounced effect on the implied labor supply elasticity.[35]

There remains the possibility that the Heckman and Mroz results differ because they are derived from different data and somewhat different populations: labor supply of white wives age 30–60 in the 1976 PSID (Mroz) may differ substantially from that of white wives age 30–44 in the 1966 NLS (Heckman) because of life-cycle and/or cohort effects. However, at this point it would be mere conjecture to make statements even about the existence of such effects, much less about whether their magnitude is sufficient to provide an explanation of the difference in results. Furthermore, any such explanation would also have to account for the difference between Mroz's results (1985) and those of Cogan (1980b). Cogan (1980b) gets an implied elasticity of 1.14 using conditional maximum likelihood – much higher than Mroz's (1985) results with the original Heckman variables – even though he, like Mroz (1985), uses the 1976 PSID (albeit for essentially all white wives regardless of age, versus Mroz's smaller group of white wives age 30–60).

The main contribution of Mroz's (1985) study is that it provides formal tests of a variety of propositions that were not subjected to serious scrutiny in previous work. Among the most important of his findings are the following: (i) there is

[35] One other consideration has to do with details about what wage equation parameter and what level of hours of work are used in calculation of the elasticities. In Table 2.27, we use 0.015 as "the" coefficient on the wife's experience variable in the wage equation, and use $H = 1300$, the approximate mean annual hours worked by *working* wives. However, one might argue that, in a given calculation, one should instead use (i) the coefficient on the experience variable in the wage equation that corresponds directly to the labor supply equation actually estimated and (ii) the *population* mean annual hours worked (by working and nonworking wives, with the latter's hours set equal to zero); indeed, most of the elasticities shown in Table 2.26 are in fact calculated in precisely this fashion [see especially the figures reported there for Heckman (1980)]. Changing either of these will in general change the implied elasticity. For example, the population mean value of H is about 740 in Mroz's (1985) data, and is 600 in the Heckman data [Heckman (1980, p. 244)]. Thus, other things being equal, using $H = 600$ or 740 rather than $H = 1300$ would increase the wage elasticity figures shown in Table 2.27 by a factor of between $1300/600 = 2.17$ and $1300/740 = 1.75$. That would certainly bring the Mroz replication results "with new variables added" closer to the original Heckman (1980) results shown in Table 2.26; but it would not change the Mroz "original Heckman variables" results very much. Note also that the difference in population mean values of H implies quite different employment rates (0.362 for the Mroz data, 0.468 for the Heckman data) coexisting alongside virtually identical mean values of hours of work for *working* women (1303 for the Mroz data, 1289 for the Heckman data). This highlights the possible importance of cohort and/or life cycle effects noted in the text.

little or no evidence that the wife's work experience is statistically endogeneous in the labor supply equation *provided* selection bias is taken into account [e.g. by inclusion of a λ variable in expressions such as (106)]; and (ii) the hypothesis of no selection bias in analyses of the labor supply of working women is rejected *provided* the wife's work experience is included in the labor supply equation [so that ignoring selection bias, e.g. omitting the λ variable in expressions such as (106), will generally lead to inconsistent estimates of labor supply parameters if work experience is included in the labor supply equation]. Conversely, (iii) if work experience is excluded from the supply equation, the hypothesis of no selection bias in the supply equation cannot be rejected; and (iv) if a selection bias term is excluded from the supply equation, the hypothesis that experience is exogenous in the supply equation is rejected. (Thus, the selection bias problem appears to manifest itself primarily through the work experience variable.) Finally: (v) the conventional Tobit specification of labor supply can be rejected in favour of the generalized Tobit ("Heckit") specification,[36] (106), with the former yielding inflated wage elasticity estimates relative to the latter; (vi) there is little or no evidence that "exogenous" income, R (defined to include husband's earnings and property income), is statistically endogenous; and (vii) correcting for taxes has a trivial effect on wage elasticity estimates, and has varying but generally small effects on estimated elasticities with respect to nonwork income.

Mroz also finds that estimated wage elasticities tend to be higher in exactly-identified labor supply functions than in overidentified labor supply functions,[37] and presents evidence favoring the latter kind of specification. Estimates of labor supply models that embody these findings (e.g. generalized Tobit estimation of overidentified labor supply equations, with or without allowance for taxes, but with correction for selection bias) generally imply a very low or even negative elasticity of labor supply with respect to wages, as shown in Table 2.28.

Six years ago, Heckman, Killingsworth and MaCurdy (1981, p. 108) commented that elasticity estimates obtained using recently developed econometric techniques had increased the mean of what might be called the "reasonable guesstimate" of the wage-elasticity of female labor supply. Work since then seems to have reduced the mean and substantially increased the variance of this

[36] The Tobit specification (in terms of Table 2.26, Procedures III, V or VII) implicitly assumes that hours of work vary continuously from zero (at a wage equal to the reservation level) to progressively larger positive amounts (at wages greater than the reservation level), with no jumps or discontinuities. In contrast, the generalized Tobit specification (in terms of Table 2.26, Procedures VII or VIII, sometimes called "Heckit") implicitly allows for a discontinuity in labor supply at the reservation wage such that hours worked are zero below the reservation level and some large amount above the reservation level. The latter approach has sometimes been characterized as a means of allowing for the labor supply discontinuities that may be induced by fixed costs of labor market entry. [For further discussion, see Cogan (1980b) and Killingsworth (1983, esp. pp. 141–148).]

[37] See footnote 32.

Table 2.28
Alternative estimates of uncompensated wage elasticity of wives' labor supply in Mroz's (1985) sensitivity analyses.

Model	Estimated elasticity (standard error)
Procedure VIII (a) – no allowance for taxes	0.09
	(0.17)
Procedure VIII (b)	
no allowance for taxes	−0.02
	(0.15)
with allowance for taxes (lbc)	−0.05
	(0.15)

Notes:
a = Variables in probit equation = age, education, exogenous income, number of children age (i) 6 or less, (ii) 5 or less, (iii) age 5–19, (iv) age 7–19, background variables (county unemployment rate, schooling of wife's parents, etc.), wife's experience, wife's experience squared, quadratic and cubic terms in wife's age and education.
Variables in wage equation = same as probit equation.
Variables in structural labor supply equation = logarithm of wife's wage, exogenous income, children (i) age 6 or less and (ii) 7–19, wife's age, wife's education.
b = Variables in probit equation = as for (a), with addition of cubic and quadratic terms in husband's age and education, family property income (family income exclusive of spouses' earnings), logarithm of husband's average hourly wage.
Variables in wage equation = same as probit equation.
Variables in structural labor supply equation = same as for (a).
lbc denotes linearized budget constraint.
For definition of Procedure VIII, see Table 2.26.
All elasticities evaluated at $H = 1300$ [= approximate mean of hours worked by working women in Mroz's (1985) sample]; see Table 2.27.

guesstimate. Regarding future research, we borrow from Samuel Gompers' characterization of union objectives, and advocate "more". Additional sensitivity analyses using a single behavioral specification, along the lines of Mroz (1985), will help identify some of the factors underlying the substantial diversity of elasticity estimates. However, as implied by our brief reference to life-cycle and/or cohort issues, studies based on alternative behavioral models – notably, life-cycle models, which have been used relatively little in empirical studies – are also likely to provide important insights. Pencavel (Chapter 1 in this Handbook) is critical of the emphasis on mere calibration – as opposed to hypothesis testing – in studies of male labor supply; if only because female labor supply elasticities have been calibrated so imprecisely, most readers are likely to agree that his comments apply just as much to female as to male labor supply.

References

Allen, R. G. D. (1938) *Mathematical analysis for economists*. London: Macmillan Press.

Altonji, J. (1986), "Intertemporal substitution in labor supply: evidence from micro data", *Journal of Political Economy*, 94 (Supplement): S176–S215.

Arrow, K. J. and M. Kurz (1970) *Public investment, the rate of return, and optimal fiscal policy*. Baltimore: Johns Hopkins University Press.

Arrufat, J. L. and A. Zabalza (1986) "Female labor supply with taxation, random preferences, and optimization errors", *Econometrica*, 54:47–64.

Ashenfelter, O. (1979) "Comment [on Manser and Brown, 1979]", in: Cynthia B. Lloyd, Emily S. Andrews and Curtis L. Gilroy, *Women in the labor market*. New York: Columbia University Press, 37–42.

Ashenfelter, O. and J. J. Heckman (1974) "The estimation of income and substitution effects in a model of family labor supply", *Econometrica*, 42:73–85.

Ashworth, J. S. and D. T. Ulph (1981) "Household models", in: C. V. Brown, ed., *Taxation and labour supply*. London: Allen & Unwin, 117–133.

Atkinson, A. B. and N. H. Stern (1981) "On labour supply and commodity demands", in: A. Deaton, ed., *Essays in the theory and measurement of consumer behaviour in honour of Sir Richard Stone*. Cambridge: Cambridge University Press, 265–296.

Atrostic, B. K. (1982) "The demand for leisure and nonpecuniary job characteristics", *American Economic Review*, 72:428–440.

Barten, A. P. (1977) "The system of consumer demand functions approach: a review", *Econometrica*, 45:23–51.

Basemann, R. (1956) "A theory of demand with variable consumer preferences", *Econometrica*, 24:47–58.

Becker, G. (1965) "A theory of the allocation of time", *Economic Journal*, 75:493–517.

Becker, G. (1974) "A theory of marriage", in: T. W. Schultz, ed., *Economics of the family*. Chicago: University of Chicago Press, 293–344.

Ben-Porath, Y. (1973) "Labor-force participation rates and the supply of labor", *Journal of Political Economy*, 81:697–704.

Bergstrom, T. (1984) "Remarks on public goods theory and the economics of the family", unpublished manuscript, Department of Economics, University of Michigan, Ann Arbor, Michigan.

Bjorn, P. A. and Q. H. Vuong (1984) "Simultaneous equations models for dummy endogenous variables: a game theoretic formulation with an application to labor force participation", unpublished manuscript, Department of Economics, California Institute of Technology, Pasadena, California.

Bjorn, P. A. and Q. H. Vuong (1985) "Econometric modeling of a Stackelberg game with an application to labor force participation", unpublished manuscript, Department of Economics, California Institute of Technology, Pasadena, California.

Blundell, R. and I. Walker (1982) "Modelling the joint determination of household labour supplies and commodity demands", *Economic Journal*, 92:351–364.

Blundell, R. and I. Walker (1983) "Estimating a life-cycle consistent model of family labor supply with cross section data", unpublished manuscript, Department of Economics, University of Manchester, Manchester, England.

Boothby, D. (1984) "The continuity of married women's labour force participation in Canada", *Canadian Journal of Economics*, 17:471–480.

Bourguignon, F. (1984) "Rationalité individuelle ou rationalité stratégique: le cas de l'offre familiale de travail", *Revue Economique*, 35:147–162.

Bourguignon, F. (1985) "Women's participation and taxation in France", in: R. Blundell and I. Walker, eds., *Unemployment, job search and labour supply*. Cambridge: Cambridge University Press.

Bowen, W. and T. A. Finegan (1969) *The economics of labor force participation*. Princeton, N.J.: Princeton University Press.

Brown, C. (1985) "An institutional model of wives' work decisions", *Industrial Relations*, 24:182–204.

Brown, A. and A. Deaton (1972) "Models of consumer behaviour: a survey", *Economic Journal*, 82:1145–1236.

Browning, M., A. Deaton and M. Irish (1985) "A profitable approach to labor supply and commodity demands over the life-cycle", *Econometrica*, 53:503–543.

Burtless, G. and D. Greenberg (1983) "Measuring the impact of NIT experiments on work effort", *Industrial and Labor Relations Review*, 36:592–605.

Burtless, G. and J. Hausman (1978) "The effect of taxation on labor supply: evaluating the Gary negative income tax experiment", *Journal of Political Economy*, 86:1103–1130.

Cain, G. (1966) *Married women in the labor force*. Chicago: University of Chicago Press.

Cain, G. (1982) "The economic analysis of labor supply: developments since Mincer", unpublished manuscript, Department of Economics, University of Wisconsin, Madison, Wisconsin.

Clark, K. B. and L. H. Summers (1981) "Demographic differences in cyclical employment variation", *Journal of Human Resources*, 16:61–79.

Clark, K. B. and L. H. Summers (1982) "Labour force participation: timing and persistence", *Review of Economic Studies*, 49 (Supplement):825–844.

Cogan, J. (1980a) "Married women's labor supply: a comparison of alternative estimation procedures", in: J. P. Smith, ed., *Female labor supply*. Princeton, N.J.: Princeton University Press, 90–118.

Cogan, J. (1980b) "Labor supply with costs of labor market entry", in: J. P. Smith, ed., *Female labor supply*. Princeton, N.J.: Princeton University Press, 327–364.

Cogan, J. (1981) "Fixed costs and labor supply", *Econometrica*, 49:945–964.

Cohen, M. S., S. A. Rea and R. I. Lerman (1970) *A micro model of labor supply*. BLS Staff Paper No. 4, U.S. Department of Labor. Washington, D.C.: U.S. Government Printing Office.

Coleman, T. (1984) "Essays on aggregate labor market business cycle fluctuations", unpublished Ph.D. dissertation, University of Chicago, Chicago, Illinois.

Corcoran, M. (1979) "Work experience, labor force withdrawals and women's wages: empirical results using the 1976 panel of income dynamics", in: C. B. Lloyd, E. S. Andrews and C. L. Gilroy, eds., *Women in the labor market*. New York: Columbia University Press.

Deaton, A. (1974) "A reconsideration of the empirical implications of additive preferences", *Economic Journal*, 84:338–348.

Deaton, A. (forthcoming) "Demand analysis", in: Z. Griliches and M. Intriligator, eds., *Handbook of econometrics*. New York: North-Holland, Vol. 3, forthcoming.

Deaton, A. and J. Muellbauer (1980) *Economics and consumer behavior*. New York: Cambridge University Press.

Deaton, A. and J. Muellbauer (1981) "Functional forms for labour supply and commodity demands with and without quantity restrictions", *Econometrica*, 49:1521–1532.

Dixit, A. (1976) *Optimization in economic theory*. Oxford: Oxford University Press.

Dooley, M. D. (1982) "Labor supply and fertility of married women: an analysis with grouped and individual data from the 1970 U.S. census", *Journal of Human Resources*, 17:499–532.

Douglas, P. H. (1934) *The theory of wages*. New York: Macmillan.

Duesenberry, J. (1952) *Income, savings and the theory of consumer behavior*. Cambridge, Mass.: Harvard University Press.

Durand, J. D. (1948) *The labor force in the U.S.* New York: Social Science Research Council.

Fisher, F. and K. Shell (1971) "Taste and quality change in the pure theory of the true cost of living index", in: Z. Griliches, ed., *Price indexes and quality change: studies in new methods of measurement*. Cambridge, Mass.: Harvard University Press.

Franz, W. (1981) "Schatzung Regionaler Arbeitsangebotsfunktionen mit Hilfe der Tobit-Methode und des Probit-verfahrens unter Berucksichtigung des sog. 'Sample Selection Bias'", Discussion Paper No. 171-81, Institut für Volkswirtschaftslehre und Statistik, University of Mannheim, Mannheim, Federal Republic of Germany.

Franz, W. and S. Kawasaki (1981) "Labor supply of married women in the Federal Republic of Germany: theory and empirical results from a new estimation procedure", *Empirical Economics*, 6:129–143.

Friedman, M. (1957) *A theory of the consumption function*. Princeton, N.J.: Princeton University Press.

Fuchs, V. (1984) "His and hers: gender differences in work and income, 1959–1979", Working Paper No. 1501, National Bureau of Economic Research, Cambridge, Massachusetts.

Goldin, C. (1980) "The work and wages of single women, 1970 to 1920", *Journal of Economic History*, 40:81–88.

Goldin, C. (1983a) "The changing economic role of women: a quantitative approach", *Journal of Interdisciplinary History*, 13:707–733.

Goldin, C. (1983b) "Life cycle labor force participation of married women: historical evidence and implications", Working Paper No. 1251, National Bureau of Economic Research, Cambridge, Massachusetts.

Goldin, C. (1984) "The historical evolution of female earnings functions and occupations", *Explorations in Economic History*, 21:1–27.

Goldin, C. (1986) "Monitoring costs and occupational segregation by sex: a historical analysis", *Journal of Labor Economics*, 4:1–27.

Goldin, C. and K. Sokoloff (1982) "Women, children, and industrialization in the early republic: evidence from the manufacturing censuses", *Journal of Economic History*, 42:741–774.

Graham, J. and C. Green (1984) "Estimating the parameters of a household production function with joint products", *Review of Economics and Statistics*, 66:277–282.

Greenberg, D. and H. Halsey (1983) "Systematic misreporting and effects of income maintenance experiments on work effort: evidence from the Seattle-Denver experiment", *Journal of Labor Economics*, 1:380–407.

Greenberg, D., R. Moffitt and J. Friedmann (1981) "Underreporting and experimental effects on work effort: evidence from the Gary income maintenance experiment", *Review of Economics and Statistics*, 63:581–589.

Gronau, R. (1977) "Leisure, home production and work—the theory of the allocation of time revisited", *Journal of Political Economy*, 85:1099–1124.

Grossbard-Shechtman, A. (1984) "A theory of allocation of time in markets for labour and marriage", *Economic Journal*, 94:863–882.

Hanoch, G. (1980) "A multivariate model of labor supply: methodology and estimation", in: J. P. Smith, ed., *Female labor supply*. Princeton, N.J.: Princeton University Press, 249–326.

Hausman, J. (1980) "The effects of wages, taxes and fixed costs on women's labor force participation", *Journal of Public Economics*, 14:161–194.

Hausman, J. (1981) "Labor supply", in: H. Aaron and J. Pechman, eds., *How taxes affect economic behavior*. Washington, D.C.: The Brookings Institution, 27–72.

Hausman, J. (1983) "Taxes and labor supply", Working Paper No. 1102, National Bureau of Economic Research, Cambridge, Massachusetts. (Forthcoming in: A. Auerbach and M. Feldstein, eds., *Handbook of public finance*. New York: North-Holland.)

Hausman, J. and P. Ruud (1984) "Family labor supply with taxes", *American Economic Review*, 74(2):242–248.

Heckman, J. (1971) "Three essays on the supply of labor and the demand for goods", unpublished Ph.D. dissertation, Department of Economics, Princeton University, Princeton, N.J.

Heckman, J. (1976a) "A life cycle model of earnings, learning and consumption", *Journal of Political Economy*, 84:S11–S44.

Heckman, J. (1976b) "The common structure of statistical models of truncation, sample selection, and limited dependent variables and a simple estimator for such models", *Annals of Economic and Social Measurement*, 5:475–492.

Heckman, J. (1978) "A partial survey of recent research on the labor supply of women", *American Economic Review*, 68 (Supplement):200–207.

Heckman, J. (1979) "Sample selection bias as a specification error", *Econometrica*, 47:153–162.

Heckman, J. (1980) "Sample selection bias as a specification error", in: J. Smith, ed., *Female labor supply*. Princeton, N.J.: Princeton University Press, 206–248.

Heckman, J., M. R. Killingsworth and T. MaCurdy (1981) "Empirical evidence on static labour supply models: a survey of recent developments", in: Z. Hornstein, J. Grice and A. Webb, eds., *The economics of the labour market*. London: Her Majesty's Stationery Office, 73–122.

Heckman, J. and T. MaCurdy (1980) "A life cycle model of female labour supply", *Review of Economic Studies*, 47:47–74.

Heckman, J. and T. MaCurdy (1982) "Corrigendum on a life cycle model of female labour supply", *Review of Economic Studies*, 49:659–660.

Heckman, J. and T. MaCurdy (1984) "Labor econometrics", in: Z. Griliches and M. Intriligator, eds., *Handbook of econometrics*. New York: North-Holland, vol. 3, forthcoming.

Heckman, J. and R. Willis (1977) "A beta-logistic model for the analysis of sequential labor force participation by married women", *Journal of Political Economy*, 85:27–58.

Heckman, J. and R. Willis (1979) "Reply to Mincer and Ofek [1979]", *Journal of Political Economy*, 87:203–211.

Hicks, J. R. (1946) *Value and capital*, 2nd ed. Oxford: Oxford University Press.

Hicks, J. R. (1965) *The theory of wages*, 2nd ed. London: Macmillan.

Hill, M. A. (1983) "Female labor force participation in developing and developed countries: consideration of the informal sector", *Review of Economics and Statistics*, 65:459–468.

Hill, M. A. (1984) "Female labor force participation in Japan: an aggregate model", *Journal of Human Resources*, 19:280–287.

Hill, M. A. (1985) "Female labor supply in Japan: implications of the informal sector for labor force participation and hours of work", unpublished manuscript, Department of Economics, Rutgers University, New Brunswick, N.J.

Horney, M. J. and M. B. McElroy (1978) "A Nash-bargained linear expenditure system", unpublished manuscript, Department of Economics, Duke University, Durham, N.C.

Hotz, J., F. Kydland and G. Sedlacek (1985) "Intertemporal preferences and labor supply", unpublished manuscript, Department of Economics, Carnegie-Mellon University, Pittsburgh, Pennsylvania.

Johnson, J. L. (1983) "Unemployment as a household labor supply decision", *Quarterly Review of Economics and Business*, 23(2):71–88.

Johnson, T. and J. Pencavel (1984) "Dynamic hours of work functions for husbands, wives and single females", *Econometrica*, 52:363–390.

Joshi, H. (1985) "Participation in paid work: multiple regression analysis of the women and employment survey", in: R. Blundell and I. Walker, eds., *Unemployment, job search and labour supply*. Cambridge: Cambridge University Press, forthcoming.

Joshi, H. and S. Owen (1984) "How long is a piece of elastic? The measurement of female activity rates in British censuses 1951–1981", Discussion Paper No. 31, Centre for Economic Policy Research, London.

Joshi, H. and S. Owen (1985) "Does elastic retract? The effect of recession on women's labour force participation", Discussion Paper No. 64, Centre for Economic Policy Research, London.

Kalachek, E. D., W. Mellow and F. Q. Raines (1978) "The male labor supply function reconsidered", *Industrial and Labor Relations Review*, 31:356–367.

Kalachek, E. D. and F. Q. Raines (1970) "Labor supply of lower-income workers", in *President's Commission on Income Maintenance Programs, Technical studies*. Washington, D.C.: U.S. Government Printing Office, 159–186.

Kapteyn, A., P. Kooreman and A. van Soest (1985) "Non-convex budget sets, institutional constraints and imposition of concavity in a flexible household labor supply model", unpublished working paper, Department of Econometrics, Tilburg University, Tilburg, The Netherlands.

Killingsworth, M. R. (1983) *Labor supply*. New York: Cambridge University Press.

Killingsworth, M. R. (1985) "A simple structural model of heterogeneous preferences and compensating wage differentials", pp. 303–17 in: R. Blundell and I. Walker, eds., *Unemployment, job search and labour supply*. Cambridge: Cambridge University Press, 303–317.

Kniesner, T. (1976) "An indirect test of complementarity in a family labor supply model", *Econometrica*, 44:651–659.

Kooreman, P. and A. Kapteyn (1984a) "Estimation of rationed and unrationed household labor supply functions using flexible functional forms", Research Memorandum 157, Department of Econometrics, Tilburg University, Tilburg, The Netherlands.

Kooreman, P. and A. Kapteyn (1984b) "A disaggregated analysis of the allocation of time within the household", Research Memorandum 153, Department of Econometrics, Tilburg University, Tilburg, The Netherlands.

Kooreman, P. and A. Kapteyn (1985) "Estimation of a game theoretic model of household labor supply", Research Memorandum 180, Department of Econometrics, Tilburg University, Tilburg, The Netherlands.

Kosters, M. (1966) "Income and substitution effects in a family labor supply model", Report No. P-3339, The Rand Corporation, Santa Monica, California.

Kosters, M. (1969) "Effects of an income tax on labor supply", in: A. C. Harberger and M. J. Bailey, eds., *The taxation of income from capital*. Washington, D.C.: The Brookings Institution, 301–324.

Layard, R., M. Barton and A. Zabalza (1980) "Married women's participation and hours", *Economica*, 47:51–72.

Layard, R. and J. Mincer, eds. (1985) "Trends in women's work, education, and family building", *Journal of Labor Economics*, 3(special edition):S1–S396.

Leibowitz, A. (1974) "Production within the household", *American Economic Review Proceedings and Papers*, 62(2):243–250.

Lewis, H. G. (1957) "Hours of work and hours of leisure", in *Industrial Relations Research Association*, *Proceedings of the ninth annual meeting*. Madison, Wisconsin: Industrial Relations Research Association, 195–206.

Leuthold, J. (1968) "An empirical study of formula income transfers and the work decision of the poor", *Journal of Human Resources*, 3:312–323.

Lillard, L. A. (1978) "Estimation of permanent and transitory response functions in panel data: a dynamic labor supply model", *Annales de l'INSEE*, 30:367–394.

Long, C. D. (1958) *The labor force under changing income and employment*. Princeton, N.J.: Princeton University Press.

Lundberg, S. (1985) "The added worker effect", *Journal of Labor Economics*, 3:11–37.

Manser, M. and M. Brown (1979) "Bargaining analyses of household decisions", in: C. B. Lloyd, E. Andrews and C. Gilroy, eds., *Women in the labor market*. New York: Columbia University Press, 3–26.

Manser, M. and M. Brown (1980) "Marriage and household decision-making: a bargaining analysis", *International Economic Review*, 21:31–44.

Marshall, A. (1920) *Principles of economics*. New York: Macmillan, 8th ed.

Martin, J. and C. Roberts (1984) *Women and employment: a lifetime perspective*. London: Her Majesty's Stationery Office.

McCabe, P. J. (1983) "Optimal leisure-effort choice with endogenously determined earnings", *Journal of Labor Economics*, 1:308–329.

McElroy, M. and M. Horney (1981) "Nash-bargained household decisions: toward a generalization of the theory of demand", *International Economic Review*, 22:333–349.

Mincer, J. (1962) "Labor force participation of married women: a study of labor supply", in *Aspects of labor economics*. Princeton, N.J.: National Bureau of Economic Research, Princeton University Press, 63–97.

Mincer, J. (1963) "Market prices, opportunity costs and income effects", in: C. F. Christ, M. Friedman, L. A. Goodman, Z. Griliches, A. C. Harberger, N. Liviatan, J. Mincer, Y. Mundlak, M. Nerlove, D. Patinkin, L. G. Telser and H. Theil, eds., *Measurement in economics*, Stanford, Calif.: Stanford University Press, 67–82.

Mincer, J. (1966) "Labor force participation and unemployment: a review of recent evidence", in: R. A. Gordon and M. S. Gordon, eds., *Prosperity and unemployment*. New York: Wiley, 73–112.

Mincer, J. and H. Ofek (1979) "The distribution of lifetime labor force participation of married women: comment", *Journal of Political Economy*, 87:197–201.

Mincer, J. and S. Polachek (1974) "Family investments in human capital: earnings of women", in: T. W. Schultz, ed., *Economics of the family: marriage, children and human capital*. New York: Columbia University Press, 397–429.

Moffitt, R. (1984a) "The estimation of a joint wage-hours labor supply model", *Journal of Labor Economics*, 2:550–566.

Moffitt, R. (1984b) "Profiles of fertility, labour supply and wages of married women: a complete life-cycle model", *Review of Economic Studies*, 51:263–278.

Moffitt, R. and K. C. Kehrer (1981) "The effect of tax and transfer programs on labor supply: the evidence from the income maintenance programs", in: R. G. Ehrenberg, ed., *Research in labor economics*. Greenwich, Conn.: JAI Press, vol. 4, 103–150.

Moffitt, R. and K. C. Kehrer (1983) "Correction", in: R. G. Ehrenberg, ed., *Research in labor economics*. Greenwich, Conn.: JAI Press, vol. 6, 452.

Mroz, T. A. (1985) "The sensitivity of an empirical model of married women's hours of work to economic and statistical assumptions", unpublished manuscript, Department of Economics, University of Chicago, Chicago, Illinois.

Mueller, D. (1981) *Public choice*. New York: Cambridge University Press.

Nakamura, A. and M. Nakamura (1981) "A comparison of the labor force behavior of married women in the United States and Canada, with special attention to the impact of income taxes", *Econometrica*, 49:451–490.

Nakamura, A. and M. Nakamura (1985a) "Dynamic models of the labor force behavior of married women which can be estimated using limited amounts of past information", *Journal of Econometrics*, 27:273–298.

Nakamura, A. and M. Nakamura (1985b) *The second paycheck: a socioeconomic analysis of earnings*. New York: Academic Press.

Nakamura, A., M. Nakamura and D. Cullen (1979) "Job opportunities, the offered wage, and the labor supply of married women", *American Economic Review*, 69:787–805.

Olsen, R. (1977) "An econometric model of family labor supply", unpublished Ph.D. dissertation, Department of Economics, University of Chicago, Chicago, Illinois.

Owen, J. (1969) *The price of leisure*. Rotterdam: Rotterdam University Press.

Owen, J. (1971) "The demand for leisure", *Journal of Political Economy*, 79:56–76.

Owen, J. (1985) *Working lives: the American work force since 1920*. Lexington, Mass.: D. C. Heath.

Pigou, A. C. (1946) *The economics of welfare*, 4th ed. London: Macmillan.

Pollak, R. (1985) "A transactions cost approach to families and households", *Journal of Economic Literature*, 23:581–608.

Pollak, R. and M. Wachter (1974) "The relevance of the household production function and its implications for the allocation of time", *Journal of Political Economy*, 83:255–277.

Ransom, M. (1982) "Estimating family labor supply models under quantity constraints", Working Paper No. 150, Industrial Relations Section, Princeton University, Princeton, New Jersey.

Ransom, M. (1985a) "The labor supply of married men: a switching regressions model", Working Paper No. 191, Industrial Relations Section, Princeton University, Princeton, New Jersey.

Ransom, M. (1985b) "A comment on consumer demand systems with binding non-negativity constraints", Working Paper No. 192, Industrial Relations Section, Princeton University, Princeton, New Jersey.

Renaud, P. S. A. and J. J. Siegers (1984) "Income and substitution effects in family labour supply", *De Economist*, 132:350–366.

Robins, P. K. (1984) "The labor supply response of twenty-year families in the Denver income maintenance experiment", *Review of Economics and Statistics*, 66:491–495.

Robinson, C. and N. Tomes (1985) "More on the labour supply of Canadian women", *Canadian Journal of Economics*, 18:156–163.

Ruffell, R. J. (1981) "Endogeneity II: direct estimation of labour supply functions with piecewise linear budget constraints", in: C. Brown, ed., *Taxation and labour supply*. London: Allen & Unwin, 101–116.

Samuelson, P. A. (1947) *Foundations of economic analysis*. Cambridge, Mass.: Harvard University Press.

Samuelson, P. A. (1956) "Social indifference curves", *Quarterly Journal of Economics*, 70:1–22.

Samuelson, P. A. (1960) "The structure of a minimum equilibrium system", in: R. W. Pfouts, ed., *Essays in economics and econometrics in honor of Harold Hotelling*. Chapel Hill, N.C.: University of North Carolina Press, 1–33.

Schoenberg, E. and P. Douglas (1937) "Studies in the supply curve of labor: the relation between average earnings in American cities and the proportion seeking employment", *Journal of Political Economy*, 45:45–62.

Schultz, T. P. (1980) "Estimating labor supply functions for married women", in: J. P. Smith, ed., *Female labor supply*. Princeton, N.J.: Princeton University Press, 25–89.

Smith, J. B. and M. Stelcner (1985) "Labour supply of married women in Canada, 1980", Working Paper No. 1985-7, Department of Economics, Concordia University, Montreal, Quebec.

Smith, J. P. (1977a) "The convergence to racial equality in women's wages", unpublished paper, The Rand Corporation, Santa Monica, California.

Smith, J. P. (1977b) "Assets, savings and labor supply", *Economic Inquiry*, 15:551–573.

Smith, J. P. (1977c) "Family labor supply over the life cycle", *Explorations in Economic Research*, 4:205–276.

Smith, J. P. (1980) "Assets and labor supply", in: J. P. Smith, ed., *Female labor supply*. Princeton, N.J.: Princeton University Press.

Smith, J. P. and M. Ward (1984) "Women's wages and work in the twentieth century", Report R-3119-HICHD, The Rand Corporation, Santa Monica, California.

Smith, J. P. and M. Ward (1985) "Time-series growth in the female labor force", *Journal of Labor Economics*, 3(Supplement):S59–S90.

Smith, R. E., ed. (1979) *The subtle revolution*. Washington, D.C.: The Urban Institute.

Smith, R. (1979) "Compensating wage differentials and public policy: a review", *Industrial and Labor Relations Review*, 32:339–352.

Smith, S. (1983) "Estimating annual hours of labor force activity", *Monthly Labor Review*, 106(2):13–22.

Sorrentino, C. (1983) "International comparisons of labor force participation, 1960–81", *Monthly Labor Review*, 106(2):23–36.

Stelcner, M. and J. Breslaw (1985) "Income taxes and the labor supply of married women in Quebec", *Southern Economic Journal*, 51:1053–1072.

Stelcner, M. and J. B. Smith (1985) "Labour supply of married women in Canada: non-convex budget constraints and the CES utility function", Working Paper No. 1985-9, Department of Economics, Concordia University, Montreal, Quebec.

Stewart, M. and C. Greenhalgh (1984) "Work history patterns and the occupational attainment of women", *Economic Journal*, 94:493–519.

Takayama, A. (1985) *Mathematical economics*, 2nd ed. New York: Cambridge University Press.

Tinbergen, J. (1956) "On the theory of income distribution", *Weltwirtschaftliches Archiv*, 77:155–173.

Trussell, T. J. and J. M. Abowd (1980) "Teenage mothers, labour force participation and wage rates", *Canadian Studies in Population*, 7:33–48.

van der Veen, A. and G. H. M. Evers (1984) "A labour-supply function for females in the Netherlands", *De Economist*, 132:367–376.

Veblen, T. (1973) *The theory of the leisure class*. Boston: Houghton Mifflin Co.

Wales, T. and A. D. Woodland (1977) "Estimation of the allocation of time for work, leisure and housework", *Econometrica*, 45:115–32.

Wales, T. and A. D. Woodland (1980) "Sample selectivity and the estimation of labor supply functions", *International Economic Review*, 21:437–468.

Wales, T. and A. D. Woodland (1983) "Estimation of consumer demand systems with binding non-negativity constraints", *Journal of Econometrics*, 21:263–285.

Watts, H., D. Poirier and C. Mallar (1977) "Sample, variables and concepts used in the analysis", in: H. Watts and A. Rees, eds., *The New Jersey income-maintenance experiment*: *Labor-Supply Response*, New York: Academic Press, vol. 2, 33–56.

Yamada, T. and T. Yamada (1984) "Part-time employment of married women and fertility in urban Japan", Working Paper No. 1474, National Bureau of Economic Research, Cambridge, Massachusetts.

Yamada, T. and T. Yamada (1985) "Part-time work vs. full-time work of married women in Japan", Working Paper No. 1608, National Bureau of Economic Research, Cambridge, Massachusetts.

Yamada, T., T. Yamada and F. Chaloupka (1985) "A multinomial logistic approach to the labor force behavior of Japanese married women", Working Paper No. 1783, National Bureau of Economic Research, Cambridge, Massachusetts.

Yatchew, A. (1985) "Labor supply in the presence of taxes: an alternative specification", *Review of Economics and Statistics*, 67:27–33.

Zabalza, A. (1983) "The CES utility function, nonlinear budget constraints and labour supply: results on female participation and hours", *Economic Journal*, 93:312–330.

Zabalza, A. and J. Arrufat (1983) "Wage differentials between married men and women in Great Britain: the depreciation effect of non-participation", Discussion Paper No. 151, Centre for Labour Economics, London School of Economics, London.

Chapter 3

MODELS OF MARITAL STATUS AND CHILDBEARING

MARK MONTGOMERY and JAMES TRUSSELL*

Princeton University

1. Introduction

One of the rites of passage for a labor economist involves the estimation of a probit model for female labor force participation. It is standard practice for the probit equation to include some indicators for a woman's marital status and the number and age distribution of her children. In estimating such a model, the labor economist veers dangerously close to a theory of household formation, childbearing, and labor supply; namely, that household formation and fertility can be safely taken as exogenous with respect to a woman's supply of hours. Whether the commission of this theory is unwitting or premeditated, we cannot say; but it is surely common enough for some exploration of the issue to be in order. In this chapter we will investigate those microeconomic models of marital status and childbearing that contain implications for female labor supply. We focus our discussion primarily on the developed countries, principally the United States, but make reference to developing country issues where these are applicable. We should note, however, that the role of economic variables as determinants of demographic behavior is often far more vivid and persuasive in developing nations than it is in the United States or Western Europe. The reader is referred to the Value of Children studies [Fawcett et al. (1974)], Ben-Porath (1980), and the volume by Schultz (1981) for an introduction.

The plan of our chapter is as follows. Section 2 contains a review for the United States of trends in those demographic variables which are strongly associated with female labor supply: age at first marriage, marital dissolution, age at first birth, the number of children born over the life cycle, and the age pattern of fertility. Demographers have uncovered pronounced empirical regularities in these variables, at least in aggregate data; in some instances the patterns are regular enough to be summarized in parsimonious model schedules. These

*We are grateful to David Bloom and Duncan Thomas for their detailed and perceptive comments on earlier drafts of this chapter. Any remaining errors are unmistakably our own.

Handbook of Labor Economics, Volume I, Edited by O. Ashenfelter and R. Layard

schedules are reviewed in Section 3. We will argue that economists have left such regularities largely unexploited; the prior information embedded in model schedules may yield efficiency gains in estimation, especially where aggregate data are concerned. Individual-level data sets on marital and fertility histories have become more numerous in recent years, and both economists and demographers have approached these histories with a common statistical framework in mind: the intervals between events are modelled with the aid of hazard functions. The detection of "stylized facts" at the level of individual data has not yet progressed as far as it has with aggregate data. We close Section 3 with a review of the recent efforts to establish regularities in micro data.

Having set out the stylized facts in Sections 2 and 3, we then turn to the microeconomic models which seek to explain these facts. Section 4 explores models of marital status, and in Section 5 the single-period models of lifetime fertility decisions are reviewed. Section 6 is concerned with the efforts of Wolpin (1984), Newman (1985a), and Hotz and Miller (1985) to extend the single-period fertility models to dynamic settings with uncertainty. We close the chapter with some conclusions, in Section 7.

2. Demographic trends and levels in the United States

When examining variations in levels of fertility among populations, demographers typically first examine differences in proportions married by age. Although childbearing is not confined to marriage, either today or in the past, rates of fertility within marriage are, with few exceptions (e.g. among blacks in the United States), much higher than those outside marriage. Hence, in this section we first examine marriage and marital dissolution before turning to fertility.

2.1. Marriage and marital dissolution

In Figure 3.1, we show the cohort trends in proportions ever marrying (among those surviving to age 15) for males and females. We can see clearly that in this century, for both sexes, the proportion ever marrying rose to a peak among the cohorts born from 1935 to 1940 and has declined[1] dramatically thereafter. These declines thus far show no signs of reversal or even leveling off. Trends in the mean age at first marriage are shown in Figure 3.2. Though they measure entirely different behavior (timing vs. level), Figures 3.1 and 3.2 are approximate mirror

[1] The experiences of recent cohorts are decidedly incomplete. Hence, when estimating summary measures for these cohorts, Schoen et al. (1985) assumed that age-specific rates for 1980 would continue to hold.

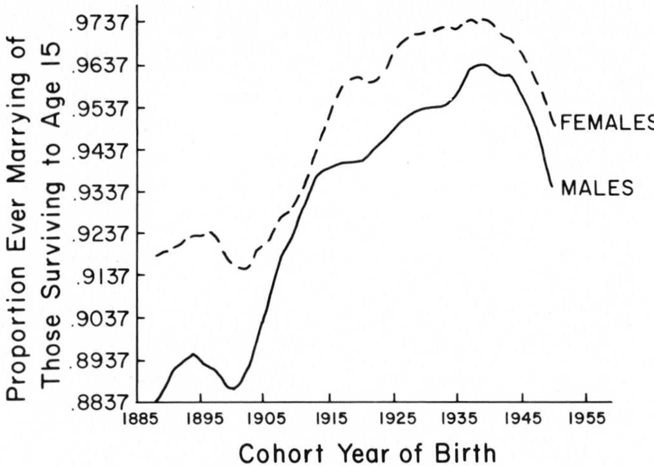

Figure 3.1. Cohort trends in the proportion ever marrying of those surviving to age 15. United States – male and female cohorts born 1888–1950. *Source*: Schoen, Urton, Woodrow and Bai (1985, Figure 1).

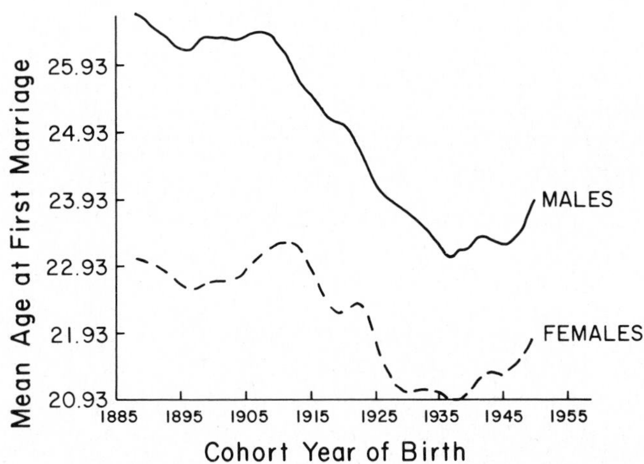

Figure 3.2. Cohort trends in the mean age at first marriage. United States – male and female cohorts born 1888–1950. *Source*: Schoen, Urton, Woodrow and Bai (1985, Figure 2).

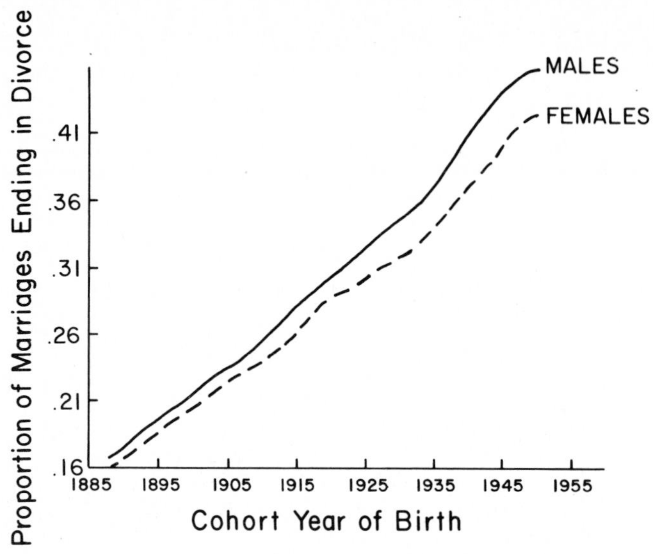

Figure 3.3. Cohort trends in the proportion of marriages ending in divorce. United States – male and female cohorts born 1888–1950. *Source*: Schoen, Urton, Woodrow and Bai (1985, Figure 3).

images. The mean age at marriage for both sexes dropped for successive cohorts born in this century until it reached a trough for the cohorts born from 1935 to 1940 and rose thereafter. The changes themselves are slightly larger for males than for females, but they are generally small, at least when compared with recent changes in a few developing countries [e.g. Malaysia, Korea, Morocco, Sri Lanka [Trussell and Reinis (forthcoming)], and China [Coale (1984)]]. For example, the proportion of females ever marrying was lowest for the 1898–1902 cohorts (91.7 percent) and highest for the 1933–42 cohorts (97.3 percent) – a difference of 5.6 percentage points. Similarly, the mean age at first marriage among females was highest for the 1908–12 cohorts (23.2) and lowest for the 1933–37 cohorts (21.0) – a difference of 2.2 years.

The changes in marital dissolution, however, have been nothing short of spectacular. Among females born before 1917, more than half their marriages ended with the death of their husbands and only about a quarter ended in divorce. In contrast, among women born in 1948–50, 42 percent of their marriages will end in divorce and 40 percent with the death of their husband [Schoen et al. (1985)]. Cohort trends in the proportions of marriages ending in divorce, displayed in Figure 3.3, show a virtually linear rise for cohorts born during the past 60 years. As can be seen from Figure 3.4, these changes in the propensities to divorce have occurred at all ages (and hence at all durations of

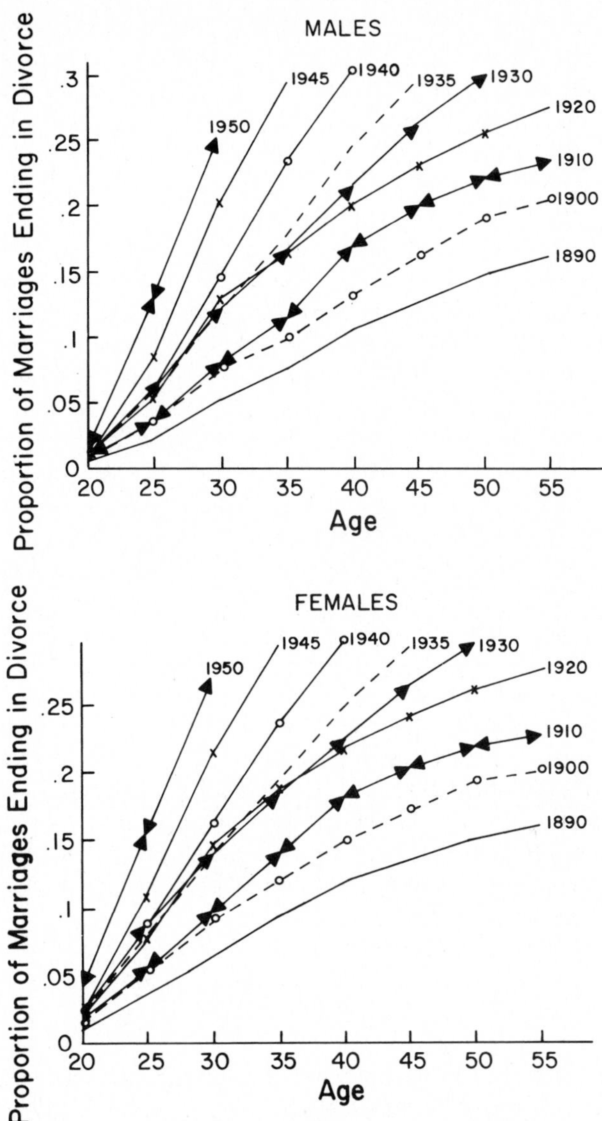

Figure 3.4. Cumulative proportion of marriages ending in divorce. United States – selected cohorts born 1890–1950. *Source*: Schoen, Urton, Woodrow and Bai (1985, Figures 5a and 5b).

marriage), so that with few exceptions, the proportions divorced by any given age are higher for each succeeding birth cohort. Divorce rates by duration since first marriage display a characteristic form, rising rapidly during the first several years of marriage to a broad plateau extending well past the tenth year of marriage [Glick and Norton (1976)].

What do these changes in nuptiality imply about trends in fertility? A full answer is clearly beyond the scope of this section, but we can sketch a few general observations. Other things being equal, we would expect that changes in the proportion ever marrying would translate directly into changes in fertility (ignoring extramarital fertility). Thus, in the absence of other changes, we might expect average fertility per woman to rise about 6 percent (5.6/91.7) from the 1898–1902 cohorts to the 1933–42 cohorts, and then fall about 2 percent (2/97.3) for the 1948–50 cohorts. What effect should the fall and later rise in the mean age at marriage have? The answer will vary depending on the assumptions. If one reasons that the reproductive span rose by 2.2 years between the 1908–12 cohorts and the 1933–37 cohorts, then we might expect an extra 2.2 years of exposure at the prime ages of childbearing to have a big increase in lifetime fertility. We could argue, on the other hand, that (ignoring marital dissolution) the 2.2 years should be added to the end of the reproductive career, thus only trivially affecting lifetime fertility. In this scenario, the propensity to bear children by duration of marriage does not change; women are married an average of 2.2 years longer before reaching age 50.

Though increases in the proportions marrying and decreases in age at marriage both would have a positive impact on lifetime fertility, the effect of increasing rates of divorce is uncertain. On the one hand, increases in the period of non-marital exposure would reduce fertility, but this effect would be counterbalanced by a tendency for women to remarry and form a new family with each new husband. On balance, we would expect the net effect on fertility of all these nuptiality changes to be small.

2.2. *Fertility*

Recent fertility behavior in the United States is captured nicely by Figure 3.5, which shows by cohort the average number of births achieved by exact ages 20, 25, 30, 35, and 40.[2] In general, the average number of children born at every age rose to a peak for the 1930–39 birth cohorts and then fell sharply thereafter. Scrutiny of Figure 3.5 reveals that changes in the average number of children born by age 20 have been relatively minor; Figure 3.5 masks, however, the dramatic shift from legitimate to illegitimate teenage fertility [O'Connell and

[2] These calculations are predicated on the assumption that all women survive through the reproductive span. Hence, the effect of mortality is eliminated.

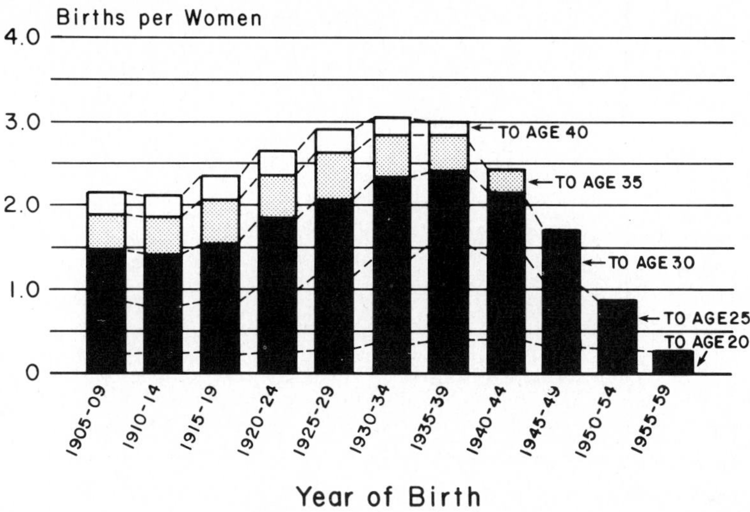

Figure 3.5. Average number of births per woman, cumulated to successive ages, for women born from 1905–09 to 1955–59: June 1980. *Source*: Rogers and O'Connell (1984, Figure 1).

Rogers (1984)]. Recent declines in the number born by age 35 or 40 (if we use our imagination to extrapolate) have been quite large. The large decline in completed family size reflects the fact that fewer and fewer women have 5, 4, or even 3 children.

Proportions of women having a first birth by exact ages 18, 20, 22, 25, 30 and 40 are displayed in Figure 3.6 for standard five-year birth cohorts of women. Changes over time have been quite pronounced. For example, the fraction of women having a child by age 20 rose from 16 percent for the 1915–19 birth cohorts to 27.7 percent for the 1940–44 birth cohorts and has fallen steadily since. At age 22 the changes are even more pronounced – an increase of 22 percentage points from the cohorts born 1910–14 to the cohorts born 1935–44. The proportion never having a child by age 40 fell from 25 percent in the earliest cohorts to 10 percent in the 1935–39 cohort. The experience of later cohorts is too incomplete to examine permanent childlessness directly, but estimates for more recent cohorts exceed 20 percent [Bloom (1982a), Bloom and Trussell (1984)].

The median age at first birth has deviated little from 22.5 years among women born from 1935 to 1954 [Rogers and O'Connell (1984)]. Projections for the younger cohorts, whose experience is incomplete, show a tendency for a recent rise [Bloom and Trussell (1984)]. Age at last birth can be reliably computed only for the older cohorts. It comes as a surprise to many to learn that the median age at last birth among women born 1905–19 was only 31.6 years; corresponding

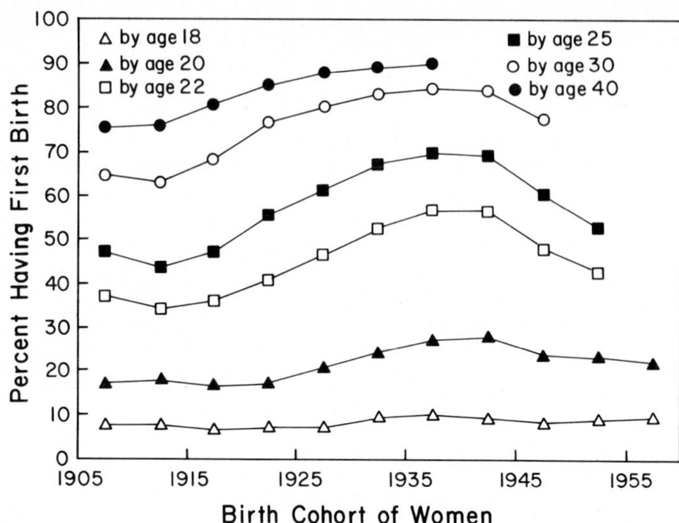

Figure 3.6. Cumulative proportion of women with first birth by given age. *Source*: Rogers and O'Connell (1984, Table A).

figures for the 1920–29 and 1930–39 cohorts are 31.4 and 29.7 years, respectively [Rogers and O'Connell (1984)].

Although some of the cohort variation in fertility observed in Figures 3.5 and 3.6 is due to cohort differences in marriage patterns, the changes in fertility are much too great to be solely attributable to nuptiality variation. The rise in fertility during the first third of the century was primarily due to big drops in the proportions of women having no births or only one birth. The decline in fertility thereafter has been overwhelmingly attributable to the revolution in contraceptive practice, though in recent years an increase in teenage sexual activity has served to keep teenage fertility rates high when rates at other ages have generally dropped markedly.

We would have sketched different pictures and reached different conclusions if we had examined trends in *period* instead of *cohort* behavior. For example, the period total fertility rate (TFR) rose from 2.1 births per woman in 1936 to a peak of 3.7 in 1957, declined to 1.7 in 1976 and has hovered around 1.8 in recent years [Heuser (1976), NCHS (1984)]. Thus, the changes in period fertility have been much more pronounced than the changes in cohort fertility. Furthermore, changes in nuptiality have had a far bigger impact on period than on cohort fertility. The period TFR remained above the peak cohort TFR level of 3.1 from 1951 through 1964. This apparent inconsistency is explained by the fact that the cohort age patterns of childbearing changed, so that the peak childbearing years for several cohorts temporarily overlapped [Ryder (1980)]. Hence, the baby boom is largely attributable to a marriage boom which started after the Second World War.

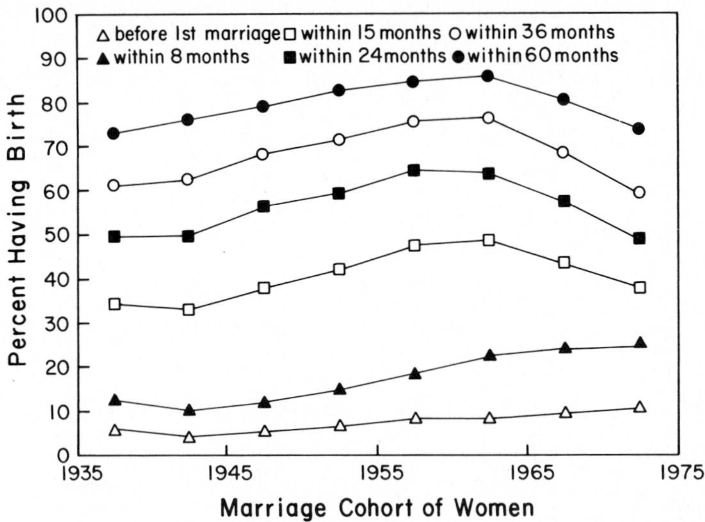

Figure 3.7. Time between first marriage and first birth. *Source*: Rogers and O'Connell (1984, Table D).

A final change worth noting here concerns the interval between marriage and first birth and subsequent interbirth intervals. In Figure 3.7 we show the interval between first marriage and first birth, by year of first marriage. We can see that since 1940, the proportion of premarital births (negative interval) has risen steadily. Likewise, the proportion with intervals of eight months or less (either born or conceived premaritally) has increased monotonically. However, if we examine only those women who bore a postmaritally conceived child, we find that there has been a pronounced postponement of marital childbearing among the two most recent marriage cohorts. For example, among women who did not bear a child within 8 months of marriage, 31 percent of the 1970–74 marriage cohort, but 55 percent of the 1960–64 marriage cohort, had a child by the time of the second wedding anniversary; comparative figures by the time of the third anniversary are 45 percent and 60 percent, respectively. We can see the same lengthening of interbirth intervals in recent years. Median interbirth intervals are displayed in Figure 3.8, for children born in standard five-year time periods.

We conclude this section with the warning that we have barely scratched the surface of demographic behavior even with respect to marriage and childbearing. There are pronounced differentials by race and education of women that have not been described [Rogers and O'Connell (1984)]. Likewise, there have been quite interesting recent changes in behavior among teenagers and among women aged 30–40 that have received considerable attention in the demographic literature [see Jones et al. (1985) and NCHS (1984)]. Finally, we have omitted detailed

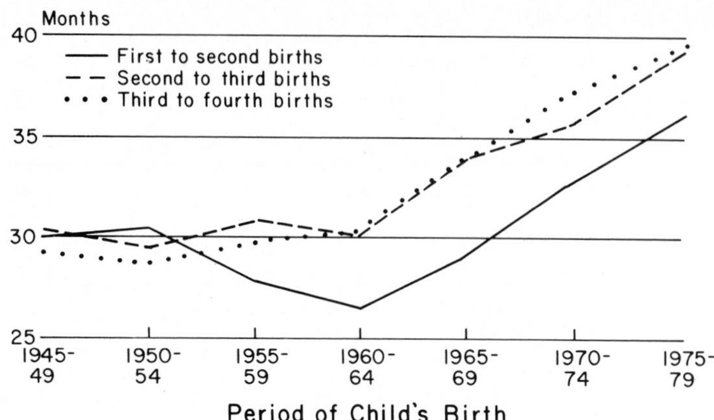

Figure 3.8. Median interval in months since birth of previous child, for births occurring from 1945–49 to 1975–79. *Source*: Rogers and O'Connell (1984, Figure 5).

consideration of the contraceptive revolution or the considerable changes in illegitimate and unwanted childbearing [see Pratt et al. (1984), Westoff and Ryder (1977)].

3. Demographic models: Empirical regularities in demographic behavior

One of the characteristics of demographic research is a search for empirical regularities, particularly regularities in the age patterns of rates of marriage, birth, and death. A product of such research is model schedules. The attention of modern demographic model-builders was drawn first to mortality, and a set of model life tables is considered an indispensible reference tool to a demographer. We do not discuss mortality models here because the link to labor economics is so tenuous.[3] Nevertheless, it is instructive to note that the philosophy that guided

[3] The first modern work in this area was an examination of historical and current life tables for developed countries thought to be reliably recorded. The resulting *Regional Model Life Tables and Stable Populations* [Coale and Demeny (1966)] set the standard for subsequent inquiry. Using graphical techniques, Coale and Demeny were able to distinguish four distinct sets of age patterns of mortality rates. For each region, model life tables are published separately by sex for expectations of life ranging from 20.0 to 80.0 in 2.5 year intervals [Coale, Demeny and Vaughan (1985)]. When constructing these models, the authors exploited a characteristic relation between male and female mortality rates as well as characteristic patterns of death rates by age. Model life tables generated by similar methods but thought to be more applicable to developing countries have recently been published by the United Nations [United Nations (1982)]. The only other widely used mortality model was developed by William Brass [Brass, 1977]. Given a "standard" schedule of probabilities of surviving to age x (the lx column of a life table), Brass constructs alternative models by expressing their logits as linear functions of the logit of the standard. His approach can be made more flexible by adding two more parameters [Zaba (1979)].

the mortality model-builders has informed the work of those who later have developed models of nuptiality and fertility: models are not final goods. The quality of a model depends on how usefully it can be exploited for empirical research.

Therefore, before proceeding, we should stop to examine the uses to which such models are applied. We emphasize that the least important function is the establishment of an empirical regularity. Rather, the empirical regularity allows the models to become an important part of the demographer's bag of methodological tools. These models have proved to be very useful in the evaluation of quality of data. Demographers, for example, would be very reluctant to accept a reported mortality pattern as being real if it deviated sharply from one of the models. A second important use has been as a building block in various procedures for estimating levels and trends of fertility, nuptiality, and especially mortality in developing countries. The interested reader is referred to *Manual X: Indirect Techniques for Demographic Estimation* for a discussion of the wide variety of estimation techniques based on demographic models [Hill, Zlotnik and Trussell (1983)]. In the remainder of this section we focus on empirical models of marriage, marital fertility, overall fertility, and birth intervals.

3.1. A model of marriage

In a seminal article, Coale (1971) noted that although age patterns of first marriage and proportions ever married differ widely across populations, there is a remarkable similarity in those patterns once adjustments have been made for location, scale, and the proportion ever experiencing the event. Figure 3.9 illustrates vividly the existence of this common pattern. In the top panel, data on proportions ever married for five populations display marked differences. The bottom panel shows these same data normalized so that the proportion ever marrying is 1.0 and adjusted to a common standardized age. The five curves are empirically indistinguishable. This same uniformity is found in age schedules of first marriage, shown in Figure 3.10. Panel (a) shows first marriage rates for two cohorts and two cross-sections. Panel (b) displays the same data after adjustments were made to the location, scale, and the proportion ever marrying. Here again the similarity is striking.

This regularity led Coale to seek a mathematical representation of age at first marriage. By trial and error, he was able to find a closed form expression for the risk of first marriage:

$$r(x) = 0.174\exp[-4.411\exp(-0.309x)], \tag{1}$$

where x is a standardized age, described in detail below. This monotonically increasing risk or hazard function accelerates rapidly from $x = 0$; by $x = 10$ it has

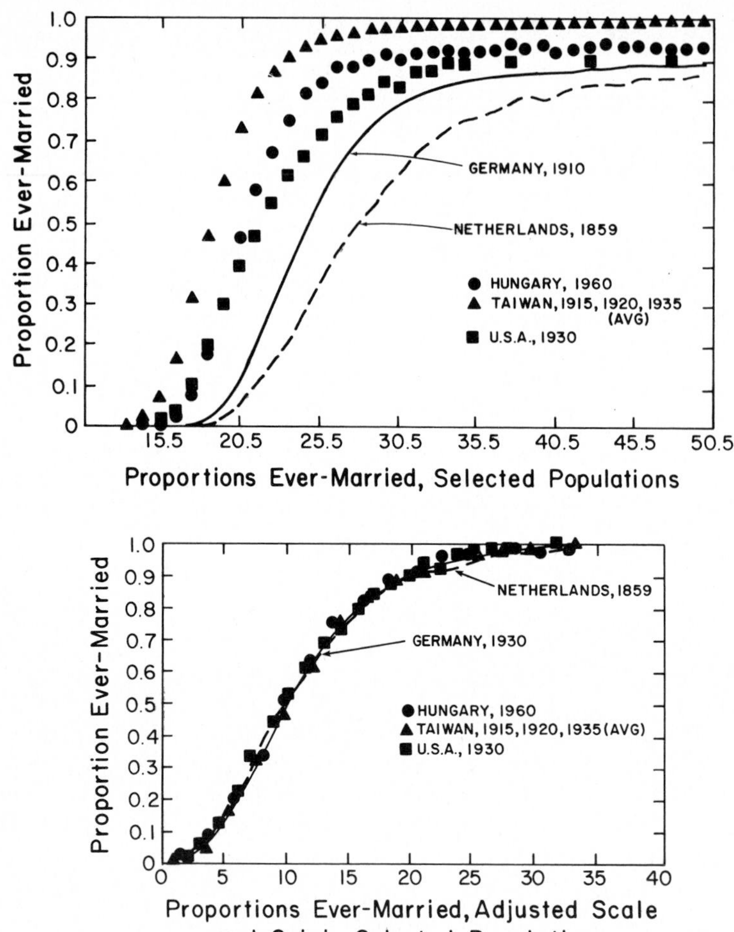

Figure 3.9. Proportions ever married by age, selected countries. *Source*: Coale (1971, Figures 3 and 4).

begun to decelerate and by $x = 20$ it is virtually flat. Later, Coale and McNeil (1972) discovered that the distribution of age at first marriage could be expressed as the convolution of a normal and three exponential delays. Unfortunately, there is no closed form expression for such a distribution, but they showed that the following analytic expression for the frequency of first marriage fits many observed nuptiality schedules remarkably well:

$$g(a|k, a_0, E) = E\cdot(1.9465/k)\exp\{(-0.174/k)(a - a_0 - 6.06k) - \exp[(-0.2881/k)(a - a_0 - 6.06k)]\}, \tag{2}$$

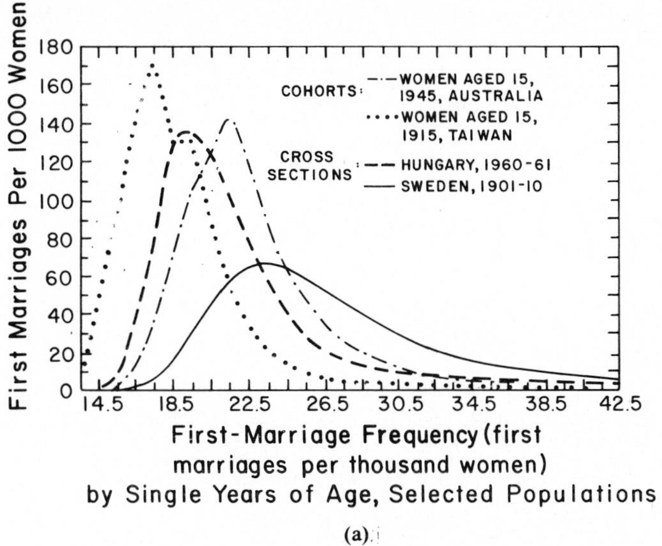

(a)

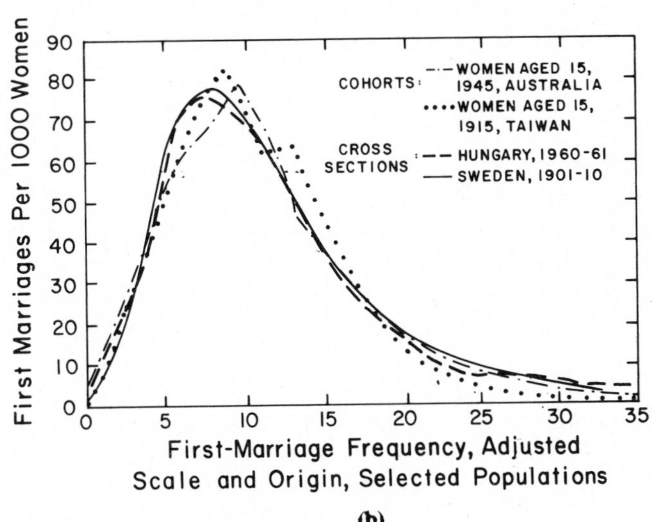

(b)

Figure 3.10. First marriage rates by age for selected countries. *Source*: Coale (1971, Figures 5 and 6).

where $g(a)\mathrm{d}a$ is the proportion of women marrying from age a to age $a+\mathrm{d}a$, E is the proportion who will ever marry, a_0 is the age at which marriage first begins, and k is a scale factor expressing the number of years of nuptiality in the given population equivalent to one year in the standard nineteenth-century Swedish population. Among those who will ever marry, the mean age at marriage is $a_0+11.36k$ and the standard deviation is $6.58k$. The standardized age x in eq.

(1) is simply $x=(a-a_0)/k$; standardization moves the origin to 0 and forces the spread to be the same as that in the standard Swedish population.

The choice of a_0 and k as the location and scale parameters is certainly valid, but somewhat arbitrary. One objection is that a_0 and k are not easily interpretable.[4] Hence, Rodriguez and Trussell (1980) transformed the model so that the location and scale parameters are the mean μ and standard deviation σ:

$$g(a|\mu,\sigma,E)=(1.2813E/\sigma)\exp\{-1.145(0.805+(a-\mu)/\sigma)$$
$$-\exp[-1.896(0.805+(a-\mu)/\sigma)]\}. \tag{3}$$

Though the integral of (3) has no closed form expression, they showed that it can be evaluated in terms of the incomplete gamma function, a fact that greatly eases computation. They also prepared a software package NUPTIAL which has been widely distributed by the World Fertility Survey (WFS). This package provides maximum likelihood estimates of the parameters and various measures of goodness of fit.

Demographers have employed the model nuptiality schedules in three ways. First, since the model is parametric, it can be estimated on a cohort that has only partially completed its nuptiality experience, and the recovered parameters can be used to forecast the remaining experience of the cohort. The important feature is that all cohorts in a cross-sectional survey are comparable, so long as one believes that the model is valid and will continue to hold. Another feature is that the location and scale parameters can be estimated from a sample of ever married women only. This property is especially important since half of the 41 WFS surveys were administered to ever married women only. An illustrative analysis of the use of the model with World Fertility Survey data is found in Trussell (1980). A second use of the model nuptiality schedule arose when it was discovered that the model also provided a good fit to first birth frequencies. Hence, it has been used as a model of first birth [Trussell, Menken and Coale (1979), Casterline and Trussell (1980), Bloom (1982a, 1982b), Trussell and Bloom (1983), Bloom and Trussell (1984)]. Estimates of μ, σ, and E for first marriage and first birth for each of six standard five-year cohorts (20–24 to 45–49) for all 41 developing countries participating in the WFS can be found in Trussell and Reinis (forthcoming). They found a strong positive association between μ and σ, so that in some cases one could use a more parsimonious two-parameter model in which the mean was a predetermined function of the standard deviation. There was, however, no association between E and σ or E and μ. A final use of the

[4]The location parameter a_0 is not the minimum age at marriage, but the age at which a consequential number of marriages first occurs. More precisely, a_0 is close to the first percentile of the distribution of age at marriage among those who will marry.

model marriage schedules, discussed more fully in a later section, is as a building block in a general model of fertility.

The marriage model described above is a one-sex model, whereas marriage is unquestionably a two-sex event. Except in polygamous societies, unmarried males can marry only unmarried females and the number of married males must always equal the number of married females; thus, we need a full and consistent two-sex model in order to forecast numbers of marriages and numbers of households. Although the two-sex problem does have a long and distinguished history in the mathematical demography literature [Schoen (1982), Pollard (1973), Pollak (1985)], no important empirical regularities have yet emerged. Nevertheless, there is one unquestionable stylized fact closely related to the two-sex problem – males on average marry females younger than themselves. Given this apparent preference, it is possible to measure changes in the tightness of the marriage market corresponding to changes in the numbers of eligible men and women at different ages [Goldman, Westoff and Hammerslough (1984)]. Such analysis of the demography of the marriage market is of interest to more than just the lovelorn. For example, Preston and Strong (1985) have argued that recent declines in age-at-marriage differences between spouses in several LDCs are due to a recent relative abundance of eligible females (caused by past changes in mortality which have altered the age distribution of the population) and not to changes in norms or tastes. In Latin America, female age at marriage has not changed but male age has fallen, while in Asia, female age at marriage has risen and male age has not changed.

3.2. *A model of marital fertility*

Henry (1961) noted that though the absolute levels are quite different, the age patterns of marital fertility are remarkably similar in populations which do not practice deliberate control of fertility in a manner that depends on parity. He said that such populations experience *natural* fertility; couples may behave in ways that reduce fertility from the potential maximum (e.g. breastfeeding), but such behavior must be independent of parity if fertility is to be deemed natural.

The age pattern of natural fertility has a characteristic concave shape. In contrast, the age schedule of marital fertility rates in populations with highly controlled fertility is convex at the older ages (above age 30). This observation led Coale (1971) to propose a simple model of marital fertility:

$$r(a) = Mn(a)\exp(m \cdot v(a)), \tag{4}$$

where $r(a)$ is the marital fertility rate from age a to age $a + \mathrm{d}a$, M is a scale factor, $n(a)$ is the age schedule of natural fertility normalized in an arbitrary

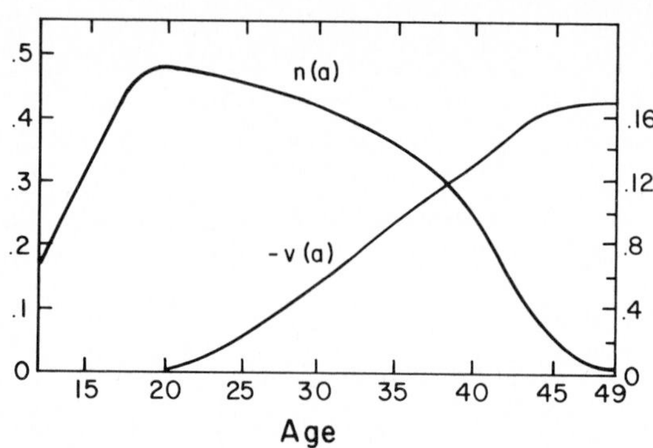

Figure 3.11. Values of $n(a)$ (natural fertility), and $v(a)$ (logarithmic departure from $n(a)$). *Source*: Coale and Trussell (1974, Figure 2).

manner, m is the level of fertility control and $v(a)$ measures the characteristic departure of controlled from natural fertility.

Coale and Trussell (1974) estimated $n(a)$ as the average of ten schedules designated by Henry as natural. Values of $v(a)$ were obtained through calculations employing published marital fertility schedules from 43 populations. First, for each population, m was set equal to 1.0 in eq. (3). Next, M was chosen to make $r(a)$ equal $n(a)$ for the age group 20–24. Finally, $v(a)$ for each of the remaining five age intervals (25–29 through 45–49) was calculated as the average value for each of the 43 populations, where the value of $v(a)$ for each population was chosen to make eq. (4) exact. Interpolation was used to obtain single-year values of $n(a)$ and $v(a)$ for ages 20–49. The resulting curves are shown in Figure 3.11.

Once the values of $n(a)$ and $v(a)$ are given, M and m can be estimated for a particular population using maximum likelihood techniques based on the following reasoning. Let the marital fertility rate at age a be constant over women. Then the waiting time to a birth is exponentially distributed, and the number of births B_a conditional on the total amount of exposure E_a is distributed as a Poisson, where the parameter of the Poisson (θ_a) is $\lambda_a E_a$. In this formulation, λ_a is simply a fertility rate, and substitution of (4) for λ_a yields the following likelihood function:

$$L = \Pi_a (Mn(a)\exp(mv(a))E_a)^{B_a} \exp(-Mn(a)\exp(mv(a))E_a)/B_a! \quad (5)$$

Maximum likelihood estimates of m and M and their standard errors can be

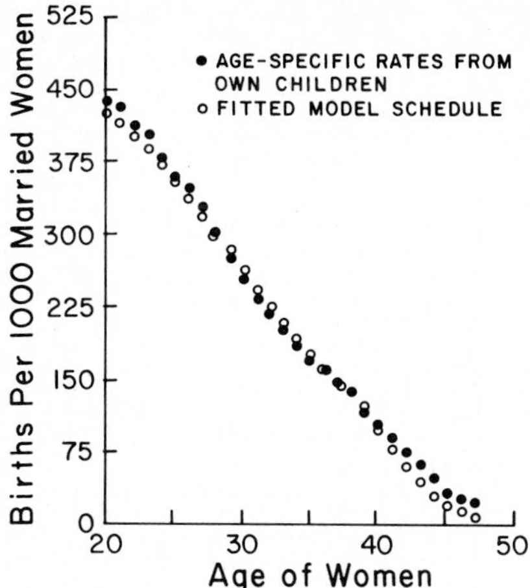

Figure 3.12. Age-specific marital fertility rates vs. fitted model schedule, Republic of Korea, 1966. *Source*: Coale and Trussell (1978, cover figure).

easily obtained using simple numerical techniques.[5] A computer program that performs such calculations has been distributed by Trussell (1982). An illustration of the fit of the model to single-year data from Korea is shown in Figure 3.12.

The model of marital fertility given by eq. (3) has found two uses in demography. Its first application was as a component in a general model of fertility described in the next section. Perhaps the more important application is its use by historical demographers and students of the demography of developing societies to detect the onset and time trend of deliberate control of fertility. One could, for example, test for evidence of deliberate parity-specific control of marital fertility in Nepal in 1970 by estimating the value of m. However, Coale and Trussell (1978) have warned that a single estimate of m is not nearly as revealing as a time series. Two examples of such time trends are shown in Figure

[5]These are also the MLEs to an equivalent hazard model. Assume that the hazard (or intensity) function describing the risk of birth is constant at each age but varies across ages. In the hazard model approach, the random variable is the *waiting time* from one birth to the next, or from a woman's birth (or marriage) to the birth of her first child. In this simple model, waiting times are distributed as piecewise exponentials, and the likelihood function can be derived in a straightforward manner. In the *counts of births* approach, the random variable is the number of births at each age, conditional on exposure at each age. The formal equivalence between the two approaches was demonstrated by Laird and Olivier (1981), who showed that hazard models with categorical covariates (including duration) could be estimated with standard packages designed to analyze contingency tables. Trussell and Hammerslough (1983) illustrate this equivalence in a paper written in a less technical manner for a demographic audience.

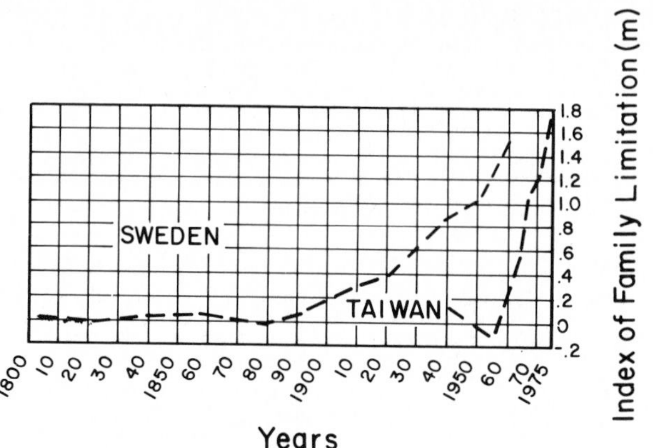

Figure 3.13. Time series of the measure of fertility control (m) for Sweden 1800–1960 and Taiwan 1940–1975. *Source*: Van de Walle and Knodel (1980).

3.13; it can be seen that the movement from uncontrolled to controlled fertility was much more rapid in Taiwan than in Sweden.

Page (1977) has shown, for selected populations at least, that the effect of voluntary control is to establish a gradient of marital fertility at each age, such that at each age women with longer durations of marriage have lower fertility. This decline in fertility with duration of marriage is well approximated by an exponential decay. Hence, the pattern by age that was found by Coale and Trussell to characterize departure from natural fertility – $v(a)$ in eq. (4) – is simply the result of the characteristic way that the distribution of married women by duration varies at different ages. There are more at the short durations among younger women and more at the long durations among older women; thus there is increasing departure of controlled from natural fertility with increasing age.

This explanation can be made more formal as follows. In a particular time period, the Page model states that marital fertility at age a and duration d can be expressed as[6]

$$r(a,d) = Tn(a)\mathrm{e}^{-sd}. \tag{6}$$

Marital fertility at age a can be obtained by integrating (6) over all durations d, where the weights would be the number of women aged a at durations of marriage d. By the second mean value theorem of integral calculus, this weighted average must equal $Tn(a)\mathrm{e}^{-sd_a}$, where d_a is a duration between zero and a. If first marriages all occurred at the mean age at marriage, then d_a would rise

[6]Note that $v(a)$ in eq. (4) is everywhere negative and d in eq. (6) is positive.

linearly with age. More generally, it can be shown that d_a rises linearly with age for those ages above the point at which most marriages have occurred [Trussell, Menken and Coale (1982)]. Indeed, the standard form of $v(a)$, shown in Figure 3.11, is virtually linear, at least for ages 25–45.

3.3. *A model of fertility*

In the two previous sections we discussed a model of nuptiality and a model of marital fertility. Coale and Trussell (1974) combined these two components into a model of fertility:

$$f(a) = Fn(a)\exp(mv(a))G(a), \tag{7}$$

where $f(a)\mathrm{d}a$ is the fertility rate from age a to age $a+\mathrm{d}a$, $G(a)$ is the proportion ever married at age a – the cumulative function of (2) up to age a – and F is a scale factor which equals $M \cdot E$ in eqs. (2) and (4). Interpreted strictly, this model ignores non-marital fertility and assumes that marriages do not dissolve. As it stands, the model has four parameters: one (F) is a level parameter, and the other three (a_0, k, and m or alternatively μ, σ, and m) determine the age pattern. To incorporate non-marital fertility, marital dissolution, and remarriage would require several additional parameters. However, such an extension seems not to be worth the effort for at least two reasons. First, eq. (7) seems to replicate many observed fertility schedules well, even when the assumptions are known to be violated, as can be seen in Figure 3.14. The model is flexible enough to be able to capture wide variations in human fertility, since age patterns are universally unimodal and skewed to the right. The parameters may not have any demographic meaning, however, even if the fit is quite good. Second, there is little point in trying to build a complicated model to fit all the minor wiggles in observed fertility rates. Indeed, model (7) was not intended for such an application. Instead, it was meant to be used as a simple way of replicating the range of human fertility schedules when devising techniques for estimating basic demographic parameters from incomplete and inaccurate data likely to be found in developing countries. The interested reader is referred to *Manual X* [Hill, Zlotnik and Trussell (1983)] for a host of such applications.

The fertility model given by (7) is one example of "proximate" or "intermediate" fertility models. Thirty years ago, Davis and Blake (1956) defined intermediate fertility variables as being those factors through which, and only through which, socioeconomic and cultural conditions could affect fertility. They identified 11 such factors, which they grouped under three categories: intercourse, conception, and gestation variables. Model (7) incorporates only two of the proximate determinants (age at entry into unions and proportions celibate, if

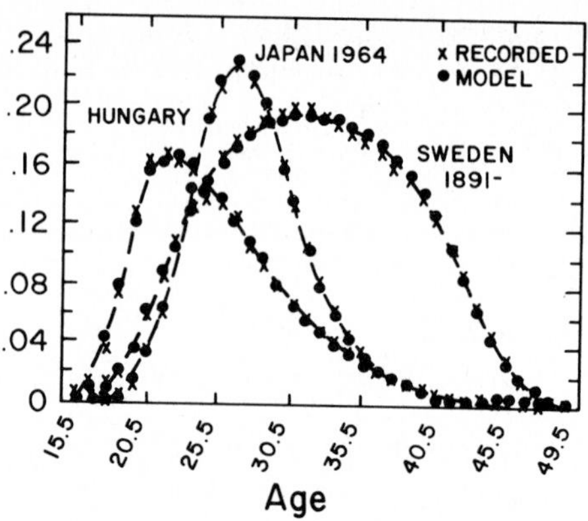

Figure 3.14. Age-specific fertility rates of three populations fitted by model fertility schedules. *Source*: Coale and Trussell (1974, Figure 3).

extramarital intercourse is ignored) by factoring fertility into the product of proportions married and marital fertility. This simple factorization has also provided the basis of indexes for analyzing historical fertility. I_f, an index of overall fertility, is the number of actual births divided by the number of births that would occur if all women experienced at each age the fertility rates of the prolific married Hutterites. I_g, an index of marital fertility, is computed as the number of marital births divided by the number that would be expected if all married women reproduced at the same rate as the Hutterites. I_m, an index of marriage, is the ratio of expected births among married women to expected births among all women, where expected births are those that would occur if Hutterite fertility rates prevailed. If one ignores extramarital fertility, then $I_f = I_g I_m$ [Coale (1973), Trussell, Menken and Coale (1982)].

Bongaarts (1978), who combined three of the Davis–Blake factors (age at entry into unions, permanent celibacy, and union dissolution and reformation) has argued that only four of the remaining eight factors are responsible for major differentials in fertility levels across populations: proportions in unions (an amalgam of three Davis–Blake factors), contraception, breastfeeding, and induced abortion. He concedes that a fifth factor, sterility, is an important determinant of fertility in some parts of Africa, but that apart from these few populations, levels of sterility do not vary much. More recent work on intermediate fertility variables, based on a micro approach, has also focused on the four factors identified by Bongaarts [Hobcraft and Little (1984)]. Both Bongaarts and Hobcraft and Little have developed methods for estimating the fertility-reducing impact of breastfeeding, abortion, contraception, and proportions not in unions. The performance of these models has been evaluated with Monte Carlo techniques in a recent review by Menken (1984). A striking empirical regularity discovered by Bongaarts is that without the inhibiting effects of the intermediate variables, potential fertility in most populations hovers around 15 children, though other work has questioned whether potential fertility does not vary more widely [Singh, Casterline and Cleland (1985)].

3.4. *A summary of empirical demographic models*

The empirical demographic models reviewed thus far share several features in common, and we pause to emphasize these characteristics.

(1) The models are descriptive. They were never intended to be anything else. No deep theory, or even shallow theory, underlies the search for these empirical regularities.[7]

(2) The models are descriptive of aggregate, not individual, behavior.

(3) Though the models can be (and have been) estimated for small samples, most applications are to samples large enough that stochastic variation can be ignored.

(4) In large samples, though the fits are generally visually quite good, formal statistical tests would nearly always reject the null hypothesis that the restricted model fits as well as an unrestricted model with a parameter for each age. We do not consider such tests really appropriate, since the purpose of these models is to capture broad empirical regularities with relatively simple models. Without recognizing the term, demographers are addicted to the principle of parsimony.

(5) Finding a mathematical expression to represent a demographic process is not an end in itself. These models are valuable because they can be used either to make inferences about behavior or, more commonly, to build a technique for estimating basic demographic indices for populations with limited or defective data.

Despite the fact that the models were first developed to summarize aggregate behavior, the vast increase in micro-level data generated by the World Fertility Survey led investigators to focus attention on individual behavior. Many new models were developed, but rather than discard the old, demographers adapted them to accept covariates. For example, consider the model of marital fertility given in eq. (4). Suppose an individual has a vector of characteristics Z_i. Then a natural extension would be to let the marital fertility rate at age a depend on the

[7]Coale and McNeil (1972) do provide an ex-post behavioral explanation for the marriage model. They showed that the model is empirically indistinguishable from a convolution of a normal and three exponential distributions. They posit that age at entry into serious dating is distributed normally. The three exponential delays correspond to the time required to meet an eligible spouse, the time from meeting to engagement, and the time from engagement to marriage. Data to test their hypothesis existed only for French women; their predictions matched the French data nearly perfectly.

vector Z_i as follows:

$$\ln_i[(r_i(a)] = \ln(M) + \ln(n(a)) + mv(a) + \beta' Z_i. \tag{8}$$

Estimation of the unknown parameters M, m, and β can be accomplished in a straightforward manner with, for example, the statistical package GLIM [Baker and Nelder (1978)]. The model of first marriage or first birth given by eq. (3) can also easily be generalized to handle individual covariates [Trussell and Bloom (1983), Bloom and Trussell (1984)].[8] At this point, the empirical work of demographers becomes virtually indistinguishable from that of labor economists; the front halves of their papers, however, will appear very different, primarily because demographers, if not actually allergic to models based on utility maximization, remain profoundly skeptical of them. Nowhere is this convergence in statistical methodologies more apparent than in the recent work on birth intervals – a topic to which we now turn.

3.5. *Birth interval models*

Differences across populations in fertility levels can logically be attributed to population differences in proportions of women exposed to the risk of pregnancy and to differences in the length of time between births when women are exposed. Exposure to risk varies primarily because the proportion of women cohabiting differs across populations, though in some populations sterilization (voluntary or involuntary) removes from exposure a significant fraction of those in sexual unions. It is not surprising that the attention of demographers has turned increasingly to the estimation of the determinants of the second factor, the length of time between births among women in unions.

Demographic work on birth intervals has been profoundly affected by mathematical models of conception and birth, particularly as explicated by Sheps and Menken (1973). One of their main contributions was to divide the interbirth interval into components (waiting time to a live-birth conception, gestation, and postpartum insusceptibility) and to analyze the variations in birth interval length attributable to each component. Their focus on childbearing as a renewal process has forced demographers to recognize the importance of sampling frames when analyzing birth interval length. For example, Sheps and Menken show that one cannot analyze only closed birth intervals because they are on average too short. Similarly, they demonstrate that if one examines birth intervals of women at a given point in time (where the total birth interval length is the sum of the interval

[8] FERTEV, a modified version of NUPTIAL that can handle covariates, is available at cost from David Bloom.

from the last birth to the survey and the interval from the survey to the next birth), then the length of intervals will be biased upward. They go on to show how unbiased estimates can be obtained from information on both closed and open intervals. These points have been explored further in recent econometric publications [Heckman and Singer (1984)].

Three different types of statistical models have been used to estimate determinants of birth interval length. The analyst may assume a particular functional form for the distribution of birth interval length (e.g. gamma), with covariates affecting the parameters of this underlying distribution. Alternatively, the interval may be divided arbitrarily into segments and the probability of giving birth in each segment may then be estimated as a function of covariates. Finally, the risk (instantaneous birth rate) may be modelled as a function of the explanatory variables. In each approach, the maximum likelihood estimates of parameters and their estimated standard errors may be obtained using standard numerical optimization techniques. The properties and therefore the advantages and disadvantages of the three types of models differ; these have been discussed in great detail in a recent review [Trussell (forthcoming)].

To conserve space, we concentrate here solely on the last class of models, in which the hazard or risk (fertility rate) is modeled as a function of the predictor variables. Consider a woman i with characteristics Z_i. Then the risk $\mu_i(d)$ of childbearing at duration d since the start of the interval is given in a very general form by

$$\ln(\mu_i(d)) = \alpha(d) + \beta(d)'Z_i(d). \tag{9}$$

In eq. (9), $\alpha(d)$ is the "underlying" hazard, and both β and Z_i are functions of d, allowing the *effect* $\beta(d)$ to change during the birth interval and the *covariates* $Z_i(d)$ to change as well. One example of a covariate which might be expected to have time-varying *effects* is breastfeeding; its fertility-suppressing effect diminishes over time. The predictor variable breastfeeding (coded as $1 =$ yes or $0 =$ no) can itself also change over time. For example, a woman may breastfeed for five months and then stop.

The likelihood function is formed from two components, each based on eq. (9). Women who are censored contribute a probability of not completing their current interval by the date of the survey. For example, if a woman's open interval is of exact duration d, then this probability is given by $\exp(-\int_0^d \mu_i(y)\,\mathrm{d}y)$. Women who give birth at exact duration d contribute the term $\mu_i(d)\exp(-\int_0^d \mu_i(y)\,\mathrm{d}y)$ to the likelihood function.

Of course, estimation cannot proceed until the functional forms for $\alpha(d)$ and $\beta(d)$ are more fully specified. The most common approach is to assume that they are step functions. The analyst first partitions the time to the next birth into discrete sub-intervals. In each of these intervals, $\alpha(d)$ or $\beta(d)$ is assumed to be constant. Sub-intervals are usually constructed so that they are relatively short (say, three months) for small values of d where the risk is changing rapidly. Model (9) then reduces to the following expression for woman i in sub-interval k with characteristics Z_{ik}:

$$\ln(\mu_{ik}) = \alpha_k + \beta_k' Z_{ik}. \tag{10}$$

As before, the effects may be allowed to vary across sub-intervals or may be constrained to be the same, in which case $\beta_k = \beta$ for all k. Of course, one may have a mixture of these two extremes, with some effects allowed to be time-dependent and others not. Similarly, the values of some covariates (such as breastfeeding) may change from one sub-interval to another while other covariates (such as ethnicity) might remain fixed. This is the model employed by Rodriguez (1984) for Colombia; Richards (1983) for Colombia and Costa Rica; Newman and McCulloch (1984) for Costa Rica; Rodriguez et al. (1984) for Bangladesh, Colombia, Indonesia, Jamaica, Jordan, Kenya, Korea, Mexico, and Sri Lanka; Trussell et al. (1985) for the Philippines, Indonesia, and Malaysia; Vaughan and Trussell (1984) for Syria; and Trussell, Vaughan and Farid (1984) for Egypt. Data for all populations were drawn from World Fertility Surveys in the respective countries.

The paper by Rodriguez (1984) is an illustrative analysis in the finest demographic tradition. He clearly explicates the model and then begins to examine the data, layer by layer, much as one would peel an onion; any reader can learn a great deal about modelling strategies from his lucid exposition. He first examines the effect of birth order and the choice of the best duration categories. He next adds age, period, and cohort as factors. Then he brings in two socioeconomic variables: childhood place of residence and mother's education. Finally, he adds breastfeeding and contraception. His final preferred model, based on an enormous amount of exploratory work and intended to be very parsimonious, contains the variables birth order, education, breastfeeding, and contraception. Of these, breastfeeding and contraception have by far the most powerful effects.

Rodriguez et al. (1984) estimated the same six-factor birth interval model for nine developing country populations. Only birth orders three through eight were examined. Length of the previous interval proved to be the most important explanatory variable (other than duration since the start of the interval), while birth order proved to be quite unimportant (except in Korea). Age, time period, and education were generally important, but their effects varied widely across populations. Both education and length of previous interval proved to have significant time-dependent effects. The importance of previous interval length and the lack of importance of birth order led the authors to view the reproductive process as an engine with built-in momentum: once started, the process seems to run by itself. Their view of reproductive behavior suggests a very important role

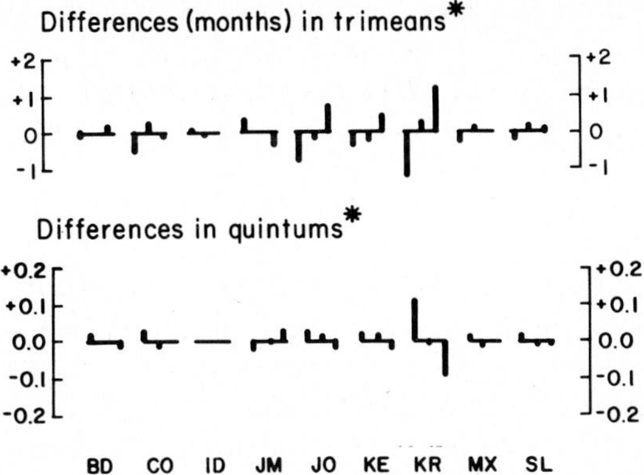

Figure 3.15. Effects of birth order on the analysis of birth intervals. (*The quintum is the proportion of birth intervals closed within 5 years from the time of the previous birth. The trimean, measured only for those who have a birth within 60 months, equals $0.25Q_{25}+0.5Q_{50}+0.25Q_{75}$, where Q_i is the ith percentile. The two-digit codes for countries represent, in order, Bangladesh, Colombia, Indonesia, Jamaica, Jordan, Kenya, Korea, Mexico, and Sri Lanka. The three categories of birth order are 3, 4–5, and 6–8.) *Source*: Rodriguez et al. (1984, Figures 5 and 6).

for the age at which women initiate childbearing. They concluded that further research needs to focus on the beginning of the reproductive career in order to determine whether the reproductive engine starts with marriage or first birth and to discover whether the determinants of age at entry into those events are also the determinants of subsequent reproductive behavior.

The fact that parity proved to have such a weak effect (see Figure 3.15) casts considerable doubt on the previously accepted notion that couples in developing countries aim at a target number of children, and that after achieving this number they cease to reproduce. This empirical regularity, along with the importance of previous interval length, are perhaps the most important stylized facts about birth interval dynamics in developing countries.[9]

Finally, Trussell et al. (1985), Vaughan and Trussell (1984), and Trussell, Vaughan and Farid (1984) have expanded the Rodriguez et al. model by explicitly including as covariates several other biological and socioeconomic factors. They discovered that the effect of previous interval length does not

[9] In a later paper, Heckman, Hotz and Walker (1985) vigorously attack these two stylized facts. They discover that (1) once unobserved heterogeneity is explicitly modeled, the length of the previous interval becomes unimportant, and (2) that parity is important. However, their model is estimated on modern Swedish data for birth intervals closed by births of orders 1, 2, and 3. Hence, whatever they find about the effect of parity is irrelevant to the work of Rodriguez et al. Their attack on the notion of a reproductive engine seems puzzling as well, since Rodriguez et al. state that the length of the previous interval is capturing persistent unobserved heterogeneity. For other discussions of unobserved heterogeneity, see below.

operate through breastfeeding and contraception; previous interval length is still a powerful predictor of current interval length even after the effects of these variables are controlled, and the effects of these two variables are not much altered by exclusion of a control for previous interval length. Length of the previous interval captures the effects of unobserved heterogeneity that persists across birth intervals. Birth order was not a significant predictor of interval length in any of these populations. Socioeconomic characteristics (male and female education, male occupation, urban residence, female work experience away from home, ethnicity, sex of previous birth) generally did not add much explanatory power to their simpler biological model (contraception, breastfeeding, age of woman, and previous interval length).

In closing this section, we hasten to emphasize that the demographic use of hazard models is not confined to the study of birth interval length. Other topics analyzed with this methodology include infant and child mortality [Trussell and Hammerslough, (1983), Martin et al. (1983)], marital dissolution [Menken et al. (1981)], contraceptive failure and discontinuation [Schirm et al. (1982), Hammerslough, (1984)], age at marriage [Michael and Tuma (1985), Trussell and Bloom (1983)], and migration [Sandefur and Scott (1981)].

3.6. Unobserved heterogeneity – a digression

In complicated non-linear models such as the hazard models discussed here, omission of a relevant variable distorts effects estimates for all variables included in the model even if the omitted variable is uncorrelated with those included. Investigators have long recognized this problem. The classical solution is to collect data on *all* variables likely to belong in the "true" model. Recent attention has focused on the recognition that some relevant variables might not even be observable. An example in birth interval analysis is the underlying fecundity of the woman (or couple), a condition not known to the investigator. The first attempts to control for the effects of unobserved heterogeneity involved specifying a distribution function for the unobservable and then mathematically "repairing" the model by integrating it out and leaving only the parameters of its distribution to be estimated. For example, Newman and McCulloch (1984) assumed that fecundity across women followed a gamma distribution. They discovered that for some cohorts, structural effects estimates changed significantly once heterogeneity was explicitly modeled.

Recent work [Heckman and Singer (1982a, 1982b)] has shown, however, that estimates of the parameters of interest in the model can vary widely depending on the particular functional form assumed for the distribution of the unobservable (e.g. normal, lognormal, beta, gamma). But the investigator surely is unlikely to know the correct functional form of a variable that is unobservable. Heckman and Singer do not leave this problem unaddressed, however. They propose a way to control for the effect of an unobserved variable without imposing a functional form on its distribution. Trussell and Richards (1985) have applied the Heckman–Singer approach in two demographic analyses – determinants of child mortality and birth interval length. In both cases, correcting for the unobservable radically altered the structural effects estimates. For the child mortality analysis, they tried two different specifications for the hazard (Weibull and Gompertz). They found that the structural parameter estimates of interest varied widely with different choices of functional form for the age pattern of mortality when the Heckman–Singer procedure was used to correct for heterogeneity, and they argue that the analyst is just as unlikely to know the correct structural mortality pattern as the correct distribution of frailty.[10]

To demonstrate that this sensitivity to choice of functional form for the hazard is not a fluke, we have conducted a similar experiment for an analysis of birth interval length. We chose two alternative forms for the hazard – log logistic and quadratic [the hazard chosen by Heckman, Hotz and Walker (1985) because it is "flexible"]. Results, shown in Table 3.1, clearly demonstrate the same instability found for the mortality analysis.

This sensitivity to the choice of functional form of the distribution of unobservables or of the hazard leaves us profoundly depressed about where next to proceed. We fear that advances in statistical technique have far outpaced our ability to collect data and our understanding of the behavioral and biological processes of interest.

4. Economic models of marital status

Any explanation of the trends and empirical regularities in demographic behavior described in Sections 2 and 3 must consider issues that go well beyond the range of microeconomic theories of the household. To pick but one example, the dramatic postponement in marriage and first birth in the United States surely reflects changes in underlying preferences as well as time-series variation in

[10] Newman and McCulloch claim that changing the distribution of the unobservable from a gamma to a lognormal did not alter the structural parameter estimates. However, their experiment was quite different from the one performed by Heckman and Singer, because they *forced* the distributions to have similar means and variances. If the parameters of the two distributions had been estimated without this restriction, their experiment would have been more illuminating and their claim that results are insensitive to the functional form chosen for the unobservable much more convincing. Nevertheless, other investigators have found that they obtain the same (qualitatively) structural parameter estimates with various choices of distributions for the unobservable [Manton, Stallard and Vaupel (1984); Ridder and Verbakel (1984)]. The lesson seems to be that the amount of sensitivity depends on the structure of the data and the complexity of the model. The challenge now is to identify when the choice of distribution of the unobservable can affect substantive results.

Table 3.1
Estimates of parameters of birth interval models with and without corrections for heterogeneity.

Hazard	No heterogeneity correction		Heterogeneity correction	
	Log-logistic	Quadratic	Log-logistic	Quadratic
Constant	−0.47	−4.53	1.12	−7.02
	(0.13)	(0.11)	(0.36)	(0.36)
Parity 2	−0.58	−0.57	−0.77	−1.32
	(0.08)	(0.09)	(0.12)	(0.19)
Parity 3–4	−1.69	−1.71	−2.08	−2.98
	(0.17)	(0.17)	(0.21)	(0.31)
Contraception	−0.51	−0.50	−0.81	−0.90
	(0.08)	(0.09)	(0.12)	(0.15)
λ	0.06	0.11	0.04	0.26
	(0.003)	(0.009)	(0.005)	(0.017)
α	3.47	−0.0015	3.21	−0.0016
	(0.21)	(0.0001)	(0.18)	(0.0002)
θ_1			−1.91	2.35
			(0.26)	(0.23)
θ_2				−3.69
				(0.34)
θ_3				−7.65
				(0.68)
− ln (likelihood)	2626	2719	2616	2662

Notes: Data drawn from the Korean Fertility Survey. All intervals in which breastfeeding occurred following last and next-to-last births between 1965 and the survey date. Log-logistic results are taken from Trussell and Richards (1984, Table 4). Heterogeneity was controlled using the Heckman–Singer non-parametric procedure.

The hazard for individual i with observed covariates X_i who belongs to unobservable covariate group j is $\mu_{ij}(t) = e^{X_i'\beta + \theta_j} h(t)$ where $h(t)$ takes the following forms:

- Log-logistic: $h(t) = \lambda\alpha(\lambda t)^{\alpha-1}/[1+(\lambda d)^{\alpha}]$.
  If $\alpha > 1$, $h(t)$ reaches a maximum at $t^* = \lambda^{-1}(\alpha-1)^{1/\alpha}$.
- Quadratic: $h(t) = \exp[\lambda t + \alpha t^2]$.
  If $\alpha < 0$, $h(t)$ reaches a maximum at $t^* = -\lambda/2\alpha$.

budget constraints. If there is a comparative advantage to the microeconomic approach, however, it lies with a focus on constraints rather than preferences; indeed, economists have traditionally had little to say about sweeping changes in tastes [although see Easterlin (1968) for an explicit model of taste formation]. In the microeconomic approach, a small set of observable, exogenous variables is selected – usually including, for instance, female wage rates – and the impact of changes in such variables on household formation and fertility is traced through with the aid of simplifying assumptions. These optimizing models are inevitably stylized; their purpose is to highlight potentially important associations and to clear the way for empirical work. Given such modest aims, it would seem natural to formulate the models with as much parsimony as is possible. Yet, as we will argue below, a place must be preserved in economic theories of demographic phenomena for the constraints on individual choice imposed both by social norms and by individual physiology. In fact it is usually straightforward to incorporate such additional constraints, and in what follows we will try to demonstrate the value of doing so.

We begin with an overview of economic models of household formation, focusing initially on age at first marriage.

4.1. *Age at first marriage*

One may draw an analogy between theories of search in the labor market and economic models of age at first marriage. It is an analogy which is strained in some respects, but enough parallels do exist to make the exercise useful. Keeley (1979) discusses marriage in the context of search theory; for an interesting recent application in a developing-country context see Boulier and Rosenzweig (1984). We will begin our discussion with the simplest case, in which marital search is conducted in a time-homogeneous environment and the time horizon for search is infinite.

The distinguishing feature of the time-homogeneous, infinite horizon case is that optimal search strategies do not change with time. We assume that the characteristics of a prospective spouse – say, a prospective husband – can be summarized in a single index ε, and that once a woman meets a prospective spouse, his value of ε is immediately all too apparent. For an investment of c in search costs each period, one offer of ε is received; the distribution from which ε is drawn is $F(\varepsilon)$ and the sequence of draws is presumed to be i.i.d. We treat the searcher's utility as linear in ε, so that alternative marital search strategies can be ranked in terms of their discounted expected value. Finally, marriages are assumed to last forever, so that the present value of a match at the time it takes place is $\varepsilon(1-D)^{-1}$, where D, $0<D<1$, is the woman's rate of discount. (Uncertainty, "intensive search", and marital dissolution will be considered in our next section.)

This benchmark example is simple enough for a constant reservation "wage" strategy to obtain [Lippman and McCall (1976a)]. That is, any marital offer valued above a threshold level ε_r is accepted, while offers below ε_r are spurned in favor of further search. Thus, for active searchers, the conditional probability of marriage at age a (given that it has not occurred before) is simply $1-F(\varepsilon_r)$, and the distribution of age at marriage generated by the model is geometric.

An implicit solution for ε_r is easily derived. The first-order condition holding for the optimal ε_r is

$$c-v^{s}=\frac{D}{1-D}\int_{\varepsilon_r}(\varepsilon-\varepsilon_r)\,\mathrm{d}F-\varepsilon_r, \tag{11}$$

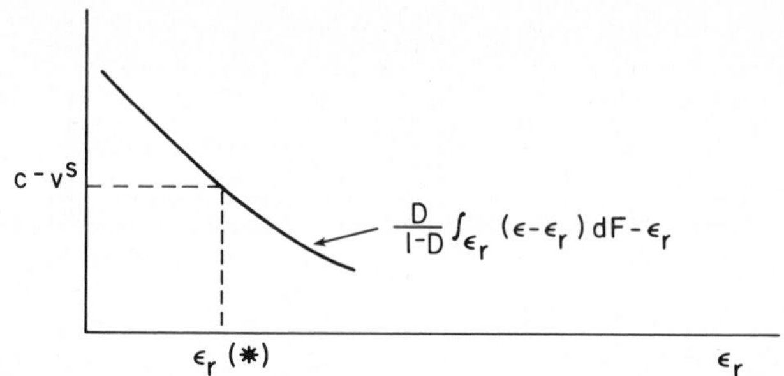

Figure 3.16. The determination of the reservation level of ε in the time-homogeneous search model [(eq. (11)].

where v^s is the per-period utility derived from being single. The right-hand side of (11) is downward sloping in ε_r; as shown in Figure 3.16, higher levels of search costs c (and lower levels of v^s) are associated with lower reservation values for ε and, hence, with a greater likelihood of early marriage.

The empirical hazard functions for marriage sketched in Section 3 are clearly not constant with respect to age, and it is natural to inquire whether the simple search framework outlined here really adds to our understanding of age at first marriage. Before we go on to generalize that framework, however, there are two points which seem worth making. The first involves the likelihood of corner solutions in search at young ages. If v^s is sufficiently large for young women, then ε_r levels may be high enough so as to effectively rule out the possibility that a match will occur. As the utility from remaining single falls with age, however, ε_r levels may decline to the point where the marriage risk becomes significant. (Note that anticipated declines in v^s constitute a departure from time homogeneity.) The age a^* at which v^s passes below a critical level for a particular woman might be thought of as her entry point into eligibility for marriage, an idea which has been formalized in the Coale and McNeil (1972) marriage model (see footnote 7). If a^* is considered a random variable, so that women pass into eligibility at different ages, then data on age at marriage in the population will be characterized by a rising empirical hazard function at young ages. Secondly, unanticipated declines in v^s – occasioned, for instance, by an unanticipated pregnancy – may reduce ε_r levels and hasten the transition into marriage. Becker, Landes and Michael (1977) have argued that such unanticipated events produce a spouse with a lower expected value of ε, and therefore may put the resulting marriage at greater risk of dissolution. Before considering such arguments, however, let us examine some useful extensions of the standard search model.

One area in which the simple search model is easily generalized has to do with the frequency of marriage offers. The notion that marriage offers arrive one per period is, of course, difficult to take seriously. A simple extension is to allow a marriage offer to arrive with probability of q per period, given an investment of c in search. Then eq. (11) is modified to

$$c - v^{s} = \frac{qD}{1-D}\int_{\varepsilon_r}(\varepsilon - \varepsilon_r)\,\mathrm{d}F - \varepsilon_r. \tag{12}$$

It is apparent from (12) that as the offer probability q rises, so does the reservation level of characteristics set by the woman, ε_r. In terms of the conditional probability of marriage, which depends on the "exit rate" $q[1-F(\varepsilon_r(q))]$, these are potentially offsetting influences. Flinn and Heckman (1983) have demonstrated that the net impact of q on the exit rate $q[1-F(\varepsilon_r)]$ depends critically on the shape of the offer distribution F. If F' is log-concave, then an increase in the frequency of offers q dominates the rise in ε_r and produces a net increase in the exit rate. For general F, however, the impact of a rise in q remains ambiguous.

In fact, demographers have long been interested in the relationship between the offer probability q and the exit rate to marriage, even though the question has seldom been posed in quite these terms. The issue has arisen in connection with what is popularly known as the "marriage squeeze" phenomenon [Espenshade (1984b)]. A marriage squeeze occurs as a result of changes in the sizes of birth cohorts which, some years later, translate into an imbalance between the sexes at marriageable ages, given the propensity for males to marry younger females. We might think of the marriage squeeze as altering the frequency of offers made to single women. Our presumption is that a fall in q will lower the risk of marriage. Yet, the full impact of a reduction in q on the exit rate to marriage depends on the endogenous response of ε_r. Marriage searchers who understand that q has fallen may compromise themselves and adjust ε_r downward; in principle, the exit rate could then either rise or fall.[11]

Particularly in small, closed populations [or "marriage circles", as Henry (1972) has defined them], anticipated declines in q with the duration of search are a central feature of the marriage market. This result occurs because, from each sex's point of view, the other side of the market from which offers are drawn becomes progressively "thinner" the longer one remains single. Let $\varepsilon_{r,a}$ represent the reservation of a searcher aged a; if q is anticipated to decline with age, then $\varepsilon_{r,a} \geq \varepsilon_{r,a+1}$. Again, however, the impact of a decline in q with age on the marital exit rate $q_a[1-F(\varepsilon_{r,a})]$ is ambiguous.

There is another mechanism by which reservation ε_r levels can decline with the age of the searcher. In societies or social groups in which marriage is highly

[11] Keeley (1979) shows that sex ratios of males to females in the marriageable ages are strong predictors of proportions married across U.S. states and SMSAs in 1960.

valued, strong normative pressures may be placed on individuals to marry by a given age A_τ. We might think of such normative sanctions as penalties imposed on individuals who continue to sample life's possibilities after A_τ. Suppose that the result of the sanction is to reduce the per-period utility derived from being single from v^s to $v^s - \Delta$ after A_τ. In terms of its effect on reservation ε levels, the imposition of a normative sanction acts much like an exhaustion of unemployment benefits in job search models [Mortensen (1977)]. That is, as A_τ is approached, we expect to see ε_r levels decline. Indeed, if the normative penalty is severe enough, a finite horizon model with A_τ periods may provide a good approximation to marital search strategies, particularly at ages near to A_τ. Lippman and McCall (1976a) show that finite horizon search models are characterized by reservation levels ε_r which decline with search duration; that is, $\varepsilon_{r,a} \geq \varepsilon_{r,a+1}$. They are also able to demonstrate that so long as A_τ remains relatively distant, the infinite horizon and finite horizon decision rules resemble each other.

It seems likely that search in the marriage market proceeds somewhat more systematically than is suggested by simple extensive-search models. In particular, a marriage searcher facing a "thin" market may have enough prior information about potential spouses to rank them and examine the best possibilities first. Salop (1973) has examined systematic search strategies when there are N potential spouses ("firms") and has derived the necessary conditions which hold for optimal strategies. He shows that the order in which potential mates are searched depends on the searcher's own prior with respect to (i) the probability that an offer will be forthcoming, and (ii) the distribution $F^j(\varepsilon)$ for the jth possibility, $j=1,\dots,N$. Salop is able to prove that $\varepsilon_{r,a}$ levels decline with search duration, just as in the finite horizon example. This result follows because, as the model is formulated, there are only N possibilities to consider. A woman who has progressively moved through the best $n<N$ of these is confronted with the following choice: either reduce the threshold level of ε for the next period or face an even less attractive search environment two periods hence. In this case it is the finite number of potential mates, rather than a finite number of time periods, which generates a decline in reservation levels of ε.

Search models therefore provide us with a host of "explanations" for a single empirical regularity: the rising risk of marriage at young ages. The first explanation has to do with transitions from corner to interior solutions. Equally plausible is the notion that anticipated declines in offer probabilities q, which occur as the other side of the market is depopulated, generate falling reservation levels. An alternative explanation is that it is the approach of a socially-defined terminal point A_τ which causes active searchers to relax their definitions of an acceptable match. Still another possibility is that reservation levels fall because the best potential partners are searched first, where the definition of "best" encompasses prior beliefs on $F^j(\varepsilon)$ and the probability that an offer might be forthcoming. Neither systematic search nor anticipated declines in q necessarily produce monotonically rising exit rates, but certainly these are both consistent with a rising risk of marriage over some age ranges.

As is the case with labor market search models, none of the hypotheses about the age pattern of $\varepsilon_{r,a}$ can be satisfactorily tested without data on accepted values of ε. A central difficulty in applying the search analogy to marriage, therefore, is the absence of a single, observed variable – like a wage rate – which can fully characterize a prospective spouse. The marriage problem is somewhat more multivariate in nature. One can imagine a list of attributes, including earnings potential but also encompassing educational attainment, religion, physical attractiveness, and age gaps, each of which has some bearing on marital decisions. Becker, Landes and Michael (1977) argue that the central propositions of search theory carry over into settings in which offer evaluations depend on more than one characteristic and preferences are not necessarily monotonic in each characteristic. However, it is difficult to see precisely how such multiple characteristics might be incorporated in empirical work.

It is particularly important in forming tests based on search theory to identify variables that influence either ε or v^{s} but not both of these quantities. Consider, for instance, the female wage rate w_{f}. One could argue that the higher is w_{f}, the higher the utility v^{s} derived from being single. But, as we will discuss below, w_{f} should also enter a woman's calculation of ε, since the value of a marriage is partly determined by the resources a woman brings to it. The point is that the net effect of an increase in w_{f} on search duration is ambiguous in theory. Boulier and Rosenzweig (1984) have noted that in certain settings the ambiguity can be resolved; for example, if no women choose to work after marriage, then that post-marriage corner solution limits the effect of w_{f} to its impact on v^{s}. However, prior information is rarely so strong, and in general it is difficult to support any prediction about women's wage rates and age at marriage.

Finally, we note that while search theory is meant to explain search intensity (for instance, corner vs. interior solutions) and reservation ε levels, the data available on marital search are – with rare exceptions – limited to information about age at marriage. Therefore, any transitions between corner and interior solutions in search go unobserved. In principle, the data issue involved in corner solutions could be resolved as it is with labor market data, that is, by defining a cutoff level of search intensity and classifying individuals who fall below that level as non-searchers. Such cutoffs are problematic enough in labor market search models; we wonder whether it is sensible to define the marital search counterpart to being "out of the labor force".

4.2. *The gains to marriage*

To this point we have not been very explicit about the manner in which searchers involved in a marriage market evaluate prospective spouses. It goes almost without saying that for a marriage to occur there must exist "gains to marriage" for both partners; to bring content to such a statement, however, we need to be more precise about the connection between the gains associated with marriage and the bargaining rules which govern the division of consumption and leisure between married partners. Our discussion begins with Manser and Brown (1980) and Becker (1973, 1985). We then go on to consider the role of uncertainty and information shocks in marriage dissolution, an area of the literature which also derives from Becker [Becker, Landes and Michael (1977)].

We begin with the following single-period problem. Suppose that a woman considering marriage has a direct utility function which depends on her own consumption x_{f}, leisure l_{f}, and a factor θ_{f} which represents the (sub-) utility derived from being married: $U = U_{\mathrm{f}}(x_{\mathrm{f}}, l_{\mathrm{f}}, \theta_{\mathrm{f}})$. Her indirect utility from remaining single ($\theta_{\mathrm{f}} \equiv 0$) is $v_{\mathrm{f}}^{\mathrm{s}} = V_{\mathrm{f}}^{\mathrm{s}}(p, w_{\mathrm{f}}, \Omega_{\mathrm{f}} + w_{\mathrm{f}}T)$, where p is a price vector, w_{f} her permanent wage, Ω_{f} the value of her assets, and T represents a time endowment. A potential husband with permanent wage w_{m} and assets Ω_{m} has $v_{\mathrm{m}}^{\mathrm{s}} = V_{\mathrm{m}}^{\mathrm{s}}(p, w_{\mathrm{m}}, \Omega_{\mathrm{m}} + w_{\mathrm{m}}T)$ as his utility in the single state. A marriage occurs if both the woman and the man can do better than $v_{\mathrm{f}}^{\mathrm{s}}$ and $v_{\mathrm{m}}^{\mathrm{s}}$, respectively, by marrying.

The set of Pareto-optimal arrangements within marriage is described by the solutions to

$$\max_{\{x_{\mathrm{f}}, l_{\mathrm{f}}, x_{\mathrm{m}}, l_{\mathrm{m}}\}} \quad U_{\mathrm{f}}(x_{\mathrm{f}}, l_{\mathrm{f}}, \theta_{\mathrm{f}})$$

subject to

$$U_{\mathrm{m}}(x_{\mathrm{m}}, l_{\mathrm{m}}, \theta_{\mathrm{m}}) = u_{\mathrm{m}},$$
$$0 \le l_{\mathrm{f}}, \quad l_{\mathrm{m}} \le T,$$
$$p'(x_{\mathrm{f}} + x_{\mathrm{m}}) + w_{\mathrm{f}} l_{\mathrm{f}} + w_{\mathrm{m}} l_{\mathrm{m}} \le \Omega_{\mathrm{f}} + \Omega_{\mathrm{m}} + (w_{\mathrm{f}} + w_{\mathrm{m}})T$$

as u_{m} is varied.

Suppose that there is a bargaining rule associated with each potential match which selects one vector $(x_{\mathrm{f}}^*, l_{\mathrm{f}}^*, x_{\mathrm{m}}^*, l_{\mathrm{m}}^*)$ from the list of Pareto-optimal possibilities. Then a necessary condition for a marriage to take place is

$$U(x_{\mathrm{f}}^*, l_{\mathrm{f}}^*, \theta_{\mathrm{f}}) \ge v_{\mathrm{f}}^{\mathrm{s}} \tag{13}$$

and

$$U(x_{\mathrm{m}}^*, l_{\mathrm{m}}^*, \theta_{\mathrm{m}}) \ge v_{\mathrm{m}}^{\mathrm{s}}. \tag{14}$$

To link condition (13) to the search theory framework discussed above, we could simply write $\varepsilon = U(x_{\mathrm{f}}^*, l_{\mathrm{f}}^*, \theta_{\mathrm{f}})$. This makes the dependence of ε on both male and female characteristics explicit. It also makes clear that the definition of $F(\varepsilon)$ depends on a variety of male and female characteristics.[12]

[12]Again, Keeley (1979) is one of the few empirical studies to investigate the characteristics of $F(\varepsilon)$ and age at marriage. He includes, for instance, the standard deviation of male education levels as a proxy for the dispersion of ε facing female marriage searchers.

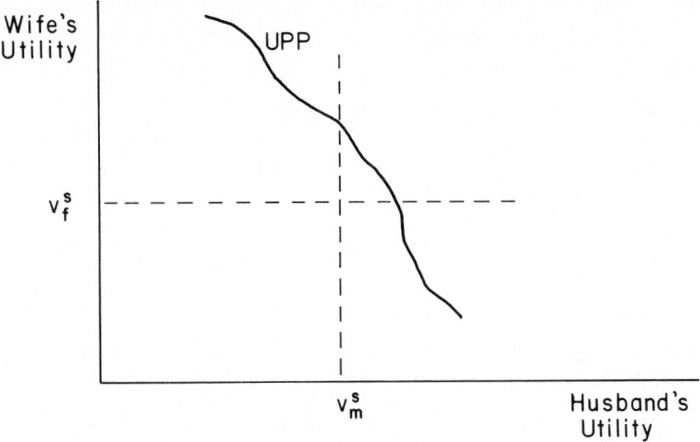

Figure 3.17. The utility-possibilities curve (UPP) for a prospective match, with associated single-state utility levels v_f^s and v_m^s.

Figure 3.17 depicts the utility-possibilities curve for a prospective match, along with the single-state utility levels v_f^s and v_m^s. As pictured, the combination of male and female preferences, resources, and the bargaining rule yields a gain to marriage. However, some arrangements *within* marriage which are Pareto optimal will never be realized, simply because these would leave one or both partners below the welfare levels attainable outside marriage.

Becker (1973, 1985) has argued that an important factor in determining the position of the utility possibilities curve – and hence the potential for gains from marriage – is the existence of goods which satisfy two properties. They (i) are difficult or impossible to obtain through market exchange, due to transactions costs, and therefore must be produced at home, and (ii) their production exhibits increasing returns to inputs of time. Point (i) suggests a reason for gains from marriage to exist even under a selfish preferences framework like the one sketched above; the notion of increasing returns is invoked to explain why spouses may specialize in different aspects of household production. In his 1985 paper Becker works through an example in which individuals possess identical Leontief preferences and also possess identical abilities to produce two household goods, x_1 and x_2. He derives the utility levels attainable in the single state and shows that by combining in a household in which one spouse specializes in x_1 and the other in x_2, with shared output, each member of the pair can do better than it is possible to do while single.

The bargaining-specialization framework has not been developed to the point of being empirically testable. Indeed, its capacity to generate testable hypotheses about the conditions under which marriage will take place seems severely limited. Manser and Brown (1980) and McElroy and Horney (1981) have isolated the central difficulty: potentially observable variables like w_f and w_m, which alter the location of the utility possibilities curve, also are likely to affect the levels of v_f^s, v_m^s *and* the relative strength of the spouses' bargaining positions. There is simply not enough structure in these models to produce sharp, empirically refutable propositions. However, the models have been useful in guiding discussions about the causes of marital dissolution.

4.3. *Marital dissolution*

The literature on marital dissolution seeks to explain two stylized facts with insights drawn from search theory and the bargaining framework outlined above. First, individuals who marry early tend to face elevated risks of marital dissolution; second, as described in Section 2, the risks of dissolution rise in the first few years of marriage to a plateau that extends past the tenth year and decline thereafter. What does the theory contribute to our understanding of these empirical regularities?

As mentioned above, when an unanticipated shock like a pregnancy lowers the utility from being single, v^s, the ensuing reduction in ε_r tends to hasten marriage; it also lowers the expected payoff to the match, $E[\varepsilon|\varepsilon \geq \varepsilon_r]$. Other things equal, this would leave a marriage close to the margin of dissolution, that is, more vulnerable to new shocks and new revelations about one's partner. In addition, individuals with high search costs c or low offer probabilities q may set lower (ε_r) standards for a marriage, and therefore may also face higher risks of dissolution. Both arguments imply that age at marriage (or, more properly, search duration) should be negatively associated with the likelihood of divorce.[13]

The decline in the divorce hazard rate with duration of marriage is well established in the empirical literature. Becker, Landes and Michael (1977) argue – and it would be hard to disagree – that information about one's spouse is still substantially incomplete at the time of marriage. Additional information accumulates rapidly in the early years of marriage, a process which may shift the realized utility possibilities curve to a point at which marriage is no longer rational for one or both partners. The early years of marriage are especially critical because one form of "marital-specific capital" – namely, children – may not yet be in place.

[13]Also note that there may be a close connection between age at marriage and the duration dependence of the divorce hazard rate. Individuals who marry early because their ε_r values are low are matched with spouses who had $\varepsilon \geq \varepsilon_r$; if ε_r goes unobserved, then the heterogeneity distributions from which individuals draw at marriage are systematically related to the age at marriage. The existence of "quality of match" heterogeneity alone induces a downward bias in estimates of the slope of the dissolution hazard; any correlation between ε and age at marriage would further muddy the findings.

One intriguing empirical application of the marital bargaining framework is the Groeneveld, Tuma and Hannan (1980) paper on the impact of negative income tax experiments on marriage dissolution. Groeneveld et al. reason that the effect of an NIT program on dissolution is indeterminate a priori. Income supplementation by itself would shift both the utility-possibilities curve within marriage and the indirect utilities v_f^s and v_m^s associated with being outside marriage. Particularly for those persons who are contemplating divorce but whose v^s levels – because of financial constraints, inabilities to borrow, etc. – are low, a new, more generous income support program might offer a one-shot opportunity to get re-established after divorcing. It is also possible, as Groeneveld et al. suggest, that the lack of stigma associated with NIT payments might influence v^s to a greater degree than a monetarily equivalent level of welfare payments. But these arguments must be balanced against the likelihood that income support might rescue otherwise floundering marriages and that support which is neutral with respect to marital status – the NIT program – should offer a weaker incentive for dissolution than programs keyed to, say, single parents (AFDC).

In light of these conflicting possibilities, the strong empirical findings in Groeneveld et al. (1980) come as something of a surprise. Using SIME/DIME data, the authors estimate a constant-hazard model[14] in which program guarantee levels are entered as explanatory variables. The findings suggest that the experimental NIT programs appeared to increase marital dissolution rates for blacks and whites (but not for Chicanos). There is a significant effect apparent even at those low guarantee levels which, in strictly financial terms, differ little from the support available through AFDC and food stamps. This last finding is consistent with the idea that welfare payments are "discounted" by potential recipients, whether because of a stigma attached to such payments or, perhaps, because of a lack of understanding of the intricacies of the welfare system.

We close this section with an observation on the anticipation of divorce as a factor influencing the length of marital search. Common sense suggests that the more uncertain one is about whether any marriage will last, the more effort one should devote to "intensive" search strategies before settling on a match. However, there is an offsetting possibility. Suppose we think of λ as representing the *exogenous* risk of a divorce in any small interval of marriage duration. Then λ is analogous to the (constant) layoff rate in models of job search and labor market turnover. In the simplest time-homogeneous, infinite horizon models of job search, an exogenous increase in λ reduces the reservation wage [Flinn and Heckman (1983)]; by analogy, an increase in the exogenous risk of divorce should reduce, rather than increase, age at marriage. The argument is simply that as λ

[14]The constant hazard assumption is employed to skirt the problem of left-censoring in the marriage duration data.

rises, the expected length of any match falls; why then continue to be so choosy about one's first partner? It seems to us that it would be difficult in an empirical sense to distinguish between two cases: one in which divorce risks are constant for a particular group, but well anticipated, and a second in which divorce risks depend on the realized level of ε in a match and therefore indirectly on age at marriage. In both cases the data would suggest an association between divorce risks and age at marriage, but that association would be left open to conflicting interpretations.

5. Economic models of fertility: One-period models

In recent years the collection of individual-level data on fertility histories has rapidly outpaced the abilities of economic models to generate interesting hypotheses about such histories. The data to be explained include age at first birth (or pregnancy), the timing of the first birth in relation to household formation, the intervals between subsequent births, and the final level of parity. It is natural to think of such data as being generated by a discrete-state, continuous-time stochastic process in which the central control variable is the time path of contraceptive use (including abstinence). Decisions about contraception can be affected or rendered moot by binding physiological constraints as well as by life cycle changes in earnings and other economic variables. Economic models which set themselves the task of explaining fertility histories as stochastic processes therefore confront an inherently dynamic or sequential decision problem under uncertainty. It is exceedingly difficult to go beyond Bellman's optimality principle in characterizing the solutions to such problems, although recent work by Wolpin (1984), Newman (1985a), and Hotz and Miller (1985) suggests that some progress can be made. We will begin our review of economic models of fertility with the modest, one-period, full-certainty models which seek to explain the number of children ever born over the life cycle – that is, the terminal level of the childbearing stochastic process. These static models are readily manipulated to produce testable propositions and, as it turns out, the economic intuitions which follow easily from them remain useful guides in more complex settings.

5.1. *Static models*

Suppose that a household's utility function depends on the number of children ever born, N, leisure time T_1, and goods consumption X, so that $U = U[N, T_1, X]$. We will assume that N is a choice variable and, for simplicity, that it is continuous. Furthermore, let the woman face a market wage w and treat husband's income Ω as exogenous. The household's time is divided between leisure, T_l, child care, T_c, and market work, T_m, so that $T_l + T_c + T_m = T$. To this point the model is utterly standard; let us focus on child care in more detail.

The care of children is assumed to require time, T_c, and money expenditures, E_c; for a household which desires $N = n$ children, T_c and E_c can be combined in different amounts to yield n "units" of child care. As the utility function is initially formulated, the household is indifferent between combinations of T_c and E_c in the provision of care to n children; without explicit preferences with respect to the quality of care, the only concern is that least-cost combinations of T_c and E_c be employed. We will return to the quality issue below.

The maximization problem may be treated in two stages. The first step is a cost minimization problem in which the number of children is held fixed at $N = n$. The second stage then involves a search over N and the remaining choice variables. The cost minimization problem summarized in (15) yields the optimal amounts of child care time and money expenditures given $N = n$:

$$\min_{T_c, E_c} wT_c + E_c \tag{15a}$$

s.t.

$$g(T_c, E_c) = n, \tag{15b}$$

where g is a child care production function. The solution to (15) is a pair of conditional demand functions $T_c(w, n)$ and $E_c(w, n)$, along with a cost function

$$C(w, n) = wT_c(w, n) + E_c(w, n),$$

with the property

$$\frac{\partial C(w, n)}{\partial w} = T_c(w, n)$$

familiar from duality theory.

The household's maximization problem now reduces to a choice over N, T_l, and X, where choices are limited by a budget constraint and the constraint on time. We combine the two constraints into one, assuming an interior solution for leisure and hours spent in the market:

$$\max U[N, T_l, X] \tag{16a}$$

s.t.

$$X + C(w, N) + wT_l - \Omega - wT = 0. \tag{16b}$$

First-order conditions are

$$\frac{\partial U}{\partial N} - \lambda \frac{\partial C}{\partial N} = 0,$$

$$\frac{\partial U}{\partial T_1} - \lambda w = 0,$$

$$\frac{\partial U}{\partial X} - \lambda = 0,$$

along with the budget constraint. Potentially testable propositions follow from the comparative statics. Consider a change in the offered wage w. We have the Slutsky equations:

$$\begin{bmatrix} \mathrm{d}N \\ \\ \mathrm{d}T_1 \\ \mathrm{d}X \\ \mathrm{d}\lambda \end{bmatrix} = \begin{bmatrix} H & \alpha \\ & \\ & \\ & \\ \alpha' & \beta \end{bmatrix} \begin{bmatrix} \lambda \dfrac{\partial^2 C}{\partial N \partial w} \mathrm{d}w \\ \lambda \mathrm{d}w \\ 0 \\ -(T_c + T_1)\mathrm{d}w + T\mathrm{d}w \end{bmatrix}$$

or

$$\begin{bmatrix} \mathrm{d}N \\ \\ \mathrm{d}T_1 \\ \mathrm{d}X \\ \mathrm{d}\lambda \end{bmatrix} = \begin{bmatrix} H & \alpha \\ & \\ & \\ & \\ \alpha' & \beta \end{bmatrix} \begin{bmatrix} \lambda \dfrac{\partial T_c}{\partial N} \mathrm{d}w \\ \lambda \mathrm{d}w \\ 0 \\ (T - T_c - T_1)\mathrm{d}w \end{bmatrix},$$

where λH is the negative semidefinite matrix (3×3) of substitution effects, α is a (3×1) column vector of income effects and β is a scalar. The (compensated) effect of a wage change on the number of children and leisure time is given by

$$\left.\frac{\mathrm{d}N}{\mathrm{d}w}\right|_c = \lambda \left\{ H_{NN} \frac{\partial T_c}{\partial N} + H_{NT_1} \right\} \gtrless 0, \tag{17}$$

$$\left.\frac{\mathrm{d}T_1}{\mathrm{d}w}\right|_c = \lambda \left\{ H_{NT_1} \frac{\partial T_c}{\partial N} + H_{T_1T_1} \right\} \gtrless 0. \tag{18}$$

There is an ambiguity in the signs of (17) and (18) because a wage change affects two shadow prices at once: the shadow price of leisure is directly affected, while the shadow price of N is affected through $\partial C/\partial N$. Both own and cross-substitution effects are therefore at work when w changes. We might assume that the own-substitution effects dominate; if that is the case, then both (17) and (18) are negative in sign.

There is no ambiguity about the compensated impact of a wage change on the total amount of time spent out of market work, $T_c + T_l$. The first term of

$$\left.\frac{\partial T_c}{\partial w}\right|_c + \left.\frac{\partial T_c}{\partial N}\frac{\mathrm{d}N}{\mathrm{d}w}\right|_c + \left.\frac{\partial T_l}{\partial w}\right|_c$$

is negative from the cost-minimization problem, while (it can easily be shown) the sum of the second and third terms is also negative. Hence, an increase in the wage induces a substitution of market time for non-market time; we know that as w rises, the sum $T_c + T_l$ must fall, but theory provides little guidance on the impact of w on the individual components of non-market time. As w rises, leisure time may be sacrificed in favor of child care time, or both components may fall together.

The theory highlights female wage rates as the key element in the opportunity cost of childbearing. What can empirical studies tell us about the sign and strength of the association? An introduction to the empirical studies that focus on female wages, male income, and lifetime fertility can be found in Schultz (1981). The results of such studies are, predictably, somewhat mixed. The key difficulty in testing for negative wage effects is a familiar one: wages are observed only for working women. If a wage effect is to be recovered, either a joint model of labor supply and fertility is required or the wage itself must be instrumented. Most studies have taken the latter course, even though the exclusion restrictions involved in the selection of instruments are quite difficult to justify. The first stage wage equation typically includes female education; in consequence, when a predicted wage is shown to vary negatively with lifetime fertility, one must wonder about whether a wage effect or an education effect has actually been isolated. Joint modeling strategies are more recent; we will review one such empirical paper [Hotz and Miller (1985)] in a later section.

To this point we have limited our discussion of the theory to the interior solutions case in which the woman participates in market work. Let us now turn to two applications of the one-period model which involve corner solutions in hours worked.

5.2. *The effect of husband's income on fertility*

Butz and Ward (1979) have estimated a version of the one-period model in which the effect of exogenous income Ω on fertility is allowed to vary with the wife's market participation. They reason that income effects will be larger when the wife is working than when she is at a corner solution in terms of market work. One rationale for this line of reasoning comes from the economic theory of choice under rationing constraints [Deaton (1981)]. Women who are not working given Ω in exogenous income, and who would continue not to work given $\Omega + \mathrm{d}\Omega$, can be thought of as "constrained" at zero hours of work. Since working hours are presumably inferior, an exogenous increase in Ω would in general induce a reduction in labor supply and an increase in home production, leisure, and fertility. But women who are already at zero hours of work cannot withdraw any further from the market. Hence, on the margin, women "constrained" to remain at a corner should exhibit less sensitivity in fertility behavior to a change in Ω than women who are not so constrained. This argument can be made rigorous; see, for instance, the approach taken by Kniesner (1976).

Butz and Ward (1979) use the insights drawn from rationing theory to specify an econometric model for aggregate fertility rates in the post-war United States. The essential idea is that the effect of male income on fertility, in the aggregate, varies with the proportion of women employed. The specification used by Butz and Ward is

$$\ln(TFR_t) = \alpha + \beta \ln(E_t WF_t) + \gamma_1 \ln(E_t \Omega_t) + \gamma_2 \ln((1 - E_t)\Omega_t) + u_t,$$

where TFR_t is the total fertility rate in period t, E_t the proportion of women employed, WF_t the female wage, and Ω_t represents male earnings. Butz and Ward recognize that E_t is endogenous and potentially correlated with the error term u_t; they use instruments in an effort to gain consistent estimates of β, γ_1, and γ_2.

Despite its simplicity, the Butz and Ward model provides a relatively good fit to the U.S. time series data. However, the use of instruments in this context deserves a brief comment. Since both TFR_t and E_t are endogenous, they presumably depend on a common set of information and constraints. The exclusion restrictions involved in the selection of instruments are therefore problematic. There is an alternative approach, perhaps more suited to micro data, which could exploit the predictions of rationing theory more rigorously. Suppose, following Deaton and Muellbauer (1981), that one could specify a pair of mutually consistent rationed and unrationed demand functions for period t employment and fertility. Changes in husband's income Ω would affect the sorting between interior and corner solutions in market work as well as fertility given employment status. In principle such a model could be estimated in a switching regressions framework, where the identifying restrictions follow directly from the specification of the demand functions.[15]

[15] Kramer and Neusser (1984) have recently taken Butz and Ward to task for specifying a model which is not homogeneous of degree zero in female wages w and male income Ω. The reformulation of the Butz–Ward model in terms of conditional demand functions would address this important criticism.

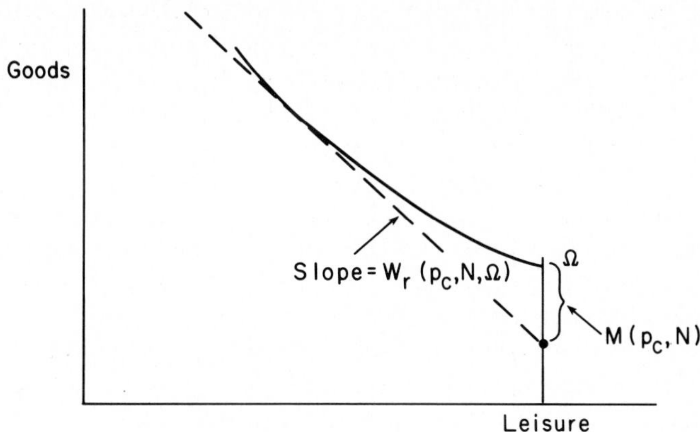

Figure 3.18. Fixed child care costs and the reservation wage.

5.3. Child care arrangements and labor supply

Let us take the number of children N as fixed and consider the short-run labor supply problem more closely. What are the implications of child care costs for the reservation wage and labor supply of married women? Heckman (1974) and Cogan (1980) set out the relevant theory.

Imagine that child care arrangements for working mothers involve only money costs and that these money costs are independent of the number of hours supplied to the market. In this setting the choice of a particular type of care is simply the result of cost minimization. Let $M(p_c, N)$ represent the cost of the optimal child care arrangement when the mother works, where p_c is a vector of prices for different types of care. (The expenditures involved in care at home given by a non-working mother are treated by netting these out from exogenous income Ω.) Figure 3.18 depicts the impact of variations in the cost of participation $M(p_c, N)$ on the reservation wage. As we would expect, increases in M arising from N or p_{c_i} increase the woman's reservation wage and discourage market participation. Moreover, the existence of child care costs induces a discontinuity in the supply of hours function as the offered wage exceeds the reservation wage.

This stylized model stands a considerable distance from the empirical facts. The ordering suggested by the model – that care prices p_c and N influence the reservation wage, but that, given a decision to work, the wage w is independent of child care arrangements – is at variance with the findings of Lehrer (forthcoming). Lehrer's empirical analyses reveal that child care arrangements are sensitive both to the mother's wage rate and to hours worked. One can imagine a number of explanations for the result. It may be that certain types of child care are not always feasible if the mother works more than part time. The possibilities for young children range from care in the home provided by one of the parents – an option chosen by nearly 36 percent of white, part-time working mothers, but only 18 percent of full-time workers [O'Connell and Rogers (1983)] – to care provided by relatives, babysitters, and formal day care centers. The money prices for arrangements involving relatives can be trivial; it seems likely, though, that the extent to which relatives could be relied upon would vary with the number of hours worked by the mother. In other words, different care arrangements are likely to be required as the mother's working hours increase; presumably these arrangements involve greater money costs.

To our knowledge, a rigorous treatment of child care modes, market participation, and hours worked has not yet been attempted. Heckman (1974) provides a good discussion of the identification issues involved. Just as in the usual labor supply model, no wage is observed for non-workers. In addition, however, there are other key prices which can go unobserved: the prices for all modes of child care for non-working mothers and the prices for all modes save the one actually chosen for working mothers. Finally, there are quality of care considerations and unobserved constraints on care modes which must be taken into account. These are challenging issues, both in terms of data and in the econometrics.

5.4. *Extensions of the static model: Child quality*

The idea of "child quality" enters fertility models to account for those characteristics of children, beyond their sheer number, which provide utility to parents. One might wonder what could be accomplished with such an elaboration of the parents' utility function. After all, a child's "quality" is not something which can be directly observed in the data; it is a derived quantity based on underlying parental preferences over child characteristics. It is not immediately obvious whether the introduction of an unobserved argument in the parents' utility function can generate testable implications for behavior. In fact, however, the concept of child quality has been exceedingly useful in explaining an empirical puzzle having to do with the effect of exogenous income on fertility.

Particularly in early work, beginning with Becker's own (1960) study, it has appeared that higher income families tend to have fewer children. One could argue about whether such studies properly separated earned from exogenous income or, as did Becker (1960), about the intervening role of contraceptive knowledge. Nevertheless, estimates of negative income effects have been common enough to cause concern, especially among those who think that the only interesting goods are normal goods. The concept of child quality, as presented in Becker (1960) and Becker and Lewis (1973), has helped to rescue the notion that "true" income effects on numbers of children are not so negative as they seem to be in the data.

It is useful to begin with a sociological explanation concerning income effects which relies on binding normative constraints. Consider the child care production function $n = g(T_c, E_c)$ of the static model presented above, a function which summarizes those technically efficient combinations of child care time and money expenditures which suffice to care for $N = n$ children. Associated with g is the cost function $C(w, N)$. Sociologists and some economists [Duesenberry (1960)] have argued that $C(w, N)$ is very much a function of social class; that is, membership in a particular social class, which we index with the variable α, imposes strong restrictions on the minimum level (and perhaps the pattern) of expenditures appropriate to the care of $N = n$ children. If that is the case, then we may write $C(w, N, \alpha)$, with $\partial C/\partial\alpha \geq 0$ and $\partial^2 C/\partial N \partial\alpha \geq 0$.

In this perspective, families in two social classes α_0 and α_1 face different constraints; in particular, the shadow price of children $\partial C/\partial N$ varies systematically with α. A possible explanation for negative income effects then follows. Exogenous income Ω and social class are surely correlated, and it is membership in social class which determines the shadow price of children. If Ω is varied in the data while α goes unobserved, estimates of the impact of Ω on N mix true income effects (α held constant) with price effects. By a simple omitted-variables argument, the true income effect would therefore tend to be underestimated.

The Becker and Lewis (1973) approach is, in its implications for the data, not really very different from this social class argument; in fact, the latter can be readily derived as a special case of the Becker–Lewis model. Rather than introduce heterogeneity into the budget constraint, Becker and Lewis incorporate preferences with respect to "child quality" in the parents' utility function. Quality, in turn, is assumed to be a function of the time and money expenditures lavished on children.

The Becker–Lewis extension of the static model is easily formalized. Suppose that there exists a joint "production" function, implicitly defined by $g(T_c, E_c; n, q) = 0$, which gives the levels of child care time and money expenditures which are minimally sufficient to care for n children at quality level q. The g function is a peculiar hybrid: it combines both household production characteristics and preference rankings concerning the (T_c, E_c) combinations which yield q units of quality.

The first stage problem, as before, is to minimize $wT_c + E_c$ subject to $g = 0$, for a given $N = n$ and $Q = q$. That yields a cost function $C(w; n, q)$, with the property $\partial C/\partial w = T_c(w; n, q)$. Becker and Lewis study a particular form of C, namely

$$C(w, N, Q) = p_0(w)N + p_1(w)Q + p_2(w)N \cdot Q,$$

where the p_i are price indices, Q is interpreted as "quality per child" and $N \cdot Q$ as "child services". This interactive form is convenient, but its main purpose is to make explicit the dependence of the shadow price of N, $\partial C/\partial N$, on the level of quality:

$$\frac{\partial C(w, N, Q)}{\partial N} = p_0(w) + p_2(w)Q.$$

Given $C(w, N, Q)$, the second stage problem is to maximize $U(X, T_1, N, Q)$ subject to a non-linear (in N and Q) budget constraint and associated constraints on time.

The essential point of the Becker–Lewis extension is a simple one. They suggest that when quality provides utility to parents, an exogenous increase in wealth $d\Omega$ tends to be channeled towards both numbers and quality. The income or wealth effect on numbers alone is therefore somewhat muted in comparison to what it would be if quality levels could be held constant. As Edlefsen (1980a) has noted, the result is immediate if we think of the issue in terms of rationing theory. Let Q be fixed at $Q(*)$, where $Q(*)$ is the level of quality which would be chosen in the full maximization problem. Then provided Q is (locally) normal and N and Q are pure substitutes, some of the increase in wealth $d\Omega$ which – in the absence of a $Q = Q(*)$ constraint – would have gone to increasing Q goes instead to increasing numbers of children. Put the other way, when quality levels can be freely chosen, income effects on N are dampened relative to the $Q = Q(*)$ case.

Rather than using rationing theory, Becker and Lewis rely on an argument about shadow prices to make their case. The shadow price of numbers of children is $\partial C(w, N, Q)/\partial N$ or $p_0(w) + p_2(w)Q$ in the special interactive form. If Q is normal, then higher income households, which intend to spend more on each child, would appear to face a higher shadow price or marginal cost for increases in numbers. In a sense, higher income induces a substitution away from numbers of children, much as in the "social class" model presented above.

The rationing-theory argument and the Becker–Lewis shadow price argument can be thought of as complementary explanations for the weak or negative estimated effects of household income on lifetime fertility. Note that the rationing-theory explanation does not rely on non-linearity in the budget constraint, so that it would continue to make sense even if $p_2(w) \equiv 0$. On the other hand, as Edlefsen (1980a) has shown, changes in the curvature of the budget constraint do alter the magnitudes of income effects relative to what they would be under an appropriately linearized constraint; non-linearity adds additional force to the rationing theory argument.

Following on Becker–Lewis, quantity–quality models have often been formulated to include an observed variable as a proxy for child quality. For instance, Becker and Tomes (1976) consider bequests (one form of E_c) as a source of utility to parents. The framework has been further generalized to consider the resources allocated to each child and parental aversion to inequality in the allocation of resources across their children, as in Behrman, Pollak and Taubman (1982). Particularly in developing countries, inequality in the provision of resources to young children can have serious consequences for their health and survival [see Chen et al. (1981) and Rosenzweig and Schultz (1982) for an investigation of sex differentials in child mortality, favoring males, in Bangladesh and India]. It is of some interest, therefore, to determine whether observed within-family inequalities result from constraints which make unequal resource allocations across children optimal in spite of parental preferences for equal provision, or whether these result directly from preferences. For instance, inequalities in educational levels across children might be attributed to child-specific differences in ability endowments; so long as ability goes unobserved, it would be difficult to say whether parents would prefer that their children be equally well educated. Indeed, as Becker and Tomes (1976) note, an unequal distribution of resources in one dimension (education) might well be counterbalanced in other dimensions (bequests). These are issues of some importance for human capital formation; the reader is referred to Behrman et al. (1982) for an excellent introduction.

5.5. *Extensions of the static model: Taste formation*

Easterlin (1968) has proposed a model of lifetime fertility in which the formation of preferences plays a central role. He suggests that the weights individuals place on material goods as sources of satisfaction, relative to numbers of children, are shaped by consumption experiences during adolescence. In particular, adolescents in families with high incomes for their household size are hypothesized to form relatively strong preferences for material goods; these tastes, once formed, then affect later fertility decisions. The Easterlin model is easily formalized. Consider a Cobb–Douglas utility function for prospective parents of generation t which takes the form:

$$U_t(X, N) = X^{\alpha_t} N^{1-\alpha_t},$$

where N is the number of children and X is a composite consumption good. The α_t parameter measures the intensity of preferences for goods relative to children among members of generation t. In the Easterlin approach,

$$\alpha_t = h(\Omega_{t-1}, N_{t-1}),$$

where Ω_{t-1} is the income of the previous generation and N_{t-1} is the family size (essentially, the number of siblings for generation t). Easterlin suggests that

$$\frac{\partial h}{\partial \Omega_{t-1}} \geq 0 \quad \text{and} \quad \frac{\partial h}{\partial N_{t-1}} \leq 0$$

and his reasoning is captured in the ratio form:

$$h(\Omega_{t-1}, N_{t-1}) = \frac{\Omega_{t-1}}{N_{t-1}}.$$

With this model of preference formation, the demand for children expressed by members of generation t is simply

$$N_t(*) = \frac{[1 - h(\Omega_{t-1}, N_{t-1})] \cdot \Omega_t}{p_t},$$

where p_t is a price index for children.

As Schultz (1981) has pointed out, the Easterlin model implies that, other things equal, parents born to large families will themselves tend to have large families. One need not rely on a particular mechanism of taste formation to make this plausible. The key to the theory, then, is the inclusion of Ω_{t-1} in the fertility demand equation. Easterlin's own work was with aggregate census data, in which several ratio measures track U.S. fertility levels over the baby boom and bust rather well. However, in tests based on micro data, the evidence in favor of including Ω_{t-1} in the demand equation is weak [Ben-Porath (1975)].

On the other hand, considerable attention has been given to another, closely related, aspect of Easterlin's theory having to do with the impact of cohort size on labor market conditions. The argument links the fertility of one generation to the labor market equilibrium conditions which will face the next generation. If large birth cohorts encounter lower wages (or greater unemployment) as they enter the labor market and such conditions persist through some portion of the reproductive life cycle, then $\Omega_t = g(N_{t-1})$ with $g' \leq 0$. This characterization of the labor market yields a demographically closed dynamic system: a relatively large birth cohort in period t will face depressed conditions in the labor market and therefore produce a relatively smaller birth cohort in period $t+1$. The dynamics are described in Lee (1974). Note that the cohort size argument is not in any way dependent on a taste formation mechanism; one generation's fertility may be linked to the fertility of the next even if preferences remain constant. Freeman (1979), Welch (1979), and Anderson (1982) have provided extensive documentation for the importance of cohort size in affecting wage levels and unemployment; the reader is referred particularly to Anderson's paper for a discussion of the issues.

5.6. Child costs and equivalence scales

It may be useful to close this section on one-period fertility models with some reflections on child costs and welfare comparisons across households which differ in composition. There is an extensive and interesting demographic literature on child costs [see Espenshade (1984a) and Lindert (1980)] which documents the money expenditures and the opportunity costs of parents' time associated with children of given characteristics. By inspecting Espenshade (1984a), for instance, one can determine, for various discount rates, precisely what is involved in raising a child and sending him through college; these figures are seldom less than appalling and invariably cast doubt on the underlying rationality of the childrearing enterprise. Nevertheless, interesting as the numbers are, they remain a mixture of exogenous prices, constraints and derived demands based on prices and constraints. One of the principal lessons from the quantity–quality approach is that total expenditures on child-related activities ought to be thought of as endogenous.

Where does this leave the issue of child costs? One response is simply that "child costs" are a function of the entire list of exogenous prices and constraints facing parents which affect $C(w, N)$ or $C(w, N, Q)$. If Q is observed, there is at least a possibility that $C(w, N, Q)$ might be identified. When Q is not observed, however, the correct interpretation of total expenditures is left open.

There is a welfare issue, closely related to the question of child costs, which has to do with equivalence scales for households which differ in composition. Let us examine the issue in the context of a simple model, following Deaton and Muellbauer (1983). The parents' direct utility function is $U(X, N)$, where X is a vector of consumption goods and N is the number of children. The expenditure function $e(p, u)$ associated with U gives, for a vector of prices p, the total expenditure required to reach utility level u. We also define a restricted expenditure function $e^*(p, u; n)$ which represents the total outlays required to attain utility u when the number of children is constrained to equal n. Then a consumer surplus measure θ,

$$\theta(p, u, n) \equiv e^*(p, u; n+1) - e^*(p, u; n),$$

is readily interpretable as the additional income which would be required to leave parents as well off with $n+1$ children as with n children. An equivalence scale ϕ expresses a similar idea in ratio form:

$$\phi(p, u, n) = \frac{e^*(p, u; n+1)}{e^*(p, u; n)}.$$

Note that for N equal to its optimal level $n(*)$, θ can be interpreted as the welfare cost of contraceptive failure. Just as in standard consumer models, preferences for children affect the levels of θ and ϕ. Therefore, parents who very much like children will require less in the way of compensation to feel as well off with $n+1$ children as with n children, given constant prices.

There has been some interest in the econometric literature concerning demand systems for goods in which demographic variables (such as the number of children) act to re-scale or translate demand function parameters [see Pollak and Wales (1981); Deaton and Muellbauer (1983)]. A key question, with implications for welfare comparisons, is whether it is possible to recover information about preferences from such systems. The demand systems are invariably estimated on goods alone, conditioning on the number and age composition of children. Pollak and Wales (1979) and Deaton and Muellbauer (1983) agree that such information is insufficient to recover θ and ϕ. This is easily seen if preferences are weakly separable. Let $U(X, N) = U^*(h(X), N)$ where h is a function which gives the sub-utility associated with a vector of goods X. With separability the relative rankings of goods bundles X are unaffected by the level of N. Therefore data on X choices alone, conditional on $N = n$, can at best identify h rather than U^*. It would seem that only a model which begins with preferences over both N and X – and which uses the joint variation of N and X in the data – can identify U^*.

If data on goods choices X alone is insufficient to make full welfare comparisons of the ϕ and θ type, is there any related welfare concept which can be tapped without recourse to an expanded (X, N) demand system? On this question Pollak and Wales (1979, 1981) and Deaton and Muellbauer (1983) have arrived at somewhat different positions. Pollak and Wales draw a distinction between "unconditional" preferences over (X, N) and "conditional" preferences over X given $N = n$; they argue that unconditional preferences are the appropriate basis for welfare comparisons. Deaton and Muellbauer concede that full welfare comparisons appear to require a joint (X, N) model. They go on to suggest, however, that the "long-run" utility associated with children can be separated, at least in principle, from the shorter-run benefits derived from goods consumption. If so, then knowledge of "conditional" preferences may provide useful information for welfare comparisons, much as the sub-utility derived from one year's consumption of goods is useful input in the consideration of life cycle welfare issues. Furthermore, Deaton and Muellbauer point out that it may be quite difficult to recover unconditional preferences, even if data on household expenditures is supplemented with information on fertility. The expenditure data are typically gathered at the level of the household, so that it is not possible to distinguish parents' consumption from that of their children. The existence of within-household public goods further complicates the issue. Hence there are formidable conceptual and empirical difficulties which, at present, appear to preclude the recovery of unconditional preferences.

6. Life cycle fertility models

Single-period fertility models certainly contribute to our understanding of individual behavior, but the gap between such stylized models and data on individual fertility histories is too wide to be easily bridged. The special features of fertility decisions have to do with uncertainty and with the fact that the arrival of a birth imposes constraints on subsequent household decisions. These issues are most naturally addressed in multiple period, sequential-decision models in which household choices are made with respect to contraceptive effort over the life cycle.

The attractiveness of the sequential-decisions setting is, at present, partly offset by the mathematical difficulties it poses for the derivation of refutable hypotheses. One can rarely get beyond the Bellman optimality principle – that is, beyond first-order conditions – without imposing structural assumptions concerning either the utility function or the constraints which are patently unrealistic. Still, as Wolpin (1984), Newman (1985a), and Hotz and Miller (1985) have shown in important recent contributions, a great deal of progress can be made if the artificial assumptions involved are judiciously chosen.

Edlefsen (1980b) has formulated an essentially static model of birth timing and spacing which serves as a useful bridge to the more complex dynamic programming approaches. His model is interesting chiefly for its attention to the life cycle budget constraint when the opportunity cost of a birth involves forgone labor market experience as well as current earnings. To put the Edlefsen approach in perspective, we should briefly review the empirical facts on discontinuous labor market participation and women's wages.

6.1. *Time costs in life cycle fertility models*

Labor market withdrawal at age a can impose both current and future costs in terms of forgone earnings if wages rise with experience. There has been some controversy in the empirical literature over just how large a wage penalty is involved when a women withdraws from the market, especially if her human capital "depreciates" during the time she is out.

Mincer and Polachek (1974) suggest that labor market withdrawal for the purpose of childbearing imposes three sorts of costs: the direct opportunity cost of forgone earnings (in the one-period framework presented earlier, this would be represented by wT_c); the loss of experience on which future wage growth is conditioned; and a depreciation of previously accumulated human capital. The Corcoran et al. (1983) paper provides empirical estimates of the rate of depreciation following withdrawal; following Mincer and Ofek (1982), it also sheds light on the rapidity with which wages "rebound" upon labor market re-entry, a

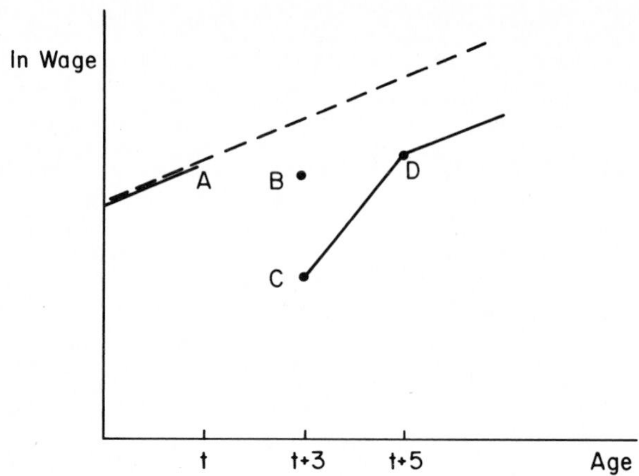

Figure 3.19. Wages for a continuously employed worker (dotted line) and the wage path for a worker who leaves the labor force at point t and returns at point $t+3$.

phenomenon which can be attributed to the restoration of previously depreciated human capital.

Corcoran et al. (1983) find that the net depreciation effect is rather small, a result which is consistent with Mincer and Ofek (1982). The implications of their findings can be seen in Figure 3.19. The top (dotted) line gives wage levels for a full time worker with continuous work experience. An interruption of three years leads to a sharp depreciation effect (that is, the re-entry wage is given by point C rather than point B) but subsequently there is an equally dramatic wage rebound; as shown in the figure, wage levels reach point D some five years after re-entry. From point D on in the life cycle, the cost of the previous three-year withdrawal is evident only in the woman's three-year gap in experience.

What implications do these findings have for theories of fertility determination? Following Edlefsen (1980b), let us consider the budget constraint for a life cycle problem when capital markets are perfect. Suppose that parents may choose the point at which childbearing begins, a_0, as well as the number of children, N. Assume that childrearing entails a full withdrawal from the labor force and that with each child there is a (fixed) period β of withdrawal, so that with N children the required span of time out of the labor force is $S \equiv \beta N$.[16] The equation which relates wages to accumulated experience is

$$\ln w(a) = \alpha + \rho E(a), \tag{19}$$

[16] Edlefsen also allows β to be a choice variable.

where $E(a)$ is accumulated experience and the wage depreciation accompanying periods out of the labor force is assumed for simplicity to be zero.

In a potential reproductive lifetime of length T, full wealth is given by

$$F(\alpha,\rho)=\int_0^T w(a)\mathrm{e}^{-ra}\mathrm{d}a=\int_0^T \mathrm{e}^{\alpha+(\rho-r)a}\mathrm{d}a, \tag{20}$$

where $\mathrm{e}^{\alpha+\rho a}$ is the wage earned at age a by a continuously employed worker and r is the rate of interest. What is the opportunity cost of a fertility strategy in which childbearing begins at age a_0 and labor market withdrawal lasts for a period of length $S=s$? Lifetime earnings under this strategy are given by the sum of three terms:

$$\int_0^{a_0}\mathrm{e}^{\alpha+(\rho-r)a}\mathrm{d}a+\int_{a_0}^{a_0+s}0\,\mathrm{d}a+\int_{a_0+s}^{T}\mathrm{e}^{\alpha+\rho(a-s)-ra}\mathrm{d}a,$$

or

$$\int_0^{a_0}\mathrm{e}^{\alpha+(\rho-r)a}\mathrm{d}a+\mathrm{e}^{-\rho s}\int_{a_0+s}^{T}\mathrm{e}^{\alpha+(\rho-r)a}\mathrm{d}a.$$

Clearly the opportunity cost of strategy (a_0,s) – that is, its claim on full wealth – is represented by

$$C(a_0,s)\equiv\int_{a_0}^{a_0+s}\mathrm{e}^{\alpha+(\rho-r)a}\mathrm{d}a+(1-\mathrm{e}^{-\rho s})\int_{a_0+s}^{T}\mathrm{e}^{\alpha+(\rho-r)a}\mathrm{d}a. \tag{21}$$

This cost function, analogous to the $C(w,N)$ cost function in the static model, is non-linear in both the initiation point a_0 and the number of children, s/β.

Note that

$$\frac{\partial C(a_0,s)}{\partial a_0}\leq 0$$

and

$$\frac{\partial C(a_0,s)}{\partial s}\geq 0.$$

These derivatives are the shadow prices of a_0 and s (ignoring money expenditures on children). The first immediately suggests that, in the absence of household preferences with respect to a_0, the age at which childbearing begins, the optimal solution for a_0 is for childbearing to begin as late as possible in the reproductive span, that is, at $a_0(*) = T - s(*)$. We would therefore need to invoke either preferences on a_0 or additional structure on the wage function to explain why first births tend to follow quickly upon marriage.[17]

The tension in a fertility model with human capital accumulation is therefore between the desire to have children first – so as to enjoy them longer – and the opportunity cost of forgone experience and earnings implied by an early childbearing strategy. A shorthand way of representing the issue is to write the objective function as $u = U^*(a_0, N, x)$, with $\partial U^*/\partial a_0 \leq 0$. At the optimum, we would have $\partial U^*/\partial a_0 = \lambda\, \partial C/\partial a_0$, where λ is the constraint multiplier.

Comparative static results in this human capital model depend on the way in which the shadow prices of a_0 and s change with the parameters of the wage function, α and ρ. Edlefsen shows

$$\frac{\partial^2 C}{\partial a_0\, \partial \alpha} \leq 0, \qquad \frac{\partial^2 C}{\partial a_0\, \partial \rho} \leq 0,$$

$$\frac{\partial^2 C}{\partial s\, \partial \alpha} \geq 0, \qquad \frac{\partial^2 C}{\partial s\, \partial \rho} \geq 0.$$

That is, the higher the level of α and ρ the greater the incentive to delay childbearing and to have fewer children.

Predictions about α, ρ, and the initiation and level of childbearing depend critically on the specification of the wage function. If wages grow exogenously with age at rate γ, for instance, then there need not be an incentive to delay childbearing. Equation (19) would be replaced by

$$\ln w(a) = \alpha + \gamma a + \rho E(a) \tag{19'}$$

and, in consequence,

$$\frac{\partial C(a_0, s)}{\partial a_0} \gtreqless 0, \quad \text{as } r \lesseqgtr \gamma.$$

If $\gamma > r$, then the optimal policy is to begin childbearing immediately. See Moffitt (1984) for a more rigorous treatment of the issues.

The fact that children of different ages receive different amounts of parental time carries further implications about wages and the opportunity costs of childbearing. Let $T_{c,a}$ represent the allocation of child care time to a child of age a, and consider fertility decisions made at point t in the parents' life cycle. The

[17]Note that if the interest rate is zero, $\partial c/\partial a_0 = 0$. In this special case, parents are indifferent to a_0.

opportunity costs of time associated with a birth in period t are

$$C(w,t)=\sum_{i=t} w(i)(1+r)^{-(i-t)}T_{c,i-t}, \tag{22}$$

where $w(i)$ is the (exogenous) wage level for age i. We expect $T_{c,a}$ to be downward-sloping in age; therefore, as Ward and Butz (1980) point out, the disincentive effect of an expected one-shot increase in wages in period t' is greater in periods near t'. That is, an expected wage increase in life cycle period five produces a relatively strong fertility disincentive for period four and a weaker disincentive (even allowing for discounting) in period one. Hotz and Miller (1985) have incorporated a simple exogenous age profile of child care in their dynamic model of fertility and labor force participation, which we will review below.

6.2. *The irreversibility of childbearing*

The arrival of a child generates a stream of demands on household resources, and parents are surely more constrained in their choices after a birth takes place than before. The accumulation of constraints on the household which is implied by childbearing has implications for other dimensions of choice as well, including labor supply. We use some simple results from the theory of rationing to draw out these implications.

Consider the "Le Châtelier" effect in the context of life cycle fertility models. As a household moves through its reproductive span, progressively adding constraints which masquerade as small children, its (compensated) responses to price changes should grow progressively smaller. That is, own-price effects will tend to be drawn in toward zero with the accumulation of constraints. In particular, the responsiveness of labor supply to the offered wage should vary with the number and age distribution of children. One might tap such a Le Chatêlier effect with a "demographically-scaled" labor supply function.

The rationing theory framework is also useful in understanding the impact of unanticipated fertility on subsequent household choices [see Rosenzweig and Wolpin (1980)]. The theory suggests that an unanticipated increase in the number of children born at age a should lead parents to reduce their consumption of goods which are (pure) substitutes and increase the consumption of complementary goods. For instance, if leisure at age $a+\Delta$ is a substitute for numbers of children born at a, then it would not be surprising to see the arrival of twins at a followed by a decrease in leisure. Similarly, if "quality" expenditures substitute for numbers, an upward shock in fertility might be following by a reduction in such expenditures.

6.3. Dynamic programming models under uncertainty

While statistical analyses of birth histories have become increasingly sophisticated [see Rodriguez et al. (1984), Newman and McCullough (1984), and Heckman, Hotz and Walker (1985)], their development has proceeded without much guidance from formal economic models of sequential decision-making under uncertainty. Most analysts would agree that any formal treatment of fertility choices over the life cycle must come to grips with a household's imperfect control over reproduction and with the "irreversible" nature of the demands imposed by children on the household. These elements are easy enough to incorporate in a descriptive sequential decisions framework; what is difficult is to draw from them some testable implications about the time path of fertility control.

Consider the following simple model of contraception over the life cycle. We suppose that household income at age a, Y_a, can be taken as exogenous and that capital markets are perfectly imperfect; that is, no savings takes place. The within-period budget constraint is

$$Y_a = X_a + pN_a,$$

where X_a represents the household's consumption of a composite commodity and p is the unit price of a child, assumed constant for simplicity.

Let the household's indirect utility index V for age a depend on the number of children present, N_a, and a function $\rho(u)$ which summarizes the disutility associated with contraceptive use at efficiency level u, where $1-u$ is the probability of conception. (The within-period budget constraint $Y_a = X_a + pN_a$ is left implicit in $V[N_a, \rho(u)]$.) To characterize the optimal path of contraceptive use over the life cycle, we first consider the household's objective function:

$$\max_{\substack{\{u_t : t \in (0,1,\ldots T),\\ \boldsymbol{u} \le u_t \le 1, \text{ for all } t\}}} E_0 \sum_{a=0}^{T} V[N_a, \rho(u_a)][1+r]^{-a} + S(N_T),$$

where $\boldsymbol{u}$ represents the household's level of fecundity ($1-\boldsymbol{u}$ is the maximum probability of conception) and $S(N_T)$ is a terminal value function, representing the utility derived over the remainder of the life cycle outside the reproductive span, given N_T children. Define

$$J[N_t, t] = \max_{\{u\}} E_t \sum_{a=t}^{T} V[N_a, \rho(u_a)][1+r]^{-a} + S(N_T)$$

so that $J[N_t, t]$ is the maximum utility which can be derived from the remaining reproductive lifetime of $T-t$ periods, conditional on $N = N_t$ children at age t.

As is usual in such problems, there is a recursive equation which describes the age path of $J[N_t, t]$. We have

$$J[N_t,t] = \max_{u_t} E_t V[N_t, \rho(u_t)][1+r]^{-t} + \max_{\{u\}} E_t \sum_{a=t+1}^{T} V[N_a, \rho(u_a))][1+r]^{-a} + S(N_T)$$

or, using the definition of u_t as one minus the likelihood of conception,

$$J[N_t,t] = \max_{u_t} E_t V[N_t, \rho(u_t)][1+r]^{-t} + \max_{\{u\}} \{u_t \cdot J[N_t, t+1] + (1-u_t) J[N_t+1, t+1]\}. \quad (23)$$

From (23), it is clear that in the absence of preferences with respect to contraceptive effort u, the optimal solutions for $\{u\}$ will be corner solutions. The difference between $J[N_t+1, t+1]$ and $J[N_t, t+1]$ gives the value of an additional child; unless these terms happen to be equal, we will have $u_t(*) = 1$ or $u_t(*) = \boldsymbol{u}$. Once preferences over u are entered into the model, however, interior solutions become a possibility.

Expression (23) characterizes an optimum; it does not directly tell us how the $u_t(*)$ control varies with changes in N_t or other parameters. It appears that in general the problem is intractable without additional structure. As Wolpin (1984) has shown, some insights can be gained by working backward from the terminal period T, but that recursive approach quickly becomes mired in complexity. Newman (1985a) takes another approach. He selects a particular functional form (the quadratic) for V and, after considerable manipulation, manages to derive a closed-form solution for $u_t(*)$. Strictly speaking, the solution holds only if the optimal sequence $\{u_t(*)\}$ is characterized by interior solutions $\boldsymbol{u} < u_t(*) < 1$ for all t; nevertheless, the Newman results are remarkable, given the complexity of the programming problem.

Newman shows that the conception hazard $1 - u_t(*)$ rises with duration since last birth, holding parity levels constant. For parents who are trying to have a birth (whose $J(N_t+1, t+1)$ is larger than $J(N_t, t+1)$), the result makes intuitive sense. For parents who are trying not to have a birth, on the other hand, the passage of time means that there are fewer fertile periods $T-t$ left over in which they will be exposed to risk. To some extent, the passage of time without a conception may allow these parents to relax their degree of contraceptive vigilance. Newman also proves that holding age (t) constant, the level of contraceptive effort should increase with an increase in realized parity. These predictions are achieved with the aid of a number of simplifying structural assumptions (among them, a household's income is assumed constant over the life cycle), but they seem reasonable and – to some degree – consistent with the birth interval data.

6.4. *Life cycle fertility models with employment*

Perhaps the most carefully integrated model of life cycle fertility and labor supply is Hotz and Miller (1985). Their model incorporates many of the elements from Ward and Butz (1980) in an explicitly dynamic decision setting under uncertainty. There are a number of areas of uncertainty considered: the time path of husband's income; the length of the fertile period; transitory shocks in the wife's wage; and the outcome of any given level of contraceptive effort. Each of these is given a stochastic specification and blended into a structural econometric model. While the Hotz and Miller analysis is the most general undertaken to date, it is not fully general. For instance, there are no savings permitted, so that the household's budget must balance each period. The wife's (permanent) wage is constant. In contrast to Newman (1985), there are no psychic or monetary costs associated with contraception, yielding an optimal path for fertility control of the "bang-bang" variety. Despite these inevitable, simplifying assumptions, however, the Hotz and Miller approach is well worth considering.

The key element in the model is the age schedule of child care time, $T_{c,a}$. The schedule is imposed exogenously on the household once a birth occurs; as Ward and Butz (1980) argue, $T_{c,a}$ should be downward sloping in the age of the child, with infants imposing the greatest demands on household time, $T_{c,0}$. A household at point t in its life cycle may have committed a portion of its time endowment to care for earlier births, leaving the remainder to be divided between leisure time and market work. The amount of time already committed is

$$T_c = \sum_{a=0} T_{c,a} n_{t-a-1}, \tag{28}$$

where n_s is the number of children born at point s in the household life cycle. Hotz and Miller study a geometrically-declining form for $T_{c,a}$ which is constrained so that there must always be some time left over for leisure ("home production") and market work. As time passes without a birth, the margin between the household's per-period time endowment and the requirements of child care begins to increase. In other words, the per-period budget set expands and with that expansion the disincentive effects associated with a next birth decline. The Hotz and Miller analysis therefore offers a structural explanation for duration dependence in birth intervals.

The labor supply component of the model resembles other single-period models in that the number and age distribution of children are entered as explanatory factors; however, Hotz and Miller allow these variables to evolve endogenously over the life cycle in response to an individual-specific, persistent fixed wage. Therefore, a correlation exists between births in years previous to year t and the unobservables governing year t labor supply. This is an innovative synthesis. Although the theoretical predictions drawn from the model are qualitative in nature (in other words, the theory does not yield a functional form for J_t) rather than explicit, as in Newman's (1985a) work, the Newman and the Hotz–Miller approaches complement each other well. The reader is referred to Newman's (1985b) thoughtful essay for further reflections on this first generation of dynamic programming models.

6.5. *Contraceptive histories*

Direct tests of the Newman and Hotz and Miller models require information on contraceptive histories. Unfortunately, such data are not available for either developed or developing countries except for relatively brief (e.g. 5-year) periods in an individual's life cycle. For the most part, then, tests based on sequential contraceptive decision models must be based on the implications of such models for birth histories. A key difficulty in forming the tests is that much of the interesting behavior occurs relatively late in the reproductive span (for instance, the characteristic switch from a concave to a convex profile of fertility rates by age) and yet it is during this time that a woman may find herself unable to conceive. It is easy to mistake systematic physiological patterns for systematic behavioral ones. A first step in avoiding this confusion is to work with contraceptive histories. Rosenzweig and Schultz (forthcoming) have begun to explore the limited contraceptive history information available in micro U.S. data sets.

7. Conclusions

It may be useful to close this review with a list of the research questions economists have posed in the area of marital status and fertility and some observations on the success with which such questions have been answered.

Much of the work in the areas of marital status and childbearing has proceeded by analogy. Theories of age at first marriage have been (loosely) informed by theories of search in the labor market. Household production models have their origins in the standard theorems of international trade. The simpler models of fertility treat childbearing as fully analogous with the purchase of durable goods at known prices. We think that it is appropriate to ask just how much has been and can be learned about marital status and childbearing from the relentless pursuit of such analogies.

The analysis of marital status is still rather underdeveloped compared to analyses of fertility given marital status. The notion that marriage and, perhaps, marriage dissolution can be analyzed in the framework of search theory seems to us to be an attractive one. Search theory has a place for many of the elements which both demographers and economists see as central to the process of marriage: uncertainty, the frequency or infrequency of marriage opportunities, a role for norms in affecting the utility of being single at a given age. Yet at this point the search framework can provide us with few empirically testable propositions. The principal stumbling block, it appears, is that relatively little can be learned from the frequencies of marriage by age alone; what is needed is additional information concerning the types of matches which occur. If a convincing test of search theory in the labor market requires data on accepted wages, a convincing test of search theory as applied to marriage must rely on the properties of accepted matches. Without such information, it is simply not possible to distinguish changes in reservation levels over the period of search from changes in offer frequencies or other relevant variables. Yet how are accepted matches to be characterized? There has been surprisingly little work on what strikes us as perhaps the central question in this area. Some progress can surely be made by treating a potential spouse's education and earnings level as the marital search counterparts to a wage offer; the econometric modeling here would be both interesting and challenging.

A pervasive theme in the economics of fertility has been the role of the female wage as an indicator of the price of time, certainly a key element in the opportunity cost of childbearing and rearing. The economic logic of the argument is impeccable; unfortunately, econometric tests of the proposition have not been nearly so convincing. There are many examples in which predicted female wages are shown to vary negatively with cumulative fertility. The wage equations, however, rely heavily on female education as a driving variable. Sociologists are certainly far from convinced that such a procedure effectively isolates a wage effect rather than an education effect, and we agree that there is room for skepticism. Analyses with actual, rather than predicted, wage rates have not succeeded in establishing a negative wage effect; perhaps the difficulty here is that, with labor supply endogenous, a joint model of fertility and labor supply is required for consistent estimation. Instrumental variables techniques [as in Schultz (1980)] may be useful in this context, but the exclusion restrictions required are seldom very appealing.

If a wage effect is to be identified, it makes sense to begin the search for it with a detailed analysis of the time spent in child care. Child care time is certainly at the heart of economic models of fertility, whether it is left implicit, as in models of completed fertility, or given explicit attention, as in the models of Butz and Ward (1980) and Hotz and Miller (1985). The substitution of market care or care provided by relatives for own (household) time is a feasible option for many households; the degree to which such substitution is undertaken may depend on the price and perceived quality of such options. Again, with the exception of Heckman (1974) and Lehrer (forthcoming), very little sophisticated work has been done on the question of child care, and yet it would seem that child care, labor force participation, and hours worked are closely intertwined. This is surely a priority area for research.

The leap from analyses of child care and labor supply at a point in the life cycle to investigations of the timing of fertility is a large one. Demographers have identified some fairly pronounced empirical regularities in the patterns of fertility by age, and it must be said that economists have not really been successful in explaining these patterns. A key difficulty here lies in the specification of the female wage function. As noted in Section 5, female wage functions which rise exogenously with age produce rather different predictions about optimal fertility timing than do wage functions which rise as a result of accumulated experience. Although the work of Mincer and Ofek (1982) and Corcoran and Duncan (1983) carries us a considerable distance, questions about discontinuous labor market experience and female wage rates are not yet fully resolved. Without a specification of the female wage function which can be agreed upon except for details, there is little hope of developing refutable predictions about the timing of fertility.

We began this review with the observation that models of female labor supply treat marital status and fertility as exogenous influences on labor force participation and the supply of hours to the market. A central theme which runs through the remainder of the chapter is that marital status, fertility, and labor supply are more properly viewed as jointly determined, each being the product of decisions made with respect to a common set of preferences and constraints; the set of constraints, in particular, evolves over the life cycle as essentially irreversible decisions are taken. It is clear from the results of Heckman et al. (1985), Newman and McCullough (1984), and Rodriguez et al. (1984) that, in the fertility dimension at least, there is every reason to suspect that unobserved variables, as well as observables, closely link decisions at one point in the life cycle to decisions at other points. A labor supply counterpart to these fertility results is found in Heckman and Macurdy (1980), in which persistent unobservables are also given a prominent role. Surely, if persistent unmeasured variables affect fertility over the life cycle and also affect labor supply over the life cycle, then the observed associations between children ever born by a given age and labor supply at that age are at least partly spurious. To put it a bit differently, if ε is the composite disturbance in a probit model of participation, then ε is very likely correlated with right-hand side variables like children ever born and marital status. To say this is not to say much that is new or much that is helpful. After all, from an empirical point of view it is difficult to judge how serious any such biases might be [see Mroz (1984)]. From the point of view of research strategy, it seems that we are left with two options. Fertility and marital status variables can of course be purged from the reduced forms of labor supply models, but at considerable cost to our understanding of actual behavior. The more difficult and potentially more rewarding alternative is to model the joint evolution of the demographic and labor supply variables, giving attention to the role of persistent unobservables. The work of Hotz and Miller (1985) is an initial step in what appears to be a very promising direction.

We would like to close this review by reminding the reader of Norman Ryder's comments (1973) on the early Becker–Lewis–Willis models. It was Ryder's point that economic models of the family are most interesting when they emphasize what is distinctive about fertility and family formation rather than what these subjects appear to share with other, more conventional areas of economic inquiry. The pervasive roles played by individual physiology, by uncertainty, by irreversibility, and by social norms set models of the family apart from other subjects of economic research. The dynamic, sequential models of contraceptive use begin to address the issues of uncertainty and irreversibility in childbearing; to this point, however, economists have hardly begun to grapple with the extra constraints imposed by normative rules and by individual physiology. These distinctive areas deserve our attention.

References

Anderson, J. (1982) "An economic-demographic model of the United States labor market", in: J. Simon and P. Lindert, eds. *Research in population economics*, 4.

Baker, R. J. and J. Nelder (1978) "The Glim system—release 3", Numerical Algorithms Group, Oxford.

Becker, G. (1960) "An economic analysis of fertility", in *Demographic and economic change in developed countries*. Princeton: Princeton University Press.

Becker, G. (1973) "A theory of marriage: part I", *Journal of Political Economy*, 81(4):813–846.

Becker, G. (1974) "A theory of marriage: part II", *Journal of Political Economy*, 82(2):S11–S26.

Becker, G. (1985) "Human capital effort, and the sexual division of labor", *Journal of Labor Economics*, 3(1):S33–S58.

Becker, G. and H. G. Lewis (1973) "On the interaction between the quantity and quality of children", *Journal of Political Economy*, 81:S279–S288.

Becker, G. and N. Tomes (1976) "Child endowments and the quantity and quality of children", *Journal of Political Economy*, 84:5143–5162.

Becker, G., E. Landes and R. Michael (1977) "An economic analysis of marital instability", *Journal of Political Economy*, 85(6):1141–1187.

Behrman, J., R. Pollak and P. Taubman (1982) "Parental preferences and provision for progeny", *Journal of Political Economy*, 90(1):52–73.

Ben-Porath, Y. (1975) "First generation effects on second generation fertility", *Demography*, 12(3):397–406.

Ben-Porath, Y. (1980) "The F-connection: families, friends and firms and the organization of exchange", *Population and Development Review*, 6(1):1–30.

Bloom, David (1982a) "What's happening to the age at first birth in the United States? A study of recent cohorts", *Demography*, 19(3):351–370.

Bloom, David (1982b) "Age patterns of women at first birth", *Genus*, 38(3–4):101–128.

Bloom, David and James Trussell (1984) "What are the determinants of delayed childbearing and permanent childlessness in the United States?", *Demography*, 21(4):591–611.

Bongaarts, John (1978) "A framework for analyzing the proximate determinants of fertility", *Population and Development Review*, 4(1):105–132.

Boulier, B. and M. Rosenzweig (1984) "Schooling, search and spouse selection: testing economic theories of marriage and household behavior", *Journal of Political Economy*, 92(4):712–732.

Brass, William (1977) "Notes on empirical mortality models", Population Bulletin of the United Nations, No. 9.

Butz, W. and M. Ward (1979) "The emergence of countercyclical U.S. fertility", *American Economic Review*, 69(3):318–328.

Casterline, John and James Trussell (1980) "Age at first birth", Comparative Studies #15, World Fertility Survey, London.

Chen, L., E. Huq, and S. D'Souza (1981) "Sex bias in the family allocation of food and health care in rural Bangladesh", *Population and Development Review*, 7(1):55–70.

Coale, Ansley (1971) "Age patterns of marriage", *Population Studies*, 25(2):193–214.

Coale, Ansley (1973) "The demographic transition reconsidered", International Union for the Scientific Study of Population, International Population Conference, Liege.

Coale, Ansley (1977) "The development of new models of nuptiality and fertility", *Population*, Numero Special:131–150.

Coale, Ansley (1984) *Rapid population change in China 1952–1982*. Washington: National Academy Press.

Coale, Ansley and Paul Demeny (1966) *Regional model life tables and stable populations*. Princeton: Princeton University Press.

Coale, Ansley, Paul Demeny and Barbara Vaughan (1985) *Regional model life tables and stable populations*, second edition. New York: Academic Press.

Coale, Ansley and Donald McNeil (1972) "The distribution by age of the frequency of first marriage in a female cohort", *Journal of the American Statistical Association*, 67:743–749.

Coale, Ansley and James Trussell (1974) "Model fertility schedules: variations in the age structure of childbearing in human populations", *Population Index*, 40(2):185–258.

Coale, Ansley and James Trussell (1978) "Technical note: finding the two parameters that specify a model schedule of marital fertility", *Population Index*, 44(2):203–213.

Coale, Ansley and Susan Watkins, eds. (1985) *The decline of fertility in Europe*. Princeton: Princeton University Press.

Cogan, J. (1980) "Labor supply with costs of labor market entry", in: J. Smith, ed., *Female labor supply*. Princeton: Princeton University Press.

Corcoran, M., G. Duncan and M. Ponza (1983) "A longitudinal analysis of white women's wages", *Journal of Human Resources*, 18(4):497–520.

Davis, Kingsley and Judith Blake (1956) "Social structure and fertility: an analytic framework", *Economics Development and Cultural Change*, IV(3):211–235.

Deaton, A. (1981) "Theoretical and empirical approaches to consumer demand under rationing", in: A. Deaton, ed., *Essays in the theory and measurement of consumer behavior*. New York: Cambridge University Press.

Deaton, A. and J. Muellbauer (1981) "Functional forms for labor supply and commodity demands with and without quantity restrictions", *Econometrica*, 49(6):1521–1532.

Deaton, A. and J. Muellbauer (1983) "On measuring child costs in poor countries", manuscript prepared for the Living Standards Measurement Study, The World Bank.

Duesenberry, J. (1960) "Comments on 'An economic analysis of fertility', by Gary Becker", in: *Demographic and economic change in developed countries*. Princeton: Princeton University Press.

Easterlin, R. (1968) *Population, labor force, and long swings in economic growth: the American experience*. New York: National Bureau of Economic Research.

Edlefsen, L. (1980a) "The quantity-quality tradeoff, the price of children, and the effect of income on fertility", manuscript.

Edlefsen, L. (1980b) "The opportunity costs of time and the numbers, timing, and spacing of births", paper presented at the September 1980 meetings of the Population Association of America.

Espenshade, T. (1984a) *Investing in children: new estimates of parental expenditures*. Washington, D.C.: Urban Institute Press.

Espenshade, T. (1984b) "Economic theories of marriage and divorce, paper presented in Household Formations session of the American Real Estate and Urban Economic Association annual meetings, Dallas, Texas, 1984.

Fawcett, J., et al. (1974) "The value of children in Asia and the United States: comparative perspectives", papers of the East–West Population Institute, No. 32.

Flinn, C. and J. Heckman (1983) "Are unemployment and out of the labor force behaviorally distinct states?", *Journal of Labor Economics*, 1(1):28–42.

Freeman, R. (1979) "The effects of demographic factors on age earnings profiles", *Journal of Human Resources*, 14(3):289–318.

Glick, Paul and Arthur Norton (1976) "Number, timing, and duration of marriages and divorces in the United States: June 1975", Current Population Reports, Series P-20, #297.

Goldman, Noreen, Charles Westoff, and Charles Hammerslough (1984) "Demography of the marriage market in the United States", *Population Index*, 50(1):5–25.

Groeneveld, L., N. Tuma, and M. Hannan (1980) "The effects of negative income tax programs on marital dissolution", *Journal of Human Resources*, 15(4):655–674.

Hammerslough, Charles (1984) "Characteristics of women who stop using contraception", *Family Planning Perspectives*, 16(1):14–18.

Heckman, J. and T. Macurdy (1980) "A life cycle model of female labor supply", *Review of Economic Studies*, 47:47–74.

Heckman, James and Burton Singer (1982a) "The identification problem in econometric models for duration data", in: W. Hildenbrand, ed., *Advances in Econometrics*. Cambridge: Cambridge University Press, 39–77.

Heckman, James and Burton Singer (1982b) "Population heterogeneity in demographic models", in: Kenneth Land and Andrei Rogers, eds., *Multidimensional mathematical demography*. New York: Academic Press, 567–599.

Heckman, James and Burton Singer (1984) "Econometric duration analysis", *Journal of Econometrics*, 24:63–132.

Heckman, James, Joseph Hotz and James Walker (1985) "New evidence on the timing and spacing of births", *American Economics Review*, 75(2):179–184.

Heckman, James (1974) "Effects of child-care programs on women's work effort", *Journal of Political Economy*, 82(2):S136–S163.

Heckman, J. and R. Willis (1975) "Estimation of a stochastic model of reproduction: an econometric approach", in: N. Terleckyi, ed., *Household production and consumption*. New York: Columbia University Press.

Henry, Louis (1961) "Some data on natural fertility", *Eugenics Quarterly*, 8(2):81–91.

Henry, L. (1972) "Nuptiality", *Theoretical Population Biology*, 3:135–152.

Heuser, Robert (1976) *Fertility tables for birth cohorts by color: United States, 1917–73*. Washington: National Center for Health Statistics.

Hill, Ken, Hania Zlotnik and James Trussell (1983) *Manual X: indirect techniques for demographic estimation*. New York: United Nations.

Hobcraft, John and Roderick Little (1984) "Fertility exposure analysis: a new method for assessing the contributions of proximate determinants to fertility differentials", *Population Studies*, 38(1):21–46.

Hotz, V. J. and R. Miller (1985) "The economics of family planning", discussion paper, Graduate School of Industrial Administration, Carnegie-Mellon University.

Jones, Elise, Jacqueline Forrest, Noreen Goldman, Stanley Henshaw, Richard Lincoln, Jeannie Rosoff, Charles Westoff, and Deirdre Wulf (1985) "Teenage pregnancy in developed countries: determinants and policy implications", *Family Planning Perspectives*, 17(2):53–62.

Keeley, M. (1977) "The economics of family formation", *Economic Inquiry*, 15:238–250.

Keeley, M. (1979) "An analysis of the age pattern of first marriage", *International Economic Review*, 20(2):527–544.

Kniesner, T. (1976) "An indirect test of complementarity in a family labor supply model", *Econometrica*, 44:651–670.

Kramer, W. and K. Neusser (1984) "The emergence of countercyclical U.S. fertility: note", *American Economic Review*, 74(1):201–202.

Laird, Nan and Donald Olivier (1981) "Covariance analysis of censored survival data using log-linear analysis techniques", *Journal of the American Statistical Association*, 76(374):231–240.

Lee, R. (1974) "The formal dynamics of controlled populations and the echo, the boom, and the bust", *Demography*, 11(4):563–585.

Lehrer, E. (1982) "Child care, female employment and fertility in the United States: an analysis of two-earner households", paper presented at the 1982 Annual Meetings of the Population Association of America, San Diego. (Forthcoming in *Demography*.)

Lindert, D. (1980) "Child costs and economic development", in: R. Easterlin, ed., *Population and economic change in developing countries*. Chicago: University of Chicago Press.

Lippman, S. and J. McCall (1976a) "The economics of job search: a survey, part I", *Economic Inquiry*, 14:155–189.

Lippman, S. and J. McCall (1976b) "The economics of job search: a survey, part II", *Economic Inquiry*, 14:347–368.

Manser, M. and M. Brown (1980) "Marriage and household decision-making: a bargaining analysis", *International Economic Review*, 1(6):31–44.

Martin, Linda, James Trussell, Florentina Salvail, and Nasra Shah (1983) "Covariates of child mortality in the Philippines, Indonesia, and Pakistan: a comparative analysis", *Population Studies*, 37(3):417–432.

McElroy, M. and M. Horney (1981) "Nash-bargained household decisions: toward a generalization of the theory of demand", *International Economic Review*, 22(2):333–349.

Menken, Jane, James Trussell, Debra Stempel, and Ozer Babakol (1981) "Proportional hazards life table models: an illustrative analysis of socio-demographic influences on marriage dissolution in the United States", *Demography*, 18(2):181–200.

Menken, Jane (1984) "Estimating proximate determinants: a discussion of the methods proposed by Bongaarts, Hobcraft and Little and Gaslonde and Carrasco", presented at an IUSSP session on Integrating Proximate Determinants into the Analysis of Fertility Levels and Trends, London, 29 April–1 May.

Michael, Robert and Nancy Tuma (1985) "Entry into marriage and parenthood by young men and women: the influence of family background", *Demography*, 22(4).

Mincer, J. and S. Polachek (1974) "Family investments in human capital: earnings of women", *Journal of Political Economy*, 82:S76–S108.

Mincer, J. and H. Ofek (1982) "Interrupted work careers", *Journal of Human Resources*, 17:3–24.

Moffitt, R. (1981) "Profiles of fertility, labor supply, and wages of married women: a complete life-cycle model", paper presented at the Annual Meetings of the Population Association of America, March.

Moffitt, R. (1984) "Optimal life-cycle profiles of fertility and labor supply", in: T. P. Schultz and K. Wolpin, eds., *Research in Population Economics*, 5:29–50.

Mortensen, D. (1977) "Unemployment insurance and job search decisions", *Industrial and Labor Relations Review*, 30(4):505–517.

Mroz, T. (1984) "The sensitivity of an empirical model of married women's hours of work to economic and statistical assumptions", NORC discussion paper 84-88.

NCHS (1984) "Advance report on final natality statistics, 1982", *Monthly Vital Statistics Report*, 33(6)(Supplement).

Neary, J. and K. Roberts (1980) "The theory of household behavior under rationing", *European Economic Review*, 13:25–42.

Newman, John and Charles McCulloch (1984) "A hazard rate approach to the timing of births", *Econometrica*, 52(4):939–961.

Newman, J. (1985a) "A stochastic dynamic model of fertility", manuscript, Department of Economics, Tulane University.

Newman, J. (1985b) "The use of dynamic fertility models", manuscript, Department of Economics, Tulane University.

O'Connell, M. and C. Rogers (1983) "Child care arrangements of working mothers: June 1982", Current Population Reports, Series P-23, Number 129, U.S. Bureau of the Census.

O'Connell, Martin and Carolyn Rogers (1984) "Out of wedlock births, premarital pregnancies, and their effect on family formation and dissolution", *Family Planning Perspectives*, 16(4):157–162.

Page, Hilary (1977) "Patterns underlying fertility schedules: a decomposition by both age and marital duration", *Population Studies*, 31(1):85–106.

Pollak, Robert (1985) "A reformulation of the two-sex problem", paper presented at the 1985 Annual Meetings of the Population Association of America, Boston, Massachusetts.

Pollak, R. and T. Wales (1979) "Welfare comparisons and equivalence scales", *American Economic Review*, 69:216–221.

Pollak, R. and T. Wales (1981) "Demographic variables in demand analysis", *Econometrica*, 49:1533–1551.

Pollard, John (1973) *Mathematical models for the growth of human populations*. Cambridge: Cambridge University Press, 82–96.

Pratt, William, William Mosher, Christine Bachrach and Marjorie Horn (1984) "Understanding U.S. fertility: findings from the national survey of family growth, cycle III", *Population Bulletin*, 39(5).

Preston, Samuel and Michael Strong (1985) "Effects of mortality declines on marriage patterns in developing countries", in: *Consequences of mortality decline*. New York: United Nations.

Richards, Toni (1983) "Comparative analysis of fertility, breastfeeding and contraception: a dynamic model", Report #22, Panel on Fertility Determinants, National Academy of Sciences, Washington.

Ridder, Geert and Wim Verbakel (1983) "On the estimation of the proportional hazards model in the presence of unobserved heterogeneity", Unpublished manuscript, Department of Actuarial Sciences and Econometrics, University of Amsterdam.

Rodriguez, German (1984) "The analysis of birth intervals using hazard models", WFS/TECH, World Fertility Survey, London.

Rodriguez, German, John Hobcraft, John McDonald, Jane Menken and James Trussell (1984) "A comparative analysis of the determinants of birth intervals", WFS Comparative Studies #30, World Fertility Survey, London.

Rodriguez, German and James Trussell (1980) "Maximum likelihood estimates of Coale's model nuptiality schedule from survey data", WFS Technical Bulletins #7, World Fertility Survey, London.

Rogers, Carolyn and Martin O'Connell (1984) "Childspacing among birth cohorts of American women: 1905 to 1959", Current Population Reports, Series P-20, #385.

Rosenzweig, M. and T. P. Schultz (1982) "Market opportunities, genetic endowments, and intrafamily resource distribution: child survival in rural India", *American Economic Review*, 72 (4):803–815.

Rosenzweig, M. and T. P. Schultz (forthcoming) "The demand for the supply of births: fertility and its life-cycle consequences", manuscript.

Rosenzweig, M. and K. Wolpin (1980) "Life cycle labor supply and fertility: a test of causality", *Journal of Political Economy*, 88:328–348.

Ryder, N. (1973) "Comment", *Journal of Political Economy*, 81(2):S65–S69.

Ryder, Norman (1980) "Components of temporal variations in American fertility", in: R. W. Hiorns, ed., *Demographic patterns in developed societies*. London: Taylor and Francs.

Sandefur, Gary and Wilbur Scott (1981) "A dynamic analysis of migration: an assessment of the effects of age, family and career variables", *Demography*, 18(3):355–368.

Salop, S. (1973) "Systematic job search and unemployment", *Review of Economic Studies*, 40:191–201.

Schirm, Allen, James Trussell, Jane Menken, and William Grady (1982) "Contraceptive failure in the United States: the impact of social, economic, and demographic factors", *Family Planning Perspectives*, 14(2):68–76.

Schoen, Robert (1982) "Generalizing the life table model to incorporate interaction between the sexes", in: Kenneth Land and Andrei Rogers, eds., *Multidimensional mathematical demography*. New York: Academic Press 385–443.

Schoen, Robert, William Urton, Karen Woodrow and John Baj (1985) "Marriage and divorce in twentieth century American cohorts", *Demography*, 22(1):101–114.

Schultz, T. Paul (1981) *The economics of population*. Reading, Mass.: Addison-Wesley.

Sheps, Mindel and Jane Menken (1973) *Mathematical models of conception and birth*. Chicago: University of Chicago Press.

Singh, Susheela, John Casterline and John Cleland (1985) "The proximate determinants of fertility: sub-national variations", *Population Studies*, 39(1):113–136.

Trussell, James and Charles Hammerslough (1983) "A hazards model analysis of the covariates of infant and child mortality in Sri Lanka", *Demography*, 20(1):1–26.

Trussell, James and Toni Richards (1984) "Correcting for unobserved heterogeneity in hazard models: an application of the Heckman-Singer model to demographic data", in Nancy Tuma, ed., *Sociological methodology 1985*. San Francisco: Jossey-Bass, 242–276.

Trussell, James, Barbara Vaughan, and Samir Farid (1984) "The determinants of birth interval length in Egypt", WFS/TECH 2320, World Fertility Survey, London.

Trussell, James, Linda Martin, Robert Feldman, James Palmore, Mercedes Concepcion, and Datin Noor Laily Bt. Dato' Abu Bakar (1985) "Determinants of birth interval length in the Philippines, Malaysia, and Indonesia: a hazard model analysis", *Demography*, 22(2):145–168.

Trussell James (1980) "Age at first marriage in Sri Lanka and Thailand", WFS Scientific Reports #13, World Fertility Survey, London.

Trussell, James (1982) "Program Mm", available from the Office of Population Research, Princeton University.

Trussell, James (forthcoming) "Estimating the determinants of birth interval length", in: John Hobcraft, ed., *Integrating proximate determinants into analyses of fertility levels and trends.*

Trussell, James, Jane Menken, and Ansley Coale (1982) "A general model for analyzing the effect of nuptiality on fertility", in: Lado Ruzicka, ed., *Nuptiality and fertility: proceedings of a conference.* Liege: Ordina Editions.

Trussell, James and David Bloom (1983) "Estimating the covariates of age at marriage and first birth", *Population Studies*, 37(3):403–416.

Trussell, James and Kia Reinis (1985) "Age at first marriage and age at first birth", WFS Comparative Studies, forthcoming, World Fertility Survey, London.

United Nations (1982) *Model life tables for developing countries*. New York: United Nations.

Van de Walle, Etienne and John Knodel (1980) "Europe's fertility transition: new evidence and lessons from today's developing world", *Population Bulletin*, 34(6):1–43.

Vaughan, Barbara and James Trussell (1984) "The determinants of birth interval length in Syria", WFS/TECH 2321, World Fertility Survey, London.

Ward, M. and W. Butz (1980) "Completed fertility and its timing", *Journal of Political Economy*, 88(5):917–940.

Welch, F. (1979) "Effects of cohort size on earnings: the baby boom babies' financial bust", *Journal of Political Economy*, 87(5):S65–S97.

Willis, R. (1973) "A new approach to the economic theory of fertility behavior", *Journal of Political Economy*, 82:S14–S64.

Wolpin, K. (1984) "An estimable dynamic stochastic model of fertility and child mortality", *Journal of Political Economy*, 92(5):852–874.

Westoff, Charles and Norman Ryder (1977) *The contraceptive revolution*. Princeton: Princeton University Press.

Zaba, Basia (1979) "The four-parameter logit life table system", *Population Studies*, 33(1):79–100.

Chapter 4

HOME PRODUCTION – A SURVEY

REUBEN GRONAU*

The Hebrew University, Jerusalem, National Opinion Research Center

1. Introduction

Neoclassical theory tends to draw a clear distinction between the theory of production and the theory of consumption. According to the traditional approach, production is undertaken by profit-seeking firms in the market, while consumption is in the domain of utility-maximizing households. The firms sell final output (goods and services) to households in exchange for inputs (labor and capital services).

This distinction became somewhat blurred in the mid-1960s. More and more economists now question the assumptions that the sole objective of firms is to maximize profits and, more important, that production decisions are confined to the market sector. The lines distinguishing the market from the home sector have always been vague in less developed countries. The "new" theory of consumption argues that even in developed countries, production at home is no less important than market production. This approach regards goods and services merely as inputs in the production process that generate utility-bearing outputs (e.g. commodities, activities, characteristics). To understand the exchange between households and firms one has to understand the factors affecting this production process.

2. Theory

Traditionally, consumers are regarded as welfare maximizers:

$$\max U = U(X_1, \dots, X_n; L) \tag{1}$$

*Support for this chapter was provided in part by the National Institute of Child Health and Human Development.

Handbook of Labor Economics, Volume I, Edited by O. Ashenfelter and R. Layard

subject to the budget constraint

$$\sum_{i=1}^{n} P_i X_i = w(T-L)+V, \tag{2}$$

where U denotes utility, X_i the ith good, P_i its price, L is "leisure" time, T the total time available (i.e. $T-L$ is work time), w is the wage rate, and V is other non-labor sources of income.[1] The necessary conditions for an optimum are well known:

$$\begin{aligned} u_i &= \partial U/\partial X_i = \lambda P_i, \\ u_L &= \partial U/\partial L = \lambda w, \end{aligned} \qquad i=1,\dots,n, \tag{3}$$

where u_i denotes the marginal utility of good i, and λ is the marginal utility of income. The marginal rate of substitution in consumption between goods i and j equals their price ratio ($u_i/u_j = P_i/P_j$), and the marginal rate of substitution between leisure and goods equals the real wage rate ($u_L/u_i = w/P_i$).

The new approach extends the traditional approach on two fronts: (a) it re-examines the assumption that market goods and services are the direct source of utility, and (b) it expands the set of constraints confronting the household. Several economists have questioned the assumption that market goods generate utilities. Lancaster (1966) argued that the source of welfare is not the goods as such, but rather their properties (or characteristics); furthermore, there does not exist a one-to-one relationship between goods and characteristics. The same characteristic (e.g. beauty) is common to many goods, and each good generates more than one characteristic. According to Lancaster, the household chooses that bundle of goods that maximizes its welfare from the desired characteristics. The demand for goods is a derived demand, and depends on the process that transforms goods into characteristics.

Becker (1965) views as the source of utility not the goods but the activities in which they service as inputs. Each activity ("commodity" in Becker's notation, e.g. a meal or a trip) is produced by combining different market goods (e.g. a meal is produced by combining foodstuffs with the capital services of kitchen appliances). The optimality of a set of goods depends both on the utility the household derives from the various commodities, and on the process whereby goods are transformed into commodities.

[1]The standard presentation usually separates consumption and labor decisions. The standard model, assuming implicitly separability of goods and leisure, consists of two parts: (a) the consumption decision $\max U = U(X_1,\dots,X_n)$ subject to a budget constraint $\sum P_i X_i = Y$, where Y denotes income $[Y = w(T-L)+V)$, and (b) the labor supply decision $\max U = U(X, L)$ subject to $X = w(T-L)+V$, where X is the composite good (for simplicity, $P_X = 1$).

On the face of it, the difference between Becker and Lancaster (ignoring the one between the nature of inputs) may seem merely semantic. But as pointed out by Pollak and Wachter (1975) and Atkinson and Stern (1979), the differences go much further; they relate to the nature of the production process converting market inputs into characteristics or commodities. The focus is on the degree of "jointness" in production: whereas Lancaster assumes perfect "jointness," Becker rules out "jointness" in production. While the characteristics approach regards goods as "public inputs," whose marginal productivity in the production of any given characteristic is not affected by its serving as inputs in the production of another characteristic, Becker's approach derives much of its analytical power from the assumption that goods serving as inputs in the production of one commodity cannot be utilized in the production of another.[2] These two extreme assumptions on "jointness" in production lead to two completely different sets of conclusions. This survey will follow (mostly) Becker's approach.[3]

Becker's second breach with traditional theory is in his definition of the relevant inputs. Following Mincer (1963), he argues that inputs serving in the production of commodities are not confined to market goods and services – no less important are the time inputs which go into this process, inputs provided by the consumer himself. The expansion of the inputs set also expands the set of constraints confronting the household. The household maximizes its welfare subject to two sets of constraints: the budget constraint and the time constraint. In effect, when the supply of labor is subject to the household decision, income and the budget constraint become endogenous variables and the household faces one ultimate constraint – the time constraint.

Formally, let us assume a one-period, one-person household. Let Z_i denote the ith commodity, where each commodity (activity) is a combination of time (T_i) and goods (X_i):[4]

$$Z_i = f_i(X_i, T_i), \quad i = 1, \ldots, m. \tag{4}$$

[2] Becker assumes that "if a good was used in producing several commodities these 'joint goods' could be fully and uniquely allocated among the commodities" (p. 495). Grossman (1971) analyzed the method of allocating these joint costs, when feasible. The Lancaster model assumes that these costs cannot be allocated uniquely.

[3] Lancaster's approach has been widely used in the analysis of hedonic prices, the differentiation of products, and the demand for modes of transport [e.g. Quandt and Baumol's (1966) "demand for abstract modes"]. It has, however, left little impact on the field of labor economics.

Muth's (1966) approach is very similar to that of Becker. However, Muth, though he recognized the importance of labor inputs at home, did not incorporate them formally in his analysis.

[4] Both X and T are vectors. X is a vector of market goods and T is a vector of time units, where it is assumed that different time units (e.g. daytime and nighttime) differ in their productivity in the production of Z_i.

The household maximizes its welfare

$$U = U(Z_1, \ldots, Z_m) \tag{5}$$

subject to two constraints: (a) the budget constraint,

$$\sum P_i X_i = Y, \tag{6}$$

and (b) the time constraint,

$$\sum T_i = T. \tag{7}$$

When the household's supply of labor is exogenously given T stands for total non-labor time and there are two separate sets of constraints (i.e. there is no way of converting time into income). The maximization of welfare (5) subject to these constraints, given the production technology (4), yields the necessary conditions for an optimum in consumption:

$$u_i = \partial U / \partial Z_i = \lambda \hat{\pi}_i, \tag{8}$$

where $\hat{\pi}_i = P_i x_i + \hat{w} t_i$ is the shadow price of commodity i, $x_i = \partial X_i / \partial Z_i$ and $t_i = \partial T_i / \partial Z_i$ are the marginal inputs of goods and time in the production of Z_i. $\hat{w}$ is the shadow price of time ($\hat{w} = \mu / \lambda$, where μ is the marginal utility of time and λ is the marginal utility of income).[5]

The optimum combination of inputs in the production of Z_i is determined by the familiar condition that the marginal rate of substitution in production equals the input price ratio:

$$\frac{\partial Z_i / \partial T_i}{\partial Z_i / \partial X_i} = \frac{x_i}{t_i} = \frac{\hat{w}}{P_i}. \tag{9}$$

The demand for goods is a derived demand. It depends on the demand for the commodity, on the share of the market input costs in total costs of producing this commodity, and on the elasticity of substitution between goods and time. The demand for commodity Z_i depends on its price, i.e. on its marginal cost of production. A crucial element in the determination of cost is the value of time for the household, i.e. the scarcity of time.

[5]The optimum condition (8) is obtained by maximizing the Lagrangian

$$L = U(Z_1, \ldots, Z_m) + \lambda\left(Y - \sum P_i X_i\right) + \mu\left(T - \sum T_i\right)$$

with respect to Z_i given the production technology (4).

Given the labor supply, time scarcity depends on the household's (or individual's) income and his non-labor time. The higher his income and the smaller his non-labor time (i.e. the greater his supply of labor), the greater the time scarcity and the shadow price of time. An increase in the shadow price of time should raise the relative price of time-intensive commodities (i.e. commodities where t_i/x_i is high) and result in a substitution of goods for time. An increase in income is therefore associated not only with an income effect but also with a price effect favoring goods-intensive commodities and increasing the demand for goods at the expense of time.[6]

When the supply of labor is part of the household decision set, income is no longer exogenous. Income can be increased by giving up consumption time. Thus, instead of the two separate constraints, (6) and (7), the household faces one constraint – the time constraint (7) – where the income–expenditures equality states

$$\sum P_i X_i = W(Z_n) + V, \tag{6'}$$

where Z_n is the activity "work in the market", and $W(Z_n)$ denotes earnings. The optimum condition for Z_n has to be modified:

$$u_n = \partial U/\partial Z_n = \lambda\left[P_n x_n + \hat{w} t_n) - W'\right], \tag{8'}$$

where $W' = \partial W(Z_n)/\partial Z_n$ is the marginal wage rate, and $\hat{w} = \mu/\lambda$ is (as before) the shadow price of time. Following convention, and measuring work in time units ($t_n = 1$), the shadow price of time equals

$$\hat{w} = W' - P_n x_n - (u_n/\lambda). \tag{10}$$

It differs from the average wage rate (w) when the average wage differs from the marginal wage, there are market inputs (e.g. transportation, child-care service) associated with a person's work, and work generates direct utility. Still, one expects the shadow price of time to increase with the average wage rate. In the case of a person working in the market one must therefore distinguish between changes in income due to a change in the wage rate, and changes originating in non-labor sources. A wage change may involve a price effect that may be as important as the income effect.[7]

[6]Strictly speaking, an increase in income and the shadow price of time will increase the demand for the goods-intensive commodity unambiguously only in a two-commodities world. When there exist more than two commodities, the outcome is ambiguous and depends on the cross elasticities of substitution between the various commodities [Atkinson and Stern (1979)].

[7]Strictly speaking, changes in non-labor income may also affect the shadow price of time if they affect the market inputs in market work (X_n) or the element of "psychic income" (u_n/λ).

Of special interest is the case where the wage does not change with the hours of work ($W' = w$), where the marginal market inputs associated with labor are negligible, and where work in the market does not involve any marginal utility or disutility.[8] In this case the value the household places on its time equals the wage rate. If, in addition, one rules out jointness in production (and, specifically, joint usage of time) and assumes that the production functions (4) are linear homogeneous (i.e. x_i and t_i depend solely on w), the price of each activity (commodity) is independent of the level of the activity and the results of the standard theory of demand apply also to the expanded model [Pollak and Wachter (1975), Atkinson and Stern (1979)]. In this case the problem can be restated as one of maximizing welfare (5) subject to the full income constraint

$$\sum \pi_i Z_i = S, \tag{11}$$

where $S = wT + V$ is full income (the income the household can generate if it spends all its time working in the market) and $\pi_i = P_i x_i + wt_i$ is exogenously given. It should, however, be emphasized that Becker's qualitative results do not depend on whether the assumptions specified above (i.e. $w = \hat{w}$ and constancy of x_i and t_i) are satisfied.

In evaluating the "new" consumption theory, and specifically, the theory of home production, one has to distinguish between its two main features: the incorporation of home time as a major determinant of household choices, and the separation of the consumption aspects from the production aspects of household behavior. Time has long been recognized as an important element in certain consumption activities (e.g. transportation). The new approach expands its role, making time a vital part of all consumption activities.

The importance of the distinction between consumption and production in household decisions is more controversial. Since "commodities" are not a measurable concept it seems only natural to combine equations (4) and (5) to express utility as a direct function of market an time inputs (X_i and T_i, respectively, where $i = 1, \ldots, n$). Given the appropriate assumptions about separability and functional form, the maximization of this expanded utility function, subject to the resources constraints, should yield results which are equivalent to those generated by the two-stage home production approach.

Becker defends his seemingly more complicated two-stage formulation, arguing that it "effectively separates objects of choice from the means used to produce them" [Michael and Becker (1973, p. 393)]. It seems, however, that this is only a partial explanation to the popularity of the new approach. The "new" consumption theory did not provide the economists with a new set of tools to analyze

[8]Note that throughout the analysis it is assumed that the utility derived from activity Z_i is independent of how it was produced. Specifically, it is independent of the time inputs involved.

economic problems.[9] Rather, it adapted a familiar language to discuss some old and many new problems in a novel fashion.[10] It re-emphasized that the household's economic decisions in the home sector extend well beyond the consumption decision, and that these decisions have important ramifications for the market sector.

The terminology of the theory of home production has been used to extend economic analysis to such diverse fields as family formation (marriage and divorce), fertility decisions, and involvement in illegal activities. It has been adapted to re-examine the demand for health, the demand for travel and transport choice, and more. Many of these applications have expanded to become research fields in their own right (e.g. the economics of the family, the economics of fertility, and the economics of crime). This survey will not cover all these spinoffs; it will focus on home production in its narrower definition, discussing inputs, shadow prices, production technology, and other aspects of the home production process.

3. The allocation of time

The theory of home production cannot escape the limitations of traditional consumption theory as the outputs (i.e. the commodities) are unobserved. Any empirical investigation based on this theory is therefore confined to the study of inputs, i.e. changes in their level and mix as a result of changes in output, prices, and productivity. Moreover, the study of inputs is hampered by the fact that data on inputs are not readily available, the output (as mentioned) cannot be measured directly, and prices (specifically the price of time) are unknown.

Consumption expenditure surveys constitute a rich source of disaggregate data on market inputs in the home production process, while the national accounting system provides the data on an aggregate level. For most countries, however, there are no official data on the allocation of time at home (the only data reported is the time spent in the market). Time budget data are, therefore, scarce, and the experience in collecting such data is limited.

There are essentially two methods of collecting time budget data: the time-diary method and the recall method; they do not necessarily yield the same results [Robinson (1983)]. The discrepancies between them increase the longer is the recall period, and depend on the object of enquiry (activities or time use).[11] Time-diary data seem to be more accurate, but collecting them is much more

[9]As did, for example, the theory of growth when it introduced the optimum control technique into the economist's arsenal.

[10]This issue will be readdressed in the summarizing section.

[11]When the interviewee is asked how much time he spent on certain activities, rather than what activities he engaged in during a certain time, the results are bound to be less accurate because there is no time constraint (e.g. daily activities usually do not add up to 24 hours).

expensive, and the researcher often has to make do with data that suffer from a large measurement error component.[12] Moreover, both kinds of data usually relate only to one person per household, and are very rarely accompanied by data on consumption.

In the absence of data on outputs one has to control for variables that affect the demand for such outputs (i.e. the household's income and demographic characteristics). Finally, only under very special circumstances is the price of time observable. In general the price of time differs from the wage rate, and one of the questions researchers have tried to answer is what is the value people place on their time, and what are the factors that affect this value.

Given the paucity of information on time use it is worth presenting some of the major patterns of the allocation of time within the household. In a recent study, Hill (1983) presents data for the United States in the mid-1970s. Comparing the time budgets of men and women by marital and employment status (Table 4.1) she found that unmarried men and women devote about the same amount of time to work (about 45 hours per week). Men spend, on average, 1.5 as many hours as women working in the market (33 vs. 22 hours), but this difference is offset by the difference in working hours at home (men spend only half the time that women do in house and yard work, child-care, shopping, and other services). Married men spend slightly more hours at work than married women (54 vs. 52 hours), but here, too, there is a significant difference in the way this time is split between work in the market and work at home. Married men spend, on average, almost 2.5 as much time at work in the market as married women (40 vs. 17 hours). Married women, on the other hand, devote about 2.5 as many hours to work at home (35 vs. 14 hours).

The total amount of work of married men and women depends largely on their market employment status. Women who are not employed work at home about 40 hours a week, about the same number of hours that full-time employed women spend in the market. However, the total number of working hours of full-time working women is almost 50 percent higher than that of their non-employed counterparts (64 vs. 44 hours). The difference between full-time working men and the non-employed is even larger. Holding the employment status constant, married women tend to work more hours than working men, the difference growing as the person's market commitments decline. These differences are, however, offset by the difference in labor force participation (and the prevalence of part-time jobs) between men and women.

[12] The most extensive time study in the United States was conducted by the Institute for Social Research at the University of Michigan in 1975/76. The results of this survey are summarized in Juster and Stafford (1983). This volume contains a series of papers discussing the methodology of the collection of time budget data. Other studies have been conducted by Walker. Time-use data are more prevalent in Europe and particularly Eastern Europe. An international comparisons of time use is contained in Szalai (1972). Time-use data have also been collected for some less developed countries (e.g. Malaysia and the Philippines).

Table 4.1
The allocation of time by sex, marital status, and employed status.

Activity	Males					Females				
		Married					Married			
	Unmarried	Work FT	Work PT	Not working	All	Unmarried	Work FT	Work PT	Not working	All
	Mean									
Work										
Labor market-related work	(32.85)	(48.62)	(28.52)	(6.60)	(40.18)	(22.17)	(39.08)	(20.94)	(3.22)	(16.73)
Market work	28.90	47.84	25.09	5.09	39.13	20.13	38.55	20.87	2.75	16.31
Education	3.95	0.78	3.43	1.51	1.05	2.04	0.53	0.07	0.47	0.42
Home-oriented work	(11.99)	(12.70)	(17.60)	(20.01)	(14.25)	(23.49)	(24.58)	(33.43)	(40.90)	(34.85)
House/yard work	8.07	7.22	13.08	14.61	8.83	16.02	16.12	22.67	26.79	22.96
Child care	0.33	1.69	1.19	0.69	1.49	2.23	2.83	3.21	6.51	4.88
Services/shopping	3.59	3.79	3.33	4.71	3.93	5.24	5.63	7.55	7.60	7.01
Total work time	(44.84)	(61.32)	(46.12)	(27.42)	(54.43)	(45.66)	(63.66)	(54.37)	(44.12)	(51.58)
Non-work										
Personal care	76.94	75.05	82.64	87.07	77.56	79.42	74.01	77.02	81.71	78.66
Organizations	2.07	2.46	5.21	3.15	2.72	3.13	2.46	2.90	3.97	3.35
Social entertainment	11.82	6.23	5.01	6.93	6.29	10.39	7.00	8.27	8.12	7.81
Active leisure	8.21	4.28	4.86	6.70	4.73	5.67	3.36	3.90	5.66	4.69
Passive leisure	24.20	18.72	24.36	37.61	22.35	23.81	17.59	21.62	24.49	21.98
Total time	168.07	168.07	168.20	168.00	168.08	168.08	168.09	168.09	168.08	168.09

Source: Hill (1983).

The scarcity of time budget data and the non-uniform definitions and methods of data collection prevent a systematic analysis of the changes in the allocation of home time over longer periods. The sketchy information available for the United States indicates that total hours of work hardly changed over the past two decades (they may have declined in the late 1960s and stabilized in the 1970s). There occurred, however, a marked change in the composition of work hours: whereas, in the case of women, work at home declined sharply, the decline being offset by an increase in work for pay, the reverse trend has taken place in the case of men. These shifts are more pronounced for the younger age-groups (25–44) than for the older ones [Juster (1983)].

It is hard to tell whether these patterns are universal. Israeli data, however, reveal similar patterns [Gronau (1976, 1977)]. Schooling has been shown to be the major determinant of labor force participation. Given the strong association between time-use patterns and employment status, Gronau (1976) investigated the effect of schooling on the allocation of time. The Israeli data indicate that in the case of married women, although work in the market increases sharply with schooling, total work time declines as schooling increases. Leisure increases with schooling, at the expense of both work and time spent on physiological needs.

Becker's theory of the allocation of time does not distinguish between activities such as cleaning, shopping, and other household chores and leisure activities. Though the line distinguishing work at home from leisure is sometimes vague, Gronau (1977) regards work at home as intermediate activity. Distinguishing home production time (work at home) from home consumption time, he defines work at home as an activity one could hire someone else to do (while it would be almost impossible to enjoy leisure vicariously). Put differently, work at home is a close substitute to work in the market in terms of the direct utility these activities generate, while there are few close market substitutes for leisure activities.

In an extreme case, work at home and work in the market are perfect substitutes – a person is indifferent to the composition of the goods and services he consumes, whether they are produced at home or purchased in the market. Formally, assuming a one-period, one-person household, the household maximizes the commodity, Z, which is a combination of goods X and consumption time L:

$$Z = Z(X, L). \tag{12}$$

The goods can either be produced at home (X_H) or purchased in the market (X_M). The two kinds of goods are perfect substitutes:

$$X = X_H + X_M. \tag{13}$$

The person can secure the goods either by selling time in the market at a fixed real wage, w:

$$X_M = wN + V, \tag{14}$$

where N denotes market work, or by producing them at home subject to diminishing marginal productivity:

$$X_H = f(H), \tag{15}$$

where H denotes work at home, and $f' > 0$, $f'' < 0$. The ultimate constraint is the time constraint:

$$L + H + N = T. \tag{16}$$

The necessary conditions for an interior optimum call for the marginal product of work at home to equal the value the person places on his time $\hat{w}$, i.e. the marginal rate of substitution between goods and consumption time. The value of time equals the wage rate ($f' = \hat{w} = w$) when the person works in the market ($N > 0$), and exceeds the wage ($f' = \hat{w} > w$) if he does not.

The two kinds of equilibrium are depicted in Figure 4.1. The concave curve $TB_0'A_0C_0$ describes the home production function (15). In the absence of market opportunities this curve describes the opportunity set facing the household. Work in the market at a constant real wage, w (described by the slope of the line

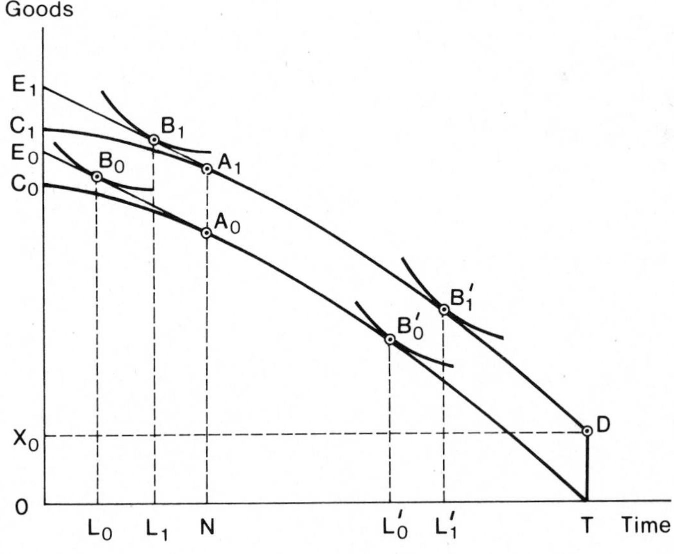

Figure 4.1

A_0E_0), allows the household to expand this set to $TB_0'A_0E_0$. Given a goods-intensive consumption technology (presented by the Z-isoquant passing through B_0), the person allocates OL_0 units of time to leisure, L_0N to work in the market, and NT to work at home. Alternatively, the consumption technology may dictate a more time-intensive combination, B_0'. In this case, the person allocates OL_0' units of time to leisure, $L_0'T$ to work at home, and does not work in the market at all. An increase in non-labor income shifts the opportunity set vertically upward (to $TDB_1'A_1E_1$). If the person works in the market, this change does not affect the equilibrium condition $f' = w$ and, hence, should not affect work at home NT. On the other hand, the increase in income is expected to increase leisure ($OL_1 > OL_0$) at the expense of market work ($L_1T < L_0T$). When the person does not work in the market, the increase in consumption time ($OL_1' > OL_0'$) has to come at the expense of work at home ($L_1'T < L_0'T$). The increase in income is associated with an increase in the shadow price of time, $\hat{w} = f'$.

An increase in the real wage, w (Figure 4.2), reduces the profitability of work at home ($N_1T < N_0T$). Its effect on consumption time and work in the market is indeterminate. The income effect tends to increase leisure, while the substitution effect favors market work.

Interpersonal differences in education may be associated not only with differences in the wage rate but also with differences in home productivity. The

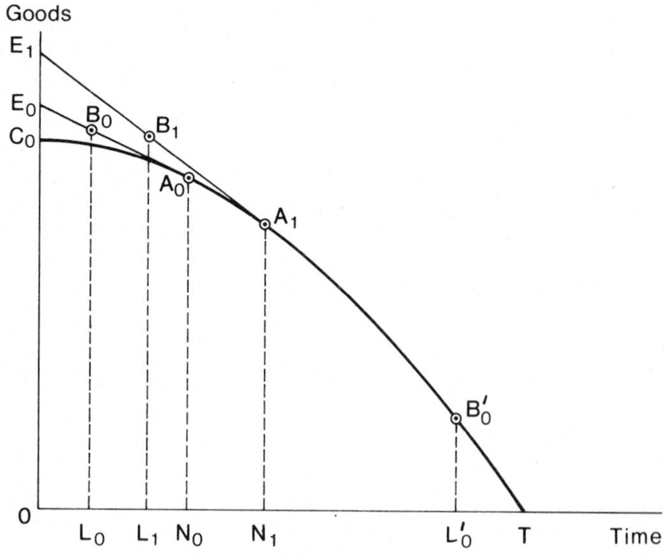

Figure 4.2

implications of such differences are, however, difficult to predict without specifying the exact nature of the change in the production or consumption technology. For example, an increase in the productivity of work at home increases real income and hence the leisure of employed persons, but its effect on work at home and in the market is indeterminate.[13]

Using data from the 1972 panel of the Michigan Study of Income Dynamics, Gronau tested his theory analyzing the allocation of time of employed and non-employed white married women. His findings are consistent with the theory: an increase in the husband's earnings reduces the work at home of the wives who are not employed but does not affect that of wives who are employed (in both cases it increases the wife's leisure). An increase in wives' wages increases their supply of labor at the expense of both work at home and leisure. (The potential wage rate does not affect work at home of the non-employed.) Education is negatively correlated with work at home of the non-employed, but does not seem to affect that of the employed.[14]

Gronau follows Becker in assuming that time inputs do not affect utility directly. Specifically, it is assumed that work at home and in the market generate the same marginal utility. Furthermore, it is assumed that intermediate commodities do not involve any direct utility and, thus, home goods and market goods can be regarded as perfect substitutes. Both assumptions prove crucial to the analysis and, subsequently, to the evaluation of the output of the home sector.

Allowing work in the market and at home to generate direct utility (i.e. psychic income) the welfare function can be rewritten [incorporating (12) and (13)]:

$$U = U(X_{\mathrm{M}} + X_{\mathrm{H}}, L, H, N). \tag{17}$$

Maximizing welfare subject to constraints (14), (15), and (16) yields the following equilibrium conditions:

$$\begin{aligned} \frac{u_L - u_N}{u_X} &= f' + \frac{u_H - u_N}{u_X} = w, && \text{when the person is employed,} \\ \frac{u_L}{u_X} &= f' + \frac{u_H}{u_X} = \hat{w}, && \text{when the person is not employed,} \end{aligned} \tag{18}$$

[13] It is often argued that an increase in home productivity always increases work at home [Chiswick (1982)]. This is true if the productivity coefficient k is multiplicative [i.e. if eq. (1) can be written $X_{\mathrm{H}} = kf(H)$]. It need not necessarily be true if the productivity change is resource saving [i.e. $X_{\mathrm{H}} = f(kH)$].

[14] Graham and Green (1984) used the 1976 wave of the Panel Study of Income Dynamics to derive the work at home function of employed white married women. Estimating a double-lag regression they find that the wife's work at home is not significantly affected by her husband's wage and schooling, but is negatively correlated with her own wage. Unfortunately, the rest of their conclusions are best treated with caution because of their extreme sensitivity to functional form. Hill (1983) employed a similar model to analyze do-it-yourself repairs and improvements in housing structures using data from the 1975/76 Time Use Study.

where u denotes marginal utility. The value placed by employed persons on their time equals $\hat{w} = w + (U_N/\lambda)$. In this case, an employed person does not equate his value of marginal productivity at home with his wage rate. The value of the marginal productivity is adjusted for the differential in the marginal utilities between work in the market and work at home.[15] An increase in non-labor income, in this case, may affect the work at home of the employed if it differentially affects the direct utilities associated with work at home and in the market.

Similarly, when maintaining the assumption that work does not involve any direct utility or disutility while relaxing the assumption that home-produced goods and market-produced goods are perfect substitutes, the conclusion that the home production of the employed is not affected by non-labor income no longer holds. In this case

$$U = U(X_{\mathrm{M}}, X_{\mathrm{H}}, L), \tag{19}$$

and at the optimum

$$\begin{aligned} (u_L/u_{X_{\mathrm{M}}}) &= (u_{X_{\mathrm{H}}}/u_{X_{\mathrm{M}}})f' = w, && \text{when the person is employed,} \\ (u_L/u_{X_{\mathrm{M}}}) &= (u_{X_{\mathrm{H}}}/u_{X_{\mathrm{M}}})f' = \hat{w} > w, && \text{when the person is not employed.} \end{aligned} \tag{20}$$

In contrast to the previous case, the value of the marginal productivity at home of the employed equals their wage rate, where this value is evaluated at the shadow price the person places on the home-produced goods. The distinction between a person who enjoys work at home per se and one who regards home-produced goods as being of higher quality, is important, as will be shown later, for the evaluation of the home sector output. There is, however, no way in which the two models can be distinguished empirically.[16]

Leisure is usually associated with the home sector (though leisure activities need not necessarily take place at home). A recent study [Stafford and Duncan (1983)] has pointed out that a considerable amount of leisure is spent on the job. According to this study, almost 10 percent of time at work is spent in formal or

[15] When $u_{\mathrm{H}} = u_N$ one obtain's Gronau's result, $f' = w$.

[16] Chiswick (1982) extends Gronau's model to analyze the case where work at home yields utility and where home goods and market goods are imperfect substitutes. Note, however, that in this case one cannot use Figure 4.1 or 4.2 unless it is assumed that the utility function is separable (i.e. that the marginal rate of substitution between goods and leisure is unaffected by the output of home goods or by the time spent working at home). Furthermore, it is incorrect to assume that home production of the non-employed will be unaffected by the changes in the real wage (i.e. by changes in the price of market goods). Graham and Green (1984) tried to estimate such a model empirically, with little success.

informal work breaks. Leisure-on-the-job thus accounts for about 10 percent of all leisure (where leisure excludes time spent on physiological needs).[17]

One aspect of time allocation that has drawn the attention of psychologists, sociologists, and economists alike is the effect children have on their parents' time use.[18] Casual observations indicate that children, and particularly young children, are associated with an increase in their mother's work at home (child care and other housework). Researchers unanimously agree that the increased time inputs in home production come at least partly at the expense of work in the market. Less well documented is the reallocation of time within the home that takes place as a result of having children. Bloch (1973) and Hill and Stafford (1980), in their study of U.S. time-use patterns, and Gronau (1976) in his study of Israeli women, agree that the time withdrawn from the market is not sufficient to compensate women for the increase in home tasks, and hence, children (and in particular preschool children) are associated with a decline in leisure. Gronau observes that Israeli married women reduce their leisure time more than they cut their work in the market, while for American women it seems [Hill and Stafford (1980)] that at least half of the increase in work at home is "financed" through a reduction in market work.

There are indications that parental and, specifically, the mother's investments in children are a key factor in the children's future careers [Leibowitz (1974)]. Does the strong positive correlation between women's education and their market commitment imply a reduced commitment to child care? Though they may differ on some of the details, all the economists who have studied this question are united in their negative answer. Hill and Stafford (1974, 1977) and Leibowitz (1974) found that the time inputs in child care and housework per child increase with education, and consequently, the higher her education the more sensitive a woman's labor supply will be to the existence of children. Lindert (1977), who found no evidence that time spent on child care increases with the wife's education, did not find any evidence of a negative relationship either. Gronau, in his study of Israeli women, found that whereas housework (controlling for children) declines with education, child care does not (education has a positive, though statistically insignificant effect).[19] In their most recent study, Hill and

[17]Stafford and Duncan (1983) claim that time diaries indicate that most data on hours of work (e.g. the CPS data) are overstated due to an inherent positive error of response, and that a substantial amount of time on the job is spent on training and leisure. They find that close to one-quarter of the time spent on the job by young workers (under 25) is spent on break-time and training, while the percentage for older workers (55–64) is less than 10 percent.

[18]In a recent paper Timmer, Eccles and O'Brien (1983) discuss the effect of parents' time use on that of their children. At this stage, however, the study of the allocation of children's time is in its initial stages.

[19]Hill and Stafford (1980) comment that the difference between their findings and those of Lindert and Gronau may be due to the fact that the latter do not allow for interactions between the number of children and education. On the other hand, Hill and Stafford, who estimate the child-care functions separately for each schooling group, base their conclusions entirely on the marginal effect of an additional child – ignoring the differences between schooling groups in the average effect (i.e. the differences in the regressions' constant terms).

Stafford (1980) reiterate their earlier conclusion that time inputs in child care increase with schooling, that these inputs decline as the child grows older, and that this decline is more pronounced in the case of the less educated.[20] In contrast with their earlier findings, Hill and Stafford detect a change in the way these increased inputs are "financed". Whereas in the 1960s the tendency of college graduates with young children was to drop out of the labor force, the 1970s witnessed an increased reluctance on the part of college-educated women to curtail their labor supply and, for these women, a larger fraction of the increase in housework and child care comes at the expense of leisure and physiological needs.

Finally, although the major burden of child care and housework is still on the woman, both the United States and Israeli studies concur that husbands, though reluctant to increase their time inputs in housework as a result of an additional child, actively help in child care, their time inputs increasing with their (or their wives') schooling.

4. The allocation of goods

The theory of home production had a major impact on the analysis of the demand for home activities, ranging from children to health. The scarcity of data that restricted the study of the allocation of time also hampered the application of the theory to the analysis of the allocation of goods and consumption patterns.

There exists a wealth of data on consumption behavior. Disaggregate data on the allocation of *both* goods and time is, however, non-existent. In its absence, researchers have to resort to data describing the allocation of goods and total non-market time. The results of the analysis of the interaction between time and goods in consumption and home production depend, therefore, to a large extent on the underlying assumptions.

Abbot and Ashenfelter (1976) investigated the interaction between home-time and goods employing the traditional model [eqs. (1) and (2)]. Examining annual aggregate time series for the United States on personal consumption expenditures, hours of work, and money wage rates for the period 1929–67, they find weak evidence that housing, transportation, and "other services" tend to be complementary with non-market time, while durables tend to be substitutable. The evidence, however, is far from conclusive, the results depending uncomfortably on functional form.

Atkinson and Stern (1979) expanded the study, adopting a home production framework. In the absence of data, they resort to a stronger set of working

[20] Hill and Stafford (1980) examine the effect of children on child care and housework. Surprisingly, they find that the differences between schooling groups in housework exceed those of child care.

assumptions on the consumption and production technology. Specifically, they assume that the utility function is of the Stone–Geary variety, that labor conveys no direct utility, and that time and goods are employed in the production of each activity in fixed proportions. Using a subsample of the U.K. 1973 Family Expenditure Survey they estimate (among other parameters) the time intensity of the activities associated with major consumption groups. The results of this exploratory study prove, however, to be poor (some basic restrictions are violated). As the authors emphasize, the study should be regarded merely as a first step in an ongoing project.

Are there scale economies in home production? The literature does not treat this question explicitly, and given that home output cannot be directly measured and that information on time inputs is very sketchy, the question seems to be insoluble. Still, a surprising amount of effort has gone into answering the related question of scale economies in consumption. It is only rarely couched in terms of home production technology, but rather in terms of adult equivalence scales. The issue at heart seems, however, to be the same one.[21]

Equivalence scales are index numbers intended to allow comparisons of welfare or real income across households of different size and composition. They are used to correct for variation of "needs" with a person's age and sex, and for scale economies in home production and consumption: "Three people do not need proportionally more bathrooms or cars than two people; buying and cooking food in bulk is cheaper; clothes can be handed down from older to younger children" [Deaton and Muellbauer (1980, p. 192)]. The estimation of these equivalence scales on the basis of the observed households' expenditure patterns has generated an extensive literature, going back to Engel's pioneering study at the end of the last century (1895).[22] The studies are unanimous in concluding that there are substantial returns to scale in consumption, but there is disagreement on their exact magnitude.[23] Unfortunately, a more thorough examination indicates that there is only little in the discussion of equivalence scales to teach us about home production technology. This examination points out some of the major shortcomings of these scales.

To demonstrate some of these limitations let us follow one of the more popular schemes, one originally suggested by Barten (1964). By this scheme, welfare depends on the adjusted quantity of goods consumed, the deflators being the

[21] One of the few exceptions are Lazear and Michael (1980) who address the problem in terms of production technology.

[22] For a survey of this literature, see Deaton and Muellbauer (1980, ch. 8).

[23] The only study claiming that home production is subject to decreasing returns is Graham and Green (1984). Typically, the BLS uses a scale where the "needs" of a three-person household can be provided at a cost that is only one-third higher than those of a two-person household, and those, in turn, are only two-thirds higher than those of a one-person household. For an analysis of the sensitivity of these estimates to the underlying theoretical assumptions see Deaton and Muellbauer (1983).

goods-specific equivalence scales M_i:

$$U = U(X_1/M_1, X_2/M_2, \ldots, X_n/M_n), \tag{21}$$

where M_1 depends on the size and age composition of the household. Utility is maximized subject to a standard budget constraint $\sum P_i X_i = Y$. It is tempting to rephrase the problem in terms of "commodities":

$$\max U = U(Z_1, \ldots, Z_n) \tag{22}$$

subject to $\sum \pi_i Z_i = Y$, where $Z_i = X_i/M_i$ and $\pi_i = M_i P_i$.

This information raises the question: Whose welfare are we measuring? Children are not one of the elements of the welfare function (22), and hence the utility derived from children is not reflected in the measurement of adult equivalence scales.[24] More important to our discussion, this formulation does not account for the time inputs going into home production and consumption. Thus, traditional equivalence scales overstate the scale economies in home production if the household shifts to a more time-intensive activity mix as it increases (for example, if activities associated with children are more time intensive than other activities). Furthermore, the household activity mix depends on both production and distribution decisions (i.e. the allocation of goods within the household), and one cannot separate empirically the two.

Similar difficulties hamper other attempts at measuring productivity in the household. Schooling and other forms of investment in human capital (health, information, on-the-job training) are a major source of increases of productivity in the market. It is of interest, therefore, to examine how much they affect home productivity. Michael (1972, 1973) examines the effect of schooling on home productivity. The increase in productivity at home reduces the shadow prices of all activities and increases the household's real income. However, it need not affect all activities identically and, hence it may result in a change in the activities' relative prices. Furthermore, it may affect differently the productivity of goods and the time inputs. Focusing on the percentage change in expenditures on good i

$$\tilde{X}_i = \tilde{Z}_i^{\mathrm{d}} - \tilde{MP}_i + wT_i\sigma[\tilde{MP}(X_i) - \tilde{MP}(T_i)], \tag{23}$$

where $\tilde{Z}_i^{\mathrm{d}}$ is the (relative) change in the demand for activity i, $\tilde{MP}_i$ the change in

[24] This issue was raised by Pollak and Wales (1979, 1981), who object for this reason to the use of equivalence scales for welfare comparisons. This formulation gave rise to another controversy which is not relevant to our discussion. Given the analogy to price indices, a lengthy discussion turned around the question to what extent can one derive the estimates of M_i from information on prices and income elasticities.

the marginal productivity in this activity, σ the elasticity of substitution between time and goods, and $\tilde{MP}(X_i)$ and $\tilde{MP}(T_i)$ the change in factor productivity. The increase in demand for Z_i depends on the increase in real income ($\tilde{MP}$), on the (full) income elasticity for this activity (η_i). Hence

$$\tilde{X}_i = \tilde{MP}\cdot\eta_i - \tilde{MP}_i + \varepsilon_i(\tilde{MP}_i - \tilde{MP}) + wT_i\sigma[\tilde{MP}(X_i) - \tilde{MP}(T_i). \quad (24)$$

In the absence of direct observations on the change of productivity, the demand for activities and the allocation of time, Michael resorts to the simplifying assumption that schooling has a neutral effect on the activity mix (i.e. $\tilde{MP} = \tilde{MP}_i$), and on the input mix [$\tilde{MP}(X_i) = \tilde{MP}(T_i)$]. In this case

$$\tilde{X}_i = \tilde{MP}(\eta_i - 1), \quad (25)$$

or in elasticity terms,

$$\varepsilon_{iE} = (\eta_i - 1)\varepsilon_{YE}, \quad (26)$$

where ε_{iE} denotes the elasticity of X_i with respect to schooling and ε_{YE} is the elasticity of real (full) income with respect to schooling. Thus, if the neutrality assumptions are satisfied, an increase in schooling will be associated with an increase in expenditures on luxuries (for which $\eta_i > 1$) and a decline in expenditures on necessities.

Using data from the 1960–61 U.S. Consumer Expenditure Survey, Michael argues that his model can quite successfully predict the direction of education's effect on consumer expenditure patterns on non-durables. Given the estimates of the schooling elasticity ε_{iE} and the income elasticity η_i, Michael attempts to estimate the elasticity of real full income with respect to schooling (holding money income constant), and his estimates range between 0.1 and 0.75. These estimates are lower than the elasticity of money income with respect to schooling. Unfortunately, these estimates are flawed because Michael erroneously uses the money income elasticities, whereas his theory deals with full income elasticities. The direction of the bias introduced by this error cannot be ascertained a priori.[25]

A partial answer to the question of the effect of schooling on home productivity can be obtained by examining the effect schooling has on the price people assign their non-market time.

[25] The bias depends on the elasticity of money income with respect to full income. In a cross section, this will depend on the source of variation between households in money income (wages, hours of work, other sources of income). Another source of bias – the fact that the estimates do not control for changes in wages and hence for substitution between time and goods – is recognized by Michael.

5. The value of time and the value of home output

The value people place on their time affects the optimum combination of inputs in home production, the price they assign to the various "commodities", and the amount of the commodities produced. Its effect is, therefore, not confined merely to the time inputs going into home production and the allocation of time at home, but is reflected in the household's supply of labor and demand for goods. The importance of the price of time for the analysis of the allocation of time within the household and the demand for goods increases the greater is the elasticity of substitution between time and goods in the production of a certain activity, the more time-intensive that activity, and the more elastic its demand.

The price of time has therefore become an important component of the analysis of time-intensive activities (such as children), and time-saving market inputs (e.g. the demand for air transport). In the field of public policy it figures prominently in the evaluation of public projects involving time saving (mostly in the field of transportation). It is, naturally, an integral part of labor supply analysis. Finally, it is a crucial component of any analysis of the value of home production.

Whereas the collection of data on the inputs going into home production involve serious technical problems, the problem involved in estimating the price of time are conceptual. In the absence of formal transactions taking place within the home, data on prices are unavailable. Instead of direct evidence one has to rely on imputations.

A first approximation for the value people assign to their time is the price they can charge for it in the marketplace, i.e. the wage rate. However, as the analysis in the previous sections indicates, the accuracy of this estimate depends on the extent to which the average wage equals the marginal wage, there are no market inputs associated with the supply of labor (e.g. transportation costs, childcare services), and work does not involve any direct utility or disutility. Furthermore, this approximation is inapplicable when the person does not work in the market.

The shadow price of time, $\hat{w}$, affects customer's choice of the optimum combination of time and market inputs [eq. (9)] and the decision whether to participate in market work or not. The imputation of this shadow price is therefore based on the observation of choices where timed is traded for goods, and the choice concerning labor force participation. Unfortunately, most often in situations where goods are traded for time, the amount of time saved is unrecorded (e.g. eating out, fast food, and time-saving home utensils). One of the few exceptions is the field of transportation.

The demand for transportation is a derived demand. The trip is basically an "intermediate activity" serving as an input in the production of the final output – at the point of destination. To produce a trip the traveller combines his own time inputs with the transport services he purchases in the market. His modal choice depends on the utility derived from travelling by the various modes and the shadow price he assigns to the trip [Gronau (1970)]. Formally, let Z_V denote the activity "visit", Z_A and Z_B the activities "trip by mode A" and "trip by mode B," and $\bar{Z}$ all other activities. The "trip" is a necessary ingredient in the production of a "visit",

$$Z_V = f_V(Z_A, Z_B, X_V, T_V), \tag{27}$$

where the "trip" in turn is produced through a combination of goods and time;

$$Z_i = f_i(X_i, T_i), \quad i = \text{A,B}. \tag{28}$$

Maximizing utility

$$U = U(Z_V, Z_A, Z_B, \bar{Z}) \tag{29}$$

subject to the time and budget constraints, yields:

$$u_i - u_V\left(\frac{\partial Z_V}{\partial Z_i}\right) = \lambda\hat{\pi}_i, \quad i = \text{A,B}, \tag{30}$$

where $u_i = \partial U/\partial Z_i$ and $\hat{\pi}_i = P_i x_i + \hat{w}t_i$. Facing a choice whether to travel by mode A or mode B, and assuming the contribution of both modes to the production of the visit is the same (i.e. $\partial Z_V/\partial Z_A = \partial Z_V/\partial Z_B$), the decision depends on the cost of travel $\hat{\pi}_i$ and the direct utility derived from travelling by mode $i(u_i)$. Mode A is preferred if

$$\hat{\pi}_A - (u_A/\lambda) < \hat{\pi}_B - (u_B/\lambda), \tag{31}$$

where u_i/λ denotes the money equivalent of the direct utility. Put differently, mode A is preferred if

$$(P_B x_B - P_A x_A) + \hat{w}(t_B - t_A) + (u_A - u_B)/\lambda > 0. \tag{32}$$

Had all three components of this equation been known, and with the appropriate assumptions about the distribution of the unobservables, the shadow price of time, $\hat{w}$, could be derived by comparing the effect of the time differential, $t_B - t_A$, on the binary choice between A and B, with that of the money cost differential, $P_B x_B - P_A x_A$.

The most serious problem plaguing the estimates of the value of time based on modal choice data is that the time and cost differential data are measured inaccurately, and that utility differentials are unknown. The errors of measurement are due to differences between the perceived time and cost differentials and the measured differentials. The difference may be due to incomplete information (in particular, information concerning the rejected alternative), interpersonal heterogeneity of costs and travel time (the measurements being based on averages), consistent biases (the variable costs of private cars are consistently underestimated), and conceptual differences.[26] These "measurement errors" can be quite substantial.[27]

Even more serious is the misspecification of the estimating function due to difficulties in quantifying the variables affecting the direct utility generated by the trip. The omission of these variables becomes a crucial factor in the estimation of the price of time. To demonstrate, let us assume that the binary choice variable D (say, choice between modes) is regressed on the time and cost variables Δt and ΔP:[28]

$$D = b_1 \Delta t + b_2 \Delta P. \tag{33}$$

If travel did not involve any direct utility, or if this utility was not correlated with time and cost of travel, one could derive an unbiased estimate of the shadow price of time comparing the time and cost coefficients ($b_1/b_2 = \text{est}\,\hat{w}$). Unfortunately, the assumption that travel does not convey direct utility seems to be unjustified. Moreover, utility (or, more often, disutility) is correlated with time of travel (utility declines as length of travel increases), and, perhaps with the fare (an increase in convenience, safety, and frequency may be reflected in higher fares).

There is no a priori way to ascertain the direction and extent of the misspecification bias (as long as the effect of the omitted variable on b_2 is not specified), but it seems that the upward bias in b_1 is dominant.

Most studies of modal choice focus on the choice of commuters.[29] The decision studied is most often the choice of mode (private car vs. public transport), and sometimes the choice of route (tollroad vs. regular road, or the use of toll bridge vs. roundabout routes). Allowing for biases, the concensus of these studies is that the shadow price of time in commuting is significantly lower than the wage rate, most studies placing it in the range of one-fifth to one-half of the wage rate. The failure to control for differences in comfort, convenience, effort, etc. results in estimates of the value of walking and waiting time which are 2.5–3.0 times higher than the estimate of the value of in-vehicle time,[30] and estimates of the value of

[26] A business air traveler asked for the time saved by using air may respond "one day", since it saved him a workday, though the measured time differential maybe only a few hours.

[27] Quarmby (1967) reports that the perceived variable operating costs of the car are only about half the true costs; Reichman (1973) shows that there are significant differences in the case of time.

[28] Most studies of modal choice use the binary logit, a few use multi-logit, probit, or discriminant analysis.

[29] There are quite a few surveys of the literature on the estimations of the value of time. For an early survey, see Harrison and Quarmby (1969). Subsequent surveys are Hensher (1976), Heggie (1976), and Bruzelius (1979).

[30] Heggie (1976) reports that weather conditions affect the value of walking and waiting time and that it seems that the direction of the journey (to and from home) may have an effect.

travel time by bus that are higher than travel by car. For the same reason, the shadow price of time is sometimes shown to increase with the length of the trip.[31] Finally, differences between gross and net wages and constrained working hours are reflected in higher estimates for value of time on interurban business trips than on personal trips.

The errors of measurements and the omission of variables need not impair the predictive power of the modal choice equation [eq. (24)]. Furthermore, since many of the public projects involving time saving are also associated with greater convenience, comfort, or safety of travel, the use of a biased estimate of the shadow price of time need not jeopardize the cost–benefit analysis.[32] However, it seems that this bias is sufficiently serious to prevent comparisons of the estimates of the value of time in commuting with other estimates of the value of time.[33]

Allowing for all reservations, the low price commuters assign to their time and the large difference between the price travellers assign to their time on business and personal trips indicates that they are not free (at least in the short run) to exchange home time for market work.[34] The wage rate will therefore be a poor approximation for the value of time at home of the employed. This approximation is especially poor in the case of the non-employed.

Traditionally, the value assigned to the time of the non-employed is their "potential" wage, i.e. the average wage of an employed person with the same observed market characteristics. This procedure raises two problems: (a) the employed may be a self-selected group that differs in its unobserved characteristics (e.g. "taste" for work in the market or career commitment) from the non-employed, and (b) even if the wage offers were known, they could hardly be used as an estimate of home productivity since these offers were implicitly rejected by those who decided to stay out of the labor force. The first of these problems is the censoring problem discussed at length by Heckman (1974), Gronau (1974), and others.

The second involves estimating a person's reservation wage, i.e. his minimum acceptable wage. Barring additional constraints (e.g. that working hours have to exceed a certain minimum), a person is assumed to join the labor force only if the wage he is offered exceeds the value of his time at home (in the absence of market opportunities). The shadow price of time of the non-employed therefore equals their reservation wage.

[31]Small time savings may have no value at all. The relationship between $\hat{w}$ and t may be discontinuous.

[32]The value of time saving is often the major benefit in public projects [Tipping (1968)].

[33]Gronau (1970), in his study of inter-city air travelers, finds that their value of time equals their wage rate.

[34]Earp, Hall and McDonald (1976) report a value of time on business trips that is twice as high as that on personal trips.

The reservation wage can be derived either directly (in answer to a question on the minimum acceptable wage), or indirectly. The indirect method infers the reservation wage from labor force participation patterns. Given a person's expected wage offer, the lower his reservation wage the greater his tendency to participate in the labor force. Put differently, given the mean wage offer of a group, the higher the participation rate the lower the mean reservation wage of the group. The information on wage offers and participation rates becomes the key to the estimation of the shadow price of time.[35] Moreover, it allows a detailed analysis of the socio-economic variables affecting the shadow price of time at home.

Gronau (1973) used data from the 1960 U.S. census to investigate the factors affecting married women's reservation wage. He found that women's education is a major determinant of housewives' value of time, but its effect is felt mainly at higher levels of education. Whereas there is no significant difference between the value of time of persons who have completed elementary or high school, the value of time of college graduates exceeds that of high school graduates by over 20 percent (the differential in the average wage of the employed is 30–40 percent). The husband's income, education, and age have a relatively small effect, and the existence of children has, as expected, a major effect on their mother's value of time. A child less than 3 years old increases this value by over 25 percent, but its effect diminishes as the child grows older. This effect is especially pronounced in the case of college graduates, and the decline in value as the child grows older is much more gradual.

The exclusion of the output of the home sector has long been recognized as the major omission in the national accounting system [Kuznets (1944)]. Given the changes that have taken place in this sector over time, and the differences in share of this sector between different economies (specifically, economies in different stages of development), this omission may bias the traditional measures of growth and international comparisons of standards of living. Not surprisingly, several attempts have been made to correct this lapse.

The value of output in the home sector, as in other non-market sectors (e.g. government), is measured by the value of the inputs. A major obstacle to the evaluation of the output is the choice of the value of time. There are essentially two methods of evaluating the productive services rendered by family members at home:

(a) evaluating time inputs at their market opportunity costs, and
(b) evaluating time inputs at the market alternative.

According to the first approach, the value of a person's time inputs at home is the price this time would have commanded in the market. The second approach

[35] Throughout this discussion it is assumed that there exists no joint production and that time inputs in a certain activity per se do not yield any direct utility. If these assumptions are relaxed, there will be no unique value of time common to all non-market activities. The value of time in a certain activity depends in this case not merely on the time scarcity but also on the marginal utility of time in that activity and on the degree of "jointness" between the activities.

evaluates such time at the price it would have cost the household to purchase the same services in the market. Both methods abound with technical and conceptual difficulties.

The major objection raised in the literature to the value of opportunity-cost method originates in the following alleged paradox [Hawrylyshyn (1976)]: "consider two housewives with equivalent family size and homes, and suppose that they are both equally good at the work, doing the same amount in the same number of hours. This suggests the output value in both cases is the same. Yet if one of them has an M.A. in microbiology with a potential wage of \$10/hour and the other is a former stenographer potentially employable at \$4/hour this method tells us the value of one's housework is 2.5 times that of the other!" The major reservation to the evaluation of time inputs using the market price of home services is "that these market prices have been explicitly rejected by the household as a true measure of its productivity. The family could have bought the home services in the market but preferred not to do so, either because it found their prices too high, or because it found their quality wanting" [Gronau (1980, p. 414)]. A secondary question is what market values should be used: an overall measure (e.g. the wage of domestic servants) for all work hours, or should one distinguish between the different tasks the homemaker performs at home and assign a different market price to each task?

Had market services and home services been perfect substitutes, and provided work at home does not involve direct utility, the conceptual problem would never crop up. In this case, any discrepancy between the opportunity cost approach and the market alternative approach would be attributed to measurement errors or to disequilibrium in the labor market. The source of the conceptual controversy is the direct utility generated by work at home and the heterogeneity of home output. The issue is a complicated one because, as has been argued in Section 3, one cannot distinguish between the case where work at home generates direct utility and the case where market services and home services are not perfect substitutes.

In the first case, the explanation of the "homemaker's paradox" lies in the fact that the micro-biologist and the stenographer must be deriving different utilities from their home and market jobs. Traditional measures of market output do not incorporate a measure of workers' "job satisfaction" and, by the same token, should not include a measure of their enjoyment from work at home. A person's market wage differs [by eq. (18)] from the value of his marginal productivity at home and should not be used to measure home outputs.[36]

[36] Note that in the Hawrylyshyn example the value of marginal productivity f' may equal 10 where the stenographer enjoys her job in the market more than does the micro-biologist, or 4 if the micro-biologist enjoys work at home more than does the stenographer, or any other value (not necessarily confined to the range 4 to 10). Note, too, that empirical studies have shown that, on average, \$10/hour micro-biologists spend less time working at home than \$4/hour stenographers.

On the other hand, if work at home and in the market are not perfect substitutes, but it is still assumed that work (at home and in the market) does not generate any direct utility, the resolution of the paradox lies in the different values the micro-biologist and the stenographer assign to their home output. The micro-biologist regards her output superior to the market substitute. She is ready to forgo $10 per hour of output, whereas other women, who place a lower value on their output, are ready to forgo much less.[37] Once we remove the assumption that home services are a homogeneous output, the market alternative approach has to be discarded. By eq. (20) the value of the marginal productivity of an employed person equals his wage rate, and his time inputs in home production should be evaluated according to this wage.[38]

There is no empirical way of telling which is the correct underlying model (both assumptions are probably correct – work at home generating direct utility and home service being non-homogeneous). Thus, there is no way of rating the two methods of evaluation of home output and, preferably, both should be used.

Given the often heated debate concerning the advantages and the disadvantages of the different methods of imputation, and the imprecise nature of the data, there is surprising unanimity on the share of the household output constitutes in total economic activity. Hawrylyshyn (1976) examined 9 studies based on U.S., U.K., and Swedish data,[39] and shows that if one uses as the value of time the net wage (rather than the gross wage), the opportunity cost method and the market alternative method yield, on average, the same estimate of the share of the home sector output in GNP – 35 percent (the estimates ranging from 32 to 39 percent).[40]

A much more important bias in the estimation of the value of the home sector may arise from the fact that almost all studies focus on the value added of the labor inputs (sometimes only the wives' labor) in the home sector, ignoring other inputs in the process. Most notably, we ignore the rewards to entrepreneurship in this "industry". A person working at his home is, in essence, self-employed, and one should, therefore, incorporate in the estimate not merely the value of his labor inputs, but also the "producer surplus". Redrawing Figure 4.1, the opportunity cost method, ignoring the decline in marginal productivity in home

[37]Note that since home output is not measurable one can phrase the same argument in terms of efficiency [Chiswick (1982)] – the micro-biologist regards herself as more efficient in home production than the stenographer.

[38]The micro-biologist may be ready to pay her physician (or hairdresser) a fee that is 2.5 as high as that paid by the stenographer to her physician, though the services seems, by all accounts, the same. Still, nobody will argue that all medical services should be assigned the same price.

[39]In a more extensive study, Goldschmidt-Clermont (1982) reports the results of over 70 studies on the value of unpaid work in the household.

[40]Studies that adopted the market alternative method, where each household function is priced separately, yield, on average, a lower value than those using the market-opportunity costs method.

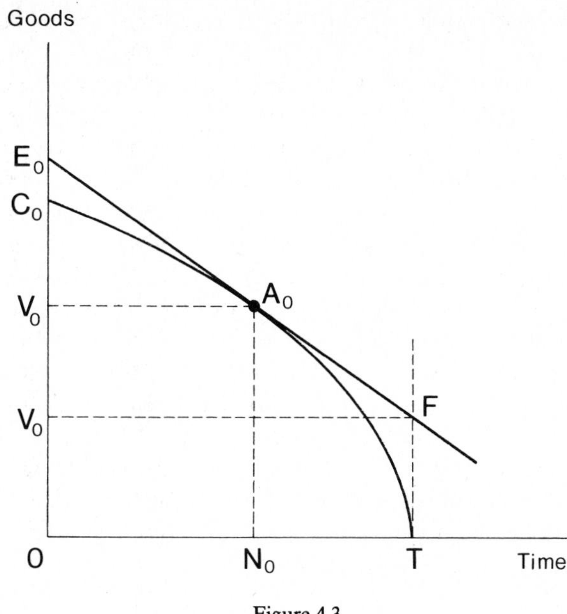

Figure 4.3

production, imputes a value of V_0V_1, whereas the value of home output is $0V_0$ (Figure 4.3).

To correct for this bias, Gronau (1980) examines the effect of the wage rate on hours of work at home of employed wives. Assuming the wage equals the value of marginal productivity at home, he generates the relationship between hours of work at home and the value of total output. By his estimates, the value of home production in 1973 equals, on average, two-thirds of the family's monthly income, and reached almost 90 percent for families with pre-school children.[41] This value by far exceeded the wife's monthly earnings. Schooling increases the wife's productivity at home; but to a smaller degree than her (or her husband's) productivity in the market. Hence, there exists a negative correlation between the husband's schooling and the share of home output in total money income. This share depends heavily on the wife's employment status. It is only one-half for families when the wife is employed and 80 percent when she is not employed. It increases with age, but peaks earlier than money earnings. Finally, these estimates are, on average, almost twice as high as those based on the opportunity cost method (the difference is even larger for families with young children).

[41] Gronau ignores the contribution of husband and children to home production.

6. Summary and evaluation

The theory of home production had a major impact on the development of the economics of human resources, generating a host of studies investigating its implications. At first glance this popularity seems to be misplaced: the theory's major elements were either quite familiar or were criticized as redundant. Thus, travel time was recognized long before Mincer's and Becker's studies as an important factor determining the demand for transport services. Admitting time into the utility function, it has been argued, one can derive all the theory's conclusions by making the appropriate separability assumptions, without recourse to the home production framework. Finally, it has been shown that the assumption of exogenous prices, a vital ingredient in traditional analysis, is very often violated in the new context of demand for "commodities".

The present survey goes only part of the way in explaining this paradox. Rather than discussing the full range of the theory's applications it focuses on home production in its narrow definition. Thus, the survey does not do justice to the theory's ramifications for the economics of fertility, health, crime, and other spinoffs. Nonetheless, the survey highlights the theory's points of strength as well as its weaknesses.

The theory played a leading role in the widening recognition of the importance of time, not only for the analysis of the demand for certain time-intensive activities, but also for analyzing the demand for all market goods and services. It shed light on a usually forgotten facet of consumption behavior, and forged a natural link between consumption and the supply of labor. But its contribution does not lie merely in pointing to the role of time in the demand for children, domestic servants, information, etc., but in reformulating this role. Even when time was recognized as affecting demand (e.g. the demand for transport services), it was implicitly treated as a variable affecting "taste". The new approach stresses the resource constraint facing the decision-maker, and its implications for the opportunity costs of time.

Without denying the effect of time on the utility of travel, the emphasis is shifted to the analysis of the price effect, where the price consists both of pecuniary costs and the cost of time. Whereas economists have little to contribute on the factors determining utility, they are comfortable with the analysis of prices. For example, whereas in the past the analysis of the effect of distance or the traveler's income on modal choice required specification of the effect of these variables on the utility of travel by the various modes, the new approach can circumvent this cardinal concept of utility by specifying the effect these variables have on the cost of time and the trip's price. There is nothing inherent in economic theory that explains why travel by bus is inferior (i.e. generates less utiles) than travel by air. However, the theory is very explicit in discussing the effect of distance on the cost of time, the effect of income on the price of time, and their implications for the relative prices of bus and air travel [Gronau (1970)]. The analysis of the cost of time gave the theory the predictive power that the earlier approach lacked.

The importance of the distinction between consumption and production is much more controversial. Pollak and Wachter (1975) show that "commodity" prices are endogenous to the system and depend on the optimum commodity mix (and hence on tastes) whenever the production function is not linear homogeneous, or when there is joint production (which is often the case when time is an input in the process). In the absence of information on "commodity" prices, one cannot estimate their demand. In this case one is better off, they suggest, to analyze the demand for inputs given input prices. Others have claimed that the distinction is barren, since all the theory's implications can be derived by incorporating time into the utility function. The criticism, though correct, seems to be misplaced.

The theory of home production has rarely been used as a guideline in an empirical study of the demand for commodities.[42] Most often, the quantity of "commodities" consumed defies measurement, and their price (even when they are exogenous) is unobserved. As the survey indicates, it was measurement problems, rather than conceptual problems, that led economists to focus on the demand for inputs.

Separability is a powerful tool in the analysis of the demand for input. But the rationale underlying the separability assumption and the distinction between different time uses is the belief that the relation between different units of time is determined by their usage. Thus, "cooking time" and "driving time" are substitutes to the extent that "eating at home" and "eating out" are substitutes, and "eating time" and "theatre time" are complements to the extent that "eating out" and "going to a play" are complements.[43] This belief is incorporated explicitly in the theory of home production.[44]

The theory of home production, rather than serving as a blueprint for empirical research, is an analytical tool. The distinction between consumption and production is essential to the analysis of work at home (as distinct from consumption time). It consequently proves important for the analysis of labor supply (in particular that of married women), and the measurement of home output.

The distinction is also important for the measurement of the returns to the investment in human capital. Market returns in the form of higher wages and

[42] Few of the exceptions can be found in the analysis of the demand for health [Grossman (1972), Rosenzweig and Schultz (1983)].

[43] Were it not for the different uses, the specification of the utility function should have been in terms of an "activity free" measure of time such as "summer time", "day time", etc.

[44] DeSerpa's paper on time allocation (1971) demonstrates the dangers of leaving these assumptions implicit.

market productivity have been shown by Leibowitz, Michael, and others to be only part (and in the case of women, perhaps even the less important part) of total returns. No less important is the effect of investment in human capital on home productivity. It affects the productivity of the investment itself [Ben-Porath (1967, 1970), Heckman (1976)], and of home production.

The theory is sometimes criticized for replacing the traditional terminology by a more complex one. But one should not scoff at the importance of language. For example, an economist may feel reluctant to assume that schooling affects the marginal utility of time and goods by the same rate, but may feel comfortable with the assumption that schooling has a neutral effect on the productivity of time and goods [Michael (1973)].

The theory of home production played a major role in the realization that economic considerations are as important in the home sector as in the market. The informal nature of the economic transactions taking place within the household hinders the detection of flows of goods and services within the home sector. In the absence of direct measurement, the distinction between consumption and production must necessarily remain conceptual. After twenty years, and in spite of the many studies it generated, the full potential of the theory has yet to be realized. With few exceptions, it has not yet served in the analysis of specific time uses. We do not know much more about the interaction between time and goods in specific activities than we did twenty years ago. For all its shortcomings, the new theory of home production has made an enormous contribution to our understanding of economic processes in the non-market sector. Its full potential has yet to be realized.

References

Abbot, M. and O. Ashenfelter, (1976) "Labor supply, commodity demand, and the allocation of time", *Review of Economic Studies*, 43:389–412.

Atkinson, A. B. and N. H. Stern, (1979) "On labor supply and commodity demands", SSRC Programme Taxation, Incentives and the Distribution of Income, No. 1.

Barten, A. P. (1964) "Family composition, prices and expenditure patterns", in: P. E. Hart et al., eds., *Econometric analysis for national economic planning*, London.

Becker, G. S. (1965) "A theory of the allocation of time", *Economics Journal* 75:493–517.

Ben-Porath, Y. (1967) "The production of human capital and the life cycle of earnings", *J.P.E.*, 75:352–365.

Ben-Porath, Y. (1970) "The production of human capital over time", in: W. Lee Hansen, ed., *Education, income, and human capital*. New York: National Bureau of Economic Research.

Bloch, F. (1973) "The allocation of time to market and non-market work within a family unit", Technical Report No. 114, Inst. Math. Studies Soc. Sci., Stanford Univ.

Bruzelius, N. (1979) *The value of travel time*. London: Croom Helm.

Chiswick, C. U. (1982) "The value of housewife's time", *Journal of Human Resources*, 17(3):413–425.

Deaton, A. and J. Muellbauer, (1980) *Economics and consumer behavior*. Cambridge: Cambridge Univ. Press.

Deaton, A. and J. Muellbauer, (1983) "On measuring child costs in poor countries", prepared for Living Standards Measurement Study, The World Bank.

DeSerpa, A. C. (1971) "A theory of the economics of time", *Economics Journal*, 81:828–846.

Earp, J. H., R. D. Hall and M. McDonald, (1976) "Modal choice behavior and the value of travel time: recent empirical evidence", in: J. G. Heggie, ed., *Modal choice and the value of travel time*. Oxford: Clarendon Press.

Engel, E. (1895) "Die Lebenkosten Belgischer Arbeiter—Familien Fruher und Jetzt", *Int. Stat. Inst. Bull.*, 9.

Goldschmidt-Clermont, L. (1982) *Unpaid work in the household*. Geneva: I.L.O.

Graham, J. W. and C. A. Green, (1984) "Estimating the parameters of a household production function with joint products", *Review of Economic Statistics*, 66(2):277–282.

Gronau, R. (1970) *The value of time in passenger transportation: the demand for air travel*, Occasional Paper No. 109. New York: National Bureau of Economic Research.

Gronau, R. (1973) "The effect of children on the housewife's value of time", *J.P.E.*, 81(2) part 2: S168–S199.

Gronau, R. (1974) "Wage comparisons, a selectivity bias", *J.P.E.*, 82(6):1119–1144.

Gronau, R. (1976) "The allocation of time of Israeli women", *J.P.E.*, 84(4) part 2:S201–S220.

Gronau, R. (1977) "Leisure, home production and work—the theory of the allocation of time revisited", *J.P.E.*, 85(6):1099–1123.

Gronau, R. (1980) "Home production—a forgotten industry", *Review of Economic Statistics*, 62(2):408–415.

Grossman, M. (1972) *The demand for health: a theoretical and empirical investigation*, Occasional Paper No. 119. New York: National Bureau of Economic Research.

Grossman, M. (1971) "The economics of joint production in the household", Report No. 7145, Center Math. Studies Bus. and Econ., Univ. Chicago.

Harrison, J. A. and D. A. Quarmby, (1972) "The value of time in transport planning: a review", in *Theoretical and practical research of time-saving*, Paris: European Conference of Ministers of Transport, 1969. Reprinted in R. Layard, ed., *Cost-benefit analysis*, London: Penguin Modern Economics Readings.

Hawrylyshyn, O. (1976) "The value of household services: a survey of empirical estimates", *Review of Income and Wealth*, 22:101–131.

Heckman, J. J. (1974) "Shadow prices, market wages, and labor supply", *Econometrica*, 42(4): 679–694.

Heckman, J. J. (1976) "A life cycle model of earnings, learning, and consumption", *J.P.E.*, 84(4) part 2:511–544.

Heggie, I. G. (1976) "A diagonistic survey of urban journey-to-work behavior", in: J. G. Heggie, ed., *Modal choice and the value of travel time*. Oxford: Clarendon Press.

Henscher, D. A. (1975) "Review of studies leading to existing value of travel time", Transportation Research Board Special Report, Washington, D.C.

Hill, C. R. and F. P. Stafford (1974) "The allocation of time to pre-school children and educational opportunity", *Journal of Human Resources*, Summer:323–341.

Hill, C. R. and F. P. Stafford, (1977) "Family background and lifetime earnings", in: F. T. Juster, ed., *The distribution of economic wellbeing*. Cambridge, Mass.: Ballinger Press.

Hill, C. R. and F. P. Stafford, (1980) "Parental care of children: time diary estimates of quantity predictability and variety", *Journal of Human Resources*, 15.

Hill, M. S. (1983) "Pattern of time use", in: F. T. Juster and F. P. Stafford, eds., *Time, goods, and well being*. The University of Michigan, Survey Research Center.

Juster, F. T. (1983) "A note on recent changes in time use", in: F. T. Juster and F. P. Stafford, eds., *Time, goods, and well being*. The University of Michigan, Survey Research Center.

Juster, F. T. and F. P. Stafford, eds. (1983) *Time, goods, and well being*. The University of Michigan, Survey Research Center.

Kuznets, S. (1944) *National income and its composition*, vol. II. New York: National Bureau of Economic Research.

Lancaster, K. J. (1966) "A new approach to consumer theory", *J.P.E.*, 74:132–157.

Lazear, E. P. and R. T. Michael, (1980) "Family size and the distribution of real per capita income", *American Economic Review*, 70(1):91–107.

Leibowitz, A. S. (1974) "Education and the allocation of women's time", in: F. T. Juster, ed., *Education, income, and human behavior*. New York: McGraw-Hill.

Lindert, P. H. (1977) "Sibling position and achievement", *Journal of Human Resources*, 12:198–219.
Michael, R. T. (1972) *The effect of education of efficiency in consumption*, Occasional Paper No. 116. New York: National Bureau of Economic Research.
Michael, R. T. (1973) "Education in nonmarket production", *J.P.E.*, 81, part 1:306–327.
Michael, R. T. and G. S. Becker (1973) "On the new theory of consumer behavior", *Swedish Journal of Economics*, 75:378–396.
Mincer, J. (1963) "Market prices, opportunity costs, and income effects", in C. Christ et al., *Measurement in economics: studies in mathematical economics and econometrics in memory of Yehuda Grunfeld*. Stanford, Calif.: Stanford University Press.
Muth, R. F. (1966) "Household production and consumer demand functions", *Econometrica*, 34:699–708.
Pollak, R. A. and M. L. Wachter (1975) "The relevance of the household production function and its implications for the allocation of time", *J.P.E.*, 83(2): 255–277.
Pollak, R. A. and T. J. Wales (1979) "Welfare comparisons and equivalence scales", *American Economic Review*, 69(2):216–221.
Pollak, R. A. and T. J. Wales (1981) "Demographic variables in demand analysis", *Econometrica*, 49(6):1533–1551.
Quandt, R. E. and W. J. Baumol (1966) "The demand for abstract transport modes: theory and measurement", *Journal of Regional Science*, 6:13–26.
Quarmby, D. A. (1967) "Choice of travel mode for the journey to work: some findings", *Journal of Transport Economic Policy*, 1(3):273–314.
Reichman, S. (1973) "Subjective time savings in interurban travel: an empirical study", *Highway Research Record*, 446: 21–27.
Reid, M. G. (1934) *Economics of household production*. New York: Wiley.
Robinson, J. P. (1983) "The validity and reliability of alternative time-use measures", in: F. T. Juster and F. P. Stafford, eds., *Time, goods and well being*. The University of Michigan, Survey Research Center.
Rosenzweig, M. R. and T. P. Schultz (1983) "Estimating the household production function: heterogeneity, the demand for health inputs, and their effect on birth weight", *J.P.E.*, 91(5):723–746.
Stafford, F. P. and G. J. Duncan (1983) "The use of time and technology by households in the United States", in: F. T. Juster and F. P. Stafford, eds., *Time, goods, and well being*. The University of Michigan, Survey Research Center.
Szalai, A. ed. (1972) *The use of time*. The Hague: Mouton.
Timmer, S. B., J. Eccles and K. O'Brien (1983) "How children use time", in: F. T. Juster and F. P. Stafford, eds., *Time, goods, and well being*. The University of Michigan, Survey Research Center.
Tipping, D. (1968) "Time savings in transport studies", *Economics Journal*, December.
Walker, K. E. (1969) "Time spent in household work by homemakers", *Family Economics Review*.
Walker, K. E. and W. H. Gauger (1973) "Time and its dollar value in household work", *Family Economics Review*, Fall:8–13.

Chapter 5

RETIREMENT FROM THE LABOR FORCE

EDWARD P. LAZEAR*

University of Chicago and National Bureau of Economic Research

1. Introduction and summary

Retirement is an important phenomenon in life-cycle labor supply. Not only does it mean a complete withdrawal from the labor force, but it also turns on a number of institutional facets such as social security and private pensions. Retirement ages have fallen steadily over the past thirty years. This chapter presents some basic facts on retirement patterns and examines some reasons for the changes in behavior over time and differences across groups. It explores a number of theoretical models and discusses empirical results. It takes a close look at pensions and social security and concludes by analyzing life-cycle savings behavior and looking at the status of retirees.

In the next few paragraphs, the most important points of the chapter are summarized. The reader should note that the examination of the literature contained herein tends to be nonjudgmental, perhaps too much so. The reason is that the goal of the chapter is to lay out the important issues in retirement behavior, rather than to draw definitive conclusions on the state of knowledge. In large part, that reflects the somewhat embryonic stage of the literature since few of the cited analyses predate the mid-1970s and most have been published in the last few years. With that in mind, let us proceed with a general overview.

A quick look at the data reveals that the most important trend among older workers in the United States is the decline in age of retirement. Since there has been a simultaneous increase in the real income of the population, an obvious conjecture is that most of this reflects an income effect that induces workers to take more leisure. Unfortunately, this simple interpretation is not supported by the international cross-section. As will be seen, the attempt to reconcile these findings by an in-depth examination of the estimates of retirement behavior is less than satisfactorily achieved.

*The assistance of Beth Asch and William Chan is gratefully acknowledged. Financial support was provided by the National Science Foundation.

Handbook of Labor Economics, Volume I, Edited by O. Ashenfelter and R. Layard

Before that is done, some definitions of retirement are considered. Because retirement may be a graduate process, with workers reducing their hours of work in a somewhat continuous fashion, the definition of retirement is ambiguous. As some have shown, the particular definition chosen can have significant effects on the conclusions. A more important question that follows relates to whether retirement, per se, should be studied separately, or merely as one rather extreme manifestation of labor supply choice. It is argued that although labor supply considerations are essential, retirement has a number of important and distinct institutional features associated with it that make it worthy of individual attention.

Before any empirical studies are examined, a number of theoretical models are considered. These vary from simple one-period work/leisure choice models, to full-blown dynamic optimization problems, where leisure at each point in the individuals lifetime depends on compensation at all other points in time. All of these models treat the compensation package as exogenous. The worker is offered a wage profile and is then allowed to choose the optimum work/leisure path. Another, more recent, strain of the literature recognizes that pensions and wages are linked by market forces. The exact nature of the compensation path may affect worker effort and under these circumstances, the worker's retirement (and labor supply decision in general), may not be determined unilaterally by the worker. An extreme manifestation of this phenomenon is mandatory retirement. Because worker effort and productivity are such important concerns to firms, and because mandatory retirement is extensive, much attention is paid to incorporating endogenous effort based compensation into the retirement analysis. In the later sections, an extension of this line of thought is applied in an attempt to explain the existence of pensions and how they may function as a form of efficient severance pay.

In the same way that the introductory facts led to somewhat contradictory conclusions, the empirical literature on the relation of retirement to social security and private pensions also yields inconsistent results. For example, some studies find that social security wealth increases the propensity to retire, while others find that the reverse is true. There are many problems in what may appear to be a simple estimation problem. For example, social security and private pensions are linked in a mechanical way to length of the work life so identification of the choice relationship separate from the technological one becomes quite difficult. Even the most thorough studies have not come to grips fully with all of the difficult issues. The results are akin to others in the labor supply literature: not only are magnitudes of the parameters often very different across studies, but there is not even complete agreement on the direction of the effects. Although there is little doubt that there are positive income effects on retirement, perhaps the strongest finding relates to substitution effects. There is agreement across studies that steeper age–pension profiles lead to delayed retirement. Put differently, for a given amount of pension wealth, sharper decreases in the actuarial value of retirement with continued work induce earlier retirement.

The discussion of pensions focuses on one empirical relationship and a number of theoretical ones. The most important empirical point is that the actuarial value of private pensions first rises, but then declines once the worker continues to work beyond a certain point. The exact pattern varies by firm and worker type, but the inverted U-shaped relation of pension value to retirement age is virtually universal.

On the theoretical side, much has been conjectured about the effects of various pension provisions on behavior. Most often, vesting and turnover are linked. Some of the folklore about these connections is actually incorrect and Section 6 takes an in-depth look at the effects of different pension provisions on worker effort and labor supply. Key here is the recognition that the market places constraints on the sum of wage and pension compensation. Once this is recognized, the usual statements are rarely valid.

A number of arguments have been made for the existence of compulsory pensions. They include taxes, firm-specific human capital, incentives, insurance, the prevention of opportunistic behavior, and sorting. None is completely satisfactory.

Finally, a brief attempt is made to describe the controversy involving the tradeoff between social security, private pensions and savings. Although some researchers have claimed that there is a strict crowding-out-effect, more recent evidence and theoretical arguments have called these earlier results into question.

2. Some basic facts on retirement

One of the most noticeable changes in recent labor force history is the significant decline in the labor force participation rate of older males. Table 5.1 reports that in 1947, males 65 years and older had a labor force participation rate of 47.8 percent, or about one-half of the labor force participation rate for males aged 35–44. By 1979, the rate was down to 20 percent or about one-fifth of the rate for males 35–44.

For females, the overall trend toward increased labor force participation swamps the effect of earlier retirement. The labor force participation rate for females 65 and older rose from 8.1 percent in 1947 to 8.3 percent in 1970. Still, the early retirement effect can be seen by looking at the ratio of labor force participation at age 65+ to labor force participation at ages 35–44. That ratio fell from 0.22 in 1947 to 0.13 in 1979. The pattern of decline has been similar for whites and nonwhites, although the decline in relative participation rates is

Table 5.1
Labor force participation rates.

Group	Year	LFPR 65+	LFPR 55–65	LFPR/LFPR 65+/35–44
Males	1947	47.8	89.6	0.49
	1954	40.5	88.7	0.41
	1959	34.2	87.4	0.35
	1964	28.0	85.6	0.29
	1969	27.2	83.4	0.28
	1974	22.4	77.4	0.23
	1979	20.0	73.0	0.21
Females	1947	8.1	24.3	0.22
	1954	9.3	30.1	0.23
	1959	10.2	36.6	0.24
	1964	10.1	40.2	0.22
	1969	9.9	43.1	0.20
	1974	8.2	40.7	0.15
	1979	8.3	41.9	0.13
White males	1954	40.4	89.2	0.41
	1979	20.1	73.6	0.21
Nonwhite males	1954	41.2	83.0	0.43
	1979	19.6	66.9	0.22
White females	1954	9.1	29.1	0.23
	1979	8.1	41.6	0.13
Nonwhite females	1954	12.2	41.2	0.21
	1979	10.6	44.3	0.16

somewhat less pronounced for nonwhite females than for white females. On the whole, the relative decline in labor force participation rates at older ages is less obvious for females than it is for males.

These statistics, when coupled with those on increased life expectancy paint a picture of increasing years spent in retirement. Even over the past 30 years, the life expectancy of older individuals has gone up slightly. In 1950, a 65-year-old male had a life expectancy of 13 years and a 70-year-old male had a life expectancy of 10 years. In 1980 those numbers were 14 and 11 years, respectively.[1]

Labor force participation behavior of the elderly varies across countries as well. A study[2] in the mid-1970s allows an examination of labor force participation by country, over time. Table 5.2 provides labor force participation rates for individuals 65 and older by selected country for 1975 and 1956.

The results hardly provide evidence that there is an income effect that works to prolong retirement. With the exception of Japan, Denmark and the United States have the highest labor force participation rates for old individuals. Both countries

[1] See Burkhauser and Turner (1982, p. 305).
[2] OECD (1977).

Table 5.2
Labor force participation rates, 65+ (in percent).

Country	1956	1975
Belgium	13.8	6.3
Denmark	20.0	19.9
Finland		8.9
France	20.7	7.1
Germany	16.5	10.0
Italy	15.6	7.1
Japan		30.7
Netherlands	13.1	6.8
Norway	20.6	
Sweden	20.5	10.9
United Kingdom	16.2	10.7
United States	23.7	14.6

have high standards of living and average income. Italy has a low labor force participation rate, but that for the Netherlands is even lower.[3]

Countries also differ in the change in labor force participation rates over time. All countries for which data are present experienced some drop in the labor force participation rates of older individuals, but the size of the drop varies significantly by country. France experienced the largest decline whereas Denmark was the most stable.

Time series evidence casually suggests that as income rises, labor force participation rates fall. But this is not borne out by cross-country comparisons, nor by the time series relation of the rate of income growth to the decline in participation rates. Evidently, other factors enter. Subsequent sections of this chapter outline some models and possible explanations for changes in retirement over time and differences across countries.

3. The definition of retirement

What is retirement? This question, which appears to have an obvious answer, becomes less obvious when examined in detail. There are a number of ways to define retirement, and the appropriateness of the definition depends in large part upon its use.

For most surveys, retirement is defined as an affirmative answer to a question like: "Are you currently retired?" The implicit definition of retirement conse-

[3] The extent to which these numbers reflect measurement rather than behavioral differences is an open question.

quently varies with the identity of the respondent. Some possible objective definitions of retirement are:

(1) The individual is out of the labor force with the intention of remaining out permanently.

(2) The individual has reduced his hours substantially from some lifetime average and intends to maintain hours at or below the current level.

(3) The individual receives some of his income as pension benefits.

(4) The individual appears on some company's retirement roll.

(5) The individual receives primary social security payments (not derivable from another's employment).

The first definition is most appropriate if one is interested in discussing patterns of labor force participation, by age, over time, or cross-sectionally. The second is useful for analyses that focus heavily on hours as well as heads in the labor force. The third is applicable when studying the well-being of various groups in the population or when trying to estimate pension costs over time or by region. The fourth is of interest when the study relates to turnover or duration of employment in general. The fifth may be the definition of choice for studies having to do with social security, its costs, benefits and cross-subsidization effects.

No concensus exists on the most fruitful way to define retirement. Murray (1972) examines the relationship between the subjective responses to the retirement question and more objective measures. Using the Retirement History Survey, she examines the relationship between hours worked and answers to the retirement question. She reports that those with zero hours and those with 35+ hours are clearly associated with responses of retired and working. But only 73 percent of those with weekly hours between 25 and 29 said that they were "partially retired". Part of this may reflect measurement error and part may be a result of substantive definitional problems. For example, an individual who currently works 25 hours per week, but plans to return to working 40 hours per week in the near future, is unlikely to call himself "partially retired". Most would agree that he is not in the same sense that a worker on layoff is not retired. This points out that retirement is not only a function of current work states, but also of past and future behavior.

There have been a number of studies that focus on the partially retired. Murray reports, however, that only 7 percent of her sub-sample of those who changed retirement status went from working to partially retired to retired. Nevertheless, the issue of partial retirement seems to be an interesting one.

Gustman and Steinmeier (1983a), also using the Retirement History Survey, find somewhat higher incidence of partial retirement. (The average incidence of partial retirement rises with the wave of the survey, reflecting changes in the age composition of the sample.) For example, slightly over one-fourth of those workers who were not retired two years earlier, but have changed status, end up as partially retired (defined subjectively).

This study adds importance to their earlier work [Gustman and Steinmeier (1982)] which estimated different earnings functions for those partially retired and those who are not. They do this because they argue that there is a strong correlation between hours of work and wages and if one ignores that some individuals partially retire, then ignoring this produces an overstatement of the decline in wages with age. They estimate that the decline can be overstated by as much as 60 percent. Still, if hours are the crucial variable, it is not clear why correcting for hours, perhaps in some nonlinear form, is not sufficient. Further, since hours of work and partial retirement are both choice variables, it is difficult to disentangle the effect of hours on wages (say, because of some productivity variation with average daily hours worked) from that of wages on hours—the traditional labor supply relationship. Their correction made for selectivity bias does not adequately address this issue. But the Gustman and Steinmeier work remains among the most thorough and informative on the issue of partial retirement.

The notion that partial retirement may be important brings up a more general issue: Why bother with retirement at all? Might it not be better merely to think in terms of life cycle labor supply, without singling out the period when hours worked falls to zero?

The answer to this question is yes and no. The advantage of thinking of retirement as just a special case of the lifetime labor supply problem is that it forces consistency on the analysis. It seems appropriate to estimate the labor supply of 55 year olds and 65 year olds within the same model, rather than making the latter appear to be a separate decision, disjoint from the former.

The disadvantage is that there are many important institutional features associated with retirement that do not pertain to early labor supply decisions. Pensions, social security, and mandatory retirement are all specific to the labor supply decision associated with retirement. Although these institutions may have effects on or be the causes of earlier labor supply behavior, it seems useful to parcel out the retirement period for special consideration.

In addition to these institutional considerations, there are theoretical reasons as well to look separately at retirement. Retirement is a period during which leisure is bunched. In the few years prior to retirement, most males work a standard work week. But after the magical date of retirement, they discontinuously drop the hours of work to zero. Why should this change in observed labor supply be so discrete? Who initiates the separation? Does it serve any function? These issues are addressed below, but their existence is another argument for treating retirement as a special phenomenon, albeit related to earlier labor supply decisions.

4. Models of retirement

4.1. *The one-period work–leisure analysis*

The easiest and most primitive models of retirement treat each year independently and think of the retirement decision as affecting one year at a time. This is easily embedded in the standard work leisure framework.

Let the worker's lifetime utility function be written as

$$U = U(L_1, X_1, L_2, X_2, \ldots, L_t, X_t), \tag{1}$$

where L_t is leisure consumed in period t and X_t is goods consumed in period t. To use the one-period framework, it is sufficient to be able to write (1) as

$$U = U_1(L_1, X_1) + U_2(L_2, X_2) + \cdots + U_t(L_t, X_t) \tag{2}$$

and to ensure that no borrowing or lending occurs. Then, each year in the individual's lifetime is treated completely separately.

This standard approach implies that a piece increase in income in any period t brings about less work in that period (leisure is a normal good). "Retirement" is defined here to occur when leisure equals the full amount of time available. A change in the wage has two effects: the increased buying power implies that more leisure should be taken, but an increase in the wage makes leisure relatively expensive. The net effect is ambiguous when leisure is a normal good.

Note that nothing is said about returning to the labor force in subsequent periods, nor is anything said about the relation of U_t to U_{t-1}. This model of leisure choice has little that is specific to the retirement decision. More will be said on this below. Within the context of this model, retirement is analyzed by examining the effects of various changes on labor force participation. Most of the studies that use this model have been interested in the effects of social security on retirement. Munnell (1974), Feldstein (1974), Boskin (1977), Pellechio (1978), Boskin and Hurd (1978), and Burtless and Hausman (1980) all make use (explicitly or implicitly) of the one-period model to examine social security effects.

Social security, it is argued, places kinks in the budget constraint. Instead of the standard budget constraint given by $\overline{AB}$ in Figure 5.1, the constraint is $ACDEB$ because of the social security earnings test. The earnings test provides that individuals receive their full social security payment of AC provided that earned income does not exceed Y_0. For each dollar earning above Y_0, 50 cents are subtracted from social security payments until earned income exceeds Y_1 when

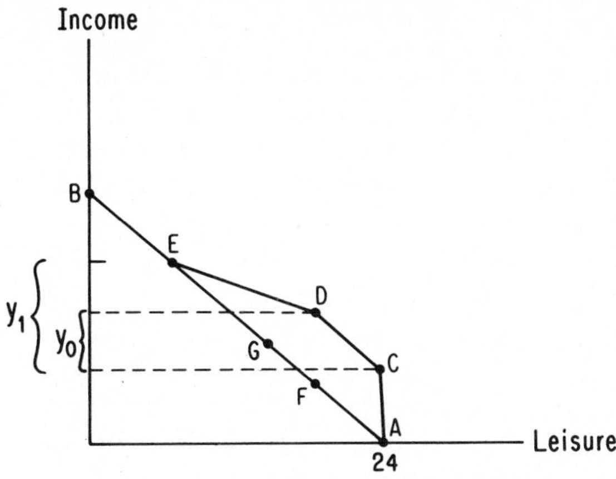

Figure 5.1

social security payments become zero. The kinked budget constraint can change behavior. All individuals who would have retired in the absence of social security continue to do do. The "income" effect of social security and reduced substitution effects of the flatter budget constraint push in that direction. Some who previously worked, however, may be induced to retire. An individual at F might now move to C. Or an individual previously at G might move to D, reducing hours of work, although not retiring completely. The interesting question, of course, is how large are these effects and the answer depends upon the distribution of preferences in the economy.

The work–leisure diagram is a useful device, but leaves many of the essential features out. Perhaps most important is how utility in time t relates to consumption of leisure and goods during other time periods. For example, the social security earnings test is not applied to individuals who are older than 72. This analysis would imply that those induced out of the labor force would re-enter at that point. This rarely happens. In order to deal with this issue, one must discuss the way that the utility function or opportunity locus changes with age.

Other issues are ignored as well. Work at earlier ages affects productivity later in life because of human capital accumulation. In the context of social security, payments upon retirement are a function of earnings and years worked before retirement. The same is true of pension plans. Additionally, depending upon how social security is financed, it may act more as a forced transfer from one point in life to another. Nonindependence of utility over time could then wipe out any income effect of social security on retirement. Clearly, a life-cycle model would enrich the analysis.

4.2. *A simple lifetime retirement model*

The simplest way to take into account life-cycle effects in the retirement decision is to use the standard demand for leisure framework. Define leisure in terms of years of nonworked time: leisure = number of years of life (T) − year of work (L)—and the wage rate, W, on the individual's annual salary. Then the workers' lifetime utility maximization problem is written as

$$\max U(\text{leisure, expenditures on goods}) \tag{3}$$

subject to the budget constraint

$$\begin{aligned}\text{expenditures on goods} &= LW \\ &= (T - \text{leisure})W. \end{aligned} \tag{3a}$$

As long as leisure is a normal good, pure changes in income imply an increase in leisure and a consequent fall in the age of retirement. A change in the annual salary implies both income and substitution effects. Increased wages make the worker richer and induce him to buy more of all normal goods, leisure included. But at the same time, the increase in the implicit price of leisure induces a substitution towards goods and away from leisure, raising the age of retirement. The net effect is ambiguous.

This simple model is obviously unsatisfactory in a number of respects. First, it assumes that the value of time in the labor market is independent of the age at which it is supplied. This is likely to be incorrect for at least two reasons. First, workers may experience exogenous changes in their productivities over the life cycle as a direct result of physical changes. Young children are less able than 25 year olds who may be more able than 82 year olds. Second, endogenous changes in productivity over the life cycle occur when individuals invest in human capital. During the initial years of life, their stock of human capital is low, but it grows with time as individuals consciously invest in themselves to increase their market value. In the final years, that stock may fall as it becomes optimal to allow it to depreciate more rapidly than it is replaced.[4]

If the value of market time varies over the life cycle, then it is preferable to work during some years rather than during others. This is true so long as the value of leisure is invariant with respect to when it is taken. But this brings up the second major difficulty with the simple model: the value of leisure may vary over time.

[4] Early models of life-cycle investment in human capital are Becker (1962) and Ben-Porath (1967).

The model arbitrarily defines nonworked years as years of retirement. But there is no obvious reason to make this arbitrary assignment. If the value of time in the market were constant over the life cycle, the individual might prefer to spread his leisure more evenly, taking off a couple of days now and then (weekends), a couple of weeks every so often (vacation), and perhaps a year once in a while (sabbatical).

However, things need not be that way. Some bunching of leisure might be preferred. There may be fixed costs to working or to taking leisure which are more effectively amortized by bunching periods of work and leisure. For example, leisure may be better in Florida, whereas work may more effectively produce income in Chicago. The fixed cost of commuting between states implies that it is optimal to bunch leisure and work to some extent to conserve on commuting costs.

Similarly, unused work skills may depreciate more rapidly than those that are constantly used. If a worker becomes "rusty" when he does not perform a given task frequently enough, then it becomes efficient to bunch periods of work together, leaving retirement as a period during which it is better to bunch leisure.

All of these factors are absent from the simple work–leisure models of retirement, but the point can be summarized succinctly: what is necessary to induce retirement is that the value of leisure rises above the value of work. This

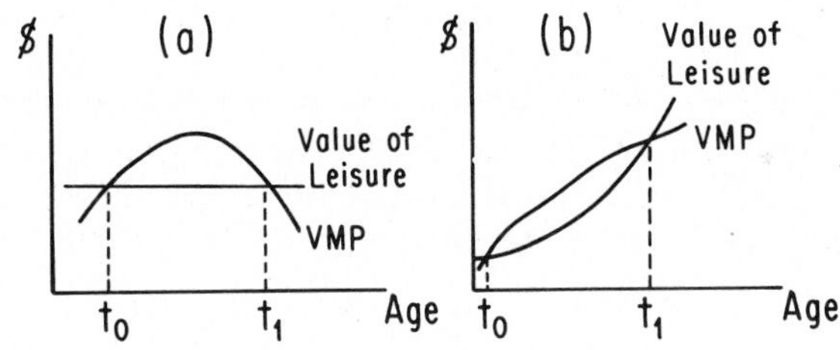

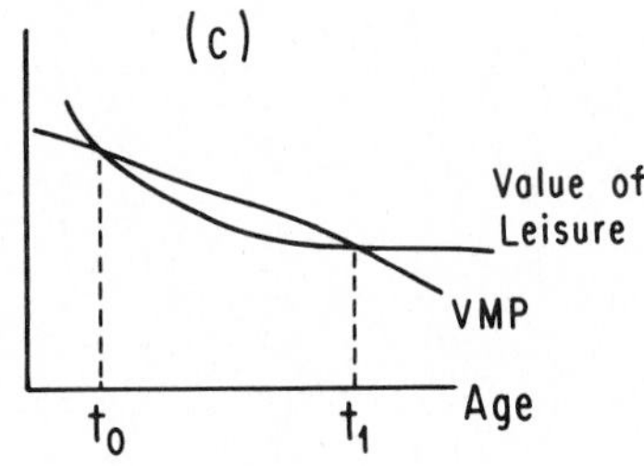

Figure 5.2

does not require that old workers be less productive than young ones. It is a statement about the relative value of time. Thus, Figures 5.2(a), (b), and (c) all induce a pattern where work begins at time t_0 and retirement begins at time t_1. Different stories can be told about each.

4.3. *More sophisticated multi-period models*

The major problem with the one-period model of retirement is the requirement of intertemporal separability in a very strong sense. Recall that this implies, among other things, that wages at other points in the work life are irrelevant for the retirement decision. It also implies that only the current pension level affects the worker's retirement decision.

Burkhauser (1976, 1979) recognized early that this simplification was likely to be misleading. In particular, he argued that pensions need not be actuarially fair in the sense that the pension value is not independent of the age of retirement. Although he did not seriously consider the reasons for this particular phenomenon, he was quick to understand that it had important implications for retirement behavior.

In the data that he examined (from a large American company), he observed that the pension value associated with early retirement often exceeded that for normal retirement. He argued that not only was the current pension value likely to affect the retirement choice, but so was the ratio of current pension benefits to those at the normal age of retirement.

Reimers (1976) generalizes the point somewhat by recognizing that it is not merely the ratio of current benefits to those received at the normal age of retirement that is relevant, but the ratio of benefits now to benefits receivable at

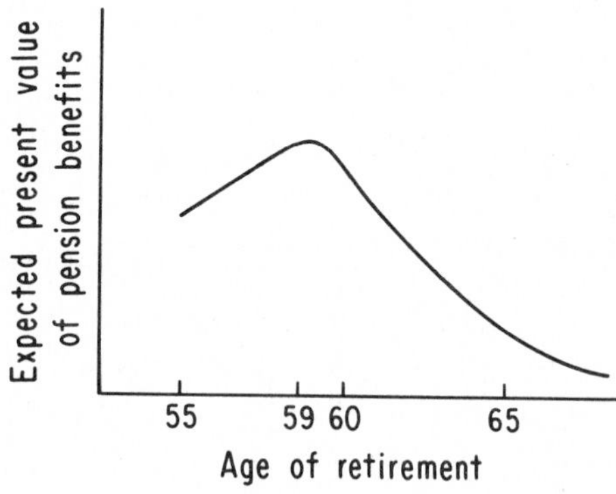

Figure 5.3

all other ages. Stated alternatively, it is the entire path of pension entitlements as a function of retirement age that must be considered.

To see this, consider Figure 5.3. It might be the case that the expected present value of pension benefits at age 65 are lower than those at age 55. This would seem to provide an incentive to retire at age 55. However, a comparison of the pension value at age 55 to that at age 59 would reveal that pension value is still increasing at age 55, providing the worker with an incentive to stay with the firm.

Bulow (1981) puts it in a somewhat different way. He points out that the true compensation at a point in time consist of two components: the current wage plus the value of the pension accrual. This notion has been used in the human capital literature as well. For example, Lazear (1976, 1979a) defines the "true" wage as the observed wage, plus the value of the wage growth that results from having worked at the firm during the current period. In an analogous way, the "true" wage can be defined as

$$\tilde{W}_t \equiv W_t + (P_t - P_{t-1}), \tag{4}$$

where $\tilde{W}_t$ is the true wage at time t, W_t is the observed wage at time t, and P_t is the expected present value of pension benefits if retirement occurs at time t. True wages are greater than the observed wage when pension value grows the additional years of work, but falls short of the observed wage when pension value is declining (e.g. beyond age 59 in Figure 5.3).

This is a convenient definition because it allows one to take account of changes in the value of fringes that are associated with work. Other studies, for example, have not limited attention to the effect of pension accrual on retirement decisions. For example, Blinder, Gordon and Wise (1980), Burkhauser (1980), Burkhauser and Quinn (1980), and Fields and Mitchell (1983b) allow accrual of social security benefits to affect the retirement decision as well. In principle, there is no reason why the true wage defined in (4) could include social security accruals as well.

When is it sufficient to examine only the true wage to determine retirement? If the entire path of $\tilde{W}_t$ is considered, then this is the relevant compensation variable for the current job. This does not imply, however, that retirement should occur when $\tilde{W}_t$ is maximized, or even when $\tilde{W}_t$ falls below the value of leisure. This is not the general solution to maximization of (1).

Two examples make this clear. In Figure 5.4(a), $\tilde{W}_t$ peaks at t_0. But at this point the value of leisure falls far short of the true wage. Even though that wage is declining, the worker is still better off by working in period $t+1$ than taking leisure. The rule that retirement should occur when the true wage is equal to the value of leisure is the one derived in Sheshinski (1978). This is correct as long as there are not multiple crossings of the paths as shown in Figure 5.4(b). Retiring at t_0 is not optimal.

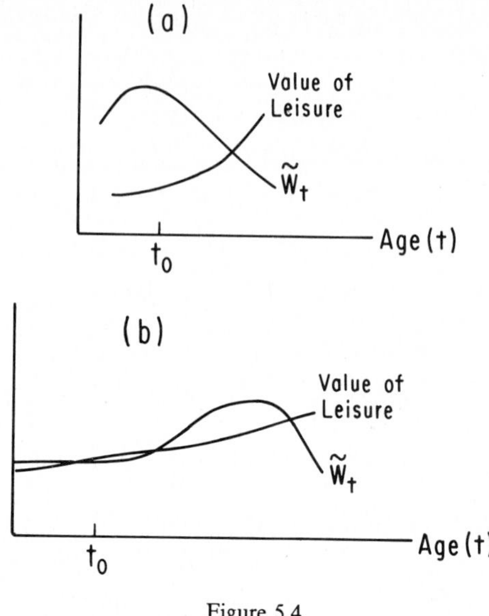

Figure 5.4

The general lifetime retirement problem can be written as a dynamic optimization problem. A continuous version of (1) has the worker maximizing

$$U = \int_0^{T'} U(L(t), X(t))e^{-\rho t}dt, \tag{5}$$

where T' is the age at death and ρ is the discount factor, subject to the following constraint:

$$\int_0^{T'} X(t)e^{-rt}dt = \int_0^{T} W(t)e^{-rt}dt + P(T), \tag{5a}$$

where r is the market interest rate, $P(T)$ is the expected present value of pension and social security benefits contingent upon the worker's retirement at T, and the worker is allowed to borrow and lend at the rate r. Retirement is defined as that date T such that $L(t) = 1$ for all $t \geq T$.

The problem in (5) is similar to the one solved by Reimers (1977) and by Boskin (1977). Burbridge and Robb (1980) set up an almost identical framework to analyze the Canadian Pension Plan. They emphasize the point that pensions need not be actuarially fair.

Little insight is gained from general models of this sort unless additional assumptions about functional form are made. This is particularly true for empirical implementation. Separability is the usual price paid.

Somewhere between the two extremes of a full life-cycle model and a simple one-period model is the type of analysis performed by Hemming (1977) and by Mitchell and Fields (1983, 1984). Mitchell and Fields devote considerable attention to the ways in which lifetime pecuniary wealth varies with date of retirement. They explicitly take into account that neither earnings nor pension benefits are independent of the date of retirement. They collapse the life-cycle problem into a single-period one by entering two arguments into the utility function: present value of expected lifetime income and years of retirement. They invoke a separability assumption and then estimate the model, using an indirect utility approach.

This kind of model captures most life-cycle aspects of the income side, but ignores the life-cycle leisure choices. It neglects any tradeoffs between leisure taken earlier in life and that bunched into a retirement period. Leisure taken at other points during the life cycle may have larger or smaller effects on lifetime wealth. If all leisure time were perfectly substitutable for all other leisure time, then the worker would take leisure in a way that maximized lifetime wealth, given the amount of leisure chosen. Without knowing anything about leisure taken over the rest of the lifetime, it would be impossible to estimate the relevant substitution parameters.

Still, the Fields and Mitchell model produces one of the more tractable empirical specifications and estimation of the model yields sensible results. As such, it appears to offer a reasonable compromise.

Other authors have incorporated additional factors to add realism to the analysis. Clark, Johnson and McDermed (1980) discuss the retirement decision in a family context. The family is an important determinant of the retirement decision in at least three ways. First, the income of the spouse affects the wealth level of the household and the demand for leisure. Second, the value of leisure might depend upon the presence of a spouse so that widows and widowers may have different retirement behavior than married individuals. Third, part of the assets of the elderly consists of returns from investments made in their children [see Willis (1981)]. Individuals with wealthy children may enjoy some transfers in old age and these transfers (or the possibility of receiving them) may affect retirement behavior.

Gotz and McCall (1980) add uncertainty to their analysis of military retirement in an attempt to explain why otherwise similar individuals choose different retirement dates. These sources of uncertainty seem important. First is uncertainty over the wage stream in the current job. Second is uncertainty over the offer that another firm makes to the worker. Third is uncertainty over the value of leisure, which may be generated by the stochastic nature of health.[5]

[5]Anderson and Burkhauser (1983)) examine the relationship between health and retirement explicitly. With mortality data from the Retirement History Survey, they argue that self-assessed health measures exaggerate the effects of health on retirement.

In a study of retirement from the military, it is important to consider the wage on the alternative job because such a large proportion of retired military personnel go on to work in the private sector. In emphasizing partial retirement, Gustmand and Steinmeier explicitly bring in the alternative wage available to workers. It is also conceivable to incorporate pension and social security benefits that accrue from the alternative job into the analysis of retirement decisions.

A final consideration is one of nonparameterized heterogeneity or, conveniently, differences in tastes for retirement. Some jobs may offer high pensions and low wages whereas others offer high wages and low pensions. Individuals who have a preference for early retirement may prefer the former and sort themselves accordingly. Asch (1983) analyzes the sorting effects of pensions on retirement decisions and argues that pensions may be used as an efficient sorting device when specific human capital is important. This is similar to the argument in Salop and Salop (1976). Mitchell and Fields (1984) address the sorting issue as well and conclude that differences in retirement behavior across individuals are in part due to differences in tastes.

4.4. *Endogenous compensation profiles and retirement*

None of the models considered makes any serious attempt to ask whether constraints on worker retirement behavior are important, why such constraints exist, what is the relation of pensions to earnings, and indeed, why are there pensions in the first place.

The most obvious constraint on worker retirement behavior is mandatory retirement, which until recently applied to about 35 percent of the work force and required that workers terminate employment usually at age 65. Recent changes in the Age Discrimination in Employment Act have raised that age to 70.

In Lazear (1979b), I consider mandatory retirement and try to explain its existence. Mandatory retirement not only seriously constrains retirement behavior, but presents a puzzle to economists because workers whom the firm is perfectly willing to employ one day are unemployable on the next. No wage adjustment takes place and many of the mandatorily retired workers are quite unhappy about being forced to retire at that point.

It turns out that the explanation of mandatory retirement brings together wages and pensions within the same framework, and takes a step toward understanding the existence of pensions. Subsequent work [Lazear (1982, 1983)] based on this theory also explains the actuarial non-neutrality of pension benefits.

The basic idea is this: the shape of the compensation profile over a worker's lifetime has two effects on behavior. First, it affects the worker's choice of hours worked, a specific case of which is the choice of retirement date. It is a standard

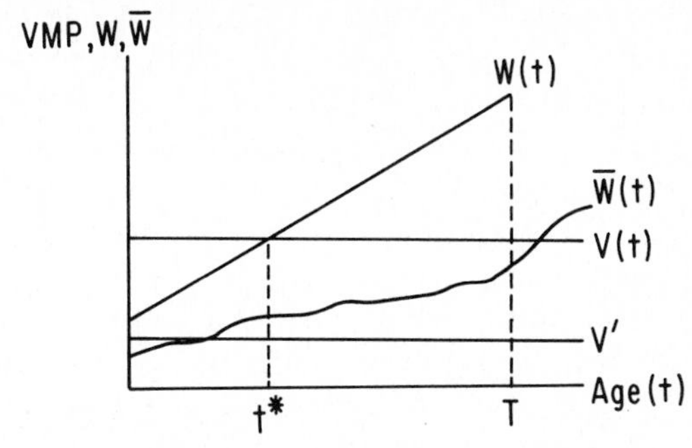

Figure 5.5

result that workers who are paid their marginal products choose to work if and only if it is efficient to do so. Second, the shape of the age–earnings profile affects the worker's productivity over the lifetime when the worker can control the level of effort that he exerts on the job.

The problem is that adjusting the age–earnings profile in a way that induces the appropriate level of effort results in a distortion of hours of work and of the retirement date.

The point is best made in the context of Figure 5.5. Suppose that a worker who performs at the efficient level of effort (the level such that the disutility from additional effort just equals the revenue from additional effort) has value of marginal product $V(t)$ over his lifetime. Suppose further that the individual's reservation wage function is given by $\overline{W}(t)$. The age at which they cross defines the date of efficient retirement, the date that the worker would voluntarily choose if he were paid V. Other wage paths are possible, however. For example, consider the wage path $W(t)$, which pays the worker less than he is worth before t^* and more than he is worth after t^*, but is selected such that the present value of stream $W(t)$ from $t=0$ to T is the same as the present value of stream $V(t)$ from $t=0$ to T.

Given perfect capital markets and no other considerations, workers would be indifferent between path $W(t)$ and $V(t)$. But two points are important. First, $W(t)$ requires "mandatory" retirement. At time T, if the worker is given the choice, he will not voluntarily retire because $W(T)>\overline{W}(T)$ even though retirement at T is efficient. Other things equal, $W(t)$ with mandatory retirement yields the worker the same marginal utility as $V(t)$ without mandatory retirement. But other things are not equal and that is the second point. Effort is not independent of the choice between paying $W(t)$ and paying $V(t)$. The reason is that the costs to the worker of losing the job depend upon the shape of the age–earnings profile. Consider a worker who is $T-1$ years old. Suppose that he considers reducing his effort level to that consistent with V' of output rather than V of output. The worst event that occurs is that he is fired. If he is earning $V(t)$, then he loses $V(T)$ as a result, but gains $\overline{W}(T)$ for his time spent as leisure. He has no incentive to work at the higher level of effort at $T-1$. However, if the worker is paid $W(t)$, termination at the end of $T-1$ costs the worker $W(T)$ and he gains only $\overline{W}(T)$. The difference, $W(T)-\overline{W}(T)$, acts as an inducement to work at the higher level of effort.

Stated intuitively, this implies that young workers exert effort not because their current wages are so high, but because, by doing so, they will be permitted to grow old in the job to enjoy high earnings later in life. Old workers must be paid a quasi-rent in order to prevent them from retiring on the job. Mandatory retirement is a consequence of changing the shape of the profile in a way which brings about efficient effort, but distorts the retirement decision.[6]

The shape of the $W(t)$ profile is determined by a number of factors. It turns out that any path that is sufficiently steep induces appropriate worker effort. But the steepness of the profile is limited by the ability of the worker to borrow, by progressive income taxes, and by the worker's trust of the firm. A firm that had nothing to lose would fire all workers after t^*. The costs involved in doing so prevent some default behavior by firms, but the steeper the profile, the greater the firm's incentive to default.

These considerations aside, there is one feature that all optimal profiles must have. In order to induce optimal effort in the last round, it is necessary that some of the worker's payment be withheld until after the final day of work. This provides some justification for a pension. A pension, which is received after completion of the work life, acts to induce appropriate effort throughout. This is true so long as the pension is at least to some extent contingent upon completion of employment.[7]

This analysis brings together voluntary retirement, mandatory retirement, earnings, and pensions. The drawback is that it is deterministic and ignores inefficiencies that result when the alternative use of the worker's time is stochastic, either for health reasons or because the worker's value to another firm cannot be anticipated perfectly.

[6] Of course, this is not the only way to provide incentives for workers to exert effort. A standard piece rate, where workers are paid their output each period, is always first best efficient when workers are risk neutral. The problem with a piece rate is that output must be measured frequently. Under certain circumstances, it is efficient to sample workers' output only infrequently. If their output has fallen below what was expected then they must be docked pay. But in order to dock them pay, the worker's wage must exceed what he can earn elsewhere or the penalty can be escaped simply by a change in employer. The age–earnings profile drawn in Figure 5.5 allows the firm to penalize the worker without inducing immediate separation. Thus, when sampling costs are large, an upward sloping age–earnings profile dominates the standard piece rate as an incentive device.

[7] Tying pensions to final salary has this effect. It turns out that this creates too strong an incentive.

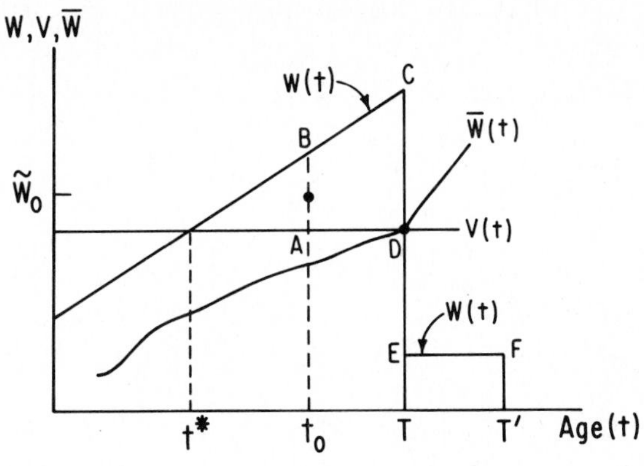

Figure 5.6

Recognition of the somewhat random nature of the alternative use of time helps fit another piece of the puzzle into place. As already discussed, pensions are rarely actuarially fair. In fact, as I have shown in Lazear (1982, 1983), the pattern of the expected present value of pension benefits with respect to age of retirement is an inverted U as shown in Figure 5.3.

The peak of the U varies with characteristics of the worker and the firm, but it is not uncommon to have the expected present value of pensions decline after age 55, the age at which many firms permit early retirement.

This pattern of declining pension value with age of retirement is easily understood in the context of Figure 5.5 once the alternative use of time is allowed to be stochastic. The intuition is this: once the worker is older than t^*, he is being paid more than he is worth. The firm would be willing to pay severance pay in order to get rid of the worker before T. In fact, if the firm agrees to pay exactly the maximum amount that it is willing to pay, then the worker's separation decision is efficient. The point is illustrated in Figure 5.6

In Figure 5.6 the worker is paid $W(t)$ over his lifetime, which includes a pension between T and T' (T' being the date of death). The problem is this: suppose that the worker's anticipated alternative value of time at t_0 was $\overline{W}(t_0)$, but that it unexpectedly rises to $\tilde{W}_0$ (either because he gets a better-than-expected outside offer or because the value of his leisure rises). It is efficient for the worker to leave because $\tilde{W}_0 > V(t_0)$, but the worker will not do so voluntarily because $W(t) > \tilde{W}_0$ for $t > t_0$.

There is a severance pay level that will induce him to leave efficiently. If the worker would have received pension equal to the present value of $EFT'T$ (hereafter, $EFT'T$) by staying until T, paying him a pension of $ABCD + EFT'T$) for a voluntary separation at t_0 induces him to leave if and only if it is efficient for him to do so. If the worker stays, he receives

$$[V(t_0)](T-T_0)+ABCD+EFT'T.$$

If he leaves, he receives

$$ABCD+EFT'T$$

from the current firm and $\tilde{W}_0(T-t_0)$ from the new employer (or as leisure). He gets more from leaving than from staying if and only if $\tilde{W}_0 > V(t_0)$, which is the efficiency criterion.

This implies that if the pension value at time t_0 exceeds that at time T in this particular fashion, the worker is induced to choose the correct retirement behavior, despite the apparent distortions caused by the tilted age–earnings profile.

Furthermore, it implies that the expected present value of pension benefits should exhibit an inverted U-shaped relation to age of retirement, with the peak occurring at age t^*.

The attempt by firms to "buy" workers into early retirement is sometimes quite explicit. This analysis shows that implicit buy-outs are also an important feature of major American pension plans.

5. Empirical results on retirement behavior

There are a large number of empirical studies on retirement. Many have already been mentioned in the section on theoretical models, but some others are entirely empirical. In this section the major findings of those studies are discussed briefly.

5.1. A brief history of the U.S. social security system

The Great Depression inspired a number of state and local governments to institute limited relief efforts, including old age pension programs. But the disparity in benefits, coupled with the limited capacity to finance the programs, led to public pressure for federal intervention. In 1934, the Committee on Economic Security was formed and its report of 1935 formed the basis for the Social Security Act, which was enacted in August 1935. The Act created an old age insurance program, an unemployment compensation program, and three grant programs for the aged, dependent children, and the blind.

Originally intended for individuals in low-paying occupations, the Act was amended in 1939 so that old age insurance was extended to elderly widows and surviving children of retired workers. At that time, the financing was set up to be a pay-as-you-go system, and the program was renamed the Old Age and Survivors Insurance program (OASI).

Extended coverage over time was presumably financed by increased payroll taxes. Most notably, the amendment of 1956 created the Disability Insurance program. Similarly, the 1965 amendment brought about Medicare and that amendment was estimated to raise the cost of the system by $6.5 million during the first year. In 1972, automatic cost-of-living increases were built into the system, but these inflated the value of benefits by more than the increase in wages during the 1970s.

In 1940, the system paid benefits to 200 000 individuals. By 1980, that number had grown to about 36 million recipients. The "solvency" of the system currently remains an issue.

5.2. *Effects of social security on retirement*

Most studies are concerned with the effects of social security pensions on the retirement decision. A few talk more generally about the effect of wages and the shape of the age–earnings profile on retirement. Among the earliest studies to look at the effect of earnings on retirement behavior are Burkhauser (1976, 1979) and Gordon and Blinder (1980). Recall that in a full life-cycle model, not only is the present value of earnings important. The actual shape of the age–earnings profile is an important determinant as well. A steeper profile is likely to encourage leisure taken early in life and later retirement than an early profile.

If there were no correlation between profile slope and present value of the earnings stream, then the effects of present value of earnings on retirement would be ambiguous. This comes directly out of the single-period model. A higher present value of earnings produces an income effect, which tends to encourage earlier retirement, and a substitution effect away from costly leisure which tends to discourage early retirement. The net effect is ambiguous.

The studies by Burkhauser and by Gordon and Blinder find a positive impact of earnings on work. Higher present value of earnings result in lower probabilities of retirement. This suggests that the substitution effect dominates the income effect.

There is another interpretation. Mincer (1974) shows that age–earnings profiles are parallel in logs as education changes. This implies that more educated, wealthier individuals have steeper age–earnings profiles in absolute levels. Steeper profiles reward work in later years relative to work in earlier years. The Burkhauser and Gordon and Blinder findings may be picking up the effect of steeper profiles on retirement rather than the effect of a lifetime income effect being swamped by lifetime substitution effects. This is especially likely since most labor supply studies suggest rather inelastic response of lifetime hours to wages, at least for men.

Many studies do not compute a present value of earnings, but merely allow the current wage to affect the retirement decision. Many of these studies find little or no effect of the current wage on retirement behavior. Studies by Cotterman (1978), Hurd and Boskin (1981), Quinn (1977), and Reimers (1977) find no effect of the current wage on retirement. However, others do find some deterrent effects of current wages on retirement. Those include Boskin (1979), Boskin and Hurd (1978), Burkhauser (1980), Burkhauser and Quinn (1980), Clark and Johnson (1980), Kotlikoff (1979), and Pellechio (1978). The ambiguity here is not surprising, given the less-than-straightforward interpretation of the current wage. Individuals with high current wages at the age of retirement are likely to have steeper profiles, reducing the probability of retirement, but also higher lifetime wealth, with ambiguous effects on the probability of retirement.

One study, Gustman and Steinmeier (1981), includes a measure of the alternative wage in the decision to retire. Since they want to focus on partial retirement, high alternative wages might induce a worker to choose another job over retirement. This is especially likely if the worker faces mandatory retirement on his original job or if the pension is set up in a way that make retirement worthwhile. The study does find a small negative effect of the estimated alternative wage on retirement.

A number of studies examine the effects of social security on retirement behavior. The early studies by Boskin (1977) and Boskin and Hurd (1978) find that the higher are eligible benefits at the time of retirement, the more likely is the individual to retire. In fact, Boskin argues that social security has been the major force in reducing labor force participation rates of older men.

Drawing inferences from these data are difficult, however, for two reasons. First, social security works on labor force behavior in a number of ways. Perhaps the largest and most direct effect is via the earnings test, which taxes the labor market earnings of social security recipients according to some specified formula. This reduces the relative price of leisure in old age. Second, individuals who continue to work make social security contributions out of their earnings, which further reduces the value of work. Third, because of the redistributive nature of social security payments, there are non-neutral lifetime income effects of the social security system. These work differently on different individuals within a generation, but also affect one generation differently from another. Some may find that lifetime wealth is increased by the system, while others may find that it decreases.

A second difficulty encountered in attempting to estimate the impact of social security on retirement includes life-cycle labor supply and identification. There are two ways that one can generate differences in benefit eligibility across individuals. The first is from exogenous changes in the social security system. This is the kind of variation that is appropriate for estimating the effects of social security on retirement. The second is from the benefit formula itself. Social security benefits depend upon earnings and employment over the work life. Individuals with higher benefit entitlements tend to be those who worked more or had higher wages in the past. This is unlikely to be uncorrelated with retirement behavior because of the ability to substitute leisure over the lifetime and also because of unobserved differences in preferences for leisure, which persist over the lifetime.

The caveats notwithstanding, it is useful to describe briefly the results of a number of the studies.

In addition to the work by Boskin, and Boskin and Hurd, Quinn (1977) and Clark, Johnson and McDermed (1980) find that eligibility for social security benefits is associated with earlier retirement. Here is perhaps the most obvious example of the effects of the benefit formula. Those old workers who are currently not entitled to benefits are likely to be ones that only recently began employment in the covered sector. They may continue to work because they have opted to take leisure early in life, or because additional work will affect their eligibility in the future. One would not want to conclude from the results of these studies that an increase in benefits or tightening of the earnings test would affect retirement in the ways estimated using this approaches.

In light of this argument, it is not surprising that Pellechio (1978, 1981), Burkhauser (1980), and Hurd and Boskin (1981) find that individuals with higher social security wealth are less likely to retire. They are likely to have been high-income, high-hours-of-work individuals in the early parts of their lives and it is not unreasonable to expect this behavior to persist in old age. Hanoch and Honig (1983) find that social security wealth, reflected by variations in the social security benefit, has a strong negative effect on participation, particularly among women. Yet persons without social security coverage at all have less of a tendency to participate. This suggests that those (women) whose benefits are most likely affected by work through the social security formula are those most anxious to participate. Fields and Mitchell (1982a) also find that social security benefits increase with the age of retirement. This is not surprising since the benefit formula is a direct function of the years of work. This reverse causality should be less important for men than women since a larger proportion of women workers have worked close to the number of years at which social security benefits vest (historically, ten years). What is more interesting is that they find that the actuarial values of those benefits increase with the age of retirement. This is the opposite of the pattern found for private pensions.

In another study, Fields and Mitchell (1982) examine the effects of various changes in social security or retirement behavior. They conclude that the policy that is likely to have the largest effect is tilting the relationship between social security benefits and age of retirement. Similarly, Blinder, Gordon and Wise (1980) argue that social security (as contrasted with private pensions) is more than actuarially fair between ages 62 and 65 (later retirement is worth more).

They conclude that social security does not discourage early retirement. They also point out that work affects entitlement so this offsets contributions made to the social security fund. (Those effects are highly nonlinear, however, taking a discrete jump at the time of vesting.) Finally, among the largest estimates come from Boskin (1977). He estimates that a reduction in the implicit tax on earnings (via the earnings test) from 50 to 33 percent would reduce the average probability of retirement by about 60 percent. These early estimates have not been replicated in any other analysis, however, and many regard them as outliers.

Hausman and Wise (1982) estimate a continuous time qualitative choice model using data from the Retirement History Survey. Their approach is to parameterize the density function on retirement by a given age. One of the strongest findings is that having a larger increment in social security benefits associated with an additional year of work significantly reduces the probability of retirement occurring in that year.

The studies that examine the effects of pensions on retirement behavior are similar in spirit and methodology because in many respects, although not all, social security is simply a public version of a private pension. As such some of the same considerations apply.

For the purpose of estimation there is one important difference: Because there are many private pension plans, one is more likely to observe differences in pension entitlements that are not simply a function of past labor force behavior than was the case with social security. This is true because plans vary dramatically across companies [see Lazear (1982)] and because even a given company's plan changes frequently. On the other hand, workers can sort themselves across companies to take advantage of the plan that best caters to their tastes. Since most jobs in the private sector are covered by the same social security system, the same kind of sorting cannot be a factor in analyses of the social security system.

One of the most important differences between pensions and social security is that pensions and wages are directly linked through constraints imposed by competition in the labor market. It is more reasonable to think of an exogenous increase in social security benefits that does not alter wages, except indirectly. The same is not true of pensions. An increase in pension benefits must be offset by a decrease in wages, unless the pension actually causes increased productivity. This relation is ignored in most studies of pensions and will be neglected here. But in the section that follows (Section 6) the relation of wages to pensions is of the essence.

5.3. *Effects of private pensions on retirement*

At the time when labor force participation of older men was falling dramatically, there was a concomitant increase in the proportion of workers covered by private pension plans. Blinder (1982) reports that the proportion of the labor force (not of retirees) covered by some private pension plan ran from 16 to 33 percent between 1950 and 1975.

Burkhauser (1976, 1979) examined data on auto workers and found that those for whom pensions declined more sharply with delayed retirement were the ones most likely to retire early. This result seems sensible. I found [Lazear (1982, 1983)] that the rate of decline in pension value with deferred retirement increases with tenure, so Burkhauser's results also imply that those workers who have worked for the firm the longest are most likely to accept early retirement.

There is evidence that supports the view that those with pensions leave the work force earlier. Gordon and Blinder (1980), Gustman and Steinmeier (1981), and Quinn (1977) find that those with pensions are more likely to leave their jobs than those without pensions. Others [Reimers (1977), Burkhauser and Quinn (1980), and Kotlikoff (1979)] find the opposite. Clark and Johnson (1980) find males with pensions are more likely, but females with private pensions are less likely to retire than those without. Hamermesh (1981) finds that pension wealth is positively associated with the probability of retirement. Mitchell and Fields (1984) combine pension and wages, arguing that what is relevant is the change in monetary wealth associated with additional years of employment, irrespective of its source. This seems the most sensible way to proceed. Like Burkhauser, they find that individuals with the lowest increase in monetary wealth with additional years of work are most likely to retire. They also examine worker sorting across plans and find that the sorting accounts for some, but not all of the variation.

It is not surprising that there is a failure to obtain uniform results across studies. Even for the same demographic group, it matters a great deal what is held constant. For example, a simple correlation between the existence of pension coverage and age of retirement is unlikely to be particularly informative. If the pension were actuarially independent of age of retirement then, other things constant, the anticipated effect would be to increase the probability of retirement. For a given wage, having a pension that is actuarially fair has no effects other than a pure income effect on leisure. It is not a subsidy to leisure now, because delayed retirement results in the same payment, just condensed into a shorter number of years.

Pension value is rarely independent of age of retirement. If pensions decline on average with delayed retirement, then this would reinforce the tendency to observe a negative correlation between pension value and age of retirement. Offsetting this, however, is the fact that wages and pensions are positively correlated [see Asch (1984) and Taubman (1982)], in part because many pension formulas depend directly upon earnings. Higher and more rapidly growing wages both act to deter retirement, via substitution away from more costly leisure. More subtle is that the existence of a pension may also be correlated with past wages, affecting the optimal path of leisure over the life cycle. Mitchell and Fields (1984) come close to taking all the effects into account, but still ignore earlier wages. Their estimates suggest that a neutral 10 percent increase in pensions or social security would bring about only a tenth of a year reduction in the age of retirement.

With the exception of Gustman and Steinmeier, distinction is rarely made between leaving the primary job and leaving the labor force. Although some pension formulas make benefits contingent upon not having another job (like the social security earnings test), relatively few do [see Banker's Trust (1975, 1980)]. The considerations that make a worker leave his job, but not the labor force, have to do with the relation of wages and benefits on the current job to those on his best alternative job. Those data are very difficult to obtain.

The major criticism of the literature on retirement is that it treats the question in more of a vacuum than is necessary. There is an enormous literature on the supply of labor and much of it is germane to the retirement question. Yet most of the work on retirement ignores other labor supply estimates and makes no attempt to link the two. There are some exceptions, but most focus on the theoretical rather than empirical linkage.

6. Pensions

Private pensions warrant significant attention for a number of reasons in any examination of retirement behavior. First, private pension coverage has grown continuously since 1950 at a substantial rate. Second, private pensions are as much a part of the retirement decision as the wage. Third, private pensions vary significantly in their coverage and their effects are by no means neutral.

Pension coverage varies by occupation, union status, and demographic characteristics of the worker. Freeman (1978) and Taubman (1982) find that union workers are more likely to be covered by pensions than otherwise similar nonunion workers. Taubman, using the 1977 Retirement History Survey, also finds that among older men, being married and white increases the probability of having a pension. The more educated are more likely to have a pension as well [Taubman (1981)]. The black–white differential in pension coverage is wiped out if earnings and education are held constant. As one might expect, among women, professionals are more likely to have a pension than are the unskilled. For the same reasons, probably having to do with lifetime labor force attachments and vesting restrictions, never-married females are more likely to have pensions than are widows. In terms of pension size, occupational variation seems to be most important here. Clerks, for example, receive less than unskilled workers, most of that reflecting the union/nonunion differential since the latter are more likely to unionize.

Pensions also vary by sector. For example, federal workers tend to enjoy more generous pension benefits than private sector employees. They tend to have more liberal early retirement benefits, retirees' benefits are fully indexed to the CPI and they do not have social security offsets. On the other hand, federal workers make explicit contributions to their pension fund, something rarely found in the private sector.[8]

Pension formulas vary substantially across firms, but there are two basic types: defined contribution and defined benefit. In the defined contribution plan, a worker and/or his employer put a specified amount into a fund on his behalf. That fund is invested in securities. When the worker retires, the value of his accumulated portfolio is assessed. Sometimes the worker receives this amount as a lump sum. More often, it is converted to an annuity, the expected present value of which equals the portfolio value at the time of retirement (or at some date near to it). The defined contribution plan is the most straightforward, but it is also relatively rare. Although a substantial proportion of the plans in this country are defined contribution plans, they cover only a small part of the work force because they predominate in smaller firms.

The vast majority of covered workers have a defined benefit pension plan. Defined benefit plans specify the annual flow of pension benefits as some function of years of service and of earnings. The "pattern" or "flat" plans make pensions a function only of years of service. These plans take the form:

$$\text{annual pension benefit} = (\text{years of service})(\$\text{ amount}).$$

These plans predominate among blue-collar workers.

Most white-collar workers, and more so as one moves up the occupational hierarchy, have the "conventional" plan. This defined-benefit plan makes the pension amount depend not only upon years of service, but also upon salary. It takes the form:

$$\text{annual pension benefit} = (\text{years of service})(\%\text{ figure})(\text{salary average}).$$

The salary average can be over any period, but it is most typically over the last five to ten years of employment. (Often the highest five out of the last ten are used.)

There are a number of questions about pensions that are of importance to retirement. Perhaps the first question is: "Why are there pensions in the first place?" A pension is a forced savings device. In a competitive labor market, one would think that firms that did not require their employees to take some of their compensation in the form of pensions would be preferred. At the very least, it would seem that pensions should be voluntary, allowing some workers to take their benefits in the form of higher wages if they desire.

[8] See Lazear and Asch (1982).

Second, what effects do pensions have on labor turnover, on worker effort, and on date of retirement? The analysis discussed in earlier sections held wages constant, treating the pension as an exogenous change. However, the pension and wage obviously are both part of the compensation of any given worker and productivity places constraints on the ways that one moves with the other.

Consider the second question first. Most analyses view the pension as exogenous and consider variations. There are some exceptions, where an attempt is made empirically to estimate the tradeoff between wages and pensions. These studies do not try seriously to determine whether the pension has any effect on behavior.

In order to understand the effects of a pension, social security or wage changes on worker behavior in equilibrium, we set up a simple framework in which the issues can be analyzed.[9] There are two primary concerns. One is worker labor supply and turnover, the other is worker effort and investment in human capital. The first is a choice over number of hours worked. The second is a choice over output per hour. To begin, simply consider a one-period model, which is then generalized to the multi-period case. What is shown is that all of the implications of the single-period model continue to hold in the multi-period case.

Workers are paid a wage, W, and are entitled to a pension, P, which may depend upon years of service, salary, and other factors. Since this is a one-period model, all that is relevant is the total time worked over the lifetime, H. (Hours and years are collapsed into this single metric.)

The worker choice over hours of work is subject to worker control. Workers trade off additional income against the utility from forgone leisure which has value $L(H)$. (This might instead reflect earnings on an alternative job.) Separability is assumed so that the analysis can be made simple and to yield unambiguous results.

The worker can affect the productivity of an hour spent at work by selecting K, thought of as the level of effort and/or human capital. If V is the value of raw labor, then K and V are normalized so that output per unit of time, H, is the sum of V and K. Thus, lifetime output is given by

$$\text{lifetime output} = (V+K)H. \tag{6}$$

Producing additional units of K also carries with it some cost. If K is thought of as effort, then the cost is the disutility of effort. If K is thought of as human capital, then the cost is the resources allocated to formal schooling, on-the-job training, or whatever was required to produce the human capital. Let the cost of production of K be given by $C(K)$.

[9]The model comes from Lazear (1983), which examines these and other issues in greater depth.

Assume that the worker's utility function has the form:

$$U = \text{income} + \text{pension} - L(H) - C(K)$$

or

$$U = HW + P - L(H) - C(K). \tag{7}$$

Then the worker's problem is to select H and K so as to maximize utility.

What is crucial to this problem is that the comparative labor market places a constraint on the sum of wages and pension. In the simplest case where all workers at a given firm are identical, the representative individual's lifetime output must equal his lifetime wage, or

$$HW + P = (V + K)H \tag{8}$$

or

$$W = V + K - P/H.$$

Equation (8) places a severe constraint on the relation of wages to pensions over the life cycle.

How does the worker behave and how does the existence of a pension affect that behavior? As we have already seen, the empirical evidence is less than unequivocal on establishing the relationship. There are theoretical reasons why this is the case, revolving around the market constraint and the issue of what varies and what is held constant.

The first point is that if the worker is fully cognizant of (8) or, more precisely, if the worker is forced to feel the bite of (8), then no matter what the structure of the pension, it cannot affect worker behavior. This is not an artifact of the one-period construct. The statement is true in a multi-period setting as well.

This is easily seen. If the worker recognizes that (8) must hold, then his general maximization problem

$$\max_{H,K} WH + P - L(H) - C(K) \tag{9}$$

becomes

$$\max_{H,K} (V + K - P/H)H + P - L(H) - C(K)$$

or

$$\max_{H,K} (V + K)H - L(H) - C(K). \tag{10}$$

This has first-order conditions

$$H = C'(K) \tag{10a}$$

and

$$(V + K) = L'(H). \tag{10b}$$

Note two things. First, the pension is irrelevant. Since what the worker receives in pension is paid for by reduced lifetime earnings, all changes are offsetting. This is a trivial result. If the firm simply takes back with one hand what it gives with the other, there can be no effect on behavior. The pension, no matter how odd the formula may appear, cannot affect behavior so long as the corresponding wage adjustments are taken into account by the worker.

Second, the problem maximized in (10) is the one that yields first-best efficiency. In (10a) the worker sets the marginal cost of effort (or human capital) equal to the value of that effort in increasing output. In (10b), he sets the marginal cost of an "hour" of work equal to the true value of an hour of work.

Although this result is a somewhat trivial one, it has important implications for the empirical work on retirement. Suppose, for example, that the market imposed the constraint implied by (8) on each worker. Then a regression of hours worked, or equivalently, years of retirement on the existence or size of the pension would reveal no effect. If lifetime wages are held constant, then this implies that $(V + K)H$, or lifetime output is higher. But whether these earnings are higher because of higher hours H, reflecting a flatter $L(H)$ function, or because of higher effort, K, reflecting a flatter $C(K)$ function makes a difference. For a given wage *per unit of time*, a higher pension implies that $V + K$ must be higher. From (10b) it is clear that hours of work should be larger and retirement should come later. Recall that Reimers, Burkhauser and Quinn, and Kotlikoff, obtained this result.

In order to obtain the result that pensions reduce the age of retirement, something else must be at work. It seems that unless there is some distortion, it is unlikely that there will be a situation where more productive workers retire earlier. It is possible only if $L'(H) < 0$, i.e. if there is a backward-bending labor supply function in the relevant range.

There are distortions that are built into compensation schedules. What was necessary to eliminate all effects of a pension (as distinguished from any other wage change) was that the worker was forced somehow to internalize (8). One way to do this would be to allow the worker to make voluntary contributions to a defined contribution pension plan. Then, each dollar contributed to the pension reduces his wages correspondingly by one dollar.

It is conceivable to argue, however, that defined benefit plans do not make this tradeoff explicit to the worker. Nor is this a mere perception on the worker's part. It results when the wage formulas or pension formulas are made independent to any one worker, even though they meet the adding up constraint for the entire firm.

Again suppose that all workers are identical. Eq. (8) tells us that for the firm to break even, it is necessary that $W = V + K - P/H$. But suppose that the firm sets $W = V + K - \overline{P/H}$, where $\overline{P/H}$ is a constant, chosen so that in equilibrium $\overline{P/H} = P^*/H^*$, where P^* and H^* are the values selected by the worker. This is a different problem from (10). Here, the worker takes the implicit pension deduction as given, no one worker having any effect on the deduction, but all workers behaving identically. This produces the kind of situation that occurs when a group of friends with similar tastes go to a restaurant and agree to split the bill. Each orders the same thing, but each individual is induced to order too much because he only pays $1/N$ of the bill (where N is the number of diners).

If pensions are structured this way, the worker might be told that his wage is

$$W = V + K - \overline{P/H}, \tag{11}$$

where $\overline{P/H}$ is the equilibrium level of pension cost per unit of time. The worker's maximization problem is no longer (10), but becomes:

$$\max_{H,K} \left(V + K - \overline{P/H}\right)H + P - L(H) - C(K). \tag{12}$$

This yields first-order conditions:

$$\frac{\partial}{\partial K} = H + \frac{\partial P}{\partial K} - C'(K) = 0 \tag{12a}$$

and

$$\frac{\partial}{\partial H} = V + K - \left(\overline{P/H}\right) + \frac{\partial P}{\partial H} - L'(H) = 0. \tag{12b}$$

Equations (12a) and (12b) allow the pension formula to depend upon the wage rate (through K) per unit of time and the amount of time worked with the firm (through H). Under certain circumstances, (12a) reduces to (10a) and (12b) reduces to (10b), which implies that the pension causes no distortion.

One such case occurs when the pension is a defined benefit pattern plan. Recall that a pattern plan depends only upon years of service and not upon the final salary, i.e.

$$P = \beta H,$$

where β is the dollar amount that accrues for each year of service. Here, $\partial P/\partial K = 0$ so (12a) reduces to (10a). Also, $\partial P/\partial H = \beta$. In equilibrium, $P = \beta H^*$, where H^* is the value chosen by each worker. Therefore, the amount by which the wage is reduced, $\overline{P/H}$, is simply $\beta H^*/H^* = \beta$. Since $\partial P/\partial H = \overline{P/H}$, (12b) reduces to (10b) and all is efficient. The pattern plan produces no distortion even when a worker can affect his own pension in a way that does not directly reduce his wage.

The same is not true of defined benefit conventional plans. Here, the formula is

$$P = \gamma WH,$$

so that the pension depends not only upon years of service with the firm, H, but also upon the annual salary, W.

The worker is induced to increase his hours of work and effort. To see this, note that now $\partial P/\partial K = (\partial P/\partial W)(\partial W/\partial K) = \gamma H$ so that (12a) becomes:

$$H = \frac{C'(K)}{1+\gamma}. \tag{13a}$$

This is not identical to (10a) unless $\gamma = 0$ (i.e. no pension). But, since

$$\begin{aligned}\overline{P/H} &= \gamma WH^*/H^* \\ &= \gamma W,\end{aligned}$$

and since $\partial P/\partial H = \gamma W$, (12a) is

$$V + K - \gamma W + \gamma W - L'(H) = 0 \tag{13b}$$

or

$$V + K = L'(H).$$

(13b) is identical to (10b).

The failure of (13a) to reduce to (10a) implies that the value of H and K are not chosen optimally. Figure 5.7 makes this clear.

The first-order conditions (10a) and (10b) are drawn in and intersect at A, yielding H_0, K_0 as the solution. Point B is the intersection of first-order conditions (13a) and (13b). Both $H_1 > H_0$ and $K_1 > K_0$ so the conventional defined benefit plan induces workers to supply too much effort and too much time to the job. The reason is analogous to the restaurant problem. The worker can increase his pension by working harder. The marginal effect of work on his pension exceeds the average amount by which his wage is reduced because he does not suffer the full consequences of his action.

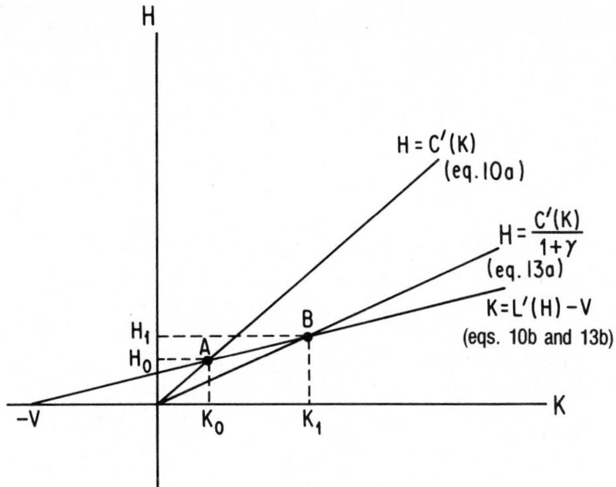

Figure 5.7

It should be reiterated that this is not a necessary consequence of a defined benefit conventional plan. The effect of the pension can always be offset by explicitly forcing the worker to recognize the constraint in (8). For example, if the worker were told that his wage would rise only by $1/(1+\gamma)$ for each dollar's worth of additional output, then all the distortions of the pension are undone. Since $\overline{P/H} = \gamma W$ in equilibrium, this is tantamount to making the worker's wage function

$$W = \frac{1}{1+\gamma}(V+K)$$

rather than

$$\begin{aligned} W &= V + K - \overline{P/H} \\ &= V + K - \gamma W. \end{aligned}$$

Then the worker's problem from (9) is

$$\max_{H,K} \left(\frac{V+K}{1+\gamma}\right) H + \gamma \left(\frac{V+K}{1+\gamma}\right) H - L(H) - C(K), \tag{14}$$

with first-order conditions:

$$\frac{\partial}{\partial K} = \frac{H}{1+\gamma} + \frac{\gamma H}{1+\gamma} - C'(K) = 0 \tag{14a}$$

or

$$H - C'(K) = 0$$

and

$$\frac{\partial}{\partial H} = \left(\frac{V+K}{1+\gamma}\right) + \gamma\left(\frac{V+K}{1+\gamma}\right) - L'(H) = 0 \tag{14b}$$

or

$$V + K = L'(H),$$

so (14a) and (14b) are identical to (10a) and (10b). An implication is that the coefficient on education, experience, and any other wage-augmenting choice variable should be smaller if the worker has a conventional pension plan. Of course, this ignores any reason for the pension in the first place.

There are a number of other provisions associated with pensions that affect labor supply in general, and retirement in particular. Perhaps the most often discussed, but not well understood is that of vesting. Pensions are generally not vested until some years of service is exceeded. Most often, that number is ten, but it is not unusual to find partial vesting at as few as five years.

It is often stated that nonvesting of pensions tends to increase the average tenure of the work force. This view comes from thinking of the pension as exogenous. But pensions that do not vest immediately are more of a cross-subsidization than anything else. It turns out that the effect of nonvesting is to shorten the tenure of "leavers", but to lengthen the tenure of "stayers". Since retirees are primarily stayers, i.e. those who are employed with the firm for a period long enough to vest, one effect of having pensions that do not immediately vest is to increase the age of retirement.[10] This is because individuals who leave the firm or labor force early in their work lives are not generally thought of as "retired" individuals.

The analysis is somewhat complicated but sufficiently important and misunderstood to consider it here. The basic intuition is that a nonvesting clause lowers

[10] The effect of nonvesting is to make few people leave with years of service close to, but less than the vesting year. This can, on average, lengthen or shorten tenure and age of retirement for that group.

the total compensation per unit of time worked below the marginal product for those who leave early. This induces them to leave even earlier. But those who stay beyond vesting find that their total compensation levels rise above marginal products, inducing longer work. Again this is not a necessary consequence. It can be offset by an appropriate (in this case, discontinuous) alteration of the wage function. But such offsetting wage functions are not observed in practice.

In order to consider the effects of vesting, it is necessary to allow for some workers to leave before the vesting date and others to stay beyond that date. The easiest way to do this is to allow for two types of individuals: the first type has alternative use of time function $L(H)$ and the second has alternative use of time function $\tilde{L}(H)$ such that $\tilde{L}'(H) > L'(H)$ for all H. Let λ of the population be of the first type and $(1-\lambda)$ be of the second type.

Let us consider a pattern plan that does not immediately vest. The simplest form of nonvesting is to assume that β, the dollar per year of service, is zero if $H < \overline{H}$. There are three cases. First, $H < \overline{H}$ and $\tilde{H} < \overline{H}$. This is the same as no pension since $\overline{P/H} = 0$ and so there is full efficiency. Second, $H > \overline{H}$ and $\tilde{H} > \overline{H}$. This is the case analyzed in eqs. (12a) and (12b) as fully vested pension benefits and it yields efficiency as well. The only interesting case arises when $H < \overline{H}$, $\tilde{H} \geq \overline{H}$ or when $H \geq \overline{H}$, $\tilde{H} < \overline{H}$.

The important feature is that there is subsidization of the stayers by the leavers and this causes a distortion. The wage paid to workers must be sufficiently low to cover the pension costs to λ of the population who are stayers. Thus, the zero profit condition that replaces (8) is

$$\lambda(WH+\beta H)+(1-\lambda)W\tilde{H} = (V+K)(\lambda H+(1-\lambda)\tilde{H}) \tag{8'}$$

or

$$W = V+K-\frac{\lambda\beta}{\lambda+(1-\lambda)(\tilde{H}/H)}.$$

Now, the maximization problem for the stayers is

$$\max_{K,H} H\left[V+K-\left(\frac{\lambda\beta}{\lambda+(1-\lambda)(\tilde{H}^*/H^*)}\right)\right]+\beta H-C(K)-L(H), \tag{10'}$$

where stars denote equilibrium values. The first-order conditions are

$$\frac{\partial}{\partial K} = H - C'(K) = 0 \tag{10'a}$$

and

$$\frac{\partial}{\partial H} = V+K+\frac{(1-\lambda)\beta}{\lambda+(1-\lambda)(\tilde{H}^*/H^*)} - L'(H) = 0. \tag{10'b}$$

Similarly, for leavers,

$$\max_{\tilde{K},\tilde{H}} \tilde{H}\left[V+\tilde{K}-\left(\frac{\lambda\beta}{\lambda+(1-\lambda)(\tilde{H}^*/H^*)}\right)\right]-C(\tilde{K})-\tilde{L}(\tilde{H}) \qquad (\tilde{10}')$$

since $\tilde{H}<\overline{H}$ so pension $=0$. The first-order conditions are

$$\frac{\partial}{\partial K}=\tilde{H}-C'(\tilde{K})=0 \qquad (\tilde{10}'\text{a})$$

and

$$\frac{\partial}{\partial \tilde{H}}=V+\tilde{K}-\frac{\lambda\beta}{\lambda+(1-\lambda)(\tilde{H}^*/H^*)}-\tilde{L}'(\tilde{H})=0. \qquad (\tilde{10}'\text{b})$$

The situation is shown in Figure 5.8.

Points Q and $\tilde{Q}$ are the efficient points for movers and stayers, respectively, and are obtained in the absence of a pension. Note that $H>\tilde{H}$ and $K>\tilde{K}$ because $L'(H)<\tilde{L}'(H)$ for all H.

In the presence of the pension that does not vest immediately, (10′a) and ($\tilde{10}$′a) are identical to (10a), but (10′b) and ($\tilde{10}$′b) shift as shown in Figure 5.8. Thus, the new equilibrium points are R and $\tilde{R}$ for movers and stayers.

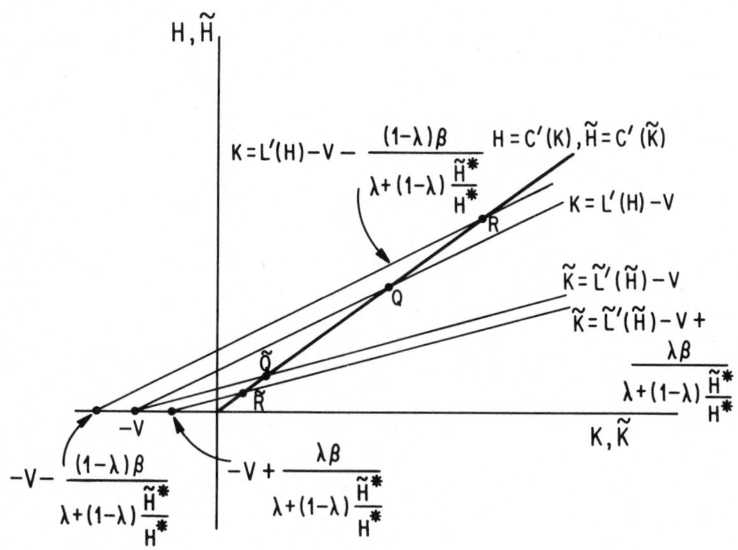

Figure 5.8

The most important result is that both H and K deviate from the efficient levels. Stayers spend too much time on the job and invest in too much human capital and effort because the marginal return to a year worked,

$$V+K+\frac{\beta(1-\lambda)}{\lambda+(1-\lambda)(\tilde{H}^{*}/H^{*})},$$

exceeds the true value of work, $V+K$. Similarly, leavers leave too early and do not invest in enough human capital and effort because the marginal return to a year worked,

$$V+\tilde{K}-\frac{\lambda\beta}{\lambda+(1-\lambda)(\tilde{H}^{*}/H^{*})},$$

is less than the true value of work, $V+\tilde{K}$.

This implies, first, that average tenure in the economy may rise or fall with the addition of an imperfect vesting provision. Although average tenure rises for those who eventually receive a pension, average tenure falls for those who do not. The effect on the average for the economy as a whole depends upon the proportion of people in each group and upon the increase and decrease for the respective groups, which depends in turn upon the slopes of $L(H)$ and $\tilde{L}(H)$. But it is indeed quite possible that average tenure falls as the result of vesting. Retirement age should rise, however, because the stayers are the individuals who show up in the retirement statistics and their average years increase. Second, since leavers subsidize stayers, one would expect some firms to cater only to leavers, offering no pension and paying wage $W=V+K$. This type of self-sorting, akin to Salop and Salop (1976), and discussed by Asch (1984), causes the nonfully vested pension equilibrium to become efficient. The reason is that firms that offer pensions obtain only stayers. Thus $\lambda=1$ and (10′b) become identical with (10b).[11]

The analysis for conventional plans is similar, has the same implications, and is not repeated here.

While on the issue of vesting, it is useful to point out here that vesting is not all that it is made out to be. There are a number of reasons, all of which derive from the definition of vesting.

A worker who is vested may leave the firm and continue to be entitled to his accrued pension benefits. But that does not imply that the worker receives a check for his pension upon separation. Under most circumstances, it merely entitles the worker to receive a pension flow, consistent with his final accrued

[11]Asch explores this mechanism both at the theoretical level and empirically.

pension level, when he reaches the firm's normal retirement age (usually 65). But the current accrued amount available at age 65 might be a very small number for various reasons.

First, accrual rates can be nonlinear and when they are, later years of employment tend to be weighted more heavily. It is not unusual, for example, to find a formula that entitles the worker to 1.5 percent of final salary times years of service up to 10 years plus 3 percent of final salary times years of service over 10. End-weighting the pension accrual can make the vesting provision unimportant.

Second, in an inflationary environment, tying the pension to final salary makes vesting at 10 years almost worthless. For example, consider a worker who begins his employment at age 25 and quits at age 35, after becoming vested. His pension is computed, based on his nominal salary at age 35. But by the time he receives it at age 65, 30 years of inflation will have occurred so that the pension flow from that job will be trivial in real terms. A defined contribution plan does not suffer this drawback because the pension flow is based upon accumulated assets valued at the market, which presumably accounts for inflation.[12]

Finally, if, as I have argued, early retirement is more lucrative than normal retirement, leaving the job before the age of early retirement precludes the possibility of taking these higher, early retirement benefits. Vesting only entitles the worker to benefits upon reaching normal retirement age.

We have not yet generated a situation where pensions actually can reduce the age of retirement yet a number of researchers (Gordon and Blinder, Gustman and Steinmeier, and Quinn) find evidence for such a relationship. In order to analyze this possibility, it is necessary to extend the simple one-period framework to the multi-period context. Let us start by showing that the period during which the pension cost is subtracted from earnings is irrelevant, again, as long as the worker is forced to be made aware of the constraint on total compensation. The basic result, that pensions cannot affect behavior if the corresponding wage adjustments are accounted for by the worker, still holds.

Tilting the age–earnings profile has no effect on behavior. This is easily seen. Consider the two periods denoted by time subscripts 1 and 2. The worker's problem is now

$$\max_{K, H_1, H_2} W_1 H_1 + W_2 H_2 + P(H_1, H_2, W_1, W_2) - C(K) - L(H_1, H_2) \tag{15}$$

subject to

$$W_1 H_1 + W_2 H_2 + P = (V + K)(H_1 + H_2) \tag{8''}$$

[12]This discussion relates to the adjustment of pension benefits before retirement to inflation. There are also post-retirement adjustments. Federal workers have full adjustment to the CPI. Clark, Allen and Sumner (1983) report that these post-retirement increases amounted to about two-fifths of the change in the CPI during the 1973–79 period.

and

$$W_1 = V + K - \theta P/H_1, \qquad W_2 = V + K - (1-\theta)P/H_2, \quad 0 \le \theta \le 1,$$

where θ is the proportion of pension costs borne in period 1. First-order conditions are

$$\begin{aligned}\frac{\partial}{\partial K} &= H_1 - \theta\frac{\partial P}{\partial K} + H_2 - (1-\theta)\frac{\partial P}{\partial K} + \frac{\partial P}{\partial K} - C'(K) = 0\\ &= H_1 + H_2 - C'(K) = 0,\end{aligned} \tag{15a}$$

$$\begin{aligned}\frac{\partial}{\partial H_1} &= V + K - \theta\frac{\partial P}{\partial H_1} - (1-\theta)\frac{\partial P}{\partial H_1} + \frac{\partial P}{\partial H_1} - \frac{\partial L}{\partial H_1} = 0\\ &= V + K - \frac{\partial L}{\partial H_1} = 0,\end{aligned} \tag{15b}$$

$$\begin{aligned}\frac{\partial}{\partial H_2} &= V + K - \theta\frac{\partial P}{\partial H_2} - (1-\theta)\frac{\partial P}{\partial H_2} + \frac{\partial P}{\partial H_2} - \frac{\partial L}{\partial H_2} = 0\\ &= V + K - \frac{\partial L}{\partial H_2} = 0.\end{aligned} \tag{15c}$$

Equations (15a)–(15c) are the two-period analogue of (10a), (10b) and bring about efficiency. Independent of the division of pension costs, i.e. for any θ, as long as the worker is aware of the competitive firm's response to his pension increase, all is internalized and efficient.

This does not imply that pensions never distort incentives. If the worker's own wage does not adjust to his own pension, but rather to the average pension on which he has only a trivial effect, then inefficiencies can result as they do in the one-period case. More fundamentally, if the "true" wage, including the value of pension accrual and other perks, does not equal marginal product, and if the worker is allowed to choose his hours, then inefficiencies result. But this point, which is analyzed in more detail in Lazear (1981), is quite independent of pensions and holds even when all compensation takes the form of a direct money wage.

How then can the pension encourage earlier retirement? The key is the way in which pension varies with years of service, H, and considering what is held constant.

It is quite straightforward to see why the simple correlation between age of retirement and pensions can be negative. Suppose that the individual's wage is independent of his pension benefit (except to the extent that it affects the mean for the firm). Think of period 1 in the two-period model as time worked between ages 25 and 45 and period 2 as time worked between age 45 and retirement. Then smaller values of H_2 can be interpreted as earlier retirement. Under these circumstances,

$$W_1 = V + K - \frac{\theta \bar{P}}{H_1^*},$$

and

$$W_2 = V + K - \frac{(1-\theta)\bar{P}}{H_2^*},$$

where $\bar{P}$ is the equilibrium pension and H_1^* and H_2^* are the equilibrium hours of work in periods 1 and 2. The worker's problem is then

$$\max_{K, H_1, H_2} \left(V + K - \frac{\theta \bar{P}}{H_1^*} \right) H_1 + \left(V + K - \frac{(1-\theta)\bar{P}}{H_2^*} \right) H_2 + P(W_1, W_2, H_1, H_2)$$
$$- C(K) - L(H_1, H_2), \tag{16}$$

with first-order conditions:

$$\frac{\partial}{\partial K} = H_1 + H_2 + \left(\frac{\partial P}{\partial W_1} + \frac{\partial P}{\partial W_2} \right) - C'(K) = 0, \tag{16a}$$

$$\frac{\partial}{\partial H_1} = V + K - \frac{\theta \bar{P}}{H_1^*} + \frac{\partial P}{\partial H_1} - \frac{\partial L}{\partial H_1} = 0, \tag{16b}$$

$$\frac{\partial}{\partial H_2} = \left(V + K - \frac{(1-\theta)\bar{P}}{H_1^*} \right) + \frac{\partial P}{\partial H_2} - \frac{\partial L}{\partial H_2} = 0. \tag{16c}$$

Equation (16c) allows us to determine sufficient conditions for a negative relationship between $\bar{P}$ and H_2. Suppose for simplicity that $L(H_1, H_2)$ is separable with $\partial L/\partial H_1, \partial L/\partial H_2 > 0$, $\partial^2 L/\partial H_t^2 > 0$, $\partial^2 L/\partial H_1 \partial H_2 = 0$. Then H_2 falls with $\bar{P}$ whenever the average "tax" on wages to pay for the pension in period 2 exceeds the increment to the pension value associated with additional work time in period 2. It is easy to imagine situations when this condition, that $[(1-\theta)\bar{P}]/H_2^* > \partial P/\partial H_2$. As θ goes to zero, the entire pension is paid for out of period 2's wages, but $\partial P/\partial H_1 > 0$ implies that accruals were made in period 1. A standard pattern plan yields this result when $\theta = 0$. Since $P = \beta(H_1^* + H_2^*)$,

$$\frac{(1-\theta)\overline{P}}{H_2^*} = \beta\left(\frac{H_1^*}{H_2^*} + 1\right).$$

But $\partial P/\partial H_2^* = \beta$ so $[(1-\theta)\overline{P}]/H^* > \partial P/\partial H_2$ and retirement occurs earlier than it would be in the absence of a pension.

It is not necessary that the pattern plan result in earlier retirement. For example, if $\theta = 1$, the opposite result is guaranteed.

There is one phenomenon that dominates the pension picture in large American firms, which ensures a negative simple relation between size or existence of a pension and age of retirement. In the average large firm, $\partial P/\partial H_2$ is negative, not positive as H_2 gets large. As individuals near the date of normal retirement, additional years of work result in lower expected pension values. For workers in firms for which this is true, (16c) implies that there must be a negative relation of pensions to age of retirement. Although it is not true of all firms, there is a large number for which $\partial P/\partial H_2 < 0$.

Evidence on this issue is available in Lazear (1982, 1983). There, two data sets were constructed, using data from the Banker's Trust (1975, 1980) on about 250 of the largest pension plans in the country, covering nearly 10 million workers. The pension formulas were programmed and the expected present value of pension benefits, contingent upon date of retirement, tenure, and salary was calculated for hypothetical individuals. Table 5.3 contains a small subset of the results.

The average (across plans) expected present value of pension benefits as a function of age of retirement is reported. For the average conventional plan, an individual who would have 20 years of tenure at the normal age of retirement finds that his pension benefit value peaks if he retires eight years before the normal age of retirement. For those with 30 and 40 years of tenure, it declines throughout. For the average pattern plan, it peaks at seven years before normal retirement for individuals who would have 20 years of tenure at the normal date. For those with 30 and 40 years of tenure, it declines throughout. The idea that $\partial P/\partial H_2$ is negative appears to be more than a mere conjecture. It is also consistent with the notion that pensions act as severance pay, buying out workers who are willing to retire early in order to save on wages that in the future will exceed the worker's marginal product.[13]

There is also some empirical evidence on the relation of pensions to tenure. Schiller and Weiss (1979) were among the first to investigate this relationship.

[13] One major potential source of error is the case of the same life tables, independent of age of retirement. As Anderson and Burkhauser (1983) have shown, the age of subsequent death is positively related to age of retirement.

Table 5.3
Average expected present value of pension benefits (1980 Bankers Trust Data) Salary = $25,000/year at normal retirement age.

Tenure at normal retirement age	20	30	40
Years before normal retirement age			
Conventional plans:			
10	55 958	107 585	158 225
9	56 822	105 111	151 713
8	57 200	101 951	144 918
7	57 081	98 212	137 902
6	56 522	94 213	130 778
5	55 604	90 176	123 844
4	54 142	85 524	116 234
3	52 165	80 656	108 553
2	49 549	75 143	100 236
1	46 903	69 863	92 429
0	43 244	63 165	79 476
Pattern plans (Benefits Independent of Salary):			
10	20 450	40 651	64 349
9	21 085	40 103	61 913
8	21 513	39 296	59 276
7	21 704	38 262	56 477
6	21 667	37 031	53 554
5	21 454	36 164	51 868
4	21 053	34 485	48 489
3	20 498	32 716	45 117
2	19 730	30 752	41 577
1	18 863	28 767	38 430
0	17 982	26 876	35 361

Source: Lazear (1983, table 3).

They find no effect on turnover for workers with less than 12 years. Mitchell (1982) finds that having a pension reduces the probability of leaving the job by about 10 percent. Wolf and Levy (1983) parameterize the turnover hazard function and infer the completed distribution of tenure from current levels of tenure. They find that median tenure is shorter for uncovered workers. They also find a bulge in the distribution of tenure after the usual vesting year.

These results are all consistent with the theory which says that those who plan to leave early shorten their stay, while those who plan to stay on lengthen their tenure with the firm. Of course, selection effects may account for much or most of the difference between covered and uncovered sectors.

The discussion of the past few pages points up the important difference between social security and pensions. Wages do not necessarily adjust fully for social security payments. Major cross-subsidization across and within generations, and differential incidence of the social security tax across sectors, imply that the effects of social security on retirement only will be estimated to be the same as those of pensions if all the relevant variables are held constant. Since it is virtually impossible to do this, pension effects are likely to incorporate different wage effects than are estimated social security effects.

Incidentally, there is a direct interaction between pensions and social security. Many pension plans subtract some function of the amount of social security benefits from the pension. Indeed, this is one reason why early retirement, before social security entitlement age, is often associated with higher present value of pension benefits.

Let us now return to the big question. Why are there pensions in the first place, and, in particular, why compulsory pensions? This question has not been answered satisfactorily in the literature and it will not be answered conclusively here. It is useful, however, to state and to evaluate briefly a few of the possible explanations.

The first and most often suggested views the pension as a tax-free savings account. This is the argument implicit in Tepper and Affleck (1974), Bulow (1981), and Black (1982), and explicit in Blinder (1982). Blinder points out that the growth of the pension system has occurred in large part since World War II, a period when taxes also rose significantly. Since interest on assets held in pension funds is exempt from tax (with some limitations), there are incentives to compensate the worker in the form of pensions. The same argument implies that pensions should be fully funded. This is because the firm can borrow at interest $r(1-t)$, where t is the tax rate and r is the nominal rate of interest. It then "lends" to pension fund at rate r because of the tax-exempt status. No matter what the debt position of the firm, it should always fully fund the pension plan (unless, of course, the borrowing rate exceeds the risk-adjusted rate obtainable in the pension portfolio divided by $1-t$; this would imply the existence of some market imperfection).

Another related argument is that the progressive nature of the tax structure makes it useful to spread income smoothly over the life cycle. Since pensions come at a time when earnings are low, there are tax savings to be had by this smoothing. Turner (1983) uses this argument in his analysis.

There are two problems with the tax argument. First, if taxes were the reason, workers should be free to choose the amount of compensation received as pension and the amount received as wages. To the extent that this makes somewhat questionable the tax-free status of the fund, it is possible that a "cafeteria" style compensation scheme would not be permitted.

Second, if taxes were the issue, one would expect all plans to be of the defined contribution type. Yet the vast majority of workers have defined benefit pension plans even though the defined contribution offers much more flexibility to the worker. This suggests that some adverse selection problem discourages the use of voluntary and flexible pensions.

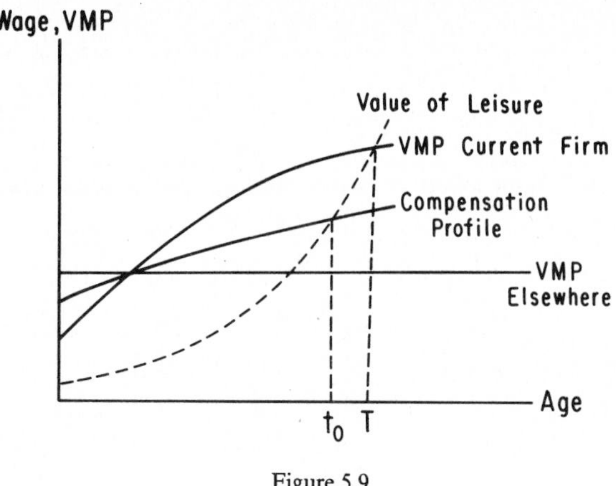

Figure 5.9

Another frequently offered explanation has to do with firm-specific human capital. The problem with investing in firm-specific human capital is that a separation initiated by either side destroys the capital of both sides. A number of authors have thought about ways to structure the compensation so as to minimize the detrimental effects.[14] One such scheme involves the use of a pension to keep workers around. If the pension is contingent upon years of employment, then working longer would produce a higher pension. This seems to be what is at work in the military, where 20-year cliff-vesting virtually assures no turnover between 10 and 20 years of service.

There are three problems with this explanation. The first is that this is a story about total compensation and need have nothing to do with pensions. The idea, first exposited in Becker (1962), is that the worker's compensation should lie somewhere between what he can get elsewhere and what he is worth to the current firm, as shown in Figure 5.9. In so doing, both the worker and the firm have an incentive to stay attached to each other. The worker receives more than his alternative wage and the firm pays less than the worker's value.

There is no need for a pension. The theory of specific capital is a theory of turnover as it relates to total compensation. There is no reason to take that compensation in the form of a pension.

On the contrary, the second difficulty with specific human capital as an explanation is that if wages are ignored, then the pension should rise with age of retirement throughout. The worker destroys less of the firm's capital by quitting at age 64 than he does by leaving at age 55. But the empirical evidence points in the opposite direction. In addition to my own, Fields and Mitchell (1984) also find that pension value declines with age of retirement.

[14] See, for example, Hall and Lazear (1984), Hashimoto (1979), and Hashimoto and Yu (1980).

Finally, if specific human capital remained important even for old workers, one would not expect to see mandatory retirement. In fact, the opposite would be the case. Mandatory retirement is necessary when compensation exceeds marginal product at the date of efficient retirement. The worker prefers to stay on because his wage exceeds his alternative use of time (which is equal to his marginal product). With specific human capital, the problem is that workers want to retire *too soon* because they receive a wage that falls short of the marginal product. In Figure 5.9, the worker would voluntarily retire at t_0. The efficient date of retirement is T. The opposite of mandatory retirement is called for here, but anti-slavery laws constrain such contracts.

A reason for pensions that has already been discussed relates to worker incentives. Holding back some compensation until after the end of the work life is necessary in an optimal contract where workers can vary their effort levels. This is the solution that results in Lazear (1979b, 1981). It helps explain why most pensions are defined benefit rather than defined contribution. Defined contribution plans are more difficult to make contingent upon satisfactory performance. Defined benefit formulas can be specified more easily in a way that makes workers who are terminated before any chosen age suffer a large penalty in reduced pension benefits. This is especially true when the pension is contingent upon final salary. Further, when the story is coupled with the notion that the pension can simultaneously act as an optimal severance pay scheme, other facts fit into place. The inverted U-shaped relation of pension present value to age of retirement is a direct implication of this theory.

Unfortunately, incentives cannot be the entire story either. First, as has already been shown, although conditioning the value of the pension on final salary does have incentive effects, it produces too much effort and labor supply. Therefore, it seems more sensible to argue that this correction serves the purpose of indexing pensions to nominal wages, rather than performing any direct incentive role.

Additionally, legal barriers place limitations on the extent to which payment of the pension can be made contingent upon satisfactory completion of the job. Although there are ways, discussed above, to make impotent the vesting requirements, it remains difficult to argue that much of the pension value is contingent upon successful completion of the job, especially near the date of retirement.

Another explanation is that pensions provide some insurance. Workers who end up having lower-than-expected productivity in old age, say due to illness, have their pensions upon which to rely. There is undoubtedly some truth to this as well, but it too raises questions. First, there are other, more direct methods of insurance. Disability benefits, often directly tied to the pension plan, are specifically designed to deal with these contingencies. Second, if pensions are insurance, it seems unreasonable to place limitations on taking them early (before age 55 or 60). Those who become ill early may be even more in need of their pensions. Third, most pensions are based upon final years' salary. Insurance is more likely to be based on permanent income, probably better estimated by an inflation adjusted career average. This is especially true when final years' earnings are adversely affected by the illness against which the pension is supposedly designed to insure.

Others have argued that a pension fund acts to prevent opportunistic behavior. This is the theme of both Bulow and Scholes (1982) and Ippolito (1983). Bulow and Scholes argue that the workers as a group possess firm-specific capital. If all of them left, the firm would be at a disadvantage. As a result, the workers are promised a pension so that they become owners in the firm and this reduces their incentives to attempt to extract too much quasi-rent.

Ippolito's argument is similar. He claims that the firm, by maintaining a not fully funded pension plan, discourages any behavior that puts the firm's survival in jeopardy. This is especially useful when the firm is unionized since unionized workers are better able to collude against management. Indeed, he finds that pensions, which are funded at 70 percent on average, tend to be more underfunded in unionized than in nonunionized firms.

These arguments have some intuitive appeal, but do not present a complete picture. Most troublesome is that there is no reason why pensions should be preferred over any other deferred compensation. The entire problem can be handled by steepening the age–earnings profile so that workers have an incentive to keep the firm viable. No pension is called for. Further, all the evidence suggests that union firms have flatter age–earnings profiles than nonunion firms, ignoring pensions.[15] Why is it optimal to offset some of the steepness introduced by pensions by flattening the age–earnings profile?

Another idea is that pensions act as a sorting device [see Asch (1984) and Salop and Salop (1976)]. The idea is that only workers know their turnover probabilities or some other measure of ability. Those who have lower ability are more likely to be separated from the firm. Those firms that pay large pensions are less attractive to these low ability, high turnover individuals.

There are two difficulties. First, a steep age–earnings profile performs the same task, giving no preference for pensions. Second, it is not optimal to sever the worker. If there are hiring costs, then forcing the worker to bear these costs through lower wages at the time of employment brings about efficient labor allocation. Additionally, there is no reason to fire workers who turn out to be of low ability. Reducing wages performs the same function and conserves on hiring costs.

One more explanation that is often given is that forced saving via a pension is desirable to workers who cannot discipline themselves. This argument is most clearly exposited by Sheffrin and Thaler (1983). The worker has "two selves": one who is responsible and thinks about the long term and another who is irresponsible and lives for today. Such explanations remain controversial, but offer some intuitive appeal.

[15]See, for example, Mincer (1983) and Perloff and Sickles (1983).

Without going into much detail, it is also useful to list some possible reasons for social security, which is a compulsory, but almost completely portable pension plan.[16] Blinder (1982) points out a few. He suggests that a government pension may be less risky than any individual private plan. Second, income tax, for the most part, depends upon current income. Social security is almost the only way to redistribute lifetime or permanent income. Third, an argument exposited by Merton (1981) is that the pay-as-you-go nature of social security allows for some intergenerational insurance of human capital. During some generations, the average worker is richer than others. This allows for the rich generation to transfer to the relatively poor. Conversely, if things turn out worse than expected, social security payments can be lowered. This is quite similar to the rationale for intergenerational transfers illustrated by the Samuelson (1958) overlapping-generations model.

One reason for making social security compulsory is to prevent moral hazard. Individuals who can opt out may believe that if they put themselves in a desperate situation in old age, others in society will feel obliged to come to their aid. It is sometimes suggested that this was the motivating force behind the founding of TIAA. Schools were bearing the burden ex post of supporting destitute retirees.

7. Retirement, savings, and consumption

Caghan (1965) was among the first to consider directly the interaction between retirement and savings. In the mid-1970s, Munnell (1974) and Feldstein (1974) revived the idea. Feldstein's findings have been the subject of controversy in Leimer and Lesnoy (1982).

The basic notion is that social security can offset private savings in two opposite ways. The first is that social security acts as a substitute for private savings in old age. This tends to reduce the amount of private savings. It increases aggregate savings, however, because some individuals are pushed beyond their desired level of savings. Only if capital markets are such that individuals can borrow at the lending rate against social security will it fail to have this effect. Then any increase in the flow of income during the retirement years could be offset by borrowing. Those who fall short of that level supplement social security with private savings up to their optima.

The second factor is that social security, by changing the cost of leisure over the life cycle, induces earlier retirement. As we have already discussed, it is not clear that this relationship even holds, but if it does, then lengthened retirement generally calls for more savings.

[16] Portability means that years of service are summed across jobs.

Feldstein found that social security had a significant depressing effect on private savings, reducing it by 30 to 50 percent. Unfortunately, his often-cited work suffered from a programming error. A redo by Leimer and Lesnoy reduced his estimates for one period and reversed the sign for another.

Munnell concludes that in the past, there has been no significant effect on savings because the two opposing forces have balanced each other. The slowdown in the decline in age of retirement, however, implies a decrease of private savings in the future from the social security effect.

Kotlikoff and Summers (1981) argue that savings to smooth out consumption over the life cycle is unimportant. They claim that intergenerational transfers account for the vast majority of aggregate U.S. capital formation. Thus, the changing patterns of retirement would have little effect on life-cycle savings.

Finally, Barro (1974) asks under what circumstances changes in government policy would be viewed by individuals as reflecting a real change, to which they respond. He argues that finiteness of life is not an issue when generations are linked through intergenerational transfers. Social security is an institutionalized transfer, but even in its absence generations are linked by private bequests from parents to children.

The intergenerational aspect brings up another issue. Some savings may be undertaken by young workers to care for elderly parents. This is likely to be most pronounced when the child is much more wealthy than his parent.

There are more general issues having to do with life-cycle savings and consumption. We have already discussed the theoretical points in the context of a life-cycle model. Two primarily empirical studies consider the status of the elderly and retired to see how they fare as compared to younger generations.

Taubman and Sickles (1982) find that it is possible to offset the standard of living of the elderly through government programs. They examine the Supplemental Social Insurance program and find that those who receive SSI experienced improved health after the program began.

Hurd and Shoven (1982) take a more general look at the standard of living among the elderly. They find that as a whole, this group is not badly off. There are a number of findings. First, they find that the per household income of the elderly increased more rapidly during the 1970s than the income per household of the rest of the population. Perhaps the most interesting finding is that the elderly are not especially vulnerable to inflation. Most of their assets are held in housing, social security, and medicine, none of which is particularly sensitive to inflation.

References

Anderson, Kathryn and Richard Burkhauser (1983) "The effect of actual mortality experience within a retirement decision model", Working Paper No. 83-W08, Vanderbilt University.

Asch, Beth (1983) "Pensions, wages and sorting: a theoretical and empirical analysis", University of Chicago.

Banker's Trust Company (1975) *1975 study of corporate pension plans*. New York: Banker's Trust.

Banker's Trust Company (1980) *1980 study of corporate pension plans*. New York: Banker's Trust.

Barro, Robert J. (1974) "Are government bonds net wealth?", *Journal of Political Economy*, November/December:1095–1117.

Becker, Gary S. (1962) "Investment in human capital: a theoretical analysis", *Journal of Political Economy*, 70:9–49.

Ben-Porath, Yoram (1967) "The production of human capital and the life cycle model of labor supply", *Journal of Political Economy*, 75:352–365.

Blinder, Alan (1982) "Private pensions and public pensions: theory and fact", NBER Working Paper No. 902.

Blinder, Alan, Roger Gordon and David Wise (1980) "Reconsidering the disincentive effects of social security", *National Tax Journal*, 33:431–442.

Boskin, Michael J. (1977) "Social security and retirement decisions", *Economic Inquiry*, 15:1–25.

Boskin, Michael and Michael D. Hurd (1978) "Effect of social security on early retirement", *Journal of Public Economy*, 10:361–377.

Bulow, Jeremy (1981) "Early retirement pension benefits", NBER Working Paper No. 654.

Bulow, Jeremy and Myron Scholes (1982) "Who owns the assets in a defined benefit pension plan?", NBER Working Paper No. 924.

Burbridge, A. John and A. L. Robb (1980) "Pensions and retirement behavior", *Canadian Journal of Economics*, 13:421–437.

Burkhauser, Richard (1976) "The early pension decision and its effect on exit from the labor market", unpublished doctoral dissertation, University of Chicago.

Burkhauser, Richard (1979) "The pension acceptance decision of older workers", *Journal of Human Resources*, 14:63–75.

Burkhauser, Richard (1980) "The early acceptance of social security: an asset maximization approach," *Industrial and Labor Relations Review*, 33:484–492.

Burkhauser, Richard and Joseph Quinn (1980) "Mandatory retirement study, part I", Urban Institute.

Burkhauser, Richard and John Turner (1982) "Labor market experience of the almost old and the implications for income support", *American Economic Review*, 72:304–308.

Burtless, G. and J. Hausman (1980) "Individual retirement decisions under an employer provided pension plan and social security", unpublished manuscript, Massachusetts Institute of Technology.

Caghan, P. (1965) "The effect of pension plans on private savings", NBER W.P. #95. New York: Columbia University Press for NBER.

Clark, Robert, Steve Allen and Daniel Sumner (1983) "Inflation and pension benefits", North Carolina State.

Clark, Robert, Thomas Johnson and Ann Archibald McDermed (1980) "Allocation of time and resources by married couples approaching retirement", *Social Security Bulletin*, 43:3–16.

Clark, Robert and Thomas Johnson (1980) "Retirement in the dual career family", North Carolina State.

Cotterman, Robert (1978) "A theoretical and empirical analysis of the labor supply of older males", unpublished doctoral dissertation, University of Chicago.

Crawford, Vincent and David Lilien (1981) "Social security and the retirement decision", *Quarterly Journal of Economics*, 96:505–529.

Ehrenberg, Ronald G. (1978) "Retirement system characteristics and compensating wage differentials in the public sector", unpublished paper, Cornell University.

Feldstein, Martin (1974) "Social security, induced retirement, and aggregate capital accumulation", *Journal of Political Economy*, 82:905–926.

Fields, Gary and Olivia Mitchell (1983) "Economic incentives to retire: a qualitative choice approach", NBER Working Paper No. 1096.

Fields, Gary and Olivia Mitchell (1982a) "Restructuring social security: how will the labor market respond?", Department of Labor.

Fields, Gary and Olivia Mitchell (1982b) "The effects of pensions and earnings on retirement: a review essay", in: R. Ehrenberg ed., *Research in labor economics*. New Haven: JAI Press.

Fields, Gary and Olivia Mitchell (1982c) "Economic determinants of the optimal retirement age: an empirical investigation", NBER Working Paper No. 876.

Freeman, Richard B. (1978) "The effect of trade unionism on fringe benefits", NBER Working Paper No. 292.

Gordon, R. and A. Blinder (1980) "Market wages, reservation wages and retirement decisions", *Journal of Public Economics*, 14:277–308.

Gotz, Glenn A. and John J. McCall (1980) "Estimating military personnel retention rates: theory and statistical method", RAND R-2541-AF.

Gustman, Alan and Thomas Steinmeier (1982) "Partial retirement and the analysis of retirement behavior", NBER Working Paper No. 1000.

Gustman, Alan and Thomas Steinmeier (1983a) "Retirement flows", NBER Working Paper No. 1069.

Gustman, Alan and Thomas Steinmeier (1983b) "A structural retirement model", unpublished manuscript, Dartmouth University.

Hall, Robert and Edward P. Lazear (1984) "The excess sensitivity of layoffs and quits to demand", *Journal of Labor Economics*, 2:233–257.

Hamermesh, Daniel (1981) "A general empirical model of life-cycle effects in consumption and retirement decisions", unpublished manuscript, Michigan State University.

Hanoch, Giora and Marjorie Honig (1983) "Retirement, wages, and labor supply of the elderly", *Journal of Labor Economics*, 1:131–151.

Hashimoto, Masanori (1979) "Bonus payments, on-the-job training, and lifetime employment in Japan", *Journal of Political Economy*, 87:1086–1104.

Hashimoto, Masanori and Ben Yu (1980) "Specific capital, employment contracts, and wage rigidity", *Bell Journal of Economics*, Autumn:536–549.

Hausman, J. and David Wise (1982) "Retirement", NBER Working Paper.

Hemming, R. C. L. (1977) "The effect of state and private pensions on retirement behavior and personal capital accumulation", *Regional Economic Studies*, 44:169–172.

Hurd, Michael D. and Michael J. Boskin (1981) "Effect of social security on retirement", NBER Working Paper No. 10.

Hurd, Michael D. and John Shoven (1982) "The impact of inflation on the financial status of the aged", 1982 conference volume, 25–27.

International Social Security Association (1976) "Implications for social security of research on aging and retirement", Report No. 9, The Hague.

Ippolito, Richard (1983) "The economic function of underfunded pension plans", U.S. Department of Labor.

Kotlikoff, Lawrence, and Daniel Smith (1984) *Pensions and the American economy*. Chicago: University of Chicago Press.

Kotlikoff, Lawrence and L. Summers (1981) "The role of intergenerational transfers in aggregate capital accumulation", *Journal of Political Economy*, 89:706–732.

Lazear, Edward P. (1976) "Age, experience and wage growth", *American Economic Review*, 66:548–558.

Lazear, Edward P. (1981) "Agency, earnings profiles, productivity, and hours restrictions", *American Economic Review*, 71:606–620.

Lazear, Edward P. (1979) "The narrowing of black/white wage differentials is illusory", *American Economic Review*, 69:553–564.

Lazear, Edward P. (1979) "Why is there mandatory retirement?", *Journal of Political Economy*, 87:1261–1264.

Lazear, Edward P. (1982) "Severance pay, pensions, and efficient mobility", NBER Working Paper No. 854.

Lazear, Edward P. (1983) "Pensions as severance pay", in: Zvi Bodie and John Shoven, eds., *Financial aspects of the U.S. pension system*. Chicago: University of Chicago Press.

Lazear, Edward P. and Beth Asch (1984) "Comparison of public and private pension plans". Washington, D.C.: American Enterprise Institute.

Leimer, Dean and Selig Lesnoy (1982) "Social security and private savings: new time-series evidence", *Journal of Political Economy*, 90:609–629.

Lingg, Barbara A. (1971) "Retired-worker beneficiaries affected by the annual earnings test in 1971", *Social Security Bulletin*, 38:22–31.

Merton, Robert (1981) "On the role of social security as a means for efficient risk-bearing in an economy where human capital is not tradeable", NBER Working Paper No. 743.

Mincer, Jacob (1974) *Schooling, experience, and earnings*. New York: NBER.

Mincer, Jacob (1983) "Union effects: wages, turnover and job training", in: R. Ehrenberg, ed., *Research in labor economics*. Greenwich, Conn.: JAI Press, 217–252.

Mitchell, Olivia M. and Gary M. Fields (1984) "The economics of retirement behavior", *Journal of Labor Economics*, 2:84–105.

Mitchell, Olivia M. (1982) "Fringe benefits and labor mobility", *Journal of Human Resources*, 17:286–298.

Munnell, Alicia Haydock (1974) *The effect of social security on personal savings*. Cambridge, Mass.: Ballinger.

Munnell, Alicia Haydock (1977) "The future of social security", Brookings Papers, Washington, D.C.

Murray, Janet (1972) "Subjective retirement", *Social Security Bulletin*, 42:20–24.

OECD (1977) *Old age pension schemes*.

Pellechio, Anthony (1978) "The effect of social security on retirement", NBER Working Paper No. 260.

Pellechio, Anthony (1981) "Social security and the decision to retire", University of Rochester.

Perloff, Jeffrey M. and Robin C. Sickles (1983) "FIML estimation of union wage, hours, and earnings differentials in the construction industry: a nonlinear limited dependent variable approach", paper presented at the Conference on the Economics of Trade Unions, NBER, Cambridge, Massachusetts.

Quinn, Joseph (1977) "Microeconomic determinants of early retirement: a cross-sectional view of white married men", *Journal of Human Resources*, 12:329–346.

Reimers, Cordelia (1977) "The timing of retirement of American men", unpublished Ph.D. Dissertation, Columbia University.

Rosenzweig, Mark and Kenneth Wolpin (1979) "An economic analysis of the extended family in a less developed country: the demand for the elderly in an uncertain environment", Yale Growth Center Discussion Paper No. 317.

Salop, Joanne and Steven Salop (1976) "Self-selection and turnover in the labor market", *Quarterly Journal of Economics*, 90:619–627.

Samuelson, P. A. (1958) "An exact consumption-loan model of interest with or without the social contrivance of money", *Journal of Political Economy*, 66:476–582.

Schillen, Bradley and Randall Weiss (1979) "The impact of private pensions on firm attachment", *Review of Economics and Statics*, 61:369–380.

Sheshinski, Eytan (1978) "A model of social security and retirement decisions", *Journal of Public Economics*, 10:337–360.

Taubman, Paul (1982) "Determinations of pension benefits", NBER Working Paper.

Taubman, Paul (1981) "Pensions and mortality", NBER Working Paper No. 811.

Taubman, Paul and Robin Sickles (1982) "Supplemental social insurance and health of the poor", NBER Working Paper No. 1062.

Tepper, Irwin (1981) "Taxation and corporate pension policy", *Journal of Finance*, 36:1–13.

Tepper, Irwin and A. R. P. Affleck (1974) "Pension plan liabilities and corporate finance strategies", *Journal of Finance*, 29:1549–1564.

Turner, John (1983) "Taxes and the structure of deferred labor compensation", U.S. Department of Labor.

U.S. Department of Labor (1980) "Handbook of labor statistics", Bulletin No. 2070.

Willis, R. J. (1981) "The direction of intergenerational transfers and demographic transitions: the Caldwell hypothesis reexamined", NORC/ERC Working Paper No. 81-3.

Wolf, Douglas and Frank Levy (1983) "Pension coverage, pension vesting, and the distribution of job tenure", in: G. Burtless and H. Aaron, eds., *Studies in Retirement Policy*. Washington, D.C.: The Brookings Institute.

Zabalza, Anthony, Christopher Pissarides and M. Barton (1980) "Social security and the choice between full-time work, part-time work and retirement", *Journal of Public Economics*, 14:245–276.

Chapter 6

DEMAND FOR EDUCATION

RICHARD B. FREEMAN

Harvard University

1. Introduction

The human capital "revolution" of the 1960s and 1970s turned the previously peripheral topic of demand for education into a major area of research for labor economists. Analysis has focused on a variety of questions relating to the role of education in an economy, individual decision-making with respect to demand for education, and social provision of education. At the *societal* level, the important questions are: What is the contribution of educated labor to national output? What is the substitutability between educated labor and other inputs in production? To what extent does demand for educated labor change with economic development and growth? And, on the wage side: How responsive are educational wage differentials to market conditions? At the level of *individual decision-makers* the questions are: How well does the economic model of investment in human capital explain individual demands for education and thus the supply of educated labor? How elastic are the supplies of workers to various educational categories? With respect to earnings, we want to know the fraction of the variance in earnings that can be explained by differences in education. Because of the significant *public* role in education markets, another important question is: What determines public funding for education?

In this chapter I examine the theoretical and empirical findings from the past two or so decades of work on these issues. The chapter shows, I believe, that we have made considerable progress along the paths developed in the late 1950s and early 1960s by T. W. Schultz, G. Becker and others on the economic analysis of demand for education.[1] While there are exceptions, the past two decades' work supports the general proposition that economic analysis of rational behavior

[1]Among the several works are Becker (1964), Schultz (1960), and Ben-Porath (1967). In a different vein is the study by Habrison and Meyers (1964) which initiated cross-country comparisons of education and economic well-being, and Krueger (1968).

Handbook of Labor Economics, Volume I, Edited by O. Ashenfelter and R. Layard

under specified market and informational conditions goes a long way to understanding the interplay between education and the economy.

The evidence on which this conclusion is based, and the specific findings on the social, individual, market, and public finance questions of concern, are presented in the remainder of this chapter. I begin with the demand for education by the society as a whole, then turn to individual decision-making and wage determination, and conclude with the issues relating to public funding.

2. Societal demand for education: Productivity

One of the fundamental issues which motivates economic analysis of education is the extent to which education contributes to national output and, in the context of economic growth, the extent to which increased educational attainment contributes to long-run increases in productivity. Put broadly, three points of view have been put forth.

(1) The human capital view that education is a productive input, whose marginal contribution can be roughly measured by wage differentials between more and less educated labor. Underlying this view is the belief that the labor market for educated workers operates in accord with the precepts of competitive economic analysis.

(2) The screening/sorting view that wage differentials overestimate the productivity gain to society from education because part of the private gain – that due to signalling one's skills to an employer – is not a social gain for levels of education beyond the minimum.

(3) The fixed coefficient-bottleneck view of education, which holds that economic growth "requires" certain quantities of various sorts of educated labor, shortages of which will cause significant bottleneck problems. As this view implies negligible elasticities of substitution among types of labor I shall consider it under that topic and focus on the human capital and screening debate here.

The human capital perspective underlies basic growth accounting. Assume that production is governed by a function

$$Q = f(E, K), \tag{1}$$

where Q = output, E = effective units of labor, where education raises effectiveness, and K = capital.

There are several ways to express effective units of labor in terms of education, depending on the educational production function. A simple widely used definition of E is:

$$E = \sum_{i \neq 0} (W_i / W_0) E_i, \tag{2}$$

where E_i = number of workers in the ith educational category, W_i = wage of workers in the ith category, and W_0 is the "numeraire" category. In (2) the productivity of workers is proportional to their wages.

Assuming that labor and capital are paid their marginal productivity, and that (1) is constant returns to scale, we obtain the basic equation of growth accounting:

$$\dot{Q} = \alpha_L \dot{E} + (1 - \alpha_L)\dot{K}, \tag{3}$$

where dots above variables refer to log differences and α_L = labor's share.

A variety of studies, pioneered by Denison, have examined the contribution of education to economic growth using variants of (3). The general finding from diverse analyses for the United States and other countries suggests that growth of education has contributed substantially to growth of output or output per worker but that education is not the "magic bullet" of economic growth. In Psacharapoulous' (1983a) review of studies for many countries, the average contribution of education to growth of output ranged from 9 to 17 percent, with larger contributions in developing countries; Bowman's (1970) summary of the evidence shows an individual country variation of the contribution of education from 2 to 28 percent. In the United States various estimates of the proportion of growth of national output due to education range from 10 to 20 percent of the observed growth rate [Denison (1962), Jorgenson and Griliches (1972), Chinloy (1980), Jorgenson (1984)].

More recent work on the contribution of education to the 1970s productivity slowdown shows that it does little to explain the slower growth of output per unit of output in the decade.[2]

The screening/sorting argument suggests that relative wages overstate relative productivities, so that the impact of additional education on output is *less* than indicated in studies based on (3). Assume that education does not increase productivity but that persons who are innately more productive than others have a comparative advantage in obtaining education. Then, all else the same, firms can use education as a means for sorting out more/less able workers, and workers will have an incentive to get educated to signal employers that they are more able. Pursuing work begun by Arrow, Spence (1974) has shown how this process can lead to an equilibrium in which education sorts out workers by ability but where increases in the mean level of education have no productive value. Consider a world with two types of workers, ables and bozos, whose native abilities vary so that employers do better hiring ables than bozos. All that is needed for employers to use schooling to sort between them is that ables get more schooling than bozos. Whether ables have 1, 6, 12 years and bozos 0, 5, 11 years is

[2]See Denison (1982) and Baily (1983).

irrelevant; any schooling beyond that which establishes the difference has no productive value. While few, if any, adherents to the screening/sorting view of education would argue that, in fact, education has no productivity effects beyond sorting, they would object to using wage differentials as a measure of gains in social productivity due to education. Following Spence's analysis a theoretical literature on screening/sorting models flourished briefly.[3]

Empirical analyses of the human capital/screening debate has been relatively sparse, in part because of the difficulty of developing clearcut tests of the two beliefs. One early attack involved comparisons of actual physical output produced by workers with different levels of education on the same job. To summarize the results somewhat facetiously, ditch-diggers with PhDs were found to be no more productive than ditch-diggers without PhDs. The obvious problem with this test is that a PhD does not ordinarily work as a ditch-digger: there is likely to be a significant negative selectivity of PhDs to digging. More generally, all contrasts of workers with different education in the same job suffer from potential problems of selectivity of the workers.

Efforts to isolate the signalling/screening effects as opposed to the general productivity effects of education have compared returns to education in sectors the market and between workers more/less likely to have significant signalling/screening effects. For example, one study [Layard and Psacharopoulos (1974)] compared rates of return to uncompleted courses with returns to completed courses. If signalling ability were important, the argument runs, dropping out should be a negative signal and the return lower per year of schooling than the return to completed education: in fact there is little or no difference. A second test has been to compare educational differences by age, on the hypothesis that signalling should become less important with age as employers learn about workers' skills by direct observation. In fact, educational earnings differentials rise with age, though the confounding of ability, on-the-job training, and schooling makes this a weak test. A third test has involved comparisons of the education of self-employed and salaried workers [Wolpin (1977)]. All else the same, self-employed (unscreened) workers should obtain less schooling than salaried workers, if screening affects the rewards to the latter. Indeed, this is what Wolpin finds in a comparison of means. While he believes the difference in means is modest, a screening proponent could argue the converse. Failure to control for family background and other factors which might also affect schooling and failure to translate the difference in schooling into impacts on rates of return lead to an inconclusive result. Approaching the problem in a different way, Taubman and Wales (1973) examined the occupational distribution of individuals at various education levels and compared them to predicted distributions based on

[3] See Arrow (1962), Layard and G. Psacharopoulos (1974), Riley (1975, 1979), Spence (1974, 1976), J. Stiglitz (1975), and Wolpin (1977).

Table 6.1
Number of cases with coefficients of differing significance in effect of education on agricultural productivity.

Absolute value of t-statistic	Positive coefficients	Negative coefficients
$t > 2$	11	0
$1 < t < 2$	15	3
$0 < t < 1$	4	3

Source: Tabulated from Jamison and Lau (1982, table 2.2) with two studies omitted due to ambiguity.

the assumption than an individual would select the occupation offering the highest income for a person with his characteristic (including ability). Their calculation suggests that the less educated are screened out of high-level occupations, raising the return to schooling by a substantial amount. At a minimum, however, they attribute 50 percent of the educational earnings differential to "true productivity differences".

An alternative effort to evaluate the impact of education on productivity has been to estimate equation (1) directly, using standard production function techniques. The "experiments" underlying the production function compare output/worker in the same industry across geographic areas, where establishments hire workers with different levels of education. The econometric problems with such studies are well-known and shall not be discussed here. When one introduces an education variable into a production function with labor and capital as other inputs, what is the coefficient on education?

In manufacturing, Griliches (1970) used indices of occupation rather than of education as the measure of labor skills and found a positive impact. Jorgenson (1987), together with a number of coworkers, put together time series data on education and estimated translog production relations for the United States, obtaining positive education effects also. The most extensive work, however, has been done in agriculture, where studies have focused on individual units as well as on aggregate data. Early aggregate studies obtained positive coefficients on education in explaining agricultural production.[4] More recent micro work summarized by Jamison and Lau (1982) have found, as Table 6.1 indicates, that education generally is a positive and at least marginally significant coefficient in the relevant production function.

In terms of labor market analysis, however, the issue is not simply whether education has a positive impact on output but whether its impact is close to the

[4] The aggregate work includes Fane (1975), Gisser (1965), Griliches (1963, 1964), Huffman (1977), Khaldi (1975), and Welch (1970).

observed wage differential. Given the confidence intervals around estimated coefficients in production functions, it is generally not possible with these types of data to reject the hypothesis of equality, but the tests have little power.

It should also be noted that at least some studies have followed the conceptual analysis of Schultz (1975), who argues that a primary impact of education is to increase the ability to deal with disequilibrium and changing circumstances and probed the black box of the education effect, with respect to how education alters speed in adopting new technologies, and responses to price incentives.[5]

Overall, while neither the studies focusing on screening/signalling nor those focusing on the direct productivity of education have yielded definitive results, the general tone of the findings is supportive of the human capital view. Screening/signalling effects are undoubtedly part of the world, but no empirical study has found them to be a major factor in the demand for education.

3. Sectoral shifts and demand for education

Economic growth and development brings with it changes in the industrial structure of an economy [Kuznets (1966)]. To the extent that industries make different use of educated labor, changes in industrial composition will change the demand for education.

Fixed coefficient input/output models have been used to analyze the link between industrial structure and demand. To focus on the effect of changes in industrial composition on demand, the models sacrifice analysis of the effect of demand responses to price changes. A typical such model starts with an equation like

$$E_i = \sum_j a_{ij} l_j X_j, \tag{4}$$

where E_i = employment "demanded" in the ith education group, a_{ij} = fixed coefficient relating number of workers in ith education category to total employment in the industry (E_j), l_j = total labor input coefficient for ith industry, X_j = output in jth industry, with $l_j = E_j / X_j$.

Taking first differences we obtain:

$$\Delta E_i = \sum_j a_{ij} \Delta l_j X_j, \tag{5}$$

or in log difference form:

$$\dot{E}_i = \sum_i \gamma_{ij} \left(\dot{l}_j + \dot{X}_j \right), \tag{6}$$

[5]See Schultz (1975), and the literature cited therein.

Table 6.2
Proportion of workers by education in different sectors, and growth of employment in those sectors, United States, 1960–1970.

	Proportion of workers with 4 years or more of college		%Δ in total employment
	1960	1970	
High education intensive sectors			
Finance, insurance and real estate	0.132	0.160	30
Business and repair services	0.081	0.110	34
Professional and related services	0.380	0.381	44
Public administration	0.087	0.134	24
Intermediate education intensive sectors			
Manufacturing	0.059	0.076	11
Transportation	0.040	0.055	14
Wholesale and retail trade	0.045	0.055	23
Entertainment and recreation services	0.061	0.085	20
Noneducation intensive sectors			
Agriculture	0.021	0.039	−52
Mining	0.070	0.098	7
Construction	0.031	0.038	14
Personal services	0.014	0.022	−9

Source: United States Bureau of the Census (1960, 1970) Census of Population, Subject Reports, *Industrial Characteristics*.

where $\gamma_{ij} = a_{ij}E_j/E_i$, the share of the work force having education of the ith type working in industry j.

For models of this type to provide reasonably valuable insight into changes in demand for education over time it is necessary that

(a) input coefficients for education groups differ greatly by industry;

(b) industry growth rates of employment (productivity and output) differ greatly; and

(c) substitution possibilities are sufficiently moderate that the assumed fixity of input coefficients is a reasonable first approximation.

As Table 6.2 indicates, assumptions (a) and (b) are consonant with the data. We can divide the economy into education-intensive and noneducation-intensive sectors, and the two sets of sectors have experienced greatly different rates of employment.

The assumption of small or essentially zero substitution possibilities is, by contrast, relatively controversial. We shall see in the next section elasticities of substitution between educated labor and other inputs, while far from infinite, are definitely nonzero, also.

The validity of the model does not, however, depend on (c) by itself, but on its interrelation with (a) and (b). When sectoral usage of educated labor differs enormously, and when growth rates of employment differ greatly, the fixed coefficient model may capture an important element in demand for education even if elasticities of substitution are non-negligible.

Empirical analysis of fixed coefficient models suggest that, in fact, this is the case. While most analyses have focused on detailed occupations rather than broad educational categories, the results can be readily translated into demand for education. The basic finding is that a sizeable proportion of the changed demand for education is attributable to changes in the composition of industries [Freeman (1977, 1980)]. It is not, however, the entire story by any means: changes in coefficients due to technology and to substitution in response to relative factor prices are also important determinants of the number of workers with different levels of education demanded and employed.

4. Substitutability between educated labor and other inputs

The elasticity of substitution between more and less educated workers (or other inputs) has been at the center of analyses of demand for educated labor for two reasons. First, as noted, because the validity of widely used "fixed coefficient" methods for forecasting educational demands or "needs" and the potential economic worth of educational planning to meet such demands or "needs" hinges critically on the size of the elasticity. The greater are actual elasticities, the less valuable are such forecasts and plans. If the elasticities are large, employers can readily substitute less educated for more educated labor, so that even accurate planning will be of little economic value. Second, the elasticity of substitution between more and less educated labor is important in analyzing the impact of changes in relative supplies of workers on the distribution of earnings. When the elasticity is high, large increases in the supply of graduates relative to nongraduates will have little effect on their relative wages. When the elasticity of substitution is small, large increases in the relative supply of graduates will cause sizeable changes in relative wages and thus will alter the distribution of earnings.

Given the critical role of the elasticity of substitution between more and less educated or skilled workers, it is not surprising that several empirical studies have sought to estimate its magnitude. Because the number of workers with varying levels of education is predetermined in any given year by supply decisions made years earlier due to the length of training, most analyses actually examine the inverse of the elasticity of substitution, the elasticity of complementarity, which measures the percentage change in relative wages due to percentage changes in

Table 6.3
Estimates of the elasticity of substitution between highly educated and less educated workers.

Study	Sample	Elasticity of substitution
Bowles (1969)	Countries	202
Johnson (1970)	States, U.S.A.	1.3
Welch (1970) (agriculture sector)	States, U.S.A.	1.4
Dougherty (1972)	States, U.S.A.	8.2
Psacharopoulos and Hinchliffe (1972)	Developed	1000
(countries)	Less developed	2.1–2.5
Tinbergen (1974)	Countries	0.6–1.2
	States	0.4–2.1
Freeman (1975)	Years, U.S.A.	1.0–2.6
Layard and Fallon (1975)	Countries	0.6–3.5
Grant (1979)	SMSAs	1.2

Note: Definitions of highly educated to less educated vary somewhat between samples. All except Layard and Fallon treat college relative to some other group. Layard and Fallon relate groups with 8 or more years to less than 8.

relative supplies. While it is reasonable to assume that supplies are fixed in analyses that treat time series data, this assumption is less defensible in comparisons across geographic regions at a point in time: within a country, the supply of educated workers to an area can migrate in response to wage differentials; across countries, differences in supply may reflect responses to differences in the rewards to education that persist over time, weakening the assumption that supplies can be taken as independent of wages. Accordingly, some studies have also used simultaneous equations techniques to estimate the relevant elasticities of substitution. In these studies demand and supply of educated labor are estimated conjointly in a system.

What is the result of these studies? What is currently known about the elasticity of substitution between more and less educated labor?

Table 6.3 summarizes the results of the most important empirical studies.

Initial work on elasticities of substitution focused on cross-sectional data, with most attention given to cross country comparisons. While the early evidence on U.S. states supported relatively moderate elasticities [Johnson (1970), Welch (1970)] the work of several analysts led many to believe that the elasticity was rather high, sufficiently so to yield practically horizontal demand curves. Bowles' book on *Planning Educational Systems for Economic Growth* produced, in particular, an elasticity between workers with some college education and those with 8 to 11 years of school of 202, and smaller but still sizeable elasticities (6 to 12) between other educational groups. With a sample of 28 states from the United States, Dougherty obtained a more moderate but still high estimate of over 8.

Psacharopoulos and Hinchliffe divided the international sample by degree of development, obtaining an essentially infinite elasticity (implying perfect substitutability at the relevant wage ratios) in the developed countries but a more modest value in the less developed countries. As the relative earnings of graduates remained constant or increased in the 1950s and 1960s, despite increased supplies of graduates from colleges and universities, these estimates were generally accepted as being in accord with reality. Some viewed them as casting serious doubt on the concept of educational bottlenecks as a barrier to economic growth and on the value of the fixed coefficient model of labor demand, then being used by the Organization for Economic Cooperation and Development, among others, to analyze the graduate and skilled worker labor markets for the purpose of educational planning.

In the 1970s, concurrent with the observed decline in the relative earnings of college graduates throughout the developed world, analysts began to re-examine these results. New estimates based on better data and models provided a very different picture of the elasticity of substitution between educated and less educated labor. Nobel-laureate Jan Tinbergen amplified the country and state analyses to take account of the likely simultaneous determination of relative wages and relative supplies in cross-sections and obtained quite different results from Bowles and Dougherty using their data sets. His elasticities ranged from 0.50 to 2.00, which were consistent with the earlier cross U.S. state work of Welch and Johnson. Freeman used time series data for the United States to estimate the effect of the growth in the number of college graduates relative to high school graduates on their relative earnings and obtained estimated elasticities of a similar magnitude, ranging from 1.0 to 2.6. Layard and Fallon examined a large cross-section of countries, with the comparable results shown in the table. Grant developed estimates in a complete translogarithmic systems equation which included capital in the analysis and obtained a value of 1.3. All told, the current evidence suggests a value of the elasticity of substitution between more and less educated labor in the range of 1.0 to 2.0. This magnitude is consistent with changes in the supply of graduates altering their relative earnings and does not invalidate the potential economic worth of educational planning based on fixed coefficient models.

A large number of additional studies on substitution among groups of workers have used occupational disaggregation. While these results show a wider range than those given for educational groups in Table 6.1, the estimates are consistent with elasticities of substitution between highly educated and less educated workers of 1–2. In the Hamermesh and Grant review of 20 estimates of elasticities of substitution between production (blue-collar) and nonproduction (white-collar) workers, the mean estimate was 2.3, with half the studies yielding estimates below 1.0 and half above that value.

The relationship between capital and more educated or skilled labor and the relationship between capital and less educated or skilled labor has also been studied as important elements in the demand for labor of varying educational qualities. The key hypothesis in this work has been that capital is less substitutable (more complementary) for educated than for less educated labor [Griliches (1969)]. If this is the case increases in capital raise the demand for educated labor relative to less educated labor and changes in the price of capital cause employers to alter employment of the less educated more than employment of the more educated. The extant evidence appears to support this hypothesis. Of the twelve studies in the Hamermesh and Grant (1979) review article, eight show capital to be more easily substituted for blue-collar labor than for white-collar labor, and half indicate that white-collar labor is actually complementary with capital, so that changes in the price of capital raise demand for white-collar labor rather than reduce it. The only study to examine labor by education also shows lower substitutability between the more educated and capital than between the less educated and capital [Grant (1981)].

With moderate elasticities of substitution between educated and less educated labor and with relatively small (or even oppositely signed) elasticities of substitution between more educated labor and capital, current evidence suggests that the elasticity of demand for educated labor is of a moderate magnitude. Analyses of the impact of economic changes or policies on employment or wages of educated labor cannot ignore the demand response to changes in wages.

5. Individual decision-making: Demand for education

At the level of individual decision-makers, the demand for education is at one and the same time the supply of educated labor and of specialized skills. This is because persons who are on the demand side of the education market are suppliers in the labor market.

Analysis of the demand for education/supply of skills by individuals was spurred by the publication of Becker's *Human Capital* in 1964. While there were valuable analyses of the economics of education prior to Becker, this work was the first to develop a complete price theoretic analysis of the individual's investment in education and derive the implications for supply of labor, salary determination, and the path of salaries over the life cycle. It is the foundation stone on which all succeeding work has been based.

At the heart of the human capital model is the notion that education is an *investment* of current time and money for future pay. While there is nothing to rule out important consumption components to education, the power of the human capital approach rests on the responses of individuals to rates of return in an investment context.

The basic idea of the model [given by Becker (1964), Ben-Porath (1967) and others] is that an individual faces the option each year of either working full time or going to school and investing in human capital (we ignore leisure, for simplicity). For workers, earnings are proportional to the amount of human capital previously accumulated:

$$W_t = \tilde{W}E_t, \tag{7}$$

where W_t = earnings, $\tilde{W}$ = rental price of human capital, and E_t = amount of human capital (effective units of labor in our previous terminology). Assuming schooling is a full-time activity, a person will have no earnings while in school but will increase his human capital according to an educational production function:

$$\Delta E_t = f(t_e) - \delta E_{t-1}, \tag{8}$$

where f is the production function translating time in school t_e into added units of human capital; E_{t-1} is last period's stock of human capital, and δ is a depreciation rate.

In this framework the cost of a year of schooling is $\tilde{W}E_t$, the *forgone earnings* while the return to schooling depends on $\tilde{W}$, $f(t_e)$, and δ, and the discount rate and the period over which returns accrue. Demand for education is higher the longer the period of accrual, the more productive is the time spent in education, and the smaller the relevant discount rate, while the depreciation of the stock of human capital has an ambiguous effect on demand.

The individual will maximize net wealth by equating the marginal cost of schooling to the marginal returns. The problem can be readily put into a formal control theory framework.

There are several points to note about this model. First is the question of the educational production function. To the extent that education is "neutral" in the sense that it raises productivity in producing further education as much as it raises wages, the model predicts rather long periods of schooling. The fact that persons have a finite work life, and thus will never invest in schooling toward the end of their lives, is not "powerful" enough to cause schooling to end in the 20–30 age period, as in fact it does. Other assumptions having to do with the cost of time (leisure) or the technology of education (a decline in productivity from school after a number of years) are needed to bring formal schooling to an end [Ben-Porath (1970)].

Second, the model has a "compensating differential" flavor in that the educational differential which follows from the investment compensates for forgone earnings early in life and is thus not a "true" indicator of inequality in earnings. An important implication, which has been picked up in ensuing analyses, is that lifetime earnings, not salaries, should be the focus of analysis. Several studies have pursued this point [Wilkinson (1966), Mattila (1982), for example].

Third, the model predicts a sharp upward slope to the age–earnings profile with zero earnings during schooling and high earnings afterwards. This insight has led analysts to detailed analyses of age–earnings profiles by expanding "human capital formation" to include on-the-job training and learning by doing or experience. The extent to which the investment explanation of the observed age-earnings profile captures reality, as opposed to more institutional lifetime contracts models, is a currently unresolved issue.

Perhaps the most important element missing from the basic model is the role of the family in education. There is a powerful positive relation between one's family background, measured by family income, occupation or education of parents, and schooling. Youths with more advantaged backgrounds go to school more than youths with less advantaged backgrounds. In his Woytinsky lecture and in ensuing work, Becker modelled this relation in terms of the demand for schooling and the supply of funds for investing in a world in which there is a rising supply curve of funds for investing in human capital. If family factors affect the "ability" of individuals to benefit from investments in education, then coming from a better home raises the individual's demand curve, and he/she will get more schooling at a higher return (see Figure 6.1). If, by contrast, family operates largely by offering youths from higher income homes a lower cost of funds for investing in human capital, then their greater amount of schooling will be associated with lower returns. The implication is that family background should affect the return to schooling as well as the amount of schooling individuals get. The proposition has not been proven or disproven in empirical analyses.

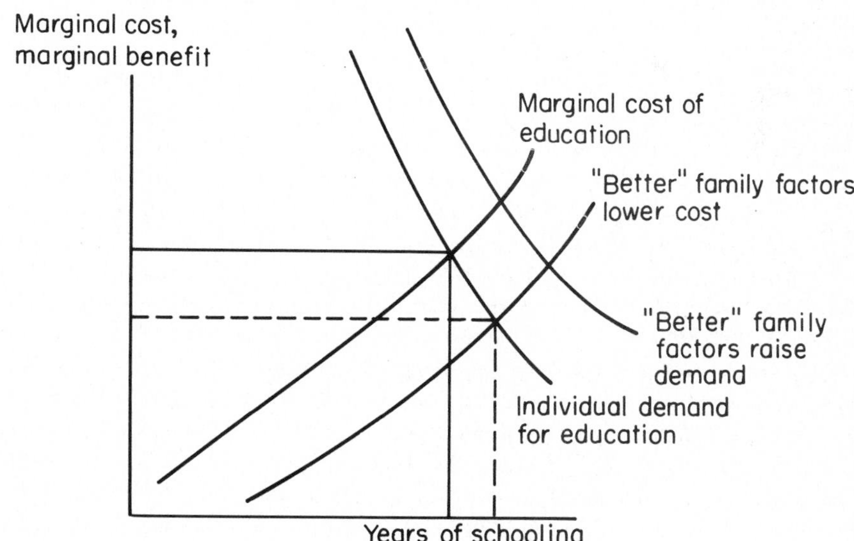

Figure 6.1

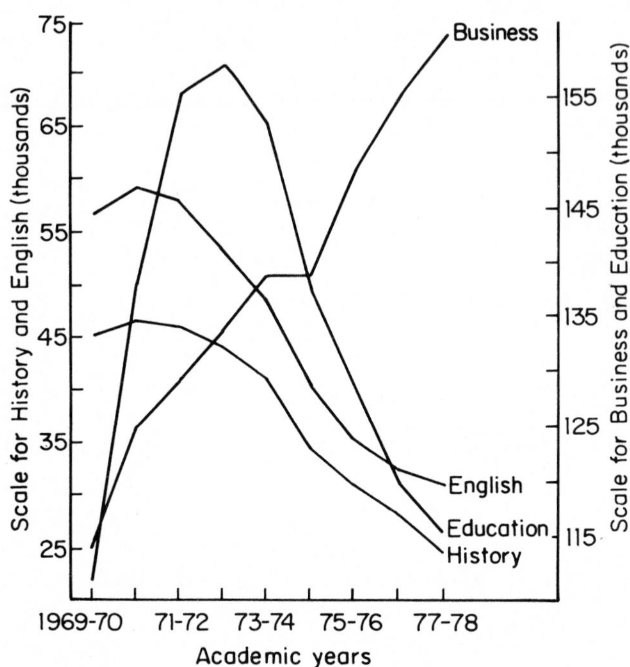

Figure 6.2. Changes over time in the supplies of educated labor. *Source*: National Center for Educational Statistics.

The investment model of the decision to pursue education has been studied extensively with generally favorable results for the key behavioral assumption: that individual decisions respond significantly to meet incentives. Much of the research has focused on time series data regarding the flow of students into diverse fields, exemplified for the United States in Figure 6.2. Some studies have analyzed the impact of the salaries of college workers relative to high school workers on the proportion of the young enrolled in college; some have focused on the effect of tuition and scholarship charges on enrollments; while others have studied the relation between salaries in specific disciplines and the relative numbers of young persons choosing to study in those areas. Several of the studies have used time series data to estimate supply elasticities, identifying supply behavior from demand behavior by the fact that, because education takes a number of years, the decision to study in a field depends on salaries and market conditions prior to the individual's graduation into the job market. Other studies

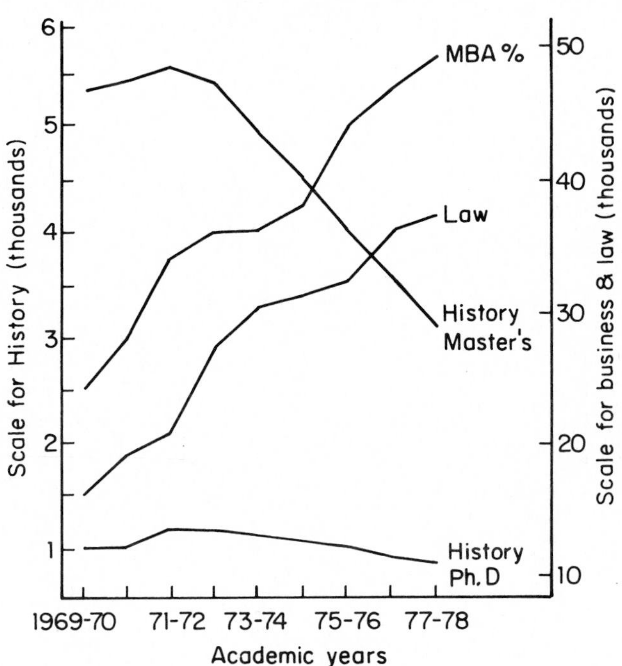

Figure 6.2, continued.

have compared the relative number of persons obtaining different levels or types of education across geographic areas to educational differentials in those areas. Because the studies focus on aggregate supply, the magnitudes of the estimated supply elasticities depend on the relative number of persons who are "on the margin" among various alternatives – that is to say, the number who, at existing pecuniary and nonpecuniary rewards to various careers, are potentially movable across fields. Since older workers have often made sizeable investments in their careers in the past, the responsive "margin" consists of the young, who are in the process of making career choices.

Another body of literature has concentrated on the decision of individuals to enroll in higher education and/or the type of education or institution they choose, using a somewhat different methodology but obtaining comparable results about the responsiveness of individuals' decisions to economic incentives.

Table 6.4 summarizes some estimates of the responsiveness of the overall supply of young persons to higher education. Panel A treats studies that have

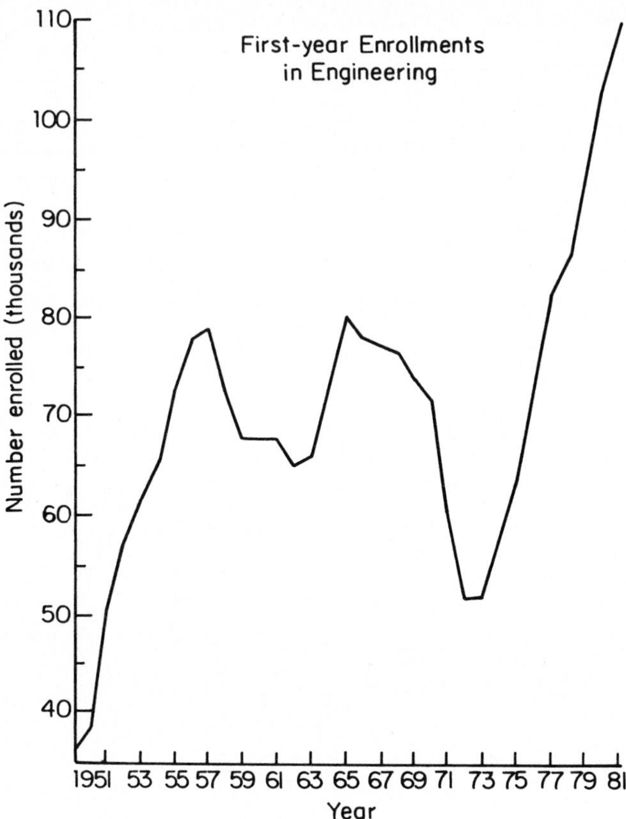

Figure 6.2, continued.

focused on the elasticity of supply to salary or wage incentives while Panel B treats studies that estimate responsiveness to tuition charges.

Despite differences in the nature of the studies, the estimates in Panel A fall into a range of around one or two. The studies for the United Kingdom are comparable to those for the United States. The Mattila study, which is the only one to estimate responses to calculated rates of return rather than starting or average salaries, yields figures analogous to studies using these measures of incentives. All told, the various studies reveal considerable responsiveness, which goes a long way to accounting for observed swings in the proportion of young persons enrolled in college in postwar years.

Table 6.4
Estimates of the supply of persons to higher education.

A. Studies of responses to salaries

Study	Sample	Elasticity response to salaries
Tinbergen (1974)	Countries	0.54–2.64
Freeman (1975)	Time series, U.S.A.	1.3–1.7
Freeman and Hansen (1982)	Time series, U.S.A.	1.82
Willis and Rosen (1979)	Individuals in NBER–Thorndike sample, U.S.A.	about 2.00
Pissarides (1979)	Time series, U.K.	1.12–1.31
Dolphin (1981)	Time series, U.K.	0.7
Mattila (1982)	Time series, U.S.A.	0.86–1.39

B. Studies of responses to tuition

Study	Sample	Response of enrollment rate per $100 change in tuition
Corazzini, Dugan and Grabowski (1963)	National cross-section	0.62
Hopkins (1963)	State cross-section	0.75
Barnes (1970)	Individual students	1.53
Radner and Miller (1966)	Individual students	0.05
Kohn, Manski and Mundel (1966)	Individual students	0.92
Hoenack (1965)	High school districts	0.71
Hoenack and Weiler (1972)	Individual students	1.46
Spies (1971)	Individual students	0.05
Campbell and Siegel (1919–64)	Time series	0.20
Bishop (1963)	Individual students	0.90

Source: Panel B from McPherson (1978).

Studies of responses to changes in tuition rates, summarized by McPherson, tell a similar story. All of the reviewed studies found that tuition affected enrollment, with a magnitude that roughly indicates that a $100 change in tuition would alter the proportion enrolled by perhaps 0.8 or so percentage points. Translated into an elasticity of response, the tuition-elasticity of enrollment is about 0.3 [McPherson (1978, p. 181)]. Since tuition is only a fraction of the salaries received by students, this low number makes intuitive sense and is, indeed, consistent with a supply elasticity of the magnitudes found in Panel A.

Finally, U.S. survey evidence provides additional support for the notion that students are highly responsive to economic rewards in decisions to enroll in college. Nearly 80 percent of freshmen surveyed by the American Council of

Education in 1977 agreed, for example, that a major reason for going to college was that it would enable them to get a better job. One-third cited "ability to make money" as a very important reason for going to college. While some may doubt the meaningfulness of these responses, they are consistent with the statistical studies cited in Table 6.4.

As for elasticities of supply to specific fields of study, a substantial literature has examined time series fluctuations in enrollment and degrees, of the type shown in Figure 6.2. Supply elasticities have been estimated for a wide variety of professional specialties. Physics [Freeman (1976)], Economics [Hansen (1980)], Engineering [Freeman (1976), Sirbu et al. (1978)], Law [Freeman (1976), Freebairn and Withers (1979), Pashigan (1977)], in the United States; teachers in the United Kingdom [Zabalza (1979)], among other areas. The principal result of this work is that supply elasticities to various professions are quite sizeable and, in conjunction with observed wage changes, explain a large proportion of the changes in degrees and enrollments of the type shown in Figure 6.2.

An important prerequisite for labor supply to be responsive to economic incentives is that decision-makers be knowledgeable about market conditions. Surveys of several thousand college students have shown them to be aware of the ranking of fields by salary, of differences in lifetime income profiles, and of recent changes in salaries, providing further support for the high estimated supply elasticities [Freeman (1971)].

Most studies distinguish between short-run and long-run elasticities of response. The short-run response is defined as the percentage change in one year's supply due to a change in economic incentives; the long-run response represents the percentage change in supply a number of years in the future assuming the new wage pattern persists. As a rough generalization, short-run supply elasticities are typically below 1.00, while long-run elasticities are in the range of 3.0–4.0. The long-run responses tend to exceed those estimated for college enrollments overall, presumably because any given field can attract persons from other college fields as well as from persons on the margin between attending college and working.

A related body of work has examined the decision of *individuals* to choose college or among colleges or other programs. Willis and Rosen (1975) estimated expected lifetime earnings for persons going to college and not going to college on the basis of a large number of ability and background indicators. They found that expected lifetime earnings gains influenced the decision to attend college. In their model persons who did not attend would have earned less then reasonably similar persons who did attend. The estimated elasticity of enrollment to earnings was about 2.00, which is remarkably similar to estimates from time series data. Lazear (1977a) used individual data to compare the amount of school obtained as an investment and the amount obtained for consumption purposes. On the basis of an individual's background and ability, returns to schools, and estimates of the cost of schooling and financial assistance, he estimated the wealth maximizing amount of education an individual should want and found it exceeded actual schooling levels. He interpreted this to imply that on the margin school attendance is "bad". While one may object to the specifics of his model and interpretation, it appears that the education-as-an-investment good interpretation of schooling attainment does better than the education-as-a-consumption good interpretation. Finally, Manski and Wise (1983) have developed conditional logit models designed to predict whether or not young people (in the National Longitudinal Study of the High School Class of 1972) apply to college, the quality of college applied, admissions, and the students' choice. Consistent with the proposition that student decisions respond to economic factors they found that local wage rates (an indicator of income forgone) had a significant negative impact on the probability of applying and that the students' choice of college was influenced by tuition, scholarships, and the like, as one would expect. In general, moreover, tuition and forgone earnings had roughly comparable effects on choices, consistent with economic rationality. Moreover, Manski and Wise concluded that most young people who rejected college were likely to have benefitted least from it and to have dropped out rather than completed it. Overall, the picture one gets is highly consistent with the model of college-going as a rational incentive decision.

In sum, while at one period of time it was possible for educationists and others to disparage the economic analysis of investment in education as unrealistic or irrelevant to actual behavior, such a view cannot now be sustained. An important outcome of the human capital revolution has been the finding that, in fact, youths respond significantly to economic incentives in their educational decisions. Indeed, the evidence indicates that among new entrants to the job market supply elasticities for educated labor are quite substantial. Because of the relative stability of the supply of older specialists, relatively few of whom go back to school to change their fields of specialization, however, elasticities of total supply are much smaller.

6. Salary determination

One of the key elements of the human capital model of demand for education is that education affects earnings. Accordingly, the education–earnings relation has been the focus of considerable work. In the simplest model of education as an investment good, one can define the return to the investment (r) by the following continuous time version of the human capital investment equation:

$$\int_0^n W_t \mathrm{e}^{-rt} = \int_s^{n_s} W_{st} \mathrm{e}^{-rt} + \int_0^S (W_{et}' - D) \mathrm{e}^{-rt} \tag{9}$$

where

W_t = wage/earnings for persons without the relevant education,
r = rate of return to investment in education,
n = number of years noneducated persons work,
W_{st} = wage/earnings for persons with education,
n_s = number of years educated persons work,
W'_{st} = wage/earnings for persons during education period,
D = direct cost of education, and
s = number of years of education.

The first term in (9) is the present value of earnings (discounted at the rate r) for persons who do not go on to education. The second term is the present value of earnings for persons with education after they graduate from school. The third term measures the earnings during school net of the direct costs of schooling. If one assumes that earnings do not change with age or experience (in practice, this means including age/experience terms in an analysis), that net earnings during school average to ero, and that educated workers retire s years later than less educated workers, (9) becomes:

$$\int_0^n W e^{-rt} = \int_s^{n+s} W_s e^{-rt} \tag{10}$$

or

$$\frac{Ws}{W} = \frac{e^{-r(n+s)} - e^{-rs}}{e^{-rn} - 1} = e^{rs}. \tag{11}$$

Taking logs, we get:

$$\log w_s = \log w + rs \ (+\text{other terms}). \tag{12}$$

This is the simplest derivation of the widely used log-earnings function in which the logarithm of earnings is regressed on years of schooling and its coefficient interpreted as a rough estimate of the initial rate of return of the investment.

In a major study of earnings determination Mincer (1974) explored various aspects of this type of equation in the context of a model which made many useful points about how post-school training affects the shape of earnings functions, the variance of earnings by age, and the like. This book was extremely influential in producing numerous "replica" studies, estimates of (12) with additional age or experience terms for various countries and settings.

In a study using 1970 Census data, Heckman and Polachek (1974) examined the fit of the log form versus that of other forms and concluded that, indeed, the log distribution offers a reasonably good fit of earnings data, compared to other "power" functions.

Virtually every study of earnings finds that years of schooling has a significant and sizeable impact on earnings. However, at the same time, every study also finds that *by itself*, years of schooling explains a relatively small part of the variance of log earnings, say 3–5 percent at most. If the human capital model rested its analysis of earnings on the link between years of schooling and earnings, it would not have had the impact on earnings analysis it did. What gives the theory its empirical power in explaining earnings is the extension to the impact of age/experience on earnings, an issue beyond the purview of this chapter.

7. Probing the education–earnings link

"But earnings studies compare different people. More educated people tend to be more able. More educated people come from higher income and status homes. Therefore, the studies overstate the education–earnings link."

The education–ability–background–earnings nexus lies at the heart of interpretations of the relation of earnings to education. Considerable effort has gone into probing the extent to which the estimated effect of education on earnings is a "true" causal effect as opposed to a spurious effect due to lack of controls for ability or background factors.

The first and most obvious way to probe the education coefficient in an earnings function is to add measures of ability and background to eq. (12). Such analyses yield a definite conclusion: education matters about as much in the presence of those measures as in their absence. For instance, an IQ measure of ability has only modest effects on earnings while measures of parental occupational status and education have, if anything, even weaker effects [Griliches (1977)]. Indeed, the background factors appear to operate largely through education, rather than on labor market rewards per se. It is this result that underlies the "radical" interpretation of education as the key institution transmitting inequality from generation to generation [Bowles and Gintis (1982)].

But... but...

If the background and ability measures are poorly measured, relative to years of schooling, the conclusions based on simply adding IQ and background measures into earnings equations may be erroneous. Perhaps better measures of ability and background would greatly change one's reading of the evidence on education's impact on earnings. Various instrumental variable and measurement models have been developed to probe this possibility. With respect to background the basic conclusion is that, while better measures of background (particularly use of family income, rather than parental occupation or education) raise the coefficient on background in earnings equations, years of schooling continues to have a sizeable significant effect on earnings. With respect to ability, the results are comparable. Instrumenting IQ or other indicators of ability on other factors raises its estimated impact but does not greatly affect the years of schooling–education link.

Concern with the effect of ability and background on earnings has led economists into an area of research previously left solely to psychologists: comparisons of blood relatives, particularly twins. The idea behind relative (twin) studies is that comparisons of persons from the same family (embryo) yield especially good controls on background and ability factors, thereby isolating the effect of education. Work on brothers by Griliches and Chamberlain (1975) found that the brother with additional schooling does, indeed, earn more than the brother with less, by amounts only modestly different from those between nonbrothers. Work by Taubman (1976) on twins, however, yielded a very different result, possibly due to sample size and measurement error. What the twins (brothers) studies essentially do is compare differences in earnings and differences in education across the groups. Because differencing reduces the true variation in education, it tends to make the measurement error or noise component of the variance in education larger relative to the genuine variance, which biases downward the coefficient.

The critical reader will have noticed an inconsistency between the analyses between this section and the preceding section. Studies of earnings typically take schooling as exogenous; in the preceding section, schooling was endogenous. As Rosen (1979) noted in his review article on human capital, making education endogenous alters the interpretation of earnings equations. Instead of tracing out the impact of education on earnings, the relation can be viewed as an envelope curve showing the covariation in the two variables due to underlying factors. It does not tell us what would happen to an individual if he/she got more education.

One way of dealing with the potential endogeneity of years of schooling is to estimate earnings equations in which schooling is instrumented on other factors as part of a two-equation system. In his Frisch lectures Griliches (1977) reports the results of various experiments of this kind. In large part because it is difficult to find identifying factors (functional form, with the log form for earnings and a linear or other nonlog form for years of schooling is too weak to yield much), the effort to estimate the effect of schooling on earnings, with education endogenous, has not yielded fruitful results. Depending on the model, one can get very different estimates.

Another way of dealing with difficulties of estimating the education–earnings relation is to examine earnings before and after a person obtains additional education. Griliches and Mason's (1972) study of men who left the armed forces contains such a longitudinal analysis. It shows reasonably similar returns to education between standard cross-section comparisons and from the before/after analysis of veterans who obtained additional schooling.

Overall, the probes into the education–earnings relation have illuminated the difficulties in making inferences from the type of data we normally analyze. At the same time, like probes into other basic empirical results in economics, they have not overturned the essential fact which serves as the starting point for the investigation: that education is causally associated with higher earnings.

8. Changes over time and market dynamics

While much analysis of earnings functions has treated the coefficient on education as a "constant", there has been considerable concern with time series changes in the impact of education, particularly of college training on earnings. Basic data on earnings by education shows a considerable decline in the premium paid college graduates in the 1970s which, combined with increases in tuition and other changes, has produced a fall in the rate of return. While there has been some controversy over the permanence and cause of the fall data from all the O.E.C.D. countries shows such a similar pattern to the United States as to indicate that this is a general phenomenon for the entire developed world (Freeman). In one sense, no one should be surprised. Higher education expanded greatly in the United States and elsewhere in the 1960s and 1970s; the large "baby boom" cohort went on to college in unprecedented numbers. Given the elasticities of substitution reported in Table 6.3, the relative earnings of college graduates could be expected, all else the same, to fall, as they did.

An important aspect of the changes in the earnings of graduates relative to nongraduates has been the incidence by age. Earnings data show that much of the decline has occurred among new entrants and young or less experienced graduates [Freeman (1975, 1976), Welch (1979)]. This has produced a striking difference between the age–earnings profile of earnings in the 1960s and in the 1970s. Among college graduates, the profile is notably steeper by age in the latter period [Freeman (1979), Welch (1979)]. Human capital explanations of age–earnings in terms of investment in post-school on-the-job training do not appear to explain this changed pattern; differences in substitution elasticities between more/less educated workers by age, do. The change in profiles highlights the difference between cross-section profiles, which compare differently aged persons at a point in time, and longitudinal profiles for the same group over time. While the longitudinal profile for graduates in the large cohorts of the 1970s shows some "catching up", over time the catch-up is not fast enough to attain the earnings for graduates in previous cohorts. This has two implications. One, that the decline in the economic value of college will continue for this group over their work life; they have suffered a major capital loss. Two, it directs our attention in evaluating returns to education to *future* market developments. Here, as elsewhere, in evaluating long-term investments, one must explicitly or implicitly forecast the future, taking account of exogenous changes in the economy and in demography and of the dynamics of the market for educated labor.

One effort to model market dynamics has focused on the training lag between the decision to enroll in school and eventual graduation into the job market. In its simplest form, the training lag leads to a two-equation cobweb type model:

$$G_{t+1} = aW^*_{t,t+1} + bX^*_{t,t+1}, \tag{13}$$

$$S_{t+1} = -\alpha G_{t+1} + Z_{t+1}, \tag{14}$$

where

G_{t+1} = number of graduates in $t+1$,
$W^*_{t,t+1}$ = salary expected in $t+1$ at time t, when the training decision is made,
$X^*_{t,t+1}$ = other conditions of the market expected in year $t+1$ at time t,
S_{t+1} = market salary in $t+1$,
Z_{t+1} = demand conditions in $t+1$.

If $W^*_{t,t+1} = W_t$, one gets the classic cobweb adjustment model, in which high initial salaries produce large entering classes, which lead to large graduate classes, which reduce salaries and so on. If $W^*_{t,t+1}$ is determined by adaptive expectations, one gets a more complex adjustment pattern. Finally, even if $W^*_{t,t+1}$ is formed by rational expectations, the market structure is such that random shocks can produce oscillations.

Empirical analysis of the market for new graduates using variants of (13)–(14), particularly of engineering, show marked oscillations (see Figure 6.2), which appear due to the internal dynamics of the market structure. The oscillations are, however, highly dampened so that continual large shocks are needed to produce the observed patterns. Moreover, it is questionable whether the oscillations are due to "cobweb" ups and downs, or to shocks in a rational expectations model. For teachers (where oscillations are less noticeable) Zarkin's (1983, 1985) analysis indicates that it is difficult with observed data to distinguish between models of these types.

There have been other changes in the education-earnings link, also. In the 1960s, the low return to education for blacks was cited in a number of articles as one of the major causes of black/white earnings inequality. Developments in the

1970s, potentially due to the Civil Rights Act of 1964 and Affirmative Action, have produced a very different pattern of educational differentials by race, particularly among the young. In 1969, for example, among 25–34 year olds the ratio of the earnings of black men with four years of college to that of black men with four years of high school was 1:21 compared to a ratio of 1:26 for all men. In 1980, the comparable ratios were: 1:35 black; 1:20 all men.[6] As the causes and consequences of this change falls more properly under the topic of economics of discrimination, I forgo further discussion here.

The key point to remember from the various analyses of changing educational premium over time is that these differentials are not "natural constants". The relative wage structure by education has shown remarkable variation over time in response to changes in supply and demand. In one sense this complicates analysis of the link from schooling to earnings. In another sense, however, it further demonstrates the power of an economic analysis of education.

9. Public finance of education

Education has long been a pre-eminent publicly funded good. The vast majority of elementary and secondary school students attend publicly funded institutions. The same is true of the vast majority of college students. The question of what determines the level of public demand for schooling has spawned a sizeable literature.

Much of this work has examined the effect of such factors as average income in an area, inequality of income, demographic factors and such cost factors as teachers salaries, expenditures per pupil, or taxes on one of two variables: spending in a locality and votes in referendum on school spending.

A typical model has three components: a utility function for the individual's benefits from school expenditures; a tax or cost burden function for the price of the good; and a political mechanism for translating individual demands into public outcomes. The utility function is a standard form, with a common assumption that persons with children have greater utility from public education than others. The tax or cost burden typically depends on the particulars of the local public finance rules and the input prices for teachers and the like. In large part because we lack a simple alternative model, Hotelling's median voter model is often invoked to rationalize the political structure and translate individual demands into public demands.[7]

[6]1959 figures taken simple mean of medians reported in United States Census of Population, 1960, *Educational Attainment*. 1979 are United States Census of Population, 1980, *United States Summary*.

[7]For some models in this vein, see Bergstrom and Goodman (1973), Denzau and MacKay (1976), Deacon and Shapiro (1975).

While different models have different interesting properties from which restrictions can be used to test relatively sophisticated issues regarding any of these three parts, the basic empirical analysis consists of multi-variate regressions of either expenditures in a community or individual votes for or against spending as a function of the relevant variables.

The principal finding of these studies is that there exists a reasonably well-defined demand curve for educational expenditures on the part of local communities. Studies of expenditures [Feldstein (1975), Inman (1978), Lovell (1978), Brown and Saks (1983)] and of voting in referendum [Rubinfeld (1976)] find positive significant income elasticities (generally less than one) and negative significant price elasticities. In addition, studies generally find that demographic variables have sizeable effects with the proportion of the population without children or of an age unlikely to have children in school likely to desire less school spending. There is a pattern in some of the studies for income elasticities to exceed price elasticities (Feldstein's is the exception).

The interface between private demand for education and public expenditures has been explored in terms of "trade-off" between public and private schooling. Some studies [Brown and Saks (1983), Peltzman (1973)] have found significant "crowding out" with expansion of public schools rendering private education or, conversely, the size of the private school sector reducing support for spending for public education. Other studies have yielded no significant results [Rubinfeld (1976), Feldstein (1975)].

10. Conclusion

This survey of research on the demand for education has shown a sizeable increase in our knowledge of the economics of education in the past two decades. While some early hopes that education and human capital more broadly defined would be the "magic bullet" for labor market and general economic analysis, explaining economic growth, income distribution, and more, have proven false, the economics of education has become safely imbedded in any serious investigation of labor market issues. The original insights of Schultz and Becker have lead us down a fertile path of research. Do we know more than we did when *Human Capital* was published in 1964? I believe the answer is yes. We know more about how education fits into an economic system. We also know more about what we do not know or cannot determine from our models and data. Both represent progress.

References

Allen, R. G. D. (1981) *Mathematical analysis for economists*. London.
American Council on Education (1966) *National norms for entering college freshman*.

American Council on Education (1974, 1979) *The American freshmen: national norms.*
Arrow, K. J. (1962) "Higher education as a filter", *Journal of Public Economics*, 2:193–216.
Baily, M. N. (1984) "A comment on Michael Darby's explanation of U.S. productivity growth", mimeo.
Baily, M. N. (1984) "Will productivity growth recover? Has it done so already?", *The American Economic Review*, 74:301–321.
Barlow, R. (1970) "Efficiency aspects of local school finance", *Journal of Political Economy*, 78:1028–1040.
Becker, G. S. (1967) "Human capital and the personal distribution of income: an analytical approach", Department of Economics, The University of Michigan.
Becker, G. S. (1964) *Human capital.* New York: National Bureau of Economic Research.
Behrman, J. and P. Taubman (1983) "The interrelationship of education across three generations", Center for Household and Family Economics, The University of Pennsylvania.
Ben-Porath, Y. (1967) "The production of human capital and the life cycle of earnings", *Journal of Political Economy*, 75:352–356.
Ben-Porath, Y. (1970) "The production of human capital over time", in: L. Hansen, ed., *Education, income and human capital.* New York: NBER, Columbia University Press.
Bergstrom, T. C. and R. P. Goodman (1973) "Private demands for public goods", *The American Economic Review*, 63(3).
Bishop, J. and J. Van Dyk (1977) "Can adults be hooked on college? Some determinants of adult college attendance", *Journal of Higher Education*, 47.
Bowles, S. (1969) *Planning educational systems for economic growth.* Cambridge, Mass.: Harvard University Press.
Bowles, S. (1972) "Schooling and inequality from generation to generation", *Journal of Political Economy*, 80(3):S219–S251.
Bowles, S. and H. Gintis (1982) *Schooling in capitalist America.* New York: Basic Books.
Bowman, M. J. (1970) "Education and economic growth", in: R. L. Johns, ed., *Economic factors affecting the financing of education in the decade ahead.*
Bowman, M. J. (1964) "Schultz, Denison, and the contribution of 'Eds' to national income growth", *Journal of Political Economy*, 72(5):450–465.
Bradford, D. F. and W. E. Oates (1974) "Suburban exploitation of central cities and governmental structure", in: H. Hochman and G. Peterson, eds., *Redistribution through public choice.* New York: Columbia University Press, 43–92.
Brown, B. W. and D. H. Saks (1983) "Spending for local public education: income distribution and the aggregation of private demands", Department of Economics, Princeton University.
Campbell, R. and B. N. Siegel (1967) "The demand for higher education in the United States, 1919–1964", *American Economic Review*, 57:482–494.
Chinloy, P. (1980) "Sources of quality change in labor input", *American Economic Review*, 70(1).
Corazzini, A., D. Dugan and H. Grabowski (1972) "Determinants and distributional aspects of enrollment in U.S. higher education", *Journal of Human Resources* 7:39–59.
Deacon, R. and P. Shapiro (1975) "Private preference for collective goods revealed through voting on referenda", *The American Economic Review*, December.
Denison, E. F. (1962) "Sources of economic growth in the United States and the alternatives before us", The Committee for Economic Development, New York.
Denison, E. F. (1967) *Why growth rates differ.* Washington: The Brookings Institution.
Denison, E. F. (1969) "Some major issues in productivity analysis: an examination of estimates by Jorgenson and Griliches", *Survey of Current Business*, 49(5):1–28.
Denison, E. F. (1979) *Accounting for United States economic growth, 1929 to 1969.* Washington, D.C.: The Brookings Institution.
Denison, E. F. (1979) *Accounting for slower economic growth: the United States in the 1970s.* Washington: The Brookings Institution.
Denzau, A. T. and R. J. Mackay (1976) "Benefit shares and majority voting", *American Economic Review*, March.
Dolphin, A. M. (1981) "The Demand for Higher Education", *The Employment Gazette*, July: 302–305.
Dougherty, C. R. S. (19XX) "Estimates of labour aggregation functions", *Journal of Political Economy*, 80(6):1101–1119.

Fairbairn, J. W. and G. Withers (1979) "Welfare effects of salary forecast error in professional labour market", *Review of Economics and Statistics*, 61:234–291.

Fallon, P. R. and P. R. G. Layard (1975) "Capital-skill complementarity, income distribution, and output accounting", *Journal of Political Economy*, April:279–302.

Fane, G. (1975) "Education and the managerial efficiency of farmers", *Review of Economics and Statistics*, 57:452–461.

Feldstein, M. S. (1975) "Wealth neutrality and local choice in public education", *The American Economy in Review*, 65(1).

Freeman, R. B. (1971) *The labor market for college-trained manpower*. Cambridge: Harvard University Press.

Freeman, R. B. (1975) "Overinvestment in college training?", *Journal of Human Resources*, Summer.

Freeman, R. B. (1975) "Legal cobwebs: a recursive model of the labor market for new lawyers", *Review of Economics and Statistics*.

Freeman, R. B. (1975) "Supply and salary adjustments to the changing science manpower market", *American Economic Review*.

Freeman, R. B. (1977) "Manpower requirements and substitution analysis of labor skills: a synthesis", in: R. Ehrenberg, ed., *Research in labor economics*. Johnson Publishers.

Freeman, R. B. (1976a) *The overeducated american*. New York: Academic Press.

Freeman, R. B. (1976b) "A cobweb model of the supply and starting salary of new engineers", *Industrial Labor Relations Review*, January.

Freeman, R. B. (1979) "The effect of demographic factors on the age-earnings profile in the U.S.", *Journal of Human Resources*, Summer.

Freeman, R. B. (1980) "An empirical analysis of the fixed coefficient manpower requirements model, 1960–1970", *Journal of Human Resources*, Spring.

Freeman, R. B. (1981) "Changing economic value of higher education in developed economies: report to the OECD", NBER Working Paper 820.

Freeman, R. B. and J. Hansen (1982) "Forecasting the changing market for college-trained workers", paper prepared for the Second Annual Policy Forum on Employability Development, Responsiveness to Changing Labor Market Demands.

Freeman, R. B. and J. H. Holloman (1976) "The declining value of college going", *Change*, September:24–31.

Freeman, R. B. and J. Leonard (1977) "Autoregressive degree patterns: evidence of endogenous cycles and the market?", Industrial Relations Research Association, Proceedings of the Thirtieth Annual Winter Meeting, 10–19.

Gintis, R. (1971) "Education, technology, and the characteristics of worker productivity", *American Economic Review*, 61:266–279.

Gisser, M. (1965) "Schooling and the farm problem", *Econometrica*, 33:582–592.

Grant, J. (1979) "Labor substitution in U.S. manufacturing", Ph.D. dissertation, Michigan State University.

Grant, J. (1981) "Separability and substitution among labor aggregates and capital", Wellesley College Working Paper #40.

Griliches, Z. (1969) "Capital skill complementarity", *Review of Economics and Statistics*, 51:465–468.

Griliches, Z. (1970) "Notes on the role of education in production functions and growth accounting", in: W. L. Hansen, ed., *Education, income and human capital. Studies in income and wealth*. New York: Columbia University Press, vol. 35.

Griliches, Z. (1977) "Estimating the return to schooling: a progress report", *Econometrica*, 45(1):1–22.

Griliches, Z. (1978) "Sibling models and data in economics: beginnings of a survey", Harvard Institute of Economic Research.

Griliches, Z. and G. Chamberlain (1975) "Unobservables with a variance-components structure: ability, schooling and the economic success of brothers", *International Economic Review*, 16(2), June.

Griliches, Z. and W. Mason (1972) "Education, income, and ability", *Journal of Political Economy*, 80.

Hamermesh, D. and J. Grant (1979) "Econometric studies of labor–labor substitution and their implications for policy", *Journal of Human Resources*, 14(4):518–542.

Hanoch, G. (1967) "An economic analysis of earnings and schooling", *Journal of Human Resources*, 2.

Hansen, W. L. et al. (1980) "Forecasting the market for new Ph.D. economists", The *American Economic Review*, 70(1):49–63.

Harbison, F. and C. Myers (1964) *Education, manpower, and economic growth*. New York: McGraw-Hill.

Heckman, J. and S. Polachek (1974) "Empirical evidence on the functional form of the earnings–schooling relationship", *Journal of the American Statistical Association*, 69.

Hopkins, T. (1974) "Higher education enrollment demand", *Economic Inquiry*, 12:53–65.

Houthakker, H. S. (1959) "Education and income", *Review of Economics and Statistics*, 41.

Huffman, W. (1977) "Allocative efficiency: The role of human capital", *Quarterly Journal of Economics*, 91:59–79.

Inman, R. P. (1978) "Testing political economy's 'as if' proposition: is the median income voter really decisive?", *Public Choice*, 33(4).

Jamison, D. and L. Lau (1982) *Farmer education and farm efficiency*. Baltimore: Johns Hopkins University Press.

Johnson, G. (1970) "The demand for labor by educational category", *Southern Economic Journal*, October:190–204.

Jorgenson, D. W. (1984) *The Contribution of education to U.S. economic growth, 1948–1973*. Cambridge, Mass.: Department of Economics, Harvard University.

Jorgenson, D. W. and Z. Griliches (1972) *The measurement of productivity*. Washington, D.C.: The Brookings Institution.

Khaldi, N. (1975) "Education and allocative efficiency in U.S. agriculture", *American Journal of Agricultural Economics*, 57:650–657.

Kohn, M., C. Manski and D. Mundel (1974) "An empirical investigation of factors which influence college going behaviors", R1470-NSF, Rand Corporation, Santa Monica, CA.

Krueger, A. O. (1968) "Factor endowments and per capita income difference among countries", *Economic Journal*, 78:641–659.

Kuznets, S. (1966) *Modern economic growth*. New Haven: Yale University Press.

Layard, P. R. G. and P. R. Fallon (19XX) "Capital-skill complementarity, income distribution and output accounting", *Journal of Political Economy*, 83(2).

Layard, R. and G. Psacharopoulos (1974) "The screening hypothesis and the returns to education", *Journal of Political Economy*, 82(5):985–998.

Lazear, E. (1977a) "Education: consumption or production?", *Journal of Political Economy*, 85(3).

Lazear, E. (1977b) "Schooling as a wage depressant", *Journal of Human Resources*, Spring.

Levhari, D. and Y. Weiss (1976) "The effect of risk and investment in human capital", *American Economic Review*, 66:221–223.

Lovell, M. C. (1978) "Spending for education: the exercise of public choice", *The Review of Economics and Statistics*, 60(4).

McPherson, X. (1978) "The demand for higher education", in: D. Brenman and C. Finn, eds., *Public policy and private higher education*. Washington, D.C.: The Brookings Institution, 181, table 3-9.

Manski, C. F. and D. Wise (1983) *College choice in America*. Cambridge, Mass.: Harvard University Press.

Mattila, J. P. (1982) "Determinants of male school enrollments: a time series analysis", *Review of Economics and Statistics*, 64:242–251.

Mincer, J. (1974) *Schooling, experience, and earnings*. New York: NBER.

Mincer, J. (1981) "Human capital and economic growth", National Bureau of Economic Research, Working Paper 803.

Pashigan, P. (1977) "The market for lawyers: the determinants of the demand for and supply of lawyers", *Journal of Law and Economics*, 20:53–86.

Peltzman, S. (1973) "The effect of government subsidies-in-kind on private expenditures: the case of higher education", *Journal of Political Economy*, 81(1):1–28.

Peterson, G. (1973) "The demand for public schooling", Urban Institute Working Paper No. 1207-28, Washington, D.C.

Psacharopoulos, G. and K. Hinchliffe (1972) "Further evidence on the elasticity of substitution among different types of educated labor", *Journal of Political Economy*, 80(4):786–791.

Psacharopoulos, G. (1983a) "The contribution of education to economic growth: international comparisons", in: J. Kendrick, ed., *International productivity comparisons*. Washington, D.C.: American Enterprise Institute.

Psacharapoulous, G. (1983b) *World Bank Research News*, 4(1):3–17.

Radner, R. and L. Miller (1975) *Demand and supply in U.S. higher education*. New York: McGraw-Hill.

Riley, J. (1975) "Competitive signalling", *Journal of Economic Theory*, 10(1):175–186.

Riley, J. (1979) "Testing the educational screening hypothesis", *Journal of Political Economy*, 87(5).

Rosen, S. (1971) "Human capital: a survey of empirical research", in: R. C. Ehrenberg, eds., *Research in labor economics*. Greenwich, Conn.: JAI Press, 3–39.

Rosen, S. (1972) "Learning and experience in the labor market", *Journal of Human Resources*.

Rubinfeld, D. L. (1976) "Voting in a local school election: a micro analysis", *The Review of Economics and Statistics*, February.

Ryder, H., F. Stafford and P. Stephan (1976) "Training and leisure over the life cycle", *International Economic Review*.

Sato, Ryuzo and K. Tetsunori (1973) "On the elasticities of substitution and complementarity", *Oxford economic papers*, 25:44–56.

Schultz, T. W. (1960) "Capital formation by education", *Journal of Political Economy*, 68(6):545–557.

Schultz, T. W. (1961) "Investment in human capital", *American Economic Review*.

Schultz, T. W. (1975) "The value of the ability to deal with disequilibria", *Journal of Economic Literature*, 13:872–876.

Selowsky, M. (1982) "The economic effects of investment in children: a survey of the quantitative evidence", in: T. E. Johnson, ed., *Child development information, and the formation of public policy: an international perspective*. Springfield, Illinois: Charles C. Thomas.

Sirbu, M. et al. (1978) "*Improved methodologies for forecasting new entrants in science and engineering*", Center for Policy Analysis Report #CPA-78-15, Center for Policy Alternatives, Cambridge.

Spence, A. M. (1974) *Market signalling: informational transfer in hiring and related screening processes*. Cambridge, Mass.: Harvard University Press.

Spence, A. M. (1976) "Competition in salaries, credentials, and signalling prerequisites for jobs", *Quarterly Journal of Economics*, 90(1):51–75.

Spies, R. (1973) *The future of private colleges: the effect of rising costs on college choice*. Princeton University: Industrial Relations Section.

Stiglitz, J. (1975) "The theory of screenings, education, and the distribution of income", *American Economic Review*, 65(3):283–300.

Taubman, P. J. (1976) "Earnings, education, genetics, and environment", *Journal of Human Resources*, 2(4):447–462.

Taubman, P. J. and T. J. Wales (1973) "Higher education, mental ability, and screening", *Journal of Political Economy*, 81(1):28–56.

Tinbergen, J. (1974) "Substitution of graduates by other labour", *Kyklos*, 27(2):217–226.

Welch, F. (1970) "Education in production", *Journal of Political Economy*, 78:764–771.

Welch, F. (1979) "Effects of cohort size on earnings: the baby boom babies' financial bust", *Journal of Political Economy*, 87.

Wilkinson, B. W. (1966) "Present values of lifetime earnings for different occupations", *Journal of Political Economy*.

Willis, R. and S. Rosen (1975) "Education and self-selection", *Journal of Political Economy*, 87:817–836.

Wolpin, K. I. (1977) "Educational screening", *American Economic Review*, 67(5):949–958.

Zabalza, A. (1979) "The determinants of teacher supply", *Review of Economic Studies*, 142:1310–1348.

Zarkin, G. (1983) "Cobweb versus rational expectations: lessons from the market for public school teachers", *Economic Letters*.

Zarkin, G. (1985) "Occupational choice: an application to the market for public school teachers", *Quarterly Journal of Economics*, 100(2):409–447.

Chapter 7

FORESTALLING THE DEMISE OF EMPIRICAL ECONOMICS: THE ROLE OF MICRODATA IN LABOR ECONOMICS RESEARCH

FRANK STAFFORD*

University of Michigan

1. Introduction

In a recent letter to the editor of *Science*, Leontief (1982) has claimed that the *American Economic Review*, and the economics profession more generally, have come to be dominated by papers in which empirical work is either weak, trivial or totally absent and in which theory, simulation, and misplaced aggregation are central. The profession of economics is characterized as unconcerned about deterioration in the quality of data sources which could be used to revitalize useful empirical work. These are serious concerns if economics is to be successful as a scientific (i.e. empirically based) field rather than a branch of applied mathematics.

In contrast to Leontief's remarks which were directed toward the entire field of economics, in this chapter it is shown that for the field of labor economics there has been a growth of new types of data, of econometric methods and practice tailored to hypothesis testing based on substantive and policy questions, and of papers with a theoretical section which is connected to the subsequent empirical work. These conclusions are based on analysis of the 759 full-length articles on labor economics subjects appearing in six major journals.

It is research based on microdata which sets labor economics apart from several other areas of economics in the extent to which theory and econometric method are used as part of a rather deliberate research program. As a recent study by Taeuber and Rockwell (1982) shows, there has been a dramatic growth in national data collection efforts in the late 1960s and the 1970s, and a large

*I would like to thank several people for helpful comments to date, namely Reuben Gronau, Bertil Holmlund, George Johnson, Gary Solon and Hal Varian. In addition, Hal Varian provided the winning margin in my first venture with microcomputers. All errors are my own responsibility. Research on this project was supported, in part, by the Industrial Institute for Economic and Social Research, Stockholm.

Handbook of Labor Economics, Volume I, Edited by O. Ashenfelter and R. Layard

number of these datasets are appropriate for labor economics research because of efforts to relate data base design to questions implied by theoretical models. These data have had a disproportionate effect on research on the supply side of labor economics with much less new work being done on the demand side. Much of this supply side work has been stimulated by the advent of a small number of large-scale sets of microdata, particularly panel data.

Was the greater availability of supply side data, in turn, the consequence of better theorizing and more policy interest in these topics? To illustrate, labor supply responses to variation in wage through time underly one of the key questions in macroeconomics: To what extent does variation in labor hours over the business cycle reflect optimizing behavior by households as they take advantage of temporary wage fluctuations to time their market work, with more hours during booms and less during recessions? To what extent is unemployment and nonparticipation in the labor market an implicit demand for leisure or a purposeful reduction in labor supply to canvass a wider set of prospective employers? Do social programs and tax laws accentuate the reduction in labor supply during economic contractions?

Although interesting labor supply questions can be listed readily, it is possible to identify just as many important demand side questions: How do inventory costs influence a firm's labor demand as product demand varies through the business cycle? Why do larger firms and certain industries pay higher wages and load their labor contract with a larger share of total compensation in the form of fringe benefits rather than direct wage payments? It is the claim of this chapter that the greater range and quality of our knowledge and theorizing on particular topics does significantly stem from the advent of large-scale micro level datasets. These datasets use individuals and households as the unit of observation and are important in explaining why, during the 1970s, about two-thirds of labor articles in major journals were on the broad subjects of labor supply and wage determination. As the existing data are worked and then reworked a type of diminishing returns will likely set in despite more elaborate econometric and theoretical machinery with which to work the data lode. To forestall the trends observed by Leontief new forms of data and observation will be required.

The contrast between data available on the supply side of the labor market versus the demand side is striking. No national probability samples exist for industrialized countries at the establishment level which can be used to characterize the microeconomic choice processes of firms in a fashion analogous to the way in which the choice process of households and individuals can be characterized. It is beyond the scope of this chapter to review the demand side data and its prospects for future development, but I believe a vastly better job can be done and that it would have a research payoff at least as great as the labor supply data have had. Perhaps new data on the demand side collected with input from researchers in the areas of industrial organization and organizational behavior will be developed during the next decade.

In this chapter we begin with a review of characteristics of papers published in selected journals (1965–83) in the field of labor economics as defined primarily by the chapter topics in this Handbook. This review demonstrates the changing character of the field in terms of topic, extent to which papers are exclusively theoretical, share of papers with a theoretical section which is meaningful and connects to the subsequent empirical endeavor, and type of data used for empirical work. Consonant with Leontief's findings we observe a growth of theoretical papers in terms of both number and share. However, it is also observed that this growth of theoretical papers does not appear to have crowded out good empirical work; if anything there seems to have been a parallel growth of both significant theoretical and empirical papers as the development of theory and data interact through time.

Section 3 of the chapter turns to a more detailed discussion of the interaction between theory, data base development and policy issues. Topics highlighted in this discussion are earnings functions and intertemporal labor supply models, including retirement and unemployment.

Section 4 discusses some of the advantages and disadvantages of different kinds of microdata, including data from social experiments which were a popular and costly type of data gathered in the United States during the 1970s. Section 4 also indicates some data based pitfalls and the weakness arising from many of the statistical tests in what can be termed second generation work on several topics. These tests often suffer from very limited power to discriminate among alternative hypotheses, but in some cases this weakness could be overcome by additional data.

2. The changing character of labor economics research, 1965–83

To characterize the changes in labor economics research all articles appearing between 1965 and 1983 in six major journals[1] were coded by topic, whether exclusively theoretical, whether, if empirical, the paper had a meaningful theoretical section, whether the paper was based on time series data, whether based on some sort of aggregate data such as census tracts[2] or states,[3] whether the paper was based on panel, experimental, or micro cross-section data, whether the data source was the Current Population Survey (CPS),[4] the Michigan Panel Study of

[1]*American Economic Review*, *Econometrica*, *Journal of Political Economy*, *Quarterly Journal of Economics*, *Review of Economics and Statistics*, and *International Economic Review*. Notes, comments and shorter papers were excluded as were *American Economic Association Proceedings*.

[2]Census tracts, school districts, SMSA, city and county data were all coded as census tract data.

[3]For research on countries outside the United States the coding was based on similar geographic areas. For example, prefectures of Japan were treated as states.

[4]Many countries have a survey which is similar or identical to the CPS and research based on such data was also coded as "CPS".

Income Dynamics (PSID), the National Longitudinal Surveys (conducted for the U.S. Labor Department by the Census Bureau, the National Opinion Research Center and the Ohio State University's Center for Human Resource Research), data from the Census, the Survey of Economic Opportunity (SEO) or some other set of microdata (all other). The coding of topic corresponds closely to the chapters in the volume.[5]

The total number of labor economics articles coded was 759, with 297 appearing between 1965 and 1974 and 462 appearing between 1975 and 1983. In Table 7.1 is presented the distribution of articles by subject for 1965–69, 1970–74, 1975–79 and 1980–83. Among broad topical areas, papers on labor supply and wage determination gained ground, particularly between 1965–69 and the 1970s. The share of papers on labor demand and on institutional structures declined throughout the period, with the exception of a modest upturn in the most recent period, 1980–83.

Some of the research trends appear to be the consequence of policy concerns. Retirement was not a subject which made an appearance in these journals until the late 1970s, when concern over funding of social security in the United States heightened interest in the topic. Similarly, the recent growth in papers devoted to labor market equilibrium, dynamic demand, and implicit contracts (included in the code of screening, signalling, and contracting),[6] can be ascribed to an interest in understanding the continued upward movement in the normal unemployment rate of most industrialized countries. Research on discrimination peaked in the 1970s at a time when government intervention for the purpose of affirmative action was the greatest but seems to have declined in most recent years as the flow of government initiatives in this area has dwindled.

Some topics seem to be largely stimulated by theoretical developments which are, in turn, at least partly stimulated by policy issues. Research on principal–agent and implicit contract models has grown recently, and this can be regarded as influencing models of retirement and unemployment. However, it can also be argued that this line of theoretical effort has, to some extent, been pushed along by policy-related interest in retirement and unemployment. A definite change in research on unemployment is a recent decline in papers on unemployment structure, and a replacement with papers devoted to establishing the idea of optimal or rational unemployment. Here theory has partly reshaped the way we think about a major policy issue.

[5]An alternative coding structure would be in terms of type of model. To illustrate, papers based on Seater's (1977) model of search as well as the original paper have a theoretical structure which is virtually identical to several of the labor supply models reviewed by Yoram Weiss in Chapter 11 of this Handbook. Yet, these papers were coded in the search category rather than a category of dynamic micro models.

[6]Again there are coding issues. Implicit contract models of retirement such as Lazear's (1979) paper were coded as having retirement as the subject rather than contracting as the subject.

Table 7.1
Articles in major journals: Labor economics subject, by year, 1965–83 (percentages in parentheses).

	1965–69	1970–74	1975–79	1980–83
Labor supply				
Population size and structure	7	14	19	10
Household production	0	11	8	8
Labor supply of men	2	5	7	6
Labor supply of women	0	3	9	6
Labor supply of others and income support disincentives of *UI*, *NIT*, taxes or other	2	7	16	15
Retirement	0	1	4	1
Educational demand	3	11	9	2
Migration	13	9	14	4
All	27 (25.0)	61 (32.0)	86 (34.0)	52 (26.0)
Labor demand				
Basic labor demand	10	11	11	10
Adjustment and dynamic demand	6	4	6	10
Minimum wage	1	2	4	4
All	17 (15.5)	17 (9.0)	21 (8.0)	24 (12.0)
Wage determination and earnings				
Earnings functions	10	22	38	17
Theoretical lifetime earnings	2	5	4	6
Compensating wage differentials	2	4	5	9
Discrimination	4	17	14	7
Income inequality (other than human capital)	9	20	22	20
Occupational choice	1	2	3	0
All	28 (25.5)	70 (37.0)	86 (34.0)	59 (29.5)
Labor market equilibrium and friction				
Specific training and turnover	1	4	3	5
Search	1	5	11	11
Unemployment structure	5	3	17	9
Cyclical movements	13	17	11	18
Screening, signalling and contracting	0	3	4	7
All	20 (18.0)	32 (17.0)	46 (18.0)	50 (25.0)
Institutional structures				
Trade unions, strikes, union wage effects	8	3	10	13
Stratification, segmentation	3	3	3	0
Public sector labor markets	3	4	1	3
All	14 (13.0)	10 (5.5)	14 (5.5)	16 (8.0)
Total	109 (100.0)	190 (100.0)	253 (100.0)	201 (100.0)

Table 7.2
Labor economics articles on major journals: Percentage distribution by type, method and data source, by year, 1965–83.

	1965–69	1970–74	1975–79	1980–83	All
Theory only, All	14	19	23	29	22
Theory only, Significant	7	12	13	15	12
Empirical with a meaningful theoretical section	17	33	36	36	33
Micro data	11	27	45	46	36
Panel	1	6	21	18	14
Experiment	0	0	2	2	1
Cross-section	10	21	21	26	21
Micro dataset					
PSID	0	0	6	7	4
NLS	0	3	10	6	6
CPS	0	1	5	6	3
SEO	0	4	4	0	2
Census (1-100, 1-100 or other)	3	5	2	0	2
All other micro datasets	8	14	18	27	18
Time series	42	27	18	16	23
Census tract	3	2	4	3	3
State	7	6	3	3	4
Other aggregate cross-section	14	16	8	4	10
Secondary data analysis	14	3	3	4	5
Significant	37	59	63	51	55
N	106	191	257	205	759

Research on institutional structures declined in the 1970–79 period but has recently experienced modest growth during 1980–83. Rather than being outside the main framework of economic theory, this newer work has applied microtheory to the analysis of unions and has made use of the data and methods developed in the broader field of labor economics, a subject to which we shall now turn.

One of the most pronounced changes in labor economics has been the growth of articles which are exclusively theoretical. Between 1965 and 1969 only about one-seventh of the papers appearing in major U.S. journals were exclusively theoretical as can be seen in Table 7.2. This share had approximately doubled by the 1980s: between 1980 and 1983, 29 percent of papers were exclusively theoretical.

The growing role of theory was not restricted to papers with an exclusively theoretical focus. Perhaps the most important change in the last twenty years has been the growth of empirical papers with a meaningful theoretical section. By this I mean papers in which there is some substantial theoretical framework which, at least in part, is an extension or reformulation of the existing standard theory of its day and which provides an interpretation of the paper's subsequent empirical work. There are obviously different standards which one could apply, and it was not required that the theoretical section be so directly connected to the empirical work that it was necessarily parameterized by the author. On the other hand, theoretical papers with a few stylized "facts" appended were not coded as "empirical with a meaningful theoretical section."

Combining papers which are exclusively theoretical with those empirical papers having a substantial theoretical section, about two-thirds of the labor economics papers in major journals in 1980–83 were theoretically based. In contrast less than one-third of the labor economics papers during 1965–69 can be characterized as theoretically based.[7] From these summary statistics it would appear that labor economics has conformed to the general pattern for all of economics reported by Leontief (1982) in his assessment of papers published in the *American Economic Review*.

A closer examination indicates a stable share of empirical papers in the range of 70–80 percent. The main decline in empirical work was in the reduced use of time series data[8] and aggregate cross-section data of various types. Secondary data analysis is defined as direct use of empirical results or tables published elsewhere, and this type of paper declined from 14 to 3 or 4 percent of all papers. As a group, the share of papers based on aggregate time series, aggregate cross-section, and secondary data analysis declined from 80 percent of all labor economics papers in 1965–69 to 30 percent in 1980–83.

The greatest attrition in terms of percentage point decline was in research using time series data. While 42 percent of all labor economics papers were based on time series in the 1965–69 period, by the 1980–83 period this had fallen to only 16 percent. The main growth in empirical papers has been in papers using microdata, particularly panel and micro cross-section data from surveys of households or individuals. In fact panel data were virtually out of the picture in 1965–69, but in the period between 1975 and 1983 they were utilized in approximately 20 percent of the papers in the sample. A few of the papers based on panel data did not employ the panel features of the dataset. Instead, the dataset was analyzed as if it were cross-sectional. Specifically, 22 percent of the papers using panel data did not exploit panel features of the dataset.

Now let us turn to a more impressionistic assessment of the research. How significant are the articles based on different methods, approaches, and data? In coding each article's "significance" I tried to be eclectic and not impose my own research priorities.

[7]The small number of papers with models simulated using hypothetical parameter values were included as theory only.

[8]Many papers involve combined aggregate cross-section and time series. For example, state data through time. Where T (the number of time periods) greatly exceeded N (the size of the cross-section) or where the main results seemed to depend on time series variation, the paper was coded as based on time series.

An article was judged significant if it was empirical and improved our understanding of how labor markets work or the actions of behavioral units within labor markets. A theoretical article was judged in terms of its empirical potential even if the article itself pointed to no evidence. To give some feeling for my coding, articles on search ended up with a high percentage with a significance code value of 1 even though few empirical articles appeared until the late 1970s. Obviously, someone who feels that search models have not been very illuminating would have coded some of these articles differently. An effort was made to judge the paper's contribution at the date it was written rather than in light of subsequent knowledge.

What has emerged is a growing use of microdata and growth of empirical papers with a substantial theoretical section. Subject to the obvious limitations of my effort to code the significance of each paper, there was a growth in the share of such papers up until 1980. From there on the share of significant papers declined. See the second to last row of Table 7.2. This decline cannot be attributed to fewer significant theoretical papers as can be seen in row 2 of Table 7.2, nor can it be attributed to a decline in the share of empirical papers with a substantial or meaningful conceptual framework as can be seen in row 3 of Table 7.2. What has occurred in this author's interpretation is a decline in the number of illuminating papers based exclusively on empirical results. In particular, I judged that 33 percent of papers were only empirical (not a theory paper and without a substantial theoretical section) and significant in 1975–79, whereas 21 percent of papers were so categorized in 1980–83.[9]

A reason for this decline in significant papers with an exclusively empirical orientation could be termed the data lode phenomenon. When a new type of data becomes available for research use as did micro cross-section and panel data during the 1970s, there appears to be a set of interesting results which will be based simply on the data without any new conceptual framework for interpretation.[10] As the data lode is worked sufficiently, diminishing returns set in to purely data based findings and perhaps eventually to innovations in or reformulations of theory.[11] This would imply that to counteract the pattern to which Leontief

[9] To illustrate the role of data based findings consider the summary offered by Duncan and Morgan (1981): "Even the most basic, descriptive findings from the PSID are surprising because they contradict many of the stereotypes built up from many years of cross-sectional analyses. The economic environment that most people face is not stable but rather quite volatile. It creates large numbers of workers and families who are occasionally poor, on welfare or in certain sectors of the labor market, but it also produces fairly small numbers who are persistently in those states. Frequent changes in family composition play a role in much of this volatility."

[10] The new data forms may give rise to complementary developments in statistical method, but it should be noted that here I have attempted to code substantive significance rather than methodological significance.

[11] Pencavel, Chapter 1 on labor supply of men in this Handbook, seems to indicate that diminishing returns can set in early in this process. New results seem to be not much better than the pioneering work on male labor supply.

objects, labor economics would have to be rejuvenated by a succession of new databases. Of course, not all new data sources can be expected to have major impacts on research. In the case of data from social experiments, only 2 percent of papers in recent years have been based on such data. See row 6 of Table 7.2.

The attrition in studies based on time series data can also be ascribed to the data lode phenomenon. Widespread availability of lower cost computing capacity and the existence of a large stock of relatively unexploited time series in the 1950s and 1960s led to extensive analysis of the basic time series data. Although new data became available with the passage of time and through the construction of new series from historical records, the basic stock had been pretty well worked, with diminishing returns to reworking the data using different methods and interpretations.

An alternative explanation for the erosion of time series as the major data source is that these data as well as aggregate cross-section data were simply displaced by microdata, which permitted better inferences for a whole range of research subjects in labor economics. In this case we would expect microdata to occupy a long standing, dominant role in labor market research rather than simply going through a cycle of rising and then falling application as diminishing returns set in.

A clear feature of microdata use is the importance of a small number of datasets. As reported by Taeuber and Rockwell (1982), there are over a hundred large-scale sets of microdata in the public domain in the United States, but about half of our sample's papers in 1975 to 1983 using microdata were written using just three data sources: the NLS, the PSID, and the CPS. The Survey of Economic Opportunity dataset collected in 1967 was quite widely used in the 1970s. In the later 1970s, of the papers using microdata, 56 percent were based on just these four datasets. During the period 1975–83, 75 percent of the papers based on panel data utilized either the NLS or the PSID. While the share of papers based on microdata accounted for by the leading datasets was substantial, there was a considerable lag in the diffusion of their use. Major use of the PSID occurred about 5–10 years after the first year of data collection (1968). Publication of papers based on panel data occurred in overnight fashion with virtually none in the sample until 1974 and an abrupt switch to a high rate of utilization from then on. Other U.S. longitudinal studies, described in Borus (1982), include the National Longitudinal Study of the High School Class of 1972, the Longitudinal Retirement History Survey and the NBER–Thondike–Hagen study.

As noted above, the data from the New Jersey–Pennsylvania, Gary, Seattle–Denver and Iowa–North Carolina income maintenance experiments have not been used a great deal. This is true even though the data, particularly those from the Seattle–Denver experiment extend over several years, include a wide array of variables and have income and wage variations which are probably much closer to being exogenous than the wage and income variations arising in a conventional set of microdata. Two explanations would appear to be that, first, the samples in the experiments are restricted to a particular (lower income) segment of the population and, second, that these data are no better for many research purposes than the previously available NLS and PSID data.[12]

Labor economics has been connected to many developments in econometics as researchers endeavored to draw inferences from the newly available datasets over the last 20 years. Only 18 of the 759 labor economics papers were coded as primarily concerned with econometric method, although many more papers were state-of-the-art applications of existing econometric method. The growth of papers emphasizing and utilizing econometric innovations grew through time as did more sophisticated uses of the data, including matching variables from other data sources to different types of microdata for the particular purposes of the research topic in question. In all, 49 papers employed a significant use of special purpose matching to a micro dataset. An illustration of this is work by Ehrenberg and Oaxaca (1976), who matched the varying unemployment system features of different states to respondents in the NLS in order to evaluate the role of benefit levels on reemployment wage and duration of unemployment spell.

To summarize, micro level data for research, particularly on labor supply, are now available in a wide variety of social surveys, including panel surveys and surveys which have been at least partly designed for the purpose of estimating specific models. These data have been used quite extensively as can be seen from the growth in the use of microdata from various sources including "all other" (see Table 7.2). Recently, there have been efforts devoted to compiling a set of data base descriptions and indexes to major social surveys. Readers interested in tracking down specific data bases can refer to these compilations. See Borus (1982). The recent Taeuber and Rockwell (1982) paper includes a time series of social surveys. Parallel to our findings on research uses of microdata it is clear that social surveys have been a growth industry. During the 1940s there are only four entries and in the 1950s this jumps to 8 entries, in the 1960s there are 32 entries and in the 1970s there are 34 entries. It should also be noted that several of the major data collection projects initiated in the 1960s were large scale panel designs in which reinterview data were collected in the 1970s.

The 1960s represented a decade during which widespread availability of low cost computing capacity occurred at the same time that there was an acceleration

[12]Another type of panel data is that from administrative records such as the Social Security Administration's Continuous Work History Sample (CWHS) and the U.S. Labor Department's Continuous Wage and Benefit History (CWBH), which has longitudinal information on earnings, benefits received and some personal characteristics. As Ashenfelter and Solon (1982) note, a common drawback of administrative data is a restricted set of variables and restricted sampling to include only sub-groups of the population eligible for benefits or program participation. Many research purposes require comparisons between enrollees (or eligibles) and nonenrollees (or ineligibles).

in the development of econometric methods. These forces also continued during the 1970s and this decade represented the further refinement and specialization of econometric method to problems of micro panel data and an enormous diffusion of micro data bases among a wide and diverse set of users in various academic settings. Thesis research in labor economics using this newly emerging technology grew at an accelerating rate in the 1970s and early 1980s.[13]

Main datasets such as the NLS and PSID became (by historical standards) very well documented for users despite the growing complexity of the file structures. In the PSID data base the complexity of the data was increased by virtue of the number of variables (over 5000 variables are in the public use data tapes) and, more importantly, by the design of parallel treatment of individuals and families. Specifically, the data are structured so that they can be used to characterize an individual's own economic history as he or she changes the connections to other individuals by splitting from or returning to a given family, and family records permit the user to define family income, family housing characteristics and other variables that can be defined for multi-person households. A unique feature of the PSID data incorporates new family units which have an original sample member giving rise to a growing sample.

An examination of the actual questionnaires used in social surveys of economic topics reveals that through time there has been considerably more complexity and sophistication in question wording and skip sequences. Studies to date show that financial compensation of respondents does not lead to obvious improvements in data quality in most circumstances as shown by Cannell (1978), and a great deal of specialized knowledge as to what types of topics and question sequences are feasible has been gained. Many data collection efforts employ standard question sequences such as those of the CPS and this permits ready comparisons across surveys.

3. The interaction between theory and data base development

There is clearly an interaction between data collection and development of theory in labor economics research. There are relatively few empty economic boxes in labor economics compared to other applied fields such as industrial organization where much of the recent theoretical developments are regarded as valuable in their own right with relatively little attention given to empirical testing to date. This probably reflects the difficulty of collecting microdata on firms and organizations, a problem which has limited some kinds of demand side research in labor economics. Virtually none of the 759 papers reviewed in the previous

[13] For a review of research based on the NLS see Daymont and Andrisani (1983).

section was based on microdata with individual firms or establishments as the unit of analysis.

In some instances theoretical models have clearly motivated data collection efforts. Prior to the advent of human capital models of lifetime earnings, most sets of microdata did not have much information on work histories of individuals. Early work on earnings functions was commonly based on years of potential labor market experience, defined in terms of age and years of formal schooling. Because the theory emphasized the importance of on-the-job training through various types of job market experience, new and on-going data collection efforts obtained extensive information on job market experience. Variables such as years of full time experience, years of part time experience, and years in military service became widely available in cross-sectional data. Panel data, in addition, allowed measurement of these variables by the researcher rather than from respondent recall.

The particular case of experience measurements for the estimation of earnings functions is a success story – so much so that it is now almost taken for granted. Yet, before experience variables were available for analysis it was claimed that labor earnings were heavily influenced simply by age and social norms about what should be paid to people of different ages. The evidence we have indicates that age has a role but one which can be interpreted by length of remaining work horizon; people nearer retirement will have a shorter period in which to recover the costs of investment in skills and will for this reason invest less. In contrast various types of work experience have effects on earnings in line with what one would judge to be the learning content on each. See Willis, Chapter 12 in this Handbook.

Differences between men and women in their work histories as measured by experience segments appear to account for perhaps 70 percent or more of the wage differences between men and women. See Cain, Chapter 13 of this Handbook, for a discussion. Experience–earnings profiles are clearly a case where data collection efforts were motivated by a conceptual framework. Moreover, the entire enterprise seems to have paid off, though some controversies remain. Does experience indicate production skills and actual output or does it also indicate such things as knowledge of how to effect organization transitions and reorganizations? In the case of male–female earnings differences one of the controversies is whether or not differences by sex in accumulated work experience are the consequence of labor market discrimination.

One can identify cases where purely data based discoveries or puzzles have led to substantial theorizing and econometric work. Two illustrations from panel data are, first, the discovery of runs patterns in data on labor force participation of women, and, second, the discovery that the duration of completed spells of unemployment is much shorter than as measured by duration from beginning of spell to survey date.

Interpretation of the apparent dependency of current labor force status on labor force status in preceding periods observed by Heckman and Willis (1977) led to efforts to determine whether this was because of fundamental effects of being in a given state or whether it was simply the consequence of differing, unobserved permanent propensities to participate.[14] One feature of this literature is that the econometric aspects of the problem seem to have absorbed most of the attention, and much of the work has continued in a rather atheoretical vein, with some connection to previously developed theories. Still, the econometric representation can be regarded as an important contribution which was initially motivated by regularities observed in the data.

The Current Population Survey involves reinterviews of the same households over a 12-month period. Using these data Kaitz (1970) discovered that by taking a sample of individuals who had completed a spell of unemployment the average duration of spell of unemployment in the United States was on the order of 4 to 5 weeks. This contrasts with the 8 weeks commonly observed during nonrecessionary times (and 14–16 weeks common during recessionary times) when one measures unemployment duration by time from beginning of spell as reported by the respondent to date of survey. This puzzle can be resolved at the descriptive level by observing that the probability of leaving unemployment declines the longer the spell of unemployment. That is, the hazard function for leaving unemployment declines monotonically, but this squarely contradicts a main implication of search theoretic models which usually show that optimizing behavior in light of a perceived, stable distribution of potential wage offers will lead to a reservation wage which declines through time. If the wage offers are sampled randomly from this distribution the probability of accepting employment will rise through time, i.e. the hazard function for leaving unemployment should rise over time.[15]

In the search literature the appeal of the theory is so strong that few students of the subject accept the apparent fact observed by Kaitz. Instead most people resolve the disparity by believing that there are unobserved individual differences in the level (and perhaps shape) of the hazard function, and that absent control of these differences one cannot identify the true structure to the time path of the probability of leaving unemployment for individuals. The data required to resolve this controversy would include panel data collected at monthly or perhaps weekly intervals for individuals during multiple spells of unemployment. Then one could identify person specific parameters of the hazard function. In this case

[14]A more general econometric model of these issues has been set out; see Heckman (1981).

[15]Note that a constant hazard function, t, in the expression $\lambda(t) = f(t)/[1 - F(t)]$ obtains in the case where $f(t)$ is an exponential density function. In a case of a constant hazard function spell to survey and spell to completion measures would coincide. If this case applied to mortality it would imply that an unbiased estimate of life expectancy could be obtained by asking a cross-section sample of individuals their age!

new data collection would have been motivated by theory which was initially stimulated by descriptive empirical findings. This example illustrates the continuing interplay of theory/method and data collection. This seems to be a healthy feature of contemporary labor economics.[16]

A significant area which highlights the interrelation between theory and data is the broad area of intertemporal labor supply. The basic theory is simple and quite appealing: intertemporal utility maximization will require individuals to exploit information on variations in their wage through time with resulting substitution effects toward more work in periods when their wage is known to be high in relation to other periods. This simple theoretical framework was used to analyse unemployment and the effects of unemployment insurance, retirement, and the other life cycle labor supply decisions. Public policy is seen as the source of changes in the price of leisure at different points of time and as the source of income variation. Armed with this simple view, a variety of empirical efforts were mounted. In each of these areas the initial model has led to empirical research which has met with anything from no success to reasonable success. In response to less than complete success, reformulations and extensions of the theory seem to be the order of the day. The two topics which will be reviewed here are unemployment and retirement.

A stylized fact which is regarded as consistent with the basic intertemporal labor supply model is the procyclical labor force participation rates and countercyclical unemployment rates for virtually all major demographic groups.[17] In this view the unemployed are simply those who choose not to work during low wage periods, but because of a dispersion of offered wages may sample some jobs (i.e. "look for work") even though their reservation wage will exceed the typical wage offer they receive. Their reservation wage, we should remember, is in this view positively influenced by the prospect of higher anticipated wages in the future.

More recently, these stylized facts have been subject to much greater scrutiny. If workers are to make a rational intertemporal choice they must have some basis for successfully forecasting future wage rates. If not they would be unable to decide whether the current period is one deserving extra work hours or fewer work hours. Work by Altonji and Ashenfelter (1980) addresses the following question: If we describe time series wage movements is it reasonable to suppose that workers can use past history to decide whether future wage rates will be higher or lower? Their findings, which should be regarded as somewhat pre-

[16]The additional work on unemployment spells has been very dependent on both new datasets and new interpretations. See, for example, Kiefer and Neumann (1981), Akerloff and Main (1981), Layard (1981), Pederson (1982) and Björklund (1983).

[17]Mincer was (one of) the original proponents of this type of interpretation of the cyclical labor force participation of married women. Recessions led to added women workers because of income declines in their families, but led to discouraged workers as they were unable to realize high wages during the temporary downturns.

liminary, indicate that "rational forecasts of future real wage rates differ by a constant from current real wage rates, and there is very little variation in these deviations with which to explain unemployment".

Recent research devoted to estimating the elasticity of substitution between leisure in different time periods from time series data has found a small substitution elasticity or one of the "wrong" sign. This result also holds in some work using disaggregated data from the 1970 U.S. Census.[18] Tests of the proposition that, in quarterly U.S. time series, people act as simple period-by-period utility maximizers cannot be rejected against the alternative hypothesis that individuals act as multiperiod maximizers.[19]

Despite the apparent lack of support for the intertemporal labor–leisure model of unemployment, this is an area in which convincing empirical work has just begun. Time series tests are of limited value because there is not that much information there to discriminate among alternative hypotheses. Moreover, theoretical models used to date seem too restrictive. To illustrate, if businesses can carry inventory how do costs of inventory influence their incentives to stabilize output, employment, and wages? Micro level models that synthesize supply and demand factors and connect to empirical analysis are probably required to illuminate the basic issue. Recent work using microdata estimates the intertemporal substitution elasticity to be about 0.2.[20]

Another approach to intertemporal labor supply research is based on a broader model which synthesizes labor supply and household portfolio choices. Here households up against a financial net worth constraint have high costs of downward adjustment for consumption commitments, such as repayment of debt for major durables. Expenditures associated with children such as food and schooling also involve substantial costs of downward adjustment.

In the presence of such consumption commitments short-run wage declines can be shown to motivate short-run market hours increases so as to maintain cash flow. The empirical work supports such a model for younger families, but for older families with positive net worth, hours of work rise during high wage periods and fall during low wage periods.[21]

The simplest labor supply models allow people to select their hours given a parametric wage. It can be argued that hours choice is, to a substantial extent, effected by job choice. However, efficient job choice is something which requires adjustment time, particularly in a world of firm-specific skills and attachment and search costs. If so, temporary wage fluctuations with a given employer can be replaced with an intertemporal, implicit contract in which hours vary and there is

[18]Altonji (1982) and Clark and Summers (1982).

[19]See Varian (1984).

[20]McCurdy (1982) reports an estimate of 0.234 based on panel data and an estimate of 0.15 based on cross-sectional data.

[21]See Dau Schmidt (1983).

an earnings level over multiple periods sufficient to meet reservation utility, that level of utility attainable in an alternative sector where wage rates and hours are stable. Workers will be induced to accept hours variations and will do so at a modest wage premium if their hours restrictions are in the form of unemployment combined with unemployment compensation. This approach appears to receive empirical support in the recent work by Abowd and Ashenfelter (1981).

Another version of this type of approach is that of Feldstein (1976) who focuses on the role of unemployment insurance in lowering the cost of varying the number of employees rather than the hours per employee to effect a variation in worker hours when output price varies. His results in Feldstein (1978) suggest that about half of the temporary unemployment rate is the consequence of the presence of the unemployment insurance system.

Before fully embracing these sorts of results it should be remembered that the regular unemployment insurance system has, in the United States, a tax rate which is substantially related, though with lags, to benefits previously paid to those laid off from the firm. In the context of the Feldstein model perfect experience rating fully eliminates the bias toward layoffs rather than variations in hours per employee. In the Abowd–Ashenfelter approach since uncertainty has a direct role in the model there could still be net social benefits of a perfectly experience rated unemployment insurance system.[22] Yet the system would lead to greater variations in work hours supplied (and demanded) through time. The important point here is that work extending the basic model has been dependent on newly available datasets, and additional data may help resolve the issue of the relative importance of some of the new features of models such as uncertainty and public policy variables.

Intertemporal labor supply models have also been the basis for recent analysis of retirement behavior. A widely observed phenomenon in industrial societies has been the growth of early retirement. The first microlevel analysis of this was by Morgan and Barfield (1969) who indicated that there appeared to be two groups of early retirees. One group planned to retire early and carried out the required work, earnings, and asset accumulation plan in the preretirement period. Another group retired early because of events which occurred (such as illness) for which they had not made provision. Part of the favorable financial status of the planners was their social security benefits.

From observing aggregate time series, the early 1970s were a time of increasing retirement of people age 62–64. In the United States this age-group had been allowed to receive benefits. As the number of beneficiaries grew relative to the number of taxpayers questions arose over the incentive effects of social security. The initial microlevel analysis was largely atemporal and based on cross-section data. Persons eligible for benefits were seen as responding to these benefits in a

[22] See the paper by Topel and Welch (1980).

myopic, single period fashion and worked less or not at all because of income effects arising from the basic guarantee and because of substitution effects embodied in the high benefit reduction rates as market earnings increased.

The second round literature was more intertemporal and emphasized social security wealth as an inducement to retire and as an inducement to less preretirement work hours and private savings. It was typically based on micro panel data. As additional work was developed in this intertemporal framework using micro panel data, several researchers discovered that added hours of market work in the preretirement period led to marginal discounted retirement's benefits – adjusted for survival probabilities – which were often substantial: in many cases the social security system could act to increase preretirement hours.[23] If this actually happened the difference in net hourly wage between those who are just prior to age of eligibility and those who had just reached the age of eligibility could be substantial. In the context of the basic intertemporal labor supply or lifetime labor supply approach the system could affect the timing more than the total hours of work over the lifetime. Sharp differences in work hours between the nearly eligible and the recently eligible could give a greatly exaggerated picture of the lifetime labor supply effects. This issue has not been fully explored and there appear to be substantial data limitations on work of this sort in the near term.[24] In one study in which marginal social security wealth is related to retirement, no significant relation is found. Mitchell and Fields conclude that "retirement is affected ambiguously by social security eligibility, by current dollar benefits, by social security wealth and change in social security wealth".[24]

Most of the work in this area has been done without employing a full life cycle theoretical model with endogenous wages and a labor–leisure choice. While such models are not easy to work with, several have been developed and analyzed yielding the following qualitative insights: (i) it is common to find that an increase in financial wealth will lead to less market time during the life cycle,[25] including early retirement; and (ii) more able individuals – those with a greater ability to learn and therefore a larger steady-state human capital stock – will have (finite) life cycles characterized by a more accentuated earnings path, later retirement and greater life cycle savings during their earnings years.[26] Greater levels of *both* private pensions and social security benefits can be associated with such an earnings and retirement plan; as a result, without controls on ability it is entirely possible to observe a *positive* relation between pension wealth or social security wealth (SSW), and later retirement.

[23] This has been observed in the work of Blinder, Gordon, and Wise (1980). See, for example, Blinder (1980, 1983).

[24] See Mitchell and Fields (1983).

[25] Heckman (1980) provides a model which illustrates this point.

[26] See Ryder, Stafford and Stephan (1976), especially the discussion on pp. 667–668. These topics are discussed by Weiss in Chapter 10 in this Handbook.

Some studies report a positive relation between SSW and length of worklife.[27] The finding of a positive relation between pensions and retirement age is also consistent with the belief that pensions can be and are used to induce workers to stay with a firm and not leave after there have been substantial firm specific investments in human capital. Here retirement is one way in which an experienced worker can leave the firm.

What are the implications of research to date on unemployment and retirement? It appears that the reformulated theories of behavior can be tested with an augmented set of variables in some of the main on-going data collection projects. Special supplements could be added to the CPS, and because of the continuing panel data collected in the PSID and NLS, new reinterviews could include variables specifically designed to test reformulated hypotheses. In fact, this feedback between testing, reformulation of theory, and new data requirements has characterized these three important datasets and probably accounts for much of their high utilization rate which we observed in Section 2.

Some of the variables suggested by the preceding discussion of retirement are indexes of market ability, characteristics of the pension plan, whether job skills are firm specific, tax treatment of social security benefits (which will in turn depend on other variables such as family structure), and measures of knowledge of the basis for retirement benefits in the public and private pension plans. Key variables suggested by the preceding discussion of unemployment are better wage measures, since changes in wage rates will be heavily influenced by measurement error in the wage itself. To this we should add measures of the household's financial wealth, measures of consumption commitments as indexed by expenditures in different categories and debt repayment.

4. Advantages and disadvantages of different types of microdata and some data based pitfalls

If panel microdata have had such an increasing role in empirical analysis why not devote resources to just a few good panel datasets and forget the rest? Much has been written on the virtues of panel data, but there are several drawbacks which would advise against the panel data only strategy. More traditional data such as micro cross-section and aggregate time series look attractive in many applications. In the United States during the late 1960s and throughout the 1970s, substantial resources were devoted to collecting and analyzing data from social experiments,[28] but as observed in Section 2, these data have received relatively

[27] See Clark and Johnson (1980) and Hamermesh (1981). In a similar vein, Blinder (1983) reports a modest *positive* effect of private pensions on probability of market work for those age 58–60.

[28] Greenberg and Halsey (1983) report that the cost of the four U.S. income maintenance experiments was over $100 million.

little use in publications in major journals. Rethinking the collection of data for social experiments is important since, in principle, one can employ decision theory and cost–benefit criteria in determining a scale of evaluation. In this section it is suggested that an extension of this perspective can be useful in obtaining rough judgements about the process of collection of nonexperimental data.

This section begins with two subsections on the advantages and disadvantages of cross-sectional microdata and panel microdata. The discussion then turns to social experiments and the possible role of international comparisons from standardized survey instruments such as the Current Population Survey.

4.1. *Advantages and disadvantages of micro cross-sections*

A major limitation of many studies based on aggregate time series is that the central endogenous and exogenous variables often all move together through time, and changes in the variables about a time trend is minor. Empirical results are often very different as a result of the inclusion or exclusion of a few observations and minor redefinitions of the variables via atheoretical changes of the lag structures. In contrast cross-sectional microdata are often characterized by many of the central variables being nearly independent of one another, including the dependent and independent variables!

In face of the low correlation among variables in microdata one is left with a quandary as to whether the real world is characterized by very great microlevel randomness in economic behavior or whether it is primarily measurement error which leads to the appearance of weak relationships.[29] For example, the topic of earnings risk has received limited illumination from microdata because one cannot tell how much true randomness there is versus measurement error. Some have rushed to infer that luck is a major determinent of lifetime earnings *because* of large unexplained variation in earnings based on microlevel earnings equations, but we know relatively little about measurement error in many of the key variables. Let us list *the problem of measurement error* is disadvantage one of cross-section microdata and label it *D1C*.

A second drawback in the use of cross-section data is that standard research practice in economics seems to be devoted to obscuring the homely nature of the actual questions used in the survey, which may be still a step (or several steps) removed from the proxy variable which is conjured up in the mind of the referee or reader of the published paper. Other social sciences have suffered from this

[29]A problem of this sort plagues microlevel research on the permanent income hypothesis where there are two sources of errors-in-variables: actual income fluctuation and survey errors. See, for example, the discussion in Holbrook and Stafford (1971, pp. 14–15).

problem, too. Presser (1983) found that "fewer than half of the (social science) articles reported anything about sampling method, response rate, the wording of even a single question, (or) year of the survey... (which is) not markedly better than the much criticized mass media".

The economics articles reviewed by Presser were clearly the outlier group with only 3.9 percent reporting the sampling method and 2.9 percent reporting any question wording. This analysis was restricted to papers based "exclusively on articles reporting data the authors themselves collected or that were collected by other individuals independent of (data collecting) organizations". Therefore, the low percentages of economics papers discussing sampling method or question wording is not just the result of greater use in economics of standard datasets collected by someone other than the author. The relatively low professional rewards to work on such matters is indexed by the fact that only 1 of the 759 U.S. papers reviewed had data concerns as a central topic, and that was a relatively general discussion of the role of data from negative income tax experiments. The gap between theoretical construct and the actual question or operationalization used in research was remarked on by Leontief (1982) and seems to apply to micro cross-section data as well. Let us label the problem of *the disparity between the theoretical variable and the actual question or question sequence* used to construct an operational index of the variable as *D2C*.

Very little work has been done to overcome these two disadvantages of micro cross-section data, but recently more studies have begun to appear on such subjects,[30] though not in the journals reviewed in Section 1. In the case of market work the usual question is on how many hours were worked for pay during the last week or month, but this method seems to have problems of several sorts with people usually reporting more hours of market work than actually took place. Studies with beepers programmed to obtain a random sample of time use show that respondents tend to exceed the 24-hour time constraint in daily time allocation[31] when asked to report directly for time spent in socially desirable activities. For people age 18–24, hours of work actually working, rather than on breaks socializing or participating in on-the-job training, are only about 68 percent of hours reported in response to a direct question about market work.[32]

If hours measurements have unknown validity and reliability this carries over to hourly wage rates which are often calculated as income per time period divided by hours worked per time period. It should be obvious that structural parameters are as likely to be biased as much or more for these reasons as for such reasons as

[30] See, for example, Mellow and Sider (1983) and Greenberg and Halsey (1983). These papers have shown not only the nature of data problems but their likely effects in drawing inferences about important research topics. The practice of using multiple indicators of variables measured with error often rests on the unwarranted premise of zero covariances among the errors.

[31] See Robinson (1984). The beeper study estimates match quite closely the estimates from repeated application of 24-hour time diaries.

[32] See Stafford and Duncan (1979).

selection bias, truncation bias, or simultaneous equation bias.[33] A favorable sign is that while detailed discussion of data problems was not prevalent in the articles I reviewed, there appears now to be more awareness of data problems and analysis limitations based purely on data quality than there was in empirical research ten years earlier. However, the broader problem requires more attention to working with observable and measurable variables in the development of theory as well as better empirical measures.

A third limitation of micro cross-section data is that there are inevitably important variables influencing any given behavior which are outside the scope of the hypothesis in question. This causes no problems if these variables can legitimately be added to the equation disturbances, but this is not defensible in most cases. To illustrate, suppose personal motivation differs across individuals, and one person is far more productive in the market than others of given education and background. Unobserved motivation variables will lead to higher potential wage rates and, if good working conditions are a normal good, people of given observed personal characteristics with higher wages can also have better working conditions – a result in apparent contradiction of hedonic labor market models of the sort discussed by Rosen in Chapter 12 of this Handbook.[34] If so, cross section data will not permit identification of the parameters of interest because increasing the sample size increases the number of parameters one for one: each new observation implies another value of the unobservable "personal motivation" parameter. Further, ad hoc inclusion of variables to measure personality seems unattractive, and complication of the theoretical model to include personality variables may lead to a model which is too complex or outside the current competence of economists. Let us label *the problem of unobserved personal differences* as it applies to cross-section data as *D3C*.

A fourth drawback of cross-section data is the limited potential to characterize market equilibrium and even individual level equilibrium.[35] The implicit or explicit framework in most studies using micro cross-section data is one of partial equilibrium with no ability to answer such questions as whether, for example, market wage rates will change in response to a government tax policy or whether an increase in those attaining a college education will drive down the returns to education and by how much.[36] For such questions aggregate data of various sorts

[33] In a paper which attempts to address this, Borjas (1979) shows how what he terms division bias can alter the sign of the labor function.

[34] Brown (1978) and Smith (1977) summarize most of the empirical findings up until the last few years.

[35] An intriguing example of individual level equilibrium is micro cross-section estimates of the income elasticity of the demand for housing. The elasticity as estimated for a sample of recent movers is much higher than for all households in a paper by Morgan (1963). One interpretation is that recent movers are more likely to have aligned actual and desired housing stock. However, recent movers may have an underlying demand elasticity which differs from the entire population.

[36] See Johnson (1970) for analysis of this question. He utilized aggregate data.

are more widely used. Let us label *the partial equilibrium nature of most work utilizing micro cross-section data* as *D4C*.

A fifth drawback of microdata in the minds of many economists is the availability of large numbers of subjective or attitudinal variables. A common assumption of economic theory is that preferences, though unknown, are stable. Theories are developed so as to place only few general restrictions on the structure of preferences. Behavior will be altered in light of changes in the opportunity set, and, because the opportunity set is defined by "hard" economic variables, it is best to work with such facts rather than subjective data. Beliefs, preferences, attitudes, and the like are better left to other disciplines. Even theories which place heavy emphasis on expectations are worked out to deduce the consequences only for observed "economic" variables.

A safer practice is probably to admit to limitations of attitudinal or perceptual variables but to avoid being doctrinaire. An illustration of this is in work on intertemporal labor supply. Wage variations are difficult to measure since wage levels are difficult to measure in the first place. Therefore, respondent reports of whether current wage is unusually high or low may be better than elaborate calculations of wage changes, and use of respondent reports of wage change was more successful in recent work by Dau Schmidt (1983). *The proliferation in the use of atheoretical attitude or preference variables* can be noted as *D5C*.

Most surveys are based on some form of geographic or area sample in order to reduce interviewer travel costs. This means that the samples are not truly random samples of the population, and there are effects of sample design on statistics derived from the sample. To illustrate, standard errors are understated and, while there are methods available to calculate the sampling influences, this is seldom done. The *cost saving departures from pure random sampling* are a limitation of many micro cross-section data, *D6C*. If the sample selection is done in a way so that probabilities of selection are not known, then, for models with an erroneous or incomplete specification, generalizing the results to a population of interest is not possible.

Inadequate sample size and lack of comparison group observations when analyzing special labor market groups such as blacks or unemployed is another disadvantage, *D7C*. In a usual cross-section only 4–10 percent are unemployed at a point in time. To remedy this it is common to design a sample of only the unemployed such as those covered and receiving benefits. However, this is a selected sample and excludes those not covered. A better but more expensive method is a screening survey applied to a random sample with lower selection rates for those who are determined to be not unemployed in the screening section.[37]

[37]A claimed drawback of PSID data is the inclusion of observations from an earlier SEO sample of poor persons. This sub-sample is selected on the general outcome of low income and can bias certain estimates. Many researchers restrict their analysis to the random sample. This sample is in fact not random either since it is based on geographic sampling procedures as noted in *D6C*.

With all these problems why are so many papers in major journals based on cross-section surveys? A part of the answer is in the information cycle suggested in Section 2: this is a relatively new form of economic data and computers provide for a period of low cost discovery which may dwindle through time. The use of microdata recalls the story of the drunk who lost his money on the dark side of the street but looked for it under the light because he could see better there. Perhaps we will keep looking at microdata because they illuminate some questions even if other questions seem more interesting. In a more positive vein, what attracts researchers to micro cross-section data?

Two main advantages of micro cross-section data are: *the flexibility provided in subset selection for hypothesis testing, A1C, and the ability to measure a large number of variables for the same individual or household which could influence behavior of these decision making units, A2C*. These two features are important because microeconomic models have been developed to interpret a wide array of individual behavior and because economic theory does not purport to have a comprehensive theory of all behaviors as they interact in the microeconomic process. Thus, for example, it becomes important to select women of a certain age who are married in studying labor supply rather than attempting a comprehensive theoretical and econometric model of labor supply (and other activities) in which adult, married females are just one case and in which, male teenagers are another and in which those nearing retirement are yet another. Normally, the medium range theoretical-econometric model will, for reasons of tractability, apply to one of these groups and one or two behaviors. As new issues arise and interest changes from one group (teenagers) to another (retirees) and from one behavior (labor supply) to another (savings) a good general-purpose, random, national probability sample can be deployed to analyze behavior without the need for time-consuming developments of a special purpose questionnaire.[38]

A parallel to the advantage of flexibility in subset selection applies to design of the survey instrument and coding categories of the variables. The basic variables should be gathered and coded in the most elemental level if costs are not prohibitive and respondents can actually report the data elements. This leads to advantages *A3C, the possibility of variable redefinition from disaggregated variables*. Again, examples are helpful. If we were gathering data for the single purpose of testing the hypothesis of the effect of transfer income of individuals on their time in market we could use a definition which appeared to suit our purposes and set out to collect these data in a survey. What we would discover in a pretest is that people cannot respond to a question which asks about transfer income but can report income received from various particular sources such as

[38]This will be true if the right variables are measured as well. A common problem in survey design is anticipating possible future uses of the data. This sometimes leads to a desire to include every conceivable variable influencing microeconomic decisions. Budget constraints and limits on respondent patience limit this if nothing else does.

unemployment insurance, food stamps and so on. Further, market work time might include travel to work and exclude on-the-job leisure, and these may be easily coded from responses in a 24-hour time diary. For the purpose of the question at hand it may be useful to define transfer income as the sum of five or six income components and to define market work to include on-the-job training time but to exclude on-the-job breaks. The next user may have a critical need to include on-the-job leisure in market work since the issue might be how many hours the person is not available for home childcare. Similarly, an aggregation of transfer income is not helpful for the researcher studying the effects of unemployment or the next trying to describe the distribution of food stamp receipts.

A limit to disaggregated variables in data archives is that some of the disaggregations may be the result of meaningless distinctions at the level of the respondent. In the United States respondents may not know whether they received regular social security benefits or supplementary security income benefits even if it is of interest to researchers and policy analysts. On the user side a limit to disaggregation can simply be the cost of performing the necessary aggregation to define meaningful variables. If there are certain standard variable aggregations which are commonly used (e.g. all transfer income) they can be in the file but this does not argue for discarding the data on elemental measures from which they were constructed.

Computer power enters the discussion in several ways. In the last fifteen years it has become easier to store strings of variables in ways which lead to faster aggregation in the process of variable redefinition. An illustration of this is found in time diary coding. One can impose a prespecified grid of, say, 10-minute intervals (i.e. 144 fixed length segments per day) or let the respondent report a chronology of activities which will typically have somewhere from 15 to 50 entries per 24-hour day each of which will require a complementary variable to record the varying time length.[39] Fifteen years ago this variable entry chronology with detailed codes per entry would create a major, almost impossible, computing problem to create an aggregation across entries into, say, 100 codes for 2000 observations. Today this is only a moderately arduous task and researchers can specify their own variable definitions based on elemental variables. These same advances in computing power make subset selection a simpler task as well.

The ability to use certain variables which can index the given dataset to other datasets and match the data can be listed as advantage *A4C*. For example, information on which SMSA of residence can allow the addition of unemployment rate and wage variables for the SMSA as variables influencing individual behavior. This has become a rather frequent practice, as noted earlier.

[39]The practice of variable length records is essential in other applications as in the PSID coding of information on varying numbers of individuals in a family unit.

4.2. *Advantages and disadvantages of panel data*

Many of the advantages and disadvantages of panel data are implicit in the discussion of econometric methods designed for panel data.[40] We can refer to advantages and disadvantages of micro level panel data with the designation used from micro cross-sectional data, replacing the *C* with a *P*. Some of the advantages of panel data turn out to be a reduction in the disadvantage present in cross-section data.

D1P: *Panel data*, it is claimed, *are more subject to measurement error than cross-section data*. One is often using change measures derived from successive observations in time, and the apparent change can be dominated by different values of the errors in successive time periods. It is for this reason that in his chapter Lewis restricts his analysis of union wage effects to studies based on cross-section data. If one postulates serially correlated measurement error, as do Duncan and Holmlund (1983), then panel data have an advantage, so one cannot conclude that panel data universally suffer more (or less) from the problem of measurement error than do cross-section data.

D2P: *The disparity between theoretical variables and the actual question or question sequence applies to panel data* as well as cross-sectional data. However, for actual change variables, such as change in assets or hours of market work one can derive these variables from simple repeated questions rather than from respondent recall. The same paucity of reports on sampling and questions describes panel data, for the most part, but since the variables defined by change measures seem to be regarded as more innovative, there tends to be more discussion of variable construction. This is just an impression I have from my review of journal articles.

D3P: *Panel data have the problem of unobserved personal characteristics, but this is usually thought to be surmountable through statistical method*. A substantial econometric literature has been developed to exploit the notion that if there are unchanging unobserved personal characteristics panel data can be used to limit their effects on estimation of other parameters. This work is illustrated by the papers by Chamberlain (1978) and Heckman (1981). In one important application, studies of compensating wage differentials seem to have had more success using panel data. Here success is defined in terms of result more in line with the a priori expectation of the theory as summarized by Rosen in Chapter 12 of this Handbook.

A limitation of the methods applied to panel data is that the person-specific effects derived in models of heterogeneity and state dependence may not really be personal characteristics but rather persistent unobserved environmental variables

[40]See *The Econometrics of Panel Data*, Institut National de la Statistique et des Etudes Economiques (1978).

such as job market characteristics, as could be the case in the analysis of youth unemployment by Ellwood (1981). Thus, unobserved variables which permanently influence behavior are still a problem though less so in panel data. Further, attention is often centered on movers or changers, who may differ from others.

D4P: Just as in micro cross-sections, *market equilibrium is seldom characterized though models of adjustment to equilibrium by price taking individuals are possible.*

D5P, *D6P*, *D7P*: Largely the same as for cross-section data. Panel data allow for a better opportunity to observe rare events since individuals are studied over a longer time period.

D8P: *Panel response rates fall through attrition and this can be a severe problem.* If response rates on the initial interview are 70 percent and as high as 90 percent on each subsequent reinterview, a panel study of work history over ten years would have mere 27 percent of the original sample by the tenth year. Certainly one can cope with some of this problem by econometric methods, but a cost is that one has to specify a valid attrition process and even if the specification is correct it will typically preempt identification of other parameters of interest. A very serious problem occurs when there is no knowledge of the characteristics of initial nonrespondents. This applies to both cross-section and panel data. There have been no major breakthroughs on the problem of getting a higher initial response rate.

D9P: *Panels require unchanged question wording and questionnaire layout in successive waves of the panel.* In implementing a panel study it is essential to have set question wording and questionnaire layout. Otherwise, changes in the values of the variables through time could arise simply because of changes in question wording. (This also applies to use of repeated cross-sections as in the measurement of unemployment from the CPS.) This point is obvious. As a practical matter there will always turn out to be problems with some questions which are discovered *after* one or more waves of panel data are collected. Should a better question replace the problem question midstream? The answer is not obvious because if there are several remaining waves one can get better questions and change measures over the remaining waves.

Also, numerous cross-sectional uses are made of data from panels. Why not just ask both the right and the wrong question sequences when a problem is discovered midstream? There are budget constraints and respondent irritation constraints. The point here for data users is that they should look at the actual question and question sequences used in different waves of a panel rather than assuming that there were no changes in wording or layout as the panel progressed.

Advantages of panel data include all of those for cross-section data and a few more.

A1P, *A2P*, *A3P*, *A4P*: Same as for cross-section. Change variables derived from panel data greatly expand the set of variables available for analysis and in subset selection. Panels allow for greater opportunities to observe changes in prices and wages.

A5P: *Dynamic models can be fit using data collected at different time points to define change* rather than respondent recall measures of the values of variables at different time points or change therein. In studying savings behavior and adjustment of financial portfolios there is some evidence by Ferber (1976) that repeated measures of assets and change therein as calculated by the researcher provide better data than respondent recall of change in assets of various types. The details of unemployment spells and work history are difficult to recall, but simple reports collected weekly (for unemployment spells) or yearly (for work history) are probably quite accurate. Note that respondent attrition and annoyance with frequent reinterviews are practical considerations which could be dominant.

A6P: *Panel designs allow several interview sessions in which to collect variables which are unchanging through time*. It is unrealistic to have a personal interview which lasts more than about one hour unless the subject matter is very salient, personally interesting and nonthreatening to the respondent. Questions asked by economists often fall on all three counts! Panel data, through the opportunity to reinterview, can be thought of as allowing a longer interview session.

A7P: *Panels can be more cost effective*. Reinterviews, particularly by telephone, are cheaper than initial sample interviews. Suppose one simply wants to estimate population means on certain variables which are subject to year-to-year or day-to-day variation. For a given research budget how many individuals should be included and how many times should each be reinterviewed? It can be shown, as in Kalton (1984) that cost-effective description can require the collection of reinterview data. Such data will permit an assessment of reliability which can be useful in various research application.

A8P: *A large on-going panel can be used to evaluate the effects of policy changes*. Do changes in the U.S. tax laws intended to reduce the marriage tax effect labor supply and marital stability? Data from on-going panels such as the NLS or PSID could be used to get an approximate answer to this question, even though panels were in place before the marriage tax was an issue of policy concern. Similar remarks hold for changes in retirement benefits which will likely occur in the U.S. social security system.

4.3. *Have social experiments been useful in labor economics?*

Social experiments conducted in the United States were based on microdata and, particularly, for the last of the four devoted to studying labor supply responses to income support, the Seattle–Denver Income Maintenance Experiment, the data structure was one of micro panel data extending over several years. The data from all social experiments were used in only about 2 percent of labor economics papers in our sample during the last ten years. What are the features of experiments that distinguish them from other sorts of microdata?

By postulating a specific, behavioral model and utilizing nonexperimental (field) survey data, one can obtain an understanding of how an individual's labor market hours change in response to changes in after-tax wage rates and lump-sum transfer payments. From such knowledge one could predict the labor market hours of households under alternative income support arrangements which differ in the extent to which they change after-tax wage rates and income guarantees. From analysis of field studies, notably large-scale household surveys, labor economists have a consensus view that adult males have a labor supply which is relatively unresponsive to changes in income or wage rates while adult women have a labor supply which is quite responsive to changes in income or wage rates. See Chapter 1 by Pencavel and Chapter 2 by Heckman and Killingsworth in this Handbook. Given this prior research, a central issue is the role of experiments.

One possible role for experiments is to verify the impression from field studies and to assure policy makers, who are unaccustomed to the ways of academic research. Policy-makers will take the experiment as clearer evidence since experiments do not require one to make a commitment to any particular structural or behavioral model. Policy-makers, it is argued, can remain agnostic or uninformed about scholarly research and can use the experiment to answer the direct question of whether a particular income support system induces people to alter their hours of market work.

If we define the traditional labor supply model as one where a single person with a temporally stable objective function faces a temporally stable, exogenous wage rate with hours of work set totally on the supply side, then the share of the labor force for whom this applies is probably very small. The NIT induced labor supply responses predicted under alternative approaches such as those suggested by the work of Ashenfelter and Abowd (1981), Ham (1980), Heckman (1974), Phelps (1970), Feldstein (1976) and Deardorff and Stafford (1976) would differ from those predicted by the traditional model. Even where hours of work predictions are similar, some of these alternative approaches highlight periods in and out of employment.

If there is uncertainty as to which theoretical approach should be used, experiments look more attractive from the perspective of policy formulation. If the policy alternative is known in terms of both type (e.g. NIT versus wage subsidy) and magnitude (e.g. guarantee $G = \$5000$, and tax rate $t = 0.5$) and the experiment covers a random assignment of those in the various labor market circumstances, one can evaluate overall labor supply effects regardless of the true

Table 7.3
Conditions for using experiments (E) or field studies (F) for policy evaluation.

		Policy alternative	
		Certain I	Uncertain II
Theory	Known	F or E (nonexperimental use of data from experiments)	F or E (nonexperimental use of data from experiments)
		III	IV
	Unknown or many	E	Neither will help much

theory. Either a total absence of theory or an abundance of competing theories seems to strengthen the case for experiments! This is summarized in Table 7.3.

When the theory is "known" and the policy is certain (Case I) the choice of experiment versus field research should be determined largely by the cost of evaluation under the two methods and the extent to which one believes that variations in exogenous variables from these two data sources really are just that. Analysis of the experimental data often employs a structural model just as does the field model. That is, experimental data may be used to fit structural models in the well-known theory–uncertain policy case, because it is believed that only the experimental treatments are likely to represent exogenous variations in the same variables reported in field surveys (Cases I and II). The use of experimental data to estimate structural models (nonexperimental use of data from experiments) characterizes much of the analysis from the experiments.[41] If the real world generated observable variations in the exogenous wage and income variables then, on a cost basis, field studies would dominate. A good deal of the debate on whether experiments are "worth it" depends on one's belief in the ability of the real world versus the experiment to generate truly exogenous variation in critical variables.

What are some of the sources of policy uncertainty? Voucher and categoric aid programs are common and combine with the cash transfer system. Some of the former programs, such as the Food Stamp Program, are income conditioned and thereby influence the effective marginal tax rate on labor income. For this reason it is often suggested that these programs be "cashed out" and blended with a

[41] See the papers reported in "The Seattle and Denver Income Maintenance Experiments," *Journal of Human Resources*, Fall 1980.

universal cash transfer system. However, various categoric programs such as those for medical problems are not so simply dealt with. These needs-based programs will likely continue, and the issue of how they interrelate with the cash part of the system has never been resolved. This leads to uneasiness about the desirability of a NIT and, in turn limits the payoff to a purely atheoretical use of the experimental data.

The results of the U.S. negative income tax experiments could be summarized by saying that they did not change people's beliefs about the mean of the subjective distribution of key labor supply parameters. The results have been in line with what has been learned from studies based on nonexperimental data. In light of a small disparity one reaction might be that experiments were not worthwhile, but to answer this question one should think of these experiments in the framework of statistical decision theory. The first two ingredients in such an approach are: (1) listing the critical parameters about which we are uncertain and relating these parameters to (2) a loss function for policy decision variables. In the case of NIT let us assume that there are two critical labor supply parameters and two policy variables, G and t. How large a sample should be drawn given some known cost per sample point? We must first begin by defining a function that relates gains to selecting G (the guarantee) and t (the tax rate) conditional on values of the unknown parameters. This can be set out with a labor supply function and an indirect utility function for the NIT recipients as is done in Burtless and Hausman (1978). The labor supply function is given as

$$h = k(w(1-t))^{a}(Y+G)^{b}, \tag{1}$$

where h = hours of market work, w = wage, Y = nonlabor income, and a and b are the critical labor supply parameters. Welfare of the recipients can be expressed as

$$V = V(w(1-t), Y+G) = \frac{k(w(1-t))^{1+a}}{1+a} + \frac{(Y+G)^{1-b}}{1-b}, \tag{2}$$

where $V(\cdot)$ is the indirect utility function or maximum utility that can be obtained given $w(1-t)$ and $Y+G$, for given values of a and b

The "taxpaying" factors give a payment, P, of

$$P = (G - twh)n \tag{3}$$

to the n recipients.[42]

[42] This is obviously an oversimplification because who is a taxpayer and who is a recipient depends on whether $G - twh$ is positive or negative for a given individual. Here we assume that all m recipients have known, identical values of w and Y and have unknown but identical values of a and b.

Substitution of (1) into (3) provides an expression for the taxpayer costs. How does one translate this into a decision theory framework to address the question of the optimal scale of evaluation? First, suppose we knew a and b with certainty. What would be the optimal values of G and t? Here it seems necessary to impose an arbitrary social welfare function. Following Orr (1976), suppose the taxpayer gets Z utils from the utility of the welfare recipients:

$$Z = Z(V), \tag{4}$$

where $Z' > 0$. One reason for this would be altruism. Another could be that the taxpayer assigns some probability that chance will place him or his heirs in the recipient category. If a and b are known, the task is to choose G and t to maximize taxpayers' net utility:

$$B = Z(V(w(1-t), Y+G; a, b)) - P(G, t; a, b). \tag{5}$$

The reason for a social experiment or survey is to provide better information about a and b. These are not really known but are given by a joint prior p.d.f. Given the joint prior p.d.f. there can be defined an expected value maximizing choice of G and t in (5). Perhaps, however, we can do better through evaluation.

A sample that costs c per observation can be drawn to carry out the evaluation. As we contemplate samples of differing sizes, we may expect to leave the mean of the joint p.d.f. on a and b unchanged but to reduce the posterior variance. The incremental gain in the maximum expected value of B as we contemplate incremental sample sizes can be compared to the marginal sampling cost, c,[43] to determine an optimal sample size. In such an analysis the scale of the program (here, n) will be important and cost–benefit analysis, could justify large evaluation expenditure of the magnitude involved for the NIT experiments ($100 million or so).

Actual implementation of the approach set out in (1)–(5) would require a computer simulation and would require some prior joint density function for a and b. Those who are skeptical of nonexperimental labor market studies would want to use a diffuse prior while others would want to use a rather tightly drawn prior. Simulation results would show a range of optimal sample sizes depending on the prior density function. An important point of such an approach is that if the posterior mean values of a and b turn out to equal the prior means, this is not the basis for concluding that the experiments were not worth it. The expected post-experimental parameter precision will be greater and the expected value of the best policy can therefore be increased above its pre-experimental value.

[43] The cost per observation also depends on a and b but we can ignore this here.

Some aspects of the above discussion of the payoff to experiments in labor economics apply to the payoff from large-scale, nonexperimental datasets (including time series). In principle, the application of econometric models to large scale datasets can inform us about structural parameters, and this information can be used for better policy making in the sense of accepting policy alternatives with smaller expected losses or in realizing that a lack of existing parameter precision implies large costs of uncertainty for specific policy choices. With experiments there is a greater focus on a *single*, *specific* policy option prior to developing the dataset. Nonexperimental datasets can inform a *wide* but *unknown* range of future private and public policy choices, making it impossible to write down an explicit function of the economic gains to additional data. There is also the problem noted above that the real world may be less likely to have truly exogenous variations in variables of interest.

From the numerous policy related topics which have been illuminated by labor economics research, one could probably rationalize the resources spent on data collection and analyses. There are usually papers which provide a useful summary of main findings and policy implications, such as the paper by Hamermesh and Grant (1979). The net payoff to additional data and analysis depends on data quality (which influences the gain in parameter precision per sample point), cost of data and processing, and the change in loss functions conditional on added parameter precision. This says that labor economics should identify and work on feasible problems with major implications for the organization of society, and this seems to have occurred to a reasonable degree from the review of subjects in Section 2.

In the context of decision theory there seems to be an important role for collection of identical datasets in several countries which differ in terms of policy. Political choices effected by chance factors, such as differences in median voter beliefs about alternative, discrete policy regimes, can be thought of as the basis for exogenous changes in major policy variables to which individual decision units respond. For example, Sweden, Japan, the United States and Canada are similar in many ways but have major differences in public policy variables such as tax treatment of married couples, deductibility of interest on home mortgages and so on. If several countries collected *identical* sets of microdata, there would be more opportunities for policy analysis as well as estimation of structural parameters of general interest. Few papers based on data of this sort have yet appeared in the labor economics literature.

4.4 *Limitations of research based on microdata*

The evolution of most research areas in labor economics has given rise to reformulations of the theory and application of more specialized econometric models. Virtually all major areas have what can be termed a second generation or even third generation literature. A common pattern is that the basic conceptual model is extended in several dimensions and work is done emphasizing one or two particular dimensions per paper.

One can be skeptical about the prospects for a substantial synthesis of the various elements of the second generation work. This is not surprising since the data actually available and perhaps even potentially available do not contain enough information to abandon the maintained or restricted hypothesis testing approach to empirical work. Specifically, many of the second generation efforts achieve identification by testing much less than the joint hypothesis for all the interesting extensions of the basic model. This implies that the power of the tests on the restricted models is less than desired.

This dilemma of low power tests could possibly be resolved in future work by using two approaches. One approach would be to develop a more complete representation of the opportunity set. To illustrate, the issue of whether fixed costs of labor force participation or preferences account for the apparent discontinuity in labor supply response [Cogan (1980)] – wherein people work substantial numbers of hours or not at all – could be resolved by actual measures of fixed time and money costs of market work rather than testing for the labor supply function parameter implications of fixed costs. Secondly, if we had better information to characterize directly the opportunity set we could employ nonparametric approaches to labor supply analysis as suggested by the recent work of Varian (1983). In that approach one obtains upper and lower bounds on preferences, and the presumption is that the range of these bounds is meaningful only if the opportunity sets facing different individuals can be represented. This nonparametric approach will preclude some of the controversies which now arise based on maintained hypotheses brought about the fact that there is a very limited set of restrictions one can place on preferences based on theory per se.

5. Conclusion

Theoretical and empirical research in labor economics has been broadened and accelerated by the advent of large-scale microdatasets. The use of these sources has allowed us to know some things with much greater certainty – as illustrated by the work on labor supply responses to social insurance and income support programs such as unemployment insurance. On the other hand, the better data have led to posing more ambitious research questions, such as: "What is the response to wage variations through time?" In some cases research has led to a realization that we cannot characterize the world in a very simple way. An important illustration is that we do not now have a clear understanding of unemployment by simply characterizing the phenomenon as a special case of labor supply. Additional breakthroughs are required on the theoretical as well as empirical side.

Another consequence of better data has been an awareness of the fact that some conceptual models have limited prospects for detailed understanding. One such area is labor supply and demand synthesis. A prototype model is the hedonic labor market model. We know much less about such supply and demand synthesis models for two reasons. First, such models are more difficult to construct since one needs a demand side theory as well as a supply side theory and secondly, such a synthesis leads to much more limited prospects for identification. One only observes the market envelope, and this reduced form approach does not permit one to capture underlying supply and demand side parameters.

Research on labor market supply and demand synthesis models is limited by the absence of good demand side information on firms. As a result many of our stylized facts have a supply side bias – we think more, for example, of the worker's fixed employment costs than the firm's fixed employment costs. Analysis of the work incentive effects of unemployment insurance centers on labor supply responses rather than to variations in wage offered by employers as product demand varies. Clearly our knowledge would be greatly improved by additional, microlevel demand side work which would fit into the substantial knowledge which has been gained on the supply side.[44]

[44]See Oi (1983), who presents an analysis of the fact that within an industry the more highly capitalized firms achieve a higher rate of capital utilization, pay higher wage rates to workers with similar observed characteristics and have a larger share of compensation in the form of non-wage benefits. This can be thought of as consistent with a labor supply and demand synthesis or hedonic equilibrium. Here longer and more predictable hours of the higher wage workers are not a simple labor supply phenomenon.

References

Abowd, John and Orley Ashenfelter (1981) "Anticipated unemployment, temporary layoffs and compensating wage differentials", in: S. Rosen, ed., *Studies in labor markets*. Chicago: University of Chicago Press.

Akerloff, George and George Main (1980) "An experience weighted measure of employment and unemployment duration", *American Economic Review*, 70:885–893.

Altonji, Joseph (1982) "The intertemporal substitution model of labour market fluctuation: an empirical analysis", *The Review of Economic Studies*. Special Issue: 783–824.

Ashenfelter, Orley and Richard Layard (1986) *Handbook of labor economics*, Amsterdam: North-Holland.

Ashenfelter, Orley and Gary Solon (1982) "Longitudinal labor market data: sources, uses, and limitations", in *What's happening to American labor force and productivity measurements*? Washington, D.C.: National Council on Employment Policy.

Barfield, Richard and James Morgan (1969) "Early retirement: the decision and the experience", Survey Research Center, University of Michigan Ann Arbor.

Björklund, Anders (1983) "Measuring the duration of unemployment: a note", *Scottish Journal of Political Economy*, 30:1975–1980.

Blinder, Alan (1983) "Public pensions and private pensions: theory and fact", W.S. Woytinsay Lecture Number 5, Department of Economics, University of Michigan Ann Arbor.

Blinder, Alan S., Roger Gordon and Donald Wise (1980) "Reconsidering the work disincentive effects of social security", *National Tax Journal* December: 431–442.

Borjas, George (1980) "The relationship between wages and weekly hours of work: the role of division bias", *Journal of Human Resources*, 5:409–423.

Borus, Michael (1982) "An inventory of longitudinal datasets of interest to economists", *Review of Public Data Use*, 10:113–126.

Brown, Charles (1980) "Equalizing differences in the labor market", *Quarterly Journal of Economics*, 94: 113–134.

Burtless, Gary and Jerry A. Hausman (1978) "The effect of taxation on labor supply: evaluating the Gary negative income tax experiment", *Journal of Political Economy*, 86:1103–1130.

Cannell, Charles (1976) *Experiments in interviewing techniques*. University of Michigan, Institute for Social Research.

Chamberlain, Gary (1978) "Omitted variable bias in panel data: estimating the returns to schooling", in *The econometrics of panel data*. Paris: Annals of the Institut National de la Statistique et des Etudes Economiques.

Clark, Kim B. and Laurence Summers (1982) "Labor force participation: timing and persistence", *Review of Economic Studies*, Special Issue: 825–844.

Clark, Robert L. and Thomas Johnson (1980) "Retirement in the dual career family", Final Report, SSA Grant No. 10-P-90543-4-02.

Cogan, John (1980) "Labor supply with costs of labor market entry", in: James P. Smith, ed. *Female labor supply*. Princeton, N.J.: Princeton University Press.

Dau Schmidt, Kenneth (1983) "The effect of consumption commitments on labor supply", Ph.D. thesis, Department of Economics, University of Michigan.

Daymont, Thomas N. and Paul J. Andrisani (1983) "The research uses of the national longitudinal surveys: an update", manuscript, Social Science Research Council, Washington, D.C.

Deardorff, Alan and Frank Stafford (1976) "Compensation of cooperating factors", *Econometrica*, 44:671–684.

Duncan, Greg and Bertil Holmlund (1983) "Was Adam Smith right after all? Another test of the theory of compensating wage differentials", *Journal of Labor Economics* 1:366–379.

Duncan, Greg and James Morgan (1981) "Longitudinal lessons from the panel study of income dynamics", Working Paper 59, Industrial Institute for Economic and Social Research, Stockholm.

Ehrenberg, Ronald and Ronald Oaxaca (1976) "Unemployment insurance duration of unemployment, and subsequent wage gain", *American Economic Review*, 66:754–766.

Ellwood, David T. (1982) "Teenage unemployment: Permanent scars or temporary blemishes?" in: Richard B. Freeman and David A. Wise, eds., *The youth labor market problems: its nature, causes and consequences*. Chicago: University of Chicago Press.

Feldstein, Martin (1976) "Temporary layoffs in the theory of unemployment", *Journal of Political Economy*, 84:937–958.

Feldstein, Martin (1978) "The effect of unemployment insurance temporary layoff unemployment", *American Economic Review*, 68:834–846.

Ferber, Robert, et al. (1964) "Validation of a national survey of consumer financial characteristics: savings accounts", *Review of Economics and Statistics* November:436–444.

Greenberg, David and Harlan Halsey "Systematic misreporting and effects of income maintenance experiments on work effort: evidence from the Seattle–Denver experiment", *Journal of Labor Economics*, 1:380–407.

Hamermesh, Daniel and James Grant (1979) "Econometric studies of labor substitution and their implications for policy", *Journal of Human Resources*, 14:518–542.

Hamermesh, Daniel S. (1981) "A general model of life cycle effects on consumption of retirement decisions", *American Economic Review*:101–113.

Heckman, James (1976) "A life cycle model of earnings, learning and consumption", *Journal of Political Economy, Essays in Honor of H. Gregg Lewis*, 84:S11–S44.

Heckman, James (1981) "Heterogeneity and state dependence", in: Sherwin Rosen, ed., *Studies in Labor Markets* Chicago: University of Chicago Press.

Heckman, James and R. Willis (1977) "A beta logistic model for the analysis of sequential labor force participation by married women", *Journal of Political Economy*, 85:27–58.

Holbrook, Robert and Frank Stafford (1971) "The propensity to consume separate types of income: a generalized permanent income hypothesis", *Econometrica*, 39:1–21.

Institute National de la Statistique et des Etudes Economiques (1978) "The econometrics of panel data", *Annals*, (Paris) 30–31.

Johnson, George (1970) "Demand for labor by educational category", *Southern Economic Journal*, 37:190–204.

Kaitz, Hyman B. (1970) "Analyzing the length of spells of unemployment", *Monthly Labor Review*, 93:11–20.

Kalton, Graham (1984) "Reliability in time use data", in: F. Thomas Juster and Frank P. Stafford, eds., *Time, goods and well-being*. Ann Arbor Michigan: Survey Research Center.

Kiefer, Nicholas M. and George R. Neumann (1981) "Structural and reduced form approaches to analyzing unemployment duration", in: Sherwin Rosen, ed., *Studies in labor markets*. Chicago: University of Chicago Press.

Klevmarken, N. Anders (1983) "Collecting data for micro analysis: experiences from the HUS pilot study", Working Paper 102, Industrial Institute for Economic and Social Research, Stockholm, Sweden.

Layard, Richard (1981) "Measuring the duration of unemployment: a note", *Scottish Journal of Political Economy*, 28:273–277.

Lazear, Edward (1979) "Why is there mandatory retirement?", *Journal of Political Economy*, 87:1261–1284.

Leontief, Wassily (1982) "Academic economics", Letter to the Editors, *Science*, 217:104–107.

McCurdy, Thomas (1982) "Interpreting empirical models of labor supply in an intertemporal framework with uncertainty", unpublished manuscript, Stanford University, Stanford.

Mellow, Wesley and Hal Sider (1983) "Accuracy of response in labor market surveys: evidence and implications", *Journal of Labor Economics*, 1:331–344.

Mitchell, Olivia and Gary Fields (1983) "The effects of pensions and earnings on retirement: a review essay", in: Ronald Ehrenberg, ed., *Research in labor economics*.

Morgan, James N. (1975) "Housing and ability to pay", *Econometrica*, 33:289–306.

Mortenson, Dale (1970) "Job search, the duration of unemployment and the Phillips curve", *American Economic Review*, 60:847–862.

Oi, Walter, (1983) "Heterogenous firms and the organization of production", *Economic Inquiry*, 21:147–171.

Orr, Larry (1976) "Income transfers as a public good", *American Economic Review*, 66:359–371.

Pederson, Peder J. (1982) "Unemployment spells and duration: a note", Working Paper 83-2, Institute of Economics, University of Aarhus.

Presser, Stanley (1983) "The use of survey data in basic research in the social sciences", mimeo, Survey Research Center, University of Michigan, Ann Arbor, Michigan.

Robinson, John (1984) "The validity and reliability of alternative time use measures", in: F. Thomas Juster and Frank P. Stafford, eds., *Time goods and well-being*. Survey Research Center, University of Michigan, Ann Arbor, Michigan.

Ryder, Harl, Frank Stafford and Paula Stephan (1976) "Labor, leisure and training over the life cycle", *International Economic Review*, 16:651–674.

Seater, John (1979) "A unified model of consumption, labor supply and job search", *Journal of Economic Theory*, 14:349–372.

Smith, Robert (1979) "Compensating wage differentials and public policy: a review", *Industrial and Labor Relations Review*, 33:339–352.

Stafford, Frank P. and Greg Duncan (1979) "The use of time and technology in the United States", in: Ronald G. Ehrenberg, Orley Ashenfelter and Ronald L. Oaxaca, eds., *Research in labor economics*. JAI Press.

Taueber, Richard C. and Richard Rockwell (1982) "National social data series: a compendium of brief descriptions", *Review of Public Data Use*, 10:23–111.

Topel, Robert and Finis Welch (1980) "Unemployment insurance: survey and extensions", *Economica*, 47:351–379.

Varian, Hal R. (1983) "Non-parametric tests of consumer behavior", *Review of Economic Studies* 50:99–100.

Varian, Hal R. (1984) Manuscript in process, Department of Economics, University of Michigan, Ann Arbor.

PART 2

DEMAND FOR LABOR

Chapter 8

THE DEMAND FOR LABOR IN THE LONG RUN

DANIEL S. HAMERMESH*

Michigan State University

1. Introduction

The demand for labor in the long run should be important to labor economists for a variety of reasons. So long as the supply of labor to an occupation, industry or area is not perfectly elastic in the long run, the nature of demand for labor in that subsector interacts with the shape of the supply function to determine the level of wages. As in the market for a commodity, so too in the market for labor the demand is an integral determinant of the price of what is exchanged.

In many cases economists are interested in the demand for labor for its own sake rather than for its effects on wage determination. In some instances, e.g. in unionized employment or where the supply of labor to a subsector is perfectly elastic, the wage can be viewed as unaffected by labor demand. In such cases knowledge of wage elasticities of labor demand allows one to infer the effects of exogenous changes in wage rates on the amount of labor employers seek to use. The impact of changes in the price of one type of labor on its employment and on the employment of other types of labor (cross-price effects) can be discovered using estimates of labor-demand relations alone. Alternatively, one can in many instances assume that the employment of workers of a particular type is fixed (and determined solely by the completely inelastic supply of such workers to the market). In those cases the demand for their labor determines the wage rate they are paid. Knowledge of the shape of the labor-demand function enables one to infer how exogenous changes in supply (due perhaps to changes in the demographic mix of the labor force or to shifts in suppliers' preferences for entering different occupations) affect the wage rate of workers in the group whose supply has shifted and in other groups too (cross-quantity effects).

Economists interested in policy questions should be concerned with issues of labor demand. The effects of any policy that changes factor prices faced by employers will depend on the structure of labor demand. Thus, to predict the

*My thanks to Orley Ashenfelter, George Borjas, George Johnson, Richard Layard, Andrew Oswald, and John Pencavel for helpful comments.

Handbook of Labor Economics, Volume I, Edited by O. Ashenfelter and R. Layard

impact of wage subsidies, payroll tax changes, investment tax credits, etc. one must have satisfactory estimates of underlying parameters. Similarly, the impact on wages of policies such as skills training or population control that change the demographic or human-capital mix of the labor force can be assessed only if one knows the underlying structure of substitution relations among groups of workers.

Bearing in mind throughout that the purpose of studying the demand for labor is to understand how exogenous changes will affect the employment and/or wage rates of a group or groups of workers, we begin this essay by examining the theory of labor demand. The theoretical discussion is divided into two parts: demand for labor in the two-factor case, and demand in the multi-factor case. In each part we first derive the results generally, then proceed to specific functional forms. In Sections 4 and 5 we point out the issues involved in estimating labor-demand relations for one type of homogeneous labor, and then summarize the state of knowledge in this area. Sections 6 and 7 perform the same tasks for the demand for labor of several types.

The focus throughout is on the relations between exogenous wage changes and the determination of employment, and between exogenous changes in inelastically supplied labor and the structure of relative wages. We ignore the possibility that firms may not maximize profits or minimize costs, and assume throughout that employers are perfect competitors in both product and labor markets. While this latter assumption may be incorrect, the analysis applies mutatis mutandis to employers who have some product-market power. Most important, we focus only on the long-run, or static theory of labor demand, and thus only on the long-run effects of exogenous changes in wage rates or labor supply. The dynamics of labor demand, particularly the role of adjustment costs and the distinction between the amount of labor used and its intensity of use (employment versus hours per period), are ignored (and left to Nickell, Chapter 9 in this Handbook). Most lags in the adjustment of labor demand to its long-run equilibrium do not appear to be very long [Hamermesh (1980)]; the slow adjustment of relative wages to exogenous shocks appears due mostly to lags in suppliers' decisions about training and mobility. That being the case, the theory of labor demand in the long run, and the estimates of parameters describing that demand, are useful in answering questions of interest to policy-makers and others who are interested in the near-term effects of various changes in the labor market.

2. Two factors – the theory

While the theoretical results on labor demand can be generalized to N factor inputs, many useful insights into the theory can be gained by examining the demand for homogeneous labor when there is only one cooperating factor, usually assumed to be capital services. Since much of the terminology of labor demand applies in the two-factor case, concentrating on it also has some pedagogical advantages. Also, many of the specific forms for the production and cost functions from which labor-demand functions are derived were initially developed for the two-factor case and make a good deal more economic sense applied to only two factors than generalized to several. The presentation here and in Section 3 goes through some derivations, but our aim is to provide a theoretical outline to link to empirical work. More complexity can be found in Varian (1978); still more is available in the essays in Fuss and McFadden (1978).

Assume that production exhibits constant returns to scale, as described by F, such that

$$Y = F(L, K), \quad F_i > 0, \quad F_{ii} < 0, \quad F_{ij} > 0, \tag{1}$$

where Y is output, and K and L are homogeneous capital and labor inputs, respectively. A firm that maximizes profits subject to a limit on costs will set the marginal value product of each factor equal to its price:

$$F_L - \lambda w = 0, \tag{2a}$$

$$F_K - \lambda r = 0, \tag{2b}$$

where w and r are the exogenous prices of labor and capital services, respectively, λ is a Lagrangean multiplier showing the extra profit generated by relaxing the cost constraint, and we assume the price of output is unity. The firm will also operate under the cost constraint:

$$C^0 - wL - rK = 0. \tag{2c}$$

The ratio of (2a) to (2b) is the familiar statement that the marginal rate of technical substitution equals the factor-price ratio for a profit-maximizing firm.

Allen (1938, p. 341) defines the elasticity of substitution between the services of capital and labor as the effect of a change in relative factor prices on relative inputs of the two factors, holding output constant. (Alternatively, it is the effect of a change in the marginal rate of technical substitution on the ratio of factor inputs, defined as an elasticity.) In this two-factor linear homogeneous case it is [see Allen (1938, pp. 342–343)]

$$\sigma = \frac{\mathrm{d}\ln(K/L)}{\mathrm{d}\ln(w/r)} = \frac{\mathrm{d}\ln(K/L)}{\mathrm{d}\ln(F_L/F_K)} = \frac{F_L F_K}{Y F_{LK}}. \tag{3}$$

The *own-wage elasticity of labor demand* at a constant output and constant r is [Allen (1938, pp. 372–373)]

$$\eta_{LL} = -[1-s]\sigma < 0, \tag{4a}$$

where $s = wL/Y$, the share of labor in total revenue. Intuitively, the constant-output elasticity of labor demand is smaller for a given technology (σ) when labor's share is greater because there is relatively less capital toward which to substitute when the wage rises. The *cross-elasticity of demand* (for capital services) is

$$\eta_{LK} = [1-s]\sigma > 0. \tag{4b}$$

[What is the intuition on the inclusion of $1-s$ in (4b)?]

Both (4a) and (4b) reflect only substitution along an isoquant. When the wage rate increases, the cost of producing a given output rises; and the price of the product will rise, reducing the quantity of output sold. The *scale effect* depends on the (absolute value) of the elasticity of product demand, η, and on the share of labor in total costs (which determines the percentage increase in price). Thus to (4a) and (4b) the scale effects must be added, so that

$$\eta'_{LL} = -[1-s]\sigma - s\eta \tag{4a'}$$

and

$$\eta'_{LK} = [1-s][\sigma-\eta]. \tag{4b'}$$

The results here and in (4a) and (4b) are the most important in the theory of labor demand. They will be proved below using the cost-function approach.

Both (4a) and (4a′) are useful, depending on the assumptions one wishes to make about the problem under study. Certainly, in an individual firm or particular industry, which can expand or contract as the wage it must pay changes, scale effects on employment demand are relevant. For an entire economy, in which output may be assumed constant at full employment, (4a) and (4b) are the correct measures of the long-run effect of changes in the wage rate on factor demand.

All of these measures assume that both factors are supplied elastically to the firm. If they are not, the increase in employment implicit in (4a′) when the wage decreases cannot be complete: the labor that is demanded may not be available; and the additional capital services whose presence raises the marginal product of labor ($F_{LK} > 0$) also may not be. In such cases the demand elasticities are reduced [see Hicks (1964, appendix)]. Though such cases may be important, we ignore them in this chapter (though we do deal with the polar case in which the wage depends upon the level of exogenous employment).

An alternative approach makes use of cost minimization subject to an output constraint. Total cost is the sum of products of the profit-maximizing input demands and the factor prices. It can be written as

$$C = C(w, r, Y), \quad C_i > 0, \quad C_{ij} > 0, \quad i, j = w, r, \tag{5}$$

since the profit-maximizing input demands were themselves functions of input prices, the level of output, and technology. By Shephard's lemma [see Varian (1978, p. 32)] the firm's demand for labor and capital at a fixed output Y can be recovered from the cost function (5) as

$$L^* = C_w \tag{6a}$$

and

$$K^* = C_r. \tag{6b}$$

Intuitively, the cost-minimizing firm uses inputs in a ratio equal to their marginal effects on costs. The forms (6) are particularly useful for estimation purposes since they specify the inputs directly as functions of the factor prices and output.

Using eqs. (6) and the result that $C(w,r,Y) = YC(w,r,1)$ if Y is linear homogeneous, the elasticity of substitution can be derived [see Sato and Koizumi (1973)] as

$$\sigma = \frac{CC_{wr}}{C_w C_r}. \tag{7}$$

Note that the elasticity of substitution derived from a cost function looks strikingly similar to that derived from a production function. Obviously they are equal, suggesting that the form one chooses to measure σ should be dictated by convenience.

The factor-demand elasticities can be computed as

$$\eta_{LL} = -[1-m]\sigma \tag{8a}$$

and

$$\eta_{LK} = [1-m]\sigma, \tag{8b}$$

where m is the share of labor in total costs. Since by assumption factors are paid their marginal products, and the production and cost functions are linear homogeneous, $m = s$, and (8a) and (8b) are equivalent to (4a) and (4b).

We are now in a position to prove (4a′) easily following Dixit (1976, p. 79). If we continue to assume constant returns to scale, we can reasonably treat the firm as an industry and write industry factor demand as

$$L = YC_w \tag{6a'}$$

and

$$K = YC_r. \tag{6b'}$$

Under competition firms equate price, p, to marginal *and* average cost:

$$p = C.$$

Noting that if markets clear, so that output equals industry demand $D(p)$, we obtain:

$$\partial L/\partial w = YC_{ww} + D'(p)C_w^2.$$

Because C is linear homogeneous, $C_{ww} = (-r/w)C_{wr}$. Substituting for C_{ww}, then from (7) for C_{wr}, and then for C_w and C_r from (6a′) and (6b′):

$$\frac{\partial L}{\partial w} = \frac{rK}{Y}\frac{\sigma L}{wC} + \frac{D'(p)L^2}{Y^2}.$$

To put this into the form of an elasticity, multiply both sides by pw/pL, and remember that $p = C$:

$$\eta_{LL} = \frac{-rK}{pY}\sigma + \frac{pD'(p)}{Y}\frac{wL}{pY} = -[1-s]\sigma - s\eta,$$

by the definition of factor shares under linear homogeneity.

The production or cost functions can also be used to define some concepts that are extremely useful when examining markets in which real factor prices are flexible and endogenous, but factor supplies are fixed (and, because of the flexibility of input prices, are fully employed). The converse of asking, as we have, what happens to the single firm's choice of inputs in response to an exogenous shift in a factor price is to ask what happens to factor prices in response to an exogenous change in factor supply. Define the *elasticity of complementarity* as the percentage responsiveness of relative factor prices to a 1 percent change in factor inputs:

$$c = \frac{\partial \ln(w/r)}{\partial \ln(K/L)}. \tag{9}$$

This is just the inverse of the definition of σ. Thus,

$$c = \frac{1}{\sigma} = \frac{C_w C_r}{CC_{wr}} = \frac{YF_{LK}}{F_L F_K}. \tag{10}$$

In the two-factor case in which the production technology is linear homogeneous, one can find the elasticities of substitution and of complementarity equally simply from production and cost functions; and, having found one of them, the other is immediately available.

Given constant marginal costs, the *elasticities of factor price* (of the wage rate and the price of capital services) are defined as

$$\varepsilon_{ww} = -[1-m]c \tag{11a}$$

and

$$\varepsilon_{rw} = [1-m]c. \tag{11b}$$

Equation (11a) states that the percentage decrease in the wage rate necessary to accommodate an increase in labor supply *with no change* in the marginal cost of the product is smaller when the share of labor in total costs is larger (because labor's contribution to costs – a decrease – must be fully offset by a rise in capital's contribution in order to meet the condition that marginal cost be held constant).

Consider now some examples of specific production and cost functions.

2.1. *Cobb–Douglas technology*

The production function is

$$Y = L^{\alpha}K^{1-\alpha}, \tag{12}$$

where α is a parameter; marginal products are

$$\frac{\partial Y}{\partial L} = \alpha\frac{Y}{L} \tag{13a}$$

and

$$\frac{\partial Y}{\partial K} = [1-\alpha]\frac{Y}{K}. \tag{13b}$$

Since the ratio of (13a) to (13b) is w/r if the firm is maximizing profits, taking logarithms and differentiating with respect to $\ln(w/r)$ yields $\sigma = 1$. Equations

(4a) and (4b) imply

$$\eta_{LL} = -[1-\alpha] \quad \text{and} \quad \eta_{LK} = 1-\alpha.$$

Minimizing total costs subject to (12), one can derive [Varian (1978, p. 15)] the demand functions for L and K, and thus the cost function. The latter reduces to

$$C(w,r,Y) = Zw^{\alpha}r^{1-\alpha}Y, \tag{14}$$

where Z is a constant. Using Shephard's lemma, one can again derive

$$\frac{L}{K} = \frac{\alpha}{1-\alpha}\frac{r}{w}. \tag{15}$$

Taking logs, the calculation that $\sigma = 1$ follows immediately. It is also clear from (15) that $c = 1$.

2.2. *Constant elasticity of substitution technology*

The linear homogeneous production function is

$$Y = [\alpha L^{\rho} + (1-\alpha)K^{\rho}]^{1/\rho}, \tag{16}$$

where α and ρ are parameters. Marginal products are[1]

$$\frac{\partial Y}{\partial L} = \alpha\left(\frac{Y}{L}\right)^{1-\rho}, \tag{17a}$$

and

$$\frac{\partial Y}{\partial K} = (1-\alpha)\left(\frac{Y}{K}\right)^{1-\rho}. \tag{17b}$$

Setting the ratio of (17a) to (17b) equal to the factor-price ratio, taking logarithms, differentiating with respect to $\ln(w/r)$, and making $\sigma \geq 0$, yields:

$$\frac{-\partial \ln(L/K)}{\partial \ln(w/r)} = \sigma = \frac{1}{[1-\rho]}. \tag{18}$$

[1] The little trick to derive (17a) and (17b) is to remember that, after having done the grubby arithmetic, the numerator is just Y raised to the power $1-\rho$.

The CES is sufficiently general that any value of $\rho < 1$ is admissible, and the relationship (18) can be used to estimate σ.

Among special cases are: (a) the Cobb–Douglas function [$\rho = 0$, as should be clear from (18)]; (b) the linear function ($\rho = 1$), in which L and K are perfect substitutes [go back to (3), and note that if $\rho = 1$, so that (16) is linear and $F_{LK} = 0$, $\sigma = \infty$]; and (c) the Leontief function ($\rho = -\infty$), in which output is the minimum function $Y = \min\{L, K\}$, and the inputs are not substitutable at all.[2] The constant-output factor-demand elasticities in each case follow immediately from the definitions and the recognition that α is labor's share of revenue if the factors are paid their marginal products.

The CES cost function can be derived [Ferguson (1969, p. 167)] as

$$C = Y\left[\alpha^{\sigma} w^{1-\sigma} + [1-\alpha]^{\sigma} r^{1-\sigma}\right]^{1/(1-\sigma)},$$

where, as before, $\sigma = 1/[1-\rho] \geq 0$. The demand for labor is

$$L = \frac{\partial C}{\partial w} = \alpha^{\sigma} w^{-\sigma} Y. \tag{19}$$

Taking the ratio of (19) to the demand for K, the elasticity of substitution can again be shown to be σ.

In both of these examples it is very straightforward to derive c first, then derive σ as its inverse. It is worth noting for later examples and for the multi-factor case that c is more easily derived from eqs. (17) and the factor-price ratio (since w/r, the outcome, appears alone), than from (19) and the demand for capital. σ is more readily derived from the cost function, since the ratio L/K appears alone. Obviously in the two-factor case the simple relation (10) allows one to obtain c or σ from the other; but the ease of obtaining c or σ initially differs depending on which function one starts with, a different that is magnified in the multi-factor case.

Two other specific functional forms, the generalized Leontief form of Diewert (1971) and the translog form [Christensen et al. (1973)], are second-order approximations to arbitrary cost or production functions. Each has the advantage over the CES function in the two-factor case that σ (or c) is not restricted to be constant, but instead depends on the values of the factor inputs or prices. In each case we examine here only the cost function.

[2] The arithmetic that demonstrates this is in Varian (1978, p. 18).

2.3. *Generalized Leontief*

$$C = Y\{a_{11}w + 2a_{12}w^{0.5}r^{0.5} + a_{22}r\}, \tag{20}$$

where the a_{ij} are parameters. Applying Shephard's lemma to (20) for each input, and taking the ratios:

$$\frac{L}{K} = \frac{a_{11} + a_{12}(w/r)^{-1/2}}{a_{22} + a_{12}(w/r)^{1/2}}. \tag{21}$$

As is easily seen from (21), in general

$$\sigma = -\,\partial \ln\left(\frac{L}{K}\right) \Big/ \partial \ln\left(\frac{w}{r}\right)$$

depends on all three parameters and the ratio w/r. Under restrictive assumptions (20) reduces to some of the examples we have already discussed. If $a_{12} = 0$, it becomes a Leontief function (since the ratio L/K is fixed). If $a_{11} = a_{22}$, it becomes a Cobb–Douglas type function.

2.4. *Translog*

$$\ln C = \ln Y + a_0 + a_1 \ln w + 0.5b_1[\ln w]^2 + b_2 \ln w \ln r + 0.5b_3[\ln r]^2 \\ + [1 - a_1]\ln r, \tag{22}$$

where the a_i and b_i are parameters. Applying Shephard's lemma to each input, and taking the ratios:

$$\frac{L}{K} = \frac{r}{w}\,\frac{a_1 + b_1 \ln w + b_2 \ln r}{[1 - a_1] + b_2 \ln w + b_3 \ln r}. \tag{23}$$

Again σ depends on all parameters and both factor prices. Under specific circumstances ($b_i = 0$ for all i), the cost function reduces to a Cobb–Douglas technology.

Both the generalized Leontief and translog functions may be useful for empirical work (see below), even when written out as in (20) and (22). Each has the virtue of allowing flexibility and containing some simpler forms as special cases. That suggests that they should supplant the Cobb–Douglas and CES functions even for empirical work involving just two inputs.

Throughout this section we have assumed the production and cost functions are linear homogeneous. This also implies they are *homothetic*: factor demand is such that the ratio of factor inputs is independent of scale at each factor-price ratio. This assumption may not always make sense. For example, large firms may be better able to function with a more capital-intensive process at given w and r than are small firms.

In the general case nonhomotheticity means that the production function *cannot* be written as

$$Y = G(F[L, K]),$$

where G is monotonic and F is linear homogeneous. Alternatively, the cost function cannot be expressed as [Varian (1978, p. 49)]: $C(w, r, Y) = C^1(Y)C^2(w, r)$, i.e. output is not separable from factor prices. Some special cases are useful for estimation; and a nonhomothetic CES-type function [Sato (1977)] and translog form [Berndt-Khaled (1979)] have been used.

3. Several factors – the theory

Mathematically the theory of demand for several factors of production is just a generalization of the theory of demand for two factors presented in the previous section. Empirically, though, the generalization requires the researcher to examine a related aspect of factor demand that is not present when the set of inputs is classified into only two distinct aggregates. The issue is illustrated when one considers a three-factor world, for example three types of labor, L_1, L_2 and L_3. One could assume that production is characterized by

$$Y = F(G(L_1, L_2), L_3), \tag{24}$$

where F and G are two-factor production functions of the kind we discussed above. The difficulty with (24) is that the aggregation of L_1 and L_2 by the function G is a completely arbitrary description of technology. Far better to devise some method that allows this particular aggregation to be a subcase whose validity can be tested. This problem, one of *separability* of some factors from other(s), provides the major reason why labor economists must be interested in multi-factor labor demand. As an example, it means that one should not, as has been done by, for example, Dougherty (1972), combine pairs of labor subaggregates by hierarchies of two-factor CES functions. Intuitively this is because changes in the amount of one type of labor in a particular subaggregate could affect the ease of substitution between two groups of labor that are arbitrarily included in another subaggregate. If so, one will draw incorrect inferences about the ease of substitution between the latter two factors (and about the cross-price demand elasticities).

Consider a firm (industry, labor market, economy) using N factors of production, $X_1,\dots, X_N$. Let the production function be

$$Y=f(X_1,\dots, X_N), \quad f_i>0, \quad f_{ii}<0. \tag{25}$$

Then the associated cost function, based on the demands for $X_1,\dots, X_N$, is

$$C=g(w_1,\dots,w_N,Y), \quad g_i>0, \tag{26}$$

where the w_i are the input prices. As in the two-factor case:

$$f_i-\lambda w_i=0, \quad i=1,\dots, N; \tag{27}$$

and, using the cost function:

$$X_i-\mu g_i=0, \quad i=1,\dots, N, \tag{28}$$

where λ and μ are Lagrangian multipliers.

The technological parameters can be defined using either the equilibrium conditions based on the production function [(25) and (27)] or those based on the cost function [(26) and (28)]. Allen (1938) used f to define the *partial elasticity of substitution*, the percentage effect of a change in w_i/w_j on X_i/X_j holding output and other input prices constant, as

$$\sigma_{ij}=\frac{Y}{X_iX_j}\frac{F_{ij}}{|F|}, \tag{29}$$

where

$$|F|=\begin{vmatrix} 0 & f_1 & \cdots & f_n \\ \vdots & & f_{ij} & \\ f_N & & & f_{NN} \end{vmatrix},$$

the bordered Hessian determinant of the equilibrium conditions (25) and (27), and F_{ij} is the cofactor of f_{ij} in F.

The definition in (29) is quite messy. An alternative definition based on the cost function is

$$\sigma_{ij}=\frac{Cg_{ij}}{g_ig_j}. \tag{30}$$

[Note the similarity to the definition of σ in (7) in the two-factor case. Note also that the definition in (30) requires knowledge only of a few derivatives of (26), unlike that of (29), which requires a complete description of the production function.]

If one differentiates the system (25) and (27) totally, the comparative-static equations are

$$[F]\begin{bmatrix} \mathrm{d}\lambda/\lambda \\ \mathrm{d}X_1 \\ \vdots \\ \mathrm{d}X_N \end{bmatrix} = \begin{bmatrix} \mathrm{d}Y \\ \mathrm{d}w_1/\lambda \\ \vdots \\ \mathrm{d}w_N/\lambda \end{bmatrix}. \tag{31}$$

Holding Y and all other w_k constant:

$$\partial X_i/\partial w_j = \frac{F_{ij}}{\lambda|F|}. \tag{32}$$

Multiplying the numerator and denominator of (32) by $w_j X_i X_j Y$:

$$\frac{\partial \ln X_i}{\partial \ln w_j} = \eta_{ij} = \frac{f_j X_j}{Y}\cdot\sigma_{ij} = s_j\sigma_{ij}, \tag{33}$$

where the last equality results from the assumptions that factors are paid their marginal products and f is linear homogeneous.[3] The η_{ij}, factor demand elasticities, can, of course, be calculated more readily using the definition of σ_{ij} based on (26).

Since $\eta_{ii} < 0$ (and thus $\sigma_{ii} < 0$), and since $\sum_j \eta_{ij} = 0$ (by the zero-degree homogeneity of factor demands in all factor prices), it must be the case that at least one $\eta_{ij} > 0$, $j \neq i$. But (and what makes the multi-factor case interesting) some of the η_{ij} may be negative for $j \neq i$.

The *partial elasticity of complementarity* between two factors is defined using the production function as

$$c_{ij} = \frac{Yf_{ij}}{f_i f_j}. \tag{34}$$

[Here the definition is just a generalization of (10).] The c_{ij} show the percentage

[3] One might wonder how, if $\eta_L = -[1-s_L]\sigma$ in the two-factor case, $\eta_{LL} = s_L\sigma_{LL}$ in the multi-factor case when we assume $N = 2$. Remembering that $s_L\sigma_{LL} + s_K\sigma_{KL} = 0$, $\eta_{LL} = -s_K\sigma_{KL}$. Since $s_K = 1 - s_L$, and σ_{KL} is just alternative notation for σ, the two representations are identical.

effect on w_i/w_j of a change in the input ratio X_i/X_j, holding marginal cost and other input quantities constant.

The c_{ij} can also be defined from the cost function [from the system of eqs. (26) and (28)] in a way exactly analogous to the definition of σ_{ij} from the production function

$$c_{ij} = \frac{C}{w_i w_j} \frac{G_{ij}}{|G|}, \tag{35}$$

where $|G|$ is the determinant of the bordered Hessian matrix that results from totally differentiating (26) and (28), and G_{ij} is the cofactor of g_{ij} in that matrix [see Sato–Koizumi (1973, p. 48)]. Note that unlike the two-factor case, in which $c = 1/\sigma$, $c_{ij} \neq 1/\sigma_{ij}$.

The result of totally differentiating (26) and (28) under the assumption that G is linear homogeneous is

$$[G]\begin{bmatrix} \mathrm{d}Y/Y \\ \mathrm{d}w_1 \\ \vdots \\ \mathrm{d}w_N \end{bmatrix} = \begin{bmatrix} Y\mathrm{d}\mu \\ \mathrm{d}X_1 \\ \vdots \\ \mathrm{d}X_N \end{bmatrix}. \tag{36}$$

Solving in (36) for $\partial w_i/\partial X_j$:

$$\frac{\partial w_i}{\partial X_j} = \frac{G_{ij}}{|G|}. \tag{37}$$

Multiply both numerator and denominator in (37) by $Cw_i w_j X_j$ to get

$$\partial \ln w_i/\partial \ln X_j = \varepsilon_{ij} = s_j c_{ij}, \tag{38}$$

the *partial elasticity of factor price i* with respect to a change in the quantity X_j.

Since $\varepsilon_{ii} = s_i c_{ii} < 0$, and $\sum_j s_j c_{ij} = 0$, $c_{ij} > 0$ for at least some factors. It is quite possible, though, that there are factors for which $\varepsilon_{ij} < 0$ for some $j \neq i$, i.e. for which an exogenous increase in the quantity of input j reduces the price of input i at a constant marginal cost.

The partial elasticities of demand and of factor prices can be used to classify pairs of factor inputs. Using the ε_{ij}, inputs i and j are said to be *q-complements* if $\varepsilon_{ij} = s_j c_{ij} > 0$, *q-substitutes* if $\varepsilon_{ij} < 0$. [Note that it is possible for all input pairs (i, j) to be q-complements.] Using the η_{ij}, inputs i and j are said to be *p-complements* if $\eta_{ij} = s_j \sigma_{ij} < 0$, *p-substitutes* if $\eta_{ij} > 0$. [Note that it is possible for all input pairs (i, j) to be p-substitutes.] If there are only two inputs, they must be q-complements and p-substitutes.[4]

The use of these definitions should be clear, but some examples may demonstrate it better. If skilled and unskilled labor are p-substitutes, one may infer that a rise in the price of skilled labor, perhaps resulting from an increase in the ceiling on payroll taxes, will increase the mix of unskilled workers in production. These two factors may also be q-complements. If so, an increase in the number of skilled workers (perhaps resulting from increased awareness of the nonpecuniary benefits of acquiring a college education) will raise the wage of unskilled workers by increasing their relative scarcity.

The concepts developed in this section can be illustrated by a number of the specific functional forms that have been used in the literature to estimate production/cost relations describing several inputs.

3.1. *Multi-factor Cobb–Douglas and CES functions*

These are just logical extensions of the two-factor cases. The N-factor Cobb–Douglas cost function can be written as

$$C = Y\prod_i w_i^{\alpha_i}, \quad \sum \alpha_i = 1. \tag{39}$$

Each $\sigma_{ij} = 1$ (just apply (30) to (39)), making this function quite uninteresting in applications where one wishes to discover the extent of p-substitutability or examine how substitution between X_i and X_j is affected by the amount of X_k used. That $c_{ij} = 1$ can be readily derived from a generalization of the argument in (13)–(15).

The N-factor CES production function is

$$Y = \left[\sum \beta_i X_i^{\rho}\right]^{1/\rho}, \quad \sum \beta_i = 1. \tag{40}$$

As with the N-factor Cobb–Douglas function, the technological parameters are not interesting:

$$c_{ij} = 1 - \rho, \quad \text{for all } i \neq j.$$

The degree of substitution within each pair of factors is restricted to be identical.

[4] A good mnemonic for these distinctions is that the q and p refer to the exogenous quantities and prices whose variation is assumed to produce changes in endogenous input prices and quantities respectively.

A slightly more interesting case is that of the two-level CES function containing M groups of inputs, each of which contains N_i individual inputs:

$$Y=\left\{\left[\sum_{1}^{N_1}\alpha_i X_i^{\rho_1}\right]^{v/\rho_1}+\cdots+\left[\sum_{N_{M-1}}^{N_M}\alpha_k X_k^{\rho_M}\right]^{v/\rho_M}\right\}^{1/v},\quad \sum_{1}^{N_M}\alpha_i=1, \tag{41}$$

where the ρ_j and v are parameters to be estimated. Equation (41) is the same as (40), except that groups of factors aggregated by CES subfunctions are themselves aggregated by a CES function with parameter v. For factors within the same subaggregate:

$$c_{ij}=1-\rho_k,\quad k=1,\ldots,M.$$

For factors in different subgroups, $c_{ij}=1-v$. While (41) is less restrictive than (40), it still imposes the assumption that the ease of substitution is the same between all pairs of factors not in the same subgroup; and it also imposes separability – substitution within a subgroup is unaffected by the amount of inputs from other subgroups.

3.2. *Generalized Leontief*

The cost function, an expanded version of (20), is

$$C=Y\sum_i\sum_j a_{ij}w_i^{0.5}w_j^{0.5},\quad a_{ij}=a_{ji}. \tag{42}$$

The technological parameters can be estimated from

$$X_i=a_{ii}+\sum_j a_{ij}\left[w_j/w_i\right]^{0.5},\quad i=1,\ldots,N. \tag{43}$$

The partial elasticities of substitution are

$$\sigma_{ij}=\frac{a_{ij}}{2\left[X_iX_js_is_j\right]^{0.5}},$$

and

$$\sigma_{ii}=\frac{a_{ii}-X_i}{2X_is_i}.$$

To derive the σ_{ij} from this functional form, one need only know those parameters that involve factors i and j.[5] A production function analogous to (42) can be used to derive the c_{ij} easily (and the σ_{ij} with great effort!).

3.3. *Translog*

In general the translog cost function is

$$\ln C = \ln Y + a_0 + \sum_i a_i \ln w_i + 0.5 \sum_i \sum_j b_{ij} \ln w_i \ln w_j, \tag{44}$$

with

$$\sum_i a_i = 1; \qquad b_{ij} = b_{ji}; \qquad \sum_i b_{ij} = 0, \quad \text{for all } j. \tag{45}$$

The first and third equalities in (45) result from the assumption that C is linear homogeneous in the w_i (proportionate increases in the w_i raise costs proportionately). By Shephard's lemma:

$$\partial \ln C / \partial \ln w_i = X_i w_i / C = s_i, \quad i = 1, \dots, N, \tag{46}$$

where both sides of the factor demand equation have been multiplied by w_i/C, and we have assumed factors receive their marginal products.

The reason for writing (46) as it is rather than as a set of factor-demand functions is that, while the latter are nonlinear in the parameters, (46) is linear:

$$s_i = a_i + \sum_{j=1}^{N} b_{ij} \ln w_j, \quad i = 1, \dots, N. \tag{47}$$

The partial elasticities of substitution are

$$\sigma_{ij} = [b_{ij} + s_i s_j]/s_i s_j, \quad i \neq j,$$

and

$$\sigma_{ij} = [b_{ii} + s_i^2 - s_i]/s_i^2.$$

The σ_{ij} can also be calculated from a translog production specification, but to do so requires using (29), and thus the determinant of what could be a large

[5] To derive σ_{ij}, perform the required differentiation and remember that $g_i = X_i$.

Table 8.1
Summary of functional forms.

Theoretical forms	Estimating forms and demand elasticities
1. Cobb–Douglas	
(a) Cost	
$C=Y^a\prod w_i^{\alpha_i};\quad a=1$ if CRS	$\ln C/Y=\sum\alpha_i\ln w_i$
(b) Production	
$Y=\prod X_i^{\beta_i};\quad \sum\beta_i=1$ if CRS	$\ln Y=\sum\beta_i\ln X_i$; $\eta_{ii}=[1-\beta_i]$;
2. CES	
(a) Cost	
$C=Y^a\left[\sum_i \alpha_i w_i^{\sigma(1-\sigma)}\right]^{1/(1-\sigma)},\quad a=1$ if CRS	$\ln X_i=a_0+\sigma\ln w_i+a\ln Y$; $\eta_{ii}=s_i\sigma$;
(b) Production	Little use
$Y=\left[\sum_i \beta_i^{\rho}X_i\right]^{b/\rho},\quad b=1$ if CRS	
3. Generalized Leontief	
(a) Cost	
$C=Y\sum\sum a_{ij}w_i^{0.5}w_j^{0.5}$, $a_{ij}=a_{ji}$	$X_i=a_{ii}+\sum_j a_{ij}[w_j/w_i]^{0.5},\quad i=1,\ldots,N$; $\eta_{ij}=\dfrac{s_j a_{ij}}{2[X_iX_js_is_j]^{0.5}}$ $\eta_{ii}=\dfrac{[a_{ii}-X_i]}{2X_i}$.
(b) Production	
$Y=\sum\sum b_{ij}X_i^{0.5}X_j^{0.5}$, $b_{ij}=b_{ji}$	$w_i=b_{ii}+\sum_j b_{ij}[X_j/X_i]^{0.5},\quad i=1,\ldots,N$ $\varepsilon_{ij}=\dfrac{s_jb_{ij}}{2[w_iw_js_is_j]^{0.5}}$ $\varepsilon_{ii}=\dfrac{b_{ii}-w_i}{2w_i}$.
4. Translog	
(a) Cost	
$\ln C/Y=a_0+\sum a_i\ln w_i+0.5\sum\sum b_{ij}\ln w_j\ln w_i$, $b_{ij}=b_{ji}$	$s_i=a_i+\sum_j b_{ij}\ln w_j,\quad i=1,\ldots,N$ $\eta_{ij}=[b_{ij}+s_is_j]/s_i$ $\eta_{ii}=[b_{ii}+s_i^2-s_i]/s_i$
(b) Production	
$\ln Y=\alpha_0+\sum\alpha_i\ln X_i+0.5\sum\sum\beta_{ij}\ln X_i\ln X_j$, $\beta_{ij}=\beta_{ji}$	$s_i=\alpha_i+\sum_j\beta_{ij}\ln X_j,\quad i=1,\ldots,N$ $\varepsilon_{ij}=[\beta_{ij}+s_is_j]/s_i$ $\varepsilon_{ii}=[\beta_{ii}+s_i^2-s_i]/s_i$

matrix. The production form is useful, though, to derive partial elasticities of complementarity.

These functional forms and the associated production functions are all summarized in Table 8.1 for the multi-factor case. (Though the Cobb–Douglas and CES should not be used when there are more than two factors, I present them here to allow their use in the two-factor case.) The relative merits of and problems with the alternative cost and production tableaux are discussed in the next sections.

4. Homogeneous labor – estimation and empirical issues

In this section we deal with the problems involved in estimating the demand for homogeneous labor. We examine how one estimates the demand parameters under the assumption that all units of labor are identical. The parameters of interest, the labor-demand elasticity and the cross-price and substitution elasticities, have been produced both in the two-factor and the multi-factor cases. We discuss both issues of how the estimating equations are to be specified, and how they are to be estimated and the results interpreted.

4.1. *Specification*

The first approach to estimation relies on the production or cost function "directly". In the case of the Cobb–Douglas function this method produces the distribution parameters. (If, for example, data on factor prices are unavailable, these parameter estimates are necessary to compute the factor-demand elasticities. If data on shares can be computed, there is no reason to estimate such a function.) Estimating a CES function directly is, an inspection of (16) shows, not easy, so the direct approach does not apply here. The generalized Leontief and translog approximations can be estimated directly (either in their cost or production function forms). Though little work has relied upon this approach, it is quite feasible in the two-factor case. In the multi-factor case the problem of multicollinearity ($N+1$ terms involving each factor of production are included in the translog approximation, N in the generalized Leontief approximation) becomes severe [but see Hansen et al. (1975)]. With more than one other factor included, direct estimation should not be done unless one arbitrarily imposes a multi-factor Cobb–Douglas technology.

The second approach uses labor-demand conditions, either from the marginal productivity condition (2a) or the Shephard condition (6a). In the simplest case, a CES function, this means estimating an equation like

$$\ln L = a_0 + \sigma \ln w_L + a_1 \ln Y, \tag{48}$$

where the a_i are parameters, with $a_1 = 1$ if the production function is characterized by constant returns to scale.[6] [Indeed, estimating (48) without constraining a_1 to equal one is the standard way of testing for constant returns to scale when estimating the labor-demand equation.] In the generalized Leontief and translog cases the amount of labor demanded is a nonlinear function of the factor prices, which makes these approaches inconvenient.

In the multi-factor case the labor-demand approach involves the estimation of an equation like

$$\ln L = \sum b_i \ln w_i + a_1 \ln Y, \quad \sum b_i = 0, \tag{49}$$

where one can test for constant returns to scale ($a_1 = 1$). Clearly, (49) should be viewed as part of a complete system of factor-demand equations; if data on all factor quantities are available, a complete system should be estimated. If not, though, (49) will provide all the necessary estimates, for

$$\partial \ln L / \partial \ln w_i = [s_i / s_L] \, \partial \ln X_i / \partial \ln w_L.$$

The multi-factor labor-demand approach provides a useful way of testing whether the condition that the demand for labor be homogeneous of degree zero in factor prices holds, and whether it is homogeneous of degree one in output. A similar approach can be used to examine a wage equation specified as a linear function of the logarithms of all factor quantities.

Yet a third approach may be called the relative factor demand method. In the two-factor CES case this just involves estimation of (18), with $\ln L/K$ as a dependent variable, from which the demand elasticities can be calculated. Some research has used this method, but none has used (21) or (23) directly.

The relative factor-demand method should not be used in the multi-factor case, for it involves the estimation of all pairs of equations like (18), in the CES case, or like (21) and (23) in the more general cases. While there is nothing inherently wrong with this approach, it prevents the imposition of the restrictions that factor demand be homogeneous of degree zero in all factor prices. Since that restriction is a postulate of the theory, the specification that prevents the researcher from imposing or at least testing it does not seem desirable.

[6] One should note that the slope parameter on $\ln w_L$ in (48) is not the usual constant-output labor-demand elasticity, and that the latter needs to be calculated from the estimate using (4a). It is also worth noting that (48) is a transformation of the equation used by Arrow et al. (1962) to estimate the elasticity of substitution in the CES function they had proposed: Under constant returns to scale (48) can be written as

$$\ln Y/L = -a_0 - \sigma w_L,$$

the form originally used to estimate σ.

The fourth approach is to estimate the demand for labor as a part of a system of equations based upon one of the approximations, like the generalized Leontief or translog forms that we discussed in Section 3. Even in the two-factor case a single equation like (47) for $i = L$ could be used, with the only parameters to be estimated being the constant term and the slope on $\ln\{w_L/w_j\}$ (since the homogeneity restrictions make an equation for the other factor redundant and the coefficients on $\ln w_L$ and $\ln w_j$ equal and of opposite sign). In the case of several factors homogeneous labor becomes one of the factors in a system of $N-1$ equations. These are the share equations for the translog approximation, or eqs. (43) for the generalized Leontief approximation.

Throughout the discussion in this section we have dealt only with methods of estimating the constant-output labor-demand elasticity. As we indicated in Section 2, in the short run, or for individual firms, sectors or industries, a change in the price of labor will induce a change in output (especially if a small industry is the unit of observation). The effect of the output change can be measured indirectly or directly. The indirect approach simply takes some extraneous estimate of the demand elasticity for the product of the industry, and uses (4a′) to derive a labor-demand elasticity that includes the scale effect. A direct approach would estimate equations like (48) and (49) but with output (Y) deleted.

4.2. *Measurement and interpretation issues*

There are many data considerations in estimating elasticities involving labor demand; we concentrate here only on problems concerning the measurement of L and w. The simpler issue is the choice of a measure of the quantity L. In the literature the alternatives have mostly been total employment and total hours. Clearly, if workers are homogeneous, working the same hours per time period, the choice is irrelevant. If they are heterogeneous along the single dimension of hours worked per time period, using number of workers to represent the quantity of labor will lead to biases if hours per worker are correlated with factor prices or output. In studies using cross-section data, in which there may be substantial heterogeneity among plants, firms or industries in hours per worker, this consideration suggests that total hours be used instead of employment. In time-series data (on which most of the estimates of demand elasticities for homogeneous labor are based) the choice is probably not important, since there is relatively little variation in hours per worker over time. However, if one is also interested in dynamics of labor demand, the choice is crucial, for there are significant differences in the rates at which employment and hours adjust to exogenous shocks (see Nickell, Chapter 9 in this Handbook).

The choice of a measure of the price of labor is more difficult. Most of the published data from developed countries are on average hourly earnings or average wage rates. A few countries publish data on compensation (employers' payments for fringes and wages per hour on the payroll). While most of the studies of the demand for homogeneous labor use one of the first two measures, none of these three is satisfactory. There are two problems: (1) variations in the measured price of labor may be the spurious result of shifts in the distribution of employment or hours among subaggregates with different labor costs, or of changes in the amount of hours worked at premium pay; and (2) data on the cost of adding one worker (or one hour of labor services) to the payroll for one hour of actual work are not available.

The first problem can be solved in studies of labor demand in the United States using the adjusted earnings series covering most of the postwar period for the private nonfarm economy. The second problem is soluble (except for labor costs resulting from inputs into training) for studies of the United States labor market beginning in 1977 by the Employment Cost Index that the Bureau of Labor Statistics has produced. Clearly, future work using aggregate data should rely upon that index. That the distinction is important is shown in Hamermesh (1983), in which a measure of labor cost per hour worked is developed and shown to lead to substantially higher own-price demand elasticities than do average hourly earnings or average compensation measures.

The second measurement issue is what variables if any should be treated as exogenous. Ideally the production or cost function, or labor-demand equation, will be embedded in an identified model including a labor supply relation. In such a case methods for estimating a system of equations are appropriate, and the problem is obviated: both the price and quantity of labor may be treated as endogenous. If a complete system cannot be specified, one may have sufficient variables that are not in the equation based on the cost or production function and that can be used to produce an instrument for the endogenous right-hand side variable. However, given the difficulty of specifying a labor supply relation in the aggregate data on which most studies of labor demand are based, it seems unlikely that a good set of variables can be found.

The choice usually boils down to whether price or quantity can be viewed as exogenous in the problem under study. In studies based on small units – plants, firms, or perhaps even geographical areas – one might well argue that supply curves to those units are nearly horizontal in the long run. If so, the wage rate may be treated as exogenous; and estimates of cost functions, labor-demand equations, or share equations based on factor prices are appropriate (for they include the wage instead of the quantity of labor as an independent variable). In studies using aggregate data this assumption has not been considered valid since Malthusian notions of labor supply were abandoned. If, as many observers believe, the supply of labor to the economy is quite inelastic even in the long run, demand parameters are best estimated using specifications that treat the quantity of labor as exogenous; production functions and variants of second-order approximations that include factor quantities as regressors should be used.

Since in reality it is unlikely that the supply of labor to the units being studied is completely elastic or inelastic, any choice other than estimating production parameters within a complete system including supply is unsatisfactory. However, since supply relations have not been estimated satisfactorily except in certain sets of cross-section and panel data, one is left to make the appropriate choice based on one's beliefs about the likely elasticity of supply to the units, the availability and quality of data, and whether factor-demand elasticities or elasticities of factor prices are of interest.

5. Homogeneous labor – results and problems

5.1. *Results with output constant and wages exogenous*

Remembering that the chief parameter of interest in analyzing the demand for homogeneous labor is the constant-output own-price elasticity of demand, let us consider a number of studies that have produced estimates of this parameter.[7] I have divided the studies into two main types depending on the specification of the equations estimated: labor-demand studies and production or cost-function studies. All of the latter use either a CES production function or a translog cost function. In the translog cost functions labor is specified as one of several factors of production (with energy, the focus of interest in these studies, included as one of the other factors).

In Table 8.2 I list the classification of the available studies of the constant-output long-run demand elasticity for labor. The estimates are of the absolute value of the own-price elasticity of demand for homogeneous labor. [The studies listed in part I.A are based on relationships like (48); since the values of s_L are unavailable for the particular samples, I present the estimates of $\eta_{LL}/(1-s_L)=\sigma$.] The estimates in the studies based on a marginal productivity condition imply a measure of the responsiveness of demand that is quite consistent with constant-output demand elasticities holding other factor prices constant of between 0.2 and 0.4 (assuming the share of labor is 2/3, and noticing that the range of most of the estimates is 0.67–1.09). Only Black and Kelejian (1970) and Drazen et al. (1984) among those studies using this approach produce estimates that imply a constant-output demand elasticity holding other factor prices constant that is well below this range. The latter may be an outlier because of the difficulties with the wage data for some of the countries; why the estimates in the former are so low is unclear.

Studies included under part I.B in Table 8.2 in most cases specify the price of capital services in a labor-demand equation that can be viewed as part of a

[7] The issues from 1975 to 1982 of a large number of journals were searched. For years before 1975 the references are taken from Hamermesh (1976). While we make no claim that our survey is exhaustive, it should give a fair representation of work on this subject.

Table 8.2
Studies of the aggregate employment-wage elasticity.

Author and source	Data and industry coverage	η_{LL}
	I. Labor demand studies	
A. Marginal productivity condition on labor (estimates of $\eta_{LL}/[1-s]$)		
Black and Kelejian (1970)	Private nonfarm, quarterly, 1948–65	0.36
Dhrymes (1969)	Private hours, quarterly, 1948–60	0.75
Drazen et al. (1984)	Manufacturing hours, quarterly, 10 OECD countries, mostly 1961–80	0.21[a]
Hamermesh (1983)	Private nonfarm, quarterly, based on labor cost, 1955–78	0.47
Liu and Hwa (1974)	Private hours, monthly, 1961–71	0.67
Lucas and Rapping (1970)	Production hours, annual, 1930–65	1.09
Rosen and Quandt (1978)	Private production hours, annual, 1930–73	0.98
B. Labor demand with price of capital		
Chow and Moore (1972)	Private hours, quarterly, 1948:IV–1967	0.37[b]
Clark and Freeman (1980)	Manufacturing quarterly, 1950–76:	
	Employment	0.33
	Hours	0.51
Nadiri (1968)	Manufacturing quarterly, 1947–64:	
	Employment	0.15
	Hours	0.19
Nickell (1981)	Manufacturing quarterly, 1958–74, United Kingdom (materials prices)	0.19
Tinsley (1971)	Private nonfarm, quarterly, 1954–65:	
	Employment	0.04[b]
	Hours	0.06[b]
C. Interrelated factor demand		
Coen and Hickman (1970)	Private hours, annual, 1924–40, 1949–65	0.18
Nadiri and Rosen (1974)	Manufacturing employment, quarterly, 1948–65:	
	Production	−0.11
	Nonproduction	0.14
Schott (1978)	British industry, annual, 1948–70:	
	Employment	0.82
	Hours	0.25
	II. Production and cost function studies	
A. CES production functions		
Brown and deCani (1963)	Private nonfarm hours, annual, 1933–58	0.47
David and van de Klundert (1965)	Private hours, annual, 1899–1960	0.32
McKinnon (1963)	2-digit SIC manufacturing, annual, 1947–58	0.29[a]
B. Translog cost functions		
Berndt and Khaled (1979)	Manufacturing, annual, 1947–71; capital, labor, energy and materials:	
	Homogeneous, neutral technology change	0.46
	Nonhomothetic, non-neutral technology change	0.17
Magnus (1979)	Enterprise sector, annual, 1950–76, Netherlands; capital, labor and energy	0.30[b]
Morrison and Berndt (1981)	Manufacturing, annual, 1952–71; capital, labor energy and materials	0.35
Pindyck (1979)	10 OECD countries, annual, 1963–73; capital, labor and energy	0.43[a]

[a] Simple average of country estimates.
[b] Estimates calculated at the sample end-point.

complete system of demand equations. The estimates have the virtue that the own-price demand elasticity is simply the coefficient of $\ln w_L$ in the equation containing $\ln L$ as the dependent variable. The estimates are substantially lower than those produced in studies in part I.A that include only the wage rate. However, when one remembers that the estimates in part I.A are of the elasticity of substitution, the two sets of estimates are in the same fairly narrow range. Only the estimates based on interrelated factor demand (part I.C in the table) are below the range implied by the estimates in parts I.A and I.B. Clark and Freeman (1980) have shown that measures of the price of capital services are much more variable than measures of wages or earnings (presumably reflecting at least in part errors of measurement). Studies of interrelated factor demand, by estimating labor and capital demand simultaneously, inherently base the estimated labor-demand elasticities in part on the responsiveness of the demand for capital to what is likely to be a poorly measured price of capital. This view suggests the studies in part I.C of the table probably shed little light on the demand parameters of interest.

Among the cost and production function studies listed under part II of Table 8.2 there is a remarkable degree of similarity in the implied constant-output labor-demand elasticity. Given the diversity of specifications, sample periods and units that are studied, the extent of agreement is astounding. These studies produce estimates that are roughly in agreement with those listed under parts I.A and I.B. Again, whether one takes information on other factor prices into account or not seems to make little difference for the estimates of the labor demand elasticity. All that is required is that one interpret one's results carefully, relating the parameter estimates back to the elasticity one is trying to estimate.

Obviously there is no one correct estimate of the constant-output elasticity of demand for homogeneous labor in the aggregate. The true value of the parameter will change over time as the underlying technology changes, and will differ among economies due to differences in technologies. However, a reading of the estimates in Table 8.2 suggests that, in developed economies in the late twentieth century, the aggregate long-run, constant-output, labor-demand elasticity lies roughly in the range 0.15–0.50. While this range is fairly wide, it does at least put some limits on the claims one might make for the ability of, for example, wage subsidies to change the relative labor intensity of production at a fixed rate of output. These limits suggest that the huge empirical literature summarized here should narrow the debate over what the likely effects would be of any change imposed on the economy that affects the demand for labor.

An examination of these empirical studies and a consideration of the problems of specification indicates that the labor-demand elasticity can be obtained from a marginal-productivity condition, from a system of factor-demand equations, from a labor-demand equation that includes other factor prices, or from a system of equations that produces estimates of the partial elasticities of substitution among several factors of production. Often data on other factor prices will not be so readily available as the wage rate. The lack of differences we have noted between studies that include other factor prices and those that do not suggest the effort devoted to obtaining series on those other prices will not result in major changes in the estimates of the labor-demand elasticity.

5.2. *Varying output or endogenous wages*

While our major interest is in the constant-output, labor-demand elasticity, it is maybe worth asking a short-run question: What is the elasticity when output can vary, that is, what is a reasonable value for η' in (4a′)? The responses to changes in wage rates under these assumptions are obviously of special interest to those concerned with short-run macroeconomic problems. One recent study [Symons and Layard (1983)] examined demand functions for six large OECD economies in which only factor prices, not output, were included as independent variables. The estimates range from 0.4 to 2.6, with four of the six being greater than one. These relatively large estimates suggest, as one should expect from comparing (4a) and (4a′), that there is more scope for an imposed rise in real wages to reduce employment when one assumes output can vary.

The discussion thus far has dealt with the demand for homogeneous labor in the aggregate. Nearly all the studies summarized treat factor prices, including the wage rate, as exogenous. Yet, as we noted in Section 4, this assumption is strictly correct only if the elasticity of labor supply is infinite, which hardly seems correct in those studies based upon data from entire economies. (It is unlikely that the private nonfarm sector can elicit more labor from households without any increase in the market price of time.) The remarkable similarity of the results discussed in this section may merely arise from the authors' use of methods that are similar, but essentially incorrect, and that fail to provide a proper test of the theory of labor demand. Studies based on units of observation to which the supply of labor can be claimed to be truly exogenous thus provide a clearer test of the predictions of the theory of labor demand.

Estimates of labor-demand elasticities for small industries, for workers within a narrowly-defined occupation, for workers within small geographical areas, or even within individual establishments, are less likely to be fraught with problems of simultaneous-equations bias than are the macro time series that underlie the studies summarized in Table 8.2. Unfortunately, relatively little attention has been paid to this problem; but those studies that have treated less aggregated data describing the demand for homogeneous labor are summarized in Table 8.3. The estimates of the constant-output, labor-demand elasticities are quite similar to those summarized in Table 8.2. This suggests that the estimated elasticities that seem to confirm the central prediction of the theory of labor demand are not entirely an artifact produced by using aggregate data.

Table 8.3
Industry studies of labor demand.

Author and source	Data and industry coverage	η_{LL}
Ashenfelter and Ehrenberg (1975)	State and local government activities, states, 1958–69	0.67[a]
Field and Grebenstein (1980)	2-digit SIC manufacturing, annual, 1947–58	0.29[a]
Freeman (1975)	U.S., university faculty, 1920–70	0.26
Hopcroft and Symons (1983)	U.K. road haulage, 1953–80, capital stock held constant	0.49
Lovell (1973)	2-digit SIC manufacturing, states, 1958	0.37[a]
McKinnon (1963)	2-digit SIC manufacturing, annual, 1947–58	0.29[a]
Sosin and Fairchild (1984)	770 Latin American firms, 1970–74	0.20
Waud (1968)	2-digit SIC manufacturing, quarterly, 1954–64	1.03[a]

[a]Weighted average of estimates, using employment weights.

One might claim that even these units of observation are not the establishments or firms upon which the theory is based. It is true that, in contrast to the myriad studies of labor supply behavior based observations on households, there is a shocking absence of research on the empirical microeconomics of labor demand. Thus the most appropriate tests of the predictions of the theory have yet to be made. For those skeptical even of the results in Table 8.3 that are based on data describing occupations or industries, an additional confirmation of the theory is provided by analyses of the effects of the minimum wage. An overwhelming body of evidence [see the summary in Brown et al. (1982)] indicates that *imposed*, and thus exogenous, changes in minimum wages induce reductions in the employment of workers in those groups whose market wages are near the minimum.

6. Heterogeneous labor – estimation and empirical issues

Most of the methods for specifying and estimating models involving several types of labor carry over from the discussion of homogeneous labor in the previous section. Yet because one is generally interested in many more parameters than in the case of homogeneous labor, there are several considerations that do not arise in that case.

6.1. *Specification*

If one assumes that there are only two types of labor, and that they are separable from nonlabor inputs, the discussion in the previous section applies and the ways of estimating substitutability between the two factors should be apparent. (But see below for some problems that arise in this case.) In most instances, though, the problem at hand involves estimating the degree of substitutability among several types of labor (and among them and other factors). In that case, as the discussion in Section 3 should make clear, the restrictive Cobb–Douglas and CES forms will not be appropriate to answer the questions under study except under highly unlikely circumstances.

Two alternatives are possible, with the choice depending on the availability of data: (1) a complete system of factor-demand equations, essentially a series of N equations with the L_i, $i=1,\dots,N$, as dependent variables, and the same set of independent variables as in (49); and (2) a system of equations based on one of the flexible approximations to a production or cost function, e.g. the generalized Leontief or translog forms, such as are shown in Table 8.1. (Whether one specifies these systems with factor prices or quantities as independent variables is another issue, which we discuss below.) Each of these approaches requires data on all factor prices and quantities. Each of the approaches using the flexible forms allows the ready inference of the partial elasticities of substitution (or of complementarity) as well as the factor-demand (factor-price) elasticities.

As in the case of homogeneous labor, one would ideally specify factor demands simultaneously with factor supplies and be able to estimate a model that obviates the need to consider whether factor prices or quantities are to be considered exogenous. However, if it is difficult to specify such a model involving homogeneous labor, it seems impossible to do so for a model that includes several types of workers. Accordingly, one must be able to argue that supplies of each type of labor are either completely inelastic or completely elastic in response to exogenous changes in demand.[8]

No satisfactory choice appears to have been made in the studies that have estimated substitution among several types of labor. For example, consider a study that seeks to examine the extent of substitutability among adult women, adult men, youths and capital. It seems reasonable to treat the quantity of adult men in the work force as exogenous, and increasingly also for adult women, but that assumption hardly makes sense for youths whose labor supply appears to be quite elastic. (The supply elasticity of capital is also a problem.) That being the case, the absence of an appropriate set of variables from which to form instruments for the wage or labor quantities used means one must accept some misspecification whether one chooses to treat wages or quantities as exogenous.

As another example, one might argue that the supplies of blue- and white-collar labor to the economy are highly elastic in the long run; but it is unlikely, given the heterogeneity among workers' abilities, that these supplies are com-

[8]Remember that this is an economic issue, not a problem of inferring the partial elasticities of substitution or complementarity. In the translog case, for example, those can always be inferred, either easily or by inverting a matrix involving all the coefficients estimated.

pletely elastic. Even if one believes they are, the long run over which they are infinitely elastic is probably longer than the quarter or year that forms the basic unit of observation of time-series studies that focus on this disaggregation of the work force. That being the case, there is no clear-cut choice dictated by theory alone about whether wages or quantities should be treated as exogenous in this example either.

The problem is not solved by estimating the cost or production parameters using aggregated cross-section data. For example, the persistence of regional wage differentials unexplained by apparent differences in amenities suggests that one cannot claim that labor of all types is supplied perfectly elastically to geographical areas. Thus, using data on metropolitan areas or other geographical subunits does not guarantee that factor prices can be considered exogenous. The same problem arises when data on industries are used: insofar as industries use industry-specific skills, the supply of labor to the industry could well be upward-sloping in the long run. The only satisfactory solution, one that has not been tried in practice, is to use data on firms or establishments as the units of observation.

In practice the best guide to the choice between treating wages or quantities as exogenous is the link between this choice and the researcher's own priors on the supply elasticities of the factors whose demand is being examined (and thus how the misspecification that is induced can be minimized). In the example involving adult females, adult males and youths the overwhelming shares of output are accounted for by the first two groups, whose supply of effort is relatively inelastic. That being so, treating factor quantities as exogenous is probably the better choice. This also means that one should focus the analysis on the elasticities of complementarity and of factor prices, which are estimated more readily using production rather than cost functions (see Section 3).

6.2. *Measurement and interpretation issues*

Whether labor subaggregates are separable from capital, or whether some groups within the labor force are separable in production from others, is of central importance in empirical work estimating substitution among heterogeneous workers. Consider first the issue of separability of labor subaggregates from capital. In many cases the available data provide no way of obtaining a measure of the price or quantity of capital services. Even if such data are available, they may be measured with much greater error than the data on wage rates or employment in each labor subgroup. If the errors of measurement are large, one might well argue the Cambridge position that the notion of trying to aggregate the capital stock in an economy, or even in a labor market, is senseless. That being the case, one must be sure that labor is separable from capital when one estimates substitution relations among labor subgroups in the absence of a measure of capital price or quantity. Otherwise, the estimates of labor–labor substitution will be biased.

A similar problem arises when one concentrates on substitution among several subgroups in the labor force and assumes that they are separable from the rest of labor. [For example, Welch and Cunningham (1978) examine substitution among three groups of young workers disaggregated by age under the assumption that the σ_{ij} of each for adult workers are identical.] The estimates of the σ_{ij} (or c_{ij}) between the pairs of labor subgroups being studied will generally be biased. The separability of the labor subgroups from capital should always be tested rather than imposed if the data permit.

Even if the labor subaggregates are separable from capital (or, if they are not separable, the biases induced by assuming separability are small), a problem of interpretation arises. Assume, for example, that the true production function is

$$Y = F(K, G[L_1, L_2]),$$

where the function G aggregates the two types of labor. Estimates based on

$$L = G(L_1, L_2), \tag{50}$$

implicitly measure substitution along an isoquant that holds L, but not necessarily Y constant. Thus, the factor-demand elasticities computed from (50) are not constant-output demand elasticities [see Berndt (1980) for a discussion of this]. They are *gross elasticities*; constant-output labor demand elasticities will differ from these, for any rise in the price of, say, L_1, will induce a reduction in L (because the price of aggregate labor has fallen). If, for example, the L-constant demand elasticity for L_1 is η_{11}^*, the constant-output demand elasticity will be

$$\eta_{11} = \eta_{11}^* + s_1 \eta_{LL}, \tag{51}$$

where η_{LL} is the constant-output elasticity of demand for all labor [see Berndt and Wood (1979)]. In general,

$$\eta_{ij} = \eta_{ij}^* + s_j \eta_{LL}.$$

The true (constant-output) demand elasticity is more negative (greater in absolute value) than the gross elasticity, η_{11}^*; and the true cross-price demand elasticities are more negative than those based on estimates of substitution using (50) as the underlying production relation.

Assuming the labor subgroups can be treated as separable from capital, there is nothing wrong with the estimates of factor-demand (or factor-price elasticities in the dual case). However, they are not the usual elasticities, and should be adjusted accordingly. Otherwise, one will underestimate own-price demand elasticities, and infer that the types of labor are greater p-substitutes than in fact they are.

Another consideration is the choice of a disaggregation of the work force. Much of the early empirical work (through the middle 1970s) focused on the distinction between production and nonproduction workers. This was dictated partly by the ready availability of time-series data on this disaggregation, partly by the belief that this distinction represented a comparison of skilled and unskilled workers. Recent work by labor economists has recognized that differences in skill (embodied human capital) between production and nonproduction workers are not very great. Also, most of the policy issues on which studies of labor demand can have a bearing involve labor subgroups disaggregated according to other criteria. Thus, most of the recent work has disaggregated the work force by age, by race or ethnicity, by sex, or by these criteria in various combinations.

Economists' interest in substitution among particular groups of labor necessitates the aggregation of workers who differ along other dimensions that are of less interest to the researcher. Care should be exercised, though, that the aggregations decided upon make sense, in that substitution toward other groups is the same for all workers within a subaggregate.[9] In practice this means that, wherever possible given the limitations of the data being used, one should test for the consistency of aggregating workers into larger groups. For example, if one is concerned about substitution among males, females and capital, one should if possible test whether the substitution between young men and females (or capital) is the same as that for older men.

The problem of deciding which disaggregation to use and the larger difficulty of deciding what we mean by a "skill" have led to efforts to circumvent the decision by defining a set of characteristics of the workers. In this view [see Welch (1969) and Rosen (1983)] each worker embodies a set of characteristics (by analogy to Lancastrian models of the demand for goods).[10] This approach has the appeal of avoiding the aggregation of what may be very dissimilar workers into a particular group; instead, it "lets the data tell" what the appropriate skill categories are, in a manner similar to factor analysis. One of its difficulties is that it has not as yet been developed enough that the powerful restrictions of production theory can be imposed on estimates using this approach. Also, for many issues that attract public interest the arbitrary disaggregations of workers by age, race, sex, etc. are of substantial importance.

[9] Indeed, one should be able to demonstrate that workers can be aggregated linearly, not merely that those within a subgroup are separable from those in other subgroups.

[10] Stapleton and Young (1983) have attempted to apply this view to the United States for 1967–77. The results support many of the findings summarized in the next section, though they are not uniformly consistent with the theory of production.

Table 8.4
Studies of substitution of production and nonproduction workers.

Study	Data and method	σ_{BK}	σ_{WK}	σ_{BW}	η_{BB}	η_{WW}
	I. Capital excluded					
A. Cost functions						
Freeman and Medoff (1982)	Manufacturing plants, 1968, 1970, and 1972, detailed industry dummy variables; CES					
	Union			0.19		
	Nonunion			0.28		
B. Production functions						
Brendt and Christensen (1974b)	Manufacturing, 1929–68; translog, 1968 elasticities			4.9	−1.63	−2.87
Dougherty (1972)	States, Census of Population, 1960; CES			4.1		
	II. Capital Included					
A. Cost functions						
Berndt and White (1978)	Manufacturing, 1947–71; translog, 1971 elasticities	0.91	1.09	3.70	−1.23	−0.72
Clark and Freeman (1977)	Manufacturing, 1950–76; translog, mean elasticities	2.10	−1.98	0.91	−0.58	−0.22
Dennis and Smith (1978)	2-digit manufacturing 1952–73; translog, mean elasticities[a]	0.14	0.38	−0.05		
Denny and Fuss (1977)	Manufacturing, 1929–68; translog, 1968 elasticities	1.50	−0.91	2.06		
Freeman and Medoff (1982)	Pooled states and 2-digit manufacturing industries, 1972; translog,					
	Union	0.94	0.53	−0.02	−0.24	−0.12
	Nonunion	0.90	1.02	0.76	−0.43	−0.61
Grant (1979)	SMSAs, Census of Population, 1970; translog,					
	Professionals and managers	0.47	0.08	0.52	−0.32	−0.18
	Sales and clericals		0.46	0.14		
Kesselman et al. (1977)	Manufacturing, 1962–71; translog, 1971 elasticities	1.28	−0.48	0.49	−0.34	−0.19
Woodbury (1978)	Manufacturing, 1929–71; translog, 1971 elasticities				−0.70	−0.52

Table 8.4 continued.

Study	Data and method	σ_{BK}	σ_{WK}	σ_{BW}	η_{BB}	η_{WW}
B. Production functions						
Berndt and Christensen (1974b)	Manufacturing, 1929–68; translog 1968 elasticities	2.92	−1.94	5.51	−2.10	−2.59
Chiswick (1978)	States, Census of Population, 1910 and 1920 manufacturing; CES professionals vs. others			2.5		
Denny and Fuss (1977)	Manufacturing, 1929–68; translog 1968 elasticities	2.86	−1.88	4.76		
Hansen et al.[b] (1975)	3- and 4-digit industries, Census of Manufactures, 1967, translog;[a]					
	highest quartile of plants			6.0	−1.3	
	lowest quartile of plants			2.0	−1.5	

[a]Estimates are medians of parameters for individual industries.
[b]Ranked by value added per manhour. Estimates are medians of parameters for individual industries.

7. Heterogeneous labor – results and problems

A summary of the parameters of interest in the studies that have examined heterogeneous labor disaggregated by occupation is shown in Table 8.4.[11] Perhaps the most consistent finding is that nonproduction workers (presumably skilled labor) are less easily substitutable for physical capital than are production workers (unskilled labor). Indeed, a number of the studies find that nonproduction workers and physical capital are *p*-complements. This supports Rosen's (1968) and Griliches' (1969) initial results on the *capital–skill complementarity hypothesis*. This finding has major implications for the employment effects of such policies as accelerated depreciation, investment tax credits and other attempts to stimulate investment in physical capital, suggesting that they will increase the demand for skilled relative to unskilled labor.

Although not uniformly observed in all studies tabulated, in most the demand elasticity for nonproduction workers is lower than that for production workers. This difference reflects what seems to be a consistent result among studies examining all the disaggregations of the labor force: the own-price demand elasticity is lower, the greater is the amount of human capital embodied in the

[11]The issues from 1979 to 1982 of a large number of journals were searched. For years before 1979 the references are taken from Hamermesh and Grant (1979).

average worker in the particular class of labor. Thus, skill per se ties employers to workers by making labor demand less sensitive to exogenous changes in wage rates.

One would like to draw some inferences about the ease of substitution of white- for blue-collar labor, and about the absolute size of the demand elasticities for each. Unfortunately, there appears to be very little agreement among the studies on these issues. Examining the table more closely, though, one notices that the estimated demand and substitution elasticities are generally higher in those studies that base them on estimates of production functions. Since inferring these parameters from production functions requires inversion of an entire matrix of parameter estimates [see eq. (29)], they will be affected by errors in any of the parameters estimated. While there is no reason to expect biases, the accumulation of errors is also to be avoided. For that reason the cost-function estimates are likely to be more reliable. The estimates shown in parts I.A and II.A are better ones to use to draw inferences about the extent of substitution among these three factors. Using them, the demand elasticities for the broad categories, white- and blue-collar labor, seem to be roughly the same magnitude as the estimates of the demand elasticity for homogeneous labor that we discussed in Section 5.

Only a few studies have disaggregated the labor force by educational attainment. Among them Grant (1979) finds that the own-price demand elasticity declines the more education is embodied in the group of workers. (This is consistent with the results on the relation of the elasticity to the skill level that we noted above.) Grant and others, including Welch (1970) and Johnson (1970), find that college and high-school graduates are p-substitutes. (These latter two studies, which estimate pairwise CES relations, are less reliable because they did not allow the level of other factor inputs to affect the measured extent of substitution within a pair of inputs. Essentially they estimate relative factor demand for many pairs of factors.) All the studies estimate the extent of substitution, and the own-price demand elasticities, to be roughly on the order of those found between white- and blue-collar workers in Table 8.4.

The disaggregations of labor used in the studies discussed above are clear-cut. In the more recent research a large variety of disaggregations, mostly involving age and/or race and/or sex, have been used. This diversity makes it rather difficult to draw many firm conclusions from the findings because of the relative lack of replication. In Table 8.5 I list the results of these studies, separating them by whether they estimate substitution elasticities or elasticities of complementarity. Among the former several results appear consistently among the studies. The estimated demand elasticities (and, though they are not shown in the table, the substitution elasticities) are much larger when produced using methods that treat factor quantities as exogenous. This result parallels what we observed in Table 8.4; even though quantities may be exogenous, deriving any substitution elasticity from estimates based on this assumption requires estimates of all the production parameters. That requirement may induce large errors when one or more of the parameters is estimated imprecisely.

The estimates of the factor-demand elasticities vary greatly among the studies. [Indeed, in Merrilees (1982) some are positive, for reasons that are not clear; but their sign casts doubt on all of Merrilees' results.] However, the demand elasticity for adult men is generally lower than that for other groups of workers. This result is another reflection of the apparently general inverse relationship between a group's average skill level and the elasticity of demand for its labor. The final generalization from the studies listed in part I of Table 8.5 is that in most of the disaggregations each factor is a *p*-substitute for the others.

As we noted in Section 6, the elasticity of supply should guide the choice about whether to treat wages or quantities as exogenous. In the case of disaggregating by age and sex, treating quantities as exogenous and deriving elasticities of complementarity and factor price is the better choice (in the absence of a well-specified model of the supply of each type of labor) if data on large geographical units are used. [Clearly, if data on a small industry or even individual establishments are used, wages should be treated as exogenous. One's belief in the validity of the theory of labor demand should be strengthened by the results of those three studies – Rosen (1968), O'Connell (1972) and King (1980) – that use these small units and find the expected negative own-price elasticities for workers in narrowly-defined occupations.] The studies presented in part II of Table 8.5 treat quantities as exogenous and estimate these elasticities for a variety of disaggregations of the labor force. As such they give a better indication of the substitution possibilities within the labor force disaggregated by age, race and sex than do those listed in part I.

In all the studies the elasticities of factor prices are fairly low. [Given the small share of output accounted for by most of the inputs, the elasticities implied by Borjas' studies and by Berger (1983) are also quite low.] They suggest that the labor market can accommodate an exogenous change in relative labor supply without much change in relative wages.[12] No generalizations about the relative magnitudes of the elasticities are possible from the studies currently available.

One intriguing result occurs in three of the four studies [Borjas (1983a), Grant-Hamermesh (1981) and Berger (1983)] that examine the issue. Adult women are *q*-substitutes for young workers. Borjas (1983a) also disaggregates the black male work force by age and finds that most of the *q*-substitutability is between women and young black men. This finding suggests that the remarkably rapid growth in the relative size of the female labor force that has occurred in many industrialized countries, including the United States, Canada and Sweden,

[12] This finding implies nothing about how *quickly* an economy can adjust to such a change. Even though the required change in relative wages may be slight, adjustment costs may be sufficiently large to lead to long periods of disequilibrium in the markets for some of the groups of labor.

Table 8.5
Studies of substitution among age and sex groups.

Category	Study	Data and method	Types of labor	σ_{ij}	η_{ii}
I. Substitution and demand elasticities					
A. Capital excluded					
Wages exogenous Cross-section	Welch and Cunningham (1978)	States, Census of Population, 1970; CES	14–15, 16–17, 18–19 Teenage Labor	All are > 0	
Pooled cross-section time series	Government of Australia (1983)	17 Australian industries, 1976–81; factor-demand equations	M < 21	All are > 0	−1.34
			F < 21		−1.80
			M 21 +		−4.58
			F 21 +		−0.59
					−2.25
Time-series	Johnson and Blakemore (1979)	Entire U.S. economy, 1970–77; CES	Average for 14 age-sex groups	1.43	
	Layard (1982)	British manufacturing, 1949–69; translog	M < 21	All are > 0 except F < 18 vs. F 18 +	−1.25
			F < 18		−0.31
			M 21 +		−0.35
			F 18 +		−1.59
B. Capital included					
Wages exogenous Time-series	Merrilees (1982)	Canada, entire economy, 1957–78; factor-demand equations	Young males	Mixed, but all involving adult male wages are < 0	0.56
			Young females		−0.44
			Adult males		−0.07
			Adult females		0.11
	Hamermesh (1982)	Entire economy, 1955–75; translog, mean elasticities	14–24	> 0	−0.59
			25 +		−0.01
Quantities exogenous Cross-section	Grant (1979)	SMSAs, Census of Population, 1970; translog	14–24	All are > 0	−9.68
			25–44		−2.72
			45 +		−2.48
Time-series	Anderson (1977)	Manufacturing, 1947–72; translog, 1972 elasticities	16–24	All are > 0	−7.14
			25–44		−3.45
			45 +		−3.99

II. Elasticities of complementarity and factor prices (quantities exogenous)				c_{ij}	ε_{ii}
A. Capital excluded					
Cross-section	Borjas (1983b)	Entire U.S. economy, microdata 1975; generalized Leontief	Blacks	All are > 0	−0.07[a]
			Hispanics		−0.64[a]
			Whites		−0.001[a]
B. Capital included					
Cross-section	Borjas (1983a)	Census of Population, 1970; generalized Leontief	Black males	All > 0 except all those involving females, and some involving Hispanics	1.02[a]
			Females		2.90[a]
			Hispanic nonmigrants		−2.66[a]
			Hispanic migrants		−11.98
			White nonmigrants		−0.03
			White migrants		1.02[a]
	Grant and Hamermesh (1981)	SMSAs, Census of Population 1970; translog	Youths	All > 0 except youths vs. F 25 +	−0.03
			Blacks 25 +		−0.43
			White M25 +		−0.13
			White F25 +		−0.19
	Grossman (1982)	SMSAs, Census of Population 1970; translog	Natives	All are < 0	−0.20
			Second generation		−0.03
			Foreign born		−0.23
Pooled cross-section,	Berger (1983)	States, U.S.,	M, 0–15 yrs. school, 0–14 experience	All are < 0	−0.51[a]
time-series		1967–74;	M, 16 + school, 0–14 experience	except young	−3.45[a]
		translog,	M, 0–15 school, 15 + experience	vs. old	−0.80[a]
		mean elasticities	M, 16 + school, 15 + experience	college grads	−1.48[a]
			F		−0.29[a]
Time-series	Freeman (1979)	Entire U.S. economy, 1950–74; translog,	M 20–34	Only M 20–34 vs. F is > 0	−0.38
			M 35–64		−0.49
		mean elasticities	F		−0.71

[a] Own-quantity elasticities of complementarity.

in the past twenty years has contributed to a decline in the equilibrium relative wage rate for young workers. To the extent that relative wages cannot adjust because of real wage floors, and thus permanent unemployment, the assumptions needed to produce estimates of q-substitutability are incorrect. However, so long as adjustment *eventually* occurs, these cross-section estimates can be used to infer that the growth of the female labor force has also contributed to the high rate of youth unemployment in these countries during this time.

Among the studies discussed in this section only a few have tested for the separability of labor from capital (and thus shed light on whether estimates of the (gross) elasticities of demand or of factor prices obtained when capital is excluded are biased). Berndt and Christensen (1974a) and Denny and Fuss (1977) examine this issue using the production-worker, nonproduction-worker disaggregation; and Grant and Hamermesh (1981) disaggregate the labor force by age, race and sex. All three studies conclude that the separability of labor from capital is not supported by the data. The findings suggest that the inclusion of the quantity or price of capital services is necessary to derive unbiased estimates of production and cost parameters even between subgroups in the labor force. The extent of the biases induced by assuming separability has not been examined, though Borjas (1983a) indicates that the a_{ij} involving labor-force subgroups change little when capital is excluded from a generalized Leontief system.[13]

There has also been very little effort made to examine whether the particular disaggregations used are correct in assuming that workers included within a subgroup are equally substitutable for workers in other subgroups. This absence is due partly to the difficulties of obtaining data on large numbers of narrowly-defined groups of workers. However, the evidence [see Grant and Hamermesh (1981)] suggesting that it is incorrect to aggregate subgroups of workers into still larger subgroups should induce greater care in future research in this area.

8. Conclusions

Research into the demand for labor over the past 50 years has focused on depicting demand in a decreasingly restrictive way as the outcome of employers' attempts at cost minimization or profit maximization. The outcome of this trend to date is a means of characterizing demand for N factors of production in a way that allows for complete flexibility in the degree of substitution within any pair of

[13] By itself, though, this shows very little, since small changes in the estimated parameters in a translog or generalized Leontief system often lead to large changes in the estimates of the underlying production or cost parameters, as the discussion in Section 3 indicates.

factors; for that flexibility to depend on the firm's output level; and for flexibility in the specification of returns to scale in production. Not only is the theory completely general: we have today the means to describe production relations empirically in a completely general manner.

Perhaps the main advantage of this increased generality is that it allows us to test whether some of the simpler specifications of labor demand describe the data well. Thus, the many studies analyzed in Section 5 suggest that the Cobb–Douglas function is not a very severe departure from reality in describing production relations between homogeneous labor and physical capital. So too, returns to scale in production functions involving homogeneous labor do not seem to differ too greatly from one.

The major advance of the last 15 years has been the ability to estimate substitution within several pairs of inputs. While such estimation is really in its childhood (partly because of the wide range of interesting choices about how to disaggregate the labor force), some results are already fairly solid. (1) Skill (human capital) and physical capital are p-complements in production; at a fixed output employers will expand their use of skilled labor when the price of capital services declines. (2) The demand for skill is also less elastic than the demand for raw labor; thus we find that the demand for more educated or more highly trained workers is less elastic than that for other workers. (3) No matter what the disaggregation, labor is not separable in production from physical capital. This finding implies that estimates of substitution among groups within the labor force should be based on models that include either the price or quantity of capital services. (4) Finally, though it is less solid a result than the other three, there is an accumulation of evidence that adult women are q-substitutes for young workers.

The theory and estimation techniques we have outlined provide many ways to estimate the degree of factor substitution and the responsiveness of factor demand (prices) to changes in factor prices (quantities). Though the appropriate specification depends upon one's beliefs about the behavior of the agents in the particular labor market, several guidelines for the analysis arise from this discussion. Where at all possible, the specification should allow the researcher sufficient flexibility to test whether simpler specifications are applicable. Where the data are available, physical capital should be included as a factor of production in the analysis along with the various types of labor.

Despite the substantial advances that have been made in analyzing the demand for labor, a remarkable amount is still unknown. We still understand very little about the absolute magnitudes of elasticities of demand, or elasticities of factor prices, for various labor-force groups. So too, the ease of substitution among groups is only now beginning to be analyzed.

More important than these lacunae in our understanding of labor demand, though, are problems induced by the failure to account for the interaction of substitution parameters with parameters describing the supply of labor-force groups. Those relatively few studies that have estimated demand relations using highly disaggregated data corroborated the basic predictions of the theory of labor demand. However, there has been far too little work that has accounted for the possibility of simultaneity between wages and quantities of labor. Since we have seen how important the specification of labor supply is to deriving estimates of production parameters, the joint estimation of substitution parameters and labor supply should be an area that will lead to substantial advances in understanding the demand for labor. Alternatively, more research is needed that estimates demand relations using data on individual firms or establishments as units of observation.

References

Allen, R. G. D. (1938) *Mathematical analysis for economists*. London: Macmillan.

Anderson, J. (1977) "Labor force age structure changes and relative wages", unpublished paper, Harvard University.

Arrow, K., H. Chenery, B. Minhas and R. Solow (1961) "Capital–labor substitution and economic efficiency", *Review of Economics and Statistics*, 43:225–250.

Ashenfelter, O. and R. Ehrenberg (1975) "The demand for labor in the public sector", in: D. Hamermesh, ed., *Labor in the public and nonprofit sectors*. Princeton, N.J.: Princeton University Press.

Berger, M. (1983) "Changes in labor force composition and male earnings: a production approach", *Journal of Human Resources*, 18:177–196.

Berndt, E. (1980) "Modelling the simultaneous demand for factors of production", in: Z. Hornstein *et al.*, eds., *The economics of the labor market*. London: HMSO.

Berndt, E. and L. Christensen (1974a) "Testing for the existence of a consistent aggregate index of labor inputs", *American Economic Review*, 64:391–404.

Berndt, E. and L. Christensen (1974b) "The specification of technology in U.S. manufacturing", unpublished paper, University of Wisconsin.

Berndt, E. and M. Khaled (1979) "Parametric productivity measurement and choice among flexible functional forms", *Journal of Political Economy*, 87:1220–1245.

Berndt, E. and C. White (1978) "Income redistribution and employment effects of rising energy prices", unpublished paper, University of British Columbia.

Berndt, E. and D. Wood (1979) "Engineering and econometric interpretations of energy–capital complementarity", *American Economic Review*, 69:342–354.

Black, S. and H. Kelejian (1970) "A macro model of the U.S. labor market", *Econometrica*, 38:712–741.

Borjas, G. (1983a) "The demographic determinants of the demand for black labor", unpublished paper, University of California–Santa Barbara.

Borjas, G. (1983b) "The substitutability of black, hispanic and white labor", *Economic Inquiry*, 21:93–106.

Brown, C., G. Gilroy and A. Kohen (1982) "The effect of the minimum wage on employment and unemployment", *Journal of Economic Literature*, 20:487–528.

Brown, M. and J. de Cani (1963) "A measure of technological employment", *Review of Economics and Statistics*, 45:386–394.

Chiswick, C. (1978) "The growth of professional occupations in U.S. manufacturing, 1900–73", in: I. Sirageldin, ed., *Research in human capital and development*. Greenwich, Conn.: JAI Press.

Chow, G. and G. Moore (1972) "An econometric model of business cycles", in: B. Hickman, ed., *Econometric models of cyclical behavior*. New York: National Bureau of Economic Research.

Christensen, L., D. Jorgenson and L. Lau (1973) "Transcendental logarithmic production frontiers", *Review of Economics and Statistics*, 55:28–45.

Clark, K. and R. Freeman (1980) "How elastic is the demand for labor?", *Review of Economics and Statistics*, 62:509–520.

Clark, K. and R. Freeman (1977) "Time-series models of the elasticity of demand for labor in manufacturing", unpublished paper, Harvard University.

Coen, R. and B. Hickman (1970) "Constrained joint estimation of factor demand and production functions", *Review of Economics and Statistics*, 52:287–300.

David, P. and T. van de Klundert (1965) "Biased efficiency growth and capital–labor substitution in the United States, 1899–1960", *American Economic Review*, 55:357–394.

Dennis, F. and V. K. Smith (1978) "A neoclassical analysis of the demand for real cash balances by firms", *Journal of Political Economy*, 86:793–814.

Denny, M. and M. Fuss (1977) "The use of approximation analysis to test for separability and the existence of consistent aggregates", *American Economic Review*, 67:404–418.

Dhrymes, P. (1969) "A model of short-run labor adjustment", in: James Duesenberry et al., eds., *The Brookings model: some further results*. Chicago: Rand McNally.

Diewert, E. (1971) "An application of the Shephard duality theorem: a generalized Leontief production function", *Journal of Political Economy*, 79:481–507.

Dixit, A. (1976) *Optimization in economic theory*. Oxford, England: Oxford.

Dougherty, C. R. S. (1972) "Estimates of labor aggregation functions", *Journal of Political Economy*, 80:1101–1119.

Drazen, A., D. Hamermesh and N. Obst (1984) "The variable employment elasticity hypothesis: theory and evidence", *Research in Labor Economics*, 6: 287–309.

Ferguson, C. (1969) *The neoclassical theory of production and distribution*. Cambridge, England: Cambridge.

Field, B. and C. Grebenstein (1980) "Capital–energy substitution in U.S. manufacturing", *Review of Economics and Statistics*, 62:207–212.

Freeman, R. (1975) "Demand for labor in a nonprofit market: university faculty", in: D. Hamermesh, ed., *Labor in the public and nonprofit sectors*. Princeton, N.J.: Princeton University Press.

Freeman, R. (1979) "The effect of demographic factors on age–earnings profiles", *Journal of Human Resources*, 14:289–318.

Freeman, R. and J. Medoff (1982) "Substitution between production labor and other inputs in unionized and nonunionized manufacturing", *Review of Economics and Statistics*, 64:220–233.

Fuss, M. and D. McFadden (1978) *Production economics: a dual approach to theory and applications*. Amsterdam: North-Holland.

Government of Australia, Bureau of Labor Market Research (1983) *Youth wages, employment and the labour force*. Canberra: Australia Government Publishing Service.

Grant, J. (1979) "Labor substitution in U.S. manufacturing", Ph.D. dissertation, Michigan State University.

Grant, J. and D. Hamermesh (1981) "Labor–market competition among youths, white women and others", *Review of Economics and Statistics*, 63:354–360.

Griliches, Z. (1969) "Capital–skill complementarity", *Review of Economics and Statistics*, 51:465–468.

Grossman, J. B. (1982) "The substitutability of natives and immigrants in production", *Review of Economics and Statistics*, 64:596–603.

Hamermesh, D. (1976) "Econometric studies of labor demand and their application to policy analysis", *Journal of Human Resources*, 11:507–525.

Hamermesh, D. (1980) "Factor market dynamics and the incidence of taxes and subsidies", *Quarterly Journal of Economics*, 95:751–764.

Hamermesh, D. (1982) "Minimum wages and the demand for labor", *Economic Inquiry*, 20:365–380.

Hamermesh, D. (1983) "New measures of labor cost: implications for demand elasticities and nominal wage growth", in: J. Triplett, ed., *The measurement of labor cost*. Chicago: University of Chicago Press.

Hamermesh, D. and J. Grant (1979) "Econometric studies of labor–labor substitution and their implications for policy", *Journal of Human Resources*, 14:518–542.

Hanson, R., B. Klotz and R. Madoo (1975) "The structure of demand for low-wage labor in U.S. manufacturing, 1967", unpublished paper, Urban Institute.

Hicks, J. R. (1964) *The theory of wages*. London: Macmillan.

Hopcroft, M. P. and J. Symons (1983) "The demand for labour schedule in the road haulage industry", Discussion Paper No. 169, Centre for Labour Economics, London School of Economics.

Johnson, G. (1970) "The demand for labor by educational category", *Southern Economic Journal*, 37:190–204.

Johnson, G. and A. Blakemore (1979) "The potential impact of employment policy on the unemployment rate consistent with non-accelerating inflation", *American Economic Review*, 69:119–123.

Kesselman, J., S. Williamson and E. Berndt (1977) "Tax credits for employment rather than investment", *American Economic Review*, 67:339–349.

King, W. (1980) "A multiple output translog cost-function estimation of academic labor services", Ph.D. dissertation, Michigan State University.

Layard, R. (1982) "Youth unemployment in Britain and the United States compared", in: R. Freeman and D. Wise, eds., *The youth labor market problem: its nature, causes and consequences*. Chicago: University of Chicago Press.

Liu, T. C. and E. C. Hwa (1974) "A monthly econometric model of the U.S. economy", *International Economic Review*, 15:328–365.

Lovell, C. A. K. (1973) "CES and VES production functions in a cross-section context", *Journal of Political Economy*, 81:705–720.

Lucas, R. E. and L. Rapping (1970) "Real wages, employment and inflation", in: Edmund Phelps, ed., *Microeconomic foundations of employment and inflation theory*. New York: W. W. Norton & Co.

Magnus, J. (1979) "Substitution between energy and non-energy inputs in the Netherlands, 1950–1976", *International Economic Review*, 20:465–484.

McKinnon, R. (1963) "Wages, capital costs and employment in manufacturing", *Econometrica*, 30:501–521.

Merrilees, W. (1982) "Labor market segmentation in Canada: an econometric approach", *Canadian Journal of Economics*, 15:458–473.

Morrison, C. and E. Berndt (1981) "Short-run labor productivity in a dynamic model", *Journal of Econometrics*, 16:339–365.

Nadiri, M. (1968) "The effect of relative prices and capacity on the demand for labor in the U.S. manufacturing sector", *Review of Economic Studies*, 35:273–288.

Nadiri, M. and S. Rosen, (1974) *A disequilibrium model of production*. New York: National Bureau of Economic Research.

Nickell, S. (1981) "An investigation of the determinants of manufacturing employment in the United Kingdom", Discussion Paper No. 105, Centre for Labour Economics, London School of Economics.

O'Connell, J. (1972) "The labor market for engineers: an alternative methodology", *Journal of Human Resources*, 7:71–86.

Pindyck, R. (1979) "Interfuel substitution and the industrial demand for energy: an international comparison", *Review of Economics and Statistics*, 61:169–179.

Rosen, H. and R. Quandt (1978) "Estimation of a disequilibrium aggregate labor market", *Review of Economics and Statistics*, 60:371–379.

Rosen, S. (1983) "A note on aggregation of skills and labor quality", *Journal of Human Resources*, 18:425–431.

Rosen, S. (1968) "Short-run employment variation on class-I railroads in the United States, 1947–1963", *Econometrica*, 36:511–529.

Sato, R. (1977) "Homothetic and nonhomothetic CES production functions", *American Economic Review*, 67:559–569.

Sato, R. and T. Koizumi (1973) "On the elasticities of substitution and complementarity", *Oxford Economic Papers*, 25:44–56.

Schott, K. (1978) "The relation between industrial research and development and factor demands", *Economic Journal*, 88:85–106.

Sosin, K. and L. Fairchild (1984) "Nonhomotheticity and technological bias in production", *Review of Economics and Statistics*, 66:44–50.

Stapleton, D. and D. Young (1983) "The effects of demographic change on the distribution of wages, 1967–1990", unpublished paper, Dartmouth College.

Symons, J. and R. Layard (1983) "Neo-classical demand for labour functions for six major economies", Discussion Paper No. 166, Centre for Labour Economics, London School of Economics.

Tinsley, P. (1971) "A variable adjustment model of labor demand", *International Economic Review*, 12:482–510.

Varian, H. (1978) *Microeconomic analysis*. New York: Norton.

Waud, R. (1968) "Man-hour behavior in U.S. manufacturing: a neoclassical interpretation", *Journal of Political Economy*, 76:511–529.

Welch, F. (1969) "Linear synthesis of skill distribution", *Journal of Human Resources*, 4:311–327.

Welch, F. (1970) "Education in production", *Journal of Political Economy*, 78:764–771.

Welch, F. and J. Cunningham (1978) "Effects of minimum wages on the level and age composition of youth employment", *Review of Economics and Statistics*, 60:140–145.

Woodbury, S. (1978) "Is the elasticity of demand for labor subject to cyclical fluctuation?", unpublished paper, University of Wisconsin.

Chapter 9

DYNAMIC MODELS OF LABOUR DEMAND

S. J. NICKELL*

London School of Economics

1. Introduction

Workers who walk out of the factory gate on a Friday afternoon will typically return through the same gate on a Monday morning, if not before. This commonplace fact is indicative of the dynamic nature of the firm's demand for labour. The typical firm does not hire its workforce afresh each day for the simple reason that it is very much cheaper not to do so. Hiring and firing generate costs for the firm over and above the weekly wage payment. As we shall see, these costs ensure that the firm's demand for labour depends not only on current exogenous factors but also on the initial size of the workforce and expectations about the future levels of such factors. The firm's demand for labour cannot, therefore, be described by a static model. This fact has, of course, been known to empirical workers in this field for a long time [see, for example, Holt et al. (1960)]. Thus, in a very thorough analysis of the response of employment to exogenous changes, Sims (1974) concludes that it takes at least a year for employment to adjust fully in response to a shift in sales, the adjustment path being illustrated in Figure 9.1. It is our purpose in this chapter to examine theoretical explanations of facts such as this[1] and to investigate the extent to which these explanations are consistent with empirical data.

In what follows, therefore, we look first at the size and structure of the "adjustment" costs imposed on the firm by turnover. This is an important issue because the structure of these costs is crucial in determining the temporal pattern

*My thanks are due to the editors, John Kennan and all the authors of the other chapters who attended the Handbook conference in Princeton in October 1983 and made valuable comments on an earlier draft. I am also grateful to the Economic and Social Research Council, the Department of Employment, the Manpower Services Commission and the Esmee Fairburn Trust for financial support.

[1]It is important to recognise that we are not simply trying to explain the fact that employment exhibits a high degree of persistence or serial correlation. This is, of course, entirely consistent with a static demand model, merely requiring that the exogenous determinants of labour demand are themselves serially correlated.

Handbook of Labor Economics, Volume I, Edited by O. Ashenfelter and R. Layard

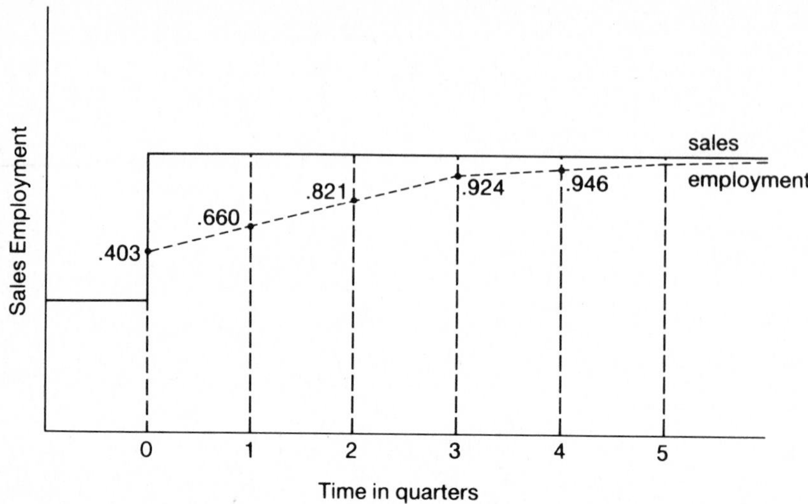

Figure 9.1. The response of employment to a change in sales. *Source*: Sims (1974, Table 6).

of labour demand in response to exogenous shocks. This is followed by analyses of a number of dynamic models of the demand for labour which will illustrate the above point. Section 4 is concerned with the formulation of empirical models and in the subsequent section we consider some of the rather limited amount of empirical work which is explicitly based on a well formulated dynamic theory.[2] We conclude with some general remarks on the directions in which research in this area might proceed.

2. The size and structure of adjustment costs

2.1. *How much does it cost to hire and fire?*

If we are going to build a dynamic model of the firm's demand for labour which is based on adjustment costs it is important that we have some idea of their size. In this section, therefore, we shall simply attempt to provide some rough notion of the orders of magnitude involved making no pretence at a comprehensive survey. Looking at hiring first, it is clear that the introduction of a new employee into a firm generates costs over and above the wage payment. These additional

[2]We shall not present a full survey of the empirical literature on labour demand which may be found in Chapter 8 by Hamermesh in this Handbook.

costs are incurred both in the act of hiring and in the consequent introduction of the new employee into the productive workforce. The former category would include expenditure on advertising and time spent on interviewing, testing and the like. The latter category would include direct expenditure on training and indirect expenditure in the form of lost output while the individual learns the job.[3] The firm may, of course, be compensated for some or all of these costs by paying a reduced wage for an initial period.

A first key issue then is the size of these costs which we shall subsume under the general heading of hiring costs. The following figures give us a rough idea of their importance. In Walter Oi's classic paper on the "quasi-fixity" of labour [Oi (1962)], he presents figures for the International Harvester Company which indicate that the average hiring plus training cost for each new employee comes to around 142 hours' pay at the average hourly rate in the company.[4] This indicates an average cost equivalent to a little over three weeks' pay but masks a very large difference between the hiring costs incurred for the unskilled labourer and the skilled manual and non-manual workforce. For example, the hiring costs for the unskilled labourer represent a mere 22 hours' pay at the unskilled rate. This latter figure compares with some more recent estimates presented in Barron et al. (1983) and based on a survey of firms in the United States in 1980. This reveals that for every unskilled/semi-skilled recruit, 8.11 employee hours are spent in the actual recruiting process and 34 employee hours are required for training/orienting in the first month. This is equivalent to a little over one week's pay in total. The enormous differential between skilled and unskilled workers in this regard is confirmed by the figures reported in Rees (1973, Table 9). These refer to hiring costs for a group of firms in the Rochester, N.Y., area in 1965–66 and indicate that in manufacturing the average hiring costs for professional, managerial and technical workers are twelve times as great as those for the unskilled and for skilled workers they are more than five times as large.

Hiring costs are, however, only one side of the coin. Further direct costs are often incurred if an employee leaves the firm. These may be minimal if the employee simply quits but can be substantial if he is laid off or fired. These costs we subsume under the generic term "firing costs" and include payments in lieu of notice, compensation for breach of contract, loss of output resulting from the lag between separation and subsequent replacement and any costs incurred because it is necessary to fulfill certain legal requirements. Returning to the International

[3] These are all essentially "internal" hiring costs. It may also be true that there exist "external" costs which are related to the rate of hiring. Thus if the rate of hiring is greater, the firm may be forced to recruit workers of a lower average quality. In so far as the firm cannot compensate for this by paying them lower wages, this must also count as a hiring cost. This effect, although possibly important, is very hard to quantify.

[4] The costs are taken from the last column of Table 1 in Oi (1962) and are the sum of Recruiting, Hiring, Orientation, Training, Tools and Materials and Intrawork Transfers. The average hourly earnings are $1.95.

Harvester data in Oi (1962), the total firing cost excluding payments for unemployment benefit comes to around 16 hours' pay at the average hourly rate.[5] Unfortunately, this figure represents an amount per new employee and since only a fraction of new employees end up as involuntary separations, it is an underestimate of the firing cost and should probably be at least doubled. Nevertheless, this is relatively minor compared with the various forms of compensation payments which are required of firms as a consequence of laying off an employee. In the United States, the experience rating system for unemployment benefit provides a link between the average level of layoffs generated by the firm and its payments into a central fund for benefits. The system is complex and also varies across States [see, for example, Brechling (1978) or Topel and Welch (1980)] but its consequence is that, for some of the time, firms can expect to pay for the unemployment benefit of workers who are laid off. So if the average unemployment duration is 6 weeks with a 50 percent replacement rate, this would amount to 3 weeks' pay. On the other hand, if a firm is already paying into the system at the maximum rate, the marginal cost of a layoff is zero. The International Harvester average payment is around one week's pay[6] but again this is *per new employee* and if, for example, the number of involuntary separations is half the number of hires, then we must double this figure.

Other countries typically do not have an experience rated benefit system but they do have other types of regulations governing the termination of employment which can make this a very expensive business. For example, in 1966 the Redundancy Payments Act was introduced in Britain and this makes employers legally liable to provide compensation for employees who are permanently laid off. Some part of this compensation comes from a central fund but some is the direct responsibility of the firm and this latter element averages out at around 5 weeks' pay. This is, of course, a legal minimum payment and Trade Unions often negotiate very much larger amounts of compensation as do executives. There are numerous other costs associated with turnover which it is even harder to quantify. Many countries have laws which lay down strict criteria for dismissals, for example, and any transgression of these rules is expensive both in terms of compensation and legal fees. Thus, for example, there are some 35 000 cases for unfair dismissal brought before Industrial Tribunals in Britain each year where average compensation and legal fees amount to around four months pay.

In general, therefore, we may argue that the costs of both hiring and firing are not trivial and may also vary dramatically between unskilled and skilled workers. The average size of these costs is not, however, the only issue at stake. Their structure is also of vital importance and this is the topic which we shall now consider.

[5]These costs are taken from the last column of Table 1 in Oi (1962) and are the sum of Terminating, Laying off and Unfilled requisitions.

[6]This is again to be found in the last column of Table 1 in Oi (1962). See also the discussion in the text.

Figure 9.2. The relationship between hiring costs and the rate of hiring.

2.2. *The structure of adjustment costs*

The question to be considered here is the functional relationship between hiring/firing costs and the rate at which accessions or separations occur. The first point to note is that voluntary quits cost less than layoffs since no contribution to unemployment benefit or redundancy compensation is required. Second, on the hiring side, it is the gross number of new employees which seems to be important not the net additions to the workforce. How, then, are hiring costs related to the rate at which hiring takes place? It is undoubtedly true that there are some cost elements which would tend to generate increasing returns in the hiring technology, particularly at low rates of hiring. The cost of advertising for two employees is the same as advertising for one and the average cost of training is certainly diminishing at the start of the range (think of lectures, for example). Some costs, on the other hand, are fixed per unit, most obviously if the firm hires from an agency. Generally speaking, for low levels of hiring it is hard to think of good reasons why hiring costs should be increasing at the margin. On the other hand, for high rates of hiring, increasing marginal costs will surely set in at some stage. If the firm takes on employees at too rapid a rate, chaos could well ensue in production as the plant is flooded with novices.

The above discussion indicates that the relationship illustrated in Figure 9.2 seems plausible. Thus we have an initial section where the average cost of hiring declines but eventually costs are increasing at the margin. Unfortunately, there is no concrete evidence on the exact shape of this relationship, in particular whether the initial non-convexities are large or small and whether the relationship remains approximately linear over a large range or the strictly convex section starts fairly early on.

Concerning firing costs, similar arguments would seem to apply. However, the arguments for initial non-convexities are much weaker and the linearity argument is correspondingly stronger particularly with regard to compensation payments.

With regard to large-scale layoffs, casual observation does seem to suggest that they are more expensive per employee since they typically involve extensive negotiation and often considerable compensation payments.

To summarise, therefore, we regard the adjustment cost structure given in Figure 9.2 as plausible with a smaller non-convexity for firing costs. There is, of course, no reason for the hiring and firing cost functions to be symmetric and the costs associated with voluntary separations we consider to be very much smaller.

Before going on to look at some formal models, one further point is worth noting. We have assumed that the firm adjusts its labour force via an active policy of hiring and firing with the assistance of voluntary separations. We have not explicitly noted the possibility that the firm could use the current wage in order to make labour force adjustments. In other words, if it wishes to generate a rise in employment it raises the wage in order to attract an increased flow of suitable applicants and similarly a reduction in employment is generated by a reduction in the wage in order to encourage quitting. On the hiring side, this type of behavior is formally the same as that already discussed since we may view the "excess" wage payments as equivalent to hiring costs. On the firing side things are a little different since the "firing" costs are now negative and there would, therefore, be every incentive for firms to utilise this kind of mechanism. The fact that layoffs occur in practice thus requires some explanation and much effort has been devoted to this and related matters in recent years. A full survey of the relevant literature on optimal contracts may be found in Hart (1983) and some interesting further thoughts are set out in Hall and Lazear (1982) and Stiglitz (1984). Suffice it to say here that optimal labour contracts may involve fixing a wage prior to the date when all relevant information becomes available, at which point employment is adjusted via a mixture of quits and layoffs. As a consequence, we shall not devote a great deal of attention to models where the firm uses the wage as a short run instrument of employment policy although, for the sake of completeness, we shall analyse one such model.

3. Dynamic theories of labour demand

In this section we shall focus on the demand for labour and, in order to do this, we make a number of simplifying assumptions to keep the exposition as straightforward as possible. We start from a gross output production function of the form:

$$y(t) = f(N(t), z(t), t),$$

where $y(t)$ is output, $N(t)$ is employment and $z(t)$ is a vector of completely flexible inputs. For the moment we ignore the hours dimension of labour input and assume all other factors can be freely adjusted. This is clearly untrue in the case of fixed capital and so we are implicitly assuming that the investment decision is separable and capital stock fluctuations are incorporated into the time argument.[7] The next step is to derive a real net revenue function $R(N(t),t)$ and this may be done for a wide variety of different assumptions concerning the general structure of the model. We consider the following cases.

(a) *Price-taking firm.*

$$p(t)R(N(t),t) = \max_{z(t)} \{ p(t)f(N(t),z(t),t) - p_z(t)z(t) \}, \tag{1}$$

where $p(t)$ is the price of output and $p_z(t)$ is the vector of input prices. Note that the right-hand-side expression is homogeneous of degree one in prices and hence R is a function of the price ratios $p_z(t)/p(t)$.

(b) *Imperfectly competitive firm.* Here we define $p(t)$ as the (exogenous) industry average output price and specify the firm's inverse demand function as $p^*(y(t), y^*(t))p(t)$, where the function p^* indicates the price of the firm's output relative to the industry average which will enable it to sell $y(t)$. $y^*(t)$ is then an exogenous index of industry demand. This is, of course, a direct generalisation of case (a) where p^* is always unity. The revenue function is now defined as

$$p(t)R(N(t),t) = \max_{z(t)} \{ p^*(f(N(t),z(t),t), y^*(t)) \\ \times p(t)f(N(t),z(t),t) - p_z(t)z(t) \}, \tag{2}$$

where again the right-hand side is homogeneous of degree one in $p(t)$ and $p_z(t)$, and thus R is now a function of the price ratios $p_z(t)/p(t)$ and the index of industry demand $y^*(t)$. For a monopoly firm $p(t)$ can be thought of as the aggregate price level, otherwise the analysis is the same. The key points to note are that in these cases, in contrast to (a), the *firm's* output price does not appear since it is not exogenous whereas the index of industry demand does influence the firm's revenue.

(c) *Demand constrained firm.* This is the situation where both the output and its price are exogenous to the firm and we thus have

$$p(t)R(N(t),t) = \max_{z(t)} \{ p(t)y(t) - p_z(t)z(t) | y(t) = f(N(t),z(t),t) \}, \tag{3}$$

[7]This may also be justified on the grounds that when decisions about employment are taken, investment plans have long since been drawn up and the capital stock may be viewed as predetermined.

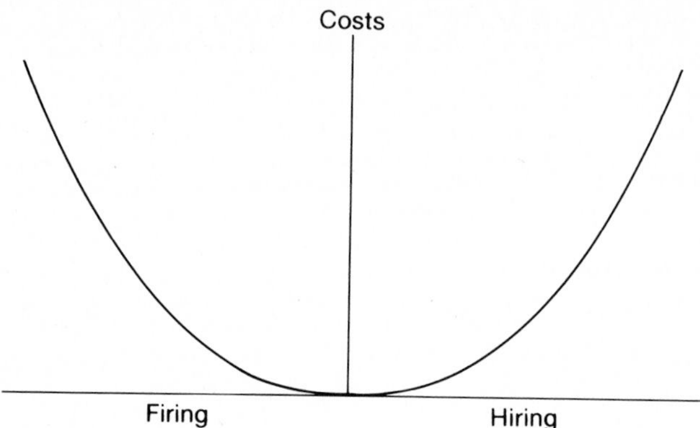

Figure 9.3. Strictly convex adjustment costs.

where R is now a function of $p_z(t)/p(t)$ and the exogenously determined level of output $y(t)$.

In all three cases we therefore have a function $p(t)R(N(t),t)$ which yields the revenue accruing to the firm for any given level of employment under the assumption that the capital stock is exogenous or predetermined and all other factors are optimally deployed. We shall now consider a series of dynamic models each of which is based on a different formulation of the adjustment cost mechanism.

3.1. *Strictly convex adjustment costs*

This is the standard model to be found in the literature[8] and assumes that the hiring/firing costs have the structure depicted in Figure 9.3. Thus, it rules out the non-convexities and linear sections which we thought of as plausible in Section 1 and forces the adjustment costs to be everywhere increasing at the margin. We shall also assume that voluntary quitting induces no direct costs and takes place mechanically at a proportional rate δ. Thus, we have adjustment costs as a function of $\dot{N}(t)+\delta N(t)$, where hiring takes place if this expression is positive and firing (involuntary separation) occurs if it is negative. This corresponds to

[8] The assumption of strictly convex adjustment costs, of which the quadratic is a special case, has been used in the employment literature by Holt et al. (1960), Tinsley (1971), Sargent (1978), Meese (1980), among others, although most of the theoretical development of the model has been in the context either of investment or of general factor demand models. Particularly worthy of note are, Eisner and Strotz (1963), Lucas (1967), (1967a), Gould (1968), Treadway (1969), (1970), (1971), (1974), Nadiri and Rosen (1969), Mortensen (1973) and Epstein (1982).

gross investment adjustment costs in the investment literature. We shall also assume, for simplicity, that these costs are additively separable (none of the results we shall discuss depends on this assumption).

Since the firm must look to the future when making employment decisions we shall endow it with point expectations concerning future values of exogenous variables. Thus, at time zero the firm will make an employment plan which it will then follow until such time as its expectations change or turn out to be incorrect. The plan is then reformulated and the firm proceeds as before. Now consider the formal problem faced by the firm at time zero. It will maximise the present value of its earnings stream given by

$$\int_0^{\infty} e^{-\phi(t)}\{p(t)R(N(t),t)-w(t)N(t)-C(x(t))\}\,dt, \tag{4}$$

where $x(t)$ satisfies

$$\dot{N}(t)=x(t)-\delta N(t), \tag{5}$$

with $N(0)$ given. $w(t)$ is the exogenously given wage and C is the adjustment cost function which has the properties $C' \gtrless 0$ as $x \gtrless 0, C''>0, C(0)=C'(0)=0$. If $r(t)$ is the rate of interest at t, then the discount factor, ϕ, is defined by

$$\phi(t)=\int_0^t r(\tau)\,d\tau. \tag{6}$$

If we think of the earnings stream as real (that is relative to some consumer price index, for example), then r can be thought of as a real discount rate. We also suppose that R has the property that $R_N>0$, $R_{NN}\leq 0$.

The formal derivation of the solution to this problem is straightforward but we prefer to use a simple economic argument to derive the appropriate conditions. Along the optimal plan it is clear that the firm can neither gain nor lose by making a slight adjustment to employment. Suppose, for example, that the firm hires one extra worker (or fires one less worker) at time t. This will induce an additional adjustment cost $C'(x(t))$ which is, of course, negative if the firm is firing at that time. Because of the assumed quitting behaviour some $e^{-\delta(\tau-t)}$ of the worker will remain at time $\tau>t$ and he or she will generate additional net earnings to the tune of $e^{-\delta(\tau-t)}(p(\tau)R_N(N(\tau),\tau)-w(\tau))$. So the total present value of the additional net earnings generated will be

$$PV=\int_t^{\infty}\exp[-(\phi(\tau)+\delta\tau-\phi(t)-\delta t)](p(\tau)R_N(N(\tau),\tau)-w(\tau))\,d\tau$$

and these must just balance the extra costs. So along the optimal path, we must have [making use of eq. (5)]

$$C'(\dot{N}(t)+\delta N(t)) = \int_t^{\infty} \exp[-(\phi(\tau)+\delta\tau-\phi(t)-\delta t)] \times (p(\tau)R_N(\tau)-w(\tau))\,\mathrm{d}\tau, \tag{7}$$

which holds for all $t \geq 0$.

This stock condition will not, in general, serve as an employment decision rule because the right-hand side is a function of the optimal employment path via the marginal revenue R_N.[9] In the particular case where $R_{NN}=0$, however, R_N is independent of employment and depends only on exogenous factors such as relative prices. This will happen, for example, in the case where we have a price-taking firm and the technology is constant returns. Under these conditions eq. (7) serves as a genuine employment decision rule and employment growth can be read off directly by solving for $\dot{N}$. This is a somewhat curious model, however, because the only thing which limits the size of the firm in equilibrium is the fact that the cost of replacing the quits is increasing at the margin as employment rises. In other words, the scale of production is limited solely by the fact that if the firm becomes too big, the hiring costs necessary to replace those who quit are simply too exorbitant [see Gould (1968) for an equivalent investment model].

Generally speaking, therefore, we must develop eq. (7) further in order to investigate the optimal employment strategy. To generate the equivalent flow condition we simply take the time derivative of (7) and using (7) itself we obtain, after some manipulation:

$$p(t)R_N(t) = w(t)+(r(t)+\delta)C'(t)-(\ddot{N}(t)+\delta\dot{N}(t))C''(t). \tag{8}$$

This is a second-order differential equation in employment which generates an infinity of paths from the given starting point $N(0)$. However, all except one of these either becomes infeasible in finite time or leads to ever increasing employment at an accelerating rate and there is thus a unique optimal path.[10] In order to look at this optimal path more closely we shall consider a particular example where all the exogenous variables are expected to remain constant. In this case prices, wages and the rate of interest are fixed and the revenue function does not shift over time, so it has the form $R(N(t))$. The stationary equilibrium level of

[9] It is also worth noting that if we divide the right-hand side of eq. (7) by $\int_t^{\infty} \exp[-(\phi(\tau)+\delta\tau-\phi(t)-\delta t)]w(\tau)\,\mathrm{d}\tau$, we obtain the employment equivalent of Tobin's marginal q less unity [see Hayashi (1982) for the corresponding investment equation]. The present value of wages used as the denominator of this q term is the price of hiring indefinitely one unit of labour which "decays" at the quit rate δ. It is thus precisely analogous to the price of a new unit of capital.

[10] This is, of course, the one satisfying the so-called transversality condition which is one of the technical necessary conditions for the solution to the problem (4), (5).

employment, N^*, therefore satisfies

$$pR_N(N^*) = w + (r+\delta)C'(\delta N^*), \tag{9}$$

which is obtained from (8). The last term differentiates this model from the standard static model and arises because of the costs associated with replacing the voluntary quits. Thus a unit increase in employment at the stationary state generates not only additional wage costs w per period but a once for all cost of C' plus a steady state increase in hiring of size δ generating a flow cost of $\delta C'$ per period. So the total increase in flow costs due to hiring is $(r+\delta)C'$. Looking at this another way, if the firm starts from an initial state where the marginal revenue product of labour is equal to the wage, it pays the firm to reduce employment somewhat because the loss in net revenue is more than compensated by the reduction in the cost of replacing the quits.

To analyse the path to the steady state we may use the phase diagram approach as follows. Making use of eq. (5), we replace (8) by the two-equation system:

$$\dot{x}(t) = \frac{1}{C''(x(t))}\{w - pR_N(N(t)) + (r+\delta)C'(x(t))\}, \tag{10a}$$

$$\dot{N}(t) = x(t) - \delta N(t). \tag{10b}$$

We may now plot the optimal path in x, N space where note that x is the hiring rate. In long-run equilibrium we have x^*, N^* satisfying

$$x^* = \delta N^*, \qquad pR_N(N^*) = w + (r+\delta)C'(x^*). \tag{11}$$

In Figure 9.4 we plot the x, N loci satisfying $\dot{x} = 0$ and $\dot{N} = 0$ and present a number of paths which satisfy eq. (8). The unique optimal path has a double headed arrow. Thus, for example, if initial employment is below N^* at $N_1(0)$ say, then the optimal strategy for the firm is to start hiring at the rate $x_1(0)$ shown on the diagram and to gradually raise employment towards N^*. It should, however, be noticed that N^* will not be attained in finite time and this is a consequence of the strict convexity of adjustment costs. However close the firm is to its equilibrium position, it always pays to spread the adjustment.

Similarly, if initial employment is too high at $N_2(0)$, the firm will gradually lay off employees at an initial rate $x_2(0)$ reducing employment towards N^*. The fact that the equilibrium is never attained suggests that there must be something akin to a partial adjustment mechanism at work here and, as Treadway (1969) demonstrates, in the neighbourhood of equilibrium the employment path is indeed described approximately by the partial adjustment equation

$$\dot{N}(t) = \lambda(N^* - N(t)). \tag{12}$$

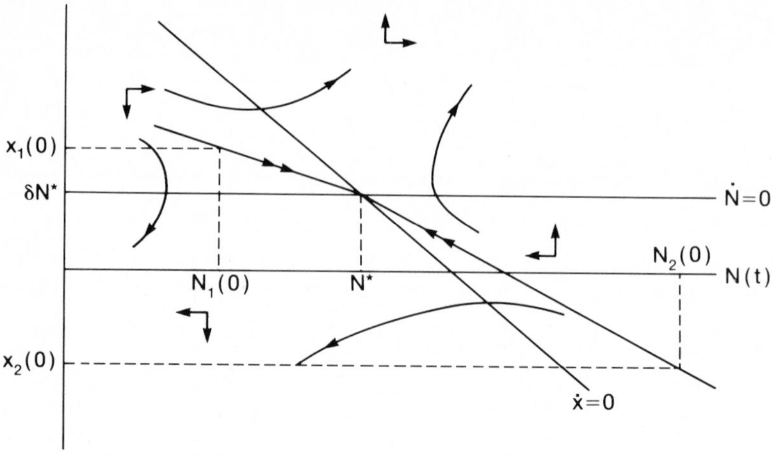

Figure 9.4. Phase diagram for eq. (8).

This is a crucial result in the sense that it may be used to provide a theoretical basis for the empirical analysis of labour demand and we shall develop it further later in the chapter. Suppose now, however, that we do not have a stationary problem. Looking back to eq. (7), it seems clear that any change in expected future prices, for example, must affect the integral on the right-hand side and will, consequently, influence current employment decisions. Suppose, for example, that the firm is initially (at time zero) in stationary equilibrium with employment N_0^* and that expectations change so that wages are expected to fall permanently at some later date t_1. Suppose that the new stationary equilibrium is $N_1^* > N_0^*$. We illustrate the firm's optimal strategy on the phase diagram in Figure 9.5 by the double headed arrow. Until time t_1, the equations describing the optimal path are those containing the current level of wages. After t_1 they contain the new lower expected wage, and so after t_1 the firm follows the standard optimal path towards N_1^*. Before t_1, however, the firm must follow one of those paths illustrated in Figure 9.4 which eventually move away from the equilibrium. The one selected is the unique path which crosses the new equilibrium path after precisely t_1 periods. The full path is thus as shown in Figure 9.5 and illustrates the crucial point that in this kind of model, an exogenous shift which is expected to occur in the future will immediately induce a change in the current employment strategy. Expectations are, therefore, of fundamental importance.

Let us now consider a more general non-static model. A convenient way of summarising such a model is in terms of the equilibrium employment level $N^*(t)$

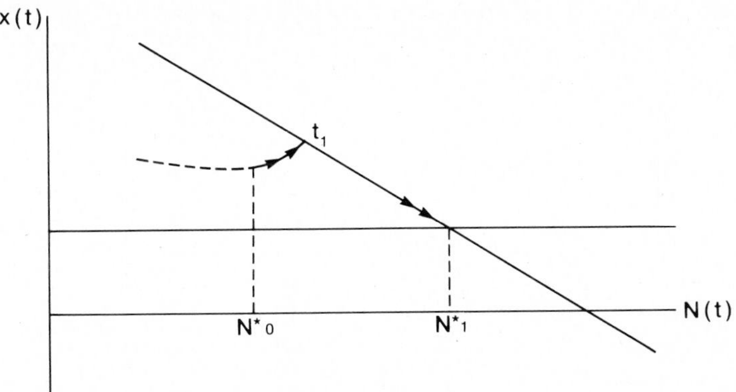

Figure 9.5. The optimal path resulting from a shift in wage expectations.

corresponding to the particular values of the exogenous variables ruling at any given moment. Thus, we may define $N^*(t)$ as that level of employment which satisfies

$$p(t)R_N(N^*(t),t)=w(t)+(r(t)+\delta)C'(\delta N^*(t)). \tag{13}$$

Thus, if we were able to ignore the last term, $N^*(t)$ would be the level of employment at t which would occur in a model without adjustment costs. Suppose $N^*(t)$ follows a cyclical path due to expected cyclical shifts either in the revenue function or in the wage. Then it is intuitively clear that the optimal employment path would have the structure illustrated in Figure 9.6. The fluctuations in $N(t)$ will track those in $N^*(t)$ but with a smaller amplitude. During the booms employment will lag behind N^* because the firm realises that the boom is not permanent and would not wish to go to the expense of hiring too many additional workers if they were to be fired only a short time later. Similarly, in slumps the firm would lay off fewer workers than in the absence of adjustment costs and would be carrying "excess" labour through the slump period. This strategy is typically referred to as labour hoarding which arises naturally in the adjustment cost framework. As we shall see, however, this is not a specific consequence of the assumption of strictly convex adjustment costs. On the other hand, one aspect of the employment behaviour described here which is a particular consequence of strict convexity is the fact that actual employment never tracks $N^*(t)$ closely. Employment will always exhibit a partial adjustment style of behaviour which implies that current employment will be some convex

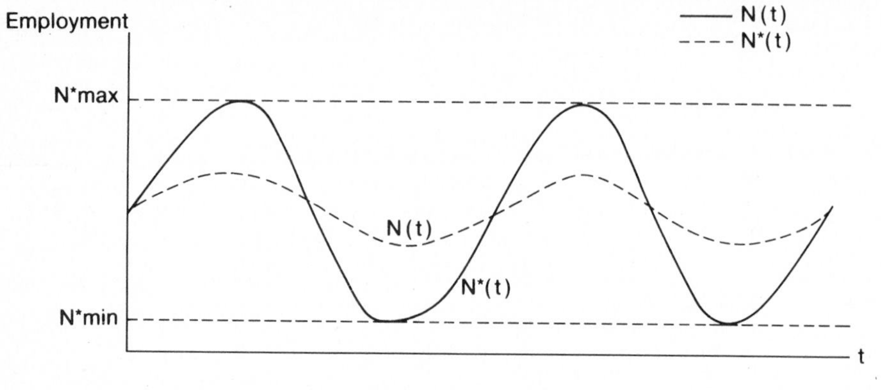

Figure 9.6. Optimal employment over a cycle (strictly convex adjustment costs).

combination of a target level and employment last period.[11] This significant property of the employment path is shared by models where the firm uses the wage as a short-run instrument of employment policy and we shall now turn to a brief consideration of such a model.

3.2. *Dynamic monopsony*

Models of this type are discussed in Mortensen (1970) and Salop (1973), for example, and typically have the following structure. The key equation is that determining the net flow of accessions or separations and this takes the form

$$\dot{N}(t) = x(w(t), w^*(t))N(t). \tag{14}$$

The function x determines the proportional rate at which employees join or leave the firm and this is increasing in the firm's wage w and decreasing in the given outside level of wages w^*. Further natural assumptions concerning the x function are $x(w^*, w^*) = 0$, $x_{11} < 0$.

The basic problem facing the firm is to determine the wage adjustments necessary to obtain the desired employment path. The firm will thus choose a

[11] When we consider a non-stationary discrete time model in preparation for the discussion of empirical work we shall be able to make this statement more precise.

wage path in order to maximise

$$\int_0^{\infty} e^{-\phi(t)}\{p(t)R(N(t),t)-w(t)N(t)\}\,dt$$

subject to the flow constraint (14). The remaining notation is the same as in the previous section. A formal derivation of the optimal strategy is straightforward but the resulting condition is somewhat opaque and so we shall proceed by using a simple economic argument. Consider first the constraint (14). This may be rewritten as

$$\frac{d}{dt}(\log N(t)) = x(w(t),w^*(t)),$$

and simple integration yields:

$$N(\tau)=\exp(X(\tau)-X(t))N(t),\quad \text{all } \tau\geq t, \tag{15}$$

where X is the integral of x given by

$$X(\tau)=\int_0^{\tau} x(w(\nu),w^*(\nu))\,d\nu. \tag{16}$$

On the optimal path, the cost of temporarily raising the wage by one unit at time t, namely $N(t)$, must just balance the net returns generated by the extra employees taken on. A unit wage increase produces $x_1N(t)$ extra workers at time t and eq. (15) then tells us that this generates $\exp(X(\tau)-X(t))x_1N(t)$ extra workers at time $\tau\geq t$. These extra employees will induce additional net revenue to the tune of $\exp(X(\tau)-X(t))x_1N(t)(p(\tau)R_N(\tau)-w(\tau))$ at time τ. The total present value of this additional net revenue just balances the cost and hence we obtain:

$$N(t)=x_1N(t)\int_t^{\infty}\exp[-(\phi(\tau)-\phi(t))+X(\tau)-X(t)]$$
$$\times(p(\tau)R_N(\tau)-w(\tau))\,d\tau, \tag{17}$$

which is the condition which must hold along the optimal path. To derive the more usual flow condition, we simply cancel $N(t)$ and take the time derivative of (17). Using (17) itself we then obtain:

$$p(t)R_N(t)=w(t)+\frac{r(t)-x(t)}{x_1(t)}+\frac{1}{x_1^2}(x_{11}\dot{w}+x_{12}\dot{w}^*), \tag{18}$$

which is the standard first-order condition for the above problem. As we have already noted, this is by no means easy to interpret, but if we consider the static problem, things become a little clearer. In such a problem p, r and w^* are fixed and the revenue function does not shift. The optimal strategy of the firm then satisfies

$$p(t)R_N(t) = w(t) + \frac{r - x(t)}{x_1(t)} + \frac{x_{11}}{x_1^2}\dot{w} \tag{19}$$

along with the flow constraint (14). In long-run equilibrium $w = w^*$ and employment, N^*, satisfies

$$pR_N(N^*) = w^* + \frac{r}{x_1(w^*, w^*)}. \tag{20}$$

First we may note that the equilibrium condition (14) differs from that generated by the static model with the addition of a positive term leading to somewhat lower employment. If we start from a position where employment is set to equate the marginal revenue product of labour with the wage, it then pays the firm to cut wages temporarily, shed a few employees and approach the equilibrium described in (20). The long-run losses due to the fact that the marginal product of labour is above the long run real wage are offset by the temporary reduction of the wage *for all workers* below w^*. Clearly, the higher is the discount rate r, the less important are the future losses in terms of present value and the stronger will be this effect.

To analyse the approach of the firm to the long-run equilibrium we may recast the necessary conditions to form a pair of differential equations in N and w. We thus have

$$\dot{N}(t) = x(w(t), w^*(t))N(t), \tag{21a}$$

$$\dot{w}(t) = -\frac{x_1^2}{x_{11}}\left(w(t) - R_N(N(t)) + \frac{r - x(t)}{x_1(t)}\right). \tag{21b}$$

We may now plot a phase diagram in N, w space and this is given in Figure 9.7. We show the N, w loci satisfying $\dot{N} = 0$, $\dot{w} = 0$ and present a number of paths satisfying (21a) and (21b). Since the initial value of employment is given, the initial wage is selected in order to move along the unique optimal path which converges on the long-run equilibrium point N^*, w^*. This is shown with the double headed arrow. So, for example, if initial employment is below N^* at $N_1(0)$, say, then the firm sets its wage at $w_1(0) > w^*$ and gradually attracts extra

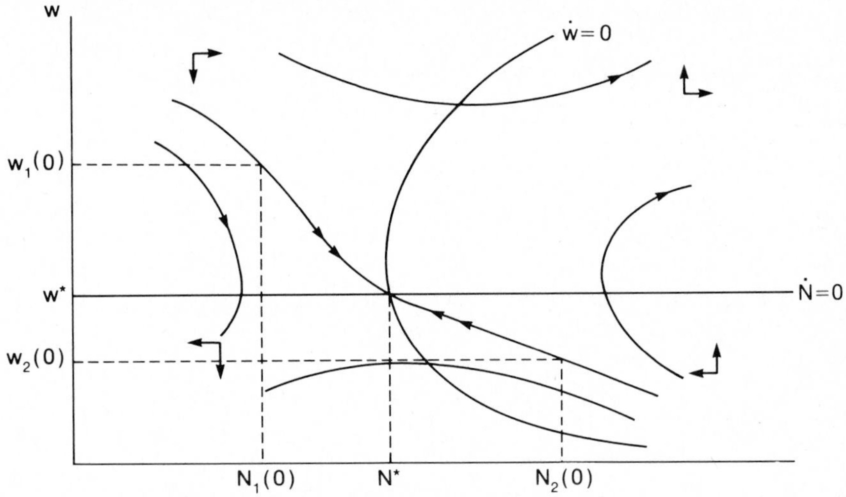

Figure 9.7. Phase diagram for eqs. (21a) and (21b).

workers while simultaneously lowering the wage slowly towards w^*. On the other hand, if initial employment is too high, at $N_2(0)$ say, then wages are set below w^* at $w_2(0)$ inducing quits. The wage is then gradually moved back up to w^*.[12]

A glance back at the phase diagram associated with the previous adjustment costs model in Figure 9.3 reveals the marked similarity between the two models and indeed it is trivial to demonstrate that in a locality of the equilibrium, the employment path in this model follows exactly the same partial adjustment process noted in eq. (12). In this sense, then, both models provide us with a satisfactory foundation for the partial adjustment model and both models generate long-run employment which is lower than that implied by a purely static model. Furthermore, the rate of discount influences the long-run employment level in exactly the same way [compare eqs. (20) and (12)]. The question we may then ask is whether it is possible to find a reasonable theoretical model which does not generate a partial adjustment mechanism in the locality of equilibrium. The answer to this question is yes, and we now consider one such model.

[12] Note that we have avoided a serious difficulty in this kind of model by our specification of the accessions/separations function, x, as a function of current wages only. A more rational specification would include the future wage path of both w and w^* in this function since a rational worker would take decisions on the basis of expected present values. This would take the firm's problem onto a higher plane of complexity without any essential change in the structure of the results. We shall not, therefore, pursue this issue.

3.3. *Linear adjustment costs*

In our discussion of the likely shape of the function relating costs to the rate of hiring and firing, it seemed to us reasonable to suppose that this function was not strictly increasing at the margin over the whole range. Indeed after some possible non-convexities, there seemed no particular reason why the function should not be linear over a considerable range. It is, therefore, important to consider the consequences of adjustment costs if they are simply linear in both hiring and firing. This kind of model has been analysed in Nickell (1978) and various extensions have been considered by Leban and Lesourne (1980).

The basic structure of the model is closely related to that where adjustment costs are strictly convex. Again we suppose mechanistic voluntary quitting at a rate δ and we have adjustment costs as a function of $\dot{N}(t)+\delta N(t)$. The difference is that their shape is that illustrated in Figure 9.8 (compare Figure 9.3). Formally, then, we have a proportional hiring rate, $a(t)$, with unit cost, α, and a proportional firing rate, $f(t)$, with unit cost, β, say, leading to adjustment costs $\alpha a(t)N(t)$ for hires and $\beta f(t)N(t)$ for fires. The firm then chooses a path of employment, hiring and firing to satisfy

$$\max\int_0^\infty \mathrm{e}^{-\phi(t)}\{p(t)R(N(t),t)-w(t)N(t)-\alpha a(t)N(t)-\beta f(t)N(t)\}\,\mathrm{d}t \tag{22}$$

s.t.

$\dot{N}(t)=(a(t)-f(t)-\delta)N(t),\quad a(t)\geq 0,\quad f(t)\geq 0,$

$N(0)$ given.

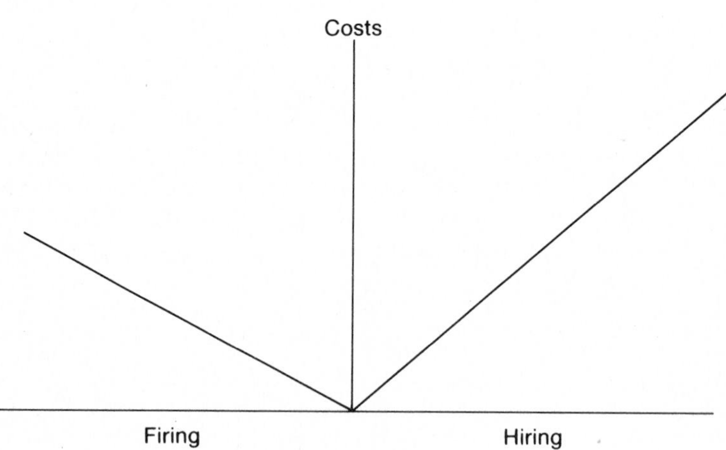

Figure 9.8. Linear adjustment costs.

The solution to this problem is a little more tricky than in previous cases but again we can derive the appropriate conditions using simple economic considerations. It is obvious, first of all, that hiring and firing will never go on simultaneously since this is a needless waste of money. Now consider hiring. It is clear that while the firm is actually hiring workers, it must be the case that the cost associated with hiring an additional worker, namely α, will balance the marginal net returns generated by this addition along the optimal path. If one additional worker is hired at t, $\mathrm{e}^{-\delta(\tau-t)}$ additional workers remain at time $\tau \geq t$ generating extra net revenue $\mathrm{e}^{-\delta(\tau-t)}(p(\tau)R_N(N(\tau),\tau)-w(\tau))$. So setting the present value of these net returns equal to the cost, α, we obtain:

$$\int_t^{\infty} \exp[-(\phi(\tau)-\phi(t)+\delta(\tau-t))][p(\tau)R_N(N(\tau),\tau)-w(\tau)]\,\mathrm{d}\tau=\alpha. \tag{23}$$

This is the key hiring equation. Furthermore, if hiring occurs over some interval, then the time derivative of this equation must also hold on that interval. Taking the time derivative and using (23) itself we obtain the simple flow condition:

$$p(t)R_N(N(t),t)=w(t)+(r(t)+\delta)\alpha. \tag{24}$$

Note that $(r+\delta)\alpha$ is the flow cost of hiring and this is added to the wage to obtain the effective price of labour.

In order to illustrate the use of these conditions, assume we have a simple static situation (p, w, r fixed, along with the revenue schedule). Suppose we start from a position $N(0)$ where this level of employment is lower than N_1^* which satisfies

$$pR_N(N_1^*)=w+(r+\delta)\alpha. \tag{25}$$

Then it is easy to show that the firm will immediately hire a group of workers equal to $N_1^*-N(0)$ and will, thereafter, hire at a rate δN_1^* in order to replace voluntary quits. The important point to note is that with linear adjustment costs, the instantaneous hiring of groups of workers can and does occur and there is no question of any form of partial adjustment to the new long-run equilibrium.

On the firing side, things are a little more complicated. Using a similar argument to that used to derive (23), when firing occurs we must have

$$\int_t^{\infty} \exp[-(\phi(\tau)-\phi(t)+\delta(\tau-t))][p(\tau)R_N(N(\tau),\tau)-w(\tau)]\,\mathrm{d}\tau=-\beta, \tag{26}$$

and if firing occurs over some interval, then we have the corresponding flow condition:

$$p(t)R_N(N(t),t) = w(t) - (r(t)+\delta)\beta. \tag{27}$$

Note first that (27) can never hold in a stationary state since such a state must involve hiring to replace the voluntary quits. It can, however, hold if, for example, real wages are rising fast enough for (27) to generate a fall in employment which is faster than δN. So what happens, in the context of a static model, if we start from a position where $N(0)$ is considerably greater than N_1^* given in (25)? The optimal strategy for the firm is to fire a group of workers and then to allow natural wastage until some time t_1 when employment has fallen to N_1^*. This is then sustained indefinitely. Eq. (26) enables us to find t_1 and the size of the group that is instantaneously fired. On the interval $(0, t_1)$, employment is given by $e^{\delta(t_1-\tau)}N_1^*$, $(0<\tau\le t_1)$ since it is declining at a proportional rate δ. Thus, eq. (26) implies:

$$\int_0^{t_1} e^{-(r+\delta)\tau}\left[pR_N\left(e^{\delta(t_1-\tau)}N_1^*\right) - w\right]d\tau$$
$$+\int_{t_1}^{\infty} e^{-(r+\delta)\tau}\left[pR_N(N_1^*) - w\right]d\tau = -\beta,$$

and using (25) to evaluate the second integral we find that t_1 must satisfy

$$\int_0^{t_1} e^{-(r+\delta)\tau}\left[pR_N\left(e^{\delta(t_1-\tau)}N_1^*\right) - w\right]d\tau = -\alpha e^{-(r+\delta)t_1} - \beta. \tag{28}$$

Consequently, the group that is fired is of size $N(0) - e^{\delta t_1}N_1^*$. Furthermore, it is trivial to show that both $\partial t_1/\partial\alpha$ and $\partial t_1/\partial\beta$ are positive indicating that a rise in either hiring or firing costs reduces the size of the group that is fired and increases the reliance of the firm on "natural wastage" to generate the appropriate employment adjustment. Indeed, it is clear that if hiring/firing costs are large enough there will be no firing at all.

The fact that the linear adjustment cost model is consistent with the instantaneous hiring and firing of groups of workers is quite an appealing property given that such events are hardly unusual. In spite of this fact, however, it does not imply myopic behaviour on the part of the firm; indeed, expectations are crucial in determining current employment policy.

Consider the following illustration where we set $\delta = 0$ to make the exposition more straightforward. Suppose the wage falls suddenly at time zero from w_1 to w_2 but is expected to rise back to w_1 at some future time t. Assuming that the wage change is large enough to induce firing at time t, then the firing eq. (26) tells us that

$$\int_t^{\infty} \mathrm{e}^{-r(\tau-t)}[pR_N(N(\tau))-w_1]\,\mathrm{d}\tau = -\beta. \tag{29}$$

Furthermore, at time zero, the hiring equation indicates that

$$\int_0^t \mathrm{e}^{-r\tau}[pR_N(N(\tau))-w_2]\,\mathrm{d}\tau + \int_t^{\infty} \mathrm{e}^{-r\tau}[pR_N(N(\tau))-w_1]\,\mathrm{d}\tau = \alpha,$$

and using (29) to evaluate the second integral we obtain:

$$\int_0^t \mathrm{e}^{-r\tau}[pR_N(N(\tau))-w_2]\,\mathrm{d}\tau = \alpha+\beta\mathrm{e}^{-rt}. \tag{30}$$

Since we have ruled out voluntary quits, it is clear that employment will remain fixed over the first interval following an initial burst of hiring. If we let this level of employment be given by N_1, then (30) indicates that

$$\int_0^t \mathrm{e}^{-r\tau}[pR_N(N_1)-w_2]\,\mathrm{d}\tau = \alpha+\beta\mathrm{e}^{-rt},$$

thus yielding:

$$pR_N(N_1) = w_2 + \frac{r(\alpha+\beta\mathrm{e}^{-rt})}{1-\mathrm{e}^{-rt}}. \tag{31}$$

This equation is very revealing since it indicates precisely how adjustment costs and the duration of the period of low real wages influence employment during that period. Indeed, if r is small, then

$$\frac{r(\alpha+\beta\mathrm{e}^{-rt})}{1-\mathrm{e}^{-rt}} \simeq \frac{\alpha+\beta}{t},$$

which indicates that the effective addition to the real wage is equal to the sum of the hiring and firing cost for the marginal worker divided by the expected length of his employment, hardly a surprising result. This does, however, give us some idea of the importance of such costs. For example, if the "boom" period is expected to last two years and both hiring and firing costs are equal to one month's salary, then this has roughly the same impact on employment as on 8 percent increase in real wages.

The most interesting aspect of this kind of model lies in its prediction about the employment behaviour of the firm in response to foreseen cyclical fluctua-

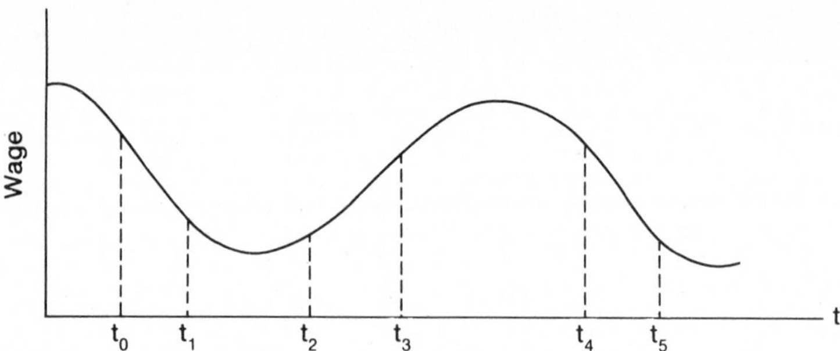

Figure 9.9. The wage cycle.

tions in an exogenous variable. Here, the contrast with the firm facing strictly convex costs of adjustment is quite striking. Again, in order to facilitate the exposition, suppose there are no voluntary quits ($\delta = 0$) and suppose that the cycles are generated by regular fluctuations in the wage, everything else remaining fixed. In order to examine the firm's employment strategy we make use of the wage cycle portrayed in Figure 9.9. It is intuitively clear that hiring will occur on the downward parts of the wage cycle and firing on the upward parts. In terms of Figure 9.9, hiring occurs on (t_0, t_1) and (t_4, t_5) and firing on (t_2, t_3). For the remainder of the time employment is fixed. How, then, is the employment path determined? On the interval (t_0, t_1), the fact that hiring takes place indicates that employment must satisfy (24), that is

$$pR_N(N(t)) = w(t) + r\alpha, \quad t_0 \le t \le t_1. \tag{32}$$

Furthermore, not only does (32) hold at t_1, but also we must have

$$\int_{t_1}^{\infty} e^{-r(t-t_1)}[pR_N(N(\tau)) - w(\tau)]\,d\tau = \alpha \tag{33}$$

from (23). Moving on to the firing interval (t_2, t_3) we must have (27) satisfied throughout and thus

$$pR_N(N(t)) = w(t) - r\beta, \quad t_2 \le t \le t_3, \tag{34}$$

and at t_2 we have

$$\int_{t_2}^{\infty} e^{-r(\tau-t_2)}[pR_N(N(\tau)) - w(\tau)]\,d\tau = -\beta. \tag{35}$$

Since $N(t)$ is constant on the interval $[t_1, t_2]$ at N_1, say, we thus have, using (35) and (33)

$$\int_{t_1}^{t_2} e^{-r(\tau - t_1)} [pR_N(N_1) - w(\tau)] \, d\tau = \alpha + \beta e^{-r(t_2 - t_1)}. \tag{36}$$

Noting that N_1 must satisfy (32) at t_1 and (34) at t_2 also gives

$$pR_N(N_1) = w(t_1) + r\alpha, \qquad pR_N(N_1) = w(t_2) - r\beta. \tag{37}$$

The three eqs. (36) and (37), then suffice to determine N_1, t_1 and t_2. Furthermore, we can also show that an increase in either α or β will lower t_1 and raise t_2 thereby lengthening the period when employment remains static at the top of the employment cycle. The period at the bottom of the employment cycle (t_3, t_4) can be determined in exactly the same fashion and lengthens in exactly the same way in response to increases in hiring or firing costs.

The key comparison we must make is between the optimal employment path in this model and that illustrated in Figure 9.6 for the case of strictly convex adjustment costs. If we define $N^*(t)$ as the level of employment generated by a static model, that is $N^*(t)$ satisfies

$$pR_N(N^*(t)) = w(t),$$

then the relationship between $N^*(t)$ and the optimal employment path is that presented in Figure 9.10. Note that during hiring and firing, the optimal path tracks $N^*(t)$ very closely although the small additional terms in (32) and (34) imply that N and N^* are not coincident. Across the boom and slump period, however, employment is constant. The key difference between this model and that described in Figure 9.6 is that in the latter case of strictly convex adjustment costs, optimal employment never tracks N^* closely. It always has a partial adjustment structure. In the linear case there are alternating regimes of more or less complete adjustment and no adjustment whatever with the positioning of these regimes depending crucially on expectations. Both models, of course, exhibit labour hoarding in the slump and in both, the amount of labour hoarding depends on the level of adjustment costs.[13] The reason for emphasizing the crucial difference between the models is that when we come to empirical work, it runs out that the only tractable model is that with strictly convex adjustment costs. If it happens to be the case that in reality adjustment costs are more or less linear over the relevant range then the strict imposition on the data of a dynamic

[13] None of these results change in essence if we allow voluntary quits. All that happens is that the hiring and firing periods are shifted and the former are lengthened with the latter being shortened. See Nickell (1978), for example.

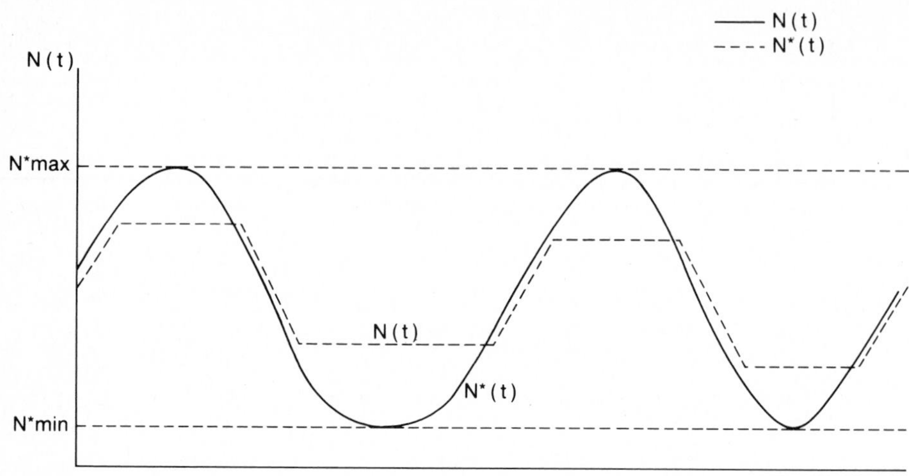

Figure 9.10. Optimal employment over the cycle (linear adjustment costs).

model derived under the assumption that such costs are strictly convex will lead to incorrect inferences being drawn. Issues of this kind will be considered at greater length in due course.

Before closing this strictly theoretical section, there are a number of other issues which must be considered. The first is the other aspect of labour input, namely hours of work, which we have ignored until now. The easiest way of incorporating this into our previous models is to redefine the revenue function R as revenue per efficiency hour worked. So if h is the number of efficiency hours, total revenue becomes Rh. Efficiency hours are *defined* to make this function linear and we would expect actual hours to be a convex function of efficiency hours because of increasing tiredness and inefficiency towards the end of the working period.[14] So if H is actual hours worked per period, then we would hypothesise the relationship between H and h to have the form shown in Figure 9.11. So we have a function:

$$H = g(h), \quad g' \geq 0, \quad g'' \geq 0, \quad g(0) = 0. \tag{38}$$

On the wage cost side, we have a relationship between earnings and hours worked of the form $w(t)W(H)$, where $W(H)$ gives us the shape of the earnings/hours function and $w(t)$ represents its general level. We expect $W(H)$ to look something like the curve portrayed in Figure 9.12. It will not pass through the origin if

[14]We ignore the probable non-convexity at very low levels of actual hours due to set-up costs since the firm never operates anywhere near this region. The non-convexity is, of course, one of the reasons for this.

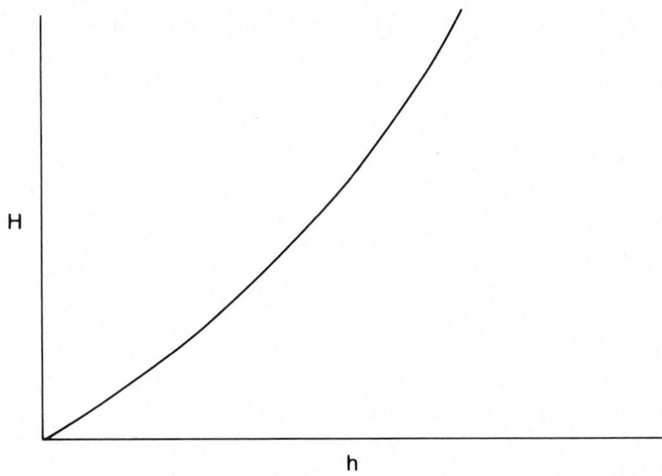

Figure 9.11. The relationship between actual hours (H) and efficiency hours (h).

there are any overhead labour costs independent of hours worked (e.g. fall-back pay, taxes levied per employee) and it will typically have a convex shape because of overtime premia and the like. The earnings/efficiency hours function is then given by

$$w^*(h) = W(g(h)),$$

where w^* is clearly "more convex" than W because of the convexity of g.

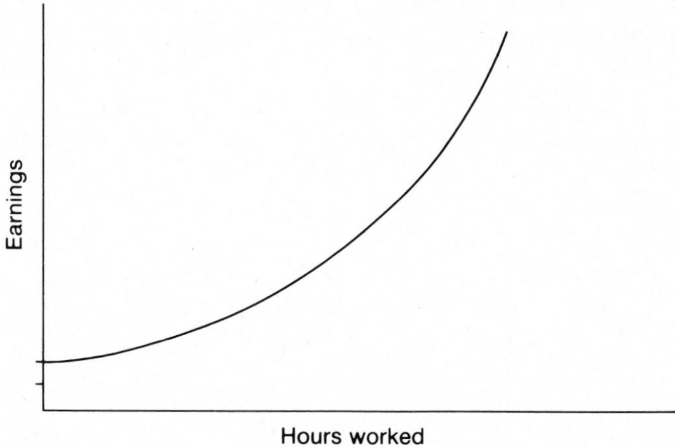

Figure 9.12. The earnings/hours function.

So in our previous problems the revenue flow accruing to the firm leaving aside adjustment costs is now given by

$$p(t)R(N(t),t)h(t)-w(t)w^*(h(t))N(t),$$

and the firm must choose h as well as N. The formal solution to the revised problem is straightforward and here we simply indicate the sort of results which ensue. The employment response to cyclical fluctuations illustrated in Figures 9.6 and 9.10 will now be somewhat attenuated and hours will fluctuate procyclically under certain reasonable conditions.[15] We shall discuss this issue further when we consider the empirical implementation of these models.

The second issue worth noting arises when we have more than one factor of production subject to costs of adjustment. In the interests of simplicity we have avoided this problem but it is clear, for example, that capital goods are subject to installation costs and it can be argued that the interaction between the investment and employment decision is too strong to be assumed away. If such factors are explicitly incorporated, then the general thrust of our previous arguments remains unaltered. In the case of strictly convex adjustment costs, the firm follows a strategy which can, in the region of long run equilibrium, be approximated by a multivariate partial adjustment mechanism. Thus, the change in employment is a function not only of the distance of employment from its equilibrium level but also of the distance of capital stock from its equilibrium level [see, for example, Mortensen (1973)]. A similar result arises in the case of linear adjustment costs where there is some degree of interaction between periods of hiring and firing and periods of investment. Such a model is analysed extensively in Leban and Lesourne (1980). Again we shall have more to say on this issue when it comes to a discussion of empirical implementation.

Finally, we shall briefly refer to the problem of non-convexities in the adjustment cost function such as those illustrated in Figure 9.2.[16] It is clear, for example, that hiring will never occur at a rate less than that which minimises the average flow cost of hiring. This point is illustrated in Figure 9.13 and any policy

[15] To avoid "perverse" movements we require

$$\frac{\mathrm{d}}{\mathrm{d}h}\left(\frac{\mathrm{d}\log w^*(h)}{\mathrm{d}\log h}\right)>0$$

and

$$\frac{\mathrm{d}}{\mathrm{d}N}\left(\frac{\mathrm{d}\log R}{\mathrm{d}\log N}\right)<0.$$

[16] The first analysis of this kind of problem is given in Rothschild (1971), although a more complete discussion may be found in Davidson and Harris (1981).

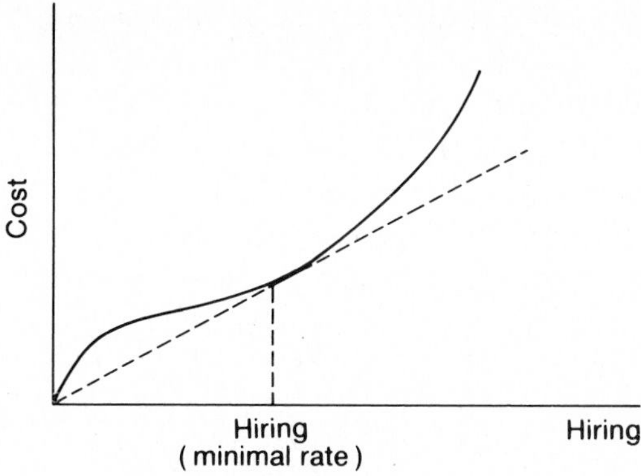

Figure 9.13. The minimal rate of hiring.

which involves hiring at a rate less than this is clearly dominated by some policy which involves hiring at the minimal rate for a shorter period in total. Indeed, by having bursts of hiring at the minimum rate, alternating with bursts of zero hiring, it is clear that the firm can approximate any continuous hiring path at less than the minimum rate as closely as it wishes. Such a policy is described in Davidson and Harris (1981) as a "chattering" policy and has the effect of "convexifying" the non-convexity. The implication of this for a discrete time description of the hiring process is that, to all intents and purposes, small initial non-convexities can be ignored since their implications would never show up in the data.[17] This completes our purely theoretical assessment of dynamic models of labour demand and we next consider the implications for empirical modelling.

4. The transition to empirical work

In this section we consider the theoretical framework of empirical models of labour demand. We begin by discussing the discrete time version of the strictly convex adjustment cost model. This is the only one which enables us to write down an employment equation which is suitable for empirical analysis although, as we have already noted, the superiority of this model as a description of reality over the alternative linear adjustment cost formulation is open to question.

Our strategy will be to write down a fairly general discrete time model and successively to approximate in order to generate a linear equation. A popular

[17]A practical example of a "chattering" policy is to hire new employees as a group at the beginning of each week or month rather than spreading them evenly throughout the interval. This will not show up in quarterly data and is, in any event, an uninteresting phenomenon.

alternative is to start from a quadratic model which immediately generates a linear demand function. This procedure does, however, mask the implications of the initial quadratic assumption and so we prefer to proceed explicitly by approximating a fairly general framework.

We begin by specifying a discrete time version of (4) where we immediately impose a quadratic structure on the adjustment costs. Thus, we have the firm maximising

$$\sum_{t=0}^{\infty} \phi(t)\Big\{ p(t)R(N(t),h(t),t) - w(t)w^*(h(t),t)N(t) - w(t)\frac{b}{2}(N(t)-N(t-1))^2\Big\},$$

where the discount factor is defined by

$$\phi(t) = \Big(\prod_{\tau}(1+r(\tau))\Big)^{-1},$$

and p = output price, N = employment, R = real revenue, w = level of wages, w^* = earnings as a function of efficiency hours and b is the adjustment cost parameter. Points worth emphasising are first, the revenue function assumes either that all other factors are variable or that the investment decision is taken completely independently. Thus, we are restricting our attention initially to the employment decision. Second, we have included hours at the outset and we have formulated the problem in terms of "efficiency" hours, h. Remember that efficiency hours are *defined* so that for a given level of employment, the addition to net revenue is the same for each efficiency hour worked. So if workers become progressively more tired, each succeeding efficiency hour is equivalent to more actual hours. Third, we have supposed that adjustment costs are fixed in wage units. This is an important element of the specification because it reflects the fact that, in reality, most adjustment costs rise in proportion to real wages (see Section 2.1). Finally, we assume point expectations.

It is convenient to rewrite the objective function in terms of real wages, $\tilde{w} = w/p$, and we obtain:

$$\sum_{t=0}^{\infty} p(t)\phi(t)\Big\{ R(N(t),h(t),t) - \tilde{w}(t)w^*(h(t),t)N(t) - \tilde{w}(t)\frac{b}{2}(N(t)-N(t-1))^2\Big\}.$$

The first-order conditions for this problem (excluding the transversality condition) are given by

$$R_N(N(t),h(t),t)-\tilde{w}(t)w^*(h(t),t)-\tilde{w}(t)b(N(t)-N(t-1))$$
$$+\frac{p(t+1)\tilde{w}(t+1)b}{p(t)(1+r(t))}(N(t+1)-N(t))=0,\quad t>0, \tag{39}$$
$$R_h(N(t),h(t),t)-\tilde{w}(t)w_h^*(h(t),t)N(t)=0,\quad t\geq 0, \tag{40}$$

with $N(0)$ given.

In order to write (39) as a linear difference equation with constant coefficients, we must clearly make a number of assumptions. First we may note that

$$\frac{p(t+1)}{p(t)(1+r(t))}\simeq\frac{1}{1+\rho},\ \text{say}, \tag{41}$$

where ρ is the real interest rate and we assume this to be constant and positive. Next we must impose some structure on the revenue function R and this we do by supposing that it has the form:

$$R(N(t),h(t),t)=R_0(t)+N(t)^{\varepsilon}h(t)\omega(t),\quad 0<\varepsilon<1. \tag{42}$$

Thus, real revenue is concave in employment, linear in efficiency hours (by definition) but has two exogenous shift factors $R_0(t)$ and $\omega(t)$. We may now define the short period equilibrium levels of hours and employment $h^*(t)$, $N^*(t)$ as the quantities which would rule in the absence of adjustment costs. These satisfy (39) and (40) setting $b=0$. Thus, using (42) we have

$$\varepsilon N^*(t)^{\varepsilon-1}h^*(t)\omega(t)=\tilde{w}(t)w^*(h^*(t),t), \tag{43}$$
$$N^*(t)^{\varepsilon}\omega(t)=\tilde{w}(t)w_h^*(h^*(t),t)N^*(t). \tag{44}$$

If we next assert that the shape of the earnings/hours relationship is not expected to change, w^* is simply a function of $h(t)$ and dividing (44) into (43) yields:

$$\varepsilon h^*(t)=w^*(h^*(t))/w_h^*(h^*(t)).$$

So, given this condition, $h^*(t)$ is a constant h^* independent of shifts in the level of wages and the revenue function.[18] The next stage is to linearise the first two

[18]See Ehrenberg (1971) for a more detailed model of long-run hours determination.

terms in (39). Noting that (44) is also satisfied by actual hours and employment $h(t)$, $N(t)$, we may obtain the following relationship between N, N^*, h and h^*, namely

$$N(t)-N^*(t)=\left[\left(w_h^*(h^*)/w_h^*(h(t))\right)^{1/(1-\varepsilon)}-1\right]N^*(t),$$

which may be linearised to obtain:

$$N(t)-N^*(t)=\alpha_1(h(t)-h^*),$$
$$\alpha_1=-\frac{N^*}{1-\varepsilon}w_{hh}^*(h^*)/w_h^*(h^*)^{1/(1-\varepsilon)}<0, \text{ by convexity of } w^*. \tag{45}$$

Turning to the non-linear terms in (39), we have

$$\begin{aligned}
&R_N(N(t),h(t),t)-\tilde{w}(t)w^*(h(t))\\
&\quad=\varepsilon N(t)^{\varepsilon-1}h(t)\omega(t)-\tilde{w}(t)w^*(h(t)), \text{ from (42)}\\
&\quad=\tilde{w}(t)w^*(h(t))\left[\varepsilon\frac{w_h^*(h(t))h(t)}{w^*(h(t))}-1\right], \text{ from (40), (42)}\\
&\quad\simeq\tilde{w}(t)w^*(h^*)\left[\varepsilon\frac{\mathrm{d}}{\mathrm{d}h}\left(\frac{w_h^*h}{w^*}\right)\right](h-h^*), \text{ linearising about } h^*\\
&\quad=\tilde{w}(t)\theta_1(h-h^*)\\
&\quad=\tilde{w}(t)\theta(N(t)-N^*(t)), \theta=\theta_1/\alpha_1, \text{ from (45)}.
\end{aligned}$$

θ will typically be negative so long as the elasticity of w^* is increasing with hours (see footnote 15). Substituting into (39) we now have the linear difference equation:

$$\theta(N(t)-N^*(t))-b(N(t)-N(t-1))+\frac{b\tilde{w}(t+1)}{(1+\rho)\tilde{w}(t)}(N(t+1)-N(t))=0.$$

In order to have constant coefficients we must assume that expected real wage growth is a constant, g, say. The final coefficient is thus $b(1+g)/(1+\rho)=b\alpha$, say. Notice that $\alpha\simeq(1+\rho-g)^{-1}$, where $\rho-g$ is the real interest rate in terms of wages. We would naturally therefore assume $0<\alpha<1$.

We have thus obtained a linear difference equation with constant coefficients which will enable us to obtain at least an approximation to the firm's optimal employment strategy. This fundamental equation is given by

$$\alpha bN(t+1)-((1+\alpha)b-\theta)N(t)+bN(t-1)=\theta N^*(t),\quad t>0, \tag{46}$$

where, from (44), we have

$$N^*(t) = \left[\omega(t)/\tilde{w}(t)w_h^*(h^*)\right]^{1/(1-\varepsilon)}. \tag{46a}$$

The solution to this kind of equation was first discussed in the economics literature by Tinsley (1971) and may be derived straightforwardly in the following way. Using the lag operator L, (46) may be written:

$$\left(\alpha bL^{-1} - ((1+\alpha)b - \theta) + bL\right)N(t) = \theta N^*(t). \tag{47}$$

Factorising the lag polynomial as

$$a_1\left(1 - a_2\lambda L^{-1}\right)(1-\lambda L),$$

we have, by comparing coefficients,

$$a_1 a_2 \lambda = -\alpha b,\ a_1\lambda = -b,\ a_1\left(1 + a_2\lambda^2\right) = -\left[(1+\alpha)b - \theta\right]. \tag{48}$$

This implies that λ is a root of the quadratic

$$\alpha b\lambda^2 - \left[(1+\alpha)b - \theta\right]\lambda + b = 0. \tag{49}$$

Given that $\theta < 0$ and $\alpha > 0, b > 0$ it is trivial to demonstrate that the roots are both positive and lie on either side of unity. In fact the stable root, μ, is given by

$$\mu = \frac{1}{2}(1+\alpha^{-1}) + \frac{|\theta|}{2\alpha b} - \left(\left[\frac{1}{2}(1+\alpha^{-1}) + \frac{|\theta|}{2\alpha b}\right]^2 - \alpha^{-1}\right)^{1/2}, \tag{50}$$

which depends only on α and $|\theta|/2b$. Indeed, since $\alpha \simeq 1$ we have

$$\mu \simeq 1 + |\theta|/2b - \left((1 + |\theta|/2b)^2 - 1\right)^{1/2}. \tag{50a}$$

Noting that (48) implies $a_1 = -b/\mu$ and $a_2 = \alpha$, (47) can be written

$$-\frac{b}{\mu}(1 - \alpha\mu L^{-1})(1 - \mu L)N(t) = \theta N^*(t)$$

or

$$N(t) = \mu N(t-1) - \frac{\mu}{b}\frac{\theta N^*(t)}{\left(1 - \alpha\mu L^{-1}\right)}.$$

Given that $-\theta\mu/b = (1-\mu)(1-\alpha\mu)$ and that $0 < \alpha\mu < 1$, this may be expanded to obtain the fundamental employment equation:

$$N(t) = \mu N(t-1) + (1-\mu)(1-\alpha\mu) \sum_{s=0}^{\infty} (\alpha\mu)^s N^*(t+s). \tag{51}$$

It is clear that this is the unique stable path satisfying (46) and is thus the optimal path (satisfying the transversality conditions). If we rewrite (51) as

$$N(t) - N(t-1) = (1-\mu)\left[(1-\alpha\mu) \sum_{s=0}^{\infty} (\alpha\mu)^s N^*(t+s) - N(t-1)\right],$$

we can see that N follows a partial adjustment process where the target is a convex combination of all future expected values of N^* with the weights forming a geometric progression. It is also clear from (50) that the "speed of adjustment", $(1-\mu)$, is decreasing in the level of adjustment costs b and consequently increases in b add relatively more weight to the future. μ is also a function of the real interest rate (via α) and of both technology parameters and the structure of the earnings/hours function (via θ).

It is straightforward to extend this model to include multiple "quasi-fixed" factors which may include the capital stock and different types of labour. If $Z(t)$ is a vector of such quasi-fixed factors and $Z^*(t)$ is the vector of factor levels which would be optimal in the absence of adjustment costs, then it may be shown that the optimal factor demand equations have the form:

$$Z(t) = VZ(t-1) + \sum_{s=0}^{\infty} (\alpha V)^s [I - \alpha V][I - V] Z^*(t+s), \tag{52}$$

where V is a stable matrix and α is defined as before [see Sargent (1978) or Nickell (1984), for example]. V is not a diagonal matrix except under highly restrictive conditions on the technology and therefore the demand for each factor is generally a function of the lagged values of all the other "quasi-fixed" factors as well as all the future Z^*'s.

Having derived the basic model, we now consider a number of particular questions which must be considered in order to make such a model operational. These questions include the specification of N^*, expectations, stochastic structure and aggregation.

4.1. *The specification of N^**

The specification of N^* clearly depends on the formulation of the revenue function R. To obtain a revenue function of the form (42), we essentially require a Cobb–Douglas technology. $N^*(t)$ is then given by (47a), where the contents of the shift variable $\omega(t)$ will depend on the assumptions made about the firm's environment. These are catalogued at the beginning of Section 3. In all cases $\omega(t)$ will contain the real prices of the variable factors plus a trend to account for technical progress and the missing capital stock. Then in the case of the imperfectly competitive firm we must also add some index of industry demand whereas with the demand constrained firm, we can simply include (exogenous) output. In this latter case it must also be noted that N^* will end up as a function only of the relative prices of all the factors including the wage. Given our Cobb–Douglas assumption, we can write N^* in log linear form[19] which suggests that it might be convenient to further approximate (51) in log form. This would give us

$$\log N(t) = \mu \log N(t-1) + (1-\mu)(1-\alpha\mu) \sum_{s=0}^{\infty} (\alpha\mu)^s \log N^*(t+s). \qquad (53)$$

An alternative to specifying N^* is to assume a revenue function which is quadratic either in the levels or the logs of all its arguments which will, of course, automatically generate a linear or log-linear form for N^*. For example, in the case of the demand constrained firm with exogenous output, the revenue function may be written as

$$p(t)R(N(t),t) = p(t)R_0(t) - c(y(t), N(t), p_z(t), t),$$

where c is the standard restricted cost function [see eq. (3)]. Some quadratic approximation to c may then be used and, indeed, c can be extended to include adjustment costs (i.e. including $\dot{N}$ in the function) and the quadratic approximation can then allow interactions between the adjustment cost terms and the other elements of the cost function [see, for example, Morrison and Berndt (1981)]. This has the advantage of representing a more flexible production relation than the Cobb–Douglas, say, and thus generally generates better results for price effects. It is, however, difficult to incorporate a serious treatment of hours worked in this kind of model and typically man-hours are treated a the labour input with a uniform price. There is little more to be said on this issue without enumerating endless specific examples and so we turn to the question of expectations.

[19] In the case of the imperfectly competitive firm, we would also require the firm to face a constant elasticity demand function. On the other hand, with the demand constrained model we may specify a CES technology while retaining log linearity.

4.2. Expectations

In our derivation of the fundamental eq. (51), we assumed point expectations. In reality, of course, there is uncertainty and the standard way of dealing with this problem is to specify the complete underlying structure of the model as quadratic. This enables us to replace all future random variables by their expectations using standard certainty equivalence results [e.g. Simon (1956) and Theil (1958)]. This is, in a sense, simply evading the issue because there is no reason whatever to believe the quadratic assumption. An alternative way of evading the issue is just to use expectations and ignore the fact that this is not optimal for non-quadratic problems. There is an extensive discussion of this problem in Malinvaud (1969) and subsequently in Nerlove (1972) who both more or less conclude that the straightforward use of expectations will not be too misleading so long as uncertainty is not large. This work has been extended in a more formal manner in Christiano (1982) which discusses the accuracy of the linear-quadratic model when it is treated as an approximation of a more general framework. More recently Pindyck (1982) and Abel (1983) have presented some results incorporating uncertainty in dynamic investment models although the form of uncertainty is rather simplistic for empirical work. Baca-Campodonico (1983), however, provides some very much more general results in a multi-factor context and includes some empirical applications. Again, however, the form of uncertainty is rather restrictive but this work indicates how it can be extended. There clearly remains much to be done in this area so for our purpose it seems best simply to use expectations of future random variables. In order to be more specific, we shall introduce the following notation:

$$\underset{t}{\mathrm{E}} N^*(t+s) = N^*(t,t+s).$$

Thus, $N^*(t,t+s)$ is the expectation formed at time t of N^* at $t+s$. To model these future expectations we must specify models for each of the exogenous variables determining N^*.

Suppose then that N^* is given by an equation of the form:

$$N^*(t) = \beta' x_1(t) + u(t), \tag{54}$$

where $x_1(t)$ is a column vector of exogenous variables such as relative prices and $u(t)$ is an unobserved random variable representing technology shocks, for example. We now need a model for $x_1(t)$ and suppose this takes the form:

$$x_1(t+1) = A_{11}(L)x_1(t) + A_{12}(L)x_2(t) + v_1(t),$$
$$x_2(t+1) = A_{21}(L)x_1(t) + A_{22}(L)x_2(t) + v_2(t),$$

where x_2 are additional variables which help to determine x_1 and $A_{ij}(L)$ are matrices of lag polynomials. In obvious notation we may combine these equations to obtain:

$$\begin{aligned} x(t+1) &= A(L)x(t)+v(t) \\ &= A_0x(t)+A_1x(t-1)+\cdots+A_2x(t-l)+v(t), \text{ say.} \end{aligned} \tag{55}$$

In order to generate the forward expectations we can stack these equations [see Sargent (1978), for example] in the following way:

$$\begin{bmatrix} x(t+1) \\ x(t) \\ \vdots \\ x(t-l+1) \end{bmatrix} = \begin{bmatrix} A_0 & A_1 & \cdots & A_l \\ I & 0 & \cdots & 0 \\ 0 & I & \cdots & 0 \\ \vdots & \vdots & \ddots & \vdots \\ 0 & 0 & I & 0 \end{bmatrix} \begin{bmatrix} x(t) \\ x(t-1) \\ \vdots \\ x(t-l) \end{bmatrix} + \begin{bmatrix} v(t) \\ 0 \\ \vdots \\ 0 \end{bmatrix}$$

or, in more concise notation,

$$X(t+1) = AX(t)+V(t). \tag{56}$$

Assuming $v(t)$ is white noise, we have

$$\underset{t}{\mathrm{E}}X(t+1) = AX(t),$$

and in general

$$\underset{t}{\mathrm{E}}X(t+s) = A^sX(t).$$

If we specify a matrix $e_1=[I,0]$ where the dimension of I equals the length of the x_1 vector, we can pick out $\mathrm{E}_t x_1(t+s)$ as

$$\underset{t}{\mathrm{E}}x_1(t+s) = e_1A^sX(t),$$

and from (54) we thus have

$$N^*(t,t+s) = \beta' e_1 A^s X(t) + \underset{t}{\mathrm{E}}u(t+s). \tag{57}$$

Substituting into (51) then yields a final equation in terms of observables of the form:

$$N(t) = \mu N(t-1)+(1-\mu)(1-\alpha\mu)\sum_{s=0}^{\infty}(\alpha\mu)^s\left(\beta' e_1 A^s X(t)+\underset{t}{\mathrm{E}}u(t+s)\right),$$

which may be simplified to

$$N(t) = \mu N(t-1) + (1-\mu)(1-\alpha\mu)\beta' e_1 (I - \alpha\mu A)^{-1} X(t) + \sum_{s=0}^{\infty} (\alpha\mu)^s \underset{t}{\mathrm{E}} u(t+s). \tag{58}$$

The final error term can only be completely specified if we assume a process for u. For example, if we have

$$u(t) = \rho u(t-1) + \varepsilon_t,$$

then the error has the form:

$$\sum_{s=0}^{\infty} (\alpha\mu)^s \underset{t}{\mathrm{E}} u(t+s) = (1-\alpha\mu\rho)^{-1} u(t).$$

This then yields a complete, non-linear, labour demand model consisting of (55) and (58). The actual labour demand equation is very tightly specified with parameters α, μ and β' and the parameters A appear in both equations. It is clear that the general structure of the model now depends crucially on the specification of the subsidiary model for the exogenous variables given by eq. (55). An obvious specification technique is simply to use vector autoregressions including as many variables as seems necessary or, indeed, feasible. There is, however, the possibility of a more sophisticated approach if we are prepared to be more precise about the economic framework. For example, Hansen and Sargent (1981) present a factor demand model for a competitive industry consisting of identical (quadratic) firms. Then the stochastic processes for the industry aggregates are themselves functions of the individual firm parameters. But aggregates such as the industry output price will appear in (55) and hence there will be a relationship between the parameters of this "sub-model" and those of the labour demand function (51). This relationship clearly tightens the model considerably although the restrictions are very sensitive to the assumed industry structure and depend crucially on the ability to aggregate in a simple fashion.

Finally, it is worth noting that a particular feature of these models is that they generate their own stochastic structure. Unfortunately, however, there are many other reasons why stochastic elements should enter other than those which are "internal" to the model and these we discuss next.

4.3. Stochastic structure

Stochastic elements can arise in these models from a variety of factors apart from those already mentioned. The largest errors will arise from the simple fact that the basic model is a far from totally accurate description of the employment process even at the individual firm level. We have already noted that if adjustment costs are linear over the relevant range, the resulting optimal strategy will not have the simple partial adjustment structure of (58). This will necessarily imply a large error if (58) is imposed on the data as well as the danger of drawing incorrect inferences if the misspecification is serious. In addition, (58) cannot be a precise representation even if adjustment costs are quadratic because of all the further approximations required in its derivation. These errors will almost certainly dominate the previously mentioned technology shocks and we have not even considered the question of aggregation to which we now turn.

4.4. Aggregation

Two basic aggregation questions must be considered. First, we look at aggregation across firms and then at aggregation across different types of labour. Suppose, for example, that we have two firms with differences in adjustment costs but identical technologies generating identical employment targets, N^*. Thus, we have, in obvious notation,

$$(1-\mu_1 L)N_1(t) = (1-\mu_1)(1-\alpha\mu_1)\sum_{s=0}^{\infty}(\alpha\mu_1)^s N^*(t,t+s),$$

$$(1-\mu_2 L)N_2(t) = (1-\mu_2)(1-\alpha\mu_2)\sum_{s=0}^{\infty}(\alpha\mu_2)^s N^*(t,t+s).$$

In order to aggregate we may simply multiply the first equation by $(1-\mu_2 L)$, the second by $(1-\mu_1 L)$ and add. This yields:

$$\begin{aligned}(1-\mu_1 L)(1-\mu_2 L)N(t) &\\ = (1-\mu_1)(1-\alpha\mu_1)\sum(\alpha\mu_1)^s(1-\mu_2 L)N^*(t,t+s) &\\ +(1-\mu_2)(1-\alpha\mu_2)\sum(\alpha\mu_2)^s(1-\mu_1 L)N^*(t,t+s). &\qquad (59)\end{aligned}$$

The first important implication of this result is that an additional lag has been added to the dependent variable. This tells us that even if the underlying model has the basic partial adjustment single lag structure, aggregation can easily generate both further lags and a corruption of the simple geometric structure of the distributed lead on N^*. Suppose, however, that μ_1 and μ_2 are close. Will the single lag model provide a good approximation? The answer to this question is a qualified yes. The single lag model with a μ value equal to $(\mu_1+\mu_2)/2$ provides a good approximation in the sense that the error is of order $(\mu_1-\mu_2)^2$. However, the geometric distributed lead becomes progressively more inaccurate as we go further into the future, the error increasing at a rate proportional to s. The consequences of this will be discussed at a later stage.

Similar implications arise with aggregation across different types of labour. If we specialise eq. (52) to simply two different types of labour with different adjustment costs, we obtain:

$$(I-VL)\begin{bmatrix} N_1(t) \\ N_2(t) \end{bmatrix} = \sum_{s=0}^{\infty} (\alpha V)^s [I-\alpha V][I-V]\begin{bmatrix} N_1^*(t,t+s) \\ N_2^*(t,t+s) \end{bmatrix}.$$

To aggregate, we note first that

$$i'\begin{bmatrix} N_1(t) \\ N_2(t) \end{bmatrix} = N(t)$$

$$= i'(I-VL)^{-1} \sum_{s=0}^{\infty} (\alpha V)^s [I-\alpha V][I-V]\begin{bmatrix} N_1^*(t,t+s) \\ N_2^*(t,t+s) \end{bmatrix},$$

where $i'=[1,1]$. We then use the fact that $(I-VL)^{-1}=(I-adj(V)L)/\det(I-VL)$ to obtain:

$$\left(1-(v_{11}+v_{22})L+(v_{11}v_{22}-v_{12}v_{21})L^2\right)N(t)$$

$$= i'(I-adj(V)L)\sum_{s}(\alpha V)^s[I-\alpha V][I-V]\begin{bmatrix} N_1^*(t,t+s) \\ N_2^*(t,t+s) \end{bmatrix}. \tag{60}$$

Again we have an additional lag on the dependent variable but, in this case, it is worth noting that the roots of this second order process can be complex which cannot occur in the previous example given in (59). Furthermore, it is very likely that there will be distinct groups of workers within the firm with very different adjustment costs (see Section 2) and, as a consequence, any equation concerned with *aggregate* employment can be expected to have at least two lags on the dependent variable as well as a coefficient structure on the distributed lead terms which is very much more complicated than simple geometric.

Other more standard aggregation problems may also arise if we are dealing with a large sector of the economy and if the relative weights of the different industries within it change over time. In particular this can lead directly to parameter instability in the aggregate equation.

4.5. *General problems*

Before we consider the empirical work in this area, it is worth running through some of the general problems and pitfalls which arise in attempting to model labour demand.

4.5.1. *Missing variables*

The missing variable problem is so standard that it is barely worth remarking. Nevertheless since there are numerous empirical papers on labour demand which use models from which key variables are omitted, it is worth listing some of the factors which it is easy to forget. In the specification of N^*, there are a number of important variables. First, whatever the assumed structure of the firm, other factor prices should appear, particularly the prices of materials and energy unless the whole analysis is carried out in a value added context. These latter prices can be ignored if a value added output price is used but if wholesale prices are used then they must be included. Furthermore, any taxes on labour paid by the firm should be added to the wage since it is clear that after-tax labour costs are the relevant price in this context.

Looking back to (46a) it is apparent that any changes in the shape of the earnings/hours relationship will influence N^*. Such changes could include shifts in the length of the regular work week, shifts in overtime premia and shifts in the relative weight accorded to payments which are independent of hours worked (e.g. some payroll taxes).

Finally there is the problem of how to deal with the capital stock if one is concerned solely with the employment relation. In the short run, the capital stock can probably be taken as predetermined, whereas in the long run the cost of capital will have a role. The standard approach is simply to make use of trend terms with which it is also hoped to pick up technical progress. This may be satisfactory in some circumstances but it clearly involves rather dangerous prior assumptions.

4.5.2. *Dynamic structure*

The basic problem here is that there is a temptation to take as the maintained hypothesis, a dynamic structure which is essentially that set out in (51). This will probably be an inadequate representation of the dynamic structure of the data for at least three reasons. First, any aggregation over labour with different adjustment costs will lead both to longer lags on the dependent variable and to a more complex lead structure on the expectation variables. Second, if firms face linear or close to linear adjustment costs we have no reason to expect a partial adjustment process and we must expect to have to use a rather more general structure for both lags and leads. Third, if uncertainty is important, this may involve a generally more cautious approach on the part of the firm which will change the dynamic structure of the employment response in rather unpredictable ways [see Muellbauer (1979)].

The implication of this is that there is no justification for imposing on the data a model with the simple dynamic structure of (51) without testing. If this is done and the data is, in fact, generated by a more complex dynamic structure, then any hypothesis testing which is done within the framework of the inadequate maintained specification will be of little consequence.

4.5.3. *The specification of the technology and environment of the firm*

In specifying the firm's technology, it is probably desirable to avoid imposing too rigid a structure which leads directly to the use of some relatively flexible function form. This is easiest to do by specifying one of the functions dual to the technology such as the cost or profit function or, in the context of a dynamic model, by working directly with the value function as described in Epstein (1981) or Epstein and Denny (1983).[20] In this latter case, however, there are problems when we allow non-static expectations.

With regard to the firm's environment, the big danger is to assume that the firm is demand constrained and that output is exogenous. This seems rather unlikely and it is almost inconceivable, for example, that a technology shock will not influence both employment and output simultaneously. Now it is, of course, perfectly legitimate to investigate employment conditional on output so long as it is remembered that output is not exogenous. This not only has implications for the treatment of current output in estimation but also for the specification of expectations. It is more or less impossible to defend an assumption of static expectations for output if it is an endogenous variable, because if employment is moving slowly towards some long run equilibrium then output is more or less certain to be expected to move in the same direction.

4.5.4. *The specification of expectations*

This is an extremely difficult problem. The specification of models for the exogenous variables determining N^* allows an embarrassment of choice since it is quite likely that there are many variables which would assist in the generation of accurate forecasts. Furthermore, the approach which leads to the labour demand model (58) assumes that agents themselves both know and use the model described by (55). This rational expectations assumption is clearly heroic and will become even more heroic if we follow the type of framework discussed in Hansen

[20] The value function is the maximised present value of net earnings.

and Sargent (1981, p. 44). The degree of arbitrariness in this area contrasts strongly with the tight specification of the labour demand itself. The problem, however, is difficult to avoid. If we simply take an equation such as (58) and ignore the structure, we must still specify all the variables in the vector $X(t)$ which will help either directly or indirectly to forecast future employment targets. There are so many possibilities that it is unlikely that anything approaching the correct specification can be achieved without considering the time series properties of the exogenous variables encapsulated in (55).

One way of avoiding the problem is to concentrate on the estimation of the first order condition (47). This is somewhat tricky [see Sargan (1982), Mendis and Muellbauer (1982), Hansen and Singleton (1982) or Pindyck and Rotemberg (1983)] and also puts a great deal of weight on the precise theoretical structure but has the great advantage of not requiring the specification of models for expectational variables. This is one of those areas where a great deal remains to be done.

5. Empirical investigations

5.1. *A general description*

In this section we shall only be concerned with those empirical investigations of labour demand where the dynamic structure is based on some coherent theoretical framework. Such papers can be divided into two main groups, those concerned essentially with the dynamic structure of interrelated factor demands and those more concerned with the treatment of expectations. Two important early pieces of work which laid out some of the groundwork in both these areas are Holt et al. (1960) and Tinsley (1971) which in their turn were based on earlier theoretical work in Simon (1956) and Theil (1958). The empirical investigation by Holt et al. specifies the firm's optimal production and employment policy in terms of a quadratic control problem and this remains the foundation of all the empirical literature. Tinsley's paper is the first to derive the fundamental labour demand equation given in eq. (51) but his treatment of expectations is essentially based on the use of trends. Sims (1974) makes use of this fundamental equation in his interesting analysis of the relationship between output and employment. He was particularly concerned with the empirical phenomenon of short-run increasing returns to labour or SRIRL: the short-run elasticity of demand for aggregate labour with respect to output is smaller than unity and less than the long run elasticity. As Sims notes, if we take the log-linear form of the fundamental eq. (53) and suppose that N^* is unit elastic in output we can obtain more or less any short or indeed long run elasticity depending on the time series process generating output. In this case (53) becomes

$$\log N(t)=a_0+\mu\log N(t-1)+(1-\mu)(1-\alpha\mu)\sum_{s=0}^{\infty}(\alpha\mu)^s\log y^*(t+s),$$

and if, for example, output, y, follows the process

$$\log y(t+1)=\rho\log y(t)+\varepsilon(t+1),\quad 0<\rho<1,$$

then the reduced form employment equation has the form:

$$\log N(t)=a_0+\mu\log N(t-1)+(1-\mu)\frac{(1-\alpha\mu)}{(1-\alpha\mu\rho)}\log y(t)$$

under rational expectations. So even in the long run, the elasticity of employment with respect to output will be estimated as $(1-\alpha\mu)/(1-\alpha\mu\rho)<1$.

The SRIRL phenomenon has been intensively investigated in Morrison and Berndt (1981) which uses a very tightly specified dynamic factor demand system based on a quadratic approximation to the restricted cost function. They assume exogenous output and static expectations but in their most general model they have five factors of production. Three are variable, namely materials, energy and unskilled labour, and two are costly to adjust, namely skilled labour and capital. The costly adjustment of skilled labour suffices to explain SRIRL (via skilled labour hoarding) but, interestingly enough, they also demonstrate that SRIRL can arise even without assuming costly labour adjustment. If capital is quasi-fixed and skilled labour is complementary with capital then SRIRL can arise in the following way. Suppose, for example, that capital is fixed and that each machine requires a skilled employee to tend it whatever the intensity of its use. When output is expanded, extra unskilled labour is hired to operate the machines more intensively and it is clear that if the elasticity of output with respect to unskilled labour is not too far below unity, the elasticity of output with respect to aggregate labour can clearly exceed unity in the short run.

One of the most sophisticated empirical investigations of a dynamic multiple factor demand model with exogenous output and static expectations is to be found in Epstein and Denny (1983). Here they derive and test an exhaustive set of restrictions implied by the adjustment-cost model of the firm using a three factor model (capital, labour and materials). They also extend the model to include non-static expectations assuming simple first-order autoregressions for the relevant variables.

Of the group of papers which concentrate on the modelling of expectations, the seminal contribution is Sargent (1978) which is based on the model of eqs. (58) and (55) [see also Kennan (1979)]. He in fact has two groups of workers, straight time and overtime, but these are separable in the quadratic production relation. The model is strictly neo-classical with real wages as the determinant of employment, capital stock being accounted for by trends. Curiously, the price variable used to normalise wages is the consumer price index which is not the relevant one for firms and materials and energy prices are ignored completely. The real wage models [corresponding to eq. (55)] are simple autoregressions and the labour demand equations have second-order lags which are induced by serially correlated technology shocks. The paper contains some interesting tests of the restrictions implied by the double appearance of the A parameters [see again (55) and (58)] which are essentially tests of rational expectations conditional on the rather restricted form of the maintained model.

This paper is extended to include the capital stock by Meese (1980) with interrelated adjustment costs. Otherwise the basic structure is identical to that of Sargent. Morrison (1983) presents one of the first interrelated factor demand systems which does not assume static expectations. As with Morrison and Berndt (1981) this is based on a quadratic approximation to the restricted cost function with exogenous output. It also assumes that labour is a completely variable factor so it is not directly relevant in the context of this chapter.

One of the problems with all these papers is that they impose the theoretically derived dynamic structure on the data without any testing. This is rather undesirable particularly as the results presented in Nickell (1984) seem to indicate that the tight dynamic structure of eq. (58) is not an adequate description of the process generating the data for reasons which we have already discussed. This paper also goes beyond the simple autoregression as a description of the processes generating the expectational variables.

Finally, we must refer to the work of Pindyck and Rotemberg (1983). Their basic strategy is to estimate the stochastic equivalent of the first-order condition (47). This indicates that at time t, the firm's choice of employment must satisfy

$$\underset{t}{\mathrm{E}}(\alpha bN(t+1))-((1+\alpha)b-\theta)N(t)+bN(t-1)=\theta N^*(t).$$

Estimation is done via an instrumental variables technique and they in fact use four inputs: equipment, structures, white-collar and blue-collar labour with the first three being costly to adjust. They specify a log quadratic restricted cost function and assume additively separable adjustment costs. As we have already noted, the great advantage of this technique is that it avoids the necessity of explicitly modelling the processes generating the exogenous variables. A drawback, however, is that it puts a great deal of weight on the theoretical structure. Mendis and Muellbauer (1982) also present some results based on the estimation of the first-order condition and compare them with those obtained using the fundamental model as exemplified by Sargent (1978). They conclude that the former is a superior framework and thus it seems that this approach is clearly worth developing.

5.2. *Some results on the dynamic structure of labour demand*

Our aim in this final section is to consider the extent to which the estimated dynamic structure of labour demand which emerges in empirical papers is consistent with such facts as we possess on real world employment adjustment costs.

The first important point to recognise is that the mere fact that a dynamic model fits the data much better than a static model does not tell us that adjustment costs are an important factor. The dynamics can arise simply because the estimated model is misspecified. Suppose, for example, that we have a true model of employment of the form:

$$\log N(t) = \mu \log N(t-1) + (1-\mu)\log N^*(t) + u(t),$$

where $0 \leq \mu < 1$ and $\log N^*(t)$ follows the first-order AR process:

$$\log N^*(t) = \rho \log N^*(t-1) + \eta(t), \quad 0 \leq \rho < 1.$$

Suppose, further, that our specification of $N^*(t)$ is poor as is quite likely to be the case. Thus, we "observe" $N^{**}(t)$, where $N^{**}(t) = N^*(t) + \varepsilon(t)$ and where $\varepsilon(t)$ is white noise. It is highly probable that both ρ and $\text{var}(\varepsilon)$ will be large. It is then easy to show that if we estimate this model by standard methods we obtain an estimate $\hat{\mu}$ which has the property:

$$\text{plim}\,\hat{\mu} = \mu + \frac{\rho(1-\mu)^2}{(1-\mu\rho)} \frac{\text{var}(N^*)\,\text{var}(\varepsilon)}{\Delta}, \quad \Delta > 0.$$

So, even if $\mu = 0$ we could still estimate a strongly dynamic model simply because we are not in a position to specify adequately the long-run determinants of employment.

This suggests that we bring our evidence on the actual size of adjustment costs to bear by considering the extent of the serial correlation which they might be expected to induce. This may then be compared with the actual serial correlation which has been estimated. Consider the quadratic adjustment cost model of Section 4. As eq. (50a) makes clear, the extent of serial correlation depends on the two parameters θ and b. Looking first at θ, we see from our discussion on p that θ is defined by the first-order Taylor expression:

$$R_N(N(t), h(t), t) - \tilde{w}(t)w^*(h(t)) \simeq \hat{w}(t)\theta(N(t) - N^*(t)),$$

where we are expanding around the equilibrium point N^* assuming hours are always adjusted optimally. To obtain some idea of the order of magnitude of θ, assume that hours are fixed and we have a stationary equilibrium. Then θ is given by

$$\theta = \frac{1}{\tilde{w}}\frac{\mathrm{d}}{\mathrm{d}n}(R_N - \tilde{w}),$$

where the derivative is evaluated at the point where $R_N = \tilde{w}$. Thus, $\theta = (1/\tilde{w})R_{NN} = R_{NN}/R_N$. So, if we have the "Cobb–Douglas" form exemplified by (42), this yields:

$$|\theta| = (1-\varepsilon)/N^*. \tag{61}$$

In the case where hours are flexible we would expect $|\theta|$ to be smaller because some of the response of $R_N - \tilde{w}$ to a change in employment is offset by the hours of shift.

Turning now to the parameter b, the first point to note is that, in the context of this model, the adjustment cost per hire/fire in period t is given by $(b\tilde{w}/2)|N(t) - N(t-1)|$. So averaging we see that the mean cost per hire/fire is $(b\tilde{w}/2)|\Delta N|$, where $|\Delta N|$ is the sample average. Let us now introduce two parameters. Define $\beta_1 = |\Delta N|/N^*$, the (average) absolute quarterly rate of employment change and β_2 = hiring (or firing) cost/$\tilde{w}$, the hiring or firing cost as a proportion of quarterly earnings. So, by definition, we have

$$\frac{b\tilde{w}}{2}|\Delta N| = \beta_2\tilde{w}$$

or

$$b = \frac{2\beta_2}{|\Delta N|} = \frac{2\beta_2}{\beta_1 N^*}. \tag{62}$$

Combining (61) and (62) we may thus obtain our key parameter $|\theta|/2b$ [see (50a)] as

$$\frac{|\theta|}{2b} = \frac{(1-\varepsilon)\beta_1}{4\beta_2}. \tag{63}$$

Let us now consider some facts. From the evidence in Section 2 it seems reasonable to suppose that for white-collar workers, hiring or firing costs are between two weeks' and two months' pay, and for blue-collar workers they are between two days' and two weeks' pay. Thus, we have $0.15 \leq \beta_2 \leq 0.67$ for white-collar workers and $0.031 \leq \beta_2 \leq 0.15$ for blue-collar workers. What of the parameter β_1 which measures the quarterly rate of employment change? It is important to recognise first of all that this parameter refers to the firm, not to the aggregate. At the level of the firm it is, of course, a considerably large number because all the up and down movements across firms will wash out in the aggregate. A reasonable range would, therefore, seem to be between 1 and 5 percent per quarter, that is $0.01 \leq \beta_1 \leq 0.05$. So, taking ε as 0.8 we have for white-collar workers $0.00075 \leq |\theta|/2b \leq 0.0167$, and for blue-collar workers $0.0033 \leq |\theta|/2b \leq 0.081$. From the formula given in (50a) this yields the following bounds on the lagged dependent variable coefficient μ:

$$\text{white-collar workers } \mu_{\min} = 0.83, \ \mu_{\max} = 0.96; \tag{64a}$$

$$\text{blue-collar workers } \mu_{\min} = 0.67, \ \mu_{\max} = 0.92. \tag{64b}$$

The first point which strikes one about these figures is that they are very high, even when adjustment costs are small. For example, even if the adjustment costs for blue-collar workers are as low as half a day's pay, the $\mu_{\min}$ parameter is 0.46 and this is essentially for fixed hours. With flexible hours it would be higher. Why does this happen? The reason is simply that for small variations in employment around the optimum, the loss of profit is a second-order magnitude since the optimum is precisely the point at which small variations in employment cause a zero loss in profit to first order. So the firm can afford to economise on adjustment costs by spreading its hiring/firing over relatively long periods. This is all the more true, of course, if there is some degree of flexibility in working hours so that they can be adjusted in the meantime.

The second striking point is that the employment dynamics for blue-collar workers and for white-collar workers can be expected to be quite different. (Note that 0.96 and 0.92 are very different numbers in this regard, since the latter implies adjustment which is approximately twice as fast as the former.) This indicates that if we were modelling aggregate employment we should expect to observe second-order lags on the dependent variable since this is the consequence of aggregating two first-order processes (see Section 4.4 on aggregation).

How then do these facts square with the results of the estimated models? The only relevant ones are those which are concerned with employment as opposed to man-hours. The dynamics of man-hours are obviously going to be some mixture of those due to employment and those due to hours. Since the latter are almost bound to respond much more quickly than the former we can expect the serial correlation in the joint variable to be much lower than that in employment alone. Precisely by how much is not clear and so the man-hour results are not very informative, at least for our purposes.

Table 9.1
Estimates of employment dynamics based on $N(t)=(\mu_1+\mu_2)N(t-1)-\mu_1\mu_2 N(t-2)\ldots$

Study	Employment variable	Parameter estimates
Sargent (1978)	U.S. employees on private non-agricultural payrolls. Seasonally unadjusted	$\mu_1=0.957$, $\mu_2=0.409$ (Table 8, $\mu_1=\delta_1, \mu_2=\rho_2$)
Meese (1980)	U.S. *production* workers on private non-agricultural payrolls. Seasonally adjusted.	$\mu_1=0.967$, $\mu_2=0$ (Table 2)
Mendis and Muellbauer (1982)	British manufacturing employment. Seasonally unadjusted. Variable in logs.	$\mu_1=0.819$, $\mu_2=0.786$ (Table 1, column b, $\mu_1=\gamma_2, \mu_2=\rho$)
Nickell (1981)	U.K. manufacturing employment. Seasonally unadjusted. Variable in logs.	$\mu_1,\mu_2=0.85\ (\cos\theta\pm i\sin\theta)$ $\theta=23.5°$ or $\pi/7.7$ (Table 2, last column)

In Table 9.1 we present some estimates of employment dynamics. These are derived from those studies which we have already noted as having an explicit dynamic theory underlying the empirical model. Several points are worth noting. First, the three studies which refer to aggregate employment (i.e. blue- and white-collar) find it necessary to specify two lags on the dependent variable. However, of these three, only Nickell justifies this by aggregation. Both Sargent and Mendis and Muellbauer justify the second lag as arising from a serially correlated unobservable. This, of course, *imposes* real roots on the second-order process, whereas complex roots very easily arise from the aggregation story.

Concerning the size of the serial correlation parameter (μ_1) it is, with the exception of Meese (1980), within the bounds suggested by eqs. (64a) and (64b), although the Sargent value is perhaps a little high when it is remembered that aggregate employment includes a significant proportion of blue-collar workers. With regard to the Meese estimate it is worth noting that when the restrictions implied by his theory are not imposed on the data (they are in fact rejected at the 5 percent level in any event), the unrestricted serial correlation parameter comes down to 0.952, although this is still rather high for the blue-collar sector.

What then can we conclude from this? First, the relatively high lagged dependent variable coefficients which are observed in empirical work on employment are generally consistent with those we might expect given our present information on the actual size of adjustment costs in reality. Second, it is worth bearing in mind that this consistency is conditional on the quadratic adjustment cost story. It is still perfectly possible that adjustment costs are, in reality, more or less linear and that the estimated lagged dependent variable coefficients are due to misspecification. Finally, differing adjustment costs for white- and blue-collar workers lead to different dynamic adjustment for the employment of these two groups and this is consistent with the second order nature of aggregate employment dynamics. Again, however, this is not the only story that can be told.

6. Summary and directions of future research

In this chapter we have considered the theoretical foundations of dynamic labour demand models focusing particularly on different possible structures of hiring and firing costs and their implications for the time path of employment. We have then considered how these models may be empirically implemented and have looked at some of the attempts to confront theoretically precise dynamic models with the data.

All existing empirical work is based on the assumption that turnover costs are quadratic since this is the only form which leads to a simple linear employment relation. Within this framework, there is clear scope for advance. The combination of a flexible technology with multiple factors and a satisfactory treatment of expectations remains elusive but is clearly the next step on the agenda. It seems particularly important to disaggregate labour into at least two different types because of the enormous differences in adjustment costs between different groups. If employment is aggregated it is surely necessary to take account of this fact in the specification of the aggregate equation. Of course, in the best of all possible worlds it would be interesting to work with firm data since there is always a feeling that aggregation over many different firms tends to mask the underlying structure, perhaps ironing out the more jagged individual firm responses. For example, individual firms sometimes open or close whole plants leading to rapid shifts in employment. We should be able to explain such activities but, at the aggregate level, they will never show up.

Finally, the question arises as to whether it is feasible or desirable to move away from the quadratic framework in empirical applications. It seems unquestionably desirable since the prior grounds for accepting quadratic adjustment costs are so thin. If, for example, we assume linear adjustment costs, then it is not possible to write down the firm's employment strategy as a simple analytic function of predetermined variables and expectations. For estimation purposes, however, this is not required. So long as we can solve numerically for the optimal strategy for any given set of parameters and variables, this is all that is needed to enable us to generate parameter estimates. This procedure, however, does throw into sharp relief one of our fundamental assumptions, namely that the firm is following a completely optimal strategy. If the econometrician requires a large computer to solve for the firm's optimal factor demand strategy in any period so, obviously, does the firm. Yet how many firms base their employment decisions on such a complex activity? Probably rather few, if any. The question then remains as to whether this is a good "as if" story or whether we must find ways of mimicking firms' rules of thumb if we are ever to model their strategies with any accuracy. This question will probably remain on the agenda for a long time to come.

References

Abel, A. B. (1983) "Optimal investment under uncertainty", *American Economic Review*: 73.

Baca-Campodonico, J. F. (1983) "Stochastic control, intertemporal duality and the investment decisions of firms", Ph.D. thesis, University of Manchester.

Barron, J. M., J. Bishop and W. C. Dunkelberg (1983) "Employer search: the interviewing and hiring of new employees", mimeo, Purdue University.

Brechling, F. (1978) "Layoffs and unemployment insurance", in: Sherwin Rosen, ed., *Low income labor markets*. Chicago University Press.

Christiano, L. J. (1982) "On the accuracy of linear-quadratic approximations", University of Chicago, Graduate School of Business, mimeo.

Davidson, R. and R. Harris (1981) "Non-convexities in continuous-time investment", *Review of Economic Studies*, April.

Ehrenberg, R. G. (1971) "Heterogeneous labor, the internal labor market, and the dynamics of the employment-hours decision", *Journal of Economic Theory*, February:85–104.

Eisner, R. and R. Strotz (1963) "Determinants of business investment", Research study two, in *Impacts of monetary policy*. Prentice-Hall.

Epstein, L. (1981) "Duality theory and functional forms for dynamic factor demands", *Review of Economic Studies*, 48.

Epstein, L. (1982) "Comparative dynamics in the adjustment-cost model of the firm", *Journal of Economic Theory*, 27.

Epstein, L. and M. Denny (1983) "The multivariate flexible accelerator model: its empirical restrictions and an application to U.S. manufacturing", *Econometrica*, May.

Gould, J. (1968) "Adjustment costs in the theory of investment of the firm", *Review of Economic Studies*, 35.

Hall, R. and E. Lazear (1982) "The excess sensitivity of layoffs and quits to demand", N.B.E.R. Working Paper No. 864.

Hansen, L. P. and K. Singleton (1982) "Generalised instrumental variables estimation of non-linear rational expectations models", *Econometrica*, September:1269–1286.

Hart, O. (1983) "Optimal labour contracts under asymmetric information: an introduction", *Review of Economic Studies*, January.

Hayashi, F. (1982) "Tobin's marginal q and average q: a neoclassical interpretation", *Econometrica*, January.

Holt, C., F. Modigliani, J. Muth and H. Simon (1960) *Planning production inventories, and work force*. Prentice-Hall.

Kennan, J. (1979) "The estimation of partial adjustment models with rational expectations", *Econometrica*, November:1441–1456.

Leban, R. and J. Lesourne (1980) "The firm's investment and employment policy through a business cycle", *European Economic Review*.

Lucas, R. (1967) "Optimal investment policy and the flexible accelerator", *International Economic Review*, 8.

Lucas, R. (1967a) "Adjustment costs and the theory of supply", *Journal of Political Economy*, August.

Malinvaud, E. (1969) "First order certainty equivalence", *Econometrica*, 37.

Meese, R. (1980) "Dynamic factor demand schedules for labour and capital under rational expectations", *Journal of Econometrics*, 14.

Mendis, L. and J. Muellbauer (1982) "Employment functions, returns to scale and expectations", mimeo, Nuffield College, Oxford.

Morrison, C. (1983) "Structural models of dynamic factor demands with non-static expectations: an empirical comparison of rational and adaptive expectations", Mimeo, Tufts University.

Morrison, C. and E. Berndt (1981) "Short run labour productivity in a dynamic model", *Journal of Econometrics*, 16.

Mortensen, D. (1970) "A theory of wage and employment dynamics", in Edmund Phelps, ed., *The microeconomic foundations of employment and inflation theory*. Norton.

Mortenson, D. (1973) "Generalized costs of adjustment and dynamic factor demand theory", *Econometrica*, 41.

Muellbauer, J. (1979) "Are employment decisions based on rational expectations", Mimeo, Birkbeck College.

Nadiri, I. and S. Rosen (1969) "Interrelated factor demand functions", *American Economic Review*, 59.

Nerlove, M. (1972) "Lags in economic behaviour", *Econometrica*, 40.

Nickell, S. (1978) "Fixed costs, employment and labour demand over the cycle", *Economica*, November.

Nickell, S. (1984) "An investigation of the determinants of manufacturing employment in the United Kingdom", *Review of Economic Studies*, October.

Oi, W. (1962) "Labor as a quasi-fixed factor", *Journal of Political Economy*, December.

Pindyck, R. and J. Rotemberg (1983) "Dynamic factor demands and the effects of energy price shocks", *Scandanavian Journal of Economics*, 85(2):223–238.

Pindyck, R. (1982) "Adjustment costs, uncertainty, and the behaviour of the firm", *American Economic Review*, 72.

Rees, A. (1973) *The economics of work and pay*. Harper and Row.

Rothschild, M. (1971) "On the cost of adjustment", *Quarterly Journal of Economics*, November:605–622.

Salop, S. (1973) "Wage differentials in a dynamic theory of the firm", *Journal of Economic Theory*, August.

Sargan, J. D. (1982) "Some problems with Muellbauer's method of specifying and estimating a rational expectations model", Discussion Paper No. 69, Centre for Econometrics and Decision Sciences, University of Florida.

Sargent, T. (1978) "Estimation of dynamic labour demand schedules under rational expectations", *Journal of Political Economy*, 86.

Simon, H. (1956) "Dynamic programming under uncertainty with a quadratic criterion function", *Econometrica*, January.

Sims, C. A. (1974) "Output and labor input in manufacturing", *Brookings Papers on Economic Activity*, 3.

Stiglitz, J. E. (1984) "Theories of wage rigidity", paper presented at the conference on Keynes' Economic Legacy, University of Delaware, January 12–13.

Theil, H. (1958) *Economic forecasts and policy*. North-Holland.

Tinsley, P. (1971) "A variable adjustment model of labor demand", *International Economic Review*, October.

Topel, R. and F. Welch (1980) "Unemployment insurance: survey and extensions", *Economica*, August.

Treadway, A. (1969) "On rational entrepreneurial behavior and the demand for investment", *Review of Economic Studies*, 36.

Treadway, A. (1970) "Adjustment costs and variable inputs in the theory of the competitive firm", *Journal of Economic Theory*, 2.

Treadway, A. (1971) "The rational multivariate flexible accelerator", *Econometrica*, 39.

Treadway, A. (1974) "The globally optimal flexible accelerator", *Journal of Economic Theory*, 7.

PART 3

WAGE STRUCTURE

Chapter 10

WAGE DETERMINANTS: A SURVEY AND REINTERPRETATION OF HUMAN CAPITAL EARNINGS FUNCTIONS

ROBERT J. WILLIS*

University of Chicago and Economic Research Center, NORC

1. Introduction

This chapter provides a survey and exposition of the development of the earnings function as an empirical tool for the analysis of the determinants of wage rates. Generically, the term "earnings function" has come to mean any regression of individual wage rates or earnings on a vector of personal, market, and environmental variables thought to influence the wage. As such, it has been applied to a wide variety of problems such as, for example, studies of discrimination by race or sex (see Chapter by Cain in this Handbook), the estimation of the "value of life" from data on job safety [Thaler and Rosen (1975)], or compensation for increased unemployment probabilities [Abowd and Ashenfelter (1981)].

The premier application, of course, is to the study of the effects of investment in schooling and on-the-job training on the level, pattern, and interpersonal distribution of life cycle earnings associated with the pioneering work on human capital by Becker (1964, 1975), Becker and Chiswick (1966), and, especially, by Mincer (1958, 1962, 1974). The bulk of this chapter is devoted to the theoretical and empirical development of the human capital earnings function during the past twenty-five years. In part, this restricted focus is justified by the importance accorded to investment in human capital as an explanation of wage differentials in the vast literature spawned by human capital theory. In addition, many of the analytical and statistical issues that arise in the estimation and interpretation of generic earnings functions also pertain to the study of other wage determinants or to tests of rivals to the human capital theory of wage determination.

*This chapter was written while the author was a member of the Economics Department, State University of New York at Stony Brook.

Handbook of Labor Economics, Volume I, Edited by O. Ashenfelter and R. Layard

The standard human capital earnings function developed by Mincer (1974) is of the form

$$\ln y = \beta_0 + \beta_1 s + \beta_2 x + \beta_3 x^2 + u.$$

The schooling coefficient, β_1, provides an estimate of the rate of return to education which is assumed to be constant in this specification. The concavity of the observed earnings profile is captured by the quadratic experience terms, x and x^2, whose coefficients, β_2 and β_3, are respectively positive and negative. Since early data sources such as Census data did not record a worker's actual labor force experience, a transformation of the worker's age was used as a proxy for his experience. Mincer uses the transformation $x = a - s - 6$, which assumes that a worker begins full-time work immediately after completing his education and that the age of school completion is $s + 6$. As an empirical tool, the Mincer earnings function has been one of the great success stories of modern labor economics. It has been used in hundreds of studies using data from virtually every historical period and country for which suitable data exist. The results of these studies reveal important empirical regularities in educational wage differentials and the life cycle pattern of earnings which are described later in this chapter.

To me, perhaps the most fascinating question concerning the human capital earnings function is why it should work so well. In a lucid survey of econometric problems that arise in estimating the returns to education, Griliches (1977, p. 1) presents a list of seven questions concerning the specification of an econometric model of earnings of this type. The fifth question is:

> Why should there be a relation like this in the first place? In other words: (a) what interpretation can be given to such an equation? (b) What interpretation can be given to the estimated [schooling] coefficient? (b) Can one expect it to be "stable" across different samples and different time periods?

He goes on to say that he will "skip lightly" over several of the questions including the fifth question which he characterizes as the "...one really hard one on this list".

In this survey, I will go into considerable detail in an attempt to deal with the set of issues raised by the "hard question" on Griliches' list. In particular, I will argue that some of the issues he raises in this question and treats later in his paper can be both clarified and simplified by a reinterpretation of the theoretical underpinnings of Mincer's earnings function within a framework which goes back to Adam Smith's theory of equalizing differences and more recently to the theory used by Friedman and Kuznets (1945) in their explanation of income differences among independent professionals. It can also be regarded as a reinterpretation of Becker's justly famous Woytinsky Lecture [Becker (1967, 1975)] which views investment in human capital as the outcome of interaction between the supply of finance and the demand for investment. Unlike Becker, who assumes that human capital is homogeneous, I assume that each job or occupation entails a particular set of skills which a worker can acquire by combining his own innate talents with an appropriate duration and curricular content of schooling. The resulting theory tends to correct an imbalance in the human capital literature which has emphasized the supply far more than the demand for human capital.

Under certain conditions labeled "equality of opportunity" and "equality of comparative advantage", the earnings function is remarkably stable in the sense that, as long as the rate of interest remains constant, the structure of educational wage differentials tends to remain constant in the long run even in the face of substantial variations in the pattern of occupational demand arising from shifts in income, product prices, and production technology. After treating this special case, I show how variations in opportunity and comparative advantage influence the empirical form of the earnings function and use the framework to interpret some of empirical literature on "ability bias".

The chapter begins by surveying the empirical estimates of the rate of return to education and the pattern of life cycle earnings in Section 2. Section 3 discusses the derivation of human capital earnings functions under the assumption of homogeneous human capital and Section 4 introduces the model of heterogeneous human capital described above. Section 5 considers theoretical and econometric issues which arise when there is inequality of opportunity and ability and closes with a discussion of empirical findings concerning ability bias. In Section 6, I briefly describe some recent literature on several topics such as signalling, implicit contracts, and specific human capital which extend or modify certain aspects of the human capital model used in the rest of the chapter. This section is followed by some concluding remarks on topics for future research.

2. Statistical earnings functions

2.1. *The theory in a nutshell*

Additional schooling entails opportunity costs in the form of forgone earnings plus direct expenses such as tuition. To induce a worker to undertake additional schooling, he must be compensated by sufficiently higher lifetime earnings. To command higher earnings, more schooled workers must be sufficiently more productive than their less schooled fellow workers. In long-run competitive equilibrium, the relationship between lifetime earnings and schooling is such that (a) the supply and demand for workers of each schooling level are equated and (b) no worker wishes to alter his schooling level.

The preceding paragraph provides a nutshell summary of the human capital theory of educational choice. In order to extend the theory to explain educational wage differentials, it is necessary to specify how variations in earnings are divided between hours of work and hourly wage rates and how wages and hours are distributed over the life cycle. The essentials of the extended theory can be stated by replacing the word "schooling" with the term "on-the-job training" in the preceding paragraph.

In fact, the development of the human capital literature has not always followed the theoretical structure just outlined. In particular, the literature often emphasizes the supply side of the theory by focusing on individual decisions to invest in human capital but neglects the demand for human capital by firms and the implications of labor market equilibrium. Even the supply-oriented studies often treat schooling and patterns of post-school investment as exogenous rather than as the outcome of optimizing decisions.

For the most part, the failure of the literature always to meet standards of full theoretical purity is explained (and to a considerable extent justified) by the pragmatic trade-offs any applied economist must make between theoretical rigor, analytic tractability, and limitations of available data and econometric methodology. In this section of the chapter I will follow the historical development of the empirical literature on the returns to education and life cycle earnings functions without attempting to interpret it within the hedonic theory outlined above. In later sections, I provide a critique of the theoretical underpinnings of some of the empirical work and then offer a fairly detailed reinterpretation of the theory which, on the one hand, is consistent with the hedonic view of labor market equilibrium and, on the other hand, provides a justification in an important special case for the major empirical formulation of earnings functions pioneered by Mincer (1974).

In this section and in most of this chapter, I will follow a convention of the earnings function literature by assuming that the life cycle pattern of hours is fixed exogenously and will treat the life cycle patterns of hourly wages and annual earnings as essentially synonymous. The neglect of labor supply considerations provides considerable analytic simplification because it (along with certain additional assumptions) enables human capital investment decisions to be treated within a wealth rather than utility maximizing framework. An unfortunate consequence of this convention is that it has led to a bifurcation of the human capital and labor supply literatures which is only slowly being bridged. (See Chapter 11 by Weiss and Chapter 1 by Pencavel, respectively, in this Handbook for surveys of the life cycle earnings and labor supply literatures.) In particular, the omission of labor supply considerations is untenable when considering the returns to human capital investments for women because of their substantial commitment to non-market household activities and the high degree of variability of market labor over the life cycle. [See, for example, Mincer and Polachek

(1974) and Chapter 4 by Gronau in this Handbook.] Consequently, the discussion in this chapter will be largely confined to male earnings.

2.2. *Statistical earnings functions*

Consider a hypothetical economy made up of workers who differ by years of schooling, s (which is assumed to begin at age 6); differ in age, t; and differ in the length of labor force experience, $x = t - s - 6$, but who are otherwise observationally identical. In this economy, data on annual earnings, y, and years of schooling may be described by a statistical earnings function

$$y = \varphi(s, x) + u, \tag{1}$$

where $\varphi(s, x)$ is the functional form that best fits the data and u is a residual with zero mean. Note that u captures the effect of any unobserved variables such as ability which influence individual productivity. For the time being, assume that u is statistically independent of s and x.

In actual data, education and earnings are positively correlated. Assume that this is true when (1) is estimated so that $\varphi(s, x)$ is positive monotonic in s. Typically, the experience profile of earnings is positively sloped through most or all of working life and concave with the growth rate of earnings being highest at early ages and slowing or even turning negative at the later stages of life. Some illustrative profiles for different schooling groups based on cross-section data from the 1960 U.S. census are presented in Figure 10.1.

In terms of the theory outlined above, the function $\varphi(s, x)$ in (1) may be interpreted as a hedonic price function in the sense of Rosen (1974) which reflects the equilibrium of the supply and demand for workers at each level of schooling and experience. In most of the following discussion I shall also assume that the economy and population are in long run, steady state equilibrium such that $\varphi(s, x)$ holds cross-sectionally in each period and, hence, also describes the longitudinal earnings path of representative individuals in each cohort, conditional on their schooling. Underlying this assumption are assumptions of zero aggregate productivity change and a constant rate of population growth with an associated stable age distribution.

2.3. *Internal rate of return*

Beginning with the early studies of investment in education by Becker (1962, 1964), Hanoch (1967), Hansen (1963) and others, statistical earnings functions like $\varphi(s, x) + u$ in (1) have been used to estimate the internal rate of return to

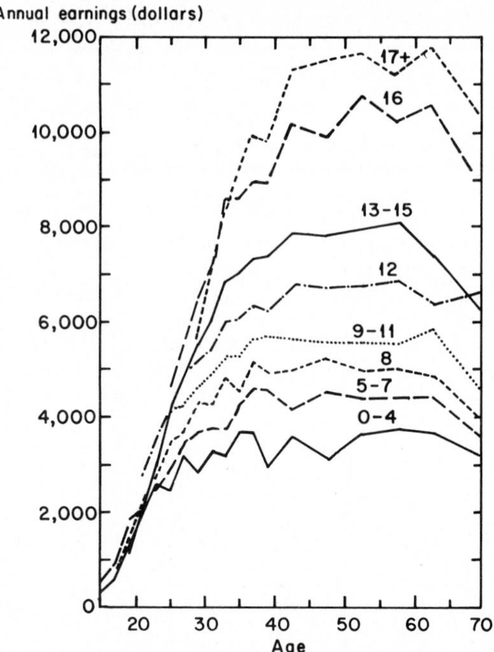

Figure 10.1. Age profiles of earnings of white, non-farm men, 1959. *Source*: Mincer (1974, Chart 4.1).

education. By definition, the marginal internal rate of return is that rate of discount, $\rho(s_1, s_2)$, such that the present value of the earnings streams net of direct costs of education which are associated with two different schooling levels, s_1 and s_2, are equated. In this section I will describe how this is done.

Ideally, the data used to estimate statistical earnings functions and the internal rate of return to education would consist of complete longitudinal life histories of the earnings of individuals beginning with their age of entry into the labor force and ending with their retirement and would also provide information about the direct costs of education such as tuition payments. Unfortunately, such ideal data are seldom available. The early studies of investment in education typically used cross-sectional census data to estimate the rate of return to education. Such data contain information on current earnings of those in the labor force, age, and years of education but no information on tuition paid, age of entry into the labor force or age of retirement. Even the more recent longitudinal data sets such as the Panel Study of Income Dynamics or the National Longitudinal Studies contain only partial life histories of selected cohorts and very limited information on direct costs of schooling. (See Chapter 7 by Stafford in this Handbook for descriptions of these data sets.)

Because of these data limitations, a more or less conventional set of simplifying assumptions have been made to permit estimates of the rate of return to education with available data. Since these assumptions also simplify the exposition, I will adopt them now and continue to use them throughout this survey unless otherwise noted. Specifically, assume that the only cost of schooling is forgone earnings, that individuals enter the labor force immediately upon the completion of schooling at age $t = 6 + s$, and that each individual's working life of n years is independent of his years of education.[1]

Given the additional assumption of a steady state with no productivity growth, the present value of the lifetime earnings of a "representative" individual with s years of education, evaluated at the age of school entry, is

$$V(s,r) = \int_0^n \varphi(s,x) \mathrm{e}^{-r(s+x)} \mathrm{d}x, \tag{2}$$

where $\varphi(s, x)$ is based on the estimated statistical earnings function and r is a discount rate.

Let $s < s + d$ be two levels of schooling, where $d > 0$, and let $\hat{\rho}(s, s+d)$ be an estimate of the marginal internal rate of return to an individual with s years of schooling who invests in an additional d years. By definition $\hat{\rho}(s, s+d)$ is the rate of discount that solves $V(s, r) = V(s+d, r)$. Using (2), it is straightforward to show that this definition implies that

$$\begin{aligned} \hat{\rho}(s, s+d) = 1/d \Big\{ &\ln\Big(\int_0^n \varphi(s+d, x) \mathrm{e}^{-r(s+d+x)} \mathrm{d}x \Big) \\ &- \ln\Big(\int_0^n \varphi(s,x) \mathrm{e}^{-r(s+x)} \mathrm{d}x \Big) \Big\}. \end{aligned} \tag{3}$$

In practice, $\hat{\rho}(s, s+d)$ is usually unique because the age–earnings profiles of two schooling groups typically only cross once when $\varphi(s, x)$ is chosen to be a smooth functional form which eliminates erratic sampling fluctuations in age–earnings profiles.

[1]As will be discussed below, a distinction is sometimes made between "private" and "social" rates of return to take into account differences between the private and social costs of schooling under public education and between the private and social benefits of schooling due to the taxation of earnings. To the extent that the tax system is proportional, the use of after-tax or before-tax earnings do not affect the rate of return if there are no fixed costs (e.g. tuition). It has also been argued by Schultz (1960) and Becker (1964) that part-time earnings of college students in the United States tend to offset the bulk of the direct costs of college so that direct costs can be ignored without seriously affecting the estimated rate of return. [However, see Parsons (1974) for a critique of this assumption.] In this case, the "conventional" set of simplifying assumptions in the text yield estimates of both the private and social rates of return.

In general, the rate of return must be calculated using numerical methods. However, there are two simpler approaches which are of interest. First, suppose that the rate of growth of earnings at any given experience level is independent of the level of experience. In this case, the earnings function in (1) can be written in the weakly separable form:

$$y = f(s)g(x) + u, \tag{4}$$

and the present value of lifetime earnings is

$$V(s,r) = f(s)\mathrm{e}^{-rs}\int_0^n g(x)\mathrm{e}^{-rx}\mathrm{d}x. \tag{5}$$

In this case it is easy to show that the estimated marginal internal rate of return to education is given by the logarithmic derivative of the statistical earnings function with respect to s. Thus, using (3)–(5), it follows that

$$\hat{\rho}(s, s+d) = [\ln(f(s+d)) - \ln(f(s))]/d. \tag{6}$$

Letting d become arbitrarily small, it is clear from (6) that the estimated return to a small increase in schooling above a given level of s is equal to the logarithmic derivative of the statistical earnings function in (4) evaluated at s. That is,

$$\frac{\mathrm{d}\ln y}{\mathrm{d}s} = \varphi_s(s,x)/\varphi(s,x) = f'(s)/f(s) = \hat{\rho}(s), \tag{7}$$

where $\hat{\rho}(s)$ is the estimated marginal internal rate of return to schooling and $\varphi_s(s)$ is the partial derivative of the earnings function.

If the profile of log earnings with respect to experience of different schooling groups are approximately parallel, this result provides a rationale for utilizing regression methods to estimate the rate of return to education. For example, let

$$\begin{aligned} \ln y &= \ln(f(s)) + \ln(g(x)) + \varepsilon \\ &= b_0 + b_1 s + b_2 s^2 + b_3 x + b_4 x^2 + \varepsilon \end{aligned} \tag{8}$$

be a regression function which is a quadratic approximation to the logarithm of the weakly separable earnings function in (4), where ε is an error term. The estimated marginal rate of return to education is then $\hat{\rho}(s) = b_1 + 2b_2 s$. Some empirical examples of this approach will be discussed below.

The logarithmic derivative of the statistical earnings function provides an estimate of $\rho(s)$ only if it is assumed, as in (4), that a given increment of schooling has the same proportional effect on earnings at all levels of experience. If this assumption is not true, Mincer (1974) has suggested a "short cut" approximate method of estimating the rate of return to schooling which avoids the need for using numerical methods. It has the added advantage that the rate of return can be estimated from data on the first ten years or so of a cohort's earnings history.

Mincer's short cut method involves the use of an "overtaking" concept. Specifically, assume that average earnings evolve according to the earnings function $y = \varphi(s, x)$ and let V_s be the present value of this earnings profile. Let $\bar{y}(s)$ be a constant level of earnings which has the same present value. Now define the overtaking experience level as $x^*(s)$ such that $\bar{y}(s) = \varphi(s, x^*(s))$.

Given these definitions, it follows that

$$V_s = \int_0^n \bar{y}(s)e^{-rx}\mathrm{d}x = \alpha\bar{y}(s)/r = \alpha\varphi(s, x^*(s))/r, \tag{9}$$

where $\alpha = (1 - e^{-rn})$. By analogy, let $x^*(s+d)$ be the overtaking level of experience for the earnings profile $\varphi(s+d, x)$ which is associated with a higher level of schooling, $s+d$. Substituting (9) into (3), the marginal internal rate of return is

$$\rho(s, s+d) = [\ln(\varphi(s+d, x^*(s+d)) - \ln(\varphi(s, x^*(s))]/d. \tag{10}$$

This expression provides an empirically useful short cut method for estimating the internal rate of return if the two overtaking levels of experience, $x^*(s)$ and $x^*(s+d)$, are known. In this case, $\rho(s, s+d)$ can be evaluated by simply plugging the average log earnings levels of the two schooling groups at their overtaking experience levels into (10). Mincer (1974) argues that the overtaking level of experience will be less than or equal to the reciprocal of the internal rate of return. For example, if the rate of return is about 10 percent, then the short cut method may be applied by evaluating (10) using the average earnings of individuals with about 8–10 years of experience.

Mincer develops the overtaking argument for a special case in which the overtaking experience level is exactly $1/\rho$ regardless of the level of schooling. The argument is as follows. Assume that individuals enter the labor force with an earnings capacity of $\bar{y}(s)$ dollars and that they invest C dollars in on-the-job training in each year after leaving school for which they pay C dollars of forgone earnings during the period of investment. The investments have a constant own rate of return of ρ percent in perpetuity. Given these assumptions, the earnings of an individual with s years of schooling and x years of experience is

$$\begin{aligned} y(s, x) &= \bar{y}(s) + \rho\int_0^x C\,\mathrm{d}t - C \\ &= \bar{y}(s) + C(\rho x - 1). \end{aligned} \tag{11}$$

If the worker is assumed to have an infinitely long working life and the discount rate is ρ, then the present value of the earnings stream in (11) is $\bar{y}(s)/\rho$ which is also the present values of a constant earnings stream of $\bar{y}(s)$. From (11), it is easy to see that $x^*(s) = 1/\rho$ is the value of x which solves $y(s, x) = \bar{y}(s)$.

Note that the growth path of earnings in (11) implies constant dollar growth (but decreasing percentage growth) as experience increases. Empirically, dollar growth in earnings tends to decrease as x increases. In this case, the constant level of earnings with the same present value as $y(s, x)$ would tend to be lower than $\bar{y}(s)$ and the overtaking point would tend to occur earlier. Thus, Mincer argues that the overtaking experience level will tend to be somewhat less than $1/\rho$.

The overtaking concept has an important implication for the distribution of individual earnings paths about the population average for individuals. In the special case described above, the earnings of all individuals with the same "earnings capacity" at school leaving [i.e. $\bar{y}(s)$] will be equal when $x = 1/\rho$ but will differ at earlier and later values of x if individuals differ in their levels of post-school investment (i.e. have different values of C). In particular, individuals with high rates of investment in on-the-job training will tend to have lower initial earnings and higher earnings growth than comparable individuals who invest at a lower rate. Thus, the variance of earnings across individuals will tend to be U-shaped with the minimum occurring at $x = 1/\rho$, assuming that initial earnings capacity and the rate of post-school investment are uncorrelated. At the minimum point, the variance of earnings is entirely a consequence variance in initial earning capacities due to differences in schooling or ability, but is independent of post-school investment. Evidence for U-shaped patterns of variance in life cycle earnings has been found by Mincer (1974), Hause (1980), and Dooley and Gottschalk (1984) among others.

2.4. *The self-selection problem*

A key assumption underlying the use of a statistical earnings function to estimate the rate of return to schooling is that it accurately represents the opportunity set faced by a typical individual (after controlling for observable exogenous characteristics such as race or sex). If it does, it is capable of answering counterfactual questions of the sort: "What would a given individual's (expected) life cycle earnings path be if he chose s_2 rather than s_1 years of school?"

From its inception, one of the major concerns of the literature on investment in human capital is the possibility that statistical earnings functions do not, in fact, correctly measure individual opportunity sets. For example, a large literature addresses the issue of the extent to which the estimated rate of return to education is upward biased because ability is unobserved and "high ability" individuals, on average, have higher schooling attainment than "low ability" individuals. [See Griliches (1977, 1979) for recent surveys of this literature.] If so, the residual, u, in (1) will be positively correlated with s and the estimated earnings function will be subject to an "ability bias" which overstates the earnings gain a person of given ability would achieve through increased schooling.

The fundamental problems are (a) that it is impossible to observe the life cycle earnings paths of the same individual who has made alternative schooling (or post-school) investments and (b) that it is impossible to observe all the variables (e.g. ability) which determine his earnings opportunities. At best, we observe the earnings path of a given individual who has chosen (or been assigned) a given level of schooling. Hence, any measure of the returns to investment must be based on the comparison of the earnings of different individuals who differ in levels of schooling.

If schooling levels (and post-school investments) were assigned at random for each ability group according to an experimental design, a statistical earnings function estimated from interpersonal differences in earnings, schooling, and experience would provide an unbiased estimate of the opportunity set of a typical individual in that group (i.e. it would provide the best estimate of the difference in life cycle earnings an individual could expect given alternative levels of schooling) because, by design, the error term, u, in (1) would be independent of s and x.

However, the basic behavioral hypothesis of economics is the hypothesis that economic agents select the most preferred alternative from their opportunity set. If the full opportunity set cannot be observed and opportunities vary across agents, then the act of optimal choice implies that market data are systematically censored and there is no guarantee that estimates based on interpersonal differences in earnings and schooling will accurately estimate the opportunity set of any individual in the population.

In the context of the literature on investment in schooling, this has come to be known as the "self-selection problem" [see Rosen (1977a), Willis and Rosen (1979), and Kenny, Lee, Maddala and Trost (1979)]. Clearly, however, the self-selection issue is ubiquitous in economics and will present difficult econometric problems in any situation in which the full opportunity set of each agent is not observed. Since many of the empirical issues, including the question of ability bias, that have arisen in the earnings function literature can be interpreted in terms of the self-selection problem various aspects of it will be discussed in detail as the survey proceeds. Before turning to these issues, it is useful first to describe some of the major empirical findings of this literature as it developed.

2.5. *Empirical internal rate of return studies*

At a gross level, the observed positive correlation between schooling and earnings provides support for (and indeed prompted) the hypothesis that education is an investment which receives a pecuniary return in the labor market [Schultz (1960,

Table 10.1
Estimates of private internal rates of return to successive levels of schooling: United States 1959.

Schooling level	5–7	8	9–11	12	13–15	16	17+
Whites/north	0.218	0.163	0.160	0.071	0.122	0.070	–
Whites/south	0.144	0.182	0.188	0.093	0.110	0.073	–

Source: Hanoch (1967, Table 3).

1961)]. This interpretation was strengthened in early studies of investment in education by Becker (1964), Hanoch (1967), Hansen (1963) and others which made calculations of the internal rate of return to education based on statistical earnings functions like $\varphi(s, x)$ in (1).

In perhaps the most thorough of the early studies, Hanoch (1967) estimated a set of internal rates of return between pairs of schooling level by race (white and non-white) and region (north and south) using cross-sectional data from the 1960 U.S. Census one-in-one thousand sample. His estimates of marginal internal rates of return, $\hat{\rho}(s_1, s_2)$, for whites by region are reproduced in Table 10.1, where s_1 is the indicated level of schooling and s_2 is the next level.

Hanoch's estimates show a clear pattern of decreasing marginal rates of return to schooling. This pattern is also evident in a number of other studies such as Hansen (1963), Becker (1964), and Mincer (1974). If correct, this pattern suggests the possibility that a redistribution of educational investment which reduced educational differentials would be efficient. However, there are a number of caveats to such a conclusion. For instance, low rates of return to graduate study may reflect the existence of substantial fellowships and scholarships which reduce the cost of schooling, but are not included in the estimation procedure. On the other hand, the high estimated rates of return to elementary school may result from ability bias. In addition, it may be noted that Mincer (1974) finds that the rate of return tends to be constant when he controls for weeks worked.

As Hanoch notes, the magnitude of the estimated rates of return in Table 10.1 appear to be similar to estimates of rates of return to physical capital estimated by Stigler (1963), but higher than the real interest rate. In rough fashion, therefore, these estimates tend to support the hypothesis that education is an investment for which individuals require compensation as opposed to the alternative hypothesis that schooling is a consumption activity for which no compensation is required.

The estimates presented in Table 10.1 are similar in magnitude to those obtained by Hansen (1963) using published data from the 1950 Census but somewhat lower than those obtained by Becker (1964) for 1940 and 1950. (Hanoch suggests that this difference may result from the crudity of the data used by Becker and from differences in estimated ages of entry into the labor force.)

Table 10.2
Time series returns to education in the United States.

Year	A. Secondary	B. Higher	C. Higher
1939	18.2	10.7	n.a.
1949	14.2	10.6	n.a.
1959	10.1	11.3	n.a.
1967	n.a.	n.a.	8.2
1968	n.a.	n.a.	8.7
1969	10.7	10.9	9.0
1970	11.3	8.8	9.0
1971	12.5	8.0	9.2
1972	11.3	7.8	8.5
1973	12.0	5.5	8.9
1974	14.8	4.8	8.5
1975	12.8	5.3	8.9
1976	11.0	5.3	8.3
1977	n.a.	n.a.	8.5
1978	n.a.	n.a.	8.5
1979	n.a.	n.a.	7.9
1980	n.a.	n.a.	8.3
1981	n.a.	n.a.	8.7
1982	n.a.	n.a.	10.2

Source: Columns A and B: Psacharopoulos (1981, Table V). Column C: Based on unpublished cross-section regressions using Current Population Survey tapes, 1968–1983, provided to author by Finis Welch. See text for additional description.

In the preface to the second edition of *Human Capital*, Becker (1975) summarizes the evidence on the time-series pattern of the rate of return to investment in education in the United States based on his own work and on the research of others as suggesting that the rate of return tended to fall from 1900 to 1940 and then remained stable through 1970. It is widely believed that the rate of return to higher education fell sharply during the 1970s. This belief is supported by a summary of estimated rates of return to education from 1939–76 presented by Psacharopoulos (1981) which is reproduced in the first two columns of Table 10.2. His summary shows that the rate of return to a secondary education has fluctuated around an average value of about 10–12 percent over the entire period. In contrast, the return to college education was virtually constant from 1939 to 1969 at about 11 percent and then began a sharp fall to about 5 percent during the 1970s.

I have been unable to find more recent rate of return estimates for higher education in published sources. Consequently, I asked Finis Welch to estimate a set of cross-sectional statistical earnings functions using micro data from the March Current Population Surveys from 1968 through 1983 which could be used to calculate rates of return to college education. The results of this exercise, which are presented in the third column of Table 10.2, provide a very different picture of recent trends in the rate of return to education than that given by the estimates summarized by Psacharopoulos.[2] According to the CPS-based estimates, the rate of return to college education stayed within a narrow range of between about 8 and 9 percent during the entire period from 1967 to 1981 and rose to a little over 10 percent in 1982.

It should be emphasized that my rate of return calculations assume that the only cost of college is forgone earnings, that the typical college student spends exactly four years in obtaining his degree, and that the cross-sectional earnings profiles of a synthetic cohort are representative of the expected life cycle earnings path of typical members of the cohort of high school seniors in each year from 1967 to 1982. Each of these assumptions is patently counterfactual and relaxing them may make a difference. For example, Freeman (1977) finds that rising college tuition costs are partly responsible for the decrease in the rate of return to college education that he found during the early 1970s. He also makes an attempt to adjust for variations in expected earnings for true cohorts.

Recently, considerable attention has been given to possible changes in the structure of earnings caused by the dramatic increase in the number of young people entering the labor force as a consequence of the post-World War II baby boom and the rapid growth in the fraction of each cohort receiving college educations [see Freeman (1975, 1976, 1977, 1979), Welch (1979), Berger (1983a, 1983b), and Murphy, Plant and Welch (1983)]. The trends in the size and composition of the labor force are illustrated in Table 10.4 below by a set of average annual growth rates of the labor force by education level since 1920 with projections to 2000. The rapid acceleration of the growth of the total labor force

[2] Professor Welch estimated regressions of log annual earnings on years of schooling and years of imputed experience in which experience is set equal to current age minus 16 for schooling less than 12 grades, age minus 17 for high school graduates, age minus 19 for 13 to 15 years of schooling and age minus 22 for 16 years and over. A variety of specifications of the functional form of this relationship were tried and a "preferred" form was chosen as the basis for the rate of return estimates presented in column C of Table 10.2. The preferred form involves a spline function which assumes that log earnings for any given schooling class grow linearly during the first 10 years of experience and follow a quadratic path thereafter. In addition, the linear spline is interacted with years of schooling to capture variations in early career earnings growth across schooling groups. Welch points out (personal correspondence, 20 December 1984) that the experience spline tracks the early career far better than the smooth quadratic popularized by Mincer. He writes: "Given this, I find it incredible that the profession sticks with the [smooth quadratic] model."

Using the preferred functional form, I calculated the estimated rate of return to a college education as follows. I first used the estimated regression coefficients to simulate life cycle paths of dollar earnings for a representative high school graduate from age 18 to 65 and a representative college graduate from age 22 to 65 and then calculated the rate of discount which brings the present value of the two simulated earnings streams into equality using the internal rate of return function in a spreadsheet program.

I am grateful to Professor Welch for supplying me with these regression estimates, but he should be held blameless for my interpretation of them.

Table 10.3
Average annual rates of growth in civilian labor force, ages 16–64.

Years	Total	By years of schooling			
		11 or less	12	13–15	16 or more
1920–30	1.63	1.18	3.12	3.11	3.21
1930–40	1.44	0.48	4.09	3.87	3.16
1940–50	1.10	−0.24	3.35	3.34	3.71
1950–60	1.16	−1.03	3.77	3.12	4.37
1960–70	1.79	−1.73	3.94	5.07	4.14
1970–80	2.46	−2.72	2.94	5.75	6.44
1980–90	1.60	−3.76	0.80	3.21	5.15
1990–2000	0.96	−6.95	−0.81	2.15	4.05

Source: Dooley and Gottschalk (1984, Table 4).

during 1970–80 is a reflection of the baby boom, while the negative growth rates of those with fewer than 11 years of education and the extremely high growth rates of those with a college education indicate the effects of the dramatic increase in educational attainments in the population during this century.

To date, there appears to be agreement that the changing age-structure has had a significant effect on the structure of earnings, but there is less agreement about the likely persistence of the earnings disadvantage and low returns of those in the large cohorts. For example, Welch (1979) suggests that the major effects on relative earnings take place in the early phase of careers while Berger (1983) argues that this finding is a consequence of Welch's econometric specification and finds evidence of greater persistence of cohort-size effects in his specification. In addition to changes in relative mean earnings, Dooley and Gottschalk (1984) show that there has been a significant increase in the variance of log earnings within schooling groups since 1970. They explain this increase, in part, as the consequence of increased post-school investment in human capital caused by expected increases in the rental rate on human capital resulting from the projected deceleration in labor force growth depicted in Table 10.3.

Rate of return studies have also been conducted in virtually every country in which at least fragmentary data on earnings by age and education exist. Results of many of these studies have been collated by Psacharopoulos (1973, 1981). His most recent summary table is presented in Table 10.4 which presents averages of marginal rate of return estimates for primary, secondary, and higher education from individual country studies. The countries are grouped by degree of economic development and by continent within the LDC category.

Table 10.4 also distinguishes "private" and "social" rates of return. The private rate of return assumes that the only cost of education is forgone earnings (because of public subsidy of direct schooling costs) and that earnings are net of taxes. The social rate of return includes the direct cost of schooling and uses before tax earnings. Psacharopoulos notes that almost all the difference between the social and private rates of return is due to the direct costs of schooling. The reason is that (estimated) taxes tend to be approximately proportional to earnings so that an increase in the tax rate tends to reduce the opportunity cost of schooling and the benefits from schooling by the same proportion, leaving the rate of return unaffected.

It is readily apparent from Table 10.4 that estimated rates of return tend to be negatively related to the degree of economic development. In general, rates of return within the Advanced country category appear to be quite comparable to estimates for the United States. It may be noted that private and social returns diverge most markedly in the LDC and Intermediate categories. For example, in her study of educational wage differentials in Turkey, Krueger (1972) argues that there appears to be an excess of highly educated workers in Turkey relative to those with intermediate level skills. She argues that this is because private incentives to obtain higher education are very strong (the estimated private rate of return is 26 percent) even though the social return appears to be below rates available on financial or physical capital investments (the estimated social rate of return is only 8.5 percent). The apparent divergence between social and private rates of return to higher education in other parts of the developing world which is indicated in Table 10.4 suggests that her argument may be generalizable.[3]

The brief survey of empirical estimates of rates of return to education in this section provides powerful support for the basic human capital hypothesis which regards education as an investment which must be compensated by higher lifetime earnings. Basically, there appears to be remarkable stability in educational wage differentials across time and space, although there are sufficient variations in both dimensions to provide fertile ground for explanation of the underlying determinants and consequences of changes in the supply and demand for human capital. I shall now turn to a rather detailed analysis and reinterpretation of the theoretical underpinnings of empirical human capital earnings functions.

[3]It should be noted that most of the studies of rates of return in the developing countries rely on data on wage and salary workers. Such workers are surely unrepresentative of the labor force as a whole. Chiswick (1976) suggests that estimates based on wage earner data which omit the large and less educated self-employed sector will tend to overstate the rate of return. However, in a study of Iranian data, Henderson (1983) found that earnings functions for wage and salary workers were essentially indistinguishable from those of the self-employed when the latter group excludes the very unskilled in the "informal" sector (e.g. shoe-shine boys, etc.).

Although I have not seen it discussed in my limited perusal of this literature, it seems to me that the measurement of earnings may be a serious problem in estimating rates of return in many LDCs because of the importance of household and non-market production in such societies. [However, see Kuznic and DaVanzo (1982) for an examination of the effects of alternative income measures on the distribution of family income in Malaysia.] It is possible that the rate of return estimates in Table 10.5 are overestimates for this reason since non-market income is likely to be of greater importance in rural areas and among the less educated.

Table 10.4
The returns to education by region and country type.

Region or country type	N	Private			Social		
		Primary	Secondary	Higher	Primary	Secondary	Higher
Africa	(9)	29	22	32	29	17	12
Asia	(8)	32	17	19	16	12	11
Latin America	(5)	24	20	23	44	17	18
LDC average	(22)	29	19	24	27	16	13
Intermediate	(8)	20	17	17	16	14	10
Advanced	(14)	[a]	14	12	[a]	10	9

[a] Not computable because of a lack of a control group of illiterates.
N = number of countries in each group.
Primary = primary educational level.
Secondary = secondary educational level.
Higher = higher educational level.
Source: Psacharopoulos (1981, Table II).

2.6. *The human capital earnings function: Empirical results*

In effect, the early rate of return studies allowed the functional form of the statistical earnings function to be dictated by the data. For example, many studies simply used tabulations of earnings by schooling by age or, when micro data was used [as in Hanoch (1967)], the regression specification was simply dictated by the best fit to the data.

A major development in the literature, initiated by Becker and Chiswick (1966) and carried to full fruition by Mincer (1974), sought to use the theory to restrict the functional form of the earnings function and thereby enhance the empirical content of the theory. This line of research attempts to integrate the theories of investment in education and on-the-job training pioneered by Becker (1964) and Mincer (1958, 1962) within an empirical framework which is compatible with more formal models of human capital accumulation such as the Ben-Porath 1967) model. This work was carried out with such ingenuity, sophistication and care by Mincer (1974), that the resulting function is often referred to as "the" human capital earnings function.

The standard human capital earnings function developed by Mincer (1974) is of the form:

$$\ln y = \beta_0 + \beta_1 s + \beta_2 x + \beta_3 x^2 + u. \tag{12}$$

Using (7), it follows that the schooling coefficient, β_1, provides an estimate of the rate of return to education which is assumed to be constant in this specification. The concavity of the observed earnings profile is captured by the quadratic experience terms, x and x^2, whose coefficients, β_2 and β_3, are respectively positive and negative. Since early data sources such as Census data did not record a worker's actual labor force experience, a transformation of the worker's age was used as a proxy for his experience. Mincer uses the transformation $x = a - s - 6$, which assumes that a worker begins full-time work immediately after completing his education and that the age of school completion is $s + 6$.

Mincer's justification for the earnings function in (12) represents a blend of theory and pragmatism. On the theoretical side, he assumes that the skills acquired by the worker through education and on-the-job training can be regarded as a stock of homogeneous human capital which influences the worker's productivity by the same amount in all lines of work for all employers. Following Becker's (1964) important distinction between firm-specific and general training, this implies that competition will force the worker (rather than the firm) to pay the costs of his training and will allow the worker (rather than the firm) to reap the returns from his accumulated investment.

The reason is that if the firm attempted to capture some of the returns from training investments, the worker could always move to another firm at a wage which reflects the full value of the human capital embodied in him. Thus, if the firm is to provide training, it will implicitly charge the worker by reducing his wages below his marginal product by the cost of training. Workers are willing to pay this implicit price because of the increase in their future earnings resulting from their increased productivity. It follows that the observed earnings of a worker at a given level of experience may be regarded as equal to the rental rate on his accumulated stock of physical capital minus the cost of his current investment.

Beginning with Ben-Porath (1967), a number of economists have attempted to characterize the life cycle earnings path that would follow from an optimal program of investment in education and on-the-job training. (See Chapter 11 by Weiss, in this Handbook, for a survey of this work.) These models commonly assume that the worker attempts to maximize the present discounted value of lifetime earnings net of the direct costs of investment. Maximization takes place subject to constraints imposed by a "human capital production function" which represents the worker's ability to transform inputs of his own time and purchased goods (e.g. tuition, time of supervisor) into outputs of human capital and by his time budget which requires him to allocate his time between "learning" and "earning".

These models have been quite successful in providing a rigorous foundation for the existence of life cycle earnings profiles which share some of the qualitative features of the Mincer earnings function in (12). Specifically, they suggest that a worker will tend to specialize in investment in the early portion of his life when his stock of human capital is low. This rationalizes specialization in education at the beginning of life. At some point, it pays the worker to combine earning with learning and he enters the labor force. Initially, the worker tends to invest at a fairly high rate so that the level of his observed earnings are low. However, as time passes, his earnings will tend to grow rapidly both because of the rate of accumulation of the stock of human capital and because the optimal level of investment decreases. Eventually, the decrease in the rate of investment combined with depreciation on the existing stock of capital may result in a cessation of earnings growth. At this point, earnings reach a maximum and they tend to decrease until the age of retirement.

Unfortunately, the optimal human capital models are very difficult to implement rigorously in empirical work. First, they typically do not have a closed form solution so that the precise functional form for life cycle earnings implied by such a model is usually not known. The Mincer earnings function in (12) may be regarded as an approximation to this unknown functional form. Second, many of the concepts underlying the model, including the concept of human capital itself, are unobservable (or, at least, not usually measured in available data). In addition to human capital, the list of unobservables includes the rental rate on human capital, the rate of discount, the functional form of the human capital production function, the inputs of time and purchased goods used in investment, and the individual-specific parameters of the production function which may be interpreted as representing the interaction of individual's "learning ability" with the home, school, and work environments where learning takes place.

The earnings function in (12) represents a pragmatic method of incorporating some of the major implications of the optimal human capital models into a simple econometric framework which can be applied to the limited information available in Census-type data. Early in his book, Mincer states his key assumption. Specifically, he says that "For simplicity the rate of return is often treated as a parameter for the individual. This amounts to assuming that a change in an individual's investment does not change his marginal (hence, average, rate of return)" [Mincer (1974, p. 7)].

He then uses this assumption in combination with an assumption about the time path of investment over the individual's life cycle to derive the earnings function in (12). In particular, assume that an individual begins with a stock of human capital of $E(0)$ at the age of school entry, $t=0$. Also assume that, at time t, he devotes a fraction, $k(t)$, of his earning capacity to investment in human capital and $1-k(t)$ to earning, and that ρ is the individual-specific rate of return. Given these assumptions, the instantaneous growth rate of his earnings capacity at time t is

$$g(t)=\rho k(t). \tag{13}$$

Thus, at time t his earning capacity is

$$E(t)=E(0)\exp\left\{\int_0^t g(\tau)\,\mathrm{d}\tau\right\} \tag{14}$$

and his actual earnings (i.e. earnings capacity minus current value of investment) is

$$y(t)=(1-k(\tau))E(\tau). \tag{15}$$

Schooling is regarded as an activity in which the individual devotes full time to investment (i.e. $k(t)=1$ for ages 6 through $6+s$). From (15), it follows that earnings capacity upon school leaving is

$$E(s)=E(0)\mathrm{e}^{\rho s}. \tag{16}$$

If no further investment took place after leaving school (i.e. $k(t)=0$ for $t>s$), the individual's life cycle earnings profile would be horizontal at a value of $y(s)=E(s)$. Taking the logarithm of both sides of (16), this implies that the schooling–earnings relationship is of the log-linear form:

$$\ln y=\ln E(0)+\rho s. \tag{17}$$

Theories of optimal human capital accumulation suggest that workers will continue to invest in on-the-job training after leaving school, but that amount of investment will tend to decline over time. The parabolic earnings function in (12) corresponds (approximately) to the assumption that the fraction of earnings capacity which is invested declines linearly during working life from an initial value of $k(0)$ at the beginning of the work career to a value of zero at the end of the career.[4] Thus, let $k(x)=k(0)-(k(0)/n)x$, where n is the length of working life. In this case, earnings capacity is

$$\begin{aligned}E(x)&=E(s)\exp\left\{\rho\int_0^x[k(0)-(k(0)/n)t]\,\mathrm{d}t\right\}\\&=E(s)\exp\{\rho k(0)x-(\rho k(0)/2n)x^2\}.\end{aligned} \tag{18}$$

Actual earnings net of investment cost are $y(x)=(1-k(x))E(x)$. Thus, (17) and (18) imply that

$$\ln y=\ln E(0)+\rho s+\rho k(0)x-(\rho k(0)/2n)x^2+\ln(1-k(x)). \tag{19}$$

Mincer treats the earnings function in (12) as an approximation to (19).

Estimates by Mincer (1974) of three alternative specifications of human capital earnings functions are presented in Table 10.5 based on data on white, non-farm men from the 1960 Census. Line 1 shows an estimate of the "schooling model" in

[4] Mincer (1974) suggests several other possible assumptions about the time path of post-school investment which lead to somewhat different functional forms for the shape of the life cycle earnings profile. However, the quadratic function in (12) has proved by far to be the most popular in part because it is the simplest to estimate and in part because alternative functional forms do not appear to be superior on statistical grounds. For example, Heckman and Polachek (1974), using a Box–Cox test find that log earnings is the preferred dependent variable. Also, it may be noted that Heckman (1976) was unable to reject an earnings function of the form in (12) against the alternative hypothesis that earnings were generated by the Ben-Porath (1967) model.

Table 10.5
Estimates of human capital earnings functions.

Equation forms	R^2
1. $\ln y = 7.58 + 0.070s$ (43.8)	0.067
2. $\ln y = 6.20 + 0.107s + 0.081x - 0.0012x^2$ (72.3) (75.5) (−55.8)	0.285
3. $\ln y = 4.87 + 0.255s - 0.0029s^2 - 0.0043xs + 0.148x - 0.0018x^2$ (23.4) (−7.1) (−31.8) (63.7) (−66.2)	0.309

y = annual earnings of white, non-farm males, 1959.
s = years of school completed.
x = years of experience measured by age-schooling-six.
t-ratios in parentheses.

Source: Mincer (1974, Table 5.1).

(17) which assumes no post-school investment. The estimated rate of return to schooling, given by the schooling coefficient, is 7 percent and the equation explains only 6.7 percent of variance in log earnings.

Omitting experience from the earnings function results in a downward bias in the schooling coefficient because schooling and experience tend to be negatively correlated due to the fact that at any given age those with more schooling of necessity have less experience. The extent of this bias is illustrated in line 2 which presents an estimate of the quadratic earnings function in (12). In this specification, the estimated rate of return rises to 10.7 percent and the coefficients of experience and experience squared imply that earnings growth is 8.1 percent at the beginning of working life and decreases continuously until it reaches zero after about 34 years of experience and becomes negative thereafter until retirement.[5] The addition of the experience terms also markedly increases the explanatory power of the regression, raising R^2 to 28.5 percent.

The earnings function in (19) assumes that all workers have the same own rate of return to investment and that they all invest the same fraction of their earnings

[5]It should be noted that the actual earnings growth of members of a given cohort of new entrants into the labor force will tend to be more rapid than the growth measured in the "synthetic" cohort of individuals from a given cross section if there is a positive trend of real wages in the economy. Sometimes, a constant growth rate of real wages is assumed in order to adjust for this bias [e.g. Ghez and Becker (1974)]. For example, if real wages are assumed to grow at 2 percent per year, the corresponding earnings function for a given cohort could be obtained by adding 2 percent to the coefficient of x in line 2 of Table 10.6. In this case, the earnings growth rate would be initially 10.2 percent and it would not fall to zero until after 42 years of experience. Note that the estimated rate of return to schooling is not affected by such an adjustment if it is assumed that the rate of wage growth is the same for all schooling groups.

The reduction in the rate of productivity change in the U.S. economy beginning in the 1970s together with evidence of changes in the wage structure by age and education discussed earlier suggest that cross-sectional data in more recent periods may be quite misleading indicators of the earnings functions faced by cohorts of current workers.

capacity at each level of experience (i.e. ρ and $k(x)$ are both constant across workers). If workers differ in these characteristics, the estimated rate of return to schooling and the growth rate of earnings may vary across schooling classes. This possibility is explored in line 3 of Table 10.5 where schooling squared and the interaction term, schooling times experience, are added to the regression. The results indicate that the marginal rate of return to schooling is decreasing. Evaluating the derivative of log earnings with respect to education at 8 years of experience yields estimates of the marginal rates as 17.4 percent at 8 years of schooling, 15.1 percent at 12 years, and 12.8 percent at 16 years. Recall that this pattern of decreasing marginal returns is similar to that found in the rate of return studies discussed in the previous section. The negative interaction term indicates some tendency for percentage earnings differentials by schooling class to converge as experience increases. However, Mincer reports that both the non-linearity in schooling and the interaction term become insignificant when a variable controlling for weeks worked is added to the regression.[6]

Earnings functions like those reported in Table 10.5, especially the form in (12) and line 2, have been estimated hundreds of times using both cross-sectional and longitudinal data sources from many countries. Almost all the earnings function estimates that I have seen indicate a concave log earnings–experience profile qualitatively similar to that implied by the earnings function in line 2 of Table 10.5. Psacharopoulous (1981) surveys estimates of the rate of return based on the schooling coefficient in earnings function regression with the following results. The average of the estimated (private) rates of return were 14.4 percent in the LDCs, 9.7 percent in the Intermediate countries, and 7.7 percent in the Advanced countries. It may be noted that these estimates are somewhat lower than the corresponding estimates obtained from direct calculation of internal rates of return which are given in Table 10.4. I am unable to provide an explanation for this.

[6]More recently, a number of economists have tended to use weekly wages (i.e. annual earnings divided by weeks worked) in place of annual earnings as the dependent variable in earnings functions [e.g. Welch (1979)]. Given the failure of most human capital models to incorporate labor supply, unemployment, or retirement as endogenous variables, the choice between these variables is somewhat arbitrary.

The argument in favor of the weekly wage is presumably that it is a better measure of the effect of schooling or experience on earnings potential and, implicitly, that earnings potential is what people seek through their investment in human capital. Heckman (1976) provides a human capital model with endogenous labor supply in which such an approach is justified formally by the assumption that human capital has the same percentage effect on both market (i.e. earning) and non-market efficiency. On the other hand, several writers have argued that the payoff to investment in (market-oriented) human capital depends on the degree to which the capital will be utilized in market activities. This argument is often made in connection with explaining male–female differences in investment incentives and market earnings [see Mincer and Polachek (1974), Barzel and Yu (1984), Becker (1985), and Rosen (1983)] but could also apply to the extent that schooling and experience influence the risks of unemployment, etc. In this case, it may be argued that annual earnings provide a better measure of the return to investment in human capital.

The emergence of longitudinal data sets has allowed economists to investigate the evolution of the life cycle earnings of individuals. In one such study, Lillard and Willis (1978) attempted to determine the extent to which cross-sectional earnings differentials persist over time. They used data from the first seven years of the Panel Study of Income Dynamics (1967–73) to estimate a standard earnings function of the form in (12) in which the residual term is assumed to be composed of a person-specific "permanent" component and a serially correlated "transitory" component. If no explanatory variables other than year dummies are included they found that about 73 percent of the total variance in log earnings is due to the permanent component and that the transitory component displays a serial correlation of about 0.4. When schooling, experience, and experience squared are added to the regression, these variables explain 33 percent of the total variance in log earnings and 44 percent of the permanent component. Their estimates suggest that most of the cross-sectional variation in earnings across individuals is persistent and that a little over half of this variance is due to "unmeasured" factors which are not captured by observed schooling and experience differentials.

Longitudinal data has also permitted a closer examination of the trade-off between earnings growth and the initial level of earnings due to differential rates of investment in on-the-job training (OJT) which are predicted by Mincer's overtaking concept which was discussed earlier. In terms of the model presented in this section, the argument is that increases in the fraction of earning capacity invested in OJT (i.e. variations in the parameter, $k(0)$) will lead to lower initial earnings and higher earnings growth. The level of earnings of individuals who differ in $k(0)$ but are otherwise alike (i.e. have identical values of ρ and $E(s)$) will tend to be equal at the overtaking level of about 8–10 years of experience. At lower experience levels, there will be a negative correlation between earnings level and the growth rate of earnings and at higher levels the correlation will be positive.

In cross-section data, this prediction can be studied only by looking at the pattern of the residual variance of log earnings with respect to experience to see if it is U-shaped and reaches a minimum near the overtaking level. (It should also be recalled that a positive correlation between initial earnings capacity, $E(s)$, and the rate of OJT investment implies that minimum variance will occur at a higher experience level and conversely for a negative correlation.) Mincer (1974) found a U-shaped pattern for individuals with 12 years of schooling but also found that the pattern was declining for those with 8 years and positive for those with 12 years of schooling. However, Dooley and Gottschalk (1984) find a U-shaped pattern for all schooling groups (with the exception of log weekly wages for college graduates) using within-cohort data from successive CPS cross-sections. Their estimates imply that minimum variance of log annual earnings tends to occur at about 23 years of experience and that the minimum for log weekly wages occurs at about 13.5 years of experience. These estimates are consistent with a weak positive correlation between initial earnings capacity and the subsequent intensity of OJT investment. The difference between the results for annual and weekly earnings is probably due to the contribution to earnings variance of relatively high levels of job turnover and other transitory shocks during the early stages of the career.

In principle, the OJT hypothesis can be examined more precisely in longitudinal data because permanent components of variance can "control" for unmeasured differences in the levels of earnings across individuals, thereby removing the correlation between initial levels and subsequent growth that confound cross-sectional estimates of overtaking. Hause (1980) exploits this aspect of longitudinal data with a small sample of Swedish white-collar workers during the early career stage and obtains results showing a substantial negative correlation between earnings levels and growth. His results indicate a (lower bound) minimum of the variance of log earnings occurs at a little over 5 years of experience and his results also suggest that variance of transitory shocks to earnings tend to be greatest in the initial years of working life and that the variance of these shocks diminish fairly rapidly. While Hause's estimates do not directly confirm the importance of OJT, they are certainly consistent with the hypothesis and no attractive alternative hypothesis has been proposed to explain such patterns of residual variance. In a somewhat similar model, Chamberlain (1978) also finds strong evidence for the OJT hypothesis using American data.

This brief survey of some of the empirical research based on human capital earnings functions has only skimmed the surface of a massive literature which utilizes this tool to study a wide variety of subjects which space constraints prevent me from describing in detail. Among these, to give a few examples, are studies of the black–white earnings differentials [e.g. Smith and Welch (1979)]; earnings differentials among other ethnic groups [e.g. Chiswick (1983a, 1983b)]; earnings of immigrants to the United States [e.g. Chiswick (1977, 1978, 1979)]; language as a form of human capital [e.g. McManus, Gould and Welch (1983)]; effects of school quality [e.g. Solmon (1975)]; evaluation of manpower training programs [e.g. Ashenfelter (1978)] and many other subjects. Another major area of research concerning the effect of ability differentials on earnings will be treated more extensively later in this chapter.

3. Homogeneous human capital models

3.1. Background

As a statistical model, the human capital earnings function developed by Mincer has provided the basis for a vast body of empirical research on the level and distribution of life cycle earnings and the returns to education. This body of work reveals some striking empirical regularities concerning the structure of wage differentials which hold over periods of time and across societies which differ dramatically in technology, patterns of demand, and forms of social and economic organization. In my view, this body of work constitutes one of the major success stories of modern labor economics.

At the same time the pragmatic character of Mincer's translation of human capital theory into an operational empirical tool has certain important drawbacks. From the point of view of individual behavior, the key assumption of human capital theory is the proposition that individuals choose to invest so as to maximize the present value of lifetime earnings. [Indeed, Rosen (1976a) argues that the entire *economic* content of human capital theory is contained in this hypothesis.][7] Mincer's derivation of the human capital earnings function which was described in the preceding section is ostensibly based on this assumption. In fact, however, both the level of schooling and the time path of post-school investment are treated as exogenous.

Moreover, as noted above, Mincer treats the rate of return to human capital (i.e. ρ) along with initial earnings capacity [i.e. $E(0)$] and the fraction of capacity invested [i.e. $k(0)$] as unobservable individual-specific constants which may vary across individuals because of differences in ability, discrimination, etc.[8] In effect, the resulting model provides an accounting scheme in which the distribution of observed earnings is related through an earnings function to the joint distribution of the observed variables, schooling and age, and the unobserved individual-specific parameters.

In this section I will describe some of the empirical and econometric difficulties that arise when individual optimization is taken into account. In order to keep the discussion simple, I will ignore post-school investment and concentrate on the schooling decision. Thus, throughout this section I assume that a given worker i with s years of schooling has constant productivity and earns a constant labor income, $y_i(s)$, from his entry into the labor force at age $s+6$ to his retirement at age $s+n+6$. Following Becker and Chiswick (1966) and Mincer (1974), this simplified model is called the "schooling model".

The argument in this section may be summarized briefly as follows. Following Rosen (1976a), I show that the wealth maximization hypothesis is inconsistent with a simple log-linear schooling–earnings relationship of the form used in Mincer's work. Then, using Rosen's adaptation of Becker's well-known

[7]Of course, the economic content of human capital theory also includes the role of human capital in production and the consequences of market equilibrium of the supply and demand for human capital.

[8]Actually, Mincer also allows the individual's rate of return parameter on schooling investments to differ from the corresponding parameter on post-school investments and also introduces another unobserved individual-specific parameter to capture depreciation or obsolecence of the accumulated human capital stock.

Woytinsky Lecture model [Becker (1967, 1975)], I show how optimal investment in schooling varies with individual "ability" and "opportunity". The term "opportunity" refers to the terms on which an individual can finance investments in human capital and the term "ability" refers to his capacity to translate investments into higher productivity. This model is shown to lead to very difficult econometric problems due to self-selection. At the end of the section, I argue that many of these difficulties can be traced to the use of the "simplifying" assumption of "homogeneous" human capital.

3.2. *Mincer's schooling model*

At the beginning of his book, Mincer (1974) proposes what amounts to two very different approaches to the derivation of a human capital earnings function. One approach, which was described in the preceding section, treats the rate of return to schooling as an individual-specific parameter. In effect, this suggests that individuals have "human capital production functions" of the log-linear form:

$$\ln y_i = \ln y_{0i} + \rho_i s_i, \tag{20}$$

where y_{0i} and ρ_i are viewed as individual-specific "ability parameters" of the ith individual. [See also (17) above.] The parameter y_{0i} may be regarded as the individual's basic earning capacity and the parameter ρ_i as his "learning ability" (i.e. his capacity to increase his labor productivity through additional schooling). Note that ρ_i also measures the ith individual's (constant) internal rate of return to investment in schooling.

If schooling is treated as exogenously determined and the model is estimated with the regression equation

$$\ln y_i = \beta_0 + \beta_1 s + u_i, \tag{21}$$

the coefficients β_0 and β_1, respectively, provide estimates of the average level of initial earnings capacity and the average value of the rate of return parameter in the population. That is, $\beta_0 = E(\ln y_i)$ and $\beta_1 = E(\rho_i)$. The residual term, u_i, is

$$u_i = (\ln y_{0i} - \ln \bar{y}_0) + (\rho_i - \bar{\rho}) s_i + \eta_i, \tag{22}$$

where $E(\ln y_{0i}) = \ln \bar{y}_0$ and $E(\rho) = \bar{\rho}$ and η_i captures the effects of measurement error and transitory income components. Note that u_i is heteroskedastic because its variance is an increasing function of schooling.

The schooling model in (21) as derived from (20) appears to be consistent with the approach used by Mincer (1974) in most of his book. However, at the beginning of the book (pp. 9–11), he proceeds to derive a log-linear earnings function in a completely different way. His derivation is as follows. Let s and $s+d$ be two levels of schooling which differ by d years and let $y(s)$ and $y(s+d)$ be two constant earning streams which are equal in present value when discounted at the market interest rate, r. From (2) it is easy to calculate that the respective present values of the two income streams are $V(s)=\alpha \mathrm{e}^{-rs}/r$ and $V(s+d)=\alpha \mathrm{e}^{-r(s+d)}/r$, where $\alpha=(1-\mathrm{e}^{-rn})$ is a correction for finite working life.

Equating these present values and rearranging, the result is

$$y = y_0 \mathrm{e}^{rs}, \tag{23}$$

where $y_0 = rV(s)$. Note that y_0 may be interpreted as the permanent labor income of a worker (adjusted for finite life) whose human wealth is $V(s)$. Taking the logarithm of both sides of (23), Mincer's "schooling function" is

$$\ln y = \ln y_0 + rs. \tag{24}$$

Clearly, the log-linear earnings functions in (20) and (24) are conceptually distinct. The function in (20) represents a hypothesis about the technology of human capital production, while (24) is simply a tautology which follows from the definition of present value. Moreover, it is also clear that the hypothesized technology in (20) is inconsistent with the hypothesis that individuals facing a given market interest rate, r, choose that level of schooling which maximizes the present value of their lifetime earnings. The problem, as Rosen (1976a) points out, is one of corner solutions. That is, given a constant internal rate of return, ρ_i, a wealth-maximizing individual will either choose zero schooling if $\rho_i < r$ or he will have an unlimited demand for schooling if $\rho_i > r$.

The corner solution problem is circumvented if it is assumed that each individual faces rising borrowing costs as he increases his investment in education. In this case, each individual invests to the point at which his marginal borrowing rate is equal to ρ_i. If all individuals faced the same schedule of borrowing rates, there would be a positive correlation between ρ_i and the level of education chosen. This possibility appears to be contradicted by the data since, if anything, the estimated marginal rate of return to education (at least in advanced countries) appears to be a decreasing function of the level of schooling as can be seen from the rate of return estimates in Tables 10.1 and 10.5 above.

3.3. *Rosen's schooling model*

In a section of his paper titled, "Education and Self-Selection", Rosen (1976a) proposes a simple reinterpretation of the schooling model which meets these theoretical objections. In effect, this model may be regarded as a simplified version of the Becker (1967, 1975) Woytinsky Lecture model or of a Ben-Porath (1967)-type model of optimal accumulation of homogeneous human capital under the conditions that post-school investment is ruled out, that the only cost of schooling is forgone earnings, and that each individual faces a constant interest rate.[9]

Let the human capital production function or "structural earnings function" for person i be

$$\ln y_i = h(s; A_i), \tag{25}$$

where A_i is a vector of exogenous variables which measure i's economic ability. For now, assume that A_i is a scalar and that higher values of A indicate higher ability (i.e. $h_A > 0$). Using (7), note that

$$\rho(s; A_i) = h_s(s; A_i) \tag{26}$$

is the marginal internal rate of return to investment in schooling. In order to have an interior solution to the problem of optimal schooling choice, assume that the marginal rate of return to schooling is decreasing (i.e. assume $h_{ss} < 0$ or, equivalently, that $\rho_s < 0$).

Following Becker (1967, 1975), assume that opportunities for financing their investments in education vary across individuals because, for example, of differential willingness or capacity of their families to support them or because of differential holdings of non-human wealth to serve as collateral for borrowing against future earning power. To stay within the wealth maximization framework, assume that person i faces a constant rate of interest,

$$r_i = r(Z_i), \tag{27}$$

at which he can borrow or lend where Z_i is a vector of exogenous variables such as family background and non-human wealth which influence his financing

[9]In his Woytinksky Lecture, Becker (1967, 1975) makes the intuitively appealing assumption that each person faces a rising supply curve of finance for educational investment. For example, some support an individual receives from his family may come in the form of a pure transfer with no opportunity cost to him, some may come in the form of loans at "low interest rates" and, if he wishes to pursue his education still further, he may have to borrow at high interest rates in the market.

It should be noted that he commits an analytical slip in his discussion by assuming wealth maximization as the individual's objective and he does not consider role of time preference. If the borrowing rate is not constant, the optimal investment problem becomes more complicated because the individual cares about the timing of the entire earnings stream, not just its present value. That is to say, it is no longer possible to appeal to the Fisher separation theorem to justify wealth-maximization as the first step in a two stage utility optimization problem in which the second stage is to choose the optimal consumption path subject to a wealth constraint. Among other things, when an individual faces a rising marginal cost of finance, subjective time preference plays a role in the investment decision. Thus, an individual with a high rate of time preference will choose less investment than another person of identical ability who faces the same financing conditions but has a lower rate of time preference. (See Chapter 11 by Weiss in this Handbook for more details.)

opportunities. For now, assume that Z_i is a scalar and that increases in Z are associated with improved (borrowing) opportunities so that $r' < 0$.

Person i's optimal schooling choice is given by the problem

$$\max V(s) = a e^{-rs} y(s)/r$$
$$\text{s.t.}$$
$$y(s) = \exp\{h(s; A_i)\}. \tag{28}$$

The first-order condition for this problem implies that the individual should continue schooling until the marginal rate of return is equal to the interest rate. That is to say, using (25) and (26), the first-order condition may be written as

$$\rho(s; A_i) = r_i = r(Z_i). \tag{29}$$

The optimal schooling choice is obtained by inverting (29) to solve for s so that

$$s = \rho^{-1}(A_i, r(Z_i)) = s(A_i, Z_i). \tag{30}$$

The individual's optimal earnings are then determined by substituting (30) back into the human capital production function in (25) to obtain:

$$\ln y = h(s(A_i, Z_i); A_i) = y(A_i, Z_i). \tag{31}$$

To aid in the discussion of this model, it is illustrated diagrammatically in Figure 10.2 for a low ability person (person 1) and a high ability person (person 2). The concave line labelled $h(s; A_1)$ is 1's human capital production function (i.e. his structural earnings function) and the concave line labelled $h(s; A_2)$ is 2's production function.

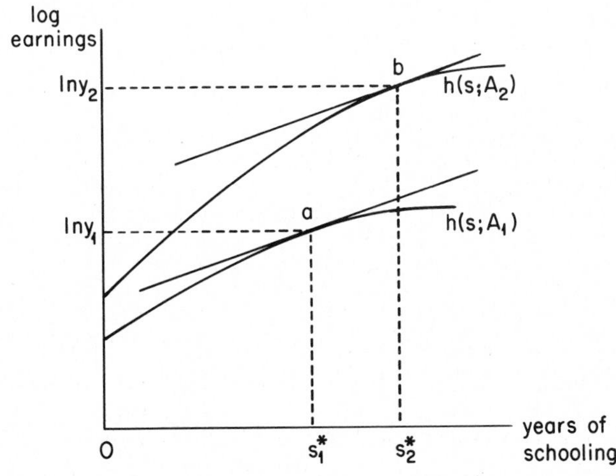

Figure 10.2. Optimal schooling choice: equal opportunity and unequal ability.

As Rosen (1977a) points out, the tautological version of Mincer's schooling function in (24) may be regarded as defining a set of iso-wealth curves in $(\ln y, s)$ space. Each curve has a slope of r_i and an intercept, $\ln y_{0i} = \ln[r_i V(s)(1 - e^{-r_i n})]$, given by an arbitrary level of the present value of lifetime earnings evaluated at the age of school entry, $V(s)$. In Figure 10.2, it is assumed that there is equality of opportunity. That is, persons 1 and 2 are assumed to face the same interest rates. Therefore both share the same family of iso-wealth curves which are given by the positively sloped straight lines.

Maximum lifetime wealth is attained at the point of tangency of each person's production function and his iso-wealth curve at points a and b for person's 1 and 2, respectively. As drawn, the high ability person chooses a higher level of schooling and has higher earnings than the low ability person. He also has a higher level of human wealth. Note that equality of opportunity implies that the allocation of educational investment is efficient because it results in equalization of marginal rates of return across individuals.

Several points can be made about the empirical implications of this model and the econometric difficulties it presents. First, the situation depicted in Figure 10.2 illustrates the problem of ability bias caused by self-selection. Clearly, an estimated rate of return from data on schooling and earnings, given by the slope of a straight line connecting points a and b, would be an overestimate of the marginal rate of return faced by either person. (Both have marginal rates equal to the common rate of interest.) In addition, the overall shape of a statistical earnings function estimated from such data would not resemble the structural earnings function of either person. Rather, the shape of the statistical earnings function, $\ln y = \ln \varphi(s) + u$, would be heavily influenced by the shape of the distribution of ability in the population.

Another point is that under conditions of equality of opportunity and ability (i.e. all persons have equal values of A and Z) optimal schooling choices and the level of earnings would be the same for everyone. Thus, data from such a population would be incapable of identifying either the structural human capital earnings function or the rate of interest.

Moreover, if ability differences are to generate variation in schooling choice, they must influence the marginal rate of return to investment. That is, suppose that increased ability has "neutral" effect in that it has an equal percentage effect on earnings potential at each schooling level [i.e. suppose that the form of the structural earnings function is $\ln y_i = A_i + h(s)$]. In this case, optimal schooling choices would be identical for all ability groups because all individuals have identical marginal rate of return functions [i.e. $\rho(s; A_i) = \rho(s)$]. Conversely, the self-selection of high ability individuals to higher levels of schooling depicted in Figure 10.2 arises because it is assumed that an increase in A has a higher percentage effect on the productivity of an individual, the more schooling he acquires ($\rho_{sA} > 0$).

From an econometric point of view, life would be easiest in the case of equality of ability and inequality of opportunity. In this case, all individuals would share identical structural earnings functions but would make different schooling choices and have different levels of earnings because they face different interest rates. For example, if all individuals have ability A_1, it is clear from Figure 10.2 that variation in the rate of interest will "trace out" the structural earnings function, $\ln y = h(s; A_1)$. In this special case, provided a suitable functional form for $h(\cdot)$ is chosen, a non-linear regression of $\ln y$ on s would suffice to identify the structural earnings function. Life would be almost as easy if ability has a neutral effect as defined above. In this case, unobserved ability differences would simply generate random residuals about the estimated earnings function of a person of average ability.

It is worth noting that this example illustrates a point made earlier concerning the fact that optimizing economic behavior tends to censor the observations an econometrician needs to identify structural economic relations. The function, $h(s; A_1)$, is identified because it is assumed that there is an "imperfection" in the capital market which prevents equalization of marginal rates of return to investment in education across workers. Thus, it is only the misallocation of resources resulting from an assumed market imperfection which permits identification. If there were perfect capital markets, we would be back to the case of no variation in s if abilities are identical or to the problem of ability bias due to self-selection if abilities are not equal.

It should be clear from this discussion that the econometric problems presented by this highly simplified model are severe. They would become still more difficult if the model is generalized to allow for post-school investment, non-constant interest rates, uncertainty, and other factors that may be important in explaining real world data. These problems are especially severe because, in practice, data on ability and on the financing opportunities available to individuals are not available. At best, some data sets contain proxies for ability in the form of IQ scores, scores on visual acuity tests, etc. and information on family income and other background variables which might proxy borrowing rates.

In the following section I argue that much of this difficulty can be traced to assumption of homogeneous human capital which is employed as a "simplification" by Becker, Mincer, and many (but not all) of the economists who have done theoretical and empirical work in human capital. In effect, the assumption of homogeneous human capital regards workers as bringing to the labor market a number of homogeneous "efficiency" units of labor which is proportional to their stock of accumulated human capital. Thus, all workers are perfect substitutes in production at ratios proportional to their endowment of efficiency units. Equivalently, the efficiency unit view assumes that a given investment in human capital increases an individual's physical productivity in all production activities by the same amount.

While this assumption is patently counterfactual, it is usually justified as a fairly innocuous simplification which enables the analyst to abstract from the details of occupational skills in order to focus on the major forces determining the distribution of earnings by schooling and age [see, for example, Becker (1975, p. 97)]. However, as I emphasized at the outset of this paper, human capital theory encompasses optimization on both sides of the market and assumes equilibration of the supply and demand for labor. If all types of labor are perfect substitutes, the demand for efficiency units of labor is perfectly elastic so that the relative wages of workers who differ in human capital stocks are fixed by technology. In order to generate variation in the amount of investment across workers, it is necessary to emphasize interpersonal differences in ability and opportunity which cause variation in the supply of human capital. This, in turn, leads to the self-selection issues discussed above.

An alternative which I explore in the following section is to drop the assumption of homogeneous human capital. The major features of Mincer's empirical analysis of human capital earnings functions emerge in an important special case of this model. Specifically, under conditions of "equality of opportunity" and "equality of comparative advantage" (a generalization of equality of ability), the simple log-linear earnings–schooling relation, the overtaking notion, and the U-shaped experience profile of residuals from the earnings function are generated by the model.

4. A model of heterogeneous human capital

4.1. *The general model*

In contrast to the homogeneous human capital model discussed above, assume that there are many types of human capital, each of which is specialized to a particular set of tasks. For convenience, I shall refer to each distinct set of tasks as an "occupation."

Initially, assume that each occupation has a rigid educational qualification in terms of the duration and curricular content of the training required to practice the occupation. For example, suppose that some occupations such as janitors and ditch diggers require no formal education. Others such as plumbers and clericals require twelve years of school, but the training received by a plumber does not qualify him as a clerical and conversely. Similarly, accountants require college degrees but are unqualified for other occupations such as chemical engineering or computer salesman which also require college degrees. For simplicity, I continue to assume that there is no process of physical or mental maturation over the life cycle and no post-school training, depreciation, or obsolescence of skills so that each person's productivity in his chosen occupation remains constant over his working life. Also, I continue to assume that there are no direct costs of schooling.

Formally, let there be $m+1$ distinct schooling–occupation categories indexed from lowest to highest training requirements by $j = 0, 1, \ldots, m$, where $s_0 = 0$ and $s_0 \leq s_1 \leq \ldots \leq s_m$ are the minimum years of schooling needed to train for each occupation. For simplicity, assume that any schooling above the minimum requirement is unproductive. In general, workers vary in their occupational abilities (i.e. in their capacity to be trained for a given occupation). Let the vector

$$l_i = (l_{0i}, \ldots, l_{mi}) \tag{32}$$

be the ability endowment of the ith worker where l_{ij} is the number of efficiency units of labor (i.e. piece rate productivity) supplied by worker i in occupation j, given that he has the requisite s_j years of schooling of the appropriate type.

The worker's opportunity set is given by a vector of potential earnings in each occupation,

$$\begin{aligned} y_i &= (y_{i0}, \ldots, y_{im}) \\ &= (w_0 l_{i0}, \ldots, w_m l_{im}), \end{aligned} \tag{33}$$

where the vector

$$w = (w_0, \ldots, w_m) \tag{34}$$

is a set of market-determined relative occupational "piece rates" or "skill prices". For example, suppose that l_{0i} measures the cubic feet of dirt worker i can dig per year if he received no education and that l_{mi} measures the number of heart transplants per year that he could perform if he became a heart surgeon, where the market piece rate is one dollar per cubic foot of dirt and w_m per heart transplant. Then he could earn $y_{0i} = l_{0i}$ per year for n years beginning at age 6 or he could earn $y_{mi} = w_m l_{mi}$ per year as a heart surgeon for n years at age $s_m + 6$.[10]

According to the human capital hypothesis, the worker chooses that occupation and associated level and type of schooling which has the highest present

[10] It is important to point out that economists typically cannot observe the physical productivity of a worker (i.e. l_{ij}) or the market piece rate per unit of productivity (i.e. w_j), but can only observe earnings which is their product (i.e. $y_{ij} = w_j l_{ij}$) because most workers are paid by time rates (e.g. hourly wage rates or annual salaries) rather than by the piece [see Pencavel (1977) and Stiglitz (1975)]. However, the relationship between worker pay and productivity that is enforced by competitive labor markets implies that it is theoretically meaningful to distinguish between physical productivity and the price per unit of product even if this distinction cannot be verified by direct observation.

value. Let the present value to person i of occupation j be

$$V_{ij} = \int_{s_j+6}^{s_j+n} y_{ij} e^{-r_i t} dt$$
$$= \alpha_i e^{-r_i s_j} y_{ij}/r_i, \quad j = 0, \ldots, m, \tag{35}$$

where i's earnings level, y_{ij}, is given by (34); r_i is his (constant) rate of discount; and $\alpha_i = (1 + e^{-r_i n})$. The worker's educations decision rule is then

$$\text{choose } s_i^* = s_k \text{ if } V_{ik} = \max(V_{i0}, \ldots, V_{im}). \tag{36}$$

Now consider the production side of the model. Within occupations, workers are assumed to be perfect substitutes in production at rates determined by their relative endowments, but they are imperfect substitutes across occupations either because they perform different tasks within firms in a given industry or because they enter into the production of different final products which are imperfectly substitutable in consumption.

Aggregate output of a composite good, Q, is given by the aggregate production function

$$Q = F(L_0, \ldots, L_m; K, t), \tag{37}$$

where

$$L = (L_0, \ldots, L_m) \tag{38}$$

is the vector of aggregate supplies of efficiency units of labor to each occupation j $(j = 0, \ldots, m)$, K is the aggregate capital stock, and t is a vector of variables summarizing the state of technology and pattern of consumer demand. For now, assume that both K and t are exogenous constants. Also assume that the dollar price per unit of Q is unity.

Let $\{1, \ldots, N\}$ be the set of workers in the economy and let $a = (a_0, \ldots, a_m)$ be an *assignment* of workers to a given schooling–occupation class such that $i \in a_j$ $(j = 0, \ldots, m)$ defines the set of workers in occupation j. Given the assignment, there are N_j workers in occupation j, where $\sum_{j=1}^{m} N_j = N$ and the aggregate supply of efficiency units to the occupation is

$$L_j = \sum_{i \in a_j} l_{ij}. \tag{39}$$

Given the vector of aggregate supplies of efficiency units of labor, L, implied by assignment a, let

$$F = (F_0, \ldots, F_m) \tag{40}$$

denote the associated vector of marginal products, where F_j is the marginal product per efficiency unit of labor in occupation j.

Labor market equilibrium is determined by the interaction of the aggregate supply and demand for workers in each occupation. Denote the market assignment in long-run competitive equilibrium by $a(w^*) = (a_0(w^*),\dots, a_m(w^*))$. The equilibrium assignment occurs when the vector of market piece rates is $w = w^*$ such that the aggregate number of efficiency units of labor in each occupation which is supplied by workers who follow the decision rule in (36) is

$$L(w^*, r) = (L_0(w^*, r),\dots, L_m(w^*, r)), \tag{41}$$

and market piece rates and marginal products per efficiency unit are equal, i.e.

$$w_j^* \geq F_j, \quad \forall j = 0,\dots, m, \tag{42}$$

where the vector $r = (r_1,\dots, r_n)$ gives the discount rates faced by each individual in the population and the equality holds in (42) for all schooling–occupation categories for which there is a positive aggregate supply in equilibrium.

At the microeconomic level, this long-run equilibrium generates data on the length of schooling (s_i^*), occupation ($i \in a_j^*$), and earnings ($y_i^* = w_j^* l_{ij}$) for each of the $i = 1,\dots, N$ individuals in the population. The schooling–earnings data generated by the market may then be described by the statistical earnings function

$$y_i = \varphi(s_i) + u_i. \tag{43}$$

In general, both $\varphi(\cdot)$ and the distribution of the error term, u, depend on production technology and the pattern of final demand which determine $F(\cdot)$, and on the distribution of ability and opportunity in the population given, respectively, by the vectors $l = (l_1,\dots, l_n)$ and $r = (r_1,\dots, r_1)$.

4.2. Non-competing groups

The model outlined above in (32)–(43) is sufficiently flexible to be capable of generating a wide variety of relationships between schooling and earnings ranging from the Mincer-type schooling function, $\ln y = \ln y_0 + rs$, in (24), to other possibilities that are in direct conflict with the spirit (if not the formalisms) of the human capital approach. Before considering the conditions under which Mincer's results arise, it is instructive to illustrate this point by considering the following example of Cairnes-Mill "non-competing groups" which lies at the opposite extreme from the human capital model in terms of its empirical implications.

Assume that any given worker in the economy can be trained for one and only one occupation, but that there is diversity across workers in the occupation for which they are suited. Thus, let the first N_0 workers have ability endowments $(l_{i0}, 0, \ldots, 0)$ for $i = 1, \ldots, N_0$; the next N_1 workers have endowments $(0, l_{i1}, 0, \ldots, 0)$; and so on. Formally, each worker chooses that occupation for which his discounted lifetime earnings are highest, but the choice is trivial. Obviously, the aggregate supplies of labor to each occupation are perfectly inelastic and lifetime earnings net of training costs are pure economic rents. Given technology and the pattern of demand for final products, the equilibrium piece rate vector, w^*, in (42) depends solely on the distribution of ability in the population.

A priori, there is no reason in this example to believe that the statistical earnings function, $\varphi(s)$, in (43) is positively sloped or even monotonic. Moreover, as the capital stock, technology, and the pattern of final demands vary, the equilibrium piece rate vector, w^*, will tend to change in both level and pattern in ways that are difficult to predict. In turn, this will lead to a change in the level and shape of $\varphi(s)$ and a change in the distribution of u.

For example, the introduction of electronic computers vastly increases the speed with which accounting analyses can be prepared. If the elasticity of demand for accounting services is sufficiently inelastic, this would tend to reduce the demand for accountants. Since the supply of labor to accounting is perfectly inelastic, this shift in demand would reduce the equilibrium piece rate per efficiency unit of labor by accountants and, hence, reduce the earning of accountants relative to earnings in other professions. Conversely, the piece rate and earnings of accountants would increase if the demand for accounting services is sufficiently elastic.

More generally, in this extreme example of "perfectly" non-competing groups, one would expect that the relationship between schooling and earnings would be highly irregular in a given economy at a given time and that it would be extremely unstable over time and across countries because of variation in technology and demand patterns. Given the overwhelming evidence that schooling and earnings are positively and monotonically related in nearly all societies in all historical periods for which there is data on schooling and earnings, it is safe to infer that the capacities of the human agent are considerably more malleable than in the example just described.

By the same token, it is possible to imagine a society in which the assignment of workers to particular types of training and to occupations is arbitrarily determined by caste, hereditary guild membership, etc. Clearly, such an arbitrary allocation rule would generate an equally arbitrary and unstable schooling–earnings relationship because, once more, the supply of labor to each occupation is perfectly inelastic. Again, the evidence is against a hypothesis of arbitrary assignment in most societies.

4.3. Perfectly equalizing differentials

In view of this discussion, it is not surprising that the strongest version of the human capital hypothesis holds under conditions of equality of opportunity and a form of equality of relative ability that I call equality of comparative advantage. In this case, the long-run supply of labor (in efficiency units) to each occupation is perfectly elastic at a piece rate which is sufficient to equalize the present value to each individual of lifetime earnings in all occupations.

This pattern of equalizing differentials generates a Mincer-type statistical earnings function:

$$\begin{aligned} \ln y_i &= \ln \varphi(s_i) + u_i \\ &= \ln y_{0i} + rs_i + A_i, \end{aligned} \tag{44}$$

where the error term, $u_i = A_i$, which is equal to person i's "absolute advantage", is homoskedastic and statistically independent of s_i. Thus, (44) can be estimated consistently by ordinary least squares even when ability differentials (i.e. differences in absolute advantage) are not observed.

In addition, this earnings function is remarkably stable in the long run under conditions of varying technology, capital stock, and demand patterns. Specifically, if the interest rate, r, remains constant, (44) remains perfectly stable for different patterns of final demand (holding resources and technology constant) and only its constant term, $\ln y_0$, shifts as technology and resources vary. Thus, a theory of heterogeneous human capital based on the hypotheses of equality of comparative advantage and equality of opportunity constitutes an extraordinarily simple and powerful theory of educational wage differentials. Moreover, when post-school investment is introduced the resulting earnings functions possess all of the properties of Mincer's human capital earnings functions.

In contrast to the relation $\ln y = \ln y_0 + rs$ in (36), which simply follows from the definition of equal present value, it is important to point out that the earnings function in (44) holds only under certain very strong conditions. Thus, a human capital theory based on the theory of perfectly equalizing differentials is eminently falsifiable with data.

The theory of equalizing differences is one of the oldest theories of wage differentials in economics, going back to Adam Smith (see Chapter 12 by Rosen in this Handbook). It is also the basic framework employed by Friedman and Kuznets (1945) in their classic study of income differences among independent professionals which was, in turn, an important precursor to the development of modern human capital theory by Becker and Mincer. Indeed, both Smith's and Friedman and Kuznets' work figure prominently in Mincer's first paper on human capital [Mincer (1958)] and clearly have deeply influenced the subsequent development of his work. Theories of the role of comparative advantage in labor markets also have a long history. Pioneering modern statements by Roy (1951) and Tinbergen (1951) have been followed by the work of Rosen (1978), Sattinger (1975, 1980), and others. Finally, as we have seen, the importance of financing opportunities has been emphasized by Becker (1967, 1975).

Despite these historical precedents, I have been unable to find a systematic exposition of the conditions under which the conventional human capital earnings function arises as the outcome of general equilibrium in the labor market, although Rosen (1977a) provides a brief description of the approach I elaborate here. Since the theory to be presented essentially duplicates the main results of Mincer's theory, I view it as a reinterpretation of his theory. The reinterpreted theory has several major advantages. First, it provides a clear and rigorous statement of the conditions under which the standard results occur. It also have certain stability properties which have not been emphasized in the past. Second, the model is a special case of a more general theory within which the empirical implications of departures from these conditions can be analyzed.

Viewed as an econometric model, (44) rests on two fundamental empirical hypotheses, one economic and the other non-economic. The economic hypothesis corresponds to the condition of *equality of opportunity* which is defined, as before, as the situation in which all individuals face a common interest rate, $r_i = r$ for all $i = i,\ldots, N$. This condition will hold if the economic system provides sufficiently good access to finance and sufficiently free entry into schools and occupations to permit the marginal rate of return to educational investment to be equalized across individuals.

The non-economic hypothesis is that humans are sufficiently alike in their basic capacities that the distribution of educational and occupational choices is not influenced by ability differences. Of course, this will be true if all individuals have identical ability endowments, $l_i = \bar{l} = (\bar{l}_0,\ldots, \bar{l}_m)$ for all $i = 1,\ldots, N$ individuals in the population. A somewhat more general condition, called *equality of comparative advantage* is that individual ability endowments are identical up to a factor of proportionality.

Specifically, there is equality of comparative advantage if

$$l_i = \mathrm{e}^{A_i}\bar{l} = \mathrm{e}^{A_i}(\bar{l}_0,\ldots, \bar{l}_m), \quad \forall i = 1,\ldots, N, \tag{45}$$

where A_i is a person-specific scalar constant which provides a one-factor (i.e. one-dimensional) measure of ability or "absolute advantage". Assume that A_i is scaled such that the mean ability level in the population is $E(A_i) = 0$ so that $\bar{l}$ is the ability vector of the average person.

The derivation of the earnings function in (44) is simple. If the potential earnings of individual i follow the pattern

$$y_{ij}/y_{i0} = \mathrm{e}^{r_i s_j}, \tag{46}$$

then, from (35), it follows that the present value of lifetime earnings is equated across all $j = 0,\ldots,m$ schooling–occupation choices faced by the individual; i.e.

$$V_{ij} = \alpha y_{ij} e^{r_i s_j / r_i} = \alpha_i y_{i0} / r_i \tag{47}$$

so that $V_{i0} = \cdots = V_{im}$, where α_i is a finite life correction defined in (35).

Given equality of opportunity and equality of comparative advantage, there exists a unique vector of relative occupational piece rates such that the earnings pattern in (46) holds for each individual in the population. From (45), equality of comparative advantage implies that $y_{ij} = w_j l_{ij} = w_j \bar{l}_j e^{A_i}$ and equality of opportunity means that $r_i = r$. Hence, the structure of potential earnings will follow the pattern in (46) for each individual if the market piece vector is $w^* = (w_0^*,\ldots,w_m^*)$, where

$$w_j^* = w_0^* (\bar{l}_0 / \bar{l}_j) \exp(r s_j) \quad \text{for } j = 0,\ldots,m. \tag{48}$$

If the vector of market piece rates is w^*, each individual will be indifferent among all potential schooling–occupation choices because each provides the same present value. When an individual is indifferent among alternative opportunities, I assume that his actual choice is random. This assumption implies that schooling choice and ability are statistically independent if w^* is the market piece rate vector and there is equality of opportunity and comparative advantage.

The piece rate w_j^* may be interpreted as the "supply price" per efficiency unit of labor in occupation k given that $w_j = w_j^*$ for all other occupations $j \neq k$. That is, if $w_k < w_k^*$ then no one will choose occupation k, and if $w_k > w_k^*$, then all individuals will choose occupation k. Hence, the long-run supply of labor to occupation k is perfectly elastic at a price of w_k^* per efficiency unit.

Since the likelihood that an individual will choose occupation k is independent of his ability, the expected earnings of a worker who chooses that occupation is $\bar{y}_j^* = \bar{a} \bar{l}_k w_k^*$, where $\bar{a} = E(e_i^A)$ is the arithmetic mean ability level of the population and $\bar{y}_j^* = E(y_k^*)$ is the arithmetic mean earnings of those who choose occupation k. Similarly, the aggregate supply of labor to occupation k is $L_k = \bar{a} \bar{l}_k N_k$, where N_k is the number of workers in the occupation.

To complete the description of long-run competitive equilibrium, we need to consider the vector of demands for labor in each occupation derived from the aggregate production function in (37). As a special case, first consider the case of homogeneous human capital. Specifically, assume that labor of each occupational type is a perfect substitute for labor of any other occupational type at a technologically determined rate. Thus, let

$$Q = F\left(\sum_{j=0}^{m} \theta_j L_k; K; t \right) = F(L; K, t), \tag{49}$$

where the θ_j's are constant parameters determined by technology and $L = \sum \theta_j L_j$ is a scalar measure of the aggregate supply of labor in efficiency units.

Given (49), the marginal product per efficiency unit of labor in occupation j is $F_j = \theta_j F'(L)$. Hence, the vector of relative marginal products in (40) is a vector of constants

$$F = (F_0, \dots, F_m) = (\theta_0, \dots, \theta_m), \tag{50}$$

and the demand for efficiency units of labor in any occupation j is perfectly elastic at a piece rate $w_j = \theta_j$.

Since the θ's are technologically determined parameters, there is no reason to assume that they will follow any particular pattern. Almost surely, the piece rate associated with the "demand price" per efficiency unit for some particular schooling–occupation choice will produce higher lifetime earnings than any other choice.[11] If so, all individuals would choose that occupation and there will be no observed variation in schooling.

Diversity in occupational choice and in the duration and curricular content of schooling depends on imperfect substitution among efficiency units of labor of different types. Given imperfect substitutability, the demand curve for efficiency units of each type of labor is downward-sloping with respect to its own piece rate. In general, the aggregate supplies of labor to each occupation will adjust so as to satisfy the equilibrium conditions in (41) and (42).

For example, suppose that all $m+1$ occupations are "necessary" in the sense that the marginal product of each type approaches infinity as its quantity approaches zero [e.g. $F(\cdot)$ is Cobb–Douglas]. In this case, the equilibrium quantities of each type of labor will be positive (i.e. $L_j^* > 0$ for all $j = 0, \dots, m$) and the equilibrium piece rates will be given by $w_j = w_j^*$ as defined in (48), where $w_0^* = F_0$ is the marginal product per efficiency unit of unschooled labor evaluated at the equilibrium vector of aggregate labor supplies $(L_0^*, \dots, L_m^*)$.

More generally, it is possible that the equilibrium supply of some schooling–occupation categories will be zero because, as its quantity approaches zero, the marginal product per efficiency unit of labor in such an occupation is less than its supply price. Typically, this will be the case if a given type of training produces a type of skill which is a close substitute in production for the skills produced by alternative types of training or if the product of that occupation is a close substitute in consumption for the products produced by individuals in other occupations. For example, accountants trained to keep ledgers by hand are close substitutes in production for accountants trained to use computers and wheelwrights produce components for a product which is a close substitute in

[11] That is, suppose that occupations j and k are both chosen by a positive number of workers. In order for this to happen, it must be the case that $w_j' = \theta_j$ and $w_k' = \theta_j$ where w_j' and w_k' are defined by (46) and θ_j and θ_k are technologically determined constants. Both of these equalities would hold only under a highly improbable coincidence.

consumption for the product produced by auto manufacturers. Given contemporary technology, the value marginal productivity of those with "obsolete" training is lower than the supply price to the occupation and the long-run equilibrium supply of labor to such an occupation is zero. However, all occupations with positive equilibrium supplies will have long-run equilibrium piece rates given by the w^* vector defined in (46).

The individual-level data generated by this model of "perfectly equalizing differentials" is determined by the equilibrium assignment vector $a^*(w^*) = (a_0^*(w^*),\dots, a_m^*(w^*))$, where w^* is the equilibrium piece rate vector defined in (48). Any given individual i is randomly assigned to schooling–occupation class j with probability $p_j = N_j^*/N$, where N_j^* is the equilibrium number of workers in occupation j implied by the relation $L_j^* = \bar{a}N_j^*$ and N is the total number of workers for $j = 0,\dots, m$. The earning of workers $i \in a_j^*(w^*)$ are given by

$$\begin{aligned} y_{ij}^* &= w_j^* l_{ij} \\ &= \left[w_0^*(\bar{l}_0/\bar{l}_j)e^{rs_j}\right]\bar{l}_j e^{A_i}, \quad \forall i \in a_j^*(w^*),\ j = 0,\dots, m, \\ &= w_0^*\bar{l}_0 e^{rs_j + A_i}, \end{aligned} \tag{51}$$

where y_{ij}^* is distributed randomly with mean $\bar{y}_j^* = \bar{a}\bar{l}_j w_0^*$ and variance var(e^{A_i}).

Taking the log of both sides of (51) yields the log-linear earnings function in (44),

$$\ln y_i = \ln y_0 + rs_i + A_i,$$

where $y_0 = w_0^*\bar{l}_0$. The present value of lifetime earnings of all individuals of the ability $V_i^* = \alpha y_0 e^{A_i}$ is the same regardless of their actual choice of schooling and occupation. The assumption of random choice among indifferent alternatives implies that A_i is homoskedastic and that there is zero covariance between A_i and s_i. Hence, a regression of schooling on log earnings will provide consistent estimates of ln y_0 and r even if ability (i.e. A_i) is unobserved.

As mentioned above, this long-run earnings function is remarkably stable as technology, the pattern of final demand, or the stock of capital change, although it may vary in the short run. For example, consider a once and for all change in technology caused by the introduction of computers such that the piece rate productivity endowment of the typical individual (for whom $A_i = 0$) changes from the vector $\bar{l}$ to the vector $\bar{l}'$, where $\bar{l}_j' > \bar{l}_j$ in certain occupations.

In the short run, assume that the number of workers in each occupation is fixed. The effect of improved technology is to increase the number of efficiency units of accounting labor which reduces the marginal product per efficiency unit or market piece rate (i.e. $w_j = F_j$ decreases because $F_{jj} < 0$). Since each accountant enjoys a ten-fold increase in the number of efficiency units of labor he possesses, the earnings of accountants, given by the product of the marginal product per efficiency unit and the number of efficiency units, may either rise or fall depending on the degree of substitutability between accounting services and other inputs. Moreover, because of cross-effects, market piece rates in other occupations also change. Types of labor which are complementary to accounting enjoy an increase in earnings and those which are substitutes suffer a decrease.

In the long run, the supply of labor to each schooling–occupation class will change in the same direction that short-run occupational earnings changed. Given equality of opportunity and comparative advantage, the vector of aggregate labor supplies $(L_0,\dots, L_m)$ and piece rate vector $(w_0,\dots, w_m)$ will adjust in the long run until the present value of each individual's potential lifetime earnings in each schooling–occupation choice are equated. Thus, from (46), this implies that the equilibrium piece rate in accounting must fall to one-tenth its previous value. Assuming that the interest rate, r, remains unchanged, the structure of occupational wage differentials continues to be described by (47) and the statistical earnings function will continue to be of the log-linear form in (44). The only change in the earnings function caused by the technological improvement will be an upward shift in the intercept which reflects the higher level of aggregate productivity.

In general, changes in technology, fluctuations in income, baby booms and busts and so on can be expected to cause short-run changes in occupational wage rates and thereby cause cross-sectional and longitudinal educational wage differentials to depart from the long-run earnings function. The precise nature of the departure depends in part on the degree of substitutability or complementarity in production of the skills supplied by different occupation–education categories. Such demand-side factors have received the most attention in recent analyses of the effects of the baby boom which were discussed earlier. (See also Chapter 8 by Hammermesh in this Handbook.)

However, the heterogeneous human capital model suggests that several supply-side factors may also be of importance. As I have developed it, the model assumes that human capital has a putty–clay structure such that the only way of altering the skill composition of the labor force is for newly trained workers with skills in high demand fields eventually to supplant older workers whose training is in areas experiencing a decline in demand. A useful extension of the model would be to incorporate the possibility of changes in occupation by workers after they have received their education.

For example, one might distinguish between "inflexible" and "flexible" educational investment. A perfectly inflexible education is one which qualifies a worker for only one occupation. That is, ex ante, the typical worker could choose to obtain any element in the vector $(\bar{l}_0,\dots,\bar{l}_m)$ but, ex post, his productivity endowment is $\bar{l}_j$ given a choice of occupation j and zero for all other occupations. In this case, changes in the skill composition of the labor force are achieved only through generational turnover and relative occupational wages will tend to fluctuate considerably as adjustment takes place. More flexible education (e.g.

liberal arts vs. vocational education?) would augment a worker's productivity in more than one occupation, thus increasing the cross-elasticity of occupational labor supplies and reducing the degree of short-run wage fluctuations.

Another supply-side factor which has received very little attention is the role of interest rate variations. The theory suggests that the supply of educated labor should be sensitive to variations in the real interest rate. It is interesting to note that the ex post real rate of interest was very low and perhaps even negative during the 1970s when the rate of return to higher education in the United States began to fall. It is too early to tell whether the current extremely high real interest rates will result in a reversal of this trend.

4.4. *Life cycle earnings growth and perfectly equalizing differentials*

What are the implications of a model of perfectly equalizing differences when post-school investment in on-the-job training is allowed? The answer comes in two parts. The first part is that the equalizing difference approach itself can say nothing about the shape of the life cycle profile. For this, one needs a model of optimal human capital accumulation such as those surveyed by Weiss in this volume. However, since the model assumes that there are many different occupations which may vary in technological possibilities for learning, it would be appropriate to assume that each occupation offers one or more optimal accumulation paths. Thus, certain occupations may be learned quickly once one has the appropriate schooling while others may require a lifetime to master.

The second part of the answer, which I shall develop below, is that most of the stability properties of the schooling function derived above hold when there is equality of comparative advantage and opportunity. In addition, the resulting set of earnings functions have all of the properties which Mincer (1974) exploited to such great advantage. In particular, under conditions similar to those assumed by Mincer, (a) the schooling coefficient in a regression of log earnings on schooling and experience will estimate the rate of return to schooling; (b) the overtaking experience level is approximately $1/r$; and (c) the variance of log earnings will tend to be U-shaped with a minimum at the "overtaking" level of experience.

The second part of the answer presumes that we have solved out for a set of optimal paths of human capital accumulation which may be chosen by those who have completed a given number of years of schooling and now are about to embark on their work careers. Without loss of generality, assume that there are m different possible paths for the $j=1,\dots,m$ different occupation–schooling categories such that

$$l_{ij}(x)=l_{ij}\exp\left\{\int_0^x g_{ij}(t)\,\mathrm{d}t\right\}, \tag{52}$$

where $l_{ij}(x)$ are the number of efficiency units of labor that individual i has accumulated in occupation j after x years of work experience and $g_{ij}(t)$ is the instantaneous growth rate of his efficiency units at time t. It is assumed that the time path of accumulation of occupational skill implied by $g_{ij}(t)$ is determined according to an optimal program that depends upon the skills embodied in individual i at the time he leaves school, on the particular characteristics of occupation j, and on his rate of discount.

Given his schooling–occupation choice and given that he follows the optimal post-school investment program for that occupation, the individual's life cycle earnings path will be given by

$$y_{ij}(x) = w_j l_{ij}(x), \tag{53}$$

where w_j is the market piece rate for that occupation. The individual then chooses an occupation–schooling category which provides the (optimized) life cycle earning path which maximizes the present value of lifetime earnings where

$$V_{ij} = \int_0^n y_{ij}(x) \mathrm{e}^{-r_i(s_j+x)} \mathrm{d}x \tag{54}$$

is the formula for the present value of earnings in occupation j with schooling level s_j for $j = 0, \ldots, m$.

As before, the case of perfectly equalizing differentials occurs when there is equality of opportunity and equality of comparative advantage. In the context of post-school investment, equality of comparative advantage means that

$$(l_{i0}(x), \ldots, l_{im}(x)) = \mathrm{e}^{A_i}(\bar{l}_0(x), \ldots, \bar{l}_m(x)). \tag{55}$$

That is, (55) implies that individuals at the same level of experience differ in occupational productivity only by a scalar factor of proportionality. In combination with (52), this also implies that each individual, regardless of his ability (i.e. regardless of A_i), will have the same path of instantaneous growth rates of earnings, given his choice of schooling and occupation.

In order to attract individuals into all occupations, the piece rate vector, $(w_0, \ldots, w_m)$, will adjust until the present value of each occupation is the same for each individual (i.e. $V_{i0} = \cdots = V_{im}$, $\forall i = 1, \ldots, N$). Given the equilibrium piece rate vector, $(w_0^*, \ldots, w_m^*)$ each individual will be indifferent among his schooling–occupation choices. Thus, the long-run supply of labor to each occupation will be perfectly elastic at an average wage rate of $y_{ij}^*(x) = w_j^* \bar{l}_j(x)$ for individuals with experience x. Hence, the experience–earnings profiles in each occupation–schooling class will tend to be stable in the long run under conditions of equality of opportunity and comparative advantage for the same reasons given earlier for the stability of the earnings–schooling relationship. However, the shape of average experience–earnings profiles within and between schooling classes may change if growth profiles differ across occupations and the occupational mix changes as a result of shifts in the pattern of labor demand.

The main features of Mincer's human capital earnings function are replicated in this model. For example, recall from (11) that the overtaking level of experience is exactly $1/r$ years if individuals make constant dollar post-school investments in on-the-job training each year. The same result holds for the model of perfectly equalizing differentials if each individual experiences linear growth in occupation-specific productivity.

Thus, consider two occupations, 1 and 2, and assume that $\bar{l}_j(x) = \bar{l}(s_j) + k_j x$ $(j = 1,2)$ is the number of efficiency units of labor in occupation j that an educationally qualified worker of average ability (i.e. $A_i = 0$) utilizes at experience level x and let $y(s_j, x) = w_j \bar{l}_j(x)$ be his earnings at that level of experience.[12] If $k_1 > k_2$, workers in occupation 1 have more rapid wage growth than workers in occupation 2. If the relative piece rate, w_1/w_2, adjusts so as to equate the present value of lifetime earnings in the two occupations, it is straightforward to show that $y_1(x) = y_2(x)$ at $x = x^* = 1/r$ (assuming an infinite working life).

In this model, the schooling coefficient in a regression of log earnings on schooling and experience provides an estimate of the rate of return to schooling (i.e. $\rho = r$) if the distribution of post-school growth opportunities is independent of duration of schooling. In this case, the data will show no interaction between schooling and experience and the distribution of the residuals from the regression will be U-shaped with a minimum at x^*. Otherwise, it is necessary to estimate the rate of return directly (i.e. by calculating it from age–earnings profiles predicted from the regression) or by using Mincer's short-cut method by comparing log earnings at the overtaking point and the distribution of residuals may follow a different pattern.

4.5. Generalizations

The Mincer earnings function can occur under conditions which are somewhat weaker than those specified in the preceding section. For example, it is not necessary to assume that each occupation has rigid schooling qualifications nor is it necessary to assume that all workers have equal comparative advantage. For simplicity, I will discuss these generalizations in the context of the schooling model with no post-school investment.

[12] Note that the worker may not utilize all of his labor because he devotes part of his time to training as in the Ben-Porath (1967) model. Alternatively, however, he may experience growth in productivity solely because of so-called "costless" learning-by-doing in which case he utilizes all of his labor potential at each point in time. Of course, since competition forces present values of all occupations to be the same, an occupation which offers better learning opportunities will force an entrant to pay for the opportunity by accepting a lower initial wage, a point made by Becker (1975).

To relax the assumption of rigid schooling qualifications, assume that each worker i of ability A_i is endowed with a separate human capital production function for each occupation j of the form $l_{ij} = h_j(s, A_i)$. Given his occupational choice, he chooses an optimal schooling level so as to equate the internal rate of return and the interest rate in the manner described by Rosen's schooling model in (26)–(31). The analogue to the assumption of equal comparative advantage in this case is that the production functions for each occupation are of the form $l_{ij} = A_i h_j(s)$ for all $i = 1,\ldots, N$ workers and all $j = 0,\ldots, m$ occupations because the internal rate of return to schooling for each occupation is independent of ability. Thus, regardless of ability, each worker in occupation j will choose the same level of schooling. Because of differences in the productivity of investment in education among occupations, the optimal schooling level will vary depending on occupational choice. The assignment of workers to occupations and the equilibrium distribution of earnings by occupation–schooling class is then determined in exactly the way described in the preceding sections.

It should also be recognized that wage differentials need not be perfectly equalizing for *all* workers in order to achieve the Mincer earnings function. All that is necessary is sufficient long-run mobility of *some* workers to maintain the equilibrium structure of educational wage differentials described in the preceding section. For example, suppose that half of the labor force has ability endowments satisfying the equal comparative advantage condition while the other half consists of individuals whose talents are completely specialized to one or another of the m occupations. Assume that the supply of efficiency units of labor to each occupation by the latter set of individuals is given by the vector $(\boldsymbol{L}_0,\ldots, \boldsymbol{L}_m)$. In this case, the supply of efficiency units of labor to occupation j is perfectly inelastic at an aggregate supply of $\boldsymbol{L}_j$ provided by those individuals whose talents are specialized to j and is perfectly elastic at a piece rate w_j^* given by (48) for any aggregate supply $L_j > \boldsymbol{L}_j$. As long as the pattern of labor demand is such that demand curves intersect the elastic portions of the occupational supply curves, the equilibrium pattern of earnings will generate the Mincer earnings function in (44).

5. Inequality of opportunity and ability

Even with the weaker conditions just described, it is not obvious on a priori grounds that one should expect the Mincer earnings function to hold exactly. In this section I will outline the implications of departures from the conditions of equality of opportunity and of comparative advantage for the equilibrium pattern of educational and occupational wage differentials. For expositional simplicity, I ignore post-school investment and concentrate on the "schooling model". The section is concluded with a brief survey of the empirical literature on "ability bias" in the returns to education.

5.1. *Inequality of opportunity*

First, consider the effect of relaxing the assumption of equality of opportunity while maintaining the assumption of equality of comparative advantage. Specifically, suppose that there is a distribution of discount rates. In this case the equilibrium labor market assignment will sort those individuals with the highest discount rates into occupations with the lowest schooling requirements, those with the next highest discount rates into occupations with the next lowest schooling requirement, and so on until those with the lowest discount rates are left to be assigned to those occupations with the highest schooling requirement.

The resulting equilibrium earnings function will be of a non-linear form:

$$\ln y_i = \varphi(s_i) + A_i, \tag{56}$$

such that $\varphi'' < 0$. Thus, the empirical earnings function will display a pattern of decreasing marginal rates of return to schooling similar to those in Hanoch's (1967) study which were reported earlier in Table 10.1. In addition, the shape as well as the level of the earnings function will tend to vary as the pattern of labor demands for each occupation shift.

These propositions are illustrated in Figures 10.3 and 10.4 for a simple example. Assume that there are three occupations $j = 1,2,3$ with schooling requirements $s_1 < s_2 < s_3$. Also assume that all individuals have identical productivity endowments, but that they differ in their discount rates. The distribution of discount rates is given in Figure 10.3.

Assume that labor demand conditions are such that one third of the labor force is in each occupation. Let the points marked $\bar{r}$ and $\underline{r}$ partition the distribution in Figure 10.3 into thirds corresponding to the areas marked A, B, and C. I first show that the equilibrium labor market assignment is such that workers for whom $r \leq \bar{r}$ choose s_1; those for whom $\underline{r} < r < \bar{r}$ choose s_2; and those for whom $r \leq \bar{r}$ choose s_3. I then show that equilibrium log earnings corresponding to this assignment is given by points a, b, and c in Figure 10.4, where the slope of the line segment ab is $\bar{r}$ and the slope of the segment bc is $\underline{r}$. Thus, the marginal rate of return to schooling is decreasing (i.e. the rate of return from s_1 to s_2 is $\bar{r}$ and from s_2 to s_3 is $\underline{r}$ where $\bar{r} > \underline{r}$).

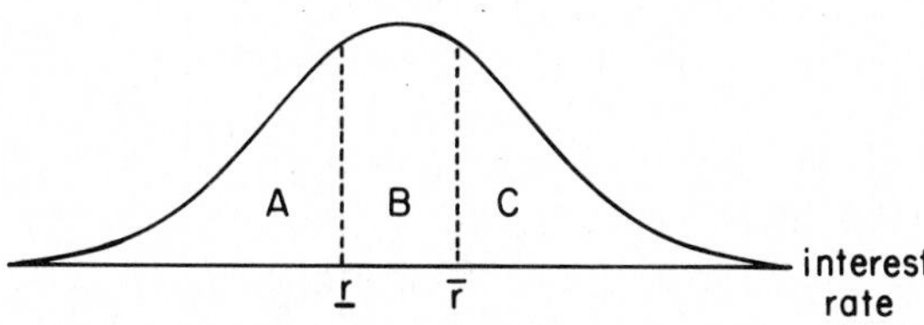

Figure 10.3. Interpersonal distribution of interest rates.

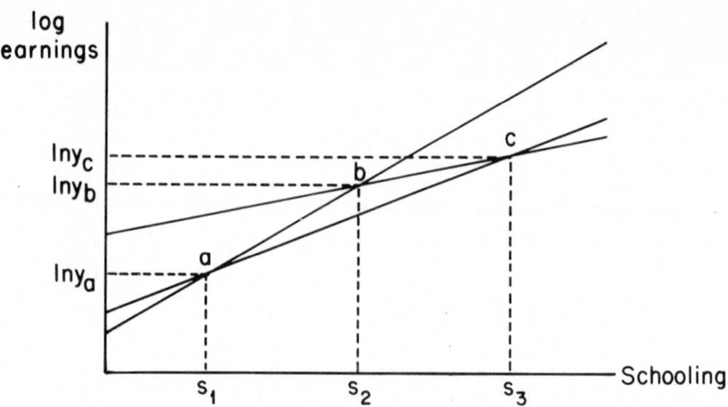

Figure 10.4. Earnings function with inequality of opportunity.

The argument is simple. Let earnings in occupation 1 be $\ln y_1 = \ln y_a$ corresponding to point a in Figure 10.4. If earnings in occupation 2 are at point b where $\ln y_2 = \ln y_b = \ln y_a + \bar{r}(s_2 - s_1)$, the marginal individual with discount rate $\bar{r}$ will receive equal present value in either occupation 1 or 2 and, hence, will be indifferent between them. Given the wage structure corresponding to points a and b, all individuals for whom $r > \bar{r}$ will prefer occupation 1 and those for whom $r < \bar{r}$ will prefer occupation 2. Thus, to maintain one third of the labor force in occupation 1, the equilibrium wage in occupation 2 must be at point b. By the same argument, the marginal individual with discount rate $\underline{r}$ will be indifferent between points b and c where $\ln y_c = \ln y_b + \underline{r}(s_3 - s_2)$ and a wage of $\ln y_3 = \ln y_c$ will lead individuals for whom $\bar{r} \leq r \leq \underline{r}$ to choose occupation 2 and those for whom $r < \underline{r}$ to choose occupation 3. Thus, the wage structure represented by points a, b, and c is the only one which will elicit a supply of one-third of the labor force to each occupation.

Note that this earnings function is sensitive to the distribution of labor demand. For example, suppose that the demand for the high skill occupation 3 increases while the demand for occupation 1 and its wage, y_a, remain constant. The wage in occupation 2 must also remain constant at point b to maintain the incentives of those previously in occupation 1 to remain while the wage in occupation 3 must rise above y_c to induce additional entrants. In the new equilibrium, the marginal rate of return to additional schooling from s_2 to s_3 will have risen.

5.2. *Inequality of ability*

In the discussions of perfectly non-competing groups and perfectly equalizing differentials, I have already described two forms of inequality of ability which have radically different implications for the shape and stability of the earnings function. There are many other possible forms of inequality of ability and a corresponding plethora of possible empirical relationships between schooling and earnings.

Beginning with Becker's (1964) early work, a major concern has been the possibility that estimates rates of return to education overstate the "true" rate of return because of a positive correlation between schooling and ability. A large literature has developed since then which attempts to test for the presence of "ability bias" and to provide estimates of the true rate of return. Implicitly, this concept of ability bias assumes that ability is essentially a one dimensional characteristic. Clearly, alternative assumptions are possible and perhaps more plausible. Strength, intelligence, agility, dexterity, visual acuity, creativity, and so on are words describing various distinct "abilities" which are thought to be of differential importance in different tasks or occupations and which are possessed, presumably, in varying levels and proportions by different workers.

In general, it is extremely difficult (some would argue impossible) to obtain direct measures of "true" abilities. At best, we have proxy measures of certain dimensions of ability such as scores in IQ tests, tests of visual acuity, etc. Despite misgivings about the meaning of test scores, early attempts to determine the extent of ability bias simply included test scores in earnings regressions. [See, for example, Taubman and Wales (1974), and Griliches and Mason (1972).] More recently, statistical methods have been developed, especially by Chamberlain and Griliches, which permit true abilities to be regarded as unobservable latent variables. This approach often requires considerable information not found in typical census-type data such as, for example, data on siblings including fraternal and identical twins. Even with unusually rich data, the capacity of economists to ascertain the extent of ability bias turns on a set of difficult issues concerning identification, treatment of errors in the measured variables, and so on. Griliches (1977, 1979) provides excellent surveys of the literature in this area together with a detailed interpretation of the statistical assumptions and empirical results in this literature. A brief synopsis of these issues and the empirical results will be given later.

In addition to the question of unobservables, there is a question of the extent to which abilities are "innate" or "acquired". In essence, this is the fundamental issue raised by the human capital concept. There is no question that there is a high degree of heterogeneity in the skills which different individuals actually possess and utilize in the performance of different occupations. However, as we have seen, if individuals are innately alike in comparative advantage, the supply of skills adjusts endogenously so as to equalize net advantages across occupations and an unbiased estimate of the rate of return to education can be obtained without controlling for ability differences in absolute advantage. This suggests that the issue of ability bias turns on the degree to which there is variation in comparative advantage which is correlated with endogenous schooling decisions.

5.3. *The Roy model*

A. D. Roy (1951) provided an early and highly innovative verbal presentation of a model of the economic implications of exogenous ability variation for the occupational choice, the structure of wages, and the distribution of earnings. In recent years the implicit mathematical structure of the Roy model has been expressed explicitly by several authors. The most complete mathematical statement of the model is probably contained in Heckman and Sedlacek (1981) who also develop its econometric implications to study the effects of minimum wage legislation on employment and wages.

The Roy model has also been extended to allow for endogenous skill acquisition through education by Willis and Rosen (1979) who used it to study issues concerning ability bias, self-selection, and the wealth maximization hypothesis in educational choice. They found that education was selective on ability, but that a one-factor representation of ability was inadequate in the data they examined.

In this section I provide a fairly detailed sketch of the Willis–Rosen version of the Roy model as a background both for discussion of their empirical findings and the findings from other investigations of the ability bias issue. For purposes of comparison with other studies, I augment the Willis–Rosen–Roy model by introducing a set of exogenous innate abilities which underlie occupation-specific abilities. However, for simplicity, I omit consideration of life cycle earnings growth which Willis–Rosen do incorporate into their model. The model of perfectly equalizing differences which leads to the Mincer earnings function (and no ability bias) is a special case of this model.

Let each individual be endowed with two exogenous innate abilities called "strength" and "intelligence" which are denoted, respectively, by ξ_1 and ξ_2. Assume that these abilities are jointly normally distributed in the population with zero means (i.e. $\mu_1 = \mu_2 = 0$), unitary variance (i.e. $\sigma_1^2 = \sigma_2^2 = 1$), and correlation ρ_{12}.

Assume that there are only two occupations, A and B, where A requires a college education and B requires a high school education. An individual's abilities are assumed to influence his occupation-specific productivity multiplicatively so that the logarithm of the occupation-specific productivities of the individual are

$$a_i = \alpha_0 + \alpha_1\xi_{1i} + \alpha_2\xi_{2i}$$

and (57)

$$b_i = \beta_0 + \beta_1\xi_{1i} + \beta_2\xi_{2i},$$

where $a_i = \ln l_{ai}$, $b_i = \ln l_{bi}$, and the α's and β's are fixed coefficients (i.e. factor loadings) which indicate the importance of each ability to occupation-specific productivity.

Given the assumption that ξ_1 and ξ_2 are jointly normal, it follows from (57) that a and b are also jointly normal with the following parameters:

$$\begin{aligned} \text{means:} \quad & \mu_a = \alpha_0,\ \mu_b = \beta_0; \\ \text{variances:} \quad & \sigma_a^2 = \alpha_1^2 + 2\alpha_1\alpha_2\rho_{12} + \alpha_2^2, \\ & \sigma_b^2 = \beta_1^2 + 2\beta_1\beta_2\rho_{12} + b_2^2; \\ \text{covariance:} \quad & \sigma_{ab} = \alpha_1\beta_1 + (\alpha_1\beta_2 + \alpha_2\beta_1)\rho_{12} + \alpha_2\beta_2. \end{aligned} \tag{58}$$

Note that the correlation between occupation-specific productivities (i.e. $\rho_{ab} = \sigma_{ab}/\sigma_a\sigma_b$) will tend to be positive if strength and intelligence are useful in both occupations even if strength and intelligence themselves are uncorrelated (i.e. $\rho_{12} = 0$).

For convenience, define

$$\begin{aligned} a_i &= \mu_a + \varepsilon_{ai}, \\ b_i &= \mu_b + \varepsilon_{bi}, \\ -\varepsilon_i &= \varepsilon_{ai} - \varepsilon_{bi}, \end{aligned} \tag{59}$$

where $\mu_a = \alpha_0$ and $\mu_b = \beta_0$ are the population means of a and b, $\varepsilon_{ai} = \alpha_1\xi_{1i} + \alpha_2\xi_{2i}$ and $\varepsilon_{bi} = \beta_1\xi_{1i} + \beta_2\xi_{2i}$. Thus, $E(\varepsilon_a) = E(\varepsilon_b) = E(\varepsilon) = 0$; $E(\varepsilon_a^2) = \sigma_a^2$; $E(\varepsilon_b^2) = \sigma_b^2$; and $E(\varepsilon_a\varepsilon_b) = \sigma_{ab}$ as defined in (58). Also, $E(\varepsilon) = 0$, $E(\varepsilon^2) = \sigma_\varepsilon^2 = \sigma_a^2 + 2\rho_{ab}\sigma_a\sigma_b + \sigma_b^2$, $E(\varepsilon\varepsilon_a) = \sigma_{\varepsilon a} = \sigma_{ab} - \sigma_a^2$, and $E(\varepsilon\varepsilon_b) = \sigma_{\varepsilon b} = \sigma_b^2 - \sigma_{ab}$.

The annual earnings of individual i are $y_i = w_a l_{ai}$ if he chooses A and $y_{bi} = w_b l_{bi}$ if he chooses B, where w_a and w_b are the market piece rates in A and B. Using (6), the rate of return to a college education for a given individual is

$$\begin{aligned} \rho_i = \rho_i(s_b, s_a) &= [\ln y_{ai} - \ln y_{bi}]/(s_a - s_b) \\ &= [\ln(w_a/w_b) + (\mu_a - \mu_b) + (\varepsilon_{ai} - \varepsilon_{bi})]/(s_a - s_b). \end{aligned} \tag{60}$$

A wealth-maximizing individual will choose to enroll in college (i.e. choose A) if $\rho_i > r_i$ and will stop at the end of high school (i.e. choose B) if $\rho_i \leq r_i$.

Define the index function

$$\begin{aligned} I_i &= (\bar{\rho} - r_i)(s_a - s_b) \\ &= (\mu_a - \mu_b) + \ln(w_a/w_b) - r_i(s_a - s_b), \end{aligned} \tag{61}$$

where $\bar{\rho}$ is the mean rate of return to college education in the population. Thus, a wealth-maximizing individual will follow the decision rule:

$$\text{choose A if } I_i > \varepsilon_i; \text{ otherwise choose B,} \tag{62}$$

where, from (59), $-\varepsilon_i = \varepsilon_{ai} - \varepsilon_{bi}$.

Clearly, the decision to choose college (i.e. A) is more likely the lower is the discount rate, r_i, and the higher is the individual's productivity in occupation A relative to occupation B (i.e. the lower is $\varepsilon_i = \varepsilon_{bi} - \varepsilon_{ai}$). In turn, the selectivity of college choice on innate ability (i.e. ξ_1 and ξ_2) depends on the relative usefulness of strength and intelligence in the two occupations, on the correlation between the two abilities in the population and on the correlation between abilities and the discount rate.

To focus on the determinants of selection on ability, assume that there is equality of opportunity (i.e. $r = r_i$ for all $i = 1,\dots, N$ individuals). The probability that an individual chosen at random from the population will choose A is then

$$\Pr(\text{choose A}) = \Pr(I/\sigma_\varepsilon > \varepsilon/\sigma_\varepsilon) = F(I/\sigma_\varepsilon), \tag{63}$$

and the probability of choosing B is $1 - F(I/\sigma_\varepsilon)$, where $F(I/\sigma_\varepsilon)$ is the c.d.f. of a standard normal distribution evaluated at I/σ_ε. Note that (63) also gives the fraction of the population who go to college and supply labor to occupation A.

If individuals were randomly assigned to schooling–occupation classes, average earnings in A and B would be $\ln \bar{y}_a = \ln w_a + \mu_a$ and $\ln \bar{y}_b = \ln w_b + \mu_b$, respectively, and the observed rate of return to college would be $\bar{\rho}$ as defined in (61). Given the decision rule in (62), the expected earnings of individuals who actually choose A and B will typically diverge from $\ln \bar{y}_a$ and $\ln \bar{y}_b$. This divergence may be called "selectivity bias" due to self-selection, although the term "bias" is fully appropriate only if our goal is to estimate the earnings potential of a randomly chosen person. In addition, the rates of return received by those who choose college will tend to be higher than $\bar{\rho}$ and the potential returns of those who did not choose college will be lower than $\bar{\rho}$.

Let $\bar{\rho}_a$ be the average rate of return to college received by those who choose A and $\bar{\rho}_b$ be the average potential rate of return that those who choose B could have received if they had gone to college. (60) implies that the distribution of rates of return is normally distributed with mean $\bar{\rho}$ and variance σ_ε^2 and (61) implies that the marginal individual who chooses college will receive a rate of return equal to the interest rate, r.

The distribution of rates of return is depicted in Figure 10.5 by a normal distribution with mean $\bar{\rho}$ and standard deviation σ_ε^2. The distribution is partitioned into two parts at the point where $\rho = r$. As drawn, most of the population chooses B (i.e. the area to the left of r) and the remaining fraction chooses A (i.e. the area to the right of r). The mean rate of return received by those who choose

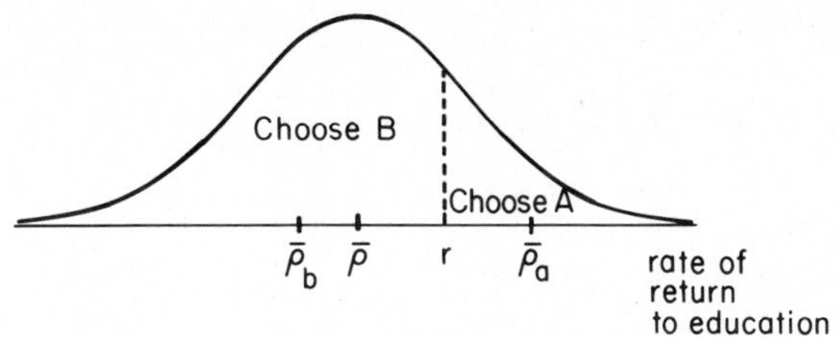

Figure 10.5. Distribution of rate of return to education.

college is indicated by $\bar{\rho}_a$ which is the mean of the right-hand portion of the normal distribution truncated at r. Similarly, the point marked $\bar{\rho}_b$ is the mean of the left-hand portion of the truncated distribution.

Mathematically, the expressions for $\bar{\rho}_a$ and $\bar{\rho}_b$ are

$$\bar{\rho}_a = \bar{\rho} - \lambda_a \geq r$$

and (64)

$$\bar{\rho}_b = \bar{\rho} - \lambda_b \leq r,$$

where the "inverse Mills ratios",

$$\lambda_a \equiv E(\varepsilon/\sigma_\varepsilon | I/\sigma_\varepsilon > \varepsilon/\sigma_\varepsilon) = -f(I/\sigma_\varepsilon)/F(I/\sigma_\varepsilon) < 0$$

and (65)

$$\lambda_b \equiv E(\varepsilon/\sigma_\varepsilon | I/\sigma_\varepsilon < \varepsilon/\sigma_\varepsilon) = f(I/\sigma_\varepsilon)/(1 - F(I/\sigma_\varepsilon) < 0,$$

are, respectively, the formulas for the means of the upper and lower tails of a truncated normal distribution [see Heckman (1979)]. Note that λ_a is always negative and λ_b is always positive. An important implication of this analysis is that $\bar{\rho}_a$, the average of the "true" rates of return received by those who go to college, is always greater than the interest rate if σ_ε^2 is non-zero.

The terms λ_a and λ_b are also important in determining the mean earnings of those who actually choose A and those who actually choose B. Expected log earnings of those who choose college is

$$\begin{aligned} \ln \hat{y}_a &= E(\ln ya | I > 0) = \ln \bar{y}_a + E(\varepsilon_a | I/\sigma_\varepsilon > \varepsilon/\sigma_\varepsilon) \\ &= \ln \bar{y}_a + (\sigma_{\varepsilon a}/\sigma_\varepsilon)\lambda_a \\ &= \ln \bar{y}_a - \alpha_\lambda \lambda_a, \end{aligned} \qquad (66)$$

and, by a parallel derivation,

$$\ln \hat{y}_b = E(\ln yb|I<0) = \ln \bar{y}_b + \beta_\lambda \lambda_b, \tag{67}$$

where the selectivity bias coefficients for A and B are, respectively,

$$\alpha_\lambda = (\sigma_a - \rho_{ab}\sigma_b)(\sigma_a/\sigma_\varepsilon)$$

and (68)

$$\beta_\lambda = (\sigma_b - \rho_{ab}\sigma_a)(\sigma_b/\sigma_\varepsilon).$$

From an economic point of view, this self-selection process produces an efficient allocation of resources in the sense that the aggregate supply of efficiency units in A is maximized for any given aggregate supply of efficiency units in B because the equilibrium assignment selects individuals according to their comparative advantage. As the demand for A rises, w_a/w_b tends to rise causing the mean of the distribution of ρ in Figure 10.5 to increase. This induces workers who were previously in B to shift to A. The sign of the "selectivity bias" on $\ln \bar{y}_a$ (i.e. α_λ) indicates whether the workers drawn from B into A tend to have lower or higher earnings potential in A than those workers previously in A. Similarly, the sign of the "selectivity bias" on $\ln \bar{y}_b$ (i.e. β_λ) indicates whether the workers drawn to A tend to have higher or lower earnings potential in B than the workers who remain in B.

If the rate of return to college is calculated by comparing the actual earnings of college and high school workers, the estimates rate of return is given by $\hat{\rho}_a = [\ln \hat{y}_a - \ln \hat{y}_b]/(s_a - s_b)$. Using (64)–(68), the estimated rate of return may be expressed as

$$\begin{aligned}\hat{\rho}_a &= \bar{\rho} - \lambda_a - \beta_\lambda(\lambda_b - \lambda_a)\\ &= \bar{\rho}_a - \beta_\lambda(\lambda_b - \lambda_a),\end{aligned} \tag{69}$$

where $\lambda_b - \lambda_a > 0$. Thus, the estimated rate of return to college will overstate the actual average return received by those who attend college (i.e. $\bar{\rho}_a$) if $\beta_\lambda < 0$ and will understate it if $\beta_\lambda > 0$. The intuition is that the average forgone earnings of those going to college is understated by the earnings of high school graduates in the former case and overstated in the latter case.

The direction of selectivity bias and its influence on the estimated rate of return to a college education depends on the underlying parameters, σ_a, σ_b, and ρ_{ab}, which describe the population distribution of productivity in the two occupations. These parameters, in turn, depend on the underlying distribution of innate ability and the role of innate ability in determining occupational productivity. Four possible patterns are described below as Cases 1 through 4.

Case 1: Equality of comparative advantage. Equality of comparative advantage holds if $\sigma_a = \sigma_b$ and $\rho_{ab} = 1$. In this case there will be no selectivity bias and the estimated rate of return will be equal to the interest rate. Specifically, recall that equality of comparative advantage holds if $(l_a, l_b) = e^{A_i}(\bar{l}_a, \bar{l}_b)$ where A_i is a scalar measure of ability with variance σ_A^2. In this case, $a_i = \ln \bar{l}_a + A_i$ and $b_i = \ln \bar{l}_a + A_i$. Thus, $\sigma_a = \sigma_b = \sigma_A$ and $\rho_{ab} = 1$ so that the bias terms, α_λ and β_λ, in (68) are zero and the estimated rate of return is equal to r. Geometrically, this corresponds to a situation in which the rate of return has zero variance across people so that the distribution of ρ in Figure 10.5 becomes degenerate at r.

In terms of innate ability, the conditions under which equality of comparative advantage holds can arise in two different ways as can be seen by examining (58). Specifically, these conditions hold if either (a) strength and ability are perfectly correlated (i.e. $\rho_{12} = 1$) and $\alpha_1 + \alpha_2 = \beta_1 + \beta_2$ or (b) strength and ability have identical percentage effects on productivity in each occupation (i.e. $\alpha_1 = \beta_i$ and $\alpha_2 = \beta_2$). Put differently, in either of these cases, economic ability will appear to be a one-dimensional factor even though, in the latter case, ability tests in a non-economic context may distinguish distinct components of ability such as strength and intelligence.

Case 2: Positive hierarchical sorting. This case arises when $\sigma_a/\sigma_b > \rho_{ab} > \sigma_b/\sigma_a$. It is called "positive hierarchical sorting" because those who go to college are drawn from the upper portion of the distribution of potential earnings in A while those who stop at high school are drawn from those in the lower portion of the distribution of potential earnings in B. Note that the parameter values for which this occurs imply that ρ_{ab} is sufficiently positive and that $\sigma_a^2 > \sigma_b^2$.

For example, suppose that $\rho_{ab} = 1$ so that there is a perfect correlation between talent in A and in B. Then the least talented person in A will be more talented than the most talented person in B. This extreme case of hierarchical sorting is illustrated in Figure 10.6 where the marginal distributions of a_i and b_i, respectively, are drawn on the horizontal and vertical axes and their joint distribution is the degenerate bivariate normal whose density lies along line dd which passes through (μ_a, μ_b) at point m and has slope σ_a/σ_b. The index function in (61), rewritten as $a = r(s_a - s_b) - \ln(w_a/w_b) + b$, is given by line II which intersects dd at point e. Anyone whose endowment point, (a_i, b_i), lies above II will achieve higher present value by choosing B and anyone whose endowment is below II will do best to choose A. Since everyone's endowments lie on *dd*, it is clear that all individuals whose endowments lie on the segment of *dd* below point e will choose B while all those whose endowments lie on the segment of *dd* above point e will choose A. The shaded areas of the two marginal distributions indicate the hierarchical sorting in labor market equilibrium.

The special case depicted in Figure 10.6 was used by Roy (1951) as a possible explanation for the tendency of the distribution of labor incomes to be more

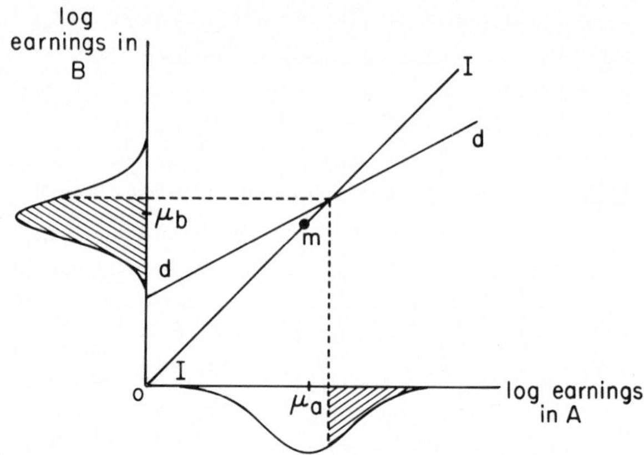

Figure 10.6. Optimal schooling choice with hierarchical sorting.

skewed than a log-normal distribution. That is, note that the overall distribution of log earnings in the diagram consists of a lower part given by the shaded area of the B distribution with variance σ_b^2 and an upper tail given by the A distribution which has a larger variance, σ_a^2, so that the composite distribution is skewed to the right.

More recently, Rosen has used a similar argument to explain the extremely high earnings of "superstars" [Rosen (1981)] and the skewed distribution of managerial salaries at successively higher levels of hierarchically structured firms [Rosen (1982)]. In both cases the argument turns on the assertion that (a) there is a one-factor distribution of ability (i.e. $\rho_{ab} = 1$) and (b) that the "scope" for talent is greater for, say, a major league baseball player than for a minor leaguer or for a corporation president compared to a middle manager (i.e. $\sigma_a > \sigma_b$). In terms of the relationship between innate abilities and occupational productivity in (57), greater "scope" for talent in A implies that $\alpha_1 + \alpha_2$ is greater than $\beta_1 + \beta_2$.

Case 3: Negative hierarchical sorting. This case corresponds to the condition $\sigma_a/\sigma_b < \rho_{ab} < \sigma_b/\sigma_a$. The negative hierarchical sorting implied by this condition would hold if there is a high positive correlation between productivities in A and B but with a greater scope for talent in the occupation which requires only a high school degree. Geometrically, the extreme form of this case would be illustrated by relabeling the axes in Figure 10.6. Needless to say, this case does not appear to be empirically important.

Case 4: Non-hierarchical sorting. The final possibility is the case of "non-hierarchical sorting" occurs when $\sigma_a/\sigma_b > \rho_{ab}$ and $\sigma_b/\sigma_a > \rho_{ab}$. This case will occur if ρ_{ab} is sufficiently small or if the scope for talent in A and B is about the same (e.g. if $\sigma_a = \sigma_b$, then $\rho_{ab} < 1$ is sufficient for non-hierarchical sorting). In this case, those who are best at B will tend to go to high school and those who are best at A will tend to go to college.

As an extreme example, suppose that innate abilities are uncorrelated (i.e. $\rho_{12} = 0$) and that only strength is useful in B and only intelligence is useful in A (i.e. $\alpha_1 = \beta_2 = 0$) so that $\rho_{ab} = 0$. Geometrically, this case would correspond to a situation in which the degenerate bivariate distribution of a and b represented by line *dd* in Figure 10.6 is replaced by an elliptical set of iso-probability contours whose major axis is horizontal. The index line, II, partitions this bivariate distribution on a slant so that the probability that individual i's comparative advantage is in A is an increasing function of a_i and the probability that his comparative advantage is in B is an increasing function of b_i. On average, the strongest workers will choose B and the most intelligent workers will choose A. Thus, average productivity of those in B will exceed μ_b and the average productivity of those in A will exceed μ_a.

5.4. *Empirical studies of ability bias*

A large and complex literature on the question of ability bias has arisen in the wake of the claim that a comparison of earnings of individuals who differ in education can be used to estimate the rate of return to investment in human capital. Since Griliches (1977, 1979) has ably reviewed all but the most recent literature in this field, I will summarize its methodology and findings very briefly in this section.

A major problem in dealing with questions concerning the role of ability and opportunity factors in determining earnings is the difficulty of finding data sets that contain information on ability and family background together with good information on individual education and earnings. To a considerable extent, economists have begun with data collected for other purposes and, in several important cases, they have resurveyed individuals who appear in existing data sets in order to add economic information. Since "opportunism" has been a dominant force in generating the data bases used to study these issues, there are often serious questions concerning the representativeness of a given sample and the comparability of variables across data sets.

Two major types of data have been used. One type provides information on psychometric mental and physical ability tests such as IQ, AFQT, tests of visual acuity and so on. These tests represent direct attempts to measure ability. Initially, such measures tended to be taken at face value and were entered directly into earnings regressions as "controls". More recently, test scores have often been regarded as "indicators" of underlying unobservable "true abilities" in latent variable models. The other major type of data uses data on siblings (i.e. brothers, dizygotic and monozygotic twins) in order to control for unobservable family effects including genetic and environmental influence which influence ability and/or opportunity. Under certain assumptions, one sibling can in effect be used as a "control" for the unmeasured family effects of the other sibling.

One example of the first type of data is the NBER-Th sample which was based on data on a sample of men who had volunteered for pilot, bombardier, and navigator programs of the Army Air Force during World War II which was originally gathered by the psychologists Robert L. Thorndike and Elizabeth Hagen. These men had taken a battery of tests of mental and physical abilities in the Air Force and were resurveyed in 1955 by Thorndike and Hagen after the war to determine their educations, occupations, and income. Later Paul Taubman and F. Thomas Juster at the National Bureau of Economic Research discovered these data and organized a resurvey of a subset of these men in 1969. The resulting data set provides information on education, income at up to five different points in the life cycle, test scores, and fairly detailed information on various measures of family background such as parental education, father's occupation, mother's work activity, and so on. As is true of most "opportunity" data sets, the individuals in the NBER-Th sample are not representative of the population. For example, they all have at least a high school education and all scored in the upper half of the AFQT ability test. These data have been used in a number of studies of earnings including Taubman and Wales (1974), Hause (1975), Lillard (1977), and Willis and Rosen (1979).

An example of the second type of data is the NRC twins sample which contains information on about 1000 monozygotic (MZ) and 900 dizygotic (DZ) twin pairs based on a National Research Council sample of white male army veterans. This data set also represents another case in which economists have resurveyed a sample which was collected for another purpose – in this case primarily for bio-medical research. Again, Paul Taubman was the economist who initiated the resurvey. More recently, Taubman and his associates have surveyed the children of these twins to study intergenerational issues.

The effect of measured ability on earnings in the NBER-Th data can be seen in Figure 10.7 which is reproduced from a descriptive study by Lillard (1977). Lillard combined individual test scores into one measure using factor analysis. This ability measure was then entered in a fully interactive manner with age and education in a third degree polynomial together with linear family background effects in a least squares earnings regression. The figure shows predicted age–earnings profiles for individuals with 12, 16, and 20 years of schooling who have sample average ability and sample average values of other variables. It also shows the earnings function for those whose measured ability is one standard deviation above or below the sample average.

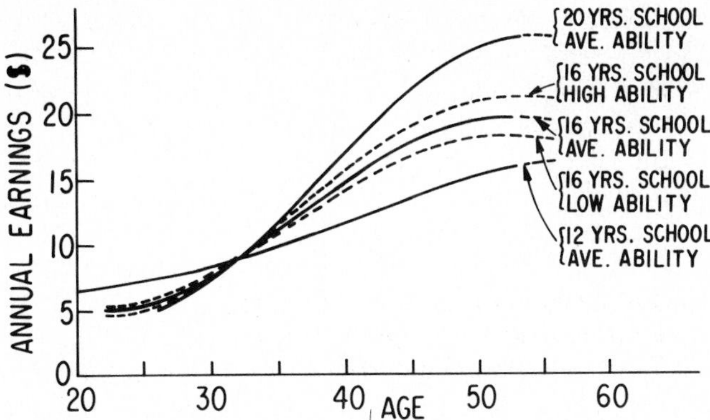

Figure 10.7. Life cycle earnings by education and ability. *Source*: Lillard (1977, Figure 1).

An important point to note from this diagram is that ability interacts positively with age (or experience). Thus, at early ages the more able earn slightly less than the less able, but by the time peak earnings are reached around age fifty the more able earn significantly more than those with less ability. Put differently, it is clear from the figure that higher levels of both ability and education are associated with higher dollar growth of income. An obvious hypothesis to explain these patterns is that the more able tend to invest more in on-the-job training or that they choose jobs with greater growth potential.

The figure also suggests that ability effects may be substantially understated in studies which rely on data for men under 35. Unfortunately, such an age limitation is characteristic of a number of data sets which have been used to study ability effects. Lillard suggests this as a possible explanation for the small magnitude of the ability effects found by Griliches and Mason (1972) and in the literature surveyed by Jenks et al. (1972). This is also a problem in the more recent series of papers by Chamberlain and Griliches [e.g. Chamberlain and Griliches (1977)] which use data from the National Longitudinal Survey of Young Men.

In the Lillard study and in a number of earlier studies, measured abilities were essentially taken at face value in the sense that they were simply entered as regressors to estimate the effect of schooling net of measured ability. There is, however, an obvious question whether tests really measure "true ability" and, if so, how well. To the extent that the measured ability measures are imperfect or incomplete representations of "true ability" there remains the possibility that the effects of schooling and experience will still be subject to ability bias even when measured ability is controlled. In addition, there are questions concerning the treatment of schooling as an endogenous choice variable which are not addressed or inadequately addressed in much of this literature.

Following Griliches (1977, 1979), the discussion of studies of ability bias can begin with a simple earnings function:

$$\ln y = \alpha + \beta s + \gamma A + u, \tag{70}$$

where β is regarded as the "true" measure of the rate of return to education and A represents a set of unmeasured variables including ability, family background, or other variables apart from schooling which are thought to influence earnings. For expositional simplicity, experience effects are assumed away. Least squares estimates which omit A will result in a biased estimate of β. Using the standard formula for omitted variable bias, the expected value of the schooling coefficient is $Eb_{ys} = \beta + \gamma b_{As}$, where $b_{As} = \text{cov}(As)/\text{var}(s)$ measures the association between schooling and the left out variable(s).

The literature surveyed by Griliches (1977, 1979) gives primary emphasis to the treatment of ability as an unobservable. Of the studies surveyed, by far the greatest degree of ability bias was found by Behrman et al. (1977) using data from the NRC twin sample which was described above. Griliches' analysis of their results provides an excellent outline of many of the theoretical and statistical issues that arise in attempts to deal with the question of ability bias. I will attempt to convey the flavor of his analysis in the following brief summary.

Behrman et al. (1977) argue that ability (and other unobservable variables determining economic success such as drive, ambition, etc.) effects may be regarded as the consequence of the genetic and environmental contribution of the family. If it is assumed that the unobserved component, A_i, of person i is a pure "family effect" which captures these genetic and environmental effects, then data on siblings, especially twin data, may be used to control for these unobservable effects and permit an unbiased estimate of β.

To illustrate this, assume that the earnings model is given by (70), that schooling is treated as exogenous and that the family effect represented by A_i can be decomposed into additive genetic and environmental components as follows:

$$A_i = G_i + E_i, \tag{71}$$

where G_i and E_i are, respectively, the genetic and environmental components which have variances σ_G^2 and σ_E^2 and covariance σ_{GE}.

The basic idea behind using sibling data is that the "within-family" return to schooling can eliminate at least part of the covariance between A and s which exists between random pairs of individuals. Thus, consider the following within-family model obtained by taking first differences of the earning function in (70):

$$\begin{aligned}\ln y_i - \ln y_{i'} &= \beta(s_i - s_{i'}) + \gamma(A_i - A_{i'}) + u_i - u_{i'} \\ &= \beta(s_i - s_{i'}) + \gamma(G_i - G_{i'}) + \gamma(E_i - E_{i'}) + u_i - u_{i'},\end{aligned} \tag{72}$$

where i and i' denote a given twin pair for $i,\ i'=1,\dots,n$ twin pairs and A_i is assumed to have the error component structure given in (71).

When it is applied to MZ twins, the within-family model can completely eliminate ability bias if it is assumed that individuals who grow up in the same family have identical environmental components and that individuals who have identical genes have identical genetic components. Given these assumptions, $E_i - E_{i'}$ and $G_i - G_{i'}$ are both zero for MZ twins. Since cov(us) is assumed to be zero, it follows that an estimate of β using data on MZ twins will be unbiased. In the case of DZ twins, the environmental component is eliminated by first differencing and the variance of the genetic component, $G_i - G_{i'}$, is considerably smaller than it would be for randomly chosen pairs.

Behrman et al. (1977) found evidence of substantial ability bias when they applied the model in (72) to data from the NRC twins sample. They first estimated β using data from random pairs and obtained an estimate of about 8 percent for β which is similar to estimates found in representative samples of the U.S. population. If individuals are chosen at random from the population, a least squares estimate of β is subject to ability bias due to covariance between A and s as explained above. When data on DZ twin pairs were used, the estimate of β fell to about 6 percent and when data on MZ twins were used it fell to only 2.7 percent. They interpreted these results as showing that a major portion of the apparent return to education is due to correlation between schooling and unmeasured family (especially genetic) components.

Griliches (1979) argues that this interpretation is suspect for two major reasons. First, it is not clear a priori that all omitted variables are purely family effects. Once individual-specific components are allowed, he shows that the within-family estimates are not necessarily less biased than estimates for randomly chosen individuals. Second, the effects of statistical problems other than unobserved ability components may be accentuated in the within-family regressions. A major example of this is the possibility that schooling is measured with error. This problem is likely to be minor when the variance of schooling is relatively large as it is in the general population. However, the noise-to-signal ratio and hence the degree of bias due to errors in variables tends to become large in the within-family regressions. Griliches argues that plausible assumptions concerning errors in the schooling measure can explain most of the differences in the estimates of the returns to schooling among random pairs, DZ twins and MZ twins found by Behrman et al.

It is important to point out that the earnings model in (70) treats schooling as exogenous and treats the coefficients α, β, and γ as constant across individuals. In contrast, as has been argued at length above, when schooling decisions are endogenous and the condition of equality of comparative advantage holds there is no bias in the least squares estimate of β because $\text{cov}(As) = 0$. However, if there is interpersonal variation in comparative advantage, there will tend to be correlation between A and s because of self-selection. Moreover, because variation in comparative advantage implies interpersonal variation in the rate of return to education, β (and the other parameters) will not be constant across individuals. Thus, β may be regarded as an estimate of the sample average of individual-specific marginal rates of return. Since individual rates of return influence schooling decisions, it follows that u will tend to be correlated with s because it contains individual deviations from β. Hence, even if "true ability" could be observed perfectly, least squares estimation of β may be subject to simultaneous equations bias.

Willis and Rosen (1979) use data from the NBER-Th sample in an attempt to deal with some of the problems presented by self-selection and unobserved ability and opportunity components. They formulate an econometric model based on the Roy model which utilizes the distinction between ability and opportunity factors emphasized in Becker's Woytinsky Lecture. Information on observed ability and opportunity variables is used to correct for selectivity on the unobservables. The model permits them to determine whether ability selection is hierarchical or non-hierarchical. It also provides evidence on the hypothesis that schooling choices are based on maximization of the present value of earnings and provides an estimate of the elasticity of college enrollment with respect to the rate of return to college education.

In the Willis–Rosen model individuals are assumed to choose that level of schooling which maximizes the present value of lifetime earnings. For reasons of computational feasibility, the choice is restricted to two schooling categories. They are labeled A for more than high school and B for high school graduate. (Recall that all members of the NBER-Th sample are at least high school graduates.)

The life cycle earnings profile of each individual, conditional on his schooling choice, is described by two parameters corresponding to an initial level and a constant growth rate of earnings. These "structural earnings functions" are

$$\begin{aligned} \ln \bar{y}_{ai} &= X_i\beta_a + u_{1i} \\ g_{ai} &= X_i\gamma_a + u_{2i}, \end{aligned} \tag{73}$$

$$\begin{aligned} \ln \bar{y}_{bi} &= X_i\beta_b + u_{3i} \\ g_{bi} &= X_i\gamma_b + u_{4i}, \end{aligned} \tag{74}$$

where $y_{ij}(x) = \bar{y}_{ij}\exp(g_{ij}x)$ is the earnings of person i at experience level x given that he has schooling level j $(=\text{A},\text{B})$. X_i is a vector of observable "ability" variables which affect the individual's initial earnings (i.e. $\bar{y}_{ij}$) and growth rate of earnings (i.e. g_{ij}) given his schooling choice j. Earnings growth is calculated as the average real growth rate of earnings between the respondent's first job (in 1946, on average) and his most recent earnings in 1969. The influence of unobservable ability variables on earning potential is captured by u_{1i} through u_{4i}.

It is important to note that neither observed nor unobserved ability components necessarily influence earnings potential in the same way in both A and B. Specifically, no restriction is placed on the variances or covariances of the unobservable components, u_1 through u_4. Similarly, the coefficients of the observable ability variables, $(\beta_a, \gamma_a, \beta_b, \gamma_b)$, may differ between A and B. It follows that the rate of return to college education may vary across individuals because of differences in both observed and unobserved components.

Opportunities to finance educational investment are also assumed to vary across individuals. Each individual is assumed to face a constant interest rate,

$$r_i = Z_i\delta + u_{5i}, \tag{75}$$

where Z_i is a vector of observable "opportunity" variables which influence the individual's rate of interest and u_{5i} reflects unobservable opportunity variables. Since there is no direct data on individual-specific discount rates, r_i is also treated as an unobservable.

The decision rule for college enrollment is obtained by defining the index function, $I_i \equiv \ln(V_{ai}/V_{bi})$, where $V_{ai} = [\bar{y}_{ai}/(r_i - g_{ai})]\exp(-r_i s)$ and $V_{bi} = \bar{y}_{bi}/(r_i - g_{bi})$, respectively, denote person i's present value of lifetime earnings if he chooses to go s years beyond high school or stop at high school graduation. (For simplicity, working life is assumed to be infinite.) Individual i will choose to enroll in college if $I_i > 0$ and otherwise will stop at high school. Using a Taylor Series approximation around the population mean values $(\bar{g}_a, \bar{g}_b, \bar{r})$ yields:

$$I_i = \alpha_0 + \alpha_1(\ln \bar{y}_{ai} - \ln \bar{y}_{bi}) + \alpha_2 g_{ai} + \alpha_3 g_{bi} + \alpha_4 r_i, \tag{76}$$

with $\alpha_1 = 1$, $\alpha_2 = 1/(\bar{r} - \bar{g}_a) > 0$, and $\alpha_3 = -1/(\bar{r} - \bar{g}_b) < 0$.

Two key assumptions are required to make this model operational. One concerns the functional form of the joint distribution of the unobservable ability and opportunity components, u_{1i} through u_{5i}. These are assumed to be normal with mean zero. No restriction is placed on the variances or covariances of these components.

The second key assumption concerns identification. Ideally, we would like to observe the effect on earnings of a change in education of a person with given ability. Since ability is not completely observable and since any given person can only choose either A or B, this ideal is unattainable. The best that we can hope for is to observe the average effect of an increase in education in a group of people in which the difference in education is uncorrelated with ability. As I pointed out earlier, this goal can be attained if opportunities (i.e. r_i) can be varied independently of abilities. Thus, to identify the effect of selection on ability it is necessary for at least one of the opportunity variables, Z_i, to differ from the ability variables, X_i.[13] In addition, if we wish to identify the effect of variation the rate of return to college on college enrollment, it is necessary for at least one X variable to differ from the Z variables.

In their paper, Willis and Rosen assume that the X and Z variables do not overlap. They associate the X variables with the battery of test scores taken by the respondents in the military. These include tests of reading, mathematics, mechanical aptitude, and dexterity. The Z variables are assumed to be a set of family background variables including father's education and occupation, mother's work experience, religion, and number of siblings. This identifying restriction emphasizes the importance of the family as a source of finance for higher education and assumes that any direct family effects on ability (e.g. genetic effects or training received within the family) are adequately captured by the test scores. While this restriction is not testable, some indirect empirical support for it is suggested by the preponderance of evidence from other studies that family background variables appear to have little direct effect on earnings, but operate primarily through their influence on schooling attainment [see Griliches (1979)]. On the other hand, the fact that the respondents were eligible for G.I. Bill educational subsidies may undercut its plausibility for the NBER-Th sample.

Willis and Rosen's estimation strategy, based on an econometric model by Lee (1977), involves three steps. First, they estimate a "reduced form probit" equation which describes the probability that an individual with observed characteristics given by (X_i, Z_i) will choose to go beyond high school. This equation is used to form an estimate of the inverse Mills ratios, λ_{ai} and λ_{bi} [which were defined in (65)], for each individual in the sample. Second, the estimated values of λ_{bi} and λ_{ai}, respectively, are entered as regressors along with X_i into the equations for the initial level and growth rate of earnings for in (73) and (74) to obtain an estimate of β_a and β_b which are corrected for selectivity bias. [See Heckman (1976) for the justification for this procedure.] As explained earlier, the estimated coefficients of λ_{ai} and λ_{bi} provide evidence on the nature of the selectivity of

[13]Actually, it is theoretically possible to correct for selectivity bias even if the X and Z variables are identical by using the fact that inverse Mills ratios are non-linear functions of these variables while the earnings parameters in (73) and (74) are assumed to be linear functions of X. However, the use of non-linearities for identification is perilous because it places very heavy reliance both on correct specification of the functional form of the unobservables and on correct specification of the structural regression.

schooling on unobserved ability components. Third, estimates of $\ln \bar{y}_{ai}$, $\ln \bar{y}_{bi}$, $\bar{g}_{ai}$, and $\bar{g}_{bi}$ are entered into a "structural probit" equation along with Z_i to obtain consistent estimates of the coefficients α_1, α_2, and α_3 in (76). Using these estimates together with estimates of $\bar{g}_a$ and $\bar{g}_b$ from sample mean growth rates, it is possible to obtain an estimate of $\bar{r}$, the mean rate of interest in the population.

Their empirical findings indicate significant non-hierarchical selection on ability equivalent to Case 4 described in Section 5.3. That is to say, individuals who enroll in college have higher lifetime earnings in A than those who did not enroll, while those who did not enroll have higher lifetime earnings in B than the enrollees would have had if they if had chosen B. The most important measured ability factor appears to be the mathematical test score which significantly increases lifetime earnings of the college educated but has little effect on the high school graduates.

From the earlier discussion of the Roy model, recall that non-hierarchical sorting implies that there is more than one distinct ability factor and that the direction of ability bias is uncertain. For the average sample member, the estimated uncorrected rate of return to college of 9 percent is lower than the corrected rate of return of 9.8 percent. On average, those who attended college had a rate of return of 9.9 percent while those who did not attend college had a return of 9.3 percent. Estimates of the average rate of discount (i.e. $\bar{r}$) range between 9.8 and 12.4 percent. Finally, at the sample mean, the estimates imply that a one percent increase in the permanent earnings of college-educated workers relative to high school graduates would increase the probability of college enrollment by about 2 percent. Alternatively, assuming four years of college, this calculation implies that an increase in the rate of return to college by one percentage point would increase college enrollment by 8 percent. This is a sizeable elasticity but it is, of course, smaller than the perfectly elastic response that would be expected under conditions of equality of opportunity and comparative advantage.

In a similar model applied to data from Project Talent, Kenny et al. (1979) find evidence of selectivity on the earnings of high school graduates but no evidence of selectivity for the college educated. However, their data do not permit estimation of corrected rates of return to college or estimation of a structural college enrollment function.

Unfortunately, it is not certain how well either the qualitative or quantitative findings reported by Willis and Rosen generalize because, apart from Kenny et al., this type of model has not been estimated with other data sets. The main reason for this is probably the scarcity of data sets that contain sufficient ability and opportunity measures and also have earnings data covering a large portion of the life cycle.

Given the complexity of the issues and the non-representative character of the data sets that have been employed in the literature on ability bias, it is difficult to reach any firm conclusions about the magnitude or even the direction of the bias in U.S. data and there seem to be few, if any, studies using non-U.S. data. My impression is that the simple Mincer-type earnings function does a surprisingly good job of estimating the returns to education even though more general econometric models suggest that the conditions of equality of opportunity and equality of comparative advantage upon which it is based are not strictly true.

6. Other topics

Throughout the chapter to this point, it has been assumed that investment in human capital raises worker productivity and that the market wage received by a worker at any point in the life cycle is equal to the value of his current marginal productivity. Both of these assumptions have been questioned in recent literature and a survey of the determinants of earnings would be seriously incomplete without mentioning them. Given the length of this survey, however, I will not be able to do them full justice with a detailed treatment.

6.1. Education and economic growth

The central question which provided the original impetus for the modern development of human capital theory was not the issue of earnings differentials by age and education which has dominated both this survey and the human capital literature since 1960. Rather, as is clear from Schultz's (1961) Presidential Address to the American Economic Association, the central question concerned the extent to which growth in the average quality of labor over time resulting from investment in human capital could help to account for the "residual" in U.S. productivity growth which growth in conventionally measured inputs of capital and labor in early studies by Solow (1957) and others left unexplained.

The answer to this question given in the "growth accounting" literature [see, for example, Dennison (1962) and Griliches (1970)] was that a considerable fraction of the residual could be explained by investment in human capital. A simple example of the basic methodology of these studies goes as follows. Assume that the relative productivity of workers in a base period who differ in education is given by their relative wages. The growth of "quality corrected" aggregate labor input in another period can then be calculated as the weighted sum of the man-hours of labor contributed by that group where the weight is given by relative base period wage of each education group. Since there has been substantial growth in the average educational attainment of the U.S. labor force over time, the growth of "quality-adjusted" aggregate labor input is more rapid than the growth of the unadjusted aggregate and the overall unexplained residual in productivity growth is reduced.

6.2. Screening and signalling

A basic assumption underlying this methodology is that an increase in educational attainment causes an increase in labor productivity. From the inception of human capital theory, a variety of critics have expressed skepticism about this causal assumption. Most frequently the skeptics, especially non-economists, argued that the higher pay received by the more educated reflects the operation of "credentialism" rather higher productivity. This line of criticism is unpersuasive to economists who ask why profit-seeking firms would choose to sacrifice profits by paying wage premia merely for "sheepskins".

In his well-known "signalling" model, Spence (1974) showed that profit-seeking firms may indeed pay wage premia to more educated individuals even if education has no effect on productivity [see also Arrow (1973)]. In addition, he shows that wealth-maximizing individuals will be willing to make educational investments because of these wage gains. Thus, he argues, it is possible for there to be a market equilibrium in which more educated workers receive higher pay even if education has no effect on worker productivity. The basis for this surprising result is the assumption that information about worker productivity is distributed asymmetrically (i.e. workers know their own productivity but firms cannot tell which workers are most productive) and that more able workers can invest in a signal more cheaply than the less able.

A simple numerical example conveys the nature of this argument [Spence (1973)]. Imagine that there are two types of workers who differ in productivity and that there are equal numbers of each type in the population. High ability workers have a marginal product of 2 and low ability workers have a marginal product of 1. Workers may choose either zero or s years of schooling at a positive cost, but schooling does not augment their productivity. With perfect information about worker productivity, employers would pay high and low ability workers wages of 2 and 1, respectively, and no worker would invest in schooling.

Now suppose that firms have no knowledge of worker productivity but that workers know their own type. If firms offer a wage of 2 to high ability workers, low ability workers have an obvious incentive to misrepresent themselves. One possible equilibrium is that firms pay the expected marginal product of a randomly chosen worker (i.e. one-half). An alternative is that high ability workers might choose to use education as a "signal" to employers of their innately higher productivity. Schooling will be a credible signal if, in fact, high ability individuals choose to invest in schooling while those with low ability do not.

This type of self-selection can occur if the cost of schooling is negatively correlated with ability. To justify this assumption, it might be assumed, for example, that high ability people can get through school with less effort than low ability people. Thus, consider the following signalling equilibrium. Assume that the direct cost of investment in schooling to high ability people is 0.5 and to low ability people is 1.5 and that firms offer a wage of 2 to educated workers and a wage of 1 to uneducated workers. The net benefit from education is equal to the wage to educated workers minus the opportunity wage to an uneducated worker minus the direct cost of education. Hence, the net benefit to education for a high ability worker is 0.5 and is −0.5 for a low ability worker. In this situation, workers self-select themselves into educational categories according to ability and firms find that the high pay given to educated workers is justified by their higher productivity. Once established, the equilibrium tends to be self-fulfilling.

The theoretical literature on signalling and screening models and aspects of the effect of asymmetric information in the labor market (and other markets) has grown rapidly since the early work of Spence and Arrow. Some of this work considers questions about the sensitivity of the results to alternative equilibrium concepts [see, for example, Riley (1975, 1979)]. The signalling model also raises questions about the efficiency of market determination of educational investment. In the simple example given above, there is clearly overinvestment in education from a social point of view since aggregate labor productivity is unaffected by education but net output is reduced by the cost of education as compared with a situation in which no education takes place. Efficiency issues become more complicated if the allocation of high and low ability workers matters. For example, suppose that low ability workers are completely unproductive if they are assigned to a "high ability" job. In this case, it is socially worthwhile to spend some resources to assign workers to the job in which they are most productive. To the extent that education plays this role, it has social productivity. [See, for example, Stiglitz (1975a).]

Signalling theories have attracted skeptics, too. For example, Becker (1975) points out that a college education is a very expensive test instrument and that it is likely that firms can find cheaper ways to determine worker ability. For example, a number of economists have explored the possibility that labor contracts can be structured in such a way that workers will self-select themselves according to their ability. If such schemes are feasible, the need for investment in a signal is eliminated. In the simple example given above, a piece rate system would suffice if worker productivity is known to the firm ex post. In more complicated situations, no first best labor contract may be feasible.

Ideally, the direction of causation between investment in education and worker productivity would be determined by empirical test. However, the signalling–human capital debate provides an extreme (and clear-cut) example of the tendency for efficient behavior to censor non-experimental economic data in such a way that information crucial to the test is removed.

The basic point is easily illustrated by considering a simple "human capital" example which parallels Spence's signalling example described above [see Spence (1981)]. In the human capital example, education causes an increase in the productivity of all workers by the same amount from a marginal product of 1 with no schooling to 2 with s years of schooling. The direct cost of schooling is 0.5 to high ability workers and 1.5 to low ability workers. As before, in the signalling example, high and low ability workers, respectively, have marginal products of 2 and 1 regardless of their schooling level and their direct costs of schooling are respectively 0.5 and 1.5. Individual ability is assumed to be unobservable (ex ante) to either firms or to the econometrician. Ex post, the average productivity of a group of workers can be observed.

Given experimental data, determination of which model is correct is perfectly straightforward. The experimenter simply randomly assigns individuals to different schooling levels and observes their average productivity ex post. If the signalling theory is correct, he would expect to find that workers in both schooling groups have an average productivity of 1.5 and, if schooling is productive, he would expect to find the average product of the uneducated and educated groups of workers to be 1 and 2, respectively. Now suppose that the econometrician must rely on market data on schooling and earnings. Note that the equilibrium distribution of workers and level of wages by educational level in the human capital and signalling examples are identical. That is, in both models low ability individuals choose zero schooling and receive a wage of 1 and high ability individuals choose s years of schooling and receive a wage of 2.

The identification issue illustrated by this example appears to be generic to tests of signalling versus human capital interpretations of educational investment. Note that any information on individual ability which is available to an econometrician is also likely to be available to firms and, therefore, would not be related to the "unobservable" ability components for which education is a signal. The issue is further complicated by the fact that the observed effect of schooling on earnings may consist of both productivity and signalling components. Thus, the empirical problem is to determine the relative importance of these components. As a consequence of these difficulties, the empirical literature on this issue is neither large nor very persuasive. [See Riley (1979) for a review and critique of earlier empirical studies.]

The main empirical tactic of any promise rests on an attempt to classify occupations in terms of an a priori view about the degree to which individual-level productivity in those occupations is observable. For example, Wolpin (1977) argues that screening by education is less important for the self-employed than for employees and then examines differences between the levels of educational attainment and the effect of schooling on earnings for the two groups. He argues that his results do not support the signalling hypothesis, but Riley (1979) argues that Wolpin's results do provide mild support for signalling if they are properly interpreted. In his own empirical work, Riley (1979) chooses a strategy which lets the data "speak for themselves" by classifying occupations into relatively screened and unscreened categories on the basis of occupation-specific earnings functions. Then some additional differences between the two groups are used as tests of the importance of screening. Riley reports some support for the screening view, but emphasizes the tentativeness of his conclusions.

6.3. *Specific human capital*

Although the important distinction between "general" and "firm-specific" investment in human capital was introduced very early in the development of human capital theory by Becker (1962, 1964) and Oi (1962), most subsequent theoretical and empirical work in the field tended to ignore the issues raised by specific capital until quite recently. The distinction between the two types of investment is simple. Purely general training received by a worker within a given firm is defined as investment which raises the potential productivity of the worker in other firms by as much as it is raised within the firm providing the training. Purely specific training raises the worker's productivity within the firm providing the training, but leaves his productivity unaffected in other firms.

As explained earlier, competition implies that workers rather than firms will tend to pay the costs and receive the returns from any general training they receive. In effect, general capital is completely embodied in the worker. Consequently, it is efficient for the worker to "own" his general capital and be free to employ it wherever it receives the highest reward. In contrast, the productivity of specific capital is jointly dependent on the productive characteristics embodied in the worker and the characteristics of other firm-specific inputs.

In this case, Becker (1962, 1964) points out that it may be inefficient for either the worker or the firm to have exclusive ownership of specific human capital. For example, if the worker pays the full cost of training and attempts to reap the full returns, the firm may inflict a capital loss on the worker by dismissing him without suffering any loss itself. Symmetrically, if the firm pays the cost of specific training and attempts to reap the returns by paying the worker his opportunity wage, the worker can without cost inflict a capital loss on the firm by quitting to work elsewhere. Becker suggested that the solution to the problem of jointness is for the worker and the firm to share both the costs and the returns so that each agent would suffer a loss if the worker–firm relationship is terminated. However, Becker was unable to provide a theory of the factors that determine the worker's and the firm's shares. Without such a theory, it is not possible to derive implications for the life cycle pattern of worker earnings. Since the theory of general training does produce such implications, it tended to provide the theoretical underpinnings for empirical studies of earnings discussed earlier in this chapter.

One of the major implications of the specific capital concept is to emphasize the importance of the duration of a worker–firm match in determining the total pay-off to the investment. Recently, this has led to renewed interest in developing theories and methods to measure the duration of jobs and to assess the determinants and implications of life cycle labor force mobility. For example, Hall (1982) has shown that "lifetime jobs" are of more importance in the United States than had commonly been believed. In a still more recent study, Randolph (1983) estimates that a typical U.S. worker has about a 50 percent chance of having a job that lasts more than half of the length of his total career in the labor force. However, he finds that the expected duration of a given job is only about 3 years because of a high exit probability in early phases of a job.

An obvious first question to be raised about specific training is how important it is empirically. Unfortunately, specific capital is no more directly observable than is general human capital. Thus, answers to this question tend either to involve classification of various types of training expense according to a priori notions about their degree of specificity or to attempt to extend the theory in order to obtain indirect evidence by testing its implications for observable behavior.

Most of the hypothesized examples of specific capital that I have run across appear to involve issues of imperfect information rather than the task-specific skills which are often conjured up when describing what human capital "really is" because the technological "know-how" involved in task-specific skills is unlikely to be unique to a given firm. For instance, possible examples of firm-specific capital include a salesman's knowledge about the characteristics and needs of the firm's clients, a middle-manager's knowledge of the firm's operating procedures, the identity of other employees who know how to fill out a given form and so on.

As another example, the costs of hiring a worker are often treated as a specific investment by the firm. Many of these costs arise because it is costly to inform potential workers of the availability of a job and also costly to screen applicants for their suitability. Similarly, many aspects of search costs incurred by workers seeking jobs can be viewed as firm specific. The concept of information about the quality of a job match as a form of specific human capital has been exploited in a theoretical model of job matching by Jovanovic (1979) which focuses on the implications of the matching process for job turnover.

Jovanovic's model assumes that the joint productivity of a given match between a firm and a worker is not known at the time of hiring by either the worker or the firm. Rather, the quality of the match is gradually revealed by the worker's productivity record on the job. As information begins to accumulate in the early phases of the job, poorly matched workers learn this fact and tend to quit in order to search for a better match. Initially, the probability (or hazard) of quitting tends to rise with tenure on the job. As time passes, however, the remaining workers tend to be those for whom the quality of the match is high relative to the expected value of alternatives and the probability of quitting tends to decrease with increased tenure. This pattern of hazard rates has been confirmed empirically by Randolph (1983) who finds that the hazard rate increases for about the first 12 months of job tenure and decreases thereafter.

In addition to exploring the empirical implications of Jovanovic's model for job turnover, Mincer and Jovanovic (1981) also examine its implications for earnings. If specific capital is important, the theory suggests that increases in job tenure, holding labor force experience constant, should have a positive effect on earnings. They find significant tenure effects which indicate that about one-third of wage growth in the early portion of the career and 20–25 percent in mid-career can be attributed to specific investment with the remainder due to general investment. [See also Bartel and Borjas (1981).] Recently, Hashimoto and Raisian (1984) have used a similar approach in an attempt to determine the relative importance of specific training in the United States and Japan. They provide evidence that expected job tenure is longer than in the United States and that the tenure-related component of wage growth in Japan tends to be relatively larger.

6.4. *Agency theories of life cycle wages*

Conventionally, it is assumed that a worker's productivity is the cause of the economic reward he receives. In an important paper, Alchian and Demsetz (1972) argue that the reverse line of causation may be equally important because of the effect of the system of compensation on worker incentives. The basic incentive problem arises because the self-interest of workers is not coincident with the interests of the firm. For example, the owners of the firm value the worker's output but do not have any direct preferences concerning the disutility of effort the worker experiences in producing that output. Conversely, the worker has no direct preferences for the output of the firm. Rather, he is concerned only with his own income and effort.

In the language of agency theory [Ross (1973)], the worker is an "agent" of the firm which is the "principal".[14] The principal's problem is to design the organization of production and system of rewards (and penalties) in such a way as to make the worker's behavior coincide with the principal's objectives subject to the constraint that the worker receives a level of utility at least as great as he could receive in his next best alternative. A large literature on "agency" theories of wage determination has arisen in the past decade. I shall only briefly describe some of the elements of this literature with special emphasis given to its implications for life cycle wage patterns. (See Chapter 14 by Parsons in this Handbook for more details on this class of problems.)

[14] However, see Carmichael (1983) for an interesting model in which the principal himself becomes an agent after the reward system has been agreed upon.

If a given worker's productivity is independent of other inputs (including the effort of other workers) and his output is easily monitored by the firm, Alchian and Demsetz point out that a piece rate system induces an efficient level of effort by the worker. However, if it is difficult to observe output or if there is "team production" (i.e. interactions in production) the worker's product cannot be used as the basis of rewards. The alternative of simply paying an hourly wage provides no incentive for the worker to expend effort.[15] To avoid shirking, the firm may expend resources in attempt to monitor the worker's effort.

As a way of reducing monitoring costs, the firm may attempt to design a compensation scheme which reduces the worker's incentive to shirk (or to engage in other misfeasances or malfeasances such as stealing). This approach was taken by Becker and Stigler (1974) and elaborated by Lazear (1979) who used it in an attempt to explain the phenomenon of mandatory retirement. (See also Chapter 5 by Lazear in this Handbook.)

Very briefly, the argument is that workers can be induced to behave "honestly" (e.g. in accord with an ex ante implicit or explicit contract specifying the level of effort) if some portion of payment to the worker is deferred and the employer follows the practice of dismissing the worker if he is discovered to violate the terms of the contract. In effect, the deferred payment acts as a performance bond because the worker loses the value of the deferred payment if he is dismissed. If the value of this loss is sufficiently high at each point in time during the period of the contract, the worker will be deterred from shirking.

Competition will ensure that the present value of a worker's productivity and the payments made to him over the period of his employment are equal. Hence, a deferred payment scheme implies that the worker will be paid less than his marginal product during the initial phases of the job and more than his marginal product later on. Given that he is being paid more than he is worth, the senior worker would prefer to continue working beyond the ex ante optimal duration of the job but the firm would lose profits if he were to do so. Thus, Lazear argues that mandatory retirement can be regarded as a contractual mechanism by which the firm enforces the optimal duration of the employment relationship.

From the viewpoint of the theory of life cycle earnings, an important implication of deferred compensation schemes is that they break the close link between the evolution of productivity and earnings which is a feature of investment in (general) human capital. The question of the relationship between productivity and wage growth is addressed by Medoff and Abraham (1980, 1981). They examine evidence based on the relationship between a worker's wages and evaluations of his performance by supervisors. They interpret this evidence as suggesting that productivity and pay are not as closely linked as is suggested by

[15] See Stiglitz (1975b) for an analysis of the trade-off between piece rates and time rates when workers are risk averse.

conventional human capital theory. In contrast, Brown (1983) finds evidence in favor of the human capital theory. He uses data from the Panel Study of Income Dynamics to examine the relationship between the importance of on-the-job training on the current job and wage growth. His results suggest that wage growth tends to be attenuated when training becomes unimportant. A clear-cut resolution of this question awaits future research.

7. Conclusion

A combination of advances in economic theory, collection of new data, and creation of new statistical and econometric techniques has been the hallmark of the development of modern labor economics. Nowhere, in my view, has this combination been more fruitful than in the analysis of the determinants of earnings. In the main, the initial insights of Becker and Mincer who first developed human capital theory have been repeatedly confirmed with data from around the world. Indeed, the reinterpretation of their theory offered in this chapter tends to strengthen this assessment. Moreover, the empirical findings have stood up remarkably well to the possibility that the return to investment in human capital is the result of innate ability differentials rather than compensation for the cost of adjustment.

The recent stress on the role of specific as opposed to general human capital and the development of agency theories of the employee–employer relationship may result in the modification of some of the received doctrine, but these theories also serve to enrich the scope of the theory by pointing toward interesting and potentially important connections between wages, job mobility, and institutional practices. Future progress in this area will hinge crucially on the development of data which links information on the individual characteristics of workers and their households with data on the firms who employ them. I see no comparable promise that the signalling hypothesis will receive a convincing test against the conventional human capital theory because of the inherent identification problem described earlier.

I believe that an important and promising area of future research lies in the further exploration of the general equilibrium interaction of the supply and demand for human capital which has begun with the recent studies of cohort size effects discussed earlier. Theoretical considerations suggest that there may be important interrelationships between changes in the age distribution due to variations in population growth, changes in the age structure of life cycle productivity due to human capital investment and the equilibrium interest rate. In addition, the underlying influence of the family and the government on the supply and demand for human capital need to be considered. Some initial explorations of these interrelationships are presented in Willis (forthcoming) in a steady-state overlapping generations model, but theoretical work on non-steady-state problems and most of the relevant empirical work awaits future research. Also, the potential for increased knowledge from international comparative studies is great. The discovery and development of new data, especially micro data, will be the key to progress in this area.

References

Abowd, John M. and Orley Ashenfelter (1981) "Anticipated unemployment, temporary layoffs, and compensating wage differentials", in: S. Rosen, ed., *Studies in labor markets*. Chicago: University of Chicago Press.

Alchian, A. and H. Demsetz (1972) "Production, information costs, and economic organization", *American Economic Review*, 62:777–795.

Arrow, Kenneth (1973) "Higher education as a filter", *Journal of Public Economics*, 2:193–216.

Ashenfelter, Orley (1978) "Estimating the effect of training programs on earnings", *Review of Economics and Statistics*, 50:47–57.

Bartel, Ann P. and George J. Borjas (1981) "Wage growth and job turnover: an empirical analysis", in: S. Rosen, ed., *Studies in labor markets*. Chicago: University of Chicago Press.

Barzel, Yoram and Ben Yu (1984) "The effect of the utilization rate on the division of labor", *Economic Inquiry*, 22(1):18–27.

Becker, Gary S. (1962) "Investment in human capital: a theoretical analysis", *Journal of Political Economy* (Supplement), 70:9–49.

Becker, Gary S. (1964) *Human capital: a theoretical analysis with special reference to education*. New York: Columbia University Press for NBER.

Becker, Gary S. (1975) *Human capital: a theoretical and empirical analysis, with special reference to education*. New York: Columbia University Press for the National Bureau of Economic Research, 2nd Edition. (1st edition, 1964.)

Becker, Gary S. (1967) *Human capital and the personal distribution of income*. Ann Arbor: University of Michigan Press.

Becker, Gary S. (1984) "The allocation of effort, specific human capital, and sexual differences in earnings and the allocation of time", *Journal of Labor Economics*.

Becker, Gary (1985) "Human capital, effort and the sexual division of labor", *Journal of Labor Economics*, 3, part 2:S33–S58.

Becker, Gary S. and Barry R. Chiswick (1966) "Education and the distribution of earnings", *American Economic Review, Proceedings*, 56:358–369.

Becker, Gary S. and George J. Stigler (1974) "Law enforcement, malfeasance, and compensation of enforcers", *Journal of Legal Studies*, 3:1–18.

Behrman, J., P. Taubman, T. Wales and Z. Hrubec (1977) "Inter- and intragenerational determination of socioeconomic success with special reference to genetic endowment and family and other environment", unpublished paper, University of Pennsylvania.

Ben-Porath, Yoram (1967) "The production of human capital and the life cycle of earnings", *Journal of Political Economy*, 75:352–365.

Berger, Mark C. (1983a) "Changes in labor force composition and male earnings: a production approach", *Journal of Human Resources*, 18:175–196.

Berger, Mark C. (1983b) "The effects of cohort size on earnings growth: a reconsideration of the evidence", Working Paper No. E-60-83, University of Kentucky.

Blaug, Mark (1976) "The empirical status of human capital theory: a slightly jaundiced survey", *Journal of Economic Literature*, 14:827–855.

Brown, James (1983) "Are those paid more really no more productive?", unpublished paper, Princeton University.

Carmichael, Lorne (1983) "The agent–agents problem: payment by relative output", *Journal of Labor Economics*, 1:50–65.

Chamberlain, Gary (1978) "Omitted variable bias in panel data: estimating the returns to schooling", *Annales de l'INSEE* (*The Econometrics of Panel Data*), 31–32:49–82.

Chamberlain, Gary and Zvi Griliches (1977) "More on brothers", in: P. Taubman, ed., *Kinometrics: the determinants of socio-economic success within and between families*. Amsterdam: North-Holland.

Chiswick, Barry R. (1977) "Sons of immigrants: are they at an earnings disadvantage?", *American Economic Review*, 67:288–325.

Chiswick, Barry R. (1978) "The effect of Americanization on the earnings of foreign-born men", *Journal of Political Economy*, 86:897–919.

Chiswick, Barry R. (1979) "The economic progress of immigrants: some apparently universal patterns", in: W. Feller, ed., *Contemporary economic problems*. Washington, D.C.: American Enterprize Institute.

Chiswick, Barry R. (1983a) "An analysis of the earnings and employment of Asian-American men", *Journal of Labor Economics*, 1:197–214.

Chiswick, Barry R. (1983b) "The earnings and human capital of American Jews", *Journal of Human Resources*, 18:313–336.

Chiswick, Carmella (1976) "On estimating earnings functions for LDC's", *Journal of Development Economics*, 67–78.

Denison, Edward F. (1962) *Sources of economic growth in the U.S.* New York: Committee for Economic Development.

Dooley, Martin D. and Peter Gottshalk (1984) "Earnings inequality among males in the United States: trends and the effect of labor force growth", *Journal of Political Economy*, 92:59–89.

Freeman, Richard B. (1975) "Overinvestment in college training", *Journal of Human Resources*, 10:287–311.

Freeman, Richard B. (1976) *The overeducated American*. New York: Academic Press.

Freeman, Richard B. (1977) "The decline in economic rewards to college education", *Review of Economics and Statistics*, 59:18–29.

Freeman, Richard B. (1979) "The effect of demographic factors on age–earnings profiles", *Journal of Human Resources*, 14:289–318.

Friedman, Milton and Simon Kuznets (1945) *Income from independent professional practice*. New York: National Bureau of Economic Research.

Ghez, Gilbert and Gary S. Becker (1974) *The allocation of time and goods over the life cycle*. New York: Columbia University Press for the National Bureau of Economic Research.

Griliches, Zvi (1970) "Notes on the role of education in production functions and growth accounting", in: W. L. Hansen, ed., *Education, income and human capital: studies in income and wealth 35*. New York: Columbia University Press for the National Bureau of Economic Research.

Griliches, Zvi (1977) "Estimating the returns to schooling: some econometric problems", *Econometrica*, 45:1–22.

Griliches, Zvi (1979) "Sibling models and data in economics: beginnings of a survey", *Journal of Political Economy* (Supplement), 87:S37–S64.

Griliches, Zvi and William M. Mason (1972) "Education, income, and ability", *Journal of Political Economy*, 80:S74–S103.

Hall, Robert E. (1982) "The importance of lifetime jobs in the U.S. economy", *American Economic Review*, 72:716–724.

Hanoch, Giora (1967) "An economic analysis of earning and schooling", *Journal of Human Resources*, 2:310–329.

Hansen, W. Lee (1963) "Total and private rates of return to investment in schooling", *Journal of Political Economy*, 71:128–140.

Hashimoto, Masanori and John Raisian (1984) "Employment tenure and on-the-job training in Japan and the United States", unpublished paper, University of Washington.

Hause, John C. (1975) "Ability and schooling as determinants of lifetime earnings, or if you're so smart, why aren't you rich?", in: F. T. Juster, ed., *Education, income and human behavior*. New York: Columbia University Press for the National Bureau of Economic Research.

Hause, John C. (1980) "The fine structure of earnings and the on-the-job training hypothesis", *Econometrica*, 38:1013–1030.

Heckman, James J. (1976) "A life-cycle model of earnings, learning, and consumption", *Journal of Political Economy* (Supplement), 84:S11–S44.

Heckman, James J. (1979) "Sample selection bias as a specification error", *Econometrica*, 47:153–162.

Heckman, James J. and Solomon Polachek (1974) "Empirical evidence on the functional form of the earnings-schooling relationship", *Journal of the American Statistical Association*, 69:350–354.

Heckman, James J. and G. Sedlacek (1981) "The impact of the minimum wage on the employment and earnings of workers in South Carolina", Minimum Wage Study Commission, Washington, D.C.

Henderson, James W. (1983) "Earnings functions for the self-employed: comment", *Journal of Development Economics*, 3:97–102.

Jencks, Christopher et al. (1972) *Inequality*. Basic Books.

Jovanovic, Boyan (1979) "Job matching and the theory of turnover", *Journal of Political Economy*, 87:972–990.

Kenny, L., L. Lee, G. S. Maddala and R. Trost (1979) "Returns to college education: an investigation of self-selection bias in project talent data", *International Economic Review*, 20:775–790.

Krueger, Ann O. (1972) "Rates of return to Turkish higher education", *Journal of Human Resources*.

Kusnic, Michael W. and Julie DaVanzo (1982) "Who are the poor in Malaysia? The sensitivity of poverty profiles to definition of income", in: Y. Ben-Porath, ed., Income distribution and the family", *Population and Development Review* (Supplement), 18:17–34.

Lazear, Edward P. (1979) "Why is there mandatory retirement", *Journal of Political Economy*, 87:1261–1284.

Lazear, Edward P. (1981) "Agency, earnings profiles, productivity and hours", *American Economic Review*, 71:606–620.

Lee, Lung Fei (1976) "Estimation of limited dependent variables models by two stage methods", Ph.D. dissertation, University of Rochester.

Lillard, Lee (1977) "Inequality: earnings vs. human wealth", *American Economic Review*, 67:42–53.

Lillard, Lee and Robert J. Willis (1978) "Dynamic aspects of earnings mobility", *Econometrica*, 46:985–1012.

McManus, Walter, William Gould and Finis Welch (1983) "Earnings of hispanic men: The role of English language proficiency", *Journal of Labor Economics*, 1:101–130.

Medoff, James L. and Katherine G. Abraham (1980) "Experience, performance, and earnings", *Quarterly Journal of Economics*, 95:703–736.

Medoff, James L. and Katherine G. Abraham (1981) "Are those paid more really more productive? The case of experience", *Journal of Human Resources*, 16:281–302.

Mincer, Jacob (1958) "Investment in human capital and personal income distribution", *Journal of Political Economy*:281–302.

Mincer, Jacob (1962) "On-the-job training: costs, returns and some implications", *Journal of Political Economy*, 70(5):50–79.

Mincer, Jacob (1984) "Labor mobility, wages, and job training", unpublished paper, Columbia University.

Mincer, Jacob and Boyan Jovanovic (1981) "Labor mobility and wages", in: S. Rosen, ed., *Studies in labor markets*. Chicago: University of Chicago Press.

Mincer, Jacob and Solomon Polachek (1974) "Family investments in human capital: earnings of women", *Journal of Political Economy* (Supplement), 82:S76–S108.

Murphy, Kevin, Mark Plant and Finis Welch (1983) "Cohort size and earnings", paper presented to the IUSSP/IASSA seminar on *Economic consequences of population composition in developed countries*, Vienna.

Oi, Walter (1962) "Labor as a quasi-fixed factor", *Journal of Political Economy*, 70:538–555.

Parsons, Donald O. (1974) "The cost of school time, foregone earnings, and human capital formation", *Journal of Political Economy*, 82:251–266.

Pencavel, John (1977) in: R. Ehrenberg, ed., *Research in labor economics*. Greenwich, Conn.: JAI Press, vol. 1, 225–258.

Psacharopoulos, George (1973) *Returns to education: an international comparison*. Joessey-Bass, Elsevier.

Psacharopoulos, George (1981) "Returns to education: an updated international comparison", *Comparative Education*, 17:321–341.

Randolph, William C. (1983) "Employment relationships: till death do us part?", Ph.D. dissertation,

State University of New York at Stony Brook.

Riley, John G. (1975) "Competitive signalling", *Journal of Economic Theory*, 10:175–186.

Riley, John G. (1979) "Testing the educational screening hypothesis", *Journal of Political Economy* (Supplement), 87:S227–S251.

Rosen, Sherwin (1974) "Hedonic prices and implicit markets: product differentiation in pure competition", *Journal of Political Economy*, 82:34–55.

Rosen, Sherwin (1977a) "Human capital: relations between education and earnings", in: M. Intriligator, ed., *Frontiers of Quantitative Economics*, Amsterdam: North-Holland, vol. 3B.

Rosen, Sherwin (1977b) "Human capital: a survey of empirical research", in: R. Ehrenberg, ed., *Research in Labor Economics*, Greenwich, Conn.: JAI Press, vol. 1.

Rosen, Sherwin (1978) "Substitution and the division of labour", *Economica*, 45:235–250.

Rosen, Sherwin (1981) "The economics of superstars", *American Economic Review*, 71:845–858.

Rosen, Sherwin (1983) "Specialization and human capital", *Journal of Labor Economics*, 1:43–49.

Rosen, Sherwin (1982) "Authority, control and the distribution of earnings", *Bell Journal of Economics and Management Science*.

Ross, Stephen (1973) "The economic theory of agency: the principal's problem", *American Economic Review*, 63:134–139.

Roy, A. D. (1951) "Some thoughts on the distribution of earnings", *Oxford Economic Papers*, 3:135–146.

Sattinger, Michael (1975) "Comparative advantage and the distribution of earnings and abilities", *Econometrica*, 43:455–468.

Sattinger, Michael (1980) *Capital and the distribution of labor earnings*. Amsterdam: North-Holland.

Schultz, T. W. (1960) "Capital formation by education", *Journal of Political Economy*, 68:571–583.

Schultz, T. W. (1961) "Investment in human capital", *American Economic Review*, 51:1–17.

Smith, James P. and Finis Welch (1979) "Inequality: race differences in the distribution of earnings". *International Economic Review*, 20:515–526.

Solmon, Lewis C. (1975) "The definition of college quality and its impact on earnings", *Explorations in Economic Research*, 2(4):537–587.

Solow, Robert M. (1957) "Technical change and the aggregate production function", *Review of Economics and Statistics*, 39.

Spence, Michael A. (1973) "Job market signalling", *Quarterly Journal of Economics*, 87:355–375.

Spence, Michael A. (1974) *Market signalling: Informational transfer in hiring and related screening processes*. Cambridge: Harvard University Press.

Spence, Michael A. (1981) "Signalling, screening, and information", in: S. Rosen, ed., *Studies in labor markets*. Chicago: University of Chicago Press.

Stigler, George J. (1963) *Capital and rates of return in manufacturing industries*. Princeton, N.J.: Princeton University Press for NBER.

Stiglitz, Joseph E. (1975a) "The theory of screening, education, and the distribution of income", *American Economic Review*, 65:283–300.

Stiglitz, Joseph E. (1975b) "Incentives, risk and information: notes towards a theory of hierarchy", *Bell Journal of Economics*, 6:552–579.

Taubman, Paul and Terence Wales (1974) *Higher education and earnings*. New York: McGraw-Hill.

Thaler, Richard and Sherwin Rosen (1975) "The value of saving a life: evidence from the labor market", in: N. Terleckyj, ed., *Household production and consumption*. New York: National Bureau of Economic Research.

Tinbergen, J. (1951) "Some remarks on the distribution of labour incomes", *International Economic Papers*, 1:195–207.

Welch, Finis (1970) "Education and production", *Journal of Political Economy*, 78:35–59.

Welch, Finis (1979) "Effects of cohort size on earnings: the baby boom's babies' financial bust", *Journal of Political Economy* (Supplement), 87:S65–S98.

Willis, Robert J. (forthcoming) "A theory of the equilibrium interest rate in an overlapping generations model: life cycles, institutions, and population growth", in: B. Arthur, R. Lee and G. Rodgers, eds., *Economic consequences of alternative population patterns*. Oxford: Oxford University Press.

Willis, Robert J. and Sherwin Rosen (1979) "Education and self-selection", *Journal of Political Economy* (Supplement), 87:S7–S36.

Wolpin, Kenneth (1977) "Education and screening", *American Economic Review*, 67:949–958.

Chapter 11

THE DETERMINATION OF LIFE CYCLE EARNINGS: A SURVEY

YORAM WEISS*

Tel Aviv University

1. Introduction

My purpose in this survey is to describe the theoretical work on the determination of life cycle earnings. The common thread in this work is the notion that workers can influence their earnings through various investment activities. A person who spends time in school or in on-the-job training sacrifices current earnings in the hope of increasing his future earning potential. Consequently, the observed life cycle earnings profiles reflect individual economic choices as well as purely technological or biological processes such as "depreciation" or "aging". Since the emergence of the influential work of Becker (1964), Mincer (1962, 1974), and Schultz (1963) this view has become widely accepted.

There is, however, considerable controversy on the market situation in which investment choices are made. As noted by Arrow (1973) and Spence (1973) the informational assumptions are particularly important. The welfare and policy implications are very different if schooling enhances productivity or is merely used as a mode of transferring income by signalling and screening. In this survey I will adhere mostly to the "human capital" approach but focus on its testable implications to individual earning profiles setting aside the aggregate and policy implications. Within this framework the discussion narrows on investments on the job.

The major stylized facts which the theory attempts to explain are: a life cycle earnings profile which is increasing at early ages and is declining towards the end of the working period. A wage profile which tends to increase over the life cycle with a weak tendency for wage reduction towards the end of the working period. An hours of work life cycle profile which is increasing at early ages and declining at older ages, with the peak occurring earlier than in the earnings or wage profiles [see Mincer (1974), Ghez and Becker (1975)]. In addition there are several

*Financial assistance from the Foerder Institute for Economic Research is gratefully acknowledged.

Handbook of Labor Economics, Volume I, Edited by O. Ashenfelter and R. Layard

important interactions between experience related earnings growth and individual characteristics such as sex, age, level of schooling, and perhaps vintage. Specifically, earnings growth (at a given level of experience) tends to be lower for women, for older workers, for workers with more years of schooling, and for workers of less recent vintages. These empirical regularities in the wage structure have been observed repeatedly at different points in time and in various countries and occupations. These findings are mostly from cross section data. However, longitudinal data, when available, also yield similar results [see Weiss and Lillard (1978), Lillard (1981)]. The observed stability of these broad patterns in the wage structure is the starting point of the human capital approach as an organizing framework. The theory attempts to explain *jointly* all the stylized facts mentioned above.

Most of the reviewed material is not new and was already covered in the excellent surveys by Rosen (1977) and Killingsworth (1983). I therefore choose to avoid both generalities and detailed enumeration of findings. Instead, my objective is to provide a relatively self-contained development of the main results in the area. I try to be quite explicit about the methods of analysis. Hopefully this will enable the readers, graduate students in particular, to reconstruct old results and produce new ones.

2. The human capital framework

The human capital approach can be applied at two different levels: at the market level it presents a set of restrictions on the equilibrium wage structure; at the individual level it analyzes the actions which workers can take to affect their current and future earnings taking market conditions as given. Most of the literature surveyed here focuses its attention on the individual experiment. A key element in the discussion is the assumed tradeoff between current and future earnings. In a complete analysis one must verify that this tradeoff indeed satisfies the restrictions imposed by market equilibrium. For this reason I begin the survey by describing the technology and the market structure in which individual decisions are embedded.

Each person in the economy is assumed to possess a certain amount of productive capacity or human capital. Human capital is not transferable but can be augmented by learning or training. The process of training generally requires individual inputs, mainly the worker's *own* time and knowledge and outside resources consisting of the knowledge and time of other workers. Outside resources can be obtained in two different ways, the worker may simply purchase the services of other knowledgeable workers or he may gain access to a job in which learning occurs jointly with work. The latter possibility arises because of the difficulties in the effective exclusion of information. In most work situations firms cannot prevent workers from learning on the job.

Firms are endowed with the technology of converting workers' time and human capital into flows of goods and new productive capacity for each of the workers. Thus, if a firm employs N workers, its inputs are specified as $K_1, K_2,\dots, K_N, h_1, h_2,\dots, h_N$, where K_i, h_i are, respectively, the human capital endowment of worker i and the time which he spends at the firm, while its outputs are specified as z, a composite good, and $\dot{K}_1, \dot{K}_2,\dots, \dot{K}_N$, where $\dot{K}_i$ is the rate of change of worker i's human capital. The addition to the earning capacity of each worker is treated as a different commodity since human capital is not transferable.

Two important simplifying assumptions are common to most of the literature:[1]

A.1.

Workers with different skills are perfect substitutes in the production of the composite good z, i.e. $z = F\left(\sum_{i=1}^{N} h_i K_i\right)$.[2]

A.2.

The amount of new earning capacity accruing to each worker depends only on his own inputs, i.e. $\dot{K}_i = G(K_i, h_i)$.

With this technology the market for work and training can be described very simply. To begin, assume that all firms are identical. Firms compete for workers by offering job opportunities. A job opportunity specifies both the wage and the time spent on the job. The worker needs to know both dimensions since the amount of human capital $\dot{K}$ which accrues to him depends on h. Since workers are distinguishable by their human capital endowment the job offer and the payment for it will depend on K. Given the terms of the contract each firm is free to select the number of workers of each type so as to maximize profits. Therefore the marginal product of a worker of type K must equal his cost, i.e. $h(K)w(K) = F'(\cdot)hK$, where $F'(\cdot)$ is common to all workers and can be defined as the rental rate of human capital, commonly denoted by R. With this payment structure the worker effectively faces an infinitely elastic demand for hours on the job. The firm can delegate the selection of hours to the worker at the equilibrium

[1]A notable exception is Mincer (1974, ch. 1). His exposition of the schooling model assumes, contrary to assumption A1 in the text that workers with different levels of schooling are essential in the production process. If (presumably) identical workers appear in the market with different levels of schooling *all* observed investment options must be equally attractive. The wage structure is then immediately determined, at the market level, by this indifference requirement. The individual investment pattern at this compensating wages equilibrium is indeterminate [see Rosen (1977)].

[2]The production function $F(\cdot)$ includes implicitly fixed factors such as capital. Assuming constant returns to scale we can interpret the short-term profits of the firm as normal profits required to compensate the fixed factors. The model outlined below therefore assumes zero profits and is thus consistent with free entry and exit of firms.

wage. The model can now be closed by determining the choice of hours by the workers given R. Workers' choices between leisure and work will fully determine the accumulation of human capital and development of wages over the life cycle. Full equilibrium is attained when R adjusts so as to make the aggregate accumulation consistent with $F'(\cdot) = R$.

The case just outlined describes the class of models which deal only with learning by doing. The distinguishing aspect is that *on-the-job* knowledge is provided freely. This does not mean that training is acquired costlessly since workers have opportunity costs to time spent on the job (i.e. the value of leisure). There is, however, an important generalization of the learning-by-doing idea which incorporates opportunity costs in the job market. According to this approach the worker can invest at a varying intensity on the job [see Becker (1975), Mincer (1974) and Killingsworth (1982)]. Such options arise either because firms differ in their capacity to provide training or because they can vary the proportions of z and $\dot{K}_i$ by shifting resources from production to training.

Similar to the ranking of workers by their human capital, K, we may introduce an index $0 \leq x \leq 1$ which ranks firms, or jobs within a firm, by the proportion of goods and training which they produce. Specifically, employing N workers with inputs $K_1, K_2, \dots, K_N, h_1, h_2, \dots, h_N$ in job x yields $(1-x)F(\sum_{i=1}^{N} K_i h_i)$ units of z and $G(K_i, h_i, x)$ units of $\dot{K}_i$ for $i = 1, 2, \dots, N$. It is assumed that for given inputs, jobs with higher x produce relatively more knowledge ($\partial G/\partial x > 0$) and less goods. The loss of output reflects the real costs of providing training due to the involvement of the various productive inputs in the training process [see Rosen (1972)]. A special case of the above technology is one in which the costs are associated solely with the shift of the trainee's own time from work to training. In this case one may write $z = F(\sum_{i=1}^{N} K_i(1-x)h_i)$ and $\dot{K}_i = G(K_i, h_i, x)$ and interpret $(1-x)h$ as time on the job spent in work and hx as time on the job spent in training [see Ben-Porath (1967)].

A contract offered to a worker type K will now specify, in addition to the wage and the duration of work, the training content of the job x. (All the variables which determine $\dot{K}$ must be included.) For any given contract the firm can decide how many workers to employ. If a positive number of workers are employed under a particular contract their marginal cost to the firm must be equal to their marginal product. Hence a worker type K employed h hours at a job type x will earn $(1-x)RKh$. Under this payment scheme the firm can delegate to the worker the choice of both x and h. From the point of view of the worker we may interpret $G(K, h, x)$ as the production function of human capital on the job and $xRKh$ as the (opportunity) costs for acquiring training. Only the costs depend on market conditions as represented by R.

Schooling activities can be treated in precisely the same manner. Each student (worker) obtains a certain amount of additional knowledge and the costs depend on the total number of students (workers). The only difference is that a negative amount of aggregate good is produced. The price facing each student (worker) is the marginal costs of his training.

Each worker can allocate his time among jobs (firms) with different x and among various schooling activities. An efficient allocation maximizes $\dot{K}$ for given K, h and given current net earning. This maximization generates an efficient frontier which may be written, for given R, as

$$Y = Y(K, \dot{K}, h), \tag{1}$$

where Y is current earnings net of explicit training costs, h is time spent at work or at school (i.e. non-leisure time), K is the amount of human capital which the worker possesses and $\dot{K}$ is the amount of new knowledge that accrues to him. The partial derivatives of Y are, respectively, positive with respect to K and negative with respect to $\dot{K}$. This reflects a basic tradeoff between current and future earnings. Choosing an activity which generates more training (or learning) reduces current earnings but enhances future earning capacity.

The current earning capacity of the worker can be defined as the maximal amount of net current earnings which is attainable given K and h. A worker who actually earns less than his earning potential is implicitly paying for acquiring knowledge. A worker may have low observed earnings, given his observed market time, either because of low earning capacity (i.e. low K) or because of high costs of investment (i.e. high $\dot{K}$). These alternatives cannot be separated empirically since neither K nor $\dot{K}$ can be directly observed. The human capital approach is in this respect reminiscent of the permanent income hypothesis. Observed behavior is guided by a variable which is observed only by the economic agents but not by the researchers.[3]

One can trace different specifications of the tradeoff in the literature to different assumptions on the function $G(K, h, x)$.

Using unified notation[4] one may cite the following.

[3] The difference from the permanent income hypotheses is that the error committed by using current earnings as a proxy for earning capacity is systematically determined by individual maximization.

[4] All of these authors except for Blinder and Weiss (1976) originally formulated their specification *without* considering variation in hours. Weizsacker (1967) and Sheshinski (1968) actually wrote

$$Y = RF(E)(1-x), \quad F'(E) > 0, \quad F''(E) < 0,$$
$$\dot{E} = x - \delta E.$$

The formula in the text is a result of the transformation $K = F(E)$. Oniki also considers a more general formulation, including direct costs. Formulation II is the Ben-Porath specification as adopted for the case of variable hours by Heckman (1976), who also includes direct costs, and Ryder, Stafford and Stephan (1976). Formulation III precisely agrees with Rosen (1976) only when hours are taken to be fixed. Blinder and Weiss (1976) actually wrote $Y = RKhg(y)$, $\dot{K} = \theta Kyh - \delta K, 0 \le y \le 1, g(0) = 1, g(1) = 0, g'(y) < 0, g''(y) < 0$. The formulation in the text is obtained by the transformation $x = 1 - g(y)$.

(I) Weizsacker (1967), Sheshinski (1968), Oniki (1968):

$$\dot{K} = g_1(K)Khx - \delta g_2(K), \qquad Y = R[hK - \dot{K}c_1(K) - \delta c_2(K)],$$
$$g_1(K) > 0, \quad g_1'(K) < 0, \quad g_2(0) = 0, \quad g_2'(K) > 0, \quad c_1(K) = 1/g_1(K),$$
$$c_2(K) = g_2(K)/g_1(K).$$

(II) Ben-Porath (1967):

$$\dot{K} = g(Khx) - \delta K, \quad Y = R(Kh - c(\dot{K} + \delta K)),$$
$$g(0) = 0, \quad g'(\cdot) > 0, \quad g''(\cdot) < 0, \quad c(\cdot) = g^{-1}(\cdot).$$

(III) Blinder and Weiss (1976), Rosen (1976):

$$\dot{K} = Khg(x) - \delta K, \qquad Y = RKhc\left(\frac{\dot{K} + \delta K}{Kh}\right),$$
$$g(0) = 0, \quad g'(\cdot) > 0, \quad g'' < 0, \quad c(\cdot) = 1 - g^{-1}(\cdot).$$

Specifications (II) and (III) imply increasing marginal costs, in terms of lost current earnings for acquiring training. In specification (I) the marginal costs for acquiring training are constant up to the boundary of feasible accumulation (where they become infinite). It is the need for individual non-purchased inputs which limits the rate of acquisition of training and produces costs of adjustment for investment in human capital at the individual level.[5]

In specifications (I) and (II), a worker who spends all his time at job x attains the same outcome as he would obtain by spending a proportion $1-x$ of his time at the job which maximizes current earnings ($x=0$) and a proportion x at the job which maximizes investment ($x=1$). That is, on-the-job training is equivalent to a *mixture* of pure work and pure training (often defined as schooling). In specification (III) a mixture of pure work and pure training requires a larger sacrifice of current earnings and is strictly dominated by the acquisition of training in one job. This built-in advantage for on-the-job training leads to increasing returns with respect to market time. That is, given K and $\dot{K}$ an increase in h increases Y more than proportionally.

In specifications (II) and (III) human capital is assumed to be self-productive. This is more pronounced in specification (III) where constant returns to scale

[5]In the theory of investment of the firm costs of adjustment are introduced somewhat artificially at the level of the firm. Since a single firm can acquire an arbitrary amount of investment goods at a fixed price, it is only the internal difficulties in implementation that can cause cost of adjustment [see Eisner and Strotz (1963)].

with respect to K are assumed. In specification (I), on the other hand, it is assumed that a large stock hinders further accumulation of earning capacity. This is in addition to the natural "depreciation of human capital" (reflected in δ) common to all models. The marginal costs for acquiring additions to the stock of human capital, in terms of forgone current earnings, are increasing in K for specification (I), unaffected by K for specification (II) and diminishing in K for specification (III).

Notice that in all the above specifications, joint concavity in K, x, and h is *not* assumed. This is due to the appearance of the products such as xhK, indicating that with higher level of K each hour of work becomes more productive (in both training and earnings). This may be interpreted as dynamic increasing returns to scale, essential to models of human capital, where an increase in current effort either reduces the costs of, or increases the benefits from, future effort.

Since neither K nor $\dot{K}$ is observable, one cannot test these different specifications directly. It is only by the implications for the observed patterns of earnings and market time that one can, perhaps, separate such alternatives. Indeed, most of the research effort, at the theoretical level, was directed to yield such testable implications. I now turn to survey these attempts.

3. The wealth maximizing model

The focus of this class of models is on the allocation of time in the market, taking the total amount of non-leisure time as predetermined. The worker is assumed to have a fixed lifetime of length T and to operate in a static economy with a perfect capital market facing a fixed rate of interest, r. The labor and training market is summarized by the tradeoff function (1). The worker's problem, then, is the choice of an optimal path of accumulation for human capital under the above conditions. Formally, the problem is stated as[6]

$$\begin{aligned} &\max_{\{x\}} \int_0^T RhK(1-x)\mathrm{e}^{-rt}\mathrm{d}t \\ &\text{s.t.} \\ &\dot{K} = G(K,h,x), \quad K(0) = K_0, \\ &0 \le x \le 1, \end{aligned} \tag{2}$$

where t is the worker's age, h is a predetermined function of t and the function $x(t)$ is the object of choice. This control problem is solved by maximizing the full

[6]The function $G(K,h,x)$ should be interpreted here as the envelope of all possible modes of generating knowledge (including investment in schooling activities). As such it may be non-differentiable with respect to x. This possibility is ignored in what follows, assuming essentially that the schooling option is identical to on the job training with $x=1$.

(discounted) earnings of the worker at each age. The full earning of the worker consists of his current earnings and the value of the additional knowledge obtained on the job. One can write full earning (the Hamiltonian function) as:

$$H(K,h,x,\psi,t) = [RhK(1-x) + \psi G(K,h,x)]\mathrm{e}^{-rt}, \tag{3}$$

where ψ is the marginal value to the worker of an additional unit of human capital. That is

$$\psi(t) = \int_t^T \mathrm{e}^{-r(\tau-t)} Rh(1-x^*) + \psi(\tau)G_K(K,h,x^*)\,\mathrm{d}\tau, \tag{4}$$

where $x^*(t)$ denotes an optimal choice for $x(t)$. By maximizing $H(\cdot)$ with respect to the control variable x, the worker takes into account the effects of investment on both current and future earnings. The optimal choice of x, if it is interior, equates the marginal cost from choosing a job with more intense training, RhK, to the marginal benefit $\psi G_x(K,x,h)$. The change in x over time is thus related to the time patterns of the endogenous variables K and ψ and to the predetermined profile of h. An increase in ψ will encourage the choice of jobs with higher training content. An increase in K will reduce the training intensity, provided that the degree of complementarity G_{Kx} is not too large. (In the analysis which follows I impose $KG_{Kx} \leq G_x$ to ensure that x is non-increasing in K, this requirement is met by the three specifications mentioned in Section 2.)

For the special case in which $h(t)$ is a constant, say 1, one can use a phase diagram (see Figure 11.1) to describe some basic qualitative aspects of the solution. The line $\dot{\psi} = 0$ in Figure 11.1 can be interpreted as the long-run (stock) demand for human capital. The line $\dot{K} = 0$ is the long-run (stock) supply for human capital. A worker with infinite life may eventually reach the long-run level of capital which equates the stock demand and supply. But life is finite and the programs which are actually followed are dominated by this constraint. Since human capital cannot be transferred the marginal value of human capital becomes zero at the end of the worker's life. This fact provides the economic incentive for an eventual reduction in the investment in human capital.

A general saddlepoint property can be noted in Figure 11.1. The system $(\dot{K}, \dot{\psi})$ is partially unstable with respect to ψ (if ψ is above the $\dot{\psi} = 0$ line, $\dot{\psi}$ is positive and vice versa) and partially stable with respect to K (if K is to the right of the $\dot{K} = 0$ line, $\dot{K}$ is negative and vice versa). This, together with the transversality condition $\psi(T) = 0$, severely limits the admissible time patterns of ψ and K. In particular no trajectory can pass through the shaded area in the figure. It follows that whenever the worker increases his earnings capacity, $\dot{K} > 0$, the shadow price of human capital must decrease, $\dot{\psi} < 0$, and hence on such intervals, observed earnings must increase (unless $x = 1$). The phase diagram also reveals

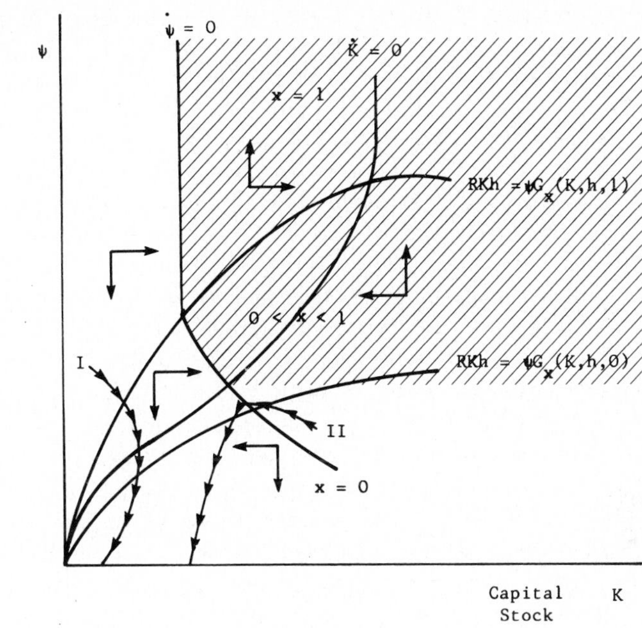

Figure 11.1

that such intervals with increasing earnings capacity, if they exist, must occur at the *beginning* of the worker's life. Trajectory I in Figure 11.1 represents the typical case.[7] Initially the worker invests at full intensity, $x=1$, then x declines, eventually reaching zero. Earning capacity increases at the range with high investment intensity and declines in the range with low investment intensity, due to a positive rate of depreciation. The increase in K and the reduction in x combine to increase observed earnings during the first part of the phase with $0<x<1$.[8]

Turning to the more special cases considered in the literature, one can make the following observations.

[7]Trajectory type II is a possible but less likely pattern. It reflects a situation in which, due to large initial stock of human capital the worker always chooses to reduce it (net investment is negative throughout the worker's life). Since a large initial K deters investment it may be optimal to postpone investment until the point in time in which K is sufficiently low. Earnings in this case will decline throughout the worker's life.

[8]Note that maximized full earnings, H^* never increases along an optimal path [provided that $h(t)$ is constant]. Specifically, the change in full earnings is proportional to actual (discounted) earnings, that is $\dot{H}=-rRKh(1-x)e^{-rt}\leq 0$.

In the Weizsacker–Sheshinski–Oniki model the region in which $0<x<1$ degenerates into a single line.[9] The control variable x can therefore obtain only three values, the two extremes, zero and one, and a steady state rate of investment corresponding to maintenance of a fixed stock for some period of time. Assuming that the initial stock is zero, the pattern of investment depends entirely on the length of the working period T. If T is short, the worker will not invest at all and his stock of human capital (and earnings) will decay throughout the worker's life. As the horizon extends it becomes profitable to invest at the maximal rate for some period then to reduce investment to the steady state level, and finally reduce it again to zero sometime before the end of life. The optimal pattern of earning therefore contains an initial increasing segment, a flat middle segment and a final decreasing segment. Sheshinski (1968) notes a turnpike property: as the duration of the horizon extends the time spent at the steady state increases, and the duration of the flat segment in earnings will be relatively longer. This simple model illustrates very clearly the role of the finite life constraint in the accumulation process.

Under the Ben-Porath and the Blinder–Weiss–Rosen specifications, the long-run (stock) demand for human capital is perfectly elastic (i.e. the $\dot{\psi}=0$ line is horizontal). The shadow price of human capital depends only on the remaining work horizon and not on the accumulated stock.[10] We can, therefore, partition the dynamic system and analyze the time pattern of ψ separately. In these cases, as the worker approaches the end of his working life, the demand price of human capital must decline monotonically, reflecting the fact that human capital will be used over a shorter period. Therefore, (gross) investment also declines monotonically (see Figure 11.2). The only difference between the models is that gross investment is measured in absolute terms, $\dot{K}+\delta K$, for the Ben-Porath specification and in proportional terms, $\dot{K}/K+\delta$, for the Blinder–Weiss–Rosen specification. As investment declines the amount (proportion) of earning capacity which is sacrificed declines. As long as net investment is positive, earnings capacity increases. These two forces combine to induce an increase in observed earnings. When net investment becomes sufficiently negative, observed earning declines. Since investment declines smoothly (and not in jumps as in the Weizsacker–Sheshinski–Oniki specification) there is no flat segment in the earning profile.

[9]As the boundary lines of the region $0<x<1$ in Figure 11.1 approach each other, the $\dot{\psi}=0$ and $\dot{K}=0$ locus in this model becomes disconnected. (Each includes a line and a disconnected point.) See Sheshinski (1968).

[10]These statements are correct for the Ben-Porath specification only in the regions where $0<x\leq 1$. For the Blinder–Weiss–Rosen specification the long-run supply of human capital is also horizontal. The same holds for the Ben-Porath specification if $\delta=0$. There is no long-run equilibrium stock (for the infinite horizon problem) in these cases.

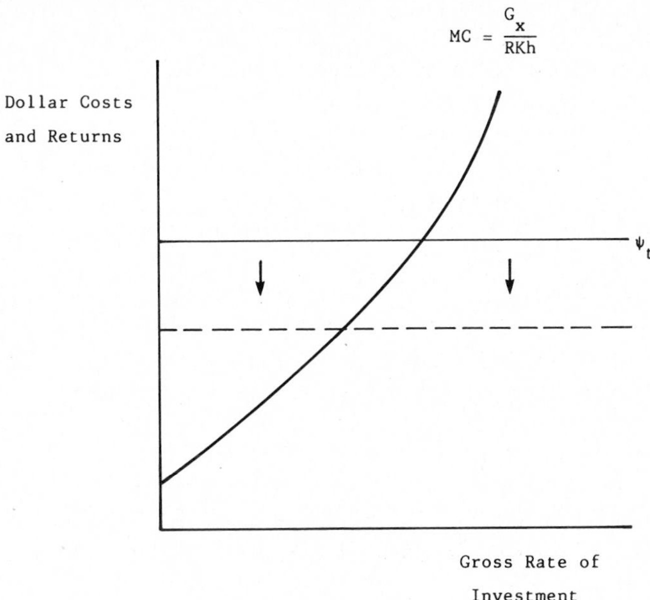

Figure 11.2

The wealth maximizing models of investment in human capital are thus capable of generating optimal patterns which imitate observed earnings profiles of full-time and continuous workers. The phenomenon of first increasing then decreasing earnings during a worker's life cycle is explained as an outcome of a voluntary economic decision, that is, a positive and declining investment rather than an exogenous natural development. This basic insight may be exploited further to explain several additional regularities in the earning structure. An important illustration is the issue of sex-related differences in earnings.

A robust empirical finding is that the (proportional) difference in male–female earnings is increasing with potential and actual work experience. To explain this phenomenon one has to relax the assumption that $h(t)$ is constant and take into account the male–female differentials in labor force participation [see Mincer and Polachek (1974)]. Consider an interruption in female labor force participation [i.e. an interval in which $h(t)=0$] due to, say, childbirth. If the interruption is unexpected it will only affect earnings after the withdrawal from the labor force. The common hypothesis is that the accumulation of human capital requires active participation of the worker in the labor-training market, that is $G(K,0,x) = -\delta K$. Therefore, human capital is actually lost and earnings capacity declines

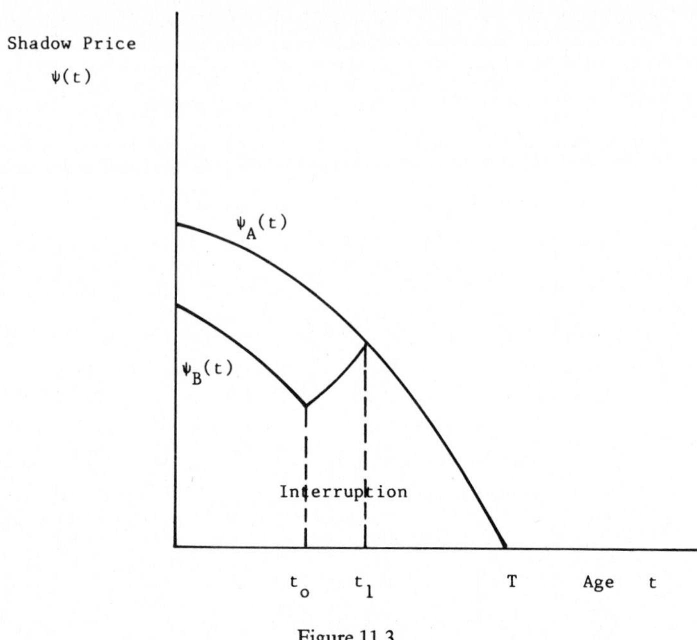

Figure 11.3

as a result of the departure from the labor force. Thus, if a woman accumulates several such episodes, an increasing gap between male and female earnings is created. To the extent that the interruption is expected it will also affect investment prior to the withdrawal from the labor force. It is convenient to apply in this case either the Ben-Porath specification [see Polachek (1975)] or the Blinder–Weiss–Rosen specification [see Weiss and Gronau (1981)], since, for these specifications, expectations are fully captured in the shadow price function $\psi(t)$. Figure 11.3 depicts the behavior of shadow price of human capital for two workers, one who participates continuously, and one who expects to withdraw during the period $[t_0, t_1]$. The two profiles $\psi_A(t)$ and $\psi_B(t)$, respectively, coincide after the interruption. However, during the interval $[t_0, t_1]$, $\psi_B(t)$ is *increasing*, reflecting the profitability of postponing investment to the time of re-entry into the labor force so as to avoid the depreciation and interest costs from unused capital. Consequently, $\psi_B(t) < \psi_A(t)$ prior to t_0, and investment will be lower. With some additional assumptions[11] the lower investment rate will be reflected in

[11] The required restrictions on tradeoff function are the same as those required for the *concavity* of the earnings (or log earnings) profiles. They involve third-order derivatives of the production, analogous to decreasing absolute (or relative) risk aversion [see Weiss and Gronau (1981) and Heckman (1976)].

lower earning growth prior to the *expected* withdrawal. This may explain why even after accounting for *past* interruptions, there is still a gap between male and female earnings growth [see Mincer and Polachek (1974)].

Another important implication of the wealth maximizing model is the potential impact of an income tax on (before-tax) earnings even when labor supply is held constant. For instance, an increase in a proportionate income tax is effectively equivalent in this model to a reduction in the interest rate. Such a change will generally encourage investment in human capital, and with some additional assumptions will be reflected in higher earnings growth [see Heckman (1976)].

In addition to these broad implications for the earnings profiles one may derive differential (or difference) equations for the observed earnings which summarize the whole process of earnings generation [see Rosen (1973)]. Such equations can be derived and their coefficients can be related to the basic parameters even when explicit solution in the extensive form $Y(t)$ is unattainable. They provide, therefore, an efficient method for distinguishing alternative specifications of the tradeoff function (1). For instance, if the tradeoff is quadratic in K and $\dot{K}$ (a special case of the Ben-Porath specification) then second-order, or higher, *linear* differential equations in observed earnings arise.[12] If one assumes the multiplicative form the tradeoff as in Blinder–Weiss–Rosen, a second-order, non-linear, differential equation in the *log* of earnings arises.

A final set of presumably testable implications of the wealth maximizing model apply to the duration of the specialization period with $x=1$. It is common to identify this period with the observed schooling period of the worker. This interpretation is questionable since knowledge is produced in schools under different conditions than on the job and a more general model is therefore required [see Johnson (1978)]. The available wealth maximizing models all predict that specialization in training, if undertaken, will occur at the *beginning* of the working life. This provides a direct test of the more general implication that investment is declining in these models.[13] Though Oniki (1968) and Weiss (1971) provide proofs of the non-optimality of postponing schooling for slightly more general models, the precise conditions required to retain the result within the context of income maximizing models are not known. It should be remarked that postponement of investment in the period of specialization is not incompatible

[12] For instance, if the function $G(\cdot)$ is specified $\dot{K}=(Kx)^{1/2}$ [setting $h(t)=1$], then $Y=R(\dot{K}-(K)^2)$ and $\ddot{Y}=2r\dot{Y}-R$. The discrete time analogue is $Y_t=(2+2r+r^2)Y_{t-1}-(1-2r+r^2)Y_{t-2}-R(1+r/2)$. The appearance of negative coefficients on lagged income also arises in more complicated examples [see Weiss (1974)]. This prediction is not supported by the findings of Ashenfelter (1978) who finds that *all* included lagged incomes (up to 5 years) have positive coefficients.

[13] Investment may be measured in a number of ways and therefore the statement that investment declines is slightly ambiguous. In the Ben-Porath specification $\dot{K}$ and "investment dollars" xK declines monotonically. This does not put a restriction on x when $\dot{K}$ is negative. In the Blinder–Weiss specification $\dot{K}/K+\delta$, and "investment time" x declines monotonically [see also Mincer (1974, ch. 5)].

with wealth maximization. If it is assumed that the intensity of investment decreases with K, then a worker with a large initial stock may find it profitable to wait until part of the existing stock depreciates.[14] Outside the scope of the model there are important potential causes for delayed investment such as changing market conditions, unknown ability (tastes) and borrowing constraints. Nevertheless, the observed life cycle pattern of investment in schooling is broadly consistent with the hypothesis of decreasing investment with age.

It is relatively easy to work out the comparative statics for the schooling period. Oniki (1968) has shown that for specification (I) (see Section 2 above), an increase in the length of the horizon or a reduction in the interest rate increases the schooling period. An increase in the initial stock reduces the duration of the schooling period but increases the final stock (attained upon exit from school). Similar results were obtained for the Ben-Porath specification [Ben-Porath (1970) and Wallace and Inhen (1975)]. A slight difference arises in the Blinder–Weiss–Rosen specification where the length of the schooling period is independent of the initial capital stock. The initial stock of human capital can be viewed as a measure of the worker's earning ability. This should be distinguished from another measure of ability, which is the worker's learning ability, usually modelled as a shift in the production function $G(\cdot)$. Such a shift is typically assumed to increase the marginal product of training and increase investment. Generally, the effect of ability on investment and on the duration of the schooling period is ambiguous. The reason is that higher ability can increase both the opportunity costs and the benefits from investment in human capital.

4. Life cycle earnings with endogenous labor supply

In this section I relax the assumption that the lifetime pattern of labor supply is predetermined. Endogenous labor supply affects the analysis in two basic ways: (1) future labor supply choices determine the utilization of human capital and thus the returns to the investment, and (2) past labor supply decisions influence

[14]A simple three-period example where

$$K_t = K_{t-1} + K_{t-1}^{\alpha} g(x_{t-1}), \quad 0<\alpha<1,$$

$$g(x_t) = ax_t - bx_t^2, \quad 0<a, \quad 0<b,$$

can be used to generate examples of postponement in investment. For instance, if $r=0$, $\delta=0.8$, $\alpha=0.8$, $a=1.65$, $b=0.15$, and $K_0=19$, the optimal policy is to set $x_0=0$ and $x_1=1$. That is, with these parameters the worker does not invest at all in the first period and specializes in investment in the second period. A milder type of postponement in investment is illustrated by trajectory II in Figure 11.1.

the current level of human capital and therefore the (opportunity) costs of investment.

It is useful to begin with a brief discussion of life cycle labor supply with exogenous wages. The worker's problem is to allocate his lifetime effort and consumption given a lifetime budget constraint. Assuming that preferences among consumption and work age profiles can be represented additively, the problem is stated as

$$\max_{\{c,h\}} \int_0^T e^{-\rho t} u(c, 1-h)\,dt$$

$$\text{s.t.} \tag{5}$$

$$\dot{A} = rA + wh - c, \quad A(0) = A_0, \quad A(T) = 0,$$

$$1 \geq h \geq 0, \quad c \geq 0,$$

where c denotes consumption, A is accumulated savings, $u(c, 1-h)$ is a current utility index, and ρ a subjective discount factor for future utilities.

An optimal allocation must maximize, at each age, full utility:[15]

$$H(A, \mu, t) = e^{-\rho t}[u(c, 1-h) + \mu \dot{A}], \tag{6}$$

where μ, the shadow price of current assets in utility terms, satisfies

$$\dot{\mu} = (\rho - r)\mu. \tag{7}$$

At an interior solution one obtains:

$$\frac{1}{\mu} u_l = w \tag{8}$$

and

$$\frac{1}{\mu} u_c = 1. \tag{9}$$

[15] The problem can be solved conveniently by *two-stage* maximization. Define the indirect utility $\phi(I, w) = \max_{c,h} u(c, 1-h)$ subject to $c = wh + I$, and observe that

$$\max_{c,h} e^{-\rho t}[u(c,h) + \mu(rA + wh - c)] = \max_I e^{-\rho t}[\phi(I, w) + \mu(rA - I)].$$

Thus at the first stage one solves an optimal savings problem. Having solved for $I(t)$ one can use the regular static supply function, where work depends on the wage rate $w(t)$ and on the non-wage income $I(t)$, to find $h(t)$.

Formally, these conditions are the *profit* maximizing conditions for a worker who produces current utility with inputs l, c (where $l=1-h$) facing the price vector $1/\mu$, 1, and w.[16] Writing the demand function for the leisure input as

$$l = D(1/\mu, w), \tag{10}$$

we recall from the theory of production that $D_2 \equiv \partial l/\partial w < 0$. Moreover, if leisure is a normal input, $D_1 \equiv \partial l/\partial(1/\mu) > 0$. Differentiating (10) with respect to the worker's age using (7), we obtain:

$$\dot{l} = D_1 \frac{r-\rho}{\mu} + D_2 \dot{w}. \tag{11}$$

This formula shows that for a fixed wage the worker will choose a decreasing (increasing) profile for labor supply if the interest rate exceeds (is below) his subjective discount factor. If $r > \rho$, then starting from a stable work profile, lifetime utility can be raised by working more in the present, investing the proceeds of the wages, then working less in the future. A rising (exogenous) wage path is associated with an increasing labor supply profile. (It is efficient to allocate effort to periods with a relatively high wage.) If $w(t)$ is single peaked and $r > \rho$, the peak in hours will precede the peak in wages during the life cycle. [See Ghez and Becker (1975), Weiss (1972), Heckman (1974), and Macurdy (1981).]

Returning to the human capital framework, let us now assume that the worker can affect his earnings capacity. The simplest type of endogeneity arises when wages respond to a process of learning by doing on the job. One can then augment the model by adding the equations

$$w(t) = RK(1-x_0) \tag{12}$$

and

$$\dot{K} = G(K, h, x_0), \tag{13}$$

where the index of training content, x, is taken as given.

An important implication of this extension is that the marginal rate of substitution between leisure and consumption generally *exceeds* the current wage [contrary to the case of exogenous wages where the marginal rate of substitution is equated to the wage; see eqs. (8) and (9)]. Specifically, in the presence of learning by doing, labor supply is determined by the condition

$$\frac{u_l}{u_c} = w + \frac{\psi}{\mu} G_h, \tag{14}$$

where ψ is now the shadow price of human capital in utility terms. This is a

[16]Note that the *current* utility index, like a production function, is arbitrary only up to linear transformation. It is only the lifetime functional $\int_0^T e^{-\rho t} u(c,l)\,dt$ that is ordinally scaled. It is therefore meaningful to assume, for instance, that $u(c,l)$ is strictly concave.

direct reflection of the fact that each hour spent on the job produces *jointly* earning and knowledge. The worker therefore takes into account both the current and future effects of his labor supply choices.

A characterization of the optimal labor supply profile and the corresponding endogenous wage profile requires some specific assumptions on the current utility index and the production function of human capital. I will illustrate here the analysis which follows from the assumptions that the utility indicator is additively separable in l and c, and the production function is given by specification (III) in Section 2. [For analyses corresponding to specifications (I) and (II), respectively, see Weiss (1972) and Killingsworth (1982).]

Under specification (III), with x predetermined at x_0, the optimal solution is characterized by the equations[17]

$$u_l(l) \leq \mu RK(1-x_0)+\psi g(x_0)K, \quad \text{with equality if } h>0, \tag{15}$$

$$u_c(c)=\mu, \tag{16}$$

$$\dot{\mu}=(\rho-r)\mu, \tag{17}$$

$$\dot{\psi}=(\rho+\delta)\psi-\mu R(1-x_0)h-\psi hg(x_0), \quad \psi(T)=0, \tag{18}$$

$$\dot{K}=g(x_0)hK-\delta K, \qquad K(0)=K_0>0. \tag{19}$$

The solution can be analyzed by a phase diagram where μK and ψK are treated as the state variables (see Figure 11.4). From eq. (15) it is seen that a straight line with a slope $-R(1-x_0)/g(x_0)$ defines combinations of these state variables which keep h constant at an interior. Therefore the $\dot{\mu K}=0$ line form straight lines. From (18) and (19) it follows that the $\dot{\psi K}=0$ line (which may have positive or negative slope) has a larger slope than any constant h line. Trajectory I in Figure 11.4 describes the typical pattern.[18] Along the optimal path h initially increases and then declines. The same holds for μK, but it starts to decline after hours have peaked. Recall that wages are proportional to K. Assuming $r>\rho$, μK will peak before K does. Hence, along trajectory I wages peak later than hours. This is the same pattern as in the case of exogenous wages.

The simple learning-by-doing model is thus capable of explaining the main stylized facts on wage and work profiles. An increase in wages followed by a

[17]It is assumed that $u_c(0)=\infty$, $u_l(0)=\infty$, therefore only a corner with $h=0, l=1$ is considered.

[18]Depending upon initial conditions the trajectory may start at a point such that both μK and h are decreasing throughout the work life. It has been shown by Driffill (1980) that a trajectory which ends with retirement (i.e. enters the $h=0$ region) cannot start below the $\dot{\mu K}=0$ locus. Thus a cycling trajectory in which μK decreases then rises and then decreases again is not optimal. The argument is based on the observation that in the Blinder–Weiss specification [see Blinder and Weiss (1976)] $K_0(\psi_0/\mu_0)$ equals lifetime earnings under the optimal policy. Thus, moving along a ray from the origin he shows that a cycling path can be replaced by one starting on the same ray which provides the same lifetime earnings but requires less lifetime disutility from work.

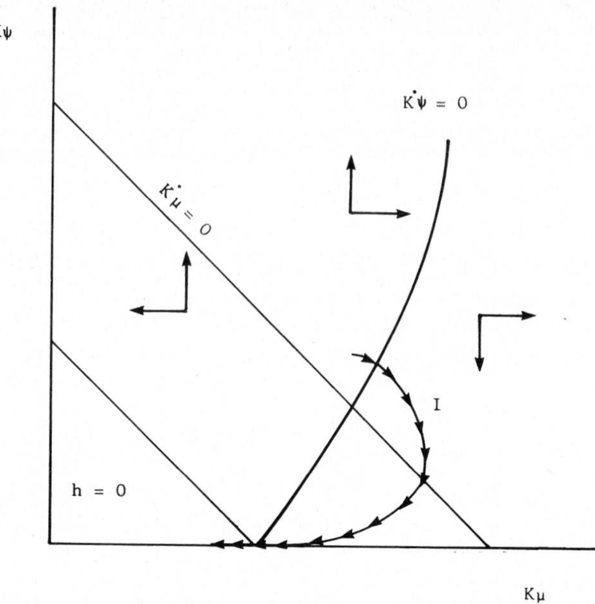

Figure 11.4

decline, an increase in hours of work followed by a decline, and a peak in hours which precedes the peak in wages [see Ghez and Becker (1975)].

The economic intuition behind these results is quite simple. The value of the investment component in work declines as the worker approaches the end of his work horizon. Thus, other things being equal, he would work more hours early in life. The high work intensity at young ages generates growth in the worker's stock of human capital. As the worker ages, hours and wage growth decline. Therefore the earning profile will first increase and then decline. The main difference from the earning maximizing models is that the patterns of accumulation are affected by the worker's *tastes*. With variable leisure, the costs of acquiring human capital (forgone leisure time) depend on the consumption state and not only on earning capacity. The production and consumption decisions cannot be separated. Consequently, taste parameters such as the subjective discount factor ρ influence the development of wages and earnings over the life cycle. If ρ is high, the worker has an incentive to work more in the future. This may lead to a pattern of increasing hours, and eliminate the final segment of reduced wages.[19]

[19] Killingsworth (1982) points out that this added flexibility is potentially beneficial. For instance, the constant decay in earnings late in life implied by the wealth maximizing model is modified to allow a variety of decay patterns when hours are flexible.

The analysis is in some respects simpler if the worker faces a variety of training options in the labor market. One may write the problem in the following form:

$$\max_{\{c,h,x\}}\left\{\int_0^T \mathrm{e}^{-\rho t}u(c,1-h)\,\mathrm{d}t+\mu_0\left[\int_0^T \mathrm{e}^{-rt}(RKh(1-x)-c)\,\mathrm{d}t+A_0\right]\right\}$$

$$\begin{aligned}&\text{s.t.}\\ &\dot{K}=G(K,h,x),\quad K(0)=K_0,\\ &0\le x\le 1,\\ &0\le h\le 1,\end{aligned}\tag{20}$$

where μ_0, the marginal utility of wealth at time 0, is a constant to be determined. Since the occupational index does not appear in the utility function directly, it will be chosen so as to maximize lifetime earnings *conditioned* on the choice of the work profile. Investment therefore is governed by the same formulas as in the income maximizing model, except that the rental rate R is replaced everywhere by its utility equivalent $\mu_0 R$. [With this modification ψ is still given by (4), and $\mu_0 RhK$ is equated to $\psi G_x(K,x,h)$ at an interior solution.]

It has been observed by Heckman (1976) that the problem can be separated further, and thus simplified if one adopts the Ben-Porath specification (specification II in Section 2) and if one further assumes that utility depends on "effective leisure", Kl, rather than on actual leisure time. Define $hx=y$, and assume that the constraints $0\le x\le 1$ and $0\le h\le 1$ are not binding, then the solution to (20) is equal to the solution of

$$\begin{aligned}&\max_{\{c,l\}}\left\{\int_0^T \mathrm{e}^{-\rho t}u(c,Kl)\,\mathrm{d}t+\mu_0\left[A_0-\int_0^T \mathrm{e}^{-rt}(RKl+c)\,\mathrm{d}t\right]\right\}\\ &\qquad+\mu_0\left[\max_{\{y\}}\int_0^T \mathrm{e}^{-rt}RK(1-y)\,\mathrm{d}t\right.\\ &\qquad\qquad\left.\text{s.t. }\dot{K}=g(Ky)-\delta K\right].\end{aligned}\tag{21}$$

Notice that the dynamic constraint is associated only with the second maximization in (21). This reflects the fact that the optimal solution for the first problem in (21) is at each age *locally independent* of K. The problem (20) can therefore be solved in stages. Given μ_0 the worker chooses an optimal investment program. This program has all the properties discussed in Section 3. In particular, for specification (II) investment is a declining function of age, and the resulting accumulation path for human capital is single peaked and concave. Taking this path of accumulation as exogenous the worker chooses an optimal consumption and leisure program. This program will have all the properties of the optimal life cycle labor supply with exogenous wages discussed above. In particular, assuming that effective leisure Kl is a normal input, it will monotonically increase if $r > \rho$ and monotonically decrease if $r < \rho$. The behavior of actual leisure time and work now follow from the exogenous pattern of K. When K peaks, then, if $r > \rho$, leisure time must increase. Therefore hours of work peak earlier than the potential wage of the worker. Finally, μ_0 is adjusted to make the two programs consistent with the lifetime wealth constraint which requires that lifetime consumption equals lifetime earnings plus initial wealth.

The studies by Ryder, Stafford and Stephan (1976) and Blinder and Weiss (1976) assume that actual leisure time appears in the utility function and admit corner solutions. Contrary to Heckman (1976) where human capital is equally productive at home and at the market and therefore future work plans have no effect on the returns from investment, these models allow the shadow price of human capital to reflect the expected intensity of labor force participation. It is shown that in a "typical" lifetime program, the worker passes through four

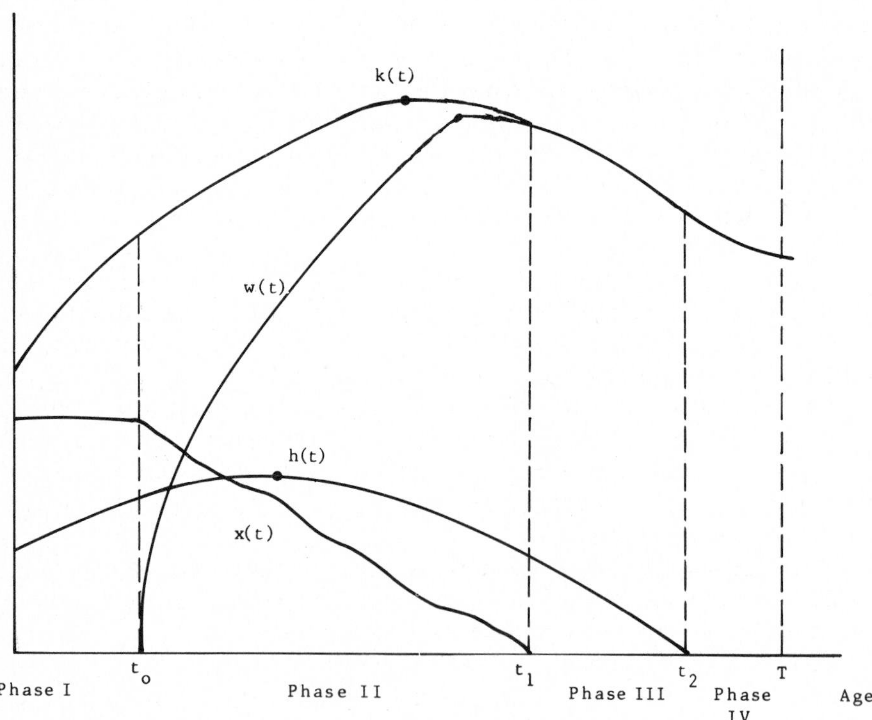

Figure 11.5. The age profiles of human capital, wages, investment and work.

different phases: schooling ($x = 1, h > 0$); on-the-job training ($0 < x < 1, h > 0$); work ($x = 0, h > 0$); and retirement ($h = 0$). Normally the phases occur in this order, though, depending on initial condition, some may not arise. The behavior of the key variables is described in Figure 11.5. Again, these patterns are similar to those predicted by the models with exogenous wages.

The main difference from the earnings maximizing models [and Heckman (1976)] is that investment as measured by $\dot{K}$ or $(\dot{K}/K)$ *increases* during the schooling phase and also in the early part of the on-the-job training phase. This is a result of the initial increase in hours of work. While in Figure 11.5, investment intensity as measured by x *declines* throughout the worker's life career, this result is only true for $\rho < r + \delta$. Generally, the incentive to postpone investment is influenced by the subjective discount factor ρ. The higher is ρ, the more likely it is that the worker consumes his leisure rather early in life and thus postpones his investment in human capital. For sufficiently high rate of impatience the worker may decide to "retire" while young. It is then quite logical that he also postpones his investment to a period close to his entry into the labor force.

For a low rate of impatience the broad patterns of the optimal work and wage plans are similar in the different available models of endogenous labor supply. This is perhaps not surprising since they were all designed to fit the same stylized facts. There are, however, some marked and unexpected differences in the comparative statics and comparative dynamics. I now proceed to survey these issues.

5. Comparative statics and dynamics

So far I have only discussed the time patterns of investment in human capital and their implications. I described models which generate optimal work and wage profiles that imitate the observed life cycle patterns. The question naturally arises, how sensitive are the time patterns of the optimal programs to changes in parameters. This issue falls under the heading of comparative dynamics. A second question relates to the impact of various parameter changes on lifetime *aggregates* such as lifetime earnings, lifetime consumption or more narrowly the total time spent in a particular phase such as "schooling". These questions fall under the heading of comparative statics.

I will illustrate some of the issues in comparative statics analysis by focusing on the effect of changes in initial wealth, A_0, on lifetime earnings and consumption. For this purpose we need to examine the determination of μ_0 in more detail. Consider first the model by Heckman (1976). Define:

$$S = \int_0^T e^{-rt} RK(1-y)\,dt, \qquad E = \int_0^T e^{rt} RKh(1-x)\,dt, \tag{22}$$

where $y = hx$. We may refer to S as lifetime income and to E as lifetime earnings. Note that S exceeds E by the present value of effective leisure which the worker "buys back". Under the two stage procedure described above, investment policy is independent of μ_0. Therefore, the supply of lifetime income as a function of μ_0 is perfectly inelastic. The demand for lifetime income,

$$\int_0^T \mathrm{e}^{-rt}(RKl + c)\,\mathrm{d}t - A_0,$$

is determined by the solution to the first maximization in (21). For a given μ_0 this maximization is equivalent to an unconstrained profit maximization at each age, and an increase in μ_0 is equivalent to a reduction in the price of output (i.e. utility). Hence with a concave utility function expenditures (i.e. $c + RKl$) must increase with $1/\mu_0$. It follows that the demand for S as a function of μ_0 is downward sloping. The level of μ_0 is determined at the intersection of the demand and supply curves.

Now consider an increase in initial wealth A_0. The supply curve for lifetime income is unaffected by this change but the demand curve shifts (parallelly) to the left. It follows immediately that S is unaffected but μ_0 declines. Under the assumption that consumption and effective leisure are normal goods both increase, at every age, as μ_0 declines, hence lifetime earnings decline and lifetime consumption increases.

Different results can arise in the models proposed by Blinder and Weiss (1976) and Ryder, Stafford and Stephan (1976). In both cases leisure is measured in time units and the utility function is additive separable in leisure and consumption. These models can be separated in a different way from the Heckman model, and the solution to problem (20) equals to the solution of

$$\begin{aligned}&\max_{\{c\}}\left[\int_0^T \mathrm{e}^{-\rho t}u(c)\,\mathrm{d}t - \mu_0\left(\int_0^T \mathrm{e}^{-rt}c\,\mathrm{d}t - A_0\right)\right]\\ &\quad + \max_{\{x,h\}}\left[\int_0^T \mathrm{e}^{-\rho t}v(1-h)\,\mathrm{d}t + \mu_0\int_0^T \mathrm{e}^{-rt}RKh(1-x)\,\mathrm{d}t\right.\\ &\qquad\qquad\qquad\qquad \left.\text{s.t. } \dot{K} = G(K,h,x)\right]. \end{aligned} \tag{23}$$

By a standard argument one can show that for each of the separate maximization problems in (23) that the value of the optimal program is *convex* in μ_0. Since the demand and supply for lifetime earnings are the derivatives of the optimized value functions of these two problems with respect to μ_0, it follows that the demand is downward sloping while the supply is upwards sloping. If it can also be shown that for every μ_0 there corresponds a *unique* E (i.e. the two curves are continuous graphs) then by the same arguments used for the Heckman (1976) formulation, μ_0 is determined by the intersection of the demand and supply curves and an increase in A_0 must lead to a reduction in lifetime earnings and in μ_0 and therefore to an increase in lifetime consumption.

A special aspect of the human capital problem is the presence of dynamic increasing returns to scale and therefore the concavity of the second maximization problem in (23) is generally *not* guaranteed. This will generally imply that the supply of lifetime earnings as a function of μ_0 need not be a continuous graph [see Brock and Dechert (1985)]. Not surprisingly, the question whether a unique level of lifetime earnings can be associated with any given μ_0 is closely related to the second-order conditions for dynamic maximization. The problem reduces to the question whether the first-order Euler or Pontryagin conditions for the second maximization in (23) identify a unique path. A well-known *sufficient* condition for uniqueness is that the corresponding Hamiltonian function be strictly concave in the control variables and that the maximized Hamiltonian is concave in the state variables [see Arrow and Kurz (1970)].

The models by Blinder and Weiss (1976) and Ryder, Stafford and Stephan (1976) do not satisfy this sufficiency condition and uniqueness cannot be guaranteed for these models.[20] Driffill (1980) has actually found a potentially wide class

[20] For the Blinder and Weiss (1976) model, the maximized Hamiltonian corresponding to the second maximization in (23) is

$$M(K,\psi) \equiv \max_{x,h}\left[v(1-h)\mathrm{e}^{-\rho t} + \mu_0 RK(1-x)h\,\mathrm{e}^{-rt} + \psi[hKg(x) - \delta K]\right]$$

and is convex in K for given ψ, since by the first-order conditions, x is independent of K and h is increasing in K, hence,

$$M_{KK} = \left[\mathrm{e}^{-rt}\mu_0 R(1-x) + \psi g(x)\right]\frac{\mathrm{d}h}{\mathrm{d}K} > 0$$

[see also McCabe (1983)]. The convexity of the Hamiltonian in the state does *not* imply that the first-order conditions identify a minimum nor does it imply that the solution is not unique. That the condition is overly strong is immediately apparent from the fact that it is not independent of positive monotone transformation in the *state* variables. For example, define a new state variable Z such that $Z^\alpha = K$, $0 < \alpha < 1$. The new Hamiltonian function is

$$M(z,\psi) \equiv \max_{x,h}\left[v(1-h)\mathrm{e}^{-\rho t} + \mu_0 Rz^\alpha(1-x)h\,\mathrm{e}^{-rt} + \psi\alpha[hzg(x) - \delta z]\right]$$

and

$$M_{ZZ} = \frac{v'(1-h)h\,\mathrm{e}^{-\rho t}}{z^2}\left[\alpha(\alpha-1)\frac{(1-x)g'(x)}{(1-x)g'(x)+g(x)} - \frac{v'(1-h)}{v''(1-h)h}\right].$$

If the optimal path is always interior [e.g. set $g'(1) = 0$, $g'(0) = \infty$, $v'(1) = 0$, $v'(0) = \infty$], then there may exist an α which yields $M_{ZZ} < 0$ along the optimal path. If such an α exists the solution to the Pontryagin conditions of the original problem is unique. Unfortunately, this sufficient condition can be verified only after a solution is found.

of cases in which an increase in initial wealth *reduces* lifetime consumption. This situation arises in the Blinder and Weiss (1976) model if the parameter configuration is such that the optimal life program starts with full time training and ends with retirement. McCabe (1983) notes that by modifying the Blinder–Weiss model, allowing effective leisure to enter the utility function [as in Heckman (1976)] uniqueness can be restored and therefore consumption *increases* with wealth.[21]

The economic explanation for these results is apparent if one considers the usual static leisure consumption problem with increasing returns (see Figure 11.6). This analogy is perfectly valid for comparative static analysis where all the dynamic effects are "maximized out". A change in initial wealth shifts the budget constraint in a way which keeps its slope constant along any vertical line. This means that with respect to leisure there is a pure income effect, and under the usual restrictions on preferences associated with normality, its consumption will increase. However, due to the increasing returns to scale the slope declines along any horizontal line. That is, holding consumption constant the increase in A leads to a *reduction* in wages. With respect to consumption both income and substitution effects operate. Since income increases but consumption becomes relatively more expensive, the income and substitution effect operate in opposite directions, and depending upon the relative strength of these effects consumption may increase or decrease. Thus, as noted by Driffill (1980), the reduction of consumption with initial wealth is a distinct possibility in any human capital model because of inherent increasing returns. The assumption of effective leisure eliminates the price effect on consumption by reducing the marginal rate of substitution together with the wage along a horizontal line. While this modifica-

[21]A very simple example will help to illustrate these general statements. Consider the static leisure consumption problem but with increasing returns to scale.

$$\max_{c,h} V = c^a + \alpha(1-h), \quad 1 > \alpha > 2a, \quad 0 < a < 1/2,$$

s.t.

$$A + h^2 = c$$

substitute for h in the objective function and differentiate to obtain

$$V_c = ac^{a-1} - (\alpha/2)(c-A)^{-1/2}$$

$$V_{cc} = a(a-1)c^{a-2} + (\alpha/4)(c-A)^{-3/2}$$

If we set $A = 0$, then, due to the restrictions on the parameters, there is an interior solution with $1 > h > 0$, $c > 0$, which satisfies $V_c = 0$ and $V_{cc} < 0$. Since $V_{cA} < 0$ it follows that $\mathrm{d}c/\mathrm{d}A|_{A=0} < 0$. Note that the auxiliary problem $\max_h \alpha(1-h) + \mu_0 h^2$ has *two* solutions when $\mu_0 = \alpha$ (i.e. $h = 0$ and $h = 1$). Finally, if the second part of utility function is changed to $\alpha(1-h)h$ (as in the effective leisure hypothesis) then $V_{CA} > 0$ and $\mathrm{d}c/\mathrm{d}A > 0$.

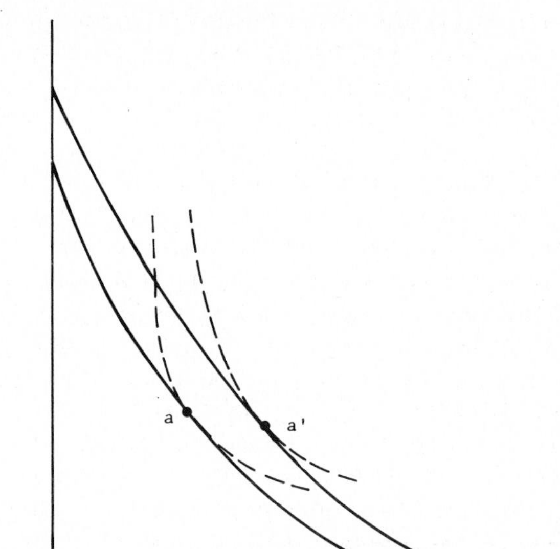

Figure 11.6

tion yields a more plausible relationship between lifetime consumption and wealth, it also has some undesirable implications. For instance, the effective leisure hypothesis is incapable of explaining the negative relationship between planned future withdrawals from the labor force and current investment. It seems that the two alternative hypotheses: that human capital, acquired at the market place, is equally productive at home and in the market [as in Heckman (1976)] or that it has no effect on home productivity [as in Blinder and Weiss (1976) and Ryder, Stafford and Stephan (1976)] are both rather extreme simplifications of the true situation.

Ryder, Stafford and Stephan (1976), who were the first to discuss the implications of the potential non-uniqueness of the solution to the Pontryagin necessary conditions, note that changes in the initial level of human capital may also cause discontinuous jumps in the optimal policy.

> A worker who starts near the "catastrophy set" but with slightly less initial human capital will find it optimal to go to work at once, do little training and retire early. If he had started with the same wealth but on the other side of the watershed with slightly more human capital it would have been optimal to start his career with training and then devote considerable time to labor continuing right to the end of his life.

Heckman (1976) derived several comparative dynamic results for his model. Some follow directly from the comparative statics exercise. For instance, the reduction in μ_0 as a result of an increase in A_0 implies that $\mu(t)$ is lower for all t and hence consumption and effective leisure will increase for every age. Heckman shows that an increase in the initial stock of human capital also reduces μ_0, and thus shifts upwards the demand for consumption and effective leisure at every age. Since investment policy in his model is completely independent of initial conditions, one can conclude that an increase in initial wealth will reduce hours of work at every age. An increase in initial human capital, on the other hand, will initially increase and later reduce labor supply.

The comparative dynamics for the investment profile in the Heckman (1976) model are the same as in the income maximizing model. This means that changes in tastes have *no* effect on the development of the worker's earning capacity. This is in sharp contrast to the models by Blinder and Weiss (1976) and Ryder, Stafford and Stephan (1976) where changes in taste parameters, such as the subjective discount factor ρ, affect investment policies in a substantive way. To analyze the effects of such a change on the optimal policy, under the Blinder and Weiss specification, consider again eqs. (15)–(19) and the added equation which determine optimal investment:

$$\begin{aligned} R\mu + \psi g'(x) &= 0, \quad \text{if } 0 < x < 1, \\ R\mu + \psi g'(x) &\leq 0, \quad \text{if } x = 0, \\ R\mu + \psi g'(x) &\geq 0, \quad \text{if } x = 1. \end{aligned} \tag{24}$$

Notice that during the phase with on-the-job trainings (i.e. $0 < x < 1$) eqs. (24), together with (15)–(19) imply an autonomous system of differential equations in x and h, with boundary conditions $x(t_1) = 1$ and $x(t_2) = 0$, where t_1 and t_2 are the (variable) points of entry and exit into this phase. Differentiating this system with respect to ρ, one obtains a new system of differential equations for the *changes* in hours of work and training intensity (h_ρ and x_ρ, respectively) which result from the increase in the subjective discount factor [see Oniki (1973) and Epstein (1978)]. The boundary conditions for this new system are $x_\rho(t_1) = x_\rho(t_2) = 0$. Evaluating the system at $\rho = 0$ it can be shown, with some added assumptions,[22] that it satisfies the following sign pattern:

$$\begin{pmatrix} \dot{h}_p \\ \dot{x}_p \end{pmatrix} = \begin{pmatrix} + & + \\ - & + \end{pmatrix} \begin{pmatrix} h_p \\ x_p \end{pmatrix} + \begin{pmatrix} +, \\ 0 \end{pmatrix}. \tag{25}$$

[22] The added conditions are

$$\frac{\mathrm{d}}{\mathrm{d}h}\left(\frac{V''(1-h)}{V'(1-h)}\right) \leq 0 \quad \text{and} \quad \frac{\mathrm{d}}{\mathrm{d}x}\left(\frac{g''(x)}{g'(x)}\right) \leq 0.$$

These conditions are also related to the concavity of the hours and wage profiles.

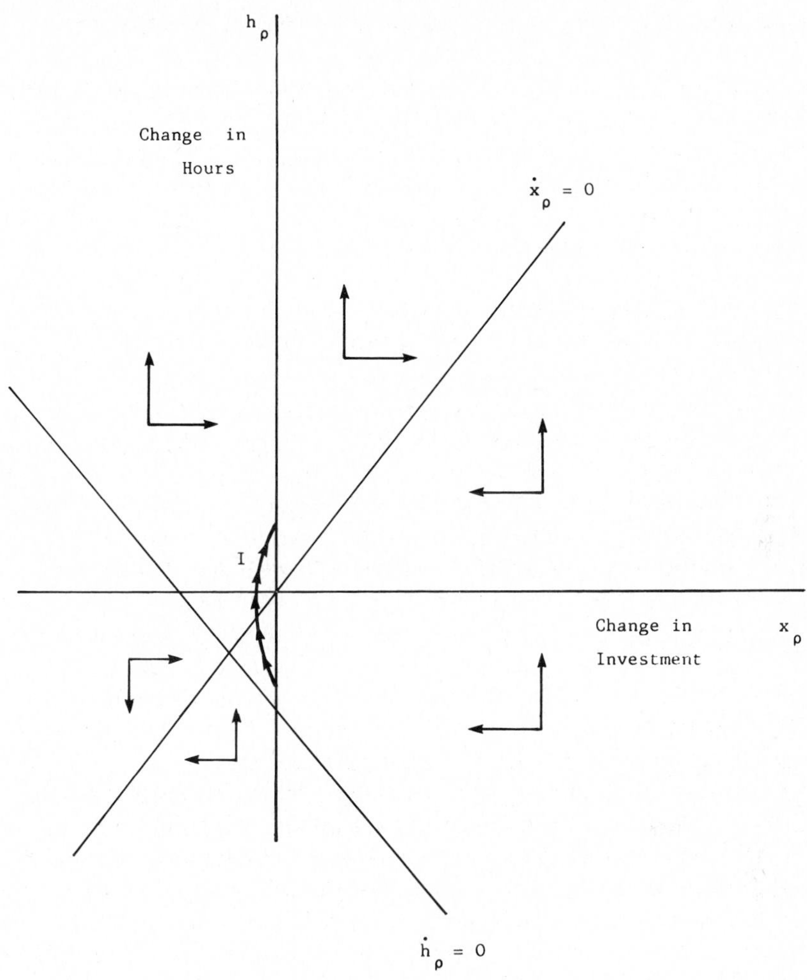

Figure 11.7

The phase diagram corresponding to (25) is presented in Figure 11.7. It is seen from examining the directional arrows that a trajectory satisfying $x_\rho(t_1) = x_\rho(t_2) = 0$ must start on the vertical axis at a point above the $\dot{h}_\rho = 0$ line and below the $\dot{x}_\rho = 0$ line, otherwise the trajectory will never return to the vertical axis. Trajectory I in Figure 11.8, therefore, describes the only admissible pattern. An increase in the subjective discount factor will reduce hours of work throughout the phase with on-the-job training. The investment intensity is initially reduced and then increased as one would expect given the incentive to postpone investment as ρ increases. The total amount of time spent at the phase with on-the-job training increases.

6. Extensions of the basic model

In this section I survey two important and related extensions of the basic model, imperfections in the capital market in the form of borrowing constraints and uncertainty with respect to the future earnings capacity of the worker. These two issues are related since potential lenders are more likely to be concerned about possible default when future earnings are random. I will follow the literature, however, and discuss each of the two issues separately.

6.1. *Borrowing constraints*

The simplest sort of borrowing constraint is one in which the worker cannot borrow to finance his educational costs but can borrow freely to finance his consumption. Such constraints were introduced into wealth maximizing models by Wallace and Inhen (1975), who impose non-negative net current earnings, and Oniki (1968), who requires that accumulated net earnings do not fall below some negative constant. Such constraints become effective only in the presence of *direct* costs of investment in human capital. It has been shown by these authors that the general time pattern of investment is not affected by such constraints, that is investment in human capital is *falling*, and a period of specialization if it occurs at all, will occur at the *beginning* of the worker's career.[23] The main difference is that the overall level of investment declines implying a lower (and with additional assumptions) flatter earnings profile.[24]

A more meaningful borrowing constraint is one which limits all borrowing, whether for consumption or training. Formally, this constraint can be written as $A(t) \geq 0$. This constraint can affect the worker in a more substantive way since it breaks the separation between consumption and investment decisions.

With the borrowing constraint the problem is restated as

$$\max_{\{x,c\}} \int_0^T \mathrm{e}^{-\rho t} u(c)\,\mathrm{d}t$$

$$\begin{aligned} &\text{s.t.} \\ &\dot{A} = rA + RKh(1-x) - c, \quad A(t) \geq 0, \quad A(0) = A_0, \quad A(T) = 0, \\ &\dot{K} = G(K, h, x), \quad K(0) = K_0. \\ &0 \leq x \leq 1, \end{aligned} \tag{26}$$

[23] In Oniki (1968) this is strictly correct only if one adopts specification I in Section 2. Under a more general specification postponement of investment may arise.

[24] Oniki (1968) performs explicit comparative statics with respect to changes in the borrowing constraint. He shows that a tightening of the constraint leads to a *reduction* in the amount of human capital accumulated in the schooling phase. (The duration of this phase may increase or decrease.)

where, as in the wealth maximizing model, $h(t)$ is predetermined. An interior optimal path is characterized by the equations

$$u'(c)-\mu=0, \tag{27}$$

$$-\mu RKh+\psi G_x=0, \tag{28}$$

$$\dot{\psi}=\rho\psi-\mu Rh(1-x)-\psi G_K, \quad \psi(T)=0, \tag{29}$$

$$\dot{\mu}=(\rho-r)\mu-\lambda, \quad \lambda\geq 0, \quad \lambda(t)A(t)=0. \tag{30}$$

Combining eqs. (29) and (30) it is seen that the shadow price of human capital in dollar terms, $\eta\equiv\psi/\mu$, satisfies

$$\dot{\eta}=(r-G_K)\eta-Rh(1-x)+\frac{\lambda}{\mu}\eta, \quad \eta(T)=0. \tag{31}$$

When the borrowing constraint is absent and $\lambda(t)\equiv 0$, eq. (31) is, of course, identical to eq. (4) in Section 2, and the optimal investment policy will maximize lifetime earnings. In the presence of the borrowing constraint the shadow price of human capital declines at a *slower* rate whenever the constraint is effective. This represents the incentive to shift investment towards periods in which an increase in investment does not require sacrifice of current consumption.

Recall that under specifications (II) and (III) in Section 2, eq. (31) involves only η and (λ/μ) [x and G_K can be eliminated using (28)]. In these cases it is still correct that η is decreasing whenever the borrowing constraint is not binding and $\lambda=0$. When the constraint is binding, η may decrease at a slower rate or increase, depending upon the parameters of the utility function. The effect of a borrowing constraint is therefore to *reduce* the shadow price of human capital at all points during and prior to the phase (or phases) in which the borrowing constraint is effective. The worker will invest less in human capital and his earning profile will be generally lower (except at early ages) and flatter.

In the presence of borrowing constraints, investment need not decline monotonically, and the period of specialization may be postponed. For instance, if the worker starts with no initial assets, it is clear that he cannot train at a full rate at the beginning of his career, even though this might be efficient in terms of the maximization of lifetime earnings. He may choose to postpone his "schooling" period to a later point and accumulate sufficient savings to support such a program.

It is interesting to note that the general shape of the earnings profile may be unaffected by the introduction of a borrowing constraint. If, for instance, $r>\rho$, then it is seen from eq. (30) that consumption will increase on an optimal path.

Hence, when the borrowing constraint is effective earnings must increase. Whenever the constraint is not effective investment declines, and earnings will increase unless net investment becomes negative. Since the borrowing constraint is likely to be effective at the beginning of the worker's life, earnings will first increase and then decline. This is the same pattern as in the absence of the borrowing constraint. However, the rate of investment and the shape of the earnings profile will strongly depend on the worker's *tastes*.[25]

A common practice in the human capital literature is to acknowledge the practical importance of borrowing constraints only to ignore them in the analysis. The discussion above suggests that if the main purpose is to explain the general qualitative aspects of earning profiles the neglect of borrowing constraints can be, perhaps, justified. If, however, one's objective is to explain the level of investment, or to identify basic parameters such as the interest rate, from observed earnings, then the omission of the borrowing constraint may lead to serious biases.

6.2. *Uncertainty*

A worker who invests in human capital faces several risks. Both future market conditions and individual circumstances (such as health) are uncertain. The worker's capacity to learn on the job and its precise training content are not known when a job is accepted. The question arises to what extent does the presence of such risks affect the incentive to invest in human capital, and what is the effect on the time pattern of investment over the life cycle.

Consider again specifications (II) and (III) of the production function in Section 2, and assume that $g(x)$ is linear. We may then reduce *both* specifications to

$$\dot{K}/K = \theta x h - \delta, \tag{32}$$

where θ can be interpreted as training efficiency and δ is the depreciation rate of

[25]A simple example is the case in which the production function is linear and the rate of depreciation is zero. That is, $\dot{K} = aKxh$ and where a and h are constants and $a > r, \rho$. In this case it can be shown that if $\rho > r$ the borrowing constraint is *always* binding, while if $r > \rho$ it can *only* be binding during the investment period [see Weiss (1972)]. Working life is divided into two phases, an investment phase in which $0 < x < 1$ and a successive non-investment phase with $x = 0$. The duration of the investment phase t_0 is determined by $a\int_{t_0}^{T} e^{-r(t-t_0)}\,dt = 1$ if $r > \rho$ (the same condition as in the absence of a borrowing constraint) and by $a\int_{t_0}^{T} e^{-\rho(t-t_0)}\,dt = 1$ if $r < \rho$. Hence, the duration of the investment period is equal or shorter, and the intensity of investment is lower when a borrowing constraint is imposed.

human capital. Assume that θ follows a random process,

$$\theta(t) = \alpha + \gamma\varepsilon(t), \tag{33}$$

where $\varepsilon(t)$ is a white noise process.[26] Then the problem facing the worker is similar to the standard investor problem facing random returns [see Merton (1971)]. As in the case of certainty the difference remains that human capital cannot be bought or sold freely, a fact which introduces constraints on the rate of accumulation and introduces a potential direct link between utility and investment. Nevertheless, as shown by Williams (1979), the same techniques apply.

The worker's problem is now to choose an optimal strategy determining c, h, and x as functions of the state variables K and A (which are random) and t. The assumed objective is the *expected* lifetime utility. If one denotes the maximized value function by $J(K, A, t)$, then the optimal strategy satisfies, at an interior solution:

$$u_c = J_A, \tag{34}$$

$$u_l = RKJ_A, \tag{35}$$

$$xh = \left(\frac{-J_K}{J_{KK}K}\right)\left(\frac{\alpha - RJ_A/J_K}{\gamma^2}\right). \tag{36}$$

(For the case of certainty I used the notation $J_A = \mu$ and $J_K = \psi$.) Conditions (34) and (35) are of the same form as under certainty, and in particular (as is generally the under specification II) the marginal rate of substitution between consumption and leisure is equated to the *potential* wage of the worker [see also Macurdy (1983)]. The numerator of the second term on the right-hand side of (36) is the criterion which determined investment under certainty. Due to the assumed linearity, a "bang-bang" solution would arise in the absence of risk. But as noted by Williams (1979), this is modified under uncertainty due to the rise of a risk premium. If $\alpha < RJ_A/J_K$, then, as under certainty, the worker will not invest in human capital (i.e. $x = 0$). This will always hold towards the end of the worker's career since the transversality condition $J_K(K, A, T) = 0$ still applies. However, if $\alpha > RJ_A/J_K$, it does not follow that the worker plunges into investment in human capital since the riskiness of this investment is taken into account. Generally, the lower is the risk (as measured by γ^2) or the lower the degree of risk aversion (as measured by $(-J_{KK}K/J_K)$ the higher will be the investment. Just as in the case of imperfect capital markets the separation

[26] The process $\varepsilon(t)$ is the continuous time analogue of a sequence of independent random variables each normally distributed with zero means and unit variances [see Karlin and Taylor (1981, ch. 15, section 14)].

between investment and consumption breaks down. The investment decisions depend on *taste* parameters which are implicit in the value function $J(\cdot)$.

Since xh depends on the realizations of a random process, it is not as meaningful to ask whether it declines with age. One can enquire, though, whether the propensity to invest *given* the realizations of human capital and assets declines with age.

A precise statement can be made if it is assumed that the utility function is of the form

$$u(c, lK) = c^{\beta_1}(lK)^{\beta_2}, \quad \beta_1 + \beta_2 < 1, \tag{37}$$

where leisure is again measured in effective units. In this case conditions (34) and (35) imply that c and lK are in fixed proportions and utility as function of consumption has constant relative risk aversion. It is possible then to solve for $J(K, A, t)$ explicitly. At an interior solution, investment in human capital (in dollars) can be written as proportional to total wealth, where the factor of proportionality depends on the relative price of human capital. That is

$$\eta Kxh = \Omega(\eta)(A + K\eta), \tag{38}$$

where $\eta \equiv (J_K/J_A)$ is the shadow price of human capital in dollar terms. Because of the assumption that leisure is measured in effective units and the specific form of the utility function (37), η depends only on t (and not on the realizations of K or A). It actually satisfies the *same* differential equation as under certainty [see Williams (1979, Appendix)] this means that η is ever decreasing. Since $\Omega(\eta)$ is an increasing function of η the conclusion is that investment in human capital as a proportion of total wealth is declining monotonically with the worker's age.

In the simple case outlined above an increase in risk, as measured by γ, reduces the propensity to invest in human capital. This may suggest that the general effect of uncertainty is to hinder the accumulation in human capital. This is not correct. In the more general model considered by Williams (1979) additional sources of uncertainty are included. In particular δ and R are also assumed random, and δ is allowed to be correlated with θ. This correlation introduces the potential for hedging against obsolesence thus encouraging the investment in human capital. In the simple two-period models [Levhari and Weiss (1974) and Williams (1978)] it is also shown that an increase in the investment in schooling may reduce the variability of earnings and total portfolio income. In such cases investment in human capital is encouraged when risk increases.

7. Specific human capital and binding labor contracts

The analysis up to this point was founded on the assumption that competition forces wages to equal the value of the marginal product which accrues to the firm.

As noted by Becker (1975) the forces of competition are often mitigated by the establishment of specific human capital. If training increases productivity within the firm more than elsewhere, then a bilateral monopoly situation arises, ex post. It is then in the interest of the parties, ex ante, to limit ex post bargaining. For this purpose they may seek a binding agreement which will set the division of the gains and the costs of the mutually beneficial investment. If it is indeed feasible to enforce such contracts the choice of the investment policy can be made jointly by the two parties, and the outcome will be independent of the division of the rents. The sharing rule can be determined, in principle, by some bargaining model, but since the transfers can take a variety of forms, there is little that can be said about the ensuing wage profiles. The fact is, however, that fully enforceable contracts are not observed in the labor market. A worker who wants to quit is rarely prevented legally or otherwise from doing so. Firms, on the other hand, do commit themselves quite often at least implicitly. This asymmetry can be exploited to put some bounds on the feasible wage profiles. Clearly, if the workers can leave the firm then the payment stream within the firm must at least match the outside opportunities of the worker. Further restrictions can be obtained if one adds asymmetry in the outside opportunities of the two parties, e.g. in the ability to rearrange payment schemes through the capital or insurance markets.

Consider the case in which a worker who joins the firm produces jointly output and knowledge which is purely specific to the firm. Suppose the worker has no access to an outside capital market and cannot rearrange the payments offered to him by the firm. At each point the worker has the option of leaving the firm, in which case his expected lifetime utility from that point on is given by $V(t, K_0)$ (V does not depend on $K(t)$ since human capital accumulated at the firm is purely specific).[27]

Suppose that the firm commits itself by offering a lifetime employment contract [with $h(t)$ set at 1 for all t] and a corresponding wage profile $w(t)$. How are the investment policy and wage profile determined? If one assumes that the bargaining between the worker and the firm leads to a *Pareto efficient* agreement, then the outcome of the bargaining process must solve

$$\begin{aligned}
&\max_{\{x,w\}} \int_0^T \mathrm{e}^{-rt}(RK(1-x)-w)\,\mathrm{d}t \\
&\text{s.t.} \qquad\qquad\qquad\qquad\qquad\qquad\qquad\qquad\qquad\qquad (39)\\
&\dot{K}=G(K,1,x), \quad K(0)=K_0, \\
&\dot{U}=\rho U-u(w), \quad U(T)=0, \quad U\geq V(t,K_0) \quad \text{for all } t,
\end{aligned}$$

where U is the discounted value of the worker's utility stream associated with

[27] It is also required that reentry into the firm is not optimal. Under static conditions and if, as assumed, experience is not transferable this will be the case [see Weiss (1971)].

$w(t)$, from t to T. That is to say, the firm's profits are maximized under the constraint that at no time can the worker's utility be improved either by quitting or by revising the investment policy and the wage offer.

It is immediately seen that the investment policy is the *same* as in the case in which human capital was perfectly general. The reason is, of course, that the collusion of the two parties allows them to jointly internalize the benefits of the investment, and it does not matter to whom the benefit accrues in the first place. The wage is determined separately by the conditions

$$-1-\mu u'(w)=0, \tag{40}$$

$$\dot{\mu}=(r-\rho)\mu-\lambda, \quad \lambda \geq 0, \quad \lambda(U-V(t,K_0))=0. \tag{41}$$

If the constraint $U \geq V(K_0, t)$ is never effective, wages are determined according to the desired *consumption* pattern of the worker. In this sense the firm acts as a bank on behalf of the worker. It follows from (40) and (41) that for $r \geq \rho$, the optimal, that is agreed upon, wage profile is *non-decreasing*.

With market imperfections there is an incentive for the provision of binding contracts even in the absence of any specific human capital. Several authors have noted that if productivity is uncertain and insurance of earnings is not available outside the firm, then a contingent wage agreement can be used to achieve risk sharing within the firm. Freeman (1977), Harris and Holmstrom (1982), and Weiss and Lillard (1983) consider extensions of the model outlined above when it is assumed that productivity both within and outside the firm evolve according to some stochastic process. If firms are assumed risk neutral, then again for $r \geq \rho$ the wage is *non-decreasing* along *any* sample path of the process. Thus in particular, average wages grow with age.

Hashimoto (1981) considers the case in which the productivity of the worker outside and inside the firm are random but not perfectly correlated. Under such circumstances it is not efficient to continue employment unless the occurrence of productivity within the firm turns out to exceed the worker's opportunity cost. The solution of the problem now requires an employment policy in addition to the wage and investment policy. If one could enforce a wage rate which is contingent on the ex post realized rents, allowing voluntary separations, given the wage rate, quits (or layoffs) will occur only if the separation is ex post efficient. (It is assumed that both parties are risk neutral.) However, since it is costly to verify the opportunities of the worker or the productivity of the firm, Hashimoto considers a non-contingent wage contract which is determined ex ante. Within a two-period model context, he shows that the predetermined wage profile will be *increasing*. The rate of increase is determined by its impact on the ex post incentives of workers to quit or firms to fire their workers. Lazear (1981) considers a similar model except that in his interpretation quitting is triggered by "shirking": a voluntary act which benefits the worker, imposes costs on the firm and leads to an immediate dismissal. In deciding whether to shirk the worker takes into account the endogenous probability that the firm terminates the contract unilaterally, sometime in the future. Lazear then shows that a Pareto efficient contract generates an upward sloping wage profile. The rise in the wage is used to discourage opportunistic behavior by the worker and, indirectly, mobility. It has been noted by several authors, e.g. Becker and Stigler (1974) and Kennan (1979), that if the worker has access to the capital market, alternative arrangements such as bonding can be used for this disciplinary purpose.

The analysis becomes considerably more complicated if one introduces variation in hours or effort. This is particularly true if effort cannot be monitored, which leads to an agency type problem. Holmstrom (1983) considers a special case where output is given by

$$Y_t = \theta + h_t + \varepsilon_t, \tag{42}$$

and the workers utility each period is

$$u_t = w_t - v(h_t), \tag{43}$$

where θ is unknown (but fixed) ability parameter, and ε_t a random transitory effect. Only output is directly observable. In equilibrium firms can infer from the workers past *output* on his ability and adjust wages correspondingly. Thus, by increasing effort the worker produces an individual specific human capital in the form of reputation. This type of human capital, however, has no direct effect on output. The model implies that effort *declines* monotonically toward zero over the life cycle. The reason is that effort is not rewarded directly, the sole return for effort is improved reputation, a return which diminishes towards the end of the work horizon.

Rogerson (1985) considers a case without learnings but with a utility function which is concave in w. The wage contract is, again, conditioned only on the outcome since effort is not observed. Because of the dynamic set-up, one can generally find more than one payment scheme which elicits the same effort and provides the same expected utility to the worker. This is accomplished by reducing utility in the present and increasing it uniformly at all future outcomes. An optimal wage contract must minimize the expected wage costs for the firm within this set. In a two-period context this leads to the condition:

$$\frac{1}{u'(w_0)} = E\left(\frac{1}{u'(w_1)}\right), \tag{44}$$

which states that the current marginal cost to the firm of increasing the worker's utility (with effort being the same) must equal the corresponding expected future cost. (It is assumed that $r=\rho$ and that the expectation is conditioned on the realized outcome at period 0.) By a direct application of Jensen's inequality it can be seen from (44) that the expected (unconditional) wages may increase or decrease depending upon the convexity of $1/u'(w)$. This is in contrast to the papers cited above which predict an increasing expected wage profile. The difference arises, in part, because of the assumed absence of quits in Rogerson's model.

To conclude, with specific human capital the wage and hours profiles are less closely tied to the accumulation of productive capacity. They also reflect the sharing of the costs and the benefits from the investment between the workers and the firm. The shares depend on the outside opportunities, mobility costs, information and attitude towards risk of the two parties. Depending upon the assumed role of these factors, one can obtain a variety of wage and work profiles. For this reason the results are considerably less robust than in the case of general human capital.

References

Arrow, K. (1973) "Higher education as a filter", *Journal of Public Economics*, 2:193–216.

Arrow, K. and K. Kurz (1970) *Public investment, the rate of return and optimal fiscal policy*, Johns Hopkins Press.

Ashenfelter, O. (1978) "Estimating the effect of training program on earnings", *The Review of Economics and Statistics*, 50:47–57.

Becker, G. (1975) *Human capital*. New York: Columbia University Press, 2nd ed.

Becker, G. and G. Stigler (1974) "Law enforcement malfeasance and compensation of enforcers", *Journal of Legal Studies*, 3:1–18.

Ben-Porath, Y. (1967) "The production of human capital and the life cycle of earnings", *Journal of Political Economy*, 75:352–365.

Ben-Porath, Y. (1970) "The production of human capital over time", in: W. Hansen, ed., *Education income and human capital*. N.B.E.R.

Blinder, A. and Y. Weiss (1976) "Human capital and labor supply: a synthesis", *Journal of Political Economy*, 84:449–472.

Brock, W. and W. Dechert (1985) "Dynamic Ramsey pricing", *International Economic Review*, 26:569–591.

Driffill, E. (1980) "Life cycle with terminal retirement", *International Economic Review*, 21:45–62.

Eisner, R. and R. Strotz (1968) "Determinants of business investment: the theoretical framework", reprinted in: A. Zellner, ed., *Reading in economic statistics and econometrics*. Little Brown.

Epstein, L. (1978) "The Le Chatalier principle in optimal control problems", *Journal of Economic Theory*, 19:103–122.

Freeman, S. (1977) "Wage trends as performance displays productive potential: a model and application to academic early retirement", *Bell Journal of Economics*, 8:419–443.

Ghez, G. and G. Becker (1975) *The allocating time and goods over the life cycle*. N.B.E.R.

Harris, M. and B. Holmstrom (1982) "A theory of wage dynamics", *Review of Economic Studies*, 49:315–353.

Hashimoto, M. (1981) "Firm specific human capital as a shared investment", *American Economic Review*, 71:475–482.

Heckman, J. (1974) "Life cycle consumption and labor supply: an explanation of the relationship between income and consumption over the life cycle", *American Economic Review*, 64:188–194.

Heckman, J. (1976) "A life cycle model of earnings learning and consumption", *Journal of Political Economy*, 84(supplement):511–544.

Holmstrom, B. (1983) "Managerial incentive problems: a dynamic perspective", in: *Essays in economics and management in honour of Lars Whalbeck*. Helsinki: Swedish School of Economics.

Johnson, T. (1978) "Time in school: the case of the prudent patron", *American Economic Review*, 68:862–872.

Karlin, S. and H. Taylor (1981) *A second course in stochastic processes*. Academic Press.

Kennan, J. (1979) "Bonding and the enforcement of labor contracts", *Economic Letters*, 3:61–66.

Killingworth, M. (1982) "'Learning by doing' and 'investment in training' a synthesis of two rival models of the life cycle", *Review of Economic Studies*, 49:263–271.

Killingworth, M. (1983) *Labor supply*. Cambridge University Press.

Lazear, E. (1981) "Agency earnings profiles productivity and hours restrictions", *American Economic Review*, 71:606–620.

Levhari, D. and Y. Weiss (1974) "The effect of risk on the investment in human capital", *American Economic Review*, 64:950–963.

Lillard, L. (1981) "Wage expectations in labor supply and the time series and cross section effects of state unemployment", Rand Corporation Report.

Macurdy, T. (1981) "An empirical model of labor supply in a life cycle setting", *Journal of Political Economy*, 89:1059–1085.

Macurdy, T. (1983) "A simple scheme for estimating an intertemporal model of labor supply and consumption in the presence of taxes and uncertainty", *International Economic Review*, 24:265–289.

McCabe, P. (1983) "Optimal leisure-effort choice with endogenously determined earnings", *Journal of Labor Economics*, 1.

Merton, R. (1971) "Optimum consumption and portfolio rules", *Journal of Economic Theory*, 3:373–413.

Mincer, J. (1962) "On the job training costs returns and some implications", *Journal of Political Economy*, 70(supplement):S50–S79.

Mincer, J. (1974) *Schooling experience and earnings*. New York: National Bureau of Economic Research.

Mincer, J. and S. Polachek (1974) "Family investment in human capital: earnings of women", *Journal of Political Economy*, 82(supplement):S76–S108.

Oniki, H. (1968) "A theoretical study on the demand for education", Ph.D. dissertation, Department of Economics, Stanford University.

Oniki, H. (1973) "Comparative dynamics (sensitivity analysis) in optimal control theory", *Journal of Economic Theory*, 6:265–283.

Polachek, S. (1975) "Differences in expected post schooling investment as determinants of market wage differentials", *International Economic Review*, 16:451–470.

Rogerson, W. (1985) "Repeated moral hazard", *Econometrica*, 53:69–76.

Rosen, S. (1972a) "Learning and experience in the labor market", *Journal of Human Resources*, 7:326–342.

Rosen, S. (1972b) "Learning as joint production", *Quarterly Journal of Economics*, 86:366–382.

Rosen, S. (1973) "Income generating functions and capital accumulation", unpublished, Department of Economics, Rochester University.

Rosen, S. (1976) "A theory of life earnings", *Journal of Political Economy*, 84(supplement):345–568.

Rosen, S. (1977) "Human capital: a survey of empirical research", in: R. Ehrenberg, ed., *Research in labor economics*. J.A.I. Press, vol. 1.

Ryder, H., E. Stafford and P. Stephan (1976) "Labor leisure and training over the life cycle", *International Economic Review*, 17:651–674.

Sheshinski, E. (1968) "On the individual's life time allocation between education and work", *Metroeconomica*, 20:42–49.

Schultz, T. (1964) *The economic value of education*. New York: Columbia University Press.

Spence, M. (1973) "Job market signalling", *Quarterly Journal of Economics*, 87:355–374.

Wallace, T. and L. Inhen (1975) "The theory of human capital accumulations with alternative loan markets", *Journal of Political Economy*, 83:157–184.

Weiss, Y. (1971) "Learning by doing and occupational specialization", *Journal of Economic Theory*, 3:189–198.

Weiss, Y. (1972) "On the optimal lifetime pattern of labor supply", *Economic Journal*, 82:1293–1315.
Weiss, Y. (1974) "Notes on income generating function", unpublished, Department of Economics, Princeton University.
Weiss, Y. and L. Lillard (1978) "Experience, vintage and time effects in the growth of earnings: American scientists 1960–1970", *Journal of Political Economy*, 86:427–446.
Weiss, Y. and R. Gronau (1981) "Expected interruptions in labor force participation and sex related differences in earnings growth", *Review of Economic Studies*, 48:607–619.
Weiss, Y. and L. Lillard (1982) "Output variability, academic contracts and waiting times for promotion", in: R. Ehrenberg, ed., *Research in labor economics*. J.A.I. Press, vol. 5, 157–188.

Chapter 12

THE THEORY OF EQUALIZING DIFFERENCES

SHERWIN ROSEN*

University of Chicago

1. Introduction

The theory of equalizing differences refers to observed wage differentials required to equalize the total monetary and nonmonetary advantages or disadvantages among work activities and among workers themselves. The basic idea originates in the first ten chapters of Book I of *The Wealth of Nations*, which is unsurpassed for the depth and breadth of analysis as well as for clarity of exposition. It remains the fundamental reference work on the subject. The topic is important for both theoretical and empirical reasons. On the conceptual level it can make legitimate claim to be *the* fundamental (long-run) market equilibrium construct in labor economics.[1] Its empirical importance lies in contributing useful understanding to the determinants of the structure of wages in the economy and for making inferences about preferences and technology from observed wage data.

As a framework of analysis, equalizing or compensating wage differentials has found its most widespread use as a theory of supply of workers to labor activities that are differentiated by various attributes – working environments, worker skills, and other job requirements. In one important class of problems these attributes refer to nonpecuniary, consumption by-products of work. Activities that offer favorable working conditions attract labor at lower than average wages, whereas jobs offering unfavorable working conditions must pay premiums as offsetting compensation in order to attract workers. Measurable job attributes on which compensating wage differentials have been shown to arise empirically include: (i) onerous working conditions, such as risks to life and health, exposure to pollution, and so forth; (ii) intercity and interregional wage differences associated with differences in climate, crime, pollution, and crowding; (iii) special

*Financial support from the National Science Foundation is gratefully acknowledged.

[1] It is also central to urban economics and to virtually all economic problems involving product differentiation and spatial considerations, e.g. see Samuelson (1983) for an elegant description of Von Thunen's theory of spatial equilibrium, which is closely related to Smith.

Handbook of Labor Economics, Volume I, Edited by O. Ashenfelter and R. Layard

work-time scheduling and related requirements, including shift work, inflexible work schedules, and possible risks of layoff and subsequent unemployment; and (iv) the composition of pay packages, including vacations, pensions, and other fringe benefits as substitutes for direct cash wage payments. Another important class of problems identifies work environments with investment rather than with consumption. This includes acquired skills necessary to perform different types of work, empirically associated with formal schooling requirements and on-the-job training. It also includes prospects for unusual lifecycle success or failure associated with the variance of possible outcomes in alternative career choices. The first class of problems is (loosely) associated with the industrial, interfirm, and regional wage structure, and the second is associated with the occupational wage structure, though there are interactions between the two.

A basic analytical symmetry leads to another, less common development of the theory as one of demand for workers with alternative traits and productive characteristics. At its most elementary level, these ideas lie behind the "efficiency units" interpretations of heterogeneous labor inputs that is useful in productivity theory and growth accounting. A much richer theory is obtained if more general and complex substitutions between productive traits of various workers are entertained, though this entire area is not yet completely understood.

This account stresses both supply and demand. It is shown that market clearing in this type of problem has a fundamentally different character than in most economic models of markets. The main point of contract with standard theory is the role of prices in achieving market equilibrium. The main point of difference is that the equilibrium achieves a matching and sorting function of allocating or assigning specific workers to specific firms. In contrast to the standard market paradigm, where the identities of traders is immaterial to final outcomes and indeed is the ultimate source of efficiency of a decentralized competitive market system, with whom and for whom one works is generally of considerable importance for achieving efficient labor allocations. Getting the most out of the resources that are available requires matching the proper type of worker with the proper type of firm: the labor market must solve a type of marriage problem of slotting workers into their proper "niche" within and between firms. Herein lies the source of my assertion concerning the fundamental nature of this equilibrium construct for labor economics.

In the general analysis to follow, a labor market transaction is viewed as a tied sale in which the worker simultaneously sells (rents) the services of his labor and buys the attributes of his job. These attributes are fixed for any one job, but may vary from job to job. Hence, the worker exercises choice over preferred job attributes by choosing the appropriate type of job and employer. On the other hand, employers simultaneously buy the services and characteristics of workers and sell the attributes of jobs offered to the market. The characteristics of a particular worker are fixed, but may differ among workers. An acceptable match occurs when the preferred choices of an employer and an employee are mutually consistent; when the worker finds the employer's job attributes to be the most desirable and the employer finds the workers productive characteristics to be the most desirable, both among all feasible choices.

The actual wage paid is therefore the sum of two conceptually distinct transactions, one for labor services and worker characteristics, and another for job attributes. The positive price the worker pays for preferred job activities is subtracted from the wage payment. The price paid by employers to induce workers to undertake onerous tasks takes the form of a wage premium, a negative price for the job, as it were. The observed distribution of wages clears both markets over all worker characteristics and job attributes. In this sense the labor market may be viewed as an implicit market in job and worker attributes. The resulting market equilibrium associates a wage with each assignment. The set of wages and the measurable attributes and characteristics associated with all such assignments are the equalizing differences observed in the market. Such associations underlie virtually all empirical estimates of wage functions estimated in actual data, and have become a focal point of modern research in labor economics. The theory of equalizing differences is helpful in interpreting these regressions and shows what inferences can be made from them concerning the preferences of workers and the technologies of firms.

The next section sketches the theory in the simplest possible case of binary choice over job consumption attributes. Before turning to that task, it should be pointed out that both the theory and applications of equalizing differences are based on the assumption of perfect information on both sides of the market. Hence, this theory (or any other) cannot possibly explain all wage variation in some specific set of data, even in the absence of measurement error.[2] The search for a job and investment in information is in many ways a search for the type of allocations described here. Hence the theory must be considered as one of longer run tendencies and of equilibrium behavior in the steady state of a more complex dynamic process.

[2] The well-known exchange between Rottenberg (1956) and Lampman (1956) is relevant here. Also see Reder (1963). In light of much subsequent research on the determinants of wages it seems fair to add the point that search, information costs, and other omitted factors sustain significant wage variability among measurably identical jobs and workers. To put it in another way, the R^2 in the typical wage regression is not large. In extremely micro-oriented data the signal-to-noise ratio is very large and it may be difficult to detect the effects under discussion. Less detailed data, e.g. from a broadly based worker survey rather than one from workers in a small number of firms in a particular local labor market, have the virtue of reducing the noise and increasing the signal. In any event, many empirical estimates of equalizing differences now appear in the literature, so there is no need to argue in the abstract.

2. Equalizing differences for work-related consumption

The pure theory and its empirical consequences are best illustrated by an example in which different types of jobs offer two different levels of some disamenity. The first rigorous analytical statement of a model of this type is found in Friedman and Kuznets (1954, chs. 3 and 4, plus appendix) restated and summarized in Friedman (1962). It is the basis on which virtually all subsequent work has proceeded.

To focus on essentials, consider a labor market in which workers are productively homogeneous (thus sorting by worker characteristics is ignored for the time being) with two types of jobs. Let D be an index of job type, with $D = 0, 1$. Jobs of type 1 are associated with some disamenity, whereas jobs of type 0 are not. To be specific, think of the disamenity as airborne particulates at the worksite. Then type 1 jobs are "dirty" (some particulates) and type 0 jobs are "clean" (no particulates). An external observer ideally would organize the data as follows. First, each job is classified by type, with a value of 1 or 0 assigned to each based on some objective measurements such as meter readings of dust or other pollutants. Second, wages w_1 and w_0 paid to workers on each type of job, as well as the number of workers employed in each is recorded. Third, specific data associated with each worker, such as nonearned income, other measures of wealth, family status, age, and other demographic variables; and data associated with each firm such as firm size, type of industry, capital intensity and so forth are also observed. The analytical task is to construct an econometrically implementable structural model that describes how the data are generated, and which identifies the underlying behavioral relationships. The rules of this game follow the standard procedures of modern economics: both workers and firms are capable of making choices and these choices are rational and privately optimal. Rational decision-making defines the behavioral structure, i.e. the demand and supply curves for each type of job.

It is possible to view these supply and demand relationships in either of two equivalent ways. Firms demand employees to work on the particular job type offered while workers supply labor to particular job types. Alternatively, workers may be viewed as demanding a particular type of job amenity, and firms may be viewed as supplying it. Clearly, both views achieve the same answer, and I shall go back and forth between them whenever it is convenient. This equivalence is due to the fact that the implicit market for the consumption attribute may itself be viewed in two equivalent ways. When the $D = 1$ job is used as the benchmark, it is natural to think of an implicit market for amenable attributes. Taking the clean job as benchmark lends itself more readily to thinking in terms of the supply and demand for labor on the disamenable job. In fact it is always possible to renormalize any analysis and speak of markets for amenities (goods) rather than disamenities (bads).[3] I normalize on the type 0 job in what follows, just because, following Smith, it is the usual practice.

2.1. Preferences, opportunities and worker choices

Preferences of a worker are defined over two types of consumption goods and can be represented by a utility function $u = u(C, D)$, where u is the utility index, C is market consumption goods purchased with money, and D is the tied consumption indicator of a job. For a given value of C it is natural to assume that $u(C,0) \geq u(C,1)$. Thus, D shifts conventional preferences and $D=1$ is not preferred to $D=0$, other things equal. The utility function allows an exact calculation of how much income or market consumption the worker must be compensated to undertake the less preferred job. Let C_0 be market consumption when $D=0$. Given C_0, define C^* as the consumption level required to achieve the same utility on a $D=1$ type job as C_0 guarantees on the $D=0$ job. Then C^* satisfies $u(C^*,1) = u(C_0,0)$. Since $D=1$ is never preferred at the same consumption level to $D=0$, other things equal, it follows that $C^* \geq C_0$. Now define the difference $Z = C^* - C_0$ as the compensating variation for $D=1$ compared with $D=0$. It is the additional compensation necessary to make the worker indifferent between the two types of jobs at a given utility index. To put it in yet another way, Z is the minimum supply or reserve price to the disamenable job.[4] Sometimes it is called a "shadow" price.

It is useful to think of utility $u(C, D)$ as defined over two continuous variables rather than over a continuous and a discrete one. Treat D as a cardinal measure, such as parts per million (ppm) particulates, even though the actual choices (for now) are qualitative. Then, for example, $D=1$ refers to some particular level, say 10 ppm, and $D=0$ refers to some lower level, say 0 ppm, and $u(C, D)$ can be regarded as a conventional description of preferences in which D is a "bad" rather than a good. Assume $u(C, D)$ is quasiconcave, so the worker's indifference curves are convex. The definition of Z (and Z') is shown in Figure 12.1. The

[3] The point is similar to the analysis of labor supply in that it is only a matter of convenience whether the analysis is cast in terms of the demand for leisure (a good) or in terms of a supply of labor (a "bad").

[4] Corresponding to the discussion above, norming on $D=1$ leads to a development in terms of the equivalent variation Z', defined by $u(C_1,1) = u(C_0 - Z',0)$. It is well known that $Z = Z'$ when both are evaluated at the same utility index; otherwise they differ by an income effect. More subtle distinctions can be made, such as the difference between Marshallian and Hicksian variations, but that is immaterial for present purposes. Some very interesting implications of these distinctions in the context of equalizing differences for health risks are presented in Cook and Graham (1977), but their analysis is applicable to a broader class of problems than risks to life.

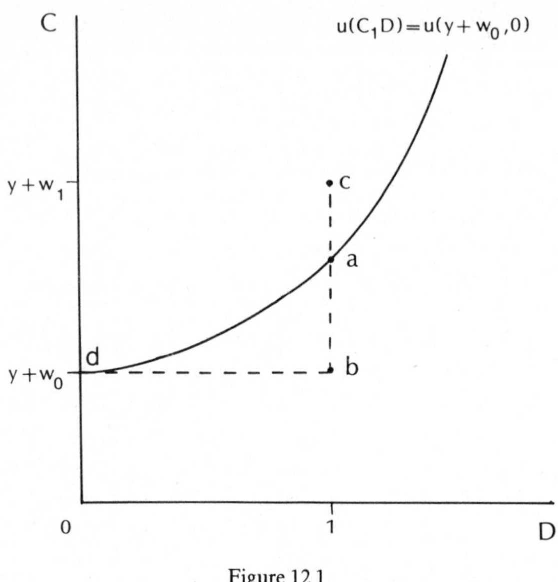

Figure 12.1

curve labeled u^* is an indifference curve and Z and Z' are measured by the vertical distance *ab*.

Competitive labor markets and binary choices imply that labor market opportunities are completely described by exactly two points in the (w, D) plane. The clean job offers point $(w_0,0)$ and the dirty one offers $(w_1,1)$. If the market is competitive we know that the worker takes these numbers as given, take it or leave it. Information on wages and working conditions (w_i, D_i) is presumably found by "comparison shopping" among alternative types of jobs.[5] If the worker also is exogenously endowed with a source of nonearned income (possibly zero) denoted by y, the consumption opportunity set is described by points c and d in Figure 12.1. Working on job type 0 commands $C_0 = y + w_0$ units of market consumption goods and $D = 0$ units of job related consumption; whereas working on job type 1 commands $C_1 = y + w_1$ unites of market consumption and $D = 1$ units of the job disamenity. Define $\Delta W = (w_1 - w_0)$ as the *market equalizing difference*. Then the $D = 1$ job offers ΔW additional units of market consumption for worse working conditions. It is the implicit market price of dirt.

A worker chooses the job type that maximizes utility: $D = 1$ is chosen if $u(\Delta W + C_0, 1) > u(C_0, 0)$ and $D = 0$ is chosen if $u(\Delta W + C_0, 0) < u(C_0, 0)$. The

[5] In the language of search theory it is easiest to think of job amenities as "search goods" rather than "experience goods" though no doubt much labor mobility at early ages is better described as experience goods.

worker is indifferent between the two if utility is the same. The rule is illustrated in Figure 12.1. As illustrated, point c lies above the indifference curve through d so $D=1$ is the preferred choice. If ΔW had been small enough so that c had fallen below the indifference curve through d, then $D=0$ would have been the preferred choice; and of course c and d would have been indifferent had they fallen on the same indifference curve.

Figure 12.1 suggests an alternative way of characterizing the worker's choice, which turns out to be more convenient and more powerful than the direct utility calculation. That $D=1$ is preferred in the figure is clearly the same thing as saying that ΔW exceeds Z. Here ΔW is just the vertical distance between points c and b, and the indifference curve shows that the worker requires Z units of additional consumption to be compensated for $D=1$ over $D=0$. If the market offers more than this increment, then $\Delta W > Z$ and utility is larger on the dirty job. A surplus value or rent is gained by the worker in the bargain. Clearly, workers choosing $D=1$ do not necessarily inherently prefer that type of work. Rather, the wage difference is sufficiently large to buy off their distaste for it. On the other hand, if $Z > \Delta W$ the opportunity cost of the better job in terms of market consumption forgone is less than the willingness to pay for it, so $D=0$ is the preferred alternative. The worse job does not offer sufficient compensation to be attractive. Consequently, choices are completely described by the rule:

$$\text{choose } D=1 \text{ or } D=0 \text{ as } \Delta W \gtrless Z. \tag{1}$$

Ties ($\Delta W = Z$) are broken by a random device, such as flipping a coin.

2.2. Market supply

The supply of labor to each type of job is defined as the number of applicants, given the relative wage prospects offered by each. Market supply functions are found by varying relatives wages and determining how choices respond, according to the individually rational behavior rule (1). Given w_0 and w_1, each individual applies to the job for which utility is maximized, so the total number of workers applying for job type D are all those for whom utility is largest there. Varying one or both of the wages and calculating how choices are affected is the conceptual experiment which maps out the market supply curves of workers to job types.

Given the equivalence between the reservation wage rule (1) and the direct utility calculation, it is clear that w_1 and w_0 need not be considered separately for ascertaining whether a worker chooses job type 0 or 1. The difference ΔW is a sufficient statistic for the problem: any combination of w_0 and w_1 which leads to the same value of ΔW leads to the same individual choices. Similarly, Z is a complete representation of preferences for this problem. Given the size of the labor force choosing between $D=0$ and $D=1$, *relative* market supply conditions are completely characterized by calculating the number of workers for whom $\Delta W > Z$ and calculating the number for whom $\Delta W < Z$. It is worth emphasizing that the differential ΔW is the relevant market price available to all workers independently of their preferences.[6] Though ΔW is the same for all workers, Z is a personal taste variable which generally varies from person to person, depending on their own circumstances and inherent preferences. It is convenient to describe differences in preferences among workers parametrically for analysis. Define $g(Z)$ as the density, in the sense of a probability density function, of tastes in the population of workers making choices and define $G(Z)$ as the cumulated density. Then for a given value of ΔW, all those choosing job type 1 satisfy the condition $\Delta W > Z$, and the fraction of workers who apply for $D=1$ must be

$$N_1^s = \int_0^{\Delta W} g(z)\,\mathrm{d}z = G(\Delta W). \tag{2}$$

The remaining fraction of workers apply for jobs of type 0. These are persons for whom $\Delta W < Z$, so

$$N_0^s = \int_{\Delta W}^{\infty} g(z)\,\mathrm{d}z = 1 - G(\Delta W). \tag{3}$$

Relative market supplies partition the distribution $g(Z)$ and assign workers to job types according to tastes. Figure 12.2 illustrates eqs. (2) and (3) for a given value of ΔW. Relative supply to $D=1$ jobs is the area under $g(Z)$ to the left of ΔW – this is eq. (2). Relative supply to $D=0$ is the area to the right of ΔW – this is eq. (3). The supply functions themselves sweep out the distribution of preferences $g(Z)$. To see this, consider a small increase in ΔW. Then the partition moves slightly to the right of what is shown in Figure 12.2. All those who previously found it optimal to choose $D=1$ certainly find it optimal to do so at a higher wage. However, those who were indifferent or had a slight net preference for $D=0$ now find the balance tipped in favor of $D=1$ instead: the choice condition (1) for this extensive margin of workers flips from $Z > \Delta W$ to $Z < \Delta W$. Finally, those who have very strong preferences against $D=1$ do not find the

[6] Notice that the size of the labor force is taken as given in this exercise and the problem is to allocate a given number of workers between job types. Fixing the number of workers to be assigned is what justifies working with ΔW alone. The total number of people to be allocated is a function of the absolute level of real wages w_1 and w_0, in the conventional manner of labor supply. A general equilibrium model is required to determine the level of wages in each market. Those details are ignored here because it is obvious that there are no difficulties in establishing the existence of an equilibrium.

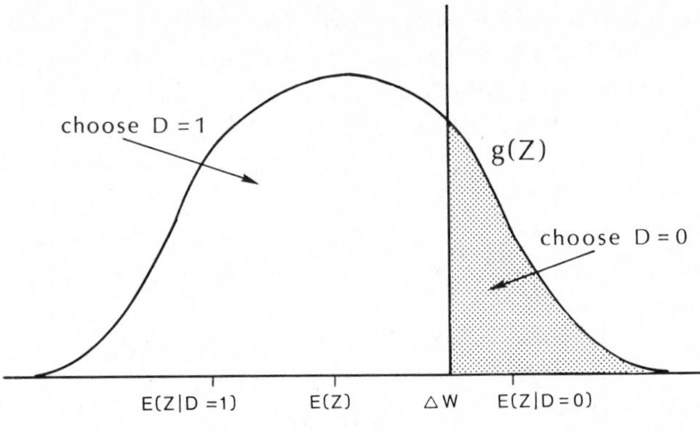

Figure 12.2

increase in wages large enough to change their minds: they remain in $D = 0$. These are all persons whose Z lies further out in the right-hand tail of $g(Z)$.

This formulation is very general in accommodating virtually all possibilities for how preferences might be distributed among workers. The following cases are instructive.

Case 1. Workers have identical reservation prices Z. Then their preferences are identical and the distribution $g(Z)$ is degenerate with a point of mass at the common value of Z and no mass elsewhere. Since $g(z)$ is a spike, the relative supply functions $G(\Delta W)$ and $1 - G(\Delta W)$ are step functions, with one step. Supply to $D = 1$ is infinitely elastic at a value of ΔW equal to the common reservation wage Z and is completely inelastic for wages either above or below it.

Case 2. The distribution $g(Z)$ is discrete over k specific values of Z, say $Z_1, Z_2, \dots, Z_k$. Then there are k distinct types of worker preferences in the population, with proportion $G(Z_j)$ having reservation prices of Z_j or less. This is an immediate generalization of case (1). The supply curve to $D = 1$ is also a step function, but it has k steps rather than one step.

Case 3. Increasing the number of values of k in case (2) and passing to the limit of a dense continuous set of subjective valuations of attributes leads to a continuous density for $g(Z)$, as depicted in Figure 12.2. If $g(Z)$ is unimodal and roughly symmetrical on either side of the mode, then the supply curve to $D = 1$ has a logistic shape when viewed from the vertical axis. There is rising supply price throughout.

Case 4. $g(Z)$ may be a mixture of discrete and continuous components. An important practical case is when a nontrivial fraction of workers are neutral toward the attribute, with $Z = 0$, and the rest are continuously distributed over $Z > 0$: a mass of workers place no value at all on dirty working conditions and are inherently indifferent to dirt while other workers have definite distaste for dirt. Such a density would appear similar to the one in Figure 12.2 with the addition of a point of mass or spike at $Z = 0$. In that case the supply curve to $D = 1$ types of jobs begins with a flat, infinitely elastic section at $\Delta W = 0$, for the fraction of workers with $Z = 0$; and is increasing thereafter to induce workers who dislike the job to choose it.

Comparing Case 1 above with the rest, these examples illustrate the general point that the elasticity of supply to $D = 1$ is decreasing in the variance or spread of the distribution $g(Z)$.

2.3. *Technology, opportunities and firm choices*

Firms must choose the job type offered to the market. This choice depends on the nature of technology, which in turn determines the relevant internal supply prices of each type of job. The optimal decision then depends on comparing relative internal supply prices with market wage opportunities and costs. The basic idea in the dirt example is that a firm can spend resources to clean up its work environment, within limits dictated by technology. The cost of doing so is compared with the wage savings on labor costs available from the fact that w_1 generally exceeds w_0. If labor cost savings exceed the cost of cleaning, the optimal strategy is to offer $D = 0$ type jobs to the market; while if cleaning costs exceed wage savings the firm chooses to offer $D = 1$ jobs to the market. In this way it is possible to characterize the firm's choice by a reservation price rule analogous to eq. (1). This general logic extends to virtually any type of attribute.

It is natural to think of the firm as engaging in a form of joint production, in which it sells a conventional good to the market and simultaneously sells a nonmarket good to its workers [an early development along these lines is found in Thompson (1968)]. Denote the market good by x and the nonmarket good by D, as above. Taking $D = 1$ as benchmark, think of particulates at the worksite as a natural by-product of x production. For example, the production of steel (x) involves smoke (D). However, production possibilities between x and D are not necessarily rigid because the firm may be able to use resources to reduce D to smaller levels. These possibilities take several forms: supplying workers with equipment and clothing that reduces exposure to pollutants, purchasing more expensive but cleaner capital, and using larger proportions of labor time to clean up the work environment as opposed to direct production of market goods. All these factors may be summarized in a joint production function $F(x, D, L) = 0$, where x and D are outputs and L is labor input. Assume $F_x > 0$, $F_D < 0$, and $F_L < 0$. Define the marginal rate of transformation between x and D by $-F_D/F_x$. Then the production possibilities curve in the (x, D) plane is an increasing function of D. Its slope gives the marginal costs of reducing D in terms of x

forgone.[7] Comparing marginal cost with wage opportunities determines whether $D=1$ or $D=0$ is the optimal choice.

An immediate and elementary but important implication is that $D=1$ must be productive if dirty jobs are ever observed in the market. For if workers demand a wage premium to work on disagreeable jobs then a firm would never find it in its self-interest to offer such jobs unless there were compensating advantages to its profitability. The production function $F(\cdot)$ shows that this benefit is extra market output x. Consequently, it is necessary that $-F_D/F_x$ is positive for at least one firm if $D=1$ type jobs are ever observed in the market. Given that the marginal rate of transformation $-F_D/F_x$ is positive for at least some firms, its magnitude clearly depends on the particular circumstances of production. For some types of work it may be very large indeed. In these cases the costs of making jobs more amenable may be extremely large. An example might be underground mining. There are virtually no circumstances under which such jobs are "pleasant". On the other hand, the marginal rate of transformation may be very small in other lines of work, for example office workers in insurance companies.

Let us analyze a specific linear technology which lends itself to a development similar to that used for workers. Suppose

$$\begin{aligned} x &= a_1 L, \quad \text{if } D=1, \\ x &= a_0 L, \quad \text{if } D=0. \end{aligned} \tag{4}$$

Define $B = a_1 - a_0$. Then imposing the restriction $B>0$ incorporates the idea that $D=1$ is productive in the sense discussed above: the efficiency of labor in x production is larger when resources are not used for cleaning up the work environment. In fact B represents the relevant marginal cost per worker of producing clean worksites in terms of forgone output x. The relevant marginal labor cost per worker to the firm's profits of providing clean jobs rather than dirty ones is just the wage difference ΔW. The firm chooses the alternative with the smallest cost. Therefore the firm's decision rule must be

$$\text{choose } D=1 \text{ or } D=0 \text{ as } B \gtrless \Delta W. \tag{5}$$

If B exceeds ΔW the foregone costs of cleaning exceed the incremental labor costs of providing clean jobs, so $D=1$ is the best choice. But if ΔW exceeds B, the cleaning costs are smaller than the wage premium of providing dirty jobs and $D=0$ is the preferred choice.

[7]It is straightforward to include other resource inputs such as capital and materials. Had we chosen to measure the job characteristic in terms of cleanliness (a good) rather than dirtiness, the production possibilities frontier would have been a more conventional downward sloping curve rather than an upward sloping one.

2.4. Market demand

The demand for workers in each type of job is a function of relative wage rates, other factor prices, demand conditions for output, and so forth. It is found by aggregating the choice rules discussed above over employers. For this exercise the size of each firm is taken as given.[8] From the development above, the two numbers B and ΔW are sufficient statistics for this problem. Let B be distributed among firms according to probability density $f(B)$, with cumulated density function $F(B)$, where the densities are taken to incorporate the size of each firm as well as its technology. Thus, for example, $F(B)$ indicates the fraction of potential jobs in the market for which firm technology is B or less (if all firms were the same size this would just be the fraction of firms with B or less). Since a firm offers $D=1$ or $D=0$ according to (5), the fraction of $D=1$ jobs offered to the market must be the sum over all firms for whom $B > \Delta W$, or

$$N_1^{\mathrm{d}} = \int_{\Delta W}^{\infty} f(B)\,\mathrm{d}B = 1 - F(\Delta W). \tag{6}$$

The fraction of $D=0$ jobs offered must be the remainder of the distribution.

Relative supplies of job types partition the distribution of technology $f(B)$, as shown in Figure 12.3. The number of dirty jobs offered to the market is the area

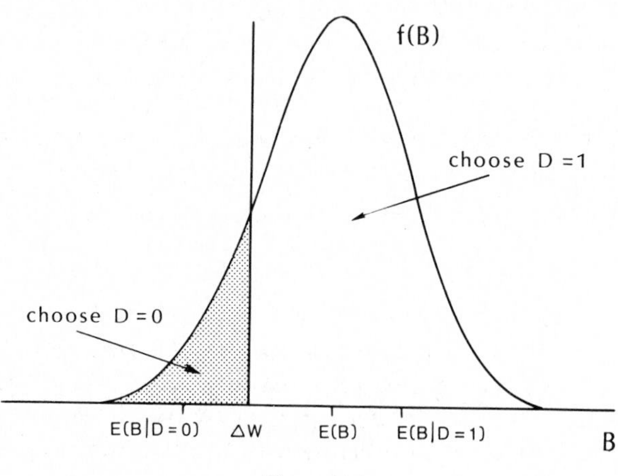

Figure 12.3

[8]Of course, a full general equilibrium analysis would determine the size distribution of firms as part of the problem, but that is taken as exogenous here. Think of what follows as an examination of the cross-section of firms in the market at the equilibrium size distribution.

under $f(B)$ to the right of ΔW, which just depicts eq. (6). The number of clean jobs offered to the market is the area under $f(B)$ to the left of ΔW. The number of jobs offered is equivalent to the demand for workers in each job type. Therefore, the demand function for workers in $D=1$ jobs sweeps out the distribution of technology. Suppose ΔW rises a little in Figure 12.3. Then all firms offering $D=0$ jobs continue to do so. Firms with values of B slightly above the old value of ΔW were previously offering $D=1$ jobs, but were close to indifferent to offering $D=0$ and now find the balance tipped in favor of supplying $D=0$ jobs. Firms for whom cleaning costs are very large continue to offer dirty jobs. The job market would show an expansion of amenable job offerings and a contraction of disamenable ones: the partition in Figure 12.3 moves to the right.

As was true of supply, this formulation accommodates a wide variety of distributions $f(B)$. For example, if all firms have the same technology the distribution degenerates to a spike and the market demand function is a downward step function with the height of the step given by the common value of B. A little experimentation will show that market demand for workers in $D=1$ jobs is decreasing in the spread or variance of the underlying distribution of technology $f(B)$, similar to the results for worker discussed above.

2.5. *Market equilibrium and selection*

Market equilibrium is defined by equality between demand and supply for workers on each type of job. This involves two things. First, the level of wages w_1 and w_0 must adjust so that the total number of workers seeking positions equals the number of positions to be filled. The principle of substitution is at work here. On the one hand, increases in the level of wages in a particular labor market increases supply by attracting job seekers from other markets and from new entrants into the labor force. On the other hand, an increase in wages reduces the amount of labor demanded through both capital-labor substitution and product substitution due to product price changes. Second, the wage differential ΔW and the relative demand for workers in $D=0$ jobs is increasing in ΔW and the relative demand for workers in $D=1$ jobs is decreasing in ΔW, so the standard stability conditions for market equilibrium are met and the equilibrium is unique. In equilibrium ΔW adjusts to make the partitions in Figures 12.2 and 12.3 conformable to each other: the area under $g(Z)$ to the left of ΔW in Figure 12.2 equals the area under $f(B)$ to the right of ΔW in Figure 12.3.

It is an immediate consequence of this construction that workers and firms are systematically matched or assigned to each other in market equilibrium. Workers found on $D=1$ jobs have the smallest distastes for D and firms offering $D=1$ employment have the largest costs of cleaning up their work environments.

Hence there is a tendency toward negative assortive matching in equilibrium.[9] Workers with larger than average values of Z are systematically found in firms with smaller than average values of B and conversely. It is precisely this feature of the labor market which distinguishes this class of problems from the standard market paradigm.

This important result may be stated more formally as follows. Let $E(Z) = \int Zg(Z)\mathrm{d}Z$ be the population average of Z over all workers making choices and let $E(B) = \int Bf(B)\mathrm{d}B$ be the mean of B over the entire population of firms. Write $E(x|y)$ as the conditional expectation of random variable x, given some particular value of the variable y. Here the relevant conditioning variables are $D=0$ or $D=1$, and the relevant random variables are Z and B.[10] Looking only at workers found on $D=1$ jobs, the choice rule (1) implies $E(Z|D=0) \geq E(Z)$ and $E(B|D=0) \leq E(B)$: workers choosing clean jobs have larger than average distates for dirt, and firms offering clean jobs have smaller than average cleaning costs.

The difference between the conditional and unconditional expectations is called a *selectivity bias* and is a convenient measure of the extent to which workers or firms found in any given job classification depart from a random sample of all workers in all firms. If there is any heterogeneity in the underlying populations, workers and firms are systematically sorted and selected among classes of jobs according to the choice rules (1) and (5), and the observations are stratified by the complex of factors that make decisions differ among the agents. Selection and stratification are ubiquitous in economics and the market for job amenities is perhaps the most elementary example of it. It should be noted that selectivity effects are the rule in virtually all spatial allocation problems. here "space" is not geographical, but rather a point in the "space of job characteristics".

Systematic selection and stratification have important consequences for the inferences that can be drawn from data about underlying tastes and technology in the population. For example, it is a common practice to survey workers at their worksites and ask them questions about what aspects of their jobs are most important to them. These surveys typically find that wages and other pecuniary considerations are not at the top of the list, and that other, nonpecuniary factors are more prominent in workers' responses. A tempting interpretation of such findings is that wages do not influence labor supply decisions to different types of jobs: in a word, that supply is inelastic. Yet this analysis suggests that consider-

[9] Since firms do not directly care about workers' tastes and workers do not directly care about firms' technologies, the *matching* is not perfectly rank order in Z and B, nor it is unique since any worker with $Z < \Delta W$ will find any firm for which $B > \Delta W$ acceptable and vice versa.

[10] These variables are random in the sense of $f(B)$ and $g(Z)$. It bears repeating that this randomness is induced by population heterogeneity, *not* by stochastic preferences or stochastic technology.

able care must be taken in drawing such inferences from qualitative survey responses.

It is clear from Figure 12.2 that if workers differ by tastes for work-related consumption then the average reservation price for workers on each job type may differ markedly from the market wage difference ΔW. Another way of saying this is that the allocation of workers to job types typically generates significant amounts of economic rent, defined as the excess return over that required to change a decision. In Figure 12.2 the average person choosing $D=1$ is far from the margin of indifference and would maintain the same choice even if ΔW changed substantially. The same thing holds true for the average worker who chose $D=0$. The difference between the reservation wage and the actual wage is the rent earned in a person's current choice. In fact the rent earned by the average person in $D=1$ is given by $\Delta W - E(Z|D=1)$, and the average rent for people found in $D=0$ is $E(Z|D=0)-\Delta W$. If these numbers are large, the typical survey respondent would identify nonmonetary considerations as more important to his job choice than wages because a change in relative wages would not affect the decision of the average person in each job category. The caution required in going from this observation to the conclusion that relative supply is inelastic is that inferences about averages don't necessarily carry over to margins: it is the weight of people at the margin of choice – the number who are close to indifferent between the two types of jobs – that determines the supply response. The relationship between averages and margins in turn depends on how tastes are distributed in the underlying population.

To illustrate some of the issues, let us work through the case where Z is normally distributed in the worker population. Write $Z=\bar{Z}+\nu$, where ν is a normal variate with mean zero and variance σ^2. $\bar{Z}$ is the unconditional (population) mean of Z. Define $\phi(x)$ as the standard normal density and write $\Phi(x)$ as the cumulative density. The proportion of workers, n_1, found in $D=1$ jobs is, from (1):

$$n_1 = \operatorname{Prob}(Z \le \Delta W) = \Pr(\bar{Z}+\nu \le \Delta W) = \Pr(\nu \le \Delta W - \bar{Z})$$
$$= \Pr\left(\frac{\nu}{\sigma} \le \frac{\Delta W - \bar{Z}}{\sigma}\right) = \Phi\left(\frac{\Delta W - \bar{Z}}{\sigma}\right). \tag{7}$$

The fraction of workers found in $D=1$ jobs at relative wage ΔW is the ordinate of the cumulated standard normal evaluated at $(\Delta W - \bar{Z})/\sigma$. Differentiating (7) with respect to ΔW and converting to an elasticity yields:

$$\varepsilon_1 = \frac{\Delta W}{n_1}\frac{\mathrm{d}n_1}{\mathrm{d}(\Delta W)} = \left(\frac{\Delta W}{\sigma}\right)\left[\phi\left(\frac{\Delta W - Z}{\sigma}\right)\Big/\Phi\left(\frac{\Delta W - \bar{Z}}{\sigma}\right)\right]. \tag{8}$$

Given ΔW, we may calculate the average value of Z among all workers found on $D=1$ jobs. This is the conditional expectation

$$\begin{aligned} E(Z|D=1) &= E(\bar{Z}+\nu|\bar{Z}+\nu \leq \Delta W) = \bar{Z} + E(\nu|\nu \leq \Delta W - \bar{Z}) \\ &= \bar{Z} + \sigma E\left(\frac{\nu}{\sigma}\middle|\frac{\nu}{\sigma} \leq \Delta W - \bar{Z}\right) \\ &= \bar{Z} - \sigma\phi\left(\frac{\Delta W - \bar{Z}}{\sigma}\right)\Big/\Phi\left(\frac{\Delta W - \bar{Z}}{\sigma}\right). \end{aligned} \tag{9}$$

The first two equalities in (9) follow from choice rule (1) and the definition $Z = \bar{Z} + \nu$, while the third and fourth equalities follow from well-known properties of the normal distribution. The ratio of ordinates Φ/ϕ is called Mill's ratio, named after the statistician who first tabulated it in the 1920s. The difference between the unconditional mean of Z and the conditional mean in (9) is the "selectivity bias". Call it S_1. Then, from (9)

$$S_1 = \sigma\phi\left(\frac{\Delta W - \bar{Z}}{\sigma}\right)\Big/\Phi\left(\frac{\Delta W - \bar{Z}}{\sigma}\right). \tag{10}$$

S_1 is a precise measure of the extent to which preferences of people found on $D=1$ jobs differ from the average among workers in all jobs. It is clear from the formula and from the construction in Figure 12.2 that S_1 is increasing in the variance of preferences in the entire population. Finally, define $\Delta W - Z$ as the rent earned by a person who chooses $D=1$. Then average rent accruing to all workers found on $D=1$ jobs must be, from (9) again

$$R_1 = \Delta W - E(Z|D=1) + \sigma\left[\frac{\Delta W - \bar{Z}}{\sigma} + \frac{\phi(\cdot)}{\Phi(\cdot)}\right].$$

Average rent among $D=1$ workers is an increasing function of the standardized wage differential and also of the variance of preferences. Of course, similar expressions may be found for workers choosing $D=0$ jobs, and also among firms offering both types of jobs.

Now in this particular example there is a partial restriction between ε_1, S_1 and R_1 because they all depend on the inverse Mill's ratio ϕ/Φ. For example, as σ^2 goes to zero S_1 and R_1 also converge to zero and ε_1 goes to infinity because population heterogeneity vanishes. At the opposite extreme, ε_1 goes to zero and S_1 and R_1 grow very large as σ^2 grows very large, i.e. as heterogeneity of preferences grows large. So indeed at these extremes qualitative survey responses do indicate something about supply elasticities. However, for intermediate values of σ^2 the situation is less clear. In fact we have, from (8) and (10), $\varepsilon_1/S_1 = (\Delta W/\sigma^2)$. The relationship between ε_1 and S_1 depends on the variance σ^2 and the typical survey response gives us little information about variances. In fact the variance of response among workers found on each job category gives us only indirect evidence on σ^2 in the whole population because of the qualitative nature of these responses and because both groups of workers are censored samples of the population.

While this example has the virtue of lending precision to calculations, readers should be cautioned that there is no particular reason to expect preferences to follow the normal distribution rather than some other one. The general point remains that information on conditional averages do not necessarily convey much information about decision-makers near the margin of choice, which determines the responsiveness of supply to relative wage movements. There is no good substitute for direct estimates of supply elasticities.

In fact most of the empirical work in this area (reviewed below) has been devoted to establishing the magnitude of the market equalizing difference ΔW in a variety of cases. Usually this is done on cross-section data for individual workers, where the wage of a worker is related to the type of job on which the person is found and to a host of other factors such as union status, race, sex, education, and experience that serve as proxies for other forces that are known to affect wages. The immediate goal of this work is to ascertain whether and to what extent the labor market provides implicit compensation for nonpecuniary attributes of work. However, it is tempting and natural to extend these estimates to other uses. For example, in the specific problem under discussion, the estimated equalizing difference for dirty jobs may assist in evaluating the monetary benefits of pollution abatement programs in the economy at large. The selection aspects of market equilibrium help delimit the possibilities for extrapolating labor market estimates to program evaluation.

The potential for using market estimates of compensating wage differentials for policy evaluation lies in the logic of cost–benefit analysis itself: benefits are valued according to a "willingness to pay" criteria, which in turn is closely related to the idea of compensating variations (the Z's) underlying the structure of worker's choices in the labor market. While such things as pollution are not directly marketed, the labor market acts as an implicit market because ΔW has the ready interpretation of a price or valuation on the disamenity. However, this price does not give a complete picture of valuations because it is a precise reading only for the set of workers who are close to the margin of choice, and as we have seen this may be much different from the average value in the population, depending on the dispersion of preferences. The logic of revealed preferences shows the difficulty. Given ΔW we know that all people in $D=1$ jobs value D no more than ΔW; otherwise they could not have chosen that type of work. We also know that people found on the $D=0$ job must place a value of at least ΔW and possibly greater on D; otherwise they would have chosen to work on dirty jobs rather than on clean ones. This is just another way of saying that rents and selection effects may exist in the market allocation of workers to jobs. But from knowledge of ΔW alone it is not possible to make inferences on the extent of such rents.[11]

Nonetheless, the estimated value of ΔW may provide a bound on the typical person's valuation of D in certain circumstances. For example, suppose the fraction of workers found in $D=1$ jobs is fairly small. Then from Figure 12.2 it follows that the average worker would be willing to pay at least as much as ΔW for pollution abatement elsewhere, since such workers now "pay" ΔW by accepting the $D=0$ job rather than the $D=1$ job. Consequently ΔW serves as a lower bound on willingness to pay in this case. That such information can be fairly limited is easily illustrated. Suppose some workers have no preferences against D; that is, their Z is zero. If the market equilibrium is such that these workers are sufficiently numerous to occupy all $D=1$ jobs, then we know that the market equalizing difference ΔW is zero, and knowing that the valuation of the typical person exceeds zero does not tell us anything that we didn't already know. Rees (1976) has stressed this point. Only if the market valuation ΔW is significantly sizable does the method provide helpful information.

By this time it almost goes without saying that similar statements apply to firms. The market price ΔW gives us some information on cleaning costs (job related pollution abatement) of firms. The cost of cleaning must be at least ΔW for those firms offering $D=1$ jobs; and it must be at most ΔW for firms offering $D=0$ jobs. This type of inference has not been used much in project evaluation, perhaps because costs of projects tend to be easier to calculate than benefits and firm's cost functions for work related attributes may be substantially different than elsewhere in the economy.

3. Generalizations

A binary choice model goes a long way toward understanding the fundamental issues raised by equalizing differences and illustrating what can be inferred from the data. However, most job attributes exhibit much more variation than that. For example, job environments differ greatly in ambiant pollution levels. A

[11] It is clear that nothing can be learned about the structure of preferences in a single cross-section because the price ΔW is the same for all people in the sample. However, a probit or logit analysis of individual choices would indicate variables that affect selection. For example, the partial effect of wealth and earnings potential (skill) increases the propensity to choose the more amenable job due to the usual income (and substitution) effects [Weiss (1976)]. Some inferences about the structure of preferences can be made if time series data are available so that changes in ΔW are observed. Then there are supply shifters in (2) and demand shifters in (6) so the problem may be modeled and estimated by the usual simultaneous equations methods.

straightforward generalization extends the model above to multinomial choices rather than binary choices. The choice rules (1) or (5) must then be put in the context of a multinomial probit or logit approach. Thus, let D take on k possible values, with $k \geq 2$. Since D is ordered, let larger values of k index larger values of D. Then k distinct markets must be considered, one for each value of D. The competitive wage in the kth market is W_k and the budget constraint for a worker is represented by k distinct points (W_j, D_j), for $j = 1, 2, \ldots, k$, in the $C-D$ plane. The worker chooses that value of j which maximizes utility. While conceptually straightforward, the problem is difficult to analyze for general utility functions because pairwise comparisons between all possible choices must be considered. A little experimentation with the equivalent of Figure 12.1 shows that the optimal choice depends not only on local curvature properties of preferences, but on global curvature as well. Nonetheless, it is clear that the ordering of optimal assignments by tastes and relative costs shown in Figures 12.2 and 12.3 are more or less preserved. Thus, with suitably regular parameterizations of preferences, the underlying taste and technology distributions are partitioned into at most k ordered regions. Workers with the largest values of Z tend to be assigned to the smallest values of j (the cleanest jobs). Firms whose cleaning costs are largest are assigned to the largest values of j and offer the dirtiest jobs to the market. The negative assortive-matching feature of market equilibrium is thereby generalized.

A marginal analysis well serves to illustrate these ideas when k is so large, and D is sufficiently divisible, that there are in infinite number of choices for all practical purposes [see Rosen (1974); Mas-Collel (1975) provides an existence theorem for markets of this type]. This analysis readily extends to a vector of attributes rather than to a single one. Represent D as a continuous variate, measured say in parts per million particulates. There remains a wage associated with every value of D, so now income possibilities for a worker are represented by a continuous function $W(D)$, which is nondecreasing if D is a disamenity. $W(D)$ is the equalizing difference function. In this conception of the problem, the market is viewed as offering a continuum of fixed packages of wages and specific job attributes that differ from job to job.

The worker maximizes utility subject to $C = W(D)$; so D is chosen to maximize $u = U(W(D), D)$. A maximum is characterized by the marginal condition $-U_D/U_C = W'(D)$. Here U_D/U_C is the marginal rate of substitution between D and consumption goods and is negative if D is disamenable. Notice the slight variance from a standard constrained maximum problem in that the *gradient* of $W(D)$ is the correct (marginal) price in the optimization calculation, not $W(D)$ itself. Notice also that $W(D)$ need not be linear, so the marginal price $W'(D)$ may vary with D. The solution is represented as a proper spatial equilibrium in Figure 12.4. The curves labeled θ^1 and θ^2 are (C, D) indifference curves for two different types of workers. The reservation price concept (Z) must be extended to functions $\theta(Z)$ for generalization beyond binary choice. $\theta(Z)$ is defined by the

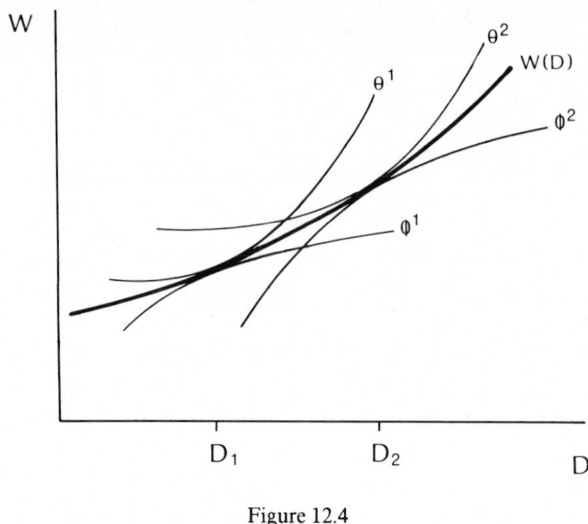

Figure 12.4

function that solves $\bar{u}=U(\theta, D)$, so it depends on the worker's preferences. Worker 1 in Figure 12.4 exhibits a greater distaste for D than worker 2 does and chooses a smaller value in equilibrium.

A similar development, where D shifts production possibilities rather than tastes, is available for firms. Since the principles of its derivation are straightforward, it is omitted. A summary of the solution is also depicted in Figure 12.4 by profit indifference curves in the (W, D) plane, labeled ϕ^1 and ϕ^2 for two different types of firms. ϕ^1 type firms find it easier to provide clean workplaces than ϕ^2 type firms do and therefore choose to offer smaller amounts of D to the market. The equilibrium assignment allocates worker taste types to firm technology types in a systematic manner. A match occurs where profit and worker indifference curves are tangent both to each other and to the common wage–amenities locus $W(D)$. That a profit indifference curve "kisses" a worker's indifference curve at the equilibrium assignment nicely summarizes the assignment and marriage aspects of the problem solved in the implicit market for job attributes.

Figure 12.4 also illustrates the revealed preferences, sorting aspects of the equilibrium assignment and shows what can be inferred from the observed market equilibrium wage–attribute locus $W(D)$. It is apparent that the gradient $W'(D)$ at any point D identifies the marginal rates of substitution only for workers and firms who happen to choose that particular value of D. When workers are approximately identical in their preferences then $W(D)$ identifies an indifference curve $\theta(D)$, and $W'(D)$ measures the relevant marginal rate of substitution for all workers. Similarly, if firms were identical and workers were different, $W(D)$ would coincide with a profit indifference curve and its gradient function would closely approximate the marginal cost function for achieving smaller values of D. $W(D)$ identifies $\phi(D)$ in this case. Figure 12.4 illustrates the general case where both firms and workers are heterogeneous, so the data are censored and selected by the optimal assignment. Thus, for example, the difference in wages between D_1 and D_2 is an understatement of the equalizing difference between these two levels of D required for type 1 workers – that is why type 1's are located at D_1 rather than at D_2; and it is an overestimate for type 2 workers, who find the wage premium sufficiently large to more than buy-off their distastes and who choose D_2 instead of D_1. Hence, if $W(D)$ is estimated over its upper range – for the largest values of D – we can confidently predict that the gradient $W'(D)$ *in that range* underestimates the average person's marginal rate of substitution, because their intrinsic distaste for D was much larger, by revealed preference. Comparable statements can be made about firms.[12]

4. Applications[13]

4.1. *Value of safety*[14]

Recent years have seen an explosion of interest in this topic that pervades many aspects of environmental legislation, workplace safety regulation, food, drug and consumer safety legislation, and so on. It is now well understood that proper cost–benefit analysis of alternative social policies requires both an estimate of the magnitude of risks involved and a money valuation of the additional safety that might be provided by the policy. Following general economic practice, the appropriate valuation of risk is the willingness to pay to reduce it. How much will a person pay to be a little safer? Let V measure this. It is defined as the marginal rate of substitution between consumption and mortality risk and is sometimes

[12] Most of the work in labor economics rests content with estimating the $W(D)$ or equivalent functions. Rosen (1974) suggests how more structural information can be obtained by utilizing the tangency conditions of equilibrium in Figure 12.4. Brown (1983) discusses the difficult econometric issues which arise from structural estimation in spatial models of this type. Extensive econometric work in urban economics using similar methods has shown that it is difficult to obtain structural estimates from a single cross-section without using many detailed and often rather arbitrary assumptions and specifications. These difficulties arise because of the stratification of agents inherent in these models. Pooled time series and cross-section data, or independent cross-sections appear to be necessary to overcome these difficulties. Such data offer more hope for structural estimation because the entire wage–attributes locus shifts over time (or across independent markets) and there is much information in these shifting loci that is not contained in movements along a given one. See, for example, Mendelsohn (1984).

[13] Ehrenberg and Smith (1982) and Hammermesh and Rees (1984) provide good general and elementary discussions of many of these topics.

[14] This exposition is based on Thaler and Rosen (1975). Linnerooth (1979) and Jones-Lee (1976) contain useful surveys of the general topic and many additional references.

called the "value of life", an unfortunately value-loaded expression. To motive this terminology, consider the following conceptual experiment. Think of a large group of N people who contemplate a project that reduces mortality probabilities by $1/N$. Then each person would be prepared to pay approximately V/N for the project. The group as a whole would pay N times this amount, or V itself. Since the project reduces mortality by $1/N$ and N people are involved, on average one statistical life is saved, and these people are prepared to pay a total of V dollars for one statistical life – the value of a life is V.

Thoroughgoing analysis of safety has been hampered by lack of direct measures of valuations V. As is usually the case in economics, it must be inferred from actual behavior of persons in risky situations. A basis for inference is provided by the common observation that people do in fact voluntarily undertake many risks in their everyday lives and do so by weighing the perceived costs and benefits of their actions. Nowhere is this so apparent as in the labor market, where we observe many jobs with substantial risks to health and longevity that pay correspondingly large wages. Test pilots and offshore oil-rig workers are ready examples. This is a straightforward application of the theory of equalizing differences. If workers find health risks distasteful, jobs that involve considerable perceived risks must effectively bribe workers to accept them by paying a wage premium. The observed wage premium and the size of the risk provide a possibility for inferring V from the risk premium.

Consider a worker with von Neuman–Morgenstern utility $(1-q)U(C)$, where q is the risk of a job and C is consumption. Differentiating this expression shows that the marginal rate of substitution between q and C is $U(C)/(1-q)U'(C)=V$. Suppose the worker has an opportunity to work in jobs of various risk classes q and that the market opportunity locus – the equalizing difference function – is $W(q)$, with $W'(q)>0$. The worker chooses q and C to maximize expected utility subject to the constraint $W(q)=C$. Substituting into the utility function and differentiating with respect to q yields the marginal condition $V=W'(q)$. Therefore the wage gradient provides an estimate of the marginal value of life V at q. The analysis in Section 3 applies virtually intact, with q replacing D – see Figure 12.4. Only if all workers had the same preferences would it be true that $W(q)$ would cover a unique indifference curve. More generally, workers have different tastes, family circumstances and wealth that makes some workers effectively more risk averse than others. Then revealed choices suggest that workers found on riskier jobs have lower values of V than those who work on safe jobs. However, if we can find the wage premium on very risky jobs (large values of q), that should serve at least as a lower bound estimate of the average value of V in the population as a whole.

Econometric estimates of $W(q)$ are obtained by regression methods. Required data are wage rates, risk-exposure of workers, and measures of personal characteristics such as schooling, experience, and other variables that are known to affect wages and which serve as statistical controls. Two types of risk measures are available for this purpose: occupational and industry risks.[15] Both are obtained from accident statistics collected by the federal government or from life insurance company records, and are matched to earnings and personal productivity data available from census survey records. Virtually all studies undertaken so far have shown that the empirical wage–risk gradient is positive, which proves the feasibility of the approach. Having said that, there is far less agreement from study to study on the magnitude of the gradient and therefore on the precise size of V. Studies using occupational risk data generally yield estimates of $W'(q)$ and therefore of V that are systematically smaller than studies using industrial risk data. The former estimates are in the vicinity of $500 000 (in 1983 dollars), whereas the latter estimates range as high as $2 million or more. The reason for these substantial differences in the estimates has not yet been resolved, but the crudeness of the risk measures available surely is an important cause. It is interesting to note that estimates inferred from observed risk-choices outside of the labor market, such as cigarette smoking and seat-belt usage, tend to corroborate some of these figures.

4.2. *Worker and job characteristics*

The theory of equalizing differences has found its earliest and most widespread use in the economic theory of discrimination which is viewed as arising from specific preferences for association with identifiable groups in the workplace. Such preferences, which in some contexts may be viewed as socially illegitimate, effectively serve to tax members of despised groups and to subsidize members of favored groups. The theory of tax incidence may then be applied to predict the distribution and size of wage differentials among workers [see Becker (1957)]. Since this theory and the many empirical studies that support it are so well known (and are surveyed elsewhere in this Handbook), I have chosen a less familiar example drawn from the market for public school teachers.[16] While specifically directed at the question of discrimination, this example broadens the scope of the theory of equalizing differences in important ways and raises issues that generally apply to all labor markets.

These studies attempt to estimate the implicit valuation of student attributes by teachers, focusing for example on the racial composition of the student body within a school. How much additional pay, if any, is required to entice a white

[15] Smith (1979) provides a good survey of studies up to that time. Viscusi (1978), Smith (1973), and Olson (1981) provide estimates from cross-industry comparisons. Sider (1983) is one of the few studies which estimates the accident production function. Ruser (1983) investigates some agency problems in workplace safety.

[16] This exposition draws mainly from the study by Antos and Rosen (1975), but several studies along similar lines appear in the literature, including Chambers (1978, 1979), Kenny (1980), and Toder (1972).

teacher to work in a school with mainly black students? How much is required to induce a black teacher to work in a white school? Answers to questions such as these have obvious relevance for estimating real educational costs indexes necessary to implement Equal Educational Opportunity legislation and to calculate the real differences in education costs across school districts. The analytical issues raised by this problem involve a nontrivial extension of the theory which has broader applicability. While teachers may have well defined preferences for schools and students of various characteristics, it is also true that schools may well have distinct preferences for various types of teachers and *their* attributes. The matching problem is therefore more complicated than was indicated in Sections 2 and 3.

Denote school characteristics by the vector S and teacher characteristics by the vector T. A teacher endowed with a particular value of T searches out a school with the desired value of S, given the wage prospects available. Similarly, a school is endowed with a particular value of S and searches for teachers with desired characteristics T, because teaching effectiveness may differ among persons with different traits for a particular composition of the student body (the endowed value of S). A match occurs when desired values of T and S by both parties are conformable with each other. It is particularly interesting that the matching problem gives rise to possibilities for trade refusal. A given teacher may desire to work at a particular school because it offers a preferred wage and student characteristic configuration. But the school may not be willing to hire that teacher if the person does not possess desirable teaching attributes T relative to someone else. Similarly, a school may desire to hire a particular teacher, but may not offer the value of S necessary to attract him. The equilibrium concept therefore must be extended to cover the joint characteristics (S, T). This implies that the equilibrium pricing mechanism must be defined over both sets of variables: $W(S, T)$ is the market clearing wage for any feasible S, T combination.

A teacher's utility function is defined over market consumption C and school attributes, as before: $u = U(C, S)$. Choice of S is found by maximizing U subject to the constraint $C = W(S, T)$, given the teacher's particular value of T and leads to the now familiar marginal conditions (assuming now that S is a "good") $W_S(S, T) = U_S/U_T$. Conditioning the choice on T is necessary for feasibility of the teacher's choice, given the definition of $W(S, T)$ and schools' demands for teacher characteristics. Therefore the S subgradient of the observed wage–attribute function measures the marginal valuation of S for those teachers who are able to choose it. The revealed preference-selectivity bias argument discussed above again applies for persons who are not located at that particular margin.

A school's choice of teachers is made on the basis of the effects of teacher traits T on educational output, represented in the education production function $E = F(T, S)$, where E is educational value-added per student. T and S strongly interact in production if the effectiveness of a teacher of given traits varies according to the characteristics of the school and students to which he is assigned. School administrators acting as agents for parents, choose teachers with traits that minimize costs given E and S (or equivalently that maximize E given costs and S). This leads to the marginal condition $W_T(S,T) = \lambda F_T(T,S)$, where λ is the marginal cost of E. The school chooses teacher attributes so that their marginal costs are proportional to their marginal products, with the caveat that choices are all conditional on the student characteristics with which the school is endowed. Therefore the T-subgradient of the observed wage–attributes function estimates the marginal productivity of T for schools who were able to hire those persons. The selectivity bias argument again applies to schools who are located at yet other margins. Clearly these ideas extend to virtually all labor market exchange as well as the teacher market per se. Production establishments tend to be stratified by worker characteristics in this type of problem.

Empirical work on this problem has concentrated on estimating the function $W(S,T)$ from cross-section data on teachers and schools. This requires information on wages paid to teachers, on the student and neighborhood characteristics of the schools they work in, and the productivity attributes of teachers. The basic unit of observation in a school–teacher pair. Wages of teachers are regressed on empirical proxies for S and T to estimate $W(T,S)$. Of the several such studies that have been published, Antos and Rosen (1975), for example, used a national random sample of schools in 1965. When S is summarized by a single dimension, the racial composition of students (measured by the proportion of black students in school), it is found that white teachers prefer to teach in schools with mainly white students. The average compensating differential was \$6 per percentage point black students for white teachers (1965 dollars) in this study. It was \$2 per percentage point white for black teachers. This suggests that it would be necessary to compensate a white teacher at least \$600 to move from an all-white school to an all black school; whereas a black teacher had to be compensated at least \$200 to move from an all-black school to an all-white one. Experimentation with other school and student characteristic variables indicated that these differentials reflect much more than only racial preferences. These indicators include measures of student ability; attendance, truancy and disciplinary problems; college-going preferences of students; and neighborhood characteristics. Regression coefficients on these additional variables typically reveal that teachers prefer to teach in schools located in more amenable neighborhoods with more able and better motivated students. For example, the wage differential between public and private schools probably reflects these factors. Teachers are willing to pay something for "a quiet life" in the form of wage reductions.

It is an unfortunate fact of life (or was in 1965) that student racial composition is highly correlated with these other attributes of students and schools. The correlation is sufficiently large that it is not possible to disentangle the separate influences of each dimension of S. An index on the entire vector is the best that can be done to summarize the data, because schools are very strongly stratified by race and other school–student attributes. Nonetheless, the sorting implications of the theory are strongly confirmed. The typical white teacher in the Antos and Rosen study required additional compensation of more than $400 to teach in schools with the characteristics of the typical black teacher. Similarly, the average black teacher required additional compensation of at least $300 to work in schools with the average characteristics of those in which white teachers were found.

4.3. *Wages and working conditions*

Several recent studies have investigated the relationship between wage rates and a diverse array of job attributes among workers. Some of these studies, like those concerning job hazards discussed above, are confined to specific attributes and to specific classes of workers and job attributes. Other studies are more broadly based.

An interesting example in the former class was the recruitment of labor for the Alaskan Pipeline, where the extreme severity of working conditions obviously called for large wage premiums. The wage offered substantially exceeded the pay available for comparable work elsewhere. It was also reported that this wage exceeded the market clearing wage and that jobs were rationed among a large group of eager applicants. Perhaps the personnel managers that set these wage rates took their cue from the Soviets, where large wage premiums are paid to voluntary labor in the permafrost areas of Siberia. Nonetheless, Soviet economists complain that the modern Soviet worker has grown soft, and that there is excessive job turnover among these workers, who return to better climates and the large cities at the first available opportunity. Evidently they are not paid enough!

The equalizing difference model is built upon the simple and intuitively compelling idea that it is the combination of wages and job attributes that constitute the relevant "price" of labor for market analysis of jobs. An important practical application occurs in the military, where wage premiums traditionally have been paid for certain conditions, such as sea duty for naval personnel and hazard pay for paratroopers and front line soldiers. The recent switch to an all-volunteer force has elevated the importance of these payments in recent years. In fact the military uses elaborate pricing schemes to recruit personnel to various positions; and these prices vary substantially among types of positions according to whether they are in short or excess supply. Not only are there special pay provisions and perquisites for the shortage positions, but the military pays selective and in some instances very large bonuses to induce reenlistment into them [Goldberg (1984), Warner and Goldberg (1984); unfortunately much of the work on military manpower remains unpublished].

Some investigators have studied differences in pay between subspecialties of professions. For example, Weisbrod (1983) noted substantial differences in earnings between lawyers specializing in public interest litigation compared to those in more traditional practice. Even after controlling for differences in age, school quality and academic performance, public interest lawyers earn some 40 percent less than others, and these differences appear to be substantial over the entire life cycle. Weisbrod argues that such differences are equalizing on preferences for public service and possibly on tastes for notoriety. Public interest lawyers also tend to be younger than the average lawyer and have larger than average probabilities of future employment in the public sector and in academic positions. Sloan (1970) shows that differences in earnings among medical specialists are largely equalizing on differential training costs and forgone earnings, while Lindsay (1971) and Lewis (1983) demonstrate that the apparent excess return to medical practice as a whole is largely accounted for by differences in hours worked between medical practitioners and comparable professionals with the same years of training.

Government service provides another interesting (and underdeveloped) application of the theory of equalizing differences [Lazear and Rosen (1980)]. State legislators, judges, and many appointed and elected officials give up substantial alternative pay to accept these positions. Some of this is undoubtedly equalizing on preferences for public service and public recognition, but another part is compensated by future private monetary rewards through the political capital built up in government service. In recent years the civil service has attempted to adjust regional pay scales for differences in costs of living, and it is well known that private industry engages in these practices in relocations of business executives among branch offices and in recruiting personnel to overseas positions.

The equalizing differences framework is also useful in analyzing personnel practices under conditions of wage and price controls. The phenomena, known as "wage drift" occurs when certain nonwage aspects of pay, such as fringe benefits and payments in kind are not controlled [Robinson (1968)]. Then competition for labor takes various nonwage forms, such as the provision of company-owned housing, paid holidays, and the like. It also takes the form of reclassifying personnel to higher paid positions through nominal changes in job titles, a phenomenon that also has been known to occur in the Civil Service.

A general approach to wage policy and labor turnover based upon deviations of offered wages from the market equilibrium wage–job attributes locus of Section 3 remains to be fully developed. In choosing an offer wage, a firm must align itself with close competitors in the market. These are firms offering similar job characteristics. We have already seen how cost considerations help determine which job attributes a firm chooses to offer to the market, and how the firm's specific location in the wage–attributes space is itself determined by economic considerations. The costs of turnover bring some extra forces to bear upon this choice. A firm for which turnover costs are large should tend to shade the wage offer, given its nonpecuniary conditions of employment, above the wage–attributes function. This makes the position relatively more attractive compared with similar jobs elsewhere, and tends to reduce labor turnover because workers accepting such positions get a "better deal" than the market offers and are reluctant to leave them. Opposite considerations apply to firms for which labor turnover is not costly. They would tend to shade their wage offers below the market equilibrium locus and turnover would be larger than average.

The probability of worker turnover in a job is therefore inversely related to the deviation between the wage paid and the wage predicted from the market equalizing wage–attributes regression line. An early study by Pencavel (1972) in a related context showed that interindustry differences in voluntary quit rates were negatively correlated with interindustry differences in wage rates and with specific human capital and other costs of turnover to firms. Other work that is consistent with this idea is presented by Hamermesh (1977), who shows that deviations of a worker's actual wage from the wage predicted by the worker's personal and job characteristics is positively correlated with various measures of job satisfaction. A related study by Freeman (1978) demonstrates that the probability of worker turnover is inversely related to self-reported measures of job satisfaction. Pencavel (1977) studies the problem of industrial morale from the point of view of its effect on worker productivity and choices made by firms to affect it. The analysis of worker absenteeism might fruitfully proceed along these lines as well.

It is intriguing to think about formal job evaluations schemes along these lines. For example, the well publicized (and widely used) system developed by Hey Associates awards point scores for each of several aspects and dimensions of jobs – their formal training requirements, responsibility and decision-making potential, stress and so forth. The scores are summed and a price is established per point awarded to arrive at the wage paid. The theory of equalizing differences makes clear that such schemes cannot be entirely determined by a priori and "scientific management" considerations, but in fact must be conditioned and disciplined by the market. For modeling purposes, one might think of a servo-mechanism response, in which jobs are re-evaluated and rescored in response to observed turnover. For example, suppose the analyst errs in awarding too few points to a particular position, resulting in a wage that effectively puts it below the market equalizing difference wage–attributes function. Then the firm will tend to find the position difficult to fill, and will observe high turnover and absenteeism when it is filled. The natural response is to reevaluate it (or possibly redefine it) and award additional points for certain attributes, which raises the wage and brings it more into line with the market. The opposite would be true for a job that was over-rated: observed turnover would be too small and the job would be brought back in line by a gradual reduction in its wage or a change in its characteristics. In equilibrium a job point evaluation system closely resembles the market equalizing difference function itself and in fact is conceptually indistinguishable from it.

A very active area of research in recent years related to the theory of equalizing differences concerns nonwage pecuniary components of pay related to fringe benefits. From the employer's point of view, the relevant cost of labor is total compensation. This not only includes wage payments, but payments associated with paid vacations, medical insurance, "free" lunches, unemployment insurance premiums, social security contributions and contributions to private pensions. Think of a "cafeteria" arrangement in which total pay is fixed but the firm makes all of these components of pay available to the worker, who chooses among them according to preferences, personal constraints on saving and so forth, along the lines of Section 2. A major element of this choice is the tax treatment of the various components, since this affects the trade-offs among them from the worker's point of view [Luskin (1978) for example]. In fact it is clear that the secular increase in the fraction of total compensation accounted for by fringe benefits is in many ways promoted by favorable tax treatment [see Miller and Scholes (1982) for an illuminating analysis of executive pay along these lines]. The analysis of pensions has occupied great attention in recent years and the literature is too large to survey here. Some aspects of the problem for government workers are discussed by Ehrenberg and Schwartz (1985).

Several broadly gauged empirical studies of equalizing differences have appeared in the last several years. Definitive research in this area has been hampered by a lack of ideal data. The basic difficulty is that personal survey records must be matched with establishment records taken from other sources and these matches may contain substantial errors in ascertaining the precise attributes of the job on which the person works. It is necessary to include proxies for workers' characteristics pertaining to skill, experience and the like in a wage equation to control for factors other than job attributes that affect wages. Earnings records and personal characteristics of workers typically come from extensive personal survey instruments. Data on job characteristics come from two main sources. One is establishment records and the *Dictionary of Occupational Titles* (DOT), which allows various job characteristics to be ascertained by occupation and industry and which can be matched to a personal record on that basis. Notice the potential measurement error in this procedure, since the worker is assigned the mean job characteristics for his particular occupation and industry, not the characteristics that are specifically applicable to his job (this is also true of the wage–risk of injury studies summarized above). The other source is self-reported working conditions by workers, largely from the *Quality of*

Employment Survey (QES) of the Institute of Survey Research. It is thought that self-reported working conditions contain subjective elements that may bias the estimates [Quinn (1979)]. Further progress in this area will require a survey design that directly matches an employer record with an employee record, but such data have so far been almost impossible to obtain and researchers have had to take more circuitous routes to make any progress at all.

An early study that uses an internally consistent data base is the Chicago Labor Market Study by Rees and Shultz (1970). Here certain subsets of job attributes (such as work at height and the weight of materials for materials handlers) could be ascertained for detailed occupations and the analysis was confined to within-occupation comparisons. While the list of job attributes is a short one in this study, very little in the way of equalizing differences for the available measures of job characteristics is found within occupations. Rees and Schultz find a systematic wage premium on journey to work. Employees traveling longer distances tend to be found on higher paying jobs. While it is implausible that an employer would be willing to pay identical workers different wages depending upon traveling distance, the result is best interpreted as a selection effect on a job search type of model: the acceptance wage in a search model should increase in commutation cost.

A more recent study on an internally consistent sample of Swedish men is reported by Duncan and Holmlund (1983), which differs in a major conceptual way from the Rees and Schultz study by including inter-occupation and industry differences as well as intra-occupational differences. They find strong positive effects of wages on dangerous and stressful working conditions, but little wage response for positions demanding hard physical labor and inflexible hours of work constraints. The finding of little effect of physical labor is consistent with the Rees and Shultz results, but on a much different sample.

Several studies have matched DOT measures of job characteristics by occupation and industry with personal survey records on wages and personal productivity characteristics. The first of these is by Lucas (1974) which describes the actual distribution of job characteristics by race and sex. Duncan (1977) presents similar tabulations from the QES data. Among other things, these studies show that males are more frequently found on jobs offering more onerous conditions of work. Lucas (1977) also matched these employment conditions to 1967 wage surveys, and found a positive wage response to onerous physical conditions of work, repetitive work and to formal training requirements of the job. Quinn (1975) found positive effects of stressful working conditions on wages in matching DOT data to the retirement history survey. Duncan (1976) found similar effects on the QES and the Panel Survey on Income Dynamics using canonical correlation methods. It is important to note that both Lucas and Duncan found that an inclusive measure of pay, including both wages and nonpecuniary working conditions, increased the rate of return to formal education, because more educated workers are more frequently found on jobs offering favorable working conditions. A more recent study by Atrostic (1983) using Bureau of Labor Statistics records of full labor compensation provides additional support to these findings about rates of return. Another study by Atrostic (1982) finds that nonpecuniary conditions of work strongly interact with labor supply decisions in addition to the well established role of money wages.

Taubman (1977) reports some related results on a somewhat different basis using the NBER–Thorndike sample, which allows for much more extensive statistical control for personal, family background and ability effects on earnings than most other sources of data. This sample does not, however, contain information on job characteristics. Instead, respondents reported the main reasons they chose their jobs. While this is not the main focus of Taubman's work, Mathios (1984) has pursued this aspect of the data, and reports effects on such variables as convenient hours, convenient location, availability of free time, challenging and interesting work, that go in the expected directions. However, other effects, such as status of the job and future financial rewards are inconsistent with equalizing differences. Mathios uses 18 different variables to capture these effects, so some collinearity and sensitivity of individual signs of effects to specification are to be expected. It remains an open question in all of these broad gauged studies of how to select regressors parsimoniously.

A well-known study by Brown (1980) introduced a useful statistical innovation into this line of work. Brown noted a possible bias in cross-section comparisons arising from a form of selection. If workers differ in their abilities and these differences are unobserved, and if the list of job attributes is incomplete, it is likely that more capable workers would be more probably found on jobs offering favorable working conditions. In fact this is a prediction of the theory [Weiss (1976), Sattinger (1977)]. For example, income effects would imply this: workers with greater earning capacity would "spend" some of it on more on-the-job consumption. This is the fundamental reason why low paying jobs tend to be the "worst" jobs. A regression of observed wages on observed personal and job characteristics would therefore capture the fact that low ability workers are more frequently found on worse jobs due to these unobserved selection effects. The estimate of the pure equalizing difference would be biased against finding such effects.

Brown dealt with this problem by using time series data and related changes in wages among persons who changed jobs to the change in their job characteristics. Nevertheless, little systematic effects of changing job characteristics on wage changes were found. That this result might be due to inadequacies of matching job characteristics with personal survey data is suggested by Duncan and Holmlund, who use a similar methodology on a conceptually superior data base and who find statistically significant effects for several classes of job indicators. A very recent study by Saffer (1984) using self reported indexes of job deterioration from the QES on a wage change specification concludes that job changes involving worse working conditions result in an increase in wages, other things equal. While the job change specification has certain statistical virtues, it also has certain conceptual difficulties, since it necessarily limits the sources of variation in the data. In particular all "between" (workers) sources of variation in the data are ignored, but the statistical bias argument suggests that only some of it should be ignored, not all of it. Furthermore, there may be additional selection problems involved with the fact that only some workers change jobs, and the reasons for these job changes are not modeled.

The most sophisticated study so far of selection along these lines is by Killingsworth (1984) who studies the white–blue-collar wage differential as an equalizing difference. Unadjusted least squares estimates show a positive differential, whereas a priori considerations appear to imply that working conditions of blue-collar workers require a premium because of more onerous conditions. Killingsworth uses a sophisticated selectivity bias statistical model to clean out the ability bias in these comparisons. These refinements turn the unadjusted equalizing difference calculation around. The unadjusted estimates apparently arise because unmeasured abilities and productivities of white-collar workers exceed, on average, that of blue-collar workers: for workers of similar latent ability, blue-collar jobs pay larger wages than white-collar jobs.

An emerging literature has investigated the extent to which measured union–nonunion wage differentials can be accounted for by differences in job characteristics. Most union contracts stipulate special pay for certain conditions, such as work at height. Duncan and Stafford (1980) originated this line of research on a more systematic basis using the Michigan Time Use Study data, where positive equalizing differences were found on the intensity of effort required by the job, the use of machinery and the inflexibility of work schedules. Union jobs are more heavily weighted toward these characteristics than nonunion jobs, so including these nonpecuniary aspects of pay in a standardized comparisons appears to account for a nontrivial fraction of the union wage differential. A methodologically similar study by Kurish (1984) on a much different data set confirms these findings for white male workers (but not for nonwhite workers), and one by Antos (1982) is consistent with the spirit of these results for the effects of unionism among white collar workers.

Finally, a long tradition in labor economics has consistently discovered size of establishment effects on earnings. The most recent and best study is by Mellow (1982) who convincingly demonstrates that statistically similar workers in large establishments earn more than those in smaller establishments. In fact these relationships carry over to top management positions as well [Murphy (1984), Rosen (1982)]. The production worker effect possibly could be equalizing on more rigid work routines and the impersonality of the work environment in large establishments, but the effects for nonproduction workers and top management suggests that these estimates may be capturing systematic differences in unobserved worker quality among establishments of different sizes.

4.4. *Equalizing differences for locational amenities*

An interesting area of research in wage theory concerns intercity and interregional wage differentials. This is a very old area of empirical inquiry in labor economics, since intercity and regional wage differences have long been observed in the U.S. data and in other countries as well. The empirical facts have been strengthened by the development of large-scale population survey data. For example, Fuchs (1967) clearly shows persistent differences in wages across regions in the United States from population census data, among workers with the same measured productivity (education, experience and the like). Wages in the South tend to be lower than elsewhere. A series of studies by Hoch (1974, 1977) attempts to decompose these differences into components reflecting differences in climate and differences in costs of living across areas. Fuchs also shows significant differences in wages among productively similar workers between cities of different sizes. That workers in larger cities appear to earn more than statistically comparable workers in smaller cities is also verified by Nordhaus and Tobin (1972), who argued that such differences are compensatory on the impersonality and difficulties of living in large cities – in a word, that people prefer to live in smaller places than in large cities, and who used them to calculate adjustments to national income measures to reflect this presumed negative aspect of economic life. The Nordhaus and Tobin study is an interesting practical example of the uses of equalizing difference estimates to adjust money income measures of economic well-being for imputing nonpecuniary amenities and changes in them over time. Liu (1975) has used multivariate statistical methods to rank cities by their "quality of life", and these methods are more generally applicable to the social indicators movement recently active in interdisciplinary social science research.

It is clear intuitively that differences in locational amenities must provoke differences in prices to attract people to less amenable areas. If workers earn the same money and have the same costs of living in a better environment compared to a poorer one, no one would choose to live in the less amenable place. Utility must be equalized in both locations and this can involve either the payment of a lower wage in the amenable place, an increase in the cost of living there or some combination of both. What is not too clear, without a model, is how utility equalization among locations show up in wage differences or in differences in site-specific prices (such as the price of land and housing) or in both.

This issue is clearly drawn in intracity models of location familiar from urban economics [see Muth (1969)]. Consider a "city" in which people commute to employment from the outlying areas to the downtown business sector. To abstract further, suppose the labor market is homogeneous in this city. Then, since the marginal product of labor is independent of where people happen to live, a single wage will clear the labor market. If all workers have identical preferences about the disamenity of commuting, then all will wish to live close to their worksites. While some of this is accommodated by greater density of dwelling units for close-in locations, limited availability of dwelling sites requires an equalizing differences on the valuation of land that is systematically decreasing in distance from the central city: people who live further out must commute longer distances and this is compensated by cheaper housing prices. It is conceptually straightforward to extend this argument to other intracity amenities, such as a hillside location, one with a lake view, access to fancy shops, and so forth. All of these locational amenities within cities get priced out in the value of land. No adjustment need occur at all in money wages. One could well imagine a similar adjustment process among cities as well as within them. For example, the price of land and housing services in highly desirable cities such as San Francisco and Los Angeles is very large relative to those cities that are less in favor, such as Detroit and Buffalo. To what extent do wages also have to adjust to equilibrate the market?

A useful analysis of this question appears in the work of Roback (1982). Ignoring intracity differences, let S index a vector of amenities that differ among cities. These might include such things as climatic differences, indexes of pollution and of crime, and also the effects of crowding. Let W be the wage paid in some city and let R be the price of land in that city. Then we expect to see equalizing differences across both the labor market and the land market: in equilibrium we should find market clearing functions $W(S)$ and $R(S)$, with the properties that $W'(S) \leq 0$ and $R'(S) \geq 0$. Wages should be nonincreasing in amenities and land rent should be nondecreasing in amenities. Roback calculates these functions in the case where workers and firm are identical.

For workers' choices it is convenient to use the properties of the indirect utility function, in which the worker optimizes consumption, labor supply and housing decisions conditional on choosing to live in location S. The indirect function is $U = U(W, R; S)$, which is increasing in W and S, and decreasing in R. This defines an indifference curve in the $W-R$ plane that has a positive slope. Given S, a higher rent must be compensated by a larger wage to keep people at the same level of welfare. This is the basic source of the difficulty in ascertaining the extent to which wages and site specific prices clear the market. Notice also that the indirect utility function implies that the $W-R$ indifference curve shifts up and to the left as S increases: for a given wage W, a person is willing to pay a larger rent in a more amenable place than in a less amenable one; or for a given rent, the worker is willing to work for a lower wage in the more amenable location to maintain utility.

A similar development for firms provides enough information to determine $W(S)$ and $R(S)$. For this purpose, assume that technology is subject to constant returns and that capital is mobile and earns the same return in all locations. The remaining two inputs are labor and land, with prices W and R, respectively. Then the unit cost function for the production of a good in location S may be written as $C(W, R, S)$. The cost function defines another $W-R$ "indifference curve" for firms. Since costs are increasing in both W and R, given S, this indifference curve has a negative slope. If the wage is large, the price of land must be smaller to produce the good at the same unit cost. The extent to which this cost-indifference curve shifts with S depends on how amenities affect production. If amenities are "productive", then costs are decreasing in S, given W and R, and the cost-indifference curve shifts up because the firm can afford to pay higher wages or higher rents in more amenable locations. If S is counterproductive (locations with lesser amenities are more productive) the cost-indifference curve shifts down; and of course it doesn't shift at all if production is independent of S.

The indirect utility functions and the cost functions allow calculation of $W(S)$ and $R(S)$ in the homogeneous case. The reason is that mobility of workers insures equalization of utility in all locations. In equilibrium it must be true that $u^* = U(W, R, S)$, where u^* is the same across all viable locations. Similarly, free mobility of firms implies that production occurs in the least cost locations. If more than one location is viable, then costs must be the same, so another equilibrium condition is $c^* = C(W, R, S)$, where c^* is a constant across all viable location S. Fix S at some arbitrary value. Then these two functions define a solution for W and R appropriate to that S, namely where the two indifference curves described above cross each other. Now fix S at a different value. This shifts the indifference curves as described above and they cross at a different value, appropriate to the new S.

More generally, the two indifference conditions in W, R and S define solutions for $W(S)$ and $R(S)$ in terms of S. For example, in the case where S is neutral in production and the cost-indifference curve does not shift in S, it is easy to see by the indifference curve construction described above that more amenable places will pay lower wages and have higher land values and these will map out or identify the cost function. Neither the wage differential nor the differences in site specific rents tell the whole story, and in fact this is a general implication of the analysis. The analysis also suggests that there must be a countervailing productivity advantage in less amenable places for their viability. For example, if the larger wages found in large cities is equalizing on the disamenity of crowding and the impersonality of city life, we expect to find that large cities offer a compensating advantage which makes production more efficient. For if not, firms located in these places could not afford to pay the higher wages necessary to attract workers to larger cities and would all move to smaller cities. Large cities would die out.

Recent empirical work in this area has concentrated on isolating the effects of intercity differences in crime rates, pollution, crowding and climate [e.g. see Rosen (1979), Roback (1982), Meyer and Leone (1977)] on wage rates. Less has been done on intercity differences in living costs and land values (however, there is a vast empirical literature in urban economics on intracity differences in house prices that follows the equalizing difference type of model). Wage studies generally find effects that go in the expected directions: wages tend to be higher for statistically comparable workers in cities with higher crime rates and greater pollution levels. They also tend to be higher in cities where climatic conditions are not as favorable an in more crowded cities. However, these effects are not sharply and precisely estimated, and tend to be sensitive to specification. Hence this evidence is much more suggestive of the direction of effects than of their precise numerical values. The probable cause of this state of affairs lies in the fact that the possible number of indicators of underlying amenity factors is very large. For example, there are at least 50 different measures of climate that could be used in a wage regression. Hence, the independent variables tend to be correlated with each other, and there is so far no statistically ideal method for dealing with multicollinearity problems in applied work. Factor analytic methods seem to offer some attractive possibilities, but existing methods are not quite suitable for this particular problem. Further work also remains to be done on the theoretical aspects of this problem, extending Roback's methods to incorporate heterogeneous preferences and technologies.

5. Further applications

5.1. *Human capital*

It is a remarkable fact that the major outline of human capital theory is found in the *Wealth of Nations*, when Smith notes that occupations requiring greater time and money expenditures on training must pay larger wages to compensate both for that expense and for the briefer duration of labor market productivity implied by it. Mincer (1958) and Becker (1964) are the fundamental modern restatements of the point. As is now well known, observed earnings differentials between schooling levels provides a basis for imputing rates of return to education. However, these concepts have much greater generality to learning opportunities and skill acquisition in the labor market as well as to the analysis of education per se [Weiss (1985)]. It is on one aspect of these largely informal, learning-by-doing features that the following account focuses, since these can be put in an equalizing differences framework. See Rosen (1977) and Willis (1985) for some surveys of the broader issues.

It is a common observation that most specific job skills are learned from work activities themselves. Formal schooling complements these investments, both by setting down a body of general knowledge and principles for students as well as teaching them how to learn. But even in the case of professional training there is no perfect substitute for apprenticeship and for work experience itself. These ideas can be captured in the equalizing difference framework in the following way [Rosen (1972)]. Think of a job as a tied package of work and learning: a worker simultaneously sells the services of his skills and jointly buys the opportunity to augment those skills. Learning potential is viewed as a by-product of the work environment, tied to a specific work activity, but varying from activity to activity and from job to job. Some jobs provide more learning opportunities and some provide less. Therein lies a margin of choice for both workers and firms.

Human capital theory suggests that a worker's incentives for capital accumulation (learning) are largest at younger ages. It is these young workers who are assigned to those jobs and work activities for which learning potential is largest. The optimal human capital investment program is implemented by a sequence of job assignments, in which workers systematically move and are promoted across jobs that offer successively smaller learning opportunities. Thus, the optimal program implies a systematic pattern of job mobility and promotions with experience. Firms accommodate this program by structuring work activities in various ways to provide greater or smaller learning options. While some learning invariably is jointly supplied with all work activity, prospects for altering learning prospects arises from reallocating experienced workers' time away from direct production and toward instructing inexperienced personnel. This is costly, because marketable output is forgone. The firm is viewed as jointly producing both marketable output and training output, summarized by a production possibilities frontier between the two. Training services are sold directly to existing employees. These transactions are implicit in wage reductions of workers who undertake training, so in this case the equalizing difference is defined over the learning opportunity connected with each job or activity.

More precisely, index the training potential of a work activity by a latent variable I. Let $P(I)$ represent the market equalizing difference, with P increasing in I and $P(0) = 0$. P is the forgone earnings paid by a worker if assigned to activity I. The more that can be learned, the higher the price paid. Let the worker be endowed with skill K, which rents for unit price R. Then the worker's observed earnings are y and $y = RK - P(I)$. This illustrates the tie-in nature of the problem. The worker sells services of value RK but buys back a learning opportunity worth $P(I)$. The worker demands learning opportunities because they increase future skills and rewards. The model is closed by specifying a

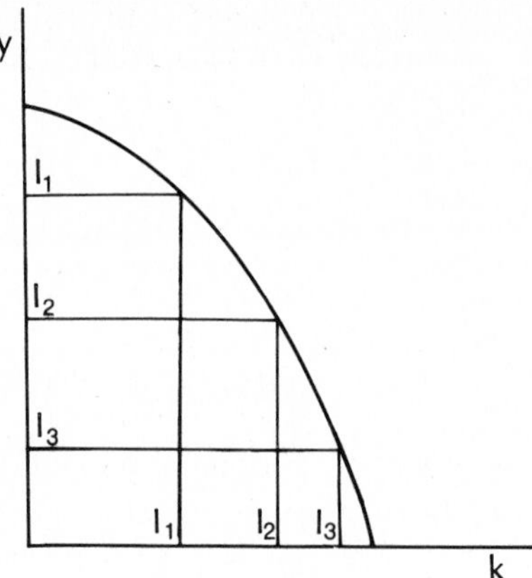

Figure 12.5.

relationship between the effect of choice of I on $\dot{K} = \mathrm{d}K/\mathrm{d}t$. This technological constraint is $\dot{K} = g(I)$, where g is an increasing function. Inverting g, expressing I as a function of $\dot{K}$ and substituting into the definition of earnings yields $y = RK - G(\dot{K})$, where G is an increasing convex function, reflecting increasing marginal costs of investment. The worker chooses a time valued function $I(t)$ and therefore $\dot{K}(t)$ – the amount of learning or investment – to maximize the present value of earnings over working life. The economics of the choice problem is illustrated in Figure 12.5. The smooth curve shown as an envelope is the function $y = RK - G(\dot{K})$ conditioned on the current value of K. The step functions that this curve envelopes represent alternative learning opportunities I, in which I is increasing in $\dot{K}$ and which cost more in terms of $P(I)$. Choice of a larger value of I is costly to produce and current earnings must fall to cover these costs. The return to choosing I is a larger value of K in the future, which expands future choices by shifting the income–investment opportunity locus upward and to the right.

For example, consider a simple example where $\dot{K} = \gamma I$, where γ is interpreted as a learning efficiency parameter. Assume that $P(I)$ is a simple quadratic function: $P(I) = I^2/2$. Then $y(t) = RK(t) - [\dot{K}(t)/\gamma]^2/2$. The discounted value of human wealth is $\int_0^N y(t)\mathrm{e}^{-rt}\mathrm{d}t$, where N is the length of working life and r is the discount rate. Then the program that maximizes human wealth [subject to an initial stock $K(0)$] equates marginal cost of investment to its marginal return [Ben-Porath (1967); Weiss (1985) considers more general models]. Marginal cost is simply the slope of the income–investment possibilities curve in Figure 12.5, or $\dot{K}(t)/\gamma^2$ in this example. The discounted marginal return of a unit of skill is the rental that will be obtained from it over its useful life. At time t this is nothing other than $(R/r)(1-e^{-r(N-t)})=Q(t)$, the present value of an annuity paying R for $(N-t)$ periods. Notice that $Q(t)$ is decreasing and concave in t. Along the optimum trajectory we have the solution $\dot{K}=\gamma^2Q(t)$: the worker's rate of learning is largest at young ages and monotonically falls over the life cycle. The sequence of learning options that implement the optimal policy is given by $I(t)=\gamma Q(t)$. Young workers are assigned to positions with the largest learning opportunities and successively shift to jobs with lesser learning possibilities as their skills increase.

An interesting selectivity aspect of this problem arises if γ is thought of as an effect that varies from person to person in the population. Some persons may have more ability to convert a given learning opportunity into useful marketable skills. A more complicated problem would specify an interaction between learning ability and previously acquired knowledge. Whatever the source of these differences, the formulas above for $\dot{K}$ and I reveal that workers with larger values of γ accumulate more human capital and are assigned to jobs with greater learning opportunities at each age. The selectivity effects in this problem arise because greater learning efficiency reduces the real price of investment to the more able, and they purchase greater amounts. This may be an important source of income inequality in the population as a whole, because human wealth at each age is increasing in γ in equilibrium.

The implied sequence of jobs suggests a "stepping stone" theory of job mobility among firms. For example, some firms might exhibit comparative advantage in producing learning opportunities. If so, they would cater mostly to young workers and provide a source of supply of experienced workers to other firms. Little empirical work has been done so far along these lines, and research on worker mobility typically follows other lines [Mortenson (1985)]. Most empirical studies in this framework have concentrated on observable life cycle earnings rather than on mobility. The basis for this is easily seen in the simple example above. If the expression for $\dot{K}$ and the implied life cycle trajectory for K is substituted into the definition of y, a closed form solution for $y(t)$ is obtained. As might be imagined, the implied functional form of $y(t)$ provides information on underlying parameters such as γ and r. These studies suggest that workers with more formal schooling are more efficient learners. They also suggest that their depreciation and obsolescence rates on human capital investment are larger than those with less schooling, implying another obvious source of selection and assignment of workers among different types of work activities [see Rosen (1977) for the references and for further discussion].

Marder and Hough (1983) use the investment activities model to study the market for medical residencies. This is one of the few studies that has attempted to estimate both demand and supply aspects of investment opportunities. The value of medical residencies is shown to increase in the investment content of the position and in the resident's expectations of future income prospects in his speciality. There is some indication of scale economies in the provision of residency positions. Studies related to this general area include Abowd (1981), who estimated tuition–school quality trade-offs among colleges in the United States. The findings indicate that higher quality and more selective schools charge higher tuition. There is also a substantial difference in the relationship between public and private colleges. It has not yet been clearly established what supports these public/private price differences in students' valuations of schools. Manski and Wise (1983) is one of the most complete studies of student–school selection and sorting in the literature, but price effects on student's choices among schools are difficult to ascertain due to the availability of scholarships and other forms of assistance.

An interesting and unproductive effect of minimum wage legislation is suggested by this type of analysis. Since a worker's observed net earnings is gross earnings capacity minus the amount "spent" on nonpecuniary aspects of the work environment, an effective minimum wage can reduce the opportunities for expenditure on job characteristics for lower productivity workers. In the case of nonpecuniary consumption items, it is conceivable that the offset is complete for workers whose productivity is close to the minimum wage. In this case, money wage payments are substituted one-for-one with such things as fringe benefits and these effectively wash out minimum wage effects, since the minimum wage does not take these other sources of pay into account [for example, see Luskin (1978) and Wessels (1980)].

For investment items of the sort discussed in this section, an effective minimum wage puts a distinct ceiling on the worker's ability to pay for on-the-job training, and this constraint is more binding the lower the worker's productivity [Rosen (1972), Welch (1978)]. A study by Hashimoto (1982) has verified these unfortunate effects empirically on the National Longitudinal Survey of young men. Minimum wage legislation not only denies on-the-job training opportunities for those who are displaced from employment, but also constrains young workers' access and opportunity to those work environments with intensive training and learning components. Part of this is probably offset by extra incentives provided to obtain training in formal school rather than on the job, but the offset cannot be complete because formal schooling is an inefficient source of training and learning for many job-specific skills.

5.2. *Uncertain prospects*

Human capital theory readily explains why earnings in occupations requiring large entry costs are larger than in those where entry is easier. Earnings differences must equalize training and educational cost differences among occupations. Another source of equalizing differences among occupations has long been noted, but has been studied far less intensively. This source relates to differences in the dispersion of outcomes among occupations. The basic idea is familiar from portfolio theory and the theory of risk aversion. If prospects for success in some field are uncertain, the mean earnings among practitioners must adjust to attract risk averse applicants. Hence, occupations in which there is greater uncertainty about possible incomes must exhibit larger mean earnings than those in which a modicum of success is virtually guaranteed.

The main point must be qualified, however, for possible biases in expectations of entrants. Of this, professional opinion differs substantially. Smith discussed the "overweening conceit" with which entrants into some trades assess their chances of success, implying systematic upward bias in the typical person's assessments about where he ultimately ranks in the distribution of outcomes. Marshall, on the other hand, held an opposite view, suggesting that persons typically underestimate their chances of success. Systematic overestimation of success probabilities by entrants increases supply into the activity, which tends to reduce the mean, whereas the opposite occurs if expectations are biased in the other direction.

This problem is perhaps most interesting at its pathological extremes, in those occupations where small numbers of practitioners dominate the trade and receive enormous rewards, whereas the majority of entrants are hardly able to make ends meet. The arts, sports, and entertainment fields provide a host of examples of this phenomenon. Large dispersion of rewards and extreme concentration at the top of the heap is best explained by scale economies in the provision of services that are inherent in the use of media, such as television, phonograph recordings, and book reproduction [see Reder (1969), Rosen (1981)]. Since the probability of rising to the top group is so uncertain, entry into these fields has many aspects of a lottery in which only a few obtain the big prizes. This lottery is tempered and made less costly by considerable turnover, especially among young entrants. As new entrants gain information that their prospects are dim, they turn to other, less risky ventures. At the opposite extreme, there are certain activities where outcomes are closely circumscribed, where most everyone achieves about the same ends, and where differences in talent have little scope to reveal themselves. These are much less risky and are more attractive to the timid.

Recent results in the economics of uncertainty shed interesting new light on this problem. Occupational choice among risky alternatives has certain conceptual similarities with the theory of option pricing in finance. The fact that a person choosing to enter a risky trade can leave it for a safer alternative if the realization turns out to be unfavorable effectively truncates downside risk. Consequently, an increase in risk of some alternative can actually increase expected utility rather than decrease it. For example, Johnson (1979a) shows that optimal sequential decisions order alternatives with respect to risk, and that it is rational to choose the job with the greatest risk first. If the outcome turns out to be very favorable, that is all to the good, and if it does not, the worker limits losses by switching to a less risky alternative. Johnson (1979b) also shows that the positive correlation between education and earnings dispersion can actually increase the expected return to schooling for these same reasons: there is greater option value to schooling if dispersion increases in this manner. Viscusi (1979) developed a similar point in the case of job hazards: if hazards among jobs are uncertain, it pays a worker to begin sampling from the unknown alternative in order to gain information on true probabilities. This general point is formalized in "two-armed bandit" problems in statistical decision theory, and has been applied to occupational choice by Miller (1984). The full market equilibrium consequences of these ideas for equalizing differences remain to be worked out.

Empirical work on equalizing differences aspects of these problems has been limited. Notice that equalizing differences are postulated as arising from uncertainty about abilities in this theory. However, we know in fact that revealed ability and talent has a large influence on personal reward in a market economy, so it is difficult to obtain precise measures of the relevant risks. Furthermore, it is not entirely clear how occupations should be defined for these purposes. On both accounts there are empirical difficulties in identifying prospective and ex ante uncertainty about the distribution from the actual ex post distribution of realizations. Two empirical studies have attempted to isolate mean–variance trade-offs. King (1974) found evidence that occupations exhibiting greater dispersion in earnings also had higher mean earnings. Johnson (1977) found strong evidence of positive correlation within education, race, sex classes. Much additional work remains to be done, especially in relating dispersion to mobility among young workers.

5.3. *Equalizing differences on working hours*

The equalizing difference framework provides an unusual perspective on the problem of labor supply. Recall that most modern labor supply analysis follows the tradition of demand theory, treating leisure similarly to all other goods: the person making choices is allowed to seek as much leisure (or supply as much labor) as desired at a competitively determined wage rate. However, many analysts have recognized that implementation of these choices might require discrete changes of jobs, since the structure of most work environments in a market economy does not allow workers to unilaterally determine hours. But if this is so there is no reason to suppose that a single wage will clear the labor market at all conceivable hours choices by all workers. Instead, it is logically necessary to consider each work–hours opportunity as a separate labor market. These various markets are linked together in much the same way as in the analysis of on-the-job amenities illustrated in Sections 2 and 3.

The fundamental analysis of this problem appears in an important paper by Lewis (1969). The point of departure is the observation that employers have definite interests in working hours of their employees. If so, the determination of working hours must be considered as a joint decision by both parties to the transaction, which is decentralized in a market setting along the lines of the analysis in Section 3. The main idea is that hours of work (or work schedules more generally) may be formally treated as nonpecuniary aspects of jobs. Then the market transaction must be viewed as a tie-in in which a firm offers a fixed wage–hours package to workers, take it or leave it, with these package deals varying from firm to firm. A worker's hours choice is exercised by choosing the firm which offers the desired amount. It is clear from the analysis of Section 3 that the market equilibrium equalizing differences function will take the form $W = W(H)$: the wage will be a function of hours demanded by the job.

That working hours are typically not a matter of indifference to employers follows from two fundamental reasons. The first has to do with coordination in production processes in which there is team production. Team production necessarily requires that hours decisions are closely coordinated among all members, and this cannot be done if each member makes a unilateral decision of how many hours to work and how to distribute them across the working day [Rosen (1978b)]. Second, there are various set up costs, or more generally quasi-fixed costs of employment [Oi (1962)] that provide a cost and profit basis for the firm to choose each component of total labor input – both the number of employees and the number of hours each one works [e.g. Fon et al. (1984)]. In fact the construction in Figure 12.4 can be made to apply to this case. Instead of thinking about the hourly wage, define the equalizing difference function $W(H)$ as total earnings paid to a worker who works exactly H hours. Then the employer's indifference curve $\phi(H)$ in Figure 12.4 is the wage–hours locus that results in a given profit level when the employment decision is optimized at each level of hours. These curves differ for various types of firms because fixed costs, set up costs and production functions differ. The construction of the worker indifference curves follow exactly the development of Section 3 with only a change in the labeling of the variables. Workers' preferences differ for the usual reasons, including differences in nonhuman wealth. In equilibrium, workers with greater tastes for work are matched to firms and jobs for which fixed costs and set up costs impel the firm to demand longer working hours. This model seems most appropriate for studying the cross-section distribution of working hours among broad classes of workers.

Little empirical work has been done on models of this type. The main advantage of the neoclassical framework is the linearity of the budget set, and the practical advantages of this are so great that they should not be given up lightly. A large component of wage variation in cross-section data arises from interpersonal differences in productivity, which effectively shift the wage–hours locus among persons in the sample. These shifts carry approximately the same income and substitution effects as the standard model, so it remains a largely open question of the extent to which the nonlinear refinements of the equalizing difference model will affect existing results. One consistent study along these lines is by Lundberg (1983) who attempts to estimate utility functions from a model of this type, but not the equalizing difference function. Kinoshita (1984) analyzes working hours of Japanese firms along these lines.

Another area where this framework may prove useful is in the analysis of work schedules. Many studies have estimated equalizing wage differences between part-time and full-time jobs, but definitive estimates remain to be computed. The analysis of flexi-time and other work schedules that more readily accommodate the demands of household production remains to be undertaken in this context (however, note the related effects estimated in the studies discussed in Section 4.3). Finally, it is well known that shift work offers wage premiums for night-time shifts [see Lucas (1970) for a theoretical model of these issues].

5.4. *Unemployment and income risk*

Smith clearly recognized the positive effect of unemployment risk on the supply price of labor, illustrating its effects on the market for construction workers. Nevertheless, the point has only recently begun to be developed by modern analysts. An important impetus for this line of research arose in unexpected quarters, namely the study of minimum wages. Elementary analysis suggests that unemployment may be an outcome of binding minimum wages, but unemployment (as distinct from employment) effects have been very difficult to find in U.S. data. A clearer picture emerges in less developed economies. An important study by Todaro (1969) noted that unemployment in urban areas in several African countries was closely correlated with minimum wages, which are substantial in many of these countries. Moreover, rural sectors are not covered and exhibit little unemployment.

Todaro proposed an elegant equalizing differences model to explain these data. Let W be the covered wage and let u be the rate of unemployment. Then $(1-u)$ is the employment rate, the probability of finding a job in the covered sector, and $(1-u)W$ is the expected wage in that sector. If wages are not allowed to clear markets something else must do so: jobs must be rationed among eager applicants by a queuing mechanism. The labor market takes on some of the features of a lottery in which workers queue up to obtain the prize of finding a position with a high wage in the covered sector. As in any queuing problem we would expect job seekers to array themselves over markets in such a way that the expected prize is equalized among them. Hence the equilibrium wage–probability tradeoff is determined by $(1-u)W=k$, where k is some constant. The probability of finding a position is lower, and unemployment is larger in those markets where the covered wage is very large. Todaro presented empirical evidence that such a model fits many of the facts of the spatial distribution of unemployment in these countries.[17]

Hall (1970), in a highly imaginative paper, extended this kind of idea to a more general theory of the spatial distribution of unemployment. The model accounts for intercity differences in unemployment along inventory theoretic lines, and is based on an observed positive partial correlation between wage rates and unemployment among cities in the United States. Hall's model explains these differences in unemployment rates as an equilibrium phenomenon. Larger wage rates support longer spells of unemployment and more frequent labor market transitions and job turnover as an equalizing difference. The wage premium is the price that firms must pay for the privilege of drawing on an inventory of potential workers in the market. The advantage of this inventory (a reserve army of the unemployed, as it were), lies in greater flexibility of employment decisions to firms facing volatile demands for their outputs, and of having a ready pool of workers available when demand and production changes require quick responses. Then equalization of expected wages across markets noted above is also an equilibrium condition on the supply side of the market.[18]

Topel (1984) takes this type of model much further by incorporating dynamic elements of mobility among local markets in response to relative demand shifts. Decomposition of demand changes into permanent and transitory components is crucial to this enterprise, since intermarket movements of labor tend to be provoked by the former, but not the latter component. While Topel's main focus is on the differential role of wage adjustments in this process for young and older workers, he finds substantial effects of specific market unemployment in sustaining higher wages, especially when unemployment compensation benefits are included in the analysis.

The theoretical issues in equalizing differences models of unemployment get more complicated when leisure and household production are brought into the analysis. For example, the equalization of expected wages model above implicitly assumes that unemployment and "leisure" have no value to workers. Consider, for example, an occupation in which work is highly seasonal and confined to five or six months of the year (e.g. fishermen in the Maritime Provinces of Canada). Write a worker's utility function as $U(C, L)$, where C is market consumption and

[17] Harris and Todaro (1970) investigate the general equilibrium effects of this idea, and Harberger (1971) analyzes its effects on social opportunity costs of labor for project evaluation. Mincer (1976) provides the most complete equilibrium analysis available for a single market.

[18] Hall (1979) constructs an equalizing difference type model of unemployment which is not easily summarized. There is a suggestion that the empirical correlation between wages and unemployment rates among cities fails when an exhaustive list of cities is included in the analysis (Hall's original analysis only included 12 large cities).

L is shorthand for leisure or nonmarket, household production. Then seasonal work implies a much larger value of the "good" L than nonseasonal work. The equalizing difference between the two requires utility equalization, not consumption equalization, so the value of C in a nonseasonal job must be greater than in a seasonal one. Since C is total market consumption, the hourly wage is $C/(1-L)$, and it cannot be shown that the hourly wage is larger (or smaller for that matter) in the seasonal job for arbitrary utility functions.[19] Hence, no equalizing difference in wage rates need be observed.

A similar issue arises independently of the leisure component, when unemployment in an activity allows workers to move easily to another activity where employment prospects are brighter. A decline in housing demand, for example, releases workers from the construction trades. Insofar as this decline is imperfectly correlated with business conditions elsewhere, many of these workers find temporary positions in other industries or in self-employment (e.g. home repair and the like). Then the equalizing difference would have to support only the costs of movement between sectors, and this might be relatively small, depending on the specificity of skills.

The situation is altered somewhat when uncertainty is brought into the picture. It is clear that a risk premium must be paid on an uncertain prospect, ceteris paribus, if workers are risk averse [e.g. see Weiss (1972)], but this too must be qualified in several ways. First is the extent to which a worker can self-insure the risk by saving and borrowing and by consumption smoothing over the life cycle. On this account, the risk premium is larger the greater the degree of imperfection in capital markets. Second is the extent to which nonmarket and market uses of time are substitutable with each other and the extent to which time uses are substitutable intertemporally. If there is enough substitution along these dimensions, then the psychic costs of risk bearing are small and the risk premium required to bear them is also small. Of course imperfect substitution will call forth a larger equalizing difference. In fact even in the atemporal case it cannot be shown that uncertainty in the wage rate in a conventional labor–leisure choice problem necessarily lowers utility. As a consequence of these considerations, economic theory puts few restrictions on the extra compensation required to bear unemployment risk, and these must be determined empirically.[20]

The most complete analysis of the problem from an equalizing differences point of view is by Ashenfelter and Abowd (1981, 1984), who treat the problem

[19] For example, suppose the utility function is $U(C-(1-L)^2)$. Then the equalizing difference function is $C=(1-L)^2+k$, where k is a constant. The equalizing hourly wage function is $w=C/(1-L)=(1-L)+k/(1-L)$ and is not monotone in $(1-L)$ – hours worked.

[20] Notice that the discussion is confined to relative risks across occupations or industries, not to risks that result from fluctuations in aggregate business conditions. It also should be noticed that the implicit contracting approach to employment risk sharing proceeds on a much different basis than equalizing differences theory, but is too complicated to be included here. See Rosen (1985) for one survey of those models.

in a distinctive and original way, related to the theory of rationing. Unemployment is considered as a constraint on work choice in which the worker cannot work as much as desired at the going hourly wage rate. Constraints of this sort result in distortions in consumer welfare that call forth compensating (or equivalent) variations analogous to the development in Section 2. However, these compensating variations are themselves uncertain in Ashenfelter and Abowd's model, which requires an additional risk premium among risk averse workers. The empirical effects of these factors on wage rates and earnings are shown to be tempered by the existence of unemployment insurance and the extent to which it is actuarially rated. Ashenfelter and Abowd find significant positive effects of the mean deviation of hours from the most preferred point, but the pure effects of risk compensation (or variance of these deviations) are not detectable in their data.

Four other studies have estimated equalizing difference on various aspects of employment risk. Hutchens (1983) finds a positive wage differential for layoff risk in longitudinal survey data, but the effects of estimated shifts in the wage–layoff equalizing differences locus among workers only partially confirm the theory. Adams (1985) matches BLS data on the time series variance of employment among industries with personal survey data and finds a positive effect of the variance in employment on wages in a cross-section of workers. Bronars (1983) uses a similar methodology to detect equalizing differences in layoff risk, matching mean and variance of layoffs by industry to worker records in the CPS. The effects of these on wages go in the proper direction, but are relatively small in magnitude.

A distinctive feature of Bronars' work is to include covariance corrections into the equalizing differences calculation. For example, consider an industry where employment requirements are negatively covariant with the general labor market. A decline in demand and employment in such an industry releases workers who more readily an find alternative positions in other expanding industries. Since the costs of search and the period of unemployment are both lower in these circumstances, firms in such industries should be able to recruit labor on more favorable terms than those in industries where demand shifts are positively covariant with the market, and where workers must bear greater personal costs of layoffs due to the unavailability of alternative market opportunities. The data show very little effects of these covariance terms, and if anything they go in the opposite direction to what theory would predict. Finally, Topel (1984) shows the importance of proper treatment of unemployment compensation in these calculations. The equalizing wage difference on unemployment rates in a worker's local labor market is shown to be strongly influenced by the extent to which unemployment insurance replaces earnings during unemployment spells. Workers for whom earnings replacements through unemployment insurance are large require little compensation in wage rates for bearing these risks. In locations where the replacement rate is lower and the insurance component is correspondingly smaller, the equalizing difference on employment risk is much larger.

6. Conclusions

Considerable progress has been made in this field in the past decade. On the empirical side of these questions, the greatest potential for further progress rests in developing more suitable sources of data on the nature of selection and matching between workers and firms. Virtually no matched worker–firm records are available for empirical research, but obviously are crucial for the precise measurement of job and personal attributes required for empirical calculations. Not only will the availability of such data produce sharper estimates of the wage–job attributes equalizing differences function, but also will allow more detailed investigations of the sorting and assignment aspects of the theory, which have not received sufficient attention in past work. Some new econometric methodology is also necessary for reducing the dimensionality of empirically relevant job attributes and for the parsimonious choice of regressors in equalizing difference functions.

On the theoretical side of these questions, much more attention must be paid to the value of workers' productivity characteristics and the nature of sorting and selection in those dimensions. Some interesting work has been done along these lines, but no specific approach has been developed far enough to illuminate these important issues.[21] Little has been done on how this aspect of the problem is linked to choice of job characteristics. Only then will we have a thorough understanding of how workers find their niche in the overall scheme of things and how all the various pieces fit together in the labor market as a whole.

References

Abowd, J. (1981) "An economic model of higher education", in: *Managing higher education: economic perspectives*. Chicago: University of Chicago Press.

Abowd, J. and O. Ashenfelter (1981) "Anticipated unemployment, temporary layoffs and compensating differentials", in: S. Rosen, ed., *Studies in labor markets*. Chicago: University of Chicago Press.

Abowd, J. (1984) "Compensating wage and earnings differentials for employer determined hours of work", University of Chicago.

Adams, J. (1985) "Persistent differences in unemployment and persistent wage differentials", *Quarterly Journal of Economics*.

Antos, J. (1982) "Union impacts on white collar compensation", Office of Research and Evaluation, U.S. Bureau of Labor Statistics.

[21] For example, Sattinger (1980), Rosen (1978a), Murphy, Plant and Welch (1983), and Heckman and Sedlecek (1984) provide alternative approaches to the problem and additional references.

Antos, J. and S. Rosen (1975) "Discrimination in the market for public school teachers", *Journal of Econometrics*.

Atrostic, B. K. (1982) "The demand for leisure and nonpecuniary job characteristics", *American Economic Review*.

Atrostic, B. K. (1983) "Alternative pay measures and labor market differentials", Office of Research and Evaluation, U.S. Bureau of Labor Statistics.

Becker, G. (1957) *The economics of discrimination*. Chicago: University of Chicago Press.

Becker, G. (1967) *Human capital*. New York: Columbia University Press.

Ben-Porath, Y. (1967) "The production of human capital and the lifecycle in earnings", *Journal of Political Economy*.

Bronars, S. (1983) "Compensating differentials and layoff risk in U.S. manufacturing industries", Ph.D. dissertation, University of Chicago.

Brown, C. (1980) "Equalizing differences in the labor market", *Quarterly Journal of Economics*.

Brown, J. (1983) "Structural estimation in implicit markets", in: J. Tripplett, ed., *The measurement of labor cost*. NBER Conference on Income and Wealth.

Chambers, J. (1978) "Educational cost differentials and the allocation of state aid for education", *Journal of Human Resources*.

Chambers, J. (1979) "A method for assessing the capacity of school personnel, the quality of their work environment and the cost of their services", School of Education, Stanford University.

Cook, P. and D. Graham (1977) "The demand for insurance and protection: the case of irreplaceable commodities", *Quarterly Journal of Economics*.

Duncan, G. (1977) "Labor market discrimination and nonpecuniary work rewards", in: T. F. Juster, ed., *The distribution of economic well-being*. NBER Studies in Income and Wealth.

Duncan, G. (1976) "Earnings functions and nonpecuniary benefits", *Journal of Human Resources*.

Duncan, G. and F. Stafford (1980) "Do union members receive compensating wage differentials?", *American Economic Review*.

Duncan, G. and B. Holmlund (1983) "Was Adam Smith right after all? Another test of the theory of compensating wage differentials", *Journal of Labor Economics*.

Ehrenberg, R. and J. Schwartz (1985) "Public sector labor markets", in: O. Ashenfelter and R. Layard, eds., *Handbook of labor economics*. North-Holland.

Ehrenberg, R. and R. Smith (1982) *Modern labor economics: theory and public policy*. Glenview, Illinois.

Fon, V., B. Boulier and R. Goldfarb (1984) "The firm's demand for daily hours of work; some unexplored implications", George Washington University.

Friedman, M. (1962) *Price theory: a provisional text*. Chicago: Aldine.

Friedman, M. and S. Kuznets (1954) *Income from independent professional practice*. New York: NBER.

Fuchs, V. (1967) "*Differentials in hourly earnings by region and city size, 1959*", NBER Occasional Paper 101, New York.

Goldberg, M. (1984) "Compensation and retention in the U.S. Navy", Ph.D. dissertation, University of Chicago.

Hall, R. (1970) "Why is the unemployment rate so high at full employment", *Brookings Papers on Economic Activity*.

Hall, R. (1979) "A theory of the natural unemployment rate and the duration of unemployment", *Journal of Monetary Economics*.

Hamermesh, D. (1977) "Economic aspects of job satisfaction", in: O. Ashenfelter and W. Oates, eds., *Essays in labor market analysis*. New York.

Hamermesh, D. and A. Rees (1984) *The economics of work and pay*. New York, 3rd ed.

Harris, J. and M. Todaro (1970) "Migration, unemployment and development: a two-sector analysis", *American Economic Review*.

Harberger, A. (1971) "The social opportunity cost of labor", *International Labor Review*.

Hashimoto, M. (1982) "Minimum wage effects on training on the job", *American Economic Review*.

Heckman, J. and G. Sedlacek (1984) "An equilibrium model of the industrial distribution of workers and wages", University of Chicago.

Hoch, I. (1971) "Climate, wages and the quality of life", in: L. Wingo and H. Evans, eds., *Public economics and the quality of life*. Baltimore.

Hoch, I. (1974) "Inter-urban differences in the quality of life", in: J. Rothenberg and R. Heggis, eds., *Transport and the urban environment*. New York.

Hutchens, R. (1983) "Layoffs and labor supply", *International Economic Review*.

Johnson, W. (1979a) "A theory of job shopping", *Quarterly Journal of Economics*.

Johnson, W. (1979b) "The demand for general and specific education with occupation mobility", *Review of Economic Studies*.

Johnson, W. (1977) "Uncertainty and the distribution of earnings", in: T. Juster, ed., *The distribution of economic well-being*. Cambridge, Mass.: NBER Studies in Income and Wealth.

Jones-Lee, M. (1976) *The value of life: an economic analysis*. London.

Kenny, L. (1980) "Compensating differentials in teachers' salaries", *Journal of Urban Economics*.

Killingsworth, M. (1984) "Heterogeneous preferences and compensating wage differentials", Rutgers University.

King, A. (1974) "Occupational choice, risk aversion and wealth", *Industrial and Labor Relations Review*.

Kinoshita, T. (1984) "A note on the supply curve of working hours", Masashi University.

Kurish, J. (1984) "Employee compensation: the impacts of and relation between compensating and union differentials", University of Hartford.

Lampman, R. (1956) "On choice in labor markets: comment", *Industrial and Labor Relations Review*.

Lazear, E. and S. Rosen (1980) "The economics of compensation for government officials", in: R. Hartman and A. Weber, eds., *The rewards of public service*. Brookings Institution.

Lewis, H. (1969) "Employer interests in employee hours of work", University of Chicago.

Lewis, H. (1963) *Unionism and relative wages in the U.S.* Chicago.

Linnerooth, J. (1979) "The value of human life: a review of the models", *Economic Inquiry*.

Liu, B. (1975) *Quality of life indicators in U.S. metropolitan areas*. Washington, D.C.: U.S. Government Printing Office.

Lindsay, C. (1971) "Measuring human capital returns", *Journal of Political Economy*.

Lucas, R. E. B. (1974) "The distribution of job characteristics", *Review of Economics and Statistics*.

Lucas, R. E. B. (1977) "Hedonic wage equations and the psychic returns to schooling", *American Economic Review*.

Lucas, R. E., Jr. (1970) "Capacity, overtime and empirical production functions", *American Economic Review*.

Luskin, D. (1978) "The economics of minimum wage laws", Ph.D. dissertation, University of Rochester.

Lundberg, S. (1983) "Involuntary unemployment as a constraint on household labor supply", Hoover Institution.

Marder, W. and D. Hough (1983) "Medical residency as investment in human capital", *Journal of Human Resources*.

Manski, C. and D. Wise (1983) *College choice in America*. Cambridge, Mass.

Mas-Colell, A. (1975) "A welfare analysis of equilibrium with differentiated commodities", *Journal of Mathematical Economics*.

Mathios, A. (1984) "Education and variation in earnings", University of Pennsylvania.

Mellow, W. (1982) "Employer size and wages", *Review of Economics and Statistics*.

Mendelsohn, R. (1984) "Estimating the structural equations of implicit markets and household production functions", *Review of Economics and Statistics*.

Meyer, J. and R. Leone (1977) "The urban disamenity revisited", in: L. Wingo and A. Evans, eds., *Public economics and the quality of life*. Baltimore.

Miller, M. and M. Scholes (1982) "Executive compensation, taxes and incentives", in: W. Sharpe and K. Cootner, eds., *Financial economics: essays in honor of Paul Cootner*. New York.

Miller, R. (1984) "Job matching and occupational choice", *Journal of Political Economy*.

Mincer, J. (1958) "Investment in human capital and the personal income distribution", *Journal of Political Economy*.

Mincer, J. (1976) "Unemployment effects of minimum wages", *Journal of Political Economy*.

Mortensen, D. (1985) "Job search and labor market analysis", in: O. Ashenfelter and R. Layard, eds., *Handbook of labor economics*. Amsterdam: North-Holland.

Murphy, K. J. (1984) "Ability, performance and compensation: a theoretical and empirical investigation of managerial labor contracts", Ph.D. dissertation, University of Chicago.

Murphy, K. M., M. Plant and F. Welch (1983) "Cohort size and earnings", University of California at Los Angeles.

Muth, R. (1969) *Cities and housing*. Chicago.

Nordhaus, W. and J. Tobin (1972) "Is growth obsolete?", in: *Economic growth*. New York: NBER.

Oi, W. (1962) "Labor as a quasi-fixed factor", *Journal of Political Economy*.

Olson, C. (1981) "An analysis of wage differentials received by workers on dangerous jobs", *Journal of Human Resources*.

Pencavel, J. (1972) "Wages, specific training and labor turnover in U.S. manufacturing industries", *International Economic Review*.

Pencavel, J. (1977) "Industrial morale", in: O. Ashenfelter and W. Oates, eds., *Essays in labor market analysis*. New York.

Quinn, J. (1975) "The microeconomics of early retirement", Ph.D. dissertation, Massachusetts Institute of Technology.

Quinn, J. (1979) "Effectiveness for work roles: employee responses to work environments", Institute for Social Research, University of Michigan.

Reder, M. (1963) "Wage structure: theory and measurement", in: *Aspects of labor economics*. New York: NBER.

Reder, M. (1969) "A partial survey of the theory of income size distribution", in: L. Soltow, ed., *Six papers on the size distribution of income and wealth*. New York: NBER.

Rees, A. (1976) "Compensating wage differentials", in: A. Skinner and T. Wilson, eds., *Essays on Adam Smith*. Cambridge.

Rees, A. and G. Schultz (1970) *Workers and wages in an urban labor market*. Chicago.

Roback, J. (1982) "Wages, rents and the quality of life", *Journal of Political Economy*.

Robinson, D. (1968) *Wage drift, fringe benefits and manpower distribution*. Paris: OECD.

Rosen, S. (1972) "Learning and experience in the labor market", *Journal of Human Resources*.

Rosen, S. (1974) "Hedonic prices and implicit markets: product differentiation in pure competition", *Journal of Political Economy*.

Rosen, S. (1977) "Human capital: a survey of empirical research", in: R. Ehrenberg, ed., *Research in labor economics*. Greenwich, Conn.: vol. 1.

Rosen, S. (1978a) "Substitution and division of labor", *Economica*.

Rosen, S. (1978b) "The supply of work schedules and employment", in: R. Clark, ed., *Work time and employment*. U.S. Government Printing Office.

Rosen, S. (1979) "On a wage based index of urban quality of life", in: P. Mieszkowski and M. Strassheim, eds., *Studies in urban economics, II*. Baltimore.

Rosen, S. (1981) "The economics of superstars", *American Economic Review*.

Rosen, S. (1982) "Authority, control and the distribution of earnings", *Bell Journal of Economics*.

Rosen, S. (1984) "Implicit contracts: a survey", University of Chicago.

Rottenberg, S. (1956) "On choice in labor markets", *Industrial and Labor Relations Review*.

Ruser, J. (1983) "Workers' compensation insurance, experience rating and occupational injuries", Ph.D. dissertation, University of Chicago.

Saffer, H. (1984) "Wages and working conditions", NBER Working Paper.

Samuelson, P. (1983) "Thunen at two hundred", *Journal of Economic Literature*.

Sattinger, M. (1977) "Compensating wage differentials", *Journal of Economic Theory*.

Sattinger, M. (1980) *Capital and the distribution of income*. Amsterdam: North-Holland.

Sider, H. (1983) "Safety and productivity in underground coal mining", *Review of Economics and Statistics*.

Sloan, F. (1970) "Lifetime earnings and physicians choice of speciality", *Industrial and Labor Relations Review*.

Smith, A. (1947) *An inquiry into the nature and causes of the wealth of nations*. Modern Library Edition.

Smith, R. (1979) "Compensating wage differentials and public policy: a review", *Industrial and Labor Relations Review*.

Smith, R. (1973) "Compensating wage differentials and hazardous work", Office of the Assistant Secretary for Policy, Evaluation and Research, U.S. Department of Labor.

Taubman, P. (1977) "Schooling, ability, nonpecuniary rewards, socioeconomic background and the lifetime distribution of earnings", in. T. Juster, ed., *The distribution of economic well-being*. Cambridge, Mass.: NBER.

Thaler, R. and S. Rosen (1975) "The value of saving a life: evidence from the labor market", in: N. Terleckyj, ed., *Household production and consumption*. New York: NBER.

Thompson, E. (1968) "The perfectly competitive production of collective goods", *Review of Economics and Statistics*.

Todaro, M. (1969) "A model of labor migration and urban unemployment in less-developed countries", *American Economic Review*.

Toder, E. (1972) "The supply of public school teachers to an urban metropolitan area", *Review of Economics and Statistics*.

Topel, R. (1984) "Equilibrium earnings, turnover and unemployment: new evidence", *Journal of Labor Economics*.

Topel, R. (1985) "Local labor markets", *Journal of Political Economy*.

Viscusi, W. (1978) "Wealth effects and earnings premiums for job hazards", *Review of Economics and Statistics*.

Viscusi, W. (1979) "Job hazards and worker quit rates: an analysis of adaptive worker behavior", *International Economic Review*.

Warner, J. and M. Goldberg (1984) "The influence of nonpecuniary factors on labor supply: the case of navy enlisted personnel", *Review of Economics and Statistics*.

Weisbrod, B. (1983) "Nonprofit and proprietary sector behavior: wage differentials and lawyers", *Journal of Labor Economics*.

Weiss, Y. (1972) "The risk element in occupational and educational choices", *Journal of Political Economy*.

Weiss, Y. (1976) "The wealth effect in occupational choice", *International Economic Review*.

Weiss, Y. (1985) "The determination of life cycle earnings: a survey", in: O. Ashenfelter and R. Layard, eds., *Handbook of labor economics*. Amsterdam: North-Holland.

Welch, F. (1978) "*Minimum wages: issues and evidence*. Washington: American Enterprise Institute.

Wessels, W. (1980) *Minimum wages, fringe benefits and working conditions*. Washington: American Enterprise Institute.

Willis, R. (1986) "Wage determinants: a survey and reinterpretation of human capital earnings functions", in: O. Ashenfelter and R. Layard, eds., *Handbook of labor economics*. Amsterdam: North-Holland.

Chapter 13

THE ECONOMIC ANALYSIS OF LABOR MARKET DISCRIMINATION: A SURVEY

GLEN G. CAIN*

University of Wisconsin-Madison

1. Introduction

This survey of the economics of labor market discrimination is motivated by two fundamental problems associated with income and wage differences among groups classified by sex, race, ethnicity, and other characteristics. The first is the inequity of long-lasting differences in economic well-being among the groups; in particular, differences in household or family income. The second is the inequity of long-lasting differences in the average wage rates among groups of workers classified by these demographic traits, when the groups may be presumed to be either equally productive or to have equal productive capacity. The second problem also raises the question of whether a labor market that pays unequal wages to equally productive workers is inefficient.

Economic discrimination is defined in terms of income differences among families and wage differences among workers. In Section 2, I discuss these definitions and present data from the United States on the income and earnings differences of blacks, Hispanics, whites, women, and men.

Section 3 surveys theories of economic discrimination in the labor market. The theories are classified into competitive and monopolistic neoclassical models with (essentially) complete information, competitive neoclassical models with imperfect information – leading to "statistical discrimination", and institutional theories. Only neoclassical models offer generalizable theories that can be rigorously tested, but I argue that these theories lack supporting empirical evidence.

*I am grateful to many persons, including most of the authors discussed in the chapter, for comments, criticisms, and corrections. Even though I did not always follow their advice, the chapter has been much improved because of their help. I am especially indebted to the following persons, who read and commented on the entire manuscript: Francine Blau, Betty Evanson, Ross Finnie, Arthur Goldberger, James Heckman, and Elizabeth Uhr. Research support was received from the Institute for Research on Poverty at the University of Wisconsin-Madison and from the U.S. Department of Health and Human Services. Any opinions expressed here are my own.

Handbook of Labor Economics, Volume I, Edited by O. Ashenfelter and R. Layard

Empirical tests of the economic theories are selectively surveyed in Section 4. Most attention in this section is, however, given to a survey of the estimations of wage (or earnings) functions for various groups of workers as a way of measuring labor market discrimination, operationally defined as differences in predicted wages (for the groups) when the prediction "holds constant" various productivity determinants of wages.

A distinction is made between marketwide estimates of labor market discrimination and estimates that apply to an individual firm. Both methods commonly use multiple regression, but they differ primarily in the specification of exogenous predictor variables – that is, variables that may be assumed to affect wages but not to reflect the process of discrimination. The statistical models of discrimination in individual firms have become widely used in recent years as evidence in court cases or other litigation stemming from antidiscrimination laws. Although the estimates of predicted wages in both firms and markets contain much useful information, there are inherent weaknesses in the models in terms of interpreting the estimates as measures of labor market discrimination.

The chapter concludes with a discussion of the policy implications of the economic research on discrimination. Data on the changes over time in comparative earnings of women and men and of black men and white men are used as a basis for discussing the role of policies in explaining and affecting these changes.

2. The definition of economic discrimination

2.1. *Concepts*

Economic discrimination is a concept that defies precise definition. One difficulty is that the intended meaning of the term differs in several contexts in which it is used. To define economic discrimination I proceed in steps and begin with two problems that span the economist's scope of interests and expertise, from the practical to the theoretical.

(1) A practical problem, based on observed and quantified outcomes in the economy and of intense concern to the public at large, is the wide disparity in income, earnings, and wage rates among a variety of demographic groups, classified by sex, race, ethnicity, and other characteristics. The disparities are systematic, persistent, and considered by most observers to be inequitable, although the definitions and sources of the inequities are often controversial. For brevity, I will refer to the group experiencing lesser economic rewards as the "minority" group and the more favored group as the "majority" group. The fact that discrimination, in the sense of disparate outcomes and inequitable treatment, has been alleged to affect many different groups complicates its conceptual definition and makes a review of empirical work overwhelming. In this chapter I

concentrate on discrimination in the United States against women, who are not a numerical minority group, and blacks. References to discrimination against certain ethnic groups, age groups, and the handicapped will sometimes be made to elucidate certain general issues.

(2) The theoretical problem, which might be purely hypothetical except that it has been motivated by the first problem, is: *Under what conditions will essentially identical goods have different prices in competitive markets*?[1] In practice, the question refers to goods that are, on average, the same and to a price difference that is sustained rather than transitory. Economic discrimination refers to a group rather than to an individual, and it is of greater concern as it persists over time. This theoretical problem may be specified more rigorously, but let us first consider its constituent parts to see its practical implications.

Discrimination in the labor market takes labor services as the good in question and the wage rate as the price. Labor services are considered "essentially identical" if they have the same productivity in the "physical" or "material" production process; a consideration that excludes the effect of the laborer on the psychic utility of his or her coworkers or employers. In fact, psychic disutility is an essential part of a useful definition of economic discrimination that was formulated by Becker (1957, rev. 1971) and which will be discussed in Section 3. If the employers, for example, feel a disutility in hiring a minority worker solely because of the worker's demographic characteristic, which, by itself, is irrelevant to the worker's physical productivity, then employers may be said to be prejudiced. As another example, if the majority group of coworkers manifest their feelings of psychic disutility by actions which curtail the minority worker's physical productivity, this outcome will still be considered discriminatory, because the operative or causal variable is the majority group's prejudices, not the minority group's productivity. Under some but not all conditions, these tastes, which reflect the prejudices of employers and workers, will lead to discrimination, defined by wages to the minority group being below what they would receive if only their physical productivity were determinant. There is, therefore, a distinction between discrimination, which refers to behavioral outcomes, and prejudice, which refers to attitudes. My point is not that tastes are the sole source of discrimination; rather that they not be allowed to define away discrimination.

The concept of physical productivity, although it excludes the psychic component, is intended to be broad and to include such characteristics of the workers as their regularity in attendance at work, dependability, cooperation, expected future productivity with the firm, and so on. A grey area occurs when there is customer contact with the workers and when it is the customers who feel the

[1] Gustav Cassel, the renowned Swedish economist, may have been the first to state this question in the context of labor market discrimination in his analysis in 1918 of why women doing similar work to men received lower wages. See the citation to Cassel along with an interesting discussion of the history of the economists' debate on labor market discrimination in Lundahl and Wadensjö (1984, pp. 8–80).

psychic disutility. Here, the distinction between physical and psychic components of production can break down. "Service with a smile is our product", may be the company's motto. It will be argued below that although customer prejudice can lead to discriminatory outcomes, it is unlikely to be a major source of the economywide disparities in the wages and incomes between minority and majority groups.

Implicit in the foregoing two concepts of economic discrimination are two subclassifications that are defined by the unit of the analysis; namely, (a) the household (or family), which is generally the appropriate unit for examining the disparity between majority and minority groups in economic well-being, usually measured by income; and (b) the individual worker, the appropriate unit for examining disparities in wage rates or earnings. In most of this survey the worker is the unit of analysis, reflecting the fact that labor market discrimination, measured by wage disparities, has been the focus of most economic-theoretical and econometric studies. Nevertheless, attention to the family as a unit and income as an outcome is important. The family is the principal matrix for a worker's choices, and an understanding of labor market discrimination requires attention to this family context. This is most clearly evident in analyzing discrimination against women. Also, our ultimate interest in labor market discrimination lies in the question of how discrimination affects the economic well-being of people, which, as noted, is most meaningfully measured for a household or family unit.

Each of the two units of observation, worker and household, may be analyzed with two general types of statistical models. In Model (I), which may apply to the short run, the outcome variable of interest – income for households or wages for workers – is compared for the two groups, holding constant certain variables that are believed (a) to affect the outcome variable (or to be relevant to the interpretation of the outcome variable), and (b) to be exogenous to the process of discrimination under study. For example, income of households may be compared, holding constant the region of residence. If region of residence is exogenous and the cost of living varies across regions, then income is a better measure of economic well-being when region is held constant in the comparison. If region of residence is endogenous to the process of discrimination, then it is probably not a proper control variable.

Model (I), which is distinguished by the use of control variables, is more important for the second definition of discrimination – wage differences for comparable workers. The comparability of the workers is with respect to their productivity, which is operationally defined by measurable characteristics of the workers that are accepted as determining productivity in the given context. Here again we require that the productivity variables that are properly held constant are exogenous to the process of discrimination under study.

Let us specify Model (I) in a form suitable for statistical estimation. Let Y_i = the outcome of the process, such as the income, earnings, or wage for the ith person; $\boldsymbol{X}_i$ = a vector of productivity characteristics of the ith person that are presumed exogenous in that they do not depend on Y nor on the particular form of economic discrimination under study; $Z_i = 1$ if the person is in the majority group and 0 if in the minority group; e_i = a random error term; and let A and $\boldsymbol{B}$ be coefficients representing the effects on Y of Z and $\boldsymbol{X}$. Assuming a linear and additive model for convenience and suppressing subscripts to avoid clutter, we have

$$Y = \boldsymbol{X}'\boldsymbol{B} + AZ + e. \tag{I}$$

Then, a regression in which we find $A > 0$ would be evidence of discrimination. The contrary case is assumed to be $A = 0$, so "reverse discrimination" ($A < 0$) is not being considered. In Model (I), the two groups designated by Z are assumed to provide "essentially identical" labor services, conditional on (holding constant) $\boldsymbol{X}$. Equivalently, we could define market discrimination, D, as

$$D = (\hat{Y}|\boldsymbol{X}, Z = 1) - (\hat{Y}|\boldsymbol{X}, Z = 0),$$

where $\hat{Y}$ is the predicted value of Y conditional on $\boldsymbol{X}$, so in the above linear and additive model, $D = A$.

Now consider Model (II), in which all X characteristics are considered endogenous, and any difference in $\boldsymbol{X}$ across groups is attributed to the process of discrimination under study. Model (II) may be appropriate for the long run, although some may consider it only the limiting case in which the group averages of all X's are equalized in the long run in a world without economic discrimination. The corresponding specification is

$$Y = CZ + u, \tag{II}$$

where u is a random error and $C > 0$ is evidence of discrimination. In this case, we can define $D = \overline{Y}_{\text{maj}} - \overline{Y}_{\text{min}}$, now using unconditional means instead of conditional means, substituting the mnemonic subscripts for the Z-values, and adopting notation suitable for describing samples instead of populations. The long-run model deliberately ignores the common distinction between the occurrence of discrimination "within" versus "prior to or outside" the labor market.

The practical problem of disparities in economic well-being, usually defined in terms of differences in household incomes, is generally addressed by Model (II). The practical-and-theoretical problem of differences in wages for equally productive workers is generally examined by Model (I). However, Model (I) may be specified as close to Model (II) as desired by restricting the set of admissible X characteristics.

An interesting and unusual feature of the economic analysis of discrimination is the attention given to the roles of tastes and nonpecuniary aspects in market transactions. The economist's treatment of tastes is, however, circumscribed. Tastes are fundamentally taken as given, and explaining their sources or how they may be changed tends to be left to the other social sciences. Instead, the economist's main objective is to determine certain behavioral outcomes that are the consequences of these tastes – specifically the disparities in employment, wages, and so on. Market outcomes become indirect measures of tastes and the focus of attention. Direct measures, such as those obtained from attitudinal surveys, which are a staple in sociology and psychology, are seldom used in economics. Despite these largely self-imposed limits of the economic analyses, the goals of predicting market outcomes and predicting the effects of policies aimed at altering these market outcomes are important and difficult.

The productivity of a given worker is also influenced by the tastes of that worker. Adherence to Model (II) implies that minority and majority groups are equal in both their productive capacity *and* their willingness to produce. Equal productive capacity refers to a common presumption of innate equality among racial and ethnic groups. Innate equality in "effective" capacity may also be assumed for women, relative to men. Thus, the biological difference in physical strength between men and women may be presumed to convey no net advantage in earnings or productive capacity to men in today's labor market. Such differences clearly lead to differential sorting into specific occupations, just as they do within a gender or racial group, but there is no necessary reason for this specialization to lead to an average wage difference across groups.

Equal willingness to produce refers to equality in tastes for market work relative to leisure when comparing racial groups and to tastes for market work relative to the combined time allocation to housework and leisure when comparing men and women. Are such tastes predetermined, or are they determined, or at least affected, by discrimination? Prior equality in tastes between men and women is often denied on the grounds that cultural and biological forces, which are presumed exogenous to the economic system (or, more narrowly, to the labor market), are the causes of a preference for market work relative to housework among men and vice versa for women. In principle, Model (I) allows any X-variable, including tastes, to be correlated with gender, because the gender effect on wages is estimated net of the X's. However, as discussed below, the choice of X's is often disputed.

Another conventional stance taken by economists in their study of discrimination is that the state of technology is given, which is the analogue in production to the assumption of given tastes in consumption. The issue arises whenever a distinctive trait of the minority group places it at some disadvantage because of the existing state of technology. In my view, if it would be costly to change the technology to accommodate the minority group, then there is no presumption of discrimination. The minority group in this industry or firm would simply be considered less productive. If the technology is not costly to change, then the market, in the absence of discrimination, should already have provided the accommodating change. Thus, lowering the height of shelves could equalize the productivity of those minority groups who tend to be shorter, and new construction offers the opportunity to build ramps instead of stairways to accommodate people in wheelchairs. Perhaps some market impediment, such as government regulations, might need to be eliminated to permit the accommodation. These issues are interesting, but they will not be discussed in this chapter. Technology is assumed to be exogenous, but, like physical strength, it is not considered an important source of average productivity differences between racial groups or between men and women.

The meaning and measure of income as an index of economic well-being and of the "wage rate" are complicated issues in any practical or empirical examination of either Model (I) or (II). For example, measuring the wage as the price of labor services must deal with distinctions between current and lifetime returns to work and between pecuniary and nonpecuniary returns and, at times, with the measure and evaluation of leisure and the rewards to housework. Some specific examples may be helpful. Black men appear to receive fewer nonpecuniary benefits from their market work than do white men [Lucas (1974)]. If so, the wage advantage of white workers would be even greater if the nonpecuniary aspects of employment were monetized and included. On the other hand, black men spend less time at work than white men. Does this compensate them for their lower wages and earnings? The usual answer is "yes" if the time not at work is voluntary and perhaps considered to be leisure, but "no" if it is "involuntary unemployment". The latter may create anxiety and distress for the unemployed person and have a zero or negative value. Another example concerns household work by women, for which the rewards are, let us assume, the income shared by the family unit. Does this income compensate women for their lower market earnings? The issue, discussed more fully below, partly depends on the degree to which women's allocation to housework and market work is voluntary, or, perhaps equivalently, the degree to which women's tastes for market and housework are exogenous.

The complexities in measuring the Y-outcomes as indicators of discrimination should not be overemphasized. Sometimes one measure is believed to understate, and another to overstate, discrimination, and yet both measures may give qualitatively similar results. Evidence for this outcome is provided below. Usually, the disparity remains whether the wage or income is used, and whether the wage is measured with or without an allowance for nonpecuniary aspects of the job.

In summary, measures of economic discrimination in the labor market are the positive coefficients, A and C, in Models (I) and (II), assuming the proper measure of Y, the suitable choice of one of the two models, and, if Model I is chosen, the suitable specification and measure of X. These qualifications and the subsequent interpretation of the coefficients and their properties all require a theoretical framework, to be discussed in Section 3.

Before presenting statistical evidence on discrimination, let us note several strengths and weaknesses of the concepts used. Their strengths include their links to market-based measurements of variables that are of intense concern to the general public as well as to the technicians who study the problem. They are robust in the face of "special cases" or individual deviations, so long as these cases and deviations are "random" with respect to the process that is modeled.

This last strength, however, may be viewed as a weakness from the perspective of various ethical or legal definitions of discrimination. When Model (I) or (II) applies to a large aggregate, such as the nationwide labor market, then a finding of no discrimination on average could be consistent with many individual cases of discrimination, so long as these were balanced by a sufficient number of cases of reverse discrimination. Lawyers and philosophers need not be put out of business by findings that A or C equal zero. [The distinctions between applying Models (I) and (II) to marketwide versus, say, individual-firm contexts will be discussed in Section 4.]

Now consider that the above economic measure of discrimination is silent about segregation. Either perfect integration or complete segregation is consistent with a finding of no discrimination. In particular, the economic definition accepts "separate but equal (wages)" as no discrimination, even though segregation may be considered noxiously discriminatory in legal and ethical senses.

Using wage differences rather than segregation indices to measure discrimination in the labor market is a corollary to my emphasis on wage discrimination rather than employment discrimination in this chapter. One justification for this emphasis, in addition to the convenience of the measurability of wages, is that when discrimination takes the form of widespread refusals to hire or promote minority workers, this should lower their relative wages. The rejected minorities must bid for jobs in less favored firms, industries, occupations, and so on. This process has been referred to as the "crowding hypothesis" [Bergmann (1974)], but my point here is that wage outcomes will reflect this reduced demand for the minority group.[2] A second justification is that wage discrimination can exist irrespective of the degree of integration or segregation in the market. Thus, wage differentials are a more fundamental measure of labor market discrimination than are employment differentials between majority and minority groups. None of these arguments for my use of wages as a basis for measuring and discussing labor market discrimination denies that employment and hiring statistics are appropriate in many practical contexts, including court cases involving discrimination.

[2]"Crowding" is an old concept. Lundahl and Wadensjö (1984, p. 73, n. 16) trace it back to John Stuart Mill, and they cite F. Y. Edgeworth and Millicent Fawcett as early twentieth-century users of the term regarding labor market discrimination against women.

2.2. Summary statistics for two concepts of economic discrimination

The first definition of economic discrimination, concerning differences in economic well-being, permits a simple measure of the differences in mean household or family income. Annual money income is assumed to be the indicator of economic well-being, and the difference will be expressed as a ratio of the minority group's income to that of the majority group.

Some comparisons of the incomes in 1981 among white, black, and Hispanic households and families are shown in Table 13.1.[3] The table is detailed, and it may be helpful to note the following highlights and interpretations.

(1) Blacks and Hispanics constitute about 17 percent of the U.S. population. The total numbers of households and families by ethnic status are shown in columns 6–8 in rows 1, 3, 5, 8, and 9. Along with other smaller minority groups, such as American Indians and certain Asian immigrant groups, about 20 percent of the U.S. population may be classified into ethnic minority groups that are often believed to be victims of economic discrimination.

(2) The average income of a black household, $14900, is 63 percent of that of a white household, which is $23700. (See row 1, columns 1–3.) On a per-person basis, the ratio is only 56 percent, reflecting the larger average size of black households, as shown in row 2, columns 3, 6, and 7. As discussed below, the ratio of black-to-white income has been fairly steady in recent years but has risen over a longer period of time.

(3) The ratios of black-to-white and Hispanic-to-white incomes tend to be around 0.6 or 0.7. The average income per member of a black family headed by a woman is, however, only 32 percent of the average income per member of a white married-couple family.[4] (Using column 2, row 6, and column 1, row 4, we obtain: $2.8/8.8 = 0.32$.) This is a large difference.

(4) Poverty status for families in 1981 was officially defined to be an annual income of $9300 or less for a family of size four and of $7300 or less for a family of size three. Thus, a substantial proportion of black and Hispanic families headed by women are poor, whereas only a small proportion of black and Hispanic married-couple families are poor. For most minority-group families, therefore, discrimination regarding family income in the United States is not so

[3] The term "white" will be used to refer to non-Hispanic whites. "Hispanic" refers to persons of Spanish origin, who may be members of any race. Persons whose origins are Mexican, Puerto Rican, Cuban, or who are from other Central or South American countries constitute most of the Hispanic group in the United States. A "household" consists of all persons who live together in a housing unit and includes one-person households. "Families" are defined as two or more persons related by blood, marriage, or adoption, and residing together.

[4] The term "female household head" refers to a household or family in which the primary earner is usually an adult woman without a husband present. The terms "householder" and "female householder," which are currently being used in the official statistics of the U.S. government, are defined in terms of the person in the household in whose name the dwelling unit is owned or rented. Statistics for households (or families) with a female householder are nearly the same as those that would apply to the older designation, female-headed households (or families).

Table 13.1
Mean annual incomes and income ratios of white, black, and Hispanic households and families, United States, 1981.

	Mean annual income ($000's) and B/W and H/W ratios[a]					Number of units (in millions) average number of persons pe unit in parentheses		
	W	B	B/W	H	H/W	W	B	H
Demographic unit	(1)	(2)	(3)	(4)	(5)	(6)	(7)	(8
1. Households[b]	$23.7	$14.9	0.63	$18.4	0.77	72.8	9.0	4.0
2. (per member)[c]	8.9	5.0	0.56	5.3	0.59	(2.67)	(2.99)	(3.4
3. Married-couple families[d]	28.7	21.9	0.76	22.1	0.77	43.3	3.2	2.3
4. (per member)	8.8	5.8	0.66	5.4	0.62	(3.27)	(3.79)	(4.0
5. Female-headed families[e]	15.3	9.8	0.61	10.8	0.70	6.6	2.6	0.7
6. (per member)	5.4	2.8	0.52	3.1	0.58	(2.84)	(3.50)	(3.4
7. Female-headed families as proportion of all families[f]						0.12	0.41	0.2
Families with primary earner working "full time":[g]								
8. Married-couple families[h]	30.5	25.9	0.85	22.3	0.73	27.8	1.9	1.5
9. Female-headed families[h]	18.0	13.4	0.74	15.9	0.88	2.5	0.8	0.2

Source: U.S. Bureau of the Census, Current Population Reports, Series P-60, No. 137, *Money Income Households, Families, and Persons in the United States*: *1981* (Washington, D.C.: U.S. GPO, 1983), Tables 13, and 19.

[a]Incomes are rounded to the nearest hundred, but the ratios are based on unrounded incomes. F example, the original mean household incomes for whites and blacks in the first row are $23 742 and $1485

[b]Households consist of all persons who live together in a housing unit and include one-person househol

[c]Mean annual income per member is money household income divided by the average size of t household. For example, for white households: $23 742/2.67 = $8892, which, rounded and expressed thousands of dollars, is 8.9.

[d]The Census Bureau defines a family as two or more persons related by blood, marriage, or adoption, a residing together. In this table, married-couple families do not include the relatively small number of famili in which the wife is listed as the owner of the housing unit. When the wife is listed as the owner, the family classified under "female householder". The term "householder" has replaced the term "headship" government tables.

[e]Does not include the relatively small number of female-headed families with a husband present.

[f]"All families" includes the relatively small number of female-headed families with a husband present.

[g]"Full time" refers to year-round, full time, defined as working 50–52 weeks for 35 or more hours per we in 1981.

[h]Median incomes are listed instead of mean incomes, which are not reported.

much a problem of poverty, at least as officially defined, as it is of inequality – their incomes are low relative to the incomes of the white majority group.

(5) One reason black and Hispanic incomes are lower is that the fraction of families headed by a woman is larger among these minority groups. If both headship status and the presence of a full-time worker are held constant, the income ratios rise to around 0.8. (See rows 7–9, columns 3 and 5.) Marital instability and slack labor markets thus appear to be important sources of

income inequality across ethnic groups in the United States. Whether marital and employment statuses should be held constant in assessing discrimination depends on the particular purposes and issues in one's analysis. As noted above, one issue is whether marital and employment statuses are affected by discrimination.

(6) This type of table is more difficult to construct for other minority groups of interest, but consider the reported incomes for the following three groups that faced discrimination in the United States in the past:

(a) persons of Italian ancestry – the largest group of immigrants to the United States in the twentieth century;

(b) persons who state their religion as Jewish, whose ancestors had immigrated predominantly from Eastern Europe; and

(c) persons of Japanese ancestry – the largest group of immigrants from Asia.

Several researchers have concluded that the average family incomes of each of these groups was, in 1970, *higher* than the average in the United States for all other white families.[5]

What adjustments to the available statistics for money income are required to measure relative economic well-being more completely? A satisfactory answer to this question would involve the resolution of philosophical and measurement problems that are beyond my capacity, but most of the issues that lend themselves to quantification or informed judgments are listed in Table 13.2. In the table the sources of inequality and the accompanying adjustments are separated into those pertaining to income receipts and those pertaining to expenditures. In measuring income receipts attention is given to (a) the measures of income from a household's assets (or wealth components); (b) the demographic unit of analysis; (c) allowances for government taxes and subsidies; and (d) allowance for survey biases.

There is not the space to discuss each of these adjustments, but two conjectures may be suggested. First, the money measures in Table 13.1 probably understate the true degree of inequality between blacks and whites, and, by extension, between majority and minority ethnic groups generally. Seven of the 10 required adjustments serve to widen the gap. Second, even descriptive statistics about "income differences" in discrimination studies are complicated.

Table 13.1 shows a static picture of income differences, and it is essential in an analysis of discrimination to describe how these differences have changed over time. The time-series data are, unfortunately, incomplete in several respects.

[5]It is more difficult to define and collect information on groups according to their ancestry and religion than it is for gender and racial classifications, so the statements in the text are more qualified. The problems of mixed or unknown ancestry, changes in one's religion, response refusals and errors, and so on appear serious, and the data on income, earnings, and wage rates have not been collected for ancestry and religion classifications as thoroughly as they have for the gender and racial groups. The sources for the research findings in the three ethnic groups referred to in the text are Greeley (1976, p. 52) and Sowell (1981, pp. 5, 126–127) for Italian-Americans, Chiswick (1983) for Jews, and Sowell (1981, pp. 5, 177–178) for Japanese-Americans.

Table 13.2
Sources of inequality in economic well-being, illustrated with a comparison of black and white families in the United States.

Source	Judgment as to whether accounting for the source would widen or narrow the conventional black–white income gap. (No adjustments needed, N.A., implies that the conventional ratio already allows for the source.)
Income receipts	
Asset ownership	
Property (income-earning)	N.A.
Property (non income-earning: car, owner-occupied house, etc.)	Widens gap (blacks have less wealth in these types of durable goods)
Human capital (wage earnings)	N.A.
Human capital (fringe benefits and nonpecuniary aspects of work)	Widens gap[a]
Defined for "household" as unit	
Adjust for family or household size	Widens gap (unless the comparison is already "per member")[b]
Adjust for multiple earners to allow for "leisure" consumption	Narrows gap (whites have 1.65 earners per family; blacks, 1.47)[c]
Allowance for government taxes, transfers, and survey bias	
Taxes	Narrows gap (reflecting the moderate degree of progressivity in the tax system)
Money transfer payments	N.A.
Nonmonetary transfer payments to nonaged persons (primarily Food Stamps, public housing, Medicaid)	Narrows gap (about 25 percent of black and 8 percent of white families receive these forms of noncash transfers)[d]
Nonmonetary transfer payments to aged persons (medical care subsidies and various tax advantages for the aged)	Widens gap[e]
Nonmonetary public benefits (parks, police service, etc.)	Widens gap[f]
Nonreported income	?
Expenditures	
Discriminatory pricing – housing, capital markets, consumer credit, etc.	Widens gap[f]
Expenditures on "regrettables" – items that do not directly produce utility, such as health maintenance, transportation to work, "waiting times"	Widens gap[f,g]

[a]Fringe benefits are generally large for jobs with higher wages and salaries. For evidence that blacks have, on average, jobs with less prestige and less pleasant working conditions, see Robert E. B. Lucas, "The Distribution of Job Characteristics," *Review of Economics and Statistics*, 56 (November 1974): 530–540.

[b]See Table 13.1.

[c]Source: Table 29 in source cited in Table 13.1.

[d]Source: U.S. Bureau of the Census, Current Population Reports, Series P-60, No. 136, *Characteristics of Households and Persons Receiving Selected Noncash Benefits, 1981* (Washington, D.C.: U.S. GPO, 1983), p. 3.

[e]Medical care subsidies are derived primarily from the Social Security system, and white persons benefit disproportionately for two reasons: (1) eligibility and payments tend to be positively related to earnings during preretirement years; (2) whites live longer. The tax advantages of the aged are generally greater for higher-income persons among the aged.

[f]A personal judgment.

[g]For a definition and application of the concept of "regrettable" expenditures, see William N. Nordhaus and James Tobin, *Is Growth Obsolete*? (National Bureau of Economic Research 50th Anniversary Colloquium, Columbia University Press, New York, 1972).

Income statistics prior to 1940 are scanty. The Census Bureau's time series of annual family income begins in 1947, and separate income statistics for blacks begin in 1967 and for Hispanics in 1972.

The income ratios are relatively stable year by year (not shown), but the change over decades is notable. To summarize the trends, several 10-year averages of the annual ratios of minority-to-majority incomes for the period since 1947 are shown in Table 13.3. The ratio of nonwhite-to-white family income rose from 0.37 in 1939, when most blacks lived in the low-income Southern region and on farms, up to 0.6 or more in the middle 1960s, when the ratio more or less stabilized. Since then it has been held down by the increasing proportion of black families headed by women, and, probably, by the relatively high unemployment levels from 1975 on.[6] Whatever the reason, progress regarding the first type of economic discrimination, family income differences, has been painfully slow.

Table 13.4 shows the earnings of workers instead of the incomes of families. To the extent that earnings measure the economic well-being of workers, the table shows economic discrimination according to the definition of discrimination that was based on disparities in well-being. According to the definition that was based on wage rate differences among comparable workers, Table 13.4 would provide a measure only if we considered the worker groups – three ethnic groups and two gender groups – to be equally productive.

In Table 13.4 ratios ranging from 0.5 to 0.7 characterize most of the comparisons between minority men and white men and between women and men within each ethnic group. However, minority women earn around 90 percent of the earnings of white women. The earnings ratios of women to men and of black men to white men are smaller for "all workers" than for "year-round, full-time workers" (hereafter, "full-time"), because women and black men are less likely to work full time. (The proportion of full-time workers to all workers is shown in parentheses in the first three columns of the last two rows. More young workers and higher unemployment among these minority groups are two sources of these lower proportions.)

Clearly, the earnings ratios for full-time workers are closer to the ratios of hourly wage rates, because the all-worker variation in hours worked in the definition of earnings – hours worked times the average wage per hour – is nearly

[6] Family income depends importantly on the number of earners per family, and this number has increased among white families relative to black families in the last 20 years. The main reason is that the percentage of all families headed by women rose from 21 percent in 1960 to 42 percent in 1980 among black families and by 8 percent to 14 percent among white families [U.S. Bureau of the Census (1983c, p. 54)]. Families headed by women tend to have fewer earners than married-couple or male-headed families. The change in work rates among wives, who are the largest and most important category of secondary earners in families, did not much affect the racial difference in earners per family. The rise in labor force participation rates of wives with husbands present was similarly rapid for both color groups from 1960 to 1981: from 30 percent to 50 percent for white wives and from 41 percent to 60 percent for black wives [U.S. Department of Labor (1982, p. 714)].

Table 13.3
Median family income ratios: Black-and-other races/white; black/white; and Hispanic/white; annual averages for five periods, 1939–1982.

Year or period[a]	Black-and-other races/white[b]	Black/white[c]	Hispanic/white[d]
1939	0.37	–	–
1947–1956	0.54	–	–
1957–1966	0.54	–	–
1967–1976	0.63	0.61	0.69[d]
1977–1982	0.62	0.57	0.68

Sources: U.S. Bureau of the Census, Current Population Reports, Series P-60, Nos. 43, 137, and 140, published in years 1964, 1983, and 1983 respectively. The full citation of No. 137, which gives the family income figures for 1947–1981 is: U.S. Bureau of the Census, Current Population Reports, Series P-60, No. 137, *Money Income of Households, Families, and Persons in the United States, 1981* (Washington, D.C.: U.S. GPO, 1983), p. 39.

[a] The years 1947–1982 are divided into four periods, and the average of the annual ratios are reported for each period. The first year for the continuous time series of annual incomes (see sources) is 1947.

[b] The category black-and-other nonwhite races is more than 90% black for most of the period and is the only category continuously available for the earlier years. Except for the recent decade or so, the trends in the ratios for nonwhites and for blacks appeared very similar, based on the scattered evidence available. In recent years, however, the proportion of blacks among the nonwhite races has declined. Also, the proportion of black families headed by women has risen most sharply during the last 10 years or so, and this has tended to make the family income statistics for blacks diverge from those of other nonwhite races.

[c] The first year in which blacks are reported separately is 1967.

[d] Family incomes of persons of Hispanic origin were first reported in the annual series in 1972; therefore, the period for the Hispanic/white ratio is 1972–1976.

eliminated. Among working women, minority women are more likely to be full-time workers, so the ratios of minority women's earnings to white women's earnings are higher for the all-worker group.

The time series of earnings ratios for full-time workers, which is shown in Table 13.5, is useful because among the available measures it comes closest to providing a comprehensive comparison for minority and majority workers of the trends in the relative price (wage) of labor services. For this interpretation, one must assume that the full-time workers remain about the same fraction of the total population of workers, or that deviations represent (a) voluntary shifts to part-time work, and (b) no systematic selection regarding workers' productivity traits, in the changing distribution of part- and full-time workers. A change in age composition could change the distribution, and, ideally, one would want to hold constant an exogenous trait like age when constructing the time series. Assuming that any group differences in these types of compositional shifts are

Table 13.4
Mean earnings, earnings ratios, and numbers of all workers and of year-round, full-time workers for men and women; whites, blacks, and Hispanics, United States, 1981.

	Numbers of all workers in millions; and year-round, full-time workers as a ratio of all workers in parentheses[a]			Mean annual earnings ($000's)[b]			(Black/white) and (Hispanic/white) earnings ratios, by gender		(Women/men) earnings ratios, by ethnicity		
	W (1)	*B* (2)	*H* (3)	*W* (4)	*B* (5)	*H* (6)	*B/W* (7)	*H/W* (8)	*W* (9)	*B* (10)	*H* (11)
All workers:									0.48	0.69	0.59
Men	58.2	5.7	3.6	$17.5	$11.6	$12.5	0.67	0.72			
Women	45.7	5.6	2.5	8.3	8.0	7.5	0.97	0.90			
Year-round, full-time workers:									0.58	0.76	0.70
Men	(0.65)	(0.58)	(0.61)	22.8	15.7	16.5	0.69	0.72			
Women	(0.44)	(0.49)	(0.45)	13.3	12.0	11.5	0.90	0.87			

Source: Table 55 in source cited in Table 13.1.
[a]A year-round, full-time worker is one who works (or is paid for) 50–52 weeks and 35 or more hours per week.
[b]Earnings are rounded to nearest hundred, but the ratios are based on unrounded earnings. For example, the earnings for white and black mén in the first row are $17453 and $11629, respectively. The use of median earnings, which are about 8 percent lower, would not much change the comparisons.

minor,[7] Table 13.5 shows gains over time in earnings ratios for black women relative to black men (column 2), black men relative to white men (column 4), and black women relative to white women (column 5). The earnings ratio of white women to white men (column 1) has been remarkably stable at around 0.6 over this 43-year span. The ratios for Hispanics (columns 3 and 6–7) are for too brief a period to measure a trend.

Further analysis of these trends will be presented later, but the following points seem evident.

(1) The ratios for the most recent period, 1975–1982, generally remain so far short of unity that "slow progress" is a fair and regrettable assessment. The exception is the remarkable rise to near-equality for black and white women, despite the fact that their earnings ratio in 1939 was the lowest one shown in the table. This rise is partly explained by the huge exodus of black women from domestic service, one of the lowest-paid occupations, and the migration of blacks

[7]The only check on these questions of compositional shift that is easily ascertained is that of the age composition. A time series of five observations from the decennial censuses from 1940 to 1980 of the percentages of the population and of the labor force that is young (age 14–24), middle-aged (25–64), and old (65 and over) show similar trends for the race and gender groups. Thus, the age factor is unlikely to be an important source of variation in the earnings-ratio trends in Table 13.5.

Table 13.5
Median-earnings ratios for year-round, full-time workers, gender and ethnicity comparisons, annual averages for four periods, 1939–1982.

	Women/men earnings ratio by ethnicity			Black/white earnings ratio		Hispanic/white earnings ratio	
Year or period[a]	White (1)	Black (2)	Hispanic (3)	Men (4)	Women (5)	Men (6)	Women (7)
1939[b]	0.61	0.51	–	0.45	0.38	–	–
1955–1966[b]	0.61	0.61	–	0.62	0.65	–	–
1967–1974[c]	0.58	0.70	–	0.68	0.83	–	–
1975–1982[d]	0.59	0.76	0.70	0.73	0.94	0.72	0.86

Sources: Various years for the P-60 Series of the Current Population Reports. See Table 13.4 for full citation.

[a]The years 1955–1982 are divided into three periods, and the average of the annual ratios are reported for each period. The first year for the continuous time series of earnings for year-round, full-time workers is 1955, but the 1940 census provides this figure for 1939.

[b]Ratios are for wage and salary earnings (excludes self-employed workers) for whites and nonwhites, who are defined as blacks and other nonwhite races in later Census publications.

[c]Ratios are for all earnings (includes self-employed workers and self-employment income) for whites and blacks. The first year for which blacks are reported separately is 1967. The black/white ratios are, on average, about 0.01 lower than the nonwhite/white ratios for men, and about 0.02 lower for women. The trends in both ratios, black/white and nonwhite/white, are virtually identical.

[d]Same as note c; also, 1975 is the first year in which earnings are reported separately for Hispanic workers.

generally from the low-income rural sector of the South to urban places. Earnings of domestic servants were understated in 1939 because of the receipt of income-in-kind payments (meals, sometimes lodging, and so on).

(2) Black earnings were relatively low in 1939, partly because of the high rate of unemployment throughout the 1930s. Black earnings rose sharply in World War II (1941–1945). The rate of increase in the men's black-to-white ratio has been slow but steady since the mid-1950s. During this period from 1955 to 1982, when real incomes were generally rising, the modest increases in the ratio have maintained roughly the same absolute difference in real earnings between blacks and whites.

(3) Blacks made relative gains between 1940 and 1960 in educational attainment and, probably, in other investments in human capital, such as health and access to better jobs by migration. In the 1960s and 1970s there were further gains in relative educational attainment and also in legal restraints on discrimination in employment.

(4) The ratio of women's earnings to men's among whites has been stable and reflects two counteracting trends: (a) more participation in the labor force by women and, associated with this, more accumulated work experience and ad-

vancement into higher occupations; (b) an increasing number of women who are new entrants or reentrants into the labor force, whose average years of experience are less than the average of the existing stock of women workers. Thus, (a) exerts a compositional effect that raises the ratio of women's earnings to men's earnings while (b) has the opposite effect [see Mallan (1982)].

The descriptive statistics presented in Tables 13.1–13.5 have shown two manifestations or definitions of economic discrimination, one dealing with incomes and another with wage rates, for three groups affected by discrimination: women, blacks, and Hispanics. The economic disparities are large and have persisted over time. The fundamental theoretical challenge is the presence and persistence of different wage rates for groups of workers for whom the assumption of equal productivity – or equal productive capacity – is maintained. The next section of the chapter surveys the economic theories that have been formulated in response to this challenge.

3. Theories of economic discrimination in the labor market

There is no shortage of theories to rationalize the existence of different wage rates for equally productive workers. What is scarce is a theory that is buttressed by empirical support. As discussed in the next section, the empirical work has seldom tested the theories. In this section I resort to informed opinion and speculative judgment about the plausibility and robustness of the theories.

Three theories of discrimination are found in the economic literature: (1) neoclassical, which include nonstochastic and stochastic versions, (2) institutional, and (3) Marxian. Only neoclassical theories, the basis for almost all the theoretical literature in the United States, will be examined in any detail. Marxian theory will not be examined, although certain components of this theory, such as exploitation, do appear in the neoclassical and institutional theories.

The neoclassical theory of discrimination is almost entirely a demand-side theory. The supply side of the labor market is effectively neutralized by the assumption that minority and majority groups of workers are equally productive (or have equal productive capacity) and have equal tastes for work. The demand side may be characterized by a competitive or monopolistic structure and by "exact" versus "stochastic" models. These characterizations define the taxonomy used below.[8]

[8] The taxonomy below, in subsections 3.1 and 3.2, of seven models was initially developed by Becker in his influential book that was published in 1957 and revised in 1971. I remind the readers of this point because "Becker's theory of discrimination" is often incorrectly identified with only one of his several models – that dealing with a competitive market and employers as agents of discrimination. The fact that I follow Becker's taxonomy in sections 3.1 and 3.2 should not be taken to mean that he would agree with my formulation of the models.

3.1. Nonstochastic competitive neoclassical models: Discrimination by consumers

Becker relabeled the abstract concept of "prejudice" into the economic concept of "tastes", and his operational definition of "tastes for discrimination" was that of a demand function; namely, a monetary offer for a good or service with, in this instance, a qualitative attribute (like race) that distinguishes it from another, otherwise identical, good or service. If the price of the labor service of the majority worker is p, then the prejudice or tastes for discrimination of a buyer are measured by an offer price, $p - d$, for the (otherwise identical) service of the minority worker. The term d is a measure of the buyer's tastes for discrimination. I use the small letter d to measure an individual agent's discrimination, and D will refer to marketwide discrimination.

Several advantages of the formulation are apparent. Discrimination has the appealing property of continuity, rather than being merely present or absent. It is potentially measurable, and the monetary units have an intuitive meaning to experts and laypersons alike – in contrast to various attitudinal scales ("like a lot"..."dislike a lot") that may or may not be scored numerically. There are explicit behavioral and even policy implications in the formulation. For example, a government subsidy to a minority-produced service could equalize the net price to consumers.

There are some disadvantages of the measure and some properties that may be either advantageous or disadvantageous depending on the question one is asking. No attention is paid to any pain or stigma felt by the victim. A lower price for one's services appears to capture the extent of victimization and to be on the same footing as a lower price owing to an inferior standard property of the good being sold. However, a black insurance salesman who offered the same policy as a white seller but sold and earned less because of customer prejudice might feel worse than if he received less because his policy offered less coverage or smaller settlements. Both price differentials could be the same, but only the former is viewed as an inequity and as a social problem.

Becker (1957, rev. 1971, p. 5) used the example of physical beauty as a qualitative attribute that leads to discrimination by demanders but is not ordinarily viewed as a social problem, either because beauty is considered legitimately productive – as it is in acting and modeling – or because discriminating in favor of this attribute is socially acceptable. On the one hand, whether discrimination in favor of an attribute is socially approved or disapproved is a datum to economists, just as we usually assume that preferences are given. Economists can still be useful if, after being informed of which attributes lead to socially disapproved discrimination, they are able to predict behavioral consequences and, ideally, suggest cost-effective remedies. On the other hand, inattention to the nonmonetary pain felt by the victim of certain types of discrimination will limit the economist's contribution to social welfare and policy analyses (to be discussed in the concluding section).

Economic analysts have generally concluded that consumer-based discrimination plays a minor role in the differences in average wages received by race and sex groups. The reasoning is as follows. Assume that black workers have the same distribution of productive skills as white workers and that consumers (who are predominantly white) are willing to pay a price, p, for a good produced by white workers. If, however, there is customer contact with the producers, the consumers consider the effective price for a good produced by black workers to be $p' = p + d$, where p is the cost of production and d is the monetary value of a white consumer's distaste for contact with black producers. (For convenience, assume temporarily that all white consumers have identical tastes.) Clearly, most goods and services are not produced with customer contact. Thus, consumers would not discriminate against, say, clothing or automobiles according to the color of the workers in clothing or automobile factories. For these goods the price would simply be p, regardless of the color of the workers.

Black workers, therefore, would specialize in the production of goods with no customer contact and, in so doing, avoid being paid a wage lower than that of an equally productive white worker, which would be the outcome if they competed with whites in, say, retail selling.[9] If the concentration of black workers in industries with no customer contact were to depress wages in these jobs, then white workers in these jobs would move – horizontally by skill level – into jobs with customer contact until wages were equalized in the two sectors. Given that the number of black workers is small relative to the number of jobs that have customer contact, all black workers would be in jobs that have no customer contact. (Realistically, some would be in the jobs with customer contact that involve nondiscriminating customers, now recognizing that consumers have varying tastes regarding contact with black workers.) The result is some degree of job segregation but no group difference in prices for labor services.

The assumptions that lead to this outcome are sufficiently plausible that consumer-based discrimination has not been assigned an important role. The market measure of discrimination, D, equals zero, even though consumers are prejudiced and job assignments among workers are affected. Thus, Becker's formulation provides the useful distinction between an ith individual agent's tastes for discrimination (with potentially varying d_i's) and market discrimination, which is an aggregate that is not the sum of its parts; here, $D = \bar{p}_{\text{maj}} - \bar{p}_{\text{min}}$. Discrimination, D, disappears even though $\sum d_i > 0$, simply because workers, in their quest to maximize their utility, will move and bring about some degree of segregation.

An outcome in which segregation reduces or eliminates market discrimination occurs in several versions of Becker's model. For this reason, Welch (1975) called Becker's theory a theory of segregation, not discrimination. Welch's point is

[9]Specialization, which is here associated with segregation, has been rigorously analyzed as a means for attaining nondiscriminatory outcomes in terms of factor payments by Stiglitz (1973, 1974).

partly semantic, but his insight is useful and may be explained briefly as follows. The source of market discrimination in Becker's model is on the demand side – the willingness of an economic agent to pay to avoid contact with members of a specific group. In a competitive model there are many employers and free mobility among economic agents, so competition enables segregation to satisfy this demand costlessly. The model assumes that mobility is costless (or nearly costless), especially in the long run.

Segregation is, therefore, a means for eliminating market discrimination, but it is not the only means. Collective action to offset the effects of discriminatory tastes or changes in those tastes can be accomplished without seriously restricting competition in markets. Indeed, common sense and casual observation indicate that an integrated society is generally more competitive. It is tempting to point to the Republic of South Africa to illustrate that segregation is not a sufficient condition to eliminate discrimination, but this country's experience is inappropriate for illustrating a competitive model. Lundahl and Wadensjö (1984, pp. 209–260) explain how a century-long pattern of private and governmental collusive arrangements have restricted competitive forces in the South African economy, with the undisguised purpose of concentrating wealth and power in the hands of the white population.

3.1.1. Discrimination by workers

Assume all workers have the same skill level. If all majority workers (whites) are prejudiced against minority workers (blacks), we may assume a white worker's wage demand for working with other white workers is w, and his wage demand for working with black workers is $(w+d)$. Clearly, employers of white workers would employ segregated work forces to pay the lower wage. Equally skilled black workers would also receive w as a consequence of competition among employers, mobility by workers, and the previously established sterilization of consumers' preferences. Integrated work forces could exist among unprejudiced white and black workers, so the worst case is when all white workers have tastes against working with black workers. But even the worst case yields only segregation among workers, not discrimination as defined by $\bar{w}_{\text{maj}} > \bar{w}_{\text{min}}$.

One could postulate various impediments to competition. For example, perhaps segregation will not permit equal wages because the black workers are too few to allow economies of scale in production, recognizing that their numbers must staff all skill levels. Rebuttal: Aside from examining the structure and technology of industrial organization to determine the plausibility of this, we should recognize the flexibility in large-scale organizations to use compartments, work in shifts, form subgroups, provide on-the-job training, and so on to achieve "effective" segregation of the workers. Remember, segregation is cost minimizing when white workers are the discriminatory agents.

Another example: Assume that black workers migrate into a region populated exclusively by prejudiced white workers. Efficient, segregated firms might take a long time to become established. Hiring and training workers entails fixed costs and, as Arrow has analyzed, these costs will retard any attempt by a firm to hire an all-black work force [Arrow (1973, pp. 20–23)]. A rebuttal should not be required because the example, although empirically relevant and interesting, should lead to a long-run equilibrium in which the work force is segregated.

Another example: Let skills vary among workers and assume that black workers have a legacy of low skills upon entering the labor market. White workers with equally low skills receive w'. Assume the technology of efficient production requires that low-skilled workers combine with complementary high-skilled workers, all of the latter being prejudiced white workers. Black workers must then receive $w'_{\text{min}} < w'_{\text{maj}}$ to compensate for (offset) the high labor costs they "impose" on their complementary factor of production – the white skilled workers. Rebuttal: Some black workers would have a particularly strong incentive to become skilled. Those who match the skilled white workers in innate ability would not only have the incentive to seek the normal (i.e. white workers') rate of return on a skill investment, but they could earn extra profits by working with low-skilled fellow black workers, because the discrimination tax, d, will not apply to them. To see the incentives involved, we can imagine that these tax savings could be shared among both skill levels of black workers and their employer, and any one of these agents would have an incentive to initiate this process. Eventually, as more black workers become skilled, the underlying source of the $(w'_{\text{maj}} - w'_{\text{min}})$ gap withers away. Again, this scenario could take a long time, and it may be empirically interesting. Finally, I argue in the next section that complementary skilled white workers correspond to employers as agents of discrimination, so the conclusions about employers also apply to complementary skilled workers.

3.1.2. *Discrimination by employers*

Two versions of employer-based discrimination in competitive markets were advanced by Becker in his analysis of racial discrimination. The first, hypothetical and pedagogic, assumed that employers all have the same prejudice against black workers (or in favor of white workers), so a uniform lower demand for black workers sets their market wage at $(w - D)$. Thus, the white workers' wages and their monetary labor costs are higher. Competition in the product market requires a uniform product price, but this can be achieved by the differential in money labor costs being compensated by a differential in money profits, which, in turn, is compensated by a differential in psychic benefits (or psychic costs – the difference depending on whether one emphasized the employer's psychic benefit from employing a white worker or the psychic cost from employing a black worker). The psychic and money forms of profits (or employer compensation) offset one another in equilibrium.

Other analysts suggested modifications of this model. Arrow (1972) obtained useful insights from an assumption that the employer's discriminatory tastes were an increasing function of the ratio of black-to-white employees, rather than being a constant that was independent of the racial composition in the firm. Arrow (1972, p. 89), Marshall (1974, p. 853), and Thurow (1975, p. 162) suggested that distaste may depend on "social distance" rather than "physical distance". If true, this would make empirical measurements complicated. For example, an employer's d might be zero for janitors but have a large negative value for professional employees. Indeed, if the owners of capital have little or no contact of any kind with the employees, the model would require that the discriminatory role shifts from employers-as-capitalists to their agents, such as managers, supervisors, foremen, or even skilled workers – all of whom are assumed to be prejudiced white persons. These interpretations of employer discrimination add realism to the model, but they do not negate Becker's central point, which was the establishment of an equilibrium differential in favor of white workers.

In a second version of Becker's model of employer discrimination in a competitive economy, tastes among employers were permitted to vary. Consider, first, the special case of just two values of d_i: low, d_1, and high, d_2. Clearly, employers with the lower value, d_1, would hire all the black workers. (I will temporarily assume that there are enough d_1 employers to hire all the black workers.) The market wage differential between white and black workers under this regime would be $D_1 = d_1$, a smaller differential than the average: $(N_1 d_1 + N_2 d_2)/(N_1 + N_2)$, where N_1 and N_2 are the numbers of employers in the two categories. Indeed, the size of d_2 is irrelevant.

Becker's insight from this model is that black workers generally benefit by a dispersion in d_i. A wider spread in the distribution of d_i could only narrow the wage gap, assuming some of the increased variance stretches the lower tail of the distribution and lowers the value of the d_i of the employer with the highest d_i required to hire all black workers. Intuitively, the upper tail is irrelevant in the setting of D because the employers with larger tastes for discrimination, $d_3 > d_2$, $d_4 > d_3$, and so on, do not bid for minority workers and they have no incentive to pay more than the existing w for majority workers. In contrast, a widening spread in the lower tail means that the new employers, with tastes $d_0 < d_1$, would now hire all the black workers. They increase the demand for black workers, and the market differential in white and black wages becomes $D_0 < D_1$.

Two plausible extensions of the dispersion effect, as just described, will tend to eliminate market discrimination entirely.

(1) First, *the lowest value of d, call this d_0, would determine the market wage differential*, even if only a small number of employers – in the limit, one per

product per market – had a value of d_i as low as d_0. Clearly, this employer would earn extra profits by hiring minority workers, benefitting monetarily from the lower wage they receive while escaping all or some of the psychic costs that would be experienced by employers with higher d_i's. Total profits could be increased by cutting prices and hiring more black workers and expanding production. Employers with $d_i > d_0$ would, correspondingly, lose business and curtail production, thereby decreasing the demand for white workers. The impersonal operation of the capital market would ensure an inflow of investment to the high-profit firms. Assuming long-run constant costs, the stopping point would be reached only when all black workers and equally paid white workers are employed by the d_0 employer(s) – perhaps in newly constructed plants, each of optimal size. White workers would lose the wage advantage they had received from discriminating employers.

(2) Second, D_0 *would become zero.* There are several routes by which the market should uncover one or more cost-minimizing employers (per product, per market) with $d_0 = 0$. Some white employers might be unprejudiced. Blacks could become employers. Capital owners, like consumers, tend to be remote from contact with employees, so their d_i's would tend to be effectively zero. (Of course, this shifts the cost-minimizing problem to that of finding managers with low d_i's.) Indeed, consumers as well as investors would have precisely these incentives of finding managers and other forms of complementary employees whose $d_0 = 0$.

In a phrase, competitive market forces, still assuming constant costs, tend to drive D toward zero. Arrow, in his analysis and reformulation of Becker's model of employer discrimination, arrived at just this conclusion: "Only the least discriminatory firms survive. Indeed, if there were any firms which did not discriminate at all, these would be the only ones to survive the competitive struggle" [Arrow (1973, p. 10)]. And, "It [Becker's model of employer discrimination] predicts the absence of the phenomenon it was designed to explain" [Arrow (1972, p. 192)].

Becker, in an article on discrimination written for the *International Encyclopedia of the Social Sciences* and published 11 years after his book, did not reach this conclusion.

> A few of the more extreme nineteenth-century advocates of a competitive market economy believed that eventually its extension and development would eliminate most economic discrimination.... Unfortunately, this has not yet taken place; discrimination exists, and at times even flourishes, in competitive economies, the position of Negroes in the United States being a clear example [Becker (1968, p. 210)].

Becker's disagreement with the previous scenario of the workings of competition is based on his view that the assumption of constant costs for a firm, even in the long run, is a polar case and not one to be accepted generally [Becker (1957, rev. ed. 1971, pp. 44–45)]. Entrepreneurial skill is an example that is sometimes suggested for a factor of production that may be inelastically supplied, even in the long run. Thus, one's judgment about the number of nondiscriminating firms that are in or that might enter the market, about the generality of entrepreneurial skills, and about the long-run elasticity of other factors all enter into one's judgment about the persistence of a discriminating cost differential in the long run under competitive conditions.

What if discrimination is redefined as nepotism and $d = d_b < 0$ is replaced by a term $d_w > 0$, now adding subscripts to distinguish discrimination against blacks from nepotism in favor of whites? This specification is examined by Goldberg (1982), who finds that a long-run differential wage advantage in favor of whites is sustained under competitive conditions. The result, which had been previously advanced and then downplayed by Arrow (1972), is correct, but in my judgment the model is not realistic.[10]

My argument begins with the observation that when a positive d_w – Goldberg's nepotism – replaces a negative d_b – Becker's discrimination – the intention is to view the tastes for whites as more than a euphemism for expressing a preference not to be associated with blacks. This intention is clarified by a dictionary definition of nepotism: "favoritism shown to one's nephews and other relatives; bestowal of patronage by reason of relationship rather than merit". As defined, nepotism is indeed real. Let us assume that only the "uncle-employers" receive nonpecuniary utility from the employment relation. Consider two cases of wage payment. In Case 1 the wage rate of "nephews" and all other workers is the same, and nephews are merely sorted into jobs where their uncles are employers. Alternatively, in Case 2 the uncles share all or some of their utility rents with their nephews by paying them a higher than competitive wage. In Case 1 the uncles earn extra rewards (profits plus utility), but they have no incentive to expand production, which would (assuming constant costs) threaten other firms, because the supply of nephews is sharply limited. In Case 2 the uncle-employers earn lower profits, but their total utility can easily be high enough to ensure their survival as employers.

Case 2 shows, therefore, that the dictionary definition of nepotism can coexist with the economic definition of nepotism, according to which nephews receive a higher wage than equally productive nonnephews (all other workers). However, to transfer this scenario of nepotism to one in which all white workers, who

[10] See Arrow (1972, pp. 91, 192). After pointing to nepotism as a source of a sustained wage differential in favor of whites, even in the absence of any differential based on tastes against blacks, Arrow commented: "But it is reasonable to postulate that any preference a firm might have for the hiring of whites per se arises as an offset to the presence of disliked blacks. That is, for a firm that has no black employees, $d_w = 0$." Furthermore, "for a firm that does not discriminate against blacks, there will also be no reason to pay anything extra for white employees" (p. 192).

constitute 85 percent of the labor force, are the equivalent of nephews (beneficiaries of nepotism) seems unrealistic. Throughout this survey, therefore, discrimination against a minority group will be viewed as the operative force.

3.2. Nonstochastic monopolistic neoclassical models: Product monopoly

A monopoly has two characteristics that permit long-run discrimination: first, a definitional uniformity in tastes, since there is only one employer; second, above-competitive profits. The former allows a d_i that will not become irrelevant because of competition, and the latter allows the sacrifice in money profits – in exchange for the psychic benefits from discrimination. Nevertheless, there are several influences in the economy at large that constrain or even eliminate the power of one or a few monopolies to sustain market discrimination.

Monopoly power in the product market does not imply monopoly power in the labor market. If the monopoly firm cannot affect wages in the labor market, it would not pay a higher wage than w to hire majority workers, nor could it pay a lower wage than w to hire minority workers. In other words, the monopoly would not be the source of discrimination, although it, like other firms with a positive d_i, would employ a segregated, all-majority work force. Were the monopoly to behave irrationally and pay higher wages to majority workers, it would create incentives for a "takeover" by investors and managers with zero d_i's. Indeed, Alchian and Kessel (1962) advanced the view that even where monopolists affect wages in their labor market, they would be unlikely to sacrifice money profits permanently by a policy of (racial) discrimination, because profit-maximizing investors would buy them out.

> But why do monopolistic enterprises discriminate... more...? One would expect that those who have a taste for discrimination... would naturally gravitate to those economic activities that, for purely pecuniary reasons, do not employ Negroes. Free choice of economic activities implies a distribution of resources that would minimize the costs of satisfying tastes for discrimination (p. 161).

Alchian and Kessel pointed out that a regulated monopolist or a government monopoly, which was constrained *not* to maximize profits, could indulge its tastes for discrimination at no loss in profits and, therefore, offer no incentive for a "takeover". Such firms could, for example, engage in nepotism and consume other nonpecuniary benefits at no cost in forgone profits, and if there were enough such firms, they could at least contribute to a marketwide discrimination differential.

It is useful to keep in mind two empirical characteristics of monopolies – now using the term as shorthand for a firm that produces a "large" share of the market. First, monopolies tend to be larger, more capital-intensive, and more likely to be unionized than the average firm. Because of this, they may pay higher wages to attract specialized skills and to ensure lower turnover. Among the workers who apply for jobs at these monopoly firms, majority workers may be the more skilled, as a result of previous discrimination from various channels. The resulting combination of hiring relatively more majority workers and paying higher wages may not be discriminatory; that is, it may be consistent with a $d_i = 0$ for the monopolist. In principle, a properly specified Model (I) would permit testing whether the firm really discriminated among equally skilled applicants, minority and majority.

Second, along with size and wealth, monopolies are often also publicly prominent. They tend to be sensitive to public relations and to their "image". In the past this sensitivity could have served to reinforce discrimination, because government and other wielders of power in the community may have been prejudiced and have influenced the monopoly. Today, our laws and professed public sentiments are against discrimination or, if neutral, condone organized pressures from minority groups on the monopolies. These forces would, if present, tend to lower the effective d_i of the monopolist below the average among employers.

In summary, monopoly firms, particularly regulated monopolies, are in theory capable of exerting some sustained discrimination in labor markets. There are, however, reasons for doubting that monopoly is a major source of marketwide discrimination.

3.2.1. Monopsony firms in labor markets

The classic case of the exploitation of labor in neoclassical economics arises under conditions of monopsony. Workers are captive in a market where there is only one employer, or where a group of employers collude and act as one buyer. Monopsony represents a rare area of common ground between neoclassical and Marxian models of the labor market.[11]

The model is well known: a single buyer of labor faces an upward-sloping supply curve of labor; equates the value of labor's marginal product (VMP) and its (rising) marginal cost; hires less labor than if the same demand for labor were generated by many competing firms; pays labor its supply (offer) price, which is lower than the price (wage) needed to induce the larger supply under competitive demand conditions; and retains the positive differential between the VMP and the wage as profit. Where two factors of production are supplied and demanded, the exploitation (measured by $[\text{VMP} - w]/w$) will be greater for the factor whose labor supply is the more inelastic. These propositions, which were presented by

[11]See Lundahl and Wadensjö (1984, pp. 49–52) for a further analysis of monopsony models of labor market discrimination and for their critique of neo-Marxist, or radical, theories as a subset of monopsony. See Cain (1976) for a brief discussion of radical theories of the labor market, including the analysis of discrimination by radical theories.

Joan Robinson (1934, pp. 301–304), provide a consistent model for discrimination simply by postulating a more inelastic supply curve of labor for minority workers. A modern application of this model is by Madden (1973).

Empirical support for the prevalence of monopsony and lower-than-competitive wages is limited [see Bunting (1962)]. Labor markets that are "one-industry towns" are increasingly uncommon, mainly because a large fraction of the population lives in larger urban places and because the automobile has greatly expanded the geographic boundaries of the labor market. Information about wage rates in geographically dispersed markets is available and only those workers "on the margin" of moving need to move to equalize wages for workers of comparable skills. Therefore, the long-run acceptance by workers of below-competitive wages presupposes a degree of immobility that is hard to accept. No doubt there are some workers who are trapped by a combination of industry-specific skills and a decline in the number of firms competing for their skills, and who suffer long-lasting exploitation. But these are not conditions that generalize to the entire labor market.

Because monopsony seems to have a limited application, it does not appear worthwhile to examine more closely the requisite proposition that the supply curve of minority workers is less elastic than the supply curve of majority workers. However, two brief points may be useful. First, if differences in the supply curve identify (in the econometric sense) a difference in exploitation, we need to satisfy ourselves that the underlying sources of this difference in supply curves are not also reasons why the workers' wages differ.

Second, regarding gender discrimination, there is a good deal of empirical evidence and theoretical support for the finding of a greater elasticity for the supply curve of women's labor than of men's labor. To be sure, this larger elasticity refers to the market, not to individual firms, but as a firm (or group of firms) becomes monopsonistic then the distinction between the supply of a factor to the labor market and the supply of a factor to the (monopsonist) firm tends to disappear. Thus, the larger labor supply elasticity of women in the labor market as a whole implies a larger elasticity to a monopsonist, and this is the opposite of the requisite condition for the exploitation of women relative to men. Again, there may be particular circumstances when this generalization does not hold. Nurses are sometimes used as an example of an occupation that faces a monopsony-employer in the form of one or a few hospitals.

3.2.2. *Labor unions as monopolies*

In Becker's model of discrimination, white workers' prejudice against black workers was not a sufficient condition to sustain a discriminatory wage differential. However, by forming a monopoly in the sale of labor to employers, white workers could enforce their tastes *and* raise their wage above the competitive level. Moreover, unlike monopsony, labor unions are widespread, supported by laws and community approval, and have been shown in many studies to have raised wages for their members above competitive levels.

Given that the union secures monopoly rents, some method of restricting entry is a necessary first step in maintaining these rents. Many analysts have pointed to the discriminatory tastes of the members as a criterion for inclusion and exclusion. Kessel (1958) added the argument that this criterion will also be useful in a second step in maintaining the rents; namely, in policing the existing members to honor the union contract, even though it would often be in their private interest to "cheat" by, say, working more for a slightly lower wage. Kessel argued that ethnic homogeneity among the members facilitates a mutual agreement to collude, making unnecessary those stronger sanctions that might be illegal or incur community disapproval. Finally, institutional research, while divided about the overall discriminatory impact of unions, documents many cases of discrimination by unions [Gould (1977), Hill (1977), Marshall (1965), Ross (1948), Northrup (1944), among many others]. Thus, the a priori case for unions as a source for labor market discrimination appears substantial.

There are, however, a number of counterarguments. First, unions have never organized a majority of the labor force in the United States, and before 1940 there were few periods during which more than 15 percent of the work force was covered by collective bargaining contracts. The wage gap between blacks and whites was larger in the pre-1940 period, although this fact by itself does not provide direct evidence on the influence of unions on the wage gap. In 1977, only around 25 percent of the labor force were union members or were covered by collective bargaining contracts [U.S. Department of Labor (1979)].

Second, membership in unions is more common among blue-collar workers, which points to a disproportionate representation among men and blacks, although within the blue-collar ranks membership is more common among skilled occupations, which points to a greater representation among white men. A larger proportion of black men were members of unions in 1977 than were white men [U.S. Department of Labor (1979)].

It is noteworthy that the few industries and occupations where unions have grown in recent years – governments, teaching, hospitals – are disproportionately composed of women or blacks. Ashenfelter (1972), whose study will be examined in the next section, concluded that the white–black wage gap among men was actually narrowed by unions as of the mid-1960s. The male–female gap was slightly widened. His study is persuasive that labor monopoly, despite many individual cases of discrimination by unions, is not a major source for the observed discriminatory differentials.

3.2.3. *Government as a monopolist*

Governments are universally monopolists in certain functions, such as providing for national defense, police and fire-fighting, and mail services, and, most importantly, as law-maker. With their power to tax and to punish, governments possess more potential monopoly power than firms and unions, although the collaboration between government and private agents may make it difficult to isolate the source of power. Moreover, governments, unlike private monopolies, need not be and seldom are guided by profit maximization goals. Granting that the majority group controls the government, there is no analytical challenge to demonstrating a theoretical case for discrimination based on government behavior. Malcolm Ross, the director of the Fair Employment Practices Commission during the 1940s, provides an example of a government law that, if it did not impose wage discrimination against blacks, at least impeded its demise. Ross's example also illustrates one expert's skepticism about the "physical-distance" theory of discrimination.

> White and Negro workers are now [1948] and have been for decades under the same plant roofs in the South. It is not the working associations to which the whites object. It is the sharing of skilled wage rates.... South Carolina...refuses by law to permit skilled Negro textile workers in the same plants with whites. But that state statute (probably unconstitutional) does permit Negro janitors and charwomen to work under the same textile plant roofs as whites. What would you say, then, that that South Carolina law is protecting – white workers from association with Negroes, or white jobs at the looms at white wages? [Ross (1948, p. 307)].

The scope, history, and literature of the government's influence on labor market discrimination are far too extensive to survey in this paper. Some discussion about government policies is reserved for the final section.

In this chapter I generally assume that government agencies do not have pervasive monopoly power regarding labor market discrimination, and that, historically, their interventions in the market have had many, but more or less offsetting, effects. In recent decades the intention of government policies has been to reduce discrimination against minorities, but the analysis is complicated by the claims that some actions, despite the beneficial intentions, turn out to worsen the problem. This criticism is frequently made about minimum wage and equal pay legislation. One fact and two theoretical-empirical points set the stage for this criticism.

Fact. The minority group is disproportionately represented in the lower tail of the distribution of productive skills, not because of an innate inferiority but because of a legacy of past inequities and prelabor-market discrimination.

Theoretical Case 1. Model (I) applies with the competitive result that minority workers receive an average pay equal to their average abilities (defined by X). However, the minimum-standards law truncates (from below) the distribution of X's among the work force, and relatively more members of the minority group are disemployed from the jobs covered by the legislation. Over the full distribution of the work force, minority workers are worse off, either because of their excess unemployment or because those disemployed from covered jobs are crowded into lower-paying jobs in the uncovered sector. Note that this case does not require any tastes for discrimination, although they would exacerbate the minorities' disadvantage (see Case 2).

Theoretical Case 2. Model (I) applies and majority workers receive a higher wage, conditioned on X, implying $A > 0$ and the existence of market discrimination. A minimum wage, w, can impede the competitive forces that encourage hiring lower-wage minority workers. Employers who might hire minority workers at a lower wage, $w - D$, are prevented from doing so. Case 2 does not require minorities to be concentrated in the lower half of the productivity distribution, but lower-skilled minority workers face the highest risk of being without a job. They are also prevented from competing for jobs that offer general on-the-job training by bidding for them with lower starting wages.

To illustrate either of the two cases, consider the following historical event, described by Ross (1948).

> During the First World War the Southern [railway] carriers lost a serious number of skilled workers to the services and munitions plants. In order to make it attractive to Negro workers to stay on the job, Secretary McAdoo as wartime transportation chief ruled that Negro railwaymen should receive the same pay as whites for the same work. This 1918 move was called "a simple act of justice," and so it was, although the far [long-run] results were anything but just.
>
> Forced to pay them the same wages as whites, the carriers lost interest in Negroes as a cheap labor supply. The white workers, for their part, began to covet the better Negro jobs. The McAdoo ruling had laid the foundation for a coalition between the carriers and the unions against Negroes in firemen's and other high-bracket positions (p. 119).

Blacks were driven out from these positions, but as Ross makes clear, the government ruling was only one part of the causal chain. Also contributing to the outcome were employer and worker prejudices, a quasi-monopolistic industry, the antiblack environment of the South, and a labor union.

3.3. *Stochastic neoclassical models and statistical discrimination*

The theoretical challenge developed in the preceding discussion of neoclassical models is to rationalize unequal pay to groups of workers who are equally productive. The comparison between groups was intended to allow within-group individual deviations from the equality between productivity and pay, which is necessary if the model of pricing is to apply to the real world. However, this stochastic feature was suppressed throughout the discussion, because the use of average values of the wages for comparisons between groups made the models equivalent to exact or nonstochastic models.

Attention to a stochastic model of wage determination, in which the worker's value to the employer is not known with certainty, offers several new insights, and more possibilities for sustained (or, at least, long-lived) group discrimination. Whether these theories are more or less persuasive than any of the others is a matter for judgment and empirical study.

Phelps (1972), Arrow (1972, 1973), and McCall (1972) were early authors. It is convenient to analyze the following model of wage determination, which is due to Phelps. Let q_i be the ith worker's true productivity, which is unknown to the employer, who must rely on some observed but imperfect indicator, y_i. The indicator may be a test score or a variable, like years of schooling, that has a more direct connection to productivity. The notation and details of the model below are shown in Aigner and Cain (1977), along with citations to various authors and statistical references.

In a simple specification that brings out the main conclusions of the approach, the relation between y and q (subscripts dropped) is

$$y = q + u, \tag{1}$$

with $E(u) = C(q, u) = 0$, $E(y) = E(q) = \alpha$, $V(u) = \sigma_u^2$, using the familiar symbols for expectation, covariance, and variance. By assuming q and u are joint-normally distributed as well as uncorrelated, we may specify a linear regression function for the reverse regression:

$$q = \alpha(1-\gamma) + \gamma y + e, \tag{2}$$

with e a well-behaved disturbance. Here γ is the coefficient of determination (r^2) between q and y; thus, $0 \leq \gamma \leq 1$, and γ measures the "reliability" of y as a measure of q.

Assuming employers pay workers according to their expected productivity, then

$$w = E(q|y) = \alpha(1-\gamma) + \gamma y. \tag{3}$$

Equations (2) and (3) reveal the obvious point that *individual* discrimination, defined as unequal pay for equally productive workers, is inevitable, given the error component, e. In contrast, *group* discrimination does not follow from this model precisely because e is considered random and has an expected value of zero for minority and majority groups.

Letting subscripts 0 and 1 refer to minority and majority groups, eq. (3) may be applied to each group. Assume temporarily that the minority and majority groups have the same mean true productivity: $\alpha = \alpha_0 = \alpha_1$, and that we compare workers with the same y-score. If we further assume that $V(q)$ is the same for both groups but that $V_0(u) > V_1(u)$, reasoning that the test instrument is more unreliable for the minority group, then $\gamma_1 > \gamma_0$, and we have

$$w_1 - w_0 = (y - \alpha)(\gamma_1 - \gamma_0). \tag{4}$$

Accordingly, for a given y-score [roughly corresponding to "holding X constant" in Model (I)], majority workers receive a higher wage than minority workers for y-scores above the mean, α, and lower wages for y-scores below the mean. Thus, group discrimination, defined by $E(w_1 - w_0) > 0$, is not present.

Clearly, postulating a lower α for minority workers would lead to their being paid a lower wage, but a lower wage for a given y-score, assuming y is a valid indicator of productivity (about which, see below), would not imply economic discrimination for the group because, on average, the minority and majority workers continue to be paid in accordance with their average productivity. In Figure 13.1, parts (a) and (b) show two cases for unequal α's. In part (a), where $\gamma_1 = \gamma_0$, the difference $\alpha_1 - \alpha_0$ is evenly distributed across all y-scores. In part (b), where $\gamma_1 > \gamma_0$, we see that the minority workers with high y-scores who are paid "too little" relative to majority workers with the same y-scores are balanced by the low-scoring minority workers who are paid "too much", relative to majority workers with the same low y-scores. As drawn in part (b), minority workers with y-scores below y' receive relatively higher wages than majority workers with the same y-score.

Nevertheless, a number of economists have claimed that this model reveals, and offers an explanation for, group discrimination. Let us examine two applications of the model. Only the second shows discrimination that is consistent with the definition adopted in this chapter.

3.3.1. *Statistical discrimination, but spurious group economic discrimination*

Thurow (1975) is one of many economists who use the term "statistical discrimination", when there is presumptively no economic discrimination. In the following example, Thurow accepts the facts of (a) a higher probability of market work by men compared with women and (b) the benefit to an employer of the higher probability. He then says:

> Any employer faced with these differences in work probabilities will practice statistical discrimination even though there are millions of women who will be in the full-time paid labor force for their entire lifetimes. *Ex ante*, he cannot tell which women will be lifetime year-around full-time employees and which women will leave the labor force or become part-time employees. Because the employer provides on-the-job-training, he will want to invest in those who are more likely to stay in the full-time labor force. If he provides training to

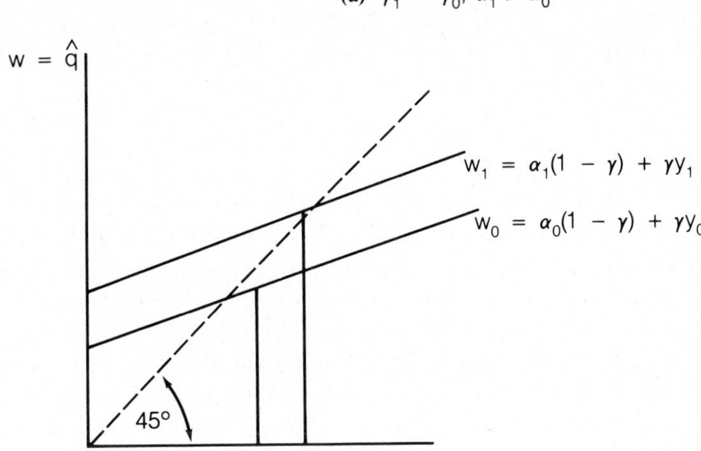

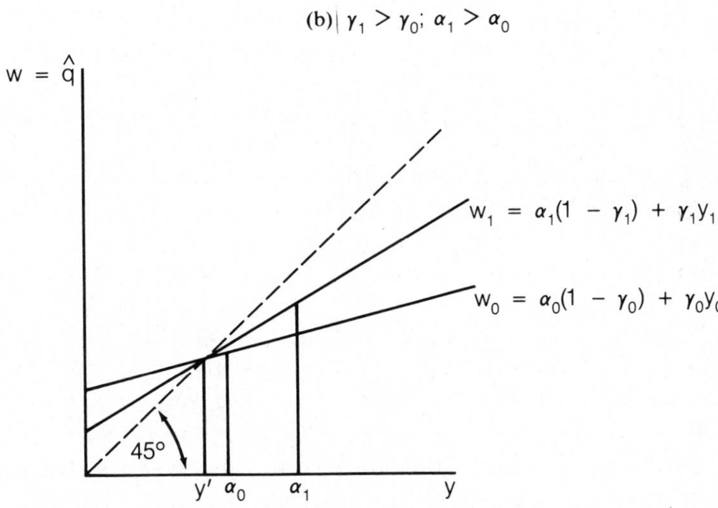

Figure 13.1. Predicted value of productivity (q) by indicator (y) for majority (1) and minority (0) workers.

> women, he is less likely to be able to recoup his investment.... The woman who will participate in the paid labor force her entire lifetime is being treated unfairly.... The net impact is discrimination against women as a group and as individuals even though there is not a basic taste for discrimination against women (p. 178).

Two points should show why this example does not imply group economic discrimination. First, Thurow correctly indicates that the women who will participate in the labor force their entire lifetimes are being treated unfairly and will be underpaid. The employers cannot know an individual's future, and they will base their wage offer partly on $\alpha_0(1-\gamma)$ – that is, partly on the known average for all women. But this is only half the story. Women who will participate for only the briefest period will be overpaid. As before, the employer, not knowing these women's true low probability of working, will rely upon the average for all women and overpay them. On average, the over- and underpayments tend to cancel out. Whether the resulting average is equal to the average for men will depend, as the next two paragraphs suggest, on whether the gender difference (here, a commitment to full-time work) is related to productivity.

Second, suppose all the workers are the same gender, that the two groups under study are persons with a college education and persons with less than a college education, and that the former have a higher probability of working on average. Thurow's entire passage could stand intact with the phrase, "persons with less than a college education", substituted for "women". Most analysts would agree that Thurow's case for group discrimination, even with the less-educated group earning less on average, loses its plausibility with this substitution.

Thurow's example inadvertently raises another interesting issue. The y-indicator in the stochastic model of wage determination is assumed to be unbiased on average, even though its reliability may differ for minority and majority workers. When, however, the y-indicator *reflects* discrimination, the model is no longer appropriate for an explanation of discrimination. In Thurow's example, the probability of working is, or could be, a reflection of discrimination. Clearly, if women or other minorities are discriminated against by not being employed, it is unsatisfactory to use the low probability of employment as an *explanation* for discrimination in the form, say, of lower wages or some other labor market outcome. This point will be discussed in Section 4, and here it serves to remind us that the choice of a y-indicator is not innocent.

3.3.2. *Statistical discrimination and actual group discrimination*

The discussion of the stochastic model up to now has not allowed the unreliability of the indicator to influence the average wage. Aigner and Cain (1977) stipulated risk aversion in the employer's utility (or profit) function and rationalized a lower average wage payment to minority workers as compensation for this undesired unreliability. A more convincing rationalization was suggested by Rothschild and Stiglitz (1982), who specified a production function that depended directly on matching the worker's q with a job assignment. In particular, both undermatching and overmatching were inefficient, so the expected output, not merely its variance, depended on matching.

Either formulation may be viewed as redefining the productivity of workers to include both the workers' physical productivity and the information workers convey about it. Does rewarding a group for their better information constitute economic discrimination against the group with less complete information? Perhaps the answer depends on the fairness of the testing system and, like the issue of the existing technology (see pp. 698–699), on how costly it is to change, and on whether its existing inadequacies for minorities reflect some market failure. The important role of the government in educating, training, certifying, and licensing workers suggests that improvements in testing minority workers may be a public good. (In fact, improvements in testing all workers may be a public good, but I focus here on discrimination between groups.)

If wage differentials are large merely because of differential test reliability, then both minority workers and employers have incentives to improve the tests and reduce this impediment to transactions. If, as is sometimes reasonable to assume, the worker knows his or her own abilities, a low-cost private-exchange method of minimizing this impediment is for workers to offer a trial period of employment to demonstrate their true productivity. The cost to the worker is a low wage during the trial period, but the benefits are higher earnings throughout the worker's subsequent career.

A trial period of working is also a device for minimizing the private and social costs of "signaling", as the term has come to be used following Spence (1973). Using Spence's model, we may assume that the test or y-score (a) has no value other than to indicate (signal) the worker's productivity, (b) is costly to obtain (as when the signal consists of an educational degree), and (c) is more costly to obtain for less productive (less able) workers. These assumptions imply that workers will choose whether to invest in the signal on the basis of their knowledge of their ability and on whether the extra pay the signal earns for them will justify its investment costs. Employers adapt to this maximizing behavior of workers by believing the signals and making their wage offers accordingly.

In Spence's model there is no guarantee that the equilibrium allocation of signaling investments among workers and, correspondingly, of workers to jobs is socially efficient, because only a "justifying" benefit/cost structure and not an "optimizing" one is required for an equilibrium. There is a tendency for too much investment in signaling; that is, Pareto-optimality could be achieved with less. Without an optimizing equilibrium there is no guarantee of a unique equilibrium. With multiple equilibria, the door is open for a benefit–cost structure that is unfavorable to a minority group compared to the majority group.

How robust is this discriminatory equilibrium? Even if one did not have faith that the competitive market would facilitate efficient signaling instruments and institutions, there remains the previously mentioned method of trial work periods based on deals struck between individual workers and employers. The strategy assumes that if the workers know enough about their ability to choose whether to invest in the signal, then they can use this knowledge to offer to work for the employer for a trial period. The strategy is better able to eliminate the Spence type of discrimination than it is to eliminate the Spence type of social inefficiency. Discrimination is eliminated if the cost to minority workers of the trial period is no higher than the cost of the majority worker's signal, even though these costs may still be higher than the socially efficient level.[12]

A recent paper by Lundberg and Startz (1983) uses certain features of both the Phelps model of unreliable indicators and the Spence theory of signaling. They derive a market failure in investment, although in contrast to Spence, too little investment occurs rather than too much. Their argument may be conveyed by reference to a commodity. Assume the commodity is produced at less quality than would be optimal, because the information about its quality cannot be conveyed perfectly. Specifically, the quality improvement could be produced at a cost that is less than the benefit, if only the quality improvement were accurately conveyed. Because the quality is imperfectly measured, however, consumers will discount the quality signal and will pay less than the costs of the optimal amount of the quality improvement. The situation is the same as in Model (3) above: employers pay γ (<1) for a unit more of y, instead of paying a full unit more as they would if y were a perfect measure of q.

Lundberg and Startz apply this argument to two groups of workers, minority and majority, and show that a less reliable signal for minority workers will lead them to underinvest relative to majority workers. Their general conclusion of underinvestment is opposite to that of Spence because of their contrasting assumptions about the benefits and costs of the investment. For Spence all or part of the benefits were merely in "signaling", whereas for Lundberg and Startz all of the benefits are in the form of enhanced productivity. For Spence, the costs of the investment varied inversely with the productive ability of the worker; for Lundberg and Startz, the costs are invariant with respect to the productive ability of the worker. Apparently, a proper mixture of the two sets of assumptions could yield optimal investment. Both models face the criticism that the employer's uncertainty about the productivity of workers may be inexpensively reduced by observing the worker's on-the-job performance.

[12]An illustration of the adaption of the Spence model to an equilibrium with no discrimination is available from the author. Also, see Riley (1975) for a critique of the robustness of Spence's conclusions about suboptimality.

Although I do not find the empirical counterparts to the models of statistical discrimination and signaling to be convincing in terms of the necessary empirical magnitudes of such variables as costs of information or in terms of behavioral patterns, what is considered convincing and realistic is a matter of judgment. Some readers may not view trial work periods as realistic. A rigid system of "tracking" newly hired workers, for example, could scuttle the strategy of trial work periods. Others may believe that government and union wage floors are pervasive and, in combination with the statistical model shown in part (b) of Figure 13.1, block the employment of minorities on a large scale. There is need for institutional knowledge and for judgments.

3.4. *Institutional theories of discrimination*

In his survey of the economics of racial discrimination, Marshall (1974) advocated an institutional theory of discrimination which, although presented as an alternative to neoclassical theories, could be viewed as a plea for more complementary attention to such factors as historical contexts, "pre-labor-market" discrimination against minorities, group bargaining, the psychological motives of the economic agents, monopoly elements, and a variety of societal factors Marshall classified as environmental. Some points are well taken, and few neoclassical economists would argue in principle against them. Others reflect certain misunderstandings. Neoclassical theory is not, for example, synonymous with perfect competition; monopolies, including labor unions and governments, are not ignored in neoclassical economics. Pre-labor-market discrimination is allowed for in Model (I), represented by group differences in X between the minority and majority workers. Many of the societal factors Marshall mentions (1974, p. 868), such as health, education, and business conditions, have all received considerable attention in the neoclassical literature.

The institutional approach sometimes cuts across several disciplines. One example is the reference to psychology and theories of adaptive behavior. Piore (1970) argues that the initial placement of disadvantaged workers into low-wage, low-status jobs creates attitudes and habits that perpetuate their low status. Arrow (1973) suggested a related model in which the psychological theory of cognitive dissonance rationalizes market exchanges that result in a suboptimal equilibrium. In essence, expectations are formed by employers about the inferiority of the group discriminated against, and the latter internalize these expectations and take actions – in particular, underinvest in human capital – which confirm those expectations. An objection to both versions of this pattern of self-injurious behavior is that the predicted behavior is obviously counter to the best interests of two key actors – the group discriminated against, whose members want to overturn the expectations, and employers, who ought to prefer to augment the supply of labor by encouraging more investment in human capital and positive attitudes towards investment and work.

Myrdal's (1944) classic work on discrimination included a similar model of feedback effects, in which economic, attitudinal, and health variables interact dynamically. An interventionist shock to any one of the variables sets in motion an upward or downward spiral of all the variables. Lundahl and Wadensjö (1984, pp. 16–18, 53) discuss Myrdal's model, including its similarity to Piore's, and point to its vulnerability to the criticism of instability. A corollary objection, similar to the one made in the preceding paragraph, is that the model's predicted consequences from a favorable shock are so obviously beneficial to the group discriminated against and to employers that it is difficult to see why the upward spiral would not quickly be initiated by group intervention. These criticisms apply, however, to the particular mathematical formulation of the model and not to the reasonable view that economic outcomes are determined by multiple causes, some of which are noneconomic, and that feedback relationships are part of reality.

If institutionalism refers to historical case studies, to details of the process by which equilibrium states (or tendencies) are reached, and to the interactions among organized and individual agents, then the approach – while not a theory, in my judgment – is always useful and sometimes indispensable. In the statistical studies that are discussed in some detail in the next section, there are often contexts in which various strata or segments of the full population are studied. The question arises: How were the individuals selected into these strata, and does the selection process either reflect discrimination or affect the interpretation we give to the analysis? For example, in studies of the effect of unions on the wage differential of black and white workers, institutional knowledge about the selection process into unions and how the process differs by race is necessary to interpret correctly the statistical estimations. Neoclassical economists are aware of the need for this information and, in one form or another, pay attention to the selection process [see Ashenfelter (1972), Becker (1959), Kessel (1958), Lewis (1959)], but they seldom have an absolute advantage in the institutional aspects of the problem. The legal and historical studies such as those of Gould (1977), Hill (1977), Marshall (1965), and Northrup (1944) are also useful.

Earlier, the institutional study by Ross (1948) was quoted to illustrate the harm done to black railway workers by the interactions of government wage-fixing (blocking the forces of wage competition), employer monopoly, Southern community prejudice, and an all-white labor union. Ross provides more institutional detail about this episode of discrimination that is worth retelling to remind those of us who work with austere models and simplified statistical specifications just how complex is the reality we are trying to capture. Ross recounts the advances made by black railway workers into the higher-paying jobs of firemen on the Southern railway carriers during World War I. Later, during two depression periods, 1921 and again in 1931, the white workers' grasp for these jobs reached an intensity that took on an all too typically American climax. I quote Ross:

> The depression of 1921 put many Negro and white workers on the street. There was violent competition to keep or grab places on any pay rolls. In 1921 there began a series of shootings from ambush at Negro firemen on Southern trains. Five were killed and eight wounded.... [In] the depression year of 1931...a Negro fireman, Clive Sims, was wounded on duty by a shot fired out of the dark beyond the track, the first of fourteen such attacks which stretched out over the next twelve months. This was not a racial outbreak in hot blood. It was a cold calculated effort to create vacancies for white firemen in the surest way possible, death, and, by stretching out the period of uncertainty and horror, to frighten away the others (pp. 119–120).

There are, as noted earlier, many theories or models that result in discriminatory outcomes. The challenge is to determine their quantitative importance. The instrument of terror, such as described above, no longer plays an important role in labor market discrimination. But even when this weapon is replaced with the milder instruments of racial and sexual harassments, we may find that the organized, sometimes conspiratorial, activities of majority workers and employers operate with a different set of rules than those we specify in our conventional economic models.

4. Empirical research on labor market discrimination

Aside from descriptive statistics, empirical research on economic discrimination may be divided into (1) tests of hypotheses suggested by the theories, such as the proposition that wage discrimination is less in competitive industries, and (2) estimation of the amount and determinants of discrimination; for example, estimating the effect of race on wages (the coefficient A) in a cross-section version of Model (I) (with productivity characteristics held constant), or estimating the change in the relative wages of minority workers over time.

4.1. Testing hypotheses suggested by theoretical models of discrimination

The hypothesis about labor market discrimination that has received the most attention is that discrimination is greater in monopolistic industries. An early empirical test is presented in Becker (1957, rev. ed. 1971, pp. 47–50). Many studies have followed.[13] I do not review this hypothesis and these studies mainly

[13] The following citations refer to studies, like Becker's, in which the proportion of minority-group employees in the firm, industry, or market is related to some measure of concentration (or degree of competitiveness): Comanor (1973), Oster (1975), and Luksetich (1979).

because I am uncomfortable with two links that connect the theory and the empirical evidence. First, I question whether product monopoly implies monopsony power in the labor market; the relevant labor market is usually a local area, and we have no assurance that monopsony power is highly correlated with the commonly used measures of monopoly, such as concentration ratios. This criticism, which applies to many of the previous studies, has been recently developed by Ashenfelter and Hannan (1986). Second, the desired theoretical measure of discrimination is the difference in minority/majority wages for equally productive workers, but most of the studies have used minority/majority employment differences (or ratios). While there is certainly interest in such employment ratios and associated measures of segregation as indicators of discrimination in the labor market, wage discrimination is not necessarily linked to segregation.

Aside from the studies of monopolies and discrimination, hypothesis testing has been, as Masters (1975, p. 19) noted, "surprisingly limited", and this type of study has produced few, if any, firm conclusions. In part this is because the theories often yield ambiguous predictions. For example, discrimination may be predicted to exist in the short run but not in the long run, but there may be no basis for determining the time required for the transition. Also, the theories suggest many economic influences, and the hypothesis test usually concentrates on one influence in isolation. The disappointing yield of most hypothesis testing may be conveyed by an examination of four studies.

(1) In his book, Reich (1981) criticized neoclassical theories of discrimination, provided tests of neoclassical hypotheses, and developed an alternative theory of discrimination that emphasized the role of class conflict between workers and capitalists. I focus solely on his test of Becker's model of employer discrimination in a competitive economy (pp. 109–163), which also appeared previously [Reich (1971)] and was discussed by Masters (1975, pp. 19–21). Reich claimed that Becker's model predicted a negative relation between (i) profits, which might more accurately be identified as the employers' return on their capital and their entrepreneurial skills, and (ii) the degree of discrimination, which is measured by and is inversely related to the ratio of blacks' wages to whites' wages, W_b/W_w, for equally productive black and white workers. An examination of Reich's analysis serves to illustrate several difficulties, listed as (a)–(c) below, in testing hypotheses.

(a) *The problem of ambiguity of theoretical predictions when, as shown in Section 3, there are many plausible outcomes, even within the neoclassical paradigm that Becker employed.* Reich claims that Becker's theory predicts that "white capitalists lose and white labor gains from racial discrimination" (1981, p. 111). This translates into a positive relation between profits and W_b/W_w. To see how this might occur, assume that white and black workers are equally productive, that their labor is inelastically supplied, that all employers have the same tastes for discrimination, and that employers' preferences for white workers lead to the ratio W_b/W_w being less than 1. Now assume that the tastes of employers change to a stronger preference for whites. This leads to a higher wage for white workers and lower money profits for employers. The decline in profits is offset by a higher psychic income to employers from their enhanced preference for white workers, thus maintaining the total returns on their capital and entrepreneurial skills.

We here encounter a distinction, not emphasized earlier, between whether the employers' preferences are pro-white or anti-black. Had the hypothesized example assumed a change in preferences by employers toward greater distaste for black workers, then W_b/W_w would still decline, but in this case W_b would fall and money profits rise – the latter offsetting a decline in the psychic income of employers. A focus on the wage ratio leaves us with an ambiguous interpretation.

There are other sources of ambiguity. The observed variables are profits and wages, and these are predicted to change in response to an unobserved change in employers' tastes. However, the observed variables may change for other reasons, with a different application or interpretation of Becker's model. Assume now that there is variation in employers' tastes for discrimination, but that the distribution of employers' tastes does not change from one period to another. If the ratio of black workers to white workers increases, Becker (1971, pp. 43–45 and 97) predicts a fall in W_b/W_w, because the employers with stronger tastes against blacks can only be induced to hire the increased number of blacks by a decline in W_b. In this case, money profits rise, offset again by a fall in the psychic income of the new employers who are hiring blacks. Thus, the predicted short-run result is a *negative* relation between profits and W_b/W_w – opposite of the implication Reich draws from Becker's theory.

(b) *The problem of ambiguity because the predictions depend on the length of the time period to which they apply and because the theory offers no guidance on the time required for certain forces to take effect.* Reich's test of the relation between profits and W_b/W_w is based on a 1960 cross-section of 48 standard metropolitan statistical areas (SMSAs). Each SMSA is designated as a separate labor market. The hypothesis Reich is testing is one that assumes that employers' tastes vary across markets and that their tastes cause the variation in W_b/W_w. In 7 of his 43 reported regressions Reich (1981, pp. 135–155) controlled statistically for the ratio of the black population to the white population in the market, so this source of variation in W_b/W_w was, in principle, neutralized in these 7 regressions. In the other 36 regressions one could argue that more black workers lower W_b/W_w and increase profits and that this negative relation is consistent with Becker's model for reasons discussed above. The simple correlation between W_b/W_w and the percentage nonwhite in the SMSA is -0.71 in Reich's sample (1981, p. 149).

In the seven regressions in which the percentage nonwhite is controlled, Reich finds a negative relation between profits and W_b/W_w, but whether this is inconsistent with Becker's model depends, as we have seen, on whether one assumes variation in pro-white or in anti-black tastes among employers. Another point is that in a cross-section any nonzero relation between profits and W_b/W_w may be viewed as a temporary disequilibrium, if the factors of production are mobile across SMSAs. Equally productive black (or white) workers would not remain in a market where they were underpaid relative to the wages available in other markets. Even though pervasive tastes against blacks by employers could lead to $W_b/W_w < 1$, the ratio should tend toward equality across markets if there is worker mobility. Alternatively, capital flows across markets will tend to equalize profit rates. If the profit variation is due to variation in employers' tastes, thereby allowing for the compensating variation in psychic income among employers, employers with the strongest tastes against blacks (or for whites) would tend to move to markets where blacks are relatively less numerous. Repeating the observation of Alchian and Kessel: "Free choice of economic activities implies a distribution of resources that would minimize the cost of satisfying tastes for discrimination" (1962, p. 161).

Neoclassical theories do not, however, tell us how long the equilibrating process will take, so tests involving SMSA data at a point in time could be thought of as either testing the competitive model or as testing the time of transition to equilibrium. Alternatively, a defender of a "sluggish" competitive model could test for the predicted equilibrating process by using SMSA data for two or more points in time.

(c) *The problem of matching the desired theoretical variables with the available empirical variables*. The hypothesis about the relation between profits and W_b/W_w for equally productive workers are actually tested by Reich by a regression between (i) a variety of measures of income inequality, such as the percentage share of all white incomes received by the top 1 percent of white families, S_1, or the Gini coefficient of white family incomes, G, and (ii) the ratio of black to white family income, Y_b/Y_w. The Gini coefficient is a commonly used measure of overall income inequality, which includes the earnings of white workers. Becker's theory of employer discrimination made no prediction about the effect of W_b/W_w on the inequality of white workers' earnings. Nor is it obvious that S_1 is a good measure of profits, because the incomes received by the richest 1 percent of families will include rents, interest payments, wage and salary earnings, and income from inherited wealth as well as current profits from businesses employing workers.[14]

The theoretical variable, W_b/W_w, may diverge from Y_b/Y_w, and Reich provided no control for the relative productivities of black and white workers by such conventional measures as the ratios of mean educational attainments, mean years of experience, and so on. Reich's control variables were measures of the

[14] It should be noted that Reich expressed interest in the relation between discrimination and overall white inequality, so my discussion is restricted to Reich's use of these inequality measures to test Becker's model.

overall occupational and industrial structure, the median family income of whites (Y_w), the percentage of the SMSA population that is black (although in only one regression were both this percentage and Y_w included), and a few others. Generally, Reich found a statistically significant negative relation between Y_b/Y_w and his profit proxies, G or S_1, which he interpreted as a refutation of Becker's model of a competitive economy and discrimination based on employers' tastes. In the light of the difficulties associated with items (a)–(c) above, I doubt that Becker's model was or can be well tested with such data.

(2) While Reich attempted to test for a relation between W_b/W_w and profits, sometimes controlling for the ratio of black workers to white workers, N_b/N_w, Landes (1968) and Flanagan (1973) drew upon Becker's theories to test for a negative relation between W_b/W_w and N_b/N_w. The justification from Becker's theory is as follows. Assume a distribution of employers' tastes for discrimination that is heterogeneous within a market and identical across markets. As we have seen, a larger N_b/N_w leads to a smaller W_b/W_w because the larger is N_b/N_w, the more are employers with stronger prejudices against blacks induced to hire black workers. The greater discrimination of these employers is manifest in a lower W_b/W_w, at least during the short run.

We have noted that mobility by black workers will tend to attenuate the negative relation between W_b/W_w and N_b/N_w, by tending to equate the ratios across markets. Also, there are institutional reasons for doubting the assumption of an identical distribution of tastes by employers across markets. Historically and in 1960, discrimination against blacks was most severe in the South, the region with the largest N_b/N_w. The legacy of slavery in the South was causal to both the discrimination and the residential location of blacks.

Scholars in other disciplines have debated how prejudice is related to N_b/N_w within a region. Perhaps prejudice is greater when N_b/N_w is greater because whites feel threatened by a larger ratio. On the other hand, perhaps the level of prejudice decreases as N_b/N_w rises because contact and familiarity erode unfavorable stereotypes and misunderstanding. In either case the level of tastes may change over time as experience with threats or with familiarity evolves. Thus, the basis for testing a version of Becker's theory that depends on identical distributions of tastes across markets appears questionable, although the empirical results of such tests are interesting on their own.

Landes (1968) found a negative correlation between W_b/W_w and N_b/N_w across all states, but the correlation was essentially zero within both the South and the non-South regions. However, this finding was secondary to Landes's main interest in the effects of antidiscrimination laws on W_b/W_w, so I examine the article by Flanagan (1973), whose main interest was to test the hypothesized negative relation between an occupation-specific W_b/W_w and an occupation-specific N_b/N_w. He used aggregated state data from the 1960 census for men in seven, and for women in five, broadly defined (one-digit) occupations. Other variables in the regressions were the black-to-white ratios of four variables – weeks worked, educational attainment, age composition, and median family income – and two nonratio variables – a dummy variable for the South and the percentage of the population that was foreign-born. No systematic relation between W_b/W_w and N_b/N_w was found. This may be evidence against Becker's theory, or it may be evidence against Flanagan's maintained assumption that the distributions of tastes of employers are identical across states, or it may be that a simultaneous relation between wages (prices) and the quantities of occupational skills prevents the identification of an effect of the quantity ratios on the wage ratios.[15]

(3) A study by Chiswick (1973) is unusual for its focus on Becker's model of workers', rather than employers', discrimination and on wage inequality among whites – a topic not treated by Becker. Essentially, Chiswick tests the hypothesis that a measure of the variance of white male incomes in a state is positively related to the percentage nonwhite in the state.

Chiswick begins with Becker's definition of worker discrimination: a wage, W, is paid to (demanded by) a white worker who works with white workers, and $(W+d)$ is paid to (demanded by) a white worker who works with black workers. As we have seen in Section 3, segregation could prevent the long-run maintenance of wage discrimination against blacks, but Chiswick argues that inequality of wages is likely to persist if some white workers have skills complementary to the skills of black workers. Chiswick offers the example of "foremen" and "laborers", presumably where whites are both foremen and laborers and blacks are only laborers (p. 1332).[16] Chiswick apparently rules out a segregated equilibrium in which there are some firms that hire only unskilled workers, who would be either all white or all black, and other firms that hire workers of both skills, who would be all white.[17]

Chiswick defines a dummy variable, X, as 1 if a white worker "works with nonwhites and ... zero if he does not" (p. 1333), and expresses the dual wage

[15] Flanagan notes the potential simultaneity problem and refers in a footnote to his consideration of it. However, not enough information is provided to determine if the simultaneity problem is adequately handled.

[16] The page numbers in parentheses in the text refer to Chiswick's article. Chiswick does not discuss the skill distribution of blacks or the possibility that blacks acquire skills. Note that if blacks acquire complementary skills, segregation could again eliminate racial discrimination in wages. Chiswick mentioned two other sources of integration in the work force besides complementarities in skills – unions and fair employment laws. The operations of these sources are not explained, except to note that they interfere with competitive market forces (p. 1332). Moreover, unions and fair employment laws are not mentioned again and play no role in Chiswick's empirical tests.

[17] Firms employing all unskilled workers will pay equal wages to black and white workers. Firms employing any white skilled workers will hire only white unskilled workers to keep their costs at a minimum, so an equilibrium requires that all firms hiring both skills to hire only white workers. All unskilled workers, white or black, would receive the same wage. But this scenario merely reflects the segregation equilibrium that Chiswick has ruled out. Thus, we need to assume, as Chiswick implicitly does, that all firms require both skills.

structure for whites as $W^* = W(1 + \mathrm{d}X)$, where W^* is the observed wage and W is the wage paid to the white worker who works only with whites. (A skill index, using a subscript for the jth skill, is omitted, and my symbols differ from Chiswick's.) The mean, $\bar{X}$, "is the proportion of the white labor force that works in an 'integrated' situation" (p. 1333), and Chiswick represents this by the percentage of nonwhites in the population, $p = (100)[N_b/(N_b + N_w)]$ (pp. 1334–1335).

The relationship between $\bar{X}$ and p may be justified by assuming that unskilled workers have tastes for discrimination, so competitive forces should lead to their segregation by race.[18] There would be no wage inequality among white unskilled workers (the laborers) within a market (or, for that matter, between markets – where a market is a state in Chiswick's formulation), at least as regards the effects of workers' tastes for discrimination. White skilled workers (foremen) would earn more if they worked in a firm with all-black unskilled workers than if they worked in an all-white firm, and labor costs would be equalized across firms by paying lower wages to black unskilled workers.

In this model and with the expectation that there are more firms with segregated unskilled workers in a state with a larger proportion of blacks, the mean wage of skilled workers should be positively correlated with p. This correlation identifies a direct test of Chiswick's model. A second direct test is the segregation of unskilled workers. I refer to these as direct tests because they involve cross-state comparisons of "first-order" effects on means and proportions rather than comparisons of "second-order" effects on within-state measures of inequality.

As noted in Section 3, the Becker-type models in which the skilled white workers have tastes for discrimination are similar to models with discriminating employers. Both agents are complementary to black labor. A long-run competitive equilibrium with discriminatory wage differentials paid to the skilled workers, like the long-run equilibrium with differential profits among employers, depends in both cases on homogeneity in the tastes of the discriminators. Or, expressed more cautiously, the tendency for discrimination to wither away depends on the existence of some nondiscriminating skilled workers (or employers) and on whether they can expand production to take advantage of their cost advantage.

Chiswick's empirical work focused on the variance of the logarithm of income for men aged 25 to 64, using midpoints of nine income classes, with an approximation for the mean of the highest, open-ended income class. This

[18] If the unskilled workers did not discriminate against each other, competitive forces would tend to make the proportion of black and white unskilled workers equal. Otherwise, either firms with more black workers would be at a competitive disadvantage – having to pay more to their skilled white workers – or blacks in firms with a larger proportion of blacks would be earning less than their counterparts in firms with a smaller proportion of blacks. See Arrow (1973, pp. 10–13) for a discussion of this case.

variable was regressed on p along with controls for several market sources of inequality in the form of variables involving the age, schooling, and weeks-worked distributions in the state and a variable defined as the rate of return on schooling in the state, which Chiswick had calculated in his previous research. Chiswick assumed that tastes for discrimination and p were uncorrelated. To make this assumption plausible, he separated the 17 Southern states from the non-Southern states. Chiswick found that white inequality was positively related to p, within both the South and non-South regions.

The causal inference seems shaky, but interpreting empirical tests that are indirect is always a matter of judgment. Here, p is an indirect measure of either the intensity of skilled workers' tastes against unskilled black workers or of the proportion of white skilled workers who receive higher wages by working with blacks, and the variance of income is an indirect measure of the skilled workers' wage inequality (since there should not be inequality among the white unskilled workers' wages). The regression for the South had only 8 degrees of freedom. In the 31 non-Southern states, there were only 13 where blacks were more than 3 percent of the population in 1960 [U.S. Bureau of the Census (1980, p. 36)]. The highest percentages, 8.0–10.0, were in the industrialized states: Illinois, Michigan, Missouri, New Jersey, New York, and Ohio. The lowest percentages, 0.1–0.9, were in relatively nonindustrialized states: Iowa, Idaho, Maine, Minnesota, Montana, New Hampshire, North Dakota, South Dakota, Utah, Vermont, and Wyoming. Thus, outside the South blacks were generally such a small proportion that it is difficult to see how they could have had much effect on white income inequality. Where they were a modest proportion, it was in states that tended to be more industrialized and densely populated.

Aside from how one might interpret Chiswick's regressions showing a positive relation between p and the variance of white incomes, I find them unconvincing as a test of Becker's model in the absence of direct information on how workers' tastes for discrimination affect (a) the segregation of workers and (b) the wages of white skilled workers who do and do not work with black unskilled workers. On this latter issue, Blau (1977, pp. 58–73) reports that in her study of labor market discrimination among several white-collar occupations, men who worked in integrated firms (with both men and women) received lower wages than men who worked in all-male firms, and she interpreted this as evidence against the hypothesis that workers' discriminatory tastes were causal to wage differentials.[19] A problem with these tests, however, is the necessary assumption that the integration measure (say, the proportion of blacks or women in a firm) is uncorrelated with the average skill level of the white or male workers whose wage is the dependent variable.

[19] In private correspondence, Chiswick cites an unpublished study by James Ragan that also uses data for individual firms and finds higher wages for whites who work in integrated firms. This finding was interpreted as supporting the Becker-type model of worker discrimination.

(4) The final example of hypothesis testing is Ashenfelter's (1972) analysis of the effect of unions on the white–black and male–female wage differences. The model of discrimination under competitive conditions, which appears fragile and difficult to test in the previous examples, is replaced here by the more robust theory of union gains and a somewhat tentative theory of racial and gender selection into unions. Specifically, it seems reasonable to assume that union-based noncompetitive wage differences across racial and gender groups can be sustained. The effect of union status on a worker's wage is estimated by a Model (I) regression function, which is applied separately to the four race–gender groups. Each of the four union effects (coefficients) is multiplied by the percentage unionized of each race–gender group to show the difference in wages across the groups that is attributable to unionism.

A numerical example is helpful. Assume that the effect of unions is to increase the wages of unionized black men by 10 percent relative to nonunion black men, while the corresponding effect for white men is 5 percent. Assume also that the proportion unionized is 20 percent for both racial groups. A first approximation to the union effect on W_b/W_w is obtained by assuming that the wages of nonunion workers, W^n, are equal to what the wages would be in the absence of unions. Let the wage ratio for nonunion workers, black-to-white, be 70/100. This can be compared to an estimated ratio for all workers, holding constant available productivity characteristics. This estimated ratio is calculated as a ratio of weighted averages of the wages of union and nonunion workers, using the percentage union, $U = 0.2$, and the percentage nonunion ($= 0.8$) as weights. Thus the estimated ratio for all workers, holding constant their productivity, is

$$\frac{\hat{W}_b}{\hat{W}_w} = \frac{(1-U)\hat{W}_b^n + U\hat{W}_b^u}{(1-U)\hat{W}_w^n + U\hat{W}_w^u} = \frac{0.8(70)+0.2(77)}{0.8(100)+0.2(105)} = \frac{71.4}{101.0} = 0.707.$$

We see in this example that unions increase the overall wage ratio by 0.007, or by 1 percent, relative to what it would be in the absence of unions.

Clearly, the overall impact of unions on the majority–minority differential by these calculations depends on the percentage of each group that is unionized and the wage effect of unionism for each group. If the union effects for both racial groups are 10 percent and the proportion unionized is 30 percent for blacks and 20 percent for whites, the same impact of unions on the black–white wage ratio would be obtained.

Calculations like these were carried out by Ashenfelter, who first obtained estimates for U, $\hat{W}^n$, and $\hat{W}^u$ for the four demographic groups. He added a refinement by computing estimates of $\hat{W}^n$ and $\hat{W}^u$ for major (one-digit) occupational groups and then summing these with weights for union and nonunion status that involve the proportion of the wage bill (total wages) received by each union-and-occupational group. Thus, instead of weighting the W's by U,

Ashenfelter used U^*, the proportion that union wages are of the total wage bill earned by whites (or blacks). The U^* values are larger than the U values, especially for blacks. The low percentage unionized of both blacks and whites in the higher-paying white-collar occupations carries a low weight for blacks relative to whites because relatively few blacks are in these occupations. Thus, although 23 percent of black workers in Ashenfelter's principal sample are union members, about 34 percent of the black wage bill is from black unionized workers. The comparable figures for whites are 23 percent and 31 percent.[20]

Using U^*, Ashenfelter concluded that "the ratio of black to white male wages may have been some 3.4 percent higher in 1967 than it would have been in the absence of all unionism" (p. 463). The ratio of female to male wages was estimated to be 1.9 percent lower than it would have been in the absence of unions (p. 453, n. 33). The 3.4 percent gain to blacks reflects a differential effect of unions in favor of blacks by about 11 percentage points – a 21 percent effect for black men and a 10 percent effect for white men (p. 450). An illustrative weighted average for men is

$$\frac{\hat{W}_{\mathrm{b}}}{\hat{W}_{\mathrm{w}}}=\frac{0.66(70)+0.34(84.7)}{0.69(100)+0.31(110.0)}=\frac{75}{103.1}=0.727,$$

which is 3.9 percent larger than the estimated wage ratio in the absence of unions, 0.7. Using the unrefined union weights, $U = 23$ percent for both blacks and whites, the weighted ratio would be 0.717, which is a little over 2 percent larger than 0.7.

These findings are evidence against the hypothesis that unionism in the United States, as measured during the 1960s, is responsible for the discriminatory wage differential in favor of whites or, with weaker evidence, in favor of men. The data on union membership by demographic groups are not controversial, and Ashenfelter provides alternative estimates of the effects of unions on wages, based on his own analysis of other data sources and on the existing literature. Overall, these checks were supportive. Ashenfelter reminds the reader that his evidence does not say that unions are nondiscriminatory; rather that they are shown to be no more discriminatory, or even less regarding blacks, than the economy as a whole.

The validity of Ashenfelter's estimates of union effects depends on two key assumptions. The first is that the estimates of union effects on union workers are either unbiased or that they are biased equally for majority and minority groups (hereafter, white and black men). The general issue concerning a bias is that

[20] These percentages are calculated using Tables 6 and 7 in Ashenfelter (1972), although I adjusted the weights in Table 7 for whites to make them sum to 1. Apparently there is an error in Table 7 for white workers, because the proportions sum to 1.072 instead of 1.00. I reduced each occupation's proportion in the table by 0.92 ($=1.00/1.072$). In my calculation of U^* I assume that the percentage unionized for private household workers and farm workers is zero for both color groups.

union status may be correlated with unmeasured productivity variables, leading to a misestimate of the true effect of unions. As stated, the bias could be positive or negative, depending on whether union workers were, holding constant the control variables in the model, less productive (owing to, say, nepotism or perhaps because unambitious workers are more attracted to unionism) or more productive (due, say, to the commitment of union workers to their trades or because employers will select high-quality workers when faced with union-imposed above-competitive wages and because high-quality workers will seek these positions). To sharpen my argument and shorten the discussion, let me assume that the net bias in the union effect is positive, and the coefficients of union status on wages, 10 percent for whites and 21 percent for blacks, are both too high. Clearly, the issue for Ashenfelter's measure of the union impact on W_b/W_w is whether the bias is larger – really, much larger – for blacks than whites.

I now argue that the bias is larger for black men and against Ashenfelter's assumption that wages of nonunion workers represent what the wages would be in the absence of unions. Assume that the jobs in the union sector are medium-paying jobs in the crafts and operative occupations for both white and black men, whereas jobs in the nonunion sector are predominantly high-paying professional, technical, managerial, and sales jobs for white men, but predominantly low-paying laborer and unskilled service jobs for black men. Skill levels of the jobs are assumed to be correlated with the skill abilities of workers, both innate and acquired. Assume that these contrasting alternatives to whites and blacks regarding nonunion jobs are entirely attributable to "pre-labor-market discrimination", which is to say that they are reflections of differential family socioeconomic backgrounds, quality and quantity of schooling, and wealth constraints on the long-term investments required for the high-paying jobs. Assume further that the distributions of innate ability (intelligence, "ambition", and so on) are identical for whites and blacks. Given these assumptions, it is reasonable to believe that if unions were nondiscriminatory then black males would be more represented in the union jobs because black workers of above-average ability are constrained from entering the highest-paying jobs but not (by assumption) from crafts and operative jobs, and they will therefore gravitate toward the better-paying crafts and operative jobs. The presence of unions restricts numbers of both blacks and whites, but the restrictions are more binding on blacks, since the excluded higher-ability white workers will have the highest occupations open to them. Thus, not only should the unionized percentages be higher for blacks in a nondiscriminatory labor market, but the effect of union status on wages will tend to be more upward-biased for blacks. The latter bias stems from the presumption that the omitted innate ability is, on average, higher for black union members than for white union members. Ashenfelter's model assumes that the occupational distribution of blacks and whites is given, and the foregoing argument suggests that it is affected by unionism.

The arguments above are admittedly speculative. An upward bias in the estimated union effect, however, has the theoretical justification that employers should respond to union-imposed high wages by upgrading their hiring and retention standards. Generally, unionized employers do have control over hiring, and they have some control over retention, at least through some probationary period before union-imposed seniority protection commences. On the other hand, arguments in favor of Ashenfelter's conclusion are the following. (a) The above scenario denied any role to labor market discrimination for the disproportionately low representation of black men in the white-collar occupations, and this denial is hard to accept. (b) For a reduction in unionism to lead to relatively more occupational upgrading among blacks than whites among the blue-collar occupations, one must assume that the general sources of labor market discrimination would not maintain the existing distribution. (c) Ashenfelter's estimated union effects on wages would have to be drastically changed to reverse his conclusion of a beneficial wage-effect for blacks among unionized workers. Recall that his union effect for blacks (21 percent) is twice that for whites (10 percent).

Finally, Ashenfelter's rejection of the hypothesis that W_b/W_w would be higher without unions is strengthened by his institutional and historical discussion about union race policies. For historical reasons, unionism is more widespread among the blue-collar occupations, and blacks are more likely to be competing for jobs requiring less skill. Thus, Ashenfelter argues that because unions of lesser-skilled workers will have more blacks in their jurisdiction, competitive forces will tend to force the unions to include blacks. Among blue-collar occupations, therefore, whites will be over-represented in the unionized skilled jobs and underrepresented in the unionized lesser-skilled jobs, relative to blacks. An overall tendency for equality in the incidence of union membership among whites and blacks is, therefore, plausible.

The remaining parameter of interest, the union-effect differential, is, however, puzzling on theoretical grounds. Ashenfelter's arguments (p. 447) about the potential power of the skilled trades to be more restrictive in controlling the supply of labor should be supported by larger union effects (rents) for the more skilled groups. This result would indeed be consistent with the a priori Marshallian arguments, found in almost every labor economics textbook, in which skilled workers face a more inelastic demand curve and therefore have more "bargaining power". As noted above, this result is not found by Ashenfelter, nor by other recent analysts of union effects. [See the studies Ashenfelter cites in his Table 3, p. 446; Johnson (1975), and others.][21] Thus, the large union

[21] To be more precise, my claim is that Ashenfelter and others have found an overall negative correlation between union effects and skill levels, even though the construction trades, airline pilots, and some other crafts have shown large union effects. Among white construction workers, incidentally, the union effects of laborers exceed those of skilled workers [see Ashenfelter (1972, Table 5, p. 450)].

effects for blacks, relative to whites, is consistent with the larger union effects for lesser-skilled blue-collar workers, but the latter union effect remains a puzzle.

4.2. *Estimating labor market discrimination*

4.2.1. *Methodological points*

Model (I) (in Section 2) is the basic model used to estimate labor market discrimination. Its widespread use along with several conventions that are customarily adopted permits a succinct summary of results, shown in Tables 13.6 and 13.7 in the next section. Unfortunately, the results are so varied that they reveal as much about our ignorance as about our knowledge of the degree of labor market discrimination against blacks and women. This variability is not really surprising in light of the theoretical vagueness that underlies most of the empirical specifications.

An inherent ambiguity, mentioned earlier (Section 2), stems from the absence of agreement on what productivity traits – the X's in Model (I) – are appropriately held constant. The criterion I suggested is that the variables held constant in Model (I) should *not* be determined by the process of discrimination under analysis. Applying the criterion requires a clear statement of the purposes of the estimations, but this is seldom provided. Perhaps the marketwide regression studies of wage discrimination are merely intended to provide a general social indicator of inequity in the economy, although this is ambiguous unless we know what counterfactual regime is being compared to the current regime. This counterfactual is usually only implicitly revealed by the set of X-variables that have been held constant, and there is seldom discussion of whether the X's are affected by labor market discrimination.[22] Predictions using the regression results are not often explored, and specific remedies or policies to deal with discrimination are seldom linked to the regression results. To clarify some of these issues, consider the following two applications of the criterion suggested above.

Case 1. Assume the analysis pertains to a given employer or firm, and that we ask whether white workers are paid more than black workers after holding constant the available productivity variables. Assume further that a panel of experts provides us with the worker characteristics that determine productivity in the firm. The productivity variables might include previous vocational training, tests of manual dexterity, age, years of schooling, and so on. To meet the above criterion, each variable should be exogenous to the employer; that is, the

[22] Blinder (1973) is exceptional in his clear distinctions between the Xs that are assumed exogenous and those that are endogenous according to current theories of labor market behavior, specifically the theory of human capital.

characteristic should not be affected by the employer's behavior. If it were, it might reflect discrimination. Thus, a variable defined as "task-specific ability" that is measured by "supervisor's rating" would be suspect, and perhaps not admissible. Clearly, the presumptive identification of supervisors with management raises suspicions about the unbiasedness of supervisors' ratings. On the other hand, if we knew that supervisors were nondiscriminatory, their ratings would provide direct evidence of the workers' productivity, which is usually difficult to obtain and certainly preferable to the indirect evidence from such variables as age and education.

Case 2. Assume the analysis pertains to the entire labor market. We ask whether white workers are paid more than black workers after holding constant an admissible set of productivity variables that are not affected by the process of discrimination under analysis. Because the entire labor market is under analysis, however, variables like "previous training" almost surely reflect previous discrimination in the labor market, so they are not admissible.

There is no simple rule in marketwide studies for determining when a variable may be appropriately held constant. Among the variables mentioned in Case 1, age is clearly exogenous. Years of schooling are appropriately held constant if we believe that the decision to attain schooling does not reflect discrimination in the labor market. Perhaps the lower education among minorities reflects societal discrimination – not labor market discrimination but "pre-labor-market discrimination". Alternatively, perhaps blacks and women perceive that higher levels of schooling yield smaller earnings for them than for white men. If this were true, then these groups may have curtailed their schooling, in which case educational attainment would reflect labor market discrimination. Determining the productivity variables that are admissible is the first step in estimating Model (I). Accurate measures of the agreed-upon variables are also needed.

Let us turn now from the conceptual issues in estimation to the mechanics of the statistical methods. The regression specifications for Model (I) that produce the estimates of labor market discrimination in the recent research literature usually involve the following assumptions and procedures.

(i) Separate regression functions are estimated for majority (hereafter white, w) and minority (hereafter black, b) groups. The equations omit the subscripts denoting the observation. The explanatory X-variables measuring productivity traits, and the B-coefficient of each X are collectively represented by $\sum BX$.

$$\hat{W}_{\mathrm{w}} = \sum B_{\mathrm{w}} X_{\mathrm{w}} \quad \text{and} \quad \overline{W}_{\mathrm{w}} = \overline{\hat{W}}_{\mathrm{w}} = \sum B_{\mathrm{w}} \overline{X}_{\mathrm{w}}, \tag{5}$$

$$\hat{W}_{\mathrm{b}} = \sum B_{\mathrm{b}} X_{\mathrm{b}} \quad \text{and} \quad \overline{W}_{\mathrm{b}} = \overline{\hat{W}}_{\mathrm{b}} = \sum B_{\mathrm{b}} \overline{X}_{\mathrm{b}}. \tag{6}$$

The caret indicates predicted value, the mean of which, $\overline{\hat{W}}$, is identically equal to the overall mean, $\overline{W}$. The intercept term in the equation is included in $\sum BX$ and may be associated with an element in the X-vector for which $X_b = X_w = 1$ for each observation.[23]

(ii) Equations (5) and (6) are used to express eq. (7), which is a particular decomposition of the difference in mean wages obtained by adding the term $\sum B_w \overline{X}_b$ to both (5) and (6) and then subtracting (6) from (5):

$$\overline{W}_w - \overline{W}_b = \sum B_w(\overline{X}_w - \overline{X}_b) + \sum \overline{X}_b(B_w - B_b). \tag{7}$$

The firm term on the right-hand side of (7) evaluates the difference in mean values of the X's at white "prices" (B_w's), and the second term evaluates the racial price differences at the mean value of the black X's. It turns out that, on average, $\overline{X}_w > \overline{X}_b$ and $B_w > B_b$; more precisely, that $\sum B_w \overline{X}_w > \sum B_b \overline{X}_b$.

(iii) The second term on the right-hand side of (7) is a conventional measure of labor market discrimination, with $B_w > B_b$ representing a higher price received by a white worker than by a black worker for the (assumed) same productivity characteristic. The first term on the right-hand side of (7) involves the racial differences in X's and does not have a clear interpretation. It may represent a source of a nondiscriminatory difference in wages, because only one price is used to evaluate different amounts of exogenous productivity characteristics. Or, it could measure the difference in wages attributable to pre-labor-market discrimination, which may explain why $\overline{X}_w > \overline{X}_b$. In any case, the conventional standard of nondiscrimination is achieved when $\hat{W}_b / \hat{W}_w = 1$, holding the X's constant.

(iv) An important reservation about the decomposition in (7) is that it is not unique. Each difference, $B_w - B_b$, in the second term is evaluated as a product with $\overline{X}_b$, but the evaluation might have used $\overline{X}_w$ or some average of $\overline{X}_b$ and $\overline{X}_w$. Similarly, the use of B_w as a weight for the first term, $\overline{X}_w - \overline{X}_b$, is also arbitrary. A different decomposition of $\overline{W}_w - \overline{W}_b$ is obtained by adding the term $\sum B_b \overline{X}_w$ to both (5) and (6) and subtracting (6) from (5):

$$\overline{W}_w - \overline{W}_b = \sum B_b(\overline{X}_w - \overline{X}_b) + \sum \overline{X}_w(B_w - B_b). \tag{7'}$$

The different standardizations shown by (7) and (7′) reflect the familiar index-number problem encountered whenever heterogeneous collections of goods

[23] Blinder (1973, pp. 438–439) separated the intercept terms from other B-coefficients and specified them as two components of discrimination. This procedure is not necessary or even helpful, because the value of the intercept term will depend on the arbitrary scaling of the X-variables. Consider, for example, the arbitrariness of defining a variable like region of residence into a set of dummy variables, where the intercept will represent the excluded region. Which region is to be excluded is arbitrary. See Jones (1983) for further discussion of the point.

(X's) are summed with two sets of prices (B's).[24] In the simplest case in which all prices are the same for both racial groups, the difference $\overline{W}_w - \overline{W}_b$ is simply equal to the first term on the right-hand side of (7), and the conceptual experiment of assigning equal X's to both racial groups leaves only the difference in intercept terms, which measures a vertical difference in $\hat{W}$ between two "parallel" linear functions. Such a difference in intercept terms is what was previously measured by the coefficients A or C on the dummy variables for group status in Models (I) and (II) in Section 2.

(v) I will rely on the following expressions for summarizing the various estimates of eqs. (5) and (6) reported in the literature:

$$\text{(i)}\quad U_r = \overline{W}_b / \overline{W}_w = \text{the unadjusted ratio,}$$

$$\text{(ii)}\quad A_r = \textstyle\sum B_b \overline{X}_w / \sum B_w \overline{X}_w = \sum B_b \overline{X}_w / \overline{W}_w,$$

which is an "adjusted ratio", obtained from either (7) or (7′). To arrive at (ii), simply set (or assume) all $\overline{X}_b$ equal to $\overline{X}_w$ to eliminate the first term of the decompositions in (7) or (7′) and to reduce the right-hand side to its discrimination component. Then divide through by $\overline{W}_w$ and simplify to express the following equation of ratios: $A_r = \overline{W}_b' / \overline{W}_w$, where $\overline{W}_b'$ is the black mean wage conditional on the black $\overline{X}$'s being set equal to the white $\overline{X}$'s. $A_r = 1$ implies no discrimination. The amount by which the controls for X have closed the gap between unity and U_r is the sometimes-used statistic

$$\text{(iii)}\quad G = [(1 - A_r)/(1 - U_r)]100,$$

called the percentage of the gap between U_r and 1 that is attributable to the difference in the X's. Thus, $1 - G$ is the percentage of the gap that is attributable to labor market discrimination.

For simplicity, I will restrict my discussion of empirical results to the adjusted and unadjusted ratios, A_r and U_r. Even here, it is somewhat arbitrary to use A_r as defined by (ii), because we could have defined

$$\text{(ii}'\text{)}\quad A_r' = \textstyle\sum B_b \overline{X}_b / \sum B_w \overline{X}_b = \overline{W}_b / \sum B_w \overline{X}_b,$$

which, like A_r, holds the $\overline{X}$'s constant and attributes the remaining differences in black and white average wages to the B's, but here the B's are multiplied by $\overline{X}_b$

[24] Blinder (1973, p. 438, n. 3) suggested that the decomposition expressed by eq. (7) is preferred to that of (7′) because he claimed that the decomposition using black prices (B_b's) as weights for the difference in X's leaves an interaction term as a residual, in contrast with the decomposition using white prices (B_w's) as weights. This is incorrect. There is no difference in the two decomposition methods in this respect.

levels. Usually A_r is presented, because the conceptual experiment of raising $\overline{X}_b$ to the levels of $\overline{X}_w$ is more appealing and more policy-relevant than lowering $\overline{X}_w$ to $\overline{X}_b$ levels as is done with A'_r. Nevertheless, it is easy to construct examples in which the regression results give qualitatively different measures of wage discrimination on the basis of A_r and A'_r. One may equal unity and the other may exceed or fall short of unity. The quantity $A_r - U_r$ may be positive, showing that the X's "explain" some of the gap (assuming $U_r < 1$), whereas $A'_r - U_r$ may be negative, showing that the gap is made even wider after controlling for the X's and using this standardization.

At the risk of belaboring the obvious, I will use the constructs of A_r and A'_r to illustrate two points. One is the potential ambiguity of these ratios as measures of discrimination, and the second is that some institutional knowledge of the process by which discrimination occurs is necessary if the statistical measures are to tell us anything.

Assume eqs. (8) and (9) refer to males (subscript m) and females (subscript f) and that the only explanatory variable, X, in the wage function is the number of young children present in the household of the worker. The wage functions, evaluated at means, are

$$\overline{W}_m = B_{0m} + B_{1m}\overline{X}_m = 10 + 1(\overline{X}_m = 2) = 12, \tag{8}$$

$$\overline{W}_f = B_{0f} + B_{1f}\overline{X}_f = 9 - 1(\overline{X}_f = 1) = 8. \tag{9}$$

In eq. (8), I assume that all men are working, that they are in families with an average of two young children, and that the presence of young children has a positive effect on the wages earned by the men. (Perhaps additional dependents lead them to work harder.) Eq. (9) is assumed to express the wage equation for employed women. I assume that half the women are employed (and thus have a market wage), that women with fewer young children are more likely to be in the labor force, and that the presence of children is negatively related to the wages of women, which is discussed below.

Clearly, $A_r = \Sigma B_f \overline{X}_m / \overline{W}_m = 7/12 = 0.58$, and $A_r - U_r = 0.58 - 0.67 = -0.09$. Thus, the unadjusted ratio is higher than the adjusted ratio. The women's wage would be less than their current wage if they had the same values of X as men, so we may conclude that discrimination is even more severe than shown by the unadjusted wages.

On the other hand, $A'_r = \overline{W}_f / \Sigma B_m \overline{X}_f = 8/11 = 0.73$, and $A'_r - U_r = 0.73 - 0.67 = 0.06$. This shows that discrimination against women would be less if men had the same values of X as women. Since the regression method shows that discrimination is both worse and better than the unadjusted wage comparisons, what should we conclude? Or, consider the following specification:

$$\overline{W}_m = 6 + 1(\overline{X}_m = 2) = 8 \tag{10}$$

and

$$\overline{W}_{\mathrm{f}} = 9 - 1(\overline{X}_{\mathrm{f}} = 1) = 8. \tag{11}$$

A_{r} ($= 0.875$) shows discrimination against women, whereas A'_{r} ($=1.14$) shows discrimination against men.

The statistical procedures cannot tell us the correct answer. Let us consider two hypothetical processes by which employers pay wages to examine how we might determine whether there is discrimination.

Case 1. Assume men and women are equally productive, but that employers discriminate against women with children, as shown in (9) or (11). Let us assume that children have no real effect on productivity of either men or women but that employers have a uniform preference for paying men with children more and women with children less. Both sets of equations, (8)–(9) and (10)–(11), show this discriminatory behavior, and constructing ratios and making decompositions do not add to our knowledge.

Equations (10)–(11) do not show a gender difference in average wages, but one could argue that the discrimination against women with children expressed in (11) is a cause of the low labor force participation of women. Assume that all women enter the labor market and that demand conditions remain the same. Then (11) becomes $\overline{W}_{\mathrm{f}} = 9 - 1(\overline{X}_{\mathrm{f}} = 2) = 7$, and U_{r} becomes $7/8 = 0.875$. The discrimination, expressed in (11) and revealed by a "potential" $U_{\mathrm{r}} < 1$ for the full population, is a cause of the fact that only half the women are working. This is a reminder that the values of the X's may reflect discrimination and are not always exogenous to the process under study.

Case 2. Assume that men and women have the same productive capacity, but women with children are less committed to market work than women with no children, and men with no children are less committed to their jobs than men with children. If these commitments reflect people's preferences about how they want to live, and if the presence of children is an accurate signal of this commitment, then there is no presumption of discrimination. The two sets of equations show the relation between productivity (commitment) and children and also show how the relation differs for men and women. Again, the ratios A'_{r} and A_{r} do not add anything useful to our knowledge.

The message is that the original data and statistical functions are mere description. Knowledge of the process by which wages are set and, perhaps, by which workers are selected into the market are necessary.

4.2.2. *A survey of selected estimated wage functions*

In contrast to the research that tests hypotheses, the studies presenting empirical estimates of labor market discrimination are numerous. Only about 20 of these studies are selected for mention in this section, and they will be summarized in two tables. Methodological issues are emphasized to aid in understanding the strengths and weaknesses of the research and its theoretical and policy content. In addition, these empirical studies contain useful descriptive statistics.

Labor market discrimination, or wage discrimination, has been defined in this paper by using Model (I) to isolate the net effect of minority-group status on wages, holding constant the productivity characteristics of the workers. Two crucial questions invariably arise: (a) Do the variables measuring productivity *reflect* discrimination? (b) Do the variables measure productivity comprehensively, aside from factors that can be assumed to be random with respect to group status? If the answer to (a) is yes, we may presume that the estimate understates discrimination. If the answer to (b) is no, the estimate of discrimination may be biased up or down. To avoid prejudging these answers, I will use the term "wage gap" rather than "wage discrimination". The wage gap will be measured by the unadjusted ratio, U_r, and by the adjusted ratio, A_r (or, rarely, A'_r).

The estimated wage gaps are based on cross-section or time-series studies, which were the classifications used in the descriptive statistics presented in Section 2. Cross-section studies generally are interpreted as representing normal or equilibrium conditions. Trends over time may be inferred from successive cross-sections, allowing for changing compositional effects (like the age distribution) or specific period effects (such as the business cycle). Trends may be directly measured in a time series by introducing time as an independent variable and determining if its effect differs for the different groups, but time-series studies are hampered by the fewness of observations. Almost all the empirical work in the published literature uses cross-sectional data, and this section will be devoted to these, leaving the few time-series studies for the final section on policy analysis.

Another classification of the studies is by the type of minority and majority groups being compared, and I will continue to focus on black–white and women–men comparisons. Some estimates of wage gaps according to national origins and religions will be briefly mentioned.

I also concentrate on studies that intend to estimate the overall wage gap, rather than on studies that focus on the differential effects on wages of particular variables, like education, years of work experience, union status, or participation in some government program. Finally, I concentrate on studies that measure the wage gap for the entire labor force, or at least for large groups in the labor force. Only limited attention is given to the many studies of the wage gap within individual firms or within occupations.

4.2.2.1. Comparisons of the earnings gap between women and men. A summary of studies of the wage gap between women and men is shown in Table 13.6. The wage is, as discussed below, the most appropriate simple measure for examining

Table 13.6
Summary of studies of ratios of women's earnings to men's earnings, unadjusted and adjusted for various characteristics of workers and jobs.

Author and year of publication[a]	Data source and population studied[b]	Measure of earnings[c]	Statistical method and explanatory variables[d]	Women's earnings as a ratio of men's	
				Observed[e] $= U_r$	Adjusted[f] $= A_r$
Gwartney and Stroup (1973)	Census, age 25+ with positive incomes	$\bar{y}$, 1959 $\bar{y}$, 1969	T, R: 1, 2 (grouped data)	0.33 0.32	0.39 0.40
Featherman and Hauser (1976)	OCG, married workers	y, 1961 1972	R, S: 1, (2), 7, 23	0.38	0.48*
Blinder (1973)	PSID, white working household heads and spouses, age 25+	w, 1969	R, S: 2, (3), 9, 12–14, 32, 34	0.54	0.54
Sawhill (1973)	CPS, wage and salary workers, age 14+	y, 1966	R: 1, 3, 10 13	0.46	0.56
Gwartney and Stroup (1973)	Census, age 25+, full-time, year-round workers	$\bar{y}_f$, 1959	T, R: 1, 2, (10)	0.56	0.58
Suter and Miller (1973)	NLS, CPS wage-and-salary workers, age 30–44	y, 1966	R, S: 1, (2), 6, 10, 23	0.39	0.62*
Roos (1981)	GSS, white workers, age 25–64	y, 1974–1977	R, S.: 1, 2, 10, 22, 23, 26, 29–31	0.46	0.63*
Fuchs (1971)	Census (1/1000 sample), nonfarm workers	w, 1959	R: 1, 2, 3, 8, 12, 25, 33	0.60	0.66
Treiman and Terrell (1975)	NLS: married workers, age 30–44: white nonwhite	y, 1966	R, S: 1, (2), 6, 7, 10, 17, 22	0.42 0.54	0.67 0.68
Cohen (1971)	Survey of working conditions, full-time nonprofessional wage-and-salary workers, age 22–64	y_f, 1969	R, S.: 1, 2, 10, 11, 16, 24, 27, 28	0.55	0.69
Blinder (1973)	PSID: white, working household heads and spouses, age 25+	w, 1969	R, S.: 1, 2, (3), 5, 9, 11–14, 21, 27, 32, 34	0.54	0.70*
Oaxaca (1973)	SEO, urban workers, age 16+ white nonwhite	w, 1967	R, S.: 1(2), 3, 7–10, 12, 13	0.65 0.67	0.72 0.69
Sanborn (1964)	Census, wage and salary workers	$\bar{y}$, 1949	T: 1, 2, 3, 10, 18, 20	0.58	0.76*
Oaxaca (1973)	SEO, urban workers, age 16+ white nonwhite	w, 1967	R, S.: 1, (2), 3, 7–10, 12, 13, 21, 25–27	0.65 0.67	0.78* 0.80*

Table 13.6 continued

Author and year of publication[a]	Data source and population studied[b]	Measure of earnings[c]	Statistical method and explanatory variables[d]	Women's earnings as a ratio of men's: Observed[e] $= U_r$	Adjusted[f] $= A_r$
Kohen and Roderick (1975)	NLS, full-time wage and salary workers, age 18–25	w_f, 1968–1969	R, S: 1, 3, 4, 7–9, 13–15		
	white			0.76	0.78
	black			0.82	0.81
Mincer and Polachek (1974)	NLS, SEO, white wage and salary workers, age 30–44	w, 1967	R, S: 1, (2), (3) 6, 11		
	married			0.66	0.80
	single			0.86	0.87
Corcoran and Duncan (1979)	PSID, working household heads, age 18–64, white	w, 1975	R, S: 1, (2), (3), 5, 6, 9, 11–13, 16, 17	0.74	0.85
Sanborn (1964)	Census, wage and salary workers	$\bar{y}$, 1949	T: 1–3, 6, 10, 16, 18–20, 24	0.58	0.88*
Malkiel and Malkiel (1973)	Professional full-time employees in one company	annual salary 1966, 1969–1971	R, S: 1, 6, 8, 16, publications, Ph.D., field	0.66*	0.77*
			above + job level[g]	0.66*	0.86*
Astin and Bayer (1972)	Survey of college faculty	annual salary	R: rank, degree, field, research output, type of college	0.78*	0.87*
Johnson and Stafford (1974)	Survey of Ph.D.s in college faculties	9-month salary	R: years since degree, field, sector, experienced (= 10 years)	0.85*	0.93*

Sources: D. J. Treiman and H. I. Hartmann, eds., *Women, Work, and Wages: Equal Pay for Jobs of Equal Value* (Washington, D.C.: National Academy Press, 1981), pp. 20–37, along with additional material and changes in the tables presented in Treiman and Hartmann.

[a]Full citations are given in the references. The same study may appear more than once in the table.

[b]Sources for the individual studies use the following shorthand terms:

Census = the decennial Census of the United States.
CPS = the Current Population Survey of the U.S. Bureau of the Census
OCG = the CPS survey of Occupational Change in a Generation, 1962 and 1972
GSS = General Social Survey, 1975–1978
SEO = Survey of Economic Opportunity, 1966–1967
NLS = National Longitudinal Survey, 1967 and subsequent years (Ohio State University)
PSID = Panel Study of Income Dynamics, 1968 and subsequent years (University of Michigan)

Terms such as "aged 25+" refer to "workers aged 25 or older", and so on.

[c]y = annual earnings (or income)
$\bar{y}$ = a group's mean (or median) annual earnings (or income)
w = wage per hour
subscript f = refers to full-time workers

[d]T = tabular standardization
R = regression analysis
S = regression analysis using separate equations for men and women

Explanatory variables are listed by number at the end of these notes. The use of parentheses around a number indicates that this variable is implicitly held constant, either because of the sample selection or because another variable effectively controls for the variable in question. For example, if only whites are sampled, then race is being held constant.

[e]U_r = the ratio of mean female earnings (or income or wage) to mean male earnings.

[f]A_r = adjusted mean-earnings ratio, which is the ratio of the conditional mean earnings of women to the mean earnings of men. The conditional mean earnings of women is the earnings predicted for women if they had the same values of the explanatory variables as do men.

[g]The term "above +" means that the explanatory variables used are the same as those in the preceding list, plus whatever new variables are listed.

*The explanatory variables include a control for the occupation of the worker. Controlling for occupation is especially likely to raise the ratio of women's to men's earnings, for reasons discussed in the text.

Explanatory variables:

1. Education
2. Age
3. Race
4. Mental ability (intelligence)
5. Formal training
6. Actual labor market experience
7. Proxy for labor market experience
8. Marital status
9. Health
10. Hours of work (annual, weekly, full-time/part-time)
11. Tenure (length of service with current employer)
12. Size of city of residence
13. Region of residence
14. SES background (parental education, occupation, income, number of siblings, migration history, ethnicity, etc.)
15. Quality of schooling
16. Absenteeism record
17. Dual burden (number of children, limits on hours of location, plans to stop work for reasons other than training, etc.)
18. Urban/rural
19. Turnover
20. Occupation (census three-digit)
21. Occupation (census one-digit)
22. Occupational prestige
23. Occupational SEI (Duncan scale of a socioeconomic index)
24. Other occupational classification or scale
25. Class of worker (self-employed, government, or private wage and salary)
26. Industry
27. Union membership
28. Type of employer (government/private, sex segregated/integrated, size of work force)
29. Supervisory status
30. Percentage female in work group
31. Median income of male incumbents
32. Local labor market conditions
33. Length of trip of work
34. Veteran status
35. Migration status

labor market discrimination between men and women, but most of the studies use earnings or incomes. For brevity, I will refer to the earnings gap. The style and much of the content of the table are taken from the compilation of studies in Treiman and Hartmann (1981). The columns denote the authors of the studies, the data sources, the measure of the dependent variable, the statistical method (usually regression analysis) and the control variables used, the unadjusted ratio, U_r, and the adjusted ratio, A_r, which is the ratio of the average predicted earnings of women to the average earnings of men. For A_r the earnings of women are usually predicted by a regression equation. When separate regressions for men and women are used, the earnings of women are predicted by assigning men's mean values for the predictor variables along with the regression coefficients from the women's equation.

The studies are listed in rough order of the size of A_r, which, although cautiously referred to as the wage gap in the sample, given the particular control variables used, is sometimes referred to as a measure of labor market discrimination. An asterisk next to the ratio indicates that some measure of occupational status was held constant. Among all the commonly used control variables, occupation is perhaps the one most "suspect" or "tainted" as being a reflection of labor market discrimination. It is an inappropriate control variable by the criterion I have proposed, although as noted above almost any variable that is subject to some choice by the individual worker and to some influence by the market may be suspect according to this criterion. Of course, occupation may have been advisedly included because the investigator wanted to measure the wage gap conditional on being in a given occupation. Thus, the asterisk is not an indicator of a defective study but rather of a study that does not measure marketwide discrimination as I have chosen to define it.

Reading down the rows of Table 13.6, we see that U_r and A_r have a similar ranking, and both range from 0.3 or 0.4 to around 0.8 or 0.9. The high figures usually refer to restricted samples. Much of the variation in these estimates may be explained in common-sense terms according to the following characteristics of the studies.

(1) *The use of earnings* (or in rare cases income) for persons in the labor force tends to give a lower ratio than the use of wage rates. The latter holds constant the unit of time for which earnings are measured. I prefer the hourly wage for gender comparisons because the amount of time spent at work will partly reflect voluntary choice. In contrast, an earnings comparison may be more useful for comparing white and black men, because working less than full-time by black men often reflects discrimination rather than voluntary choices.

(2) *Samples that represent the full population* generally show a smaller ratio. There is no necessary reason for this pattern; rather, the restricted samples happen to be for groups where the gap is narrower, such as for young age groups, for single women, or for certain occupations or industries. The wage gap is

narrow for young people, and it widens with age. This could mean that there is little discrimination by gender for young people and that the widened gap among older workers merely reflects the voluntary choices of women and men to specialize later on in housework or market work, respectively. Or it could mean that discrimination takes the form of providing women fewer chances for promotion or for on-the-job training. If it is the latter, then some part of the lesser market work (and more housework) by women may reflect market discrimination.

(3) *Black women* tend to have a higher U_r and A_r than white women. Again, the research challenge is to determine the extent to which this is attributable to differential discrimination on the demand side compared with the difference in supply-side characteristics between white and black women. Keep in mind that certain supply-side factors, such as the century-long commitment of black women to market work, their lower probability of marriage, and their higher probability of marital dissolution are all plausible reflections of the labor market discrimination faced by black men.[25] Thus, the low earnings of black men are in part a cause of the high work rates of black wives and, perhaps of the lower proportion of black adults who are married.

(4) *Adding more control variables* usually raises A_r, and there is a noteworthy pattern to this. Various "pre-labor-market" controls, such as education, age, family background, and residential location, are all very similar for men and women, unlike the case of white men compared to black men. Standardizing the women's predicted earnings with men's mean values for these control variables can hardly close the gap by much. Thus, Blinder shows no difference between U_r and A_r (both equal 0.54) when he holds constant age, health, residence, and family background. Nor would education have made much difference, because the means for men and women in his sample are about the same. These pre-labor-market variables often differ substantially between blacks and whites, however, so controlling for them does raise A_r relative to U_r, as we shall see in Table 13.7.

The variables that reflect work experience, such as the number of years spent in the labor force and the worker's tenure with a firm have, on the other hand, substantially different mean values for men and women. When Blinder added tenure, union status, and a one-digit occupational classification, the A_r rose to 0.70 (from a $U_r = 0.54$). A strong point of Blinder's study is his distinction between variables that are reasonably viewed as being exogenous to the process of labor market discrimination from the variables that are likely to reflect labor market discrimination.

[25] The percentage of black women who had ever been married tends to be slightly lower than this percentage among white women, holding age constant. The percentage of black women who were divorced or separated at the time of the surveys is two to three times as large as this percentage among white women, holding age constant. These statistics refer to the years 1970 and 1982. See U.S. Bureau of the Census (1983c, pp. 33, 44–45).

(5) *Using a wage rate as the dependent variable and controlling for years of experience* usually raises A_r, as is illustrated by Corcoran and Duncan and by Mincer and Polachek (M&P). Both studies measure a relatively narrow definition of discrimination in which the years of experience of the workers are carefully controlled. In these studies the A_r's rise to 0.80 and 0.85 for married persons and to 0.87 for single persons. These ratios are almost as close to unity as those for which occupation is controlled (Sanborn, Malkiel and Malkiel, Astin and Bayer, and Johnson and Stafford). However, if tenure is a reflection of discrimination – "last hired, first fired" – and if years of experience are less for women because of the lower wage offered to them, then tenure and experience are in the same category as occupation; that is, invalid control variables because they reflect discrimination.

M&P deal with the endogeneity of experience in one of their models by substituting the predicted value of experience in place of actual experience in the wage equation for women. [This technique is also used by Zabalza and Arrufat (1983), who estimate the wage difference between women and men in Great Britain.] The validity of this technique, however, depends crucially on two assumptions. (1) There is at least one variable in the equation predicting experience that is excluded from the equation predicting wages. (2) The excluded variable, which serves to identify the "experience effect" in the wage equation, does not reflect labor market discrimination. The key predictor variable that is excluded from the wage equation and included in the experience equation is the woman's number of children. Are the above two assumptions satisfied? The question is debatable, but I believe the presence and number of children shifts the issue of discrimination onto another dimension of what are simultaneously determined behavioral outcomes: time in market work, time in housework, numbers of children, occupational choices and career plans, and so on.

Polachek (1979) does treat experience and occupation similarly, because he views both as simultaneously chosen by women in view of their greater commitment to housework and their lesser commitment to market work compared to men. Polachek argues that women will choose occupations that facilitate their intended short and intermittent stays in the labor market; specifically, occupations with relatively flat age–earnings profiles that do not offer the large rewards to experience as do occupations that provide relatively steeply rising age–earnings profiles and which tend to be male-dominated. The theory of Polachek and M&P of the time allocations to work over the life cycle offers an explanation for why market experience is less for women and also for why women's wage returns to experience are less – that is, why their age–earnings profile is flatter.

Figure 13.2 clarifies these ideas. Consider the three age–earnings paths, *DF*, *EG*, and *DH*, drawn linearly to simplify the exposition. Equally productive workers, who start at age A_0 and who retire no later than A_n, may be assumed to be indifferent between occupations with the age–earnings profile *DH* or *EG* because, let us assume, the present values of the two streams of earnings are the

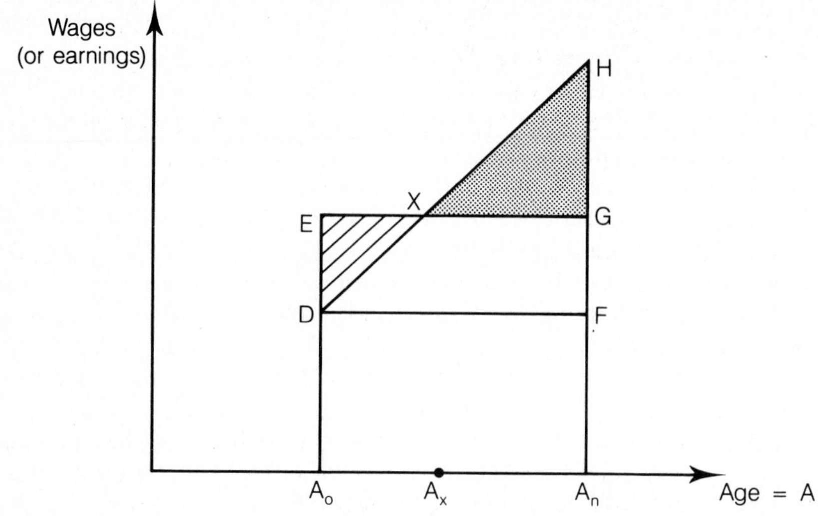

Figure 13.2. Three hypothetical age–earnings profiles. A_0 = age at which worker enters labor force; A_n = retirement age; EG, DH = two age–earnings profiles chosen by equally productive workers; DF = age–earnings profile chosen by a worker who has chosen to invest less in earnings capacity (or human capital).

same. The cross-hatched area, DEX, is drawn to be smaller than XGH to allow for the discounting of future receipts.

If the equally productive workers are men and women, the M&P theory is that women will choose EG instead of DH because they are less likely to want to stay in their job continually (from ages A_0 to A_n), and they will prefer the higher wages in EG up to age A_x instead of choosing the DH path. This part of the M&P theory would not, by itself, be supported empirically: we do not observe women earning higher wages than men between ages A_0 to A_x. A second part of the theory offers a supply and demand explanation for why women's profiles will be like *DF* instead of *EG*. On the demand side the claim is that employers generally prefer workers who are willing to work continually and who are willing to accept the *DH* profiles (and the on-the-job investment that *DH* implies). This decreases the demand for the *EG* workers and lowers their earnings profile. On the supply side, the choice by women to work intermittently implies that they will not invest as much in marketable human capital, because they will have fewer years to receive returns on their investment. This lowers the earnings path still further, say to *DF*.

Thus, the supply-side argument for lower earnings paths for women is that they invest less. However, when the investment is measured by years of schooling, we do not observe important differences between men and women. The argument sometimes shifts to an emphasis on less observable variables, such as the intensity of investment in schooling or in on-the-job training. See the comments by June O'Neill, below.

In principle, these sorts of assumptions about gender behavior can rationalize an A_r of 0.85 and explain away the remaining gap of 0.15 by references to "measurement error" and other sources of omitted productivity variables that, if corrected, would show men to be more productive. In summary, the argument is that the lesser investment, lesser experience, greater time in housework, and lower occupational attainments of women (a) are voluntary choices made by women and (b) are choices that causally precede the gender difference in the demand structure. But because our economic theories and statistical techniques cannot tell us what is or is not voluntary, I doubt that the computations of A_r's will measure labor market discrimination in any fundamental sense.

Perhaps the most emphatic argument in support of the "voluntary view" is presented in a series of papers by O'Neill (1983a, 1983b, 1984). Her discussion of the lower occupational status of women is replete with references to choices (from 1983b):

> The investment component of schooling ... varies by subject matter. Women have traditionally chosen majors such as education, arts, and humanities, which have lower pecuniary returns than subjects such as business or science (p. 19).
>
> Since many women continue to be responsible for a disproportionate share of household maintenance and child care even after they enter employment, they are likely to evaluate certain job characteristics differently than men...[so] predominantly female occupations were much more likely to offer part-time work and less likely to require very long work weeks (p. 19).
>
> ... there is a strong element of personal choice in the occupations held by women... the dominant variables explaining whether a woman is in a typically female occupation were those describing plans and expectations held five years

earlier. Women who said they planned to be a homemaker at age 35, who had children, were married, and who did not attend college, were more likely to be in stereotypically female occupations (p. 22).

Women who five years earlier said they planned to work at age 35 and desired to be working in a male-typed occupation, who attended college, and majored in a scientific subject, were in fact highly likely to be in male-dominated occupations. These findings would appear to contradict the presumption that barriers to entry are the primary reason why women are poorly represented in many occupations (p. 22).

Notice that none of these arguments, which emphasize choice rather than discrimination, is persuasive if discrimination is believed to be causal to the choice of majors, to the time devoted to housework, to the employers' offers of part- versus full-time jobs, and to the "plans and expectations" women had at ages 19–29 regarding their career at age 35. In other words, if labor market discrimination does restrict the quality of jobs and wages available to women, it is reasonable to believe that this affects their plans and expectations regarding school majors, fertility, and their time allocation to home and market sectors. The last quote by O'Neill seems to say that, for example, (a) if a woman who received a degree in electrical engineering is working as an electrical engineer, then (b) the poor representation of women in electrical engineering is not to be considered evidence for discrimination against women ("barriers to entry") in that occupation. It seems to me that (b) does not follow from (a).

(6) *Restricting the sample to unmarried women and men* usually shows higher values of U_r and A_r, as is illustrated by the ratios 0.86–0.87 reported by M&P. Studies that compare single women to either single men or all men might be viewed as providing a purer measure of gender discrimination by avoiding the troublesome issue of the dual career that is associated with married women. Unfortunately, the issue remains. The never-married single women tend to be young, under 25 or so, and the U_r for young people is relatively high (see the Kohen and Roderick entry in Table 13.6). However, a ratio that is less than 1 may reflect the employers' expectations that the women are likely to marry and to be less committed to their jobs than men of the same age. If the sample were restricted to never-married women in their 40s or older, for whom a strong commitment to market work may be presumed, the sample would be relatively small and probably selective of women who were either unusually dedicated to a career or unusually adverse to marriage. Arguments could be made that these women would be likely to earn more, or less, than men who are comparable in the conventional characteristics used in earnings functions. Indeed, single men tend to earn less than married men, holding constant conventional variables. A full understanding of these selective traits determining marital status involves more than just economics.

(7) *Restricting the comparison to a narrowly selected group of jobs* tends to produce higher U_r and A_r ratios, as is illustrated by Malkiel and Malkiel (1973). This study is the only one in Table 13.6 for a single company, and I will have more to say about this type of sampling restriction later. Also, it is not only a sample of a relatively narrowly defined occupational group – all college-educated professionals who work for a particular research firm – but it offers a control over "job level", which further narrowly defines the tasks, duties, and responsibilities of the employees. By controlling for job level, the adjusted ratio rises from 0.77 to 0.86. This is evidence for the claim made earlier that with a sufficiently narrowly defined job almost all ratios would be unity. Indeed, if not, companies would risk violating the law. Finally, the study offers a rather striking example of the importance of the method of standardization. The conventional A_r is equal to $\hat{\overline{W}}_f/\overline{W}_m$, and an alternative is $A'_r = \overline{W}_f/\hat{\overline{W}}_m$. The alternative adjusted ratios in the Malkiel and Malkiel study are 0.85 (instead of 0.77) and 0.99 (instead of 0.86). The 0.99 ratio was the one emphasized by Malkiel and Malkiel and used by O'Neill (1984, pp. 79–82).

4.2.2.2. Black – white earnings gap for men. The empirical measurements of wage discrimination between blacks and whites in the United States involve the same procedures as those just described for men and women, but there are differences in results and interpretations. I focus on men in the racial comparison in order to separate this from the gender factor. A difference in the normative interpretation is that the wage ratios for women-to-men, U_r and A_r, that are less than one may be rationalized by claiming that women choose to specialize in home production. No such alternative employment is credible for black men. Furthermore, even if women suffered lower market wages because of discrimination, they might recover all or part of these losses by marrying men, who are the favored group. Consideration of total household income for comparisons between men and women will be discussed in the last section.

The unadjusted wage ratios for black and white men shown in Table 13.7 are similar to those for women-to-men in Table 13.6, if we restrict the comparisons to large populations and exclude the comparisons for young people and for selected occupations. The average U_r is 0.58 in the black-to-white male ratios and 0.55 for women-to-men. The increase in the adjusted ratios, $A_r - U_r$, is, however, generally larger for the race ratios in Table 13.7 than those for the gender ratios in Table 13.6, if we exclude the comparisons with asterisks where occupation is held constant. The average increase in A_r relative to U_r is about 0.16 (0.74–0.58) for men, black-to-white, and about 0.09 (0.65–0.56) for women-to-men. Despite the crudity of these comparisons – they are not confined to comparisons with similar variables held constant, for example – we may conclude that holding constant the usual available productivity variables has a larger effect in reducing the wage gap between black and white men. The reason, mentioned earlier, is that the usual

Table 13.7
Summary of studies of ratios of black men's earnings to white men's earnings, unadjusted and adjusted for various characteristics of workers and jobs.

Author and year of publication[a]	Data source and population studied[b]	Measure of earnings[c]	Statistical method and explanatory variables[d]	Blacks' earnings as a ratio of whites'	
				Observed[e]	Adjusted[f]
Masters (1975)	Census (1/1000 sample), blacks, non-Hispanic whites, age 17–64, worked in 1959, civilian, nonstudent	y, 1959	R, S: 1, 2, 12, 13, 25	0.50	0.59
			above +10[g]	0.50	0.80
	Same as above but for non-South	y, 1959	R, S: 1, 2, 12 13, 25	0.64	0.61
			above +10[g]	0.64	0.74
Blinder (1973)	PSID, white and black working household heads	w, 1969	R, S: 2, 9, 12–14, 32, 34	0.49	0.64
			above +1, 5, 11, 21, 27[g]	0.49	0.80*
Masters (1975)	SEO, blacks, non-Hispanic whites, age 17–64, worked in 1966, civilian, nonstudent	y, 1966	R, S: 1, 2, 12, 13, 25	0.55	0.66
			above +10[g]	0.55	0.72
	Same as above but for non-South		R, S: 1, 2, 12, 13, 25	0.68	0.75
Duncan (1968)	OOC, native, nonfarm, 25–64	y, 1961	R, S: 1, 4, 8	0.46	0.68
			above +4[g]	0.46	0.75
Corcoran and Duncan (1979)	PSID, household heads, worked 500 hours or more, age 18–64	w, 1975	R, S: 1, (2), 5, 6, 9, 11–13, 16, 17	0.77	0.89
Flanagan (1974)	NLS, men 15–25 or 46–60	w, 1967	R, S: 1, (2), 5, 6, 8, 9, 11, 13, 26, 35		
	Age 46–60			0.58	0.84
	Age 15–25			0.72	0.94

Sources: Full citations of the original studies are in the bibliography. In some cases the adjusted ratios that are shown in this table do not appear in the original studies or appear in a different form.
Note: All footnotes are identical to the footnotes in Table 13.6.

control variables generally represent either exogenous characteristics, like age, or pre-labor-market characteristics, like years of schooling, and these types of variables tend to be more similar for men and women than they are for whites and blacks.

Blinder's (1973) comparisons are again instructive. His control for exogenous variables made no difference in the women/men ratios; both U_r and A_r equal 0.54, but the same control variables raised the black/white ratios from 0.49 to 0.64.

The 1979 study by Corcoran and Duncan (C&D) is also interesting, and some comments about it serve to raise several general points. The unadjusted ratio,

$U_r = 0.77$, is the highest in Table 13.7. C&D use a wage rate rather than earnings as the dependent variable, and they exclude workers who worked less than 500 hours during the survey year. Both restrictions raise the black/white ratio, because black men are likely to suffer more unemployment, including unemployment for 10 months or longer. Recall that restricting women/men comparisons to full-time workers (or controlling for hours worked) was primarily justified on grounds that the frequency of part-time jobs among women was often voluntary. This is seldom true among prime-age black men.

C&D also restrict their sample to men who are are household heads, and there is likely to be some selectivity bias here that raises the wage ratio above what it would be for the full population of black and white male workers. A smaller proportion of black men aged 18–64 are household heads compared to white men of these ages; the wages of those who are not household heads in both races are lower than the wages of heads of households; the wage ratio of blacks-to-whites among men who are not household heads is slightly less than 0.77; and household headship may reflect labor market discrimination.[26] Therefore, the black-to-white wage ratio for all men would be less than 0.77.

The adjusted ratio in the C&D study is 0.89, also high relative to other A_r's. The control variables include years of experience which, given a control for years of schooling, is representing age and therefore almost purely exogenous. Let us assume, for the sake of argument, that years of schooling, city size, region of residence, and health, are exogenous. The remaining control variables, formal training and tenure with one's current employer are, however, likely to reflect labor market discrimination.

The ratios by Blinder and by C&D are virtually the lower and upper bounds in Table 13.7. The other studies suggest several additional methodological issues, but I will be brief. Masters' studies (1975) show the importance of the South/non-South differential. More recent data in the C&D study show that this differential is still important, although smaller. Masters clearly brings out the effect of controlling for time worked, because each of the A_r's for the "above + 10" comparisons (see the fourth and sixth columns) allows only the additional control for weeks worked, and these A_r's are much larger. Finally, although I do not show them, there are some striking differences between the A_r and A'_r ratios in Masters' study.

[26]Among men aged 18–64, which is the population frame for Corcoran and Duncan, 79 percent of white men and 58 percent of black men were household heads at the time of the Census Bureau's survey in 1981 [U.S. Bureau of the Census (1983a, P-20, No. 372, Table 2)]. The incomes of year-round full-time workers who are male heads of households is about 25 percent higher than for similar workers who are not heads of households. The ratio of black-to-white income for men who were not household heads in 1981 is around 0.70 for all workers and 0.76 for full-time workers [U.S. Bureau of the Census (1983b, P-60, No. 137, Tables 44 and 55)]. Income figures are used instead of earnings because earnings are not reported for persons classified by their relationship to the household head.

The study by the sociologist Otis Dudley Duncan (1968) may have been the first to use separate regressions and to construct the "decompositions" of wage (or income) differences. Economists usually cite later studies by economists for these procedures.

Flanagan's studies show the frequently observed result that black/white wage ratios are relatively high for young workers, which was also true for the gender ratios. However, the smaller ratio among older men surely does not reflect a voluntary choice by black men to work less in market employment, as might be claimed for women. On the other hand, so-called "vintage effects" may be revealed in the different wage ratios for younger and older black and white groups, whereby the current period's larger ratio for young workers may reflect a true long-run improvement in the relative earnings capacities of black men – perhaps reflecting, in turn, recent improvements in the quality and quantity of education. Welch (1973) and Smith and Welch (1977, 1978) have stressed this source of a vintage effect. Others have emphasized the civil rights movement in the last 20 years, a reduction in discrimination in society, and the increase in antidiscriminatory legislation, all of which may be having a larger positive effect on young blacks than on older blacks [see Freeman (1981)].

Clearly, current wages of young blacks and whites cannot conclusively reveal a lifetime comparison. Cohort analyses of previous generations show that only part of the improvement in wage ratios among previous generations of young people is sustained. See Freeman (1973a), Chiswick (1974, pp. 116–118), Smith and Welch (1978), and Hoffman (1979).

4.2.2.3. The earnings gap for other ethnic groups. The nationality group in the United States that has received the most attention in discrimination studies in recent years is Hispanics, which consists predominantly of persons with Mexican, Puerto Rican, and Cuban ancestry, in that order. There is not the space to review the empirical estimates of Model (I) for these groups and to display a corresponding table. Nevertheless, some new and interesting methodological issues may be mentioned briefly in connection with the general finding that relatively small unadjusted wage ratios (U_r), Hispanic-to-white, coexist with relatively large adjusted ratios (A_r). ("White" refers to non-Hispanic white.) For example, Reimers (1983) finds that U_r for Mexican Americans (hereafter Mexicans) relative to whites is about 0.70, whereas the adjusted ratio after fitting separate Model (I)-type regressions is about 0.94. See also Abowd and Killingsworth (1982) and Grenier (1984) for similar results. Adjusted ratios of 0.9 or higher imply a minor role for labor market discrimination.

There are four main sources for the increases from U_r to A_r in these studies: (1) Age differences: Hispanics tend to be younger than whites, so part of the wage difference is explained by this exogenous variable. (2) Education differences: Hispanics, particularly Mexicans and Puerto Ricans, have substantially lower average educational levels. (3) Immigration status, as measured by years in the United States. (4) Language, as measured, for example, by a categorical variable defined as the ability to speak and understand English. All these controls seem reasonable, but let us critically examine the last three and raise again the point that definitive empirical measures of wage discrimination require knowledge about the underlying processes and institutions.

Education. Assume that education contributes to one's earnings capacity in skilled jobs but not in unskilled jobs. If this were true, then the fact that, say, Mexicans have a low average years-of-schooling-completed (ED) should not place them at an earnings disadvantage relative to whites in the unskilled jobs, even though whites in these jobs may have a larger mean ED, perhaps because of school attendance laws in the U.S. Nevertheless, the usual regression procedure, with ED entered linearly in the earnings regression, will tend to assign a lower predicted wage to Mexicans relative to whites in these unskilled jobs. Actual discrimination in these jobs may be masked. The following simple hypothetical example brings out this point. Assume that only ED, among the observable variables, has a systematic effect on wages, and that the distribution of wages (W) and ED is as shown in Panel A of Table 13.8. There are two examples each of distributions for whites and Hispanics, which permit four possible calculations of U_r and A_r. To obtain A_r with the data of example 1, we obtain the average predicted wages for Hispanics and whites:

$$\hat{W}_w = -0.46 + 0.357ED, \quad \text{so } \overline{W} = -0.46 + 0.357(\overline{ED} = 11.93) = 3.80 \tag{12}$$

and

$$\hat{W}_h = -0.60 + 0.375ED, \quad \text{so } \overline{W} = -0.60 + 0.375(\overline{ED} = 8) = 2.40. \tag{13}$$

The corresponding regression equations using example 2 data are

$$\hat{W}_w = 0.025 + 0.322ED, \quad \text{so } \overline{W} = 0.025 + 0.322(\overline{ED} = 11.73) = 3.80 \tag{14}$$

and

$$\hat{W}_h = -0.300 + 0.313ED, \quad \text{so } \overline{W} = -0.300 + 0.313(\overline{ED} = 8) = 2.20. \tag{15}$$

The A_r and A'_r formulas, using (12)–(15), give us the A_r entries in Panel B of Table 13.8.

The data have been constructed to reveal wage discrimination against Hispanics that is *assumed* among unskilled workers, who are all classified with low levels of ED – an average of 4 for Hispanics and an average of either 4 or 5 for whites. In example 1 of Hispanic data there is no discrimination among the higher ED

Table 13.8
Hypothetical distribution of years of schooling (ED) and wages (W) among whites and Hispanics and resulting comparisons of unadjusted and adjusted wage ratios

Panel A. Distribution

Years of schooling (ED)	Whites				Hispanics			
	Example 1		Example 2		Example 1		Example 2	
	Number	Wage	Number	Wage	Number	Wage	Number	Wage
4	1	\$2	3	\$2	3	\$1	3	\$1
5	1	2						
6	1	2						
12	7	3	7	3	1	3	1	3
16	5	6	5	6	1	6	1	5
Number	15		15		5		5	
Means	$\overline{ED}=11.93$ $\overline{W}=\$3.80$		$\overline{ED}=11.73$ $\overline{W}=\$3.80$		$\overline{ED}=8$ $\overline{W}=\$2.40$		$\overline{ED}=8$ $\overline{W}=\$2.20$	

Panel B: Comparisons of unadjusted (U_r) and adjusted (F_h, A_r, A'_r) wage ratios*

White distribution	Hispanic distribution: Example 1				Example 2			
	U_r	F_h	A_r	A'_r	U_r	F_h	A_r	A'_r
Example 1	0.63		1.02	1.00	0.58		1.02	0.94
Example 2	0.63	0.70	0.99	0.93	0.58	0.67	0.88	0.85

Source: Hypothetical numbers.
Definitions and explanations of ratios in Panel B:

$U_r = \overline{W}_h / \overline{W}_w$.

$A_r = \hat{W}_h / \overline{W}_w = \Sigma b_h \overline{X}_w / \overline{W}_w$.

$A'_r = \overline{W}_h / \hat{W}_w = \overline{W}_h / \Sigma b_w \overline{X}_h$.

F_h for example 2 of whites with example 1 of Hispanics:
$F_h = (3/5)(1/2)+(1/5)(1)+(1/5)(1) = 0.70.$

F_h for example 2 of whites with example 2 of Hispanics:
$F_h = (3/5)(1/2)+(1/5)(1)+(1/5)(5/6) = 0.67.$

categories, and in example 2 there is discrimination for the college ($ED=16$) category – a wage ratio of $5/6 = 0.83$.

The unadjusted wage ratios with the data reveal typical values: 0.63 and 0.58. An exact measure of wage discrimination, given the assumptions used in constructing the data, is available with example 2 of the white data and both sets of the Hispanic data. This measure, expressed as a ratio, will be labeled F_h to indicate that the ratio is based on a "free functional form" (using categorical variables for each level of ED) and that it uses Hispanic numbers of workers as weights. It is calculated as follows: With example 2 of the white data, we see that 3 of the 5 Hispanics have the same ED as whites and earn only half as much. With example 1 of the Hispanic data, the other two Hispanic workers with higher ED earn the same as whites with the same ED values. F_h is the Hispanic/white wage ratio, adjusted for *ED* values in each of the three *ED* categories.

$$F_{\mathrm{h}} = (3/5)(1/2) + (1/5)(3/3) + (1/5)(6/6) = 0.70.$$

No functional form has been imposed on the *ED/W* relation, and the wage comparisons at each *ED* level are weighted by the relative frequencies in the Hispanic distribution.[27]

The main conclusions from Table 13.8 are that the A_{r} and A'_{r} ratios show either minimal or no discrimination, despite its "constructed" presence, and that the sources of the discrepancy are the incorrect linear relation between *ED* and *W* and the disparity in numbers of observations in the categories – few Hispanics in the higher *ED* categories and relatively few whites in the low *ED* category. The example is oversimplified, of course, but the problem it reveals with the typical econometric estimation for Hispanics, particularly Mexicans, is, I believe, worth considering. The general issue is that a trait, in this case *ED*, may vary in its validity as an indicator of productivity over certain ranges of the variable and in certain work situations.

Immigration. Years since arrival in the United States may be an indicator of productivity, because the variable may represent English-language skills, labor market information (including investments in job mobility), and various aspects of cultural assimilation that may enhance workers' productivity in their contacts with supervisors, co-workers, customers, and so on. If the lack of cultural assimilation has nothing to do with one's productivity and everything to do with discrimination, the variable loses its appeal as a control variable on this account, although it retains its appeal on the other two accounts.

Language skills. As a control variable, language skills may be partially contaminated by simultaneity if the skills depend on the type of job available to the worker, on the relationship to one's co-workers, and on other outcomes of the labor market. In one study the variable was highly correlated with "place of birth" and "number of years spent in the U.S." and the latter variables were omitted from the regression. The author [Grenier (1984, p. 42)] commented: "One consequence of these omissions, however, is that estimated coefficients of the language variables may include some effects of these other variables."

In addition to the study and measurement of discrimination regarding Hispanics, there have been a few econometric and historical-institutional studies

[27] Using white relative frequencies, we have $F_{\mathrm{w}} = (3/15)(1/2) + (7/15)(3/3) + (5/15)(6/6) = 0.80$, but even this moderate measure of discrimination is not appropriate to describe the situation of Hispanics in this hypothetical example, where 60 percent (3 of 5) are experiencing a large measure of discrimination. A more appropriate use of the *F*-ratio for whites is to define

$$F'_{\mathrm{w}} = (3/15)(2/1) + (7/15)(3/3) + (5/15)(6/6) = 1.20,$$

which shows that the large (two-to-one) wage advantage of the unskilled whites raises their overall wages relative to Hispanics by 20 percent, holding education constant. Finally, if we assume, with example 1 data for whites, that the *ED* levels of 4, 5, and 6 provide no productivity differences among these workers, then F_{h} and the other *F*-ratios would be defined exactly as they are for the example 2 data for whites.

of several European and Asian nationality groups and various religious groups. One important result of these studies is that for many ethnic groups, the ratio of their earnings to those for a more broadly defined white group (sometimes as narrow as those with an English ancestry) is larger than one. This was found, for example, for Catholic Irish-Americans [Greeley (1976, p. 52), and (1981, pp. 110–120)], Japanese-Americans [Petersen (1978), Sowell (1981)], and Jews [Chiswick (1983), Sowell (1981)]. The current advantaged status of these groups has been explained by particular historical and institutional developments, rather than as revealing "reverse discrimination", and these explanations persuade me of the value of this method of analysis.

In a study of the relation between the larger religious groups and earnings, Tomes (1984) found small and statistically insignificant effects among Catholic, Protestant, and "None/Other" categories.[28] He also found no statistically significant difference among various Protestant denominations. Tomes provides a useful distinction between estimates with purely exogenous variables held constant – family background, age (and age squared), and location of residence – and estimates in which potential "outcome" variables, like education and self-employment, were additional control variables. Another interesting feature of this study was the distinction between one's current religious affiliation and that of one's upbringing. Current affiliation is, to some extent, endogenous, and there were some interesting, although not startling, differences in the estimates when the two definitions of religious affiliation were used.

4.2.3. *Empirical studies of wage discrimination in individual firms and "reverse regression"*

A brief examination of the econometric analysis of discrimination in individual firms is useful for three reasons. First, discrimination by firms, identified singly, has come under close scrutiny by various groups in society, mainly as a result of antidiscrimination laws and executive orders. Regression analyses of the Model (I) type are frequently offered as evidence in court cases and other litigation proceedings stemming from these laws and regulations.[29] Discrimination in firms may consist of the differential treatment of majority and minority groups in hiring, placement, wages, promotion, layoffs, and in other ways. I will refer only to wage discrimination in this discussion.

A second reason for interest in these studies is that they have the advantages, relative to marketwide studies, of explicit and well-defined objectives and

[28] Tomes found relatively large positive effects for Jews, but this group was numerically small in his sample and the differences were sometimes not statistically significant.

[29] See Baldus and Cole (1980), Finkelstein (1980), and Fisher (1980) for a discussion of statistical analyses in court cases of discrimination and for extensive citations. An example of an econometric study of wage discrimination in a single firm, listed in Table 13.6, is that by Malkiel and Malkiel (1973), although this study was not used in litigation proceedings.

straightforward procedures. The analysts' objectives are usually to support their clients, and the objective of the court is to use these studies to determine whether an employer is guilty or innocent. The procedures involve a Model (I)-type regression in which the employer's criteria for wage payments may be specified in detail, and those criteria that are correlated with race or gender can be explicitly included in the estimation model. Moreover, many characteristics associated with the workers' productivity may be clearly exogenous to the employer, even though they are not exogenous to the market as a whole. Regression analyses with nationwide samples usually suffer from ambiguities and vagueness about both their objectives and model specifications.

A third reason for our attention is the innovative use of "reverse regression", which raises some interesting methodological points even if, as I will argue, it does not offer a preferred model for estimating wage discrimination. Indeed, this section will examine only this aspect of the studies of individual firms. The actual analyses are often buried in trial proceedings, and there is no space to present them here. More important, I believe that studies of discrimination by single firms do not provide useful measures of marketwide discrimination, which is my main interest. The reason is that the samples are based on company records, and the selection rules for inclusion in the sample are seldom known. The companies studied in court cases are not a random sample of all companies, and their recruitment policies do not pretend to yield random samples.

Company records generally apply to a single industry and a few occupations, and the question of how market discrimination affects the distribution of minority workers in the industry and occupation is not examined. More generally, no valid conclusions about discrimination can be reached without attention to the company's recruitment or selection procedures. For example, perhaps the company has a reputation for discrimination against women that restricts the pool of female applicants. Maybe only a small number of newcomers to the community constitute this pool. The statistical analyst usually deals with the employees on board or, at best, with persons who have applied to the company. A famous study by Conway and Roberts (1983) of alleged salary discrimination against women in a large bank, for example, involved a sample of 274 employees, of whom only 37 are women. Under these circumstances, generalizing about discrimination in the market as a whole on the basis of studies of one or several companies is not valid.

Studies by Roberts (1980) and by Conway and Roberts have given prominence to the statistical model known as "reverse regression" (hereafter *RR*).[30] The term refers to "reversing" the Model (I) regression in which the wage, W, is regressed

[30]A large number of articles on reverse regression in discrimination analyses appeared around the time and soon after Roberts's article (1980), and a symposium on the issue appears in *Journal of Business and Economic Statistics*, vol. 1, January 1983. My understanding of the issues owes much to Arthur S. Goldberger, and my discussion is based on Goldberger (1984), but I am solely responsible for any errors in this section.

on a vector of productivity variables, $\boldsymbol{X}$, and a minority/majority-status variable, Z. In RR, $\boldsymbol{X}$ is in effect regressed on W and Z. Assume Z refers to gender. One motivation for RR may lie in the question it addresses: "Holding wages constant, are men less qualified than women?" This reverses the customary question in direct regression: "Holding qualifications (the X's) constant, are men paid more than women?"

Another motivation for RR is the classic problem, in regression analysis, of errors in the independent variables. Given the regression, $\hat{W} = a + bX$, in which X contains random measurement error but wherein the regression is otherwise correctly specified, RR – here, $\hat{X} = c + dW$ – permits the coefficients b and $1/d$ to give boundaries on the true linear relation between W and the correctly measured X. When $\boldsymbol{X}$ is a collection of variables, the dependent variable in RR may either be (a) each individual X-component regressed against W and Z in a system of equations, or (b) the fitted part of the direct regression for the case in which $Z = 0$, specifically, $\hat{W} = \boldsymbol{X'B}$. Thus, $\boldsymbol{X'B}$ is regressed on W and Z in RR. I will sometimes simply refer to $\boldsymbol{X}$ as the "dependent variable" in RR.

The initial appeal of RR is the reasonable proposition that the econometrician's usual set of productivity variables, $\boldsymbol{X}$, is not a perfect measure of a worker's productivity. Assuming that W is a function of "true productivity", X^*, the following model may be specified:

$$W = X^* + AZ + v, \quad \text{where } Z = 1 \text{ for men and } Z = 0 \text{ for women}; \tag{16}$$

$$X^* = GZ + u, \quad \text{where } G > 0; \tag{17}$$

$$X = X^* + e. \tag{18}$$

By eq. (16) the wage is a function of true productivity, X^*, which is unobserved by the econometrician. Holding X^* constant, $A = 0$ implies no discrimination against women, and $A > 0$ implies discrimination against women. Equation (17) says that men are more productive than women; this assumption will be maintained throughout this discussion. Equation (18) says that X is a fallible measure of X^*. The usual assumptions about the error terms are that v, u, and e are independent of each other; that v and e are independent of X^* and Z; and that u is independent of Z.

Assume that the econometrician estimates the direct regression:

$$W = BX + CZ + v'. \tag{19}$$

It follows from (16)–(18) that C is an upwardly biased estimate of the true relation, A. Assuming $A = 0$, C will be greater than zero, implying discrimination against women when none exists. [The algebra and further discussion of these qualitative results are found in Goldberger (1984).] In eq. (19), X^* is an omitted variable, as revealed by the assumed correct wage eq. (16). By (17), X^* is systematically related to gender. Thus, positive values of Z in (19) partly represent "more" X^* in addition to representing "maleness" (since $Z=1$ for men). Therefore, the coefficient C will be positive owing to the relation of X^* to Z even if the true male effect, A, is zero. Clearly, C is more upwardly biased as G is larger in (17) and as the variance of e is larger (implying that X is a less accurate measure of X^*) in (18).

At first glance, eqs. (16)–(18) may seem so plausible that the systematic upward bias of C in (19) seems incontrovertible. The first glance is misleading. There is no basis for assuming that the employer pays according to "true productivity", X^*. On the contrary, we should expect that the systematic basis on which employers pay their workers is a basis of observable variables. A random error term should also be included to allow for miscellaneous factors that may be assumed unrelated to gender. This latter point reintroduces the earlier argument that in a discrimination case, any systematic productivity trait that is correlated with minority-group status should be included in the employer's list of the X-variables. These assumptions effectively restore to legitimacy either eq. (19), for the case of a single X-variable, or eq. (20), as written below, with multiple X-variables:

$$W = \boldsymbol{X}'\boldsymbol{B} + CZ + v'. \tag{20}$$

We may further assume that there is generally a positive relation between $\boldsymbol{X}$ and Z in the sense that the men's mean of the X-vector, weighted by their "prices" – the B-vector – is larger than that for women, that is

$$E(\boldsymbol{X}'_{\mathrm{m}})\boldsymbol{B} > E(\boldsymbol{X}'_{\mathrm{w}})\boldsymbol{B}. \tag{21}$$

This inequality is the analogue of (17), which expressed the assumption that men are more productive than women. Given the assumption that the X's are positively correlated with X^*, (21) implies $G > 0$ in (17), and conversely. However, (17) and (21) do not imply that the expected value of X^*, holding constant the observable X's, is greater for men than for women, and without this assumption there is no basis for assuming that C is upwardly biased in (20).

Despite the assumed correctness of (17) and (21), the direct regression of (20) gives an unbiased estimate of the gender (male) coefficient. Equation (20) has the virtue of focusing attention on the explicit measure of alleged discrimination, W, and of leading all the interested parties – the econometrician, the defendant employer, the plaintiff, and the adjudicator – to address the same questions raised earlier in this chapter about Model (I):

(a) Are the variables in $\boldsymbol{X}$ proper control variables; that is, are they exogenous with respect to the employer's behavior?

(b) Are there omitted productivity variables that are systematically related to gender?

It should be clear that eq. (20), which expresses an observable relation and is to be analyzed in conjunction with an inquiry into questions (a) and (b), allows for the model expressed as eq. (16) to be a special case. As mentioned earlier, X^* could be assumed to be an omitted variable and, given (17)–(18), the upward bias in C follows. But there is no reason to believe that any such concept as "true productivity" will be operational. Furthermore, if X^* is redefined to be the employer's "assessed productivity" [see Roberts (1980), Conway and Roberts (1983)], then we return to the reasonable expectation (or requirement) that the employers simply point out which criteria in their assessment have a net correlation with gender – that is, a correlation that persists after controlling for the observable X's. Again, a straightforward analysis of "omitted variable" bias in eq. (20) could provide a qualitative answer about the direction of bias in C. The direct regression associated with (20) leads us to focus attention on specific sources of any bias. This has more appeal to me than a model in which the wage is presumed to be determined by "true" (or "assessed") productivity combined with the presumption that male superiority regarding that productivity is maintained after holding constant observable measures of productivity. These presumptions prejudge the very issue that is to be investigated, and these presumptions are precisely what eqs. (16)–(18) embody.

The model in eqs. (16)–(18) has two multivariate analogues that have been analyzed by Goldberger (1984). In one, each X-variable in the vector of observed indicators, $\boldsymbol{X}$, is assumed to be a fallible measure of the corresponding element in a vector of unobserved true productivity determinants, $\boldsymbol{X}^*$. In this case RR is not necessarily superior to direct regression even though one may assume, analogous to (17), that

$$\boldsymbol{X}^* = \boldsymbol{H}Z + \boldsymbol{u}, \tag{17a}$$

with all elements of $\boldsymbol{H} > 0$.

In the other multivariate model the X-vector is assumed to provide multiple indicators of a single X^*, so (18) becomes

$$\boldsymbol{X} = \boldsymbol{D}X^* + \boldsymbol{e}. \tag{18a}$$

Let a representative indicator be X_j. The RR for the j-indicator is

$$\hat{X}_j = c_j + d_j W + f_j Z, \tag{18b}$$

and the estimator, A^*, of the gender coefficient in the true wage equation, (16), is $A_j^* = -f_j/d_j$.

This multiple-indicator model is said to be the one "stochastic specification under which reverse regression provides a valid estimator" of the gender coefficient [Goldberger (1984, p. 314)]. Because each indicator of $\boldsymbol{X}$ is assumed to provide a consistent estimator of the true gender coefficient, these implied restrictions on the different estimators can be tested. Few such tests have been tried, and those few are hardly supportive of the model [see Goldberger (1984), Green and Ferber (1984)].

One of the questionable assumptions of the multiple-indicator model as it applies to gender discrimination is that each indicator, X_j in $\boldsymbol{X}$, is independent of gender, holding constant X^*. This assumption is associated with eq. (18a), where $\boldsymbol{e}$ is assumed to be independent of gender, or with eq. (18) in the classical errors-in-variable model with one independent variable. To illustrate why this assumption and the implied restrictions on the coefficients in (18b) are not likely to hold, consider an $\boldsymbol{X}$ that has the following four elements, which are positively correlated with true (or assessed) productivity, X^*, but which differ in their correlation with gender: $X_1 =$ verbal test score; $X_2 =$ mathematics test score; $X_3 =$ manual dexterity; $X_4 =$ physical strength.

The gender correlations will reflect, let us assume, an advantage of women over men in verbal ability and manual dexterity and an advantage of men over women in mathematical ability and physical strength, which are gender-linked relationships that have been generally found [see Anastasi (1969, p. 421)]. To keep the statistical relations simple, assume that each element of $\boldsymbol{D}$ is the same. Then if a nondiscriminating employer hires men and women at a specified wage, we should observe that women's low scores on X_2 and X_4 will tend to be compensated by higher scores on X_1 and X_3, and conversely for men. The dependence of $\boldsymbol{e}$ with gender ($= Z$) in (18a) will induce different *signs* of the f_j in (18b). In particular, with $Z = 1$ for men, f_1 and f_3 will tend to be negative and f_2 and f_4 will tend to be positive. With d_j positive, the estimators of the true gender effect, A_j^*, will not all have the same sign.

The reasons why the multiple-indicator model is invalid in this example are, I believe, realistic and prevalent; specifically, the presence of some gender-linked productivity traits that favor women, the fact that employee productivity typically involves multiple skills, and the fact that employers recognize that skills (and traits) are typically compensating (or substitutable).[31]

[31]A hypothetical example of substitutable gender-linked traits that brings out these statistical points is available from the author. It should be noted that a model in which wages are determined by gender-linked traits, $\boldsymbol{X}$, along with an assumption that other traits, holding constant $\boldsymbol{X}$, are uncorrelated with gender simply illustrates the model in eq. (20), which is the same as the "multiple cause model" that Goldberger (1984) discusses.

5. Policy implications and conclusions

5.1. *Explaining and judging discrimination: The diversity of cases*

This chapter began with the normative issue of equity in outcomes measuring economic well-being among racial, ethnic, and gender groups. Inequities appear to be widespread, and our economic theories of why they persist are only moderately helpful.

At one extreme, the outcomes experienced by earlier immigrants to the United States suggest an optimistic view of both the ethical and the scientific judgments about the workings of the economy generally and of labor markets more particularly.[32] Although discrimination against early immigrant groups was not analyzed in this chapter, the references to the achievements of immigrants who were Irish Catholics, Italians (mainly from southern Italy), Japanese, and Jews (mainly from eastern Europe) seem to show a pattern in which groups who were initially "have nots" in the United States and who faced discrimination gradually attained an equal economic status to whites whose ancestry was Anglo-Saxon Protestant and who were the "haves". Such an evolution is consistent with a neoclassical view of the workings of competitive markets, assuming that the productive capacities of the different ethnic groups are equal and that the economy is sufficiently competitive.

A more specific application of economic principles to an analysis of discrimination involves Hispanic Americans, who are mainly recent immigrants. Their lower relative earnings may be rationalized by a theory of the determinants of earnings that assigns important roles to information about the labor market, to facility in the English language, and to education, measured by years of schooling. Such theories are qualitatively supported by empirical evidence. Whether the evidence shows that the quantitative gap in earnings between Hispanic and non-Hispanic whites is explained by these theories is not clear to me.

The difference in market earnings between men and women can be rationalized by economic theories of the gains from specialization and investment in human capital, combined with an assumption of voluntary choices by women to specialize in the home sector. This earnings gap, particularly between white men and women, is one of the largest and most time-persistent of the comparisons discussed in this paper (see Table 13.5).

In another paper [Cain (1985)] I have suggested that the theory of voluntary choice regarding labor market activities should lead to equality in *total incomes*

[32] Hispanic immigrants are considered to be recent immigrants, and most blacks who came to the United States were not voluntary immigrants, so these two groups are not included in the group referred to as the earlier immigrants.

received by men and women, if not to equality in *labor market wages*. I assume equality in women's and men's productive capacity, in the nonpecuniary aspects of their work, and in their leisure consumption. I then test for the equality in income received by assuming that husbands and wives share their household income equally while married. Even with this assumption women were found to have a substantially lower present value of lifetime income than men: the ratios were between 0.7 and 0.9 (depending on various assumptions). These are, however, closer to unity than the usual measure of women-to-men ratios of wages, as reported in Table 13.6.

I also examined the total time spent in housework and market work combined for men and women. The data are weak, but the available evidence suggests near equality among husbands and wives [Cain (1984b)]. It is not clear how the inclusion of men and women without spouses present would affect this comparison. More women than men are likely to head single-parent families, and many of these women have the double burden of market work combined with a heavy workload at home, especially child care. On the other hand, those female heads-of-household who are recipients of public welfare tend not to work much in the market; indeed, the conditions of their welfare receipt discourage market work. Men who are single-parent heads-of-households are not likely to be on welfare. Another important unknown factor in my attempted comprehensive measure of economic well-being is the nonpecuniary utility (or disutility) that men and women obtain from their work.

The wages, earnings, and incomes of black workers and black households are substantially less than those of whites, and the conventional human capital variables, such as education, training, and health care leave much of the difference unexplained. Even if they explained more, the question would then be: Why is the market for such human capital investments functioning so poorly that blacks continue to be shortchanged? If whites find it profitable – in terms of higher earnings and better jobs – to make these investments, why are blacks' opportunities for these investments so curtailed? If the answer is not labor market discrimination, is it discrimination in the capital markets that supply funds or other sources of human capital investments? It is not scientifically satisfactory for economists to argue that labor market discrimination is minimal if they then have no explanation for how discrimination in capital markets creates and sustains the inequities we measure in the labor market.

The case of blacks in the United States appears to offer the strongest evidence for the reality of labor market discrimination and, given existing economic theories, for flaws in the competitive functioning of the market. In these respects, the case of blacks is at the other end of the spectrum from that of non-Hispanic early-immigrant groups. Economic discrimination, whether measured by average family incomes or by comparing wages when exogenous productivity factors have been held constant, is substantial for blacks and is nonexistent or insubstantial for various former-immigrant white (and some Oriental) groups. For those groups, but not for blacks, the market has virtually eliminated the differences in economic attainment that were present decades ago.

5.2. *The effects of discrimination on total output*

The foregoing remarks refer to descriptive statistics, including regression analyses of earnings functions, and to the normative issue of equity. Let us turn to positive economics and the tasks of analysis, prediction, and explanation. One issue that has not been much studied is the implications of discrimination for economic efficiency as measured by total social income. I have elsewhere [Cain (1985)] addressed this question regarding discrimination against women, and my conclusions were embarrassingly thin. The neoclassical economist's convention, and perhaps it is an obligation, to take tastes – individual preferences – as given prevents the automatic translation of "different prices (wages) for the same good (labor)" into a loss in total social income (or total utility).[33] In a competitive economy in which tastes are the fundamental cause of discrimination there is no presumptive case for inefficiency.

Perhaps the underlying atomistic competitive model with only private (internalized) benefits and costs is too narrow. Alexis (1973, p. 297) distinguishes between discrimination, in which the discriminator is indifferent "to the welfare of the avoided [black] person", and racism, where "the decision maker is not indifferent to the relative economic status of nonpreferred persons". Alexis's point may be extended to posit racist discrimination as a public "good" among the majority group, and this could explain the persistence of labor market discrimination. However, it is difficult to reconcile the idea of racism as a public good with the proliferation during the last 30 years of antidiscriminatory legislation and court decisions, which ought to reflect the public's externalities regarding discrimination. On the other hand, there have also been numerous references in recent American politics to the "silent majority" among whites, who oppose the pro-civil-rights legislation. The purely political aspects of this topic are well beyond the scope of this chapter. The issue of externalities is not, but I do not pursue it.

Discrimination that results from private and government monopolies deserves further study, particularly if the term monopoly is extended to include collusive action that deprives minorities of access to various opportunities, some of which, like housing, may be only indirectly related to labor markets. Akerlof (1976)

[33]Ambiguities about total welfare when tastes for discrimination are part of a person's utility function are discussed by Thurow (1969, pp. 116–138), Toikka (1976), and Lundahl and Wadensjö (1984, pp. 81–108).

analyzes several models illustrating collusion, including conspiratorial acts and intimidation, that are sources of the oppression of minorities. Even if I am correct in my judgment that monopoly is not the predominant source of discriminatory wage differences, this does not imply that the benefits from attacking this source are less than the associated costs.

Aside from monopoly, the standard cases of market failure that point to inefficiencies that might be overcome through government intervention do not emerge from economic theories of discrimination. Perhaps an exception is the externalities of information concerning the productive capacities of minorities. Tests, licenses, certifications, and other such signals are used extensively in labor markets, and the private costs of obtaining accurate information about workers' productivity may be high relative to the private benefits, which are not necessarily appropriable as a private good. Clearly, those who believe in the equality of productive capacities across the groups under study will be more likely to believe in the benefits of more scientific information about productive capacities. The history of the stereotypes of inferiority among ethnic minorities in the United States is too familiar to cite, and the demise of these stereotypes regarding the earlier immigrant groups is part of the latter's success story.

In the main, however, I was not able to extract efficiency losses from the economic theories of discrimination [Cain (1985)], which reflects my agnostic view of these theories expressed in Section 3. Something is amiss. Discrimination in its many forms, not only economic, is widely believed to suppress the achievements of the minority group with no fully offsetting gains to the majority group. The economists that I know agree on this, yet conventional economic theories do not, to my knowledge, explain or analyze this widely shared belief.

Economists have prescribed limits for themselves in many policy spheres. Economics does not distinguish among the ethical merits of different tastes; between, say preferences for physical attractiveness or for race. As economists we have nothing to say about the justness of laws that prohibit an employer from refusing to hire someone on the basis of color but that permit hiring on the basis of physical attractiveness. As citizens we may, of course, have strong opinions about such matters.

5.3. *Measuring the impact of policies*

A more promising role for economic analysis lies in the measurements and methods that permit prediction. Empirical regularities, such as time trends, may be established and be useful even in the absence of fully developed theories. At a minimum, the measurements provide valuable data for monitoring progress or regress regarding discrimination.

A more ambitious form of prediction is that concerning policy instruments. The policies available to government may be classified into three categories: (a) macroeconomic (mainly monetary and fiscal policies affecting aggregate demand), (b) income transfers, and (c) microeconomic structural labor market policies. I discuss only the third. Supply-side structural policies typically comprise education and training programs. They have tended to be directed to low-income workers, with no special targeting to workers of a particular race or gender. In this regard, the supply-side policies tend to differ from the demand-side policies. Microeconomic demand-side policies might also be general, such as public employment programs or wage subsidies for unemployed and low-income workers, but the demand policies that have received most attention are those that directly forbid discrimination or promote preferential treatment of minority workers in hiring, placement, pay, or employment security. Preferential treatment is also called affirmative action.

Research aimed at evaluating these policies is abundant and controversial. See, for example, the proceedings of a conference on the labor market effects of antidiscrimination legislation that appeared in the *Industrial and Labor Relations Review* (vol. 29, July 1976). The essential difficulty in evaluating these programs is the classic problem of trying to make inferences from an uncontrolled experiment. We observe an outcome for a group of workers, some of whom participated in the program or, alternatively, had the program imposed on them. To establish causality between program status and the outcome, the factors that selected the workers into the program must be either (a) known and controlled for in the evaluation, or (b) known to be unrelated to the outcome.

It is difficult to know enough about the selection process and about all the causes of the outcome to justify either (a) or (b). Random assignment would satisfy condition (b), but this selection procedure is rare. Legislators and courts, therefore, seldom rely on the research of economists to determine the fate of government programs.

Decades of empirical research on labor markets, much of it like the research reported in Section 4, can be helpful in estimating the effects of a variety of policy variables on the earnings of workers, even if the research does not provide conclusive answers. Customarily we use cross-sectional data for empirical work, although the policy question is invariably one of predicting a change over time.

The implications for policy from cross-sectional research arose in the previous section. Some variables may be only minimally affected by policy, like "years since immigration" among the existing stock of immigrants; some partly affected, like "years of schooling"; and some almost wholly affected, like "participation in a government training program". Policies related to the cross-sectional findings will not be discussed, but some of the issues about how the above-mentioned variables affect outcomes in the labor market appear in time-series analyses of discrimination, which is the final topic of this chapter.

5.4. Results of time-series analyses

For my purposes the essential facts from time-series data that pertain to economic discrimination have been revealed by Table 13.5 in Section 2. This table shows two major challenges. One is the near-constant ratio of women's-to-men's wages over a 40-year period, using the data on earnings of year-round, full-time workers. The second is the slow increase in the ratio of black-to-white wages among men, which in 1982 was only 0.72. These trends in wages could be usefully supplemented with an analysis of trends in other measures of attainment in the labor market, including occupational attainment, labor force participation, and employment/unemployment rates, but space limitations preclude more than brief remarks.

The sharp increase in labor force participation rates (LFPRs) by women and the moderate decrease in LFPRs of men during the last 40 years have brought men and women into closer equality with respect to the quantity of time spent in market work, although men still spend about twice as many hours of their adult life in market work as do women [Cain (1984a)].

The increase in LFPRs for women has been the result of two trends which, as noted in Section 3, have contrasting effects on the trend in average wages of women: (a) women who work are working more continuously and for more years of their adulthood; (b) a larger fraction of women are entering and reentering the work force. Trend (a) should increase the average wage, because the wage should increase with experience and seniority. Trend (b) probably decreases the average wage because the composition of workers is altered by the influx of women with less-than-average experience – referred to as "adverse selection". The "adverse selection" hypothesis is strongly advocated by Smith and Ward (1984), but see Fuchs (1984) for counter arguments and Mallan (1982) for counter evidence.[34]

The LFPRs of men between the ages of 50 and 65 have declined during the last 20 years or so. Are these early retirements and disability-related retirements concentrated among low-wage workers? The substitution effect of wages on labor supply suggests a yes answer, but the income effect suggests otherwise. Retirement may be considered a "luxury good" that is selected by workers with above-average incomes. The net result of these contrasting effects on the trends among men needs to be studied.

The changing composition of the male labor force has also been examined in analyzing trends in wages of men, black and white. Butler and Heckman (1977)

[34]Further counter evidence to Smith and Ward is Maloney's finding that the wages of husbands and wives who work in every year covered by the Michigan Panel Study of Income Dynamics show declining women-to-men ratios from 1975 through 1980 [Maloney (1983, pp. 135–139)]. These data may, of course, simply reflect the contrasting age/earnings profiles shown in Figure 13.2. Whether the declining ratios imply labor market discrimination depends on whether they reflect voluntary choices of these wives to commit less effort than their husbands to the market sector.

Table 13.9
Median money incomes and income ratios for black and white male workers, 1948–1982, in constant 1982 dollars

Year	White median$	Black median$	Ratio B/W	Year	White median$	Black median$	Ratio B/W
1948	$10064	$5465	0.54	1965	$16185	$8710	0.54
1949	10006	4844	0.48	1966	16631	9212	0.55
1950	10862	5899	0.54	1967	16901	9653	0.57
1951	11524	6346	0.55	1968	17388	10551	0.61
1952	11837	6487	0.55	1969	17812	10508	0.59
1953	12237	6760	0.55	1970	17428	10490	0.60
1954	12080	6011	0.50	1971	17248	10351	0.60
1955	12776	6724	0.53	1972	18029	11100	0.62
1956	13558	7113	0.52	1973	18360	11551	0.63
1957	13402	7096	0.53	1974	17330	11135	0.64
1958	13275	6614	0.50	1975	16679	10511	0.63
1959	13937	6561	0.47	1976	16849	10540	0.63
1960	14003	7367	0.53	1977	16889	10326	0.61
1961	14290	7385	0.52	1978	16945	10796	0.64
1962	14859	7318	0.49	1979	16363	10604	0.65
1963	15151	7874	0.52	1980	15612	9786	0.63
1964	15361	8708	0.57	1981	15172	9624	0.63
				1982	14748	9493	0.64

Source: U.S. Bureau of the Census, Current Population Reports, Series P-60, No. 142, *Money Income of Households, Families, and Persons in the Unites States: 1982* (Washington, D.C.: U.S. GPO, 1984), Table 40.

suggested that part of the rise in the ratio of black-to-white wages through the 1960s and into the early 1970s could be attributable to a selection of higher-earning workers among blacks, relative to whites. Their argument is as follows. Black men's LFPRs have declined more than have the LFPRs of white men. Assume that the men who drop out of the labor force tend to be low earners. The black male labor force would then have relatively fewer of the low earners remaining, and the average earnings of blacks – which is measured only for those in the labor force – will rise relative to that of whites.

The issue is not resolved, and it illustrates themes that I wish to stress in this survey: the need for closer attention to descriptive economic statistics about the labor market statuses of majority and minority groups, and the need to specify the purposes of one's analysis. A problem in charting trends is that the use of broad population groups may introduce exogenous compositional changes (like the age distribution) that should be held constant, while narrowing the comparison to various subgroups may reflect selection according to an endogenous characteristic (like full-time work status) that should not be held constant.

Table 13.9 shows another version of the black-to-white comparison among men, but this time for all men who worked, rather than for year-round, full-time workers, as in Table 13.5. Table 13.9 shows the time series for money incomes in constant 1982 dollars for each year, 1948–1982. (The trend in money income is very similar to the trend in money earnings.) The dollar figures show the striking reversal from 1973 on, of the long-term growth in real incomes for both groups that prevailed from 1948 to 1973.

The overall picture regarding the black-to-white (B/W) ratios in Table 13.9 is similar to that summarized in Table 13.5, but the year-by-year statistics bring out more clearly the three periods of stability and change in the B/W ratios: 1948–1965, stability; 1966–1974, growth; 1975–1982, stability. Presumably a theory or an empirical evaluation of specific hypotheses about labor market discrimination against blacks should be able to explain these stylized facts.

Freeman (1981) discusses three main contending explanations, in addition to the Butler–Heckman hypothesis about selectivity in the composition of the populations. One is that the B/W ratio is pro-cyclical – rising during periods of prosperity, when unemployment is low, and falling during recessions. This is consistent with its growth in 1966–1974, when labor markets were relatively tight, and with the ratios that are low relative to surrounding years in the recession troughs of 1949, 1954, and 1958. However, the hypothesis is not supported by the stability of the ratios throughout the period of 1948–1965, when unemployment rates were relatively low, or by the behavior of the ratios in the later recession troughs, 1961, 1971, 1975, and 1982.

A second hypothesis is that the B/W ratios were affected by the surge of legal measures that may be said to have begun with an Executive Order in 1961 (No. 10925) that reinforced a somewhat dormant ban on discrimination by firms doing business with the federal government, followed by the Civil Rights Act of 1964 and subsequent legislation. Measuring the impact of these various forms of government intervention is difficult, however. How does one quantify the resources devoted to the intervention? How do we separate the effects of the legislation from the effects of the political and social climates that fostered the legislation? It is no surprise that the attempted evaluations of the legislation have not been conclusive.

A third hypothesis to explain the time series of black-to-white earnings ratios focuses on education, where this may be interpreted narrowly as years of schooling completed or broadly as a general indicator of human capital, including qualitative aspects of schooling as well as the training, information, and mobility that are affected by schooling. In either case, the emphasis is on the supply side of the labor market and the relative increases in the human capital of black men.

The role of education in this stream of research has had a curious history. Early quantitative studies based on the 1940, 1950, and 1960 censuses consistently showed two rather pessimistic regularities about male workers: (a) holding age constant, the B/W earnings ratio generally declined as years-of-schooling increased; (b) holding years of schooling constant, the B/W ratio generally declined as age increased. See Zeman (1955) as quoted in Becker, (1971,

Table 13.10
Median years of schooling completed and schooling ratios, white and black men, various populations, 1940–1980.

Year	Population, by age and labor force status	Median years of educational attainment		
		White	Black	Ratio B/W
1940	All males 25+	8.6	5.7	0.66
	Males, 25–59	10.3	7.0	0.68
1950	All males 25+	9.3	6.8	0.73
	Males 25–29	12.0	8.6	0.72
1952	Males, 18+ in civilian labor force	10.8	7.2	0.67
1959	Males, 18+ in civilian labor force	11.9	8.3	0.70
1970	All males 25+	12.2	9.9	0.81
	Males, 25–29	12.6	12.2	0.97
	Males, 18+ in civilian labor force	12.1	11.1	0.89
1980	All males 25+	12.5	12.0	0.96
	Males, 25–29	12.9	12.6	0.98
	Males, 18+ in civilian labor force	12.7	12.2	0.96

Sources: "All males" and "Males, 25–29": U.S. Bureau of the Census, *Statistical Abstract of the United States: 1982–83*, 103rd edition (Washington, D.C.: U.S. GPO, 1983) p. 143; "Males, 18+ in civilian labor force", U.S. Department of Labor, *Handbook of Labor Statistics 1978*, Bulletin 2000 (Washington, D.C.: U.S. GPO, 1979) p. 68; "Males, 16+ in civilian labor force", U.S. Department of Labor, Bureau of Labor Statistics, *Handbook of Labor Statistics*, Bulletin 2175 (Washington, D.C.: U.S. GPO, 1981), pp. 152–153.

p. 111) for 1940, Anderson (1955) and Freeman (1973b, p. 85) for 1950, and Hanoch (1967) for 1960.

At face value, (a) implies that an equal growth in educational attainment over time would widen the B/W difference in earnings. However, the increase in educational attainment by black men has exceeded that of white men, particularly between 1960 and 1980 (see Table 13.10). This period includes, but does not coincide with, the period of the rise in the earnings ratios, 1967–1974. By 1980 the B/W differences in median educational attainments had been virtually eliminated, although there may well remain differences in the quality of schooling.

In addition to the relative increase in the quantity of schooling obtained by blacks, a new development in research findings in the 1970s re-emphasized the importance of schooling. Recent studies show that the wage returns to schooling were becoming more equalized between blacks and whites, although this was mainly true for the young age groups and those with some college [see Smith and Welch (1977), Freeman (1977)]. Like the vintage hypothesis regarding age effects, these new and higher education effects for black men relative to white men remain to be tested in the years to come.

This brief survey of proposed explanations for the trend in black-to-white male earnings illustrates the tentativeness of empirical regularities regarding labor market discrimination and the consequent difficulty in drawing policy implications. Estimated relations from cross-sections at different times show widely varying results, and the time series, with relatively few observations and many competing hypotheses, do not yield firm empirical regularities either.

5.5. *Final word*

The economics of discrimination is a particularly complex subject. My judgment is that the theories of discrimination have been useful for providing definitions and for suggesting measurements of discrimination but not for providing convincing explanations of the phenomenon nor of its patterns. The econometric work has also been useful, but to my eyes more so for its descriptive content than for testing hypotheses or for providing estimates of causal relations.

References

Abowd, John M. and Mark Killingsworth (1982) "Employment, wages, and earnings of Hispanics in the federal and non-federal sectors: methodological issues and their empirical consequences", in: G. Borjas and M. Tienda, eds., *Hispanic labor conference*. Washington, D.C.: National Commission on Employment Policy. (Subsequently published in G. J. Borjas and M. Tienda, eds., *Hispanics in the U.S. Economy*. Orlando, Fla.: Academic Press, (1985, 77–125.)

Aigner, Dennis J. and Glen G. Cain (1977) "Statistical theories of discrimination in the labor market", *Industrial and Labor Relations Review*, 30:175–187.

Akerlof, George A. (1976) "The economics of caste and of the rat race and other woeful tales", *Quarterly Journal of Economics*, 94:599–617.

Alchian, Armen A. and Reuben Kessel (1962) "Competition, monopoly and the pursuit of pecuniary gain", in: *Aspects of labor economics*, Conference Volume of the Universities-National Bureau Committee for Economic Research. Princeton, N.J.: Princeton University Press, 156–175.

Alexis, Marcus (1973) "A theory of labor market discrimination with interdependent utilities", *American Economic Review*, 63:296–302

Anastasi, Anne (1969) "Differential psychology", in: *Encyclopedia Britannica*. Chicago: Encyclopedia Britannica, Inc., William Benton, vol. 7.

Anderson, C. Arnold (1955) "Regional and racial differences in the relation between income and education", *The school review*, 63:38–45.

Arrow, Kenneth (1972) "Models of job discrimination", and "Some mathematical models of race in the labor market", in: A. H. Pascal, ed., *Racial discrimination in economic life*. Lexington, Mass.: Lexington Books, 83–102 and 187–204.

Arrow, Kenneth (1973) "The theory of discrimination", in: O. A. Ashenfelter and A. Rees, eds., *Discrimination in labor markets*. Princeton, N.J.: Princeton University Press, 3–33.

Ashenfelter, Orley (1972) "Racial discrimination and trade unions", *Journal of Political Economy*, 80:435–464.

Ashenfelter, Orley and Timothy Hannan (1986) "Sex discrimination and product market competition: the case of the banking industry", *Quarterly Journal of Economics*, 101: 149–173.

Astin, Helen S. and Alan E. Bayer (1972) "Sex discrimination in academe", *Educational Record*, 53:101–118.

Baldus, D. C. and J. W. L. Cole (1980) *Statistical proof of discrimination*. New York: McGraw Hill.

Becker, Gary S. (1971) *The economics of discrimination*. Chicago: The University of Chicago Press. (Original edition, 1957.)

Becker, Gary S. (1959) "Union restrictions on entry", in: P. D. Bradley, ed., *The public stake in union power*. Charlottesville, Va.: University of Virginia Press, 209–224.

Becker, Gary S. (1968) "Discrimination, economic", in: D. L. Sills, ed., *International encyclopedia of the social sciences*. New York: Macmillan and Free Press, vol. 4, 208–210. (Reprint edition, 1972.)

Bergmann, Barbara R. (1974) "Occupational segregation, wages and profits when employers discriminate by race or sex", *Eastern Economic Journal*, 1:103–110.

Blau, Francine D. (1977) *Equal pay in the office*. Lexington, Mass.: D.C. Heath and Co.

Blinder, Alan S. (1973) "Wage discrimination: reduced form and structural variables", *Journal of Human Resources*, 8:436–455.

Bunting, Robert L. (1962) *Employer concentration in local labor markets*. Chapel Hill: University of North Carolina Press.

Butler, Richard and James J. Heckman (1977) "Government's impact on the labor market status of black Americans: a critical review", in: *Equal rights and industrial relations*. Madison, Wis.: University of Wisconsin, Industrial Relations Research Association, 235–281.

Cain, Glen G. (1976) "The challenge of segmented labor market theories to orthodox theory: a survey", *Journal of Economic Literature*, 14:1215–1257.

Cain, Glen G. (1984a) "Lifetime measures of labor supply of men and women", Discussion Paper No. 749-84, Institute for Research on Poverty, University of Wisconsin-Madison.

Cain, Glen G. (1984b) "Women and work: trends in time spent in housework", Discussion Paper No. 745-84, Institute for Research on Poverty, University of Wisconsin-Madison.

Cain, Glen G. (1985) "Welfare economics of policies toward women", *Journal of Labor Economics*, 3, part II:375–396.

Chiswick, Barry R. (1973) "Racial discrimination in the labor market: a test of alternative hypotheses", *Journal of Political Economy*, 81:1330–1352.

Chiswick, Barry R. (1974) *Income inequality*. New York: National Bureau of Economic Research, distributed by Columbia University Press.

Chiswick, Barry R. (1983) "The earnings and human capital of American Jews", *Journal of Human Resources*, 18:313–336.

Cohen, Malcolm S. (1971) "Sex differences in compensation", *Journal of Human Resources*, 6:434–447.

Comanor, William S. (1973) "Racial discrimination in American industry", *Economica*, 40:363–378.

Conway, Delores A. and Harry V. Roberts (1983) "Reverse regression, fairness and employment discrimination", *Journal of Business and Economic Statistics*, 1:75–85.

Corcoran, Mary and Greg J. Duncan (1979) "Work history, labor force attachment, and earnings differences between the races and sexes", *Journal of Human Resources*, 14:497–520.

Duncan, Otis Dudley (1968) "Inheritance of poverty or inheritance of race?", in: D. P. Moynihan, ed., *On understanding poverty*. New York: Basic Books, 85–110.

Featherman, David L. and Robert M. Hauser (1976) "Sexual inequalities and socioeconomic achievement in the U.S., 1962–1973", *American Sociological Review*, 41:462–483.

Finkelstein, Michael O. (1980) "The judicial reception of multiple regression studies in race and sex discrimination cases", *Columbia Law Review*, 80:737–754.

Fisher, Franklin M. (1980) "Multiple regression in legal proceedings", *Columbia Law Review*, 80:702–736.

Flanagan, Robert J. (1973) "Racial wage discrimination and employment segregation", *Journal of Human Resources*, 8:465–471.

Flanagan, Robert J. (1974) "Labor force experience, job turnover, and racial wage differentials", *Review of Economics and Statistics*, 56:521–529.

Freeman, Richard B. (1973a) "Decline of labor market discrimination and economic analysis", *American Economic Review*, 63:280–286.

Freeman, Richard B. (1973b) "Comment", in: O. Ashenfelter and A. Rees, eds., *Discrimination in labor markets*. Princeton, N.J.: Princeton University Press, 82–87.

Freeman, Richard B. (1977) *Black elite: the new market for highly qualified black Americans*. New York: McGraw-Hill.

Freeman, Richard B. (1981) "Black progress after 1964: who has gained and why?", in: S. Rosen, ed., *Studies in labor markets*. Chicago: University of Chicago Press, 247–294.

Fuchs, Victor R. (1971) "Differences in hourly earnings between men and women", *Monthly Labor Review*, 94:9–15.

Fuchs, Victor R. (1984) "His and hers: gender differences in work and income, 1959–1979", Working Paper No. 1501, National Bureau of Economic Research, Cambridge, Mass. Forthcoming in *Journal of Labor Economics*.

Goldberg, Matthew S. (1982) "Discrimination, nepotism, and long-run wage differentials", *Quarterly Journal of Economics*, 96:307–319.

Goldberger, Arthur S. (1984) "Reverse regression and salary discrimination", *Journal of Human Resources*, 19:293–318.

Gould, William B. (1977) *Black workers in white unions: job discrimination in the United States*. Ithaca, N.Y.: Cornell University Press.

Greeley, Andrew M. (1976) *Ethnicity, denomination and inequality*. Beverly Hills, Calif.: Sage Publications.

Greeley, Andrew M. (1981) *The Irish Americans*. New York: Harper and Row.

Green, Carol A. and Marianne A. Ferber (1984) "Employment discrimination: an empirical test of forward versus reverse regression", *Journal of Human Resources*, 19:557–569.

Grenier, Gilles (1984) "The effect of language characteristics on the wage of Hispanic-American males", *Journal of Human Resources*, 19:35–52.

Gwartney, James D. and Richard Stroup (1973) "Measurement of employment discrimination according to sex", *Southern Economic Journal*, 39:575–587.

Hanoch, Gloria (1967) "An economic analysis of earnings and schooling", *Journal of Human Resources*, 2:310–329.

Hill, Herbert (1977) *Black labor and the American legal system*. Washington, D.C.: The Bureau of National Affairs.

Hoffman, Saul (1979) "Black-white life cycle earnings differences and the vintage hypothesis: a longitudinal analysis", *American Economic Review*, 69:855–867.

Johnson, George E. (1975) "Economic analysis of trade unionism", *American Economic Review, Papers and Proceedings*, 65:23–28.

Johnson, George E. and Frank P. Stafford (1974) "The earnings and promotion of women faculty", *American Economic Review*, 64:888–903.

Jones, F. L. (1983) "On decomposing the wage gap: a critical comment on Blinder's method", *Journal of Human Resources*, 18:126–130.

Kessel, Reuben A. (1958) "Price discrimination in medicine", *Journal of Law and Economics*, 1:20–53.

Kohen, Andrew and Roger Roderick (1975) "The effect of race and sex discrimination on early career earnings", unpublished paper, Center for Human Resource Research, Ohio State University, Columbus, Ohio.

Landes, William (1968) "The economics of fair employment laws", *Journal of Political Economy*, 76:507–552.

Lewis, H. Gregg (1959) "Competitive and monopoly unionism", in: P. D. Bradley, ed., *The public stake in union power*. Charlottesville, Va.: University of Virginia Press, 181–208.

Lucas, Robert E. B. (1974) "The distribution of job characteristics", *Review of Economics and Statistics*, 56:530–540.

Luksetich, W. A. (1979) "Market power and sex discrimination in white-collar employment", *Review of Social Economy*, 37:211–224.

Lundahl, Mats and Eskil Wadensjö (1984) *Unequal treatment: a study in the neo-classical theory of discrimination*. London: Croom Helm.

Lundberg, Shelly J. and Richard Startz (1983) "Private discrimination and social intervention in competitive labor markets", *American Economic Review*, 73:340–347.

Madden, Janice F. (1973) *The economics of sex discrimination*. Lexington, Mass.: D.C. Heath and Co.

Malkiel, Burton G. and Judith A. Malkiel (1973) "Male-female pay differentials in professional employment", *American Economic Review*, 63:693–705.

Mallan, Lucy B. (1982) "Labor force participation, work experience, and the pay gap between men and women", *Journal of Human Resources*, 17:437–448.

Maloney, Timothy J. (1983) "The cyclical labor supply response of married women and disequilibrium unemployment", unpublished Ph.D. dissertation, Department of Economics, University of Wisconsin-Madison.

Marshall, F. Ray (1965) *The Negro and organized labor*. New York: John Wiley.

Marshall, F. Ray (1974) "The economics of racial discrimination: a survey", *Journal of Economic Literature*, 12:849–871.

Masters, Stanley H. (1975) *Black–white income differentials*. New York: Academic Press.

McCall, John J. (1972) "The simple mathematics of information, job search, and prejudice", in: A. Pascal, ed., *Racial discrimination in economic life*. Lexington, Mass.: Lexington Books, 205–224.

Mincer, Jacob and Solomon Polachek (1974) "Family investments in human capital earnings of women", *Journal of Political Economy*, 82, part 2:S76–S108.

Myrdal, Gunnar (1944) *An American dilemma*. New York: Harpers.

Northrup, Herbert R. (1944) *Organized labor and the Negro*. New York: Harpers.

Oaxaca, Ronald L. (1973) "Male–female wage differentials in urban labor markets", *International Economic Review*, 14:693–709.

O'Neill, June (1983a) "The determinants and wage effects of occupational segregation", working paper, Urban Institute, Washington, D.C.

O'Neill, June (1983b) "The trend in sex differentials in wages", paper presented at the Conference on Trends in Women's Work, Education, and Family Building, Urban Institute, Washington, D.C.

O'Neill, June (1984) "Earnings differentials: empirical evidence and causes", in: G. Schmid and R. Weitzel, eds., *Sex discrimination and equal opportunity*. London: Gower Publishing Co., 69–91.

Oster, Sylvia M. (1975) "Industry differences in discrimination against women", *Quarterly Journal of Economics*, 89:215–229.

Petersen, William (1978) "Chinese Americans and Japanese Americans", in: T. Sowell, ed., *Essays and data on American ethnic groups*. Washington, D.C.: The Urban Institute, 65–106.

Phelps, Edmund S. (1972) "The statistical theory of racism and sexism", *American Economic Review*, 62:659–661.

Piore, Michael J. (1970) "Jobs and training", in: S. H. Beer, ed., *The State and the Poor*. Cambridge, Mass.: Winthrop Press, 53–83.

Polachek, Solomon W. (1979) "Occupational segregation among women: theory, evidence, and prognosis", in: C. B. Lloyd, E. S. Andrews and C. L. Gilroy, eds., *Women in the Labor Market*. New York: Columbia University Press, 137–157.

Reich, Michael (1971) "The economics of racism", in: David M. Gordon, ed., *Problems in economy: an urban perspective*. Lexington, Mass.: D.C. Heath and Co., 107–113.

Reich, Michael (1981) *Racial inequality*. Princeton, N.J.: Princeton University Press.

Reimers, Cordelia W. (1983) "Labor market discrimination against hispanic and black men", *Review of Economics and Statistics*, 65:570–579.

Riley, John G. (1975) "Competitive signaling", *Journal of Economic Theory*, 10:174–186.

Roberts, Harry V. (1980) "Statistical biases in the measurement of employment discrimination", in: E. R. Livernash, eds., *Comparable worth: issues and alternatives*, Washington, D.C.: Equal Employment Advisory Council, 173–195.

Robinson, Joan (1934) *The economics of imperfect competition*. London: Macmillan.

Roos, Patricia A. (1981) "Sex stratification in the workplace: male–female differences in economic returns to occupations", *Social Science Research*, 10:195–224.

Ross, Malcolm (1948) *All manner of men*. New York: Reynal and Hitchcock.

Rothschild, Michael and Joseph E. Stiglitz (1982) "A model of employment outcomes illustrating the effect of the structure of information on the level and the distribution of income", *Economics Letters*, 10:231–236.

Sanborn, Henry (1964) "Pay differences between men and women", *Industrial and Labor Relations Review*, 17:534–550.

Sawhill, Isabel (1973) "The economics of discrimination against women: some new findings", *Journal of Human Resources*, 8:383–396.

Smith, James P. and Michael P. Ward (1984) "Women's wages and work in the twentieth century", Report R-3119-NICHD, RAND, Santa Monica, Calif.

Smith, James P. and Finis Welch (1977) "Black–white male wage ratios: 1960–1970", *American Economic Review*, 67:323–338.

Smith, James P. and Finis Welch (1978) "Race differences in earnings: a survey and new evidence", unpublished ms., R-2295-NSF, RAND, Santa Monica, Calif.

Sowell, Thomas (1981) *Ethnic Americans*. New York: Basic Books.

Spence, A. Michael (1973) "Job market signaling", *Quarterly Journal of Economics*, 87:355–374.

Stiglitz, Joseph E. (1973) "Approaches to the economics of discrimination", *American Economic Review, Papers and Proceedings*, 63:287–295.

Stiglitz, Joseph E. (1974) "Theories of discrimination and economic policy", in: G. M. von Furstenberg, A. R. Horowitz, and B. Harrison, eds., *Patterns of racial discrimination. Volume B: employment and income*. Lexington, Mass.: D.C. Heath and Co., 5–26.

Suter, Larry E. and Herman P. Miller (1973) "Income differences between men and career women", *American Journal of Sociology*, 78:962–974.

Thurow, Lester C. (1969) *Poverty and discrimination*. Washington, D.C.: The Brookings Institution.

Thurow, Lester C. (1975) *Generating inequality*. New York: Basic Books.

Toikka, Richard S. (1976) "The welfare implications of Becker's discrimination coefficient", *Journal of Economic Theory*, 13:472–477.

Tomes, Nigel (1984) "The effects of religion and denomination on earnings and the returns to human capital", *Journal of Human Resources*, 19:472–488.

Treiman, Donald J. and Heidi I. Hartmann, eds. (1981) *Women, work, and wages: equal pay for jobs of equal value*. Washington, D.C.: National Academy Press.

Treiman, Donald J. and Kermit Terrell (1975) "Sex and the process of status attainment: a comparison of working women and men", *American Sociological Review*, 40:174–200.

U.S. Bureau of the Census (1980) *Statistical abstract of the United States, 1980*. Washington, D.C.: U.S. GPO, 101st ed.

U.S. Bureau of the Census (1983a) Current population reports, Series P-20, No. 372, *Marital status and living arrangements, March 1981*. Washington, D.C.: U.S. GPO.

U.S. Bureau of the Census (1983b) "Current population reports", Series P-60, No. 137, *Money income of households, families, and persons in the United States: 1981*. Washington, D.C.: U.S. GPO.

U.S. Bureau of the Census (1983c) *Statistical abstract of the United States, 1984*. Washington, D.C.: U.S. GPO, 104th ed.

U.S. Bureau of the Census (1984) "Current population reports", Series P-60, No. 142, *Money income of households, families, and persons in the United States: 1982*. Washington, D.C.: U.S. GPO.

U.S. Department of Labor, Bureau of Labor Statistics (1979) *Earnings and other characteristics of organized labor, May 1977*, Report 556. Washington, D.C.: U.S. GPO.

U.S. Department of Labor, Bureau of Labor Statistics (1982) *Labor force statistics derived from the current population survey: a databook, Volume I*, Bulletin 2096. Washington, D.C.: U.S. GPO.

Welch, Finis (1973) "Education and racial discrimination", in: O. A. Ashenfelter and A. Rees, eds., *Discrimination in labor markets*. Princeton, N.J.: Princeton University Press, 43–81.

Welch, Finis (1975) "Human capital theory: education, discrimination, and life cycles", *American Economic Review*, 65:63–73.

Zabalza, Anthony and J. L. Arrufat (1983) "Wage differences between married men and married women in Great Britain: the depreciation effect of nonparticipation", unpublished Discussion Paper No. 151, Centre for Labour Economics, London School of Economics.

Zeman, Mordechai (1955) "A quantitative analysis of white–nonwhite income differentials in the United States in 1939", unpublished Ph.D. dissertation, University of Chicago.

INDEX